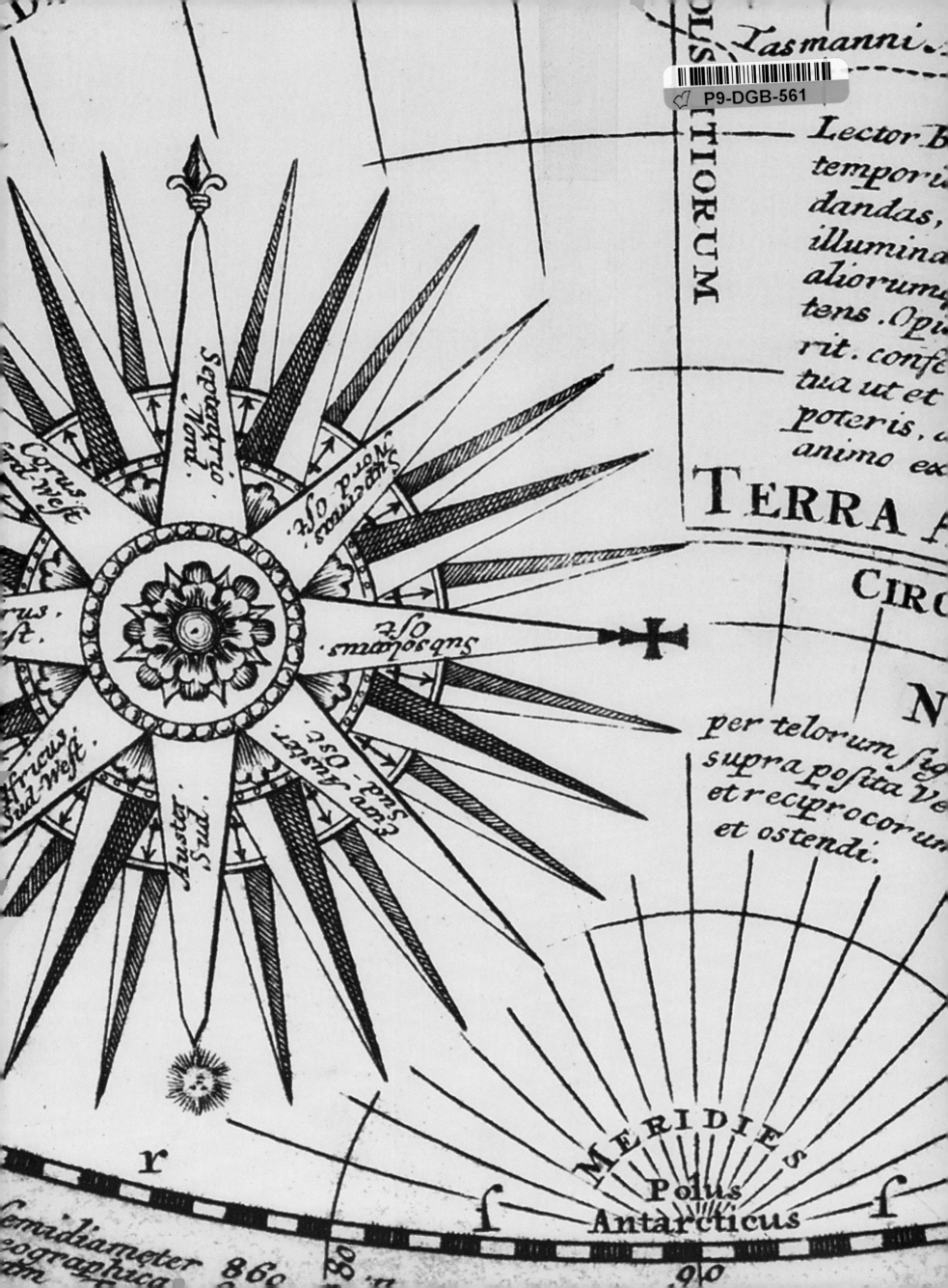

DK ATLAS OF WORLD HISTORY

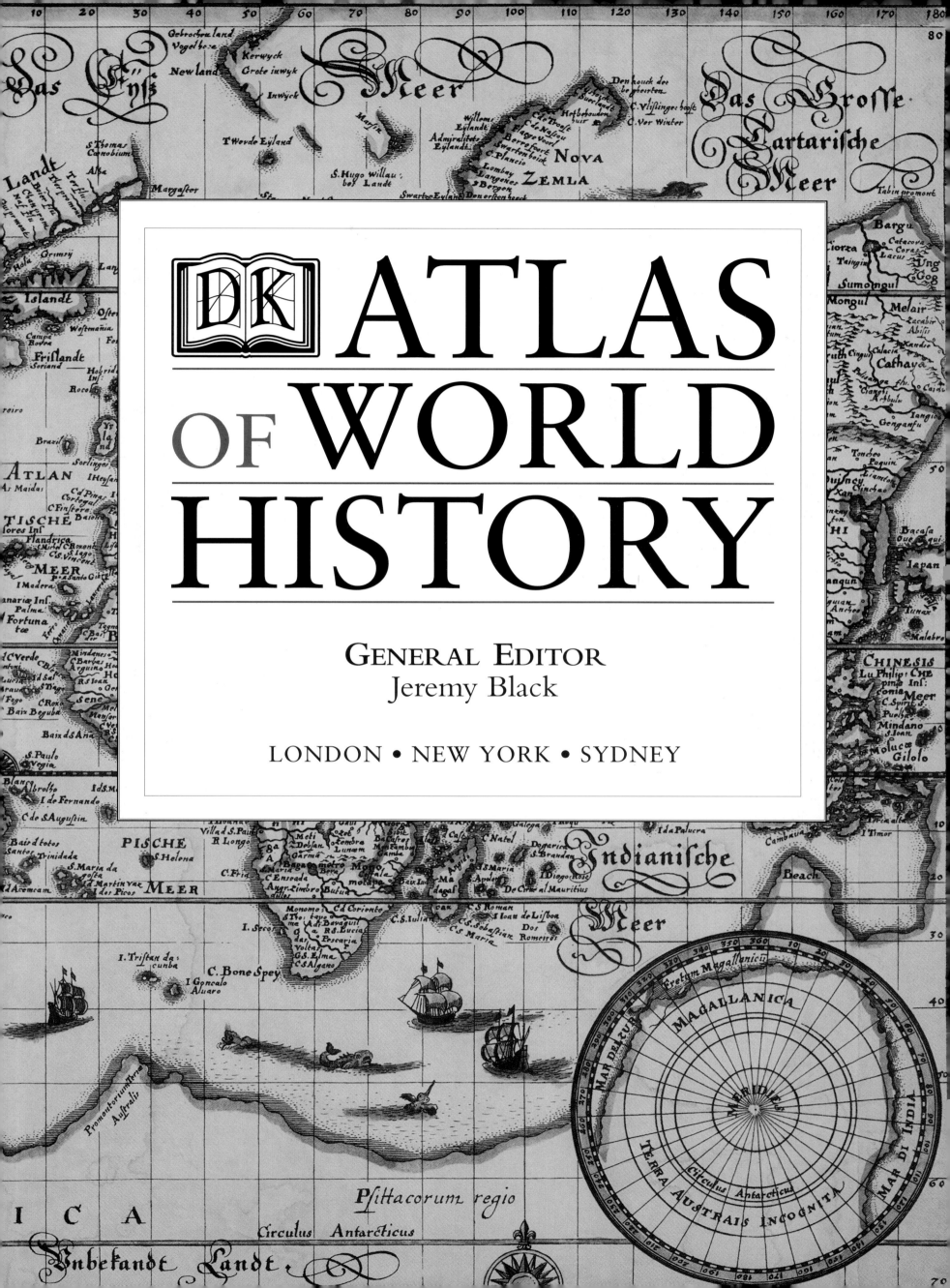

DK ATLAS OF WORLD HISTORY

GENERAL EDITOR
Jeremy Black

LONDON · NEW YORK · SYDNEY

A DORLING KINDERSLEY PUBLISHING BOOK
www.dk.com

CONSULTANTS

GENERAL EDITOR Professor Jeremy Black, Department of History, University of Exeter, UK

WORLD HISTORY

Professor Jerry Bentley, Department of History, University of Hawaii, USA
Professor James Chambers, Department of History, Texas Christian University, USA
Dr. John France, Department of History, University of Swansea, UK
Dr. Guy Halsall, Department of History, Birkbeck College, London, UK
Dr. Chris Scarre, The MacDonald Institute, Cambridge, UK
H. P. Willmott, Royal Military Academy, Sandhurst, UK

NORTH AMERICA

Professor Donald S. Frazier, Department of History, McMurray University, Texas, USA
Professor Ross Hassig, Department of Anthropology, Oklahoma State University, USA
Dr. Kendrick Oliver, Department of History, University of Southampton, UK
Professor George Raudzens, Department of History, Macquarie University, Sydney, Australia
Dr. Brian Ward, Department of History, University of Florida, USA

SOUTH AMERICA

Dr. Edwin F. Early, Department of Economics, University of Plymouth, UK
Dr. Anthony McFarlane, Department of History, University of Warwick, UK
D.r Nicholas James, Cambridge, UK
Professor Neil Whitehead, Department of Anthropology, University of Wisconsin, USA

AFRICA

Professor John Thornton, Department of History, Millersville University, USA

EUROPE

Professor Richard Britnell, Department of History, University of Durham, UK
Dr. Michael Broers, School of History, University of Leeds, UK
Professor Brian Davies, Department of History, University of Texas, USA

EUROPE (continued)

Professor Michael Jones, Department of History, University of Nottingham, UK
Dr. Don McRaild, Department of History, University of Sunderland
Dr. Susan Rose, Department of History, Roehampton Institute, London, UK
Professor Peter Waldron, Department of History, University of Sunderland, UK
Dr. Peter Wilson, Department of History, University of Sunderland, UK
Professor Spencer Tucker, Department of History, Virginia Military Institute, USA
Professor Edward M. Yates, Department of Geography, King's College, London, UK

WEST ASIA

Dr. Ahron Bregman, Webster University, Regent's College, London, UK
Professor Ian Netton, School of Arabic Studies, University of Leeds, UK
Sajjad Rizvi, Department of Oriental Studies, Cambridge University, UK

SOUTH AND SOUTHEAST ASIA

Professor Joseph E. Schwartzberg, Department of Geography, University of Minnesota, USA
Dr. Sunil Kumar, Department of Medieval History, University of New Delhi, India

NORTH AND EAST ASIA

Professor Gina Barnes, Department of East Asian Studies, University of Durham, UK

AUSTRALASIA AND OCEANIA

Dr. Steven Roger Fischer, Institute of Polynesian Languages and Literatures, Auckland, New Zealand

The publishers would like to acknowledge additional contributions and advice from the following people: Professor Richard Overy, Professor Geoffrey Parker, Gordon Marsden, Professor Kenneth Kiple, Paul Keeler.

DORLING KINDERSLEY CARTOGRAPHY

EDITOR-IN-CHIEF Andrew Heritage

MANAGING EDITOR Lisa Thomas

SENIOR EDITOR Ferdie McDonald

PROJECT EDITORS Margaret Hynes, Elizabeth Wyse, Ailsa Heritage, Caroline Chapman, Debra Clapson, Wim Jenkins

US EDITOR Chuck Wills

ADDITIONAL EDITORIAL ASSISTANCE Louise Keane, Adele Rackley, Sam Atkinson

SENIOR MANAGING ART EDITOR Philip Lord

PRINCIPAL DESIGNER Nicola Liddiard

PROJECT ART EDITORS Rhonda Fisher, Carol Ann Davis, Karen Gregory

CARTOGRAPHIC MANAGER David Roberts

SENIOR CARTOGRAPHIC EDITOR Roger Bullen

CARTOGRAPHIC DESIGN John Plumer

DIGITAL MAPS CREATED BY Rob Stokes

PROJECT CARTOGRAPHERS Pamela Alford, James Anderson, Dale Buckton, Tony Chambers, Jan Clark, Tom Coulson, Martin Darlison, Jeremy Hepworth, Chris Jackson, Julia Lunn, John Plumer, Alka Ranger, Ann Stephenson, Julie Turner, Peter Winfield

ADDITIONAL CARTOGRAPHY Advanced Illustration Ltd., Arcadia Ltd., Lovell Johns Ltd.

HISTORICAL CARTOGRAPHIC CONSULTANT András Bereznay

PICTURE RESEARCH Deborah Pownall, Louise Thomas

INDEXING Julia Lynch, Janet Smy, Jo Russ, Sophie Park, Ruth Duxbury, Zoë Ellinson

DATABASE CONSULTANT Simon Lewis

SYSTEMS MANAGER Philip Rowles

PRODUCTION David Proffit

Picture information: *p.1* Andreas Cellarius, rector of the Latin school at Hoorn in northern Holland, produced this map of the eastern hemisphere in 1708 as part of his exquisite atlas of the heavens, *Atlas Coelestis; seu Harmonia Macrocosmica*. The map illustrates the seasons of the year and the various climate zones from pole to pole. *pp.2–3* Produced in 1646, by Matthaüs Merian, a Swiss engraver. The geography in the map is based on world maps using the influential Mercator projection, produced by the Dutch Blaeu family, a dynasty of master cartographers. *p.5* This 1598 Dutch engraving shows a cartographer at work, probably Rogerius Bullenius.

INTRODUCTION

WE SEE OURSELVES in the mirror of the past, and in this mirror we see how
we have created our world, and where we have come from. The *DK Atlas of
World History* offers a history of the world relevant as we start a new Millennium
and as we look back to consider how we have got here.

An international team of experts was assembled and
given the task of producing an atlas that would make
sense for all parts of the world. Unlike other works
of this type, we have sought to avoid a Eurocentric
approach to history. To achieve this, we have combined
a comprehensive global overview of world history
in Part One, with more detailed narratives of the
development of each of the world's regions in Part Two.

This is not the only new feature of this atlas. Again,
unlike most historical atlases, this is a work that puts
maps first. This is not simply a book with maps, but
represents an integrated cartographic approach. The maps
have been created using the most modern techniques
and accurate digital data, drawing on the established
state-of-the-art skills of Dorling Kindersley as innovative
map publishers. In addition, the atlas includes numerous
examples of historical maps, setting past views of the
world in contrast with modern knowledge.

The atlas is structured so that readers can look at
history from a number of different angles: global,
thematic, regional, and chronological. This offers a rich
variety of approaches which allows the reader to form
a comprehensive picture of the past.

The inclusion of past maps, both European and non-
European, is valuable, as it reminds us that there are, and
have been, many different ways of describing the world.
Ours is not the only way to consider space, place, and
the world.

The pages in this atlas are portraits of an alien world.
A range of devices has been used to relate this lost realm
to our own: the distribution of sites and cultures, political
borders and structures, areas of cultural influence and
political control, with arrows indicating the movements

of peoples and the spread of technologies and ideas.
Frequently, explanatory annotations have been added to
the maps. Beyond the maps themselves, each page offers
texts, chronological timelines, and carefully chosen
pictures to built up as complete an impression of each
period or historical episode as possible. This is not
intended as a visual dictionary of dates – dates merely
provide the historian with a skeletal framework, signposts
on the journey into the past. *The DK Atlas of World
History* is, rather, about geography and about the
continuous processes of change.

Change through time is multifaceted: political and
economic, demographic and social, cultural and
ecological. This atlas attempts to cover all these features,
although the extent to which historical developments
can be mapped varies, with to the quality and nature of
the sources and research available. Yet, benefiting from
a wide range of talent, this atlas pushes forward the
geography of the past as never before. It includes maps
of familiar episodes from history and many more never
previously described in cartographic form.

Mapping episodes through time demands dynamic
narrative tools. The digital mapmaking techniques used
in this atlas make it possible to offer exciting and
informative perspectives and projections. The earth can
be seen from any viewpoint, creating explanatory yet
accurate formats for the visualization of historical stories.
The rigid orthodoxy of the north-oriented map is, after
all, a relatively recent – and European – invention.

This atlas is produced with an awareness of the
relationship between geography and history. It is up-to-
date and of its time, not an atlas for all time, but the best
possible at the start of the new Millennium.

Jeremy Black, June 1999

CONTENTS

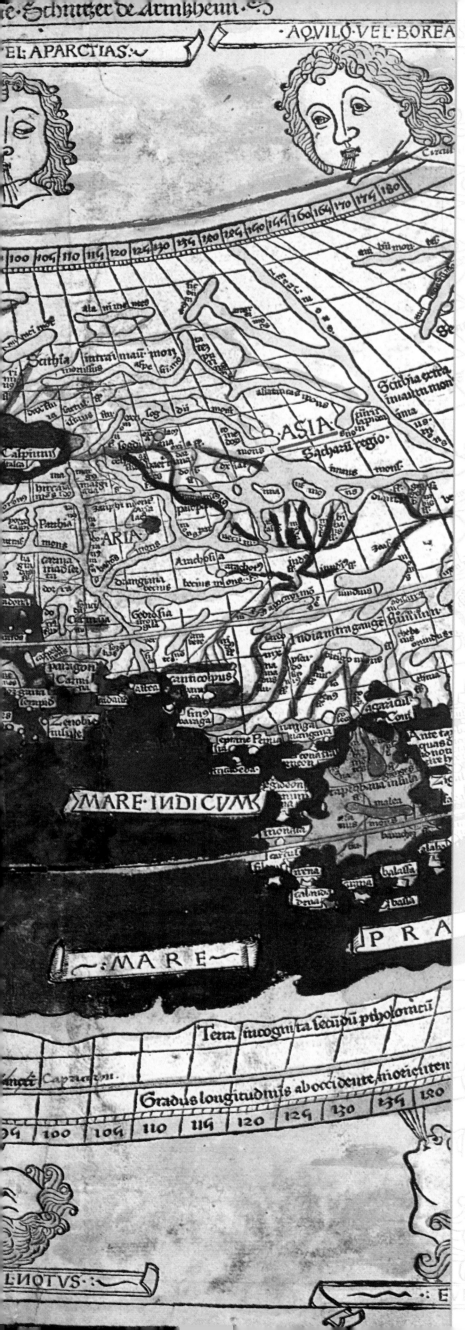

PART ONE

ERAS OF WORLD HISTORY

GLOBAL CITIZENS at the beginning of the 3rd millennium are uniquely able to regard their world both as a totality and as a sum of its constituent parts. The first section of this Atlas presents history on a global basis, comprising a series of chronological overviews of the world across the last twenty millennia. These maps portray the changing map of the world and its cultures from ancient times down to the present day, accompanied by summaries of regional developments. Features highlighting the main technological advances of the period are complemented by maps or views of the world produced at the time. Each overview is followed by pages which examine aspects of the changing global scene – political, economic, religious, or demographic – which had a global impact during that period.

The Greek polymath Ptolemy wrote his famous *Guide to Geography* in the 2nd century CE, and his conclusions about the map of the world held sway until the 16th century. This woodcut map of the Ptolemaic world – incorporating Africa, Europe, and Asia – was published in 1486.

THE EARLY HISTORY OF HUMANITY

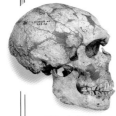

This skull comes from the Neanderthal burial site at La Ferrassie, southwest France.

THE AUSTRALOPITHECINES, OR SOUTHERN APES, which emerged in Africa c.4 million years ago, possessed many apelike characteristics, but crucially had evolved the ability to walk upright. The oldest of these species, *Australopithecus afarensis*, which is represented by the find of a skeleton of a small adult female, known as "Lucy," from the Hadar region of Ethiopia, may be ancestral to the earliest species of *Homo* (man), which emerged some 2.5 million years ago. The increased brain capacity of *Homo* was matched by the ability to make tools and control fire, vital cultural developments which enabled human ancestors to exploit a wide range of foods and colonize marginal environments. Fully modern humans, distinguished by their refined tool-making skills, resourcefulness, and ingenuity, were able to withstand the ravages of the last Ice Age and reach the most remote corners of the globe.

Neanderthals

The Neanderthals, a separate and distinct branch of the *Homo* genus, evolved in Europe and West Asia about 120,000 years ago, surviving until up to 35,000 years ago. They had powerful heavy skeletons, with a projecting jaw, and broad nose and brow ridge, and their brains were the same size as those of fully modern humans. They adapted to a wide range of habitats and harsh climates. Neanderthal burials are clear evidence that they had developed cultural rituals.

The Neanderthal burial at Kebana in Israel is c.60,000 years old. The discovery of burials, often with items intended to equip the deceased for the afterlife, led to a revision of the view that Neanderthals were both brutal and primitive.

Human ancestors

The genus *Australopithecus* evolved in eastern and southern Africa between 4 and 1.7 million years ago. Australopithecines were small and sturdy, with apelike bodies, but they had mastered bipedalism, as finds of fossilized footprints, at least 4 million years old, from Laetolil in Tanzania testify. Four major Australopithecine species, classified by variations in their skulls and teeth, have been identified. The earliest known fossils of the *Homo* genus date to 2.5 million years ago. They are distinguished by larger brain size, rounded skulls, and a distinctively human formation to the hips and pelvis.

The virtually complete skeleton of a fully mature adult female, known as "Lucy," found at Hadar in Ethiopia, is c.3.4 million years old and belongs to the oldest known species of Australopithecines.

Prehistoric technology

The first crucial development in the history of early technology was the appearance, about 1.3 million years ago, of stone handaxes, used for butchering hides, cutting wood, and preparing plant foods. Around 100,000 years ago, stone tools, shaped by striking flakes from the core, started to be made. Composite tools, where points, blades and scrapers were mounted in wooden or bone hafts developed c.45,000 years ago.

Recent discoveries of a new australopithecine (A. bahrelchazali) stretch the geographical range 2,350 miles west of Great Rift Valley

Hadar Find site of "Lucy," skeleton of an adult female *Australopithecus afarensis*, dated to c.3.4 million years ago

Limited remains of first hominid *Australopithecus anamensis* dating to c.4.2 million years ago

First finds of *Australopithecus boisei* c.2.7–1.7 million years ago

1 Hominid ancestors

Australopithecus remains
◇ afarensis
◇ africanus
◇ boisei
◇ robustus

The skull of the "Taung child," is c.2.5 million years old. It was discovered in 1924 and revolutionized theories about human evolution.

Stone handaxes, such as these examples from Hoxne in eastern England dating to at least 100,000 years ago, were made by chipping away flakes to create a sharp cutting edge. They became standard implements throughout Africa, Asia, and Europe.

The evolution of hominids

Hominid evolution is still a matter of dispute. The australopithecines, the earliest hominids, evolved some 4 million years ago. The oldest species (*Australopithecus afarensis*) may be ancestral to the earliest species of *Homo*, the precursors of modern humans, which evolved some 2.5 million years ago. Alternatively, *Homo* may have evolved separately.

By around 30,000 years ago, tools and weapons had become infinitely more sophisticated, adapted both the environment and methods of hunting, as demonstrated by the detailed carving and attention to function on these bone spearheads.

Human evolution

c.4.2 million years ago: *Australopithecus anamensis*: limited remains of bipedal hominid found on shores of Lake Rudolf	c.3 million years ago: *Australopithecus africanus*: notable for powerful build of upper body	c.2.5 million years ago: *Homo habilis*: large brain in relation to body size. Average male height, 1.32 m	c.2 million years ago: *Australopithecus robustus*: hand bones indicate anatomical ability to make stone tools	c.1 million years ago: Earliest evidence of the use of fire	c.900,000 years ago: Earliest evidence of hominids in Asia	c.120,000 years ago: Neanderthals: short-limbed, thick-bodied. Average male height, 1.65 m	c.35,000 years ago: First fully modern humans in Europe; disappearance of Neanderthals

4,000,000 BP — 3,000,000 BP — 2,000,000 BP — 1,000,000 BP — present

c.3.8 million years ago: *Australopithecus afarensis*: based on find of "Lucy" skeleton at Hadar, Ethiopia. Average male height, 1.5 m	c.2.6 million years ago: *Australopithecus boisei* with massive chewing muscles. Earliest finds of stone stools.	c.1.8 million years ago: *Homo erectus*: distinguished by long limbs. Average male height, 1.77 m	c.850,000 years ago: Hominids reach Europe from Africa	c.800,000 years ago: Archaic *Homo sapiens*; Average male height, 1.75 m	c.100,000 years ago: *Homo sapiens* (anatomically modern humans); earliest evidence in Africa

The emergence of modern humans

The first representative of the *Homo* genus, *Homo habilis* ("handy man"), emerged about 2.5 million years ago and was distinguished by the ability to make and use tools. *Homo erectus*, which appeared about 1.7 million years ago, had a still larger brain capacity, tall, long-legged physique and ability to walk fully upright, and adapted successfully to a wide range of environments, spreading from Africa to Asia and Europe over the next million years. The earliest fossil remains of fully modern humans, *Homo sapiens sapiens,* found in Africa, date to c.100,000 years ago. Resourceful and inventive, modern humans colonized the most marginal regions, and became the sole surviving human species.

Fossils of *Homo habilis* were discovered in the Olduvai Gorge in the 1960s, and are dated to 2.5 million years ago.

The fossils found at Koobi Fora in Kenya, dating to 1.7 million years ago, are amongst the earliest finds of *Homo erectus*, and clearly demonstrate a marked increase in brain size.

Modern humans reached Europe from Africa c.35,000 years ago, and replaced the Neanderthal population. This skull was found at the site of Predmosti in eastern Europe.

SEE ALSO:

North America: pp.120–121

South America: pp.142–143

Africa: pp.160–161

Europe: pp.174–175

West Asia: pp.220–221

South and Southeast Asia: pp.240–241

North and East Asia: pp.258–259

Australasia and Oceania: pp.278–279

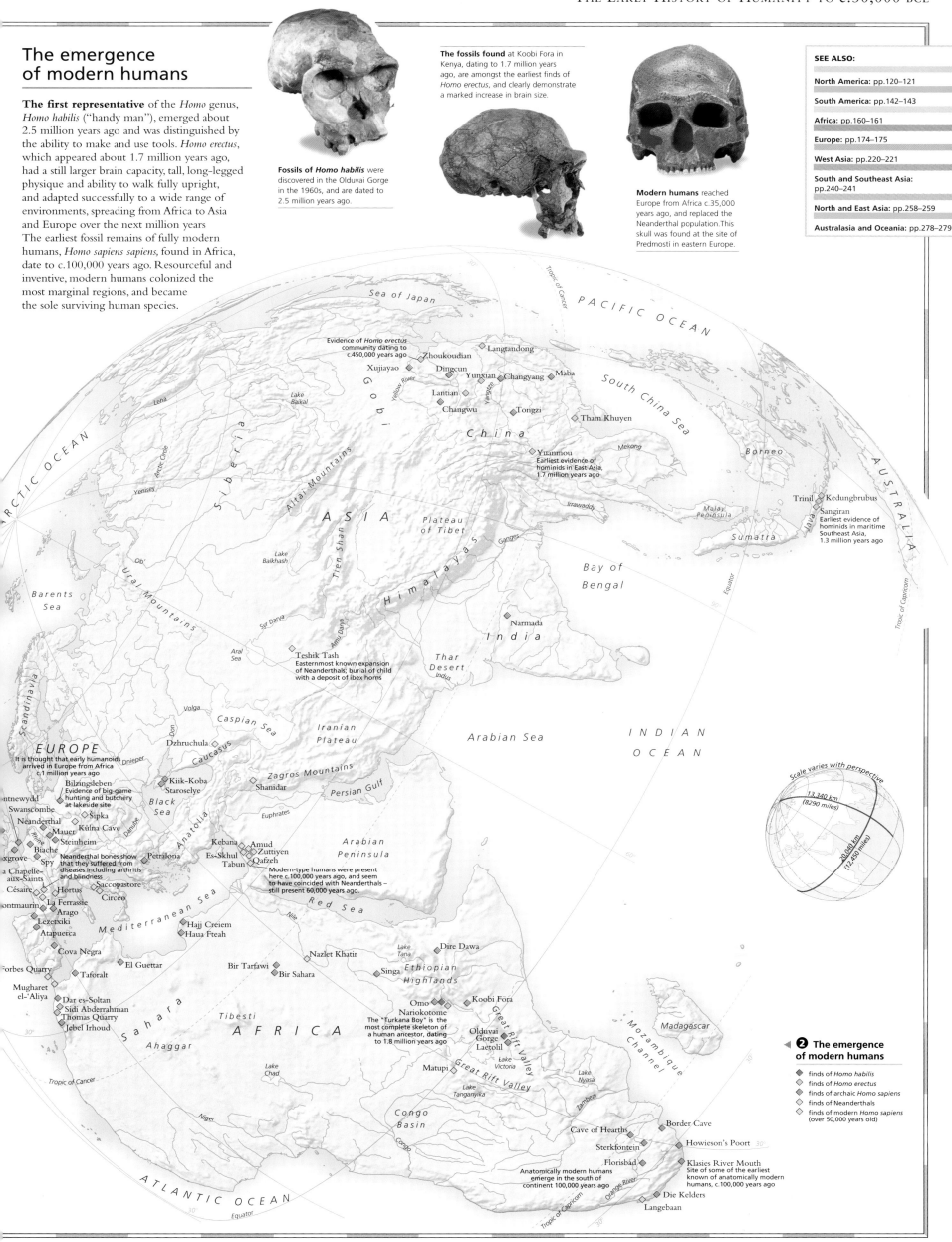

2 The emergence of modern humans

- ◆ finds of *Homo habilis*
- ◆ finds of *Homo erectus*
- ◆ finds of archaic *Homo sapiens*
- ◇ finds of Neanderthals
- ◇ finds of modern *Homo sapiens* (over 50,000 years old)

Evidence of Homo erectus community dating to c.450,000 years ago

Yuanmou Earliest evidence of hominids in East Asia, 1.7 million years ago

Sangiran Earliest evidence of hominids in maritime Southeast Asia, 1.3 million years ago

Teshik Tash Easternmost known expansion of Neanderthals; burial of child with a deposit of ibex horns

EUROPE It is thought that early humanoids arrived in Europe from Africa c.1 million years ago

Bilzingsleben Evidence of big-game hunting and butchery at lakeside site

Neanderthal bones show that they suffered from diseases including arthritis and blindness

Modern-type humans were present here c.100,000 years ago, and seem to have coincided with Neanderthals – still present 60,000 years ago

Nariokotome The "Turkana Boy" is the most complete skeleton of a human ancestor, dating to 1.8 million years ago

Anatomically modern humans emerge in the south of continent 100,000 years ago

Klasies River Mouth Site of some of the earliest known of anatomically modern humans, c.100,000 years ago

Scale varies with perspective
13,340 km (8290 miles)
20,040 km (12,450 miles)

THE WORLD FROM PREHISTORY TO 10,000 BCE

FULLY MODERN HUMANS evolved in Africa between 200,000 and 100,000 years ago. With their tool-making skills and abilities to communicate and organize themselves into groups, these early hunter-gatherers were uniquely well-equipped to explore and settle new environments. By 30,000 years ago, they had colonized much of the globe. When the last Ice Age reached its peak 20,000 years ago, they were forced to adapt; they refined their tool technology, enabling them to fully exploit the depleted resources, and used sturdy shelters and warm clothing to survive the harsh conditions. As the temperatures rose and the ice sheets retreated, plants and animals became more abundant and new areas were settled. By 9000 BCE larger populations and intense hunting had contributed to the near-extinction of large mammals, such as mastodons and mammoths. In the Near East, groups of hunter-gatherers were living in permanent settlements, harvesting wild cereals and experimenting with the domestication of local animals. The transition to agriculture was under way.

MESOLITHIC MAN AND THE ENVIRONMENT

Mesolithic peoples, whether semi-settled in one location or constantly on the move in search of food, would have carried a detailed mental map of important local landmarks. Precious water or food sources may have become centers of cultic activity, as in the rock painting below. Though its meaning is far from clear, the wavy vertical lines seem to represent cascades of water. The painting may even be a representation of a specific sacred site.

This painting discovered at Kalhotia in Central India seems to show a lizard or crocodile, cascades, a stream, and people carrying bundles of stone-tipped arrows.

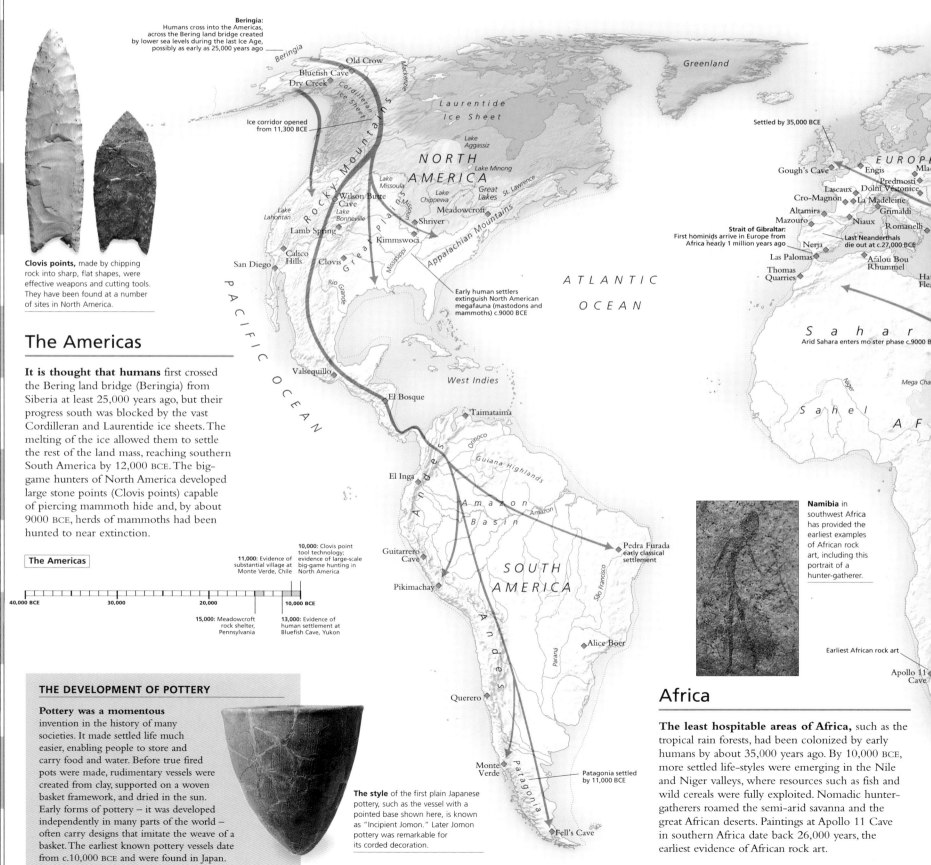

Clovis points, made by chipping rock into sharp, flat shapes, were effective weapons and cutting tools. They have been found at a number of sites in North America.

The Americas

It is thought that humans first crossed the Bering land bridge (Beringia) from Siberia at least 25,000 years ago, but their progress south was blocked by the vast Cordilleran and Laurentide ice sheets. The melting of the ice allowed them to settle the rest of the land mass, reaching southern South America by 12,000 BCE. The big-game hunters of North America developed large stone points (Clovis points) capable of piercing mammoth hide and, by about 9000 BCE, herds of mammoths had been hunted to near extinction.

The Americas

40,000 BCE — 30,000 — 20,000 — 10,000 BCE

10,000: Clovis point tool technology; evidence of large-scale big-game hunting in North America

11,000: Evidence of substantial village at Monte Verde, Chile

15,000: Meadowcroft rock shelter, Pennsylvania

13,000: Evidence of human settlement at Bluefish Cave, Yukon

Map labels

Beringia: Humans cross into the Americas, across the Bering land bridge created by lower sea levels during the last Ice Age, possibly as early as 25,000 years ago

Ice corridor opened from 11,300 BCE

Old Crow
Bluefish Cave
Dry Creek
Mackenzie
Greenland
Laurentide Ice Sheet
Cordilleran Ice Sheet
Rocky Mountains
Lake Aggassiz
Lake Minong
NORTH AMERICA
Lake Missoula
Lake Chippewa
Great Lakes
St. Lawrence
Wilson Butte Cave
Meadowcroft
Lake Lahontan
Lake Bonneville
Shriver
Lamb Spring
Kimmswoci
Appalachian Mountains
Calico Hills
Clovis
San Diego
Great Plains
Missouri
Mississippi
Rio Grande
Early human settlers extinguish North American megafauna (mastodons and mammoths) c.9000 BCE
PACIFIC OCEAN
ATLANTIC OCEAN
Valsequillo
West Indies
El Bosque
Taimataima
EUROPE
Settled by 35,000 BCE
Gough's Cave
Engis
Mla
Lascaux
Predmosti
Dolní Vestonice
Cro-Magnon
La Madeleine
Altamira
Mazouro
Grimaldi
Niaux
Romanelli
Strait of Gibraltar: First hominids arrive in Europe from Africa nearly 1 million years ago
Last Neanderthals die out at c.27,000 BCE
Nerja
Las Palomas
Afalou Bou Rhummel
Thomas Quarries
Ha
Fle
Sahara
Arid Sahara enters moister phase c.9000 B
Mega Cha
Niger
Sahel
AF
Orinoco
Guiana Highlands
El Inga
Andes
Amazon Basin
Amazon
Guitarrero Cave
Pedra Furada early classical settlement
SOUTH AMERICA
São Francisco
Pikimachay
Namibia in southwest Africa has provided the earliest examples of African rock art, including this portrait of a hunter-gatherer.
Alice Boer
Paraná
Earliest African rock art
Apollo 11 Cave
Quereo
Monte Verde
Patagonia settled by 11,000 BCE
Patagonia
Fell's Cave

THE DEVELOPMENT OF POTTERY

Pottery was a momentous invention in the history of many societies. It made settled life much easier, enabling people to store and carry food and water. Before true fired pots were made, rudimentary vessels were created from clay, supported on a woven basket framework, and dried in the sun. Early forms of pottery – it was developed independently in many parts of the world – often carry designs that imitate the weave of a basket. The earliest known pottery vessels date from c.10,000 BCE and were found in Japan.

The style of the first plain Japanese pottery, such as the vessel with a pointed base shown here, is known as "Incipient Jomon." Later Jomon pottery was remarkable for its corded decoration.

Africa

The least hospitable areas of Africa, such as the tropical rain forests, had been colonized by early humans by about 35,000 years ago. By 10,000 BCE, more settled life-styles were emerging in the Nile and Niger valleys, where resources such as fish and wild cereals were fully exploited. Nomadic hunter-gatherers roamed the semi-arid savanna and the great African deserts. Paintings at Apollo 11 Cave in southern Africa date back 26,000 years, the earliest evidence of African rock art.

Portable art objects – sculptures and engravings of animals, like these reindeer, on bone and antler, or small stone slabs or plaques – were being produced in Europe by 25,000 years ago.

Europe

Settled by modern humans by about 35,000 BCE, Ice Age conditions over much of Europe tested their ingenuity; wood, bone, hide, and antler were all used to build a range of shelters, and new tools – bows and arrows, spear throwers, and harpoons – were used to hunt big game. As the climate stabilized, some sites were occupied year-round, while others were used by seasonal hunters.

West Asia

The world's earliest known burial, at Qafzeh Cave in Israel, dates back 100,000 years and is evidence that complex forms of social organization had already begun to evolve in this region. By 13,000 BCE people from Wadi en-Natuf, also in Israel, were intensively harvesting, grinding, and storing the abundant wild grains which grew there. It was in this region that agriculture was soon to develop.

This bone and shell necklace was one of the personal items found at a burial in Mugharet el-Kebara in Israel.

SEE ALSO:

North America: pp.118–119

South America: pp.144–145

Africa: pp.158–159

Europe: pp.174–175

West Asia: pp.220–221

South and Southeast Asia: pp.240–241

North and East Asia: pp.258–259

Australasia and Oceania: pp.280–281

Europe

35,000: Fully modern humans settle continent. Extinction of Neanderthals. New tool technology

10,000: Retreat of glaciers; temperate deciduous woodland spreads northward. Rich array of marine and land resources

110,000 BCE   90,000   70,000   50,000   30,000   10,000 BCE

120,000: Neanderthals present from western Europe to Central Asia

10,000: Large mammals, such as woolly rhinoceros, giant deer, and mammoth gradually become extinct

West and South Asia

100,000: World's first known burial at Qafzeh Cave, Israel

40,000: Neanderthals still present alongside modern humans in southwest Asia

13,000: Intensive harvesting of wild cereals by Natufian people, Israel

11,000: Dogs domesticated in Middle East; the world's first domesticated animals

110,000 BCE   90,000   70,000   50,000   30,000   10,000 BCE

45,000: Aurignacian flint tool technology developed in Israel and spreads across southern Europe

17,000: Evidence of wild cereal gathering in the Middle East

12,000: First use of grindstones in Middle East

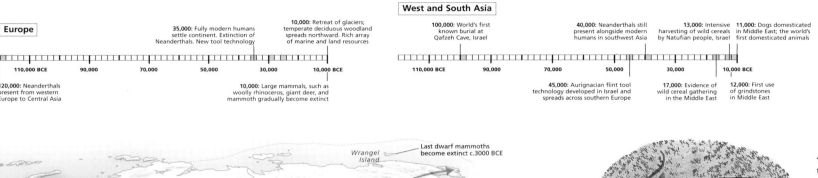

Last dwarf mammoths become extinct c.3000 BCE

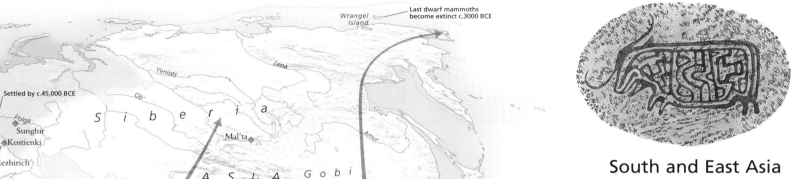

The paintings in the rock shelters at Bhimbetka in Central India date from c.10,000 BCE. They include this remarkable buffalo, shown here in an artist's rendition.

South and East Asia

At the end of the last Ice Age sea levels rose, and an abundance of plants, animals, and seafood proliferated. Seafood played a very important part in the Asian diet at this time, and many hunter-gatherer groups settled around coasts and estuaries. The Jomon people exploited the summer fish stocks of Honshu island in Japan, and, in about 10,000 BCE, were the first people in the world to make pottery.

East Asia

90,000: First evidence for modern humans

40,000: First stone tools, of chert, made in island Southeast Asia

11,000: Earliest portable art in China – engraved antler found in Longyn Cave

110,000 BCE   90,000   70,000   50,000   30,000   10,000 BCE

60,000: Fully modern humans established throughout Southeast Asia

10,000: Earliest known pottery vessels in the world, from Honshu, Japan

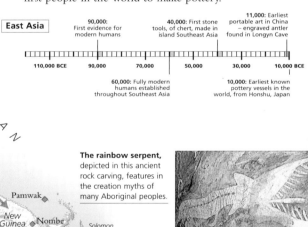

The rainbow serpent, depicted in this ancient rock carving, features in the creation myths of many Aboriginal peoples.

Australasia

Early humans first reached Australia about 60,000 years ago. Although sea levels were low, Australia was not joined to Southeast Asia at this time, so the first settlers must have used boats to cross 60 km of open sea. Early sites were clustered along the coasts and rivers but rising sea levels at the end of the last Ice Age forced settlers inland.

The spread of modern humans

→ possible colonization route
◆ major site 50,000–12,000 BCE
extent of ice sheet 18,000 BCE
extent of ice sheet 10,000 BCE
coastline 18,000 BCE
ancient river
ancient lake

Africa

70,000: Evidence of burials at site of Klasies River Mouth, southern Africa

30,000: New tool technology; development of microliths

26,000: Painted rock slabs at Apollo 11 Cave, Namibia

110,000 BCE   90,000   70,000   50,000   30,000   10,000 BCE

100,000: Earliest evidence of modern humans in eastern and southern Africa

42,000: Red ocher being mined from Lion Cave, southern Africa; probably used for body decoration

20,000: Terra-cotta figurines from Algeria. Engraved objects from Border Cave, South Africa

45,000: World's first known rock art, from Panaramitee, South Australia

16,000: Extinction of giant marsupials caused by changing climate

110,000 BCE   90,000   70,000   50,000   30,000   10,000 BCE

Australasia

60,000: Settlement of Australia by groups from Southeast Asia

20,000: Settlement extends to southern coast of Tasmania

Settled by c.45,000 BCE

First evidence of human burials

Olduvai Gorge: Site of first discoveries of *Australopithecus boisei* and *Homo habilis*, dating from c.2.5 million years ago

Migration of early modern humans begins c.150,000 years ago

Southern Africa: From c.120,000 years ago, early hominids colonize more marginal areas of Africa

First settled c.60,000 BCE

East Asia: Earliest evidence for hominid colonization dates to c.1.7 million years ago

Earliest settlers c.40,000 BCE

Earliest evidence of use of boats

Australia: Fully modern humans colonize Australia from Southeast Asia, from c.60,000 years ago; they utilize land bridges created by lowered sea levels during last Ice Age

Earliest evidence of human cremation c.26,000 BCE

Labels on map: Wrangel Island, Lena, Yenisey, Ob, Siberia, Volga, Sunghir, Pushkari, Kostienki, Mezhirich, Black Sea Lake, Caspian Sea, Aral Sea, ASIA, Gobi, Mal'ta, Amur, Yellow River, Zhoukoudian, Japan, Honshu, Hoshino, Fukui, Yangtze, Lake Konya, Shanidar, Tigris, Euphrates, Himalayas, Yuanmou, Ganges, Indus, Maba, Nazlet Khatir, Nile, Arabian Peninsula, India, Bhimbetka, Patne, Mekong, PACIFIC OCEAN, Philippine Islands, Lake Galla, Tabon Cave, Sunda, Niah Cave, Borneo, Pamwak, Sumatra, New Guinea, Nombe, Solomon Islands, Java, Kosipe, Sahul, Lake Carpentaria, Olduvai Gorge, Kisese, Lake Victoria, Great Rift Valley, INDIAN OCEAN, Madagascar, Lake Makgadikgadi, Koolan, Cuckadoo, Puritjarra, Kenniff Cave, Australia, Koonalda Cave, Lake Nawait, Panaramitee, Lake Mungo, Darling, Arumvale, Keilor, Kow Swamp, Lion Cave, Border Cave, Klasies River Mouth, Kahari Desert, Tasmania, New Zealand, Beginner's Luck Cave, Bone Cave

15

THE SETTLING OF THE GLOBE

This figure of a mammoth, carved from an animal's shoulder bone, dates from the last Ice Age.

THE MELTING OF THE GLACIERS at the end of the last Ice Age radically transformed the global environment; as the climate changed, with warmer temperatures and increased rainfall, food sources became more abundant and diverse, and populations increased. Hunters and gatherers could use the technological and survival skills acquired during the Ice Age to colonize new areas and adapt to more plentiful food supplies. In many regions, hunters began to live together in larger, more sedentary communities, working cooperatively and evolving more specialized roles within the group. Rituals and symbols were used to reinforce group identity – the beginnings of truly modern behavior.

Survival strategies

The rapidly changing environments of the postglacial world required a wide range of adaptations. In some regions, such as eastern Europe and North America, plentiful supplies of big game meant that hunters could depend on a specialized diet of mammoth, mastodon, or bison. In other regions, such as the fertile river valleys of the Middle East and North Africa, wild cereals – the ancestors of cultivated grains – were harvested. In Europe, a varied diet encompassed game, edible plants, and fish and shellfish, evidenced by deposits of discarded shells, or middens. Climate and local resources influenced the building of shelters; a wide range of materials was used, from mud and stone to timber and hides. Some shelters were portable, used by hunters following migrating herds; in other areas plentiful food supplies meant that permanent villages could be built.

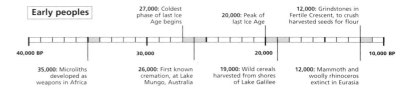

Early peoples			
	27,000: Coldest phase of last Ice Age begins	20,000: Peak of last Ice Age	12,000: Grindstones in Fertile Crescent, to crush harvested seeds for flour
40,000 BP	30,000	20,000	10,000 BP
35,000: Microliths developed as weapons in Africa	26,000: First known cremation, at Lake Mungo, Australia	19,000: Wild cereals harvested from shores of Lake Galilee	12,000: Mammoth and woolly rhinoceros extinct in Eurasia

Ukraine

On the treeless, windswept steppes of the Ukraine, mammoth-hunters, lacking wood, used the remains of their prey to build shelters. They constructed the walls from mammoth bones, which were then covered with animal hides, anchored down in high winds by heavy mammoth jawbones.

Israel

The El Wad cave on the eastern Mediterranean coast was used as a shelter by hunters stalking fallow deer in the nearby hills. The site may have been used during the summer months. The cave has been occupied many times in the past 100,000 years.

France

At Pincevent, in the Seine Valley, hunters following migrating herds of reindeer camped from midsummer to midwinter in portable tents, made of wooden poles covered by animal skins.

❶ **Different ways of life c.10,000 BCE**

uninhabited and/or marginally inhabited areas

◇ early settlement site

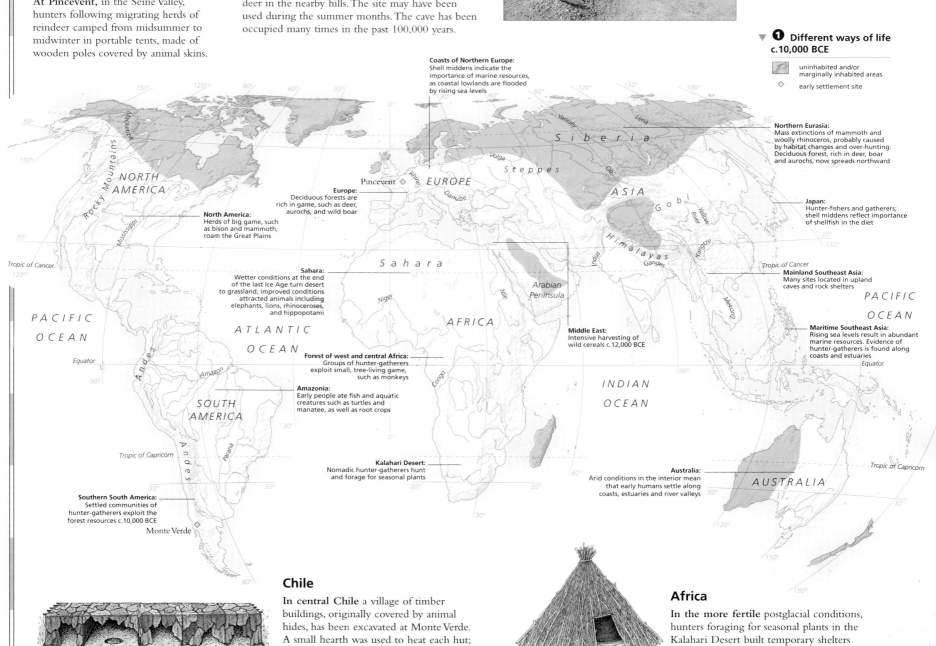

Coasts of Northern Europe: Shell middens indicate the importance of marine resources, as coastal lowlands are flooded by rising sea levels

Northern Eurasia: Mass extinctions of mammoth and woolly rhinoceros, probably caused by habitat changes and over-hunting. Deciduous forest, rich in deer, boar and aurochs, now spreads northward

Europe: Deciduous forests are rich in game, such as deer, aurochs, and wild boar

Japan: Hunter-fishers and gatherers; shell middens reflect importance of shellfish in the diet

North America: Herds of big game, such as bison and mammoth, roam the Great Plains

Mainland Southeast Asia: Many sites located in upland caves and rock shelters

Sahara: Wetter conditions at the end of the last Ice Age turn desert to grassland; improved conditions attracted animals including elephants, lions, rhinoceroses, and hippopotami

Middle East: Intensive harvesting of wild cereals c.12,000 BCE

Maritime Southeast Asia: Rising sea levels result in abundant marine resources. Evidence of hunter-gatherers is found along coasts and estuaries

Forest of west and central Africa: Groups of hunter-gatherers exploit small, tree-living game, such as monkeys

Amazonia: Early people ate fish and aquatic creatures such as turtles and manatee, as well as root crops

Kalahari Desert: Nomadic hunter-gatherers hunt and forage for seasonal plants

Australia: Arid conditions in the interior mean that early humans settle along coasts, estuaries and river valleys

Southern South America: Settled communities of hunter-gatherers exploit the forest resources c.10,000 BCE
Monte Verde

Chile

In central Chile a village of timber buildings, originally covered by animal hides, has been excavated at Monte Verde. A small hearth was used to heat each hut; communal hearths were used for cooking.

Africa

In the more fertile postglacial conditions, hunters foraging for seasonal plants in the Kalahari Desert built temporary shelters from brushwood branches.

Paleolithic art

The art of the last Ice Age and its aftermath, ranging from painted caves to engraved and finely carved objects and clay sculptures, is found in many parts of the world. Since much of this art is probably associated with religious rituals concerned with hunting, fertility, and the initiation of the young, it is a testament to the increasing complexity and sophistication of human society. One of the greatest flowerings of paleolithic art is undoubtedly the extraordinary painted caves of southwestern Europe, but there is evidence of a wide range of different regional artistic traditions, from the ocher-decorated rock shelters of Kisesse in East Africa to the rock art of Bhimbetka in South Asia, which dates to the coldest phase of the last Ice Age.

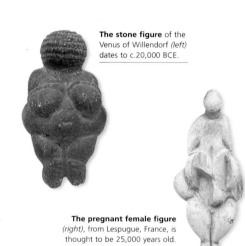

In the caves of southwest Europe, animals such as bison are depicted with grace and fluidity.

Hand stencils often dominate the part of the cave in which they are found. The red pigments could be made from either iron oxide or red ocher.

Hand paintings

Stencils of hands, made by blowing a spray of powdered pigment over the outstretched hand, are found on cave walls in both western Europe and Australia. The stencils may be associated with initiation rites – children's footprints have also been found in the European caves.

SEE ALSO:

North America: pp.116–117

South America: pp.140–141

Africa: pp.154–155

Europe: pp.170–171

West Asia: pp.216–217

South and Southeast Asia: pp.236–237

North and East Asia: pp.254–255

Australasia and Oceania: pp.276–277

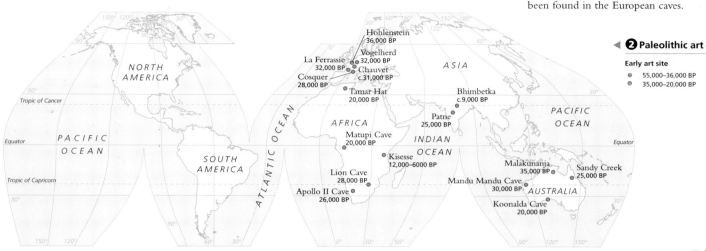

◀ **②** **Paleolithic art**

Early art site
- 55,000–36,000 BP
- 35,000–20,000 BP

Hohlenstein 36,000 BP
Vogelherd 32,000 BP
La Ferrassie 32,000 BP
Cosquer 28,000 BP
Chauvet c.31,000 BP
Tamar Hat 20,000 BP
Bhimbetka c.9,000 BP
Patne 25,000 BP
Matupi Cave 20,000 BP
Kisesse 12,000–6000 BP
Lion Cave 28,000 BP
Apollo II Cave 26,000 BP
Malakumanja 35,000 BP
Mandu Mandu Cave 30,000 BP
Sandy Creek 25,000 BP
Koonalda Cave 20,000 BP

European cave paintings

The caves of southwestern Europe, with their vibrant paintings of bison, deer, oxen, and horses, and bas-relief and clay sculptures, are unique. These images, often found in the darkest and most inaccessible parts of the caves, may have acted as forms of hunting magic or illustrated myths and traditions.

Portable art

Small plaques of engraved antler and bone, decorated ornaments of amber and ivory – including pendants and beads – and carved figurines of both animals and humans are found throughout Europe. Highly stylized female figurines *(right)* are possibly representations of the mother goddess, and may have been associated with fertility rituals.

The stone figure of the Venus of Willendorf *(left)* dates to c.20,000 BCE.

The pregnant female figure *(right)*, from Lespugue, France, is thought to be 25,000 years old. It is carved from mammoth ivory.

④ **Venus figurines in Europe** ▼

◇ important find of Venus figurines

▼ **❸** **Painted caves and rock art**

◇ important rock art site

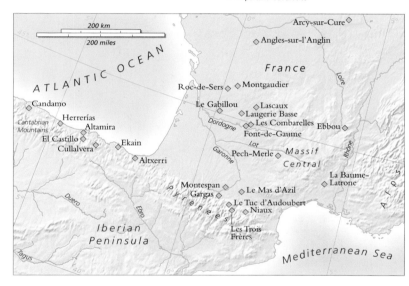

Australia

The oldest rock engravings in the world, from Panaramitee, date to 45,000 BCE. Australian rock paintings and engravings are widespread; most designs are abstract, using lines, dots, crescents, and spirals. Some are thought to represent kangaroo and bird tracks.

Some of the earliest examples of Aboriginal rock carvings or petroglyphs – here in the form of circles and stars – are found at Wilpena Sacred Canyon in southern Australia.

▲ **⑤** **Australian rock art**

◇ Panaramittee style rock engraving
▨ major rock art region

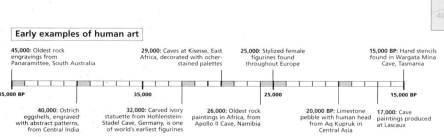

Early examples of human art

45,000: Oldest rock engravings from Panaramitee, South Australia
29,000: Caves at Kisesse, East Africa, decorated with ocher-stained palettes
25,000: Stylized female figurines found throughout Europe
15,000 BP: Hand stencils found in Wargata Mina Cave, Tasmania

45,000 BP — 35,000 — 25,000 — 15,000 BP

40,000: Ostrich eggshells, engraved with abstract patterns, from Central India
32,000: Carved ivory statuette from Hohlenstein-Stadel Cave, Germany, is one of world's earliest figurines
26,000: Oldest rock paintings in Africa, from Apollo II Cave, Namibia
20,000 BP: Limestone pebble with human head from Aq Kupruk in Central Asia
17,000: Cave paintings produced at Lascaux

THE WORLD 10,000–5000 BCE

IN THE MORE HOSPITABLE CLIMATE and terrain of the post-glacial world, groups of hunter-gatherers began to experiment with the domestication of wild cereals and animals. By 7000 BCE, farming was the main means of subsistence in West Asia, although hunter-gathering remained the most common form of subsistence elsewhere. Over the next 5000 years farming became established independently in other areas. The impact of the agricultural revolution on early societies was immense. Farming could support much larger populations, so settlement sizes increased significantly. Larger communities generated new demands and possibilities, and a class of specialized craftsmen evolved. Trade in raw materials and manufactured goods increased contact between farming communities. Communal ventures, such as irrigation, encouraged cooperation. All these developments paved the way for the much larger cities and states which were soon to follow.

THE FIRST USE OF METAL

The discovery that metals can be isolated from ore-bearing rocks by heating appears to have been made independently in West Asia and southeastern Europe between 7000–5000 BCE. Copper, gold, and lead, all soft metals that melt at relatively low temperatures, were the first metals in use. In early copper-using societies, most copper objects were decorative items that denoted the status of the owner: tools made from the new material could not compete with those of flint and stone.

This horned bull fashioned from sheet gold is one of a pair from a rich set of grave goods unearthed at a cemetery in Varna, southeast Europe.

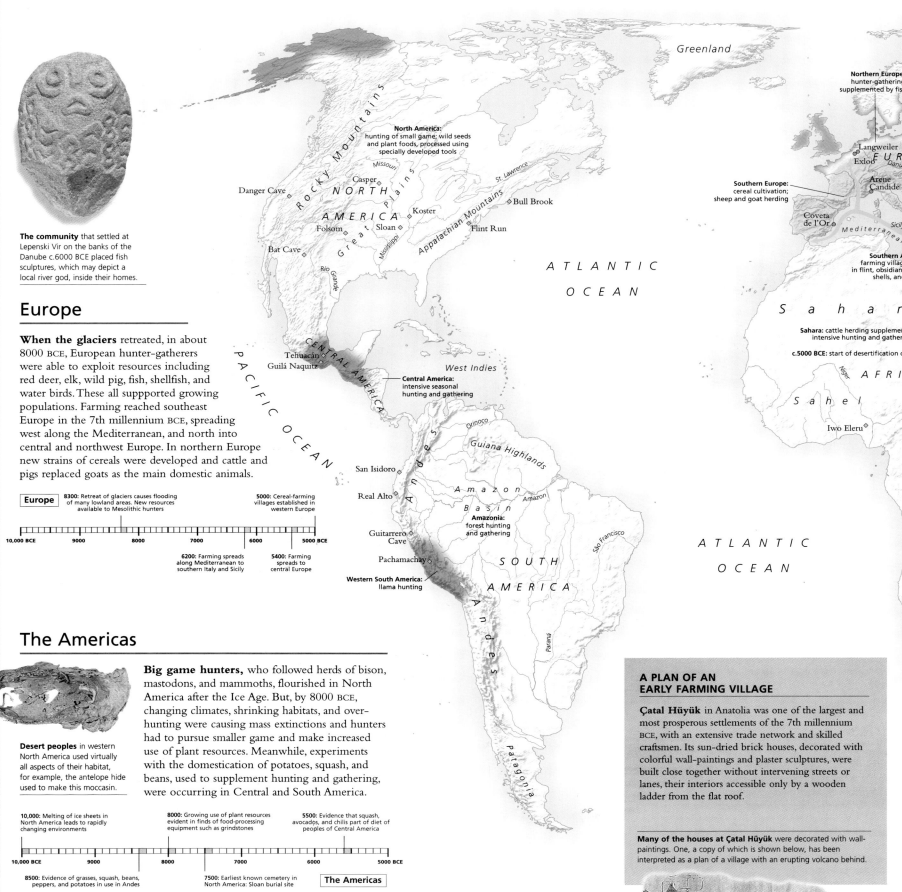

The community that settled at Lepenski Vir on the banks of the Danube c.6000 BCE placed fish sculptures, which may depict a local river god, inside their homes.

Europe

When the glaciers retreated, in about 8000 BCE, European hunter-gatherers were able to exploit resources including red deer, elk, wild pig, fish, shellfish, and water birds. These all supported growing populations. Farming reached southeast Europe in the 7th millennium BCE, spreading west along the Mediterranean, and north into central and northwest Europe. In northern Europe new strains of cereals were developed and cattle and pigs replaced goats as the main domestic animals.

Europe

8300: Retreat of glaciers causes flooding of many lowland areas. New resources available to Mesolithic hunters

5000: Cereal-farming villages established in western Europe

| 10,000 BCE | 9000 | 8000 | 7000 | 6000 | 5000 BCE |

6200: Farming spreads along Mediterranean to southern Italy and Sicily

5400: Farming spreads to central Europe

The Americas

Big game hunters, who followed herds of bison, mastodons, and mammoths, flourished in North America after the Ice Age. But, by 8000 BCE, changing climates, shrinking habitats, and over-hunting were causing mass extinctions and hunters had to pursue smaller game and make increased use of plant resources. Meanwhile, experiments with the domestication of potatoes, squash, and beans, used to supplement hunting and gathering, were occurring in Central and South America.

Desert peoples in western North America used virtually all aspects of their habitat, for example, the antelope hide used to make this moccasin.

10,000: Melting of ice sheets in North America leads to rapidly changing environments

8000: Growing use of plant resources evident in finds of food-processing equipment such as grindstones

5500: Evidence that squash, avocados, and chilis part of diet of peoples of Central America

| 10,000 BCE | 9000 | 8000 | 7000 | 6000 | 5000 BCE |

8500: Evidence of grasses, squash, beans, peppers, and potatoes in use in Andes

7500: Earliest known cemetery in North America: Sloan burial site

The Americas

Map labels

Greenland

North America: hunting of small game; wild seeds and plant foods, processed using specially developed tools

Northern Europe: hunter-gathering supplemented by fishing

Rocky Mountains

Missouri

Danger Cave

Casper

NORTH AMERICA

Great Plains

St. Lawrence

Bull Brook

Langweiler

Exloo

EUROP

Danube

Koster

Appalachian Mountains

Flint Run

Arene Candide

Lepens

Folsom

Sloan

Bat Cave

Rio Grande

Mississippi

Coveta de l'Or

Mediterranean Sea

Sicily

Southern Europe: cereal cultivation; sheep and goat herding

Southern Anatolia: farming villages trade in flint, obsidian, timber shells, and coppe

ATLANTIC OCEAN

Sahar

PACIFIC OCEAN

Tehuacán

Guilá Naquitz

CENTRAL AMERICA

West Indies

Central America: intensive seasonal hunting and gathering

Sahara: cattle herding supplemented by intensive hunting and gathering

c.5000 BCE: start of desertification of Sahar

AFRICA

Sahel

Iwo Eleru

Orinoco

Guiana Highlands

San Isidoro

Real Alto

Andes

Amazon Basin

Amazon

Amazonia: forest hunting and gathering

São Francisco

Guitarrero Cave

Pachamachay

Western South America: llama hunting

SOUTH AMERICA

ATLANTIC OCEAN

Andes

Paraná

Patagonia

A PLAN OF AN EARLY FARMING VILLAGE

Çatal Hüyük in Anatolia was one of the largest and most prosperous settlements of the 7th millennium BCE, with an extensive trade network and skilled craftsmen. Its sun-dried brick houses, decorated with colorful wall-paintings and plaster sculptures, were built close together without intervening streets or lanes, their interiors accessible only by a wooden ladder from the flat roof.

Many of the houses at Çatal Hüyük were decorated with wall-paintings. One, a copy of which is shown below, has been interpreted as a plan of a village with an erupting volcano behind.

West Asia

The world's earliest farmers settled in the fertile arc of land stretching from the Persian Gulf to the eastern Mediterranean. Large-seeded grains were domesticated in Jericho by 8000 BCE. Villages of mud-brick houses appeared in Anatolia, and in Central Mesopotamia by the 7th millennium BCE and craftsmen were smelting copper and lead by 6000 BCE. By 5500 BCE the farmers of southern Mesopotamia were irrigating arid land to improve crop yields.

Terra-cotta figurines of goddesses with swollen abdomens were found at Çatal Hüyük, suggesting a fertility cult.

West Asia

9000: Wheat (einkorn) harvested in Mesopotamia

8000: First fully domesticated cereals harvested in Jericho

7000: Goat becomes main domesticated animal throughout region. Foundation of settlement of Çatal Hüyük, Anatolia

6000: At Hassuna in northern Mesopotamia; painted pottery and copper and lead smelting

6500: Earliest known Old World textiles (linen) from Çatal Hüyük

5500: Ubaid culture of southern Mesopotamia harnesses spring floods of Euphrates for irrigation

East Asia

In northern China, agriculture dates back to c.7000 BCE. At farming villages such as Banpo, millet was cultivated and kept in grain storage pits, and there is evidence that pigs and dogs were domesticated. In a separate development, rice cultivation was initiated in the lowlands of the Yangtze delta, probably by 6000 BCE. In Japan, the Jomon people lived by hunting, fishing, and gathering in the well-stocked mountains and coastal waters. Although the Japanese were making pottery by 10,500 BCE, their way of life would remain based on hunting and gathering for several thousand years.

The people of Banpo were producing and firing pottery such as this cord-scored amphora by the 5th millennium BCE.

East Asia

9000: Limestone caves in central China give evidence of hunting, fishing, and gathering way of life

c.5000: Hunting and fishing villages in Yangtze River Delta begin cultivating rice

5000: Jade imported into northern Manchuria from Central Asia or Siberia

6500: "Jomon" pottery spreads throughout southern Japanese archipelago

SEE ALSO:

North America: pp.120–121

South America: pp.144–145

Africa: pp.158–159

Europe: pp.174–175

West Asia: pp.220–221

South and Southeast Asia: pp.240–241

North and East Asia: pp.258–259

Australasia and Oceania: pp.280–281

South and Southeast Asia

The first South Asian farmers were cultivating wheat and barley in the fertile highlands of northern India by the 5th millennium BCE. At the same time there was a gradual transition from hunting to farming, primarily rice, to the south of the Ganges Valley. In Southeast Asia, post-glacial rises in sea levels created many new islands and estuaries with a marked increase in maritime resources. By c.2000 BCE farming had gradually become established in this region.

South and Southeast Asia

7000: Evidence of drainage and cultivation in the highlands of New Guinea

6000: Pottery in grave goods from Mehrgarh indicates trade with Central Asia

6000: First pottery production in mainland Southeast Asia

At Mehrgarh in the Baluchi highlands, burials took place in open spaces within the settlement; the dead were often accompanied by personal ornaments including bone, shell, and limestone beads.

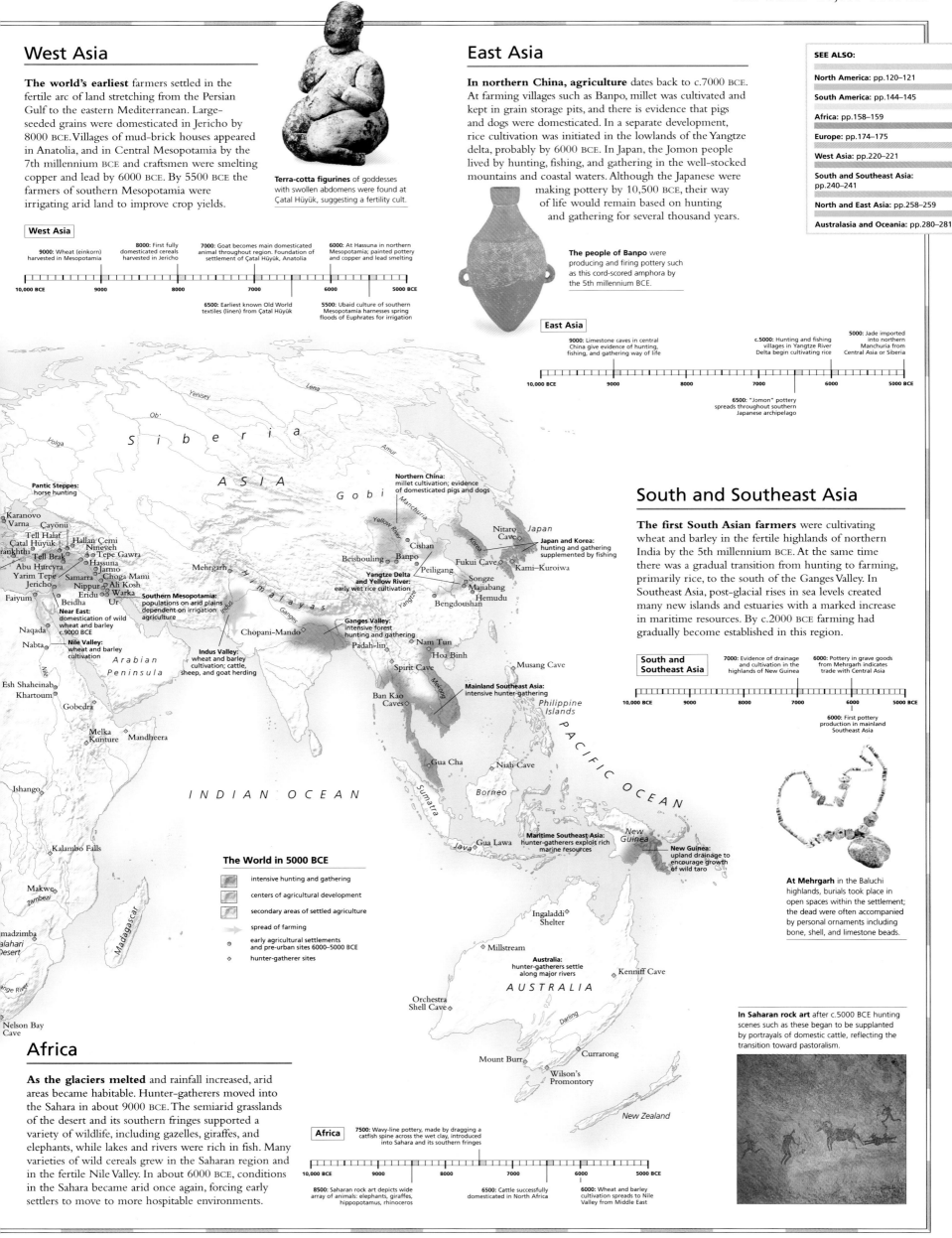

The World in 5000 BCE

- intensive hunting and gathering
- centers of agricultural development
- secondary areas of settled agriculture
- spread of farming
- early agricultural settlements and pre-urban sites 6000–5000 BCE
- hunter-gatherer sites

In Saharan rock art after c.5000 BCE hunting scenes such as these began to be supplanted by portrayals of domestic cattle, reflecting the transition toward pastoralism.

Africa

As the glaciers melted and rainfall increased, arid areas became habitable. Hunter-gatherers moved into the Sahara in about 9000 BCE. The semiarid grasslands of the desert and its southern fringes supported a variety of wildlife, including gazelles, giraffes, and elephants, while lakes and rivers were rich in fish. Many varieties of wild cereals grew in the Saharan region and in the fertile Nile Valley. In about 6000 BCE, conditions in the Sahara became arid once again, forcing early settlers to move to more hospitable environments.

Africa

7500: Wavy-line pottery, made by dragging a catfish spine across the wet clay, introduced into Sahara and its southern fringes

8500: Saharan rock art depicts wide array of animals: elephants, giraffes, hippopotamus, rhinoceros

6500: Cattle successfully domesticated in North Africa

6000: Wheat and barley cultivation spreads to Nile Valley from Middle East

THE ADVENT OF AGRICULTURE

Fragments of Egyptian wavy line pottery, decorated with a fish spine from c.7000 BCE

THE APPEARANCE OF FARMING transformed the face of the Earth. It was not merely a change in subsistence – in many regions a necessity caused by over-hunting, limited natural resources, and population growth – it also transformed the way in which our ancestors lived. Agriculture, and the vastly greater crop yields it produced, enabled large groups of people to live in permanent villages, surrounded by material goods and equipment. Specialized craftsmen produced these goods, supported by the community as a whole – the beginnings of social differentiation. These developments led ultimately to the emergence of the first cities, but in 5000 BCE only a limited number of regions were fully dependent on agriculture. In many parts of the globe, small-scale farming was being used to supplement hunting and gathering – the first steps in the gradual transition to the sedentary agricultural way of life.

The agricultural revolution

The advent of farming brought large groups of people together into settled communities. Not only could food production be made more efficient, but animals could be tended communally, and food surpluses used to support villagers through the winter months. Some members of the community were therefore able to develop craft skills, engage in long-distance trade, and experiment with technology, such as pottery kilns, gold, and copper metallurgy and, by c.5500 BCE, irrigation. But sedentary coexistence also exposed people to infectious disease; the settlement of Çatal Hüyük, for example, was plagued by malaria.

Stone querns, dating to about 6000 years ago, were used by farmers for grinding grain into flour, which could then be kept in storage pits.

Ways of life

The exceptional productivity of the major cultivated species, in particular cereals, was vital to the viability of early farming villages. Cereals can be kept as a year-round resource, providing a staple supplement to more seasonal foods, thus creating a total dependence on farming. An inevitable, and necessary, by-product of this settled way of life was pottery – pottery containers could be used for both storing and cooking the harvested food. The technique of hand-modeling and firing clay pots evolved independently in many regions. Molds, wheels, and kilns were later innovations, and became the province of specialized craftsmen.

The earliest pottery had a round-based shape (right), and was sometimes decorated with incisions or impressions. A characteristic later vessel from western Europe was the flat-based beaker (left), again decorated with incisions, In other regions of Europe, notably the southeast, painted decoration was also used.

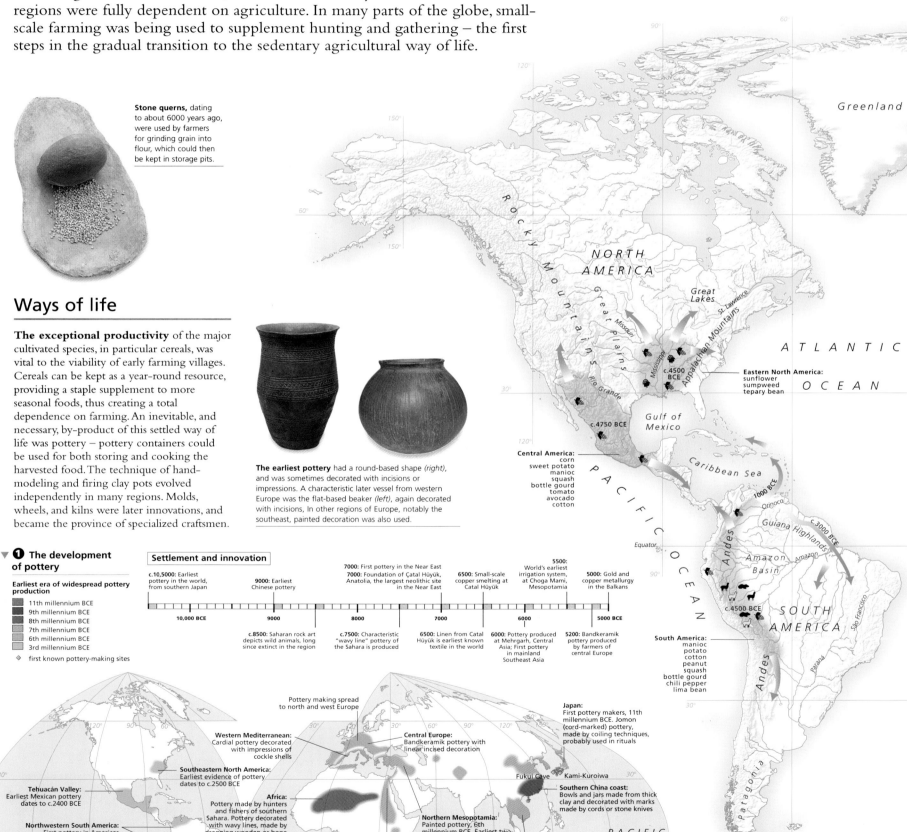

▼ ❶ The development of pottery

Earliest era of widespread pottery production

- ■ 11th millennium BCE
- ■ 9th millennium BCE
- ■ 8th millennium BCE
- ■ 7th millennium BCE
- ■ 6th millennium BCE
- ■ 3rd millennium BCE
- ◇ first known pottery-making sites

Settlement and innovation

c.10,5000: Earliest pottery in the world, from southern Japan

9000: Earliest Chinese pottery

7000: First pottery in the Near East
7000: Foundation of Çatal Hüyük, Anatolia, the largest neolithic site in the Near East

6500: Small-scale copper smelting at Çatal Hüyük

5500: World's earliest irrigation system, at Choga Mami, Mesopotamia

5000: Gold and copper metallurgy in the Balkans

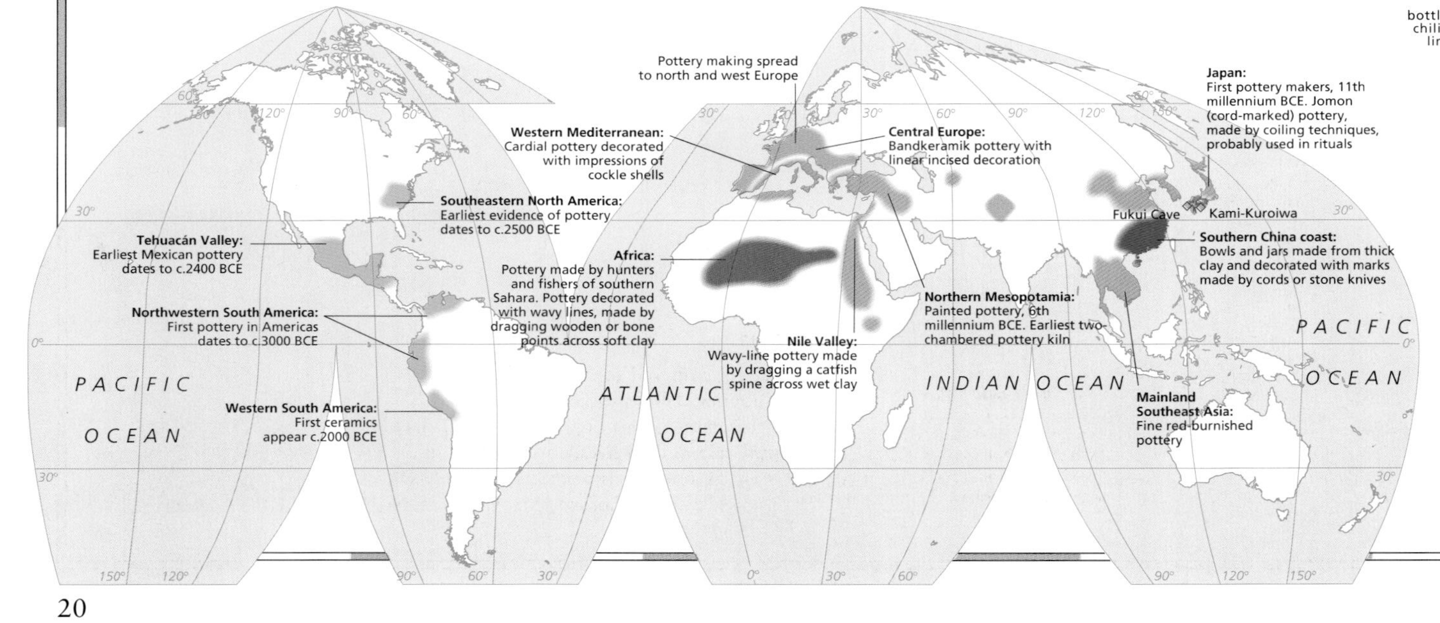

c.8500: Saharan rock art depicts wild animals, long since extinct in the region

c.7500: Characteristic "wavy line" pottery of the Sahara is produced

6500: Linen from Çatal Hüyük is earliest known textile in the world

6000: Pottery produced at Mehrgarh, Central Asia; First pottery in mainland Southeast Asia

5200: Bandkeramik pottery produced by farmers of central Europe

(timeline: 10,000 BCE — 9000 — 8000 — 7000 — 6000 — 5000 BCE)

Eastern North America: sunflower sumpweed tepary bean

Central America: corn sweet potato manioc squash bottle gourd tomato avocado cotton

South America: manioc potato cotton peanut squash bottle gourd chili pepper lima bean

c.4500 BCE
c.4750 BCE
1000 BCE
c.3000 BCE
c.4500 BCE

Map labels: Greenland, NORTH AMERICA, Rocky Mountains, Great Plains, Great Lakes, St. Lawrence, Appalachian Mountains, Mississippi, Missouri, Rio Grande, Gulf of Mexico, Caribbean Sea, Orinoco, Guiana Highlands, Amazon Basin, Amazon, Andes, SOUTH AMERICA, Paraná, São Francisco, Patagonia, Equator, ATLANTIC OCEAN, PACIFIC OCEAN

Pottery making spread to north and west Europe

Japan: First pottery makers, 11th millennium BCE. Jomon (cord-marked) pottery, made by coiling techniques, probably used in rituals

Western Mediterranean: Cardial pottery decorated with impressions of cockle shells

Central Europe: Bandkeramik pottery with linear incised decoration

Southeastern North America: Earliest evidence of pottery dates to c.2500 BCE

Tehuacán Valley: Earliest Mexican pottery dates to c.2400 BCE

Africa: Pottery made by hunters and fishers of southern Sahara. Pottery decorated with wavy lines, made by dragging wooden or bone points across soft clay

Southern China coast: Bowls and jars made from thick clay and decorated with marks made by cords or stone knives

Fukui Cave   Kami-Kuroiwa

Northwestern South America: First pottery in Americas dates to c.3000 BCE

Western South America: First ceramics appear c.2000 BCE

Nile Valley: Wavy-line pottery made by dragging a catfish spine across wet clay

Northern Mesopotamia: Painted pottery, 6th millennium BCE. Earliest two-chambered pottery kiln

Mainland Southeast Asia: Fine red-burnished pottery

Map labels: PACIFIC OCEAN, ATLANTIC OCEAN, INDIAN OCEAN, PACIFIC OCEAN

Domestication

Domestication, a process of selecting and propagating beneficial traits in wild crops, occurred independently in a number of areas at different times, principally in the subtropical zone. Each region developed a dependence on different staple crops: wheat and barley in the Middle East and South Asia; millet and rice in China and Southeast Asia; corn in the Americas. Animals were also domesticated, and a process of selective breeding gradually enhanced useful traits. Sheep and goats, native to West and Central Asia, were domesticated for their meat, milk, hides and wool. Cattle were domesticated all over Eurasia, and eventually used to pull plows, thus increasing plant yields.

The early pastoral farmers of the Sahara made a number of paintings on rocks and in caves, depicting the animals they herded. Cattle are an important feature of these early paintings, some dating from 6000 BCE.

Wild einkorn has brittle stalks, which make it difficult to harvest and transport.

Domestic einkorn, has larger seeds and a tougher stalk than its wild form. It needs to be threshed in order for the seeds to disperse.

SEE ALSO:

North America: pp.120–121

South America: pp.144–145

Africa: pp.158–159

Europe: pp.174–175

West Asia: pp.220–221

South and Southeast Asia: pp.240–241

North and East Asia: pp.258–259

Australasia and Oceania: pp.280–281

c.9000: Einkorn wheat grown in northern Syria: first evidence of true cultivation

c.7000: Farming in northern India; barley is main crop

c.6500: Farming spreads to Balkans from Near East

c.6000: Farming spreads to Nile Valley from Near East

c.4500: Cultivation of corn in eastern North America

c.4000: Plants domesticated in sub-Saharan Africa

c.8500: Rice domesticated in southern China

c.7750: Broomcorn and foxtail millets domesticated on North China Plain

c.6500: Cattle domesticated in Saharan region

c.4750: First evidence of plant and animal domestication in Central America

c.4500: Evidence of agriculture in south-central Andes

Stages in domestication

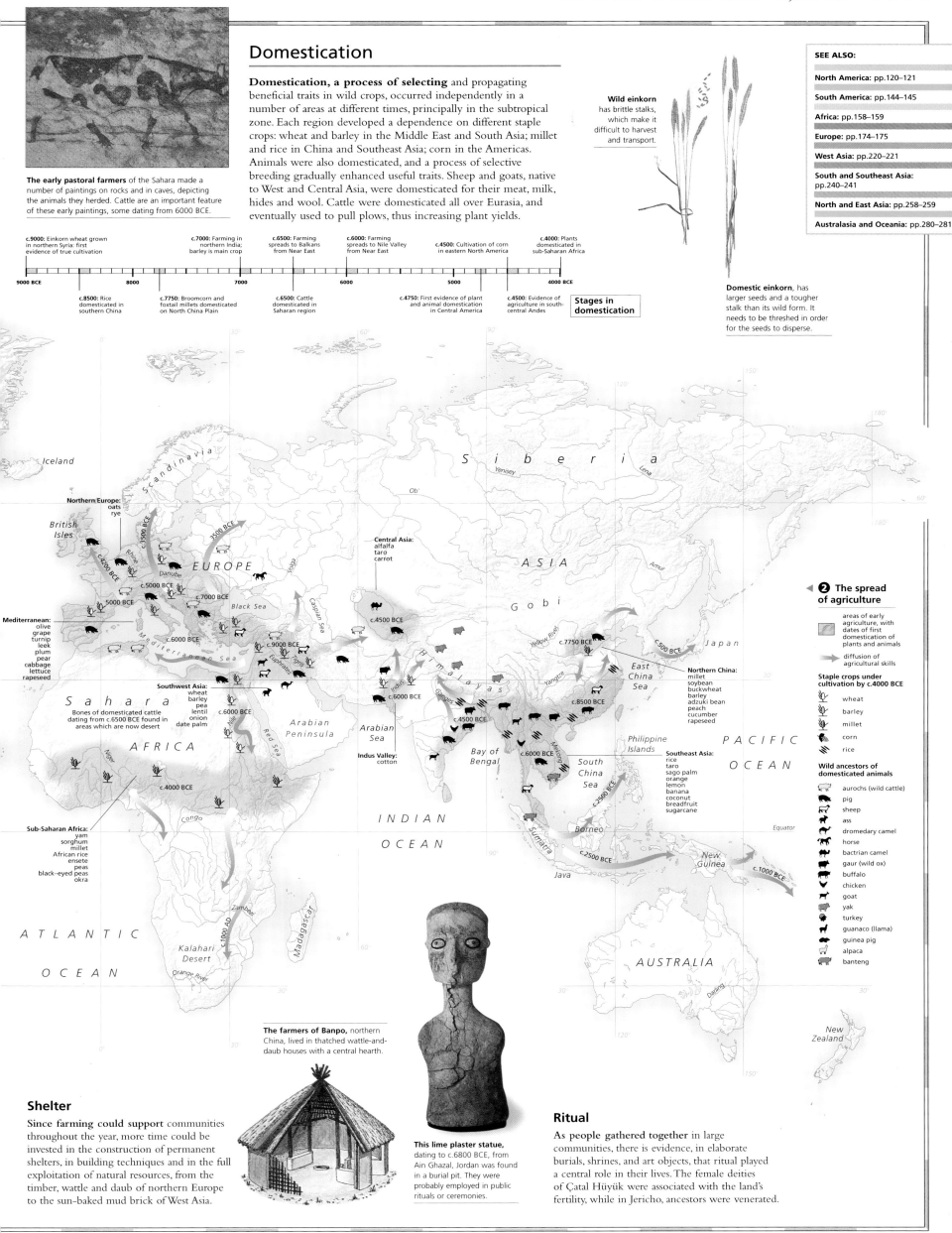

Northern Europe: oats, rye

British Isles

Central Asia: alfalfa, taro, carrot

Mediterranean: olive, grape, turnip, leek, plum, pear, cabbage, lettuce, rapeseed

Southwest Asia: wheat, barley, pea, lentil, onion, date palm

Sahara Bones of domesticated cattle dating from c.6500 BCE found in areas which are now desert

Sub-Saharan Africa: yam, sorghum, millet, African rice, ensete, peas, black-eyed peas, okra

Indus Valley: cotton

Northern China: millet, soybean, buckwheat, barley, adzuki bean, peach, cucumber, rapeseed

Southeast Asia: rice, taro, sago palm, orange, lemon, banana, coconut, breadfruit, sugarcane

2 The spread of agriculture

- areas of early agriculture, with dates of first domestication of plants and animals
- diffusion of agricultural skills

Staple crops under cultivation by c.4000 BCE
- wheat
- barley
- millet
- corn
- rice

Wild ancestors of domesticated animals
- aurochs (wild cattle)
- pig
- sheep
- ass
- dromedary camel
- horse
- bactrian camel
- gaur (wild ox)
- buffalo
- chicken
- goat
- yak
- turkey
- guanaco (llama)
- guinea pig
- alpaca
- banteng

Shelter

Since farming could support communities throughout the year, more time could be invested in the construction of permanent shelters, in building techniques and in the full exploitation of natural resources, from the timber, wattle and daub of northern Europe to the sun-baked mud brick of West Asia.

The farmers of Banpo, northern China, lived in thatched wattle-and-daub houses with a central hearth.

This lime plaster statue, dating to c.6800 BCE, from Ain Ghazal, Jordan was found in a burial pit. They were probably employed in public rituals or ceremonies.

Ritual

As people gathered together in large communities, there is evidence, in elaborate burials, shrines, and art objects, that ritual played a central role in their lives. The female deities of Çatal Hüyük were associated with the land's fertility, while in Jericho, ancestors were venerated.

THE WORLD 5000–2500 BCE

THE FERTILE VALLEYS of the Nile, Tigris, Euphrates, Indus, and Yellow rivers were able to support very large populations, and it was here that the great urban civilizations of the ancient world emerged. Although cities developed independently in several regions, they shared certain characteristics. Urban societies were hierarchical, with complex labor divisions. They were administered, economically and spiritually, by an elite literate class, and in some cases, were subject to a divine monarch. Monuments came to symbolize and represent the powers of the ruling elite. Elsewhere, farming communities came together to create ritual centers or burial sites, while craftsmen experimented with new materials and techniques, such as copper and bronze casting, and glazed pottery. All these developments indicate that urban and non-urban societies were attaining a high degree of social organization.

EARLY PERCEPTIONS OF THE COSMOS

The stone circles and alignments of northwestern Europe are extraordinary prehistoric monuments which have mystified successive generations. Astronomical observations are central to the ritual purpose of these structures; at many monuments, stones are arranged to be illuminated by the Sun only on certain days, such as the winter or summer solstice.

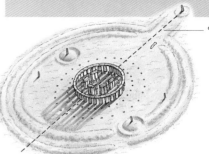

central axis

Stonehenge became the preeminent ritual center of southern Britain c.2500 BCE. The rising sun on midsummer's day shines along the central axis of the site, but little is known of the ritual enacted there.

WHEELED VEHICLES

The origin of the wheel is uncertain; humans probably first made use of rotary motion in log rollers, and then in the potter's wheel. Wheeled vehicles were known in southwest Asia by 3500 BCE – a Sumerian pictograph from this period depicts a sledge equipped with wheels – and their use had spread to Europe and India by 3000 BCE. Early vehicles were probably ox-drawn, two-wheeled carts, on wheels formed from planks of wood secured with crosspieces.

This ceramic model of a two-wheeled bullock cart is from a grave at Harappa in the Indus Valley.

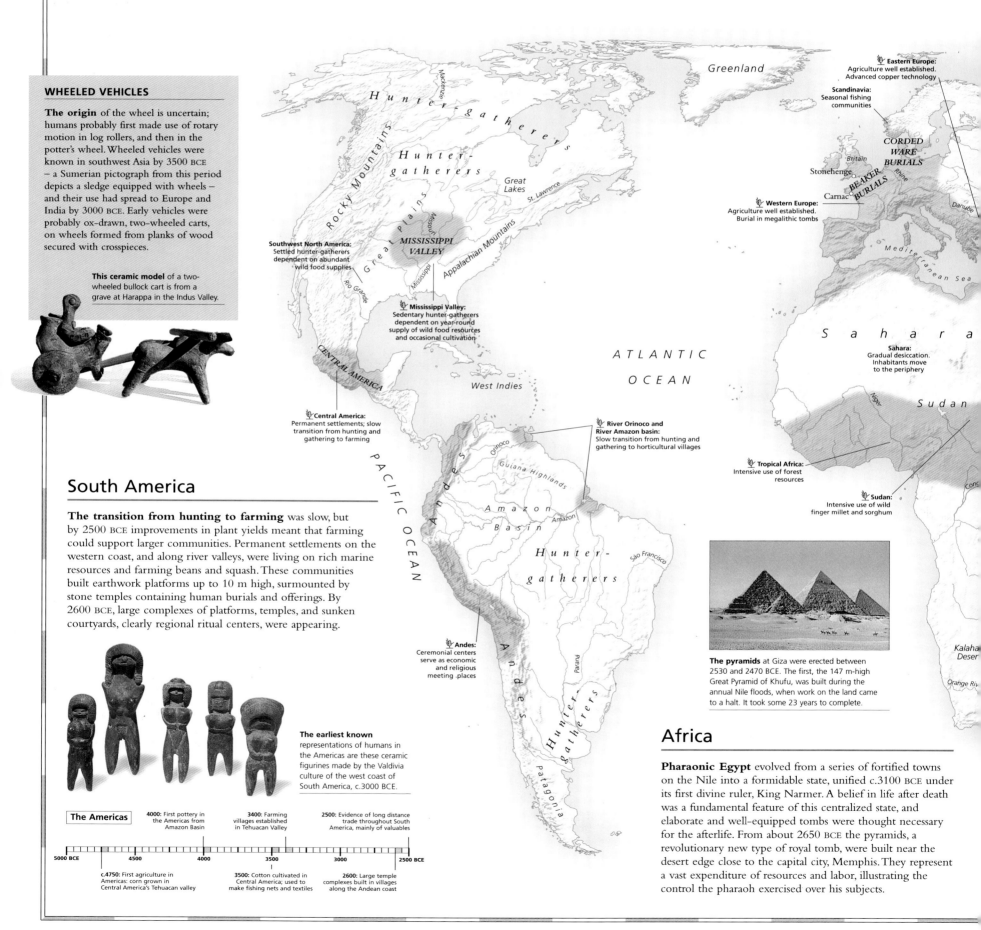

Eastern Europe: Agriculture well established. Advanced copper technology

Scandinavia: Seasonal fishing communities

CORDED WARE BURIALS

BEAKER BURIALS

Britain

Stonehenge

Carnac

Western Europe: Agriculture well established. Burial in megalithic tombs

Southwest North America: Settled hunter-gatherers dependent on abundant wild food supplies

MISSISSIPPI VALLEY

Mississippi Valley: Sedentary hunter-gatherers dependent on year-round supply of wild food resources and occasional cultivation

CENTRAL AMERICA

Central America: Permanent settlements; slow transition from hunting and gathering to farming

River Orinoco and River Amazon basin: Slow transition from hunting and gathering to horticultural villages

Sahara: Gradual desiccation. Inhabitants move to the periphery

Tropical Africa: Intensive use of forest resources

Sudan: Intensive use of wild finger millet and sorghum

Andes: Ceremonial centers serve as economic and religious meeting places

Greenland

ATLANTIC OCEAN

West Indies

PACIFIC OCEAN

Amazon Basin

Hunter-gatherers

Hunter-gatherers

Patagonia

Sahara

Sudan

Kalahari Desert

Orange River

Mediterranean Sea

South America

The transition from hunting to farming was slow, but by 2500 BCE improvements in plant yields meant that farming could support larger communities. Permanent settlements on the western coast, and along river valleys, were living on rich marine resources and farming beans and squash. These communities built earthwork platforms up to 10 m high, surmounted by stone temples containing human burials and offerings. By 2600 BCE, large complexes of platforms, temples, and sunken courtyards, clearly regional ritual centers, were appearing.

The earliest known representations of humans in the Americas are these ceramic figurines made by the Valdivia culture of the west coast of South America, c.3000 BCE.

The pyramids at Giza were erected between 2530 and 2470 BCE. The first, the 147 m-high Great Pyramid of Khufu, was built during the annual Nile floods, when work on the land came to a halt. It took some 23 years to complete.

Africa

Pharaonic Egypt evolved from a series of fortified towns on the Nile into a formidable state, unified c.3100 BCE under its first divine ruler, King Narmer. A belief in life after death was a fundamental feature of this centralized state, and elaborate and well-equipped tombs were thought necessary for the afterlife. From about 2650 BCE the pyramids, a revolutionary new type of royal tomb, were built near the desert edge close to the capital city, Memphis. They represent a vast expenditure of resources and labor, illustrating the control the pharaoh exercised over his subjects.

The Americas	4000: First pottery in the Americas from Amazon Basin	3400: Farming villages established in Tehuacan Valley	2500: Evidence of long distance trade throughout South America, mainly of valuables

5000 BCE	4500	4000	3500	3000	2500 BCE

c.4750: First agriculture in Americas: corn grown in Central America's Tehuacan valley

3500: Cotton cultivated in Central America; used to make fishing nets and textiles

2600: Large temple complexes built in villages along the Andean coast

Europe

Elaborate burials, from the megalithic tombs of northern Europe to the large cemeteries of central and eastern Europe, indicate an increasing level of social organization among the scattered farming communities of the European continent. By the 3rd millennium BCE small farming communities were gathering to build defensive enclosures and to create regional centers. Stone circles, such as Stonehenge, or stone avenues, such as Carnac, were major communal undertakings which acted as social, economic, and ritual centers.

Skara Brae is a magnificently preserved Stone Age village on the Orkneys. The village consists of one-room houses of undressed stone, with paved walkways between them and a drainage system.

SEE ALSO:

North America: pp.120–121

South America: pp.144–145

Africa: pp.158–159

Europe: pp.174–175

West Asia: pp.220–221

South and Southeast Asia: pp.240–241

North and East Asia: pp.258–259

Australasia and Oceania: pp.280–281

Europe

4500: Large cemeteries, for example on the western coast of the Black Sea, contain rich burials with elaborate gold jewelry

3800: Ditched enclosures around settlements in Central Europe create defended villages

3200: Stone circles and rows of standing stones built throughout northern and western Europe

c.5000: Metallurgy discovered in south-eastern Europe

c.4500: In western Europe, megalithic (large stone) chamber tombs, built as communal burial places

2900: Earliest burials containing Corded Ware pottery in northern and Central Europe

East Asia

As the early farming villages of China became more prosperous, new skills emerged. Farmers of the Longshan culture of eastern China invented the potter's wheel and were making eggshell-thin vessels by 3000 BCE; 250 years later they were raising silkworms and weaving silk. By 3000 BCE there was a marked difference between rich and poor burials, and walled settlements were appearing. The more complex social organization that these developments indicate was soon to lead to China's first urban civilization, the Shang.

This Kui (a pitcher with three hollow legs) is typical of Longshan pottery from the late 3rd millennium BCE.

East Asia

c.4000: Planned villages in northern China, with distinct residential, workshop, and burial areas

3000: First evidence of farming (millet cultivation) in Korea

2500: Banshan culture of western China produces boldly painted burial urns

c.3000: Potter's wheel invented during formative phase of Longshan culture of eastern China

2750: First Chinese bronze artefacts

South Asia

By 2500 BCE, an urban civilization had developed in the Indus Valley, dominated by Harappa and Mohenjo-Daro. At its height, the latter had a population of about 40,000. A network of residential streets, houses made with standardized bricks and sophisticated drains running into main sewers, overlooked by the "citadel," the religious and ceremonial focus of the city. Merchandise was traded as far afield as Mesopotamia.

The Harappans developed a pictographic form of writing which they used mainly on sealstones.

South Asia

5000: Evidence of use of pottery vessels at Mehrgarh and other Indus Valley settlements

2500: True cities emerge in Indus Valley. Cultural uniformity throughout Indus plain. Evidence of trade links with Central Asia and Mesopotamia

4500: Introduction of irrigation techniques in Indus Valley increases size and prosperity of farming settlements

3500: Indus Valley lowlands settled by farmers; walled towns develop

The royal standard of Ur depicts the Sumerian ruler at war and in peacetime. The panels are crafted in lapis lazuli and shell from as far away as Afghanistan.

West Asia

Mesopotamia's fertile floodplains were the crucible of the urban revolution. Uruk, the first city-state, evolved c.3500 BCE. The early cities of Mesopotamia were built around the raised mud-brick temple complex. The temple administered much of the city's land and livestock and a priestly elite was responsible for recording and storing produce. The temple accounting system led to pictographic writing by c.3250 BCE.

Map labels

Hunter-gatherers
Hunter-gatherers
Lena
Yenisey
Ob'
Aral Sea
Siberia
Hunter-gatherers
Gobi
Amur
Pontic Steppes: Cereal cultivation
Livestock herding
PIT GRAVE CULTURE
Caspian Sea
Black Sea
River Yenisey: Cereal cultivation
Yellow River Valley: Barley and millet cultivation
Korea
Japan: Hunter-gathering and fishing
Japan
Hattushash
Tell Brak
Mesopotamia
Tigris
Euphrates
Iranian Plateau: scattered trading cities
Yellow River
Yangshao
LONGSHAN CULTURE
Susa
Uruk SUMER
Ur
Mehrgarh
Mohenjo-Daro
Indus
Harappa
Himalayas
Yangtze
China
Giza
Memphis
Saqqara
OLD KINGDOM OF EGYPT
INDUS VALLEY
Ganges
Ganges Valley: Wet rice cultivation
Yangtze Delta: Wet rice cultivation
Nile
Arabian Peninsula
Kachhi: Wheat and barley cultivation
Deccan: Cattle pastoralists
Coastal Vietnam: Rice-farming villages, domesticated animals, bronze tools and ornaments
Philippine Islands
PACIFIC OCEAN
Upper Nile Valley: Wheat and barley cultivation
Sumatra
Borneo
New Guinea
Java
Maritime Southeast Asia: Slow transition from hunting and gathering to farming
Hunter-gatherers
Madagascar
Zambezi
INDIAN OCEAN
Hunter-gatherers Australia
Darling

The world in 2500 BCE

- transition from hunting and gathering to agriculture
- agricultural areas
- urban areas
- urban hinterland

New Zealand

Africa

3400: First walled towns appear in Egypt

3000: First evidence of hieroglyphic writing system

2530: Construction of Great Pyramid of Khufu, the largest of the Eyptian pyramids, at Giza

3100: King Narmer unifies Upper and Lower Egypt, and becomes first pharaoh. City of Memphis is founded

2650: The step pyramid of Zoser, the first Egyptian pyramid, is built at Saqqara

West Asia

c.3250: Pictographic clay tablets from Tell Brak: earliest evidence of writing

2500: City-states present throughout Mesopotamia and Levant

3500: Emergence of Uruk, the first city-state

2500: Rich array of grave goods at Royal Graves at Ur indicate extensive trade links

TRADE AND THE FIRST CITIES

This Egyptian ivory label is inscribed with the name of King Djet (c.3000 BCE).

BY 2500 BCE, CITIES WERE ESTABLISHED in three major centers: the Nile Valley, Mesopotamia, and the Indus Valley, with a scattering of other cities across the intervening terrain. The culmination of a long process of settlement and expansion – some early cities had populations tens of thousands strong – the first urban civilizations all relied on rich agricultural lands to support their growth. In each case, lack of the most important natural resources – timber, metal, and stone – forced these urban civilizations to establish trading networks which ultimately extended from the Hindu Kush to the Mediterranean. They imported a diverse range of goods: metals and precious stones, such as lapis lazuli, gold, and turquoise, met the demands of the growing social elites for luxury goods; diorite, limestone, and timber were needed for the monumental construction programs which were an integral part of urban life. Where trading contacts led, cultural influence followed, and cities soon began to develop in the trading hinterlands of the Iranian Plateau and Anatolia.

Ur: a trading city

The ancient city of Ur, was the capital of a south Mesopotamian empire toward the end of the 3rd millennium. It was a major economic center, with extensive trade links extending as far as Dilmun (Bahrain) and the cities of the Indus. Ships laden with gold, copper, timber, ivory, and precious stones had access to the Persian Gulf via canals which linked the city to the Euphrates. Archives of clay tablets record, in minute detail, transactions and ships' cargoes. The wealth this trade generated is reflected in the grandiose buildings which adorned the city, most notably the ziggurat dedicated to the city's deity, Ur-Nammu, and in the lavishly furnished burials of Ur's so-called "Royal Graves."

Cities and trade

c.3500: Rise of city-state of Uruk

c.3100: Sumerian trading post at Habuba Kabira, Syria. Sumerian merchants have their own quarters in Persian city of Godin Tepe

c.2500: City of Ur in southern Mesopotamia is a major center of trade and manufacture

c.2500: Indus Valley trading colony of Shortughai, 1000 km from Harappa, supplies tin and lapis lazuli

c.3300: First walled towns in Egypt: Hieraconpolis and Naqada

c.3100: City of Byblos is founded on the Levantine coast

c.2500: The city of Ebla in western Mesopotamia begins to trade with Mediterranean peoples

3500 BCE — 3000 — 2500 BCE

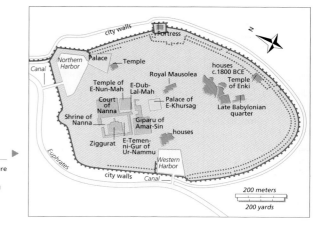

① Ur
- sacred enclosure
- royal palace
- other building
- inner walls
- outer walls

200 meters / 200 yards

Transportation

The long-distance trading networks of the ancient world required revolutionary developments in transportation. Much of the trade was maritime; the cities of Mesopotamia all had access, via rivers and canals, to the Persian Gulf and Indus Valley, and there is ample evidence for trade along the Gulf coast and Arabian Sea to the mouth of the Indus. The timber boats of the Nile, depicted carrying great columns of granite and alabaster, are known from tomb reliefs, models, and burials. Overland trade was dependent on newly-domesticated beasts of burden, such as donkeys and camels. Wheeled carts, pulled by oxen and bullocks, were also used.

A high-prowed reed boat can be seen on this impression from a cylinder seal from Uruk, dating to the 4th millennium BCE. The boat is being used to transport a priest or ruler, probably as part of a religious procession.

Egyptian culture was based on and around the Nile River, which offered the most effective means of transport. Some of the earliest vessels with sails were developed in Egypt.

This copper model from Tell Agrab, Mesopotamia, shows a two-wheeled chariot drawn by onagers, a type of wild donkey. Wheeled vehicles were used for both trade and warfare.

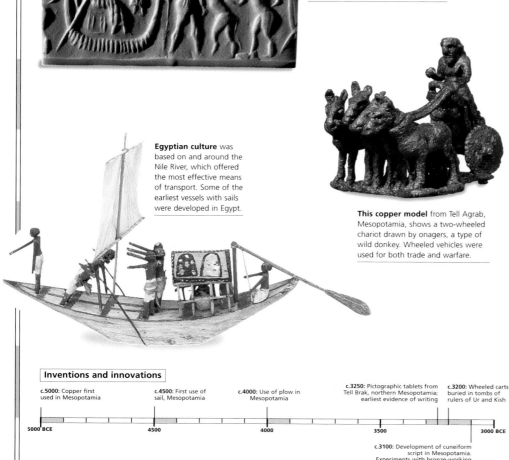

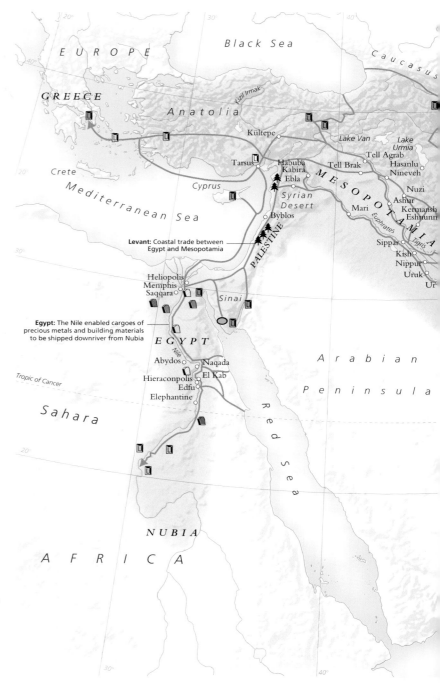

Levant: Coastal trade between Egypt and Mesopotamia

Egypt: The Nile enabled cargoes of precious metals and building materials to be shipped downriver from Nubia

Inventions and innovations

c.5000: Copper first used in Mesopotamia

c.4500: First use of sail, Mesopotamia

c.4000: Use of plow in Mesopotamia

c.3250: Pictographic tablets from Tell Brak, northern Mesopotamia; earliest evidence of writing

c.3200: Wheeled carts buried in tombs of rulers of Ur and Kish

5000 BCE — 4500 — 4000 — 3500 — 3000 BCE

c.3100: Development of cuneiform script in Mesopotamia. Experiments with bronze-working

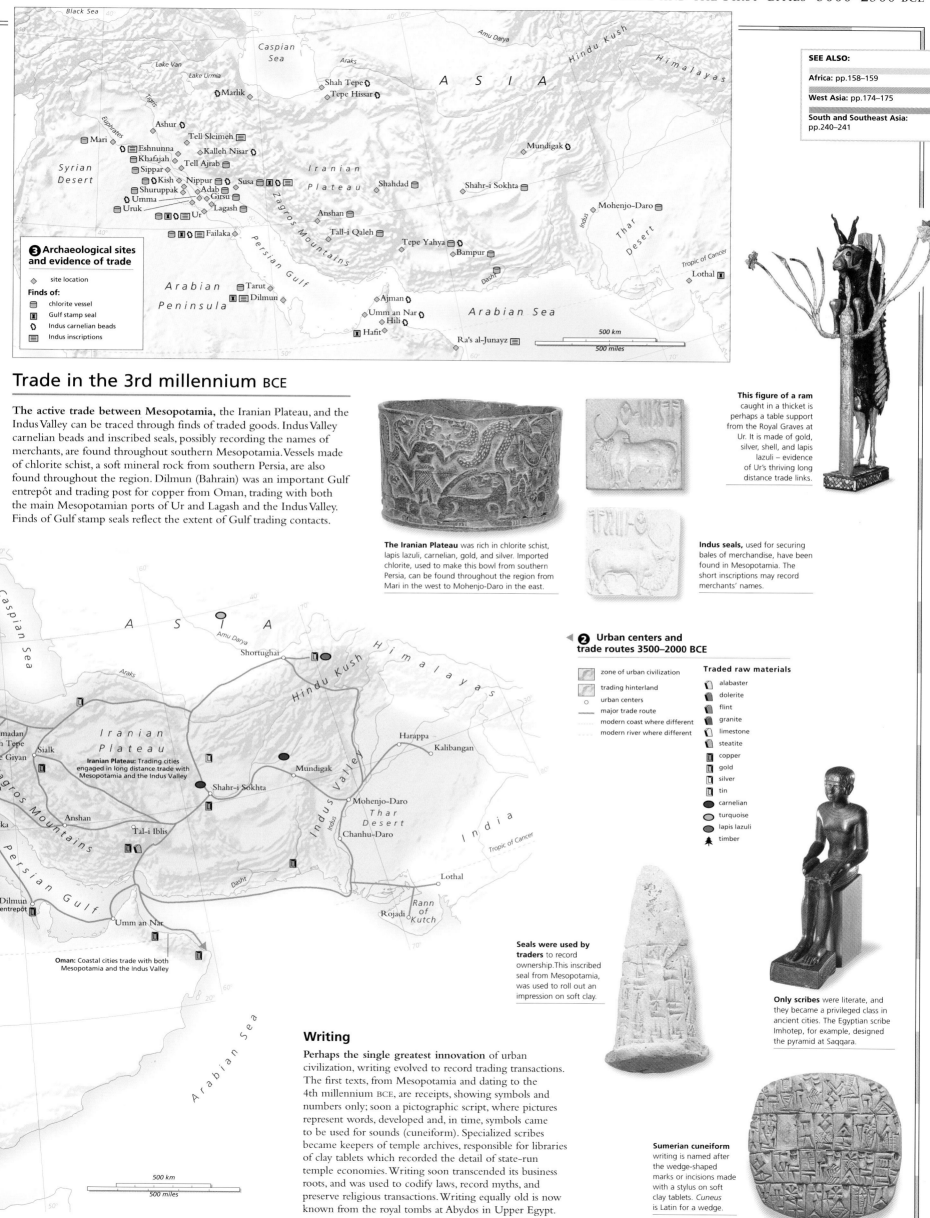

SEE ALSO:

Africa: pp.158–159

West Asia: pp.174–175

South and Southeast Asia:
pp.240–241

❸ Archaeological sites and evidence of trade

◇ site location

Finds of:

▱ chlorite vessel

▣ Gulf stamp seal

◊ Indus carnelian beads

▤ Indus inscriptions

Trade in the 3rd millennium BCE

The active trade between Mesopotamia, the Iranian Plateau, and the Indus Valley can be traced through finds of traded goods. Indus Valley carnelian beads and inscribed seals, possibly recording the names of merchants, are found throughout southern Mesopotamia. Vessels made of chlorite schist, a soft mineral rock from southern Persia, are also found throughout the region. Dilmun (Bahrain) was an important Gulf entrepôt and trading post for copper from Oman, trading with both the main Mesopotamian ports of Ur and Lagash and the Indus Valley. Finds of Gulf stamp seals reflect the extent of Gulf trading contacts.

The Iranian Plateau was rich in chlorite schist, lapis lazuli, carnelian, gold, and silver. Imported chlorite, used to make this bowl from southern Persia, can be found throughout the region from Mari in the west to Mohenjo-Daro in the east.

This figure of a ram caught in a thicket is perhaps a table support from the Royal Graves at Ur. It is made of gold, silver, shell, and lapis lazuli – evidence of Ur's thriving long distance trade links.

Indus seals, used for securing bales of merchandise, have been found in Mesopotamia. The short inscriptions may record merchants' names.

❷ Urban centers and trade routes 3500–2000 BCE

▦ zone of urban civilization

▨ trading hinterland

○ urban centers

— major trade route

---- modern coast where different

---- modern river where different

Traded raw materials

▰ alabaster

▰ dolerite

▰ flint

▰ granite

▰ limestone

▰ steatite

▰ copper

▰ gold

▰ silver

▰ tin

● carnelian

● turquoise

● lapis lazuli

🌲 timber

Iranian Plateau: Trading cities engaged in long distance trade with Mesopotamia and the Indus Valley

Oman: Coastal cities trade with both Mesopotamia and the Indus Valley

Seals were used by traders to record ownership. This inscribed seal from Mesopotamia, was used to roll out an impression on soft clay.

Only scribes were literate, and they became a privileged class in ancient cities. The Egyptian scribe Imhotep, for example, designed the pyramid at Saqqara.

Writing

Perhaps the single greatest innovation of urban civilization, writing evolved to record trading transactions. The first texts, from Mesopotamia and dating to the 4th millennium BCE, are receipts, showing symbols and numbers only; soon a pictographic script, where pictures represent words, developed and, in time, symbols came to be used for sounds (cuneiform). Specialized scribes became keepers of temple archives, responsible for libraries of clay tablets which recorded the detail of state-run temple economies. Writing soon transcended its business roots, and was used to codify laws, record myths, and preserve religious transactions. Writing equally old is now known from the royal tombs at Abydos in Upper Egypt.

Sumerian cuneiform writing is named after the wedge-shaped marks or incisions made with a stylus on soft clay tablets. *Cuneus* is Latin for a wedge.

THE WORLD 2500–1250 BCE

AS THE FIRST CITIES expanded and proliferated, states developed, populations grew, and economic pressures increased. Rivalry for territory and power made the early states increasingly militaristic, and warfare, weapons, and diplomacy are conspicuous in the archaeology of this period. As these early societies became more stratified, distinct classes – warriors, priests, scribes, craftspeople, laborers – began to emerge. The great wealth of rulers and the social elite is reflected in the rich array of grave goods found in their burials. Urban civilizations still covered only a tiny fraction of the Earth's surface; in Europe, scattered agricultural communities were becoming more sophisticated, developing metallurgy and trade, and beginning to compete for land and resources. Hunter-gatherer groups still thrived in many areas, and many islands in the Pacific were yet to be settled at this time.

SUN SYMBOLISM

Symbolic representations of the Sun, suggestive of life, fertility, and creation, are found in almost all cultures. During this period in Egypt, the sun god Ra was the dominant figure among the high gods, his enhanced status culminating in the brief solar monotheism under Pharaoh Akhenaton c.1350 BCE. In Scandinavia, ritual finds such as the sun chariot found in a bog at Trundholm (*below*) attest to monotheistic sun worship and fertility rites in the region during the Bronze Age.

This bronze wheeled model of a horse drawing a disc, which dates to c.1650 BCE, may depict the sun's progress across the heavens.

The World in 1250 BCE

- New Kingdom Egypt
- Hittites
- Mitanni
- Elam
- Shang China
- Mycenaean civilization
- areas of transition from hunting and gathering to agriculture
- other urbanized regions

Major bronze-using regions c.1250 BCE

- Andronovo steppe cultures
- Bronze Age Europe
- Mainland Southeast Asia
- → colonization of Pacific from c.1500 BCE

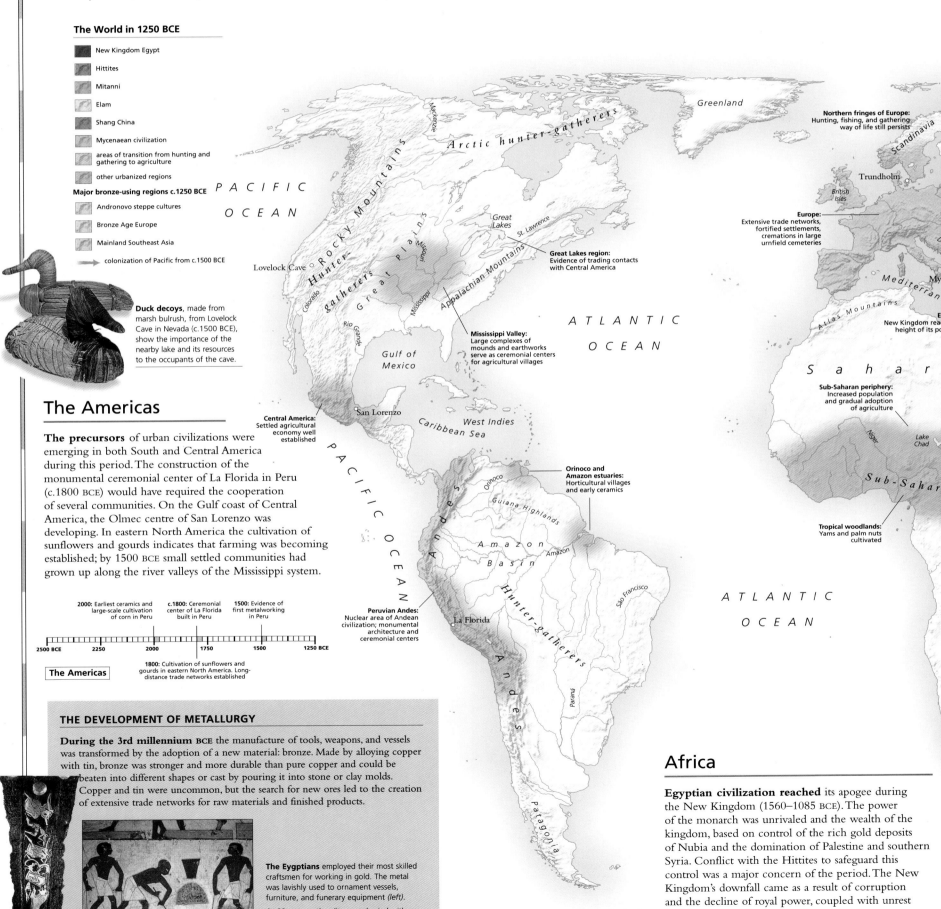

Duck decoys, made from marsh bulrush, from Lovelock Cave in Nevada (c.1500 BCE), show the importance of the nearby lake and its resources to the occupants of the cave.

Great Lakes region: Evidence of trading contacts with Central America

Mississippi Valley: Large complexes of mounds and earthworks serve as ceremonial centers for agricultural villages

Central America: Settled agricultural economy well established

Orinoco and Amazon estuaries: Horticultural villages and early ceramics

Peruvian Andes: Nuclear area of Andean civilization; monumental architecture and ceremonial centers

Northern fringes of Europe: Hunting, fishing, and gathering way of life still persists

Europe: Extensive trade networks, fortified settlements, cremations in large urnfield cemeteries

Egypt: New Kingdom reaching height of its power

Sub-Saharan periphery: Increased population and gradual adoption of agriculture

Tropical woodlands: Yams and palm nuts cultivated

The Americas

The precursors of urban civilizations were emerging in both South and Central America during this period. The construction of the monumental ceremonial center of La Florida in Peru (c.1800 BCE) would have required the cooperation of several communities. On the Gulf coast of Central America, the Olmec centre of San Lorenzo was developing. In eastern North America the cultivation of sunflowers and gourds indicates that farming was becoming established; by 1500 BCE small settled communities had grown up along the river valleys of the Mississippi system.

| 2000: Earliest ceramics and large-scale cultivation of corn in Peru | c.1800: Ceremonial center of La Florida built in Peru | 1500: Evidence of first metalworking in Peru |

2500 BCE — 2250 — 2000 — 1750 — 1500 — 1250 BCE

1800: Cultivation of sunflowers and gourds in eastern North America. Long-distance trade networks established

The Americas

THE DEVELOPMENT OF METALLURGY

During the 3rd millennium BCE the manufacture of tools, weapons, and vessels was transformed by the adoption of a new material: bronze. Made by alloying copper with tin, bronze was stronger and more durable than pure copper and could be beaten into different shapes or cast by pouring it into stone or clay molds. Copper and tin were uncommon, but the search for new ores led to the creation of extensive trade networks for raw materials and finished products.

The Egyptians employed their most skilled craftsmen for working in gold. The metal was lavishly used to ornament vessels, furniture, and funerary equipment (*left*).

At Mycenae, the elite were buried with an opulent array of metal goods. This dagger blade (*far left*) (1600–1550 BCE) of bronze inlaid with silver portrays a lion hunt.

Africa

Egyptian civilization reached its apogee during the New Kingdom (1560–1085 BCE). The power of the monarch was unrivaled and the wealth of the kingdom, based on control of the rich gold deposits of Nubia and the domination of Palestine and southern Syria. Conflict with the Hittites to safeguard this control was a major concern of the period. The New Kingdom's downfall came as a result of corruption and the decline of royal power, coupled with unrest in Palestine, and foreign attacks on Egypt.

Europe

European field systems and settlements, ranging from hillforts to island villages, indicate that increased pressures on land were causing conflict. New types of bronze weapons show the emergence of a warrior elite. The palace of Knossos on Crete marked the appearance of the first Mediterranean state, and on the mainland, the small, palace-based cities of Mycenaean Greece grew wealthy on east Mediterranean trade, but were all sacked or abandoned by the 12th century BCE.

Many aspects of Minoan life are depicted in the colorful frescoes at Knossos, a recurring theme being the acrobatic bull-leaping game on which a religious cult was possibly centered.

Europe

2300: Bronze technology reaches Europe	**2000:** Fortified settlements appear in Central and Eastern Europe	**1550:** Mycenaeans become dominant power on Greek mainland

2500 BCE — 2250 — 2000 — 1750 — 1500 — 1250 BCE

2000: Minoan civilization becomes established on island of Crete; palace of Knossos is built

1650: Linear A script comes into use on Crete

West Asia

Northern Mesopotamia was dominated by a number of city-states, such as Ashur and Mari, which centered on palaces and religious complexes. The palace administered each city's long-distance trade and tribute, and recorded these transactions on archives of clay tablets. In the 18th century BCE, the city-state of Babylon gained temporary control of the region. In central Anatolia, the Hittites ruled a powerful kingdom from their fortified citadel at Hattushash. Their attempts to gain control over the wealthy trading cities of the Levant brought them into conflict with Egypt.

This gold figurine of a Hittite king dates to c.1400 BCE.

West Asia

2300: City-states of southern Mesopotamia temporarily united under Sargon of Agade	**1775:** Construction of palace of Zimri-Lim at Mari. Palace archive contained 17,500 clay tablets	**1650:** Emergence of Hittite kingdom, with capital at Hattushash	**1500:** Period of endemic warfare between Hittites, Egyptians, and Mitanni of northern Mesopotamia

2500 BCE — 2250 — 2000 — 1750 — 1500 — 1250 BCE

1760: City-state of Babylon gains political hegemony over northern Mesopotamia

1600: Phoenicians start to use Canaanite script – the first alphabetic script

1290: Battle of Kadesh: Egypt versus the Hittites

SEE ALSO:

North America: pp.120–121

South America: pp.144–145

Africa: pp.158–159

Europe: pp.174–175

West Asia: pp.220–221

South and Southeast Asia: pp.240–241

North and East Asia: pp.258–259

Australasia and Oceania: pp.280–281

East Asia

The urban civilization of Shang China developed in about 1800 BCE in the middle valley of the Yellow River. The Shang dynasty exercised an absolute power reflected in their incredibly rich burials. Yet this absolute power was based on the labor of farmers who cultivated beans and millet with tools of wood and stone. Elsewhere, in Southeast Asia, the transition to farming was slow, although agricultural villages in Thailand were producing bronze vessels using similar techniques to the Chinese.

Chinese mastery of bronze casting is evident in the exquisite vessels, created primarily for ceremonial use, that often accompanied the wealthy elite into the grave.

East Asia

1800: Emergence of Shang dynasty in middle valley of Yellow River	**1500:** Evidence of bronze-working in mainland Southeast Asia	**1400:** Anyang succeeds Zhengzhou as the Shang capital

2500 BCE — 2250 — 2000 — 1750 — 1500 — 1250 BCE

2500: First domesticated animals and pottery in island Southeast Asia

1900 BCE: First Chinese city founded at Erlitou on the Yellow River

1800: First bronze vessels cast from ceramic molds

1400: First written inscriptions appear on oracle bones, which were used as a process of divination

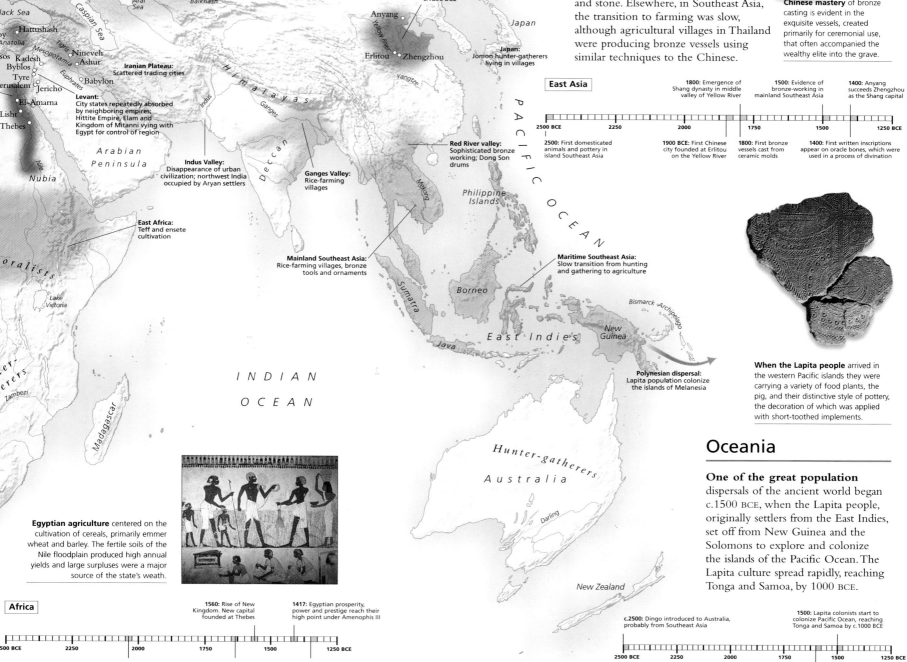

(Map labels:)
Arctic hunter-gatherers · Yenisey · Lena · Ob · Volga · Siberia · Lake Baikal · Amur · Steppes · **Andronovo steppe cultures:** Cattle herders and seasonal nomads · Aral Sea · Lake Balkhash · Gobi · **China:** Longshan groups form basis of Shang state c.1800 BCE · Anyang · Japan · Erlitou · Zhengzhou · **Japan:** Jomon hunter-gatherers living in villages · Yellow River · Yangtze · Black Sea · Troy · Hattushash · Anatolia · Caspian Sea · Nineveh · Ashur · **Iranian Plateau:** Scattered trading cities · Knossos · Kadesh · Mesopotamia · Tigris · Euphrates · Byblos · Tyre · Babylon · Jerusalem · Jericho · El-Amarna · El-Lisht · Thebes · **Levant:** City states repeatedly absorbed by neighboring empires; Hittite Empire, Elam and Kingdom of Mitanni vying with Egypt for control of region · Nile · Nubia · Arabian Peninsula · Himalayas · Indus · Ganges · Deccan · **Indus Valley:** Disappearance of urban civilization; northwest India occupied by Aryan settlers · **Ganges Valley:** Rice-farming villages · **Red River valley:** Sophisticated bronze working; Dong Son drums · PACIFIC OCEAN · Japan · **East Africa:** Teff and ensete cultivation · pastoralists · Lake Victoria · Zambezi · hunter-gatherers · Madagascar · INDIAN OCEAN · **Mainland Southeast Asia:** Rice-farming villages, bronze tools and ornaments · **Maritime Southeast Asia:** Slow transition from hunting and gathering to agriculture · Philippine Islands · Mekong · Sumatra · Borneo · Java · East Indies · New Guinea · Bismarck Archipelago · **Polynesian dispersal:** Lapita population colonize the islands of Melanesia · Hunter-gatherers Australia · Darling · New Zealand

When the Lapita people arrived in the western Pacific islands they were carrying a variety of food plants, the pig, and their distinctive style of pottery, the decoration of which was applied with short-toothed implements.

Oceania

One of the great population dispersals of the ancient world began c.1500 BCE, when the Lapita people, originally settlers from the East Indies, set off from New Guinea and the Solomons to explore and colonize the islands of the Pacific Ocean. The Lapita culture spread rapidly, reaching Tonga and Samoa, by 1000 BCE.

Egyptian agriculture centered on the cultivation of cereals, primarily emmer wheat and barley. The fertile soils of the Nile floodplain produced high annual yields and large surpluses were a major source of the state's wealth.

Africa

1560: Rise of New Kingdom. New capital founded at Thebes	**1417:** Egyptian prosperity, power and prestige reach their high point under Amenophis III	

2500 BCE — 2250 — 2000 — 1750 — 1500 — 1250 BCE

2040: Egypt reunited under Middle Kingdom pharaohs after period of dominance by nobles. New capital is founded at El-Lisht

1633: Much of Egypt ruled by the Hyksos, an Asiatic people

1350: Pharaoh Akhenaton introduces sun worship in Egypt

Oceania

c.2500: Dingo introduced to Australia, probably from Southeast Asia	**1500:** Lapita colonists start to colonize Pacific Ocean, reaching Tonga and Samoa by c.1000 BCE

2500 BCE — 2250 — 2000 — 1750 — 1500 — 1250 BCE

c.1600: Earliest examples of Lapita pottery in Bismarck Archipelago

THE GROWTH OF THE CITY

Pharaoh Akhenaten
(1379–1362 BCE) was
the founder of the new
city of El-Amarna.

OVER THE COURSE OF 2000 YEARS from c.3500 BCE, cities evolved in many different ways, reflecting the culture from which they emerged, outside pressures, and the preoccupations of their rulers. Yet, in a period of increasing social stratification, all cities represented the gulf between the ruler and the ruled, the sacred and the secular. They were physically, and symbolically, dominated by the palaces of the ruling elite, and by temples and religious precincts. The elaborate monuments of these early centers, clearly segregated from the houses and workshops of the laboring classes, symbolized the absolute power wielded by royal dynasties, priests, and the aristocracy. But the *status quo* was underpinned by a relentless quest for new territory and greater wealth; ultimately, this urge to expand was to evolve into imperialism.

The urban heartland

By 1250 BCE, zones of urbanism extended from the Mediterranean to China. The early expansion of urban civilization in southern Mesopotamia had created a swathe of cities, from Ur to Mycenae, which thrived on trade and contact, supplemented by the levying of taxes, tolls, and tribute. Rivalry for control of key cities was endemic. While Egypt was also vying for political and economic control of the region, the cities of the Nile were stately religious and dynastic centers, adorned by magnificent temples, palaces, and cities of the dead. The distant cities of Shang China were strictly segregated – symbolic of a stratified society where the great wealth and luxury of the few rested on a simple farming base.

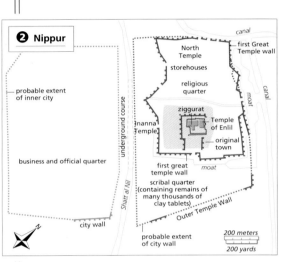

❷ Nippur

probable extent of inner city

business and official quarter

city wall

canal

first Great Temple wall

North Temple

storehouses

religious quarter

ziggurat

Inanna Temple

Temple of Enlil

original town

first great temple wall

scribal quarter (containing remains of many thousands of clay tablets)

Outer Temple Wall

underground course

Shatt al Nil

moat

moat

probable extent of city wall

200 meters
200 yards

A ruler's power
was legitimized by
the foundation of
cities and temples,
as this sculpture of
a Babylonian king
carrying building
materials shows.

Nippur

Center of the worship of Enlil, the chief deity of the Sumerian pantheon, Nippur retained its importance over three millennia. Located on the Shatt al Nil, an ancient course of the Euphrates, the city was first occupied in c.4000 BCE. In c.2100 BCE, Ur-Nammu, ruler of the city-state of Ur, legitimized his role as Enlil's earthly representative by building the first temple and ziggurat to the deity. The temple was subsequently destroyed and rebuilt at least three times. The remains of the extensive religious quarter encompass a large scribal district as well as a temple to Inanna, queen of heaven.

A map of the city of Nippur – probably the oldest plan in the world – was found on a clay tablet from the site dating to c.1500 BCE. The two lines on the far left denote the Euphrates River; adjoining lines show one wall of the city.

❶ Urbanism 1250 BCE

urban area of the Old World, c.1250 BCE

area of secondary urbanization, with date

extent of Indus civilization c.5000–2500 BCE

major city

EUROPE

Volga

Caspian Sea

Caucasus

Black Sea

Elburz Mountains

Danube

Europe: Urbanism spreads in early centuries CE with Roman imperialism

c.750 BCE

Hattushash

Alaca Hüyük

Northern Greece c.750 BCE

Troy Acemhüyük

Kanesh

Carchemish

Persia c.500 BCE

Italy c.750 BCE

Aegean Sea

Beyçesultan

Anatolia

Taurus Mountains

Tell Brak

Mycenae

Athens

Karahüyük

Aleppo

MESOPOTAMIA

Tigris

Pylos

Tiryns

Miletus

Ugarit

Mari

Euphrates

Eshnunna

Zagros

Knossos

Mallia

Qadesh

Byblos

Syrian

Kish

Nippur

Susa

Phaistos

Zakro

Hazor

Desert

Babylon

Uruk

Lagash

Lachish

Megiddo

Larsa

Ur

Mediterranean Sea

Buto

Pi-Ramesse

Arabian

Sais

Bubastis

Peninsula

Memphis

Heliopolis

El-Lisht

Phoenicia c.750 BCE

EGYPT

El-Amarna

Arabian Peninsula: Harsh desert terrain is sparsely populated by desert pastoralists

Thebes

Luxor

Edfu

Nile

Red Sea

Tropic of Cancer

Southern Arabia c.500 BCE

Sculpted lions flank the "Lion Gate," a major entrance into the city of Hattushash. In the 14th century BCE the fortifications of Hattushash were extended and strengthened, as befitted its status as an important imperial capital.

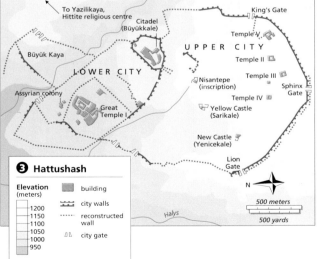

To Yazilikaya, Hittite religious centre

King's Gate

Citadel (Büyükkale)

Temple V

Büyük Kaya

UPPER CITY

Temple II

LOWER CITY

Temple III

Nisantepe (inscription)

Sphinx Gate

Assyrian colony

Temple IV

Yellow Castle (Sarikale)

Great Temple I

New Castle (Yenicekale)

Lion Gate

N

❸ Hattushash

Elevation (meters)

1200
1150
1100
1050
1000
950

building

city walls

reconstructed wall

city gate

Halys

500 meters
500 yards

Hattushash

The Hittite kingdom, which emerged from the conquest of a number of Anatolian city states in the 17th century BCE, adopted the site of Hattushash (Boğazköy) as its capital. Situated at the head of a fertile river valley, the citadel, Büyükkale, was the core of the old city. By c.1400 BCE the walls had been extended to encompass the "Upper City," and Hattushash had been adorned with a series of grandiose monuments – five temples and a palace within the citadel with a large pillared audience hall and a royal archive of 3000 clay tablets. The city walls, which stood on stone-faced ramparts, with projecting towers and twin-towered gateways, made Hattushash one of the most strongly fortified cities in the Middle East.

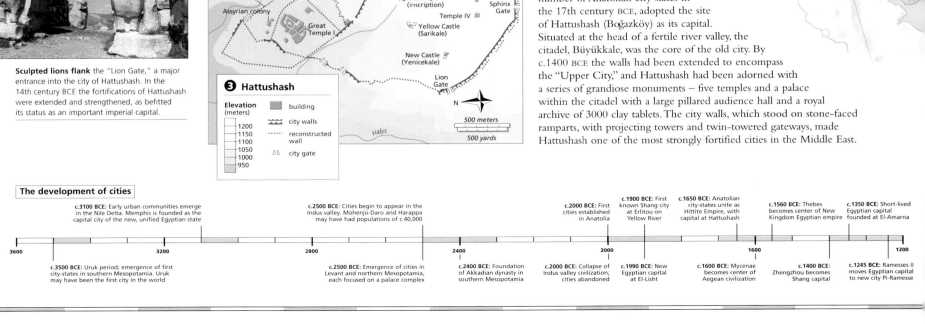

The development of cities

c.3100 BCE: Early urban communities emerge in the Nile Delta. Memphis is founded as the capital city of the new, unified Egyptian state

c.2500 BCE: Cities begin to appear in the Indus valley. Mohenjo-Daro and Harappa may have had populations of c.40,000

c.2000 BCE: First cities established in Anatolia

c.1900 BCE: First known Shang city at Erlitou on Yellow River

c.1650 BCE: Anatolian city-states unite as Hittite Empire, with capital at Hattushash

c.1560 BCE: Thebes becomes center of New Kingdom Egyptian empire

c.1350 BCE: Short-lived Egyptian capital founded at El-Amarna

3600   3200   2800   2400   2000   1600   1200

c.3500 BCE: Uruk period; emergence of first city-states in southern Mesopotamia. Uruk may have been the first city in the world

c.2500 BCE: Emergence of cities in Levant and northern Mesopotamia, each focused on a palace complex

c.2400 BCE: Foundation of Akkadian dynasty in southern Mesopotamia

c.2000 BCE: Collapse of Indus valley civilization; cities abandoned

c.1990 BCE: New Egyptian capital at El-Lisht

c.1600 BCE: Mycenae becomes center of Aegean civilization

c.1400 BCE: Zhengzhou becomes Shang capital

c.1245 BCE: Ramesses II moves Egyptian capital to new city Pi-Ramesse

Zhengzhou

The Shang dynasty ruled in the middle valley of the Yellow River from c.1800 BCE. Remains of Shang cities, rich tombs and luxury artifacts all indicate the presence of a highly sophisticated urban elite. Zhengzhou, one of successive Shang capitals, was founded c.1700 BCE. It consists of a roughly square enclosure, surrounded by 4 mile-long, 11 yd-high rammed earth walls. Within these walls stood the palace and ritual altar, dwelling places, storage pits for grain, pottery, and oracle bones (a means of divination, used by the Shang to consult their ancestors) and pits for human sacrifices. Outside the walls stood the residential areas, and specialist workshops producing fine artifacts in bone, bronze, and pottery.

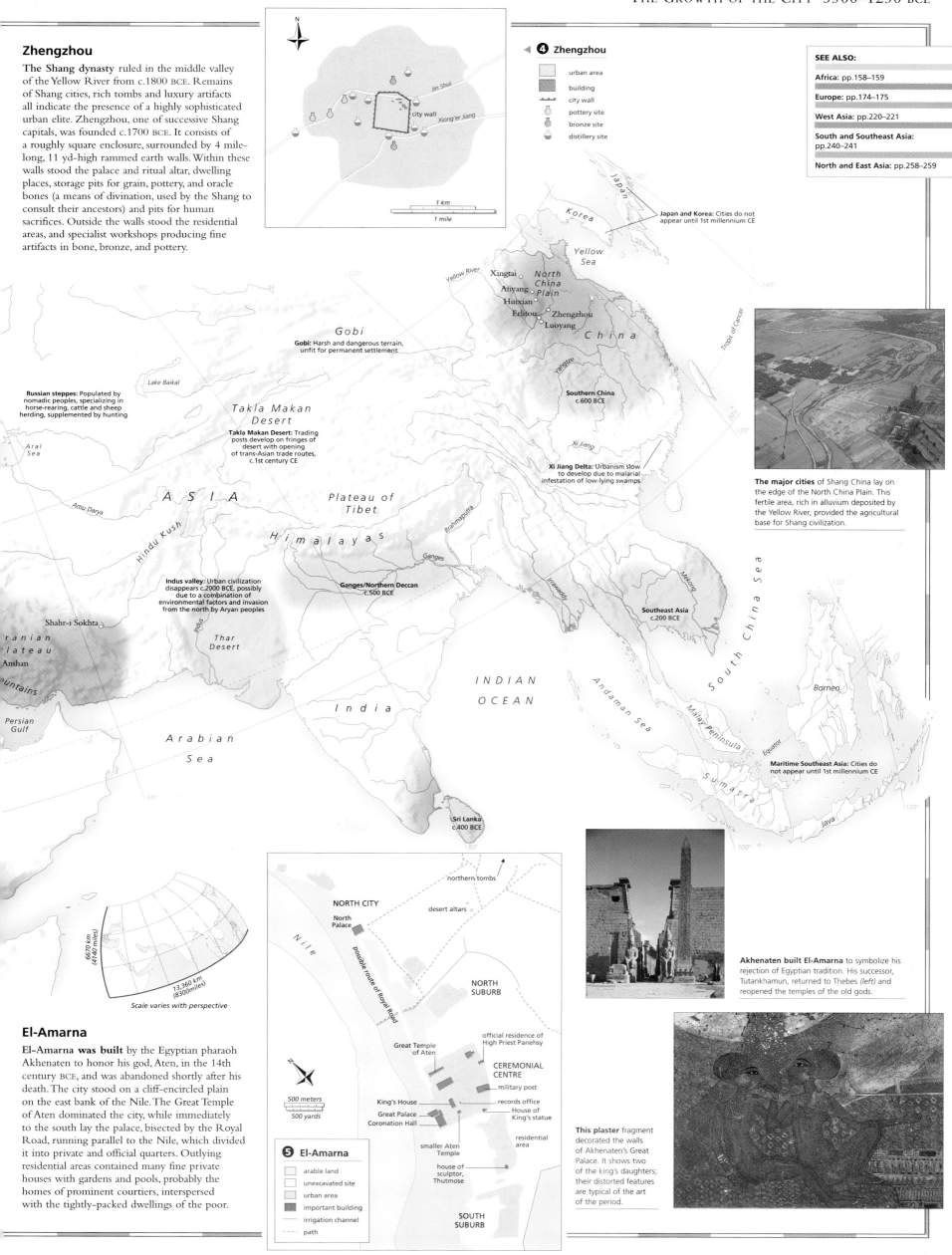

④ Zhengzhou

- urban area
- building
- city wall
- pottery site
- bronze site
- distillery site

SEE ALSO:

Africa: pp.158–159

Europe: pp.174–175

West Asia: pp.220–221

South and Southeast Asia: pp.240–241

North and East Asia: pp.258–259

Japan and Korea: Cities do not appear until 1st millennium CE

Gobi: Harsh and dangerous terrain, unfit for permanent settlement

Russian steppes: Populated by nomadic peoples, specializing in horse-rearing, cattle and sheep herding, supplemented by hunting

Takla Makan Desert: Trading posts develop on fringes of desert with opening of trans-Asian trade routes, c.1st century CE

Xi Jiang Delta: Urbanism slow to develop due to malarial infestation of low-lying swamps

Indus valley: Urban civilization disappears c.2000 BCE, possibly due to a combination of environmental factors and invasion from the north by Aryan peoples

Southern China c.600 BCE

Ganges/Northern Deccan c.500 BCE

Southeast Asia c.200 BCE

Maritime Southeast Asia: Cities do not appear until 1st millennium CE

Sri Lanka c.400 BCE

Scale varies with perspective

The major cities of Shang China lay on the edge of the North China Plain. This fertile area, rich in alluvium deposited by the Yellow River, provided the agricultural base for Shang civilization.

Akhenaten built El-Amarna to symbolize his rejection of Egyptian tradition. His successor, Tutankhamun, returned to Thebes (left) and reopened the temples of the old gods.

El-Amarna

El-Amarna was built by the Egyptian pharaoh Akhenaten to honor his god, Aten, in the 14th century BCE, and was abandoned shortly after his death. The city stood on a cliff-encircled plain on the east bank of the Nile. The Great Temple of Aten dominated the city, while immediately to the south lay the palace, bisected by the Royal Road, running parallel to the Nile, which divided it into private and official quarters. Outlying residential areas contained many fine private houses with gardens and pools, probably the homes of prominent courtiers, interspersed with the tightly-packed dwellings of the poor.

⑤ El-Amarna

- arable land
- unexcavated site
- urban area
- important building
- irrigation channel
- path

This plaster fragment decorated the walls of Akhenaten's Great Palace. It shows two of the king's daughters; their distorted features are typical of the art of the period.

29

THE WORLD 1250–750 BCE

THE INEXORABLE RIVALRIES between the cities and states of the Old World and incursions by nomadic tribes created a shifting pattern of allegiance and control within West Asia. The Assyrians formed the world's first large empire, and ruled their territory with ruthless efficiency, utilizing cavalry and new iron technology to fashion more effective weapons and armor. In both Europe and Asia iron revolutionized weapons, tools, and agricultural implements. More efficient farming produced higher crop yields and supported larger populations. Long-distance trade networks disseminated political and cultural influences across Europe and along the Mediterranean shores, but many areas remained unaffected. The first major centers of the Americas, the Chavín in Peru and the Olmec in Central America, developed in isolation, evolving the art styles, religious motifs, and ceremonies which were to imbue the civilizations that succeeded them.

North America

The first great Mexican civilization, the Olmec, emerged in the coastal lowlands southwest of Yucatán in about 1200 BCE. The Olmec founded a number of ceremonial centers, notably at San Lorenzo and La Venta. They also established trade networks in commodities such as obsidian, jade, and basalt which extended far to the north and west. To the northeast, the peoples of the Adena culture, based along the Ohio River from about 1000–300 BCE, constructed burial chambers beneath earthen mounds.

At San Lorenzo, the Olmec sculpted remarkable stone monuments, including colossal basalt heads with characteristic flat faces, thickened lips, and protective helmets.

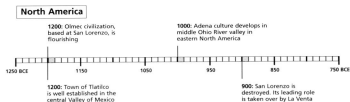

North America

1200: Olmec civilization, based at San Lorenzo, is flourishing

1000: Adena culture develops in middle Ohio River valley in eastern North America

1250 BCE — 1150 — 1050 — 950 — 850 — 750 BCE

1200: Town of Tlatilco is well established in the central Valley of Mexico

900: San Lorenzo is destroyed. Its leading role is taken over by La Venta

The World in 750 BCE

- Greek cities and territories
- Phoenician cities and territories
- small Chinese states under the Eastern Zhou dynasty

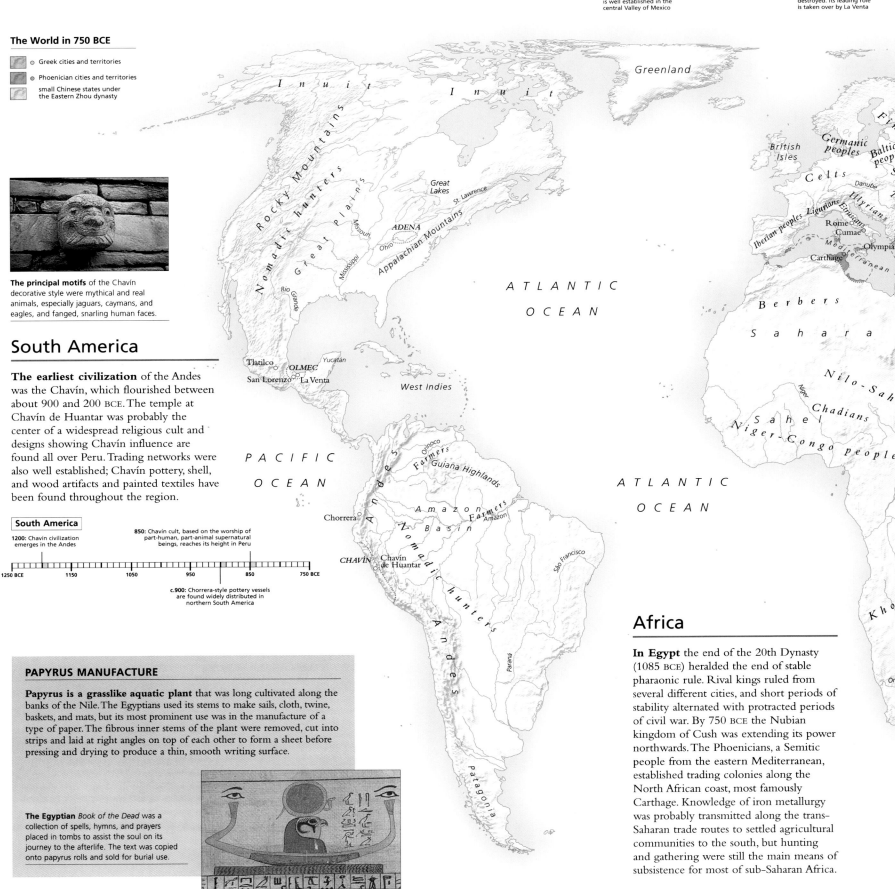

The principal motifs of the Chavín decorative style were mythical and real animals, especially jaguars, caymans, and eagles, and fanged, snarling human faces.

South America

The earliest civilization of the Andes was the Chavín, which flourished between about 900 and 200 BCE. The temple at Chavín de Huantar was probably the center of a widespread religious cult and designs showing Chavín influence are found all over Peru. Trading networks were also well established; Chavín pottery, shell, and wood artifacts and painted textiles have been found throughout the region.

South America

1200: Chavín civilization emerges in the Andes

850: Chavín cult, based on the worship of part-human, part-animal supernatural beings, reaches its height in Peru

1250 BCE — 1150 — 1050 — 950 — 850 — 750 BCE

c.900: Chorrera-style pottery vessels are found widely distributed in northern South America

PAPYRUS MANUFACTURE

Papyrus is a grasslike aquatic plant that was long cultivated along the banks of the Nile. The Egyptians used its stems to make sails, cloth, twine, baskets, and mats, but its most prominent use was in the manufacture of a type of paper. The fibrous inner stems of the plant were removed, cut into strips and laid at right angles on top of each other to form a sheet before pressing and drying to produce a thin, smooth writing surface.

The Egyptian Book of the Dead was a collection of spells, hymns, and prayers placed in tombs to assist the soul on its journey to the afterlife. The text was copied onto papyrus rolls and sold for burial use.

Africa

In Egypt the end of the 20th Dynasty (1085 BCE) heralded the end of stable pharaonic rule. Rival kings ruled from several different cities, and short periods of stability alternated with protracted periods of civil war. By 750 BCE the Nubian kingdom of Cush was extending its power northwards. The Phoenicians, a Semitic people from the eastern Mediterranean, established trading colonies along the North African coast, most famously Carthage. Knowledge of iron metallurgy was probably transmitted along the trans-Saharan trade routes to settled agricultural communities to the south, but hunting and gathering were still the main means of subsistence for most of sub-Saharan Africa.

Europe

Independent city-states were founded throughout Greece and western Asia Minor. The establishment of trade links with Italy and the Levant increased prosperity and population and colonists began to build Greek trading cities along the shores of the Mediterranean. In Italy, the Etruscans built fortified hilltop cities and established extensive trade links with Africa and Europe. Iron metallurgy, established in Central Europe by 1000 BCE, had reached the British Isles by the 8th century. Iron was used to make sophisticated weapons and tools.

After the fall of Mycenean Greece in the 12th century, various powers vied for control of the east Mediterranean. Naval battles were fought between fleets of long, narrow oared vessels built for speed and maneuverability, such as the Greek galley depicted on this pot.

BABYLONIAN ASTRONOMY

The Babylonians were one of the earliest peoples to make a systematic, scientific study of the skies. Their records go back to c.1800 BCE and accumulated over centuries. By 1000 BCE they were able to predict lunar eclipses and within two or three hundred years, the path of the Sun and some of the planets had been plotted with considerable accuracy. These astronomical records contributed to the later flowering of western astronomy.

This bronze model of the solar system is from Lake Sevan in Armenia. It dates from 10th–9th century BCE.

SEE ALSO:

North America: pp.120–121

South America: pp.144–145

Africa: pp.160–161

Europe: pp.176–177

West Asia: pp.222–223

South and Southeast Asia: pp.240–243

North and East Asia: pp.258–259

Australasia and Oceania: pp.280–281

Europe

| 1150: Collapse of Mycenean Greece | 1000: Colonists from mainland Greece settle coast of Asia Minor and islands of eastern Aegean | 900: End of dark ages in Greece | 800: Rise of Etruscan city-states in Central Italy | 776: First Pan-Hellenic athletics festival held at the Sanctuary of Zeus, Olympia |

1250 BCE — 1150 — 1050 — 950 — 850 — 750 BCE

| 1200: New Urnfield culture emerges in Danube area. Named after tradition of placing cremated ashes in urns in large communal burial fields | c.1000: Iron-working reaches Central Europe from the Near East | 850: Earliest village on Rome's Palatine Hill | 800: First phase of Celtic Iron Age named after cemetery at Hallstatt in Austria |

West Asia

Power struggles between the established empires of the West Asia created opportunities for infiltration by barbarian tribes, such as the Medes, Chaldeans, Philistines, Hebrews, and Phrygians, who attempted to seize power. The Hebrews under King David briefly created a kingdom which united Palestine and Syria, but it collapsed after the rule of Solomon (966–926 BCE). From the 9th century BCE, the dominant power in the region was Assyria, originally based in the Tigris valley. By the 8th century BCE the Assyrian Empire, extended from the Levant to the Persian Gulf. Subject peoples were ruled by provincial governors and resistance was ruthlessly suppressed. Only the Armenian kingdom of Urartu remained beyond Assyrian control.

Assyrian kings plowed the proceeds of their military conquests into the building of vast temples and palaces at Nimrud and Nineveh. Booty acquired during the campaigns, like this ivory panel of a sphinx, enriched many palace furnishings.

West Asia

| 1200: Collapse of the Hittite Empire | c.1100: Syria and Palestine settled by nomadic tribes | c.1000: King David unites Israel and Judaea, with its capital city at Jerusalem | 900: Kingdom of Urartu established in Armenia resists Assyrian expansion |

1250 BCE — 1150 — 1050 — 950 — 850 — 750 BCE

| c.1200: Jewish exodus from Egypt and settlement in Palestine | c.1000: Phoenicians dominate trade of Levant and develop an alphabetic script | 950: Foundation of the Assyrian Empire |

The need to preserve the body from decay through mummification was an integral part of the Egyptian belief in a life after death. This anthropomorphic case belonged to Shepenmut, Priestess of Thebes, who was buried around 800 BCE.

Zhou rulers maintained Shang cultural traditions, including ancestor worship. Food and drink were offered in bronze ritual vessels, often shaped into bizarre combinations of animal forms.

East Asia

In China the Zhou dynasty succeeded the Shang in the 11th century BCE, heralding a period of stability until the 8th century when central authority collapsed, former fiefs rose up against the Zhou, and China split into separate kingdoms. Bronze technology for weapons and ornaments reached the Korean peninsula from Manchuria in about 1000 BCE.

Africa

| 1166: Death of Rameses III, Egypt's last great pharaoh. | 945: Civil war in Eygpt. By mid-8th century, Egypt divided into several small states | c.750: Kingdom of Cush extends power and influence northward |

1250 BCE — 1150 — 1050 — 950 — 850 — 750 BCE

| 1085: End of 20th Dynasty and Egyptian New Kingdom | c.900: Foundation of Nubian kingdom of Cush | 814: Foundation of Phoenician colony of Carthage |

East Asia

| 1027: Zhou dynasty replaces Shang in China | 1000: Chinese bronze casting reaches level of craftsmanship unrivaled elsewhere at this period |

1250 BCE — 1150 — 1050 — 950 — 850 — 750 BCE

| c.1000: Wet rice cultivation introduced to Korea from China | c.770: Western Zhou period ends with collapse of centralized power |

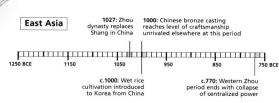

WRITING, COUNTING, AND CALENDARS

The Greek inscription *(above)* is an offering of thanks to Asclepius, the god of healing.

THE INTERTWINED DEVELOPMENT of writing and counting was closely related to the advent of agriculture and the need to record and tally stored goods, livestock, and commercial transactions. The precursors of the first known writing and numerical systems were clay counting tokens, used in Sumeria from c.3400 BCE to record quantities of stored goods. They were eventually sealed in clay envelopes, and marked on the outside with signs indicating their contents – the first written symbols. Within a thousand years, writing and numerical systems had spread throughout West Asia (they evolved separately in China and Central America), bringing a revolutionary change in human consciousness. The ability to count in abstract enabled humans to measure, assess, record, and evaluate their world – calendrical systems, weights and measures, coinage, astronomical calculations, and geometry all followed. Writing became a powerful tool of government, a means of communicating over increasing distances, codifying laws, and recording myths and history.

The evolution and spread of major scripts

The earliest symbolic records, of economic transactions, were used in Sumeria from c.3400 BCE, and gradually evolved into a pictographic script, where pictures represented words. Cuneiform writing (made by impressing a wet clay tablet with a stylus) was used to record a variety of languages, and spread throughout West Asia. The system eventually became more complex, and written symbols also came to stand for concepts or sounds. Egyptian hieroglyphics probably developed under Sumerian influence, though the system was unique. Chinese pictographic writing developed independently, as did the Zapotec and Maya systems in Central America. Ugaritic alphabetic cuneiform (c.1400 BCE) was the precursor of the Phoenician alphabet, adapted by the Greeks in the 8th century BCE.

This inscription in Egyptian hieratic is a record of a trading transaction. Hieratic was a form of cursive script, written with ink and a reed brush.

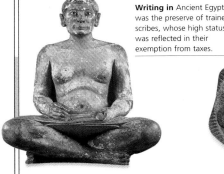

Writing in Ancient Egypt was the preserve of trained scribes, whose high status was reflected in their exemption from taxes.

This glyph from Central America, represents the word "grass."

Oracle bones, the earliest examples of writing from Shang dynasty China, record predictions made by interpreting cracks in the bones.

The inscriptions on this black basalt pillar are the most complete example of the law code of Hammurabi, king of Babylonia (c.1790–1750 BCE), who is depicted on the top of the pillar.

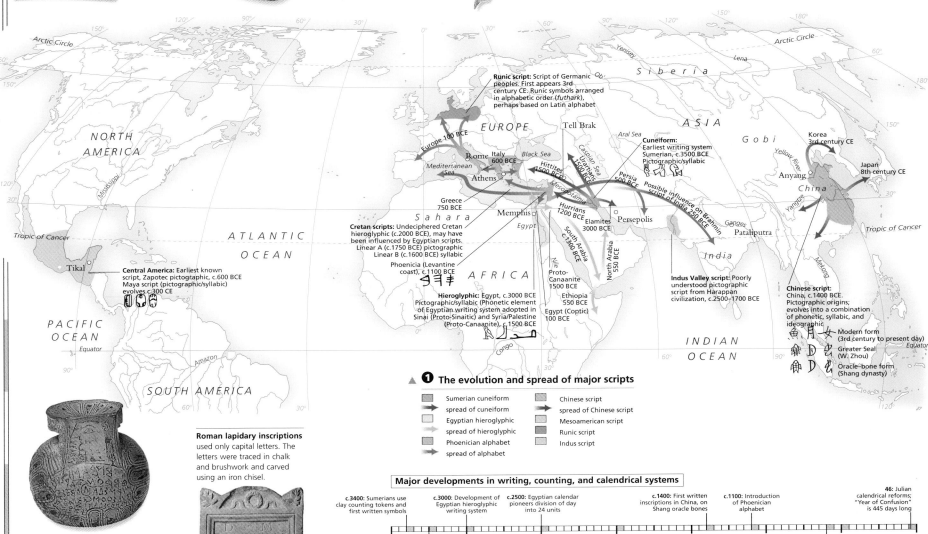

Runic script: Script of Germanic peoples. First appears 3rd century CE. Runic symbols arranged in alphabetic order (*futhark*), perhaps based on Latin alphabet

Cuneiform: Earliest writing system Sumerian, c.3500 BCE. Pictographic/syllabic

Cretan scripts: Undeciphered Cretan hieroglyphic (c.2000 BCE), may have been influenced by Egyptian scripts. Linear A (c.1750 BCE) pictographic Linear B (c.1600 BCE) syllabic

Central America: Earliest known script, Zapotec pictographic, c.600 BCE Maya script (pictographic/syllabic) evolves c.300 CE

Hieroglyphic: Egypt, c.3000 BCE Pictographic/syllabic (Phonetic element of Egyptian writing system adopted in Sinai (Proto-Sinaitic) and Syria/Palestine (Proto-Canaanite), c.1500 BCE

Indus Valley script: Poorly understood pictographic script from Harappan civilization, c.2500–1700 BCE

Chinese script: China, c.1400 BCE. Pictographic origins; evolves into a combination of phonetic, syllabic, and ideographic

Modern form (3rd century to present day)
Greater Seal (W. Zhou)
Oracle-bone form (Shang dynasty)

① The evolution and spread of major scripts

- Sumerian cuneiform
- spread of cuneiform
- Egyptian hieroglyphic
- spread of hieroglyphic
- Phoenician alphabet
- spread of alphabet
- Chinese script
- spread of Chinese script
- Mesoamerican script
- Runic script
- Indus script

Central America: Earliest known script, Zapotec pictographic, c.600 BCE

Roman lapidary inscriptions used only capital letters. The letters were traced in chalk and brushwork and carved using an iron chisel.

This perfume jar from Corinth in Greece is inscribed in the alphabetic script which was adapted from the Phoenician, and used in Greece from the 8th century BCE.

Major developments in writing, counting, and calendrical systems

c.3400: Sumerians use clay counting tokens and first written symbols

c.3000: Development of Egyptian hieroglyphic writing system

c.2500: Egyptian calendar pioneers division of day into 24 units

c.1400: First written inscriptions in China, on Shang oracle bones

c.1100: Introduction of Phoenician alphabet

46: Julian calendrical reforms; "Year of Confusion" is 445 days long

3500 BCE   3000 BCE   2500 BCE   2000 BCE   1500 BCE   1000 BCE   500 BCE   1 CE

c.3250: Earliest writing in the world; clay pictographic tablets from Tell Brak, Syria

c.2000: Appearance of Cretan hieroglyphic writing

c.600: First Greek coins
c.600: First Central American script (Zapotec)

c.500: Hebrews evolve use of 7-day weeks
c.500: First coins used in China

SEE ALSO:

North America: pp.122–123

South America: pp.146–147

West Asia: pp.222–223

North and East Asia: pp.258–259

The evolution of numerical systems

Wooden tally sticks were used over 30,000 years ago, probably to record numbers of animals killed. From c.3400 BCE the Sumerians used clay counting tokens of various sizes and shapes to represent order of magnitude, and evolved the first written numbering system. As humans count using their fingers and toes, most systems used base 10, while Mayans, Aztecs, and Celts chose base 20. The Sumerian and Babylonian use of base 60 (still evident in our use of 60 minutes and seconds, and 360 degrees) remains mysterious. Alphabetic counting systems, used by Greeks, Hebrews, and Arabs, wrote numbers by using letters. The concept of zero, and the positional numbering system, was an Indian invention.

The Rhind mathematical papyrus dates to c.1575 BCE. It demonstrates that the Egyptians had some understanding of the properties of right-angled triangles.

This Babylonian mathematical text with cuneiform numbers dates to c.500 BCE. The use of the sexagesimal system was an important factor in the development of Babylonian astronomy.

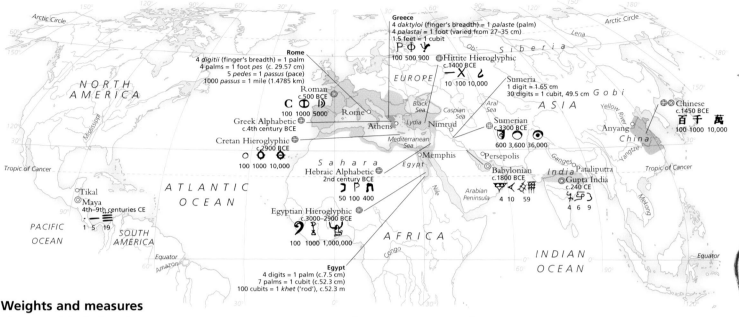

❷ The evolution of numerical systems

Earliest known date of counting system

Numerical system		Regions	
⊕	additive		Roman
⊗	multiplicative		Hittite
○	positional		Egyptian
Base			Greek
●	Base 10		Hebraic
◐	Base 20		Gupta India
○	Base 60		Chinese

Heracles is shown stringing a bow on this Theban coin (c.446–426 BCE).

Weights and measures

The parts of the body, such as the fingers, palms, and toes, were used by all ancient civilizations for shorter units of measurement. Greater distances reflect the nature of the civilization; the Roman *passus* (1.6 m) reflects the Romans' road system and marching armies, the Greek stadion originates in the length of an athletic race track.

Bronze scales, using a simple balance system, were used extensively in Ancient Rome. Weights were verified by officials.

Mesopotamian weights were calculated according to the sexagesimal system. This 1st-millennium BCE relief from Nimrud, Iraq, shows tribute being weighed.

Coinage

As trade networks expanded, barter, which depended on long negotiations, became increasingly inconvenient. The need for an agreed system of equivalences of value led to the invention of coins, metal objects with a constant weight, marked with the official stamp of a public authority. The Greeks of Lydia developed the system in the 7th century BCE, and it was rapidly adopted elsewhere.

This Athenian coin is known as a tetradrachm (479 BCE). The owl was a symbol of Athena.

This early Egyptian counting stick was found with pieces of metal, used as money.

The evolution of calendrical systems

The development of calendars was linked to religion and the need to predict days of ritual significance, such as the summer solstice. Calendrical systems developed through astronomical observation and record-keeping, and were dependent on both writing and numeracy. All calendars had to resolve the incommensurate cycles of days, lunations and solar years, usually by intercalating extra days or months at regular intervals. Eras were assessed by different means, most commonly from the regnal years of monarchy, or from the year of birth of significant individuals, such as Buddha or Christ.

Fragments of a bronze Celtic lunisolar calendar have been found at Coligny, France. Pegs may have been inserted into holes to mark the passage of the days.

Light penetrates the neolithic tomb at Newgrange in Ireland at sunrise on 21 December, an example of the astronomical significance of many stone alignments.

The Babylonians made systematic observations of the setting and rising of the planet Venus at the city of Kish, recorded on the Venus tablet (c.1700 BCE).

❸ The evolution and spread of calendrical systems

- ● lunar (months are kept in step with lunar cycle by intercalating days)
- ◐ solar (lunar cycle is ignored; years are kept in step with the Sun by intercalating days)
- ◑ lunisolar (month are geared to lunar cycle; extra months are intercalated to key year synchronized with sun)
- □ wandering year (fixed number of days; lunar and solar cycles abandoned)
- ⋯ extent of Roman Empire in 2nd century CE

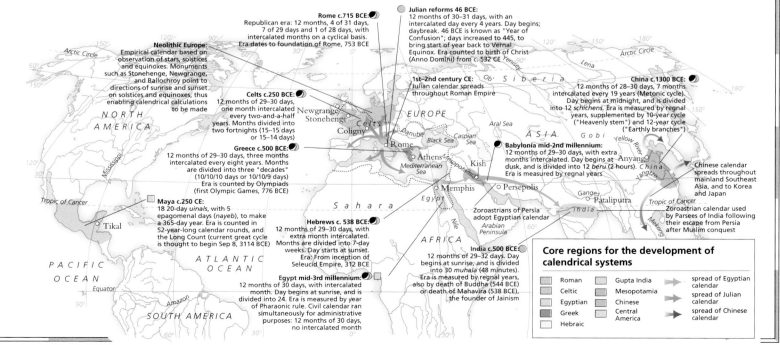

Core regions for the development of calendrical systems

Roman		Gupta India	→ spread of Egyptian calendar
Celtic		Mesopotamia	
Egyptian		Chinese	⇒ spread of Julian calendar
Greek		Central America	
Hebraic			⟹ spread of Chinese calendar

THE WORLD 750–500 BCE

THE CIVILIZATIONS OF EURASIA, although they only occupied a small portion of the Earth's surface, now lay in a more or less continuous belt from the Mediterranean to China. Both trade and cultural contact were well-established; understanding of iron metallurgy had spread from the Middle East as far as China, and by the 6th century BCE Chinese silk was beginning to appear in Europe, marking the beginning of 1,500 years of trans-Asian trade. All these civilizations, however, were increasingly subjected to incursions by tribes of nomadic pastoralists who were rapidly spreading across Central Asia, eastern Europe, and Siberia. By 500 BCE, the Classical Age in Greece – a high point in the history of western civilization – was beginning. It was to have a profound impact on European political institutions, art, architecture, drama, and philosophy. In 505 BCE, the *polis* of Athens initiated radical political reforms and became the birthplace of democracy.

Europe

As the city-states of Greece became more prosperous, their civic pride was expressed through magnificent buildings. Greek colonies, which stretched from the Black Sea to the Iberian Peninsula, were major trading centers, importing raw materials and food supplies in exchange for manufactures, such as pottery. The expanding European population moved into more marginal areas, using iron tools for land clearance and agriculture. Northern Europe was occupied by Celtic and Germanic peoples, whose tribal societies centered on princely graves and hill-top fortresses.

Revelry is a common theme in the tomb frescoes of the Etruscans, whose urban civilization reached its height in 6th-century BCE Italy.

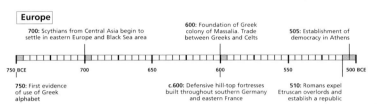

Europe

700: Scythians from Central Asia begin to settle in eastern Europe and Black Sea area

600: Foundation of Greek colony of Massalia. Trade between Greeks and Celts

505: Establishment of democracy in Athens

750: First evidence of use of Greek alphabet

c.600: Defensive hill-top fortresses built throughout southern Germany and eastern France

510: Romans expel Etruscan overlords and establish a republic

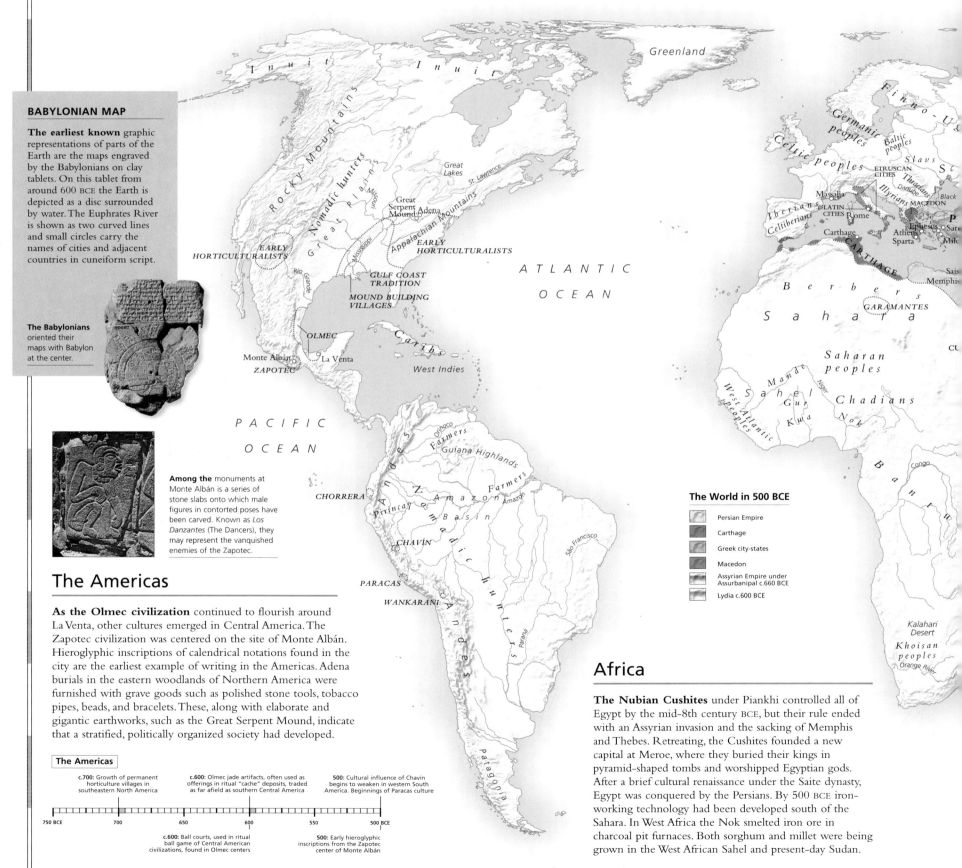

BABYLONIAN MAP

The earliest known graphic representations of parts of the Earth are the maps engraved by the Babylonians on clay tablets. On this tablet from around 600 BCE the Earth is depicted as a disc surrounded by water. The Euphrates River is shown as two curved lines and small circles carry the names of cities and adjacent countries in cuneiform script.

The Babylonians oriented their maps with Babylon at the center.

Among the monuments at Monte Albán is a series of stone slabs onto which male figures in contorted poses have been carved. Known as *Los Danzantes* (The Dancers), they may represent the vanquished enemies of the Zapotec.

The Americas

As the Olmec civilization continued to flourish around La Venta, other cultures emerged in Central America. The Zapotec civilization was centered on the site of Monte Albán. Hieroglyphic inscriptions of calendrical notations found in the city are the earliest example of writing in the Americas. Adena burials in the eastern woodlands of Northern America were furnished with grave goods such as polished stone tools, tobacco pipes, beads, and bracelets. These, along with elaborate and gigantic earthworks, such as the Great Serpent Mound, indicate that a stratified, politically organized society had developed.

The Americas

c.700: Growth of permanent horticulture villages in southeastern North America

c.600: Olmec jade artifacts, often used as offerings in ritual "cache" deposits, traded as far afield as southern Central America

500: Cultural influence of Chavin begins to weaken in western South America. Beginnings of Paracas culture

c.600: Ball courts, used in ritual ball game of Central American civilizations, found in Olmec centers

500: Early hieroglyphic inscriptions from the Zapotec center of Monte Albán

The World in 500 BCE

- Persian Empire
- Carthage
- Greek city-states
- Macedon
- Assyrian Empire under Assurbanipal c.660 BCE
- Lydia c.600 BCE

Africa

The Nubian Cushites under Piankhi controlled all of Egypt by the mid-8th century BCE, but their rule ended with an Assyrian invasion and the sacking of Memphis and Thebes. Retreating, the Cushites founded a new capital at Meroe, where they buried their kings in pyramid-shaped tombs and worshipped Egyptian gods. After a brief cultural renaissance under the Saite dynasty, Egypt was conquered by the Persians. By 500 BCE iron-working technology had been developed south of the Sahara. In West Africa the Nok smelted iron ore in charcoal pit furnaces. Both sorghum and millet were being grown in the West African Sahel and present-day Sudan.

THE FIRST COINS

The use of metals to make payments can be traced back more than 4000 years, but standardization and certification in the form of coinage did not arrive until the 7th century BCE. The first coins were issued by the Lydians of western Anatolia. They consisted of bean-sized pieces of electrum – a natural alloy of gold and silver – with punchmarks testifying to their weight and therefore their value in payments. By 570 BCE coinage had spread west to Greece and east to Persia. It was invented independently in China and India c.500 BCE.

The first Chinese coins, introduced c.500 BCE, were miniature bronze hoes or spades (*left*), copies of the tools that previously had been used for barter. Early Greek coins carried stamped designs, many derived from the animal world (*right*).

West Asia

Assyria's enemies united to overthrow the empire in 612 BCE, and for a brief period Babylon again enjoyed ascendancy in Mesopotamia. This changed with the arrival of the Medes and Persians, Indo-Europeans from Central Asia. In 550 BCE the Persian king, Cyrus the Great, defeated the Medes and united the two peoples, founding the Achaemenid Empire, which became the largest state the world had yet seen, stretching from the Nile to the Indus. A later Persian ruler, Darius I, consolidated imperial rule: subject peoples were divided into provinces, or satrapies; taxes were levied and the construction of the Royal Road from Sardis to Susa facilitated fast, efficient communications.

The king is the focus of the decoration of the palace at Persepolis, ceremonial capital of the Achaemenid Persians. Reliefs depict his court and processions of tribute-bearers from his empire.

SEE ALSO:

North America: pp.120–121

South America: pp.144–145

Africa: pp.158–159

Europe: pp.176–179

West Asia: pp.222–223

South and Southeast Asia: pp.240–243

North and East Asia: pp.258–259

Australasia and Oceania: pp.280–281

West Asia

700: Nomadic Scythians begin to establish permanent settlements on western steppes

c.663: Assyrian Empire reaches greatest extent with sack of Thebes in Egypt

604: Nebuchadnezzar II rebuilds Babylon and captures Jerusalem

539: Cyrus takes Babylon, and Babylonian Empire, without bloodshed

612: Nineveh and Nimrud are sacked by Babylonians and Medes; end of Assyrian Empire

c.550: Cyrus the Great of Persia defeats Medes and founds Achaemenid Empire

521: Persian Empire reaches greatest extent, under Darius I

750 BCE | 700 | 650 | 600 | 550 | 500 BCE

East Asia

With the beginning of the Eastern Zhou period in 770 BCE, China experienced several centuries of conflict as many former vassals of the Zhou competed for supremacy. This was a period of technological and cultural change. The widespread use of iron tools improved the productivity of the land and led to a marked population increase. At the same time new ideas stimulated feverish intellectual debate. The teaching of Confucius was a practical, ethical guide to good government and social behavior, while Taoism was a philosophy based on a mystical faith in natural forces.

During this period Chinese chariots were elaborately decorated to enhance their appearance in battle. This bronze bull's head chariot fitting is inlaid with gold.

East Asia

c.650: Introduction of iron technology to China. Silk painting, lacquerwork, and ceramics become highly skilled

605: Birth of Lao-tzu, founder of Taoism

551: Birth of Confucius

c.500: Bronze coinage introduced in China

750 BCE | 700 | 650 | 600 | 550 | 500 BCE

c.500: Iron-casting used to manufacture huge quantities of tools and weapons in China

In India, early traditions, dating back before 2000 BCE, evolved into Hinduism. This stone statue portrays an early deity, Surya, the sun god.

South Asia

From about 1500 BCE the peoples of central north India began to adopt a sedentary life and expanded eastward to settle the Ganges plain. By the 7th century BCE, a patchwork of small states had emerged in northern India. Some were tribal republics, others absolute monarchies, but their common roots – apparent in the Hindu religion and the caste system – underpinned their religious and social organization. The Afghan region of Gandhara and the Indus Valley were absorbed into the Persian Empire in the late 6th century BCE.

From Meroe, the Cushites were able to maintain their rule over the middle Nile until the 4th century CE, while Egypt suffered a series of invasions. This stone ram lies among the ruins of a Meroitic temple at Naqa.

Africa

747: Rule of Egypt by Nubians

671: Assyrian king, Esarhaddon, captures Egyptian capital, Memphis

600: Nubian capital moves to Meroe

c.500: Darius I of Persia completes construction of a canal linking Nile and Red Sea

750 BCE | 700 | 650 | 600 | 550 | 500 BCE

663: Egypt regains independence under 26th Dynasty, which rules from Sais in the Nile Delta until 525 BCE

525: Egypt becomes part of Persian Empire

South Asia

c.600: 16 Aryan kingdoms are spread across northern India

c.540: Birth of Mahavira, founder of Jain religion

750 BCE | 700 | 650 | 600 | 550 | 500 BCE

c.566: Birth of Buddha, who forsakes life of a nobleman to seek enlightenment through asceticism and good conduct

533: Kingdom of Gandhara becomes satrapy of Persia

THE ORIGINS OF ORGANIZED RELIGION

The development of a priestly class, as here at Sumer, was central in the organization of religious practice as a core social activity.

THE 6TH CENTURY BCE has been called an axial period in the development of religion. Judaism, Hinduism, and Taoism were well established. Reformers such as Deutero-Isaiah, Mahavira, Siddhartha Gautama, and Confucius were at work. Around the Mediterranean, a melting-pot of local cults was forming the roots of European Classical civilization, while in the Americas the first urban cultures brought with them organized religion. And frequently, it was the adoption by political rulers of a particular religion which would ensure its longevity and evolution – as in Buddhism, Confucianism, and, later, Christianity – into a world religion.

The development of organized religion

Zoroastrian worship focused on a supreme being, Ahura Mazda, who was widely worshiped at fire altars.

The development of organized religions was linked to the emergence of urban civilization. The earliest known state religion was that of Sumer in the 3rd millennium BCE, and the oldest coherent mythology was that of Egypt, from the 2nd millennium BCE. By the 1st millennium a range of common characteristics and practices had emerged from local cults to acquire the trappings of organized religion: shamans became priests; myth became doctrine; sacrifice became ceremony; ancestor worship was celebrated in increasingly rich and elaborate burial practices and grandiose monumental architecture.

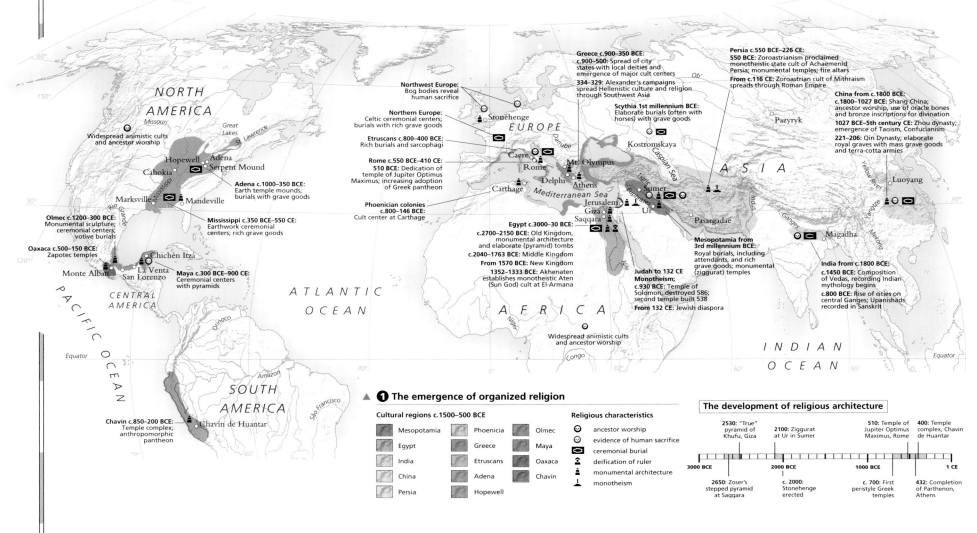

① The emergence of organized religion

Cultural regions c.1500–500 BCE

Mesopotamia	Phoenicia	Olmec
Egypt	Greece	Maya
India	Etruscans	Oaxaca
China	Adena	Chavin
Persia	Hopewell	

Religious characteristics

- ancestor worship
- evidence of human sacrifice
- ceremonial burial
- deification of ruler
- monumental architecture
- monotheism

The development of religious architecture

2530: "True" pyramid of Khufu, Giza — 2100: Ziggurat at Ur in Sumer — 510: Temple of Jupiter Optimus Maximus, Rome — 400: Temple complex, Chavin de Huantar

3000 BCE — 2000 BCE — 1000 BCE — 1 CE

2650: Zoser's stepped pyramid at Saqqara — c. 2000: Stonehenge erected — c. 700: First peristyle Greek temples — 432: Completion of Parthenon, Athens

Early religion in South Asia

A *trimurti* at the Temple of Shiva at Elephanta depicts the three principal Hindu divinities, Shiva, Vishnu, and Brahma.

The religion of the ancient Aryan tribes is known largely from the hymns of the *Rig Veda*, and the *Vedas*, *Brahmanas*, and *Upanishads*. It focused on sacrifices to a pantheon of deities and semigods quite different to those of today. From its core region in Brahmavarta, Vedic Hinduism spread over much of India before the rise of Buddhism and Jainism, both of which developed in northeastern India in reaction to the excesses of Aryan religious practices. These faiths emphasized *ahimsa* (nonviolence), meditation, and the suppression of desire for worldly possessions.

② Religions of South Asia

UDICHYA broad cultural region recognised by ancient Aryans

MAGADHA other regions

Yamuna sacred river

core area of Buddhism and Jainism

Ashokan rock and pillar edicts

Early religion in South Asia

c.1550: Aryans overwhelm Indus valley civilization and settle northern India

6th century: Life of Mahavira, founder of Jainism

566: Birth of Siddhartha Gautama, founder of Buddhism

322: Chandragupta founds Mauryan dynasty

1400 BCE — 1000 — 600 — 200 BCE

c.800: Rise of urban culture in Ganges valley

c.600: Rise to dominance of Magadha

272–232: Reign of Ashoka, who promulgates Buddhism as state religion

Legendary descent of the Buddha from heaven

563: Birthplace

534: Great Renunciation

483: Attainment of Nirvana

528: Attainment of Enlightenment

528: Sermon in the Deer Park

Religions of the Mediterranean

The Mediterranean world in the 1st millennium BCE was the home of a range of discrete cultures, each supporting its own religious beliefs. However, many of these shared striking similarities in mythology, the character and nature of their pantheons of gods, and in religious practice and observance. Rivalry, warfare, and trade created an interaction of influences and cross-fertilizations, and with the rise of Classical Greece, Hellenistic culture, and then Rome, certain local beliefs and practices became widespread.

Zeus (Jupiter for the Romans) was the supreme Greek deity.

Greece

The Greek mythological pantheon, developed during the Mycenaean period, was described by writers such as Homer and became, during the Classic Greek period, a central force in Greek life. Each city-state worshiped favored cults, but the emergence of oracles and other cult centers (such as Mount Olympus) codified a pan-Hellenic religious tradition which was spread widely by colonization and the campaigns of Alexander the Great (*see pp.40–41*).

SEE ALSO:

Africa: pp.160–161

Europe: pp.174–179

West Asia: pp.220–221

South and Southeast Asia: pp.242–243

North and East Asia: pp.258–259

❸ **The Mediterranean cults** ▶

Cult centers
- ◉ Egyptian
- ◉ Greek
- ○ other
- Ares   main divinity worshipped
- → spread of the cult of Cybele
- → spread of the Greek Pantheon
- → spread of Mithraism

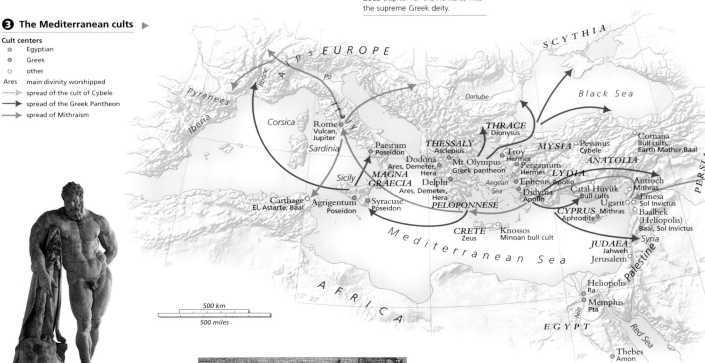

The demigod Heracles (Hercules in Latin) formed part of the Greek mythological pantheon adopted by the Romans.

Rome

Rome's pantheon was largely adopted from that of Greece, although certain local cults gained popularity as the empire grew. One of the most widespread was that of Mithras, which spread from Persia to Syria, then throughout the empire; eventually the most influential was Christianity.

A dead man kneels before Anubis, goddess of mummification. Life after death was central to Egyptian theology, celebrated through a series of elaborate rituals.

Egypt

A detailed mythology and pantheon permeated Ancient Egyptian life and thought, and is recorded abundantly in votive statuary and hieroglyphic tomb paintings. The hierarchy and character of Egyptian cosmology probably influenced the development of the Mycenaean and Greek pantheon.

This Mycenaean ritual sprinkler takes the form of a bull's head.

Judaism

Originating around 1200 BCE with the worship of Jahweh, Judaism remained almost unique in being monotheistic. Formalized as a state religion of Israel during the reign of David (c.1000 BCE), the religion survived exile and persecution to form the seedbed of Christianity.

The Jewish candelabra *(menorah)* symbolizes the eternal light *(ner tamid)* which burned in the first Temple of Solomon.

Bull cults

Bull worshipping was widespread in the Mediterranean region, from Çatal Hüyük (c.7000 BCE) to the famous Minos cult in Crete (from c.2000 BCE); bulls also played a significant role in Egyptian and Greek mythology.

Taoism and Confucianism

Taoism developed during the Zhou dynasty as the most widespread of Chinese religions. Based on the worship of ancestors, nature spirits, and sacred places, it was codified by Lao-tzu (605–520 BCE). The philosopher Confucius (551–479 BCE) promulgated a system of filial observance, learning, obedience, and selflessness which became central to Chinese imperial policy and governance. Followers such as Mencius (c.370–300 BCE) ensured that his teachings survived the Warring States period (403–221 BCE).

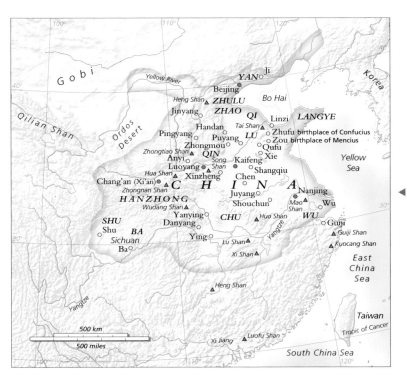

❹ **Taoism and Confucianism**

- ▨ Chinese cultural area c.220 BCE
- YAN   region associated with development of Taoism
- ▲ mountain sacred to Taoism

Centers of Confucianism
- ○ Imperial capital
- ● Qin state capital by c.220 BCE

The teachings of Confucius ensured that even the most lowly could, by ability, correct behavior, and hard work, aspire to high office.

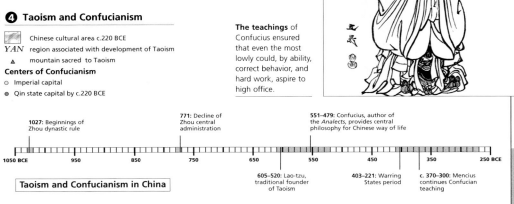

771: Decline of Zhou central administration

1027: Beginnings of Zhou dynastic rule

551–479: Confucius, author of the *Analects*, provides central philosophy for Chinese way of life

605–520: Lao-tzu, traditional founder of Taoism

403–221: Warring States period

c. 370–300: Mencius continues Confucian teaching

Taoism and Confucianism in China

THE WORLD 500–250 BCE

THE 5TH CENTURY BCE was an age of enlightened and innovative thought. It was the climax of the Classical Age in Greece, a period that was remarkable for its art, philosophy, drama, architecture, and political theory. At the same time the Buddhist religion, based on the precepts of renouncing all material desires as practiced by Siddhartha Gautama (c.566–486 BCE), was spreading throughout the Indian subcontinent. In China, the teachings of Confucius (551–479 BCE) were concerned with ethical conduct and propriety in human relations. Yet the ensuing centuries were a time of conflict and conquest. From 331–323 BCE Alexander the Great's military conquests created an empire which stretched from Macedon to the Indus. From c.272 BCE the emperor Ashoka absorbed most of the Indian subcontinent into his empire, while in China the Warring States period was a time of violent turmoil.

The shrine of Delphi was the site of the Pythian Games, one of four great athletic festivals that brought Greeks together at set intervals of years.

Europe

In the 5th century BCE, Greece reached the pinnacle of the Classical Age. Athens' conflict with Sparta in the Peloponnesian Wars weakened the Greek city-states, which in the 4th century fell to Philip of Macedon. Under his son, Alexander the Great, who conquered the Persian Empire, Greece became a great imperial power. In Italy, by 264 BCE, Rome was poised to become a world power.

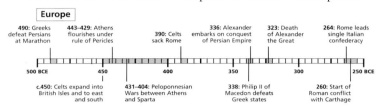

Europe

490: Greeks defeat Persians at Marathon | 443–429: Athens flourishes under rule of Pericles | 390: Celts sack Rome | 336: Alexander embarks on conquest of Persian Empire | 323: Death of Alexander the Great | 264: Rome leads single Italian confederacy

500 BCE — 450 — 400 — 350 — 300 — 250 BCE

c.450: Celts expand into British Isles and to east and south | 431–404: Peloponnesian Wars between Athens and Sparta | 338: Philip II of Macedon defeats Greek states | 260: Start of Roman conflict with Carthage

THE ARCHIMEDEAN SCREW

Named after Archimedes, the Greek mathematician (287–212 BCE), the Archimedean screw is one of the earliest devices for raising water. It was probably invented in the 7th or 8th century BCE in Mesopotamia. Consisting of a spiral screw revolving inside a close-fitting cylinder, it has been widely used over the centuries for irrigation and land drainage.

This Egyptian terra-cotta figurine from c.30 BCE shows a slave driving an Archimedean screw by means of a treadmill.

Textiles are one of the earliest and greatest art forms in the Andean region. This strikingly embroidered alpaca-wool piece shows the complex imagery of the Paracas culture.

The Americas

As the influence of Chavín culture waned, distinct local cultures began to emerge in South America. At Paracas in southern Peru cemeteries have been found containing thousands of mummified bodies, wrapped in colored woven textiles, decorated with mythical beasts and deities which bear a strong Chavín imprint. In North America the Hopewell culture of the eastern woodlands succeeded the Adena, continuing earlier traditions of building elaborate burial mounds and large earthworks.

The Americas

c.500: Paracas culture of southern Peru, famed for brightly colored textiles, emerges | c.350: Beginnings of Nazca culture in southern Peru

500 BCE — 450 — 400 — 350 — 300 — 250 BCE

c.400: Early Zapotec culture flourishing around city of Monte Albán | c.300: Hopewell culture in eastern North America develops traditions of earlier Adena culture

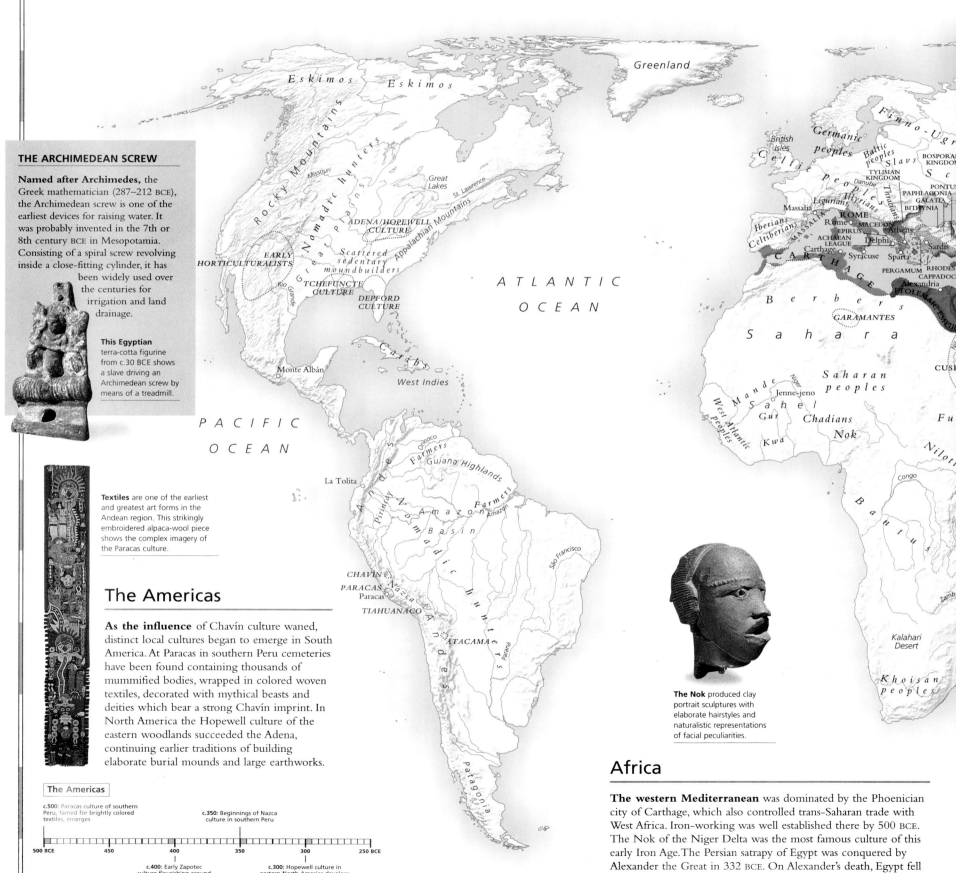

The Nok produced clay portrait sculptures with elaborate hairstyles and naturalistic representations of facial peculiarities.

Africa

The western Mediterranean was dominated by the Phoenician city of Carthage, which also controlled trans-Saharan trade with West Africa. Iron-working was well established there by 500 BCE. The Nok of the Niger Delta was the most famous culture of this early Iron Age. The Persian satrapy of Egypt was conquered by Alexander the Great in 332 BCE. On Alexander's death, Egypt fell to his successor, Ptolemy, who founded the Ptolemaic dynasty.

SEE ALSO:

North America: pp.120–121

South America: pp.144–147

Africa: pp.158–161

Europe: pp.176–179

West Asia: pp.222–223

South and Southeast Asia: pp.240–243

North and East Asia: pp.258–259

Australasia and Oceania: pp.280–281

MAPPING THE FIXED STARS

Ancient astronomers had noticed that the Sun, Moon, and planets did not remain stationary relative to the "fixed" stars. Instead, over the course of a year, they seemed to pass through a region in the sky occupied by twelve specific constellations that we now call the zodiac, from a Greek term meaning "circle of animals." The zodiacal signs appear to have been a Babylonian invention: their first appearance is on a cuneiform horoscope from c.410 BCE.

The twelve signs of the zodiac border a procession of horses and musicians on this 4th-century BCE fresco from a Thracian tomb.

West Asia

In 490 BCE Darius I of Persia sent a punitive expedition against Athens and other cities that had helped Greek cities in Asia Minor to rebel, but it was defeated at Marathon. Over the next century, the Persian empire was weakened by strife and rebellion. In 331 BCE Alexander the Great of Macedon defeated Darius III and brought the Persian Empire to an end. In 323 BCE, Alexander's vast empire was divided among three successors. Most of West Asia became part of the Seleucid Empire. Small local kingdoms were ruled by ethnic or mixed Greek dynasties.

Following his untimely death at the age of 32, Alexander the Great remained a legendary figure in the ancient world. This detail of a 1st-century BCE mosaic from Pompeii shows the young king in battle against the Persians at Issus in 333 BCE.

West Asia

- 490: Persian expedition to Greece is defeated at Marathon
- 480: Darius I is succeeded by his son Xerxes, who invades Greece and is defeated at Salamis, Plataea, and Mycale
- 331: Alexander the Great's victory at the battle of Gaugamela brings Achaemenid Persian Empire to an end
- 312: Seleucus gains control of Persia, Syria, and much of Asia Minor; founds the Seleucid dynasty
- 276–272: Ptolemaic Empire expands into Syria during war with Seleucids

(timeline: 500 BCE — 450 — 400 — 350 — 250 BCE)

East Asia

From about 1000 BCE, nomads reared cattle, goats, and sheep, supplemented by farming and hunting, on the Russian steppe. Contemporary burial sites in the Altai Mountains contain leather, wood, fur, textiles, a wooden wagon, and tattooed bodies. Steppe chieftains may have acted as middlemen in trade between China and Europe. From 403–221 BCE, China was locked in internal conflict, with seven major states competing for supremacy. By the 4th century BCE the Qin were starting to assert control over the whole region.

Mythical combat was a favored theme in the art of the hunting and herding peoples of the Altai region. On this wooden carving, a stag is gripped in the jaws of a griffin.

East Asia

- c.450: Burials at Pazyryk and Noin Ula in Siberia give insight into life of steppe nomads
- c.480: Death of Confucius, who developed humanistic ethical system
- 403: Beginning of Warring States period in China
- 400: Iron-working introduced to Korea
- c.350: The crossbow invented in China
- c.350: Qin state develops new political and economic system based on strict system of rewards and punishments
- 256: Qin takes Luoyang area

(timeline: 500 BCE — 450 — 400 — 350 — 300 — 250 BCE)

Ashoka recorded his understanding of the moral teachings of Buddhism by inscribing edicts on pillars and stones at suitable sites throughout India, including the Great Stupa at Sanchi.

South Asia

During the 5th century BCE the states of the Ganges plain were eventually absorbed into the kingdom of Magadha. Shortly after Alexander's invasion of northwest India in 327 BCE, Chandragupta Maurya seized the throne and began to expand the empire. By the time of Ashoka (297–232 BCE), the Mauryans ruled most of the subcontinent. Ashoka became repelled by warfare and converted to Buddhism, which, under his patronage, became a major force in India, and beyond.

South Asia

- 327: Alexander the Great occupies northwest India
- 320: Chandragupta Maurya controls Magadha kingdom and advances towards Indus and Central India
- 272: Ashoka seizes throne and embarks on further imperial conquests
- 260: Ashoka converts to Buddhism

(timeline: 500 BCE — 450 — 400 — 350 — 300 — 250 BCE)

The World in 250 BCE

- Qin Empire
- Carthage
- Massalia
- Greek city-states
- Macedon
- Mauryan Empire
- Seleucid Empire
- Ptolemaic Empire
- Empire of Alexander the Great 323 BCE

Africa

- c.500: First iron-working in sub-Saharan Africa. Beginning of period of Nok culture in Niger Delta
- c.500: Iron-using Bantus begin to spread from Niger to East African lakes region and down west coast of Africa
- 332: Alexander the Great conquers Egypt. He lays the foundations of Alexandria
- 302: Ptolemy I declares himself king of Egypt. The Ptolemies took pharaonic titles and worshipped Egyptian deities
- c.250: Settlement of Jenne-jeno is founded on inland Niger Delta

(timeline: 500 BCE — 450 — 400 — 350 — 300 — 250 BCE)

Map labels: Palaeosiberians, Yenisey, Lena, Ob', Samoyeds, Siberia, Tungus, Turks, Amur, steppes, Scythians, Caucasus peoples, Caspian Sea, Altai Mountains, Pazyryk, Noin Ula, EMPIRE OF THE XIONGNU, Hun tribal confederacy, Gobi, Ainu, Japan, CHOSON, Korea, Japanese Is, Xianyang, Luoyang, Yellow River, QIN EMPIRE, unified with Qin 221 BCE, Yangtze, Tibetans, Sinitic peoples, GRAECO-BACTRIA, Bactra, SELEUCID EMPIRE, Taxila, Seleucia, Ecbatana, Babylon, Persepolis, ARMENIA, MEDIA, ATROPATENE, Antioch, Damascus, Gaugamela, Arabs, Arabian Peninsula, Semites, Kushites, Meroe, HIMYARITES, MAURYAN EMPIRE, Ujjain, Sanchi, Pataliputra, Mon-Khmer peoples, Chams, Mekong, SMALL STATES, Malays, Sumatra, Borneo, Java, Malays, Philippine Islands, PACIFIC OCEAN, INDIAN OCEAN, Madagascar, Papuans, New Guinea, Australian Aborigines, Darling, New Zealand

THE EMPIRE OF ALEXANDER

Alexander the Great, (356–323 BCE), was king of Macedonia and conqueror of a great Afro-Eurasian empire.

THE CONQUESTS OF ALEXANDER took Greek armies to Egypt, Mesopotamia, the Hindu Kush, and India's western borders, and forced Achaemenid Persia, the most powerful empire in the world, into submission. This extraordinary and audacious military feat, accomplished in just ten years, was to create a truly cosmopolitan civilization. Hellenism permeated the cultures of West Asia: some Hellenistic kingdoms survived into the 1st century CE, while Greek remained the official language in many parts of West Asia until the 8th and 9th centuries CE; cities founded in the aftermath of Alexander's conquests, perpetuated the ideals of Greek civilization – some, such as Alexandria, Kandahar, and Tashkent, survive to this day. Ultimately, Alexander opened up new horizons; his followers encountered different peoples and cultures and established trade routes which linked the Mediterranean with East Africa, India, and Asia.

The battle between the Greeks and Persians is depicted with vigorous, high-relief realism on this sarcophagus, found at Sidon.

The conquests of Alexander

Alexander succeeded to the Macedonian throne after the assassination of his father, Philip, in 336 BCE. He crossed into Asia in 334 BCE, defeated the Persian provincial army at Granicus and liberated the old Greek cities of Asia Minor. After a brief sojourn in Egypt, he won a spectacular victory over the Persian emperor, Darius III, at Issus and pursued him into Persia, taking the cities of Babylon, Susa, and Persepolis. He pressed on to Bactria and Sogdiana, the eastern outposts of the Persian Empire, and crossed the Hindu Kush. At the Hyphasis River (Beas) his army refused to go farther. He died in Babylon in 323 BCE, aged 32.

① The Empire of Alexander ▶

    Empire of Alexander
    dependent regions
    independent states
    → route of Alexander the Great
    → route of Nearchus
    → return route of Craterus
    ✗ major battle
    — Persian Royal Road

Scale varies with perspective
3330 km (2070 miles)
8900 km (5530 miles)

This 1st-century Roman mosaic (based possibly on a Macedonian original) shows Darius III, the Persian emperor, at the battle of Issus (333 BCE). His crushing defeat allowed Alexander to conquer the western half of the Persian Empire.

Hellenistic cities of West Asia

The most magnificent West Asian Hellenistic foundation was Pergamum, capital of the Attalid dynasty (282 to 133 BCE). Adorned by a new school of baroque architecture, characterized by its ornate and heavy style, the city had a spectacular theater and an impressive library, second only to Alexandria.

"The Dying Gaul" is a copy of one of the statues erected in Pergamum to commemorate the turning back of a Gaulish invasion in 241 BCE.

(map region labels)

Aral Sea
CHORASM
Steppes
Ural
Don
Volga
Caspian Sea
SCYTHIA
Dnieper
Dniester
Olbia
Tyras
Sea of Azov
Crimea
Theodosia
Panticapaeum
Caucasus
COLCHIS
Cyrus
Phasis
Araxes
Black Sea
Istrus
Danube
Odessus
Apollonia
Sinope
Amisus
Trapezus
ARMENIA
Elburz Moun
MARI
Spring 333 BCE: Over 30 cities in Lycia surrender to Alexander; he reaches Gordium, where he cuts Gordian Knot, said to be sign he will rule all Asia
1 Oct 331 BCE: Alexander's second battle with Darius III, whose army includes elephants and scythe-wheeled chariots. Victory for Alexander signals effective end of Persian Empire
Philippopolis
Byzantium
Nicomedia
PAPHLAGONIA
Heraclea
Halys
GALATIA
CAPPADOCIA
MED
Ecbatana
THRACE
BITHYNIA
Ancyra
Gordium
Melitene
Nisibis
Nineveh
Arbela
Gaugamela 331
ILLYRIA
Lissus
May 334 BCE: Alexander visits Troy, where he appropriates so-called sword of Achilles
Pella
Granicus 334
Troy
MYSIA
Asia Minor
PHRYGIA
Tyana
Carrhae
MESOPOTAMIA
Feb 324 BCE: Returns to S Mass marriage of Gr soldiers to Persian br
Adriatic Sea
Epidamnus
MACEDONIA
Aegae
Pergamum
Sardis
LYDIA
Apamea
LYCAONIA
Lystra
PISIDIA
CILICIA
Issus 333
Tarsus
Nicephorium
Euphrates
Tigris
BABYLON
Aegean Sea
Corfu
EPIRUS
AETOLIA
HELLAS
Thebes
Athens
Smyrna
Ephesus
Priene
Miletus
CARIA
Aphrodisias
Perge
Side
ISAURIA
Nagidus
Aradus
Salamis
Heliopolis
Emesa
Palmyra
SYRIA
Syrian Desert
Babylon
Corinth
Halicarnassus
Cnidus
LYCIA
Xanthus
Cyprus
Byblos
Sidon
Damascus
Sparta
Rhodes
Paphos
PHOENICIA
Nov 333 BCE: Alexander's first meeting in battle with Darius III. Persian army taken by surprise, suffer heavy losses, and Darius flees
Tyre 332
Samaria
PALESTINE
Nov 331 BCE: Following surrender of Babylon, Alexander enters city in triumph
10 Jun 323 BCE: Alexander dies in Babylon
CRETE
Knossos
Jerusalem
Gaza
Mediterranean Sea
Sep–Nov 332 BCE: Siege of key Persian fortress of Gaza. Alexander wounded by catapult bolt
Alexandria
Pelusium
Cyrene
Paraetonium
Heliopolis
Sinai
Memphis
Midwinter 331 BCE: Alexander visits oracle of Ammon at Siwa; kinship with Ammon-Zeus proclaimed
Oxyrhynchus
Sanctuary of Ammon (Siwa Oasis)
Sahara
EGYPT
Thebes
Nile
Red Sea
Syene
Tropic of Cancer
ITALY

The growth of Macedonian power

359: Philip starts rise to power, and begins to extend Macedonian territory
342: Philip master of Thrace; one of conquered cities renamed Philippopolis
336: Philip is succeeded by his son Alexander
333: Persian king Darius III is defeated at Issus
326: Alexander reaches Taxila; prevented from advancing into India by revolt of his troops

| 360 BCE | 350 | 340 | 330 | 320 BCE |

359: Philip II takes title of king; birth of his son Alexander
346: War in Central Greece ends in uneasy peace between Philip and Athens
338: Battle of Chaeronea; Philip II defeats Greek states
332: Alexander founds the city of Alexandria in northern Egypt
331: Decisive defeat of the Persians at battle of Gaugamela
323: Death of Alexander

SEE ALSO:
Africa: pp.160–161
Europe: pp.176–179
West Asia pp.222–225
South and Southeast Asia: pp.240–241

Gobi
Yellow River
Atlai Mountains
Lake Balkhash
Tien Shan
Takla Makan Desert
Plateau of Tibet
Brahmaputra
Himalayas
Jaxartes
Tashkent
Autumn 329 BCE: Greeks use Maracanda as forward base for raids into surrounding regions. Revolt by conquered peoples harshly repressed
Alexandria Eschate (Kokand)
Spring 328 BCE: Capture of Sogdian Rock
Spring 327 BCE: Alexander marries Roxanne, daughter of Sogdian baron, Oxyartes
Maracanda (Samarkand)
Sogdian Rock
Oxus
Bukhara
Nautaca
SOGDIANA
Aornos 327
Drapsaca
Winter 327 BCE: Campaigns in Swat valley
Spring 326 BCE: Leading army of some 80,000 troops and 30,000 camp-followers, Alexander crosses Indus and marches on Taxila
Alexandria ad Oxum (Ai Khanoum)
PARAPAMISUS
Taxila
Bucephala
Bactra
BACTRIA
Hydaspes 326
Sangela
Kara Kum
Alexandria (Merv)
Spring 329 BCE: Alexander crosses Hindu Kush
Hindu Kush
Sep 326 BCE: At Hyphasis River, Greek troops refuse to go any further. Army turns back
May 326 BCE: Death of Alexander's horse, Bucephalus. City founded in his memory
Meshed
330
Susia
ARIA
MALAVA
Bojnurd
Artacoana
Alexandria Areion (Herat)
HYRCANIA
Alexandria Arachoton (Kandahar)
ARACHOSIA
Opiana
Nov 326 BCE: Army passes through Punjab and Sind, ruthlessly crushing all resistance
Hecatompylos
DRANGIANA
PARTHIA
Quetta
Thar Desert
Summer 330 BCE: In pursuit of retreating Darius, Alexander passes through Caspian Gates (rocky defile guarded by Persian fortress). Discovers Darius dying, murdered by conspiring Persian commanders
Caspian Gates
Great Salt Desert
Nad-i-Ali
Indus
INDIA
PAETACENE
Iranian Plateau
Gabae
CARMANIA
Pattala
GEDROSIA
Kokala
PERSIS
Zagros Mountains
Pasargadae
Pura
325
Persepolis
Alexandria (Gulashkird)
324
Persian Gates
Harmozia
Gwadar
Autumn 325 BCE: Alexander leads troops through Makran desert, where heat and thirst cause terrible loss of life. Rest of the army makes wide detour around the desert, under the leadership of Craterus
30 Jan 330 BCE: Alexander reaches Persepolis; army sacks city. Royal palace later put to torch by Alexander and troops
Gulf of Oman
Arabian Sea
Persian Gulf
Jan 330 BCE: Alexander attempts to go through Persian Gates (a pass through Zagros Mountains). When ambushed by Persians, Alexander leads army up steep, narrow track to surprise enemy from the rear
325 BCE: Alexander's fleet, built to descend the Indus, is brought back to the Persian Gulf by Nearchus
Arabian Peninsula

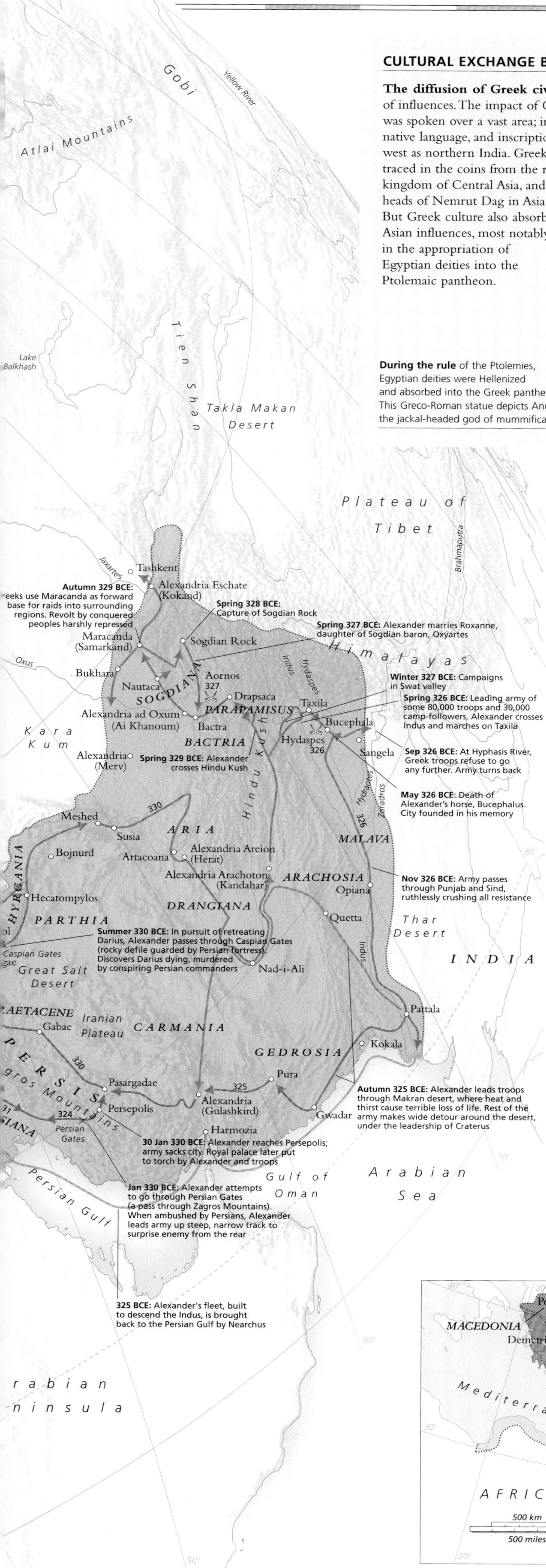

CULTURAL EXCHANGE BETWEEN GREECE AND ASIA

The diffusion of Greek civilization resulted in a rich interplay of influences. The impact of Greek culture was extensive. Greek was spoken over a vast area; in Egypt it started to replace the native language, and inscriptions in Greek are found as far west as northern India. Greek styles of portraiture can be traced in the coins from the remote Greco-Bactrian kingdom of Central Asia, and in the massive sculptured heads of Nemrut Dag in Asia Minor. But Greek culture also absorbed West Asian influences, most notably in the appropriation of Egyptian deities into the Ptolemaic pantheon.

During the rule of the Ptolemies, Egyptian deities were Hellenized and absorbed into the Greek pantheon. This Greco-Roman statue depicts Anubis, the jackal-headed god of mummification.

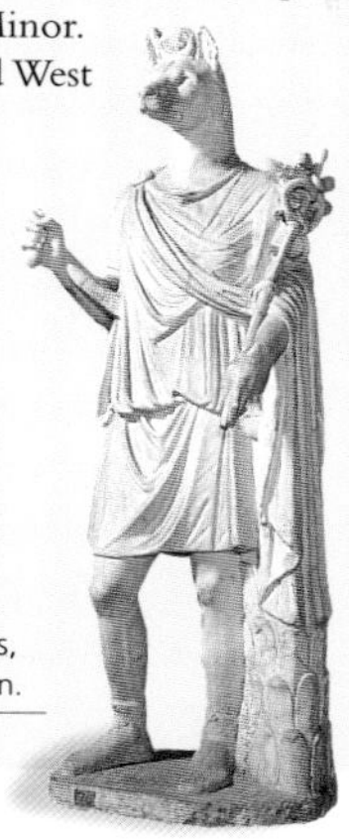

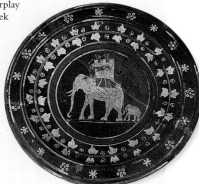

War elephants, depicted here on an Italian plate, were brought back to the Mediterranean by Greeks who had fought against them in India. The fighting tower on the elephant's back was possibly a Greek invention.

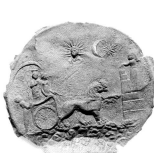

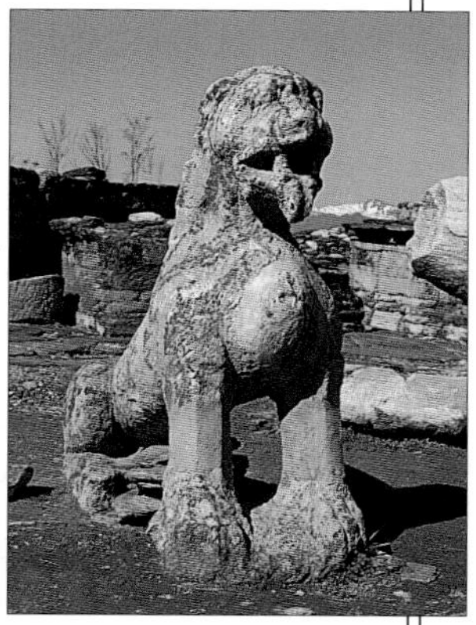

Hellenism in the East

One of the most remote outposts of Hellenism was the city of Ai Khanoum (probably known in its day as Alexandria ad Oxum), on the borders of modern Russia and Afghanistan. It had all the characteristic features of a Greek city: agora, acropolis, temples, gymnasium, and library. The ruined temple of Cybele, however, suggests that oriental rites were used in the worship of the goddess. A Greek inscription found in the city records one of the maxims of the famous oracle at Delphi, some 3,700 miles away.

A silver disc from the temple of Cybele at Ai Khanoum shows a Hellenized version of the goddess riding in a chariot with a Persian priest standing at a fire altar.

This Hellenistic statue of a lion stands in the ruins of Buthara in present-day Pakistan.

The Alexandrian legacy

Alexander's death precipitated destructive wars between his Macedonian generals. Eventually, his empire was divided between three main dynasties. The Ptolemies ruled in Egypt until 30 BCE, and established a stable kingdom with its capital at Alexandria. The Antigonids, based in Macedonia, dominated the affairs of Greece. The Seleucids, who ruled over Syria and Babylon, lost much of their original territory in the east to independent Hellenistic kingdoms such as Bactria, while Pergamum came to dominate Asia Minor.

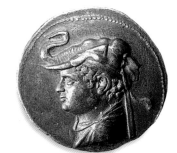

On this Bactrian coin, King Demetrios is portrayed wearing the symbolic elephant scalp that appeared on similar coins of Alexander after his eastern conquests.

Hellenistic empires and kingdoms

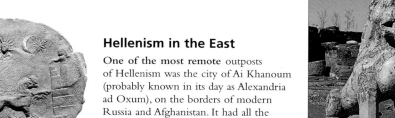

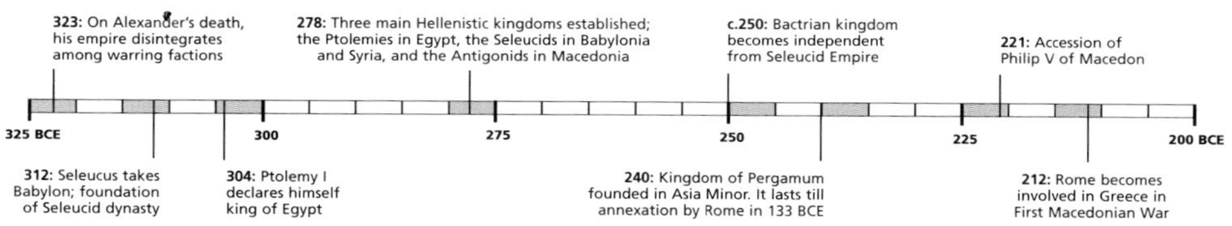

323: On Alexander's death, his empire disintegrates among warring factions
278: Three main Hellenistic kingdoms established; the Ptolemies in Egypt, the Seleucids in Babylonia and Syria, and the Antigonids in Macedonia
c.250: Bactrian kingdom becomes independent from Seleucid Empire
221: Accession of Philip V of Macedon
325 BCE
300
275
250
225
200 BCE
312: Seleucus takes Babylon; foundation of Seleucid dynasty
304: Ptolemy I declares himself king of Egypt
240: Kingdom of Pergamum founded in Asia Minor. It lasts till annexation by Rome in 133 BCE
212: Rome becomes involved in Greece in First Macedonian War

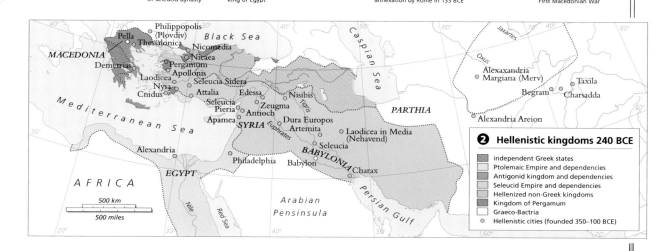

Philippopolis (Plovdiv)
Black Sea
Pella
Thessalonica
Nicomedia
MACEDONIA
Nicaea
Demetrias
Pergamum
Apollonis
Laodicea
Seleucia Sidera
Nysa
Cnidus
Attalia
Edessa
Nisibis
Seleucia Pieria
Zeugma
Antioch
Apamea
SYRIA
Dura Europos
Artemita
Caspian Sea
PARTHIA
Mediterranean Sea
Laodicea in Media (Nehavend)
Seleucia
Alexandria
Philadelphia
Babylon
BABYLONIA
Charax
EGYPT
AFRICA
Nile
Red Sea
Arabian Pensinsula
Persian Gulf
Jaxartes
Oxus
Alexaxandria Margiana (Merv)
Taxila
Begram
Charsadda
Alexandria Areion
500 km
500 miles
2 Hellenistic kingdoms 240 BCE
independent Greek states
Ptolemaic Empire and dependencies
Antigonid kingdom and dependencies
Seleucid Empire and dependencies
Hellenized non-Greek kingdoms
Kingdom of Pergamum
Graeco-Bactria
Hellenistic cities (founded 350–100 BCE)

THE WORLD 250 BCE – 1 CE

BY 1 CE HALF THE GLOBAL population, which had reached about 250 million, lived within three major empires - Rome, Parthia, and Han China. With the addition of the developing kingdoms of northern India and Southeast Asia, urban civilization now existed in a wide swathe across the Old World, from the Iberian Peninsula in the west to Korea in the east, surrounded by nomadic pastoralists, farmers, and increasingly marginalized hunter-gatherers. The opening up of the Silk Road in the 1st century BCE and the discovery of monsoon trade routes across the Indian Ocean led to an unprecedented degree of contact between empires, disseminating both religious and cultural influences. In the New World the increasingly sophisticated Nazca and Moche cultures were developing in Peru, while Teotihuacán in Mexico was poised to become one of the world's most populous cities.

Europe

The Ara Pacis (Altar of Peace) was set up in Rome in 9 BCE to commemorate the pacification of Gaul and Iberia by the Emperor Augustus.

Following the defeat of Carthage in the 2nd century BCE, Rome embarked on a program of expansion, which extended control to Greek territories in the east and Gaul to the north. In the 1st century BCE, a period of civil wars and rule by military dictators threatened the unity of the growing empire. In 27 BCE Octavian assumed imperial power (and the title Augustus), reuniting the Roman world and ushering in two centuries of stability and prosperity.

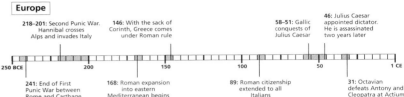

Europe

- 218–201: Second Punic War. Hannibal crosses Alps and invades Italy
- 146: With the sack of Corinth, Greece comes under Roman rule
- 58–51: Gallic conquests of Julius Caesar
- 46: Julius Caesar appointed dictator. He is assassinated two years later
- 241: End of First Punic War between Rome and Carthage
- 168: Roman expansion into eastern Mediterranean begins
- 89: Roman citizenship extended to all Italians
- 31: Octavian defeats Antony and Cleopatra at Actium

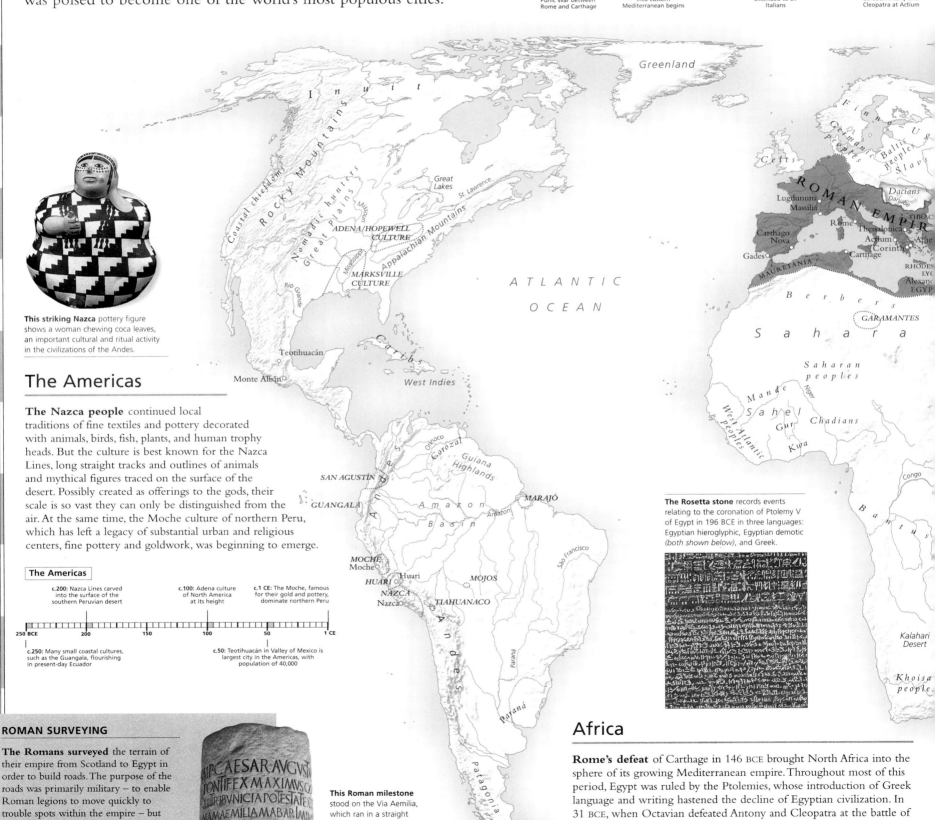

This striking Nazca pottery figure shows a woman chewing coca leaves, an important cultural and ritual activity in the civilizations of the Andes.

The Americas

The Nazca people continued local traditions of fine textiles and pottery decorated with animals, birds, fish, plants, and human trophy heads. But the culture is best known for the Nazca Lines, long straight tracks and outlines of animals and mythical figures traced on the surface of the desert. Possibly created as offerings to the gods, their scale is so vast they can only be distinguished from the air. At the same time, the Moche culture of northern Peru, which has left a legacy of substantial urban and religious centers, fine pottery and goldwork, was beginning to emerge.

The Americas

- c.200: Nazca Lines carved into the surface of the southern Peruvian desert
- c.100: Adena culture of North America at its height
- c.1 CE: The Moche, famous for their gold and pottery, dominate northern Peru
- c.250: Many small coastal cultures, such as the Guangala, flourishing in present-day Ecuador
- c.50: Teotihuacán in Valley of Mexico is largest city in the Americas, with population of 40,000

The Rosetta stone records events relating to the coronation of Ptolemy V of Egypt in 196 BCE in three languages: Egyptian hieroglyphic, Egyptian demotic (both shown below), and Greek.

ROMAN SURVEYING

The Romans surveyed the terrain of their empire from Scotland to Egypt in order to build roads. The purpose of the roads was primarily military – to enable Roman legions to move quickly to trouble spots within the empire – but they also carried local commercial traffic. Distances were measured in thousands of paces (*mille passuum*) – hence the word mile – and milestones were placed at regular intervals. The Roman mile was about 1,680 yards (1,540 meters).

This Roman milestone stood on the Via Aemilia, which ran in a straight line across northern Italy. The inscription records road repairs undertaken in the reign of Augustus (27 BCE–14 CE).

Africa

Rome's defeat of Carthage in 146 BCE brought North Africa into the sphere of its growing Mediterranean empire. Throughout most of this period, Egypt was ruled by the Ptolemies, whose introduction of Greek language and writing hastened the decline of Egyptian civilization. In 31 BCE, when Octavian defeated Antony and Cleopatra at the battle of Actium, Egypt became a Roman province destined to serve as Rome's granary. To the south the kingdom of Meroe prospered, exporting frankincense to Rome along the Red Sea. The Bantus continued their progress into southern Africa, introducing agriculture and iron-working.

West Asia

Following the secession of Bactria, Sogdiana, and Parthia from Seleucid rule in the mid-3rd century BCE, the nomadic Parthians took advantage of the upheaval to extend their territory. By the early 1st century BCE, their empire included Mesopotamia and stretched from Syria to Bactria. With their heavily armored cavalry, the Parthians withstood the might of Rome at the battle of Carrhae (53 BCE), halting Rome's eastern expansion. The Parthian Empire lasted 500 years, growing wealthy from its control of the Silk Road linking China and Rome.

This ivory rhyton (horn-shaped drinking cup) was found at Nisa, the early capital of the Parthians after they expanded south from their homelands east of the Caspian Sea.

West Asia

247: Arsaces founds the Arsacid, or Parthian, dynasty

171: Mithridates I founds Parthian Empire

141: Parthians control Mesopotamia following capture of the old Seleucid capital, Seleucia-on-the-Tigris

53: Defeat of Roman infantry at the battle of Carrhae in northern Syria

124: Accession of Mithridates III. Parthian Empire reaches greatest extent

90: Ctesiphon established as Parthian capital

40: Rome recognizes Herod the Great as ruler of Judaea

East Asia

The Qin unified China in 221 BCE, their leader taking the title "First Emperor" and introducing a harsh, centralized, bureaucratic regime. His death in 210 was followed by widespread revolts. By 206 the Han dynasty under Gao Zu had taken power. The Han, too, presided over a highly centralized bureaucracy, their state monopoly on iron and salt, combined with the opening up of the Silk Road to Central Asia, ensuring their prosperity.

Shi Huangdi, the Qin First Emperor, imposed his autocratic rule through military force. A symbolic army of thousands of life-sized, terra-cotta soldiers was assembled to guard his tomb.

East Asia

210: Death of Shi Huangdi leads to revolts throughout Qin Empire

206: Han dynasty, under Gao Zu, assumes control

119: State monopoly on iron-working established

108: Chinese take military control of Korea

55: Xiongnu confederacy breaks up; southern group becomes tributary of Han China

221: Great Wall built as protection against northern nomadic incursions

136: Confucianism becomes state religion of China

c.112: Opening up of Silk Road across Central Asia

SEE ALSO:

North America: pp.120–121

South America: pp.144–145

Africa: pp.160–161

Europe: pp.178–179

West Asia: pp.224–225

South and Southeast Asia: pp.240–243

North and East Asia: pp.258–261

Australasia and Oceania: pp.280–281

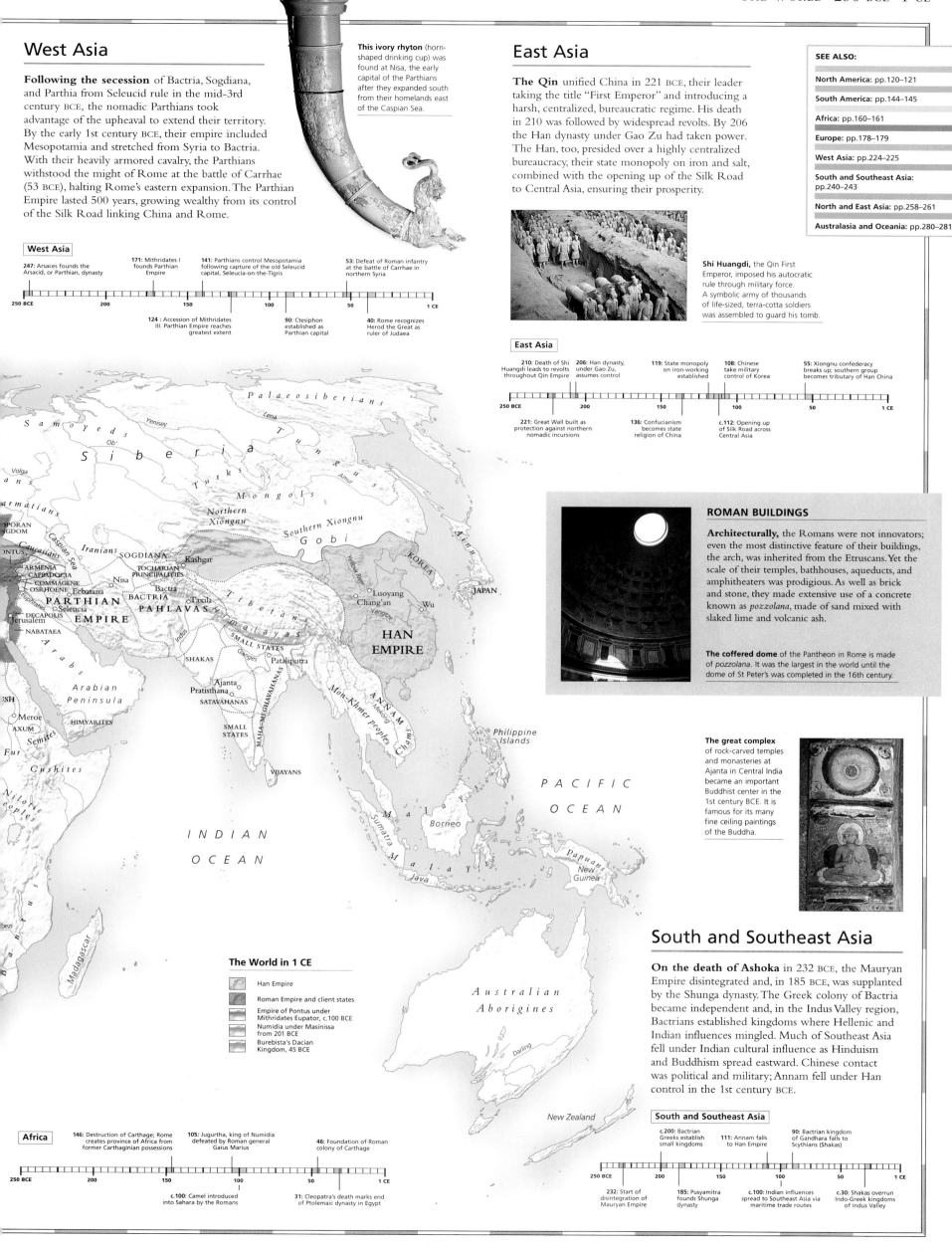

ROMAN BUILDINGS

Architecturally, the Romans were not innovators; even the most distinctive feature of their buildings, the arch, was inherited from the Etruscans. Yet the scale of their temples, bathhouses, aqueducts, and amphitheaters was prodigious. As well as brick and stone, they made extensive use of a concrete known as *pozzolana*, made of sand mixed with slaked lime and volcanic ash.

The coffered dome of the Pantheon in Rome is made of *pozzolana*. It was the largest in the world until the dome of St Peter's was completed in the 16th century.

The great complex of rock-carved temples and monasteries at Ajanta in Central India became an important Buddhist center in the 1st century BCE. It is famous for its many fine ceiling paintings of the Buddha.

South and Southeast Asia

On the death of Ashoka in 232 BCE, the Mauryan Empire disintegrated and, in 185 BCE, was supplanted by the Shunga dynasty. The Greek colony of Bactria became independent and, in the Indus Valley region, Bactrians established kingdoms where Hellenic and Indian influences mingled. Much of Southeast Asia fell under Indian cultural influence as Hinduism and Buddhism spread eastward. Chinese contact was political and military; Annam fell under Han control in the 1st century BCE.

The World in 1 CE

- Han Empire
- Roman Empire and client states
- Empire of Pontus under Mithridates Eupator, c.100 BCE
- Numidia under Masinissa from 201 BCE
- Burebista's Dacian Kingdom, 45 BCE

Africa

146: Destruction of Carthage; Rome creates province of Africa from former Carthaginian possessions

105: Jugurtha, king of Numidia defeated by Roman general Gaius Marius

46: Foundation of Roman colony of Carthage

c.100: Camel introduced into Sahara by the Romans

31: Cleopatra's death marks end of Ptolemaic dynasty in Egypt

South and Southeast Asia

c.200: Bactrian Greeks establish small kingdoms

111: Annam falls to Han Empire

90: Bactrian kingdom of Gandhara falls to Scythians (Shakas)

232: Start of disintegration of Mauryan Empire

185: Pusyamitra founds Shunga dynasty

c.100: Indian influences spread to Southeast Asia via maritime trade routes

c.30: Shakas overrun Indo-Greek kingdoms of Indus Valley

TRADE IN THE CLASSICAL WORLD

Fine Chinese silks from this period, lightweight and of high value, have been found throughout Eurasia, as far west as Egypt and Greece.

BY THE BEGINNING of the 1st millennium CE, a series of commercial and political networks had evolved which combined to form a nexus of trade which linked the eastern shores of the Atlantic Ocean, the Indian Ocean, and the western shores of the Pacific. At its extremes this network linked the Roman Empire, centered on the Mediterranean, and the land-based Han Empire of China. As the commercial and territorial influences of these two power bases spread beyond their political domains, so outlying regions were drawn into the web, from sub-Saharan Africa to the East Indies. However, the most important link to emerge was the Silk Road which spanned Asia, threading through the mountain ranges and deserts of the Central Asian landmass, and along which a chain of powerful trading cities and states came into being.

Han China and the wider world

Decorated Han votive mirrors were used as diplomatic gifts by the Chinese, and have been found as far away as Siberia, the Caucasus, and southern Russia.

The Han Dynasty, which emerged to take over the territorial extent of the Qin Empire from 206 BCE, was largely self-sufficient. Trade was not regarded as an imperial concern, although desirable goods were drawn into Han markets by successive middlemen on the empire's fringes – spices from South and Southeast Asia, trepang (dried sea cucumber) and mother-of-pearl from the East Indies and, with the extension of the empire into Central Asia, the swift cavalry horses of Ferghana became highly prized. Conversely, Chinese products such as silk and lacquerware commanded high prices across Asia.

The nimble "Horses of Heaven" from Ferghana provided the Chinese with the style of cavalry needed to keep the Xiongnu at bay.

Han trade
(in approximate order of value)

Exports	Imports
silk	horses
lacquerware	spices
	precious stones

The Classical world

141: Wudi expands Han power into Central Asia	**60:** Establishment of Kushan Empire	**c.150:** Ptolemy publishes first World Atlas	**200:** Han dynasty collapses	**396:** Roman Empire divided into eastern and western halves		

200 BCE — 100 BCE — 1 CE — 100 — 200 — 300 — 400

31: Roman victory at Actium consolidates control of eastern Mediterranean	**117:** Roman Empire at greatest extent	**224:** Beginning of Sassanian control in Persia	**238:** First Germanic incursions into Roman Empire	**370:** Huns enter Europe

Roman trade

Rome, in contrast to Han China, was an empire largely dependent on trade. Rome's imports were prodigious. A single currency, common citizenship, low customs barriers, and the development of a broadly secure network of roads, inland waterways, harbors, and sea-routes provided a hub of commerce which drew in produce from far beyond the imperial boundaries.

The popular Roman taste for combat with exotic wild animals in the arena saw bears, bulls, and boars being imported from northern Europe, lions and tigers from Asia, crocodiles from Egypt, and rhinoceros, hippopotami, and a variety of large cats from sub-Saharan Africa.

Roman trade
(in approximate order of value)

Exports	Imports
gold	food
silver	slaves
wine	animals
olive oil	spices
glassware	silk
	incense
	ivory
	cotton

The Romans built many ports and harbors around the Mediterranean, elaborate complexes with lighthouses and docks, which serviced the Roman maritime trading network.

Knowledge of Classical Eurasia

Although there is no evidence of direct contact between Rome and the Han Empire, there was extensive knowledge of the general shape of Classical Eurasia. The Greek geographer Strabo gave a detailed description of the known world in his 17-volume *Geography* (c.20 CE) and by 150 CE the Alexandrian Ptolemy's *Geography* formally laid out the topography of Eurasia. His world view (*below*) names Sinae (China), Taprobane (Sri Lanka), and Sera Metropolis (Chang'an).

Reconstruction of Ptolemy's map of Classical Eurasia

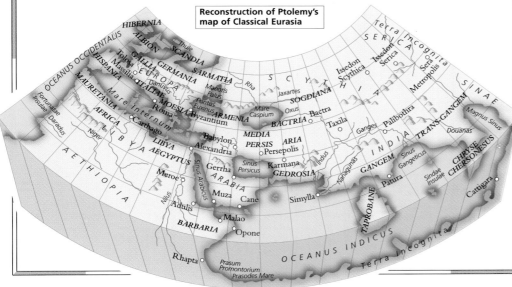

Central Asian trade

The opening of the Silk Road saw the growth of a string of powerful cities and states which thrived, controlling the trade which passed through them. The greatest of these was the Parthian Empire of Persia (247 BCE–244 CE), while to the north Transoxiana, Bactria, and the Kushan Empire of modern Uzbekistan straddled the region in which the Silk Road converged and intersected with routes traveling north from India through the Hindu Kush, and on to the Caspian Sea and the river routes of Scythia.

The Silk Road

The campaigns by the Qin First Emperor, Shi Huangdi, and his Han successor Wudi against the nomadic Xiongnu opened a series of routes which traversed Central Asia, remaining the principal east-west trade route for centuries. The Silk Road linked Samarkand in the west with Anxi in the east; a summer route went north of the Tien Shan range, while the main route split to skirt the Takla Makan.

SEE ALSO:
Africa: pp.160–161
Europe: pp.180–181
West Asia: pp.224–225
South and Southeast Asia: pp.240–241
North and East Asia: pp.260–261

Fortified cities such as Jiaohei were established as *caravanserais* around the hostile wastes of the Takla Makan Desert.

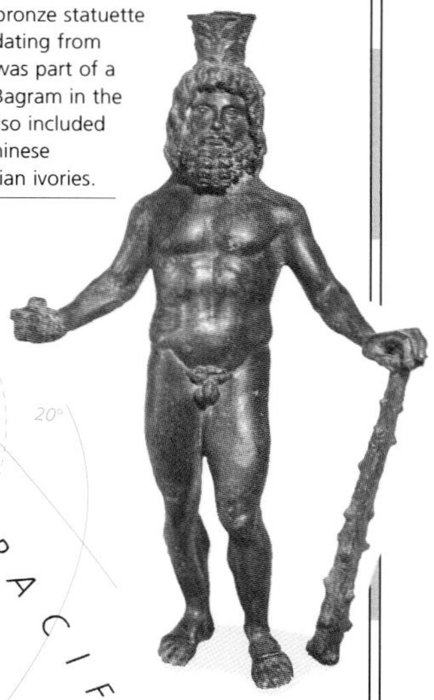

This Greco-Roman bronze statuette of Serapis-Hercules, dating from 1st–4th century CE, was part of a hoard discovered at Bagram in the Hindu Kush, which also included Roman glassware, Chinese lacquerware, and Indian ivories.

① Eurasian and African trade c.1 CE

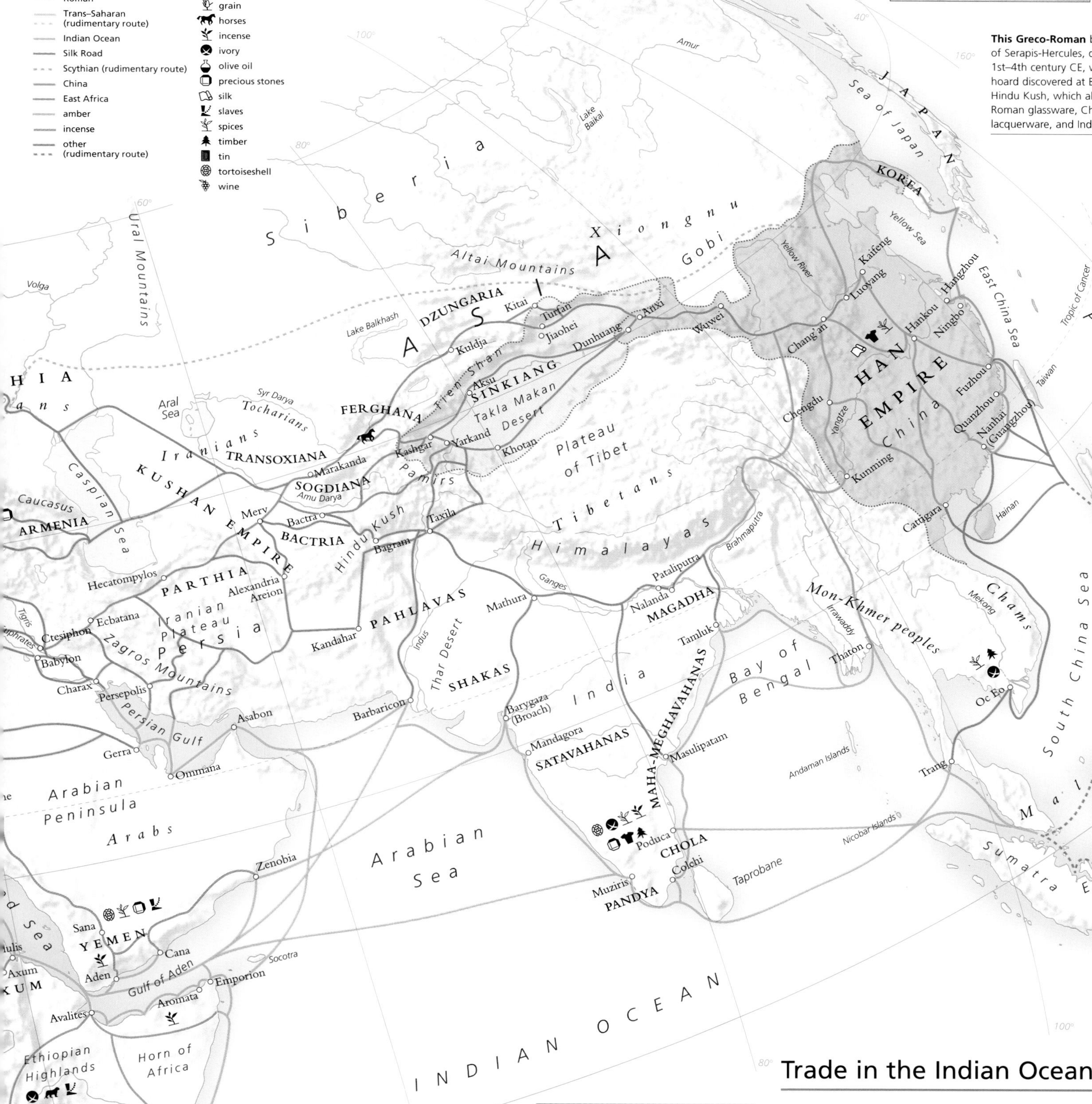

Roman Empire and client states
Han Empire
Sinkiang (Han protectorate 73–94 CE)

Trade routes
Roman
Trans–Saharan (rudimentary route)
Indian Ocean
Silk Road
Scythian (rudimentary route)
China
East Africa
amber
incense
other (rudimentary route)

Goods traded
amber
animals
clothing
gold
silver
grain
horses
incense
ivory
olive oil
precious stones
silk
slaves
spices
timber
tin
tortoiseshell
wine

Trade in the Indian Ocean

Maritime trade routes in the Indian Ocean provided important links between the Roman Mediterranean, East Africa, the Persian Gulf, India, Taprobane (Sri Lanka) and beyond into the East Indies. Greek barges hugged the coasts, but lateen-rigged dhows, propelled by the regular seasonal pattern of the monsoon winds, were the first craft to move beyond coastal trade to establish direct routes across the ocean between major trading markets. The rich variety of goods they transported was described in a Greek manual from the 1st century CE, the *Periplus of the Erythraean Sea*; hoards of Roman coins have been found in southern India, Southeast Asia, and East Africa, while silks and spices from South and East Asia were transported westward.

Cana, on the southern coast of the Arabian Peninsula, one of numerous fortified *entrepôts* which ringed the Indian Ocean, flourished on the local trade in incense.

Scale varies with perspective
7720 km (4490 miles)
17,810 km (11,070 miles)

Map labels: Sea of Okhotsk, Kurile Islands, Amur, Lake Baikal, Sea of Japan, JAPAN, KOREA, Yellow Sea, East China Sea, PACIFIC OCEAN, Philippine Islands, Tropic of Cancer, Taiwan, Hainan, Luzon, Siberia, Altai Mountains, Xiongnu, Gobi, DZUNGARIA, Kitai, Turfan, Jiaohei, Anxi, Kuldja, Aksu, Dunhuang, Wuwei, Tien Shan, SINKIANG, Takla Makan Desert, Yellow River, Kaifeng, Luoyang, Hangzhou, Hankou, Ningbo, Chang'an, HAN EMPIRE, China, Fuzhou, Chengdu, Yangtze, Quanzhou, Nanhai (Guangzhou), Kunming, FERGHANA, Kashgar, Yarkand, Khotan, Plateau of Tibet, Tibetans, Himalayas, Brahmaputra, Canigara, Chams, Mekong, Mon-Khmer peoples, Irrawaddy, Oc Eo, Trang, South China Sea, Malays, Borneo, Celebes, Moluccas, Sumatra, EAST INDIES, Java, Java Sea, Equator, Ural Mountains, Volga, Aral Sea, Syr Darya, Tocharians, TRANSOXIANA, Marakanda, SOGDIANA, Amu Darya, KUSHAN EMPIRE, Iranians, Merv, Bactra, BACTRIA, Hindu Kush, Bagram, Taxila, Caspian Sea, Caucasus, ARMENIA, PARTHIA, Hecatompylos, Iranian Plateau, Persia, Alexandria Areion, Kandahar, PAHLAVAS, Indus, Thar Desert, SHAKAS, Mathura, Ganges, Pataliputra, Nalanda, MAGADHA, Tamluk, Tigris, Euphrates, Ctesiphon, Ecbatana, Babylon, Zagros Mountains, Charax, Persepolis, Persian Gulf, Gerra, Ommana, Asabon, Barbaricon, Barygaza (Broach), Mandagora, SATAVAHANAS, MAHA-MEGHAVAHANAS, Masulipatam, Bay of Bengal, Andaman Islands, Nicobar Islands, Arabian Peninsula, Arabs, Arabian Sea, Zenobia, Poduca, CHOLA, Colchi, Taprobane, Muziris, PANDYA, India, Sana, YEMEN, Cana, Socotra, Aden, Gulf of Aden, Emporion, Aromata, INDIAN OCEAN, Axum, Avalites, Ethiopian Highlands, Maji, Cushites, Horn of Africa, Sarapion, Pemba, Zanzibar, Lake Victoria

THE WORLD 1–250 CE

AS THE EMPIRES OF THE OLD WORLD expanded, the protection of their borders and far-flung imperial outposts became an urgent priority. Increasing threats from the mounted nomadic pastoralists of Asia, the Germanic tribes of Eastern Europe, and the Berbers of North Africa stretched resources to the limit, weakening Roman control, and leading to economic and social chaos. The empire of Han China collapsed in 220 CE, a victim of famine, floods, insurgency, and the growing power of regional warlords. By the early 3rd century CE, pressures on Rome's eastern borders precipitated a stormy century of civil wars, dynastic disputes, and army revolts. Against this troubled backdrop a new religion, Christianity, was beginning to spread throughout the Roman world. Originating with the teachings of Jesus of Nazareth in Palestine, the new religion proved remarkably resistant to Roman persecution.

Marcus Aurelius was one of the most conscientious Roman emperors: a Stoic philosopher and tireless campaigner on the German frontier.

Europe

In the 2nd century CE the Roman Empire stretched from West Asia to the Atlantic, united by one language, one coinage, a system of well-paved roads, and protected by fortified frontiers. The empire prospered under strong emperors, but stresses began to appear. Conflict over the imperial succession undermined central authority, leading to civil wars between rivals, economic breakdown, and revolts by the army. Pressure on imperial frontiers, especially from the Germanic tribes to the east of the Rhine, stretched the empire's resources, leading to inflation, famine, disease, and lawlessness.

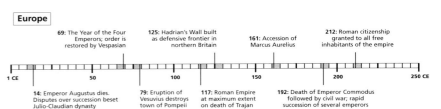

Europe

69: The Year of the Four Emperors; order is restored by Vespasian
125: Hadrian's Wall built as defensive frontier in northern Britain
161: Accession of Marcus Aurelius
212: Roman citizenship granted to all free inhabitants of the empire

| 1 CE | 50 | 100 | 150 | 200 | 250 CE |

14: Emperor Augustus dies. Disputes over succession beset Julio-Claudian dynasty
79: Eruption of Vesuvius destroys town of Pompeii
117: Roman Empire at maximum extent on death of Trajan
192: Death of Emperor Commodus followed by civil war; rapid succession of several emperors

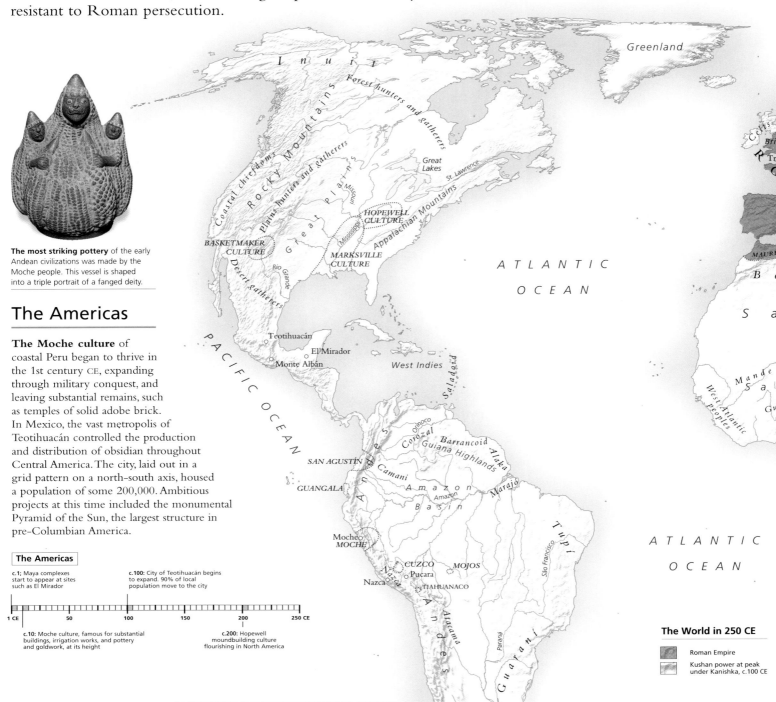

The most striking pottery of the early Andean civilizations was made by the Moche people. This vessel is shaped into a triple portrait of a fanged deity.

The Americas

The Moche culture of coastal Peru began to thrive in the 1st century CE, expanding through military conquest, and leaving substantial remains, such as temples of solid adobe brick. In Mexico, the vast metropolis of Teotihuacán controlled the production and distribution of obsidian throughout Central America. The city, laid out in a grid pattern on a north-south axis, housed a population of some 200,000. Ambitious projects at this time included the monumental Pyramid of the Sun, the largest structure in pre-Columbian America.

The Americas

c.1: Maya complexes start to appear at sites such as El Mirador
c.100: City of Teotihuacán begins to expand. 90% of local population move to the city

| 1 CE | 50 | 100 | 150 | 200 | 250 CE |

c.10: Moche culture, famous for substantial buildings, irrigation works, and pottery and goldwork, at its height
c.200: Hopewell moundbuilding culture flourishing in North America

The World in 250 CE

Roman Empire

Kushan power at peak under Kanishka, c.100 CE

THE FIRST PAPER

The traditional date for the invention of paper is 105 CE, but lightweight felted material for writing had been made in China for some time before then. The pulp was made of scraps of bark, bamboo, and hemp, finely chopped and boiled with wood ash. As techniques improved, paper replaced expensive silk and cumbersome wooden tablets.

A Chinese worker lifts a mesh screen covered with a thin layer of pulp that will drain and dry to form a sheet of paper.

Africa

Under Roman rule, Egypt experienced a remarkable economic recovery. As ancient Egyptian cults and traditions declined, Christianity found converts among the Egyptians. To the west, the Romans extended their control to the Berber kingdoms of Numidia and Mauretania. The fertile coastal plains were fully exploited, but the southern borders of Roman territory were under constant threat of Berber invasion. By 100 CE the Red Sea kingdom of Axum, its wealth based on control of the incense trade, had become a major power.

The ruined city of Petra contains remarkable rock-cut tombs. It was annexed by Rome in 106 as capital of the province of Arabia.

West Asia

In the 1st century CE the Parthian Empire was torn by internal dissent and dynastic struggles. Between 114 and 198, the Romans invaded three times, sacking the cities of Seleucia and Ctesiphon. In 224 Ardashir Papakan defeated his Parthian overlords and founded the Sassanian dynasty. He introduced a centralized administration, and transformed vassal kingdoms into provinces, ruled by Sassanian princes. His son Shapur repelled the Romans and made Sassanian Persia the most stable power of late antiquity.

70: Romans suppress Jewish revolt and destroy temple in Jerusalem

c.150: Petra, a major trading post for incense, at height of prosperity

165: Avidius Cassius sacks Seleucia and Ctesiphon

224: Sassanians take over Parthian Empire

1 CE   50   100   150   200   250 CE

West Asia

114: Trajan annexes Armenia, takes Seleucia and reaches Persian Gulf

c.132: Second Jewish revolt precipitates diaspora

197: Septimius Severus sails down Euphrates to invade Parthian Empire

East Asia

In 25 CE, after a brief interregnum, Han emperors regained control of China, but their rule depended on the support of powerful landowners. The capital moved to Luoyang, and eastern and southern China exerted greater political influence. In the early 3rd century the empire, beset by rebellions and feuds, collapsed. Regional warlords carved out three new kingdoms and China remained fragmented for over 300 years. With the decline of the Han, small local states, notably Koguryo and Silla, took control of Korea.

This model horse and trap was found among the goods in the grave of a high-ranking officer of the Han period.

East Asia

9: Wang Mang seizes throne, founding short-lived Xin dynasty

159: Han imperial family feuds hand effective power to court eunuchs

c.220: Collapse of Han dynasty; replaced by three kingdoms: Shu, Wu, and Wei

1 CE   50   100   150   200   250 CE

25: Han reassert control over China, but their power is limited

184: Rising of the Yellow Turbans, an insurgent group, in China

c.200: Emergence of native states in Korea

SEE ALSO:

North America: pp.120–121

South America: pp.144–145

Africa: pp.160–161

Europe: pp.180–181

West Asia: pp.224–225

South and Southeast Asia: pp.240–243

North and East Asia: pp.260–261

Australasia and Oceania: pp.280–281

MOSAIC OF THE NILE IN FLOOD

The Romans drew maps, but unfortunately only a few fragments carved on stone survive. Some others have come down to us through medieval copies. One highly imaginative representation of the contemporary world that has been preserved is this mosaic of a panoramic view of *The Nile in Flood* found at Praeneste, near Rome.

The Nile River was of great importance to Rome: its fertile floodplain was a major source of grain for feeding the city.

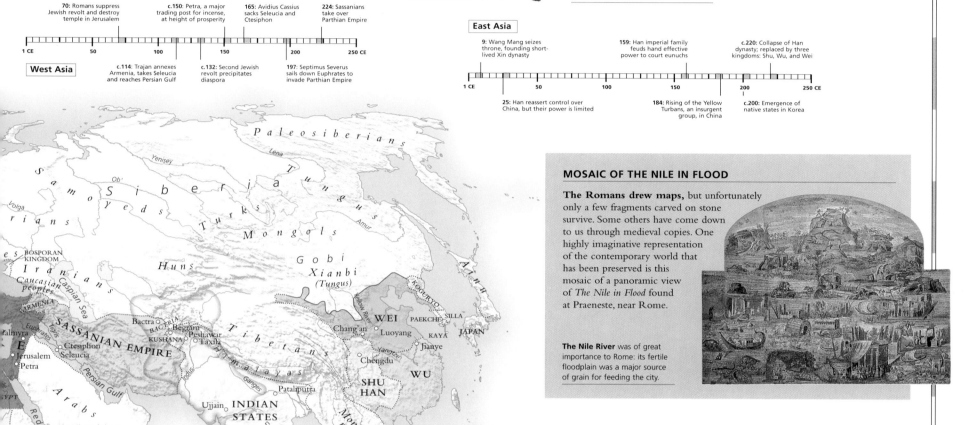

South Asia

In the 1st century CE the nomadic Yuezhi were pushed westward from the borders of China. One of the tribes, the Kushans, united the others, moved into Bactria, and from there expanded into northern India, founding their capital at Peshawar. The Kingdom of Kushana crumbled at the end of the 2nd century, when native peoples – the Tamils of southern India and the Satavahanas of the Deccan – were beginning to assert their power.

The Kushans' wealth came from their control of east–west trade routes. This ivory plaque was part of a famous hoard found at Begram, which contained artifacts from Rome, Africa, India, and China.

Egyptian mummy cases took on a curious hybrid appearance under Roman rule. The portrait on this 2nd-century example shows the Romans' Hellenistic taste in art.

Africa

c.50: Kingdom of Axum starts to emerge

c.100: Alexandria emerges as a center of Christian scholarship, seat of one of the earliest Christian bishoprics

c.150: Christianity starts to spread westward to Roman provinces of Numidia and Mauretania

1 CE   50   100   150   200   250 CE

44: Mauretania annexed by Rome

69: Romans defeat powerful Saharan kingdom of Garamantes, but do not absorb it into empire

South Asia

99: Indian embassy to court of Trajan in Rome, probably to announce Kushan conquests

c.102: Death of Kushans' greatest ruler, Kanishka

c.200: Cities appear for first time on Deccan plateau

1 CE   50   100   150   200   250 CE

c.60: Kushans, under Kadphises I, unite Yuezhi tribes and advance into northern India

c.150: Kushans become Persian vassals

THE EMERGENCE OF GLOBAL RELIGIONS

This 7th-century silver plaque from Hexham, England is thought to depict a Christian saint.

BY 250 CE CERTAIN OLD WORLD religions *(see pp.36–37)* had spread far beyond their areas of origin to become substantial bodies of faith. In the west, the Roman taste for monotheistic Mithraism, derived from Persian Zoroastrianism, spread throughout the empire; but in its wake the cult of Christianity was becoming firmly established. Further, the Roman suppression of the Jewish revolt in 132 CE had caused a diaspora through much of the empire. In South Asia, Hinduism became deeply rooted throughout the subcontinent as Dravidians and tribal peoples adopted the practices of their Aryan conquerors; meanwhile Buddhism was spread overland to Central Asia and China and beyond by missionaries of various sectarian schools.

Mithraism, Judaism, and Christianity

The worship of Mithras was arduous and limited to males; it was popular among the Roman legions, spreading to the corners of the empire. Its monotheism paved the way for Christianity which, in parallel to the Jewish diaspora, spread to centers throughout the empire. This was inaugurated by the missionary journeys of St. Paul, in the 1st century CE. By the time of Diocletian's persecutions (304 CE) centers had been established in Asia Minor, Mesopotamia, and around the Mediterranean. The fusion of Christian theology with the ethical concerns of Greek philosophy gave it intellectual respectability; and when Constantine (306–337) adopted the faith, Christianity became the official religion of the empire.

This 5th-century pottery amphora is decorated with two versions of the Christian cross, which became the most widely used symbol of the religion.

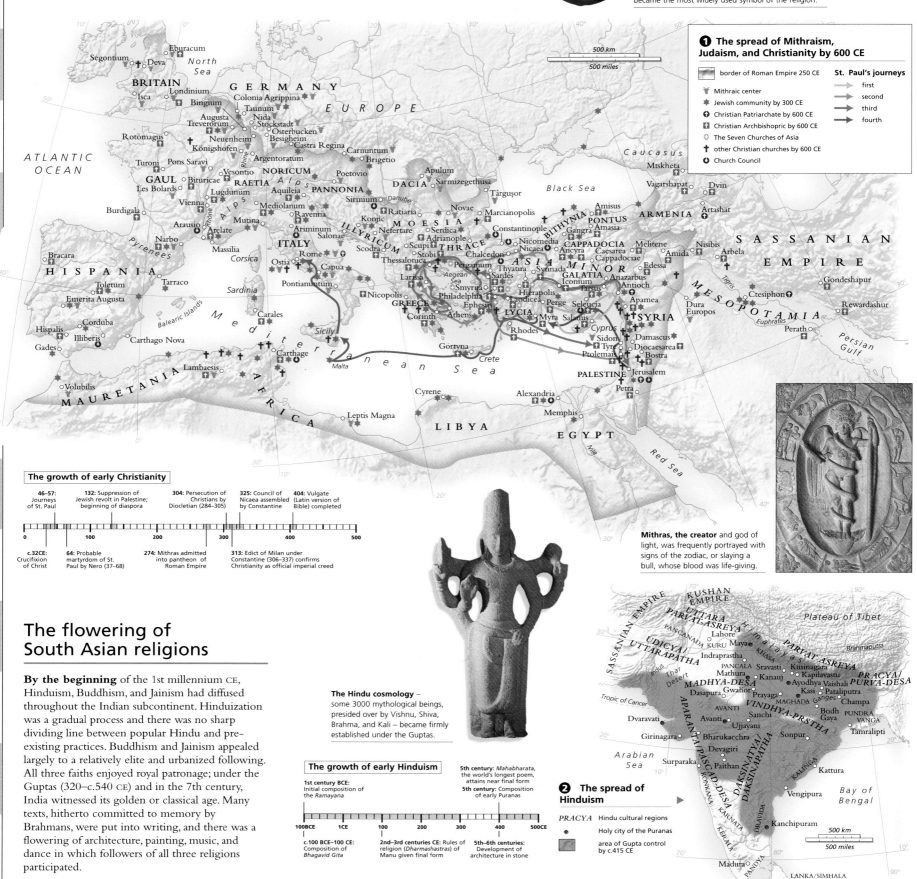

The flowering of South Asian religions

By the beginning of the 1st millennium CE, Hinduism, Buddhism, and Jainism had diffused throughout the Indian subcontinent. Hinduization was a gradual process and there was no sharp dividing line between popular Hindu and pre-existing practices. Buddhism and Jainism appealed largely to a relatively elite and urbanized following. All three faiths enjoyed royal patronage; under the Guptas (320–c.540 CE) and in the 7th century, India witnessed its golden or classical age. Many texts, hitherto committed to memory by Brahmans, were put into writing, and there was a flowering of architecture, painting, music, and dance in which followers of all three religions participated.

The Hindu cosmology – some 3000 mythological beings, presided over by Vishnu, Shiva, Brahma, and Kali – became firmly established under the Guptas.

Mithras, the creator and god of light, was frequently portrayed with signs of the zodiac, or slaying a bull, whose blood was life-giving.

The growth of early Christianity

46–57: Journeys of St. Paul	**132:** Suppression of Jewish revolt in Palestine; beginning of diaspora	**304:** Persecution of Christians by Diocletian (284–305)	**325:** Council of Nicaea assembled by Constantine	**404:** Vulgate (Latin version of Bible) completed

0 — 100 — 200 — 300 — 400 — 500

c.32CE: Crucifixion of Christ	**64:** Probable martyrdom of St. Paul by Nero (37–68)	**274:** Mithras admitted into pantheon of Roman Empire	**313:** Edict of Milan under Constantine (306–337) confirms Christianity as official imperial creed

The growth of early Hinduism

1st century BCE: Initial composition of the *Ramayana*	**5th century:** *Mahabharata*, the world's longest poem, attains near final form **5th century:** Composition of early Puranas

100BCE — 1CE — 100 — 200 — 300 — 400 — 500CE

c.100 BCE–100 CE: Composition of *Bhagavid Gita*	**2nd–3rd centuries CE:** Rules of religion (*Dharmashastras*) of Manu given final form	**5th–6th centuries:** Development of architecture in stone

❶ The spread of Mithraism, Judaism, and Christianity by 600 CE

- border of Roman Empire 250 CE
- Mithraic center
- Jewish community by 300 CE
- Christian Patriarchate by 600 CE
- Christian Archbishopric by 600 CE
- The Seven Churches of Asia
- other Christian churches by 600 CE
- Church Council

St. Paul's journeys
- first
- second
- third
- fourth

❷ The spread of Hinduism

- *PRACYA* Hindu cultural regions
- Holy city of the Puranas
- area of Gupta control by c.415 CE

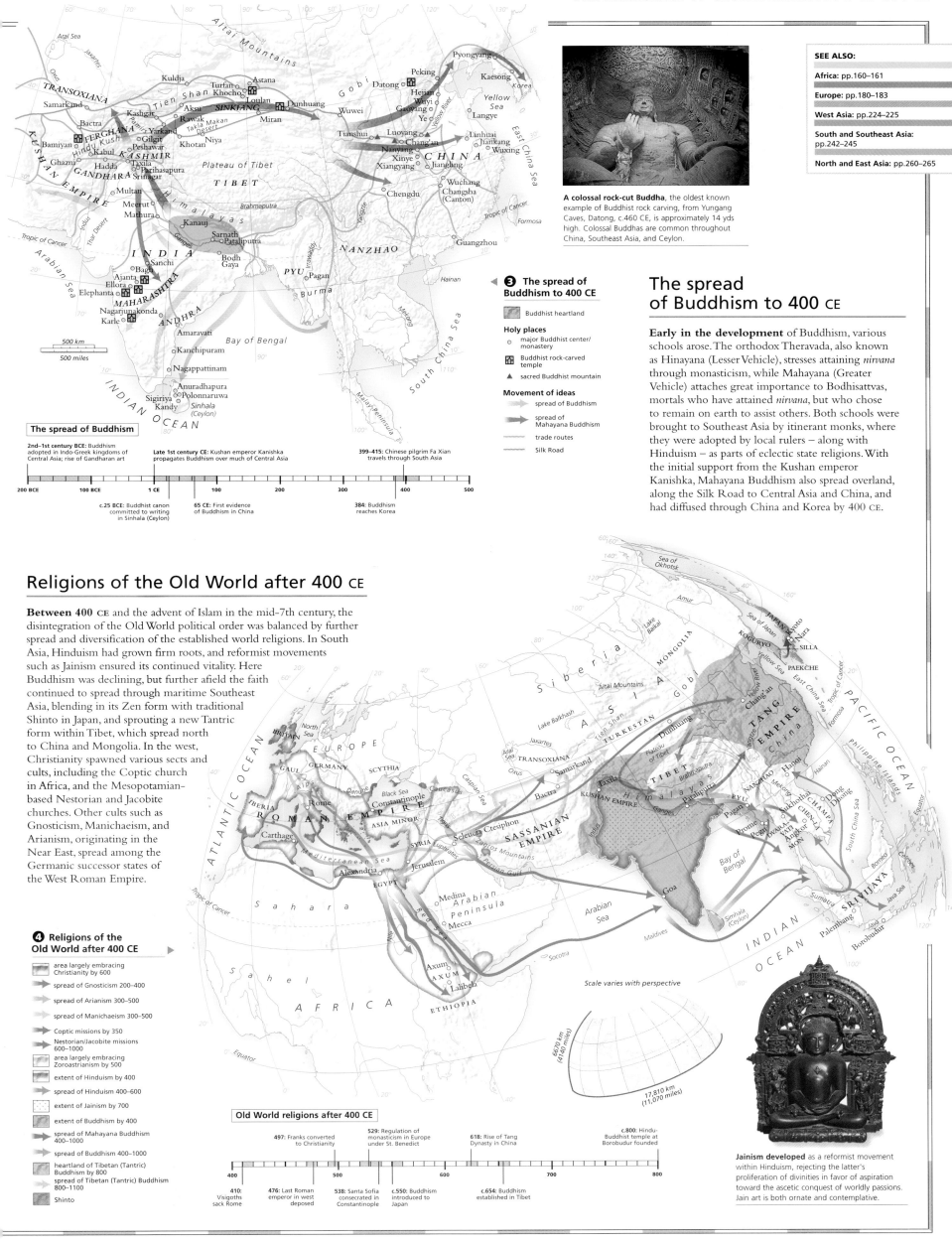

SEE ALSO:

Africa: pp.160–161

Europe: pp.180–183

West Asia: pp.224–225

South and Southeast Asia: pp.242–245

North and East Asia: pp.260–265

A colossal rock-cut Buddha, the oldest known example of Buddhist rock carving, from Yungang Caves, Datong, c.460 CE, is approximately 14 yds high. Colossal Buddhas are common throughout China, Southeast Asia, and Ceylon.

❸ The spread of Buddhism to 400 CE

Buddhist heartland

Holy places
- ○ major Buddhist center/monastery
- ⊞ Buddhist rock-carved temple
- ▲ sacred Buddhist mountain

Movement of ideas
- → spread of Buddhism
- → spread of Mahayana Buddhism
- — trade routes
- — Silk Road

The spread of Buddhism to 400 CE

Early in the development of Buddhism, various schools arose. The orthodox Theravada, also known as Hinayana (Lesser Vehicle), stresses attaining *nirvana* through monasticism, while Mahayana (Greater Vehicle) attaches great importance to Bodhisattvas, mortals who have attained *nirvana*, but who chose to remain on earth to assist others. Both schools were brought to Southeast Asia by itinerant monks, where they were adopted by local rulers – along with Hinduism – as parts of eclectic state religions. With the initial support from the Kushan emperor Kanishka, Mahayana Buddhism also spread overland, along the Silk Road to Central Asia and China, and had diffused through China and Korea by 400 CE.

The spread of Buddhism

2nd–1st century BCE: Buddhism adopted in Indo-Greek kingdoms of Central Asia; rise of Gandharan art

Late 1st century CE: Kushan emperor Kanishka propagates Buddhism over much of Central Asia

399–415: Chinese pilgrim Fa Xian travels through South Asia

c.25 BCE: Buddhist canon committed to writing in Sinhala (Ceylon)

65 CE: First evidence of Buddhism in China

384: Buddhism reaches Korea

200 BCE — 100 BCE — 1 CE — 100 — 200 — 300 — 400 — 500

Religions of the Old World after 400 CE

Between 400 CE and the advent of Islam in the mid-7th century, the disintegration of the Old World political order was balanced by further spread and diversification of the established world religions. In South Asia, Hinduism had grown firm roots, and reformist movements such as Jainism ensured its continued vitality. Here Buddhism was declining, but further afield the faith continued to spread through maritime Southeast Asia, blending in its Zen form with traditional Shinto in Japan, and sprouting a new Tantric form within Tibet, which spread north to China and Mongolia. In the west, Christianity spawned various sects and cults, including the Coptic church in Africa, and the Mesopotamian-based Nestorian and Jacobite churches. Other cults such as Gnosticism, Manichaeism, and Arianism, originating in the Near East, spread among the Germanic successor states of the West Roman Empire.

❹ Religions of the Old World after 400 CE

- area largely embracing Christianity by 600
- → spread of Gnosticism 200–400
- → spread of Arianism 300–500
- → spread of Manichaeism 300–500
- → Coptic missions by 350
- → Nestorian/Jacobite missions 600–1000
- area largely embracing Zoroastrianism by 500
- extent of Hinduism by 400
- → spread of Hinduism 400–600
- extent of Jainism by 700
- extent of Buddhism by 400
- → spread of Mahayana Buddhism 400–1000
- → spread of Buddhism 400–1000
- heartland of Tibetan (Tantric) Buddhism by 800
- → spread of Tibetan (Tantric) Buddhism 800–1100
- Shinto

Scale varies with perspective

Old World religions after 400 CE

497: Franks converted to Christianity

529: Regulation of monasticism in Europe under St. Benedict

618: Rise of Tang Dynasty in China

c.800: Hindu-Buddhist temple at Borobudur founded

400 — 500 — 600 — 700 — 800

410: Visigoths sack Rome

476: Last Roman emperor in west deposed

538: Santa Sofia consecrated in Constantinople

c.550: Buddhism introduced to Japan

c.654: Buddhism established in Tibet

Jainism developed as a reformist movement within Hinduism, rejecting the latter's proliferation of divinities in favor of aspiration toward the ascetic conquest of worldly passions. Jain art is both ornate and contemplative.

THE WORLD 250–500

BY 500, MIGRATIONS IN ASIA AND EUROPE had so weakened the civilizations of the Old World that only the East Roman Empire and Sassanian Persia survived. Asian nomads broke the power of the Chinese and destroyed India's Gupta Empire. The Huns even invaded Europe, where the Romans repulsed them, but only with the aid of their Gothic allies. Rome relied increasingly on the aid of the Goths and other Germanic peoples, who settled within the empire and, as central authority waned, carved out new kingdoms for themselves. In contrast to the collapsing empires of the Old World, the great urban civilizations of Central America, Teotihuacán, the Maya, and the Zapotecs, were beginning to flourish.

Much of the best late Roman sculpture is found in the carving of Christian scenes on sarcophagi.

Europe

In 284, **Diocletian** divided the Roman Empire into eastern and western halves. With the advent of Christianity and the establishment of Constantinople as a new capital in 324, the empire's center of gravity shifted eastward. Meanwhile, Germanic and Slav peoples, living on Rome's northern borders, infiltrated imperial territory, at times peacefully, often by force. The Western Empire collapsed in 476 to be replaced by a series of Germanic kingdoms, and the mantle of empire passed to Constantinople in the east.

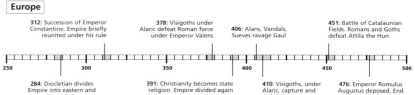

Europe

312: Succession of Emperor Constantine. Empire briefly reunited under his rule

378: Visigoths under Alaric defeat Roman force under Emperor Valens

406: Alans, Vandals, Sueves ravage Gaul

451: Battle of Catalaunian Fields. Romans and Goths defeat Attila the Hun

284: Diocletian divides Empire into eastern and western halves

391: Christianity becomes state religion. Empire divided again

410: Visigoths, under Alaric, capture and sack Rome

476: Emperor Romulus Augustus deposed. End of Western Empire

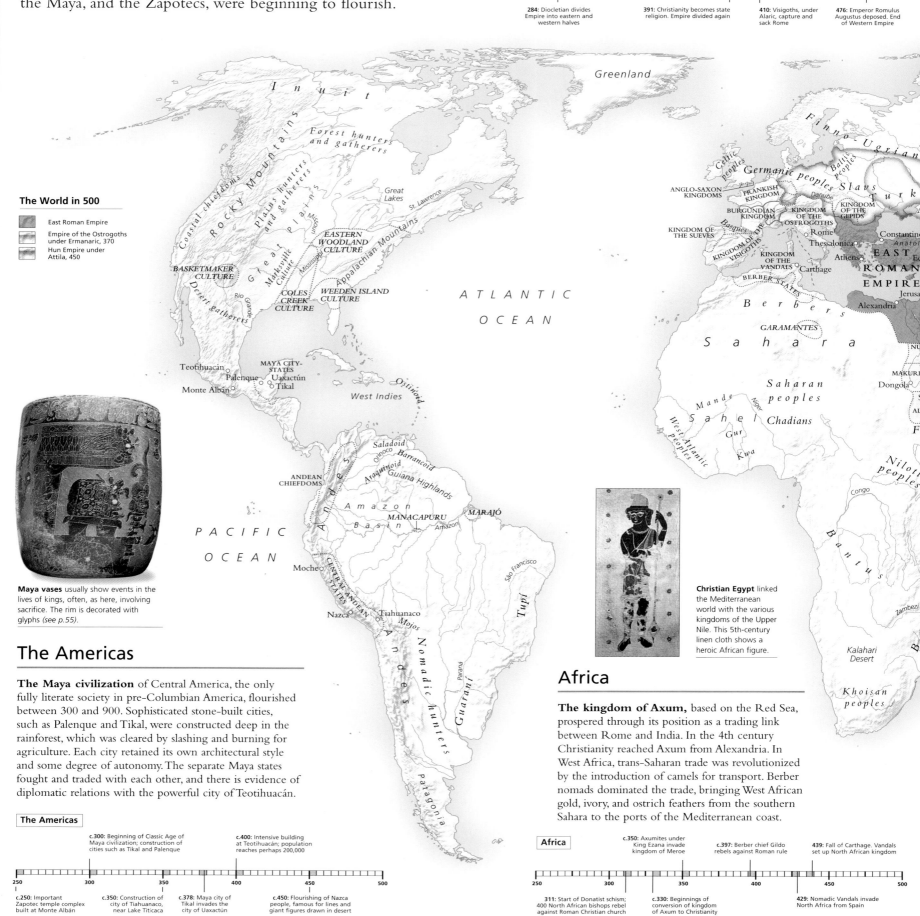

The World in 500

- East Roman Empire
- Empire of the Ostrogoths under Ermanaric, 370
- Hun Empire under Attila, 450

Maya vases usually show events in the lives of kings, often, as here, involving sacrifice. The rim is decorated with glyphs (see p.55).

Christian Egypt linked the Mediterranean world with the various kingdoms of the Upper Nile. This 5th-century linen cloth shows a heroic African figure.

The Americas

The Maya civilization of Central America, the only fully literate society in pre-Columbian America, flourished between 300 and 900. Sophisticated stone-built cities, such as Palenque and Tikal, were constructed deep in the rainforest, which was cleared by slashing and burning for agriculture. Each city retained its own architectural style and some degree of autonomy. The separate Maya states fought and traded with each other, and there is evidence of diplomatic relations with the powerful city of Teotihuacán.

The Americas

c.300: Beginning of Classic Age of Maya civilization; construction of cities such as Tikal and Palenque

c.400: Intensive building at Teotihuacán; population reaches perhaps 200,000

c.250: Important Zapotec temple complex built at Monte Albán

c.350: Construction of city of Tiahuanaco, near Lake Titicaca

c.378: Maya city of Tikal invades the city of Uaxactún

c.450: Flourishing of Nazca people, famous for lines and giant figures drawn in desert

Africa

The kingdom of Axum, based on the Red Sea, prospered through its position as a trading link between Rome and India. In the 4th century Christianity reached Axum from Alexandria. In West Africa, trans-Saharan trade was revolutionized by the introduction of camels for transport. Berber nomads dominated the trade, bringing West African gold, ivory, and ostrich feathers from the southern Sahara to the ports of the Mediterranean coast.

Africa

c.350: Axumites under King Ezana invade kingdom of Meroe

c.397: Berber chief Gildo rebels against Roman rule

439: Fall of Carthage. Vandals set up North African kingdom

311: Start of Donatist schism; 400 North African bishops rebel against Roman Christian church

c.330: Beginnings of conversion of kingdom of Axum to Christianity

429: Nomadic Vandals invade North Africa from Spain

THE STIRRUP

Most technological advances in equipment for horsemen were developed by the nomadic peoples of Central Asia, where the horse had first been domesticated. The Scythians may have used leather loops as a kind of stirrup as early as 400 BCE, although these were probably just an aid for mounting. Rigid metal stirrups, which provided a stable platform for warriors to fight effectively from horseback, were adopted some time before 400 CE in China, from where their use spread across Central Asia to Europe.

This Chinese ceramic figurine of a hunter attacked by a lion demonstrates one of the advantages of the stirrup as the rider turns to deal with his aggressor.

West Asia

By the end of the 4th century, Sassanian Persia stretched from the Euphrates to the Indus. Social stability was maintained by an elaborate and efficient bureaucracy, a healthy economy based primarily on agriculture, and widespread adherence to Zoroastrianism, the state religion. The Sassanians posed a major threat to Roman interests in Asia, and for 200 years there was conflict with the Roman Empire, especially over Armenia. In the 5th century Persia had to withstand incursions by eastern nomads, notably the Hephthalites or "White Huns," but survived intact.

A Sassanian Shahanshah (King of Kings), probably Bahram V, who ruled from 421 to 439, demonstrates his authority (and prowess as a lion-hunter) on this magnificent silver dish.

SEE ALSO:

North America: pp.120–123

South America: pp.144–147

Africa: pp.160–161

Europe: pp.180–183

West Asia: pp.224–225

South and Southeast Asia: pp.242–245

North and East Asia: pp.260–261

Australasia and Oceania: pp.280–281

West Asia

296: Sassanians occupy Armenia and defeat Roman emperor Galerius. Treaty ensures peace for next 40 years

337: Shapur II embarks on new warfare against Romans

c.450: Hephthalites attack northeastern borders of Sassanian Empire

260: At Edessa, Sassanians under Shapur I defeat and capture Roman emperor, Valerian

309: Accession of Shapur II. Persian borders are threatened by nomads

484: Hephthalites defeat and kill Sassanian ruler, but the empire survives

250 300 350 400 450 500

MOSAIC MAP OF JERUSALEM

The sites associated with the life of Christ all lay within the East Roman Empire. Jerusalem, as the scene of Christ's Passion, was a major center of pilgrimage and source of relics from the 4th century onward. The city was depicted in great detail in a 6th-century mosaic found at Madaba in Jordan: a bird's-eye view of the city that indicates all the important churches and pilgrimage sites.

The Madaba map shows clearly the central colonnade which dates from Hadrian's rebuilding of Jerusalem in the 2nd century CE.

China's many Buddhist monasteries of this period have all been destroyed. Only the vast cave-temples, built with imperial patronage, such as this one at Longmen near Luoyang, have survived.

This fresco of two heavenly maidens decorated Kassapa's 5th-century fortified mountaintop palace at Sigiriya in Ceylon.

South Asia

The Gupta dynasty grew in power and influence throughout the 4th century to dominate northern India. Sanskrit literature, poetry, sculpture, and architecture all flourished under the Hindu Guptas. It was also an age noted for its religious tolerance. In the mid-5th century, however, the Hephthalites advanced into Gupta territory, ending India's "golden age." In Ceylon, meanwhile, Buddhism became established as the dominant faith.

South Asia

c.415: High point in career of Kalidasa, one of India's greatest poets and playwrights

c.500: Collapse of Gupta Empire under renewed Hephthalite attacks

320: Expansion of Gupta family, from Magadha, heralds start of Gupta dynasty

376: Gupta rule reaches its greatest extent under Chandra Gupta II

495: Death of Kassapa, self-appointed god-king of Sigiriya in Ceylon

250 300 350 400 450 500

East Asia

After a period of fragmentation, China was briefly re-united in 280 under the Jin; but when nomads sacked Chang'an in 316, the Eastern Jin dynasty moved to Nanjing. They retained control over southern China, but the north suffered successive invasions by steppe nomads. In this climate of political uncertainty, Buddhism flourished and the monastic life grew in appeal. Japan's Yamato state emerged in the 4th century, gradually gaining hegemony over the south of the country.

East Asia

c.300: Emergence of Yamato state in Osaka region of Japan

420: Song rule in southern China: start of period of the Southern Dynasties

c.490: Northern Wei capital moved to Luoyang

280: Sima Yan, leader of the Jin dynasty, unites China

291: Steppe peoples from beyond Great Wall allowed to settle within empire

386: Toba Wei reunify northern China, intermarry with Chinese, and adopt Chinese culture

479: Rule of southern China passes to the Qi dynasty

250 300 350 400 450 500

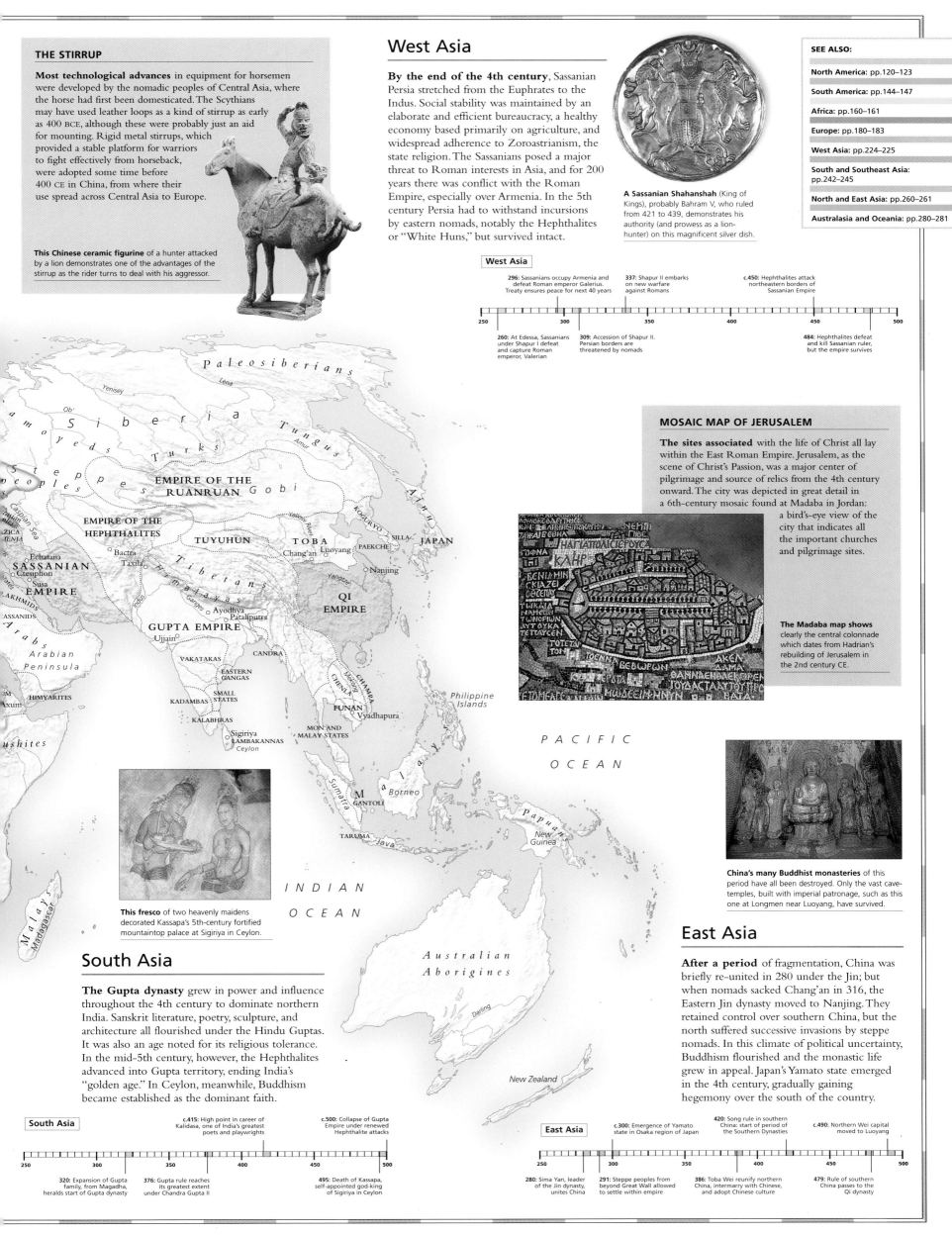

Map labels: Paleosiberians; Siberia; Samoyeds; Tungus; Turks; Steppe peoples; EMPIRE OF THE RUANRUAN; Gobi; EMPIRE OF THE HEPHTHALITES; TUYUHUN; TOBA; Chang'an; Luoyang; Nanjing; KOGURYO; SILLA; PAEKCHE; JAPAN; Yangtze; QI EMPIRE; Tibetans; Himalayas; Bactra; Taxila; SASSANIAN EMPIRE; Ecbatana; Ctesiphon; Susa; AKHMIDS; ASSANIDS; Arabs; Arabian Peninsula; HIMYARITES; Axum; Kushites; GUPTA EMPIRE; Ujjain; Ganges; Ayodhya; Pataliputra; VAKATAKAS; EASTERN GANGAS; CANDRA; SMALL STATES; KADAMBAS; KALABHRAS; Sigiriya; LAMBAKANNAS; Ceylon; CHENLA; CHAMPA; FUNAN; Vyadhapura; MON AND MALAY STATES; Sumatra; Borneo; GANTOLI; TARUMA; Java; Malays; Madagascar; Philippine Islands; New Guinea; Papuan; PACIFIC OCEAN; INDIAN OCEAN; Australian Aborigines; Darling; New Zealand

MIGRATIONS AND INVASIONS

The half-Vandal general Stilicho was regent during the reign of the child emperor Honorius.

THE GERMANIC PEOPLES who migrated into the Roman Empire during the 5th century were seeking to share in the fruits of empire, not to destroy it. They were spurred to move west in search of land by a combination of factors: famine, population pressure, and the prospects of a better standard of living. Rome initially accepted "barbarian" recruits into its depleted army as *foederati* (federates), and allowed them to retain their own leaders and laws. But when the Romans opposed the settlement of large groups or refused to reward them for their services, the results could be disastrous: campaigns of plunder, sacked cities, and the breakdown of imperial control.

Turmoil in Italy

From the late 4th century, the West Roman Empire was plagued by disputes over the imperial succession, which led to factionalism and civil wars. These were very destructive of Roman manpower and led to the recruitment of large numbers of barbarians under their own leaders. Emperors were often pawns in the power struggles of generals. Many of these, such as the half-Vandal Stilicho and the Suevian Ricimer, were of Germanic origin.

Honorius succeeded his father, Theodosius, as western emperor in 395 while still a child. He lived in comfortable seclusion while senior ministers governed.

Turmoil in Italy

324: Constantine becomes sole ruler	391: Theodosius makes Christianity religion of the Empire	402: Imperial court moved to Ravenna	476: Child emperor, Romulus Augustulus, deposed by Odoacer, "King of Italy"
300 — 350 — 400 — 450 — 500			
395: Theodosius dies; West Roman Empire left to child emperor Honorius	410: Sack of Rome by Visigoths	455: Accession of Libius Severus, puppet emperor controlled by Ricimer	

The aims of the migrations

The peoples who invaded the Roman Empire in the 4th and 5th centuries were driven by a variety of motives. Some, like Alaric's Visigoths, sought official acceptance by the Roman authorities. Others, such as the peoples of the Great Migration of 406, were intent on finding land anywhere and by any means. The only invaders bent purely on destruction and plunder were the Huns. As steppe nomads, the Huns' strength lay in their mobility and their skill with bow, lance, and saber. They were able to smash the overstretched imperial defenses, but were repulsed when Goths and Romans joined forces against them. The Romans relied more and more on Gothic military support, and it was the Goths who emerged as the first inheritors of the Empire's western territories.

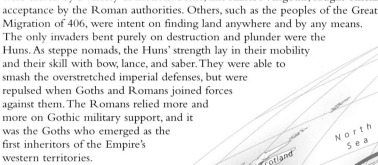

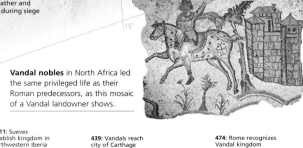
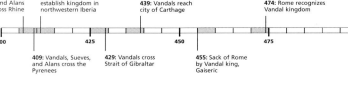

c.410: Romans abandon Britain

402: Capital of West Roman Empire moved to Ravenna

452: Attila persuaded to leave Roman Empire

453: On death of Attila, Empire of the Huns collapses

EMPIRE OF THE HUNS c.420

Visigoths from 382

Ostrogoths from 450

410: Visigoths sack Rome
455: Vandals sack Rome

410: Death of Alaric; Visigoths abandon plan to invade Africa

KINGDOM OF THE VISIGOTHS c.418

414: Athaulf, leader of the Visigoths, marries Galla Placidia, daughter of late Emperor Theodosius. She had been captured during sack of Rome

KINGDOM OF THE BURGUNDIANS c.443

WEST ROMAN EMPIRE from 395

430: City of Hippo taken by Vandals. St. Augustine, church father and bishop of the city, dies during siege

429: Gaiseric leads Vandals into North Africa

Vandal nobles in North Africa led the same privileged life as their Roman predecessors, as this mosaic of a Vandal landowner shows.

The Great Migration

At Christmas 406, vast hordes of Vandals, Sueves, and Alans overwhelmed the imperial defenses and poured across the Rhine River into Gaul, where they greatly disrupted settled life. They then moved in a southwesterly direction and eventually reached the Iberian Peninsula. The Vandals pressed on to North Africa, crossing the Strait of Gibraltar in 429, while the Sueves and Alans set up kingdoms in Iberia.

The Great Migration

406: Vandals, Sueves, and Alans cross Rhine	c.411: Sueves establish kingdom in northwestern Iberia	439: Vandals reach city of Carthage	474: Rome recognizes Vandal kingdom
400 — 425 — 450 — 475 — 500			
409: Vandals, Sueves, and Alans cross the Pyrenees	429: Vandals cross Strait of Gibraltar	455: Sack of Rome by Vandal king, Gaiseric	

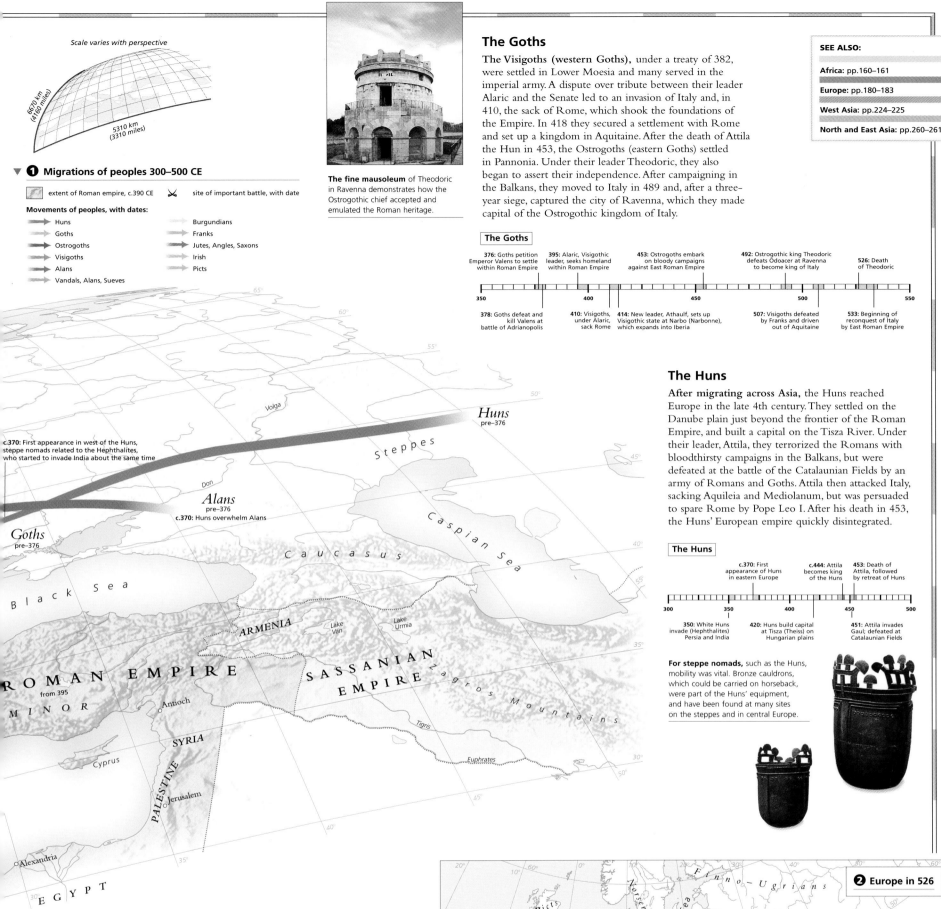

Scale varies with perspective

6670 km
(4160 miles)

5310 km
(3310 miles)

❶ Migrations of peoples 300–500 CE

extent of Roman empire, c.390 CE	✗ site of important battle, with date

Movements of peoples, with dates:

➤ Huns	➤ Burgundians
➤ Goths	➤ Franks
➤ Ostrogoths	➤ Jutes, Angles, Saxons
➤ Visigoths	➤ Irish
➤ Alans	➤ Picts
➤ Vandals, Alans, Sueves	

The fine mausoleum of Theodoric in Ravenna demonstrates how the Ostrogothic chief accepted and emulated the Roman heritage.

The Goths

The Visigoths (western Goths), under a treaty of 382, were settled in Lower Moesia and many served in the imperial army. A dispute over tribute between their leader Alaric and the Senate led to an invasion of Italy and, in 410, the sack of Rome, which shook the foundations of the Empire. In 418 they secured a settlement with Rome and set up a kingdom in Aquitaine. After the death of Attila the Hun in 453, the Ostrogoths (eastern Goths) settled in Pannonia. Under their leader Theodoric, they also began to assert their independence. After campaigning in the Balkans, they moved to Italy in 489 and, after a three-year siege, captured the city of Ravenna, which they made capital of the Ostrogothic kingdom of Italy.

SEE ALSO:

Africa: pp.160–161

Europe: pp.180–183

West Asia: pp.224–225

North and East Asia: pp.260–261

The Goths

376: Goths petition Emperor Valens to settle within Roman Empire	395: Alaric, Visigothic leader, seeks homeland within Roman Empire	453: Ostrogoths embark on bloody campaigns against East Roman Empire	492: Ostrogothic king Theodoric defeats Odoacer at Ravenna to become king of Italy	526: Death of Theodoric
350	**400**	**450**	**500**	**550**
378: Goths defeat and kill Valens at battle of Adrianopolis	410: Visigoths, under Alaric, sack Rome	414: New leader, Athaulf, sets up Visigothic state at Narbo (Narbonne), which expands into Iberia	507: Visigoths defeated by Franks and driven out of Aquitaine	533: Beginning of reconquest of Italy by East Roman Empire

The Huns

After migrating across Asia, the Huns reached Europe in the late 4th century. They settled on the Danube plain just beyond the frontier of the Roman Empire, and built a capital on the Tisza River. Under their leader, Attila, they terrorized the Romans with bloodthirsty campaigns in the Balkans, but were defeated at the battle of the Catalaunian Fields by an army of Romans and Goths. Attila then attacked Italy, sacking Aquileia and Mediolanum, but was persuaded to spare Rome by Pope Leo I. After his death in 453, the Huns' European empire quickly disintegrated.

The Huns

c.370: First appearance of Huns in eastern Europe	c.444: Attila becomes king of the Huns	453: Death of Attila, followed by retreat of Huns
300 **350**	**400**	**450** **500**
350: White Huns (Hephthalites) invade Persia and India	420: Huns build capital at Tisza (Theiss) on Hungarian plains	451: Attila invades Gaul; defeated at Catalaunian Fields

For steppe nomads, such as the Huns, mobility was vital. Bronze cauldrons, which could be carried on horseback, were part of the Huns' equipment, and have been found at many sites on the steppes and in central Europe.

The inheritors of Western Europe

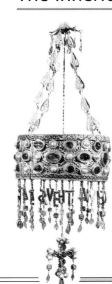

By 526, the waves of migrations had redrawn the map of Western Europe. The Ostrogoths, under their charismatic leader Theodoric, controlled Italy, while the Visigoths had captured most of the Iberian Peninsula. The Vandals were established in North Africa, the Sueves in Galicia, and the Burgundians, who crossed the Rhine c.400, had settled in southeast France. The most enduring of the many Germanic kingdoms, however, would prove to be that of the Franks, founded in 456 by Clovis, which laid the foundations of modern France and Germany.

The magnificent votive crown of the 7th-century king Reccesuinth illustrates the importance of Christianity in Iberia under the Visigoths. Their rule lasted from the 5th century to the Arab conquest of 711.

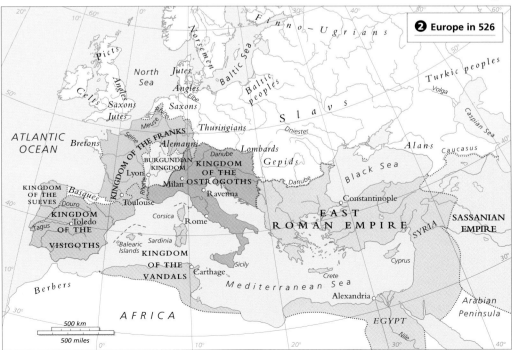

❷ Europe in 526

THE WORLD 500–750

THE RAPID RECOVERY of the ancient world from the onslaught of invading nomads is evident in the rise of two great empires in West Asia and China. The new religion of Islam was based on the teachings of Muhammad, an Arabian merchant from Mecca. Fired by a zeal for conquest and conversion, Islamic armies overran West Asia and North Africa, and by 750 had created an empire that stretched from the Indus to Spain. Under the Tang dynasty, Chinese civilization reached new heights; Tang control penetrated deep into Central Asia and Chinese cultural influence was widespread. In the Americas, the Maya remained the most advanced civilization, though their small city-states did not have the far-reaching influence of the great city of Teotihuacán.

The Byzantines were the champions of Christianity. This mosaic shows Emperor Justinian as God's representative on Earth.

Europe

The Franks became the most powerful of all Rome's Germanic successors. United under Clovis I, their overlordship was extended to the south of France and east of the Rhine. Constantinople was the Christian capital of the Byzantine Empire. The Emperor Justinian (527–65) reconquered North Africa and much of Italy, briefly creating an empire stretching from Spain to Persia. Over the next two centuries much of this territory was lost to Islam and, in the Balkans, to Slavic invaders.

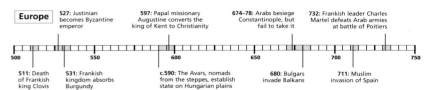

Europe	527: Justinian becomes Byzantine emperor	597: Papal missionary Augustine converts the king of Kent to Christianity	674–78: Arabs besiege Constantinople, but fail to take it	732: Frankish leader Charles Martel defeats Arab armies at battle of Poitiers
500	550	600	650	700 750
511: Death of Frankish king Clovis	531: Frankish kingdom absorbs Burgundy	c.590: The Avars, nomads from the steppes, establish state on Hungarian plains	680: Bulgars invade Balkans	711: Muslim invasion of Spain

The World in 750

	Tang Empire
	Byzantine Empire
	Umayyad Caliphate
	Kök Türk Empire 551–572
	East Roman Empire 554–565
	Horsha's Empire c.640
	Avar Empire c.595

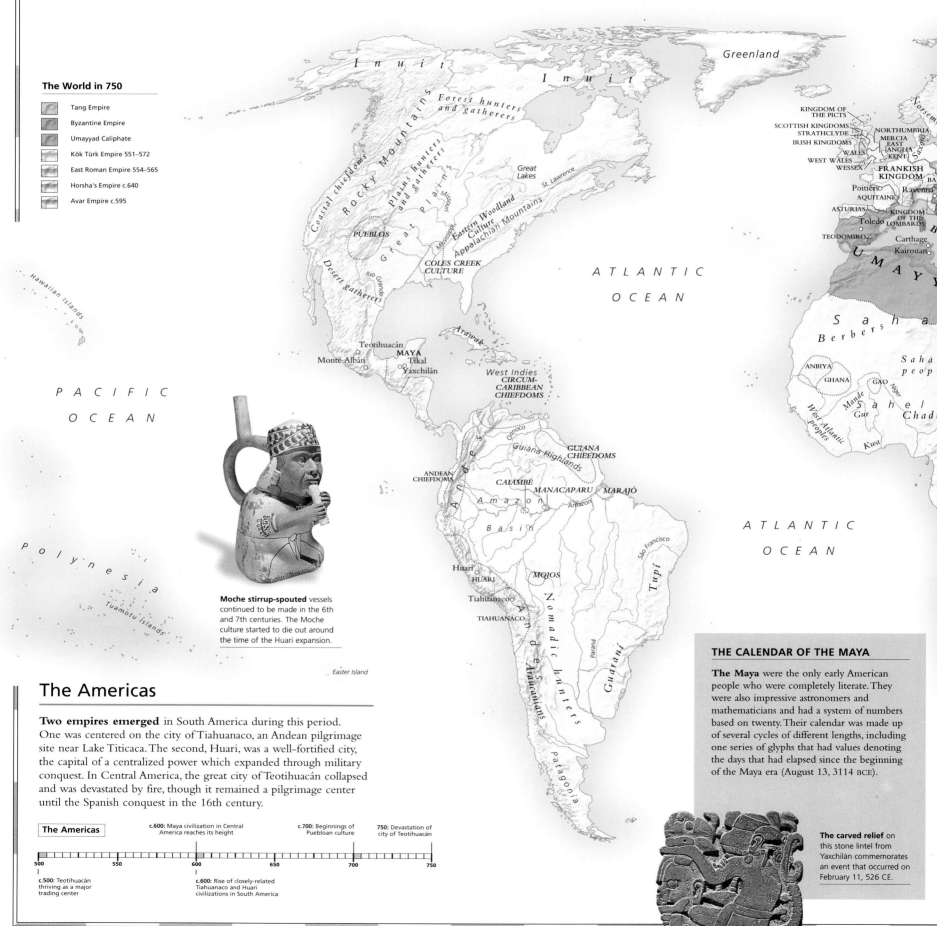

Moche stirrup-spouted vessels continued to be made in the 6th and 7th centuries. The Moche culture started to die out around the time of the Huari expansion.

The Americas

Two empires emerged in South America during this period. One was centered on the city of Tiahuanaco, an Andean pilgrimage site near Lake Titicaca. The second, Huari, was a well-fortified city, the capital of a centralized power which expanded through military conquest. In Central America, the great city of Teotihuacán collapsed and was devastated by fire, though it remained a pilgrimage center until the Spanish conquest in the 16th century.

The Americas	c.600: Maya civilization in Central America reaches its height	c.700: Beginnings of Puebloan culture	750: Devastation of city of Teotihuacán
500	550	600 650	700 750
c.500: Teotihuacán thriving as a major trading center		c.600: Rise of closely-related Tiahuanaco and Huari civilizations in South America	

THE CALENDAR OF THE MAYA

The Maya were the only early American people who were completely literate. They were also impressive astronomers and mathematicians and had a system of numbers based on twenty. Their calendar was made up of several cycles of different lengths, including one series of glyphs that had values denoting the days that had elapsed since the beginning of the Maya era (August 13, 3114 BCE).

The carved relief on this stone lintel from Yaxchilán commemorates an event that occurred on February 11, 526 CE.

West Asia

In the 7th century the whole of West Asia was overrun by Arabian armies, soldiers of Islam inspired to conquer and convert by the new religion founded by Muhammad. They were able to exploit the weaknesses of the two great powers in the region, the Sassanians and the Byzantines. Sassanian Persia had reached its peak under Khosrau I (531–79), who invaded Byzantine Syria and captured Antioch. But continuing conflict with the Byzantines led to a crushing defeat at Nineveh in 628.

The Dome of the Rock in Jerusalem was built in 692 over the ruins of the Jewish Temple. It is sacred to Islam as the site of Muhammad's journey to heaven.

CLASSICAL ARAB WORLD MAPS

When the Arabs took over much of the Greek-speaking eastern Mediterranean, they seized on the classical scholarship of Alexandria, including the famous *Geography* of Ptolemy *(see p.44).* Though no maps from this period survive, it seems that, while the map-making tradition died out in the west, it was kept alive by Arab scholars, albeit in the academic style of this later world map.

Al-Istakhri's world map, from the 10th century, uses a Ptolemaic projection, but with south at the top.

SEE ALSO:

North America: pp.122–123

South America: pp.142–145

Africa: pp.162–163

Europe: pp.182–185

West Asia: pp.226–227

South and Southeast Asia: pp.242–245

North and East Asia: pp.262–265

Australasia and Oceania: pp.280–281

West Asia

531: Beginning of reign of Sassanian ruler, Khosrau I Anohshirvanh

570: Prophet Muhammad born in Mecca

622: The Hegira: Muhammad and his followers move to Medina; start of Islamic era

628: Defeat of Sassanians by Byzantine emperor Heraclius

637: Arabian armies capture Sassanian capital, Ctesiphon

656: Arabians overrun Persia

661: Start of Umayyad dynasty. Damascus is center of Islamic empire

674–78: Arabian siege of Constantinople

698: Arabs capture Carthage

711: Islamic armies cross the Strait of Gibraltar and conquer Spain

500 550 600 650 700 750

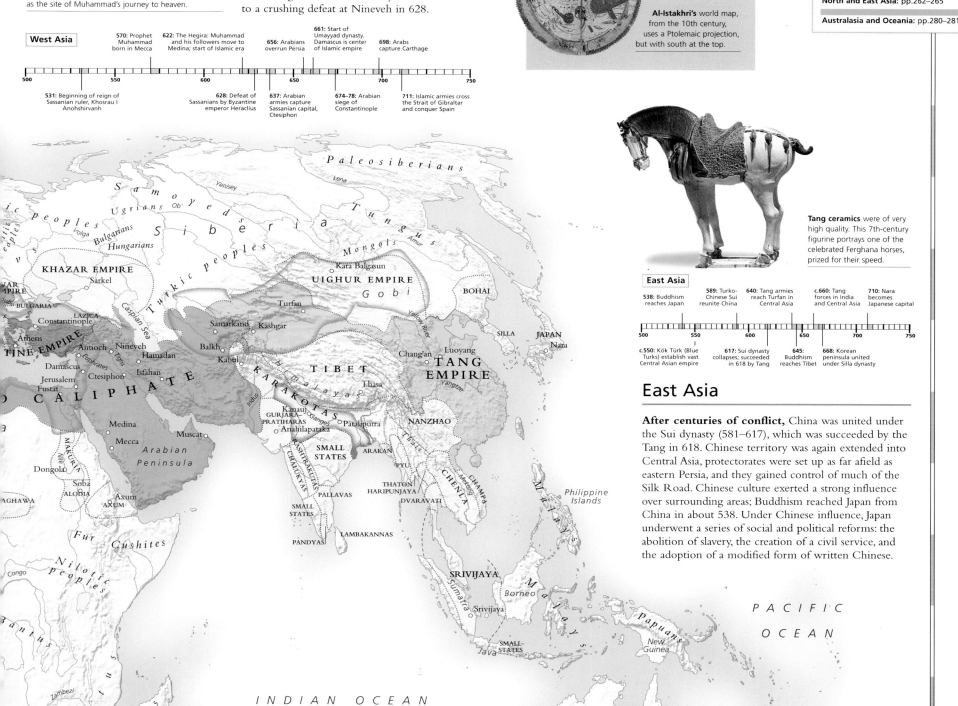

Tang ceramics were of very high quality. This 7th-century figurine portrays one of the celebrated Ferghana horses, prized for their speed.

East Asia

538: Buddhism reaches Japan

589: Turko-Chinese Sui reunite China

640: Tang armies reach Turfan in Central Asia

c.660: Tang forces in India and Central Asia

710: Nara becomes Japanese capital

c.550: Kök Türk (Blue Turks) establish vast Central Asian empire

617: Sui dynasty collapses; succeeded in 618 by Tang

645: Buddhism reaches Tibet

668: Korean peninsula united under Silla dynasty

500 550 600 650 700 750

East Asia

After centuries of conflict, China was united under the Sui dynasty (581–617), which was succeeded by the Tang in 618. Chinese territory was again extended into Central Asia, protectorates were set up as far afield as eastern Persia, and they gained control of much of the Silk Road. Chinese culture exerted a strong influence over surrounding areas; Buddhism reached Japan from China in about 538. Under Chinese influence, Japan underwent a series of social and political reforms: the abolition of slavery, the creation of a civil service, and the adoption of a modified form of written Chinese.

Oceania

The island of Fiji was first settled around 1500 BCE, and it was there and in nearby islands that Polynesian culture developed. Descendants of these first settlers would eventually colonize the whole Pacific Ocean. The Polynesians sailed across the open ocean in twin-hulled outrigger canoes, using sails and paddles, with only their knowledge of the skies, winds, and ocean currents to guide them. By 400 CE they had reached Easter Island and the Hawaiian Islands, but did not colonize New Zealand until about 700.

Oceania

c.600: Polynesian colonists settle the Tuamotu Islands

c.650: Easter Islanders start to build *ahus,* sacred stone platforms

c.700: Polynesians reach North Island of New Zealand

500 550 600 650 700 750

This greenstone *heitiki* is a traditional ornament of the Maori, one of the most recent cultures of Polynesia.

THE IMPACT OF ISLAM

This richly-decorated copy of the Koran dates from 704.

THE RAPID SPREAD OF ISLAM was one of the most decisive developments of the medieval period. The Arabian Peninsula was conquered for Islam within ten years, and following the death of Muhammad in 632, the expansion of Islam continued unabated. By the early 8th century, Arab armies fired by the concept of *jihad* (holy war) had reached the borders of India in the east and were invading Spain in the west. With the establishment of the Abbasid Caliphate, by 750 the Muslim realm was second only to that of China in extent and cultural sophistication. The Caliphate controlled Eurasian trade on land and by sea – trade which would spread the faith further afield, deep into Africa, across the Indian Ocean, and north into Central Asia, over the subsequent centuries.

The early history of the Caliphate

Muhammad's first successors – who became known as caliphs – were early disciples (Companions of the Prophet): Abu Bakr (632–34), 'Umar (634–44), and 'Uthman, who was murdered in 656. The authority of 'Uthman's successor Ali – Muhammad's cousin and son-in-law – was challenged by 'Uthman's family, the Umayyads. Ali was murdered in 661, and the Umayyads gained power as caliphs; their supporters were known as Sunnites. A minority of Muslims, however, known as Shi'a, saw the descendants of Ali (the Imams) as the true successors of the Prophet. This fundamental division within the faith continues to this day.

Harun al-Rashid, the great Abbasid caliph, reigned from 786 to 809. This illustration shows him in an episode from the *1001 Nights* with a barber in a Turkish Bath.

The spread of Islam 623–751

The Great Mosque at Kairouan is one of the oldest surviving Islamic buildings. It was begun in 670, shortly after Arab armies had swept through the Byzantine possessions along the North African coast.

Muhammad's vision of the Archangel Gabriel in about 610 began a process of revelation, enshrined in the Koran, the holy book which lies at the heart of Islam. His opposition to polytheism and adherence to a strict code of observation and conduct led to hostility in Mecca, and his withdrawal to Medina (the Hegira) in 622. Here the first Muslim state was established. By 630, with an army of 10,000 followers, he reentered Mecca, and began the conquest of Arabia. Conversion swelled the Muslim ranks, and Muhammad's work was continued after his death in 632 by his disciples. Within a century the heartland of Eurasia was dominated by Islam. Although Muslim warriors believed it their duty to conquer in the name of Islam, conquered peoples, especially Christians and Jews, were treated with tolerance.

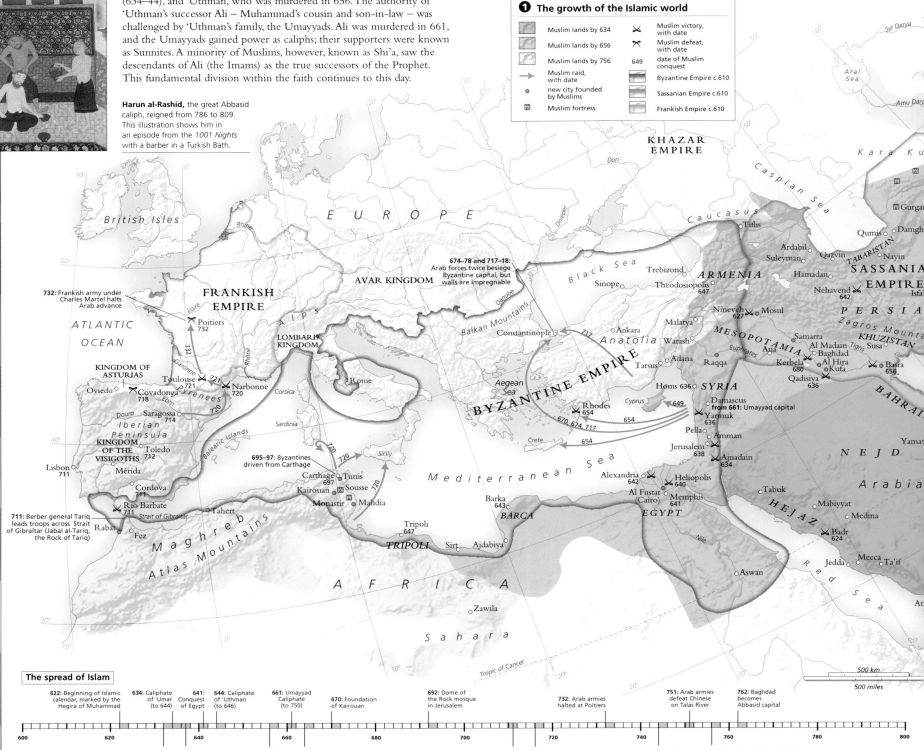

① The growth of the Islamic world

- Muslim lands by 634
- Muslim lands by 656
- Muslim lands by 756
- → Muslim raid, with date
- ● new city founded by Muslims
- 🏰 Muslim fortress
- ✕ Muslim victory, with date
- ✕ Muslim defeat, with date
- 649 date of Muslim conquest
- Byzantine Empire c.610
- Sassanian Empire c.610
- Frankish Empire c.610

(Map labels include:) KHAZAR EMPIRE, Kara Ku, Aral Sea, Amu Dar, Syr Darya, Caspian Sea, Gurgan, Qumis, Damgh, EUROPE, British Isles, Rhine, Don, Dnieper, Caucasus, Tiflis, Ardabil, Qazvin, Nayin, TABARISTAN, SASSANIA EMPIRE, PERSIA, Suleyman, Hamadan, Nehavend 642, Isfa, KHUZISTAN, Zagros Mount, AVAR KINGDOM, Danube, Black Sea, Trebizond, ARMENIA, Sinope, Theodosiopolis 647, Nineveh 627, Mosul, MESOPOTAMIA, Samarra, Al Madain, Baghdad, Tigris, Susa, **674–78 and 717–18:** Arab forces twice besiege Byzantine capital, but walls are impregnable, **732:** Frankish army under Charles Martel halts Arab advance, FRANKISH EMPIRE, Loire, Poitiers 732, Alps, LOMBARD KINGDOM, Balkan Mountains, Constantinople, 717, Ankara, Anatolia, Warash, Malatya, Adana, Raqqa, Ana, Al Hira 680, Kerbela, Qadisiya 636, Basra 656, Kufa, ATLANTIC OCEAN, KINGDOM OF ASTURIAS, Toulouse 721, Narbonne 720, Rome, Tarsus, Aegean Sea, BYZANTINE EMPIRE, Hâms 636, SYRIA, Damascus from 661: Umayyad capital, Yarmuk 636, Pella, BAHRA, Oviedo, Covadonga 718, Pyrenees, 720, Corsica, Rhodes 654, Cyprus 649, 654, Amman, Jerusalem 638, Ajnadain 634, Yama, Saragossa 714, Douro, Iberian Peninsula, KINGDOM OF THE VISIGOTHS, Toledo 712, 670, 674, 717, Crete, 654, NEJD, Lisbon 711, Mérida, Sardinia, Sicily, **695–97:** Byzantines driven from Carthage, Heliopolis 640, Alexandria 642, Al Fustat (Cairo) 641, Memphis, Arabia, Tabuk, Mabiyyat, Medina, Cordova 711, Río Barbate 711, Strait of Gibraltar, Tahert, Carthage 697, Tunis, Kairouan, Sousse, Monastir, Mahdia, Barka 643, BARCA, EGYPT, Nile, HEJAZ, Badr 624, **711:** Berber general Tariq leads troops across Strait of Gibraltar (Jabal al-Tariq, the Rock of Tariq), Rabat, Fez, Maghreb, Atlas Mountains, Tripoli 647, Sirt, Ajdabiya, TRIPOLI, Mediterranean Sea, Jedda, Mecca, Ta'if, AFRICA, Aswan, Red Sea, Zawila, Sahara

(Scale:) 500 km / 500 miles
Tropic of Cancer

The spread of Islam

622: Beginning of Islamic calendar, marked by the Hegira of Muhammad	
632: Death of Muhammad; succession of Abu Bakr (to 634)	
634: Caliphate of 'Umar (to 644)	
637: Conquest of Mesopotamia	
641: Conquest of Egypt	
644: Caliphate of 'Uthman (to 646)	
656: Imamate of Ali (to 661)	
661: Umayyad Caliphate (to 750)	
664: Conquest of Kabul	
670: Foundation of Kairouan	
692: Dome of the Rock mosque in Jerusalem	
711: Invasion of Iberian Peninsula by Tariq; rapid conquest of Visigothic kingdom	
718: Christian victory at battle of Covadonga halts Muslim advance in Iberian Peninsula	
732: Arab armies halted at Poitiers	
744: Abbasid Caliphate established	
751: Arab armies defeat Chinese on Talas River	
756: Breakaway Umayyad Emirate established at Cordova (to 1031); claims status of caliphate in 928	
762: Baghdad becomes Abbasid capital	

(Timeline: 600, 620, 640, 660, 680, 700, 720, 740, 760, 780, 800)

Preaching and teaching spread the Arabic language throughout the Islamic world. This 13th-century Persian illustration shows a preacher in the mosque at Samarkand.

The impact of the Islamic advance

Water-wheels for irrigation were introduced wherever the Arabs settled. This example stands at Hamah in Syria. The Arabs also introduced Asian fruits, such as peaches and apricots.

The Islamic imprint 1000–1200

By 1000, the Islamic world had become broadly divided into two caliphates: the Abbasids, based at Baghdad, and, in the west, the Umayyads (a branch of the Abbasids' predecessors), who ruled the Iberian Peninsula. So extensive were the Abbasid domains that many subsidiary rulers wielded local power in varying degrees and were able to found autonomous dynasties. Further, the movement of peoples into the Islamic world caused further decentralization of power. In the west, the Berbers gradually established a string of local dynasties along the Maghreb coast. The Shi'ite Fatimids emerged in North Africa, conquered Egypt, and claimed caliphate status; but the most significant blow to the Abbasid Caliphate was the invasion of the Seljuk Turks from Central Asia, who moved across southwest Asia, conquered Baghdad and drove back the frontiers of the Byzantine Empire, eventually occupying Anatolia.

SEE ALSO:

Africa: pp.162–163

Europe: pp.186–187

West Asia: pp.226–227

South and Southeast Asia: pp.242–243

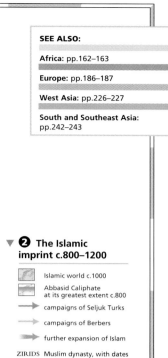

② The Islamic imprint c.800–1200

- Islamic world c.1000
- Abbasid Caliphate at its greatest extent c.800
- → campaigns of Seljuk Turks
- → campaigns of Berbers
- → further expansion of Islam
- ZIRIDS Muslim dynasty, with dates

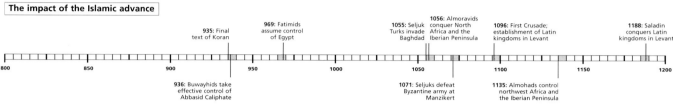

935: Final text of Koran
969: Fatimids assume control of Egypt
1055: Seljuk Turks invade Baghdad
1056: Almoravids conquer North Africa and the Iberian Peninsula
1096: First Crusade; establishment of Latin kingdoms in Levant
1188: Saladin conquers Latin kingdoms in Levant

936: Buwayhids take effective control of Abbasid Caliphate
1071: Seljuks defeat Byzantine army at Manzikert
1135: Almohads control northwest Africa and the Iberian Peninsula

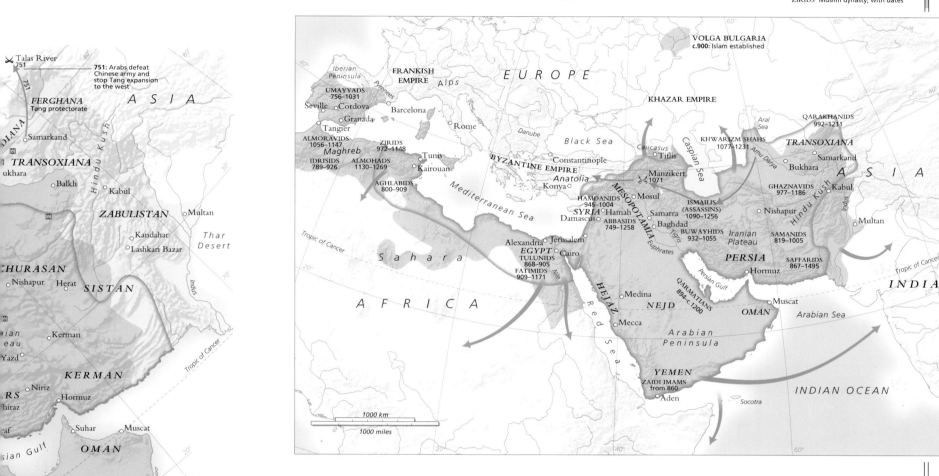

Samarra: an Islamic city

Founded by the Abbasid caliph al-Mu'tasim, Samarra was the Abbasid capital from 836–892, and grew to sprawl some 25 miles (40 km) along the east bank of the Tigris. The new city was based around earlier settlements; it was not walled, and was organized into residential cantonments arranged around central features such as palaces and mosques, and included luxurious facilities such as racetracks and a gigantic 11.6 square miles game reserve. Later caliphs added substantial areas, notably al-Mu'tasim's successor al-Mutawakkil, who built a new center to the north, Ja'fariyya. The Abbasid court returned to its original capital at Baghdad after the death of the eighth caliph, al-Mu'tamid.

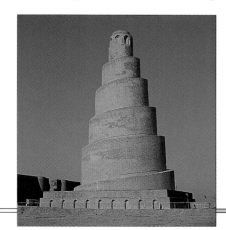

The spiral minaret of the Great Mosque of al-Mutawakkil at Samarra is one of the few standing remains of the city.

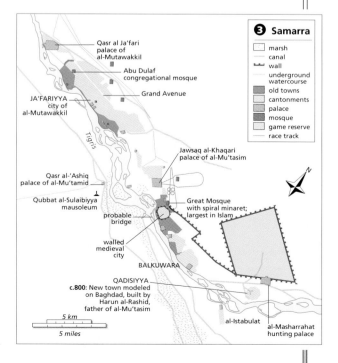

③ Samarra

- marsh
- canal
- wall
- underground watercourse
- old towns
- cantonments
- palace
- mosque
- game reserve
- race track

Qasr al Ja'fari palace of al-Mutawakkil
Abu Dulaf congregational mosque
Grand Avenue
JA'FARIYYA city of al-Mutawakkil
Jawsaq al-Khaqari palace of al-Mu'tasim
Qasr al-'Ashiq palace of al-Mu'tamid
Qubbat al-Sulaibiyya mausoleum
probable bridge
Great Mosque with spiral minaret; largest in Islam
walled medieval city
BALKUWARA
QADISIYYA c.800: New town modeled on Baghdad, built by Harun al-Rashid, father of al-Mu'tasim
al-Istabulat
al-Masharrahat hunting palace

THE WORLD 750–1000

THE DISINTEGRATION OF GREAT EMPIRES and conflicts between warring dynasties were widespread throughout the 9th and 10th centuries. In Europe, Charlemagne was crowned western Emperor in 800, but his Frankish Empire was broken apart by disputes over inheritance. The Abbasid Caliphate, based in Baghdad, could not maintain central control over the vast Islamic world. New Islamic dynasties, such as the Fatimids of northern Africa, broke away from Baghdad's authority. In China, the mighty Tang Empire split into small warring states while in Central America, the Maya were in decline. In contrast to this political fragmentation, powerful new states developed in many parts of the world: the Khmers in Southeast Asia, Koryo in Korea, the Toltecs in Mexico, Ghana and Kanem-Bornu in Africa, and Kievan Rus in Eastern Europe.

Ireland suffered badly from Viking raids in the 9th and 10th centuries, so monasteries built distinctive round towers, such as these at Glendalough, as lookouts and refuges.

Europe

Charlemagne, king of the Franks, incorporated most of Western Europe into a single dominion. After disputes over his inheritance, the kingdom was divided into three parts. Henry I, the Saxon successor, extended his influence over the German duchies and conquered Italy. His son, Otto I, defeated the Magyars and was crowned Holy Roman Emperor. In the west, the Carolingian Empire and the British Isles fell prey to Viking raiders.

Europe

752: Lombards capture Ravenna	800: Charlemagne crowned Holy Roman Emperor by the pope in Rome	884: Kiev becomes capital of new Russian state	896: Danish raiders besiege Paris	996: Start of war between Byzantines, led by Emperor Basil II, and Bulgaria
774: Charlemagne defeats Lombards in Italy	827: Crete and Sicily occupied by Saracen (Arab) raiders	843: Treaty of Verdun divides Carolingian empire into three	885: Saxon ruler, Alfred the Great, reconquers London from Vikings	955: Otto I defeats Magyars and halts expansion of Hungary

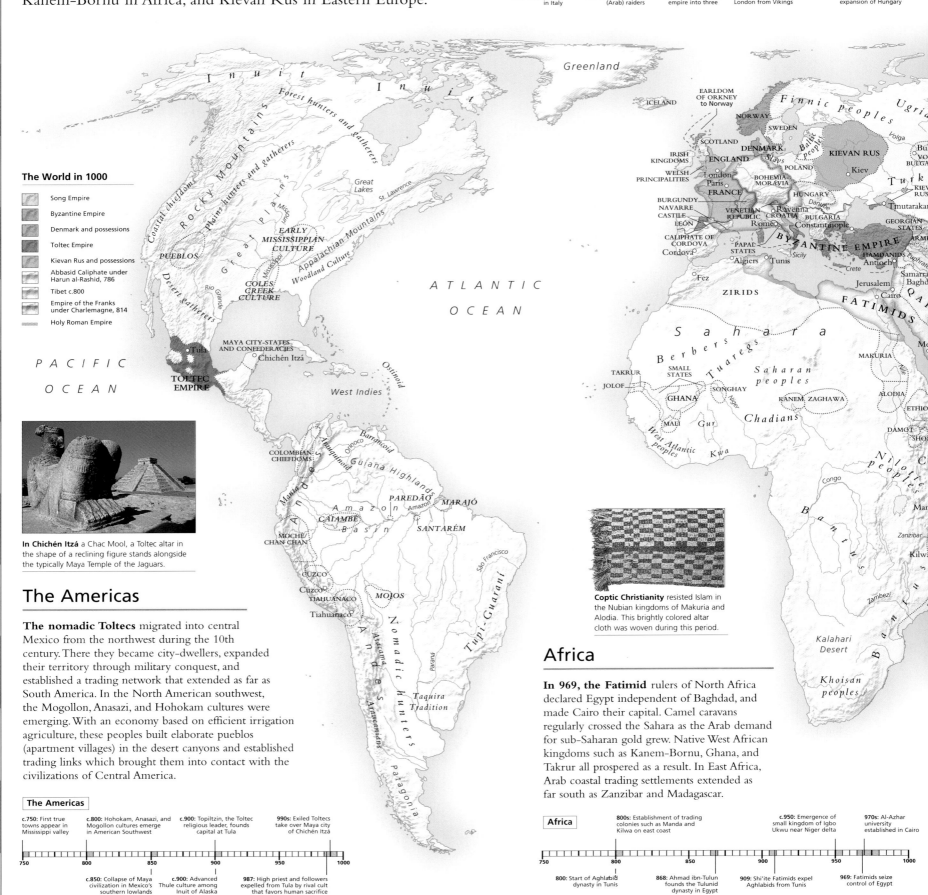

The World in 1000

- Song Empire
- Byzantine Empire
- Denmark and possessions
- Toltec Empire
- Kievan Rus and possessions
- Abbasid Caliphate under Harun al-Rashid, 786
- Tibet c.800
- Empire of the Franks under Charlemagne, 814
- Holy Roman Empire

In Chichén Itzá a Chac Mool, a Toltec altar in the shape of a reclining figure stands alongside the typically Maya Temple of the Jaguars.

The Americas

The nomadic Toltecs migrated into central Mexico from the northwest during the 10th century. There they became city-dwellers, expanded their territory through military conquest, and established a trading network that extended as far as South America. In the North American southwest, the Mogollon, Anasazi, and Hohokam cultures were emerging. With an economy based on efficient irrigation agriculture, these peoples built elaborate pueblos (apartment villages) in the desert canyons and established trading links which brought them into contact with the civilizations of Central America.

The Americas

c.750: First true towns appear in Mississippi valley	c.800: Hohokam, Anasazi, and Mogollon cultures emerge in American Southwest	c.900: Topiltzin, the Toltec religious leader, founds capital at Tula	990s: Exiled Toltecs take over Maya city of Chichén Itzá
	c.850: Collapse of Maya civilization in Mexico's southern lowlands	c.900: Advanced Thule culture among Inuit of Alaska	987: High priest and followers expelled from Tula by rival cult that favors human sacrifice

Coptic Christianity resisted Islam in the Nubian kingdoms of Makuria and Alodia. This brightly colored altar cloth was woven during this period.

Africa

In 969, the Fatimid rulers of North Africa declared Egypt independent of Baghdad, and made Cairo their capital. Camel caravans regularly crossed the Sahara as the Arab demand for sub-Saharan gold grew. Native West African kingdoms such as Kanem-Bornu, Ghana, and Takrur all prospered as a result. In East Africa, Arab coastal trading settlements extended as far south as Zanzibar and Madagascar.

Africa

	800s: Establishment of trading colonies such as Manda and Kilwa on east coast	c.950: Emergence of small kingdom of Igbo Ukwu near Niger delta	970s: Al-Azhar university established in Cairo
800: Start of Aghlabid dynasty in Tunis	868: Ahmad ibn-Tulun founds the Tulunid dynasty in Egypt	909: Shi'ite Fatimids expel Aghlabids from Tunis	969: Fatimids seize control of Egypt

PRINTING IN CHINA

The Chinese had been experimenting with ways of reproducing writing and illustrations for centuries, before they made their greatest breakthrough under the Tang in the 8th century. Carving characters and pictures in reverse onto wooden blocks was a time-consuming process, but it allowed many hundreds of copies to made before the wood's surface became too worn. All kinds of documents – from religious texts to tax receipts – were printed by this method.

The earliest printed document that can be dated with certainty is *The Diamond Sutra*, a work of Buddhist doctrine printed on a scroll, produced in 868.

After the fervor of the 7th-century *jihads*, many Arab tribes subsequently turned against one another as they competed to rule the various parts of the Islamic world.

West Asia

The Abbasid dynasty came to power in 750. Though the arts, culture, and trade flourished under their rule, disagreements over the succession meant that their authority was not universally recognized. Even in Baghdad the caliphs became figureheads, real power being in the hands of Turkish mercenary or slave troops and Persian administrators. Under a new dynasty of Macedonian rulers (867–1081) the Byzantine Empire reached its apogee, and came into conflict with the Arabs to the east. Byzantine troops regained control of most of Anatolia and, in 969, reconquered Antioch.

SEE ALSO:

North America: pp.122–123

South America: pp.144–145

Africa: pp.162–163

Europe: pp.184–185

West Asia: pp.226–227

South and Southeast Asia: pp.244–245

North and East Asia: pp.262–265

Australasia and Oceania: pp.280–281

West Asia

750: Umayyad Caliphate is overthrown and succeeded by the Abbasid dynasty

786: Under Caliph Harun al-Rashid Baghdad becomes center of arts and learning

863: Byzantines annihilate Arab forces to stem Muslim advance in Anatolia

945: Persian Buwayhids conquer Baghdad but allow caliph to reign as figurehead

976: Byzantine forces threaten to take Jerusalem

762: Abbasid capital founded at Baghdad

836: Baghdad terrorized by Turkish slave troops; Abbasid Caliph al-Mutasim builds new capital at Samarra

936: Caliphs of Baghdad lose effective power; caliphate under control of Turkish troops

(timeline: 750 — 800 — 850 — 900 — 950 — 1000)

ARAB STAR MAPS

Arab scientists and mathematicians were the finest in the world, and their astronomers added greatly to our knowledge of the heavens during this period. As well as using the night sky to set a course at sea and help them cross the desert, the Arabs continued to name stars and map constellations in the tradition of Ptolemy and other Greek astronomers. Many stars, such as Aldebaran, Rigel, and Rasalgethi, are still known by their Arab names.

The constellation of Andromeda is one of many attractive illustrations in *The Book of the Fixed Stars* compiled by Abd al-Rahman ibn Umar al-Sufi in the 10th century. The individual stars forming the constellation are shown in red.

(map labels: Paleosiberians, Lena, Samoyeds, Yenisey, Ob, Tungus, Siberia, Mongols, Amur, peoples, KHITAN EMPIRE, Gobi, Linhuang, QARAKHANIDS, Uighurs, Tanguts, Kaesong, JAPAN, Samarkand, Dunhuang, Yellow River, KORYO, Kyoto, GHAZNAVIDS, KASHMIR, Kaifeng, Ghazni, HINDU SHAHIS, TIBET, Chang'an, QARMATIS, HIMALAYAS, Yangtze, UWAYHIDS, GURJARA-PRATIHARAS, SONG EMPIRE, SMALL STATES, CHAHAMANAS, BHAUMAS, Ganges, PARAMARAS, NANZHAO, TIANS, CHANDELLAS, KALACURIS, CHAULUKYAS, PALAS, ABHIRAS, SMALL STATES, PAGAN, ARAKAN, Arabian Peninsula, Godavari, EASTERN GANGAS, ANNAM, Kalyani, Krishna, PEGU, THATON, CHAMPA, MEN, CHALUKYAS, EASTERN CHALUKYAS, HARIPUNJAYA, DVARAVATI, KHMER, Angkor, Philippine Islands, SMALL STATES, CHOLAS, Ceylon, LAMBAKANNAS, PACIFIC OCEAN, INDIAN OCEAN, SRIVIJAYA, Borneo, Palembang, Papua, New Guinea, EAST JAVA KINGDOM, Borobudur, Java, Australian Aborigines, Darling, New Zealand)

Buddhism affected all aspects of life in Tang China, the Buddha assuming Chinese features, as in this wall painting from Dunhuang.

This bronze of the god Shiva was made under the Chola dynasty. In this period cults of individual Hindu deities grew in popularity.

South and Southeast Asia

In the north, the Islamic kingdom of the Afghan ruler Mahmud of Ghazni stretched from the Oxus to the Indus, while states such as Gurjara-Pratiharas and the Buddhist Palas vied for the Ganges plain. To the south, the Tamil Cholas and the Chalukyas fought over the Godavari and Krishna rivers. Chola conquests expanded to include Ceylon and parts of the Malay Peninsula.

South and Southeast Asia

802: Angkorian dynasty founded by King Jayavarman II

889: Khmer King Indravarman I begins construction of Angkor

997: Mahmud of Ghazni extends rule into northwest India

c.800: Construction of Buddhist temple at Borobudur, Java

886: Chola dynasty rules much of southern India

c.900: Gurjara-Pratiharas dominates northern India

962: Foundation of Afghan Ghaznavid dynasty

(timeline: 750 — 800 — 850 — 900 — 950 — 1000)

East Asia

Threats of internal rebellion in the middle of the 8th century weakened the Tang dynasty's control of China. As a result the empire became more inward looking and the political and economic center of gravity began to shift south to the Yangtze valley. The Tang dynasty eventually collapsed after massive peasant uprisings in the 9th century, and China split into ten separate states until 960–79, when it was reunified under the Song. Both Korea and Japan were governed by strong, centralized Buddhist dynasties.

East Asia

751: Defeat of Chinese by Muslim forces at battle of Talas River

794: Kyoto becomes capital of Japan

868: *The Diamond Sutra*, world's oldest surviving printed work

935: Foundation of kingdom of Koryo in Korea

979: Song establish power in China

756: Rebel general An Lushan captures Chang'an

763: Tang China is invaded by Tibetans

870s: Peasant uprisings throughout Tang China

907: End of the Tang dynasty

970: Paper money introduced by Chinese government

(timeline: 750 — 800 — 850 — 900 — 950 — 1000)

EXPLORERS OF THE OCEANS

In the 1st millennium CE, three peoples surpassed all others as navigators of the world's oceans: the Vikings, the Arabs, and the Polynesians. The traders and raiders of Scandinavia created the fast, efficient Viking longship, which took them along the rivers of Russia to the Black Sea, and across the Atlantic Ocean to Iceland and North America. The Arabs were already accomplished seafarers; the discovery, in the 8th century, of the sea route to China via the Strait of Malacca heralded a new era of long-distance trade, and Arab ships sailed to the East Indies, East Africa, and China. Perhaps the most extraordinary seafarers of all were the Polynesians, who by 1000 CE had completed the colonization of all the islands of the Pacific.

The stylized image of a ship decorates this early Viking coin, which was minted at Hedeby in the 9th century.

These 12th-century walrus ivory chesspieces are from Lewis in the Outer Hebrides. The islands were settled by Norwegians in the 9th and 10th centuries, but remained a regular target for Viking raids.

NORTH AMERICA

Region visited for timber by Greenland settlers

St Lawrence

VINLAND

c.1000: Site of small Norse settlement, occupied for about 20 years

L'Anse aux Meadows

Newfoundland

Most southerly region visited by Vikings – so named for vines growing there

The Viking world

Harsh northern conditions drove the Vikings to sail in search of new lands and resources. At first they dominated their Baltic neighbors, taking tribute in the form of amber, wax, fish, ivory, and furs. Norwegians and Danes exploited weaknesses in France, England, and Ireland, using their fast, maneuverable longships to conduct lightning raids, exacting tribute, conquering, and colonizing. Eventually, in a quest for land, they crossed the Atlantic, reaching Iceland in 860 and Newfoundland c.1000. Swedish traders penetrated the navigable rivers of Russia to dominate the lucrative trade with Constantinople and the Arab world. Varangians (as these eastern Vikings were called) founded Kievan Rus, the first Russian state, and their fighting qualities were recognized by the Byzantine emperors, who employed them as their elite mercenary guard.

800 km
800 miles

Viking longships were oar-powered, ranging from 17–33 yds in length. Their light, flexible hulls "rode" the waves and made them ideal for raiding in shallow, coastal waters.

Viking voyages

793: Vikings plunder island monastery of Lindisfarne off northeast coast of England

845: Vikings sack Paris; exact tribute from Franks

866: Vikings take York

c.900: Norwegians settle in Scotland and northwest England

c.1000: Voyages from Greenland to Newfoundland and coast of North America

700　　800　　900　　1000　　1100

c.789: First recorded Viking raid on England; first raids on Ireland and Scotland recorded in 795

839: Swedes travel through Russia to Constantinople

862: Novgorod founded by Rurik the Viking

c.930: Viking settlement of Iceland complete

986: Erik the Red begins settlement of Greenland

1042: End of Danish rule in England

The Polynesians

The first wave of colonization of the Pacific, between 2000 and 1500 BCE, took settlers from New Guinea and neighboring islands as far as the Fiji Islands. From there, they sailed on to the Tonga and Samoa groups. In about 200 BCE, the Polynesians embarked on a series of far longer voyages, crossing vast tracts of empty ocean to settle the Marquesas, the Society Islands, Hawaii, Rapa Nui (Easter Island), and New Zealand. By about 1000 CE they had discovered almost every island in the Pacific. They sailed in double-hulled canoes, laden with seed plants, chickens, and pigs. The canoes could tack into the wind, and they probably navigated by observing the sun and the stars, the direction of prevailing winds, and the flight patterns of homing birds.

Polynesian voyages 1500 BCE–1000 CE

c.1500 BCE: Earliest evidence of colonization of Fiji – by makers of incised Lapita pottery

c.500 BCE: On Samoa, Lapita style of pottery is replaced by plain, undecorated bowls

c.200 BCE: Polynesians reach Marquesas Islands from Samoa

c.400 CE: Polynesians reach Hawaiian Islands

c.700 CE: Earliest temple platforms (ahu) built on Rapa Nui (Easter Island)

1500 BCE　　1000 BCE　　500 BCE　　1 CE　　500 CE　　1000 CE

c.1300 BCE: Colonization of Tonga

c.1000 BCE: Distinct Polynesian culture starts to emerge in Fiji, Tonga, and Samoa

c.300 CE: Settlement of Rapa Nui (Easter Island)

c.400 CE: Colonization of Society Islands

c.700 CE: Ancestors of Maori reach Aotearoa (New Zealand)

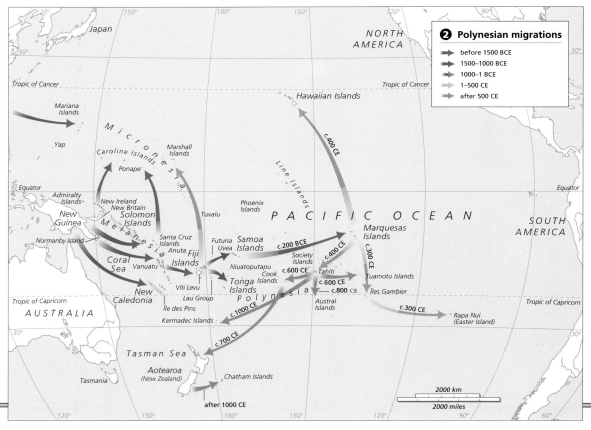

Japan

NORTH AMERICA

2 Polynesian migrations
- before 1500 BCE
- 1500–1000 BCE
- 1000–1 BCE
- 1–500 CE
- after 500 CE

Tropic of Cancer

Hawaiian Islands

c.400 CE

Mariana Islands

Yap

Micronesia

Caroline Islands

Marshall Islands

Ponape

Equator

Line Islands

PACIFIC OCEAN

SOUTH AMERICA

Admiralty Islands

New Ireland New Britain

Solomon Islands

Tuvalu

Phoenix Islands

New Guinea

Melanesia

Normanby Island

Santa Cruz Islands

Anuta

Futuna Uvea

Samoa Islands

Marquesas Islands

c.200 BCE

c.400 CE

c.300 CE

Coral Sea

Vanuatu

Fiji Islands

Niuatoputapu

Cook Islands

Society Islands

Tahiti

c.600 CE

c.600 CE

c.800 CE

Tuamotu Islands

Îles Gambier

New Caledonia

Viti Levu

Lau Group

Tonga Islands

Polynesia

c.1000 CE

Austral Islands

c.300 CE

Rapa Nui (Easter Island)

Île des Pins

Tropic of Capricorn

AUSTRALIA

Kermadec Islands

c.700 CE

Tasman Sea

Tasmania

Aotearoa (New Zealand)

after 1000 CE

Chatham Islands

2000 km
2000 miles

On their epic ocean voyages, the Polynesians used twin-hulled canoes, similar to the one in this 19th-century engraving, up to 33 yds long. Canoes with an outrigger, attached to the hull and kept to windward for balance, were probably for inshore sailing and shorter voyages. Both types of vessel could be powered by oars or sails.

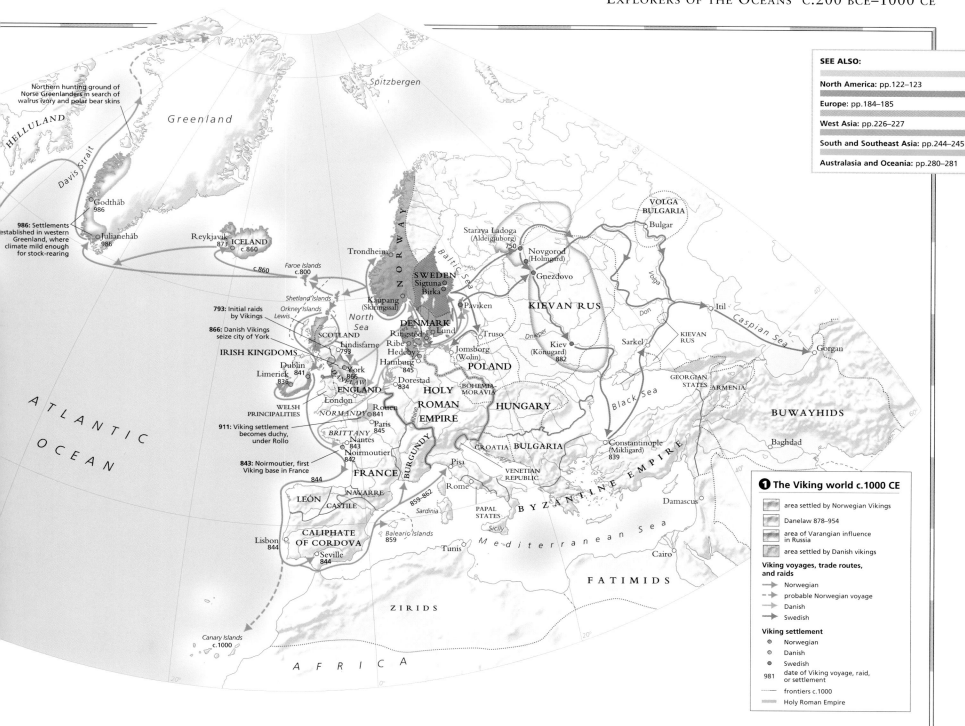

SEE ALSO:

North America: pp.122–123

Europe: pp.184–185

West Asia: pp.226–227

South and Southeast Asia: pp.244–245

Australasia and Oceania: pp.280–281

Northern hunting ground of Norse Greenlanders in search of walrus ivory and polar bear skins

Godthåb 986

986: Settlements established in western Greenland, where climate mild enough for stock-rearing

Julianehåb 986

Reykjavik 873 ICELAND c.860

793: Initial raids by Vikings

866: Danish Vikings seize city of York

911: Viking settlement becomes duchy, under Rollo

843: Noirmoutier, first Viking base in France

❶ The Viking world c.1000 CE

- area settled by Norwegian Vikings
- Danelaw 878–954
- area of Varangian influence in Russia
- area settled by Danish vikings

Viking voyages, trade routes, and raids
- → Norwegian
- ⇢ probable Norwegian voyage
- → Danish
- → Swedish

Viking settlement
- ⊙ Norwegian
- ⊙ Danish
- ⊙ Swedish
- 981 date of Viking voyage, raid, or settlement
- ---- frontiers c.1000
- ▬ Holy Roman Empire

Arab traders in the Indian Ocean

The Arabs used the wind systems of the monsoon to propel their ships eastward from the Persian Gulf in November and to return them westward in the summer. In the 8th century, Arab traders discovered the sea route to Guangzhou (Canton) by way of the Malabar Coast, the Strait of Malacca, and Hanoi, a journey of 120 days, which nevertheless could take between 18 months and three years. The Arabs exported iron, wool, incense, and bullion in return for silk and spices. When the fall of the Tang Empire disrupted trade with China c.1000 CE, the Arabs turned to the East Indies, and Islam consequently became well established in the the islands of Southeast Asia. They also navigated the East African coast to Zanzibar and Madagascar, where they met the Malays who had colonized the island some 300 years earlier.

An Indian ship is depicted in an Arab manuscript of 1238. It has a square-rigged sail, suitable for running with the strong monsoonal winds, well known from the 1st century CE. The capacious hold could carry both passengers and cargo, essential for thriving Indian Ocean trade routes from the 8th century CE.

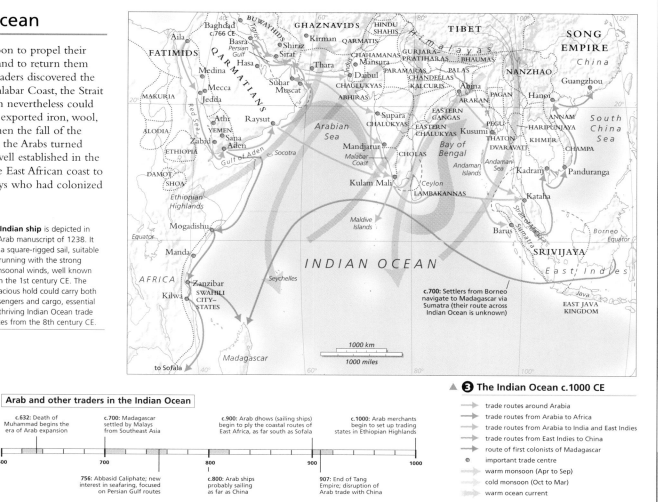

c.700: Settlers from Borneo navigate to Madagascar via Sumatra (their route across Indian Ocean is unknown)

❸ The Indian Ocean c.1000 CE

- ⟶ trade routes around Arabia
- ⟶ trade routes from Arabia to Africa
- ⟶ trade routes from Arabia to India and East Indies
- ⟶ trade routes from East Indies to China
- ⟶ route of first colonists of Madagascar
- ● important trade centre
- ⟶ warm monsoon (Apr to Sep)
- ⟶ cold monsoon (Oct to Mar)
- ⟶ warm ocean current

Arab and other traders in the Indian Ocean

c.632: Death of Muhammad begins the era of Arab expansion

c.700: Madagascar settled by Malays from Southeast Asia

c.900: Arab dhows (sailing ships) begin to ply the coastal routes of East Africa, as far south as Sofala

c.1000: Arab merchants begin to set up trading states in Ethiopian Highlands

756: Abbasid Caliphate; new interest in seafaring, focused on Persian Gulf routes

c.800: Arab ships probably sailing as far as China

907: End of Tang Empire; disruption of Arab trade with China

THE WORLD 1000–1200

IN MANY PARTS OF THE WORLD conflict over territory and religion was intense. This was a time when the Christian West was recovering from the tumult that followed the fall of Rome. As marginal land was cleared for agriculture, the population expanded. Trade routes crossed Europe and a mercantile economy developed and prospered. Yet the resurgence of Christian Europe brought it into direct confrontation with Islam when it launched the Crusades to regain the Holy Land. This ultimately proved a failure, but in Spain and Portugal the Christian reconquest made intermittent progress. To the east, the states of northern India fell to Muslim invaders, and Buddhism was finally driven from the subcontinent. In China the Song Empire shrank under pressure from powerful nomadic peoples to the north, such as the Xixia and the Jin.

The power of the Church was expressed in new cathedrals built first in the Romanesque and then in the Gothic style, typified by the soaring façade of Chartres.

Europe

The assimilation in the 11th century of Poland, Hungary, and the Scandinavian kingdoms into the realm of Western Christianity brought it to a new peak of power and influence. As Western Europeans began to wrest control of the Mediterranean from the Arabs and Byzantines, a new era of prosperity based on trade began. Italian merchants became middlemen in Byzantine trade, and north Italian towns, such as Venice, Genoa, and Pisa, prospered. Elsewhere, forests and marginal land were cleared for agriculture, populations grew, and new towns were founded.

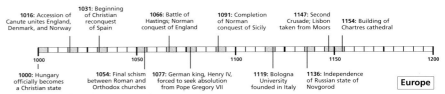

1016: Accession of Canute unites England, Denmark, and Norway
1031: Beginning of Christian reconquest of Spain
1066: Battle of Hastings; Norman conquest of England
1091: Completion of Norman conquest of Sicily
1147: Second Crusade; Lisbon taken from Moors
1154: Building of Chartres cathedral

1000: Hungary officially becomes a Christian state
1054: Final schism between Roman and Orthodox churches
1077: German king, Henry IV, forced to seek absolution from Pope Gregory VII
1119: Bologna University founded in Italy
1136: Independence of Russian state of Novgorod

Europe

AL-IDRISI'S WORLD MAP

Islamic geographers led the world in medieval times. Al-Idrisi (1100–65) was a Moroccan in the service of Roger II of Sicily. The island had been under Arab rule in the 10th century and became a meeting point of two cultures where much of the knowledge of the Islamic world was transmitted to the Christian West.

Al-Idrisi's map shows the lasting influence of Ptolemy (see p.44). However, he oriented his maps, as did most contemporary Islamic geographers, with the south at the top.

The Americas

The Chimú rose to prominence in the 11th century with the construction of their capital at Chan Chan. This powerful empire, ruled by semi-divine kings, expanded by military conquest. Subject territories, linked by an advanced road system, were kept under tight economic control. In Central America, the Toltec city of Tula was sacked by Chichimec tribesmen from northwest Mexico. In turn the Chichimec established a number of small city-states, which engaged in constant, internecine warfare. North America's first true towns arose in the fertile Mississippi valley, while in the harsher climate of the arid southwest magnificent cliff dwellings were built.

The Anasazi was the most widespread of the Pueblo farming cultures of the American Southwest. Roads linked their impressive canyon villages, where they produced fine black and white pottery.

The Americas

c.1000: Leif Ericson, son of Eric the Red, sets sail from Greenland and reaches North America
c.1100: Anasazi people of Southwest build fortified cliff dwellings at Mesa Verde and Chaco Canyon
c.1200: Incas, led by Manco Capac, enter and settle in Andean valley near Cuzco

c.1050: Settlements of mound-builders of Mississippi valley expand to become true towns
1121: Bishop Eirik visits North America from Greenland
c.1175: Toltec capital, Tula, is sacked by Chichimec

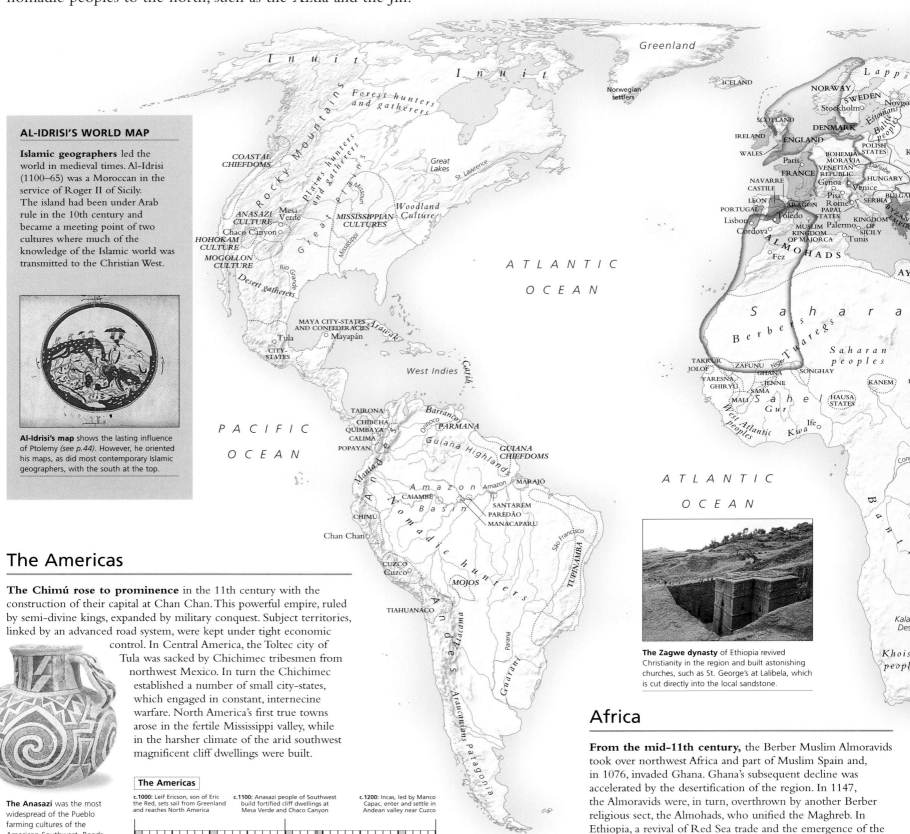

The Zagwe dynasty of Ethiopia revived Christianity in the region and built astonishing churches, such as St. George's at Lalibela, which is cut directly into the local sandstone.

Africa

From the mid-11th century, the Berber Muslim Almoravids took over northwest Africa and part of Muslim Spain and, in 1076, invaded Ghana. Ghana's subsequent decline was accelerated by the desertification of the region. In 1147, the Almoravids were, in turn, overthrown by another Berber religious sect, the Almohads, who unified the Maghreb. In Ethiopia, a revival of Red Sea trade and the emergence of the Zagwe dynasty in 1150, led to a more expansionist, prosperous era. In Egypt, the military leader Saladin became ruler in 1174, ending the Fatimid dynasty and founding that of the Ayyubids.

WINDMILLS

Wind power had been harnessed in various different ways, notably in Persia and China, for grinding corn and raising water. But it was not until the 12th century that the windmill started to take on its familiar European form. The mills of northern Europe differed from earlier versions in that the shaft turned horizontally rather than vertically and the sails were turned so that they kept facing the wind. The first northern European mills were simple post-mills. These evolved gradually into bulkier tower mills with rotating caps.

In Europe windmills were used only for grinding corn up until the 15th century, as illustrated in this English woodcut from c.1340. Their power was then adapted for tasks such as land drainage, particularly in Holland.

West Asia

Byzantium's resurgence under Basil II did not last, and in the 11th century most of the empire's Asian lands fell to the Seljuk Turks. The Islamic Turks, originally from Central Asia, established themselves in Baghdad in 1055. As "men of the sword," they formed a partnership with the Persians and Arabs, the "men of the law." Tens of thousands of

Europeans answered Pope Urban II's call in 1095 to recapture Jerusalem for Christendom. In 1099 the holy city was taken and the Crusaders set up states in Antioch, Edessa, Tripoli, and Jerusalem. In the following century, Muslim leaders, notably Saladin, founder of the Ayyubid dynasty in Egypt, embarked on a campaign of reconquest.

The capture of Antioch in 1098 was one of the first Christian successes on the First Crusade. The strongly fortified city held out for seven months.

SEE ALSO:

North America: pp.122–123

South America: pp.146–147

Africa: pp.162–163

Europe: pp.186–187

West Asia: pp.228–229

South and Southeast Asia: pp.244–245

North and East Asia: pp.262–265

West Asia

1055: Seljuk Turks capture Baghdad	1099: Jerusalem captured by Crusaders	1174: Founding of Ayyubid Sultanate in Egypt	1187: Saladin recaptures Jerusalem

1000 — 1050 — 1100 — 1150 — 1200

| 1025: Death of great Byzantine emperor, Basil II | 1071: Seljuk Turks defeat Byzantines at Manzikert | 1144: Fall of Edessa to Muslims | 1188: Crusader states reduced to coastal enclaves by Saladin |

East Asia

By 1110, Song China was the most advanced, prosperous, and populous state in the world. However the Song alliance with the Manchurian Jin to dislodge the hostile Liao from their northern border, fatally weakened the Song Empire. The Jin overran northern China and the Song were forced to regroup in the southeast, defensive and hostile to outside influences. In Japan, the emperors lost power to the Fujiwara family in the mid-12th century. A period of violent interclan warfare followed, ending with the victory of the Minamoto clan.

This Song scroll gives a vivid depiction of the bustling street life and prosperity of Kaifeng in the 12th century. In 1105 the city's population had risen to 260,000.

East Asia

1005: Song China becomes subject state of northern Liao kingdom, with capital at Beijing	1125: Liao defeated by Jin from Manchuria	1191: Zen Buddhist order founded in Japan

1000 — 1050 — 1100 — 1150 — 1200

| c.1045: Movable type printing invented in China | 1130: Song capital moves to Hangzhou | 1192: Minamoto Yoritomo becomes Shogun and forms military government in Japan |

The Khmer Empire was at its height in the 11th and 12th centuries. The artistic brilliance of the court, evident in these carvings decorating a temple at Angkor Wat, was in marked contrast to the conditions of the mass of the population.

South and Southeast Asia

Northern India was repeatedly invaded by the Ghazni Muslims of Afghanistan. In 1186 the last Ghazni ruler was deposed by the Turkish leader, Muhammad al Ghur, who continued to wage holy war in the region. Southeastern India was dominated by the Chola dynasty, who controlled the sea route between West Asia and China. The two most powerful states of Southeast Asia, the Khmer Empire and the kingdom of Pagan, both enjoyed an artistic golden age.

The World in 1200

- Byzantine Empire
- England and possessions
- Venetian Republic
- Holy Roman Empire
- Almoravid Empire 1120
- Great Seljuk Empire 1071
- possessions of Canute 1028–1035

Africa

1048: Fatimids lose control of Ifriqiya (Libya)	c.1110: Onset of serious desiccation of Sahel region	1147: Almohads established in Morocco and southern Spain	1171: Shi'ite Fatimid dynasty in Egypt suppressed by Saladin

1000 — 1050 — 1100 — 1150 — 1200

| 1076: Ghana falls to Almoravids | 1128: Almohads start takeover of Almoravid dominions | 1150: Zagwe dynasty established in Ethiopia |

South and Southeast Asia

1014: Rajendra I becomes ruler of the Cholas of southeastern India	1018: Rajendra conquers Ceylon	1113: Accession of Suryavarman II, powerful warrior king of the Khmer	1152: Temple of Angkor Wat completed	1191: Muhammad al Ghur defeats Rajput clans

1000 — 1050 — 1100 — 1150 — 1200

| c.1000: First Muslim raids into northern India, led by Sultan Muhammad of Ghazni | 1044: Establishment of first Burmese state at Pagan | 1077: Chola merchants send embassy to China | 1186: Raids by Muhammad al Ghur herald end of Buddhism in northern India |

THE AGE OF THE CRUSADES

The idealism of a devout Crusader is captured in this 13th-century drawing.

THE IDEA OF A HOLY WAR was never part of the doctrine of the early Christian church. This changed in 1095, when Pope Urban II made an impassioned speech at Clermont, urging French barons and knights to go to the aid of the beleaguered Christians of the Byzantine Empire. In return, they were promised indulgences. When they got to the Holy Land and captured Jerusalem in 1099, the aims of the Crusaders became rather less spiritual. Those rewarded with land tried to recreate the society of feudal Europe, but there was always a shortage of manpower to maintain the Crusader states in their precarious two centuries of existence. Nevertheless, the crusading ideal became firmly established in European consciousness, and there were many subsequent expeditions to defend or recapture Jerusalem, but none was as successful as the first.

The most devout and determined of all the crusading kings of Europe was Louis IX of France (St. Louis). He sailed on two Crusades, once to invade Egypt, the second time to convert the King of Tunis. Both ended in disaster. In 1270, Louis and his men were struck down by disease as they camped before Tunis. Louis himself died. Here his coffin is being loaded on a ship to be carried back to France.

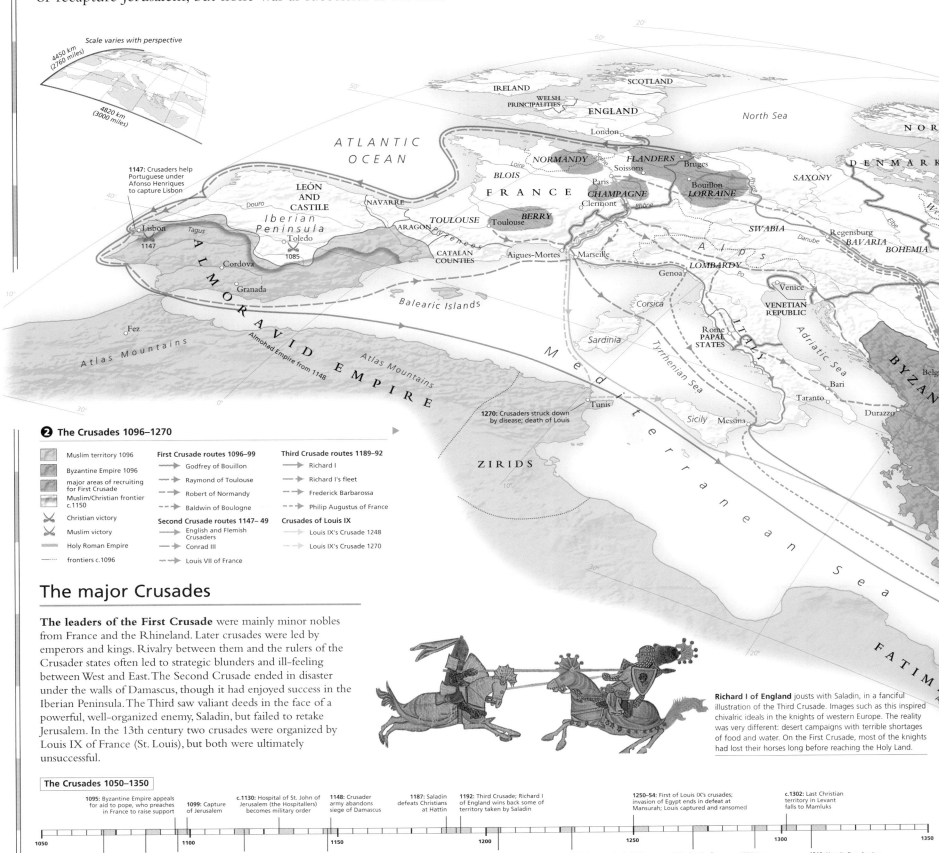

Scale varies with perspective

4450 km (2760 miles)
4820 km (3000 miles)

② The Crusades 1096–1270 ▶

	Muslim territory 1096
	Byzantine Empire 1096
	major areas of recruiting for First Crusade
	Muslim/Christian frontier c.1150
✕	Christian victory
✕	Muslim victory
▬	Holy Roman Empire
┄	frontiers c.1096

First Crusade routes 1096–99
→ Godfrey of Bouillon
→ Raymond of Toulouse
⇢ Robert of Normandy
⇢ Baldwin of Boulogne

Second Crusade routes 1147–49
→ English and Flemish Crusaders
→ Conrad III
⇢ Louis VII of France

Third Crusade routes 1189–92
→ Richard I
→ Richard I's fleet
⇢ Frederick Barbarossa
⇢ Philip Augustus of France

Crusades of Louis IX
→ Louis IX's Crusade 1248
→ Louis IX's Crusade 1270

Map labels: IRELAND, SCOTLAND, WELSH PRINCIPALITIES, ENGLAND, London, North Sea, NORMANDY, FLANDERS, Bruges, DENMARK, NOR..., BLOIS, Soissons, SAXONY, Paris, CHAMPAGNE, Clermont, BOUILLON, LORRAINE, FRANCE, Loire, Rhine, BERRY, SWABIA, Regensburg, BAVARIA, BOHEMIA, NAVARRE, TOULOUSE, Toulouse, ARAGON, Pyrenees, Aigues-Mortes, Marseille, ALPS, LOMBARDY, Danube, Elbe, LEÓN AND CASTILE, Iberian Peninsula, Toledo, CATALAN COUNTIES, Genoa, Po, Corsica, VENETIAN REPUBLIC, Venice, ATLANTIC OCEAN, 1147: Crusaders help Portuguese under Afonso Henriques to capture Lisbon, Lisbon, 1147, Douro, Tagus, Cordova, 1085, Granada, Balearic Islands, Rome, PAPAL STATES, ITALY, Sardinia, Tyrrhenian Sea, Adriatic Sea, Bari, Taranto, Durazzo, BYZAN..., Belgr..., Fez, Atlas Mountains, ALMORAVID EMPIRE, Almohad Empire from 1148, ZIRIDS, Tunis, 1270: Crusaders struck down by disease; death of Louis, Sicily, Messina, Mediterranean Sea, FATIMI..., 1095

The major Crusades

The leaders of the First Crusade were mainly minor nobles from France and the Rhineland. Later crusades were led by emperors and kings. Rivalry between them and the rulers of the Crusader states often led to strategic blunders and ill-feeling between West and East. The Second Crusade ended in disaster under the walls of Damascus, though it had enjoyed success in the Iberian Peninsula. The Third saw valiant deeds in the face of a powerful, well-organized enemy, Saladin, but failed to retake Jerusalem. In the 13th century two crusades were organized by Louis IX of France (St. Louis), but both were ultimately unsuccessful.

Richard I of England jousts with Saladin, in a fanciful illustration of the Third Crusade. Images such as this inspired chivalric ideals in the knights of western Europe. The reality was very different: desert campaigns with terrible shortages of food and water. On the First Crusade, most of the knights had lost their horses long before reaching the Holy Land.

The Crusades 1050–1350

1095: Byzantine Empire appeals for aid to pope, who preaches in France to raise support
1099: Capture of Jerusalem
c.1130: Hospital of St. John of Jerusalem (the Hospitallers) becomes military order
1148: Crusader army abandons siege of Damascus
1187: Saladin defeats Christians at Hattin
1192: Third Crusade; Richard I of England wins back some of territory taken by Saladin
1250–54: First of Louis IX's crusades; invasion of Egypt ends in defeat at Mansurah; Louis captured and ransomed
c.1302: Last Christian territory in Levant falls to Mamluks

1071: Turks defeat Byzantines at battle of Manzikert
1085: Alfonso VI of León takes Toledo
1096: First wave of Crusaders departs
c.1118: Crusading order of Knights Templar founded
1147: Second Crusade; Emperor Conrad defeated by Turks at Dorylaeum
1204: Fourth Crusade never reaches Holy Land; Crusaders take Constantinople
1229: Emperor Frederick II regains control of Jerusalem through diplomacy
1270: Death of Louis IX outside walls of Tunis
1291: Loss of Acre
1310: Hospitallers, having taken Rhodes, make it their headquarters

1050   1100   1150   1200   1250   1300   1350

The boundaries of Christianity and Islam

In the 9th and 10th centuries, the boundaries between the Islamic and Christian worlds shifted very little. A new threat to Christianity came in the mid-11th century with the advance of the Seljuk Turks, newly converted to Islam and effective rulers of the Abbasid Caliphate after reaching Baghdad in 1055. Following their victory over the Byzantines in 1071 at Manzikert, they won control of almost all Asia Minor, home to former Christian subjects of the Byzantine Empire. In the Iberian Peninsula, however, the Christian kingdoms won back land from the Muslims in the course of the 11th century.

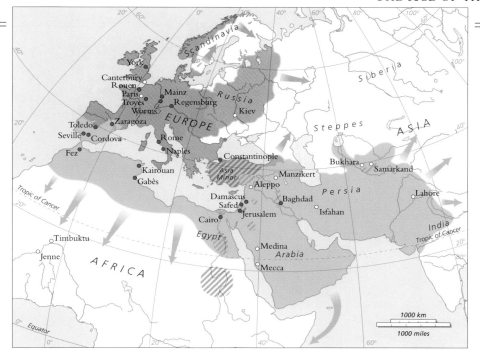

SEE ALSO:

Africa: pp.162–163

Europe: pp.186–187

West Asia: pp.228–229

❶ Islam and Christianity c.1090

- Muslim lands
- Greek Christians (Orthodox)
- Roman Church (under papal authority)
- Greek Christians in Muslim lands
- other Christians
- direction of Muslim expansion
- direction of Greek Christian expansion
- direction of Roman Church expansion
- city with important Jewish community

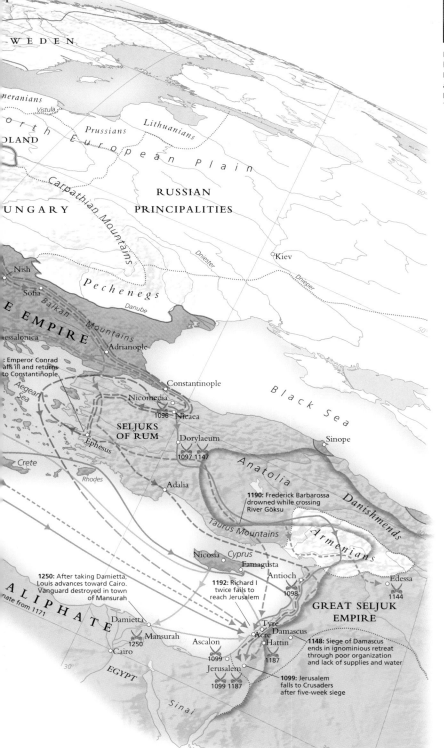

Godfrey of Bouillon leads the attack on Jerusalem in 1099. After all the hardship and the long journey there, the capture of the Holy City was hailed as a miracle. It was followed by the murder or brutal eviction of many of the city's Muslims and Jews.

Krak des Chevaliers was one of many heavily fortified Crusader castles. Manned by the Hospitallers, it held out against Saladin's forces, but fell to the Mamluks in 1271 after a month's siege.

Crusader states in the Holy Land

How the Crusaders' conquests should be ruled was not considered until after Jerusalem had fallen. The solution – a feudal kingdom of Jerusalem buttressed by the counties of Edessa, Tripoli, and Antioch – alienated the Byzantines, who had hoped to regain their former territories. Jerusalem was always a weak state with a small population, heavily dependent on supplies and recruits from western Christendom. When a strong Islamic ruler such as Saladin emerged, the colonists had little hope against a determined Muslim onslaught. They held on to the coast through the 13th century, but in 1291, Acre, the last major city in Christian hands, fell to the Mamluks of Egypt.

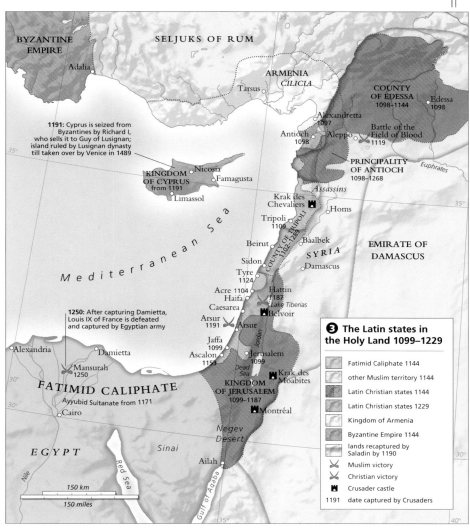

❸ The Latin states in the Holy Land 1099–1229

- Fatimid Caliphate 1144
- other Muslim territory 1144
- Latin Christian states 1144
- Latin Christian states 1229
- Kingdom of Armenia
- Byzantine Empire 1144
- lands recaptured by Saladin by 1190
- Muslim victory
- Christian victory
- Crusader castle
- 1191 date captured by Crusaders

1191: Cyprus is seized from Byzantines by Richard I, who sells it to Guy of Lusignan; island ruled by Lusignan dynasty till taken over by Venice in 1489

1250: After capturing Damietta, Louis IX of France is defeated and captured by Egyptian army

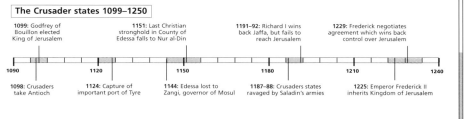

The Crusader states 1099–1250

1099: Godfrey of Bouillon elected King of Jerusalem

1151: Last Christian stronghold in County of Edessa falls to Nur al-Din

1191–92: Richard I wins back Jaffa, but fails to reach Jerusalem

1229: Frederick negotiates agreement which wins back control over Jerusalem

1098: Crusaders take Antioch

1124: Capture of important port of Tyre

1144: Edessa lost to Zangi, governor of Mosul

1187–88: Crusaders states ravaged by Saladin's armies

1225: Emperor Frederick II inherits Kingdom of Jerusalem

THE WORLD 1200–1300

IN THE 13TH CENTURY Mongol horsemen burst out of their Central Asian homeland and conquered a vast swathe of the Eurasian landmass. By 1300, they had divided their conquests into four large empires that stretched from China to eastern Europe. Mongol campaigns brought devastation, particularly to China and the Islamic states of southwest Asia but, once all resistance had been crushed, merchants, ambassadors, and other travelers were able to move safely through the Mongol realms. Though the old political order of the Islamic world, centered on the Abbasid Caliphate and Baghdad, was swept away, the influence of Islam continued to spread as many Mongols adopted the religion. Powerful new Muslim states also emerged in Mamluk Egypt and the Sultanate of Delhi. Europe remained on the defensive in the face of the Mongols and Islam, but city-states such as Venice and Genoa prospered through increased trading links with the East.

The port of Venice was the richest city in western Europe. This illustration shows Marco Polo with his father and uncle setting off in 1271 on the first stage of their incredible journey to the court of the Great Khan.

Europe

The feudal monarchies of England and France consolidated large regional states, but conflict between popes and emperors prevented any similar process in Italy and Germany. In Spain, Christian forces took Córdoba and Seville, leaving only the small kingdom of Granada in Moorish control. In eastern Europe, the Mongols of the Golden Horde collected tribute from the Russian principalities. Western Europe, in contrast, prospered economically as Italian merchants linked northern lands to the commerce of the Mediterranean basin.

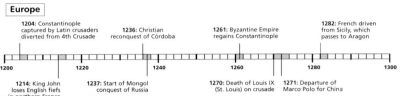

Europe

1204: Constantinople captured by Latin crusaders diverted from 4th Crusade	1236: Christian reconquest of Córdoba	1261: Byzantine Empire regains Constantinople	1282: French driven from Sicily, which passes to Aragon

1200 — 1220 — 1240 — 1260 — 1280 — 1300

| 1214: King John loses English fiefs in northern France | 1237: Start of Mongol conquest of Russia | 1270: Death of Louis IX (St. Louis) on crusade | 1271: Departure of Marco Polo for China |

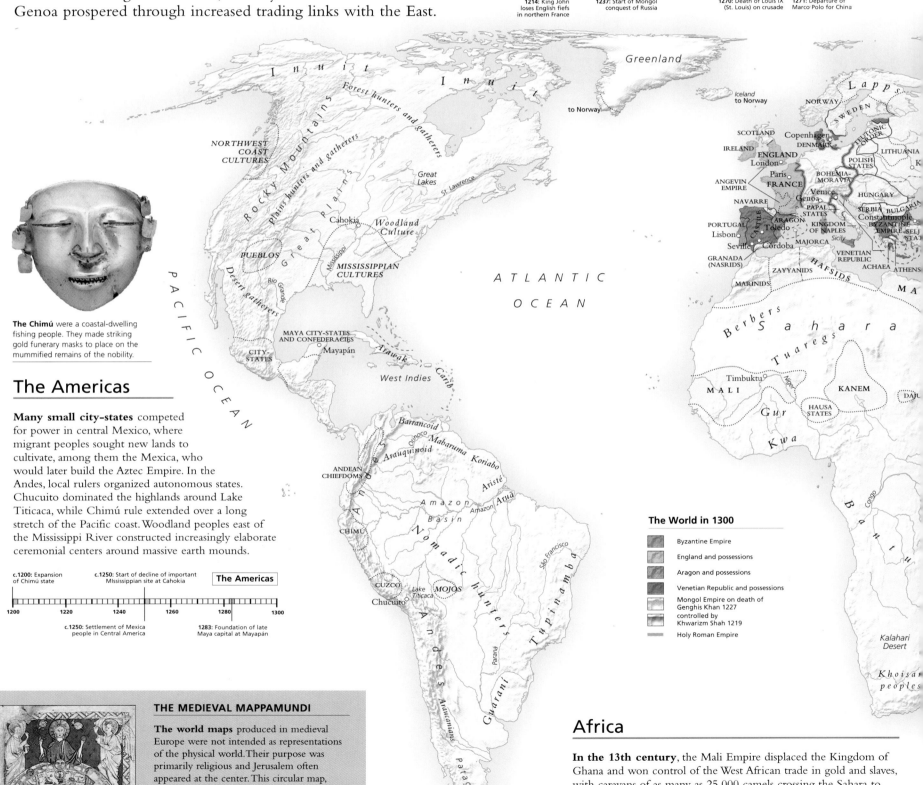

The Chimú were a coastal-dwelling fishing people. They made striking gold funerary masks to place on the mummified remains of the nobility.

The Americas

Many small city-states competed for power in central Mexico, where migrant peoples sought new lands to cultivate, among them the Mexica, who would later build the Aztec Empire. In the Andes, local rulers organized autonomous states. Chucuito dominated the highlands around Lake Titicaca, while Chimú rule extended over a long stretch of the Pacific coast. Woodland peoples east of the Mississippi River constructed increasingly elaborate ceremonial centers around massive earth mounds.

| c.1200: Expansion of Chimú state | c.1250: Start of decline of important Mississippian site at Cahokia | **The Americas** |

1200 — 1220 — 1240 — 1260 — 1280 — 1300

| c.1250: Settlement of Mexica people in Central America | 1283: Foundation of late Maya capital at Mayapán |

The World in 1300

- Byzantine Empire
- England and possessions
- Aragon and possessions
- Venetian Republic and possessions
- Mongol Empire on death of Genghis Khan 1227
- controlled by Khwarizm Shah 1219
- Holy Roman Empire

THE MEDIEVAL MAPPAMUNDI

The world maps produced in medieval Europe were not intended as representations of the physical world. Their purpose was primarily religious and Jerusalem often appeared at the center. This circular map, oriented with Asia at the top, is full of Christian symbolism, and is decorated with grotesque faces and mythical beasts.

A 13th-century English psalter contains this tiny world map or *mappamundi*, which measures just 4 inches across.

Africa

In the 13th century, the Mali Empire displaced the Kingdom of Ghana and won control of the West African trade in gold and slaves, with caravans of as many as 25,000 camels crossing the Sahara to North Africa. Meanwhile, the Swahili city-states on the East African coast exported goods through the trading networks of the Indian Ocean. Rulers of Mali and the Swahili city-states adopted Islam and built mosques and religious schools. Islam did not reach central and southern Africa, but the trade it generated led to the establishment of wealthy inland states such as the Kingdom of Great Zimbabwe.

West Asia

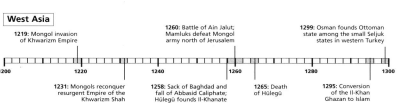

This luster tile from 13th-century Persia is decorated with a verse from the Koran. The Mongols were too few to impose their beliefs on the peoples they conquered. Instead, many of them became Muslims.

In 1258 the Mongols sacked Baghdad and overthrew the Abbasid Caliphate. Their leaders established themselves as Il-Khans, nominally subordinate to the Great Khan in China. Their empire extended almost to the Mediterranean, where their westward expansion was halted by the Mamluks of Egypt. By 1300 most Mongols of the Il-Khanate had embraced Islam, as had many of their fellow Mongols of the Golden Horde. Meanwhile, the Seljuks and other Turkic peoples consolidated their position in formerly Byzantine territory by establishing regional states.

THE MAGNETIC COMPASS

The Chinese had long known that a floating magnetized needle always points in the same direction. Their sailors started to make regular use of this fact in about 1100. By the 13th century, the magnetic compass was probably in widespread use among the Arab navigators of the Indian Ocean. In Europe, a written account of its principles appeared as early as 1190.

In the 13th century the Chinese simply floated a magnetized needle on water. This boxed compass is an early example.

SEE ALSO:

North America: pp.122–123

South America: pp.146–147

Africa: pp.162–163

Europe: pp.186–191

West Asia: pp.228–229

South and Southeast Asia: pp.244–245

North and East Asia: pp.262–265

West Asia

1219: Mongol invasion of Khwarizm Empire
1260: Battle of Ain Jalut; Mamluks defeat Mongol army north of Jerusalem
1299: Osman founds Ottoman state among the small Seljuk states in western Turkey

1200   1220   1240   1260   1280   1300

1231: Mongols reconquer resurgent Empire of the Khwarizm Shah
1258: Sack of Baghdad and fall of Abbasid Caliphate; Hülegü founds Il-Khanate
1265: Death of Hülegü
1295: Conversion of the Il-Khan Ghazan to Islam

North and East Asia

Genghis Khan invaded northern China in 1211, but the Southern Song Empire fell only after a long campaign (1260-79) directed by Kublai Khan. China was the richest of all the Mongol conquests. Kublai became emperor and founded the Yuan dynasty. He appointed many foreigners to govern the empire and fostered both maritime and overland trade with other lands throughout East Asia. From Korea (Koryo) the Mongols made two failed attempts to invade Japan.

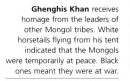

Ghenghis Khan receives homage from the leaders of other Mongol tribes. White horsetails flying from his tent indicated that the Mongols were temporarily at peace. Black ones meant they were at war.

North and East Asia

1206: Temujin named Genghis Khan
1233: Mongols take Jin capital, Kaifeng
1264: Kublai elected Great Khan
1279: Foundation of Yuan dynasty
1294: Death of Kublai

1200   1220   1240   1260   1280   1300

1211: Mongols begin conquest of northern China
1274: First Mongol attempt to invade Japan
1292: Departure of Marco Polo from China

South and Southeast Asia

In 1206 Qutb al-din, leader of the Islamic raiders who had terrorized northern India for the past 30 years, fixed the capital of a new sultanate at Delhi. The Sultanate suffered occasional Mongol raids, while the Mongols made repeated forays from China into Annam and Pagan, without ever gaining secure control of the region. They also launched a massive seaborne attack on Java, but their tactics were ineffective in the island's tropical jungles.

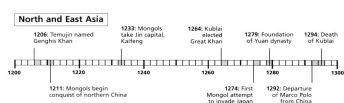

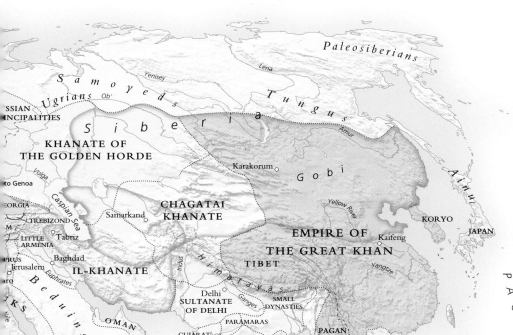

The spectacular royal enclosure of Great Zimbabwe was rebuilt many times between the 11th and the 15th century. The kings owed their wealth to trade in cattle, gold, and copper.

The Qutb Minar minaret rises beside the Quwwat-al-Islam mosque in Delhi. Begun in 1199, it became a powerful symbol of Islamic rule in northern India.

Africa

1228: Start of collapse of Almohad Empire in North Africa
c.1250: Building of stone mosques in Swahili city-states
1270: Expansion of Christian Kingdom of Ethiopia

1200   1220   1240   1260   1280   1300

1230: Establishment of the Mali Empire by Sundiata
1250: Mamluk military caste takes over Egypt
1255: Death of Sundiata
1269: Marinids inflict final defeat on Almohads in Morocco

1206: Foundation of Sultanate of Delhi
1258: First Mongol expedition to Annam
1288: Kublai Khan gives up attempt to subdue Annam and Champa

1200   1220   1240   1260   1280   1300

South and Southeast Asia

1293: Failed Mongol invasion of Java

Map labels:
Paleosiberians, Samoyeds, Ugrians, Tungus, Siberia, RUSSIAN PRINCIPALITIES, KHANATE OF THE GOLDEN HORDE, to Genoa, Volga, GEORGIA, Caspian Sea, TREBIZOND, LITTLE ARMENIA, CYPRUS, Tabriz, Baghdad, Jerusalem, IL-KHANATE, TURKS, Beduin, Euphrates, Tigris, Arabian Peninsula, OMAN, RASULIDS, YEMEN, ETHIOPIA, IFAT, HADYA, DAWARO, BALI, Cushites, TERLACUSTRINE STATES, SWAHILI CITY-STATES, Zambezi, Malays, Madagascar, GREAT ZIMBABWE, Great Zimbabwe, Lena, Yenisey, Ob', CHAGATAI KHANATE, Samarkand, Karakorum, Gobi, Amur, Yellow River, Indus, Himalayas, TIBET, EMPIRE OF THE GREAT KHAN, Kaifeng, Yangtze, KORYO, JAPAN, Ainu, Delhi, SULTANATE OF DELHI, SMALL DYNASTIES, Ganges, PARAMARAS, GUJARAT, YADAVAS, EASTERN GANGAS, KAKATIYAS, HOYSALAS, PANDYAS, CERAS, SMALL STATES vassals to Pandyas, ARAKAN, PAGAN, PEGU, CHIENGMAI PHAYAO, SUKHOTHAI, LAVO, KHMER, LAOS, Mekong, ANNAM, CHAMPA, MALAY STATES, Borneo, Sumatra, East Indies, Java, MAJAPAHIT, Borneo, PACIFIC OCEAN, Philippine Islands, Papuans, New Guinea, INDIAN OCEAN, Australian Aborigines, Darling, Maoris, New Zealand

THE AGE OF THE MONGOLS

Genghis Khan – the title means "universal ruler" – was born Temujin, son of a minor Mongol chief.

THE NOMADIC HERDSMEN of the Mongolian steppe traded livestock, horses, and hides with the settled agricultural civilization of China to the south, but relations between the two were usually marked by hostility and suspicion. By the 13th century, the Chinese empire had become weak and fragmented. Into this power vacuum burst the Mongols, a fierce race of skilled horsemen, their normally warring tribes united under the inspired leadership of Genghis Khan. Genghis did not seek war at all costs; he first gave his enemies a chance to submit – on his terms. If they refused, he unleashed a campaign of terror, sacking cities and massacring entire populations. Although at first the Mongols numbered no more than a million, their ranks were swelled by Turks, Arabs, and other subject peoples. Genghis's successors extended his conquests across Asia and deep into Europe, but his empire then split into four khanates. By 1400, the Mongols were a divided and weakened force and most of their conquests had been lost.

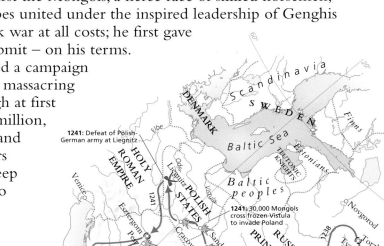

Genghis Khan, preceded by Jebe, one of his most trusted commanders, leads a cavalry charge. Jebe and another great general, Sübedei, made the astonishing raid into Russia in 1222 that first made Europe aware of the Mongols' existence.

Caravan routes across Central Asia thrived in the climate of law and order imposed by Mongol rule. This illustration from the Catalan Atlas of 1375 shows a group of European merchants riding along the Silk Road.

The Mongol peace

The Mongols' chief aim was always to exact tribute from conquered peoples, but they also brought long periods of peace; travelers were able to cross Eurasia in safety along the old Silk Road. In the reign of Genghis Khan's grandson Möngke (1251–59) it was said that a virgin with a pot of gold on her head could walk unmolested across his empire. The two most famous travelers to benefit from the Mongol peace were the Venetian merchant Marco Polo, who claimed to have spent 17 years in the employment of Kublai Khan, and Ibn Battuta, a Muslim legal scholar from Tangier in Morocco, who also traveled as far as China.

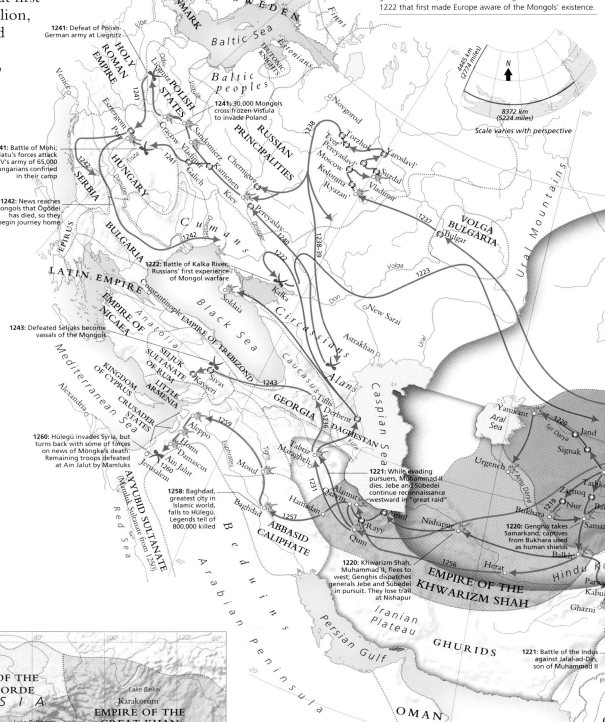

1241: Defeat of Polish-German army at Liegnitz

1241: 30,000 Mongols cross frozen Vistula to invade Poland

1241: Battle of Mohi; Batu's forces attack Béla IV's army of 65,000 Hungarians confined in their camp

1242: News reaches Mongols that Ögödei has died, so they begin journey home

1222: Battle of Kalka River; Russians' first experience of Mongol warfare

1243: Defeated Seljuks become vassals of the Mongols

1260: Hülegü invades Syria, but turns back with some of forces on news of Möngke's death. Remaining troops defeated at Ain Jalut by Mamluks

1258: Baghdad, greatest city in Islamic world, falls to Hülegü. Legends tell of 800,000 killed

1221: While evading pursuers, Muhammad II dies. Jebe and Sübedei continue reconnaissance westward in "great raid"

1220: Khwarizm Shah, Muhammad II, flees to west; Genghis dispatches generals Jebe and Sübedei in pursuit. They lose trail at Nishapur

1220: Genghis takes Samarkand; captives from Bukhara used as human shields

1221: Battle of the Indus against Jalal-ad-Din, son of Muhammad II

N

4445 km (2774 miles)

8372 km (5224 miles)

Scale varies with perspective

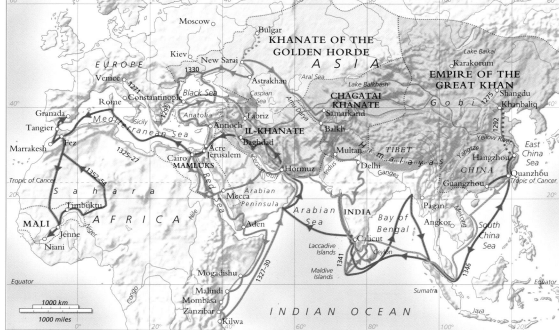

② Eurasia and Africa c.1300

route of Marco Polo
1271 — 1295

route of Ibn Battuta
1325 — 1345

⋯ disputed journeys of Ibn Battuta

— Silk Road

The Mongol peace

1235: Walled city built at Karakorum as fixed Mongol capital

1275: Marco Polo reaches Kublai's summer palace at Shangdu (Xanadu)

1325: Ibn Battuta's first pilgrimage to Mecca

1345–46: Ibn Battuta visits Southeast Asia and China

1225 · 1250 · 1275 · 1300 · 1325 · 1350

1264: Kublai defeats rival for title of Great Khan, ending civil war

1266: Kublai founds new capital at Khanbaliq (Beijing)

1292: Marco Polo given task of escorting Mongol princess to Hormuz

1334–41: Ibn Battuta serves as *qadi* (judge) in Delhi

The Mongol conquests

In less than 20 years, in a series of conquests without parallel in history, Genghis Khan shattered the Muslim states of Central Asia, overran northern China, and sent troops on a lightning raid into Russia. Genghis's immediate successor was his third son Ögödei, whose reign as Great Khan saw the destruction of the Jin and Khwarizm empires, continued fighting with Song China, and an invasion of Europe that reached Hungary and Poland. The conquest of the Song was completed by Kublai Khan, a grandson of Genghis, who became emperor of China, while Kublai's brother, Hülegü, founder of the Il-Khanate, destroyed the Abbasid Caliphate, sacking the great Islamic city of Baghdad. The first setback to Mongol expansion came at the hands of the Mamluks, who, in 1260, prevented their advance into Egypt at Ain Jalut.

At the siege of Hezhou in 1258–59, Mongol horsemen tried unsuccessfully to cross the Yangtze on a pontoon bridge of boats. The conquest of Song China was accomplished only after many protracted sieges.

Mongol conquests of the 13th century

1206: Mongols united by Genghis Khan
1211: First invasion of Jin Empire
1219: Genghis attacks Khwarizm
1227: Death of Genghis
1229: Ögödei elected Great Khan
1242: Batu founds Golden Horde
1258: Sack of Baghdad
1260: Hülegü invades Syria; Mongols suffer first major defeat at Ain Jalut
1279: Last Song resistance crushed
1281: Second failed invasion of Japan
1294: Death of Kublai

1200 1220 1240 1260 1280 1300

SEE ALSO:

Europe: pp.188–189

West Asia: pp.228–229

South and Southeast Asia: pp.244–245

North and East Asia: pp.262–265

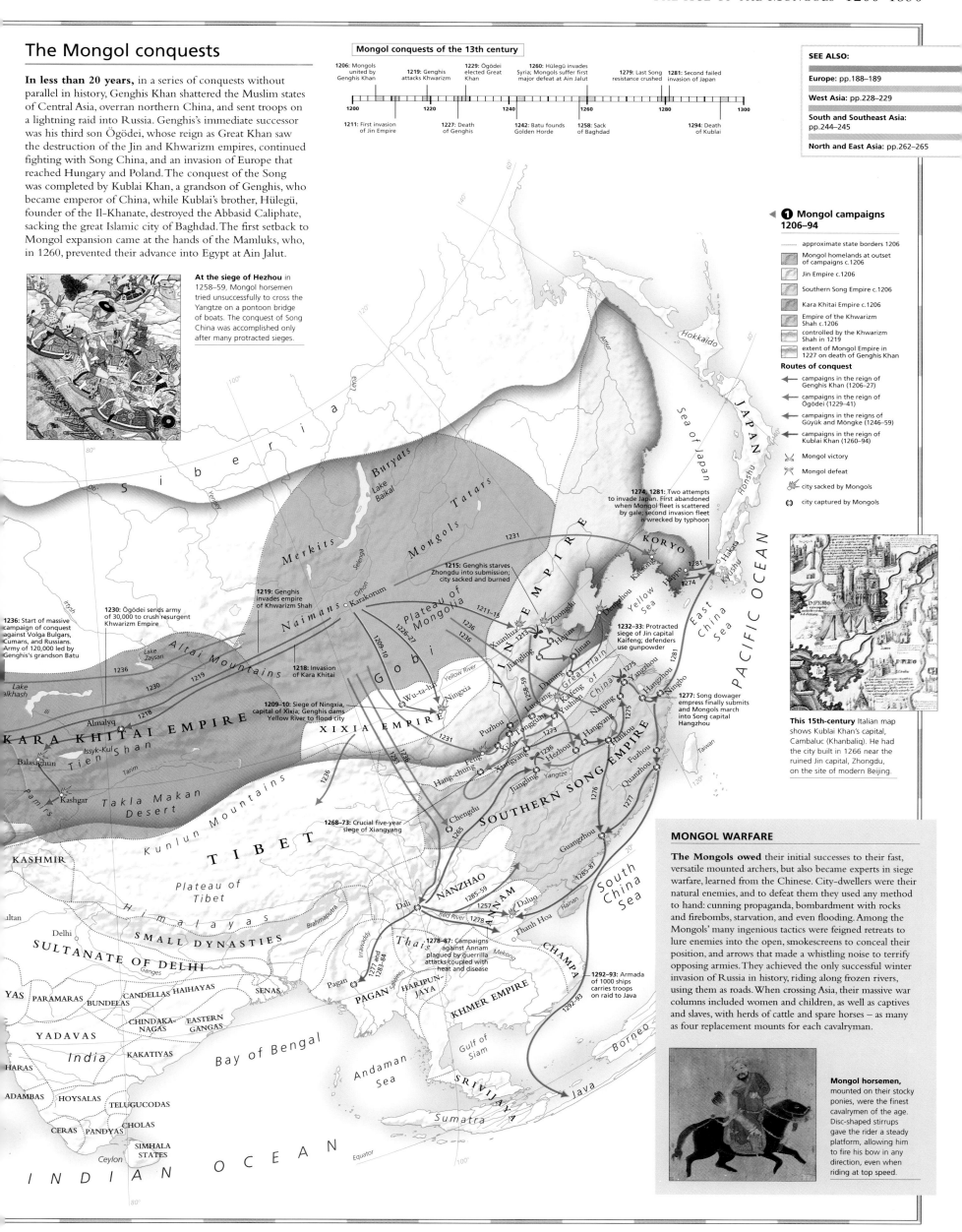

◀ ❶ Mongol campaigns 1206–94

- ········· approximate state borders 1206
- Mongol homelands at outset of campaigns c.1206
- Jin Empire c.1206
- Southern Song Empire c.1206
- Kara Khitai Empire c.1206
- Empire of the Khwarizm Shah c.1206
- controlled by the Khwarizm Shah in 1219
- extent of Mongol Empire in 1227 on death of Genghis Khan

Routes of conquest
- → campaigns in the reign of Genghis Khan (1206–27)
- → campaigns in the reign of Ögödei (1229–41)
- → campaigns in the reigns of Güyük and Möngke (1246–59)
- → campaigns in the reign of Kublai Khan (1260–94)
- ⚔ Mongol victory
- ⚔ Mongol defeat
- ✸ city sacked by Mongols
- ⟨⟩ city captured by Mongols

This 15th-century Italian map shows Kublai Khan's capital, Cambaluc (Khanbaliq). He had the city built in 1266 near the ruined Jin capital, Zhongdu, on the site of modern Beijing.

MONGOL WARFARE

The Mongols owed their initial successes to their fast, versatile mounted archers, but also became experts in siege warfare, learned from the Chinese. City-dwellers were their natural enemies, and to defeat them they used any method to hand: cunning propaganda, bombardment with rocks and firebombs, starvation, and even flooding. Among the Mongols' many ingenious tactics were feigned retreats to lure enemies into the open, smokescreens to conceal their position, and arrows that made a whistling noise to terrify opposing armies. They achieved the only successful winter invasion of Russia in history, riding along frozen rivers, using them as roads. When crossing Asia, their massive war columns included women and children, as well as captives and slaves, with herds of cattle and spare horses – as many as four replacement mounts for each cavalryman.

Mongol horsemen, mounted on their stocky ponies, were the finest cavalrymen of the age. Disc-shaped stirrups gave the rider a steady platform, allowing him to fire his bow in any direction, even when riding at top speed.

THE WORLD 1300–1400

DURING THE 14TH CENTURY epidemics of bubonic plague swept across the Old World from China and Korea to the west coast of Europe. Dramatic demographic decline led to economic and social disruption that weakened states throughout Eurasia and North Africa. In addition, the onset of the so-called "Little Ice Age," which would last till the 19th century, brought bad weather and poor harvests to many of the regions affected by plague. The Mongol empires, which had dominated Eurasia since the conquests of Genghis Khan in the 13th century, began to disintegrate, though the Khanate of the Golden Horde maintained its hegemony in southern Russia into the 15th century. In both China and Persia the Mongols were assimilated into the local population, but in China, a new dynasty, the Ming, introduced a Han Chinese aristocratic regime.

The Black Death reached Europe from Asia in 1347. In three years it probably killed one third of the population. The fear it generated is captured in this image of Death strangling a plague victim.

Europe

Europe struggled to recover from the social and economic disruption caused by the Black Death. Scarcity of labor led peasants and workers to seek improved conditions and higher wages, but landlords and employers resisted their demands, provoking many revolts in western Europe. France suffered too from the military campaigns of the Hundred Years' War, fueled by the dynastic ambitions of English kings. Religious differences also brought disorder. Rival popes residing in Rome and Avignon both claimed authority over the Catholic Church, while in England the Lollards challenged the authority and doctrine of the Church itself.

| Europe | 1312: Order of Knights Templar suppressed by pope | 1337: Beginning of the Hundred Years' War | 1346: English defeat French at Battle of Crécy | 1378: Beginning of Great Schism in Catholic church | 1381: Peasants' Revolt in England |

1300 1320 1340 1360 1380 1400

1309: Pope takes up residence at Avignon
1347: Arrival of bubonic plague in Italy
1358: The Jacquerie, uprising against nobility in France
1397: Union of Kalmar; Norway, Denmark, and Sweden united under a single monarch

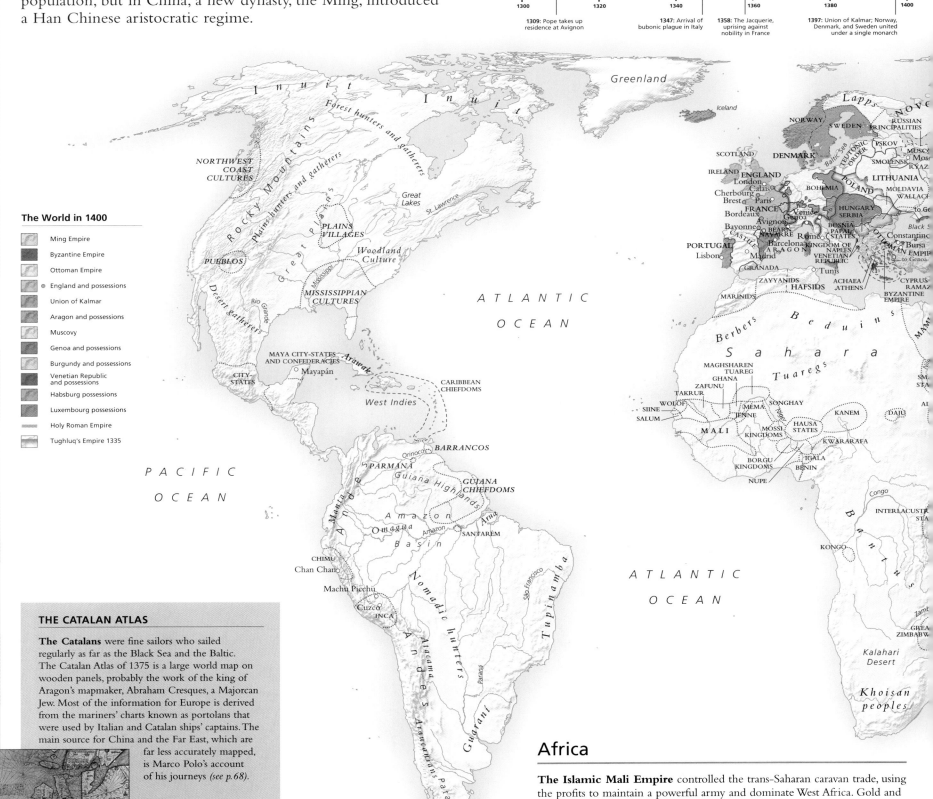

The World in 1400

- Ming Empire
- Byzantine Empire
- Ottoman Empire
- England and possessions
- Union of Kalmar
- Aragon and possessions
- Muscovy
- Genoa and possessions
- Burgundy and possessions
- Venetian Republic and possessions
- Habsburg possessions
- Luxembourg possessions
- Holy Roman Empire
- Tughluq's Empire 1335

THE CATALAN ATLAS

The Catalans were fine sailors who sailed regularly as far as the Black Sea and the Baltic. The Catalan Atlas of 1375 is a large world map on wooden panels, probably the work of the king of Aragon's mapmaker, Abraham Cresques, a Majorcan Jew. Most of the information for Europe is derived from the mariners' charts known as portolans that were used by Italian and Catalan ships' captains. The main source for China and the Far East, which are far less accurately mapped, is Marco Polo's account of his journeys *(see p.68)*.

The Catalan map gives a comprehensive and accurate picture of the coastline and ports of Europe and North Africa.

Africa

The Islamic Mali Empire controlled the trans-Saharan caravan trade, using the profits to maintain a powerful army and dominate West Africa. Gold and slaves went north in exchange for salt, textiles, horses, and manufactured goods. Tales of the wealth of Mali spread to Europe and West Asia, especially after the ostentatious pilgrimage to Mecca made by one of the country's most powerful rulers, Mansa Musa. Many smaller states emerged in the region as rulers sought to ensure a regular supply of trade goods. The Swahili cities of East Africa were not hit by plague, but commercial traffic declined as their trading partners in Asia experienced social and economic disruption.

West Asia

During the late 14th century the Turkish warrior chieftain Timur (Tamerlane), who claimed descent from Genghis Khan, carved out a vast Central Asian empire, and built himself a magnificent capital at Samarkand. Timur invaded India and sacked the city of Delhi, and he was planning an invasion of China when he died in 1405. One other empire expanded during this period – that of the Ottoman Turks, who seized Anatolia and encroached on Byzantine holdings in southeastern Europe. By 1400 the once-mighty Byzantine Empire consisted of Constantinople and a few coastal regions in Greece and western Anatolia that maintained maritime links with the capital.

Timur's ambition and cruelty revived memories of Genghis Khan. He instilled fear into conquered peoples and opponents of his rule by building towers studded with the severed heads of his victims.

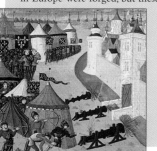
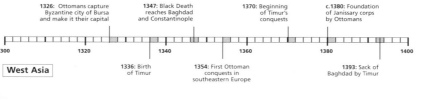

West Asia

1326: Ottomans capture Byzantine city of Bursa and make it their capital
1347: Black Death reaches Baghdad and Constantinople
1370: Beginning of Timur's conquests
c.1380: Foundation of Janissary corps by Ottomans
1336: Birth of Timur
1354: First Ottoman conquests in southeastern Europe
1393: Sack of Baghdad by Timur
1300 1320 1340 1360 1380 1400

East Asia

Plague, floods, and famine all contributed to the buildup of Chinese resentment at Mongol rule. Local uprisings became increasingly frequent, culminating in 1356 in a rebellion in southeastern China, which carried Zhu Yuanzhang, founder of the Ming dynasty, to power. War with the Mongols continued for some years, but the Chinese drove them back to their original homelands in the north. Japan had successfully resisted Mongol attempts at invasion, but their own Kamakura shogunate collapsed in 1333. The new shoguns of the Ashikaga family never succeeded in exercising the same degree of control over the country.

The Ming emperors restored Chinese values after a century of Mongol rule. This statue portrays a guardian of the spirit world.

East Asia

1335: Rebellions against Mongol rule in China
1351: Massive flooding of Yellow River
1392: Foundation of Yi dynasty in Korea
1336: Foundation of Ashikaga shogunate in Japan
1368: Establishment of the Ming dynasty
1300 1320 1340 1360 1380 1400

South and Southeast Asia

In India, the Sultanate of Delhi reached its greatest extent in the reign of Tughluq, but by the end of the century had lost control of most of the peninsula. The small kingdoms of mainland Southeast Asia all maintained diplomatic and commercial links with Ming China. The new Thai kingdom of Siam proved especially skillful in its dealings with its powerful neighbor to the north. During the 14th century island Southeast Asia fell increasingly under the influence of the Majapahit empire based in Java. A Javanese navy, financed by taxes levied on the lucrative trade in spices, patrolled the waters of the archipelago and controlled maritime trade.

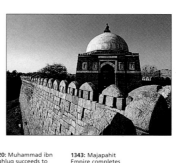

The marble dome of Tughluq's mausoleum rises above the ramparts of the fortified city he built at Delhi in 1321.

Mansa Musa, ruler of Mali, is depicted on the Catalan Atlas of 1375. Europeans were in awe of his reported wealth and the splendor of his court.

Africa

1331: Ibn Battuta's voyage to the Swahili cities of East Africa
1344: Ethiopia at its height at death of ruler Amde Sion
c.1390: Formation of the kingdom of Kongo
1324: Pilgrimage to Mecca by Mansa Musa of Mali
1347: Marinids take Tunis
1352: Ibn Battuta's travels to the Mali Empire
1300 1320 1340 1360 1380 1400

South and Southeast Asia

1320: Muhammad ibn Tughluq succeeds to Sultanate of Delhi
1343: Majapahit Empire completes conquest of Bali
1378: Sukhothai becomes vassal of Siam and is gradually absorbed
c.1350: Founding of Ayutthaya, capital of new kingdom of Siam
1398: Delhi sacked by Timur
1300 1320 1340 1360 1380 1300

Map Labels

Paleosiberians
Samoyeds
Ugrians
Siberia
Lena
Yenisey
Ob
Tungus
Amur
KHANATE OF THE GOLDEN HORDE
KHANATE OF THE OIRATS
Gobi
TREBIZOND
Caspian Sea
Ardabil
SULKADIR
Samarkand
CHAGATAI KHANATE
Yellow River
Beijing
KOREA
JAPAN
MING EMPIRE
Baghdad
EMPIRE OF TIMUR
TIBET
KASHMIR
Himalayas
Yangtze
Bedouins
HARIRS
MEDINA
SHARIFS OF MECCA
Mecca
Arabian Peninsula
OMAN
Delhi
SIND
SULTANATE OF DELHI
Ganges
SHARQIS
MALLA
SMALL STATES
BENGAL
SHAN STATES
CHIENGMAI
ANNAM
KHANDESH
SMALL STATES
ARAKAN
EASTERN GANGAS
JAVA
LAOS
TOUNGOO
BAHMANI KINGDOM
TELINGANA
REDDIS
PEGU
Mekong
CHAMPA
RASULIDS
SUKHOTHAI
SIAM
Ayutthaya
CAMBODIA
ETHIOPIA
IFAT
VIJAYANAGAR
SMALL STATES
Philippine Islands
SIDAMA STATES
Cushites
SWAHILI CITY-STATES
PACIFIC OCEAN
Borneo
MALAY STATES
Malays
Madagascar
INDIAN OCEAN
PAJAJARAN
MAJAPAHIT
Java
Bali
Papuans
New Guinea
Australian Aborigines
Darling
New Zealand
Maoris

TRADE AND BIOLOGICAL DIFFUSION

CAMPAIGNS OF IMPERIAL EXPANSION, mass migration, cross-cultural trade, and long-distance travel all facilitated the spread of agricultural crops, domesticated animals, and diseases throughout much of the Old World. From 500 to 1500 CE, an array of historical processes helped introduce biological species to new regions and peoples. Chinese rulers extended their authority south of the Yangtze River; Muslim armies pushed into India, Persia, and North Africa; Bantu-speaking peoples migrated throughout most of sub-Saharan Africa; Muslim merchants pursued commercial opportunities throughout the Indian Ocean basin and across the Sahara; and missionaries, pilgrims, diplomats, administrators, and other travelers ventured throughout Eurasia and North Africa. Biological exchanges resulting from these changes profoundly influenced the development of societies throughout the eastern hemisphere.

The peripatetic black rat, at home in a wide range of human environments, was the host for plague-carrying fleas.

Skulls, crossbones, and other images of death were frequently represented in both religious and secular art during the period of the so-called "Black Death."

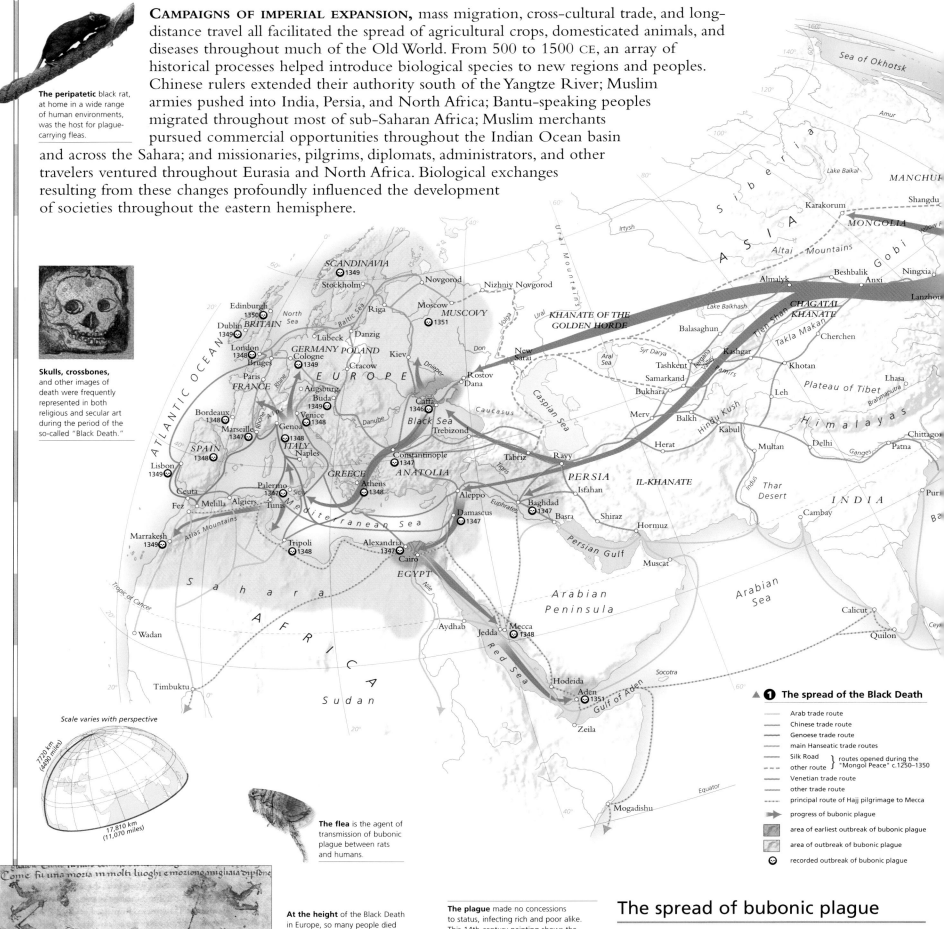

① The spread of the Black Death

- Arab trade route
- Chinese trade route
- Genoese trade route
- main Hanseatic trade routes
- Silk Road ⎫ routes opened during the
- other route ⎭ "Mongol Peace" c.1250–1350
- Venetian trade route
- other trade route
- principal route of Hajj pilgrimage to Mecca
- ➤ progress of bubonic plague
- area of earliest outbreak of bubonic plague
- area of outbreak of bubonic plague
- ☺ recorded outbreak of bubonic plague

Scale varies with perspective

7720 km (4480 miles)

17,810 km (11,070 miles)

The flea is the agent of transmission of bubonic plague between rats and humans.

At the height of the Black Death in Europe, so many people died daily that it was impossible to bury them all separately. The bodies were buried together in mass graves, usually outside the settlement walls. This manuscript illustration shows plague victims carried off by agents of Death.

The plague made no concessions to status, infecting rich and poor alike. This 14th-century painting shows the deathbed of Queen Anne of Bohemia, wife of King Richard II of England.

The spread of bubonic plague

Bubonic plague has long maintained an endemic presence in rodent communities in both Yunnan in southwest China and the Great Lakes region of East Africa. In the early 14th century, Mongol armies helped infected fleas spread from Yunnan to the rest of China. In 1331 an outbreak of plague reportedly carried away 90% of the population in parts of northeast China, and by the 1350s there were widely scattered epidemics throughout China. From China, bubonic plague spread rapidly west along the Silk Roads of Central Asia. By 1346 it had reached the Black Sea. Muslim merchants carried it south and west to southwest Asia, Egypt, and North Africa, while Italian merchants carried it west to Italy and then to northern and western Europe, where it became known as the Black Death. Up to one-third of Europe's population is thought to have died in this one episode.

The spread of plague during the 14th century

1320: Outbreak of plague in Yunnan province

1330: Plague reaches northeastern China

1348: Black Death hits Greece, Italy, France, Spain, Britain, and North Africa

1351: Black Death reaches much of northern Europe

1310   1320   1330   1340   1350   1360

1320–30: Mongol armies help spread plague throughout China

1346: Plague reaches coast of Black Sea

1349: Black Death arrives in central Europe

The changing balance of world population

The spread of diseases and agricultural crops decisively influenced population levels throughout the Old World. In sub-Saharan Africa, for example, bananas grew well in forested regions that did not favor yams and millet, the earliest staples of Bantu cultivators. In 500 CE the population of sub-Saharan Africa was about 12 million, but following the spread of bananas it rose to 20 million by 1000 and 35.5 million by 1500. The spread of fast-ripening rice in China fueled an even more dramatic demographic surge: from 60 million in 1000, when fast-ripening rice went north from Vietnam to the Yangtze river valley, the Chinese population climbed to 100 million in 1100 and 115 million in 1200. However, beginning in the 14th century, bubonic plague raced through densely-populated lands from China to Morocco, thinning human numbers with drastic effect. By 1400, China's population had fallen to about 70 million.

SEE ALSO:

Africa: pp.162–163

Europe: pp.188–193

West Asia: pp.228–229

North and East Asia: pp.262–263

Many people were displaced by the depopulation of the Black Death and the societal changes that it wrought. Those reduced to begging often sought alms at the doors of churches or other religious foundations.

Some towns and villages suffered such depredations in population during the Black Death that they were abandoned by those who were left. The ruined church (left) is one of few remnants of the former village of Calceby, in the fenlands of eastern England.

❷ Distribution of world population c.1400 ▼

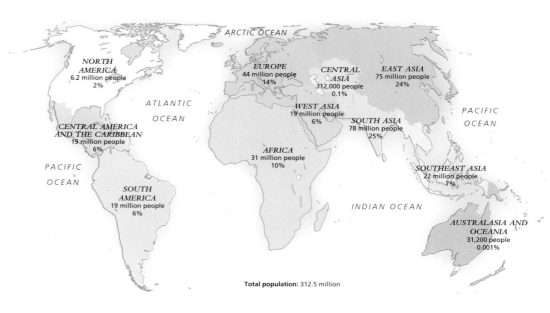

Total population: 312.5 million

❸ The diffusion of staple crops to c.1500 ▶

Original source areas (pre-700)
- bananas
- sugarcane
- cotton
- sorghum

Spread of crops c.700–1500
- spread of bananas
- spread of sugarcane
- spread of cotton
- spread of sorghum

Areas to which crops had spread by 1500
- bananas
- sugarcane
- cotton
- sorghum

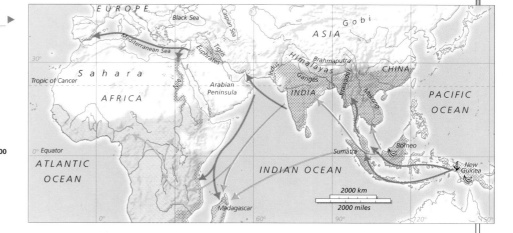

Sugar cane was taken westward to Europe from India from c.600 CE. This 16th-century engraving of a Sicilian sugar mill shows raw sugar being transformed into sugar loaves.

The diffusion of staple crops

A massive diffusion of agricultural crops took place between about 700 and 1400 CE. Most crops spread from tropical or subtropical lands in South and Southeast Asia to the more temperate regions of the eastern hemisphere. Many crops moved with the aid of Muslim merchants, administrators, diplomats, soldiers, missionaries, pilgrims, and other travelers who visited lands from Morocco and Spain to Java and southern China. Sugar cane, native to New Guinea, arrived in the Mediterranean basin as a result of this biological diffusion, along with hard wheat, eggplants, spinach, artichokes, lemons, and limes. Other crops that dispersed widely during this era included rice, sorghum, bananas, coconuts, watermelons, oranges, mangoes, cotton, indigo, and henna.

THE WORLD 1400–1500

BY 1500 MOST OF THE EASTERN HEMISPHERE had recovered from the depopulation caused by the Black Death in the 14th century. China began the 15th century by sponsoring naval expeditions in the Indian Ocean, but in the 1430s the Ming rulers ended these voyages and concentrated on their land empire. In Southwest Asia, two Turkish peoples established strong empires – the Ottomans in Anatolia and the Safavids in Persia. European states, meanwhile, were starting to build central governments with standing armies and gunpowder weapons. In the course of the 15th century Portuguese mariners settled the Atlantic islands, explored the west coast of Africa, and completed a sea voyage to India. It was, however, a Spanish expedition under the Genoese Columbus that crossed the Atlantic to make contact with the Americas, where the Aztec and Inca empires ruled over complex organized agricultural societies.

North America

The Aztec Empire reached its height in the late 1400s, exacting heavy tribute from the small city-states it had conquered. Through trade, Aztec influence reached far beyond the borders of the empire, extending across most of Central America as far as the Pueblo farmers north of the Rio Grande. In the woodlands around the Mississippi River, mound-building peoples maintained sizeable communities based on the cultivation of corn.

Human sacrifice to the sun god Huitzilopochtli was the core of the Aztec religion. Thousands of prisoners might be killed in a single ceremony.

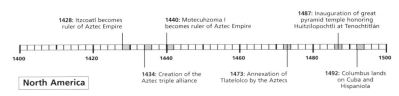

1428: Itzcoatl becomes ruler of Aztec Empire
1440: Motecuhzoma I becomes ruler of Aztec Empire
1487: Inauguration of great pyramid temple honoring Huitzilopochtli at Tenochtitlán

| North America |

1434: Creation of the Aztec triple alliance
1473: Annexation of Tlatelolco by the Aztecs
1492: Columbus lands on Cuba and Hispaniola

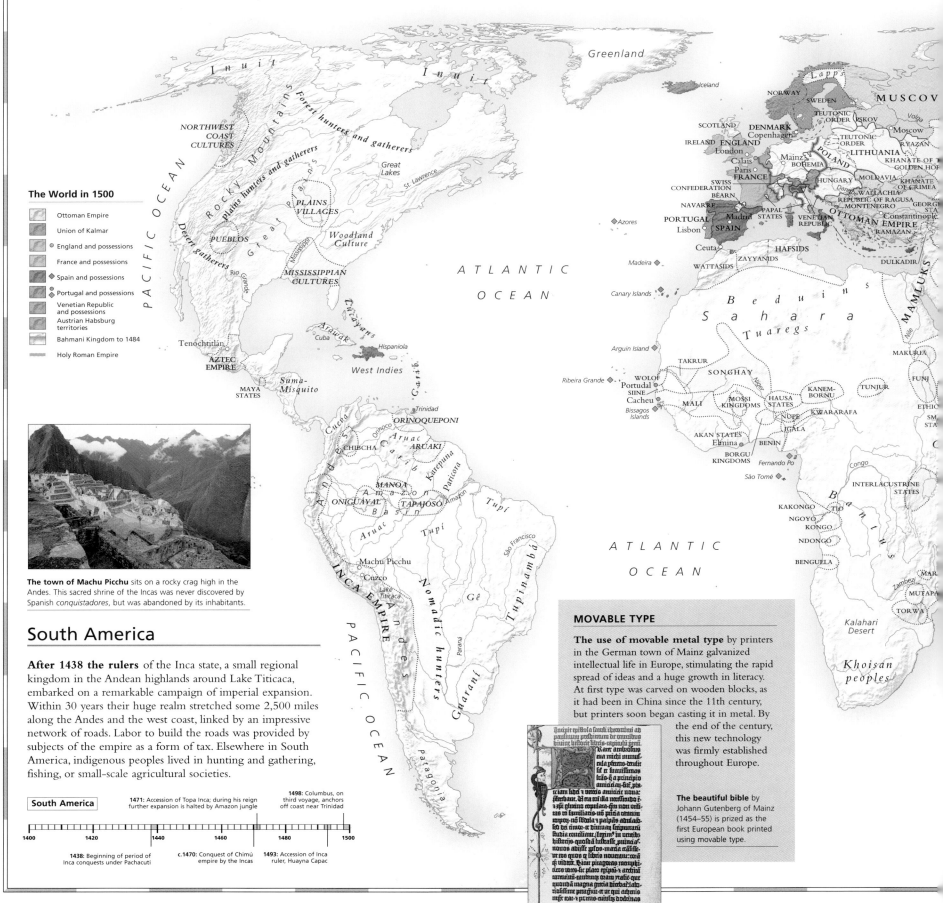

The World in 1500

- Ottoman Empire
- Union of Kalmar
- England and possessions
- France and possessions
- Spain and possessions
- Portugal and possessions
- Venetian Republic and possessions
- Austrian Habsburg territories
- Bahmani Kingdom to 1484
- Holy Roman Empire

The town of Machu Picchu sits on a rocky crag high in the Andes. This sacred shrine of the Incas was never discovered by Spanish *conquistadores*, but was abandoned by its inhabitants.

South America

After 1438 the rulers of the Inca state, a small regional kingdom in the Andean highlands around Lake Titicaca, embarked on a remarkable campaign of imperial expansion. Within 30 years their huge realm stretched some 2,500 miles along the Andes and the west coast, linked by an impressive network of roads. Labor to build the roads was provided by subjects of the empire as a form of tax. Elsewhere in South America, indigenous peoples lived in hunting and gathering, fishing, or small-scale agricultural societies.

| South America |

1471: Accession of Topa Inca; during his reign further expansion is halted by Amazon jungle
1498: Columbus, on third voyage, anchors off coast near Trinidad

1438: Beginning of period of Inca conquests under Pachacuti
c.1470: Conquest of Chimú empire by the Incas
1493: Accession of Inca ruler, Huayna Capac

MOVABLE TYPE

The use of movable metal type by printers in the German town of Mainz galvanized intellectual life in Europe, stimulating the rapid spread of ideas and a huge growth in literacy. At first type was carved on wooden blocks, as it had been in China since the 11th century, but printers soon began casting it in metal. By the end of the century, this new technology was firmly established throughout Europe.

The beautiful bible by Johann Gutenberg of Mainz (1454–55) is prized as the first European book printed using movable type.

Europe

Sixtus IV, elected in 1471, was typical of the popes of the Renaissance. A worldly, nepotistic prince, he commissioned great works of art and architecture, including the Sistine Chapel.

The 15th century saw the start of the Renaissance, a flowering of architecture, art, and humanist idealism inspired by Classical models. The city-states of Italy were the cultural leaders of Europe, but political power was shifting toward the "new monarchs," who created strong, centralized kingdoms in England, France, and Spain. Poland dominated eastern Europe, but here the future lay with Muscovy, where Ivan III launched Russian expansion to the east and south and in 1472 assumed the title of "tsar."

MARTIN BEHAIM'S GLOBE

Martin Behaim was a geographer of Nuremberg who visited Portugal and sailed down the west coast of Africa with Portuguese mariners in the 1480s. His globe, produced in 1490–92, is the oldest surviving globe in the world. Since he knew nothing of the existence of America, he depicted the island of "Cipangu" (Japan) and the east Asian mainland directly across the Atlantic from western Europe.

Martin Behaim's globe gives a very good picture of how Columbus must have imagined the world before he set sail across the Atlantic Ocean.

Europe

1415: English defeat French at Agincourt	1429: English siege of Orléans relieved by Joan of Arc	1454: Peace of Lodi ends wars in Italy	1480: Muscovy throws off Mongol yoke	1492: Muslim Granada falls to Spain

1400 — 1420 — 1440 — 1460 — 1480 — 1500

1417: End of Schism in Catholic church	1453: Fall of Bordeaux to France ends Hundred Years' War	1469: Marriage of Ferdinand of Aragon and Isabella of Castile	1494: Invasion of Italy by Charles VIII of France

West Asia

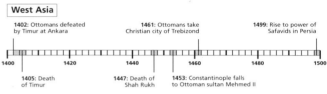

The fall of Constantinople removed the major Christian stronghold barring Islam's spread to the west. The small defending force of Byzantines and Italians was no match for the besieging army of 100,000.

When Timur died in 1405, his empire was divided among his four sons. After a series of quarrels, Shah Rukh, who inherited the eastern part, presided over an era of peace, in which the arts and architecture flourished. The Shaybanids, who expanded south across the Syr Darya, were descendants of Genghis Khan. However, a new power was rising that would eclipse the Mongol dynasties that vied to control Persia – the Shi'ite Safavids. In the west, the Ottoman Turks, led by Sultan Mehmed II ("the Conqueror") and aided by powerful cannons, took Constantinople in 1453 and put an end to the Byzantine Empire.

West Asia

1402: Ottomans defeated by Timur at Ankara	1461: Ottomans take Christian city of Trebizond	1499: Rise to power of Safavids in Persia

1400 — 1420 — 1440 — 1460 — 1480 — 1500

1405: Death of Timur	1447: Death of Shah Rukh	1453: Constantinople falls to Ottoman sultan Mehmed II

This painting on silk shows the courtyards of the Forbidden City, the compound of the imperial palace at the center of Beijing. The Ming capital was moved north from Nanjing to Beijing in 1421 during Yung Luo's campaign against the Mongols.

East and Southeast Asia

The Ming dynasty consolidated its hold on China, rebuilding the Great Wall to prevent raids by Mongol Oirats to the north. After Zheng He's epic but costly voyages in the Indian Ocean, the Ming rulers adopted a policy of self-sufficiency, discouraging travel and trade. In contrast to this defensive, inward-looking attitude, Southeast Asia thrived on trade. The most important entrepôt was Malacca. By 1500 its population was about 50,000, and it was reported that 84 languages could be heard in the city's streets.

East and Southeast Asia

c.1400: Foundation of Malacca	1424: End of long Ming campaign against Mongols	1445: Conversion of Malacca to Islam	1472: Birth of Neoconfucian philosopher Wang Yangming

1400 — 1420 — 1440 — 1460 — 1480 — 1500

1405: Beginning of Zheng He's voyages in Indian Ocean	1449: Mongols defeat Chinese and capture emperor	1471: Annamites expand to south by invading Champa

This bronze statue of a Portuguese soldier was made in Benin, one of Portugal's West African trading partners.

Africa

Between the 1460s and 1490s the Songhay ruler Sunni Ali conquered Mali and took over the Saharan caravan trade. Meanwhile, the Portuguese explored the west coast, where African rulers, seeing opportunities for trade, laid the foundations for the small kingdoms of Akan and Benin. Sailors from the Swahili city-states in East Africa helped Vasco da Gama understand the local monsoon winds and complete his voyage to India.

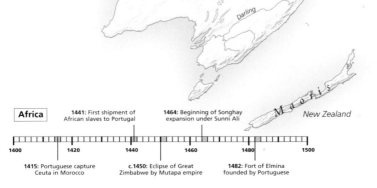

Africa

1441: First shipment of African slaves to Portugal	1464: Beginning of Songhay expansion under Sunni Ali	

1400 — 1420 — 1440 — 1460 — 1480 — 1500

1415: Portuguese capture Ceuta in Morocco	c.1450: Eclipse of Great Zimbabwe by Mutapa empire	1482: Fort of Elmina founded by Portuguese

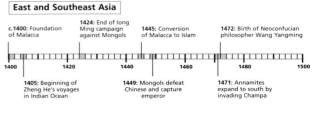

GLOBAL KNOWLEDGE

Knowledge of the world and its peoples was colored by hearsay and travelers' tales.

THE GLOBAL WORLD VIEW is a relatively modern concept. The Americas were unknown to Old World Eurasia until 500 years ago, and each of the major cultural regions had discrete world views of varying extents. Each region had developed its own means of subsistence, and technologies which were direct responses to their immediate environment. In Eurasia, ideas, faiths, and technical achievements were spread by trade, migration, and cultural or political expansion; thus the imprint of Buddhism, Christianity, and Islam was widespread, and technical ideas as diverse as printing and gunpowder, originating in East Asia, had reached Europe. Mapping in one form or another was used by all cultures as a means of recording geographical information and knowledge, although pathfinding and navigation was usually a matter of handed-down knowledge, experience, and word of mouth.

❶ Global economies and technologies c.1500

Principal economies

- hunting and gathering
- herding/pastoralism
- hand cultivation
- plow cultivation
- hand cultivation and hunting and gathering
- slash and burn farming
- terraced farming
- uninhabited

The Americas

Both the Aztecs of Central America and the Incas of the Andes were still in the process of consolidating their young empires when the first Europeans arrived. Although there is evidence in both regions of extensive trading contacts, geographical obstacles (deserts, jungle) and relative immaturity meant their worlds were closely defined.

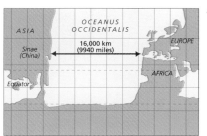

❷ The Americas ▲

- Aztec Empire
- known world 1500
- Inca Empire
- known world 1500

The size of the globe

The rediscovery of Classical texts was an important stimulus to the development of technology, science, and the arts, which flowered in the European Renaissance. European cartographers began to build a more detailed world map, using the works of Classical geographers such as Strabo and Ptolemy. The voyage of Bartolomeu Dias (1487–88) around the Cape of Good Hope established the limits of Africa; but in 1492, when Columbus made landfall in the Caribbean four weeks after leaving the Canary Islands, he assumed he had reached China (Cathay) rather than the West Indies. Although the circumnavigation by Magellan and del Cano some 30 years later (1519–22) dispelled many uncertainties, the accurate charting of the world's oceans and coasts would not be completed until the 20th century.

◀ **❽ The Ptolemaic map of the world**

◀ **❾ The Behaim map of the world 1492**

→ Marco Polo 1271–75
Marco Polo assumed he had travelled 16,000 miles instead of 7000 miles

❿ The modern map of the world

Coasts charted by
- 1500
- 1600
- 1700
- 1800
- 1900

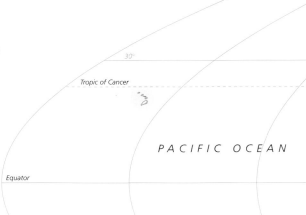

❶ Global economies and technologies c.1500

Significant technologies

• draft animals
- buffalo
- oxen
- horse/mule
- camel
- elephant
- llama/alpaca

• transport
- wheeled vehicles
- dragged vehicles

• hydraulics
- canals
- aqueducts
- irrigation

• architecture
- temporary shelters
- post and lintel
- barrel vaulting
- groin vaulting

• navigation
- riverine
- coastal
- oceanic
- lodestone/compass

• warfare
- thrown missiles
- archery
- gunpowder

• power
- windmills
- watermills

X technology not developed

• recording of knowledge
- knowledge recorded in writing
- knowledge preserved orally
- empirical cartographic tradition

The Muslim World

The most extensive and cosmopolitan of the Old World cultures, by 1500 Islam straddled large extents of three continents, stretching from the islands of the southwest Pacific to the shores of the Atlantic. Knowledge acquired from trade and travel underpinned much Muslim cultural hegemony and scholarship.

❸ The Muslim world ▲

- Muslim heartland
- known world 1500

❻ South Asia ▼

- South Asian states
- known world 1500

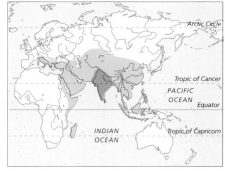

South Asia

In 1500, India was about to become subject to Muslim (Mughal) rule. Nevertheless its position on the crossroads of trade across the Indian Ocean, and overland routes from East and Southeast Asia, dated back many centuries, and its exports were known in Europe. Although essentially inward-looking, South Asian rulers and scholars had an extensive knowledge of the Old World.

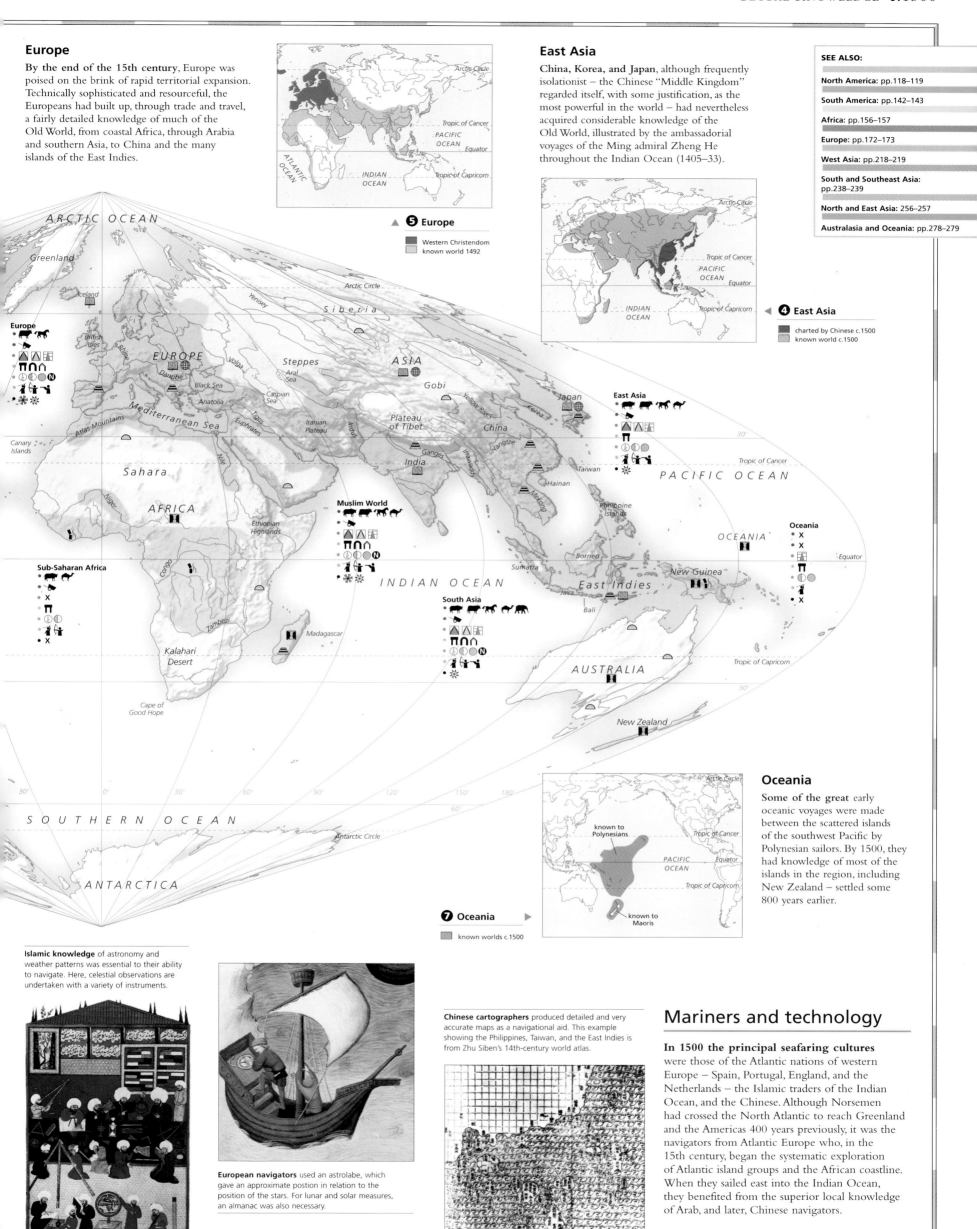

Europe

By the end of the 15th century, Europe was poised on the brink of rapid territorial expansion. Technically sophisticated and resourceful, the Europeans had built up, through trade and travel, a fairly detailed knowledge of much of the Old World, from coastal Africa, through Arabia and southern Asia, to China and the many islands of the East Indies.

East Asia

China, Korea, and Japan, although frequently isolationist – the Chinese "Middle Kingdom" regarded itself, with some justification, as the most powerful in the world – had nevertheless acquired considerable knowledge of the Old World, illustrated by the ambassadorial voyages of the Ming admiral Zheng He throughout the Indian Ocean (1405–33).

SEE ALSO:

North America: pp.118–119

South America: pp.142–143

Africa: pp.156–157

Europe: pp.172–173

West Asia: pp.218–219

South and Southeast Asia: pp.238–239

North and East Asia: 256–257

Australasia and Oceania: pp.278–279

5 Europe
- Western Christendom
- known world 1492

4 East Asia
- charted by Chinese c.1500
- known world c.1500

Oceania

Some of the great early oceanic voyages were made between the scattered islands of the southwest Pacific by Polynesian sailors. By 1500, they had knowledge of most of the islands in the region, including New Zealand – settled some 800 years earlier.

7 Oceania
- known worlds c.1500

known to Polynesians

known to Maoris

Islamic knowledge of astronomy and weather patterns was essential to their ability to navigate. Here, celestial observations are undertaken with a variety of instruments.

European navigators used an astrolabe, which gave an approximate postion in relation to the position of the stars. For lunar and solar measures, an almanac was also necessary.

Chinese cartographers produced detailed and very accurate maps as a navigational aid. This example showing the Philippines, Taiwan, and the East Indies is from Zhu Siben's 14th-century world atlas.

Mariners and technology

In 1500 the principal seafaring cultures were those of the Atlantic nations of western Europe – Spain, Portugal, England, and the Netherlands – the Islamic traders of the Indian Ocean, and the Chinese. Although Norsemen had crossed the North Atlantic to reach Greenland and the Americas 400 years previously, it was the navigators from Atlantic Europe who, in the 15th century, began the systematic exploration of Atlantic island groups and the African coastline. When they sailed east into the Indian Ocean, they benefited from the superior local knowledge of Arab, and later, Chinese navigators.

THE WORLD 1500–1600

IN THE 16TH CENTURY Spain seized a vast land empire that encompassed much of South and Central America, the West Indies, and the Philippine Islands. Meanwhile, the Portuguese acquired a largely maritime empire stretching from Brazil to Malacca and Macao. Ferdinand Magellan, a Portuguese in the service of Spain, demonstrated that all the world's oceans were linked and sea lanes were established through the Indian, Atlantic, and Pacific oceans, creating for the first time a genuinely global trading network. Although the Portuguese traded with the Ming Empire and Japan, cultural contact between Europeans and East Asia was limited. In Africa, too, European impact barely extended beyond the coast. Missionaries took the Catholic faith to distant parts of the Spanish and Portuguese empires, but in Europe the Church of Rome faced the threat of the Reformation, while Catholic kingdoms fought to stem Ottoman expansion in the Mediterranean and into the Habsburg lands of Central Europe.

Europe

The **Protestant Reformation** dominated 16th-century Europe. Rulers in Scandinavia, England, Scotland, and many German states abandoned the Roman church and took over monasteries and the running of church affairs. In France Protestants fought Catholics in a debilitating round of civil wars (1562–98) and religion was a major factor in the Dutch revolt against Spanish rule in 1565. The kings of Spain championed Catholicism and promoted missions worldwide. In the east, Russia's tsars extended their empire to the Caspian Sea and western Siberia.

Spanish troops raid a convoy in a scene typical of the atrocities of the Dutch Wars of Independence.

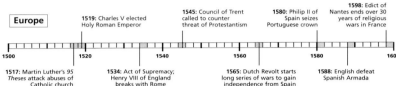

Europe					
	1519: Charles V elected Holy Roman Emperor	**1545:** Council of Trent called to counter threat of Protestantism	**1580:** Philip II of Spain seizes Portuguese crown		**1598:** Edict of Nantes ends over 30 years of religious wars in France
1500	**1520**	**1540**	**1560**	**1580**	**1600**
1517: Martin Luther's 95 Theses attack abuses of Catholic church	**1534:** Act of Supremacy; Henry VIII of England breaks with Rome		**1565:** Dutch Revolt starts long series of wars to gain independence from Spain	**1588:** English defeat Spanish Armada	

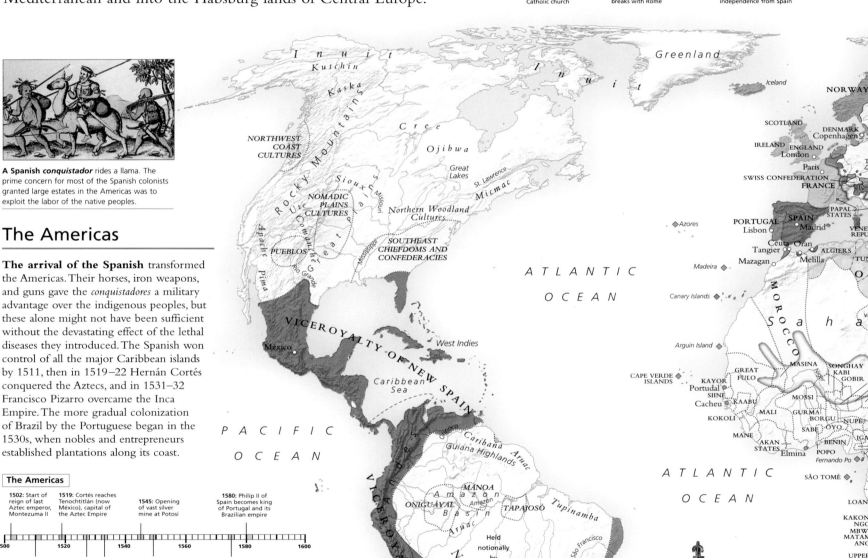

A Spanish *conquistador* rides a llama. The prime concern for most of the Spanish colonists granted large estates in the Americas was to exploit the labor of the native peoples.

The Americas

The arrival of the Spanish transformed the Americas. Their horses, iron weapons, and guns gave the *conquistadores* a military advantage over the indigenous peoples, but these alone might not have been sufficient without the devastating effect of the lethal diseases they introduced. The Spanish won control of all the major Caribbean islands by 1511, then in 1519–22 Hernán Cortés conquered the Aztecs, and in 1531–32 Francisco Pizarro overcame the Inca Empire. The more gradual colonization of Brazil by the Portuguese began in the 1530s, when nobles and entrepreneurs established plantations along its coast.

The Americas					
1502: Start of reign of last Aztec emperor, Montezuma II	**1519:** Cortés reaches Tenochtitlán (now México), capital of the Aztec Empire	**1545:** Opening of vast silver mine at Potosí		**1580:** Philip II of Spain becomes king of Portugal and its Brazilian empire	
1500	**1520**	**1540**	**1560**	**1580**	**1600**
1510: First African slaves brought to Americas	**1527:** Death of Inca emperor Huayna Capac ignites civil war	**1533:** Pizarro captures Inca capital Cuzco	**1549:** Portuguese royal government established in Brazil	**c.1575:** Brazil becomes world's largest sugar producer	

SHIPS OF THE AGE OF EXPLORATION

The ships used by Columbus and other European explorers at the end of the 16th century were usually small caravels between 60 and 200 tons. Square-rigged on the main- and foremasts, they had a lateen sail on the mizzen mast for tacking against the wind. However, once the Spanish and Portuguese had learned to use the trade winds of the Atlantic and Indian oceans, they built huge square-rigged carracks with high castles in the stern. With a laden weight of up to 1,600 tons, they were designed to maximize the cargoes of spices and precious metals shipped back from the East Indies and the Americas.

Columbus made his first crossing of the Atlantic in a square-rigged caravel similar to the model below.

This cast bronze horse and rider is an impressive example of the stylized sculpture of Benin.

Africa

While most of North Africa fell to the Ottoman Empire, Morocco remained an independent champion of Islam, dealing a mortal blow to Portuguese expansion in the region and conquering Songhay to gain control of the valuable trans-Saharan caravan trade. Many of the small West African states had trade links both with Morocco and the Portuguese, who established a fortified trading post at Elmina.

West Asia

In the 16th century the Ottoman Empire expanded into Southwest Asia, North Africa, and southeastern Europe. The Ottoman navy was the preeminent power in the Mediterranean until its defeat by a Christian fleet at Lepanto in 1571, and Muslim vessels dominated the region's shipping. Ottoman rulers clashed constantly with the Safavids in Persia, and in the late 16th and early 17th centuries the two empires fought for control of Mesopotamia and the Caucasus. Many earlier Ottoman gains were reversed during the reign of Shah Abbas the Great, the Safavid ruler from 1588 to 1629.

Suleiman the Magnificent extended Ottoman rule far into southeastern Europe. In this miniature, he is seen receiving homage from his many Christian vassals.

West Asia

1507: Portuguese victory over Ottoman and Arab fleet at Diu
1514: Ottomans victory over Safavids at Chaldiran
1520: Suleiman the Magnificent becomes Ottoman sultan
1526: Battle of Mohács; Ottomans crush Hungarian army
1566: Suleiman succeeded by Selim II
1571: Battle of Lepanto; Ottoman navy defeated by united Christian fleet off Greek coast
1587: Isfahan becomes capital of Safavid Empire
1588: Abbas I the Great becomes Safavid shah

1500 1520 1540 1560 1580 1600

THE NEW WORLD BY ABRAHAM ORTELIUS

Abraham Ortelius was a mapseller from Antwerp whose *Theatrum Orbis Terrarum* of 1570 is considered the first modern atlas. He was not an original cartographer, but he traveled widely in search of reliable sources and his atlas sold well throughout Europe for over 40 years. His map of the New World was a fairly accurate summary of European explorers' knowledge of the Americas and the Pacific. The vast southern continent, *Terra Australis*, a relic of the Classical geography of Claudius Ptolemy, was a feature of most maps of the period. It includes Tierra del Fuego and part of the coast of New Guinea, but the rest is pure conjecture. Ortelius was a contemporary of Gerardus Mercator. Between them, the two great mapmakers did much to shift the center of European cartography from Italy to the Low Countries.

The map gives a fairly accurate picture of Central America and the Caribbean; however, many parts of America had still not been explored by Europeans at all.

SEE ALSO:

North America: pp.124–125

South America: pp.146–149

Africa: pp.162–163

Europe: pp.194–195

West Asia: pp.230–231

South and Southeast Asia: pp.244–247

North and East Asia: pp.264–267

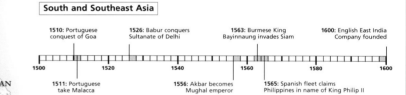

South and Southeast Asia

South and Southeast Asia

1510: Portuguese conquest of Goa
1511: Portuguese take Malacca
1526: Babur conquers Sultanate of Delhi
1556: Akbar becomes Mughal emperor
1563: Burmese King Bayinnaung invades Siam
1565: Spanish fleet claims Philippines in name of King Philip II
1600: English East India Company founded

1500 1520 1540 1560 1580 1600

In 1523 the **Chagatai Turk Babur** invaded northern India, founding the Mughal dynasty of Islamic rulers. The empire was consolidated by Babur's grandson, Akbar. Mughal rulers concentrated on their land empire and agriculture, allowing the Portuguese to maintain coastal trading posts and a flourishing colony at Goa. Portugal also conquered Malacca and the "Spice Islands" of the Moluccas. The dominant power in mainland Southeast Asia was Burma, which reached its largest extent under King Bayinnaung, who conquered Siam and Laos and installed puppet rulers.

The richest prize for European merchants in South and Southeast Asia was control of the valuable spice trade. This French illustration shows the pepper harvest in southern India.

The World in 1600

- Ming Empire
- Ottoman Empire
- Spain and possessions
- Portugal and possessions (ruled by Kings of Spain 1580–1640)
- England and possessions
- Austrian Habsburg territories
- France
- Denmark and possessions
- Venetian Republic and possessions
- United Provinces (fighting for independence from Spain)
- Dutch (United Provinces) possessions
- Mughal Empire at Akbar's accession, 1556
- under Burmese control, 1575
- Songhay to 1590
- Holy Roman Empire

Africa

c.1500: Establishment of forest states of Oyo and Benin
1505: First Portuguese trading posts in East Africa
1517: Ottomans conquer Mamluks in Egypt
1546: Songhay destroys Mali Empire
1570: Establishment of Portuguese colony in Angola
1578: Moroccans crush invading Portuguese
1591: Songhay Empire falls to Morocco

1500 1520 1540 1560 1580 1600

THE AGE OF EUROPEAN EXPANSION

The Portuguese
Vasco da Gama was the first European navigator to reach India by sea.

THE 16TH CENTURY saw the expansion of several of the great European nations far beyond their continental limits. Explorers searching for new sources of luxury goods and precious metals began to open up new territories which monarchs such as Philip II of Spain quickly built up into great empires in the "New World." The Spanish and Portuguese, inspired by the voyages of Columbus and da Gama, led the way, closely followed by the Dutch and the English. The explorers were aided by technological advances in shipbuilding, navigational equipment, and cartography. At the start of the 16th century, the Americas were virtually unknown to Europeans; by 1700, outposts of a greater European empire had been established almost everywhere the explorers landed.

European voyages of expansion and discovery

Spain and Portugal were the leaders of world exploration in the 16th century. In search of maritime trade routes to Asia, the Portuguese found sea lanes through the Atlantic and Indian oceans to India. By 1512, fortified trading posts were in place at Goa and Malacca, and they had reached the "Spice Islands" of the Moluccas in eastern Indonesia. The Spanish, taking a westward route, found the Caribbean islands and the Americas instead. Magellan's three-year global circumnavigation revealed a western route through the Strait of Magellan and across the Pacific Ocean. English and French mariners sought northern passages to Asian markets and their voyages paved the way for the establishment of European settlements in North America.

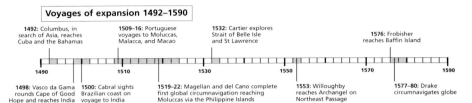

Voyages of expansion 1492–1590

1492: Columbus, in search of Asia, reaches Cuba and the Bahamas

1509–16: Portuguese voyages to Moluccas, Malacca, and Macao

1532: Cartier explores Strait of Belle Isle and St Lawrence

1576: Frobisher reaches Baffin Island

1490   1510   1530   1550   1570   1590

1498: Vasco da Gama rounds Cape of Good Hope and reaches India

1500: Cabral sights Brazilian coast on voyage to India

1519–22: Magellan and del Cano complete first global circumnavigation reaching Moluccas via the Philippine Islands

1553: Willoughby reaches Archangel on Northeast Passage

1577–80: Drake circumnavigates globe

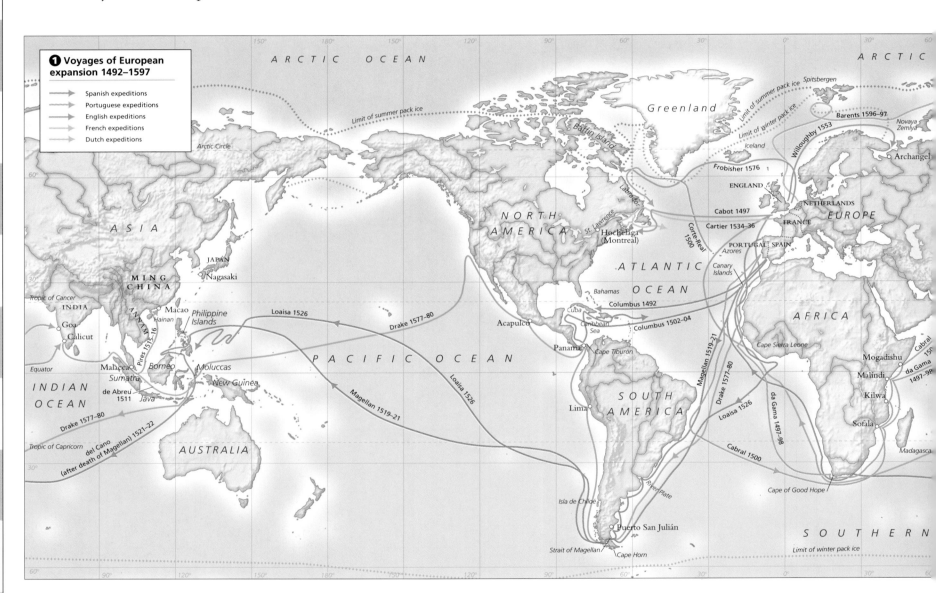

❶ Voyages of European expansion 1492–1597

➤ Spanish expeditions
➤ Portuguese expeditions
➤ English expeditions
➤ French expeditions
➤ Dutch expeditions

Magellan's global circumnavigation was so extraordinary that contemporary artists portrayed him abetted on his voyage by both the latest navigational technology and weaponry, and by mythical creatures such as monsters and mermaids. He was killed by hostile local people in the Philippine Islands in 1521.

EAST MEETS WEST

Europeans and the peoples they encountered in the East had much to learn from one another. Jesuit missionaries were particularly successful at establishing links between China and Japan and the West. During the 1580s, the Jesuit Matteo Ricci informed the Chinese emperor and his court about many European inventions. He presented them with elaborate clocks and taught them about astronomical equipment and weapons such as cannon. His primary purpose was to convert the Chinese to Christianity, using European scientific advances to demonstrate the superiority of European religion. Despite his efforts to accommodate Chinese culture – including the celebration of the mass in Chinese – large-scale conversion eluded him. But much future scientific endeavor was due to these cultural contacts: the revival of Chinese mathematics, the development of the suspension bridge, and early Western experiments in electrostatics and magnetism.

The arrival of Portuguese merchants in Japan is shown below by a Japanese artist. From the mid-16th century, Portuguese traders provided a link between a hostile China and Japan and St. Francis Xavier began a mission to gain new Christian converts. They were soon perceived as a threat to Japanese security and ships which landed were ordered to be confiscated and their crews executed.

❷ Biological exchanges ▶

Origin and movement of plants and animals

- 🐗 from Europe
- 🔴 from America
- ⬤ from Asia

Plants and animals
- 🍌 bananas
- 🌶 chili peppers
- 🐎 horses
- 🌽 corn
- 🌿 manioc
- 🥜 peanuts
- 🥔 potatoes
- 🌾 rice
- ↓ sugarcane
- 🍠 sweet potatoes
- ○ tomatoes
- 🌾 wheat
- 🌱 yams

Diseases
- ➤ bubonic plague
- ➤ diphtheria, influenza, measles, smallpox, and whooping cough
- ➤ syphilis

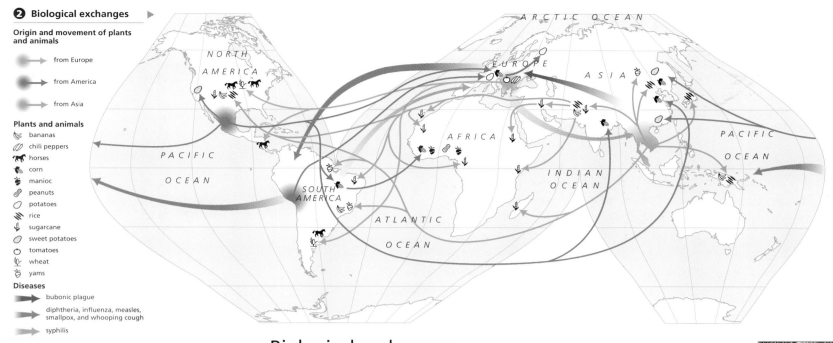

SEE ALSO:

North America: pp.118–119, 122–123

South America: pp.142–143, 148–149

Africa: pp.156–157, 162–163

South and Southeast Asia: pp.238–239, 246–247

North and East Asia: pp.256–257

Australasia and Oceania: pp.278–279

Biological exchanges

The plantain, a herb with medicinal properties, was known as "Englishman's foot" by native North Americans who believed it would grow only where the English had trodden.

European expansion had a profound biological impact. Travelers transported numerous species of fruits, vegetables, and animals from the Americas to Europe. At the same time, settlers introduced European species to the Americas and Oceania. Horses, pigs, and cattle were transported to the western hemisphere where, without natural predators, their numbers increased spectacularly. The settlers consciously introduced food crops, such as wheat, grapes, apples, peaches, and citrus fruits. Some plants, such as nettles, dandelions, and other weeds were inadvertently dispersed by the winds or on the coats of animals. European expansion also led to a spread of European diseases. Vast numbers of indigenous American peoples died from measles and smallpox, which broke out in massive epidemics among populations with no natural or acquired immunity. During the 16th century, syphilis – thought now to be the result of the fusion of two similar diseases from Europe and the New World – killed a million Europeans.

Many more indigenous Americans were killed by smallpox and measles than were slaughtered by the colonizers. Up to 90% of the total population may have perished from European diseases.

❸ The Spanish Empire in 1600 ▶

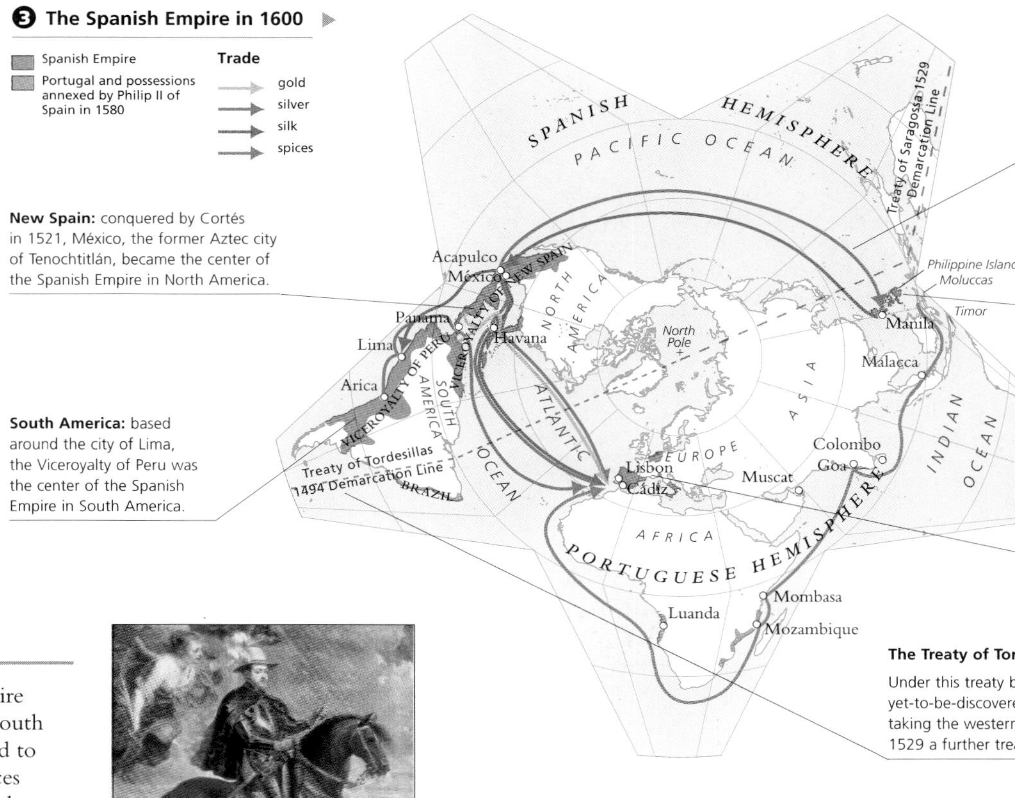

- ▨ Spanish Empire
- ▨ Portugal and possessions annexed by Philip II of Spain in 1580

Trade
- → gold
- → silver
- → silk
- → spices

New Spain: conquered by Cortés in 1521, México, the former Aztec city of Tenochtitlán, became the center of the Spanish Empire in North America.

South America: based around the city of Lima, the Viceroyalty of Peru was the center of the Spanish Empire in South America.

The Manila galleon: brought silver once a year from Acapulco in New Spain to Manila. The silver was used to buy silk, porcelain, and lacquerware which were transported back to New Spain and then to Spain.

The Philippine Islands: first discovered in 1521 by Magellan and claimed for Spain. A governorship and Spanish settlement of the Philippines began in 1565.

Europe: by 1600, the Spanish Empire in Europe included Portugal, Flanders, Naples, and Sicily.

The Treaty of Tordesillas (1494)

Under this treaty between Spain and Portugal, the yet-to-be-discovered world was divided, with Spain taking the western portion and Portugal the east. In 1529 a further treaty divided the eastern hemisphere.

The Spanish Empire

By the end of the 16th century the Spanish Empire included Central America, the West Indies, western South America, and most of the Philippine Islands. The need to safeguard the new lands, their precious natural resources and the new trading networks which evolved, led to the development of a colonial administration of unparalleled scope. Royal authority was vested in the twin institutions of *audiencias*, with political, administrative, and judicial functions, and a series of viceroys, who acted primarily as powerful governors, though they possessed no judicial powers. All information relating to government in the Spanish territories was controlled by specially created councils, the Council of Castile and the Council of the Indies, which met regularly to ensure communication between Spain and the distant possessions of the Spanish Empire.

The New World empire Philip II inherited from his father, Charles V, was greatly expanded after 1580 following the annexation of Portugal, which added Brazil and the East Indies.

The Expansion of the Spanish Empire

- **1494:** Treaty of Tordesillas divides western hemisphere between Spain and Portugal
- **1493:** Columbus establishes first Spanish settlement in western hemisphere
- **1509:** Spanish settlement of mainland Central America begins
- **1519–21:** Cortés conquers Aztec Empire
- **1532–40:** Pizarro conquers Inca Empire
- **1540s:** Potosí becomes greatest single source of silver in the world
- **1564:** System of Atlantic convoys established
- **1565–75:** Spanish conquest of Philippine Islands
- **1571:** Foundation of Manila
- **1580:** Union of Spanish and Portuguese crowns
- **1590:** Silver shipped to Manila almost equal in value to Atlantic trade

1480 · 1500 · 1520 · 1540 · 1560 · 1580 · 1600

(left-hand inset map labels)

OCEAN

Limit of summer pack ice

Arctic Circle

ASIA

JAPAN
Nagasaki

MING CHINA
Macao
Hainan

Tropic of Cancer

INDIA
Goa
Calicut

Philippine Islands
Magellan 1519–21

Pires 1515–16
Malacca
Sumatra
Borneo   Moluccas
de Abreu 1511   Java

Loaisa 1526
Drake 1577–80

Equator

New Guinea

Drake 1577–80

del Cano (after death of Magellan) 1521–22

AUSTRALIA

Tropic of Capricorn

30°

60°

90°   120°   150°

(central projection map labels)

SPANISH HEMISPHERE
PACIFIC OCEAN
Treaty of Saragossa 1529 Demarcation Line

Acapulco
México / NEW SPAIN
NORTH AMERICA
North Pole
ASIA

Panama
Havana
Lima   VICEROYALTY OF PERU
Arica   SOUTH AMERICA

Treaty of Tordesillas 1494 Demarcation Line
BRAZIL
ATLANTIC OCEAN

EUROPE
Lisbon   Cádiz
Muscat
Colombo   Goa
INDIAN OCEAN

Manila
Malacca
Timor
Philippine Islands
Moluccas

AFRICA
Luanda
Mombasa
Mozambique

PORTUGUESE HEMISPHERE

THE WORLD 1600–1700

DURING THE 17TH CENTURY Dutch, British, and French mariners followed Iberians into the world's seas. All three lands established colonies in North America, and all entered the trade networks of the Indian Ocean. British and French mariners searched for a northeast and a northwest passage from Europe to Asia and, although unsuccessful, their efforts expanded their understanding of the world's geography. Dutch incursions into the East Indies began to erode the dominance of the Portuguese empire in this region. Trade between Europe, Africa, North America, and South America pushed the Atlantic Ocean basin toward economic integration, while European trade in the Indian Ocean linked European and Asian markets.

Many European rulers believed that they governed by divine right. Louis XIV of France is here portrayed in a classical fashion which reflects both his supreme power and his belief in his godlike status.

Europe

The ramifications of the Protestant Reformation complicated political affairs in western and Central Europe. The Thirty Years' War (1618–48) ravaged much of Germany, but the Peace of Westphalia that ended the war established a system of states based on a balance of power. This system did not eliminate conflict but maintained relative stability until the French Revolution. The Russian Empire expanded to reach the Pacific Ocean by the mid-17th century as Cossacks and other adventurers established forts throughout Siberia while searching for furs.

Europe

1618: Start of Thirty Years' War
1643: Louis XIV becomes King of France
1648: Thirty Years' War ended by Peace of Westphalia
1682: Peter the Great becomes tsar of Russia

1600 — 1620 — 1640 — 1660 — 1680 — 1700

1611: Accession of Gustavus Adolphus signals Swedish expansion
1649: Execution of Charles I of England
1683: Siege of Vienna ends in Ottoman defeat

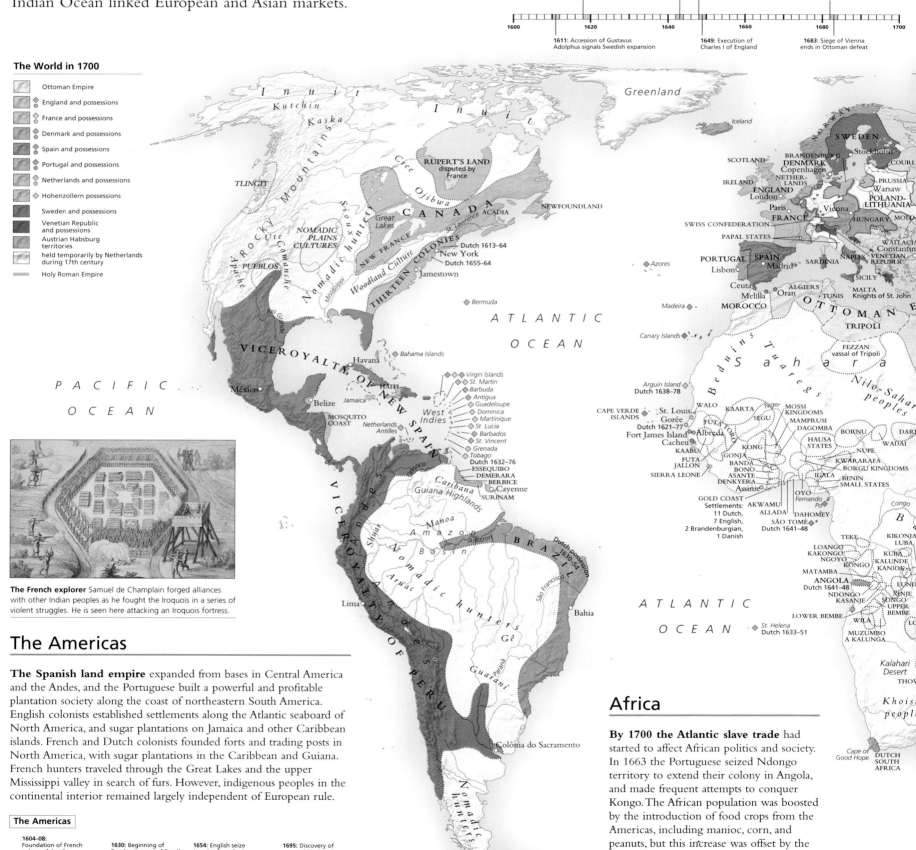

The World in 1700

- Ottoman Empire
- England and possessions
- France and possessions
- Denmark and possessions
- Spain and possessions
- Portugal and possessions
- Netherlands and possessions
- Hohenzollern possessions
- Sweden and possessions
- Venetian Republic and possessions
- Austrian Habsburg territories
- held temporarily by Netherlands during 17th century
- Holy Roman Empire

The French explorer Samuel de Champlain forged alliances with other Indian peoples as he fought the Iroquois in a series of violent struggles. He is seen here attacking an Iroquois fortress.

The Americas

The Spanish land empire expanded from bases in Central America and the Andes, and the Portuguese built a powerful and profitable plantation society along the coast of northeastern South America. English colonists established settlements along the Atlantic seaboard of North America, and sugar plantations on Jamaica and other Caribbean islands. French and Dutch colonists founded forts and trading posts in North America, with sugar plantations in the Caribbean and Guiana. French hunters traveled through the Great Lakes and the upper Mississippi valley in search of furs. However, indigenous peoples in the continental interior remained largely independent of European rule.

The Americas

1604–08: Foundation of French colony of Acadia
1630: Beginning of Dutch conquest of Brazil
1654: English seize Jamaica from Spain
1695: Discovery of gold in Brazil

1600 — 1620 — 1640 — 1660 — 1680 — 1700

1607: Foundation of English colony at Jamestown
1630: Foundation of English Massachusetts Bay colony
1664: English seizure of Dutch colony of New Amsterdam; renamed New York

Africa

By 1700 the Atlantic slave trade had started to affect African politics and society. In 1663 the Portuguese seized Ndongo territory to extend their colony in Angola, and made frequent attempts to conquer Kongo. The African population was boosted by the introduction of food crops from the Americas, including manioc, corn, and peanuts, but this increase was offset by the export of two million slaves from Africa — mainly to the Americas — during the 17th century. States such as Asante, Dahomey, and Oyo raided their neighbors in search of slaves to exchange for European guns.

OPTICAL INSTRUMENTS

The development of telescopes and microscopes geatly advanced human knowledge of both distant objects and those too small to see with the naked eye during the 17th century. The refracting telescope, using a combination of lenses, was first used for observation of the Moon and distant universe by Galileo in 1609. Newton's reflecting telescope, using lenses and mirrors, gave a still clearer picture of the stars and planets. In 1683, Anton van Leeuwenhoek made the first high-powered precision microscope.

A model of Newton's reflecting telescope, made in 1668.

East Asia

In 1644 a Manchu army toppled the Ming dynasty, entered Beijing, and established the Qing dynasty (1644–1911). By the 1680s they had consolidated their hold on southern China, conquered the island of Formosa, and extended Chinese influence far into North and Central Asia. The Qing adapted to Chinese ways and largely preserved the Ming administrative structure. In Japan, the Tokugawa dynasty imposed a central government for the first time. Foreign trade was strictly controlled by both the Chinese and Japanese, confined mainly to Macao in China and Nagasaki in Japan.

The Qing dynasty began their rule with great energy, encouraging many projects for the improvement of their new lands. These workers are building a new dike constructed from timber and brushwood.

SEE ALSO:

North America: pp.126–127

South America: pp.148–149

Africa: pp.164–165

Europe: pp.196–197

West Asia: pp.230–231

South and Southeast Asia: pp.244–245

North and East Asia: pp.268–269

Australasia and Oceania: pp.278–279

East Asia

1603: Establishment of Tokugawa dynasty in Japan
1633: Closure of Japan by Tokugawa shoguns
1644: Manchu forces topple the Ming and establish the Qing dynasty
1654: Kangxi becomes Qing emperor
1683: Conquest of Formosa by Kangxi
1689: Treaty of Nerchinsk between Russia and China; Russians withdraw from Amur basin

JOAN BLAEU'S EASTERN HEMISPHERE

During the 17th century, Dutch mariners and merchants pushed forward the boundaries of the world known to Europeans. Willem Blaeu and his son Joan were official cartographers to the Dutch East India Company (VOC), publishing maps and charts based on the most up-to-date and accurate information provided by explorers, as well as a series of world atlases.

The eastern hemisphere of Joan Blaeu's *Nova et accuratissima totius terrarum orbis tabula*, was first published in his *Atlas Major* in 1662. The map presents a familiar view of Africa, Europe, and most of Asia, although Australia is shown only sketchily.

The Taj Mahal was built by the Mughal emperor Shah Jahan as a mausoleum for his beloved wife, Mumtaz. Exquisitely conceived on a massive scale, it also reflects the great power and wealth of the Mughals.

South and Southeast Asia

Mughal territory was extended by Shah Jahan during the mid-17th century but the empire was increasingly riven by religious intolerance, leading to instability. English and Dutch trading companies consolidated their possessions in the Indian Ocean. The English East India Company built forts and trading posts along the coasts of India, while the Dutch East India Company established headquarters on Java to control the production and distribution of spices from the Moluccas, increasingly taking over territory held by the expansionist sultanate of Mataram.

South and Southeast Asia

1619: Dutch found Batavia as center of trading empire in Southeast Asia
1627: Shah Jahan becomes Mughal emperor
1641: Dutch conquest of Malacca
1658: Aurangzeb becomes Mughal emperor
1663: Dutch complete expulsion of Portuguese from Ceylon
1679: Fleeing Manchus settle in Mekong Delta
1691: South Cambodia organized into two provinces of Annam

Fort Jesus near Mombasa was built by the Portuguese in 1593. It was lost in 1698 following persistent raids by Omani Arabs on Portuguese possessions in East Africa.

1619: African slaves taken to the English colony at Jamestown
1641: Dutch capture Portuguese possessions in Angola
1652: Establishment of Dutch colony at the Cape of Good Hope
1665: Portuguese defeat Kongo at Battle of Mbwila.
1670: Angola gives up attempt to conquer Kongo after defeat of Portuguese army
1698: Omani Arabs capture Mombasa

Africa

TRADING IN HUMAN LIVES

Hugh Crow was a Liverpool trader who made a fortune from slaves in the early 19th century.

THE USE OF SLAVES seems to have been endemic in most human societies. Normally taken as prisoners of war, slaves were also acquired as a form of tribute. The establishment of European colonies and overseas empires between the 16th and 19th centuries saw the creation of a slave trade on an industrial scale, a commerce which laid the foundations for inter-global trading networks. Trading concerns such as the English and Dutch East India companies developed trade on a larger scale than ever before; but it was the need to supply labor for the plantations of the Americas which led to the greatest movement of peoples across the face of the earth.

The Atlantic slave trade

From the late 15th to the early 19th century, European merchants – especially the British and Portuguese – carried on a massive trade in African slaves across the Atlantic. As well as utilizing the established sources of slaves from the Central and West African kingdoms, they also raided coastal areas of West Africa for additional supplies of slaves. European manufactured goods, especially guns, were exchanged for slaves destined to work as agricultural laborers on plantations in the Caribbean and the tropical Americas. Slaves transported to the western hemisphere may have numbered 12 million or more.

Conditions on the terrible "Middle Passage" from the slave ports of West Africa to the New World improved little over the centuries, although the death rate declined because journey times decreased significantly. Between four and five million people are thought to have perished before reaching the Americas.

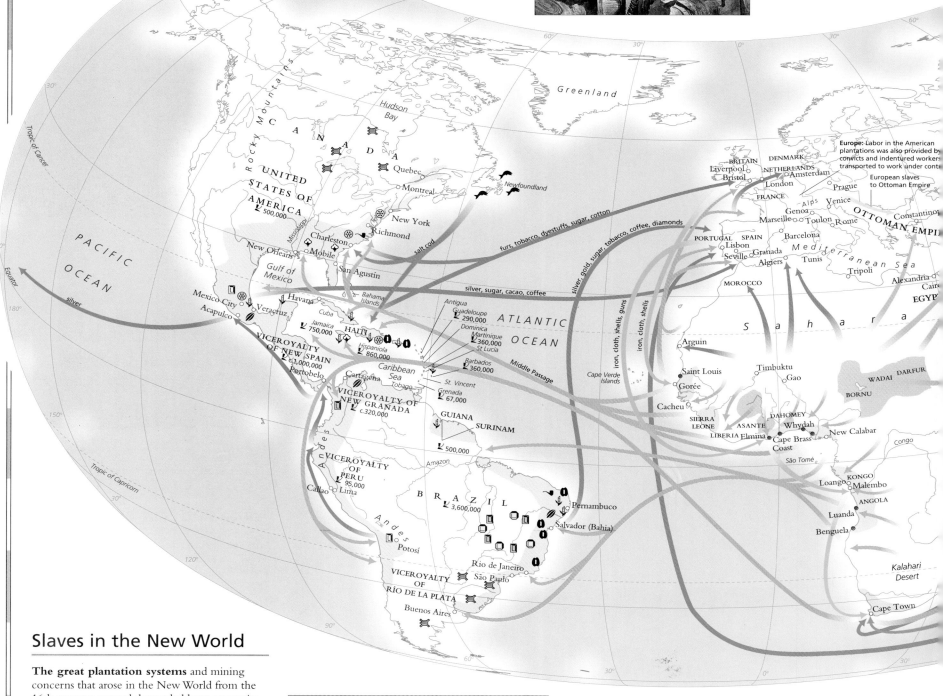

Slaves in the New World

The great plantation systems and mining concerns that arose in the New World from the 16th century onward demanded large reservoirs of labor. Though the Spanish and Portuguese initially used enslaved indigenous people, they soon required a more reliable source of labor. The Portuguese began bringing African slaves to the Caribbean and Brazil in the early 16th century. The cotton plantations of the southern US, which boomed in the early 19th century, were a key factor in sustaining the Atlantic trade.

Slaves planting sugarcane cuttings in specially-prepared plots on an Antiguan plantation in 1823 illustrate the labor-intensiveness of plantation agriculture. As European colonies, the Caribbean islands concentrated on cash crops such as sugar, coffee, and spices.

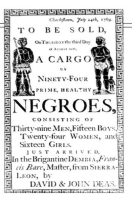

Slaves were sold at auction at ports such as Charleston, South Carolina. They swelled the population of southern North America: in the early 18th century, they comprised more than half of South Carolina's population

Other slave trades

By the 9th and 10th centuries, a number of complex slave-trading routes were in existence in Europe and the Near East. Viking and Russian merchants traded in slaves from the Balkans who were often sold to harems in southern Spain and North Africa. The Baghdad Caliphate drew slaves from western Europe via the ports of Venice, Prague, and Marseille, and Slavic and Turkic slaves from eastern Europe and Central Asia. In the 13th century, the Mongols sold slaves at Karakorum and in the Volga region. There was long-standing commerce in African slaves – primarily from East Africa before European mariners entered the slave trade. Between the 9th and 19th centuries Muslim merchants may have transported as many as 14 million across the Sahara by camel caravan and through East African ports, principally to destinations in the Indian Ocean basin.

This illustration from a 13th-century Arabic manuscript shows Africans and Europeans for sale at a slave market. Arab slave traders drew slaves from much of mainland Europe, Central Asia, and Africa.

SEE ALSO:

North America: pp.126–127, 130–131

South America: pp.148–149

Africa: pp.162–165

Slave trades

	1502: Introduction of African slaves to the Caribbean		1739: Stono rebellion in South Carolina	1791: Slave revolt in Haiti	1804: Foundation of independent Haitian state	1867: Last known arrival of a slave ship in Cuba

1450 — 1500 — 1550 — 1600 — 1650 — 1700 — 1750 — 1800 — 1850 — 1900

1479: Treaty of Alcaçovas permits Portuguese importation of slaves into Spain
1522: First American slave revolt in Hispaniola
1685: French *Code Noir* restricts slavery in French Caribbean colonies
1807: Slave trade outlawed in Britain
1850: Effective end of slave trade in Brazil
1863: Emancipation proclamation frees slaves in Confederate states*

* 13th Amendment to the Constitution (passed 1865) ended slavery in full in the US

❶ The world slave trade 1400–1860

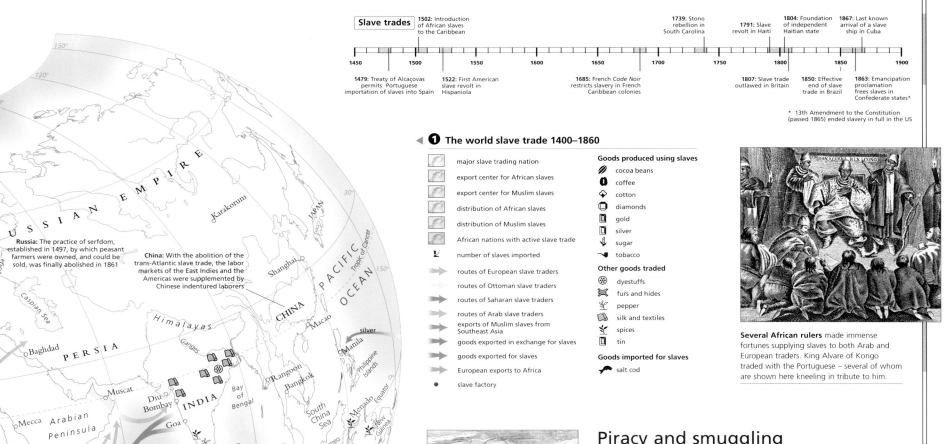

- major slave trading nation
- export center for African slaves
- export center for Muslim slaves
- distribution of African slaves
- distribution of Muslim slaves
- African nations with active slave trade
- number of slaves imported
- routes of European slave traders
- routes of Ottoman slave traders
- routes of Saharan slave traders
- routes of Arab slave traders
- exports of Muslim slaves from Southeast Asia
- goods exported in exchange for slaves
- goods exported for slaves
- European exports to Africa
- slave factory

Goods produced using slaves
- cocoa beans
- coffee
- cotton
- diamonds
- gold
- silver
- sugar
- tobacco

Other goods traded
- dyestuffs
- furs and hides
- pepper
- silk and textiles
- spices
- tin

Goods imported for slaves
- salt cod

Russia: The practice of serfdom, established in 1497, by which peasant farmers were owned, and could be sold, was finally abolished in 1861

China: With the abolition of the trans-Atlantic slave trade, the labor markets of the East Indies and the Americas were supplemented by Chinese indentured laborers

Several African rulers made immense fortunes supplying slaves to both Arab and European traders. King Alvare of Kongo traded with the Portuguese – several of whom are shown here kneeling in tribute to him.

Piracy and smuggling

High volumes of trade in lucrative commodities created abundant opportunities for piracy, privateering, and smuggling. Predators were most active in relatively unpoliced Caribbean and American waters. The numerous tiny islands, hidden harbors, and dense, tropical vegetation – and the access it provided to valuable cargoes of sugar, rum, silver, and slaves – made the Caribbean a notorious hotspot for piracy and smuggling. Some predators were privateers who worked with the blessing of their home governments, such as Sir Francis Drake, but most maritime predators were freelance pirates, who selected their victims without discrimination.

Henry Morgan was a Welsh buccaneer who made a number of successful raids on Spanish ships and territory in the late 17th century – the most devastating being the destruction of Panamá in 1671.

This iron headcollar was one of number of cruel devices designed for the restraint of slaves.

❷ Piracy in the Caribbean in the 16th and 17th centuries ▷

Routes of privateers
- John Hawkins 1562
- John Hawkins 1565
- John Hawkins 1567
- Sir Francis Drake 1571
- Sir Francis Drake 1572–73
- Sir Francis Drake 1577–80
- Sir Francis Drake 1585–86
- Piet Heyn 1623–28
- Edward Mansvelt 1665
- Francois l'Olonnois 1667
- Henry Morgan 1668
- Henry Morgan 1669
- Henry Morgan 1670
- treasure ship seized
- sack or capture of island or city (colour shows privateer)
- conflict with Spain

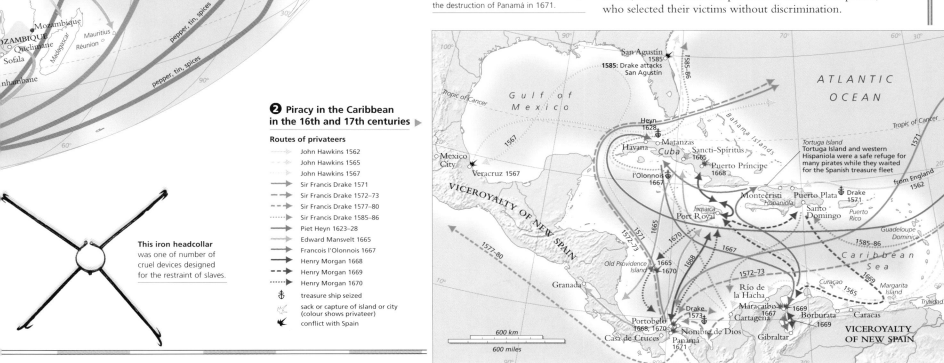

THE WORLD 1700–1800

FROM THE BEGINNING of the 18th century, new ideas in science, philosophy, and political organization fueled change throughout the world. Popular reaction against the *ancien régime* in both France and North America led to the overthrow of the ruling governments. Improvements in agricultural techniques and land reform increased food production, and the population – especially in Europe – began to expand rapidly. Technological innovations in Europe led to the beginning of the Industrial Revolution and consequent urban growth. The expansion of European influence and territorial possessions throughout the world continued apace, with explorers charting the scattered islands of the Pacific and Britain establishing its power in India and Australia.

On January 21, 1793, the French king, Louis XVI, was guillotined in front of a huge Parisian crowd. His wife, Marie Antoinette, was executed later in the year.

Europe

Throughout Europe, government became more powerful, especially in the Russia of Peter the Great and the Prussia of Frederick the Great. In France, Bourbon monarchy had reached its peak during the reign of Louis XIV (1643–1715). Revolutionary ideas unleashed by the "enlightenment," combined with political relaxation, created an incendiary situation, leading in 1789 to the French Revolution whose effects reverberated throughout Europe.

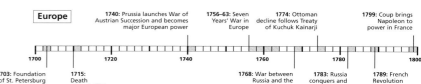

Europe					
	1740: Prussia launches War of Austrian Succession and becomes major European power	1756–63: Seven Years' War in Europe	1774: Ottoman decline follows Treaty of Kuchuk Kainarji	1799: Coup brings Napoleon to power in France	
1700	1720	1740	1760	1780	1800
1703: Foundation of St. Petersburg by Peter the Great	1715: Death of Louis XIV		1768: War between Russia and the Ottomans	1783: Russia conquers and annexes Crimea	1789: French Revolution begins

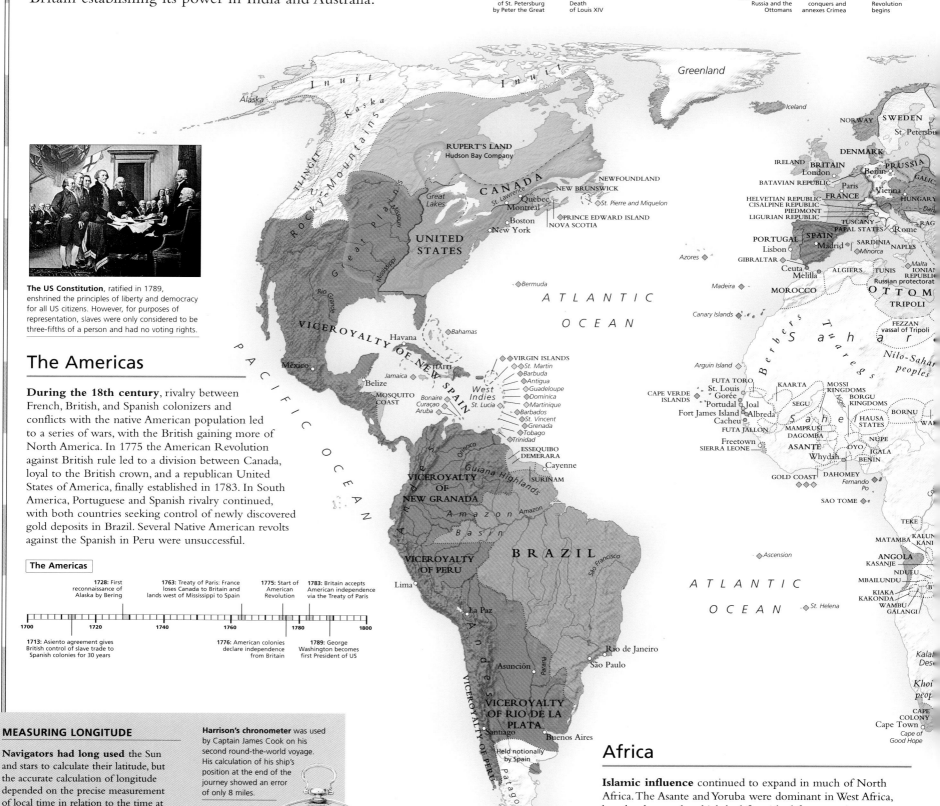

The US Constitution, ratified in 1789, enshrined the principles of liberty and democracy for all US citizens. However, for purposes of representation, slaves were only considered to be three-fifths of a person and had no voting rights.

The Americas

During the 18th century, rivalry between French, British, and Spanish colonizers and conflicts with the native American population led to a series of wars, with the British gaining more of North America. In 1775 the American Revolution against British rule led to a division between Canada, loyal to the British crown, and a republican United States of America, finally established in 1783. In South America, Portuguese and Spanish rivalry continued, with both countries seeking control of newly discovered gold deposits in Brazil. Several Native American revolts against the Spanish in Peru were unsuccessful.

The Americas					
	1728: First reconnaissance of Alaska by Bering	1763: Treaty of Paris: France loses Canada to Britain and lands west of Mississippi to Spain	1775: Start of American Revolution	1783: Britain accepts American independence via the Treaty of Paris	
1700	1720	1740	1760	1780	1800
1713: Asiento agreement gives British control of slave trade to Spanish colonies for 30 years			1776: American colonies declare independence from Britain	1789: George Washington becomes first President of US	

MEASURING LONGITUDE

Navigators had long used the Sun and stars to calculate their latitude, but the accurate calculation of longitude depended on the precise measurement of local time in relation to the time at the Greenwich meridian. The invention by John Harrison of an accurate ship's chronometer in 1762 enabled navigators to calculate their position far more precisely, greatly reducing the risk of shipwrecks, and shortening journey times.

Harrison's chronometer was used by Captain James Cook on his second round-the-world voyage. His calculation of his ship's position at the end of the journey showed an error of only 8 miles.

Africa

Islamic influence continued to expand in much of North Africa. The Asante and Yoruba were dominant in West Africa, but the slave trade which had flourished for centuries throughout much of Africa was internationalized and greatly magnified by European influence in this period. Over 13.5 million people left Africa as slaves during the 1700s. West Africans and Angolans were shipped to the New World – especially Brazil – and northern Africa traded with the Ottoman Empire. In southern Africa, Dutch and British colonists struggled for supremacy against organized Xhosa resistance.

CAPTAIN COOK'S MAP OF NEW ZEALAND

Until the 18th century Oceania and the South Seas remained a mystery to most navigators. The English sailor Captain James Cook made three exploratory voyages to the South Pacific between 1768 and 1779. This map of New Zealand was made on Cook's first voyage. His ship, the *Endeavour*, traced the coast to make this remarkably accurate map.

Cook's map was the first accurate representation of New Zealand and copies were issued to map publishers all over Europe.

By the late 18th century, many Indian rulers, such as the Nawab of Bengal, had assigned administrative powers to the British.

South and West Asia

The Persians under Nadir Shah began to challenge the Ottomans and pushed eastward into Mughal India, even sacking the city of Delhi in 1739. By the middle of the 18th century, the Marathas were emerging as successors to the Mughals, but they were comprehensively defeated by an Afghan army at Panipat in 1761. By the end of the century, the British East India Company had established firm control over much of India via a series of effective military campaigns.

South and West Asia timeline:

- 1707: Death of Aurangzeb heralds decline of Mughal power in India
- 1722–36: Subjugation of Afghans by Persia
- 1736: Nadir Shah becomes Shah of Persia
- 1747: Foundation of Afghanistan by Ahmad Khan Abdali
- 1757: Robert Clive defeats Bengalis at battle of Plassey
- 1761: British destroy French power in India following seizure of Pondicherry
- 1765: Bengal comes under British control
- 1775: First Anglo-Maratha war
- 1786: Start of Qadjar dynasty in Persia
- 1799: Conquest of Mysore ends challenge to British power in southern India
- 1796: British conquest of coastal Ceylon

East Asia, Southeast Asia, and Oceania

The Qing dynasty extended its empire to include a protectorate over Tibet and the conquest of Xiankiang (Dzungaria) by 1760. By 1790, the Chinese population had virtually tripled to 300 million. Trade in tea, porcelain, and silk with Russia and the West boosted the economy, and Manchu China was able to resist European incursion. The kingdoms of Southeast Asia were frequently at war, and subject to invasion by the Chinese, as with Burma in 1765–69. Though the Portuguese and Dutch had set up trading ports, much of the East Indies had yet to be formally colonized.

East Asia, Southeast Asia, and Oceania timeline:

- 1716: Start of Kyoho era in Japan
- 1751: Tibet, Dzungaria, and the Tarim Basin overrun by the Chinese
- 1752: Start of Konbaung dynasty in Burma
- 1755: Alaungpaya founds Rangoon and reunites Burma
- 1765–69: Manchus invade Burma
- 1768: Captain James Cook starts exploration of Pacific
- 1774: Nguyen Anh becomes emperor of Vietnam
- 1788: First British settlement at Botany Bay in Australia

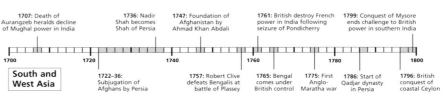

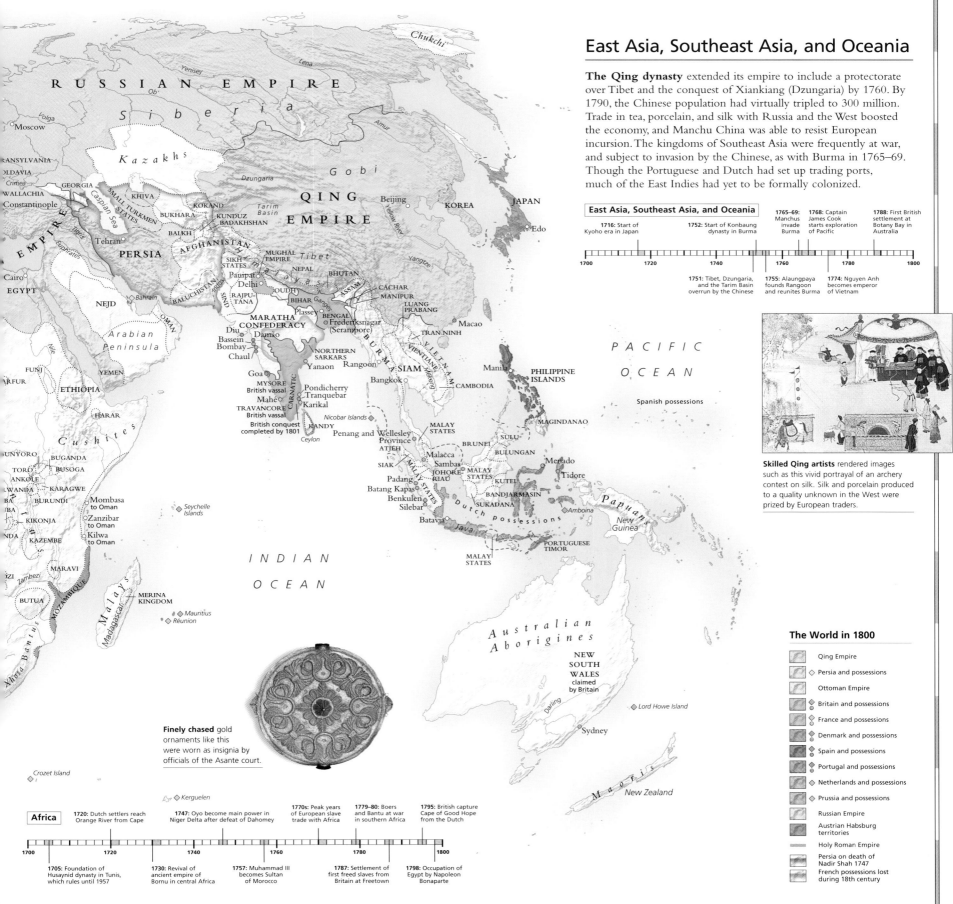

Finely chased gold ornaments like this were worn as insignia by officials of the Asante court.

Skilled Qing artists rendered images such as this vivid portrayal of an archery contest on silk. Silk and porcelain produced to a quality unknown in the West were prized by European traders.

The World in 1800

- Qing Empire
- Persia and possessions
- Ottoman Empire
- Britain and possessions
- France and possessions
- Denmark and possessions
- Spain and possessions
- Portugal and possessions
- Netherlands and possessions
- Prussia and possessions
- Russian Empire
- Austrian Habsburg territories
- Holy Roman Empire
- Persia on death of Nadir Shah 1747
- French possessions lost during 18th century

Africa timeline:

- 1705: Foundation of Husaynid dynasty in Tunis, which rules until 1957
- 1720: Dutch settlers reach Orange River from Cape
- 1730: Revival of ancient empire of Bornu in central Africa
- 1747: Oyo become main power in Niger Delta after defeat of Dahomey
- 1757: Muhammad III becomes Sultan of Morocco
- 1770s: Peak years of European slave trade with Africa
- 1779–80: Boers and Bantu at war in southern Africa
- 1787: Settlement of first freed slaves from Britain at Freetown
- 1795: British capture Cape of Good Hope from the Dutch
- 1798: Occupation of Egypt by Napoleon Bonaparte

EMPIRE AND REVOLUTION

João V, king of Portugal from 1706–50, used most of the gold imported from his colonies in Brazil to finance his own grandiose building schemes.

RAPID POPULATION GROWTH, the creation of the first industrial societies, the maturing of Europe's American colonies, and new ideas about statehood and freedom of the individual, combined to create an overwhelming demand for political change in the late 18th century. Royal tax demands to finance expensive wars, and their often harsh attempts to control imperial subjects, became major focuses of discontent. The success of the Americans in their rebellion against British rule, and the total rejection of royal authority in favor of representative government during the French Revolution, had profound repercussions throughout Europe, with the revolutionary flame lit on numerous occasions from the 1790s onward.

❷ An era of revolution 1768–1868 ▶

- area gaining independence from imperial control c.1750–1850
- area resisting imperial control or expansion c.1750–1850
- Britain and possessions
- Netherlands and possessions
- Spain and possessions
- France and possessions
- Portugal and possessions
- Denmark and possessions
- Russia and possessions
- ▲ independence achieved following war or revolution with date of independence
- European revolution or uprising 1750–1830 with date
- European revolution or uprising after 1830 with date
- area affected by 1848 revolutions
- important non-European uprising with date

War on a global scale

With the acquisition of new territories overseas during the 18th century, the major European powers often transferred their local conflicts to a far wider arena. The Seven Years' War (1756–63) was fought in the colonies as well as in Europe, with Britain able to take control of the Atlantic and defeat the French in North America. A few years later, however, French support for the American rebels and the resurgence of French naval power thwarted Britain's attempts to hold on to its American colonies. The position was reversed in India, where British victory at Plassey in 1757 gave her vital control of the state of Bengal, and enabled the rapid expansion of British India.

The signing of the Treaty of Paris in 1763 ended seven years of bitter fighting between Britain and France in North America. Great celebrations were held in London's Green Park to mark the agreement.

The export of European conflict

1743: King George's War between Britain and France in North America lasts until 1748
1754: French-Indian War between France and Indian allies and Britain
1757: British victory at battle of Plassey in northern India
1760: End of French resistance in North America; Britain gains control of much of French America

1740 — 1750 — 1760 — 1770

1744: Britain and France join Carnatic War in India
1756: Start of Seven Years' War in Europe parallels conflict in North America
1758: British take Senegal in West Africa from French
1758–61: British victorious over French at Fort St. David and Pondicherry in India
1763: Treaty of Paris ends Seven Years' War

❶ The European empires and the first world wars ▼

- Britain and possessions c.1750
- Dutch possessions c.1750
- Spain and possessions c.1750
- France and possessions c.1750
- Portugal and possessions c.1750
- Denmark and possessions c.1750
- Russia and possessions c.1750
- maximum area of French control in India c.1751
- ceded to Spain 1763
- ceded to Britain by 1766
- maximum area of British control in India by 1815
- ◇ Dutch acquisition
- ◇ British acquisition
- ◇ French acquisition
- ◇ Spanish acquisition
- ◇ Portuguese acquisition
- ◇ Russian acquisition
- ◇ Danish acquisition
- ⚔ colonial conflict
- ✕ battle, with date

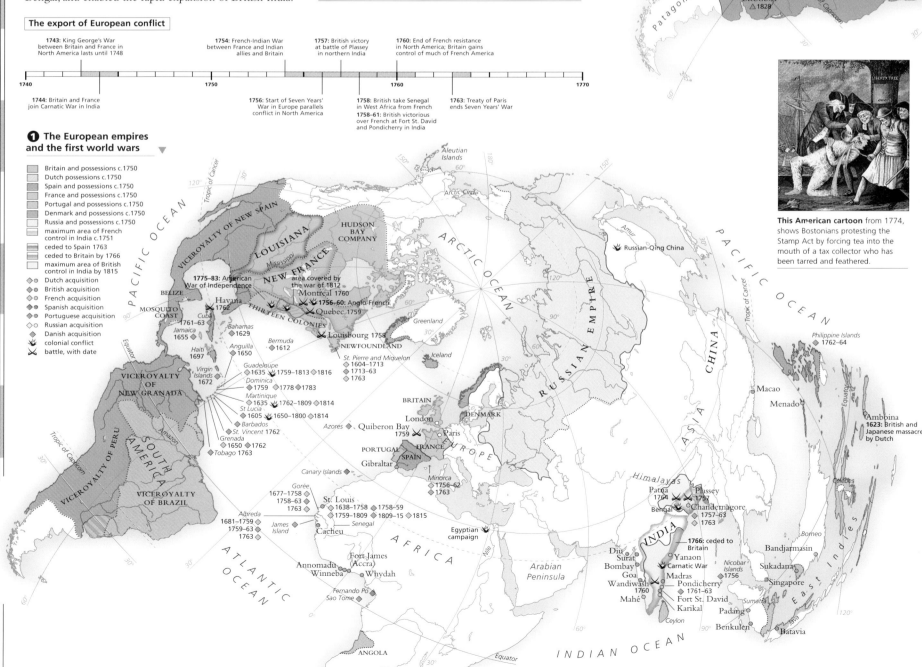

This American cartoon from 1774, shows Bostonians protesting the Stamp Act by forcing tea into the mouth of a tax collector who has been tarred and feathered.

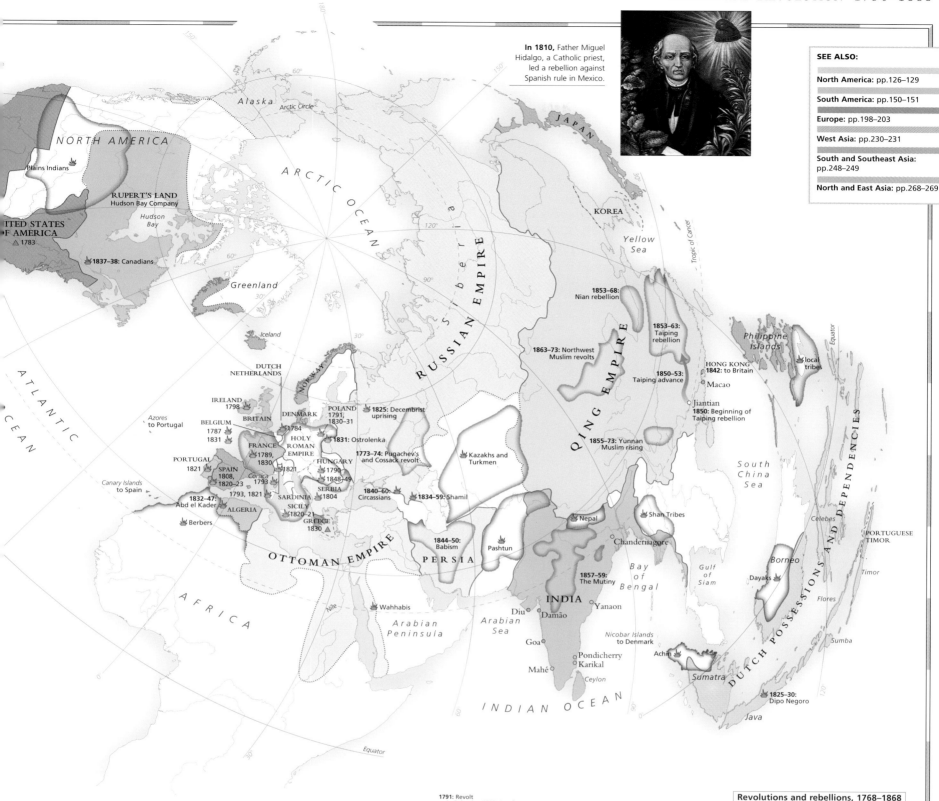

In 1810, Father Miguel Hidalgo, a Catholic priest, led a rebellion against Spanish rule in Mexico.

SEE ALSO:

North America: pp.126–129

South America: pp.150–151

Europe: pp.198–203

West Asia: pp.230–231

South and Southeast Asia: pp.248–249

North and East Asia: pp.268–269

The era of revolution

The first serious challenges to absolutist monarchy and exploitative imperial rule came in the late 18th century, with Pugachev's revolt in Russia, the American Revolution against British colonial rule, and most influentially, the French Revolution of 1789. Uprisings continued in central and eastern Europe into the early 19th century, and the 1808 revolution in Spain spilled over into Spanish America, where a series of successful independence campaigns began in 1810. Periodic attempts to reestablish the old regime were continually met by risings, culminating in the "year of revolutions" in 1848, when the fall of Louis Philippe in France inspired uprisings across most of Europe.

Revolutions and rebellions, 1768–1868

1773: Risings in southeast Russia led by Pugachev
1768: Revolt in Geneva
1775: Start of American War of Independence
1784: Risings in Dutch Netherlands
1791: Revolt in Poland
1791: Revolution in Haiti
1789: Start of French Revolution
1790: Revolt in Hungary
1793: Revolt in Sardinia
1793: Rebellion in Corsica
1798: Revolt in Ireland
1804: Revolt in Serbia
1808: Revolution in Spain
1810: Start of revolutions in Spanish America: by 1826 all Spanish colonies in South America have gained independence
1848: Year of revolution in Europe
1850s: Taiping rebellions and control in China
1850s: Muslim rebellions in China
1853–68: Nian rebellion in China

Delacroix's famous painting *Liberty on the Barricades*, became a banner of inspiration to French (and other European) revolutionary movements during the 19th century.

❸ The revolution in Haiti

Haiti: a post-revolutionary state

In 1791, fired by the French Revolution, slaves in the prosperous French colony of Saint-Domingue rebelled, and by 1794, slavery was abolished. In 1801, rebel forces entered Spanish Santo Domingo, briefly uniting the whole island. Intervention by British and French forces failed to stop Haiti declaring its independence in 1804.

Toussaint l'Ouverture, a former slave, led the revolt of 1791, but did not declare Haiti fully independent. As a concession, he was appointed governor-general by the French in 1801. When French troops were sent to the island in 1802, Toussaint was forced to make terms with the commander of the invasion force. Subsequently betrayed, he died in prison in France in 1803.

THE WORLD 1800–1850

THE AFTERMATH OF THE FRENCH and American revolutions and the Napoleonic wars led to a new nationalism and demands for democracy and freedom. The colonial regimes of South America were overthrown, and in Europe, Belgium and Greece gained independence. The US and northern Europe were transformed by the Industrial Revolution, as mass production and transportation led to an economic boom. There were mass movements of peoples to the expanding cities or to new lives abroad. Hunger for raw materials to feed industry and the desire to dominate world markets was soon to lead to unprecedented colonial expansion. In the US, Australia, and New Zealand, indigenous peoples were fighting a futile battle for their homelands.

A series of major innovations put Britain at the forefront of industrial development. The Nielsen hot blast process, invented in 1824, made iron smelting more efficient.

Europe

The Napoleonic Empire convulsed the established European order, abolishing states and national institutions. While liberals preached democracy, the ruling class responded with repressive measures to restrict freedom of speech and political expression. By the late 1840s civil unrest in the growing cities, bad harvests, and economic crisis led to open rebellion. In 1848, Louis Philippe of France was forced to abdicate, and revolution broke out throughout Europe.

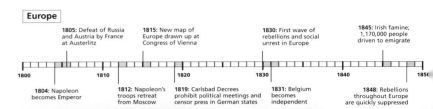

Europe

| 1800 | 1810 | 1820 | 1830 | 1840 | 1850 |

1805: Defeat of Russia and Austria by France at Austerlitz
1815: New map of Europe drawn up at Congress of Vienna
1830: First wave of rebellions and social unrest in Europe
1845: Irish famine; 1,170,000 people driven to emigrate

1804: Napoleon becomes Emperor
1812: Napoleon's troops retreat from Moscow
1819: Carlsbad Decrees prohibit political meetings and censor press in German states
1831: Belgium becomes independent
1848: Rebellions throughout Europe are quickly suppressed

North America

The acquisition of new territories opened up the vast interior of North America to new settlement. Settlers pushing across the plains in search of fertile land and new wealth came into bloody conflict with Native Americans who, equipped with both horses and guns, proved to be formidable foes. The mechanization of agriculture increased exports of wheat, tobacco, and cotton and as the economy prospered, cities expanded and immigrants arrived in great numbers.

The intensive plantation economy of the southern US was dependent on slave labor to pick cotton and harvest tobacco.

North America

| 1800 | 1810 | 1820 | 1830 | 1840 | 1850 |

1819: Parts of Spanish Florida conquered by US
1836: Texans rebel against Mexican rule and declare Republic of Texas
1849: California Gold Rush

1803: France sells territory between Mississippi and Rockies in Louisiana Purchase
1821: Mexico gains independence from Spanish colonists
1846–48: US victory in war with Mexico which cedes New Mexico and California to US

South America

When Spain was cut off from her colonies by the Napoleonic wars, nationalist forces took advantage of the resulting disorder and weakness of the colonial regimes. Argentina's struggle for independence was led by José de San Martín, who marched an army across the Andes to liberate Chile and Peru from royalist control. Simón Bolívar led Venezuela and New Granada to independence, and helped found the new republic of Bolivia in 1825.

The Venezuelan Simón Bolívar (1783–1830) was known as the "liberator of South America."

South America

| 1800 | 1810 | 1820 | 1830 | 1840 | 1850 |

1810: Argentina declares independence from Spain
1821: Bolivar secures Venezuelan independence

1817: San Martin wins a decisive victory over the Spanish and liberates Chile
1822: Empire of Brazil becomes independent from Portugal

RAILROADS

The steam locomotive was first developed in Britain in the early 19th century to haul heavy industrial loads. By 1830, engines were being used to pull cars on iron rails and the first steam railroad – from Stockton to Darlington – had opened. By 1850, railroads had been built throughout Britain and were being introduced throughout its empire.

The steam engine Locomotion, built by Robert Stephenson and Co., hauled the first train at the opening of the Stockton-to-Darlington railroad in 1825.

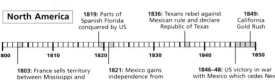

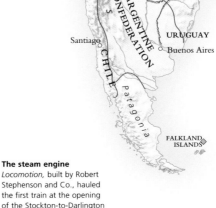

Africa

In sub-Saharan West Africa several Islamic leaders waged *jihad* against neighboring states. Under the Ottoman leader, Muhammad Ali, the viceroyalty of Egypt extended south to incorporate Sudan. The French invasion of Algeria in 1830 led to a war of resistance, led by Abd al-Qadir. In southeastern Africa, conflict broke out between different tribal groups (the *mfecane*) as natural resources became scarce. Shaka, the Zulu leader, established a united kingdom in southern Africa. In the late 1830s the "Great Trek" of the Boers from Cape Colony extended European influence into the African interior.

East and Southeast Asia

In the early 19th century, British merchants began to exploit the Chinese desire for Indian opium. As the trade flourished and the problem of opium addiction grew, the Chinese authorities attempted to stamp out the trade. The British objected and the first Opium War ensued. Japan, ruled by the inward-looking, Tokugawa shogunate for the last two centuries, remained closed to all foreigners, except a small Dutch trading community.

Superior firepower such as that displayed by the merchant steamer *Nemesis* enabled the British to overwhelm the wooden junks used by the Chinese in the first Opium War.

GEOLOGICAL MAPS

In the 19th century newly-discovered fossil remains were used to classify rocks and determine the sequence of geological strata. Geographical names were often used in the naming of rock types; for example, the Jura Mountains gave their name to the dinosaur-bearing Jurassic rocks.

Geologists used cross sections to map the age of rocks. This one is taken from the Reverend William Buckland's *Bridgewater Treatise on Mineralogy and Geology.*

SEE ALSO:

North America: pp.128–131

South America: pp.150–151

Africa: pp.166–167

Europe: pp.200–205

West Asia: pp.232–233

South and Southeast Asia: pp.248–249

North and East Asia: pp.268–271

Australasia and Oceania: pp.282–285

East and Southeast Asia

1804: Russian envoy fails to agree commercial treaty with Japan

1819: Stamford Raffles, of the British East India company, founds Singapore

1837: Tokugawa Ieyoshi succeeds Ienari as Japanese shogun

1839–42: First Opium War in China

1800 — 1810 — 1820 — 1830 — 1840 — 1850

1802: Gia-Long proclaimed emperor of united Annam (Vietnam)

1834: Monopoly of China trade by East India Company abolished

1842: Treaty of Nanjing. Hong Kong ceded to British and five ports opened to foreign trade

Australasia and Oceania

New Zealand and Australia became British colonies in the first half of the 19th century. In Australia, settlement spread from the penal colony at Port Jackson, now part of Sydney. As settlers founded towns at Adelaide, Melbourne, and Perth, they expropriated Aboriginal lands, and infected the people with fatal diseases, destroying local Aboriginal communities.

The Treaty of Waitangi allowed the Maori to maintain control over their lands while ceding the sovereignty of New Zealand to Britain, an unequal exchange which soon led to resentment and further wars.

Australasia and Oceania

1810: Kamehameha I unites Hawaiian islands

1825: Dutch annex western New Guinea

1840: British takeover of New Zealand under Treaty of Waitangi

1800 — 1810 — 1820 — 1830 — 1840 — 1850

1829: Britain annexes the whole continent of Australia

1835–36: British found Melbourne and Adelaide

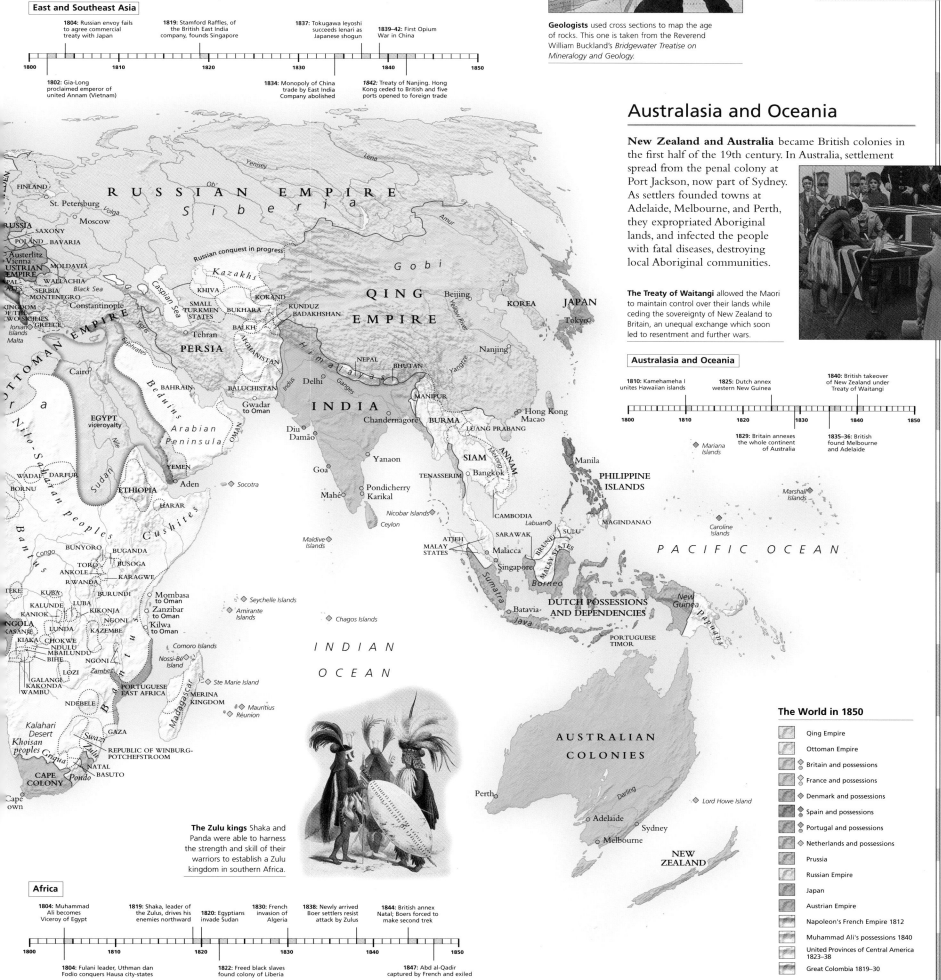

The Zulu kings Shaka and Panda were able to harness the strength and skill of their warriors to establish a Zulu kingdom in southern Africa.

The World in 1850

- Qing Empire
- Ottoman Empire
- Britain and possessions
- France and possessions
- Denmark and possessions
- Spain and possessions
- Portugal and possessions
- Netherlands and possessions
- Prussia
- Russian Empire
- Japan
- Austrian Empire
- Napoleon's French Empire 1812
- Muhammad Ali's possessions 1840
- United Provinces of Central America 1823–38
- Great Colombia 1819–30

Africa

1804: Muhammad Ali becomes Viceroy of Egypt

1819: Shaka, leader of the Zulus, drives his enemies northward

1820: Egyptians invade Sudan

1830: French invasion of Algeria

1838: Newly arrived Boer settlers resist attack by Zulus

1844: British annex Natal; Boers forced to make second trek

1800 — 1810 — 1820 — 1830 — 1840 — 1850

1804: Fulani leader, Uthman dan Fodio conquers Hausa city-states

1822: Freed black slaves found colony of Liberia

1847: Abd al-Qadir captured by French and exiled

THE WORLD'S ECONOMIC REVOLUTION

Innovative new constructions of the late-19th century included the Eiffel Tower, built in 1889.

IN THE FIRST HALF of the 19th century, world trade and industry was dominated by Britain; by the 1870s, the industrial balance was shifting in favor other nations, especially Germany, France, Russia, and the US, with rapid industrialization occurring throughout most of Europe by the end of the century. A stable currency, a standard (i.e., the price of gold) against which the currency's value could be measured, and an effective private banking system were seen as essential to the growth and success of every industrializing nation. The major industrial nations also began to invest heavily overseas. Their aims were the discovery and exploitation of cheaper raw materials, balanced by the development of overseas markets for their products.

The impact of the Industrial Revolution

The introduction of steam to oceangoing ships decreased journey times, and increased reliability because ships were no longer reliant on the wind.

World industrial output from 1870–1914 increased at an extraordinary rate: coal production by as much as 650%; steel by 2500%; steam engine capacity by over 350%. Technology revolutionized the world economy: the invention of refrigerated ships meant that meat, fruit, and other perishables could be shipped to Europe from as far away as New Zealand; sewing machines and power looms allowed the mass production of textiles and clothing; telephones, telegraphs, and railroads made communications faster.

The opening of the Suez Canal in 1869, linking the Red Sea to the Mediterranean, reduced the journey time from Europe to India by 50%.

By the 1880s almost all of the US was connected by long-distance rail networks including the Illinois Central Railroad (below).

❶ The impact of technology on the world trading system 1870–1910 ▶

Improvements in communications
- ░░░ most highly industrialized nations
- ▒▒▒ industrializing nations
- ▓▓▓ major industrial regions c.1914

- ─── major rail networks c.1914
- ⟶ North Atlantic shipping route
- ─── other shipping route
- ─── underwater telegraph cable route

Location of manufacturing industry
- ⚙ heavy machinery
- ⚙ iron and steel
- ▯ textile production

Export markets opened up by technology
- 🐂 beef cattle
- 🐑 lamb and mutton
- ○ fruit

Major cash crops
- ◉ coffee
- ◈ cotton
- ◊ rubber
- ⬇ sugarcane
- ❦ tea

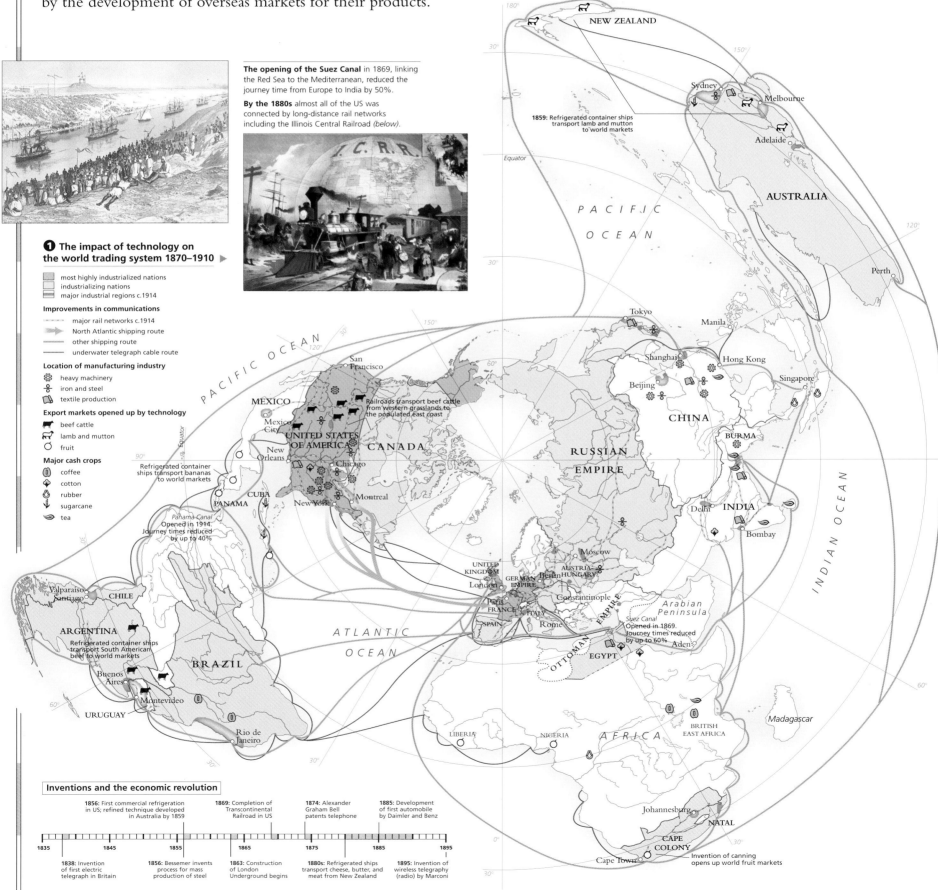

The opening of the Suez Canal in 1869, linking the Red Sea to the Mediterranean, reduced the journey time from Europe to India by 50%.

1859: Refrigerated container ships transport lamb and mutton to world markets

Railroads transport beef cattle from western grasslands to the populated east coast

Refrigerated container ships transport bananas to world markets

Panama Canal Opened in 1914. Journey times reduced by up to 40%

Refrigerated container ships transport South American beef to world markets

Suez Canal Opened in 1869. Journey times reduced by up to 60%

Invention of canning opens up world fruit markets

Inventions and the economic revolution

1856: First commercial refrigeration in US; refined technique developed in Australia by 1859

1869: Completion of Transcontinental Railroad in US

1874: Alexander Graham Bell patents telephone

1885: Development of first automobile by Daimler and Benz

1838: Invention of first electric telegraph in Britain

1856: Bessemer invents process for mass production of steel

1863: Construction of London Underground begins

1880s: Refrigerated ships transport cheese, butter, and meat from New Zealand

1895: Invention of wireless telegraphy (radio) by Marconi

The great mineral rush

The search for new sources of minerals, both precious and functional, reached new heights of intensity in the industrial 19th century. New finds of gold and diamonds in the US, Canada, Australia, and South Africa fueled the so-called gold and diamond rushes of the later 19th century. Though individuals could pan for gold in the Australian and North American rushes, the depth of gold and diamond deposits in South Africa meant that they could only be fully exploited with mechanical diggers owned by mining companies.

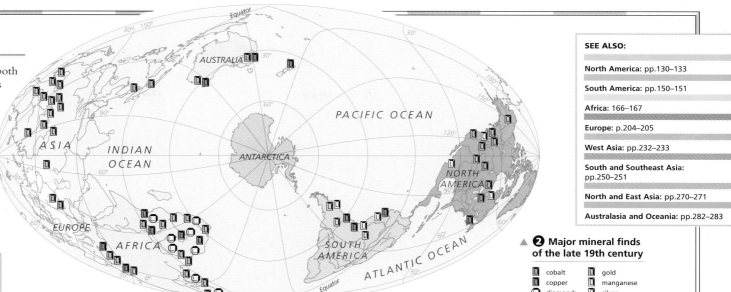

SEE ALSO:

North America: pp.130–133

South America: pp.150–151

Africa: 166–167

Europe: p.204–205

West Asia: pp.232–233

South and Southeast Asia: pp.250–251

North and East Asia: pp.270–271

Australasia and Oceania: pp.282–283

▲ ❷ **Major mineral finds of the late 19th century**

cobalt	gold
copper	manganese
diamonds	silver
iron ore	tin

❹ **The Yukon and Klondike gold rushes**

- major gold strike
- settlement or fort

In the rush for instant riches miners such as this man, panning for gold in British Columbia in 1900, were prepared to undergo extreme hardship.

The Klondike and Yukon gold rushes

Gold was first discovered near the Pacific coast of Alaska in 1880 by the explorers Juneau and Harris. The mid-1890s saw frenzied activity along the Yukon river and its tributaries, with an influx of many thousands of prospectors into one of the world's most desolate regions. Though Dawson City and other settlements grew up to supply the miners, the boom had receded by 1899.

Boom towns sprang up rapidly during the Yukon gold rush. Such was the passion for gold that even the city streets were dug up by eager prospectors.

Gold and diamond rushes

1849–50: Comstock Lode found near Virginia City, Nevada

1851: Rich gold deposits found in southern Australia

1869: Discovery of "Star of South Africa" diamond sets off diamond rush

1896–98: Yukon and Klondike gold rushes

1840 — 1850 — 1860 — 1870 — 1880 — 1890 — 1900

1848: California Gold Rush starts neaer Sutter's Mill on the Sacramento River

1858: Gold discovered on Fraser River, northwest Canada

1867: Diamonds found at Kimberley, north of Cape Colony, South Africa

1876–78: Gold found near Black Hills of Dakota Territory

1886: Deeps seams of gold discovered on the Witwatersrand, South Africa

---

The politics of cotton

In the 1870s woven cotton in India was still produced on a local scale, by individuals, rather than factories, and traded at local markets *(above)*.

❺ **The politics of cotton** ▽

- raw cotton from US to Britain
- cotton textiles to India
- raw cotton from India to Britain
- cotton producing region
- textile town
- major cotton-producing states

Cotton production was an early beneficiary of the Industrial Revolution. Eli Whitney's invention of the cotton gin led to a huge increase in the volume of cotton that could be processed; the invention of the power loom industrialized the weaving of cotton textiles. Britain's colonies in India and America supplied raw cotton for the cotton towns of Lancashire and Yorkshire; even with American independence, the southern states continued to provide much of Britain's cotton. The economic and political importance of cotton to the US was reflected in the Confederate states' decision to use it as a bargaining tool during their struggle for international recognition following secession in 1861. The ploy failed as a strategy; during the Civil War, Britain turned to India for its raw cotton supplies. British cloth woven with Indian cotton was then exported back to India, a policy which benefited British producers, while keeping the Indian textile industry at a local level until the end of the 19th century.

◀ ❹ **The cotton towns of Lancashire and Yorkshire**

- cotton town
- Peel textile firm
- major railroad c.1850
- major canal

Cotton production in Lancashire

With plentiful water to power new machinery, Lancashire had developed as a major cotton-weaving center by the late 18th century. Textile towns such as Stockport, Blackburn, and Cromford, often containing several firms, grew up in the area around Manchester, which acted as a major market for finished cloth.

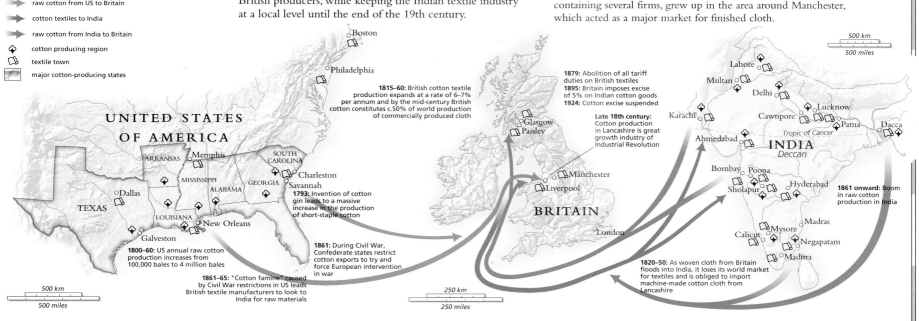

1815–60: British cotton textile production expands at a rate of 6–7% per annum and by the mid-century British cotton constitutes c.50% of world production of commercially produced cloth

1793: Invention of cotton gin leads to a massive increase in the production of short-staple cotton

1800–60: US annual raw cotton production increases from 100,000 bales to 4 million bales

1861: During Civil War, Confederate states restrict cotton exports to try and force European intervention in war

1861–65: "Cotton famine" caused by Civil War restrictions in US leads British textile manufacturers to look to India for raw materials

1879: Abolition of all tariff duties on British textiles
1895: Britain imposes excise of 5% on Indian cotton goods
1924: Cotton excise suspended

Late 18th century: Cotton production in Lancashire is great growth industry of Industrial Revolution

1861 onward: Boom in raw cotton production in India

1820–50: As woven cloth from Britain floods into India, it loses its world market for textiles and is obliged to import machine-made cotton cloth from Lancashire

THE WORLD 1850–1900

BY 1900 THE EUROPEAN POPULATION had more than doubled to 420 million, while the population of the US had reached 90 million. Industry and commerce were booming, and both Europe and the US were traversed by rail networks. The major European powers were extending their economic and political influence to the very ends of the globe, while fierce rivalries and competition were being enacted on the international as well as the domestic scene. Within two decades the European powers had colonized virtually the whole of the African continent, the British had claimed India for the Crown, and the western powers had exploited the fatal weaknesses of China's crumbling Qing dynasty to penetrate deep into the heart of Asia.

Kaiser Wilhelm II was determined to establish Germany as Europe's leading military power.

Europe

The emergence of new states, the rise of nationalism, and growing economic and political power led to rivalry and conflict. Expansionist Russia's activities in the Balkans led in 1854 to the Crimean War, between a Franco-British-Turkish alliance and Russia. In 1870 Bismarck, prime minister of Prussia, goaded the French into war; the French defeat led to the collapse of the Second Empire, providing the final impetus to the creation of the new German and Italian nations.

Europe

1854–56: Franco-British-Turkish alliance victorious against Russians in Crimea	**1862:** Otto von Bismarck prime minister of Prussia	**1870:** Franco-Prussian war; Prussian victory leads to collapse of Second Empire	**1887:** Bulgaria, independent of Ottoman empire, becomes leading Balkan state

1861: Abolition of serfdom in Russia	**1867:** Dual monarchy of Austria-Hungary established	**1871:** Rome becomes capital of united Italy; King Wilhelm I of Prussia declared German emperor	**1896:** Revival of Olympic Games at Athens, Greece

CAMPAIGN MAPS

During the American Civil War, new printing technology combined with up-to-date information from correspondents on the battlefields allowed US newspapers to produce simplified campaign maps to explain the stages of the war to a fascinated public.

THE FIGHT AT CAMPBELL'S STATION.

This map shows the battle of Campbell's Station, Tennessee, as witnessed from the Union position by the *New York Tribune's* correspondent, Elias Smith.

The final push to populate the western US occurred in the latter half of the 19th century. Settlers and their wagon trains braved sometimes horrific conditions to claim new lands in the west.

The Americas

In 1860-1 eleven southern states, fearful that the North was about to abolish slavery, left the Union and formed the Confederacy, beginning a conflict in which over 600,000 soldiers lost their lives. Following the Civil War, the US became the fastest growing economy in the world, its population swollen by waves of immigrants. In South America, economic prosperity, especially from the export of meat and rubber, was enjoyed by the ruling elite, while border disputes bedeviled the new republics.

The Americas

	1864–70: Paraguayan War: Brazil, Argentina, and Uruguay defeat Paraguay	**1879–83:** War of Pacific; Chile, Peru, and Bolivia fight for control of Atacama Desert	
1861–65: US Civil War			

1858: Mexican Civil War between conservatives and liberals	**1867:** Canada becomes a British dominion	**1876:** Battle of Little Bighorn; Sioux warriors kill 250 US soldiers	**1898:** Spanish-American War. US occupies Cuba and gains control of Philippines

The World in 1900

- Ottoman Empire
- Britain and possessions
- France and possessions
- Denmark and possessions
- Spain and possessions
- Portugal and possessions
- Netherlands and possessions
- German Empire and possessions
- Russian Empire and possessions
- Japan and possessions
- Italy and possessions
- US and possessions
- Confederate States 1861–65

East Asia

Agrarian unrest in China in the 1850s led to rebellion and famine. Western powers were quick to exploit internal dissent, carving out spheres of influence and annexing territory. A wave of xenophobia led to the Boxer Rebellion of 1900. Western troops were sent to China and concessions were extracted from the weak government. In Japan, the overthrow of the Tokugawa shogunate in 1868 was followed by industrial and economic modernization.

From the late 19th century, the newly-modernized Japan reopened its doors to foreign trade.

East Asia

1850: Taiping Rebellion begins in Guangxi province

1860: British and French occupy Beijing

1871: Abolition of feudalism in Japan

1900: Boxer Rebellion: Christian missions and western legations attacked

1853: Rebels capture Nanjing – recaptured a year later

1868: Overthrow of Tokugawa shogunate

1877–79: Famine in northern China leaves at least 10 million dead

1894–95: Japanese overwhelm Chinese forces and annex Taiwan

South Asia

The railroad station in Bombay was opened in 1887. The style and scale of the building reflected the great self-confidence of India's British rulers.

By 1850 the British East India Company emerged as the major power on the subcontinent. Hostility to the British, combined with suspicions about their attitude to India's traditional faiths, led to the Mutiny of 1857–59. Following the Mutiny, the British took administrative control of India, developed an extensive rail network, and began to industrialize the Indian economy.

South Asia

1878–79: Second Afghan War; British invade Afghanistan, which is coming under Russian influence

1885: Foundation of Indian National Congress

1857: Outbreak of Indian Mutiny

1876: Queen Victoria declared Empress of India, and a Viceroy appointed as her representative

1885–86: Third Burmese War leads to British annexation of Burma

SEE ALSO:

North America: pp.128–133

South America: pp.150–151

Africa: pp.166–167

Europe: pp.202–207

West Asia: pp.232–233

South and Southeast Asia: pp.248–251

North and East Asia: pp.268–270

Australasia and Oceania: pp.282–285

THE TELEPHONE

The telephone was invented in 1876 by the Scottish-born inventor and speech therapist Alexander Graham Bell. His device used a thin diaphragm to convert vibrations from the human voice into electrical signals. These were then reconverted into sound waves. Within a few years of its invention, the telephone had been installed in many city homes in Europe and the US.

This view of Broadway in 1880 shows its skyline crisscrossed by telegraph and telephone wires.

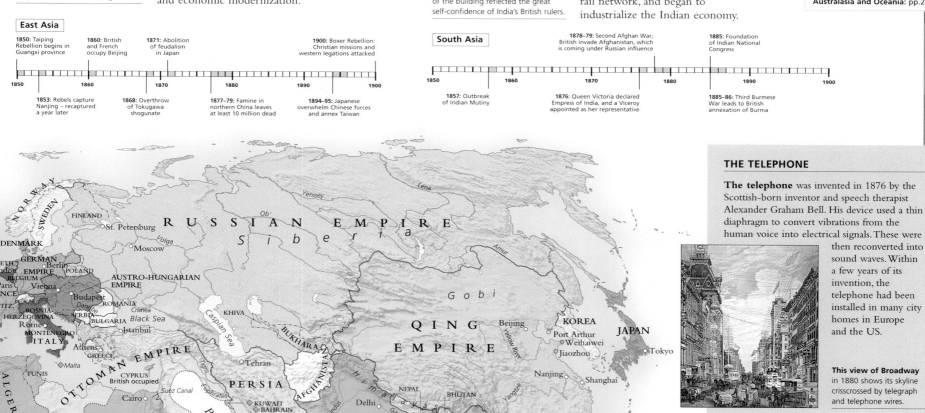

Africa

In 1850 Africa was a patchwork of kingdoms and states, mostly unknown to Europeans. But, by 1900, the major European powers had seized virtually the entire continent. Rivalries between European nations were played out in Africa as colonizing countries raced for territory, raw materials, and new markets. In 1898, open war between France and the British in the White Nile region was only just averted. In 1899, the Boer War, a bitter struggle between the British and Afrikaaners, began.

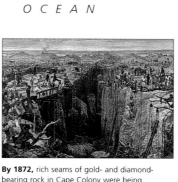

By 1872, rich seams of gold- and diamond-bearing rock in Cape Colony were being heavily mined by European prospectors.

Africa

1869: Opening of Suez Canal

1880: White Boers have appropriated most habitable land in Cape Colony

1896: Abyssinia defeats Italians at Adowa

1899: Boer War begins

1863: Al-Hajj 'Umar clashes with French in Senegal Valley and creates a Muslim empire

1879: Zulu War with British; Zulus defeated

1882: British invade and occupy Egypt

1893: French conquer Dahomey

1898: British and French clash at Fashoda

THE ERA OF WESTERN IMPERIALISM

This *Punch* cartoon from 1890 depicts Germany as an eagle, with Africa as her prey. The caption reads, "On the Swoop."

THE LAST TWENTY YEARS of the 19th century saw unprecedented competition by the major European nations for control of territory overseas. The balance of imperial power was changing: having lost their American empires, Spain and Portugal were no longer preeminent. From the 1830s, France began to build a new empire, and Britain continued to acquire new lands throughout the century. Newly unified Italy and Germany sought to bolster their nation status from the 1880s with their own empires. Africa was the most fiercely contested prize in this race to absorb the nonindustrialized world, but much of Southeast Asia and Oceania was also appropriated in this period. Even the US, historically the champion of anticolonial movements, began to expand across the Pacific.

Other nations were frequently critical of the behavior of European imperialists in Africa. This German cartoon (*left*) has the caption: "Even the lions weep at the way the native Africans are treated by the French."

Many British officials in India maintained rituals of extreme formality (*below*), rather than adapting to native patterns of behavior.

The scramble for Africa

The race for European political control Africa began in the early 1880s. The Berlin Conference of 1884–85, convened to discuss rival European claims to Africa, was the starting point for the "scramble." Some governments worked through commercial companies; elsewhere, land was independently annexed by these companies; sometimes Africans actually invited Europeans in. In most cases, however, European political control was directly imposed by conquest. By 1914, Africa was fully partitioned along lines that bore little relation to cultural or linguistic traditions.

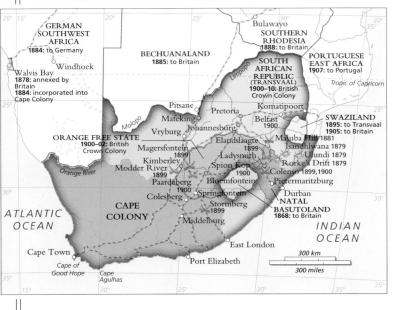

Colonial administrators often required extreme obeisance from the people they controlled. A local Moroccan sultan is shown here kneeling before a French colonel.

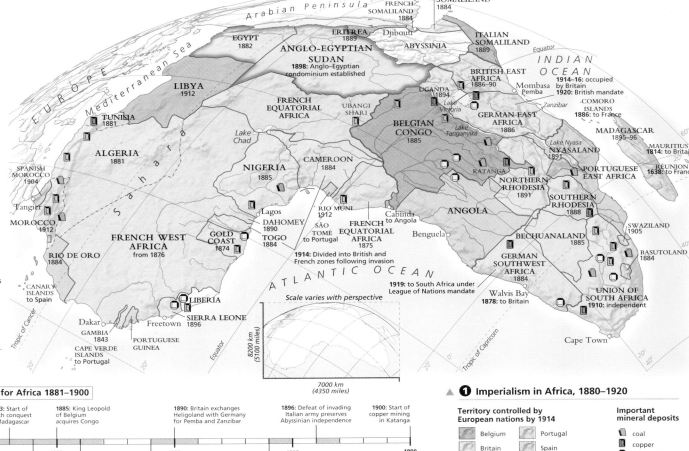

Scale varies with perspective

8200 km (5100 miles)

7000 km (4350 miles)

① **Imperialism in Africa, 1880–1920**

Territory controlled by European nations by 1914

Belgium	Portugal
Britain	Spain
France	nominally Ottoman, under British control
Germany	1882 date of taking control
Italy	—— borders in 1914

Important mineral deposits

- coal
- copper
- diamonds
- gold

The scramble for Africa 1881–1900

1881: French occupation of Tunisia
1883: Start of French conquest of Madagascar
1885: King Leopold of Belgium acquires Congo
1890: Britain exchanges Heligoland with Germany for Pemba and Zanzibar
1896: Defeat of invading Italian army preserves Abyssinian independence
1900: Start of copper mining in Katanga

1880 — 1885 — 1890 — 1895 — 1900

1882: Revolt in Egypt prompts occupation by British
1884: Germany acquires South West Africa, Togo, and Cameroon
1886: Germany and Britain divide up East Africa
1889: Establishment of first Italian colony in Eritrea
1889: Cecil Rhodes' British South Africa Company begins colonization of Rhodesia
1894: Uganda occupied by Britain

The struggle for South Africa

The British, with political control, the Afrikaners (Boers) – the first European settlers – and the Zulus all fought for control of South Africa in the 19th century. Seeking political autonomy, the Boers moved to found their own republics. The success of Transvaal, which grew rich from gold, led to annexation by Britain in 1877. British invasion of Zulu territory led to the First Zulu War, and British defeat, although this was swiftly reversed. In 1881, Boers in Transvaal rebelled against British rule, to set up the South African Republic. In 1899, the second Anglo–Boer war, broke out, lasting until 1902. The former Boer Republics became part of the British Empire as part of the Peace of Vereeniging.

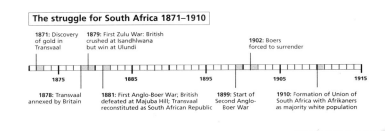

It took more than 300,000 British soldiers five years to subdue 75,000 heavily-armed Boers, who were skilled in guerrilla and siege tactic,and had intimate knowledge of the terrain.

② **The struggle for South Africa, 1854–1914**

- Cape Colony and Natal 1854
- territory under British control 1895
- South African Republic 1895
- Orange Free State 1895
- ⚔ battle in Zulu wars

Boer War 1899–1902

- ⚔ Afrikaner (Boer) victory
- ⚔ British victory
- ● Afrikaner sieges
- --- Union of South Africa boundary 1910
- ---- railroad

The struggle for South Africa 1871–1910

1871: Discovery of gold in Transvaal
1879: First Zulu War: British crushed at Isandhlwana but win at Ulundi
1902: Boers forced to surrender

1875 — 1885 — 1895 — 1905 — 1915

1878: Transvaal annexed by Britain
1881: First Anglo-Boer War; British defeated at Majuba Hill; Transvaal reconstituted as South African Republic
1899: Start of Second Anglo-Boer War
1910: Formation of Union of South Africa with Afrikaners as majority white population

Imperialism in Southeast Asia

Though the Dutch East Indian Empire had existed since the early 17th century, much of Southeast Asia was not colonized until the mid-19th century. Moving east from India, British ambitions concentrated on Burma, the Malay Peninsula, and north Borneo. Renewed French interest in empire-building began in earnest with the capture of Saigon in 1858 following a concerted naval effort. By 1893, France controlled Tongking, Laos, Annam, and Cambodia, collectively known as Indochina.

SEE ALSO:

North America: pp.132–133

Africa: pp.166–167

Europe: pp.202–203, p.206

West Asia: pp.232–233

South and Southeast Asia: pp.250–251

North and East Asia: pp.268–271

Australasia and Oceania: pp.282–283

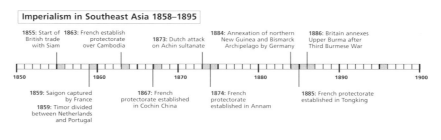

Imperialism in Southeast Asia 1858–1895

- 1855: Start of British trade with Siam
- 1859: Saigon captured by France
- 1859: Timor divided between Netherlands and Portugal
- 1863: French establish protectorate over Cambodia
- 1867: French protectorate established in Cochin China
- 1873: Dutch attack on Achin sultanate
- 1874: French protectorate established in Annam
- 1884: Annexation of northern New Guinea and Bismarck Archipelago by Germany
- 1885: French protectorate established in Tongking
- 1886: Britain annexes Upper Burma after Third Burmese War

1850 — 1860 — 1870 — 1880 — 1890 — 1900

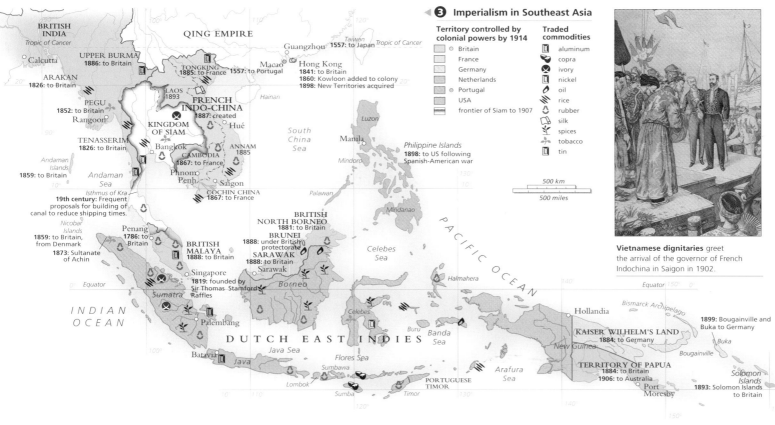

③ Imperialism in Southeast Asia

Territory controlled by colonial powers by 1914
- Britain
- France
- Germany
- Netherlands
- Portugal
- USA
- frontier of Siam to 1907

Traded commodities
- aluminum
- copra
- ivory
- nickel
- oil
- rice
- rubber
- silk
- spices
- tobacco
- tin

500 km
500 miles

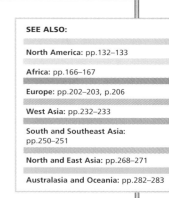

Vietnamese dignitaries greet the arrival of the governor of French Indochina in Saigon in 1902.

The Malay Peninsula became a British possession in 1888. Vast rubber plantations provided a firm economic basis for imperial control.

Reactions to imperialism

The aggressive scramble for empire provoked determined armed resistance across Africa and Asia. Local peoples rose up to repel the European intruders – for example against the British in Sudan, the Italians in Libya, and the Dutch in Sumatra – but in most cases they had to submit when faced by superior firepower. One exception was the defeat of the Italians at Adowa in Abyssinia in 1896. Imperialist meddling in countries such as China and Persia led to rebellions against the governments of the day, and the tottering Russian Empire faced a major revolt in Central Asia in 1916.

1000 km
1000 miles

The Boxers were one of the antigovernment societies which emerged in China at the end of the 19th century. Resolutely anti-Western, they attacked communities and property, especially railroads and installations being built by Europeans. The siege of the European legations in Beijing was ended by an international expedition.

④ Movements against colonial rule, 1880–1920

Anti-colonial uprisings and incidents
- anti-British
- anti-Dutch
- anti-French
- anti-German
- anti-Italian
- anti-Portugal
- anti-Russian
- anti-Spanish
- anti-US

Other partly anti-western rebellions
- Persia
- area of Chinese revolution 1911–12
- boundary at 1914

THE WORLD 1900–1925

THE IMPERIAL AND MILITARY RIVALRY between Britain and France, and Germany and Austria-Hungary led, in 1914, to World War I, which left millions dead and redrew the map of Europe. The Habsburg and Ottoman empires broke up, leading to the emergence of a number of smaller nation states, while the end of the Ottoman Empire also created a territorial crisis in the Middle East. In 1917, the Russian Empire collapsed in revolution and civil war, to be transformed by the victorious Bolsheviks into the world's first Communist empire. The US's participation in the war confirmed its status as a world power, cemented by the central role played by President Wilson at the Versailles Conference, and by the nation's increasing economic dominance.

German soldiers wearing gas masks emerge from a dugout. Troops on both sides endured terrible conditions in the trench warfare which dominated the war in France.

Europe

Most countries in Europe and their colonies took part in World War I, which was fought on a scale unimagined in the 19th century. Years of rivalry between the major European powers, France, Britain and Germany had created an incendiary situation, finally touched off by a crisis in the Balkans. The Versailles Settlement of 1919 altered the balance of power in Europe irrevocably, setting up the conditions for a second European war 20 years later.

Europe

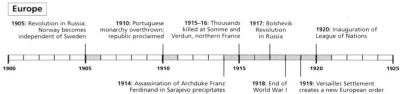

1905: Revolution in Russia; Norway becomes independent of Sweden
1910: Portuguese monarchy overthrown; republic proclaimed
1915–16: Thousands killed at Somme and Verdun, northern France
1917: Bolshevik Revolution in Russia
1920: Inauguration of League of Nations

1900 — 1905 — 1910 — 1915 — 1920 — 1925

1914: Assassination of Archduke Franz Ferdinand in Sarajevo precipitates start of World War I
1918: End of World War I
1919: Versailles Settlement creates a new European order

RADIO

Radio technology was first invented by Guglielmo Marconi in 1894. In 1901 he was able to send Morse Code messages across the Atlantic, and by 1920 the first commercial radio station was set up in Pittsburgh. By the mid-1920s, radio was established as an immensely effective means of mass communication.

This radio, advertised using the famous fox terrier listening to "His Master's Voice," dates from the 1920s.

Bi-Acoustic Radio
It's "HIS MASTER'S VOICE" of the air!

Revelers mourn the passing of the Volstead Act in 1919, prohibiting the sale of alcohol in the US. Alcohol sales merely went underground, creating a profitable black market presided over by an organized criminal network.

The Americas

By 1925, the US was the world's most powerful industrial nation. Its international standing was greatly enhanced by involvement in World War I and the Treaty of Versailles of 1918, although after 1920 there was a marked return to isolation from Europe. In Mexico, Central and South America, revolt against the old rural elites ushered in a new social order and an increasingly urban society.

The Americas

1910: Start of Mexican revolution
1919: US Senate rejects entry into League of Nations
1920: US refuses to ratify Paris treaties and withdraws into isolation

1900 — 1905 — 1910 — 1915 — 1920 — 1925

1903: Panama Canal Zone ceded to US
1914: Opening of Panama Canal joins Atlantic and Pacific oceans
1917: US declares war on Germany and its allies
1921: US restricts immigration

The World in 1925

- Turkey
- Britain and possessions
- France and possessions
- Denmark and possessions
- Spain and possessions
- Portugal and possessions
- Netherlands and possessions
- Germany
- USSR
- Japanese Empire
- Norway and possessions
- Belgium and possessions
- Italy and possessions
- New Zealand and possessions
- Australia and possessions
- US and possessions

Map labels

Alaska
Greenland
ICELAND in personal union with Denmark
BRITAI
IRISH FREE STATE
Aleutian Islands
CANADA
NEWFOUNDLAND
Rocky Mountains
Great Lakes
Ottawa
St. Lawrence
St. Pierre and Miquelon
UNITED STATES OF AMERICA
Chicago
Pittsburgh
New York
Washington DC
Missouri
Mississippi
Appalachian Mountains
Los Angeles
Rio Grande
Bermuda
ATLANTIC OCEAN
SPA
PORTUGAL
Lisbon
Madr
Gibraltar
Tangier international
SPANISH MOROCCO
Madeira
MOROCC
Azores
Canary Islands
IFNI
RIO DE ORO
S
Hawaiian Islands
MEXICO
Mexico City
Havana
Bahamas
Turks and Caicos Islands
DOMINICAN REPUBLIC
Puerto Rico
VIRGIN ISLANDS
CUBA
HAITI
Jamaica
LEEWARD ISLANDS
BRITISH HONDURAS
HONDURAS
St. Martin
Guadeloupe
GUATEMALA
Martinique
EL SALVADOR
NICARAGUA
Curaçao
BARBADOS
WINDWARD ISLANDS
COSTA RICA
CANAL ZONE
TRINIDAD AND TOBAGO
PANAMA
VENEZUELA
BRITISH GUIANA
DUTCH GUIANA
FRENCH GUIANA
COLOMBIA
Guiana Highlands
Orinoco
CAPE VERDE ISLANDS
GAMBIA
PORTUGUESE GUINEA
SIERRA LEONE
LIBERIA
FRENC
PACIFIC OCEAN
Christmas Island
Galapagos Islands to Ecuador
ECUADOR
Amazon
Amazon Basin
PERU
BRAZIL
São Francisco
Lima
BOLIVIA
Ascension
ATLANTIC OCEAN
ST. HELENA
Phoenix Islands
WESTERN SAMOA New Zealand mandate
AMERICAN SAMOA
French Polynesia
Cook Islands
Tonga
PARAGUAY
Paraná
Rio de Janeiro
São Paulo
Pitcairn Island
CHILE
Andes
Santiago
Buenos Aires
URUGUAY
ARGENTINA
Kermadec Islands
Patagonia
FALKLAND ISLANDS

Kemal Atatürk was the first leader of the new Turkish republic. From 1923–38 he radically overhauled Ottoman institutions to bring Turkey into the modern age.

West Asia

In 1918, the Ottoman Empire collapsed after more than 400 years. A new Turkish republic was inaugurated in 1923. In the post-war period much of the former Ottoman Empire, including Transjordan, Syria, and Iraq was controlled by Britain and France. A new Arab nationalism was becoming more strident, resulting in numerous political disturbances.

West Asia

1912–13: Ottomans lose most of their European lands in Balkan Wars	**1915:** Allied attack on Gallipoli	**1917:** Balfour Declaration commits Britain to creation of Jewish state in Palestine

1900   1905   1910   1915   1920   1925

1908: Ottoman sultan deposed in Young Turk Revolution
1914: Ottomans ally with Germany and Austria after Britan, France and Russia declare war
1918: Collapse of Ottoman Empire
1923: Foundation of modern Turkey by Kemal Atatürk

A Soviet propaganda poster encourages peasants to invest their savings in state projects. Much policy at this time was aimed at exerting control over the peasants.

Northeast Asia

Much of North and East Asia was destabilized by the collapse of the Chinese Empire into civil war in 1911, and the Russian Revolution of 1917. The victorious Bolsheviks hoped for the spread of revolution in other countries. Meanwhile, Japanese expansionism was rewarded by territorial gains in Siberia, China, and the Pacific islands.

Northeast Asia

1910: Japanese annexation of Korea	**1914:** Japan takes over many German colonies in the Pacific	**1918–20:** Japan occupies part of Manchuria and Siberia

1900   1905   1910   1915   1920   1925

1904–05: Russo-Japanese War; series of Russian defeats
1911: Qing dynasty overthrown by Sun Yat Sen's nationalists and Republic of China declared
1922: Washington Naval Agreement limits Japanese naval power in the Pacific

SEE ALSO:

North America: pp.132–133

South America: pp.152–153

Africa: pp.166–167

Europe: pp.206–207

West Asia: pp.232–233

South and Southeast Asia: pp.250–251

North and East Asia: pp.270–271

Australasia and Oceania: pp.284–285

ROAD MAPS

The growth in automobile use, a burgeoning road network and an increasingly mobile population, necessitated the creation of a new type of road map, more detailed than any made previously.

The cover of this 1920s road map emphasizes the link between car usage and leisure pursuits.

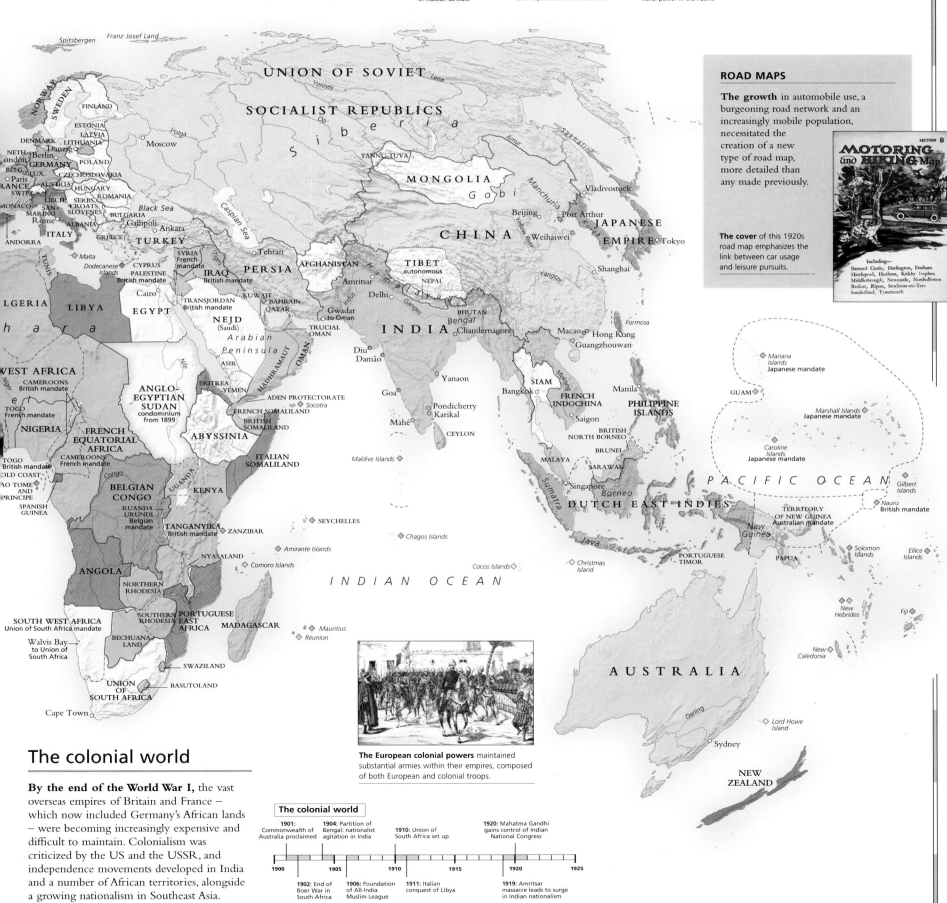

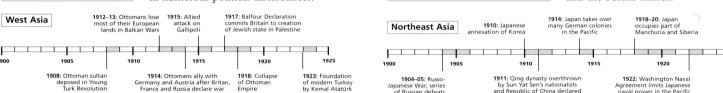

The European colonial powers maintained substantial armies within their empires, composed of both European and colonial troops.

The colonial world

By the end of the World War I, the vast overseas empires of Britain and France – which now included Germany's African lands – were becoming increasingly expensive and difficult to maintain. Colonialism was criticized by the US and the USSR, and independence movements developed in India and a number of African territories, alongside a growing nationalism in Southeast Asia.

The colonial world

1901: Commonwealth of Australia proclaimed	**1904:** Partition of Bengal: nationalist agitation in India	**1910:** Union of South Africa set up	**1920:** Mahatma Gandhi gains control of Indian National Congress

1900   1905   1910   1915   1920   1925

1902: End of Boer War in South Africa
1906: Foundation of All-India Muslim League
1911: Italian conquest of Libya
1919: Amritsar massacre leads to surge in Indian nationalism

GLOBAL MIGRATION

The Japanese shipping line *Osaka Shoshen Kaisha* carried thousands of immigrants to the US.

THE TECHNICAL INNOVATIONS of the Industrial Revolution made the 19th-century world seem a much smaller place. Railroads could quickly transport large human cargoes across continents, the Suez and Panama canals reduced travel times – sometimes by as much as 50%, and ships became larger, faster, and more seaworthy. The mechanization and centralization of industry required the concentration of labor on a scale never seen before. At the same time, the European imperial powers were exploiting their tropical possessions for economic benefit. Cash crops, grown on large plantations, needed a plentiful supply of labour as well. Political upheaval, wars, and economic hardship provided the most dramatic impetus to emigration – especially in the Russian Empire and Central Europe, and in southeastern China.

Migration in the 19th century

More than 80 million people emigrated from their country of origin during the 19th and early 20th centuries. Over half of them moved across the Atlantic to North and South America. The end of the American Civil War in 1865, and the opening up of Native American land to settlers saw the greatest period of immigration to the US and Canada. In the Russian Empire, movement was eastward from European Russia into Siberia and the Caspian region. Europeans moved south and east to take up employment in the colonies, while indentured laborers traveled to the Americas, Africa, and Southeast Asia.

Pogroms, or riots against Jews were frequent in late 19th-century Russia. Many fled following the riots; others were formally expelled from designated areas such as St. Petersburg *(above)*.

❶ World migration c.1860–1920

Transatlantic migration
- → to North America
- → to South America and the Caribbean
- → to Europe from the Americas

Other European migration
- → to Australia and New Zealand
- → to North Africa

Asian migration
- → to the Americas and Australia
- → Russian migration into Siberia
- → Indian intercolonial migration
- ---- transcontinental railroad
- major exporters of people
- major importers of people

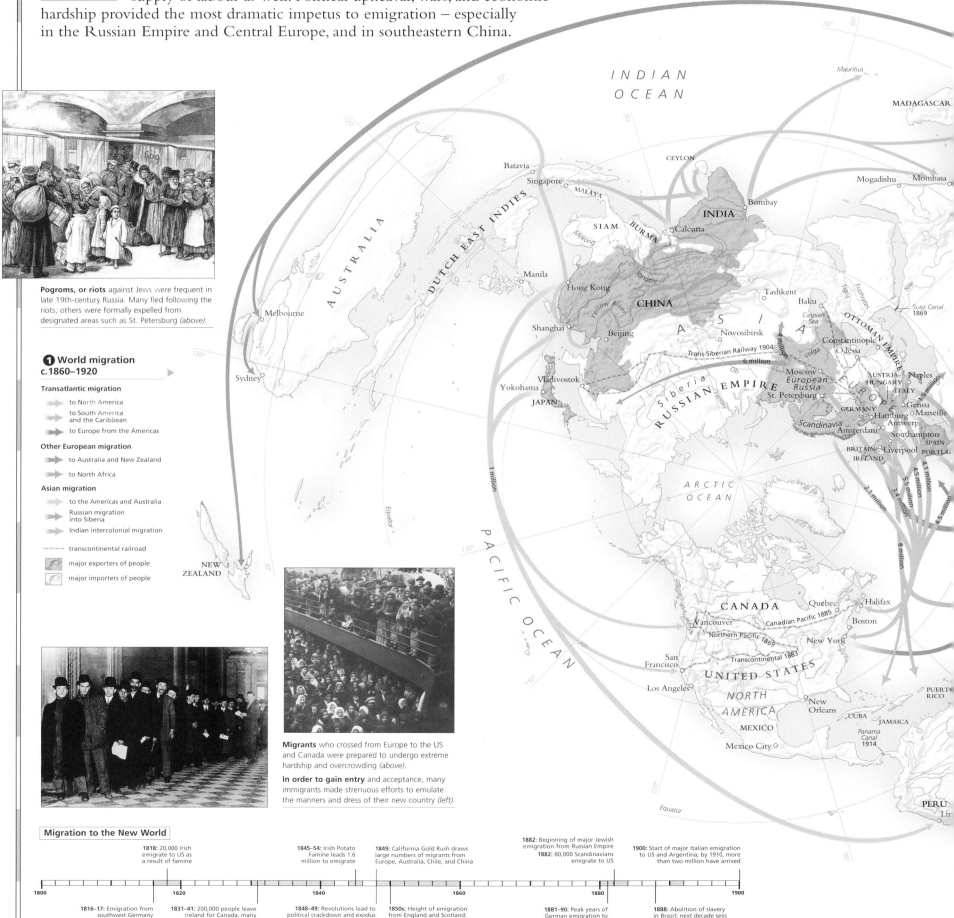

Migrants who crossed from Europe to the US and Canada were prepared to undergo extreme hardship and overcrowding *(above)*.

In order to gain entry and acceptance, many immigrants made strenuous efforts to emulate the manners and dress of their new country *(left)*.

Migration to the New World

1818: 20,000 Irish emigrate to US as a result of famine

1845–54: Irish Potato Famine leads 1.6 million to emigrate

1849: California Gold Rush draws large numbers of migrants from Europe, Australia, Chile, and China

1882: Beginning of major Jewish emigration from Russian Empire

1882: 80,000 Scandinavians emigrate to US

1900: Start of major Italian emigration to US and Argentina; by 1910, more than two million have arrived

| 1800 | 1820 | 1840 | 1860 | 1880 | 1900 |

1816–17: Emigration from southwest Germany following Napoleonic wars

1831–41: 200,000 people leave Ireland for Canada, many traveling on to the US

1848–49: Revolutions lead to political crackdown and exodus of democrats from Central Europe

1850s: Height of emigration from England and Scotland: more than 50,000 per year

1881–90: Peak years of German emigration to US (1,300,000)

1888: Abolition of slavery in Brazil; next decade sees over a million immigrants

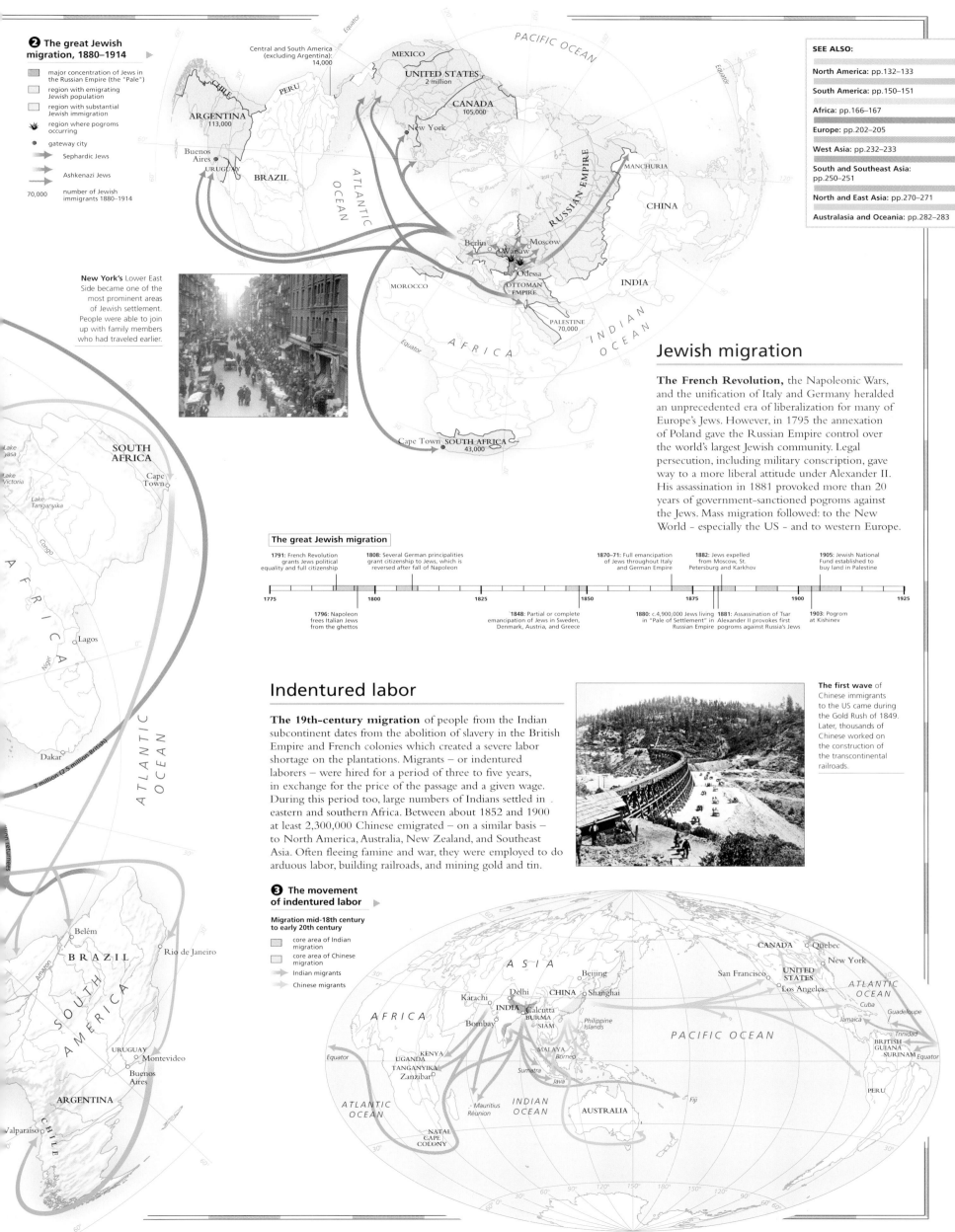

❷ The great Jewish migration, 1880–1914

- major concentration of Jews in the Russian Empire (the "Pale")
- region with emigrating Jewish population
- region with substantial Jewish immigration
- ❀ region where pogroms occurring
- ● gateway city
- ➤ Sephardic Jews
- ➤ Ashkenazi Jews
- 70,000 number of Jewish immigrants 1880–1914

New York's Lower East Side became one of the most prominent areas of Jewish settlement. People were able to join up with family members who had traveled earlier.

Jewish migration

The French Revolution, the Napoleonic Wars, and the unification of Italy and Germany heralded an unprecedented era of liberalization for many of Europe's Jews. However, in 1795 the annexation of Poland gave the Russian Empire control over the world's largest Jewish community. Legal persecution, including military conscription, gave way to a more liberal attitude under Alexander II. His assassination in 1881 provoked more than 20 years of government-sanctioned pogroms against the Jews. Mass migration followed: to the New World – especially the US – and to western Europe.

The great Jewish migration

1791: French Revolution grants Jews political equality and full citizenship	**1808:** Several German principalities grant citizenship to Jews, which is reversed after fall of Napoleon		**1870–71:** Full emancipation of Jews throughout Italy and German Empire	**1882:** Jews expelled from Moscow, St. Petersburg and Karkhov	**1905:** Jewish National Fund established to buy land in Palestine

1775   1800   1825   1850   1875   1900   1925

1796: Napoleon frees Italian Jews from the ghettos

1848: Partial or complete emancipation of Jews in Sweden, Denmark, Austria, and Greece

1880: c.4,900,000 Jews living in "Pale of Settlement" in Russian Empire

1881: Assassination of Tsar Alexander II provokes first pogroms against Russia's Jews

1903: Pogrom at Kishinev

Indentured labor

The 19th-century migration of people from the Indian subcontinent dates from the abolition of slavery in the British Empire and French colonies which created a severe labor shortage on the plantations. Migrants – or indentured laborers – were hired for a period of three to five years, in exchange for the price of the passage and a given wage. During this period too, large numbers of Indians settled in eastern and southern Africa. Between about 1852 and 1900 at least 2,300,000 Chinese emigrated – on a similar basis – to North America, Australia, New Zealand, and Southeast Asia. Often fleeing famine and war, they were employed to do arduous labor, building railroads, and mining gold and tin.

The first wave of Chinese immigrants to the US came during the Gold Rush of 1849. Later, thousands of Chinese worked on the construction of the transcontinental railroads.

❸ The movement of indentured labor

Migration mid-18th century to early 20th century

- core area of Indian migration
- core area of Chinese migration
- ➤ Indian migrants
- ➤ Chinese migrants

SEE ALSO:

North America: pp.132–133

South America: pp.150–151

Africa: pp.166–167

Europe: pp.202–205

West Asia: pp.232–233

South and Southeast Asia: pp.250–251

North and East Asia: pp.270–271

Australasia and Oceania: pp.282–283

THE WORLD 1925–1950

THOUGH THE PARTIES to the Versailles Treaty of 1919, which followed World War I, hoped for stability, the League of Nations, set up in 1919, proved ineffective. By 1939 expansionist nationalism in Germany, Italy, and Japan led once more to war on a massive scale. World War II devastated Europe, Asia, and the USSR, killing more than 50 million people – among them perhaps 21 million Soviet citizens and more than six million Jewish civilians. The real victors of the war were the US and the USSR, who emerged as the world's most powerful nations. The great empires of Britain and France began to fragment under the financial strain of war and the rise of independence movements in their territories, beginning with India in 1947.

Adolf Hitler used vast rallies such as this one at Nuremberg to muster his followers and show the world the strength of his popular support.

Europe

Germany's humiliation at Versailles, alongside economic depression, created the conditions for a revival of aggressive German nationalism. In its efforts to create a greater Germany, Hitler's Nazi party seized much of continental Europe and launched a policy of genocide against European Jews. Only with US intervention and a resurgent Soviet Union was their advance finally halted.

Europe

1925: Josef Stalin comes to power in USSR	**1933:** Hitler becomes Chancellor in Germany	**1936:** Great Terror in the USSR

1939: Britain and France declare war on Germany after invasion of Poland — **1945:** German surrender ends war in Europe — **1948:** Communists take over in Czechoslovakia and Hungary

1925 — 1930 — 1935 — 1940 — 1945 — 1950

1931: Collapse of central European banks leads to major recession — **1936:** Spanish Civil War begins — **1938:** German invasion of Czechoslovakia — **1942:** Hitler starts mass extermination of Jews — **1948–49:** Berlin airlift to counter Soviet blockade of the city

SCHEMATIC MAPS

The subway and metro maps produced in the 1930s are some of the simplest, yet most sophisticated maps ever produced. Using bold, clearly differentiated colored lines for routes, and clear symbols to represent stations, they made no attempt to reproduce distances accurately, and showed direction only roughly. This schematic approach helped travelers to identify their destination and the quickest way to reach it.

The London Underground map devised by Harry Beck in 1931 and printed in 1933 is one of the most famous topological maps. Its design is based on electrical circuit diagrams.

The Americas

The Wall Street Crash of 1929 plunged the US into a severe depression. Only with the war effort was the economy rejuvenated: the mobilization of industry established the US as the world's leading military and industrial power. In South and Central America, a number of states sought to diversify their economies and gain control over valuable mineral reserves in neighbouring countries. The Chaco War between Bolivia and Paraguay was the most serious of these conflicts prior to World War I.

Eva Perón was the charismatic wife of the Argentinian president Juan Perón. Her immense popularity helped to mask the ruthlessness of his regime.

The Americas

1930: Military revolution in Brazil — **1933:** Franklin Roosevelt's New Deal begins — **1945:** United Nations established in New York — **1946:** Juan Perón comes to power in Argentina

1925 — 1930 — 1935 — 1940 — 1945 — 1950

1929: Wall Street Crash starts Great Depression — **1932–35:** Paraguay defeats Bolivia in Chaco War — **1941:** US enters war following Japanese air attack on Pearl Harbor — **1947:** Marshall Plan drawn up to aid recovery in western Europe

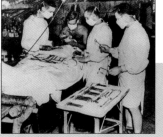

Among the first to benefit from antibiotics were US troops wounded in the Pacific theater of World War II.

ANTIBIOTICS

The discovery of penicillin in 1928 led to the creation of antibiotics, powerful drugs which were able to combat epidemic diseases such as tuberculosis. Over-prescription has led to many bacteria developing antibiotic immunity, prompting a search for new agents to combat disease.

South and East Asia

Gandhi's strategy against British rule in India was based on non-violent civil disobedience.

Japanese expansionism during the 1930s led to war with China in 1937, and in 1941 Japan's bombing of Pearl Harbor forced US entry into World War II. Chinese Communist and Nationalist forces held the Japanese at bay; after the war the Communists overwhelmed their former allies. In India the move to independence became irresistible following the war. In 1947 the British withdrew and the separate nations of India and Pakistan were created.

Southeast Asia and Oceania

In 1942–42 Japanese forces rapidly overran European troops throughout Southeast Asia, in a campaign of "liberation." Their eventual defeat by Allied forces nevertheless precipitated a widespread reluctance to return to colonial rule among the peoples of the region.

The mighty Japanese fleet was eventually destroyed by US planes launched from aircraft carriers.

SEE ALSO:

North America: pp.134–137

South America: pp.152–153

Africa: pp.168–169

Europe: pp.208–209

West Asia: pp.232–235

South and Southeast Asia: pp.250–251

North and East Asia: pp.272–273

Australasia and Oceania: pp.282–285

South and East Asia

1925: Civil war in China
1926: Chiang Kai-shek begins Chinese reunification
1934: Start of the Chinese Communists' "Long March" to Yan'an
1936: Japan signs anti-Comintern pact with Germany
1937: War between China and Japan
1939: Russo-Japanese neutrality pact
1942: Japanese control much of South and East Asia; arrest of Congress leaders in India
1945: Atomic bombs at Hiroshima and Nagasaki force Japanese surrender
1947: India and Pakistan gain independence
1949: Mao Zedong and Chinese Communists win Chinese Civil War

Southeast Asia and Oceania

1926–27: Rebellion against Dutch rule in Java and Sumatra
1932: End of absolute monarchy in Siam (renamed Thailand in 1939)
1942: Indonesia, Indochina, Malaya, the Philippines, New Guinea and Singapore seized by Japan
1942: US navy halts Japanese expansion at battle of Midway in the Pacific
1945: Ho Chi Minh proclaims independent Vietnam
1946: Philippines become independent
1949: Indonesia gains independence from the Dutch

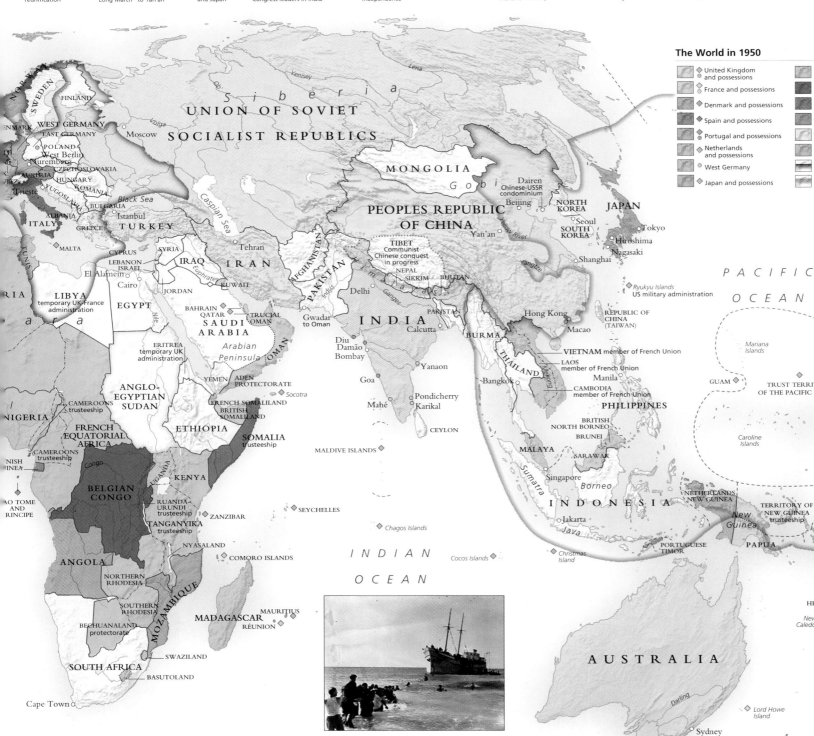

The World in 1950

- United Kingdom and possessions
- France and possessions
- Denmark and possessions
- Spain and possessions
- Portugal and possessions
- Netherlands and possessions
- West Germany
- Japan and possessions
- Norway and possessions
- Belgium and possessions
- Italy and possessions
- New Zealand and possessions
- Australia and possessions
- US and possessions
- controlled by European Axis powers Nov 15 1942
- controlled by Japan Nov 15 1942

Africa and West Asia

At the end of World War I Britain and France gained control over much of North Africa and West Asia – especially the oil-producing nations. In World War II the Horn of Africa and North Africa became battlegrounds; Italian and German forces were eventually defeated. A new state of Israel was proclaimed for the survivors of Nazi Germany's genocide of European Jews in 1948. Conflict over Israel's disputed territorial boundaries remained unresolved for over 50 years.

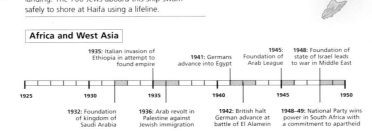

In 1948 the UK blockaded the seas around Israel to prevent ships carrying Jewish refugees from landing. The 700 Jews aboard this ship swam safely to shore at Haifa using a lifeline.

Africa and West Asia

1932: Foundation of kingdom of Saudi Arabia
1935: Italian invasion of Ethiopia in attempt to found empire
1936: Arab revolt in Palestine against Jewish immigration
1941: Germans advance into Egypt
1942: British halt German advance at battle of El Alamein
1945: Foundation of Arab League
1948: Foundation of state of Israel leads to war in Middle East
1948–49: National Party wins power in South Africa with a commitment to apartheid

WORLD WAR II

Adolf Hitler's National Socialist (NAZI) party was underpinned by extreme nationalism and racism, enforced though a police state.

WORLD WAR II was a protracted struggle by a host of Allied nations to contain, and eventually destroy, the political, economic, social, and territorial ambitions of the Axis, a small group of extreme nationalist (fascist) states led by Germany and Japan. The struggle led to the mobilization of manpower and economic might on an unprecedented scale, a deployment of forces on land, sea, and air globally, and the prosecution of war far beyond the front line, deep into the civilian hinterland in all theaters. For these reasons it has been called a "Total War." Its human costs were enormous, variously estimated at between 50 and 60 million dead, and its conclusion – with the detonation of two atomic bombs over Japan – heralded the Nuclear Age.

World War II, 1939–41

Until May 1941 Japan and Germany fought and won localized conflicts: in a series of campaigns they conquered and denied isolated enemies the opportunity to gather support and mobilize potentially far superior resources. In summer 1941, with Britain isolated but for its empire, the German invasion of the Soviet Union and the Japanese move into Southeast Asia marked the point at which their separate conflicts changed and came together. Japan's provocation of the US and Germany's failure in Russia marked the end of Axis successes and the advent of global warfare.

The war to December 1941

Sep 1939: Invasion of Poland by Germany and Soviet Union

Jun 1940: Italy declares war on Britain and France

Jun 1941: Germany invades the Soviet Union (Operation Barbarossa)

Dec 1941: Japan attacks Pearl Harbor; US enters the war

Jan 1940   Jan 1941   Jan 1942

Sep 1939: Britain and France declare war on Germany

Jun 1940: German troops enter Paris; fall of France

Jul–Oct 1940: Battle of Britain waged in air over southern England

Jul 1941: Soviet Union and Britain sign pact of mutual assistance

Dec 1941: Germany declares war on US

Japan's campaigns in Asia aimed to destroy British, US, and Dutch influence and create a "Greater East Asian Co-Prosperity Sphere" in the region.

❶ World War II, Sep 1939–Dec 1941

— political boundaries in 1939
▨ Axis and its allies in Mar 1940
▨ Allies in May 1940
▨ Allies by Dec 1941
— Axis territorial expansion by Jun 1940
— Axis territorial expansion by Dec 1941
◆ Axis satellites following the German invasion of France, May 1940
☐ neutral state

Major battles: Dec 1941–Jul 1943

1	Moscow	Dec 1941	8	Milne Bay	Aug 1942
2	Singapore	Feb 1942	9	Guadalcanal	Aug 1942–Feb 1943
3	Lashio	Apr 1942	10	El Alamein	Oct–Nov 1942
4	Kalewa	May 1942	11	Stalingrad	Oct 1942–Feb 1943
5	Corregidor	May 1942	12	Tunis	Apr–May 1943
6	Coral Sea	May 1942	13	Kursk	Jun–Aug 1943
7	Midway	Jun 1942	14	Minsk	Jun–Aug 1943

World War II, 1941–43

By late 1942 Germany and Japan were isolated and besieged; they had to win the wars they had initiated or suffer defeat by the the massive forces ranged against them. Despite initial successes, their undoing was ensured by November 1942 with Anglo-American success in North Africa, the Soviet counter-offensive at Stalingrad, and US victories off Guadalcanal. By summer 1943 Allied consolidation in the Mediterranean, Soviet victory at Kursk and Japanese reverses at Guadalcanal and Milne Bay fatally compromised the Axis positions.

❷ World War II, Dec 1941–Jul 1943

— extent of Axis powers Dec 1942
▨ Allies Jul 1943
▨ Axis powers Jul 1943
☐ neutral state
● Allied base
● Axis base
⚔ major battle

The war to July 1943

Feb 1942: Surrender of British forces to Japan in Singapore

Aug 1942: US bombing raids over Europe begin

Oct–Nov 1942: British defeat Germans at El Alamein

Feb 1942   Jan 1943   Apr 1943

Mar 1942: Dutch surrender East Indies to Japan

Sep 1942: Start of German siege of Stalingrad (ends Jan 1943)

Jan 1943: Roosevelt and Churchill meet at Casablanca

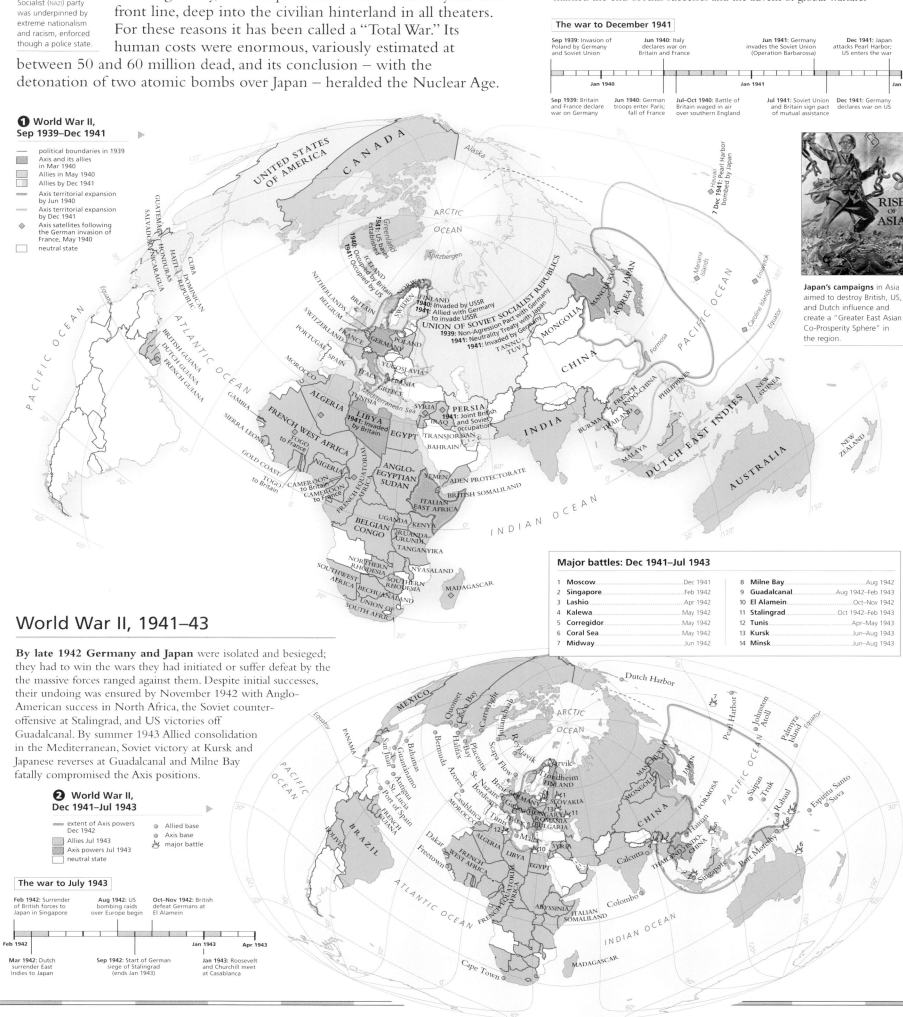

World War II, 1943–45

In 1943 Allied success was piecemeal and attritional; after June 1944 they achieved increasing depth of penetration and permanency of conquest. The Axis suffered escalating losses on the front line and in their heartlands. By August 1944 Germany's "Fortress Europe" was breached by the Soviets in Central Europe, and by Anglo-American forces in Italy and Normandy, while US victory in the Philippine Sea fatally split Japan's "Greater East Asian Co-Prosperity Sphere." However, Axis tenacity and the Allied insistence upon unconditional surrender, meant that peace would only be achieved with the devastation of Europe and Japan.

SEE ALSO:

Europe: pp.210–211

West Asia: pp.234–235

South and Southeast Asia: pp.250–251

North and East Asia: pp.272–273

July 1943 to the end of the war

Jul 1943: Allied forces land in Sicily

Sep 1943: Italy surrenders to Allies; German forces occupy Milan and Rome

Aug 1944: Allied forces liberate Paris

Oct 1944: Battle of Leyte Gulf against Japan

May 1945: Germany surrenders

Aug 1945: Atomic bombs exploded over Hiroshima and Nagasaki

Jul 1943 — Jan 1944 — Jan 1945 — Oct 1945

Oct 1943: Italy declares war on Germany

Nov 1943: Roosevelt, Stalin, and Churchill meet at Tehran

Jun 1944: D-Day: Allied landings in Normandy

Nov 1944: US begins direct aerial bombing of Japan

May 1945: Berlin surrenders to the Red Army

Sep 1945: Formal Japanese surrender

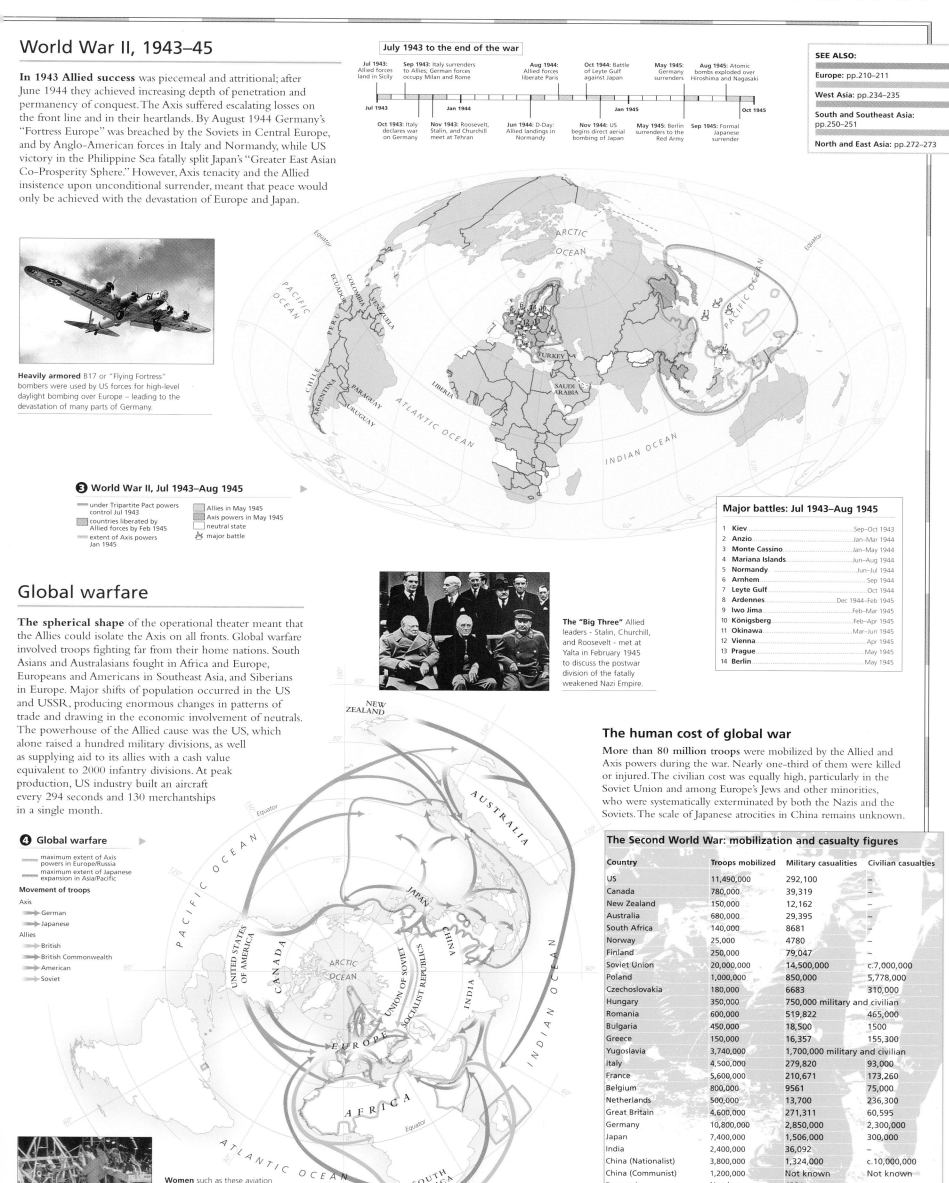

Heavily armored B17 or "Flying Fortress" bombers were used by US forces for high-level daylight bombing over Europe – leading to the devastation of many parts of Germany.

❸ World War II, Jul 1943–Aug 1945

- under Tripartite Pact powers control Jul 1943
- countries liberated by Allied forces by Feb 1945
- extent of Axis powers Jan 1945
- Allies in May 1945
- Axis powers in May 1945
- neutral state
- major battle

Major battles: Jul 1943–Aug 1945

1	Kiev	Sep–Oct 1943
2	Anzio	Jan–Jun 1944
3	Monte Cassino	Jan–May 1944
4	Mariana Islands	Jun–Aug 1944
5	Normandy	Jun–Jul 1944
6	Arnhem	Sep 1944
7	Leyte Gulf	Oct 1944
8	Ardennes	Dec 1944–Feb 1945
9	Iwo Jima	Feb–Mar 1945
10	Königsberg	Feb–Apr 1945
11	Okinawa	Mar–Jun 1945
12	Vienna	Apr 1945
13	Prague	May 1945
14	Berlin	May 1945

Global warfare

The spherical shape of the operational theater meant that the Allies could not isolate the Axis on all fronts. Global warfare involved troops fighting far from their home nations. South Asians and Australasians fought in Africa and Europe, Europeans and Americans in Southeast Asia, and Siberians in Europe. Major shifts of population occurred in the US and USSR, producing enormous changes in patterns of trade and drawing in the economic involvement of neutrals. The powerhouse of the Allied cause was the US, which alone raised a hundred military divisions, as well as supplying aid to its allies with a cash value equivalent to 2000 infantry divisions. At peak production, US industry built an aircraft every 294 seconds and 130 merchantships in a single month.

The "Big Three" Allied leaders - Stalin, Churchill, and Roosevelt - met at Yalta in February 1945 to discuss the postwar division of the fatally weakened Nazi Empire.

❹ Global warfare

- maximum extent of Axis powers in Europe/Russia
- maximum extent of Japanese expansion in Asia/Pacific

Movement of troops

Axis
- German
- Japanese

Allies
- British
- British Commonwealth
- American
- Soviet

The human cost of global war

More than 80 million troops were mobilized by the Allied and Axis powers during the war. Nearly one-third of them were killed or injured. The civilian cost was equally high, particularly in the Soviet Union and among Europe's Jews and other minorities, who were systematically exterminated by both the Nazis and the Soviets. The scale of Japanese atrocities in China remains unknown.

The Second World War: mobilization and casualty figures

Country	Troops mobilized	Military casualties	Civilian casualties
US	11,490,000	292,100	–
Canada	780,000	39,319	–
New Zealand	150,000	12,162	–
Australia	680,000	29,395	–
South Africa	140,000	8681	–
Norway	25,000	4780	–
Finland	250,000	79,047	–
Soviet Union	20,000,000	14,500,000	c.7,000,000
Poland	1,000,000	850,000	5,778,000
Czechoslovakia	180,000	6683	310,000
Hungary	350,000	750,000 military and civilian	
Romania	600,000	519,822	465,000
Bulgaria	450,000	18,500	1500
Greece	150,000	16,357	155,300
Yugoslavia	3,740,000	1,700,000 military and civilian	
Italy	4,500,000	279,820	93,000
France	5,600,000	210,671	173,260
Belgium	800,000	9561	75,000
Netherlands	500,000	13,700	236,300
Great Britain	4,600,000	271,311	60,595
Germany	10,800,000	2,850,000	2,300,000
Japan	7,400,000	1,506,000	300,000
India	2,400,000	36,092	–
China (Nationalist)	3,800,000	1,324,000	c.10,000,000
China (Communist)	1,200,000	Not known	Not known
Denmark	Not known	4339	–
Spain	Not known	23,000 military and civilian	

Women such as these aviation engineers were enormously important to the booming US defence industry.

THE WORLD 1950–1975

WORLD POLITICS IN THE ERA following the close of World War II were defined by the tense relationship between the US and the USSR. The "Cold War" between democratic capitalism and Communism saw each side constantly attempting to contain and subvert the other. The Korean War (1950–55), the Cuban Missile Crisis of 1962, and the Vietnam War (1954–75), as well as many smaller conflicts – particularly in Central America and Africa – were all manifestations of the Cold War. Though no nuclear weapons were ever used in anger, both sides built up huge nuclear arsenals whose potential for mass destruction acted as a deterrent to conflict on a global scale.

Europe

During the Soviet era the May Day parade in Moscow's Red Square became the focus for the USSR's display of its military might. Weapons such as these ballistic rockets were wheeled through the streets.

The **1950s and 1960s** were a period of widespread prosperity and political stability in Western Europe, faltering only in the early 1970s. West Germany, banned from keeping a large army, rebuilt its shattered economy and infrastructure with stunning success. Eastern Europe was overshadowed by Soviet Communism, which restricted both economic development and the personal freedom of its citizens.

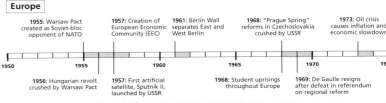

Europe

- **1955:** Warsaw Pact created as Soviet-bloc opponent of NATO
- **1956:** Hungarian revolt crushed by Warsaw Pact
- **1957:** Creation of European Economic Community (EEC)
- **1957:** First artificial satellite, Sputnik II, launched by USSR
- **1961:** Berlin Wall separates East and West Berlin
- **1968:** "Prague Spring" reforms in Czechoslovakia crushed by USSR
- **1968:** Student uprisings throughout Europe
- **1969:** De Gaulle resigns after defeat in referendum on regional reform
- **1973:** Oil crisis causes inflation and economic slowdown

SATELLITE IMAGERY

With space technology came the ability to keep artificial satellites in permanent orbit around the Earth. They are used to carry transmitters for telecommunications, as aids to navigation, and as bases for space exploration. The data picked up by sensors can be digitally combined to create images of the Earth.

This satellite image of North and South America shows both vegetation cover and weather conditions at the time at which it was taken.

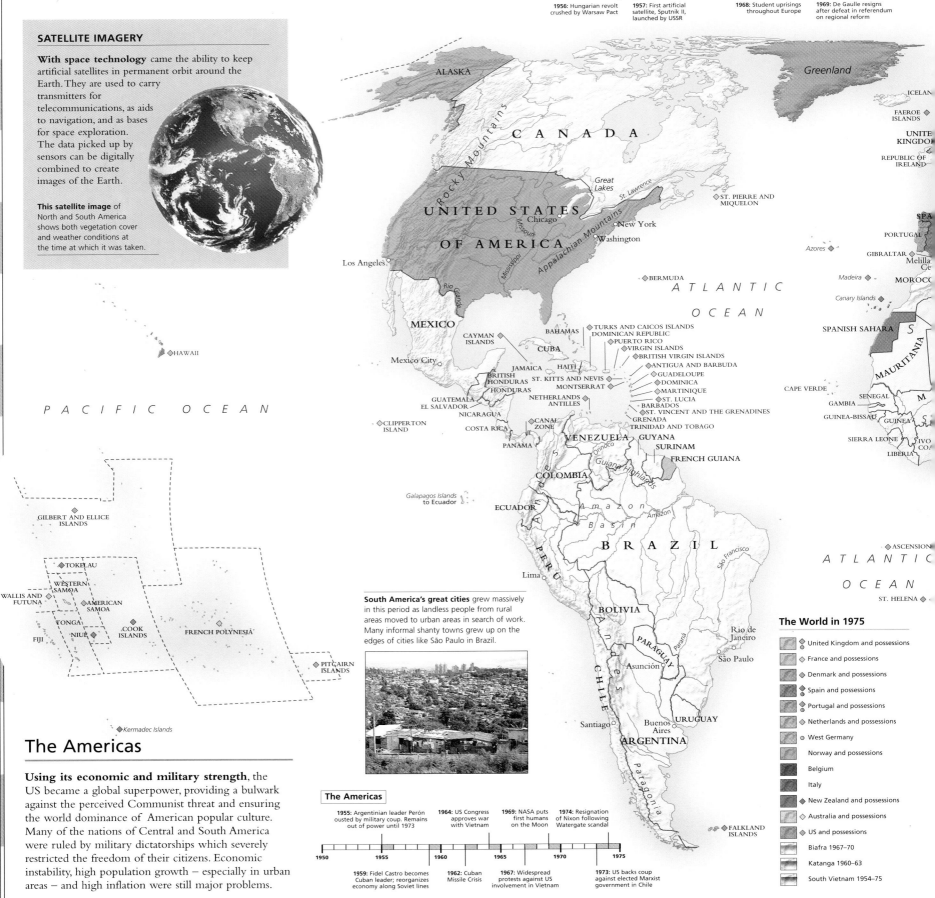

South America's great cities grew massively in this period as landless people from rural areas moved to urban areas in search of work. Many informal shanty towns grew up on the edges of cities like São Paulo in Brazil.

The Americas

Using its economic and military strength, the US became a global superpower, providing a bulwark against the perceived Communist threat and ensuring the world dominance of American popular culture. Many of the nations of Central and South America were ruled by military dictatorships which severely restricted the freedom of their citizens. Economic instability, high population growth – especially in urban areas – and high inflation were still major problems.

The Americas

- **1955:** Argentinian leader Perón ousted by military coup. Remains out of power until 1973
- **1959:** Fidel Castro becomes Cuban leader; reorganizes economy along Soviet lines
- **1964:** US Congress approves war with Vietnam
- **1962:** Cuban Missile Crisis
- **1967:** Widespread protests against US involvement in Vietnam
- **1969:** NASA puts first humans on the Moon
- **1973:** US backs coup against elected Marxist government in Chile
- **1974:** Resignation of Nixon following Watergate scandal

The World in 1975

- United Kingdom and possessions
- France and possessions
- Denmark and possessions
- Spain and possessions
- Portugal and possessions
- Netherlands and possessions
- West Germany
- Norway and possessions
- Belgium
- Italy
- New Zealand and possessions
- Australia and possessions
- US and possessions
- Biafra 1967–70
- Katanga 1960–63
- South Vietnam 1954–75

Intense rivalry between Israel and Egypt led in June 1967 to the Six Day War. Superior Israeli air power routed the Egyptian air force and the ground forces of Egypt, Jordan, Iraq, and Syria.

West and South Asia

Israel, supported by Western powers, fought a series of wars with its Arab neighbors to define its boundaries. The exploitation of extensive oil reserves brought immense wealth to the undeveloped Arabian Peninsula. Relations between India and Pakistan were strained by territorial disputes, and in 1971, the geographical separation of Pakistan proved unsustainable, with East Pakistan becoming Bangladesh.

West and South Asia

1952: First Indian general election won by Congress Party

1956: Pakistan constituted as Islamic Republic

1965: India–Pakistan War over sovreignty of Kashmir

1971: Pakistan divides; East Pakistan becomes Bangladesh

1973: OPEC restricts flow of oil to world markets

1950 — 1955 — 1960 — 1965 — 1970 — 1975

1961: Foundation of Organization of the Petroleum Exporting Countries (OPEC)

1967: Israel defeats Egypt and other Arab nations in Six Day War

1973: Arab states fail to defeat Israel in Yom Kippur War

East and Southeast Asia

In China and mainland Southeast Asia, power passed to native Communist movements. Mao Zedong's Communist China became a superpower to rival the USSR, while the US intervened in Korea and Vietnam in response to the perceived threat of Communism. Japan began rebuilding its economy with American aid to become, by the mid-1970s, one of the world's richest nations. From 1950 onward, mainland Southeast Asia was destabilized by Cold War-inspired conflict: in Laos, Vietnam, and Cambodia.

The political thoughts of Mao Zedong were published as the "Little Red Book" and distributed to all Communist Party members.

East and Southeast Asia

1950: Outbreak of Korean War

1958: Start of Mao's "Great Leap Forward" in China

1965: US troops sent to Vietnam – bombing of North begins

1975: US-backed South Vietnam regime falls

1950 — 1955 — 1960 — 1965 — 1970 — 1975

1954: Independence of Laos, Cambodia, and North and South Vietnam

1962: US military advisors sent to assist South Vietnamese regime

1966–70: Mao Zedong imposes Cultural Revolution in China

SEE ALSO:

North America: pp.136–137

South America: pp.152–153

Africa: pp.168–169

Europe: pp.212–213

West Asia: pp.234–235

South and Southeast Asia: pp.250–253

North and East Asia: pp.274–275

Australasia and Oceania: pp.284–285

THE MICROCHIP

The miniaturization of transistors and other electronic components, allowed complete electronic circuits to be created on a single slice of silicon about the size of a human fingernail. The first microprocessor chip, the Intel 4004, was produced in the USA in 1971.

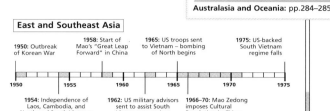

Most modern electronic devices use a number of integrated circuits like this.

Africa's post-colonial era provided rich pickings for a series of corrupt military dictators such as President Mobutu, who ruled Zaire from 1965–97.

Africa

A succession of former colonies became independent from 1957 onward; by 1975, 41 African counties had become independent. Few were fully prepared for the demands of independence, and many countries remained pawns in the Cold War, armed by the opposing powers, and fighting wars on behalf of their conflicting ideologies.

Africa

1956: UK fails to block Egypt's nationalization of Suez Canal

1960: Fifteen African countries gain independence; South Africa leaves Commonwealth

1964: Nelson Mandela, leader of ANC, jailed in South Africa

1975: Angola and Mozambique gain independence from Portugal

1950 — 1955 — 1960 — 1965 — 1970 — 1975

1954: Algerian uprising against French rule

1957: Ghana becomes first British colony to achieve independence

1960: Katanga province secedes from Republic of Congo (Zaire); UN intervention follows

1967–70: Civil war in Nigeria over secession of oil-rich east (Biafra). Over one million die

THE COLD WAR

Spies, such as the Rosenbergs, executed in 1953 for passing US nuclear secrets to the USSR, were endemic during the Cold War.

FROM THE MEETING OF US AND SOVIET FORCES on the Elbe River in April 1945 came a division of Europe and a confrontation between the former allies which would last for almost five decades. Defensive needs – for the US the security of Western Europe, for the USSR a buffer zone in Eastern Europe – which appeared to each other to be of offensive intents, overlaid by ideological, political, and economic rivalries. Thus the Cold War took shape, with the US committed to a policy of containment and attrition by all means just short of open conflict, and the USSR intent on supporting anti-Western revolutionary movements throughout the world. Strategic and armed stalemate gave rise to détente in the 1970s, but only the collapse of Soviet system in 1989–91 ended the Cold War.

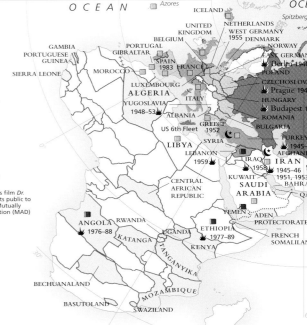

The Cuban missile crisis 1961–62

The Cold War's most dangerous single episode arose from the Castro Revolution (1956–59) and subsequent US–Cuban estrangement. Castro's alignment with the Eastern bloc provided the USSR with an opportunity to offset its strategic inferiority by the creation of Cuban bases from which missiles could strike at the heart of the continental US. This was forestalled by a US blockade, and a stand-off following which the Soviets were forced to withdraw their missiles.

Cold warriors J. F. Kennedy and Nikita Khrushchev underestimated each other's strength and determination when they met in Vienna in 1961. By 1962 they had taken the world to the verge of nuclear conflict during the Cuban missile crisis.

Cold War crises 1956–64

1956–59: Cuban Revolution under Fidel Castro

1957: USSR launches first space satellite

1961: Increasing US involvement in Vietnam

Apr 1961: USSR launches first manned space flight

1962: Cuban missile crisis

1964: Kubrick's film *Dr. Strangelove* alerts public to dangers of Mutually Assured Destruction (MAD)

1956 1958 1960 1962 1964

Scale varies with perspective

4990 km (3100 miles)

4440 km (2760 miles)

★ Apr 1961: CIA-backed invasion force of Cuban exiles aborted at Bay of Pigs

2 The Cuban missile crisis 1961-62

- potential range of Soviet missiles (1100 miles)
- US blockade zone
- ⊕ Soviet missile and jet base
- ⊕ US air base
- ⚓ US naval base

NATO and the Warsaw Pact

Deepening US-Soviet hostility, plus Western Europe's patent inability to defend itself, led to the creation of the North Atlantic Treaty Organization (NATO) in April 1949; in effect, the US provided guarantee of Western Europe's security. The latter's continuing war-weariness saw a buildup of US forces in Europe, and contributed to the decision to permit West Germany to have armed forces, admitting the nation to NATO in 1955. This in turn prompted the USSR and its satellite countries in Eastern Europe to form the Warsaw Pact. The building of the Berlin Wall in 1961 consolidated the "Iron Curtain" which divided Europe into two zones – East and West – until 1989.

On June 23, 1948, the Soviet army blockaded the Western-controlled sectors of Berlin, forcing the Allied powers to mount a massive airlift to supply the beleaguered enclave.

The Cold War in Europe 1947–68

1948: Berlin airlift following Soviet blockade of Berlin

1948: Soviet-sponsored regimes established in Czechoslovakia and Hungary

1955: Formation of Warsaw Pact

1957: Treaty of Rome; basis of European Economic Community

1968: Reforms in Czechoslovakia suppressed by Soviets

1950 1955 1960 1965

1947: Marshall Plan for US economic aid to Europe

1955: West Germany admitted to NATO

1956: Uprisings in Poland and Hungary crushed by Soviets

1961: Berlin Wall built

3 The Cold War in Europe

- original NATO members in 1949
- later NATO members (with dates)
- Warsaw Pact members in 1955
- neutral states

500 km

500 miles

① The alliances of the Cold War

US, allies, and satellite states

- US and original NATO 1949
- later NATO
- NATO dependencies 1960
- other nations allied to the Western bloc by treaty
- ☪ CENTO Pact 1959
- major US and NATO overseas bases

USSR and allies

- USSR
- Warsaw Pact 1955
- Communist satellite states
- China
- ⚓ major Soviet overseas base
- ⚓ Cold War flashpoint
- major US fleet

From the early **1960s** the Western allies depended increasingly on long-range nuclear-powered submarines to deliver missiles in the event of war. With the development of Trident submarines in the 1980s the range extended to 4,500 miles, a key factor in the Strategic Arms Reduction (START) negotiations of 1982–91.

SEE ALSO:

North America: pp.138–139

South America: pp.152–153

Africa: pp.168–169

Europe: pp.212–215

West Asia: pp.234–235

South and Southeast Asia: pp.252–253

North and East Asia: pp.274–275

Australasia and Oceania: pp.284–285

Strategic manoeuvres in the Cold War

1947: Truman Doctrine seeks "containment" of USSR
1949: Formation of NATO
1972: SALT I strategic arms limitation talks
1979: SALT II arms limitation agreement signed
1990: NATO and Warsaw Pact agree on conventional arms limitation in Europe

1945 1955 1965 1975 1985 1995

1945: Yalta Conference; division between Allies; origins of Cold War
1955: Formation of Warsaw Pact
1989–90: Collapse of Communism in Europe
1991: US and USSR sign START arms reduction treaty

The strategic balance

In the Cold War's first decade the US sought to contain the threat of global Communism by a series of regional treaties and alliances backed by economic and military strength. But by 1960, with a rift in Sino-Soviet relations splitting the Communist bloc, and as the simultaneous process of decolonization (endorsed by the US) deprived its European NATO allies of their global outreach, so the theater of the Cold War shifted from Europe to the developing world. Here a series of conflicts from Cuba to Vietnam saw both the US and the Communist world frequently fighting a war by proxy.

The Korean War 1950–53

Reluctantly sanctioned by the USSR, North Korea's invasion of the south in June 1950 was immediately seen as a test of US global credibility. The challenge was initially countered by a US-led UN force, which was met in turn by Chinese intervention. Thereafter the front stabilized around the prewar border. The US, confronted by the need to garrison Europe, and by a reluctance to carry the war beyond Korea's borders, accepted a policy of defensive self-restraint, which formed the basis of the Western Allies' Limited War doctrine.

THE ARMS RACE

As the Cold War arms race began, the US held technological, numerical, and positional advantages over the Soviet Union. In the 1960s, as US vulnerability increased, deterrence shifted from bombers to a triad built around submarine- and land-based intercontinental missiles (ICBMs). With the USSR acquiring ICBM capability by the late 1960s, both superpowers faced the future with secure second-strikes: MAD (Mutually Assured Destruction). This situation, and the development of multiple-warhead (MRV, MIRV) technology threatened a new round in the arms race. The 1970s saw ceilings on missile and warhead numbers, and antimissile defences (ABM) were limited (SALT I in 1972, and SALT II in 1979). The brief period of détente gave way to perhaps the most dangerous phase of the Cold War, one that witnessed ABM revival with the Strategic Defence Initiative (SDI, Star Wars) which only ended with the collapse of the USSR in 1991.

The Korean War effectively ended in stalemate in July 1953, with the partition of Korea into a Communist North and a nominally democratic South along an armistice line straddling the 38th parallel. This border has remained a heavily armed military frontier ever since. These South Korean troops were photographed in 1996.

▲ **④ The Korean War 1950–53**

- area controlled by North Korean forces Sep 15 1950
- front line Sep 15 1950
- US forces Sep 16–Oct 24 1950
- Chinese forces Oct 1950
- front line Nov 24 1950
- front line Jan 25 1951
- cease-fire line Jul 27 1953

The Angolan Civil War 1975–88

By the 1970s Soviet naval and airlift capacity enabled it to give active support to anti-Western revolution globally. However, its major efforts in Africa, in Angola (1976–88) and Ethiopia (1977–89), were conducted by proxy via Cuba. In Angola, the three main organizations which had fought to end Portuguese rule were bitterly hostile to each other, and by 1975 there was a three-way civil war, the Marxist MPLA initially clearing the FNLA and UNITA from the north. The Soviets sustained the MPLA with Cuban troops, while the Western powers, through South Africa, secured southern borders in support of UNITA. The conflict lasted until 1988, the Cubans, MPLA and South Africa concluding an uneasy ceasefire. Throughout the struggle, UNITA dominated most of Angola through guerrilla warfare, but 50,000 Cuban troops ensured the survival of the MPLA.

Ideological indoctrination by both East and West during the Cold War conflicts in the developing world was enforced irrespective of sex or age. The image of the child soldier is an enduring legacy of these conflicts in Africa.

⑤ The Angolan Civil War from 1975

- under FNLA control 1975
- under MPLA control 1975
- under UNITA control 1975
- area of MPLA control by mid-1976
- area under UNITA control by mid-1976
- Cuban troops and Soviet aid to MPLA from 1975
- area of effective South African occupation
- South African attacks in support of UNITA 1976–88
- limit of UNITA guerrilla activity 1976–92

THE WORLD · THE MODERN AGE

WITH THE CLOSE OF THE COLD WAR IN 1989, a new world order emerged. Rivalry between the US and the USSR ended, as the latter broke up in 1991, and the former Eastern bloc was opened up to the West and free-market forces, although Russia itself suffered crises of confidence. In the Middle East, disputes between Israel and its neighbors remained unresolved, while Islamic fundamentalism in Iran and Saddam Hussein's aggressive militarism in Iraq kept much of the region on constant standby for war. In Southeast Asia, massive investment during the 1980s fed an economic boom which proved unsustainable, plunging the region into depression in the late 1990s. South Africa's all-embracing elections of 1994 were a triumph for democracy in Africa, but as the century closed, Central Africa was becoming enveloped in regional war.

The Berlin Wall, hated symbol of division between East and West, was torn down in 1989, and Germany's two halves were reunited the following year.

Europe

While Western Europe progressed toward economic and political unity under the European Union (EU), eastern Europe was still economically constrained by Soviet Communism. But in 1989 popular movements rejected Communism, fracturing first the Eastern bloc and in 1991, the USSR itself. The fragmentation boiled over into civil war, notably in Yugoslavia and Georgia, where conflicts were fueled by ethnic nationalism.

Europe

1985: Mikhail Gorbachev becomes Soviet leader; moves to end Cold War	**1990:** East and West Germany reunited **1991:** Breakup of USSR **1995:** Ceasefire agreed in Bosnia and Herzegovina; UN troops remain

1975 1980 1985 1990 1995 2000

1975: General Franco dies in Spain. He is replaced by King Juan Carlos — **1989:** End of Communism in Poland, Hungary, Czechoslovakia, Romania, East Germany, and Bulgaria — **1991:** Start of civil war in Yugoslavia

REMOTE-SENSED MAPPING

The detailed data collected by sensor-bearing satellites can be used to map changing geographic patterns. Examples include climatic conditions, soils, vegetation, pollution, and levels of urbanization.

An infrared satellite image of Buenos Aires taken from a French *SPOT* satellite shows densely populated urban areas in blue, vegetation in red, and water – including the River Plate – in black.

The Modern World

- Turkey
- United Kingdom and possessions
- France and possessions
- Denmark and possessions
- Spain and possessions
- Portugal and possessions
- Netherlands and possessions
- Russian Federation
- Japan and possessions
- Norway and possessions
- India and possessions
- Italy
- New Zealand and possessions
- Australia and possessions
- US and possessions

B-H   Bosnia and Herzegovina

The traditional lifestyles of peoples such as the Yanomami of Brazil were under ever greater threat from the destruction of the rain forest and encroaching urbanization.

The Americas

From the end of the 1970s the states of Central and South America began to shed their repressive regimes and move towards democracy. Economic instability, high population growth, and chronic inflation remained major problems. The US maintained its economic dominance and position as a world power-broker, retaining a hostility to Communism until 1985, when moves by a reforming USSR paved the way for a new world order.

The Americas

1982: Falklands War between UK and Argentina	**1987:** US and USSR agree to limit intermediate nuclear weapons	**1991:** UN-brokered peace ends 10-year civil war in El Salvador

1975 1980 1985 1990 1995 2000

1979: Start of civil war in Nicaragua between Sandinistas and US-backed Contras — **1989:** Democracy restored in Chile as Pinochet steps down — **1991–92:** USSR ends preferential trade agreement with Cuba; US tightens blockade

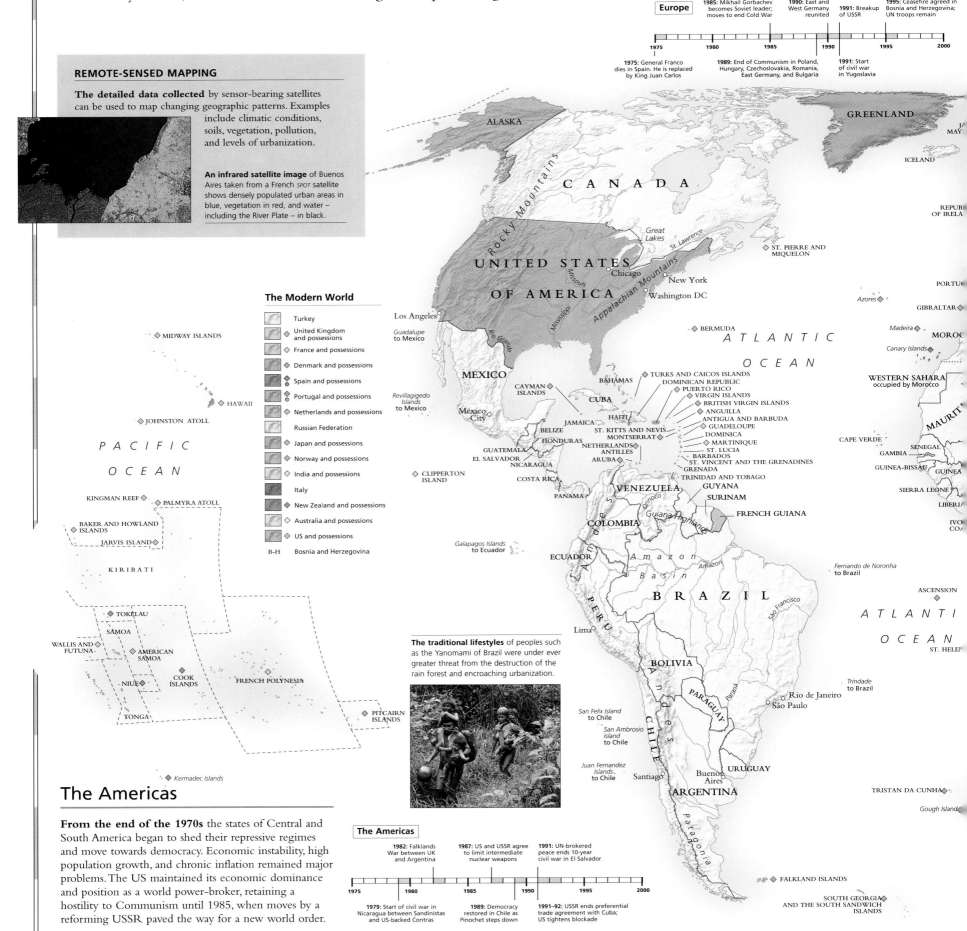

West and South Asia

Conflict continued throughout the Middle East, paralleled by a resurgence of a more fundamentalist form of Islam, especially in Iran. This led in turn to a destabilization of much of the western region, affecting particularly Lebanon, nearby Iraq, and Syria, and leading to a number of wars. Disputes over the boundaries between Israel and its neighbors, and Palestinian self-government proved difficult to resolve.

In 1979, an Islamic revolution led by the Ayatollah Khomeini overthrew the corrupt regime of the Shah of Iran. Iran became an Islamic state, vilifying the West, governed by religious laws, and ruthlessly suppressing political opposition.

West and South Asia

1979: Islamic revolution in Iran	**1980:** Start of Iran–Iraq War	**1984:** Assassination of Indira Gandhi by Sikh bodyguards	**1989:** USSR withdraws from Afghanistan	**1990:** Iraqi invasion of Kuwait sparks Gulf War	**1995:** Israeli-PLO agreement extends Palestinian self-rule within the West Bank

1975 — 1980 — 1985 — 1990 — 1995 — 2000

1977: Start of Middle East peace process	**1979:** Soviet invasion of Afghanistan	**1988:** End of Iran–Iraq War	**1996:** Taliban forces capture Kabul

East and Southeast Asia

From the late 1970s, China sought closer links with the West and began a program of industrial expansion. Calls for greater democracy were halted in 1989 following the massacre of students in Tiananmen Square. The Japanese economy boomed and Pacific Rim economies such as South Korea, Taiwan, Singapore, and Indonesia saw unprecedented industrial growth until an economic collapse in the late 1990s.

Cheaper labor costs led many firms to relocate their production to factories in China and Southeast Asia during the 1980s. These women are making toys for a Western firm in a factory near Guangzhou.

East and Southeast Asia

	1989: Crushing of pro-democracy demonstrators in Beijing	**1998:** Economic crisis in Indonesia leads to overthrow of government

1975 — 1980 — 1985 — 1990 — 1995 — 2000

1975: Indonesia annexes East Timor	**1979:** Vietnamese invasion of Cambodia ousts Pol Pot	**1997:** Hong Kong returned to Chinese rule

SEE ALSO:

North America: pp.136–137

South America: pp.152–153

Africa: pp.168–169

Europe: pp.214–215

West Asia: pp.234–235

South and Southeast Asia: pp.252–253

North and East Asia: pp.274–275

Australasia and Oceania: pp.284–285

THE COMPUTER AGE

Computer technology has revolutionized the way in which business is conducted internationally. Information can be transmitted in seconds and decisions made with equal speed across continents and time zones.

Brokers in a trading office have access to information from across the world via their computers.

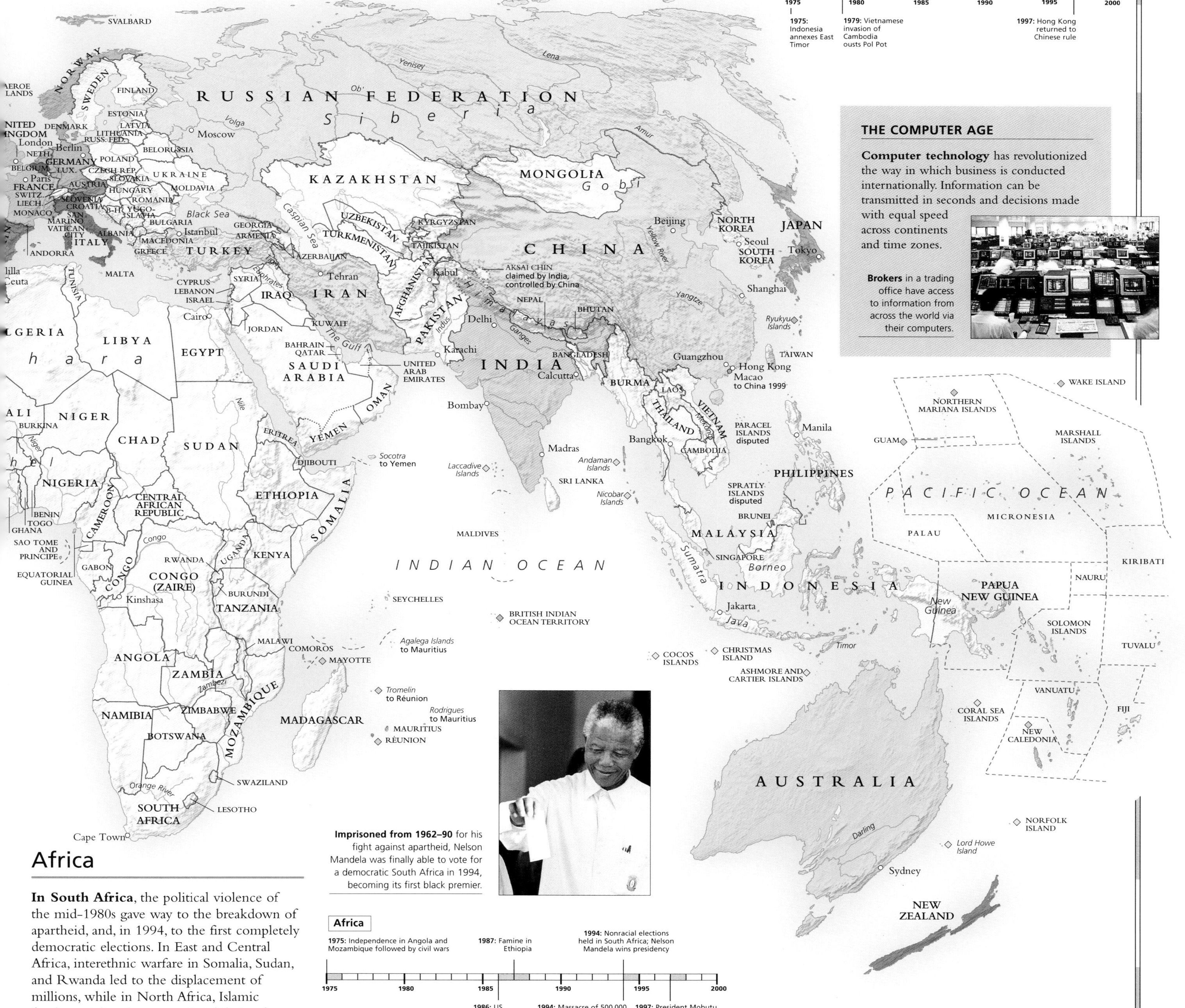

Imprisoned from 1962–90 for his fight against apartheid, Nelson Mandela was finally able to vote for a democratic South Africa in 1994, becoming its first black premier.

Africa

In South Africa, the political violence of the mid-1980s gave way to the breakdown of apartheid, and, in 1994, to the first completely democratic elections. In East and Central Africa, interethnic warfare in Somalia, Sudan, and Rwanda led to the displacement of millions, while in North Africa, Islamic fundamentalism became a destabilizing force.

Africa

1975: Independence in Angola and Mozambique followed by civil wars	**1987:** Famine in Ethiopia	**1994:** Nonracial elections held in South Africa; Nelson Mandela wins presidency

1975 — 1980 — 1985 — 1990 — 1995 — 2000

	1986: US bombs Libya	**1994:** Massacre of 500,000 Tutsis by Hutu in Rwanda	**1997:** President Mobutu overthrown in Zaire

Map labels (reading order):

SVALBARD · NORWAY · SWEDEN · FINLAND · AEROE LANDS · UNITED KINGDOM · London · DENMARK · Berlin · NETH. · GERMANY · POLAND · BELORUSSIA · ESTONIA · LATVIA · LITHUANIA · RUSS. FED. · Moscow · RUSSIAN FEDERATION · Siberia · Ob' · Yenisey · Lena · Amur · Paris · FRANCE · BELGIUM · LUX. · CZECH REP. · SLOVAKIA · UKRAINE · Volga · SWITZ. · LIECH. · AUSTRIA · HUNGARY · MOLDAVIA · ROMANIA · SLOVENIA · CROATIA · YUGOSLAVIA · MONACO · SAN MARINO · VATICAN CITY · ITALY · BOSNIA-HERZ. · BULGARIA · Black Sea · Istanbul · GEORGIA · ARMENIA · AZERBAIJAN · KAZAKHSTAN · MONGOLIA · Gobi · ANDORRA · ALBANIA · MACEDONIA · GREECE · TURKEY · Caspian Sea · TURKMENISTAN · UZBEKISTAN · KYRGYZSTAN · TAJIKISTAN · Beijing · NORTH KOREA · JAPAN · Tokyo · Seoul · SOUTH KOREA · CHINA · Yellow River · Shanghai · Yangtze · Ryukyu Islands · MALTA · CYPRUS · LEBANON · ISRAEL · SYRIA · Euphrates · Tehran · AFGHANISTAN · Kabul · AKSAI CHIN claimed by India, controlled by China · NEPAL · BHUTAN · lilla Ceuta · TUNISIA · Cairo · JORDAN · IRAQ · IRAN · KUWAIT · PAKISTAN · Himalayas · Ganges · Delhi · Indus · TAIWAN · ALGERIA · LIBYA · EGYPT · Sahara · Nile · BAHRAIN · QATAR · SAUDI ARABIA · UNITED ARAB EMIRATES · The Gulf · Karachi · INDIA · Calcutta · BANGLADESH · BURMA · Guangzhou · Hong Kong · Macao to China 1999 · WAKE ISLAND · MALI · NIGER · CHAD · SUDAN · Sahel · ERITREA · YEMEN · OMAN · Socotra to Yemen · Bombay · Madras · Laccadive Islands · SRI LANKA · Andaman Islands · Nicobar Islands · LAOS · THAILAND · VIETNAM · Mekong · PARACEL ISLANDS disputed · Manila · NORTHERN MARIANA ISLANDS · GUAM · MARSHALL ISLANDS · BURKINA · NIGERIA · BENIN · TOGO · GHANA · SAO TOME AND PRINCIPE · EQUATORIAL GUINEA · GABON · CAMEROON · CENTRAL AFRICAN REPUBLIC · ETHIOPIA · SOMALIA · Bangkok · CAMBODIA · PHILIPPINES · SPRATLY ISLANDS disputed · MALAYSIA · BRUNEI · PALAU · MICRONESIA · PACIFIC OCEAN · KIRIBATI · Congo · RWANDA · BURUNDI · UGANDA · KENYA · TANZANIA · Kinshasa · CONGO (ZAIRE) · MALDIVES · INDIAN OCEAN · SEYCHELLES · BRITISH INDIAN OCEAN TERRITORY · Sumatra · SINGAPORE · Borneo · INDONESIA · Jakarta · Java · New Guinea · PAPUA NEW GUINEA · NAURU · SOLOMON ISLANDS · TUVALU · ANGOLA · ZAMBIA · MALAWI · COMOROS · Agalega Islands to Mauritius · MAYOTTE · Timor · COCOS ISLANDS · CHRISTMAS ISLAND · ASHMORE AND CARTIER ISLANDS · VANUATU · NAMIBIA · ZIMBABWE · BOTSWANA · MOZAMBIQUE · Zambezi · MADAGASCAR · Tromelin to Réunion · Rodrigues to Mauritius · MAURITIUS · RÉUNION · CORAL SEA ISLANDS · NEW CALEDONIA · FIJI · Orange River · SWAZILAND · SOUTH AFRICA · LESOTHO · Cape Town · AUSTRALIA · Darling · NORFOLK ISLAND · Lord Howe Island · Sydney · NEW ZEALAND

HIDDEN WORLDS OF TODAY

THE WORLD ECONOMY at the end of the 20th century was dominated increasingly by investment trends and corporate business strategies determined at transcontinental and global rather than national levels. The World Trade Organization (WTO) formed in 1995 and enshrining liberal free-trade principles, found itself tackling disputes as likely to be between trade blocs as between individual countries. The phenomenon of globalization was made possible, and greatly reinforced, by digital technology and the rapid growth of telecommunications. At the same time, links of ethnic origin, cultural affinity, or religious identity were the defining characteristics of communities transcending national boundaries – such as the Islamic world. Across Europe, the trend toward economic integration was accompanied by some devolution of government, to meet demands for autonomy within existing states.

The production of illegal drugs occurs globally. These examples of 'kef' (cannabis) and opium were made in Morocco.

The Greater African Nation

The African diaspora in the Americas, originating with the slave trade in the 16th–18th centuries, is today over 80 million strong. Only the Caribbean states have majority black populations, but African Americans in the US are the world's fourth largest black community and in the world top ten. The UK's black minority is a more recent result of post-war immigration, as is Portugal's. The black community has few political ties internationally, but a shared sense of identity and awareness of their African roots.

Dancers celebrate the Carnival in Rio de Janeiro, a spectacular celebration of the city's vibrant cultural mix.

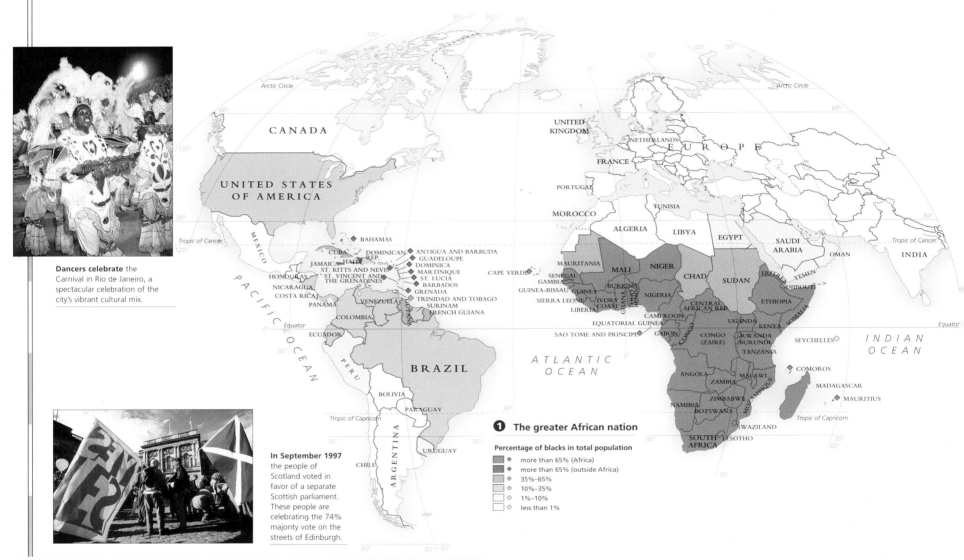

❶ The greater African nation

Percentage of blacks in total population

- ◇ more than 65% (Africa)
- ◇ more than 65% (outside Africa)
- ◇ 35%–65%
- ◇ 10%–35%
- ◇ 1%–10%
- ◇ less than 1%

In September 1997 the people of Scotland voted in favor of a separate Scottish parliament. These people are celebrating the 74% majority vote on the streets of Edinburgh.

Devolution in Europe

Europe's new nation states of the 1990s emerged from the demise of the Soviet Union, the "velvet divorce" of Czechs from Slovaks, and the bloody breakup of the former socialist Yugoslavia. Unresolved separatist aspirations persisted, notably among Albanian-speakers under Serbian rule in Kosovo, while Bosnia now barely exists beyond its separate Serb and Muslim-Croat "entities." Within the European Union, the archetype of "supranational" integration, a federal system like Germany's gave substantial autonomy to state government. Belgium, riven by rivalries between the Flemish and the francophone Walloons, opted to devolve power to the regions – as did Spain, albeit not far enough for more militant Basques, while even centralist France held out special status plans for Corsica, and in Italy a separatist Northern League became a political force.

❷ Devolution and statehood in Europe

- ▢ new state since 1990
- ▢◇ a degree of devolution acknowledged
- ▨ substantial ethnic groups without their own state
- ◔ pressure for greater self-determination

Serbian persecution of ethnic Albanians in the Kosovo region of the rump state of Yugoslavia led, in early 1999 to air strikes against Serbia by NATO and the murder or exodus of hundreds of thousands of refugees, "ethnically cleansed" from their former homes.

The pan-Islamic world

Sunni Islam is the dominant tradition in the Muslim world, under regimes ranging from secular states and conservative Gulf sheikdoms to the extreme militancy of the Afghani Taliban. Iran is the major contemporary Shi'a power – and the Iranian revolution the inspiration for Shi'a militancy elsewhere. Outside Iran, however, only Azerbaijan, Bahrain, and parts of Iraq have Shi'a majorities, and even in Bahrain and Iraq it is Sunnis who hold power. Assad's regime in Syria is based on the Alawite minority, who follow a variant of Shi'a Islam.

The Muslim requirement for prayer to Mecca several times daily continues despite the restrictions posed by modern urban life. These Egyptian Muslims are praying in the middle of an Alexandria street.

SEE ALSO:

North America: pp.138–139

South America: p152–153

Africa: pp.168–169

Europe: pp.214–215

West Asia: pp.234–235

South and Southeast Asia: pp.252–253

North and East Asia: pp.274–275

❸ The pan–Islamic World

Percentage of Muslims in population
- 91–100%
- 51–90%
- 21–50%
- 6–20%
- 1–5%
- less than 1%

Official status of Islam
- ☾ formally designated Islamic republic
- ◐ secular state where population is more then 50% Muslim
- Ⓘ established religion is Islam
- ✳ membership of Organization of the Islamic Conference (OIC)
- ⚜ active conflict over militant Islam

The subterranean world of organized crime

Ease of travel and speed of communication encouraged the spread of organized crime syndicates far beyond national borders. As business became globalized, so too was corruption in business and finance; traditional industries such as narcotics, prostitution, gambling, extortion, and money-laundering were transformed into global industries. Law enforcement had some successes in curtailing the Italian and US mafia, but the collapse of Communism in the Soviet Union created conditions in which a Russian mafia grew rapidly, becoming established across Eurasia and America. The big drug cartels, dealing in cocaine or heroin, fought for control of the production and distribution channels to the rich markets of North America and Europe. Profits, "laundered" through other businesses and exploiting the confidentiality of banking systems, were used to acquire increasing political influence and protection.

This "Internet Cafe" in Taiwan, offers diners access to the Internet while they eat.

THE WORLD WIDE WEB

Wide-area computer networking, developed originally for sharing information between academic institutions, expanded to become a worldwide Internet whose user numbers exploded in the 1990s. The big stimulus to its popular success was the creation of a graphical interface for "surfing" hyperlinked sites on what became known as the World Wide Web. The opportunities for anonymity, the use of encrypted communications, and the problems of authentication and copyright protection posed great difficulties for policing and control.

❹ The world of organized crime

Narcotics production and trafficking
- cannabis production
- cocaine production
- heroin production
- heroin and cannabis production
- → heroin trafficking
- → cocaine trafficking
- → cannabis trafficking

Major centers for criminal organizations
- ◆ Mafia
- ◇ Triads
- ✎ major center for drug-related crime
- ▱ drug transit centers
- — "Golden Triangle"
- Ⓢ major center for money laundering
- ⊛ murder rate greater than 8 per 100,000, with figure

Extent of international organized crime
- Italian Mafia
- Chinese Triads
- Jamaican Posses
- Russian Mafia
- Colombian cartels
- Japanese Yakuzas
- United States Cosa Nostra
- Turkish Mafia

PART TWO

REGIONAL HISTORY

INHABITANTS OF EACH PART of the globe view the history of the world through the lens of their regional heritage. The second section of this atlas presents the chronological story of eight principal geographic regions: North America, South America, Africa, Europe, West Asia, South and Southeast Asia, North and East Asia and, finally, Australasia and Oceania. Each regional narrative is prefaced by a map which examines its historical geography. This is followed by pages covering the exploration and mapping of the area, showing how it came to be known in its present form. Thereafter, the maps are organized to present the continuous historical development of each region through time.

By the 18th century, the modern world map was clearly emerging. This map, produced by the Dutch cartographer, Matthias Seutter in 1730, combines a series of detailed projections of the various hemispheres, with compass points depicted as a variety of different windheads.

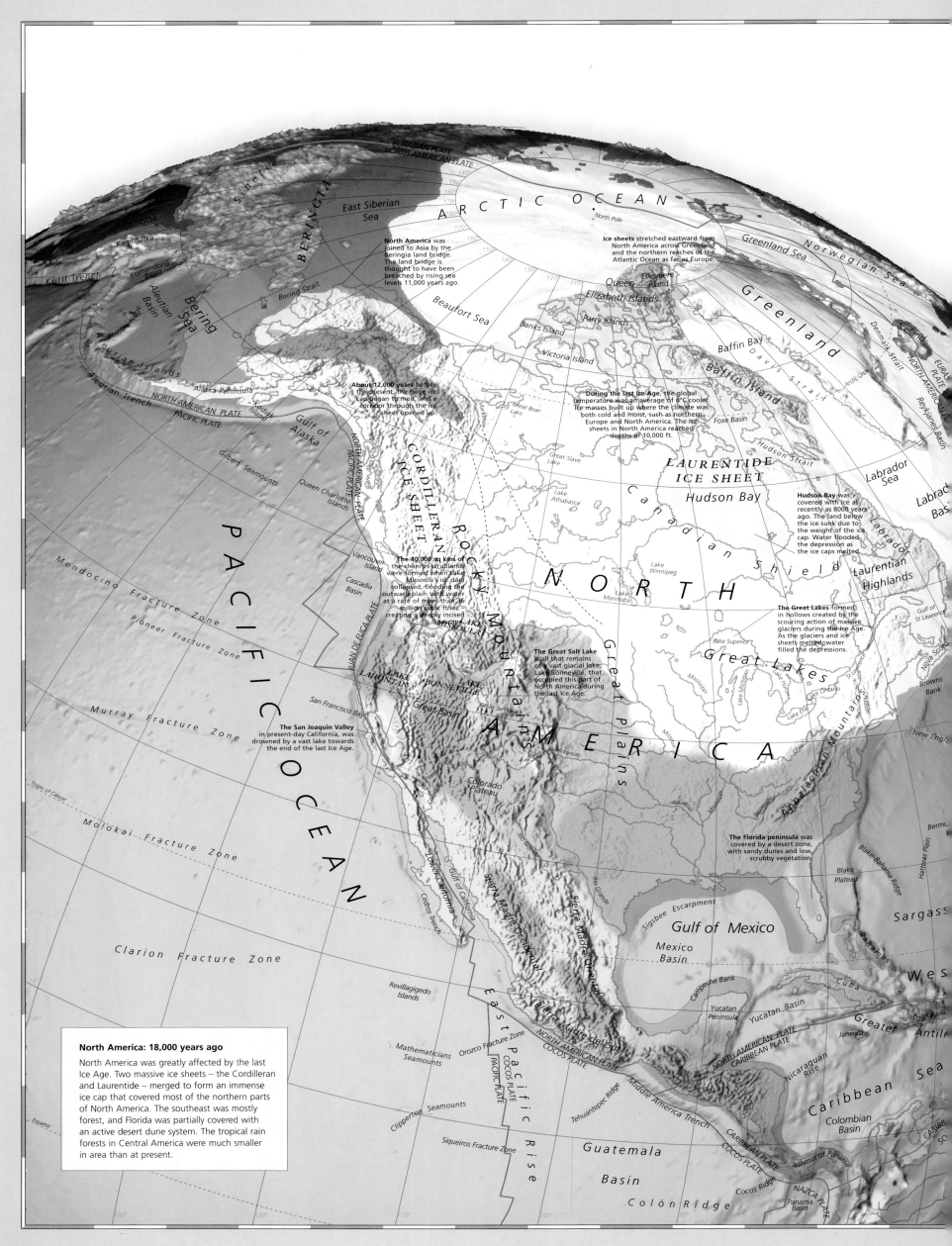

EURASIAN PLATE
NORTH AMERICAN PLATE

ARCTIC OCEAN

North Pole

Ice sheets stretched eastward from
North America across Greenland
and the northern reaches of the
Atlantic Ocean as far as Europe.

Greenland Sea

Norwegian Sea

Siberia

East Siberian
Sea

BERINGIA

Iceland

Denmark Strait

EURASIAN PLATE
NORTH AMERICAN PLATE

Reykjanes Basin

Sea of
Okhotsk

Kamchatka

North America was
joined to Asia by the
Beringia land bridge.
The land bridge is
thought to have been
breached by rising sea
levels 11,000 years ago.

Bering Strait

Queen
Elizabeth Islands

Ellesmere
Island

Greenland

Komandorskaya
Basin

Kuril Trench

Aleutian
Basin

Bowers Ridge

Bering
Sea

Beaufort Sea

Banks Island

Parry Islands

Baffin Bay

Davis Strait

Baffin Island

Arctic Circle

Gilbert Seamounts

Aleutian Islands

Alaska Peninsula

NORTH AMERICAN PLATE
PACIFIC PLATE

Kodiak
Island

Gulf of
Alaska

Yukon

Victoria Island

Great Bear
Lake

Mackenzie

Foxe Basin

Hudson Strait

Labrador
Sea

Labrad
Bas

About 12,000 years before
the present, the huge ice
cap began to melt, and a
corridor through the ice
sheet opened up.

During the last Ice Age, the global
temperature was an average of 6°C cooler.
Ice masses built up where the climate was
both cold and moist, such as northern
Europe and North America. The ice
sheets in North America reached
depths of 10,000 ft.

**LAURENTIDE
ICE SHEET**

Hudson Bay

Hudson Bay was
covered with ice as
recently as 8000 years
ago. The land below
the ice sunk due to
the weight of the ice
cap. Water flooded
the depression as
the ice caps melted.

Queen Charlotte
Islands

NORTH AMERICAN PLATE
PACIFIC PLATE

CORDILLERAN
ICE SHEET

ROCKY

Great Slave
Lake

Lake
Athabasca

Gulf of
St Lawrence

Nova Scot

PACIFIC

Mendocino Fracture Zone

Pioneer Fracture Zone

Vancouver
Island

Cascadia
Basin

JUAN DE FUCA PLATE

Mountains

The 40,000 sq kms of
the channeled scrublands
were formed when Lake
Missoula's ice dam
collapsed, flooding the
outwash plain with water
at a rate of more than 36
million cubic feet,
creating a deeply incised
landscape.

Columbia

LAKE
MISSOULA

Missouri

Lake
Winnipeg

Lake
Manitoba

N O R T H

Laurentian
Highlands

The Great Lakes formed
in hollows created by the
scouring action of massive
glaciers during the Ice Age.
As the glaciers and ice
sheets melted, water
filled the depressions.

Great Plains

Canadian Shield

Browns
Bank

Murray Fracture Zone

San Francisco Bay

LAKE
LAHONTAN

LAKE
BONNEVILLE

LAKE

Great Basin

Great Salt Lake

The Great Salt Lake
is all that remains
of a vast glacial lake,
Lake Bonneville, that
occupied this part of
North America during
the last Ice Age.

Lake Superior

Lake Michigan

Great Lakes

Lake Huron

Lake
Erie

Lake Ontario

New Engle

A M E R I C A

OCEAN

The San Joaquin Valley
in present-day California, was
drowned by a vast lake towards
the end of the last Ice Age.

Colorado
Plateau

Arkansas

Missouri

Ohio

Appalachian Mountains

Tropic of Cancer

Molokai Fracture Zone

Rio Grande

Lower California

Colorado

Arkansas

Mississippi

The Florida peninsula was
covered by a desert zone,
with sandy dunes and low,
scrubby vegetation.

Blake
Plateau

Blake-Bahama Ridge

Sargass

Bermu

Clarion Fracture Zone

Cedros Trench

Gulf of California

Sierra Madre Occidental

Sigsbee Escarpment

Gulf of Mexico

Mexico
Basin

Campeche Bank

Bahamas

Cuba

Greater

West

Revillagigedo
Islands

Sierra Madre del Sur

Sierra Madre Oriental

Yucatan
Peninsula

Yucatan Basin

Jamaica

Antil

Mathematicians
Seamounts

Orozco Fracture Zone

East Pacific Rise

NORTH AMERICAN PLATE
COCOS PLATE

PACIFIC PLATE
COCOS PLATE

Tehuantepec Ridge

Middle America Trench

Nicaraguan
Rise

**Caribbean
Sea**

Colombian
Basin

Equator

Clipperton Seamounts

Pacific Rise

CARIBBEAN PLATE
COCOS PLATE

Cocos Ridge

Isthmus of Panama

NAZCA
PLATE

CARIBBE

Siqueiros Fracture Zone

**Guatemala
Basin**

Colón Ridge

Panama
Basin

North America: 18,000 years ago

North America was greatly affected by the last
Ice Age. Two massive ice sheets – the Cordilleran
and Laurentide – merged to form an immense
ice cap that covered most of the northern parts
of North America. The southeast was mostly
forest, and Florida was partially covered with
an active desert dune system. The tropical rain
forests in Central America were much smaller
in area than at present.

Vegetation type

- ice cap and glacier
- tundra
- polar and alpine desert
- semidesert or sparsely vegetated
- grassland
- forest or open woodland
- tropical rain forest
- temperate desert
- tropical desert
- coastline (present-day)
- coastline (18,000 years ago)

NORTH AMERICA
REGIONAL HISTORY

THE HISTORICAL LANDSCAPE

HUMANS FIRST ENTERED NORTH AMERICA FROM SIBERIA some 30,000 years ago. They migrated over the land bridge across the Bering Strait and, as the ice receded, moved south, into the rich gamelands of the Great Plains and onward to eventually populate Central and South America. As the ice melted and sea levels rose, these early settlers and their new homeland became isolated from Eurasia, and would remain so until the second millennium CE. The low population level and abundance of foods meant that sedentary agricultural life evolved only sporadically, some groups sustaining a hunting and gathering way of life to the present day. During this period of isolation, unique ecological, genetic, and social patterns emerged which proved disastrously fragile when challenged by the first European colonists in the 15th century CE. Within 500 years the indigenous cultures of North America had been destroyed or marginalized by waves of migrants from the Old World who, with astonishing energy and ferocity, transformed the continent into the World's foremost economic, industrial, and political power.

At the heart of the continent, it was the plains which provided homelands for Native North Americans, displaced and driven west by European immigrants.

The gigantic basin drained by the Mississippi, spanning the entire tract between the Appalachians and the Rockies, provided a suitable environment for some of the first agricultural communities.

The Central American mountain plateaus and uplands were where some of the earliest complex civilizations in North America developed. A combination of favorable climate and fertile land allowed plants to be cultivated and early agriculture to develop.

NORTH AMERICA
EXPLORATION AND MAPPING

Lewis *(above)* and Clark led an epic expedition to explore the west in 1805–06.

FOR MANY CENTURIES North America was untouched by contact with other continents. Viking seafarers en route from Iceland and Greenland made landfall at Newfoundland over 1,000 years ago, but their settlements were short-lived and their area of operation quite limited. Not until the early 16th century was the presence of a vast continent across the Atlantic fully accepted, and knowledge about it remained fragmentary. Once Europeans began to investigate North America, they were able to draw heavily on information from indigenous peoples, and use their preexisting trails to explore the continent.

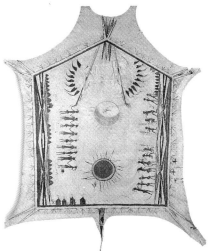

This map of three villages showing their positions relative to the Sun and Moon was painted on a cured buffalo skin by members of the Qapaw tribe.

Native American maps

The indigenous peoples of North and Central America had detailed knowledge of the continent long before the first European expeditions. Much knowledge was undoubtedly passed on orally. But the location of early petroglyph maps carved on rocks suggests that they may have been produced as guides for traveling hunters, and to define territorial boundaries. Later maps – sometimes produced at the request of Europeans – reveal an intimate knowledge of the landscape and principles of space and distance. Several tribes used maps to show the long history of their tenure of the land when they were fighting for territory during the Indian removals of the 19th century.

Early European explorers

Though the first Europeans to visit North America were 10th-century Vikings, European exploration began in earnest in the late 15th century when improvements in shipping made the longer exploratory voyages of Columbus and Cabot viable. By the mid-16th century Spanish-sponsored expeditions in search of gold and territory founded settlements in Florida, Central America, and the Caribbean, and explored the lands of the southeast and southwest. Meanwhile, English and French expeditions traced the Atlantic coast in detail, moving north in search of new routes to Asia.

❶ The first European explorers of North America

Norse expeditions
- Bjarni Herjolfsson 985–86
- Leif Eriksson 1003
- Thorvald Eriksson 1005–12

Spanish and Portuguese expeditions
- Christopher Columbus 1492–93
- Miguel Corte-Real 1501,1502
- Christopher Columbus 1502–04
- Hernán Cortés 1519–21
- Juan Ponce de León 1513
- Panfilo de Narváez and Álvar Núñez Cabeza de Vaca 1528–36
- Francisco de Ulloa 1539–40
- Hernando de Soto 1539–43
- Francisco Vázquez de Coronado and Garcia Lopez de Cardeñas 1540–42
- Sebastián Vizcaino 1602–03

English expeditions
- John Cabot 1497
- Martin Frobisher 1576–77
- Francis Drake 1579
- John Davis 1585–87
- Henry Hudson 1610–11

French expeditions
- Giovanni da Verrazano 1524
- Jacques Cartier 1535–36
- Samuel de Champlain 1604–07
- ○ European settlement 1608 and date of foundation

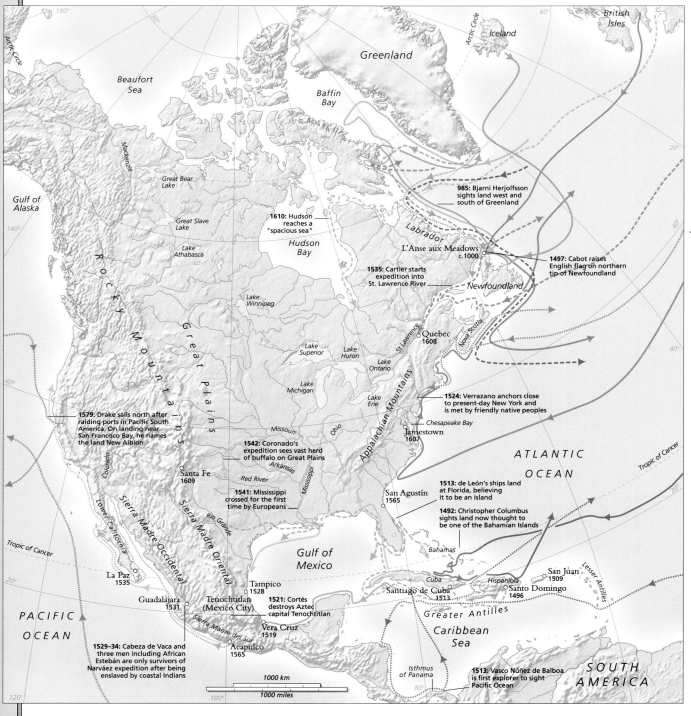

985: Bjarni Herjolfsson sights land west and south of Greenland

1610: Hudson reaches a "spacious sea"

1535: Cartier starts expedition into St. Lawrence River

L'Anse aux Meadows c.1000

1497: Cabot raises English flag on northern tip of Newfoundland

1524: Verrazano anchors close to present-day New York and is met by friendly native peoples

1579: Drake sails north after raiding ports in Pacific South America. On landing near San Francisco Bay, he names the land New Albion

1542: Coronado's expedition sees vast herd of buffalo on Great Plains

1541: Mississippi crossed for the first time by Europeans

1513: de León's ships land at Florida, believing it to be an island

1492: Christopher Columbus sights land now thought to be one of the Bahamian Islands

1521: Cortés destroys Aztec capital Tenochtitlan

1529–34: Cabeza de Vaca and three men including African Estebán are only survivors of Narváez expedition after being enslaved by coastal Indians

1513: Vasco Núñez de Balboa is first explorer to sight Pacific Ocean

Santa Fe 1609
Quebec 1608
Jamestown 1607
San Agustín 1565
San Juan 1509
Santo Domingo 1496
Santiago de Cuba 1513
La Paz 1535
Tampico 1528
Guadalajara 1531
Tenochtitlan (Mexico City)
Vera Cruz 1519
Acapulco 1565

1000 km
1000 miles

This map of Florida and Chesapeake Bay *(above)* was painted in the late 16th century. The spatial relationships are very inaccurate, with the Caribbean islands depicted much too far to the north.

European explorers were astonished by the quantity of wildlife they encountered in North America *(left)*. Fur-bearing animals such as beavers were quickly exploited for their pelts.

15th- and 16th-century European expeditions

1497: Cabot lands on Newfoundland

1501: Miguel Corte-Real enslaves 50 Indians from Beothuk

1524: Verrazano sails up Atlantic coast as far as Nova Scotia

1539–43: De Soto explores southeastern North America

1490 | 1500 | 1510 | 1520 | 1530 | 1540

1492: Columbus lands in the Bahamas thinking he has reached Asia

1513: Ponce de León traces coast of Florida

1528: Cabeza de Vaca explores Gulf of Mexico and southwest

1534: Cartier begins exploration of St. Lawrence

Exploring the eastern interior

The rich Atlantic fisheries and the bounteous wildlife of the northeast were magnets for European hunters and fishermen, and many of the earliest settlements were fur-trading posts. Samuel de Champlain, aided by Iroquois and Montagnais, explored the St. Lawrence River and the Great Lakes, while Hudson and Davis ventured further west into Canada's great bays. Other expeditions were undertaken for missionary purposes, including Jolliet's Mississippian journey, where he was accompanied by Father Marquette. During the late 17th and early 18th centuries, several expeditions sought routes through the Appalachians, which would open up the Midwest to settlers.

One of America's great frontiersmen, Daniel Boone, is shown here leading a group of settlers through the Cumberland Gap, a pass through the Appalachian system which provided a route to the West.

② Journeys into the North American interior 1600–1775 ▶

British expeditions
→ John Smith 1608
→ Thomas Batts and Robert Fallam 1671
→ James Needham and Gabriel Arthur 1673
→ Dr. Henry Woodward 1674, 1685

French expeditions
→ Samuel de Champlain 1609–16
→ Medart Chouart des Groseillers and Pierre-Esprit Radisson 1659–1660
→ Father Claude Allouez 1665–67
→ Father Charles Albanel 1671–72
→ Louis Jolliet and Jacques Marquette 1672–73
→ René-Robert Cavelier Sieur de La Salle 1684–87
→ Louis Hennepin 1680
→ Chaussegros de Léry 1729

Dutch expeditions
→ Arnout Viele 1682–84
→ Johannes Rosebloom 1685–87

American expeditions
→ Christopher Gist 1750–51
→ Thomas Walker 1750
→ Daniel Boone 1769–71

By the late 17th century knowledge of the east coast of North America had improved significantly. This plate from Visscher's *Atlas Contractus* of 1671 shows the Atlantic coast from New England south as far as Chesapeake Bay. Detail of the lands further west and the Great Lakes remained limited.

1671: Guided by Indians, Batts and Fallam become first Europeans to cross Appalachians and reach Mississippi watershed

1750: Walker reaches Cumberland Gap, the gateway to Kentucky

1607: Settlement founded by 120 colonists from England

200 km
200 miles

17th- and 18th-century expeditions in eastern North America

1609–13: Champlain explores St. Lawrence and eastern Great Lakes	**1665–67:** Father Allouez explores Great Lakes

1673: Jolliet and Marquette explore Mississippi and Illinois Rivers

1752: John Finley realizes that Cumberland Gap is gateway to Kentucky lowlands

1607–08: John Smith leads colonizing expeditions in Virginia

1673: Needham and Arthur follow Occaneechee Path across Appalachians

1682: La Salle follows Mississippi to its mouth

1729: de Léry makes first proper survey of Allegheny and upper Ohio Rivers

1600 1650 1700 1750

Charting the West

The rapid expansion of the US created the need to survey and quantify the vast territories of the new nation. Lewis and Clark's famous cross-continental expedition was funded by Congress at the express request of President Jefferson. Fremont conducted his reconnaissance of the west under the auspices of the US Army's Corps of Topographical Engineers. The highly competitive railroad surveys of the 1850s were inspired by economic and political considerations, while Clarence King's survey of the western deserts was motivated primarily by scientific curiosity.

An illustration from Lieutenant Fremont's *Memoirs* shows members of his Great Basin survey team camped on the shores of the Pyramid Lake. The lake was later surveyed in detail by Clarence King.

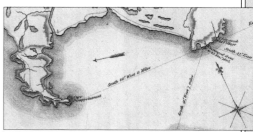

Lewis and Clark kept a series of illustrated notebooks on their westward journey. This map shows the mouth of the Columbia River.

③ 19th-century exploration and surveys of the US and Canada ▶

Individual expeditions
→ Meriwether Lewis and Wiliam Clark 1805–07
→ Lt. Zebulon M. Pike 1806–07
→ Major Stephen Long 1819–20
→ Lt. John Franklin 1820–21
→ Lt. John Franklin 1825–27
→ Lt. John C. Fremont 1842–44
→ Lt. William Emory 1846
→ Lt. James Simpson and Capt. Lorenzo Sitgreaves 1849–51
→ Lt. John Palliser 1857–59

Other expeditions and surveys
→ Russian expeditions to Alaska 1816–65
→ Western Railroad surveys 1853–55
→ Western Union Telegraph survey 1865–67
→ Canadian Yukon Exploring expedition 1887–89

Survey areas
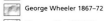 Henry Hind 1857–58
George Wheeler 1867–72
Clarence King 1867–73

Scale varies with perspective
7780 km (4830 miles)
5480 km (3400 miles)

This watercolor of the Kanab Desert was painted by a member of the US Geological Survey team in 1880.

Surveys in the north and west

1819: Artists on Long's expedition across Great Plains record landscape and wildlife

1821: Ill-fated expedition by Franklin along Yellowknife and Coppermine Rivers

1849–51: Simpson and Sitgreaves reveal ancient societies in southwest

1853–55: Series of surveys to find best route for railroad to the Pacific

1805–06: Lewis and Clark explore new land acquired in the Louisiana Purchase and reach Pacific coast

1816: Start of Russian exploration of Alaska

1842: Fremont begins series of expeditions to map American west and encourage settlement

1846: Emory surveys Spanish territory during Mexican War

1857–72: Wheeler produces first contour maps of southwest

1800 1810 1820 1830 1840 1850 1860 1870

EARLY PEOPLES OF NORTH AMERICA

The Hopewell
produced beautifully made grave offerings for burial with their dead, such as this hand, carved from a flat sheet of mica.

THE FIRST PEOPLE to settle North America are thought to have crossed over from Asia during the last Ice Age – more than 25,000 years ago. They probably spread out initially along the Pacific coast, only moving further north and southeast when the glaciers began to melt about 15,000 years ago. By about 11,000 BCE, significant hunting activities were taking place further south and many of the largest mammals, such as the woolly mammoth, may have become extinct through hunting. Once humans were established in Central America, they quickly became more sedentary, simple village structures evolving within a small time frame into far more complex societies. The archaeological evidence left by the Olmec and Zapotec in Central America, and the burial mounds of the Adena and Hopewell of the American Southeast reveal sophisticated societies.

The hunter-gatherers

Hunter-gatherers recorded events in their lives on the walls of caves. This series of images from Cueva Flecha in Lower California, shows humans and animals pierced by spears – perhaps as a result of conflict with other groups in the area.

The first peoples of North and Central America banded together in egalitarian, extended-family groups, living by hunting and gathering. They eventually become specialized and adapted to the continent's various ecological niches: plains, mountains, deserts, woodlands, river valleys, and coastal areas. Specially adapted spear points and other weaponry reveal the major prey species in different culture areas. The fine "Clovis-pointed" spearheads were used by plains hunters to kill bison, barbed harpoon heads were developed by coastal peoples for spearing marine creatures; and darts with stone heads were thrown by the basin and mountain dwellers at the wildfowl which provided them with the bulk of their diet.

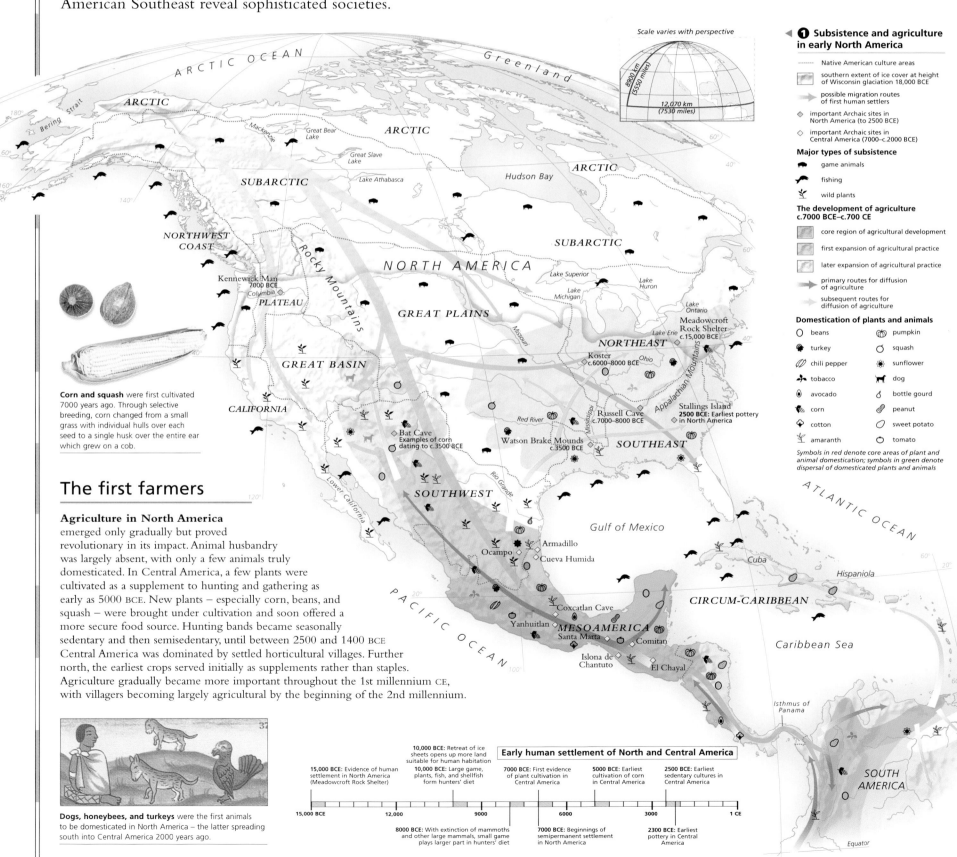

① Subsistence and agriculture in early North America

- ········· Native American culture areas
- ▭ southern extent of ice cover at height of Wisconsin glaciation 18,000 BCE
- ➝ possible migration routes of first human settlers
- ◇ important Archaic sites in North America (to 2500 BCE)
- ◇ important Archaic sites in Central America (7000–c.2000 BCE)

Major types of subsistence
- 🦌 game animals
- 🐟 fishing
- 🌿 wild plants

The development of agriculture c.7000 BCE–c.700 CE
- ▭ core region of agricultural development
- ▭ first expansion of agricultural practice
- ▭ later expansion of agricultural practice
- ➝ primary routes for diffusion of agriculture
- ➝ subsequent routes for diffusion of agriculture

Domestication of plants and animals
○ beans	pumpkin
turkey	squash
chili pepper	sunflower
tobacco	dog
avocado	bottle gourd
corn	peanut
cotton	sweet potato
amaranth	tomato

Symbols in red denote core areas of plant and animal domestication; symbols in green denote dispersal of domesticated plants and animals

Corn and squash were first cultivated 7000 years ago. Through selective breeding, corn changed from a small grass with individual hulls over each seed to a single husk over the entire ear which grew on a cob.

The first farmers

Agriculture in North America
emerged only gradually but proved revolutionary in its impact. Animal husbandry was largely absent, with only a few animals truly domesticated. In Central America, a few plants were cultivated as a supplement to hunting and gathering as early as 5000 BCE. New plants – especially corn, beans, and squash – were brought under cultivation and soon offered a more secure food source. Hunting bands became seasonally sedentary and then semisedentary, until between 2500 and 1400 BCE Central America was dominated by settled horticultural villages. Further north, the earliest crops served initially as supplements rather than staples. Agriculture gradually became more important throughout the 1st millennium CE, with villagers becoming largely agricultural by the beginning of the 2nd millennium.

Dogs, honeybees, and turkeys were the first animals to be domesticated in North America – the latter spreading south into Central America 2000 years ago.

Early human settlement of North and Central America

15,000 BCE: Evidence of human settlement in North America (Meadowcroft Rock Shelter)

10,000 BCE: Retreat of ice sheets opens up more land suitable for human habitation

10,000 BCE: Large game, plants, fish, and shellfish form hunters' diet

7000 BCE: First evidence of plant cultivation in Central America

5000 BCE: Earliest cultivation of corn in Central America

2500 BCE: Earliest sedentary cultures in Central America

8000 BCE: With extinction of mammoths and other large mammals, small game plays larger part in hunters' diet

7000 BCE: Beginnings of semipermanent settlement in North America

2300 BCE: Earliest pottery in Central America

| 15,000 BCE | 12,000 | 9000 | 6000 | 3000 | 1 CE |

Early civilizations of Central America

With the establishment of village life, the earliest complex settlements occurred in the tropical lowlands from the Gulf of Mexico across the Isthmus of Tehuantepec to the Pacific coast of present-day Guatemala. Increasingly sophisticated societies were made possible by new crops and productive soils. The Olmec civilization – widely regarded as the mother culture of Central America – emerged on the Gulf Coast c.1150 BCE and persisted as an important culture until 400 BCE. Slightly later than the Olmecs, the Valley of Oaxaca witnessed the development of a sophisticated society, and by 500 BCE, complex chiefdoms or early states dominated the three interconnected valleys of central Oaxaca. At their juncture, the Zapotecs built the hilltop city of Monte Albán which would dominate the region for over 1000 years. Further south, Kaminalijuyú emerged by c.500 BCE, but a nearby volcanic eruption c.250–200 BCE, and consequent mass migration, deprived the site of much of the population in the southern part of its trading area. In the highlands south of Yucatan, the Maya civilization was starting to emerge as early as 1000 BCE.

This Olmec ceremonial adze from La Venta is carved from the pale green jade typical of the site.

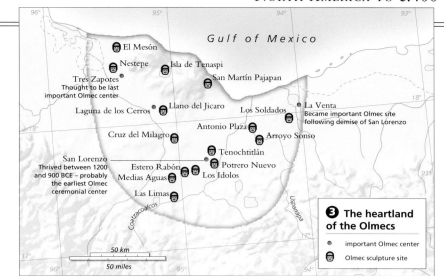

❸ The heartland of the Olmecs

- important Olmec center
- Olmec sculpture site

El Mesón
Nestepe
Isla de Tenaspi
Tres Zapotes — *Thought to be last important Olmec center*
San Martín Pajapan
Llano del Jicaro
Los Soldados
La Venta — *Became important Olmec site following demise of San Lorenzo*
Laguna de los Cerros
Antonio Plaza
Arroyo Sonso
Cruz del Milagro
Tenochtitlán
San Lorenzo — *Thrived between 1200 and 900 BCE – probably the earliest Olmec ceremonial center*
Estero Rabón
Potrero Nuevo
Medias Aguas
Los Idolos
Las Limas

50 km
50 miles

The Olmecs

The earliest civilization in Central America, the Olmecs initiated the Mesoamerican pantheon of gods, gave rise to kings and classes, and fought wars, as well as trading over vast distances and heavily influencing other cultures. They built elaborate platforms and mounds, made fine ceramics, worked precious stone, engaged in complex and sophisticated stone sculpture, established the Mesoamerican calendar, and invented the syllabary writing system. By 500–400 BCE, the Olmecs began withdrawing into their homeland and, though remaining an intellectually vibrant culture throughout the 1st millennium BCE, ceased to influence groups elsewhere directly.

❷ Early civilizations of Central America

- area of Olmec influence
- area of Maya influence c.1000 BCE
- additional area of Maya influence c.800 BCE
- area of Zapotec influence

◆ site settled by, or influenced by the Olmecs
◆ other sites from formative period
→ main Olmec trade routes

Mineral resources
- basalt
- obsidian
- iron ore (magnetite)
- serpentine
- green jade

Pavón
El Opéno
Chupicuaro
El Trapiche
El Viejon
Tlatilco
Cuicuilco
Tlapacoya
Remojadas
Gualupita
Cerro de las Mesas
Becan
Chalcatzingo
Las Bocas
Taxla
Cuello
Capacha
Tres Zapotes
Laguna de los Cerros
El Mirador
Mezcala
Oxtotitlán Cave
San José Mogote
La Venta
Balancán
Uaxactún
Barton Ramie
Juxtlahuaca Cave
San Lorenzo
Tikal
Xunantunich
San Jerónimo
Zanja
Monte Alban
Dainzú
Chiapa de Corzo
Seibal
Altar de Sacrificios
Valley of Oaxaca
Cerro de la Bomba
Santa Cruz
Xoc
Boca de Río
Playa de los Muertos
Padre Piedra
Los Naranjos
Pijijiapan
Yojoa
Kaminalijuyú
Copán
Aquiles Serdán
Izapa
Yarumela
Altamira
San Isidro Piedra Parada
La Victoria
Abaj Takalik
Las Victorias
La Blanca
Ilopango
Chalchuapa

Sierra Madre Oriental
Sierra Madre del Sur
Gulf of Mexico
Yucatan Peninsula
Isthmus of Tehuantepec
PACIFIC OCEAN

Dzibilchaltún
Chichén Itzá
Maní

250 km
250 miles

Early civilizations of North and Central America

c.1150: Start of Olmec civilization
800: Evidence that Maya beginning to spread northward into Yucatan peninsula
500: Settlement of Monte Albán
400: Beginning of Olmec decline

1200 BCE — 1000 — 800 — 600 — 400 — 200 BCE

1100: Establishment of Poverty Point in present-day Louisiana, an early nonagrarian settlement
700: Start of Adena culture
c.250: El Mirador, the largest early Maya city flourishing. Sites, such as Becan, fortified

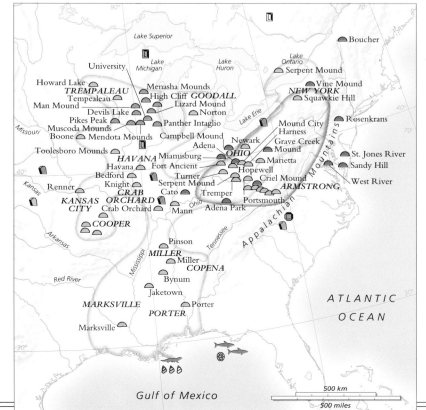

❹ Moundbuilders of eastern North America c.700 BCE–c.400 CE

- Adena heartland
- Adena site
- Hopewell area of influence
- *OHIO* Hopewell cultural area
- Hopewell burial mound site
- effigy mound site

Resources traded by the Hopewell
- chert
- chlorite
- obsidian
- silver
- copper
- galena
- mica crystals
- olive shell
- tulip shell
- whelks
- turtle
- alligator
- barracuda
- shark

Lake Superior
Boucher
University
Serpent Mound
Howard Lake
TREMPEALEAU
Vine Mound
NEW YORK
Menasha Mounds
High Cliff *GOODALL*
Squawkie Hill
Man Mound
Lizard Mound
Norton
Devils Lake
Rosenkrans
Pikes Peak
Panther Intaglio
Muscoda Mounds
Mound City
Boone
Mendota Mounds
Harness
Campbell Mound
Grave Creek Mound
Toolesboro Mounds
Adena
Newark
St. Jones River
HAVANA
Miamisburg
Marietta
Sandy Hill
Havana
Fort Ancient
OHIO
Hopewell
Bedford
Criel Mound
West River
Knight
Turner
Serpent Mound
ARMSTRONG
CRAB
Cato
Tremper
KANSAS CITY
ORCHARD
Crab Orchard
Mann
Adena Park
Portsmouth
Renner
COOPER
Pinson
MILLER
Miller
COPENA
Bynum
Jaketown
MARKSVILLE
Porter
PORTER
Marksville

Appalachian Mountains
ATLANTIC OCEAN
Gulf of Mexico

500 km
500 miles

The moundbuilders of the eastern river valleys

The Adena culture was found in the upper Ohio valley as early as 700 BCE. Settlements were centered on burial mounds and extensive earthworks. Their grave goods included jewelry made from imported copper, carved tablets, and tubular pipes – which provide evidence of the early cultivation of tobacco *(see Map 1)*. The Hopewell culture had emerged by c.100 CE, and spread throughout the Mississippi Valley, sustained by small-scale agriculture. They created a complex and far-reaching trade network to source the many raw materials – including obsidian, quartz, shells, teeth, and copper – used in their characteristic animal and bird sculptures. Elements of Hopewell culture appear to have been adopted by many other Indian groups.

The Hopewell produced many objects in the shape of animals including birds, beavers, and bears. The frog adorns a platform effigy pipe; tobacco was placed in a bowl in its back and inhaled through the hole in the front of the pipe.

CITIES AND EMPIRES

Hollow pottery dogs, typical of the highly realistic ceramics of western Mexico, are common grave offerings.

CENTRAL AMERICA was split into Mexican and Maya areas, between which there were some major differences, including languages, writing systems, and art and architectural styles. City-states dominated both areas: in the Maya area these tended to be small, multicity regional polities or autonomous cities, while Mexico was dominated by a series of empires. The peoples of southern North America were turning to sedentary agriculture and establishing settled communities. Several overlapping cultures settled the desert southwest, including the Hohokam, Anasazi, and Mogollon. In the southeast, larger settlements in the Mississippi Valley replaced the Hopewell by 800 CE.

Central American civilizations 400–1400

Teotihuacan emerged as the capital of the first major empire in the 1st century CE and influenced cities throughout Mexico and Guatemala, spreading ideas and innovations. The multiethnic city reached a population of 125,000–200,000 by 500, exporting goods to the rest of Central America. By 550, Teotihuacan was in decline, and by 750, the city was largely abandoned. The resulting political vacuum encouraged the rise of several independent, fortified hilltop cities from about 650, including Cacaxtla and Xochicalco. All had extensive trade links and varying degrees of contact with other cultures. Centred at Tula, the Toltec Empire emerged in the 10th century. The Toltecs were traders, trading as far south as Costa Rica and north into the desert. Drought undermined Tula's agriculture and by 1168, it was abandoned.

Teotihuacan was centrally planned, laid out in a grid, and dominated by huge pyramids which would have held temples on their summits. It traded over much of Central America, dealing in obsidian products, ceramics, stone carvings, and featherwork.

These massive basalt figures stand on top of the central pyramid at Tula, the Toltec capital. The city reached a peak population of 60,000 inhabitants, with an equal number in the immediate hinterland.

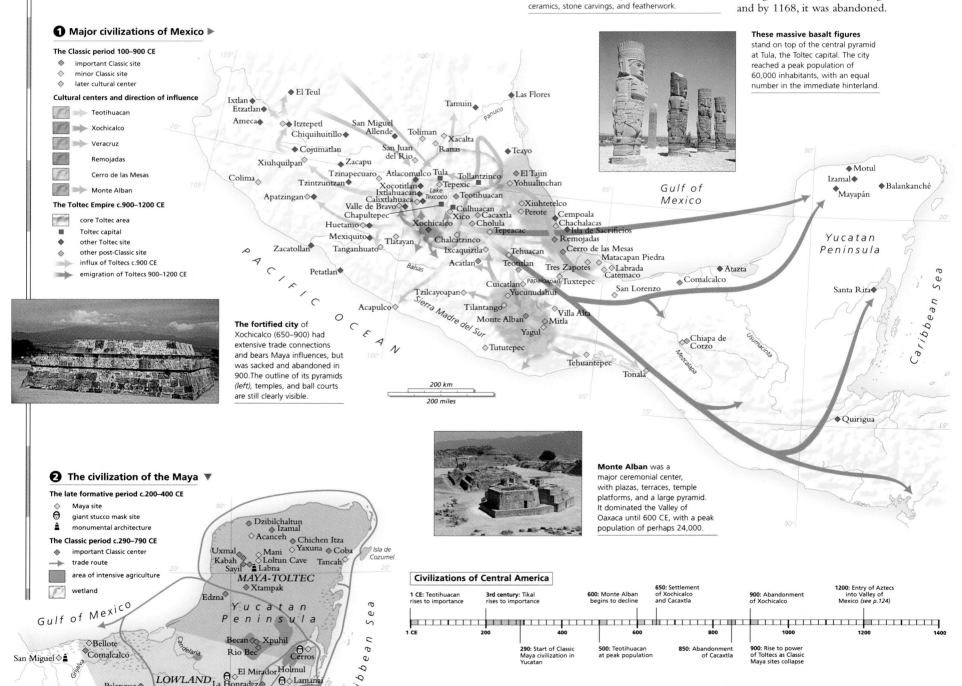

① Major civilizations of Mexico ▶

The Classic period 100–900 CE
◆ important Classic site
◇ minor Classic site
◇ later cultural center

Cultural centers and direction of influence
▨ Teotihuacan
▨ Xochicalco
▨ Veracruz
▨ Remojadas
▨ Cerro de las Mesas
▨ Monte Alban

The Toltec Empire c.900–1200 CE
▢ core Toltec area
■ Toltec capital
◆ other Toltec site
◇ other post-Classic site
→ influx of Toltecs c.900 CE
→ emigration of Toltecs 900–1200 CE

The fortified city of Xochicalco (650–900) had extensive trade connections and bears Maya influences, but was sacked and abandoned in 900. The outline of its pyramids (left), temples, and ball courts are still clearly visible.

Monte Alban was a major ceremonial center, with plazas, terraces, temple platforms, and a large pyramid. It dominated the Valley of Oaxaca until 600 CE, with a peak population of perhaps 24,000.

② The civilization of the Maya ▼

The late formative period c.200–400 CE
◇ Maya site
☺ giant stucco mask site
▲ monumental architecture

The Classic period c.290–790 CE
◆ important Classic center
→ trade route
▨ area of intensive agriculture
▨ wetland

Civilizations of Central America						
1 CE: Teotihuacan rises to importance	**3rd century:** Tikal rises to importance		**600:** Monte Alban begins to decline	**650:** Settlement of Xochicalco and Cacaxtla	**900:** Abandonment of Xochicalco	**1200:** Entry of Aztecs into Valley of Mexico (see p.124)

290: Start of Classic Maya civilization in Yucatan

500: Teotihuacan at peak population

850: Abandonment of Cacaxtla

900: Rise to power of Toltecs as Classic Maya sites collapse

The city-states of the Maya

The jungle of Guatemala and Yucatan became the center for the florescence of Maya civilization. Many city-states emerged, sometimes linked by elite marriages and sometimes by descent, but political ties were few and fleeting. The Classic Maya civilization is thought to be the first fully literate culture of the Americas, developing a hieroglyphic writing system. Classic Maya cities were characterized by their massive size and structural complexity. Following 700, many cities were abandoned and the focus of Maya civilization shifted to the northern lowlands.

The corbelled Arch of Labna in northern Yucatan dates from the late Classic period. Its intricate reliefs and massive size typify Maya architecture during this period.

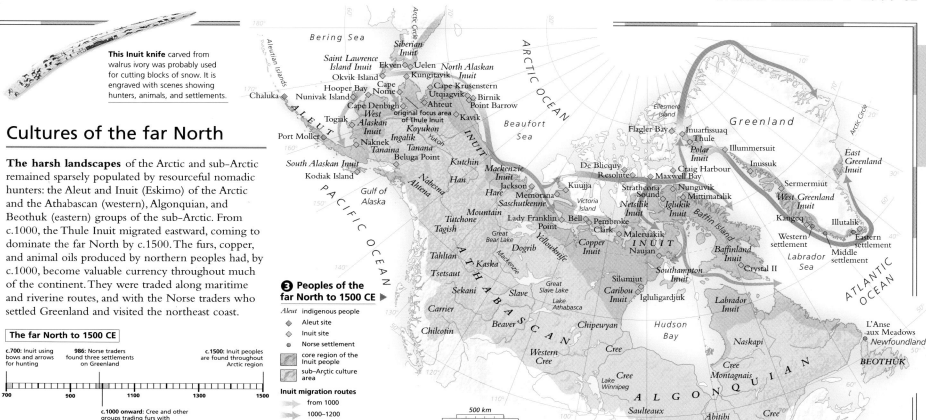

This Inuit knife carved from walrus ivory was probably used for cutting blocks of snow. It is engraved with scenes showing hunters, animals, and settlements.

Cultures of the far North

The harsh landscapes of the Arctic and sub-Arctic remained sparsely populated by resourceful nomadic hunters: the Aleut and Inuit (Eskimo) of the Arctic and the Athabascan (western), Algonquian, and Beothuk (eastern) groups of the sub-Arctic. From c.1000, the Thule Inuit migrated eastward, coming to dominate the far North by c.1500. The furs, copper, and animal oils produced by northern peoples had, by c.1000, become valuable currency throughout much of the continent. They were traded along maritime and riverine routes, and with the Norse traders who settled Greenland and visited the northeast coast.

❸ Peoples of the far North to 1500 CE ▶

Aleut indigenous people
◆ Aleut site
◇ Inuit site
○ Norse settlement
▨ core region of the Inuit people
▨ sub-Arctic culture area

Inuit migration routes
→ from 1000
⇒ 1000–1200
⇛ 1200–1500

The far North to 1500 CE

c.700: Inuit using bows and arrows for hunting
986: Norse traders found three settlements on Greenland
c.1500: Inuit peoples are found throughout Arctic region

c.1000 onward: Cree and other groups trading furs with southern peoples for grain

The American Southwest

In the Southwest, sedentary ways of life increased throughout the 1st millennium CE, producing villages and cliff dwellings, such those of the Hohokam in Arizona, after 1000, and regional polities such as Chaco Canyon and Casas Grandes. The Hohokam developed irrigation systems to allow them to grow maize in the arid semidesert and built multistoried pueblos: storehouses and dwellings of stone or adobe sometimes with ball courts and low platform mounds. The Anasazi and Mogollon peoples left evidence of pueblos constructed for defensive purposes – probably to counter other hostile groups who entered the area from c.1300. Increasing aridity caused a decline in the southwest after 1250 leaving only dispersed puebloan groups.

The Mimbres branch of the Mogollon culture produced spectacular pottery, usually for burial purposes. The pots, adorned with geometric designs, were often ritually "killed" by having a hole drilled through their base.

Settlement in the Southwest to 1500

100: Emergence of Hohokam and Mogollon cultures
800: Mimbres pottery starts to be made by Mogollon
1050: Pueblos built for defensive purposes by Anasazi
1200: Peak of importance of Chaco Canyon

c.950: Flourishing pueblo culture in Southwest
1100: Construction of the Cliff Palace at Mesa Verde
1350: Most Anasazi pueblos abandoned – probably due to drought

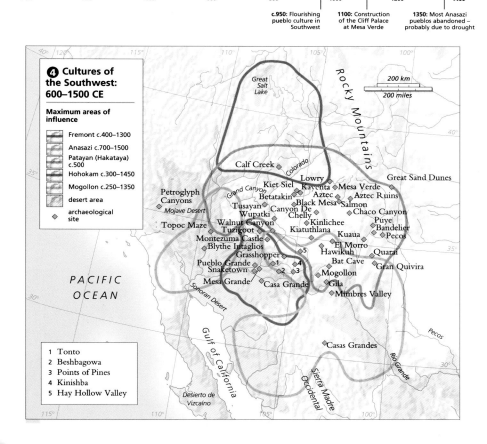

❹ Cultures of the Southwest: 600–1500 CE

Maximum areas of influence
▨ Fremont c.400–1300
▨ Anasazi c.700–1500
▨ Patayan (Hakataya) c.500
▨ Hohokam c.300–1450
▨ Mogollon c.250–1350
▨ desert area
◆ archaeological site

1 Tonto
2 Beshbagowa
3 Points of Pines
4 Kinishba
5 Hay Hollow Valley

The American South and Mississippi Valley

In eastern North America there were improvements in agricultural technology, and crops such as beans and new varieties of corn were imported from Mexico. There was a developmental hiatus for about 400 years following the decline of the Hopewell trading empire but from c.800, settlements grew larger until, in around 1000, the Mississippian chiefdoms emerged, leading to more regional integration and significantly greater social differentiation. Many centers, including sites such as Etowah and Moundville, became regional foci, with the largest being Cahokia, with a peak population of 15,000.

❺ Mississippian cultures of eastern North America

Areas of influence and temple mound sites
⌂ Middle Mississippian
⌂ South Appalachian
⌂ Fort Ancient
▨ extent of secondary Mississippian influence
⌂ Plaquemine Mississippian
⌂ Caddoan Mississippian
⌂ Oneota
◆ other site

This sculpted soapstone pipe from the Spiro mound site is thought to depict a warrior beheading his victim.

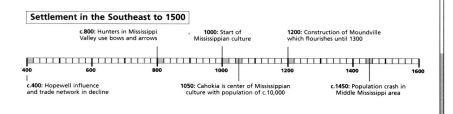

Settlement in the Southeast to 1500

c.800: Hunters in Mississippi Valley use bows and arrows
1000: Start of Mississippian culture
1200: Construction of Moundville which flourishes until 1300

c.400: Hopewell influence and trade network in decline
1050: Cahokia is center of Mississippian culture with population of c.10,000
c.1450: Population crash in Middle Mississippi area

COMPETING EMPIRES

Quetzalcoatl, the god of wind, was one of a pantheon of gods worshiped by the Aztecs.

UNTIL THE EUROPEAN INCURSIONS of the late 15th century, North and Central America remained largely untouched by contacts with other continents. Spanish explorers and traders, seeking new routes and markets, first reconnoitred the Caribbean islands and Central America, returning later to claim Mexico, the Caribbean and much of the southern half of America as new territory for the Spanish crown. One of their most significant conquests was the Aztec Empire that dominated central Mexico. Elsewhere European impact was slight during the 16th century; they passed through, leaving little of their own cultures behind, save for animals, such as horses, that transformed native lives, and diseases that decimated populations.

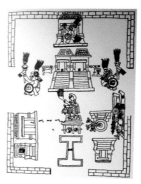

The Great Temple dominated the central plaza of Tenochtitlan. The northern temple *(left)* was dedicated to Tlaloc, god of rain and the southern temple *(right)* to the Aztec patron god of war, Huitzilopochtli.

The Aztec Empire

The Aztecs entered the already highly urbanized Valley of Mexico around 1200, establishing their island capital of Tenochtitlan on Lake Texcoco in 1325, and overthrowing their imperial masters, the Tepanecs, in 1428 to begin their own empire. By 1519, the Aztec Empire controlled most of central Mexico as well as the Maya areas of further east. The Aztecs presided over a collection of city-states which remained autonomous except for their tributary obligations to the Aztecs. The Aztec Empire maintained a state of constant military activity which served to provide a flow of tributes from neighboring states.

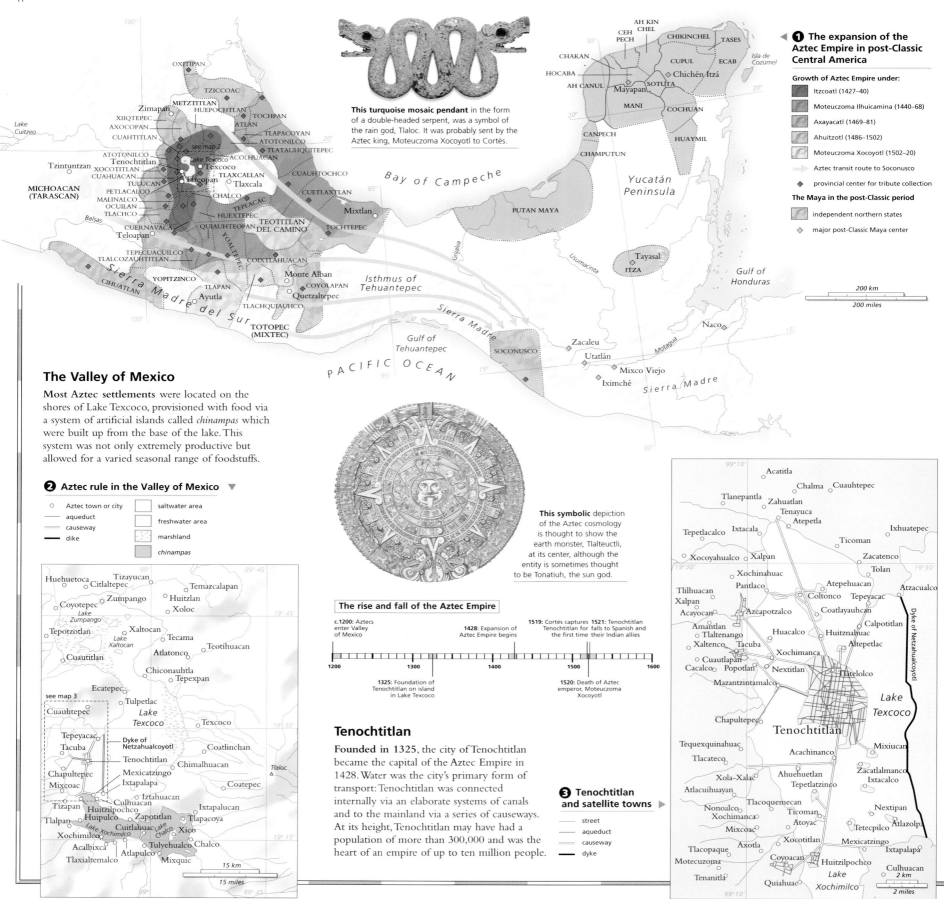

This turquoise mosaic pendant in the form of a double-headed serpent, was a symbol of the rain god, Tlaloc. It was probably sent by the Aztec king, Moteuczoma Xocoyotl to Cortés.

❶ The expansion of the Aztec Empire in post-Classic Central America

Growth of Aztec Empire under:

- Itzcoatl (1427–40)
- Moteuczoma Ilhuicamina (1440–68)
- Axayacatl (1469–81)
- Ahuitzotl (1486–1502)
- Moteuczoma Xocoyotl (1502–20)
- ⟶ Aztec transit route to Soconusco
- ◆ provincial center for tribute collection

The Maya in the post-Classic period

- independent northern states
- ◇ major post-Classic Maya center

The Valley of Mexico

Most Aztec settlements were located on the shores of Lake Texcoco, provisioned with food via a system of artificial islands called *chinampas* which were built up from the base of the lake. This system was not only extremely productive but allowed for a varied seasonal range of foodstuffs.

❷ Aztec rule in the Valley of Mexico

- ○ Aztec town or city
- aqueduct
- causeway
- dike
- saltwater area
- freshwater area
- marshland
- chinampas

This symbolic depiction of the Aztec cosmology is thought to show the earth monster, Tlalteuctli, at its center, although the entity is sometimes thought to be Tonatiuh, the sun god.

The rise and fall of the Aztec Empire

c.1200: Aztecs enter Valley of Mexico		1428: Expansion of Aztec Empire begins	1519: Cortés captures Tenochtitlan for the first time	1521: Tenochtitlan falls to Spanish and their Indian allies

1325: Foundation of Tenochtitlan on island in Lake Texcoco

1520: Death of Aztec emperor, Moteuczoma Xocoyotl

Tenochtitlan

Founded in 1325, the city of Tenochtitlan became the capital of the Aztec Empire in 1428. Water was the city's primary form of transport: Tenochtitlan was connected internally via an elaborate systems of canals and to the mainland via a series of causeways. At its height, Tenochtitlan may have had a population of more than 300,000 and was the heart of an empire of up to ten million people.

❸ Tenochtitlan and satellite towns

- street
- aqueduct
- causeway
- dyke

European exploration and conquest

Some of the earliest evidence of Spanish incursions into Mexico and North America is in the form of religious buildings. The church of St. Francis at Tlaxcala dates from 1521.

The Spanish first visited the Gulf of Mexico and the Caribbean in the late 1400s and early 1500s, quickly conquering the West Indies, whose people were enslaved or impressed into forced labor and devastated by European diseases such as smallpox. The first formal expedition to Mexico, led by Córdoba, reached the Yucatán Peninsula in 1517. In 1518, Grijalva landed on the Vera Cruz coast, trading with the natives and giving Aztec emissaries their first glimpse of Europeans. The rest of the 16th century saw the replacement of Indian leaders with Spanish, the substitution of Christianity for Indian religions, and the imposition of Spanish rule in Central America. Major entries were made into North America – in the southeast by expeditions, such as de Soto's in 1539–42, and in the southwest by Coronado in 1540, leading to the initial conquest of New Mexico and the founding of Santa Fe in 1609.

Spanish colonizing expeditions in the New World

1	Sebastian de Ocampo	1508
2	Juan Ponce de León	1508 and 1512
3	Juan de Esquival	1509
4	Diego Velasquez	1511
5	Vasco Núñez de Balboa	1513–14
6	Pedrarias Dávila	1514–19
7	Hernández de Córdoba, Juan de Grijalva, Alonso Álvarez de Peneda, and Francisco de Garay	1517–23
8	Pedrarias Dávila	1519
9	Hernan Cortés	1519
10	Gonzalo de Sandoval	1521
11	Luis Marin	1521–24
12	Francisco Orozco	1521
13	Francisco Gordillo and Pedro de Quexos	1521
14	Pedro de Alvarado	1522
15	Hernan Cortés	1522
16	Cristóbal de Olid	1522
17	Gil Gonzalez Dávila and Andres Nino	1522–23
18	Pedro de Alvarado	1523–24
19	Cristóbal de Olid	1524
20	Francisco Hernández de Córdoba	1524
21	Estaban Gomez	1524–25
22	Lucas Vázquez de Ayllón	1526
23	The Montejos	1527
24	Pánfilo de Narváez and Álvar Núñez Cabeza de Vaca	1528
25	Nuño de Guzmán and Cristóbal de Oñate	1529
26	Hurtado de Mendoza, Becerra, Grijalva, Cortés, Tapia, Ulloa, Alarcon	1532–42
27	Hernando de Soto	1539–42
28	Francisco Vázquez de Coronado	1540
29	The Montejos	1545
30	Francisco de Ibarra	1554
31	Pedro Menéndez de Avilés	1565
32	Juan de Oñate	1595
33	Sebastián Vizcaíno	1596

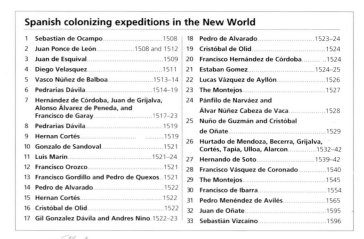

San Agustín, Florida, was founded by Pedro Menéndez de Avilés in 1565. Its massive coastal fort, the Castillo de San Marcos was a classic example of 16th-century military technology.

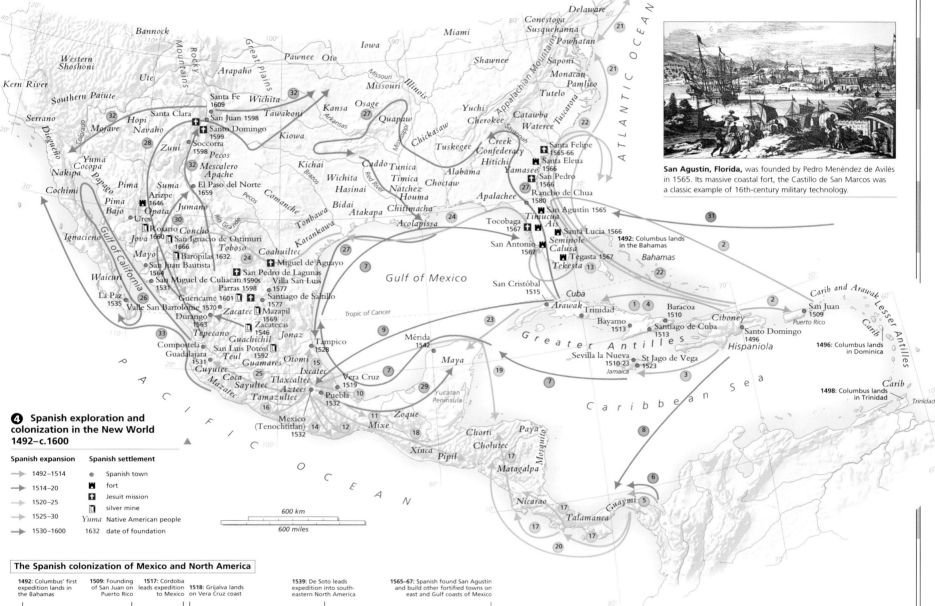

❹ Spanish exploration and colonization in the New World 1492–c.1600

Spanish expansion	Spanish settlement
⟶ 1492–1514	● Spanish town
⟶ 1514–20	▣ fort
⟶ 1520–25	▣ Jesuit mission
⟶ 1525–30	▣ silver mine
⟶ 1530–1600	*Yuma* Native American people
	1632 date of foundation

600 km / 600 miles

The Spanish colonization of Mexico and North America

1492: Columbus' first expedition lands in the Bahamas

1496: Foundation of Santo Domingo on Hispaniola

1509: Founding of San Juan on Puerto Rico

1517: Córdoba leads expedition to Mexico

1518: Grijalva lands on Vera Cruz coast

1519–21: Cortés' expedition into Mexico leads to collapse of Aztec Empire

1539: De Soto leads expedition into southeastern North America

1540: Coronado leads expedition into southwestern North America

1565–67: Spanish found San Agustin and build other fortified towns on east and Gulf coasts of Mexico

1560s: Jesuit missions established in the Southeast (Florida) and in the Southwest

(timeline: 1490 · 1510 · 1530 · 1550 · 1570)

The conquest of the Aztecs

In 1519, Hernan Cortés, sponsored by the Governor of Cuba, landed on the Vera Cruz coast with about 450 soldiers. Forging alliances with the Totonacs and the Tlaxcaltecs, he was able to seize the Aztec capital, Tenochtitlan, in November 1519. Governor Velasquez then attempted to punish Cortés for disobeying his orders, sending a force to retrieve him which ultimately led to his being forced out of Tenochtitlan, but he was able to maintain his alliances with groups such as the Chalcas and the Acolhua. In 1520 Cortés again led expeditions around the Valley of Mexico and beseiged Tenochtitlan, defeating the Aztecs in August 1521.

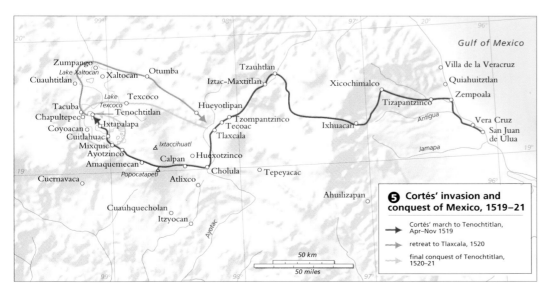

❺ Cortés' invasion and conquest of Mexico, 1519–21

⟶ Cortés' march to Tenochtitlan, Apr–Nov 1519
⟶ retreat to Tlaxcala, 1520
⟶ final conquest of Tenochtitlan, 1520–21

50 km / 50 miles

While Cortés claimed victory for Spain, the battles against the Aztecs were actually won by his tens of thousands of Indian allies. With several major allied groups, no one group was able to take power and Cortés reaped the benefits.

FROM COLONIZATION TO INDEPENDENCE

George Washington, the first US president, came to prominence in the Anglo-French conflicts of the 1750s.

FROM THE EARLY 17TH CENTURY, British, French, and Dutch migrants settled along the Atlantic seaboard and in the Gulf of St. Lawrence. As they grew in numbers, they displaced Native American peoples from their lands. Though the French were able to form mutually beneficial alliances with local peoples, relationships elsewhere were characterized by conflict, and by 1759, most of the surviving Native Americans had been driven westward. By the second half of the 18th century, the British emerged as the major political power in North America. By 1775, and with the elimination of French power in Canada, the American desire for self-determination led to revolution and the creation of an independent United States of America by 1783.

European colonial settlement 1600–1750

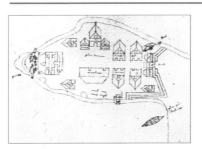

The site of Montreal was first visited by Jacques Cartier in 1535. In 1642, when this map was drawn, the first French settlement was set up.

During the 17th century, the British established a string of Atlantic colonies with a population that grew to about a million settlers, including African slaves. They produced and exported tobacco, timber, fish, and food, and ran a thriving colonial merchant fleet that dominated Atlantic trade, along with sugar colonies in the West Indies. To the north and west, a small number of French settlers forged strong alliances with native peoples, traded in fur, and established an arc of territories designed to stop further British expansion.

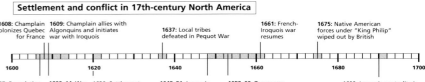

Settlement and conflict in 17th-century North America

1608: Champlain colonizes Quebec for France	**1609:** Champlain allies with Algonquins and initiates war with Iroquois	**1637:** Local tribes defeated in Pequot War	**1661:** French-Iroquois war resumes	**1675:** Native American forces under "King Philip" wiped out by British

1600	1620	1640	1660	1680	1700

1607: Foundation of Jamestown	**1609–14:** War between English and Powhatan	**1620:** Settlement of New England begins	**1648–51:** Iroquois destroy French allies, the Huron	**1653–60:** Temporary French-Iroquois peace	**1690:** Iroquois neutrality is followed by alliance to British

European traders made use of the fur trade routes established by native peoples. In 1670, the Hudson's Bay Company established fur "factories" to tap the fur trade of the far interior.

Changing populations

The population composition of North America changed radically with the European incursion. Indigenous peoples succumbed to European diseases such as plague and measles, and to the settlers' superior firepower and ability to organize themselves quickly. Only small numbers of Africans were brought to North America as slaves in the 17th century, but the growth of labor-intensive plantation agriculture in the south and the West Indies led to the burgeoning of the Atlantic slave trade.

◀ ❶ The colonization of North America to 1750

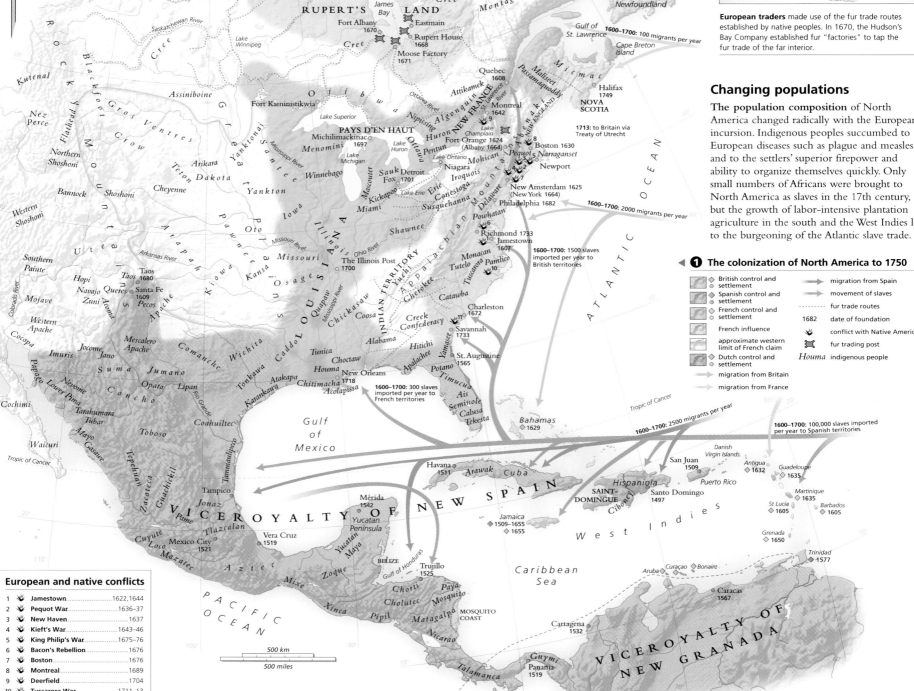

British control and settlement	migration from Spain
Spanish control and settlement	movement of slaves
French control and settlement	fur trade routes
French influence	1682 — date of foundation
approximate western limit of French claim	conflict with Native Americans
Dutch control and settlement	fur trading post
migration from Britain	Houma — indigenous people
migration from France	

European and native conflicts

1	Jamestown	1622, 1644
2	Pequot War	1636–37
3	New Haven	1637
4	Kieft's War	1643–46
5	King Philip's War	1675–76
6	Bacon's Rebellion	1676
7	Boston	1676
8	Montreal	1689
9	Deerfield	1704
10	Tuscarora War	1711–13
11	Yamasee War	1715–28

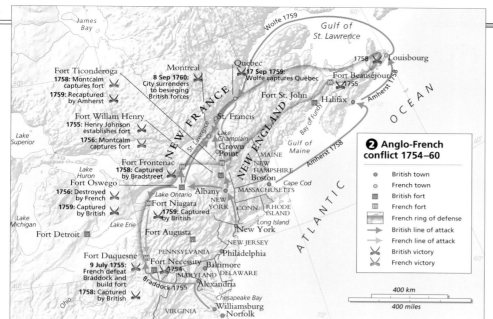

Fort Ticonderoga
1758: Montcalm
captures fort
1759: Recaptured
by Amherst

Competition for North America 1690–1761

Conflict between France and Britain in North America at first mirrored the wars of Louis XIV in Europe in the 1690s. In the late 1730s Britain and Spain clashed in the Spanish colonies. Serious fighting between the British and French resumed in 1744–48, but the decisive struggle for the continent occurred between 1754–61. In July 1755, General Braddock, aided by provincial troops including George Washington, marched on Fort Duquesne but was repelled by the French. It took the full weight of the British army until 1759 to gain ascendancy over the French and their native allies. General Wolfe's capture of Quebec in September 1759 was followed by the surrender of Montreal. With peace agreed at the Treaty of Paris in 1763, Britain became the dominant colonial power in the New World.

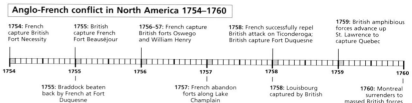

Anglo-French conflict in North America 1754–1760

1754: French capture British Fort Necessity	**1755:** British capture French Fort Beauséjour
1756–57: French capture British forts Oswego and William Henry	**1758:** French successfully repel British attack on Ticonderoga; British capture Fort Duquesne
1759: British amphibious forces advance up St. Lawrence to capture Quebec	

1755: Braddock beaten back by French at Fort Duquesne
1757: French abandon forts along Lake Champlain
1758: Louisbourg captured by British
1760: Montreal surrenders to massed British forces

② Anglo-French conflict 1754–60
- British town
- French town
- British fort
- French fort
- French ring of defense
- British line of attack
- French line of attack
- British victory
- French victory

400 km / 400 miles

The brief but fierce battle for Quebec in September 1759, claimed the lives of the commanders of both sides: the British General Wolfe (*left*), and the French Marquis de Montcalm the following day. Final victory belonged to the British who had been advancing up the Gulf of St. Lawrence for over a year.

The Revolutionary War 1775–1783

By the 1760s, the inhabitants of the British colonies had grown rapidly in population, wealth, and self-confidence and were increasingly resistant to conventional methods of colonial control, such as taxation. In addition, the British government was perceived to be keeping all the fruits of victory against the French for itself, including the Canadian fur trade and the western lands. In 1775, the first shots of the Revolutionary War were fired near Boston. Almost all of the early campaigns ended in stalemate: British forces were superior in numbers and weaponry, but the Patriots gained support with every campaign as the struggle moved south. The American victory at Saratoga in 1777 convinced the French government to support the Americans with troops and ships. Later the Dutch and Spanish also joined against Britain. In 1781 George Washington forced General Cornwallis to surrender at Yorktown, Virginia, and the new nation was secure.

③ The American Revolutionary War
- The Thirteen Colonies, 1775
- The United States, 1783
- British movements
- French movements
- US movements
- British victory
- French victory
- US victory
- indecisive outcome
- fort

Scale varies with perspective

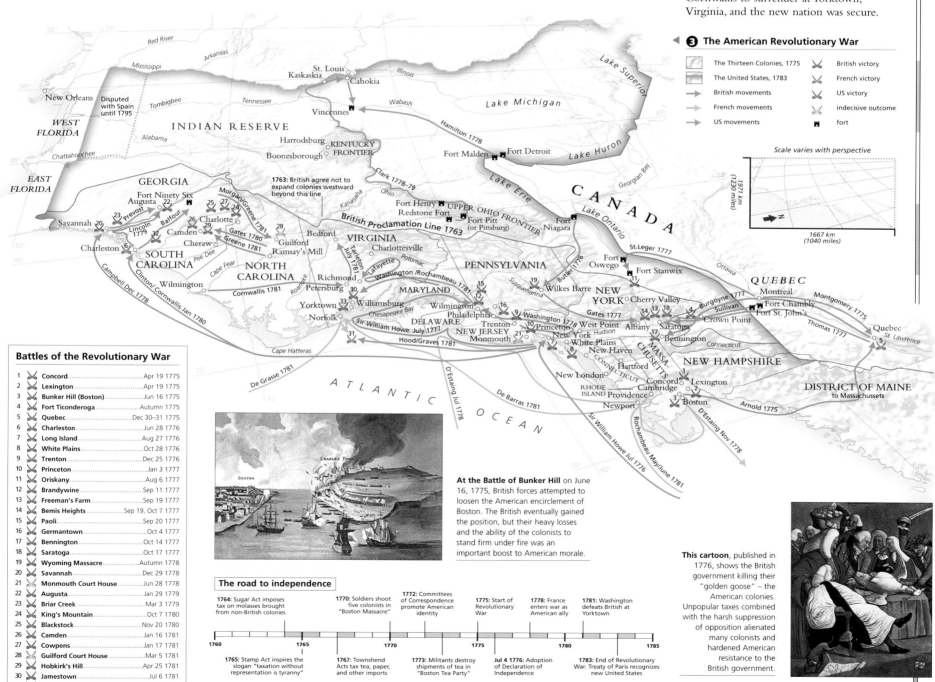

Battles of the Revolutionary War

1	Concord	Apr 19 1775
2	Lexington	Apr 19 1775
3	Bunker Hill (Boston)	Jun 16 1775
4	Fort Ticonderoga	Autumn 1775
5	Quebec	Dec 30–31 1775
6	Charleston	Jun 28 1776
7	Long Island	Aug 27 1776
8	White Plains	Oct 28 1776
9	Trenton	Dec 25 1776
10	Princeton	Jan 3 1777
11	Oriskany	Aug 6 1777
12	Brandywine	Sep 11 1777
13	Freeman's Farm	Sep 19 1777
14	Bemis Heights	Sep 19, Oct 7 1777
15	Paoli	Sep 20 1777
16	Germantown	Oct 4 1777
17	Bennington	Oct 14 1777
18	Saratoga	Oct 17 1777
19	Wyoming Massacre	Autumn 1778
20	Savannah	Dec 29 1778
21	Monmouth Court House	Jun 28 1778
22	Augusta	Jan 29 1779
23	Briar Creek	Mar 3 1779
24	King's Mountain	Oct 7 1780
25	Blackstock	Nov 20 1780
26	Camden	Jan 16 1781
27	Cowpens	Jan 17 1781
28	Guilford Court House	Mar 5 1781
29	Hobkirk's Hill	Apr 25 1781
30	Jamestown	Jul 6 1781
31	Virginia Capes	Sep 5 1781
32	Eutaw Springs	Sep 8 1781
33	Yorktown	Oct 19 1781

At the Battle of Bunker Hill on June 16, 1775, British forces attempted to loosen the American encirclement of Boston. The British eventually gained the position, but their heavy losses and the ability of the colonists to stand firm under fire was an important boost to American morale.

The road to independence

1764: Sugar Act imposes tax on molasses brought from non-British colonies	**1770:** Soldiers shoot five colonists in "Boston Massacre"
1772: Committees of Correspondence promote American identity	**1775:** Start of Revolutionary War
1778: France enters war as American ally	**1781:** Washington defeats British at Yorktown

1765: Stamp Act inspires the slogan "taxation without representation is tyranny"
1767: Townshend Acts tax tea, paper, and other imports
1773: Militants destroy shipments of tea in "Boston Tea Party"
Jul 4 1776: Adoption of Declaration of Independence
1783: End of Revolutionary War. Treaty of Paris recognizes new United States

This cartoon, published in 1776, shows the British government killing their "golden goose" – the American colonies. Unpopular taxes combined with the harsh suppression of opposition alienated many colonists and hardened American resistance to the British government.

BUILDING NEW NATIONS

Thomas Jefferson was the principal author of the Declaration of Independence and the third US president.

BY 1783, THE NEWLY-FORMED United States of America operated under the Articles of Confederation and had a border which soon extended as far as the Mississippi, causing considerable alarm among its Native American, Spanish, and Canadian neighbors. In the War of 1812, Canada successfully fended off invasion by the United States, but remained fearful of the growing power to its south. In Mexico and Central America, Creole dissenters launched a disastrous war for independence from Spain starting in 1810. Mexico plunged into a bloody race war that killed hundreds of thousands and wrecked the colonial infrastructure. The nations of Central America and Mexico became independent during the 1820s, though greatly weakened from their former colonial status.

The growth of the US

The Louisiana Purchase of 1803 added to the US a huge swathe of western lands formerly controlled by France. After the War of 1812, all hope of annexing Canada was abandoned, and the US began the great push westward.

The consolidation of western lands encouraged millions of pioneers to forge new lives in the West. The spirit of aggressive progress which drove settlers westward soon became known as "manifest destiny".

Settlers poured into the Great Plains, the Pacific Northwest, and the northern periphery of the Republic of Mexico, including Texas and California. The Santa Fe trail, open for trade by 1823, brought New Mexico under US influence. By mid-century, the US boasted an extensive communications network. Steamboat traffic dominated the riverine highway system, augmented by canals and railroads running cross-country.

② North America 1783–1905: struggles for nationhood and the seizing of the West

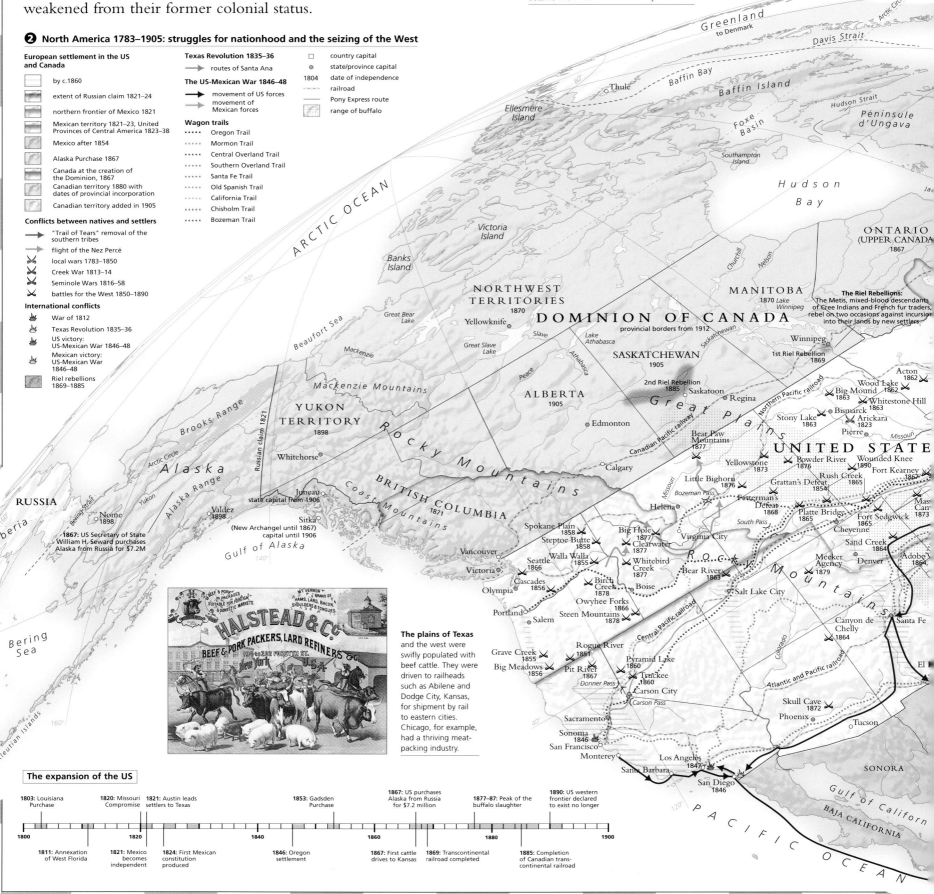

The plains of Texas and the west were swiftly populated with beef cattle. They were driven to railheads such as Abilene and Dodge City, Kansas, for shipment by rail to eastern cities. Chicago, for example, had a thriving meat-packing industry.

Territorial conflict and US expansion

Although involved in conflicts with Britain over the boundary with Canada, the US managed to solve these issues peacefully. A weak, divided Mexico, however, feared US territorial demands, especially after President Andrew Jackson offered to purchase Texas. By 1835 the Texans had seceded. Suspicion between the US and Mexico turned quickly to crisis, and in 1846, to war. In 1848 Mexico yielded about a third of its territory to the US as terms of peace, and descended into civil war. The cession of the northern Oregon Country by Britain in 1846 and James Gadsden's 1853 purchase of 30,000 square miles south of the Gila river from Mexico, completed the westward expansion of the US. The last piece of continental land added to the US was the northwestern territory of Alaska in 1867.

Destruction of Native Americans

From the 1790s, Native Americans were removed from their Eastern homelands and forced to migrate west of the Mississippi River. Some, like the Seminole in Florida, resisted stoutly. The settlement of the West from the 1860s was met with serious armed resistance from Native Americans. With the final loss of their lands, traditional societies were reorganized so as to pave the way for their integration into the national population.

Sitting Bull *(above)*, chief of the Teton tribe of the Lakota (Sioux) nation, attempts to retain a homeland in the western lands and predicted the deaths of Custer and his men at the Battle of Little Bighorn.

White Cloud *(left)* was chief of the Iowa tribe, who pursued a semisedentary agricultural existence alongside their hunting and battle activities. In 1836, the Iowa ceded their lands to the US and moved to a reservation on what is now the Kansas-Nebraska border.

In the latter half of the 19th century, western Canada and the US prioritized the building of transcontinental railroads. These opened up the West to hunters who killed millions of buffalo for their hides, almost destroying the North American herd by the end of the century.

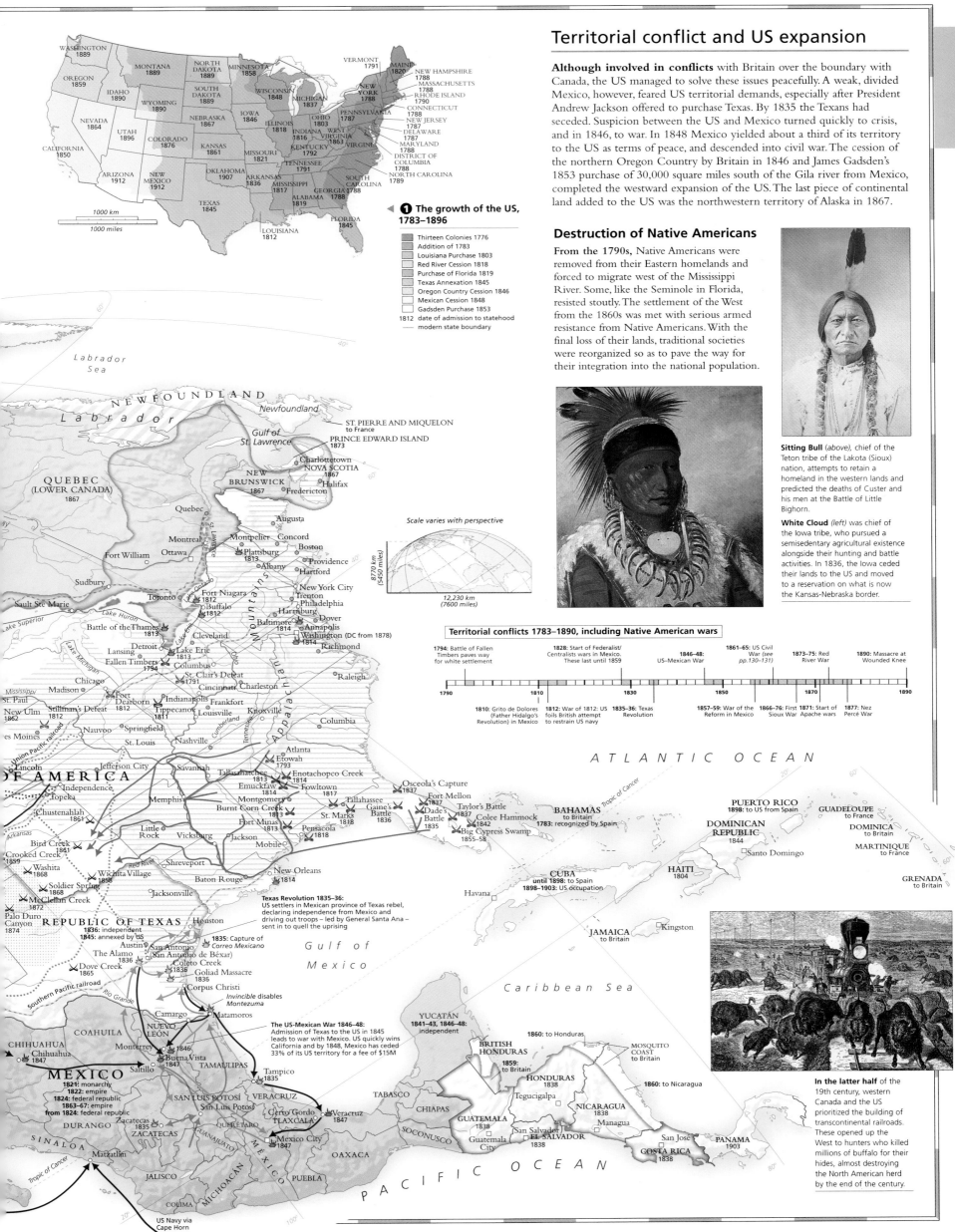

◀ ❶ **The growth of the US, 1783–1896**

- ▢ Thirteen Colonies 1776
- ▢ Addition of 1783
- ▢ Louisiana Purchase 1803
- ▢ Red River Cession 1818
- ▢ Purchase of Florida 1819
- ▢ Texas Annexation 1845
- ▢ Oregon Country Cession 1846
- ▢ Mexican Cession 1848
- ▢ Gadsden Purchase 1853
- 1812 date of admission to statehood
- — modern state boundary

Scale varies with perspective

8770 km (5450 miles)
12,230 km (7600 miles)

Territorial conflicts 1783–1890, including Native American wars

1794: Battle of Fallen Timbers paves way for white settlement
1828: Start of Federalist/Centralists wars in Mexico. These last until 1859
1846–48: US–Mexican War
1861–65: US Civil War *(see pp.130–131)*
1873–75: Red River War
1890: Massacre at Wounded Knee

1790 — 1810 — 1830 — 1850 — 1870 — 1890

1810: Grito de Dolores (Father Hidalgo's Revolution) in Mexico
1812: War of 1812: US foils British attempt to restrain US navy
1835–36: Texas Revolution
1857–59: War of the Reform in Mexico
1866–76: First Sioux War
1871: Start of Apache wars
1877: Nez Percé War

Texas Revolution 1835–36:
US settlers in Mexican province of Texas rebel, declaring independence from Mexico and driving out troops – led by General Santa Ana – sent in to quell the uprising

The US-Mexican War 1846–48:
Admission of Texas to the US in 1845 leads to war with Mexico. US quickly wins California and by 1848, Mexico has ceded 33% of its US territory for a fee of $15M

1836: independent
1845: annexed by US

1821: monarchy
1822: empire
1824: federal republic
1863–67: empire
from 1824: federal republic

BAHAMAS to Britain
1783: recognized by Spain
CUBA until 1898: to Spain
1898–1903: US occupation
JAMAICA to Britain
HAITI 1804
PUERTO RICO **1898:** to US from Spain
DOMINICAN REPUBLIC 1844
GUADELOUPE to France
DOMINICA to Britain
MARTINIQUE to France
GRENADA to Britain

1860: to Honduras
BRITISH HONDURAS
1859: to Britain
MOSQUITO COAST to Britain
1860: to Nicaragua
HONDURAS 1838
NICARAGUA 1838
GUATEMALA 1838
EL SALVADOR 1838
COSTA RICA 1838
PANAMA 1903
YUCATÁN 1841–43, 1846–48: independent

THE AMERICAN CIVIL WAR

Abraham Lincoln's 1863 Emancipation Proclamation freed the slaves of the south.

BETWEEN INDEPENDENCE in 1776 and 1860 there developed within the United States two very different regional societies. In the North there emerged an industrialized society, committed to liberal banking and credit systems, and protective tariffs. The south was a less populous agrarian society opposed to the sale of public land in the Midwest, high duties, and restrictions upon the institution of slavery. Moreover, the libertarian North increasingly resented Southern political and judicial overrepresentation. The Democratic Party held the two parts together until 1859; its split, and the election of a Republican president committed to opposing the spread of slavery, provoked the Union's collapse – even before Lincoln's inauguration, seven southern states had seceded, and war became inevitable.

The cotton gin invented by Eli Whitney in 1793 enabled the swift processing of short-staple cotton. Cotton production increased massively in the southern states, with a resultant rise in the number of slaves required to work the burgeoning plantations.

❻ The Civil War to the fall of Vicksburg Apr 1861–Jul 1863 ▶

- Union states 1861
- Confederate states 1861
- Union front line to Dec 1861
- Union front line to Dec 1862
- → Union movement
- → Confederate movement
- Union fort
- Confederate fort
- Union naval blockade
- ⚔ Union victory
- ⚔ Confederate victory
- Apr 12 1865 date of battle or attack

An unequal nation

By 1860 the US was composed of 18 "free" states – mainly in the North, and 15 "slave" states – mainly in the South. On the issue of slavery, as well as economics, the expanding nation was divided. Industry and finance dominated the North which also had 71% of the population, 81% of bank deposits, 72% of railroad mileage, and 85% of the country's factories. The South concentrated on farming, in particular on the production of cotton, tobacco, and sugar for export to Europe. In 1850, 347,000 Southern families out of a total population of 6,000,000 were slaveowners. The West was developing an agricultural economy, but produced a greater variety of crops, and sold most of its produce to the North.

◀ ❶ 1820: the Missouri Compromise

- free states
- free territories
- slave states
- territories where slavery legal

▼ ❷ 1850: a new compromise

- free states
- free territories
- slave states
- territories where slavery legal

▼ ❸ 1854: the Kansas-Nebraska Act

- free states
- free territories
- slave states
- territories where slavery legal
- territories newly opened to slavery 1854
- area not subject to standard territorial laws

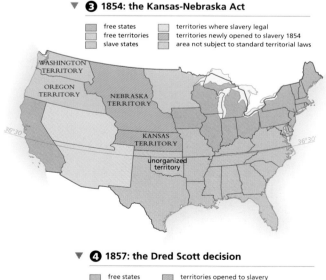

Industrial production fueled the growth of Northern cities such as Chicago, seen here in the 1860s. The Southern states, largely dependent on agriculture, remained far less economically developed.

Compromises on the road to civil war

The addition of Missouri in 1820 was the first extension of Union territory west of the Mississippi. The question of whether slavery should be allowed in the new state was settled by the so-called Missouri Compromise, with an artificial limit of 36° 30' marking the boundary between slave and free territory. In 1854 the Kansas–Nebraska Act established two new territories and proposed to allow territorial legislatures to decide the issue of slavery. The Dred Scott decision of 1857 – in which a slave who had been taken west by his master claimed that he was free because slavery was not legal in the new territory – led to the ruling that slavery could not be excluded from new territories.

▼ ❺ North versus South: the state of the Union in 1861

- Union states
- Confederate states
- slavery legal
- → major slave trade routes
- Jan 1861 date of secession from the Union

Resources and industry
- southern cotton belt
- northern corn belt
- coal
- iron ore
- precious metal
- textile production
- manufacturing city

▼ ❹ 1857: the Dred Scott decision

- free states
- slave states
- territories opened to slavery
- area not subject to standard territorial laws

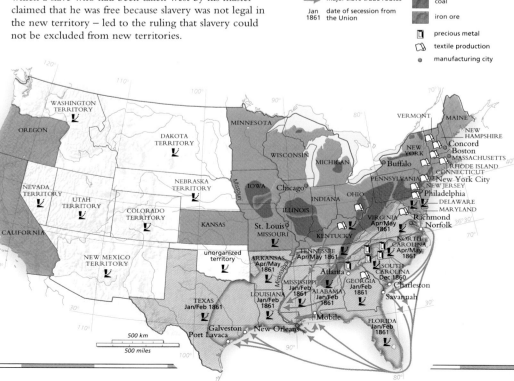

The Civil War 1861–65

In 1860, seven Southern states, fearing restrictions on slavery, seceded from the US. By 1861, they had been joined by four more and became known as the Confederacy. The remaining 23 so-called Union states remained loyal to the US. In April 1861, an attack on Fort Sumter in Charleston Harbor started a war for which neither side was prepared. The Civil War became a war of exhaustion. The superior demographic, industrial, and positional resources of the North, combined with sea power that ensured the Confederacy's isolation, slowly destroyed the capacity and will of the Confederacy to wage war. The Confederacy rarely tried to carry the war to the North, meeting crushing defeat at Gettysburg in July 1863. For the most part it waged a defensive war in order to sap the will of the Union. Certainly by 1864 war-weariness had set in in the North, but the successes of the 1864 campaign ensured Lincoln's reelection and sealed the South's defeat.

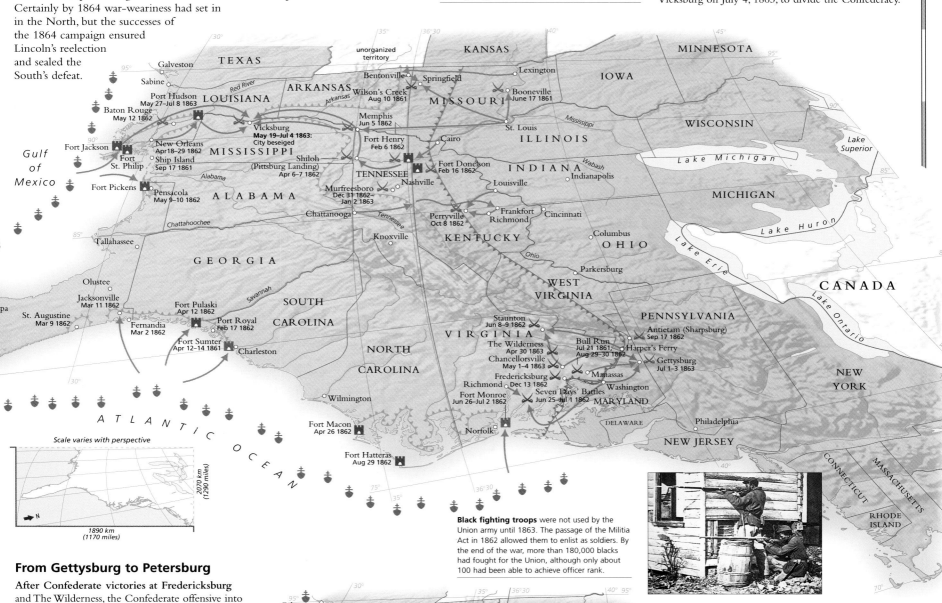

The Civil War was among the first wars to be recorded using photography. Field photographers such as Matthew Brady were able to record the true horrors of battles such as Gettysburg, the dead from which are seen above.

The Civil War to the fall of Vicksburg

During 1861–62 Union forces lost a series of battles to an enemy with superior military skills. However, the Northern naval blockade began to cut off both Southern exports and essential supplies. With no Confederate offensive on the upper Ohio which might have split the Union, the North was able to undertake offensives against the Confederate capital, Richmond, Virginia, and along the Tennessee and Mississippi. Repulsed before Richmond and obliged thereafter to move directly against the city, Union forces secured Memphis and New Orleans, capturing Vicksburg on July 4, 1863, to divide the Confederacy.

Black fighting troops were not used by the Union army until 1863. The passage of the Militia Act in 1862 allowed them to enlist as soldiers. By the end of the war, more than 180,000 blacks had fought for the Union, although only about 100 had been able to achieve officer rank.

From Gettysburg to Petersburg

After Confederate victories at Fredericksburg and The Wilderness, the Confederate offensive into Pennsylvania was defeated at Gettysburg, on the same day as Vicksburg fell. Thereafter on the defensive, Confederate armies were increasingly outnumbered: with Grant's appointment as commander, they were also increasingly outfought. Grant undertook an offensive against Richmond that broke the Confederate freedom of action in a series of battles and the siege of Petersburg: at the same time, Sherman's army broke into Georgia and South Carolina. With defeat in front of Petersburg, Confederate resistance collapsed in April 1865.

Ulysses S. Grant was appointed supreme commander of the Union forces in 1864.

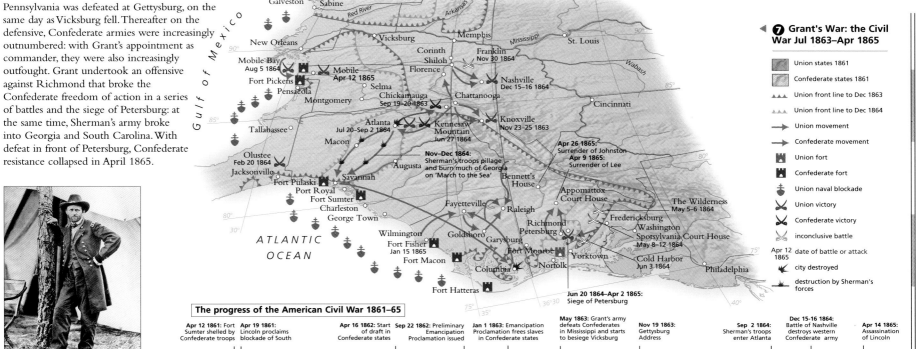

◀ **7 Grant's War: the Civil War Jul 1863–Apr 1865**

- Union states 1861
- Confederate states 1861
- Union front line to Dec 1863
- Union front line to Dec 1864
- → Union movement
- → Confederate movement
- Union fort
- Confederate fort
- Union naval blockade
- Union victory
- Confederate victory
- inconclusive battle
- **Apr 12 1865** date of battle or attack
- city destroyed
- destruction by Sherman's forces

The progress of the American Civil War 1861–65

Apr 12 1861	Fort Sumter shelled by Confederate troops
Apr 19 1861	Lincoln proclaims blockade of South
Sep 16 1862	Start of draft in Confederate states
Apr 16 1862	Preliminary Emancipation Proclamation issued
Sep 22 1862	Emancipation Proclamation frees slaves in Confederate states
Jan 1 1863	Grant's army defeats Confederates in Mississippi and starts to besiege Vicksburg
May 1863	Gettysburg Address
Nov 19 1863	Sherman's troops enter Atlanta
Sep 2 1864	Battle of Nashville destroys western Confederate army
Dec 15-16 1864	Assassination of Lincoln
Apr 14 1865	

Apr 15 1861	President Lincoln issues call for troops
Apr 6-7 1862	Battle of Shiloh: heavy casualties on both sides
May 1 1862	Union fleet captures New Orleans
Dec 13 1862	Severe Union defeat at Fredericksburg
Mar 3 1863	Draft law passed in North
Jul 1-3 1863	Confederate defeat at battle of Gettysburg
Jul 4 1863	Vicksburg captured by Union troops
Nov 15 1864	Sherman begins "March to the Sea"
Apr 9 1965	Lee surrenders to Grant at Appomattox

1861 1862 1863 1864 1865

NORTH AMERICA 1865–1920

The Statue of Liberty came to symbolize the hope and freedom offered by the US.

THE NATIONS OF NORTH AMERICA focused on the development of their own resources after 1865. The US worked to reconstruct itself after the Civil War and, like Canada, concentrated on the completion of transcontinental railroads to further exploit the continent's immense resources. Abroad, the US extended its influence in Central America and west across the Pacific, gaining new territory and economic advantage. In Mexico, Benito Juárez and his Republican forces felled the regime of Maximilian, ushering in a period of relative calm. Under Porfirio Díaz, Mexico attracted foreign investment and immigration, but its population remained brutally suppressed.

Industrialization and urbanization

US manufacturing techniques and machinery were refined throughout the second half of the 19th century.

The growth of the railroads and industrialization transformed the North American landscape. The economic boom turned the continent into a magnet for immigration: thousands came to its shores seeking a better life. Inventions and innovations abounded; cities arose across the continent, supporting factories that had expanded rapidly because of the demands of the American Civil War. The new industrial cities became pressure cookers of societal and political discontent, with often bloody confrontations between organized labor, police, and even the military.

Theodore Roosevelt, president 1901–09, presided over the economic boom of the early 20th century.

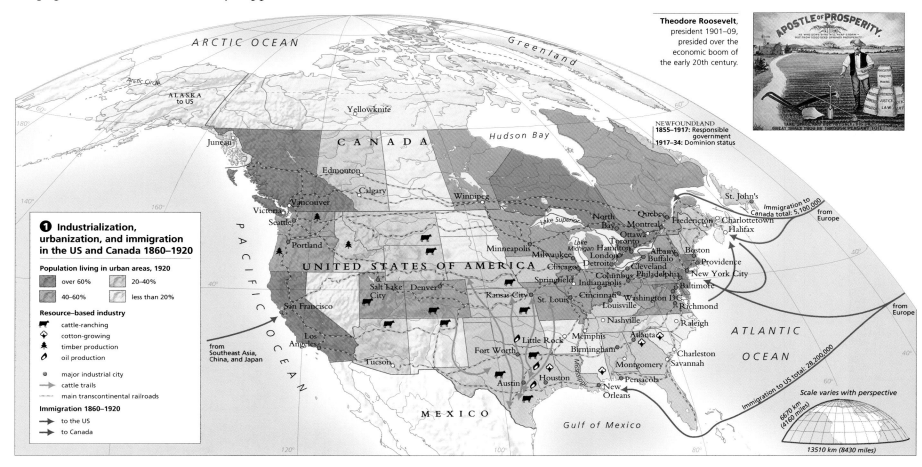

① Industrialization, urbanization, and immigration in the US and Canada 1860–1920

Population living in urban areas, 1920

- over 60%
- 40–60%
- 20–40%
- less than 20%

Resource-based industry

- cattle-ranching
- cotton-growing
- timber production
- oil production
- major industrial city
- cattle trails
- main transcontinental railroads

Immigration 1860–1920

- to the US
- to Canada

NEWFOUNDLAND
1855–1917: Responsible government
1917–34: Dominion status

Immigration to Canada total: 5,100,000 from Europe

Immigration to US total: 28,200,000

from Europe

Scale varies with perspective

6670 km (4160 miles)

13510 km (8430 miles)

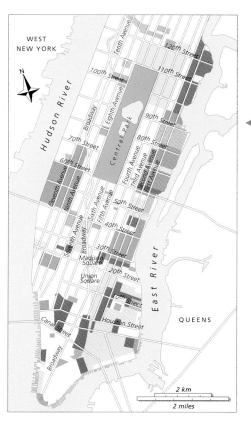

WEST NEW YORK

② Ethnic neighborhoods in Manhattan c.1920

- African-American
- Chinese
- Czech, Hungarian
- French
- German
- Irish
- Italian
- Jewish
- Scandinavian, Finnish
- Syrian, Turkish, Armenian, Greek

QUEENS

2 km
2 miles

New York

New York City's Ellis Island was the point of entry for millions of immigrants between 1892 and 1920. Many people remained within the city, finding comfort and support in the ethnic neighborhoods which had grown up there. By the 1920s, the diversity of nationalities on Manhattan was a reflection of the diverse strains that made up the population of the US.

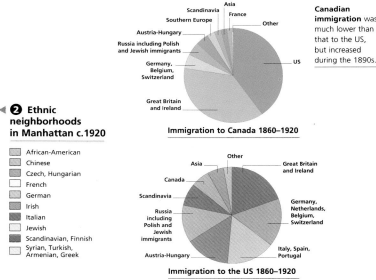

Canadian immigration was much lower than that to the US, but increased during the 1890s.

Immigration to Canada 1860–1920

Immigration to the US 1860–1920

The era of mass migration

During the 19th century nearly 50 million immigrants swelled the populations of Canada and the US. Immigration was initially from northern Europe: Germany, Scandinavia, Britain, and Ireland. From the 1880s, the bulk of migrants came from eastern and southern Europe. Most settlers were lured by the economic opportunities offered by the Americas, but others sought freedom from religious persecution and political uncertainty. After World War I, immigration was severely curtailed.

The majority of new arrivals to the Americas were able to gain entry. Only about 2% were refused entryy.

The US: 1865–1914

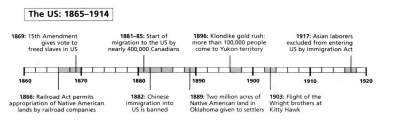

1869: 15th Amendment gives vote to freed slaves in US

1881–85: Start of migration to the US by nearly 400,000 Canadians

1896: Klondike gold rush: more than 100,000 people come to Yukon territory

1917: Asian laborers excluded from entering US by Immigration Act

1866: Railroad Act permits appropriation of Native American lands by railroad companies

1882: Chinese immigration into US is banned

1889: Two million acres of Native American land in Oklahoma given to settlers

1903: Flight of the Wright brothers at Kitty Hawk

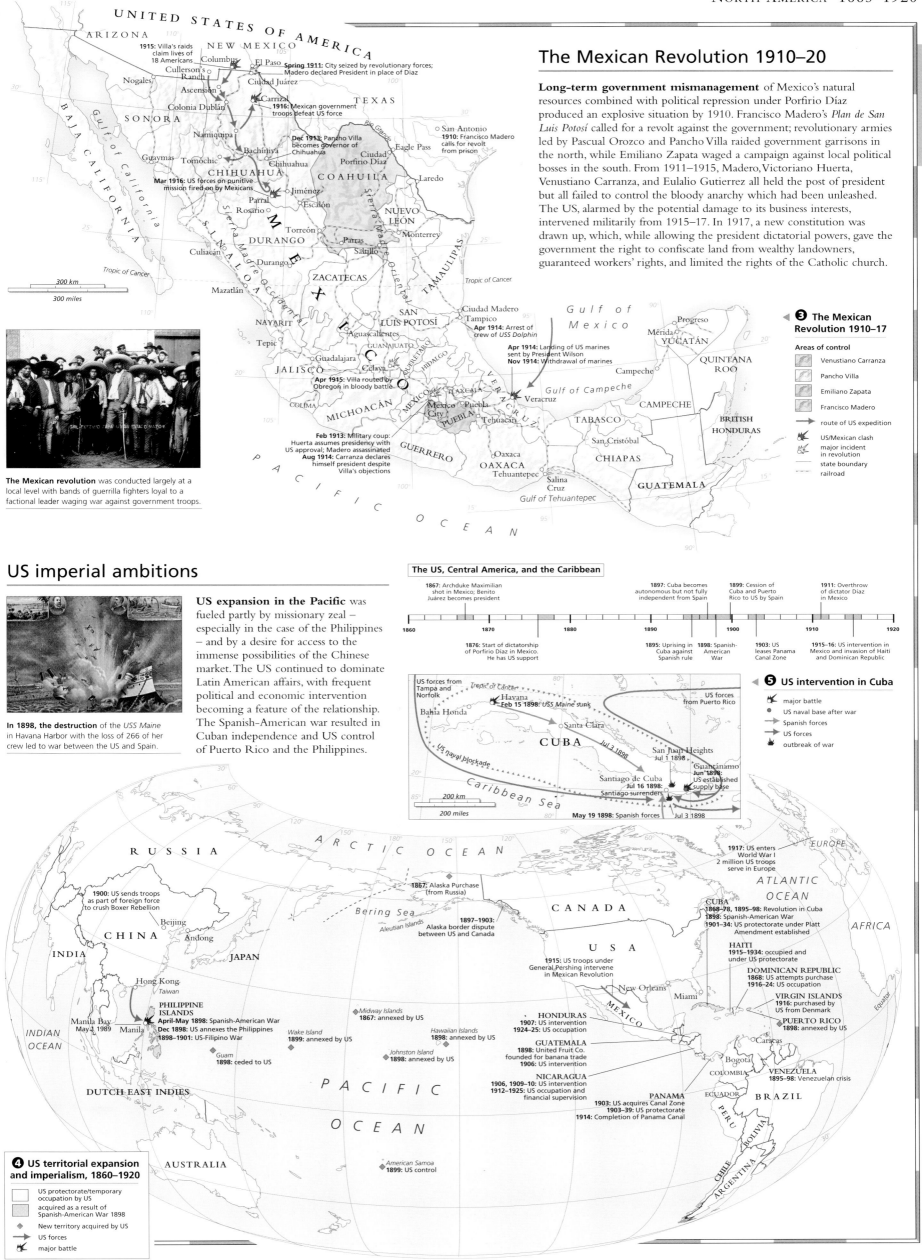

The Mexican Revolution 1910–20

Long-term government mismanagement of Mexico's natural resources combined with political repression under Porfirio Díaz produced an explosive situation by 1910. Francisco Madero's *Plan de San Luis Potosí* called for a revolt against the government; revolutionary armies led by Pascual Orozco and Pancho Villa raided government garrisons in the north, while Emiliano Zapata waged a campaign against local political bosses in the south. From 1911–1915, Madero, Victoriano Huerta, Venustiano Carranza, and Eulalio Gutierrez all held the post of president but all failed to control the bloody anarchy which had been unleashed. The US, alarmed by the potential damage to its business interests, intervened militarily from 1915–17. In 1917, a new constitution was drawn up, which, while allowing the president dictatorial powers, gave the government the right to confiscate land from wealthy landowners, guaranteed workers' rights, and limited the rights of the Catholic church.

The Mexican revolution was conducted largely at a local level with bands of guerrilla fighters loyal to a factional leader waging war against government troops.

❸ The Mexican Revolution 1910–17

Areas of control
- Venustiano Carranza
- Pancho Villa
- Emiliano Zapata
- Francisco Madero
- → route of US expedition
- US/Mexican clash
- major incident in revolution
- state boundary
- railroad

US imperial ambitions

US expansion in the Pacific was fueled partly by missionary zeal – especially in the case of the Philippines – and by a desire for access to the immense possibilities of the Chinese market. The US continued to dominate Latin American affairs, with frequent political and economic intervention becoming a feature of the relationship. The Spanish-American war resulted in Cuban independence and US control of Puerto Rico and the Philippines.

In 1898, the destruction of the USS Maine in Havana Harbor with the loss of 266 of her crew led to war between the US and Spain.

The US, Central America, and the Caribbean

1867: Archduke Maximilian shot in Mexico; Benito Juárez becomes president
1876: Start of dictatorship of Porfirio Díaz in Mexico. He has US support
1895: Uprising in Cuba against Spanish rule
1897: Cuba becomes autonomous but not fully independent from Spain
1898: Spanish-American War
1899: Cession of Cuba and Puerto Rico to US by Spain
1903: US leases Panama Canal Zone
1911: Overthrow of dictator Díaz in Mexico
1915–16: US intervention in Mexico and invasion of Haiti and Dominican Republic

❺ US intervention in Cuba
- major battle
- US naval base after war
- Spanish forces
- US forces
- outbreak of war

Feb 15 1898: USS Maine sunk
Jul 1 1898 – San Juan Heights
Jul 3 1898
Jul 16 1898: Santiago surrenders
May 19 1898: Spanish forces
Jun 1898: US established supply base (Guantánamo)

❹ US territorial expansion and imperialism, 1860–1920
- US protectorate/temporary occupation by US
- acquired as a result of Spanish-American War 1898
- ◆ New territory acquired by US
- → US forces
- major battle

AN ERA OF BOOM AND BUST

INVOLVEMENT IN WORLD WAR I confirmed the US's position as a world power in the first quarter of the century. Immigration greatly magnified the population, but during the 1920s, laws were enacted to control the tide of European settlers. The economy grew quickly, but the boom proved vulnerable and in 1929 the stock market collapsed. Between 1930 and 1932, the number of unemployed rose from 4 million to between 12 and 15 million – 25% of the total workforce. The Republican government, which had promoted the boom and was blamed for the crash, was rejected by the electorate, leading to the political dominance of a Democrat, Franklin Delano Roosevelt, for 13 years.

The industrial boom

This Model-A Ford was the successor to the Model-T Ford, the first car to be built using production line techniques and initially produced only in black. By the 1930s, Henry Ford achieved his dream of "a car so low in price that no man making a good salary will be unable to afford one."

The early 1920s saw a massive growth in US production. Traditional industries such as iron and steel were in relative decline, but automobiles, petrochemicals, construction, and the service industries grew rapidly, as did speculation on the stock market. But the boom was built on shaky foundations. High rates of small business failure in the 1920s gave the first signs of fragility and it was clear that production was outstripping consumption. Paper fortunes that had accrued in stocks and shares were wiped out by the Wall Street Crash of 1929.

The depression and the New Deal

The stock market crash of 1929 shattered millions of dreams and left many Americans destitute. Farmers were particularly hard hit, as banks withdrew funding. So were black people in both cities and rural areas. The Roosevelt administration devised a series of relief programs known as the "New Deal" to restart the economy and provide new jobs. Though millions of dollars of federal funding were spent on relief, 20% of Americans were still unemployed in 1939. Not until World War II did the economy recover.

The Works Progress Administration (WPA) provided work relief for 8.5 million unemployed. Projects included the building and repair of roads, bridges, schools, and hospitals.

❶ Major US industries c.1925

- iron and steel
- meat processing
- oil and gas
- textile production
- timber
- vehicle manufacture
- coalfield
- major industrial city

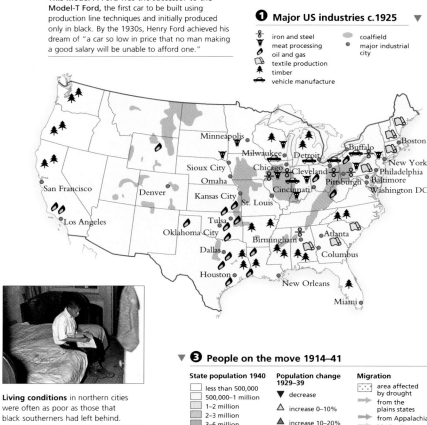

Living conditions in northern cities were often as poor as those that black southerners had left behind.

▼ ❸ People on the move 1914–41

State population 1940	Population change 1929–39	Migration
less than 500,000	▼ decrease	area affected by drought
500,000–1 million	△ increase 0–10%	from the plains states
1–2 million	△ increase 10–20%	from Appalachia
2–3 million	▲ increase over 20%	black migrants from South
3–6 million		other
over 6 million		

▲ ❷ The impact of the Great Depression 1933–34

Unemployed	Families receiving relief
less than 10%	less than 10%
11–15%	10–15%
16–25%	over 15%
over 25%	

Migration in the US, 1914–41

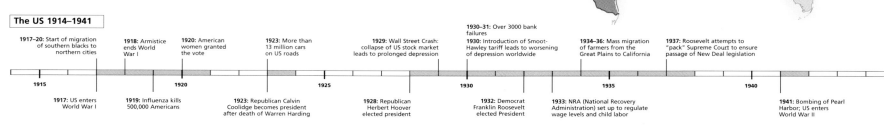

Refugees from the Dust Bowl carry only the bare essentials as they walk towards Los Angeles in search of work (1939).

By the 1920s, more than 50% of Americans lived in urban areas. From 1917–20, more than 400,000 rural black southerners moved to northern cities, and 600,000 more went in the 1920s. In the mid-1930s, farmers from the drought-affected plains states abandoned their farms by the thousands and moved west – primarily to California's cities and valleys. Appalachia also saw a mass transference of people north to Indiana and Ohio and west to California.

The US 1914–1941

1917–20: Start of migration of southern blacks to northern cities

1918: Armistice ends World War I

1920: American women granted the vote

1923: More than 13 million cars on US roads

1929: Wall Street Crash: collapse of US stock market leads to prolonged depression

1930–31: Over 3000 bank failures

1930: Introduction of Smoot-Hawley tariff leads to worsening of depression worldwide

1934–36: Mass migration of farmers from the Great Plains to California

1937: Roosevelt attempts to "pack" Supreme Court to ensure passage of New Deal legislation

1915 1920 1925 1930 1935 1940 1945

1917: US enters World War I

1919: Influenza kills 500,000 Americans

1923: Republican Calvin Coolidge becomes president after death of Warren Harding

1928: Republican Herbert Hoover elected president

1932: Democrat Franklin Roosevelt elected President

1933: NRA (National Recovery Administration) set up to regulate wage levels and child labor

1941: Bombing of Pearl Harbor; US enters World War II

Popular culture in the US

Developments in technology during World War I improved communications throughout the US. By the 1920s virtually all of the nation was connected to the Bell Telephone network. Radio sets enabled news and information to reach even isolated areas. The movies became the first mass entertainment industry. From small beginnings in the early 1900s, by the 1930s, the film industry in Hollywood was exporting its glamorous products worldwide. During the Depression, cheap movie tickets kept audience numbers buoyant despite an initial downturn. Professional sports such as football, baseball, and boxing became of national interest for the first time, with huge attendances and highly paid celebrities.

❹ The major Hollywood studios in 1919

- ⭐ Nestor
- ⭐ Famous Players – Lasky Clater Paramount
- ⭐ National Film Corporation of America
- ⭐ Metro
- ⭐ Chaplin
- ⭐ Brunton
- ⭐ Fox
- ⭐ D.W. Griffith
- ⭐ Vitagraph
- ⭐ Mack Sennett
- ⭐ Universal
- ⭐ Ince
- ⭐ Goldwyn

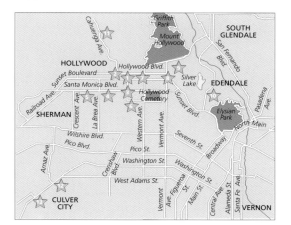

By 1919, most of the major movie studios had established themselves to the north of Los Angeles. Hollywood became the heart of the world motion picture industry and a magnet for all aspiring filmmakers.

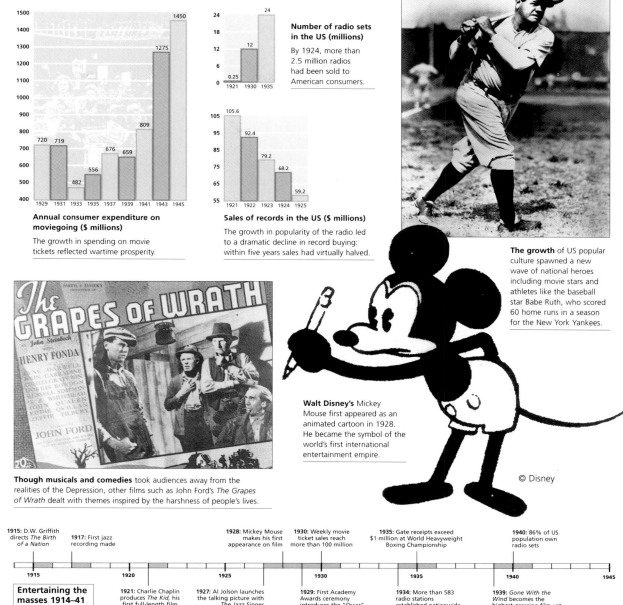

Number of radio sets in the US (millions)
By 1924, more than 2.5 million radios had been sold to American consumers.

Annual consumer expenditure on moviegoing ($ millions)
The growth in spending on movie tickets reflected wartime prosperity.

Sales of records in the US ($ millions)
The growth in popularity of the radio led to a dramatic decline in record buying: within five years sales had virtually halved.

The growth of US popular culture spawned a new wave of national heroes including movie stars and athletes like the baseball star Babe Ruth, who scored 60 home runs in a season for the New York Yankees.

Though musicals and comedies took audiences away from the realities of the Depression, other films such as John Ford's *The Grapes of Wrath* dealt with themes inspired by the harshness of people's lives.

Walt Disney's Mickey Mouse first appeared as an animated cartoon in 1928. He became the symbol of the world's first international entertainment empire.

© Disney

Entertaining the masses 1914–41

- **1915:** D.W. Griffith directs *The Birth of a Nation*
- **1917:** First jazz recording made
- **1921:** Charlie Chaplin produces *The Kid*, his first full-length film
- **1927:** Al Jolson launches the talking picture with *The Jazz Singer*
- **1928:** Mickey Mouse makes his first appearance on film
- **1929:** First Academy Awards ceremony introduces the "Oscar"
- **1930:** Weekly movie ticket sales reach more than 100 million
- **1934:** More than 583 radio stations established nationwide
- **1935:** Gate receipts exceed $1 million at World Heavyweight Boxing Championship
- **1939:** *Gone With the Wind* becomes the highest-grossing film yet
- **1940:** 86% of US population own radio sets

(timeline: 1915 1920 1925 1930 1935 1940 1945)

THE FDR EFFECT

The political complexion of the US altered radically during the 1930s. Hoover's Republican party, so dominant at the height of the 20s boom, was routed by the Democrats in 1932. The patrician Franklin Delano Roosevelt attracted a "New Deal coalition" of Blacks, women, labor groups, and southern whites which dominated American politics for over 30 years.

Roosevelt spoke regularly to the American people via his "fireside chats" which were broadcast on national radio.

❺ Presidential elections

- ⬜ Republican
- ⬛ Democrat

1928
1932 1936
1940 1944

Intolerance

This period, particularly the 1920s, was marked by diverse displays of intolerance against perceived threats to the "American Way of Life." "New" immigrants, black migration, the increased freedom of women, and economic instability all fueled anxieties. The prohibition of alcohol, immigration "Quota Acts," and the formation of the FBI in response to the "Red Scare" of 1919–20 and the fear of Communism, were official responses to this new intolerance. Other – unofficial – reactions included race riots in the southern states and Midwest, and the revival of the white supremacist Ku Klux Klan, whose membership increased to more than two million in the 1920s.

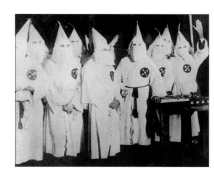

The growth of the Ku Klux Klan in this period was largely an expression of insecurity among small-town White Anglo-Saxon Protestants toward a multitude of apparent threats to their power and influence.

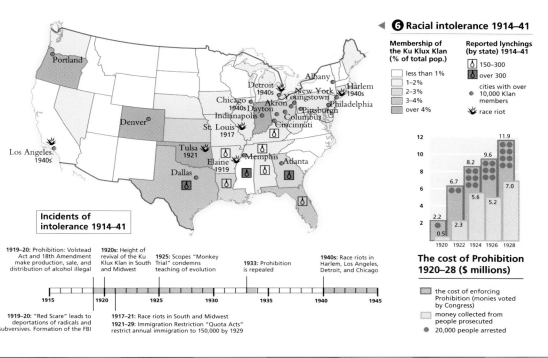

❻ Racial intolerance 1914–41

Membership of the Ku Klux Klan (% of total pop.)
- ⬜ less than 1%
- 1–2%
- 2–3%
- 3–4%
- over 4%

Reported lynchings (by state) 1914–41
- 150–300
- over 300
- cities with over 10,000 Klan members
- race riot

The cost of Prohibition 1920–28 ($ millions)
- ▢ the cost of enforcing Prohibition (monies voted by Congress)
- ▢ money collected from people prosecuted
- ● 20,000 people arrested

Incidents of intolerance 1914–41

- **1919–20:** Prohibition: Volstead Act and 18th Amendment make production, sale, and distribution of alcohol illegal
- **1920s:** Height of revival of the Ku Klux Klan in South and Midwest
- **1925:** Scopes "Monkey Trial" condemns teaching of evolution
- **1933:** Prohibition is repealed
- **1940s:** Race riots in Harlem, Los Angeles, Detroit, and Chicago
- **1919–20:** "Red Scare" leads to deportations of radicals and subversives. Formation of the FBI
- **1917–21:** Race riots in South and Midwest
- **1921–29:** Immigration Restriction "Quota Acts" restrict annual immigration to 150,000 by 1929

(timeline: 1915 1920 1925 1930 1935 1940 1945)

SOCIETIES IN TRANSITION

Martin Luther King, Jnr. harnessed the spontaneous protests of the 1950s to create a massive civil rights movement.

IN THE 1950s, THE UNITED STATES was labeled "the affluent society." This phrase reflected the experience of unprecedented economic prosperity and social progress in the years since World War II ended the Great Depression. Most Americans enjoyed rising incomes on the back of the postwar boom. The quality of life was further enhanced by the availability of new consumer goods, new leisure opportunities, and suburban housing. The people of Mexico, Central America, and the Caribbean continued to have a much lower standard of living than the US and Canada. And within the US, itself, not all regions and social groups experienced equal advances in affluence and status.

Postwar prosperity in the US

The idealized family unit, headed by a male breadwinner, became a favorite image for advertisers and politicians during the 1950s.

The economic stimulus provided by the war and, later, the arms race with the Soviet Union were key factors in creating the affluence of the immediate postwar decades. As manufacturing switched to a peacetime mode, consumer durables flowed into the domestic marketplace. Consumerism generated a flourishing service sector. America's position at the hub of the international trading system gave her access to foreign markets and raw materials crucial to economic success. The boom ended in the early 1970s, with the Vietnam War and the energy crisis producing prolonged inflation and recession. Europe and Japan were also challenging American economic dominance.

❶ Average family income by region, 1949

Rocky Mountains $13,857 · Far West $15,416 · Great Plains $12,635 · Great Lakes $14,997 · New England $13,328 · Mid-Atlantic $15,122 · Southwest $11,656 · Southeast $8856

By no means all of the US benefited from the prosperity of the postwar period. While California and the industrial north boomed, the South in particular remained depressed, with an average income only half that of other parts of the US.

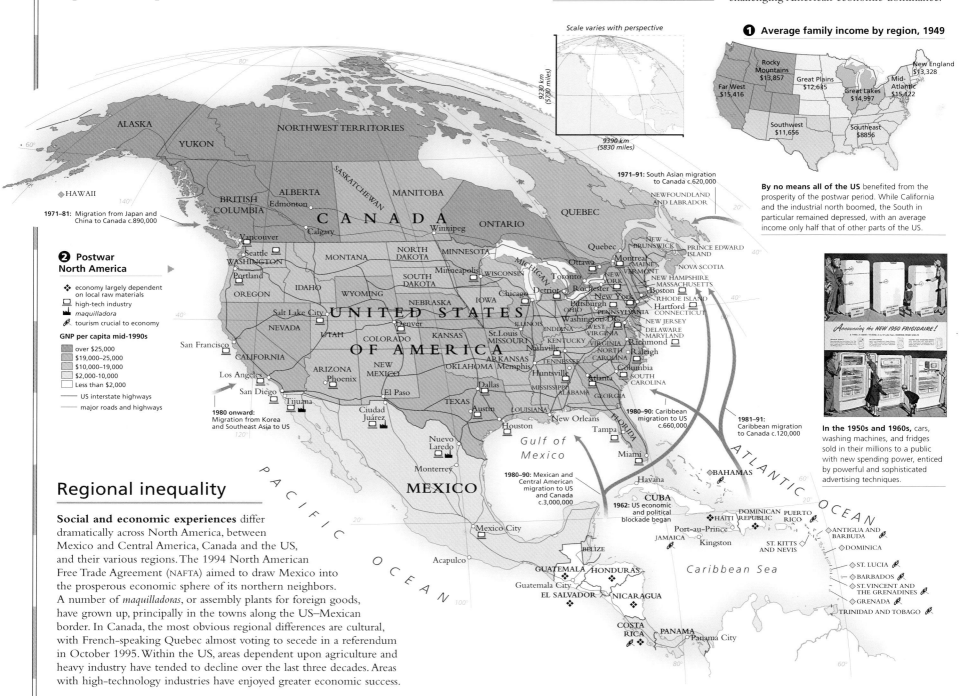

Scale varies with perspective
9230 km (5730 miles)
9390 km (5830 miles)

1971–81: Migration from Japan and China to Canada c.890,000

1971–91: South Asian migration to Canada c.620,000

❷ Postwar North America

- ❖ economy largely dependent on local raw materials
- ⌂ high-tech industry
- *maquilladora*
- 🏖 tourism crucial to economy

GNP per capita mid-1990s
- over $25,000
- $19,000–25,000
- $10,000–19,000
- $2,000–10,000
- Less than $2,000
- ▬▬ US interstate highways
- ─── major roads and highways

1980 onward: Migration from Korea and Southeast Asia to US

1980–90: Mexican and Central American migration to US and Canada c.3,000,000

1962: US economic and political blockade began

1980–90: Caribbean migration to US c.660,000

1981–91: Caribbean migration to Canada c.120,000

In the 1950s and 1960s, cars, washing machines, and fridges sold in their millions to a public with new spending power, enticed by powerful and sophisticated advertising techniques.

Regional inequality

Social and economic experiences differ dramatically across North America, between Mexico and Central America, Canada and the US, and their various regions. The 1994 North American Free Trade Agreement (NAFTA) aimed to draw Mexico into the prosperous economic sphere of its northern neighbors. A number of *maquilladoras*, or assembly plants for foreign goods, have grown up, principally in the towns along the US–Mexican border. In Canada, the most obvious regional differences are cultural, with French-speaking Quebec almost voting to secede in a referendum in October 1995. Within the US, areas dependent upon agriculture and heavy industry have tended to decline over the last three decades. Areas with high-technology industries have enjoyed greater economic success.

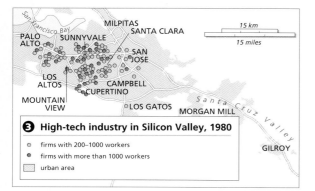

❸ High-tech industry in Silicon Valley, 1980

- ○ firms with 200–1000 workers
- ● firms with more than 1000 workers
- ▢ urban area

SILICON VALLEY

Without specific locational needs, many high-tech firms were able to site their businesses in nonurban areas in the South and West, helping to revitalize the economy of these regions. Silicon Valley near San Francisco, California, contains one of the world's highest concentrations of computing and electronic industries. Initially, many high-tech manufacturers relied upon contracts from the US military, but the age of the personal computer has allowed these manufacturers to play a key role in sustaining American exports and growth.

New high-tech industries including aerospace and electronics, as at Silicon Valley (right), grew up in the late 1970s to fill the gaps left by the decline of traditional US heavy industries.

Changes in urban life

As black Americans migrated from the rural South to urban centers in the 1940s and 1950s, many whites abandoned city life for the suburbs. These areas became increasingly detached from the cities; instead of petitioning for access to the cities' municipal facilities, postwar suburban residents fought fiercely against annexation proposals. The tax dollars of prosperous whites were no longer available to maintain the city infrastructure. The financial crisis was made worse by the decline of traditional US industries, and many of America's cities sank into crisis during the 1960s and 1970s. Housing stock deteriorated, roads were not repaired, and poverty, crime, and racial tension were common features of many urban areas in the US. Poverty was not confined to the inner cities: people in rural areas in the deep South and the Appalachians were some of the most deprived in the US.

The centers of many of America's great cities declined physically as people move to the suburbs. Old housing stock was torn down but not replaced, and the infrastructure declined through lack of funding.

The new suburbs provided a safe haven away from the cities. Mortgage assistance was readily available to those wishing to move to suburban areas. Until the 1960s, money was siphoned into the suburbs by federal housing officials, who simultaneously denied loans to people still living in urban areas.

The growth of the suburbs

The 1950s saw the growth of suburban America. New construction techniques lowered the cost of new homes, and expressways improved access to and from urban centers. In the postwar era, cities like Chicago absorbed ever more of their surrounding areas.

4 Chicago: 1850–1969

Urban growth
- 1850
- 1875
- 1900
- 1925
- 1950
- 1969

MCHENRY COUNTY, LAKE COUNTY, ILLINOIS, KANE COUNTY, DU PAGE COUNTY, Chicago, COOK COUNTY, KENDALL COUNTY, WILL COUNTY, Lake Michigan, INDIANA, LAKE COUNTY, PORTER COUNTY

20 km / 20 miles

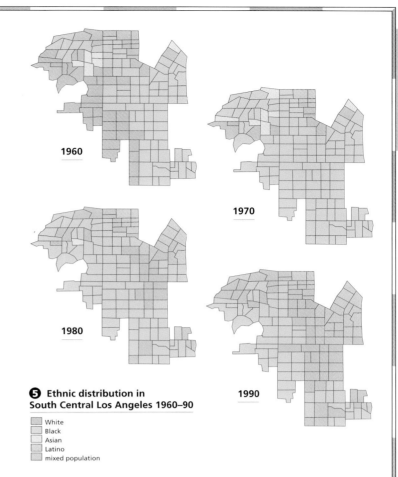

5 Ethnic distribution in South Central Los Angeles 1960–90

- White
- Black
- Asian
- Latino
- mixed population

1960 · 1970 · 1980 · 1990

Poverty and ethnic balance in inner city Los Angeles

Los Angeles demonstrates how wealth and poverty live separate lives in postwar urban America. The central neighborhoods in an otherwise prosperous city have a massively disproportionate number of poor residents, with an ethnic mix in constant flux. In 1960, a substantial white population remained in South Central Los Angeles. By 1970, whites had largely left the area, which had a now predominantly black population. Twenty years later, Latinos formed a majority in many South Central neighborhoods.

Civil Rights and other protest movements

1955: Bus boycott against segregation in Montgomery, Alabama

1961: Student freedom riders go into South to protest against segregation

1963: March on Washington led by Martin Luther King, Jr.

1965: Voting Rights Act increases number of black voters; Watts Riots in Los Angeles

1968: Assassination of Martin Luther King, Jr. sparks riots in 124 US cities

1970: Four students killed at Kent State University, Ohio in protest over US involvement in Cambodia

1955 · 1960 · 1965 · 1970 · 1975

1957: Martin Luther King, Jr. heads coordinated resistance movement

1964: Civil Rights Act forbids segregation in public places

1966: Race riots in Atlanta

1968: Riots and protests follow Democrat rally in Chicago

1969: 250,000 people march on Washington in protest against war in Vietnam

1974: High Court gives go-ahead to busing for integration of US schools

WASHINGTON, OREGON, MONTANA, NORTH DAKOTA, MINNESOTA, IDAHO, WYOMING, SOUTH DAKOTA, WISCONSIN, MICHIGAN, MAINE, VERMONT, NEW HAMPSHIRE, NEW YORK, MASS., R.I., CONN., CALIFORNIA, NEVADA, UTAH, COLORADO, NEBRASKA, IOWA, ILLINOIS, INDIANA, OHIO, PENN., N.J., DELAWARE, MARYLAND, WEST VIRGINIA, KANSAS, MISSOURI, KENTUCKY, VIRGINIA, ARIZONA, NEW MEXICO, OKLAHOMA, ARKANSAS, TENNESSEE, NORTH CAROLINA, SOUTH CAROLINA, MISSISSIPPI, ALABAMA, GEORGIA, LOUISIANA, TEXAS, FLORIDA

1970: Four students at Kent State University shot in protest over US entry into Cambodia

Aug 1967: Woodstock

San Francisco 1966
1967: "Summer of Love"
1969: Anti-war protest
Fresno 1967
Santa Barbara
1970: Bank burned by antiwar protestors
Los Angeles
Aug 1965: Watts riots leave 34 dead
Oakland 1966
Phoenix 1967
Tucson 1967

Des Moines
1969: Student protest
Omaha 1968
Milwaukee 1966
Detroit 1963, 1968
1967: Riots leave 43 dead
Rochester 1964, 1967
Albany
Boston 1967
New York 1968
Jul 1964: Riots in Harlem
Apr 1968: 5000 students in protest at Columbia University
Newark
1967: Riots leave 25 dead
Chicago 1964, 1966, 1967
Cleveland 1966, 1967
Kent 1970
Pittsburgh 1968
Philadelphia 1964, 1968
Cincinnati 1967
Dayton 1966
Baltimore 1968
Washington DC 1968
Oct 1967, Nov 1969: Antiwar protest
Kansas City 1968
St Louis 1967
Richmond 1968
VIRGINIA 38% 52%
Nashville 1967
1968: Martin Luther King Jr. assassinated
Wichita 1967
Greensboro 1968
Raleigh 1968
NORTH CAROLINA 44% 43%
Knoxville 1967-68
Charlotte 1968
Memphis 1968
Little Rock 1968
ARKANSAS 42% 81%
Birmingham 1955, 1963
MISSISSIPPI 6% 60%
Selma 1967
Anniston
Atlanta 1967
GEORGIA 28% 64%
SOUTH CAROLINA 33% 45%
Montgomery
ALABAMA 18% 54%
LOUISIANA 32% 56%
Jackson 1962, 1967
1970: Two students killed at Jackson State University
New Orleans 1967
Mobile 1968
Tallahassee 1967
FLORIDA 51% 54%
Tampa 1967
Miami 1966
Houston 1967

In August 1969, 400,000 people gathered at a farm near Bethel in upstate New York to form the "Woodstock Nation," at a music festival which was also a celebration of peaceful, antiestablishment coexistence.

Moves for freedom

The opportunities presented by postwar America were denied to many black Americans, particularly in the still-segregated South, where they were prevented by whites from voting. Inspired by decolonization movements abroad, and aided by a 1954 Supreme Court judgement that segregation was unconstitutional, black Americans began to challenge discrimination. In 1955, a bus boycott in Montgomery, Alabama forced the bus company to end segregation. The success inspired similar protests throughout the South. In 1964 and 1965, the US Congress passed legislation banning racial discrimination and protecting the democratic rights of all Americans. The 1960s also saw a rise in political consciousness among other groups; protests against the Vietnam War grew in number throughout the late 1960s, as did the movement for women's rights.

A woman prays for peace in Birmingham, Alabama, during a Civil Rights protest in May 1963, as fellow demonstrators dance and sing behind her.

6 Protest movements and urban unrest of the 1960s

- ☀ antiwar protest
- ✳ center of civil rights activity
- ⚘ urban unrest/race riot

GEORGIA 28% 64% Percentage of the black population of voting age registered to vote: before the Voting Rights Act of 1965, in 1971

Blacks as a % of state population
- more than 30
- 20–30
- 15–20
- 7–15
- less than 7

THE USA: GROWTH OF A SUPERPOWER

John F. Kennedy, a charismatic and popular US president, was assassinated in 1963.

THE JAPANESE ATTACK on Pearl Harbor in December 1941 and the subsequent US entry into World War II marked the beginning of a new era in America's role in the world. Thereafter, through alliances, military interventions, and trade, the United States exerted a powerful influence over the lives of other nations. While the US and Canada remained stable and prosperous, Central America and the Caribbean struggled for democracy and autonomy in the postwar period. Although challenged by the Cuban Revolution in 1959, the US continued to exercise power in the region, often through support for military dictatorships.

America and the world

During World War II, the US established a large number of military bases around the world. With the onset of the Cold War with the Soviet Union in the late 1940s, those bases had renewed importance. The Cold War also encouraged the Americans to form alliances with other nations. The North Atlantic Treaty Organization (NATO) was formed in 1949. After the Vietnam War, the US retreated from an active international role. The Soviet invasion of Afghanistan in 1979, however, revived the Cold War for another decade. With the collapse of the Soviet Union in 1991, the United States was left as the only superpower.

1 Strategic alliances 1948–89

US collective defense treaties
- NATO from 1983
- Rio Treaty by 1975
- ANZUS Pact 1951
- Southeast Asia Collective Defense Treaty 1954
- Bilateral defense treaties (Japan 1960; South Korea 1953; Philippines 1951; Taiwan 1954)
- US troops on active service
- COMECON members
- other Communist states 1977
- Military Air Transit Rights, Eastern Hemisphere

US involvement in world affairs 1950–90

| 1950 | 1955: US intervention in Iran | 1958: Eisenhower Doctrine commits US to prevent spread of Communism in Middle East | 1973: US withdraws troops from Vietnam | 1979: Iran hostage crisis | 1990: US sends troops to The Gulf in response to Saddam Hussein's invasion of Kuwait |

1950: Korean War | **1950:** Start of US involvement in Vietnam | **1960** | **1961:** Cuban Missile Crisis | **1970** | **1973:** US assists in right-wing coup in Chile | **1978:** US-brokered peace deal between Egypt and Israel | **1980** | **1983:** US intervention in Grenada | **1990**

US involvement was crucial to Allied success in World War II, with campaigns in the Pacific and support both on the ground and in the air in Europe. At the end of the war, US troops liberated a number of Nazi concentration camps and prisoner-of-war camps (*above*).

US soldiers with a Viet Cong suspect during the Vietnam War (1950–73), the longest and most costly of US attempts to contain the perceived Communist threat during the Cold War.

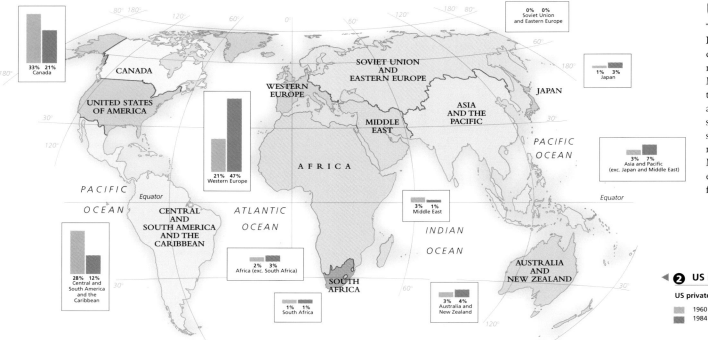

0% 0%
Soviet Union and Eastern Europe

33% 21% Canada

1% 3% Japan

21% 47% Western Europe

3% 7% Asia and Pacific (exc. Japan and Middle East)

3% 1% Middle East

28% 12% Central and South America and the Caribbean

2% 3% Africa (exc. South Africa)

1% 1% South Africa

3% 4% Australia and New Zealand

US investment overseas

During the Cold War, investment overseas was seen as a way to bind other nations to the capitalist sphere. The Marshall Plan of 1948 aimed both to aid the postwar recovery of Western Europe and reduce the chances of Communist subversion. American firms also tried to secure access to valuable raw materials, most importantly oil in the Middle East. More recently, US companies sought to exploit cheap foreign labor by establishing factories overseas, threatening jobs at home.

◄ 2 US investment overseas

US private direct investment abroad
- 1960
- 1984

The decline of the Democratic South

The migration of Southern blacks to northern cities in the 1940s and 1950s (in part due to the mechanization of cotton farming) killed off most of the remaining cotton plantations in the South, which had depended on their cheap labor, leading to a decline in the Southern economy. In the North, black Americans became an important political constituency. The Democratic Party tried to reconcile its desire for their votes with its desire for the continued support of white Southerners who traditionally voted Democrat. By the late 1960s, after the Civil Rights legislation of President Lyndon Johnson, many Southerners abandoned their traditional commitment to the Democratic Party.

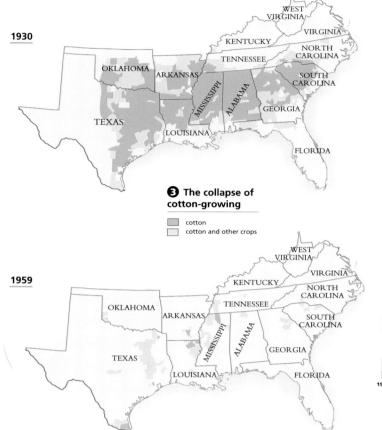

1930

1959

❸ **The collapse of cotton-growing**

- cotton
- cotton and other crops

KEY ELECTIONS 1948–96

In 1948 Democrat President Harry Truman won a shock victory over the Republican Thomas Dewey. However, the success of the pro-segregationist States Rights Party indicated that the Democrats might have problems maintaining the support of both blacks and Southerners, and in 1968 the Democrats lost every Southern state except Texas. Though Republicans held the Presidency throughout the 1980s, the elections of 1992 and 1996 proved that the Democrats could still win despite a largely Republican South.

The *Chicago Daily Tribune* was so confident of the outcome of the 1948 US presidential elections that the paper was printed without confirmation of the results, leaving the victorious Democratic candidate Harry Truman to revel in the premature headline.

1948

1968

Alaska ◆
Hawaii ◆

1996

Alaska ◆
Hawaii ◆

❹ **Presidential elections**

States won by each party

- Republicans
- Democrats
- States Rights
- American Independent

US election results 1944–96

1944: Roosevelt (Democrat) elected for a fourth term but dies in April 1945

1948: Roosevelt's successor, Truman (Democrat) is surprise winner

1952: Eisenhower (Republican) wins election

1956: Eisenhower wins second term

1960: Kennedy (Democrat) elected President

1963: Assassination of Kennedy. Johnson becomes President. Reelected in 1964

1968: Nixon (Republican) elected. Reelected 1972

1974: Nixon resigns over Watergate scandal. Replaced by Gerald Ford

1976: Jimmy Carter (Democrat) elected

1980: Ronald Reagan (Republican) wins. Wins second term in 1984

1988: George Bush (Republican) wins

1992: Bill Clinton (Democrat) elected. Wins second term in 1996

1944 · 1952 · 1960 · 1968 · 1976 · 1984 · 1992

US intervention in Central America

Historically the US has acted to prevent instability and protect its business interests in Central America. During the Cold War, America's concern intensified, with the fear of Communist subversion in its own backyard. In 1954, US agents organized the downfall of a left-wing government in Guatemala. In 1962, a crisis over Soviet nuclear arms in Cuba (*see p.108*) almost caused nuclear war. During the 1980s, President Reagan acted against leftists in Grenada and Nicaragua. After the Cold War, the drugs trade presents a major reason for continued American involvement in the region.

❺ **US intervention in Central America and the Caribbean** ▼

🏃 Cuban-sponsored guerilla activities 1959–68
■ US intervention

The Sandinista revolution of 1978 put an end to more than 40 years of military dictatorship in Nicaragua. The left-wing Sandinistas were distrusted by the US which sponsored Contra guerrillas based in Honduras (*left*) against the government.

In 1989, 23,000 US troops invaded Panama, arresting its ruler General Manuel Noriega (*above*) on drug trafficking charges. He was replaced by Guillermo Endara, a US-approved choice.

UNITED STATES OF AMERICA

ATLANTIC OCEAN

Gulf of Mexico

US exploitation of cheap Mexican labor in free trade zone (see p.136)

Tropic of Cancer

MEXICO
1980s: Serious economic difficulties
■ **1993–94:** NAFTA creates free-trade community of US, Mexico, and Canada

BAHAMAS

CUBA
1961: Attempted invasion at Bay of Pigs by US-supported forces
1962: Cuban Missile Crisis
Apr–Sep 1980: Muriel boatlift: Migration of thousandsof Cubans to US
1990: Severe economic distress following withdrawal of Soviet aid

■ **1954:** Military, with US backing, topples democratic government pledged to land and social reforms
1961: Appearance of revolutionaries
1968–70: US ambassador and military advisors killed by rebels
1980s–90s: Ongoing guerrilla activity

BELIZE
GUATEMALA
HONDURAS
EL SALVADOR
NICARAGUA

■ **1978–90:** Staging area for anti-Sandinista rebel army (Contras) organized and financed by US

Guantanamo Bay to US

JAMAICA

HAITI
1991: Ongoing unrest; military coup ousts elected government

DOMINICAN REPUBLIC
1961: Assassination of President Trujillo
■ **1965:** US President Johnson intervenes with 22,000 troops

PUERTO RICO to US

Caribbean Sea

1960s: The "model" of the Alliance for Progress
1970: First revolutionaries appear
1991: Right-wing government and opposition leaders sign unbrokered peace treaty
■ **1990s:** Continued reliance on US aid; heavy influence of US ambassador

COSTA RICA

1961: FSLN (Sandinista) rebels appear
1978: Sandinista revolution
■ **1982–83:** US finances guerrilla army fighting leftist Sandinista government
1990: Anti-Sandinista coalition wins election

PANAMA
1959, 1964: Anti-US riots
1978: Panama Canal Treaties
■ **Dec 1989:** US invades Panama to capture General Noriega

Scale varies with perspective

5000 km (3110 miles)

5550 km (3450 miles)

PACIFIC OCEAN

ST. KITTS AND NEVIS

ANTIGUA AND BARBUDA

DOMINICA

ST. VINCENT AND THE GRENADINES · ST. LUCIA

Caracas

GRENADA
Oct 1983: Radical left-wing government overthrown by US intervention

BARBADOS

TRINIDAD AND TOBAGO

COLOMBIA 🌿
1980s/1990s: Flow of drugs to US causes serious crime

VENEZUELA 🌿

ECUADOR

GUYANA

SOUTH AMERICA
REGIONAL HISTORY

THE HISTORICAL LANDSCAPE

THE LAST CONTINENT – APART FROM ANTARCTICA – to be colonized by humans (the first settlers arrived from North America no more than 20,000 years ago), South America remains a realm of harsh extremes of climate, environment, and human society. The cordillera spine of the Andes was the heartland of the first complex societies and civilizations. Early settlers spread through the fertile tracts of the Amazon Basin, but few ventured to the sterile salt pans of the Atacama Desert – one of the driest places on Earth – or Patagonia – one of the least hospitable. European contact in the 16th century brought, as elsewhere in the Americas, the decline of indigenous cultures. Although here widespread intermarriage and the enforced importation of African slaves to work on plantations created an extraordinarily varied genetic, linguistic, and cultural pool. The continent struggled free of European colonialism in the 19th century only to be confronted by the challenge of economic, social, and political modernization, which was met with varying success. This process brought wealth for some, marginalization for many – especially in the continent's burgeoning but scattered centers of population – and a threat to the global ecosystem, as the resources of the Amazonian wilderness were increasingly placed under pressure.

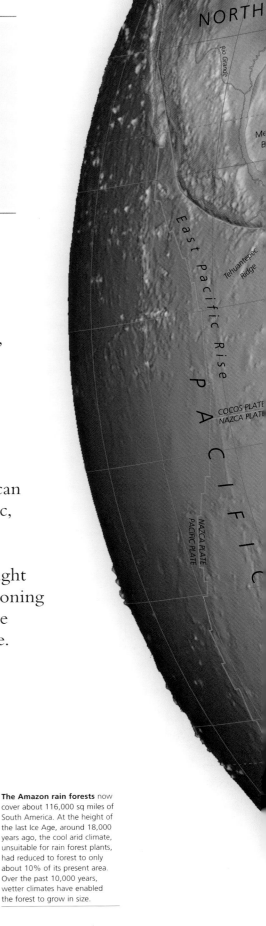

The Andes were one of the sites of the earliest agricultural civilizations in South America, perhaps as many as 10,000 years ago. The mountains and temperate climate provided a wide range of habitats for wild plants. Tubers – such as potatoes and sweet potatoes – grew naturally and were simple to cultivate.

The Amazon rain forests now cover about 116,000 sq miles of South America. At the height of the last Ice Age, around 18,000 years ago, the cool arid climate, unsuitable for rain forest plants, had reduced to forest to only about 10% of its present area. Over the past 10,000 years, wetter climates have enabled the forest to grow in size.

The flat grassland plains of the pampas of southeastern South America were mainly desert during the era covered by the map (*opposite*). Higher levels of moisture have allowed grasslands to develop, but the area remains dry, and has always been a region of low human population.

Vegetation type

- ice cap and glacier
- tundra
- polar and alpine desert
- semi-desert or sparsely vegetated
- grassland
- forest or open woodland
- tropical rain forest
- temperate desert
- tropical desert
- coastline (present day)
- coastline (18,000 years ago)

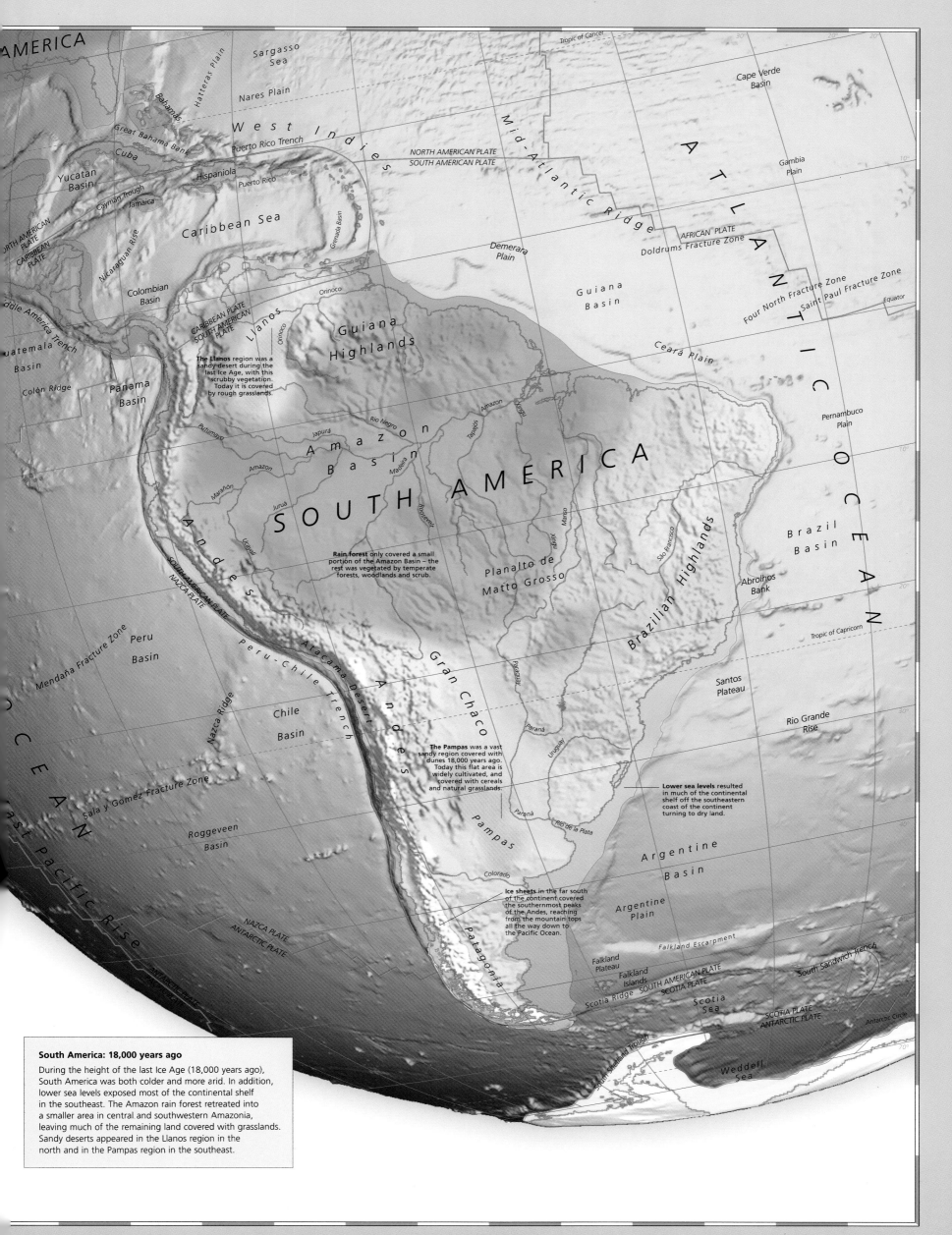

AMERICA

Sargasso
Sea

Nares Plain

Hatteras Plain

West   I n d i e s

Tropic of Cancer

Cape Verde
Basin

Mid-Atlantic Ridge

Bahamas

Great Bahama Bank

Puerto Rico Trench

NORTH AMERICAN PLATE
SOUTH AMERICAN PLATE

A T L A N T I C

Cuba

Yucatan
Basin

Hispaniola

Puerto Rico

Gambia
Plain

Cayman Trough

Jamaica

AFRICAN PLATE

Doldrums Fracture Zone

Caribbean Sea

Demerara
Plain

Grenada Basin

NORTH AMERICAN
PLATE

CARIBBEAN
PLATE

Nicaraguan Rise

Colombian
Basin

Orinoco

Guiana
Basin

Four North Fracture Zone

Saint Paul Fracture Zone

Equator

Middle America Trench

Guatemala
Basin

Colón Ridge

Panama
Basin

CARIBBEAN PLATE
SOUTH AMERICAN
PLATE

Llanos

Orinoco

Guiana
Highlands

Ceará Plain

The Llanos region was a
sandy desert during the
last Ice Age, with this
scrubby vegetation.
Today it is covered
by rough grasslands.

Putumayo

Rio Negro

Amazon

Xingu

Demerara
Plain

Pernambuco
Plain

Japurá

A m a z o n

Amazon

Madeira

Marañón

Amazon

Juruá

Tapajós

SOUTH AMERICA

B a s i n

Roosevelt

São Francisco

Brazilian Highlands

Brazil
Basin

A T L A N T I C   O C E A N

Mendaña Fracture Zone

Peru
Basin

SOUTH AMERICAN PLATE
NAZCA PLATE

A n d e s

Ucayali

Rain forest only covered a small
portion of the Amazon Basin – the
rest was vegetated by temperate
forests, woodlands and scrub.

Planalto de
Matto Grosso

Manço

Abrolhos
Bank

Atacama Desert

Andes

Peru-Chile Trench

Gran Chaco

Paraguay

Tropic of Capricorn

Nazca Ridge

Chile
Basin

Santos
Plateau

Rio Grande
Rise

P A C I F I C   O C E A N

Sala y Gomez Fracture Zone

The Pampas was a vast
sandy region covered with
dunes 18,000 years ago.
Today this flat area is
widely cultivated, and
covered with cereals
and natural grasslands.

Paraná

Uruguay

Paraná

Lower sea levels resulted
in much of the continental
shelf off the southeastern
coast of the continent
turning to dry land.

Roggeveen
Basin

Colorado

Río de la Plata

P a m p a s

Argentine
Basin

East Pacific Rise

NAZCA PLATE
ANTARCTIC PLATE

Ice sheets in the far south
of the continent covered
the southernmost peaks
of the Andes, reaching
from the mountain tops
all the way down to
the Pacific Ocean.

Argentine
Plain

Patagonia

Falkland Escarpment

Falkland
Plateau

Falkland
Islands

SOUTH AMERICAN PLATE
SCOTIA PLATE

South Sandwich Trench

ANTARCTIC PLATE

Scotia Ridge   SOUTH AMERICAN PLATE

Scotia
Sea

SCOTIA PLATE
ANTARCTIC PLATE

Antarctic Circle

South Shetland Trough

Weddell
Sea

South America: 18,000 years ago

During the height of the last Ice Age (18,000 years ago),
South America was both colder and more arid. In addition,
lower sea levels exposed most of the continental shelf
in the southeast. The Amazon rain forest retreated into
a smaller area in central and southwestern Amazonia,
leaving much of the remaining land covered with grasslands.
Sandy deserts appeared in the Llanos region in the
north and in the Pampas region in the southeast.

SOUTH AMERICA
EXPLORATION AND MAPPING

The name America was coined to honor Amerigo Vespucci, an Italian explorer in the service of Portugal.

THOUGH THE INCAS left no maps, their Andean empire's extensive road system was testimony to their topographical skills. It was a long time before any Europeans had a similar understanding of the continent. When Columbus first sighted the South American coast in 1498, he realized he had found a continental landmass, but thought it was part of Asia. This was disproved by the voyages of Vespucci and others along the Atlantic coast, culminating in Ferdinand Magellan's reaching the Pacific in 1520.

In the wake of Pizarro's conquest of Peru and theft of the Incas' gold, many explorers were fired by dreams of instant riches. The net products of most expeditions, however, were the alienation of native tribes and the spread of European killer diseases. From the mid-17th century to the late 18th century, when serious scientific surveys began, exploration was largely the preserve of intrepid missionaries, notably the Jesuits, and slave-raiders from Brazil.

European conquerors and explorers

Throughout the first two decades of the 16th century Portuguese and Spanish explorers of the Atlantic coast sailed into every wide estuary in the hope that it would prove to be a passage to the Indies. Magellan eventually demonstrated that such a route existed, but it proved impracticable for the purpose of trade with the East. As a result, the Atlantic coastal regions of the continent were soon well understood and mapped, further information coming from Portuguese traders who sailed there in search of brazil wood, a tree that produced a valuable red dye and gave its name to the region. In the Andes, Pizarro, Benalcázar, and their fellow *conquistadores* were able to follow the well-maintained roads of the Inca Empire; but in most other parts of the continent, expeditions were forced back by hostile indigenous peoples, trackless swamps and forests, or impassable rapids.

This detail from a map of South America produced by John Rotz in 1542 shows Native Americans carrying logs of brazil wood for trade with Europeans.

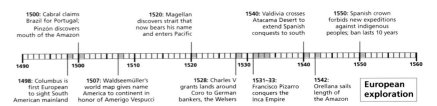

1490 1500 1510 1520 1530 1540 1550 1560

1500: Cabral claims Brazil for Portugal; Pinzón discovers mouth of the Amazon

1520: Magellan discovers strait that now bears his name and enters Pacific

1540: Valdivia crosses Atacama Desert to extend Spanish conquests to south

1550: Spanish crown forbids new expeditions against indigenous peoples; ban lasts 10 years

1498: Columbus is first European to sight South American mainland

1507: Waldseemüller's world map gives name America to continent in honor of Amerigo Vespucci

1528: Charles V grants lands around Coro to German bankers, the Welsers

1531–33: Francisco Pizarro conquers the Inca Empire

1542: Orellana sails length of the Amazon

European exploration

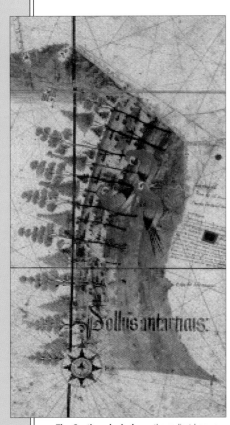

The Cantino planisphere, the earliest known map showing South America, was produced in Lisbon in 1502. It shows part of Brazil and the line agreed by the Treaty of Tordesillas in 1494, dividing the world between Portugal and Spain.

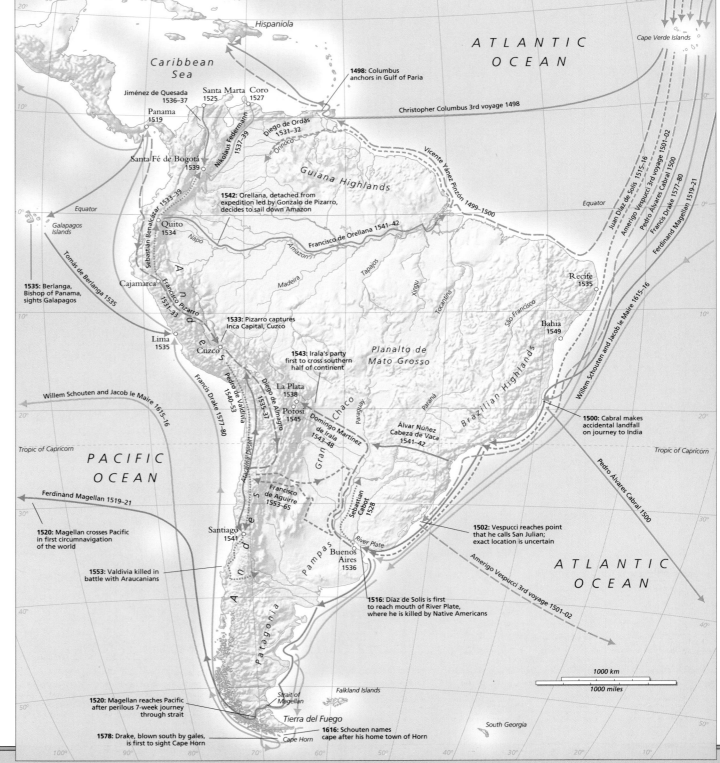

① First European explorers of South America ▶

Principal journeys

→ Spanish expedition
→ Portuguese expedition
→ German expedition
→ English expedition
→ Dutch expedition

Recife 1535 European settlement and date of foundation

(Map labels:)

Hispaniola
Caribbean Sea
ATLANTIC OCEAN
Cape Verde Islands
1498: Columbus anchors in Gulf of Paria
Jiménez de Quesada 1536–37
Santa Marta 1525
Coro 1527
Panama 1519
Nikolaus Federmann 1537–39
Diego de Ordás 1531–32
Orinoco
Christopher Columbus 3rd voyage 1498
Guiana Highlands
Vicente Yáñez Pinzón 1499–1500
Santa Fé de Bogotá 1539
1542: Orellana, detached from expedition led by Gonzalo de Pizarro, decides to sail down Amazon
Juan Díaz de Solís 1515–16
Amerigo Vespucci 3rd voyage 1501–02
Pedro Álvares Cabral 1500
Francis Drake 1577–80
Ferdinand Magellan 1519–21
Equator
Galapagos Islands
Quito 1534
Napo
Francisco de Orellana 1541–42
Amazon
Tapajos
Equator
Sebastián Benalcázar 1533–39
Madeira
Xingu
Recife 1535
Tomás de Berlanga 1535
1535: Berlanga, Bishop of Panama, sights Galapagos
Cajamarca
Francisco Pizarro 1531–33
São Francisco
Bahia 1549
Willem Schouten and Jacob le Maire 1615–16
1533: Pizarro captures Inca Capital, Cuzco
Lima 1535
Cuzco
1543: Irala's party first to cross southern half of continent
Planalto de Mato Grosso
La Plata 1538
Diego de Almagro 1535–37
Potosí 1545
Domingo Martínez de Irala 1543–48
Gran Chaco
Paraguay
Álvar Núñez Cabeza de Vaca 1541–42
Brazilian Highlands
1500: Cabral makes accidental landfall on journey to India
Pedro de Valdivia 1540–53
Francis Drake 1577–80
Atacama Desert
Paraná
Sebastián Cabot 1528
Pedro Álvares Cabral 1500
Tropic of Capricorn
PACIFIC OCEAN
Ferdinand Magellan 1519–21
1520: Magellan crosses Pacific in first circumnavigation of the world
Francisco de Aguirre 1553–65
Santiago 1541
Pampas
River Plate
Buenos Aires 1536
1502: Vespucci reaches point that he calls San Julian; exact location is uncertain
Amerigo Vespucci 3rd voyage 1501–02
ATLANTIC OCEAN
1553: Valdivia killed in battle with Araucanians
1516: Díaz de Solís is first to reach mouth of River Plate, where he is killed by Native Americans
Andes
Patagonia
1000 km
1000 miles
1520: Magellan reaches Pacific after perilous 7-week journey through strait
Strait of Magellan
Falkland Islands
1616: Schouten names cape after his home town of Horn
South Georgia
Tierra del Fuego
1578: Drake, blown south by gales, is first to sight Cape Horn
Cape Horn

Jesuit missions in the interior

Spanish Jesuits created frontier settlements – often of three or four thousand people – known as *reducciones*. These had their own churches, workshops, foundries, even armories, and lands where the Native Americans grew crops and raised herds of cattle. Money was not used, but the Jesuits traded with local Spanish settlers, who envied their success, especially among the Guaraní tribes. For the authorities, however, the *reducciones* formed a defense against Portuguese encroachment on Spanish lands; Native Americans fought many battles with the slave-raiders from São Paulo known as Paulistas or *mamelucos*.

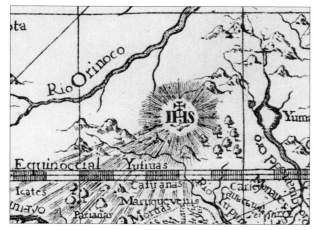

From the 17th century, most serious exploration and mapping of the interior of South America was the work of missionaries. This detail is from a map of the Amazon compiled by Samuel Fritz, a Bohemian-born Jesuit, and published in 1707. Note the Jesuits' IHS monogram above the Equator.

❷ South America 1750 ▶

Areas colonized
- Spanish by 1650
- Spanish by 1750
- Portuguese by 1650
- Portuguese by 1750
- Dutch
- French

Missionary activity
- principal areas of Jesuit *reducciones*
- other major Jesuit missions
- major Franciscan missions
- *CHACO* 1732   *reduccion* with date of foundation
- 1630–32   active between these dates

Exploration of the interior
- → Jesuits
- → Franciscans
- → Paulista raids

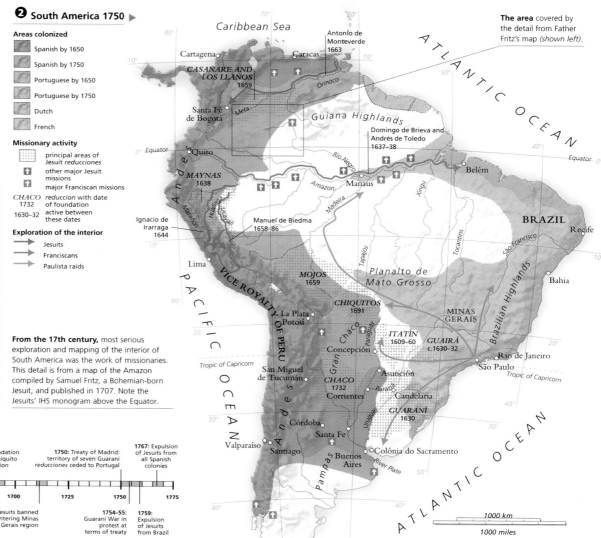

The area covered by the detail from Father Fritz's map *(shown left)*.

The Jesuits in South America

1550: First Jesuits reach Brazil	**1607:** Jesuits found province of Paraguay around Asunción	**1641:** Indians and Jesuits defeat slave-raiders from São Paulo on Uruguay River	**1649:** Viceroy grants *reducciones* virtual independence	**1690:** Foundation of first Chiquito *reduccion*	**1750:** Treaty of Madrid: territory of seven Guaraní *reducciones* ceded to Portugal	**1767:** Expulsion of Jesuits from all Spanish colonies	

1550 1575 1600 1625 1650 1675 1700 1725 1750 1775

1573: Rules drawn up for planning Jesuit towns	**1631:** Father Ruiz de Montoya descends Paraná River with 12,000 Indians to escape slave-raiders	**1640s:** Long-running quarrel between Jesuits and governor of Asunción	**1711:** Jesuits banned from entering Minas Gerais region	**1754–55:** Guaraní War in protest at terms of treaty	**1759:** Expulsion of Jesuits from Brazil

Later scientific exploration

Humboldt endured far greater hardship than this studio portrait suggests, as he traveled with French botanist, Aimé Bonpland, by canoe and on foot through the rainforests of the Orinoco.

For three centuries, the colonial authorities in South America did little to encourage scientific exploration. In the 19th century, however, scientists of all kinds began to explore the peaks of the Andes, the Amazon Basin, and even the wilds of Patagonia. The Prussian Alexander von Humboldt amassed unparalleled data on the geography, geology, meteorology, and natural history of South America. He mapped the course of the Casiquiare, a most unusual river in that it links the Amazon and Orinoco drainage basins. Of later travelers, the most famous was Charles Darwin, whose observations as a young naturalist aboard *HMS Beagle* in 1831–36 would inspire his theory of evolution expounded in *On the Origin of Species*. The French paleontologist Alcide d'Orbigny, who spent eight years studying the continent's microfossils, published the first detailed physical map of South America in 1842.

❸ Scientific explorers

Humboldt's journey
Aug 1799 ——— Mar 1803

Darwin's journey
Feb 1832 ——— Sep 1835

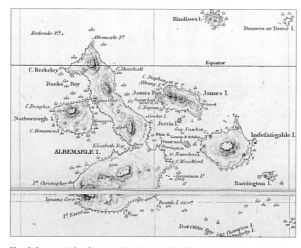

The Galapagos Islands are a volcanic group that lies on the equator. This chart was drawn by the officers of the *Beagle*, who were surveying the coast of South America for the British Navy. Darwin's interest was aroused by the peculiarities of the islands' fauna, such as the giant tortoises, which had evolved slightly different forms on each of the main islands, and the curious marine iguanas.

Large-billed seed-eating finch

Insectivorous warbler finch

The finches Darwin collected on the Galapagos Islands later provided powerful evidence for his theory of natural selection. Several closely related species had diverged from a common ancestor to occupy the various ecological niches on the islands.

Scientific exploration

1802: Humboldt climbs to record height on the mountain of Chimborazo; correctly attributes altitude sickness to lack of oxygen	**1826–34:** D'Orbigny studies continent's fossil-bearing strata	**1835:** Darwin encounters unique island fauna of the Galapagos Islands	**1859:** Naturalist Henry Bates returns to England with 8,000 insects new to science after 11 years in Amazon region		

1725 1750 1775 1800 1825 1850 1875 1900

1735: Expedition to Quito led by French scientist La Condamine to test sphericity of the Earth	**1783:** Spanish crown sponsors botanical expedition to South American colonies	**1832:** Darwin discovers fossils of giant mammals near Bahía Blanca, including *Megatherium*	**1835–44:** Guiana region explored by Sir Robert Schomburgk, who fixes boundary of British colony	**1872:** German Wilhelm Reiss scales Cotopaxi, which Humboldt had pronounced unclimbable

EARLY CULTURES OF SOUTH AMERICA

SOUTH AMERICA WAS COLONIZED by settlers from the north, possibly more than 20,000 years ago. Within 10,000 years, hunter-gatherers had reached its southern tip and, by 5000 BCE, were beginning to exploit local resources, such as corn, manioc, and potatoes. Successful agriculture led to growing populations and increasingly stratified societies. The distinctive temple mounds of Peru appeared by c.2500 BCE, and characteristic elements of South American religious iconography were disseminated all over Peru from the site of Chavín de Huantar, from c.1200 BCE. By 300 CE, Peru was dominated by two major civilizations: the Nazca and the more expansionist Moche.

The Bahía people of coastal Ecuador made clay sculptures such as this figure holding a swaddled child.

The earliest settlements

The first South American settlers were hunter-gatherers, exploiting the big game which flourished following the last Ice Age. Spearheads and darts found at Fell's Cave indicate that this way of life had reached the far south of the continent by 10,000 BCE. In Chile, the site of Monte Verde (c.11,000 BCE) is a village of timber huts draped with animal hides. Finds of medicinal plants from the Andes, potato peelings, digging sticks, wooden bowls, and mortars, reveal an intimate knowledge of plant resources which supplemented a diet of small game and mastodon.

Monte Verde, the earliest known settlement in the southern half of the continent, is thought to have existed by at least 11,000 BCE. Stone tools found there include devices for chopping, scraping, and pounding (left).

Earliest settlements in South America

c.20,000 BCE: Linguistic and DNA evidence indicates first settlers arrived in South America

c.11,000 BCE: Evidence of settlement at Monte Verde in present-day Chile

c.2500 BCE: Masonry building and temple architecture at sites such as Aspero and Kotosh

c.1750 BCE: Massive ceremonial architecture at Sechin Alto

20,000 BCE — 16,000 — 12,000 — 8000 — 4000 BCE

10,000 BCE: Evidence of hunter-gatherers at site of Fell's Cave, Patagonia

6000 BCE: Corn is cultivated in Ecuador

3000 BCE: Cotton cultivated in Central Andes. Large village settlements begin to appear

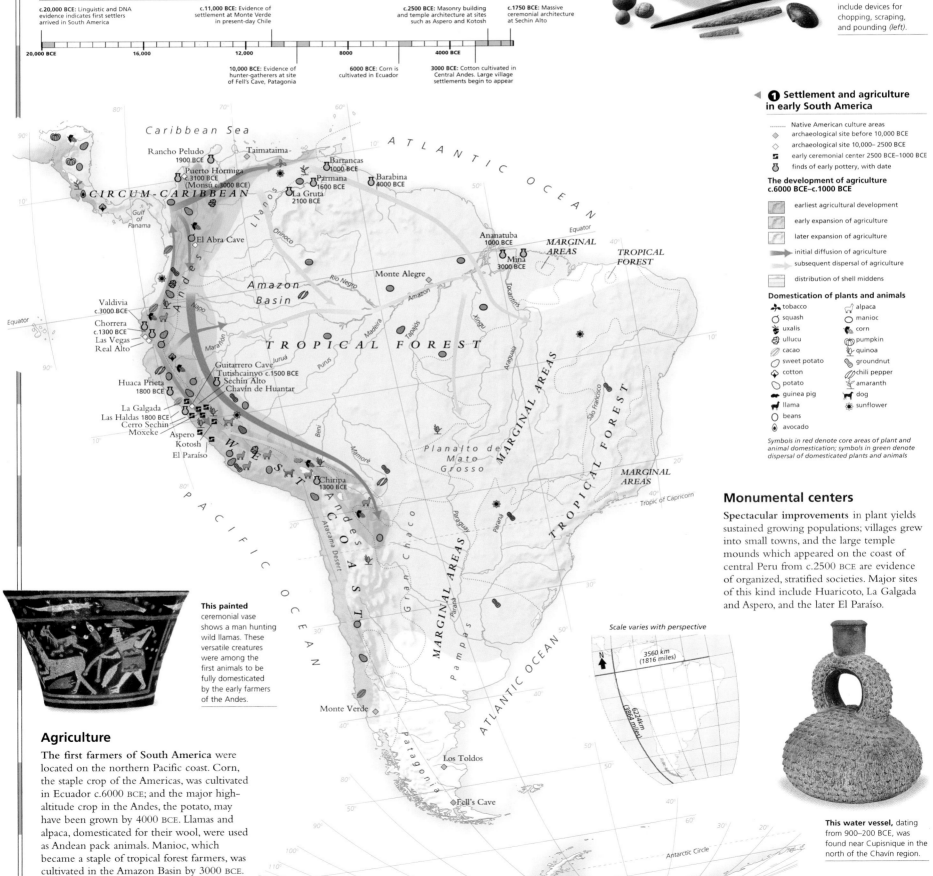

① Settlement and agriculture in early South America

.... Native American culture areas

◇ archaeological site before 10,000 BCE

◇ archaeological site 10,000– 2500 BCE

⌂ early ceremonial center 2500 BCE–1000 BCE

⌂ finds of early pottery, with date

The development of agriculture c.6000 BCE–c.1000 BCE

▨ earliest agricultural development

▨ early expansion of agriculture

▨ later expansion of agriculture

➤ initial diffusion of agriculture

➤ subsequent dispersal of agriculture

▨ distribution of shell middens

Domestication of plants and animals

tobacco	alpaca
squash	manioc
uxalis	corn
ullucu	pumpkin
cacao	quinoa
sweet potato	groundnut
cotton	chili pepper
potato	amaranth
guinea pig	dog
llama	sunflower
beans	
avocado	

Symbols in red denote core areas of plant and animal domestication; symbols in green denote dispersal of domesticated plants and animals

Monumental centers

Spectacular improvements in plant yields sustained growing populations; villages grew into small towns, and the large temple mounds which appeared on the coast of central Peru from c.2500 BCE are evidence of organized, stratified societies. Major sites of this kind include Huaricoto, La Galgada and Aspero, and the later El Paraíso.

Scale varies with perspective

N
3560 km (1816 miles)
6224km (3864 miles)

This painted ceremonial vase shows a man hunting wild llamas. These versatile creatures were among the first animals to be fully domesticated by the early farmers of the Andes.

Agriculture

The first farmers of South America were located on the northern Pacific coast. Corn, the staple crop of the Americas, was cultivated in Ecuador c.6000 BCE; and the major high-altitude crop in the Andes, the potato, may have been grown by 4000 BCE. Llamas and alpaca, domesticated for their wool, were used as Andean pack animals. Manioc, which became a staple of tropical forest farmers, was cultivated in the Amazon Basin by 3000 BCE.

This water vessel, dating from 900–200 BCE, was found near Cupisnique in the north of the Chavin region.

The peoples of the Amazon Basin and the Atlantic coast

Rock shelters and flaked stone tools dating to c.10,000 BCE provide the earliest evidence of settlement east of the Andes. The transition from hunting and gathering to agriculture – principally the cultivation of manioc – probably began c.3000 BCE. Large shell middens at the mouths of the Amazon and Orinoco rivers contain remains of pottery dating to c.5000 BCE – far earlier than the first pottery of Peru. When corn was introduced into the river flood plains in the 1st millennium BCE, populations expanded and hierarchical societies (chiefdoms) developed. Drainage earthworks on the Llanos de Mojos suggest that large populations were cooperating to farm the landscape.

② Early settlement of Amazonia and eastern South America

◇ early archaeological site 12,000–6000 BCE
⬯ early ceramic site 5000–1000 BCE
⬠ early lithic site
⬭ earthworks and hydrological systems
⬬ shell midden

The cultures of Peru 1300 BCE–600 CE

The most influential culture of the middle Andes was that of the Chavín, which flourished at and around the major religious center of Chavín de Huantar between 850 BCE and 200 BCE. The Chavín were distinguished by the sophistication of their architecture and sculptural style and by technological developments including the building of canals. As Chavín influence waned, from c.200 BCE, many distinctive regional cultures developed in the Andean highlands. Coastal Peru, however, was dominated by two major civilizations, Nazca in the south, and Moche in the north. As these cultures developed a strong identity, military rivalries intensified, paving the way for the appearance of other major states from 500 CE including Tiahuanaco and Huari.

Large cemeteries in the Paracas region contained thousands of mummified bodies wrapped in colorful wool. The motif of a large-eyed deity, the Occulate Being, on these textiles shows a strong affinity with the Chavín deity, known as the Smiling God.

④ Coastal Peru c.600 BCE–600 CE

▧ Paracas cultural region c. 600–350 BCE
◇ major Paracas sites
▨ Ecuadorian cultural region c.500 BCE–500 CE
▨ Lima cultural region c.400 BCE–500 CE
▨ Nazca cultural region c.350 BCE–450 CE
▨ earliest Moche sites c.1 CE
▨ Moche cultural region c.1–600 CE
▨ Recuay cultural region c.500 CE
▽ irrigated river valley

Moche

Moche culture was centered on the capital of Moche, dominated by the famous Temple of the Sun, a massive structure of solid adobe 40 m high. The Moche state was powerful, well-organized, and expanded by military conquest. Mass labor was organized to participate in major public works and civil engineering projects and the construction of "royal" tombs.

The stirrup-spout on this drinking vessel is a typical feature of Moche pottery, as is the maryelously realistic and sensitive modeling of the facial features.

Nazca

Based on the south coast of Peru, Nazca culture is famous for its superb and graphic pottery, textiles, and above all, the enigmatic "Nazca lines," straight, geometric, or figurative designs etched onto the surface of the desert, possibly as offerings to the gods.

This aerial view shows Nazca lines etched into the shape of a hummingbird. Some of these images can be over 100 m across.

③ Chavín culture

▧ Chavín heartland
◇ early Chavín sites, 2000–850 BCE
◇ Chavín sites, 850–200 BCE
→ trade route

The Chavín

Chavín de Huantar (c.1200–200 BCE), with its large stone sculptures and grand temples, became a cult center. Chavín motifs, in architecture, textiles, pottery, and goldwork, are found throughout Peru.

Cultures of Peru 1300 BCE–1 CE

850 BCE: Florescence of Chavín de Huantar; Chavín style widely disseminated

500 BCE: Paracas culture in southern Peru produces textiles woven with Chavín-style images

c.1 CE: Emergence of Moche culture of coastal Peru

1400 BCE · 1200 · 1000 · 800 · 600 · 400 · 200 · 1 CE

1300 BCE: Cerro Sechin is earliest central Andean site with Chavín-style iconography

200 BCE: Regional cultures begin to appear in central Andes

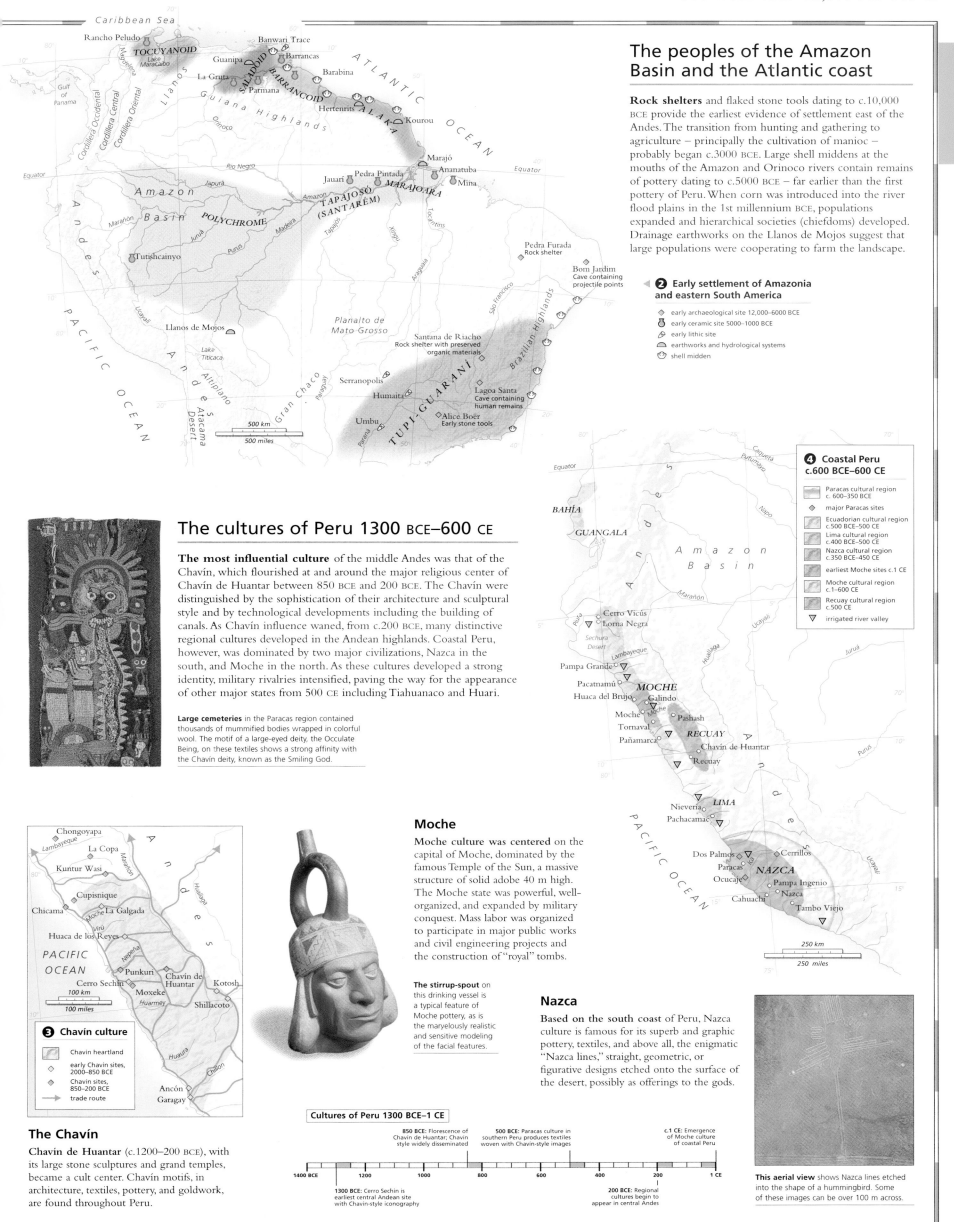

THE EMPIRES OF SOUTH AMERICA

THE EMPIRES WHICH DOMINATED the Andes between 500 and 1450, Tiahuanaco, Huari, and Chimú, were important precursors of the Inca, laying down the religious and social foundations, and the authoritarian government which were to serve the Inca so well. The Inca Empire (1438–1532) was the greatest state in South America exercising stringent control over its subjects through taxation, forced labor, compulsory migration, and military service. With its unyielding hierarchy and ill-defined line of succession, the empire was fatally weakened by a leadership crisis at the very point when Pizarro arrived in 1532, and was unable to prevent its own destruction at the hands of the Spanish *conquistadores*.

This gold knife in the form of a Chimú (or Sicán) sun god dates from c.1100 CE. The body is decorated with turquoises.

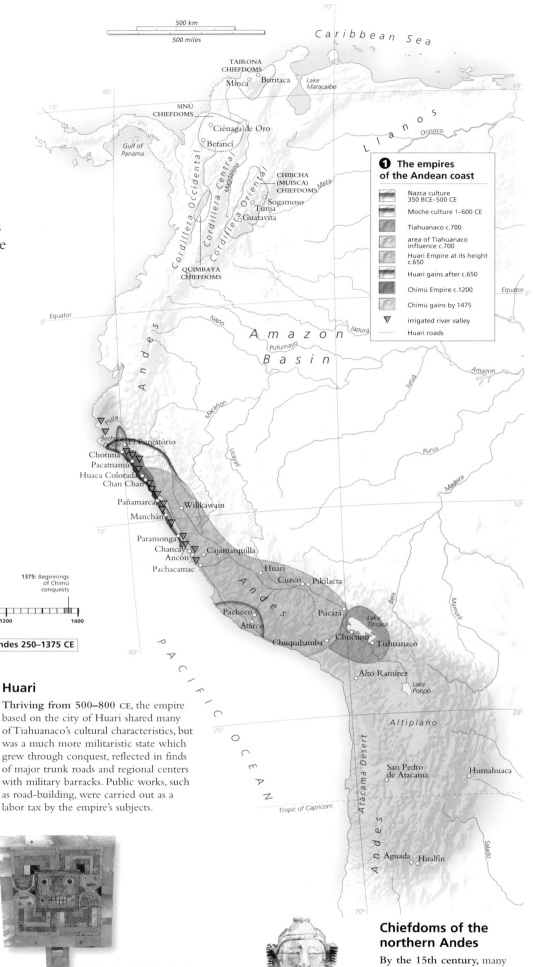

❶ The empires of the Andean coast

- Nazca culture 350 BCE–500 CE
- Moche culture 1–600 CE
- Tiahuanaco c.700
- area of Tiahuanaco influence c.700
- Huari Empire at its height c.650
- Huari gains after c.650
- Chimú Empire c.1200
- Chimú gains by 1475
- ▽ irrigated river valley
- Huari roads

Empires of the Andean coast 250–1375

The empires of Tiahuanaco and Huari, which together dominated the Andes from 500 CE, shared a similar art style, and probably the same religion. The city of Tiahuanaco, on the windswept Altiplano of modern Bolivia, was a major pilgrimage center, and its cultural influence diffused throughout the south-central Andes from 500–1000. The contemporary Huari Empire, which controlled the coast around present-day Lima, was, by contrast, centralized and militaristic, expanding its influence through conquest. The Inca owed most to their direct predecessor, the Chimú Empire of the northern Andes, with its efficient administration, colonial expansionism, and stress on an effective communication system.

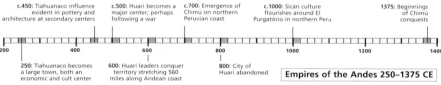

c.450: Tiahuanaco influence evident in pottery and architecture at secondary centers

c.500: Huari becomes a major center; perhaps following a war

c.700: Emergence of Chimú on northern Peruvian coast

c.1000: Sicán culture flourishes around El Purgatório in northern Peru

1375: Beginnings of Chimú conquests

250: Tiahuanaco becomes a large town, both an economic and cult center

600: Huari leaders conquer territory stretching 560 miles along Andean coast

800: City of Huari abandoned

Empires of the Andes 250–1375 CE

Tiahuanaco

By 500 CE the city of Tiahuanaco on Lake Titicaca's southeastern shore had become a major population center, housing up to 40,000 people, and a focus of pilgrimage for the entire Andean region. It was dominated by palaces and a cult center, consisting of temples, monumental gateways, and large monolithic sculptures. The city's iconography, with its symbolism of water, sun, and weather, spread throughout the south-central Andes.

Carved from a single slab of andesite, the Gateway of the Sun at Tiahuanaco is a representation of the cosmos, with the creator god at the center of the frieze.

Huari

Thriving from 500–800 CE, the empire based on the city of Huari shared many of Tiahuanaco's cultural characteristics, but was a much more militaristic state which grew through conquest, reflected in finds of major trunk roads and regional centers with military barracks. Public works, such as road-building, were carried out as a labor tax by the empire's subjects.

The back of this Huari hand mirror contains a central face, with small heads at each side. The reflecting surface is of pyrite and the mosaic back of a variety of stones of contrasting texture and color.

Chimú

The Chimú Empire which ruled over the coast of northern Peru (c.700–1476) was centered on the capital of Chan Chan. A series of great royal compounds within the city served as both the palaces and tombs of ten successive monarchs. The empire stretched for 1,600 miles along the Peruvian coast, administered by a series of regional centers.

The Chimú people were skilled metalworkers, producing a wide variety of ceremonial objects such as this gold dove with turquoise eyes.

Chiefdoms of the northern Andes

By the 15th century, many peoples of the northern Andes were organized into chiefdoms, based on large villages, supported by wetland farming, and capable of mobilizing sizable armies. Their gold-working skills gave rise to myths of "El Dorado" (*see p.149*). Gold and copper resources were exploited by efficient mining operations — an indication of their impressive organizational ability.

This small figure reflects the intricate casting and polishing typical of the goldsmiths of the Quimbaya chiefdoms. They also produced masks, spear tips, pendants, and helmets

② South America c.1500

- ···· border of Inca Empire
- high civilization
- chiefdoms
- tropical forest farming villages
- other farming villages
- nomadic hunter-gatherers
- *Ona* indigenous people

The peoples of South America c.1500

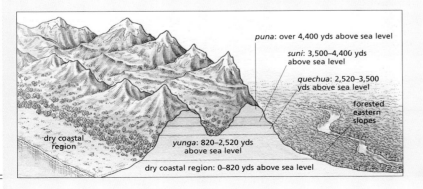

A great diversity of indigenous cultures existed in South America by the start of the 16th century, ranging from the high civilization of the Incas to the hunter-gatherers of Patagonia. Large populations lived along the Amazon, the upper river dominated by the Omagua people, its lower reaches controlled by the warlike Tapajosó. Many chiefdoms held sway over huge areas, some extracting forced labor from subject peoples, who were often engaged on extensive building projects. Ancestor cults, based on the mummified bodies of chiefs, were widespread.

The golden raft, bearing a godlike figure surrounded by attendants, is a detailed example of a *tunjo* or offering piece, produced by the Muisca (Chibcha) people of the northeastern Andes.

This stylized carving in the shape of a tree is etched on a hillside in the coastal desert above present-day Paracas.

THE VERTICAL ECONOMY OF THE ANDES

The rugged terrain of the Andes provided a series of contiguous, but contrasting environments, fully exploited by the Incas and their predecessors. High, treeless, grassy plains (the *puna*) were used for grazing llamas. Below this, at heights up to 4,400 yds above sea level, lay the *suni*, where potatoes and tubers could be cultivated. Corn, squash, fruits, and cocoa grew in lower, frost-free valleys (the *quechua*), while the lower slopes of the mountains (the *yunga*) were planted with peppers, coca plants, and other fruits. Sources of shellfish and fish from the ocean were periodically disrupted by El Niño, an irregular climatic disturbance which warmed the ocean, leading to torrential rains and disastrous flooding.

puna: over 4,400 yds above sea level

suni: 3,500–4,400 yds above sea level

quechua: 2,520–3,500 yds above sea level

forested eastern slopes

yunga: 820–2,520 yds above sea level

dry coastal region

dry coastal region: 0–820 yds above sea level

The Inca Empire

The Inca emerged, in less than a century, as the preeminent state in South America; from 1470 they ruled vast territories from their capital, Cuzco. Their hierarchical society, ruled by the Sapa Inca (believed to be descended from the sun), depended on the mass organization of labor. Adult men were liable for forced labor, and worked in the fields, on public works (terracing, building, mining), and served in the army. An extensive road network, interspersed with way stations and regional centers, bound the empire together. Yet this complex bureaucracy had no form of writing, although arithmetic records were used for administration, tribute, and taxation.

The Inca *quipumayoc*, or grand treasurer, is shown holding a *quipu*, a device made of knotted strings, used to record administrative matters and sacred histories. Information was encoded in the colors of the strings and the style of the knots.

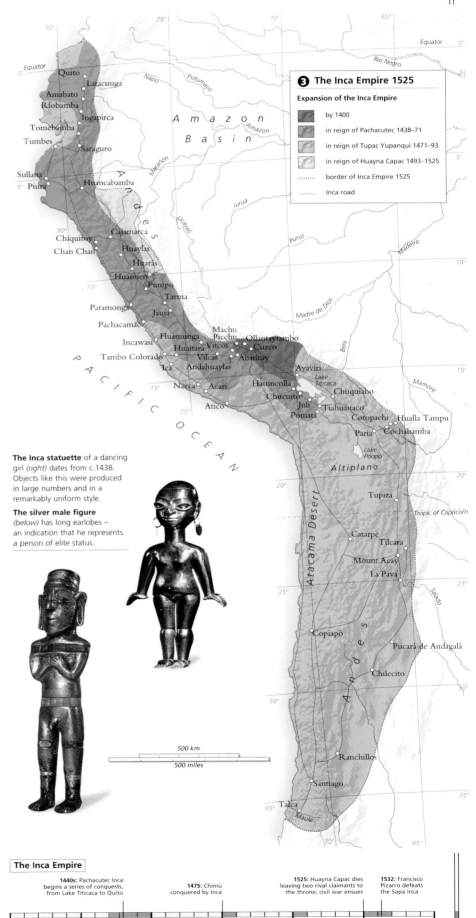

③ The Inca Empire 1525

Expansion of the Inca Empire

- by 1400
- in reign of Pachacutec 1438–71
- in reign of Tupac Yupanqui 1471–93
- in reign of Huayna Capac 1493–1525
- ···· border of Inca Empire 1525
- Inca road

The Inca statuette of a dancing girl *(right)* dates from c.1438. Objects like this were produced in large numbers and in a remarkably uniform style.

The silver male figure *(below)* has long earlobes – an indication that he represents a person of elite status.

The Inca Empire

1440s: Pachacutec Inca begins a series of conquests, from Lake Titicaca to Quito	**1475:** Chimú conquered by Inca
	1525: Huayna Capac dies leaving two rival claimants to the throne; civil war ensues
	1532: Francisco Pizarro defeats the Sapa Inca

1400 — 1425 — 1450 — 1475 — 1500 — 1525 — 1550

1438: Incas rise to power; attack Lake Titicaca basin, and establish upland empire

1500: Protracted military campaigns at northern and southern extremes of empire lead to establishment of second capital at Tomebamba

COLONIAL SOUTH AMERICA

Christianity in South America blended with local traditions to produce colorful spectacles such as this 18th-century Corpus Christi procession in Cuzco.

IN THEIR CONQUEST of South America, the Spanish were so driven by the quest for gold and silver that it took the *conquistadores* less than ten years to take over the rich, organized states of the Andes. The Portuguese were slower to settle Brazil, first trading with the Indians, then turning to sugar production. Wherever Europeans settled, the native population declined rapidly, mainly through lack of resistance to alien diseases. There were also periodic wars against the colonists. Large cattle stations that destroyed native arable smallholdings were a further factor in their decline. Emigration to South America from both Spain and Portugal was light; settlers mixed with the natives, creating a mixed-race *mestizo* population. To make up for shortages in labor, they imported African slaves. Catholic missionaries, notably the Jesuits, were active throughout the colonial era, often defending the rights of the Indians against the settlers. Both colonial empires collapsed in the 19th century, but the religion and languages of the conquerors survived.

The silver mine at Potosí was the prime source of revenue to the Spanish crown between 1550 and 1650. At first the native population supplied all the labor and technology. The silver was extracted using mercury, mined at Huancavelica.

The conquest of Peru

In 1531 Francisco Pizarro sailed from Panama to conquer Peru. By the time the expedition had penetrated inland to Cajamarca, where the reigning Inca, Atahualpa, and 40,000 men were camped, Pizarro had only 180 men. Yet he succeeded in capturing Atahualpa, whom he held for ransom. When this was paid, Atahualpa was executed, and the *conquistadores* moved on to capture the Inca capital, Cuzco. The Incas were in awe of the Spanish horses and guns, but this astonishing feat of conquest would have been impossible had the Inca Empire not been weakened by a smallpox epidemic and civil war.

Atahualpa was given a summary trial by Pizarro and then garrotted, or – as this contemporary Inca illustration shows – beheaded.

① Pizarro's conquest of the Inca Empire

→ 1524 expedition
→ 1526 expedition
→ 1531–33 expedition
···· extent of Inca Empire
1526 date of foundation

② Spanish South America

■ Spanish territory before 1650
■ Spanish territory after 1650
□ region disputed by Spain and Portugal up to 1777
□ Jesuit mission states, with dates
···· border with Brazil by Treaty of Madrid 1750
--- border with Brazil where modified by Treaty of San Ildefonso 1777
○ Portuguese settlement
▣ gold   ⚘ drugs
▣ silver   ⬡ hides
▣ copper   ◈ cocoa
▣ mercury

Inca ornaments, such as this gold llama, are very rare because most were melted down and shipped to Spain.

Spanish South America

Spain ruled her American colonies through two great viceroyalties, New Spain (centered on Mexico) and Peru. The viceroys' principal duty was to guarantee a steady flow of bullion for the Spanish Crown. When booty from the native empires was exhausted, the colonists turned to the region's mineral resources, using forced native labor *(mita)* to extract precious metals, in particular silver. Smaller administrative units called *audiencias* were presided over by a judge who enacted the complex laws devised in Spain for the running of the colonies. Attempts to expand the empire were thwarted in the south by the fierce Araucanian people, elsewhere by the inhospitable nature of the terrain.

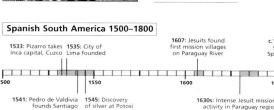

The founder of Spain's South American empire, Pizarro was an aging soldier of fortune. Some of his own lieutenants rebelled against him and he was killed in a riot in Lima in 1541.

Spanish South America 1500–1800

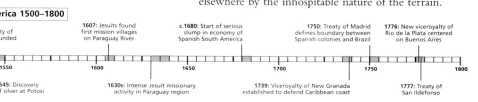

1533: Pizarro takes Inca capital, Cuzco
1535: City of Lima founded
1607: Jesuits found first mission villages on Paraguay River
c.1680: Start of serious slump in economy of Spanish South America
1750: Treaty of Madrid defines boundary between Spanish colonies and Brazil
1776: New viceroyalty of Río de la Plata centered on Buenos Aires

1541: Pedro de Valdivia founds Santiago
1545: Discovery of silver at Potosí
1630s: Intense Jesuit missionary activity in Paraguay region
1739: Viceroyalty of New Granada established to defend Caribbean coast
1777: Treaty of San Ildefonso

Portuguese South America

Brazil was formally claimed by Portugal in 1500. There were no conspicuous mineral resources, so colonization depended on agriculture. In the 1530s, in an attempt to encourage settlement, João III made grants of land to 12 hereditary "captains," each captaincy consisting of 50 leagues of coastline. Some failed completely and little of the coastal plain was settled before 1549 when a royal governor-general was sent to Bahia. The captaincy system continued, but the colonists' fortunes changed with the success of sugar. The native population living near the coast had been almost wiped out by disease and wars. The few that remained had no wish to labor on sugar plantations, so slaves were imported from Africa. In the 18th century, a gold boom opened up the Minas Gerais region, but apart from slave-raiders hunting for natives and prospectors searching for gold and diamonds, penetration of the interior was limited.

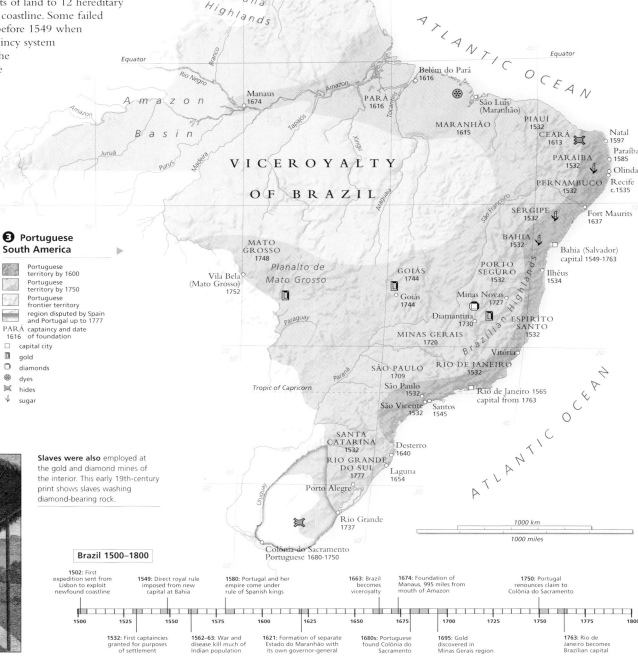

❸ Portuguese South America ▶

- Portuguese territory by 1600
- Portuguese territory by 1750
- Portuguese frontier territory
- region disputed by Spain and Portugal up to 1777

PARÁ 1616 captaincy and date of foundation
- □ capital city
- gold
- diamonds
- dyes
- hides
- sugar

Between 1550 and 1800, some 2.5 million African slaves were taken to Brazil, more than 70% of them to work for the sugar plantations and mills which were the backbone of the economy.

Slaves were also employed at the gold and diamond mines of the interior. This early 19th-century print shows slaves washing diamond-bearing rock.

VICEROYALTY OF BRAZIL

Brazil 1500–1800

1502: First expedition sent from Lisbon to exploit newfound coastline
1549: Direct royal rule imposed from new capital at Bahia
1580: Portugal and her empire come under rule of Spanish kings
1663: Brazil becomes viceroyalty
1674: Foundation of Manaus, 995 miles from mouth of Amazon
1750: Portugal renounces claim to Colónia do Sacramento

1500 | 1525 | 1550 | 1575 | 1600 | 1625 | 1650 | 1675 | 1700 | 1725 | 1750 | 1775 | 1800

1532: First captaincies granted for purposes of settlement
1562–63: War and disease kill much of Indian population
1621: Formation of separate Estado do Maranhão with its own governor-general
1680s: Portuguese found Colónia do Sacramento
1695: Gold discovered in Minas Gerais region
1763: Rio de Janeiro becomes Brazilian capital

THE SEARCH FOR EL DORADO

From the 1530s until well into the 17th century, fantastic tales of the kingdom of El Dorado (the gilded man) inspired many foolhardy expeditions through the Andes, the Orinoco basin, and the Guiana Highlands. The English sea captain Walter Raleigh twice sailed to the Orinoco, but both his voyages ended in failure, and on the second in 1617 his teenaged son was killed by the Spanish.

The legend of El Dorado took many forms. The most persistent was of a chieftain so rich that he was regularly painted in gold by his subjects.

Other colonial powers

For 150 years Portugal's hold on Brazil was far from secure. The French, who traded along the coast with the natives, made several attempts to found colonies. In the first half of the 17th century, the defense of Portuguese colonies was neglected by the ruling Spanish kings. This allowed the Dutch to capture a long stretch of the northeast coast. They were finally expelled in 1654 and had to be content, like the English and French, with a small colony in the Guianas.

Dutch Brazil thrived under the governorship of Prince Maurits of Nassau (1636–44), when many new towns were built. The artist Franz Post painted idealized views of the colony during this period. This detail shows the slave quarters on a plantation.

▼ ❹ Brazil and the Guianas c.1640

- Portuguese possession and settlement
- Dutch possession and settlement
- French possession and settlement
- temporary French colonies in Brazil

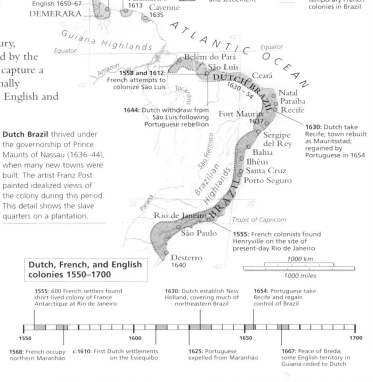

1558 and 1612: French attempts to colonize São Luís
1644: Dutch withdraw from São Luís following Portuguese rebellion
1630: Dutch take Recife; town rebuilt as Mauritsstad; regained by Portuguese in 1654
1555: French colonists found Henryville on the site of present-day Rio de Janeiro

Dutch, French, and English colonies 1550–1700

1555: 600 French settlers found short-lived colony of France Antarctique at Rio de Janeiro
1630: Dutch establish New Holland, covering much of northeastern Brazil
1654: Portuguese take Recife and regain control of Brazil

1550 | 1600 | 1650 | 1700

1568: French occupy northern Maranhão
c.1610: First Dutch settlements on the Essequibo
1625: Portuguese expelled from Maranhão
1667: Peace of Breda; some English territory in Guiana ceded to Dutch

THE AGE OF INDEPENDENCE

Pedro I became the emperor of an independent Brazil in 1822, when his father and the royal family returned from exile to Portugal.

AFTER THREE CENTURIES of rule by Spain, the colonial families of South America began to demand more autonomy. When Spain was invaded by Napoleon in 1808, it was cut off from its empire, and in 1810 several colonies established independent ruling juntas. The struggle for independence lasted until 1826, when the last Spanish troops departed. The heroic deeds of the Liberators, Simón Bolívar, José de San Martín, and others passed into legend, but the task of forming new republics proved harder. Liberals and Conservatives fought numerous civil wars and military dictators ran countries as their personal fiefs. The economies of the new states were dominated by foreign trading powers, especially Britain. Brazil gained its independence from Portugal more peacefully, a result of the royal family's flight to Brazil in 1807. The two states separated when they returned to Portugal in 1822.

The liberation of Spanish South America

The wars of liberation were fought between patriots and those who remained loyal to the Spanish crown. The longest struggle was that of Simón Bolívar in his native Venezuela and neighboring Colombia. The first states to achieve independence were Paraguay and Argentina, from where in 1817 José de San Martín led an army over the Andes to help liberate Chile. Bolívar's campaigns regained momentum in 1818–22 in a triumphal progress from Venezuela to Ecuador. The armies of liberation from north and south then joined forces for the liberation of Peru and, in honor of Bolívar, Upper Peru was renamed Bolivia.

The llanero lancers from the plains of Venezuela were praised by Bolívar as his "cossacks." They continually harrassed the army sent from Spain in 1815 to oppose the liberation movement.

Bolívar enters Caracas in triumph in 1829 after putting down the uprising of his former lieutenant Antonio Páez. But it was Páez who became dictator of the new republic of Venezuela on Bolívar's death in 1830.

The break-up of Great Colombia

The personality of Simón Bolívar and the need for military unity in confronting the Spanish created the republic of Great Colombia. It proved an unwieldy state with a very remote capital at Bogotá. Commercial links and communications between the three former Spanish colonies of New Granada, Venezuela, and Quito (Ecuador) were very limited, and in 1830, the year of Bolívar's death, they became separate states under the leadership of generals Santander, Páez, and Flores respectively.

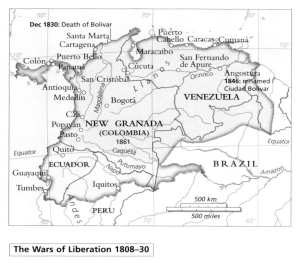

❷ **The dissolution of Great Colombia**

- Republic of Great Colombia 1819–30
- New Granada 1830
- Ecuador 1830
- Venezuela 1830
- present-day international borders

❶ **The independence of South America 1810–30**

Spanish territory in South America 1810

VICEROYALTY OF NEW GRANADA — Spanish administrative region

1821 — date of independence of new state

Principal campaigns of liberators

- Bolívar 1812–14
- O'Higgins 1817–18
- San Martín 1817–18
- Bolívar 1819
- San Martín 1820–22
- Sucre 1821–22
- Bolívar 1822
- Bolívar 1823–26
- Sucre 1824
- ✕ victory for armies of liberation
- ✕ defeat for armies of liberation

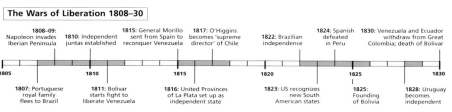

The Wars of Liberation 1808–30

1808–09: Napoleon invades Iberian Peninsula
1810: Independent juntas established
1815: General Morillo sent from Spain to reconquer Venezuela
1817: O'Higgins becomes 'supreme director' of Chile
1822: Brazilian independence
1824: Spanish defeated in Peru
1830: Venezuela and Ecuador withdraw from Great Colombia; death of Bolívar

1807: Portuguese royal family flees to Brazil
1811: Bolívar starts fight to liberate Venezuela
1816: United Provinces of La Plata set up as independent state
1823: US recognizes new South American states
1825: Founding of Bolivia
1828: Uruguay becomes independent

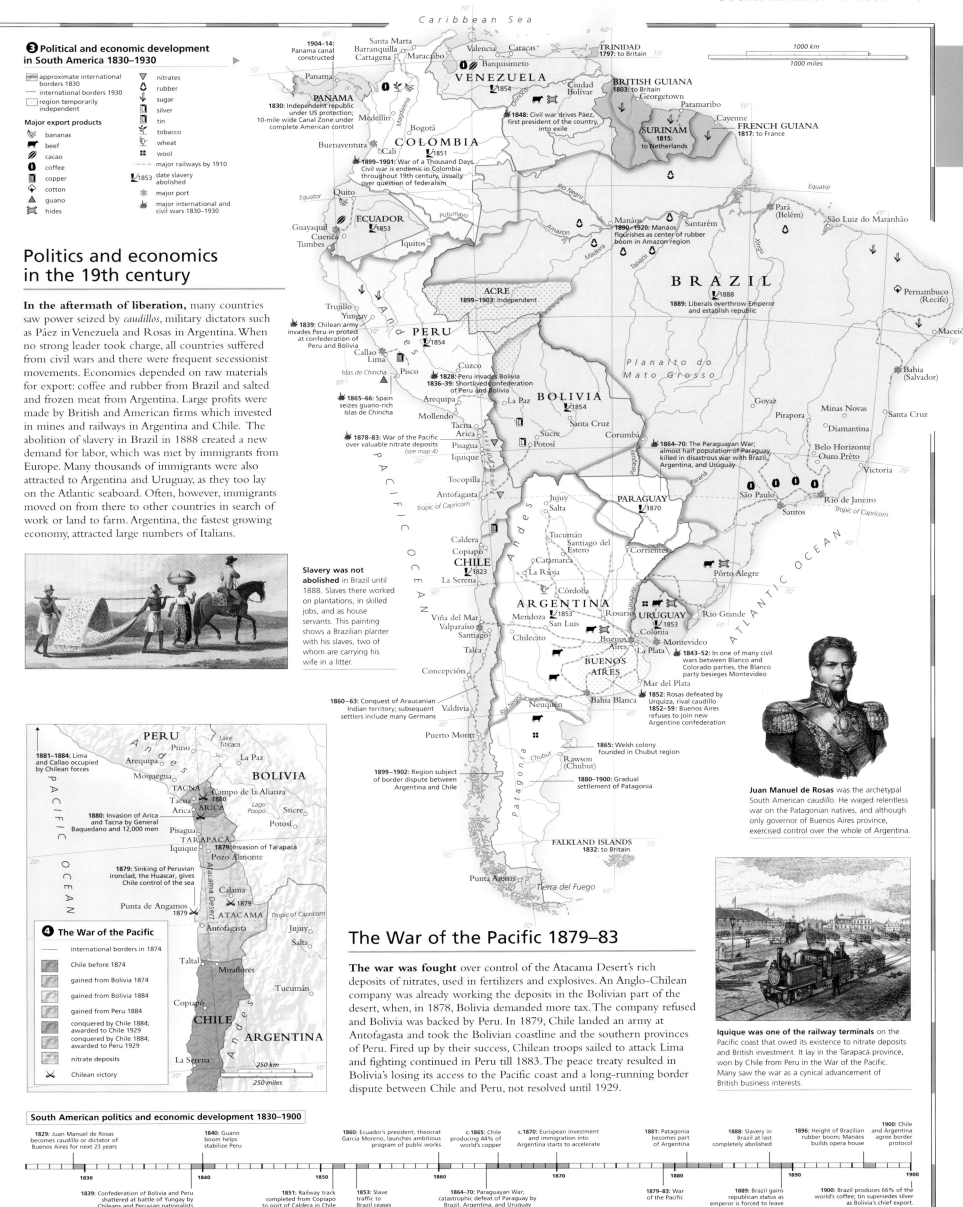

❸ Political and economic development in South America 1830–1930 ▶

- approximate international borders 1830
- international borders 1930
- region temporarily independent

Major export products
- 🍌 bananas
- 🐄 beef
- cacao
- ☕ coffee
- copper
- cotton
- guano
- hides
- ▽ nitrates
- ▽ rubber
- sugar
- silver
- tin
- tobacco
- wheat
- wool
- --- major railways by 1910
- ⚡1853 date slavery abolished
- ✳ major port
- ⚔ major international and civil wars 1830–1930

Politics and economics in the 19th century

In the aftermath of liberation, many countries saw power seized by *caudillos*, military dictators such as Páez in Venezuela and Rosas in Argentina. When no strong leader took charge, all countries suffered from civil wars and there were frequent secessionist movements. Economies depended on raw materials for export: coffee and rubber from Brazil and salted and frozen meat from Argentina. Large profits were made by British and American firms which invested in mines and railways in Argentina and Chile. The abolition of slavery in Brazil in 1888 created a new demand for labor, which was met by immigrants from Europe. Many thousands of immigrants were also attracted to Argentina and Uruguay, as they too lay on the Atlantic seaboard. Often, however, immigrants moved on from there to other countries in search of work or land to farm. Argentina, the fastest growing economy, attracted large numbers of Italians.

Slavery was not abolished in Brazil until 1888. Slaves there worked on plantations, in skilled jobs, and as house servants. This painting shows a Brazilian planter with his slaves, two of whom are carrying his wife in a litter.

Juan Manuel de Rosas was the archetypal South American *caudillo*. He waged relentless war on the Patagonian natives, and although only governor of Buenos Aires province, exercised control over the whole of Argentina.

Map labels

Caribbean Sea

Santa Marta, Barranquilla, Cartagena, Maracaibo, Valencia, Caracas, Barquisimeto, Ciudad Bolívar
TRINIDAD 1797: to Britain
PANAMA 1830: Independent republic under US protection; 10-mile wide Canal Zone under complete American control
1904–14: Panama canal constructed
VENEZUELA 1854
1848: Civil war drives Páez, first president of the country, into exile
BRITISH GUIANA 1803: to Britain, Georgetown
SURINAM 1815: to Netherlands, Paramaribo
FRENCH GUIANA 1817: to France, Cayenne
Medellín, Bogotá, Cali, Buenaventura
COLOMBIA 1851
1899–1901: War of a Thousand Days. Civil war is endemic in Colombia throughout 19th century, usually over question of federalism
Quito, Guayaquil, Cuenca, Tumbes
ECUADOR 1853
Iquitos
Pará (Belém), Santarém, São Luiz do Maranhão
Manáos 1890–1920: Manáos flourishes as center of rubber boom in Amazon region
ACRE 1899–1903: Independent
BRAZIL 1888
1889: Liberals overthrow Emperor and establish republic
Pernambuco (Recife)
Maceió
Bahia (Salvador)
Trujillo, Yungay
1839: Chilean army invades Peru in protest at confederation of Peru and Bolivia
PERU 1854
1828: Peru invades Bolivia
1836–39: Shortlived confederation of Peru and Bolivia
1865–66: Spain seizes guano-rich Islas de Chincha
Cuzco, Arequipa, Mollendo, Tacna, Arica, Pisagua, Iquique, Tocopilla, Antofagasta
1878–83: War of the Pacific over valuable nitrate deposits (see map 4)
La Paz, Sucre, Santa Cruz, Corumbá, Potosí
BOLIVIA 1854
Planalto do Mato Grosso
Goyaz, Piropora, Minas Novas, Santa Cruz, Diamantina, Belo Horizonte, Ouro Prêto, Victoria
1864–70: The Paraguayan War; almost half population of Paraguay killed in disastrous war with Brazil, Argentina, and Uruguay
São Paulo, Santos, Rio de Janeiro
PARAGUAY 1870
Jujuy, Salta, Tucumán, Santiago del Estero, Corrientes, Catamarca, La Rioja, Córdoba
CHILE 1823
Caldera, Copiapó, La Serena, Viña del Mar, Valparaíso, Santiago, Talca, Concepción, Chilecito, Mendoza, San Luis, Rosario
ARGENTINA 1853
URUGUAY 1853
Colonia, Montevideo, La Plata, Rio Grande, Pôrto Alegre
BUENOS AIRES
1843–52: In one of many civil wars between Blanco and Colorado parties, the Blanco party besieges Montevideo
1852: Rosas defeated by Urquiza, rival caudillo
1852–59: Buenos Aires refuses to join new Argentine confederation
Mar del Plata, Bahía Blanca
1860–63: Conquest of Araucanian Indian territory; subsequent settlers include many Germans
Valdivia, Neuquén, Puerto Montt
1865: Welsh colony founded in Chubut region
1899–1902: Region subject of border dispute between Argentina and Chile
1880–1900: Gradual settlement of Patagonia
Rawson (Chubut)
Patagonia
FALKLAND ISLANDS 1832: to Britain
Punta Arenas, Tierra del Fuego

The War of the Pacific 1879–83

The war was fought over control of the Atacama Desert's rich deposits of nitrates, used in fertilizers and explosives. An Anglo-Chilean company was already working the deposits in the Bolivian part of the desert, when, in 1878, Bolivia demanded more tax. The company refused and Bolivia was backed by Peru. In 1879, Chile landed an army at Antofagasta and took the Bolivian coastline and the southern provinces of Peru. Fired up by their success, Chilean troops sailed to attack Lima and fighting continued in Peru till 1883. The peace treaty resulted in Bolivia's losing its access to the Pacific coast and a long-running border dispute between Chile and Peru, not resolved until 1929.

Iquique was one of the railway terminals on the Pacific coast that owed its existence to nitrate deposits and British investment. It lay in the Tarapacá province, won by Chile from Peru in the War of the Pacific. Many saw the war as a cynical advancement of British business interests.

War of the Pacific map (inset 4)

1881–1884: Lima and Callao occupied by Chilean forces
Puno, Arequipa, Moquegua
TACNA Tacna, Arica
ARICA 1880: Campo de la Alianza
1880: Invasion of Arica and Tacna by General Baquedano and 12,000 men
Lake Titicaca, La Paz, Lago Poopó, Sucre, Potosí
BOLIVIA
Pisagua, Iquique
TARAPACÁ 1879: Invasion of Tarapacá
Pozo Almonte
1879: Sinking of Peruvian ironclad, the Huascar, gives Chile control of the sea
Calama
Punta de Angamos 1879
ATACAMA 1879
Atacama Desert
Antofagasta, Taltal, Miraflores, Jujuy, Salta, Tucumán, Copiapó, La Serena
CHILE
ARGENTINA

❹ The War of the Pacific
- international borders in 1874
- Chile before 1874
- gained from Bolivia 1874
- gained from Bolivia 1884
- gained from Peru 1884
- conquered by Chile 1884; awarded to Chile 1929
- conquered by Chile 1884; awarded to Peru 1929
- nitrate deposits
- ⚔ Chilean victory

Timeline: South American politics and economic development 1830–1900

1829: Juan Manuel de Rosas becomes *caudillo* or dictator of Buenos Aires for next 23 years
1839: Confederation of Bolivia and Peru shattered at battle of Yungay by Chileans and Peruvian nationalists
1840: Guano boom helps stabilize Peru
1851: Railway track completed from Copiapó to port of Caldera in Chile
1853: Slave traffic to Brazil ceases
1860: Ecuador's president, theocrat García Moreno, launches ambitious program of public works
c.1865: Chile producing 44% of world's copper
1864–70: Paraguayan War; catastrophic defeat of Paraguay by Brazil, Argentina, and Uruguay
c.1870: European investment and immigration into Argentina starts to accelerate
1879–83: War of the Pacific
1881: Patagonia becomes part of Argentina
1888: Slavery in Brazil at last completely abolished
1889: Brazil gains republican status as emperor is forced to leave
1896: Height of Brazilian rubber boom; Manáos builds opera house
1900: Chile and Argentina agree border protocol
1900: Brazil produces 66% of world's coffee; tin supersedes silver as Bolivia's chief export

1830 · 1840 · 1850 · 1860 · 1870 · 1880 · 1890 · 1900

MODERN SOUTH AMERICA

Augusto Pinochet headed Chile's military government from 1974 to 1990.

POLITICAL AND ECONOMIC instability arose in South America as a result of the great depression of the 1930s. Various factors, including a sharp rise in population and rapid urbanization and industrialization, exerted great pressures on the weak democratic institutions of most nations. Opposition to the conservative status quo was pronounced among intellectuals, students, and trade unionists. In the late 1960s social conflicts and ideological battles shook governments. The crisis sent many countries toward repression and a new kind of conservative authoritarianism arose. In the 1980s, South American countries turned toward democracy and freer markets. Throughout the century, long-standing border disputes remained, but few flared up like the Chaco War of 1932–35.

South America: from instability to democracy

Founded in 1970, the Shining Path, the Peruvian revolutionary movement, asserts its authority in Ayacucho in 1989, by defiantly parading through the city's streets.

South America suffered the full force of the global recession of the 1930s. Populist governments shifted toward economic nationalism, energetically promoting industrial development. By the late 1950s economic and social progress had ushered in greater democracy. The impact of the Communist-inspired Cuban Revolution threatened the status quo. The US, fearing the spread of communism, pledged $10 billion in aid, but massive population growth cancelled out the benefits of the grants. With increased conflict between leftist guerrillas and the ruling elite, military regimes, backed by the US, assumed power in order to contain social unrest. The tide of military rule receded in the early 1980s.

Political development from 1930

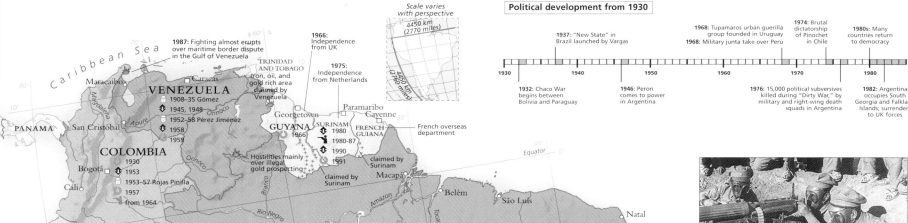

1937: "New State" in Brazil launched by Vargas
1968: Tupamaros urban guerilla group founded in Uruguay
1968: Military junta take over Peru
1974: Brutal dictatorship of Pinochet in Chile
1980s: Many countries return to democracy

1932: Chaco War begins between Bolivia and Paraguay
1946: Peron comes to power in Argentina
1976: 15,000 political subversives killed during "Dirty War," by military and right-wing death squads in Argentina
1982: Argentina occupies South Georgia and Falkland Islands; surrenders to UK forces

(timeline 1930 1940 1950 1960 1970 1980)

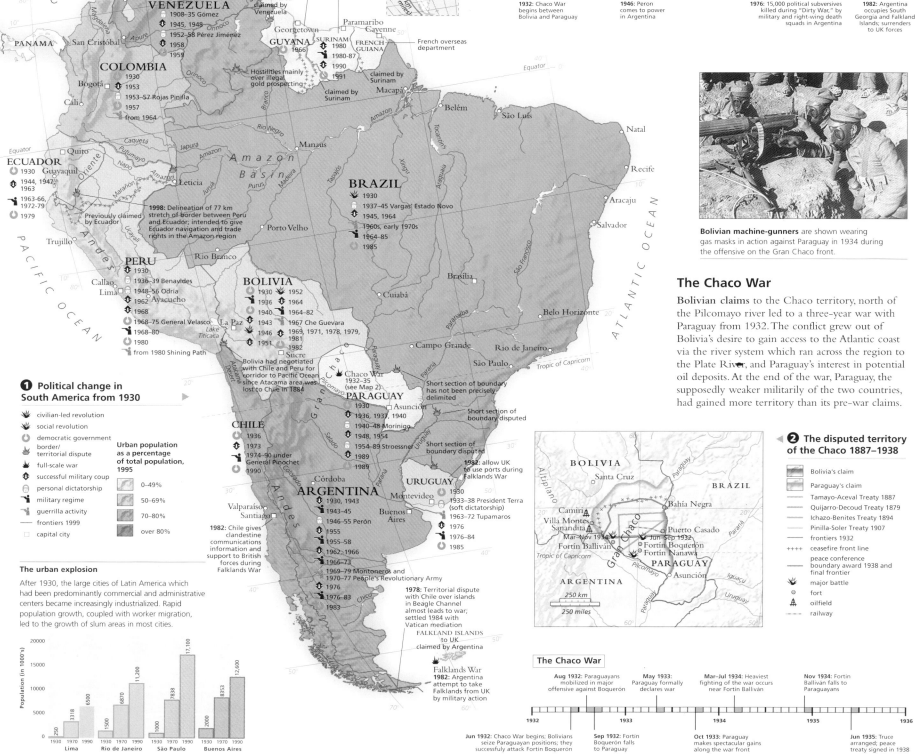

Scale varies with perspective
4450 km (2770 miles)

1987: Fighting almost erupts over maritime border dispute in the Gulf of Venezuela

1966: Independence from UK

1975: Independence from Netherlands

TRINIDAD AND TOBAGO
Iron, oil, and gold rich area claimed by Venezuela

Caribbean Sea

Maracaibo
Caracas
VENEZUELA
1908–35 Gómez
1945, 1948
1952–58 Pérez Jiménez
1958
1959

PANAMA
San Cristóbal
Apure
Orinoco
Georgetown
Paramaribo
Cayenne
GUYANA **SURINAM** **FRENCH GUIANA**
1966
1980
1980-87
1990
1991

French overseas department

COLOMBIA
1930
1953
1953–57 Rojas Pinilla
1957
from 1964

Bogotá
Cali

Hostilities mainly over illegal gold prospecting
claimed by Surinam
claimed by Surinam
Macapá
Equator

ECUADOR
1930 Guayaquil
1944, 1947, 1963
1963-66, 1972-79
1979

Quito
Oriente
Napo
Marañón

Previously claimed by Ecuador

Belém
São Luís
Natal

1998: Delineation of 77 km stretch of border between Peru and Ecuador; intended to give Ecuador navigation and trade rights in the Amazon region

Leticia
Manaus
Amazon Basin
Porto Velho
Recife

PACIFIC OCEAN

Trujillo

Río Branco

PERU
1930
1936–39 Benavides
1948–56 Odría
1962 Ayacucho
1968
1968–75 General Velasco
1968–80
1980
from 1980 Shining Path

Callao
Lima
La Paz
Lake Titicaca

BRAZIL
1930
1937–45 Vargas' Estado Novo
1945, 1964
1960s, early 1970s
1964–85
1985

Aracaju
Salvador
Brasília
Cuiabá
Belo Horizonte
Campo Grande
Rio de Janeiro
São Paulo
Tropic of Capricorn

ATLANTIC OCEAN

BOLIVIA
1930 1952
1936 1964
1940 1964–82
1943 1967 Che Guevara
1946 1969, 1971, 1978, 1979, 1981
1951 1982

Sucre
Bolivia had negotiated with Chile and Peru for corridor to Pacific Ocean since Atacama area was lost to Chile in 1884

Chaco War 1932–35 (see Map 2)

Short section of boundary has not been precisely delimited

PARAGUAY
1930
1936, 1937, 1940
1940–48 Morínigo
1948, 1954
1954–89 Stroessner
1989
1989

Asunción

Short section of boundary disputed

Short section of boundary disputed

1982: allow UK to use ports during Falklands War

CHILE
1936
1973
1974–90 under General Pinochet
1990

Córdoba

URUGUAY
1930
1933–38 President Terra (soft dictatorship)
1963–72 Tupamaros
1976
1976–84
1985

Valparaíso
Santiago
ARGENTINA
1930, 1943
1943–45
1946–55 Perón
1955
1955–58
1962, 1966
1966–73
1969–79 Montoneros and 1970–77 People's Revolutionary Army
1976
1976–83
1983

Montevideo
Buenos Aires

1982: Chile gives clandestine communications information and support to British forces during Falklands War

1978: Territorial dispute with Chile over islands in Beagle Channel almost leads to war; settled 1984 with Vatican mediation

FALKLAND ISLANDS to UK claimed by Argentina

Falklands War
1982: Argentina attempt to take Falklands from UK by military action

① Political change in South America from 1930

- ☠ civilian-led revolution
- ⚑ social revolution
- ↻ democratic government
- border/territorial dispute
- ⚔ full-scale war
- ✦ successful military coup
- personal dictatorship
- military regime
- guerrilla activity
- — frontiers 1999
- □ capital city

Urban population as a percentage of total population, 1995
- 0–49%
- 50–69%
- 70–80%
- over 80%

The urban explosion

After 1930, the large cities of Latin America which had been predominantly commercial and administrative centers became increasingly industrialized. Rapid population growth, coupled with worker migration, led to the growth of slum areas in most cities.

Population (in 1000's)
20000 15000 10000 5000 0

Lima: 250 (1930), 3318 (1970), 6500 (1990)
Rio de Janeiro: 1500 (1930), 6870 (1970), 11,200 (1990)
São Paulo: 1600 (1930), 7838 (1970), 17,100 (1990)
Buenos Aires: 2000 (1930), 8353 (1970), 12,600 (1990)

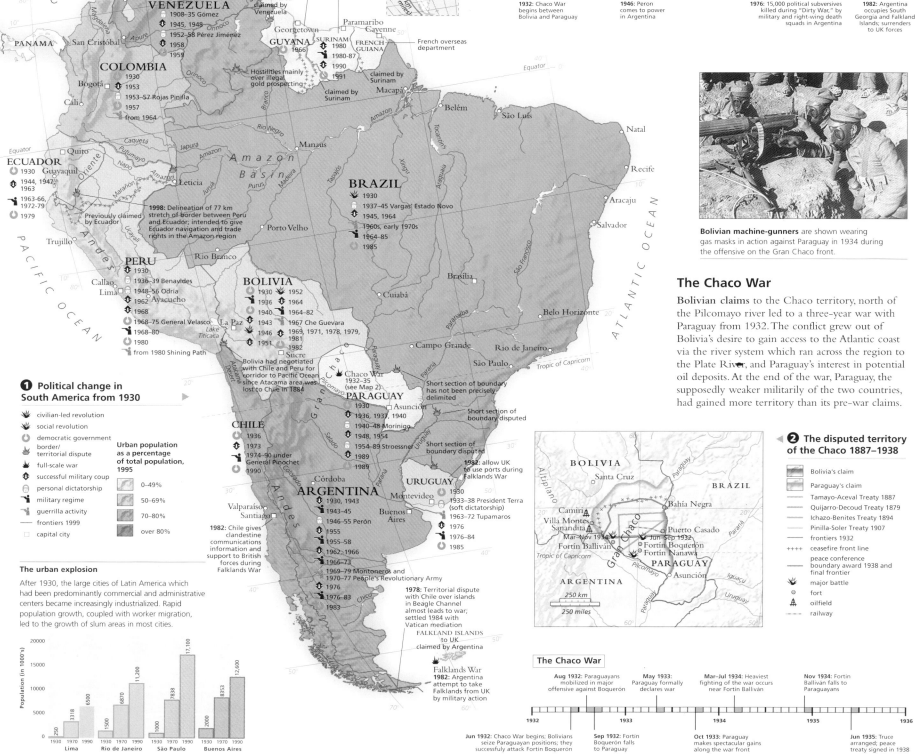

Bolivian machine-gunners are shown wearing gas masks in action against Paraguay in 1934 during the offensive on the Gran Chaco front.

The Chaco War

Bolivian claims to the Chaco territory, north of the Pilcomayo river led to a three-year war with Paraguay from 1932. The conflict grew out of Bolivia's desire to gain access to the Atlantic coast via the river system which ran across the region to the Plate River, and Paraguay's interest in potential oil deposits. At the end of the war, Paraguay, the supposedly weaker militarily of the two countries, had gained more territory than its pre-war claims.

② The disputed territory of the Chaco 1887–1938

BOLIVIA
Santa Cruz
Camiri
Villa Montes
Sanandita
Mar-Nov 1934
Fortín Ballivián
Jun-Sep 1932
Fortín Boquerón
Fortín Nanawa
Tropic of Capricorn
PARAGUAY
ARGENTINA
Puerto Casado
Bahía Negra
BRAZIL
Asunción
Pilcomayo
Paraná
Uruguay
Iguazú
250 km
250 miles

- Bolivia's claim
- Paraguay's claim
- Tamayo-Aceval Treaty 1887
- Quijarro-Decoud Treaty 1879
- Ichazo-Benites Treaty 1894
- Pinilla-Soler Treaty 1907
- frontiers 1932
- ++++ ceasefire front line
- peace conference
- boundary award 1938 and final frontier
- ⚔ major battle
- ○ fort
- ⚒ oilfield
- ---- railway

The Chaco War

Aug 1932: Paraguayans mobilized in major offensive against Boquerón
May 1933: Paraguay formally declares war
Mar-Jul 1934: Heaviest fighting of the war occurs near Fortín Ballivián
Nov 1934: Fortín Ballivián falls to Paraguayans

(timeline 1932 1933 1934 1935 1936)

Jun 1932: Chaco War begins; Bolivians seize Paraguayan positions; they successfully attack Fortín Boquerón
Sep 1932: Fortín Boquerón falls to Paraguay
Oct 1933: Paraguay makes spectacular gains along the war front
Jun 1935: Truce arranged; peace treaty signed in 1938

Economic development

After 1930, many South American nations adopted industrial development policies in an attempt to restructure economies which had relied upon the production of raw materials. Trade tariffs were imposed from the 1940s to accelerate industrialization while high inflation was tolerated in the hope of maintaining a strong demand for goods and services. Manufacturing industries became concentrated in a number of locations, yet income distribution remained unequal. More open economies from the 1980s attracted foreign and domestic investment. Economic reforms in the 1990s, which were aimed at defeating spiraling inflation, saw the privatization of many state-run enterprises.

③ Industry and resources in modern South America

Industry		Agricultural resources		Mineral resources	
	aerospace		cattle		bauxite (aluminium)
	car/vehicle manufacture		cocoa		copper
	chemicals		corn (maize)		diamonds
	electronics		cotton		gold
	engineering		coffee		iron ore
	finance		fishing		lead
	food processing (includes brewing, fish processing, meat processing, and sugar processing)		fruit		manganese
			oil palms		nickel
	gas		peanuts		silver
	hi-tech industry		rubber		tin
	iron and steel		sheep		coal field
	metal refining		shellfish		gasfield
	narcotics		soya beans		oilfield
	oil		sugar cane		
	pharmaceuticals		vineyards		
	printing and publishing		wheat		
	shipbuilding				
	textiles				
	timber processing				
	tobacco processing				
	main industrial areas				

Gross national product per capita 1998

less than $1000
$1000–$2500
$2501–$4500
$4501–$7000
$7001–$10,000

Development and deforestation in Amazonia

In the 1950s, the Brazilian government attempted to alleviate poverty among landless rural populations by granting resettlement plots along new roads in the Amazonian rain forest. From the 1960s, the government pursued vigorous economic policies which encouraged the development of the region. Subsidies and tax incentives made the clearing of Amazonia especially profitable for large land-holders involved in cattle ranching, and these farms were responsible for the destruction of 80% of the forest. By 1998, 12% of Brazil's rainforest had been cleared.

1964: Plans for highway network throughout Amazon Basin

1978: Trans-Amazon Highway completed, it extends 5000 km from Recife to Peruvian border

1981: United States provides $1.5 billion for conversion of forest land into pastures in Brazil

1960 — 1970 — 1980 — 1990

1953: SUDAM established to manage government granted settlement plots

1967: Daniel Ludwig sets up Jari Project in north Brazil; includes a wood-pulp plant and rice growing

1992: United Nations Conference on the Environment in Rio de Janeiro; natives granted title to one million hectares in Amazonia

Economic development of the Brazilian rainforest from 1960

④ Development and deforestation in Amazonia

Environmental issues

tropical forests
forest under medium / high threat
deforested areas

Transportation network

major Amazonian railway
major Amazonian road

Mineral resources

bauxite (aluminium)
gold
copper
iron ore
manganese
nickel
tin

Development programs

development area with type of development

A child harvests the coca crop in Colombia, where the shrub thrives in the tropical climate. Coca has been traditionally chewed by the people of Andean South America to cope with altitude sickness.

Scientists believed that gas released during the burning of the Brazilian rain forest contributed to global warming. Burning resulted in the release of carbon dioxide which the destroyed forest could not absorb to produce free oxygen.

Semi-skilled assembly line work, as in this car manufacturing plant in Argentina, was the main type of employment offered by foreign multinational corporations to South American workers in the 1990s.

⑤ The drugs trade

coca-growing areas
poppy-growing areas
provinces of Colombia
border 1999

The narcotics trade

From the 1970s, Latin America began to ship massive quantities of cocaine to its main overseas market, the United States. The Andean countries: Bolivia, Colombia, and Peru produced the coca leaf from which cocaine was derived, and the trade was organized and directed by the Medellín and Cali drugs cartels in Colombia. International intervention did little to depress the profits of drug barons, who later diversified into poppy growing in Colombia, for the production of heroin.

AFRICA
REGIONAL HISTORY

THE HISTORICAL LANDSCAPE

THE GEOGRAPHY AND CLIMATE OF AFRICA has, to possibly a greater extent than in any other continent, determined its role in world history. The earliest human remains have been found here in the arid geological block faults of the Great Rift Valley and southern Africa. Although unaffected by the glaciation of the last Ice Age, attendant climatic changes witnessed a transformation of the Sahara from a desert during the Ice Age, into a belt of temperate grassland, inhabited by herds of game and groups of hunter–gatherers by 8000 years ago. By around 4000 BCE, the process of desiccation began which continues today, effectively isolating sub-Saharan Africa from the Mediterranean. Only the Nile Valley provided a link, and here one of the world's oldest civilizations emerged. South of the Sahara, a wide range of isolated cultures developed, their nature determined largely by their environment, linked by rich nonliterate oral traditions. The plateau nature of much of Africa, and the desert and jungle which dominate much of the landscape, meant that Africa was the last continent (excepting Antarctica) to be colonized by Europeans, and their brief and callous century of tenancy left a legacy of underdevelopment and political strife.

The Great Rift Valley was home to one of the earliest known human ancestors, *Australopithecus afarensis*, 3.8 million years ago. Modern humans (*Homo sapiens*) evolved here about 100,000 years ago before migrating to Asia and Australasia, Europe, and finally the Americas.

The Sahara covers much of northern Africa, although sand dunes account for only a quarter of the desert's area. The rest is made up of barren, rock-strewn surfaces. Desert has existed in this part of Africa for almost five million years, and the harsh climate and inhospitable landscape have prevented the establishment of permanent settlements.

The Nile River winds its way across the hostile Sahara to the Mediterranean Sea, flanked by fertile floodplains. Humans have inhabited the Nile region since the early Stone Age, making use of the fertile soils that have built up as a result the annual flooding of the river.

Vegetation type

- semidesert or sparsely vegetated
- grassland
- forest or open woodland
- tropical rain forest
- tropical desert (18,000 years ago)
- desert (8000 years ago)
- coastline (present-day)
- coastline (18,000 years ago)

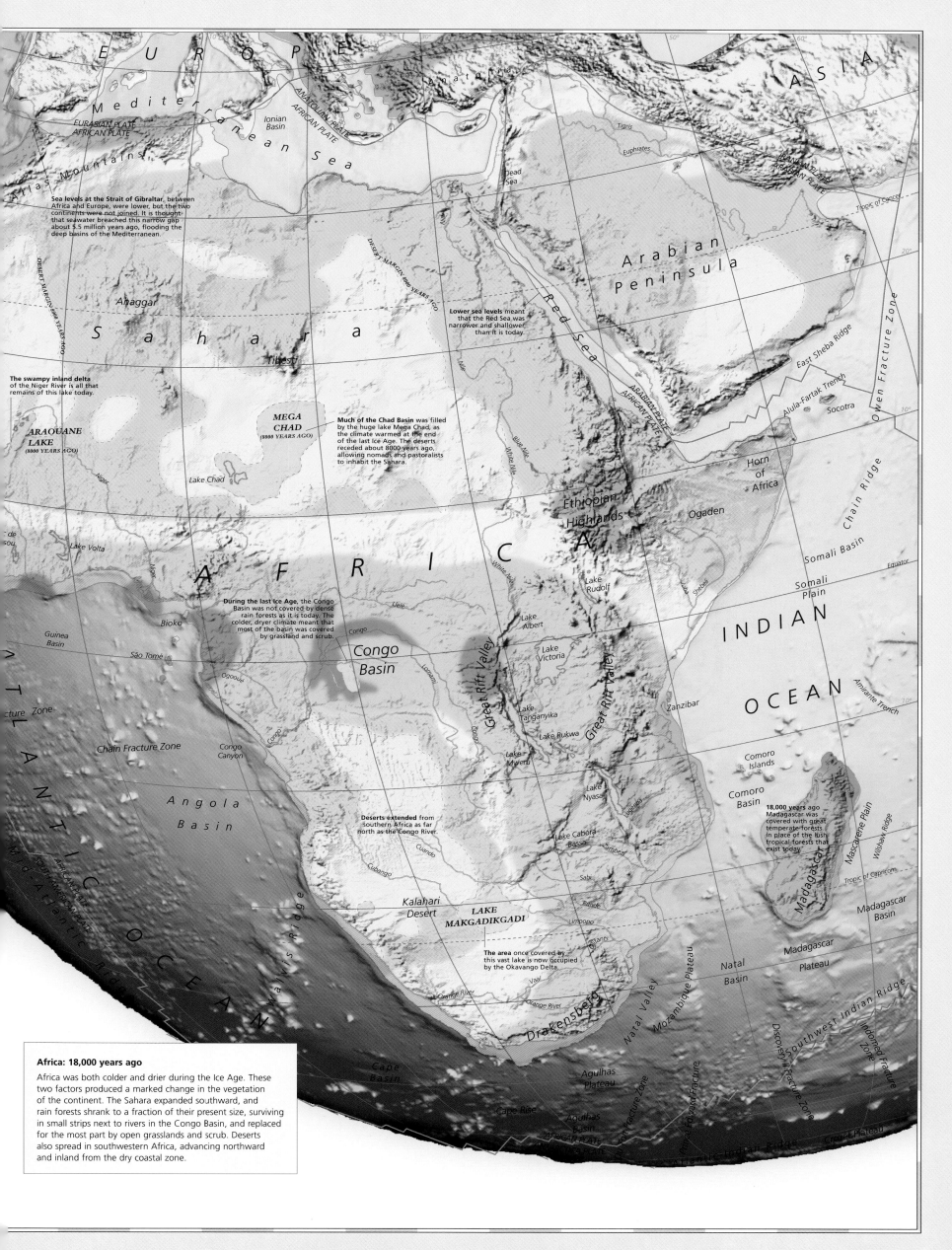

Sea levels at the Strait of Gibraltar, between Africa and Europe, were lower, but the two continents were not joined. It is thought that seawater breached this narrow gap about 5.5 million years ago, flooding the deep basins of the Mediterranean.

The swampy inland delta of the Niger River is all that remains of this lake today.

ARAOUANE LAKE
(8000 YEARS AGO)

MEGA CHAD
(8000 YEARS AGO)

Much of the Chad Basin was filled by the huge lake Mega Chad, as the climate warmed at the end of the last Ice Age. The deserts receded about 8000 years ago, allowing nomads and pastoralists to inhabit the Sahara.

Lower sea levels meant that the Red Sea was narrower and shallower than it is today.

During the last Ice Age, the Congo Basin was not covered by dense rain forests as it is today. The colder, drier climate meant that most of the basin was covered by grassland and scrub.

Deserts extended from southern Africa as far north as the Congo River.

18,000 years ago Madagascar was covered with great temperate forests in place of the lush tropical forests that exist today.

The area once covered by this vast lake is now occupied by the Okavango Delta.

Africa: 18,000 years ago

Africa was both colder and drier during the Ice Age. These two factors produced a marked change in the vegetation of the continent. The Sahara expanded southward, and rain forests shrank to a fraction of their present size, surviving in small strips next to rivers in the Congo Basin, and replaced for the most part by open grasslands and scrub. Deserts also spread in southwestern Africa, advancing northward and inland from the dry coastal zone.

AFRICA

EXPLORATION AND MAPPING

To stake a territorial claim, Portuguese sailors would place a stone cross (padrão) on the African shore.

IN THE ABSENCE OF A WRITTEN historical record, little is known of early local knowledge of Africa south of the Sahara. Writing in the 5th century BCE, the Greek historian Herodotus reported an attempt by a Phoenician crew to circumnavigate the continent in 600 BCE. By 150 CE, the Greek geographer Ptolemy had mapped the area north of the line between Mombasa and the Canary Islands (see p.44). From 600 CE Arab merchants crisscrossed the Sahara establishing Muslim settlements. Several trading nations of Europe had secured coastal toeholds by 1600; however, by 1800, the African land mass remained relatively uncharted. The great 19th-century explorers of the interior meticulously recorded those features they encountered.

MEDIEVAL ACCOUNTS OF THE INTERIOR OF WEST AFRICA

Though the West Africans did not have maps, travelers in the region built up a considerable store of topographic information. It was this knowledge that Arabs and later the Portuguese tapped as their source for maps of the interior. Al-Idrisi, in 1154 reported a single river in West Africa. The Egyptian geographer al-'Umari had an account of a Nile of the Blacks which divided into two rivers, one flowing to the ocean, the other to the East African Nile via Lake Chad. Writing in 1456, a Portuguese squire called Diogo Gomes recounted the testimony of Buquer, an African merchant, who talked of a great river called Emin. The reports of Mandinka merchants in 1585 agreed with Buquer's account and gave additional detail.

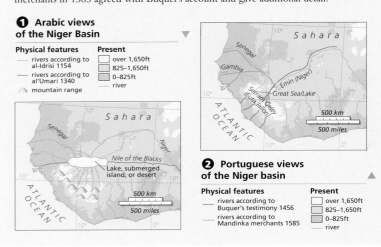

❶ Arabic views of the Niger Basin

Physical features	Present
— rivers according to al-Idrisi 1154	☐ over 1,650ft
— rivers according to al'Umari 1340	☐ 825–1,650ft
⋀ mountain range	☐ 0–825ft
	— river

❷ Portuguese views of the Niger basin

Physical features	Present
— rivers according to Buquer's testimony 1456	☐ over 1,650ft
— rivers according to Mandinka merchants 1585	☐ 825–1,650ft
	☐ 0–825ft
	— river

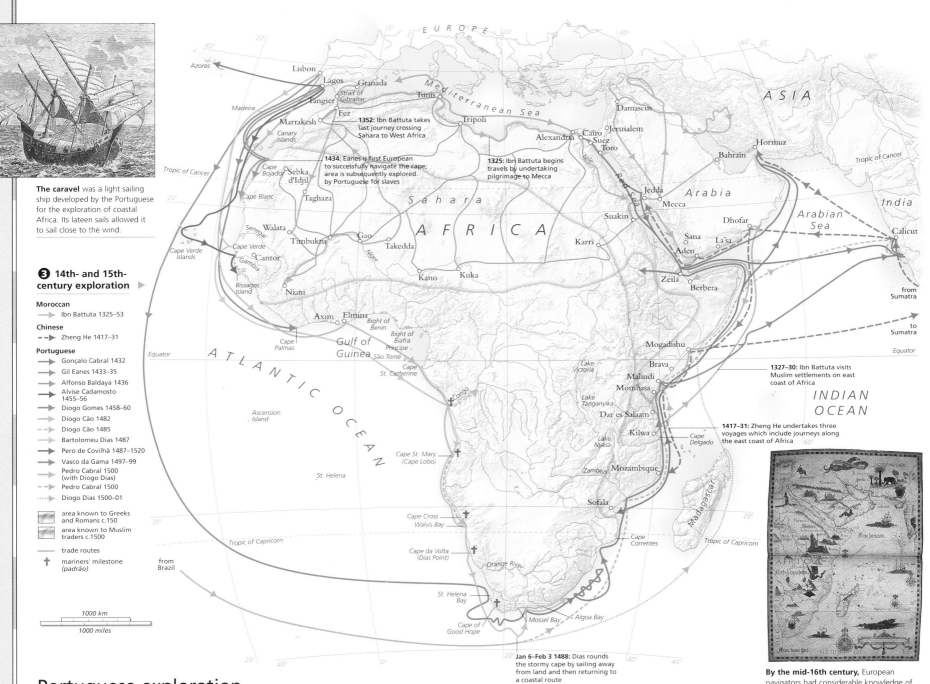

The caravel was a light sailing ship developed by the Portuguese for the exploration of coastal Africa. Its lateen sails allowed it to sail close to the wind.

❸ 14th- and 15th-century exploration

Moroccan
→ Ibn Battuta 1325–53

Chinese
– – ➤ Zheng He 1417–31

Portuguese
→ Gonçalo Cabral 1432
→ Gil Eanes 1433–35
→ Alfonso Baldaya 1436
➤ Alvise Cadamosto 1455–56
→ Diogo Gomes 1458–60
→ Diogo Cão 1482
→ Diogo Cão 1485
→ Bartolomeu Dias 1487
➤ Pero de Covilhã 1487–1520
→ Vasco da Gama 1497–99
– – ➤ Pedro Cabral 1500 (with Diogo Dias)
– – ➤ Pedro Cabral 1500
······ Diogo Dias 1500–01

▨ area known to Greeks and Romans c.150
▨ area known to Muslim traders c.1500
— trade routes
✝ mariners' milestone (padrão)

1352: Ibn Battuta takes last journey crossing Sahara to West Africa

1434: Eanes is first European to successfully navigate the cape; area is subsequently explored by Portuguese for slaves

1325: Ibn Battuta begins travels by undertaking pilgrimage to Mecca

1327–30: Ibn Battuta visits Muslim settlements on east coast of Africa

1417–31: Zheng He undertakes three voyages which include journeys along the east coast of Africa

Jan 6–Feb 3 1488: Dias rounds the stormy cape by sailing away from land and then returning to a coastal route

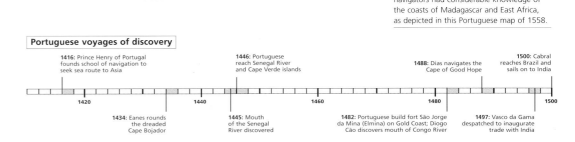

By the mid-16th century, European navigators had considerable knowledge of the coasts of Madagascar and East Africa, as depicted in this Portuguese map of 1558.

Portuguese exploration

Systematic voyages of discovery were undertaken by the Portuguese along the western coast of Africa. These and later expeditions were made in the hope both of making contact with the gold-producing centers known to exist in West Africa and of establishing a trade route to India around the tip of the continent. In consequence, the lower reaches of the rivers Gambia and Senegal were explored, contact was made with the Empire of Mali, and the Cape Verde Islands were discovered.

Portuguese voyages of discovery

1416: Prince Henry of Portugal founds school of navigation to seek sea route to Asia

1446: Portuguese reach Senegal River and Cape Verde islands

1488: Dias navigates the Cape of Good Hope

1500: Cabral reaches Brazil and sails on to India

1434: Eanes rounds the dreaded Cape Bojador

1445: Mouth of the Senegal River discovered

1482: Portuguese build fort São Jorge da Mina (Elmina) on Gold Coast; Diogo Cão discovers mouth of Congo River

1497: Vasco da Gama despatched to inaugurate trade with India

| 1420 | 1440 | 1460 | 1480 | 1500 |

Exploration of the African interior

The European exploration of the African interior is largely the story of the search for the sources of some of the world's greatest rivers. The Scottish explorer, James Bruce toured Ethiopia between 1768 and 1773, discovering the source of the Blue Nile in 1772. Systematic exploration may be said to have begun in 1778, under the auspices of the African Association, a group of English scientists and scholars. In 1795 the association sponsored Mungo Park's first journey to West Africa; he investigated the Gambia River and reached the Niger, showing that it flowed eastward. British exploration intensified in the first half of the 19th century culminating in John Hanning Speke's triumphant discovery of the source of the Nile at Ripon Falls, Lake Victoria, in 1862. In anticipation of the scramble for territorial control, a number of continental Europeans also embarked on investigative expeditions.

French explorer René Caillié made this sketch of Timbuktu in 1828, when he fulfilled his great ambition to visit the Saharan city and secured a 10,000-franc prize for his efforts. The sum had been offered by the Société Géographique to the first European to return from the city.

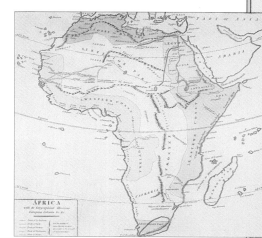

The 19th century saw the systematic and scientific exploration of the African interior. As a result, cartographers were reluctant to represent uncertain data. Published in 1808, this map of Africa shows less information than its more speculative predecessors.

④ 19th-century exploration ▶

British
➤ James Bruce 1768–73
➤ Mungo Park 1795–96
➤ Mungo Park 1805–06
➤ Hugh Clapperton, Dixon Denham, and Walter Oudney 1821–25
➤ Hugh Clapperton and Richard Lander 1825–27
➤ David Livingstone 1841–53
➤ David Livingstone 1849
➤ David Livingstone 1853–56
➤ David Livingstone 1866–73
➤ Samuel and Florence Baker 1861–65
➤ Henry Stanley 1871–89
➤ Mary Kingsley 1895

French
➤ René Caillié 1827–28
➤ Pierre Savorgnan de Brazza 1875–78
➤ Jean-Baptiste Marchand 1897–98

German
➤ Heinrich Barth 1850–55

Italian
➤ Vittorio Bottego 1892–97

Portuguese
➤ Alexandre Serpa Pinto 1877–79

Swedish
➤ Charles Andersson 1853–59

⑤ Tracking the Nile
➤ Richard Burton and John Speke 1856–59
➤ John Speke 1858
➤ John Speke and James Grant 1860–63
➤ Samuel and Florence Baker 1863–65

John Hanning Speke journeyed with Richard Burton in 1856–59. In 1862, James Grant and Speke came across the source of the Nile at Lake Victoria.

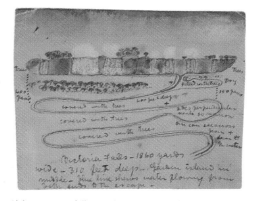

Livingstone carefully noted the dimensions of those physical features he encountered. He annotated this map of Victoria Falls with precise measurements and descriptive detail.

The source of the Nile

The quest for the source of the Nile captured the imagination of 19th-century Europe. The adventure stimulated intellectual debate and provoked fierce personal jealousies. After Speke had identified the source as Ripon Falls, Lake Victoria, he endured many attempts to discredit his discovery. The political and economic importance of the region made it the objective of rival imperialists.

Sir Henry Morton Stanley, the British-American journalist, was sent to Africa by the *New York Herald* in 1871 to find David Livingstone, of whom nothing had been heard for several months. In the 1880s he helped create Léopold's Congo Free State.

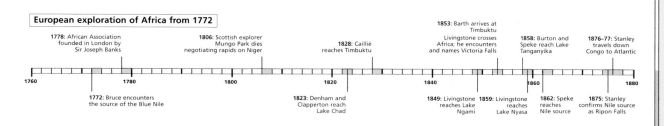

European exploration of Africa from 1772

1760 — 1772: Bruce encounters the source of the Blue Nile — 1778: African Association founded in London by Sir Joseph Banks — 1780 — 1800 — 1806: Scottish explorer Mungo Park dies negotiating rapids on Niger — 1820 — 1823: Denham and Clapperton reach Lake Chad — 1828: Caillié reaches Timbuktu — 1840 — 1849: Livingstone reaches Lake Ngami — 1853: Barth arrives at Timbuktu; Livingstone crosses Africa; he encounters and names Victoria Falls — 1859: Livingstone reaches Lake Nyasa — 1858: Burton and Speke reach Lake Tanganyika — 1860 — 1862: Speke reaches Nile source — 1875: Stanley confirms Nile source as Ripon Falls — 1876–77: Stanley travels down Congo to Atlantic — 1880

THE EARLY HISTORY OF AFRICA

Hatshepsut seized the throne in Egypt from her stepson and reigned from 1472 to 1458 BCE.

THREE EVENTS contributed to the growth and spread of farming in Africa: the spread of cattle pastoralism in the Sahara, the domestication of indigenous crops further south, and the introduction of West Asian livestock and cereals to Egypt. Asian wheat and barley spread along the Mediterranean coast, down the Nile Valley to the Sudan, and the Ethiopian Highlands. Drier conditions from 3000 BCE forced Saharan pastoralists to migrate to the Nile Valley, where from 5000 BCE crops had thrived in fertile soil deposited by annual floods. Egypt thereafter emerged as a powerful state, organized conventionally into 30 "Dynasties," broken down into three "Kingdoms" separated by two "Intermediate Periods" of disunity and instability.

The development of agriculture

From 4000 BCE bulrush millet was cultivated alongside sorghum in southern Sudan.

Both the herding of wild cattle in the Sahara and the cultivation of indigenous plants farther south began c.6000 BCE. From 5000 BCE, Asian wheat and barley were grown in Egypt. By 2000 BCE pastoralism was widespread north of the Equator. Farming and herding south of the Equator however, were impeded by dense forests and the presence of the parasitic tsetse fly. As a result, pastoralism progressed only slowly down the east coast, reaching southern Africa by 1000 CE.

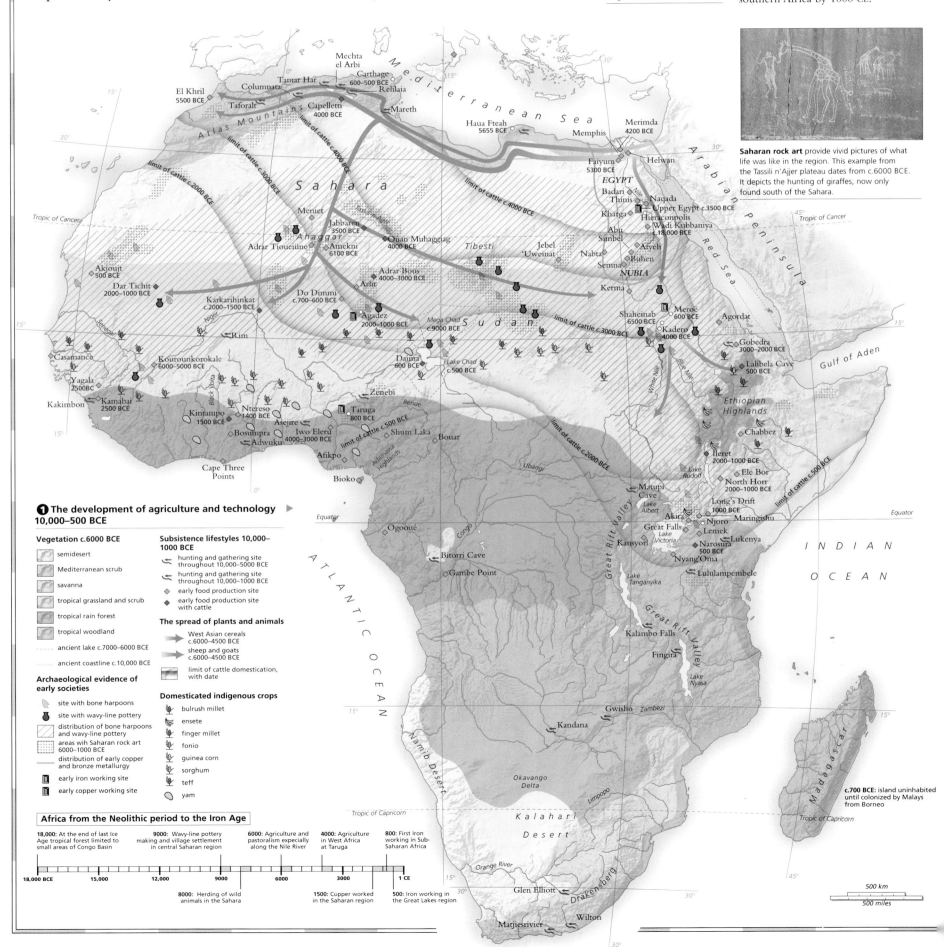

Saharan rock art provide vivid pictures of what life was like in the region. This example from the Tassili n'Ajjer plateau dates from c.6000 BCE. It depicts the hunting of giraffes, now only found south of the Sahara.

❶ The development of agriculture and technology ▶
10,000–500 BCE

Vegetation c.6000 BCE
- semidesert
- Mediterranean scrub
- savanna
- tropical grassland and scrub
- tropical rain forest
- tropical woodland
- ---- ancient lake c.7000–6000 BCE
- ····· ancient coastline c.10,000 BCE

Archaeological evidence of early societies
- site with bone harpoons
- site with wavy-line pottery
- distribution of bone harpoons and wavy-line pottery
- areas wih Saharan rock art 6000–1000 BCE
- distribution of early copper and bronze metallurgy
- early iron working site
- early copper working site

Subsistence lifestyles 10,000–1000 BCE
- hunting and gathering site throughout 10,000–5000 BCE
- hunting and gathering site throughout 10,000–1000 BCE
- early food production site
- early food production site with cattle

The spread of plants and animals
- West Asian cereals c.6000–4500 BCE
- sheep and goats c.6000–4500 BCE
- limit of cattle domestication, with date

Domesticated indigenous crops
- bulrush millet
- ensete
- finger millet
- fonio
- guinea corn
- sorghum
- teff
- yam

c.700 BCE: island uninhabited until colonized by Malays from Borneo

Africa from the Neolithic period to the Iron Age

18,000: At the end of last Ice Age tropical forest limited to small areas of Congo Basin	**9000:** Wavy-line pottery making and village settlement in central Saharan region	**6000:** Agriculture and pastoralism expecially along the Nile River	**4000:** Agriculture in West Africa at Taruga	**800:** First Iron working in Sub-Saharan Africa

| 18,000 BCE | 15,000 | 12,000 | 9000 | 6000 | 3000 | 1 CE |

8000: Herding of wild animals in the Sahara **1500:** Copper worked in the Saharan region **500:** Iron working in the Great Lakes region

500 km
500 miles

② Predynastic Egypt c.5000–3000 BCE

- Confederacy of Thinis c.3500–3000 BCE
- Confederacy of Nubt c.3500–3000 BCE
- Confederacy of Nekhen c.3500–3000 BCE
- predynastic kingdom of Hieraconpolis
- military expansion of Hieraconpolis
- ○ early predynastic site
- △ middle predynastic site
- ▽ middle predynastic Nubian site
- ◇ late predynastic site
- ◇ late predynastic Nubian site
- oasis

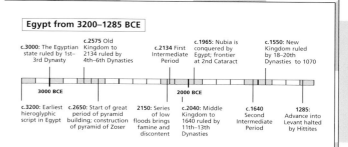

Egypt from 3200–1285 BCE

c.3000: The Egyptian state ruled by 1st–3rd Dynasty

c.2575 Old Kingdom to 2134 ruled by 4th–6th Dynasties

c.2134 First Intermediate Period

c.1965: Nubia is conquered by Egypt; frontier at 2nd Cataract

c.1550: New Kingdom ruled by 18–20th Dynasties to 1070

3000 BCE — 2000 BCE

c.3200: Earliest hieroglyphic script in Egypt

c.2650: Start of great period of pyramid building; construction of pyramid of Zoser

2150: Series of low floods brings famine and discontent

c.2040: Middle Kingdom to 1640 ruled by 11th–13th Dynasties

c.1640 Second Intermediate Period

1285: Advance into Levant halted by Hittites

The growth of Egypt 3500–2134 BCE

From 5000 BCE settled communities of farmers in the Nile valley gradually coalesced into urban centers under local rulers who developed efficient administrations. Menes of the 1st Dynasty established the Egyptian state c.3000 BCE. From this time the use of hieroglyphic writing spread and Memphis was founded. With greater centralization of power the Old Kingdom emerged and the building of the great pyramids, which served as royal burial places, began. From 2400 BCE royal power began to decline and by 2034 BCE the Old Kingdom was divided between two rival dynasties in Upper and Lower Egypt. The 94 years of political instability which followed, became known as the First Intermediate Period.

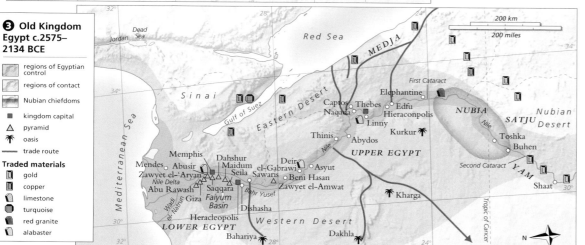

③ Old Kingdom Egypt c.2575–2134 BCE

- regions of Egyptian control
- regions of contact
- Nubian chiefdoms
- ■ kingdom capital
- △ pyramid
- oasis
- — trade route

Traded materials
- gold
- copper
- limestone
- turquoise
- red granite
- alabaster

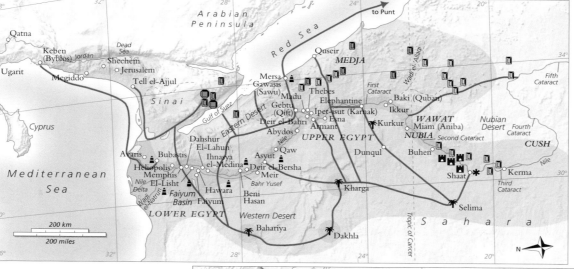

④ Middle Kingdom Egypt c.2040–1640 BCE ▶

- regions of Egyptian control
- regions of contact
- ✳ trading center
- Nubian fort
- Middle Kingdom temple
- oasis
- — trade route

Traded materials
- gold
- copper
- turquoise

The step pyramid of Zoser dating from c.2700 BCE was the earliest pyramid built in Egypt. Its construction required the large-scale mobilization of thousands of workers

Hatshepsut's temple at Deir el-Bahri was built c.1473 BCE. A fine example of architecture from the 18th Dynasty, the building has a series of colonnades and courts on three levels.

Expansion and division in Egypt

The governors of Thebes emerged from the First Intermediate Period as rulers of Upper Egypt. They later successfully challenged Lower Egypt for control of the entire region, and the Middle Kingdom was established by c.2040 BCE. Its army and administration systematically enriched Egypt's economy by dominating, and eventually annexing, Wawat and northern Cush. The Second Intermediate saw Nubia lost from Egyptian control, and the division of the Nile Delta region into several kingdoms. From 1640 BCE much of Egypt was ruled by the Hyksos from the Mediterranean coast. They were later expelled by Ahmose, king of Thebes, who became the first ruler of the New Kingdom. During the New Kingdom Egypt embarked on a policy of expansion both north and south which made it the major commercial power in the ancient world. By 1000 BCE, however, the New Kingdom was in decline.

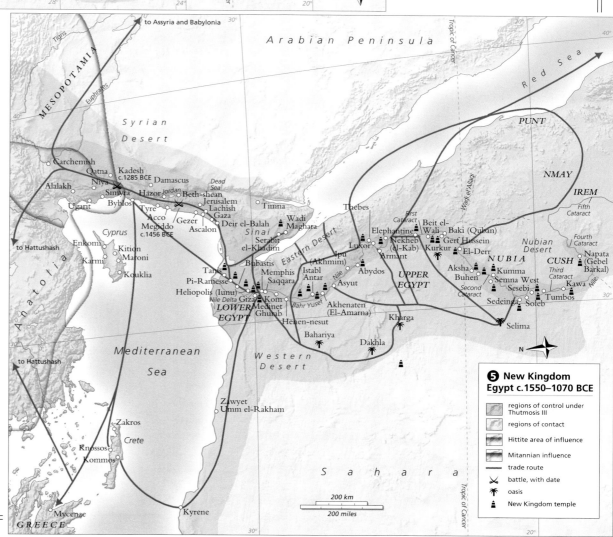

⑤ New Kingdom Egypt c.1550–1070 BCE

- regions of control under Thutmosis III
- regions of contact
- Hittite area of influence
- Mitannian influence
- — trade route
- ✕ battle, with date
- oasis
- New Kingdom temple

THE SPREAD OF COMPLEX SOCIETIES

The Nok culture of West Africa was noted for its terracotta sculptures.

ALTHOUGH TRADE ROUTES connected sub-Saharan Africa to the Mediterranean civilizations of the north, the two regions developed very much in isolation. The southward migrations of Bantu-speakers from 2000 BCE may have contributed to the diffusion of settled agriculture in sub-Saharan Africa. Sheep-herding and ironworking spread south at a later date. The Nok of West Africa were smelting iron by 600 BCE. In North Africa, the rich lands of the Mediterranean coast and Egypt attracted foreign invaders, including the Greeks and Romans. However, from 300 BCE, powerful native states also emerged in the region, notably Axum, which dominated the Red Sea, and the Berber states which competed with Rome for the lands of northwest Africa.

The spread of ironworking

The earliest evidence for ironworking south of the Sahara is found at the settlements of the Nok culture in West Africa, including Taruga and Samun Dukiya and dates from c.600 BCE. By 300 BCE, ironworking had spread as far south as the Congo river. From 1 CE, dates from sites on the subequatorial west coast correspond with those in East Africa. It is possible, therefore, that iron smelting diffused southward along two separate routes: one along the eastern part of the continent and the other along the west. In addition to its use for tools such as hoes, axes, knives, and spears, iron was also a luxury trade item, and helped to sustain intercommunity relations in the sub-Saharan region.

Paintings of chariots are found along the great African overland trade routes. They may provide evidence for the transport of ironworking to sub-Saharan Africa.

The Bantu influence

From their homeland in modern-day Nigeria on Africa's west coast, the Bantu-speaking peoples dispersed along eastern and western routes into the equatorial rain forests and then on to southern Africa during the 2nd millennium BCE. The migrating Bantu cleared forests and engaged in mixed farming. From the late 1st century BCE, their knowledge of ironworking gave them a distinct advantage over hunter-gatherers such as the Khoisan people. They established an economic basis for new societies which could sustain greater populations than those based on hunting and gathering. Thus, the period from 500 BCE to 1000 CE saw the transfer of Bantu traditions to much of sub-Saharan Africa.

During the first millennium BCE the Bantu settled in villages on the edge of the rain forest in Central Africa, engaging in mixed farming.

The development of iron technology and social organization

c.600 BCE: First known ironworking in Nok region	**c.400 BCE:** Beginnings of ironworking in Ethiopian Highlands	**c. 200 BCE:** Earliest settlement in Jenne	**c.1 CE:** Sheep herded by Khoisans in southern Africa	**c.400 CE:** Jenne a substantial city with population of 12,000	**c.600 CE:** Cattle and ironworking widespread in southern Africa

600 BCE	400	200	1 CE	200	400	600 CE

c.300 BCE: Berber states begin to emerge in North Africa

c.300 CE: Bantu cereal cultivators in southeast Africa begin to herd cattle

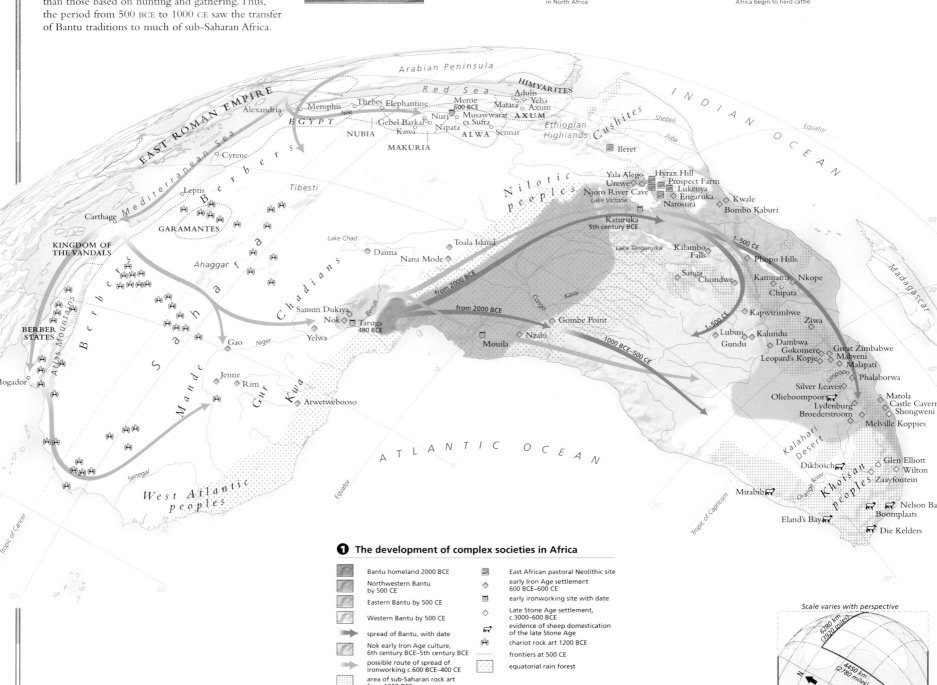

① The development of complex societies in Africa

- Bantu homeland 2000 BCE
- Northwestern Bantu by 500 CE
- Eastern Bantu by 500 CE
- Western Bantu by 500 CE
- → spread of Bantu, with date
- Nok early Iron Age culture, 6th century BCE–5th century BCE
- → possible route of spread of ironworking c.600 BCE–400 CE
- area of sub-Saharan rock art from 1000 BCE
- East African pastoral Neolithic site
- ◇ early Iron Age settlement 600 BCE–600 CE
- early ironworking site with date
- ◇ Late Stone Age settlement, c.3000–600 BCE
- evidence of sheep domestication of the late Stone Age
- chariot rock art 1200 BCE
- ····· frontiers at 500 CE
- equatorial rain forest

Scale varies with perspective

6280 km (3920 miles)
4450 km (2780 miles)

Berber states in North Africa

From 300 BCE, the Berber inhabitants of North Africa, including the Mauri, Masaesyli, and Massyli, began to form states, building cities and developing administrative structures. In alliance with Rome, the kingdoms were largely united to form Numidia by Masinissa of the Massyli in 201 BCE. Masinissa's grandson Jugurtha later incited war with Rome and was defeated in 104 BCE. His territory was subsequently absorbed into the Roman Empire as a client state. In 33 BCE King Boccus II of the Mauri willed his kingdom to the empire thus completing the annexation of the region. The entire North African coast supplied Rome with agricultural products, primarily wheat and olives; cities on the coast, such as Carthage, were centers of exchange.

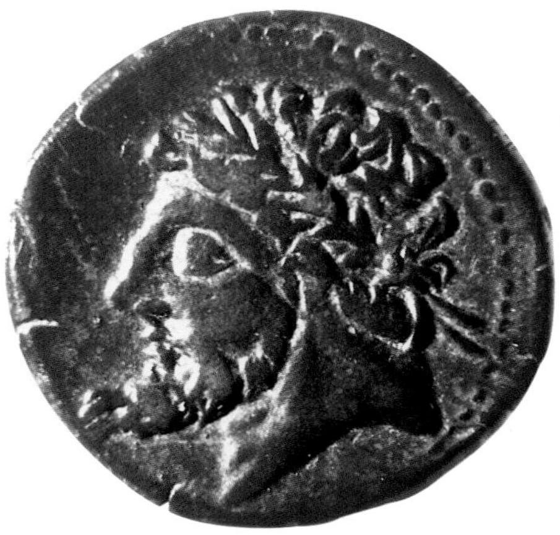

The Berber states issued their own coinage. This coin dating from the 2nd century BCE depicts Jugurtha, ruler of Numidia from 118 BCE until his defeat at the hands of the Romans in 104 BCE.

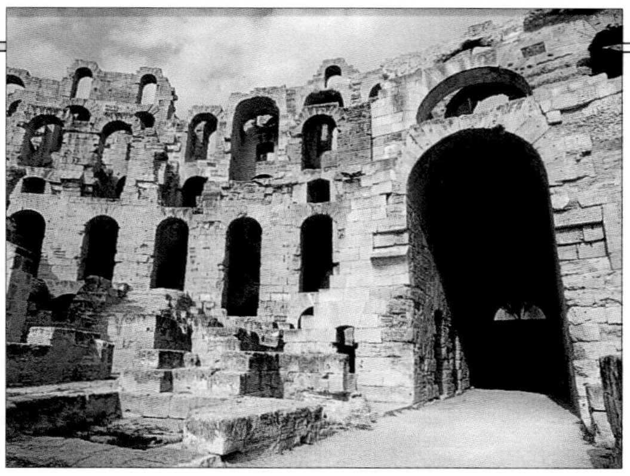

An enduring consequence of the Roman Empire was the spread of the Latin language and Roman architecture. As towns sprang up in North Africa, they acquired characteristic features of Roman cities and architecture, such as this Roman amphitheater at Thysdrus in present-day Tunisia. Built in 300 CE, the building could seat 50,000 people.

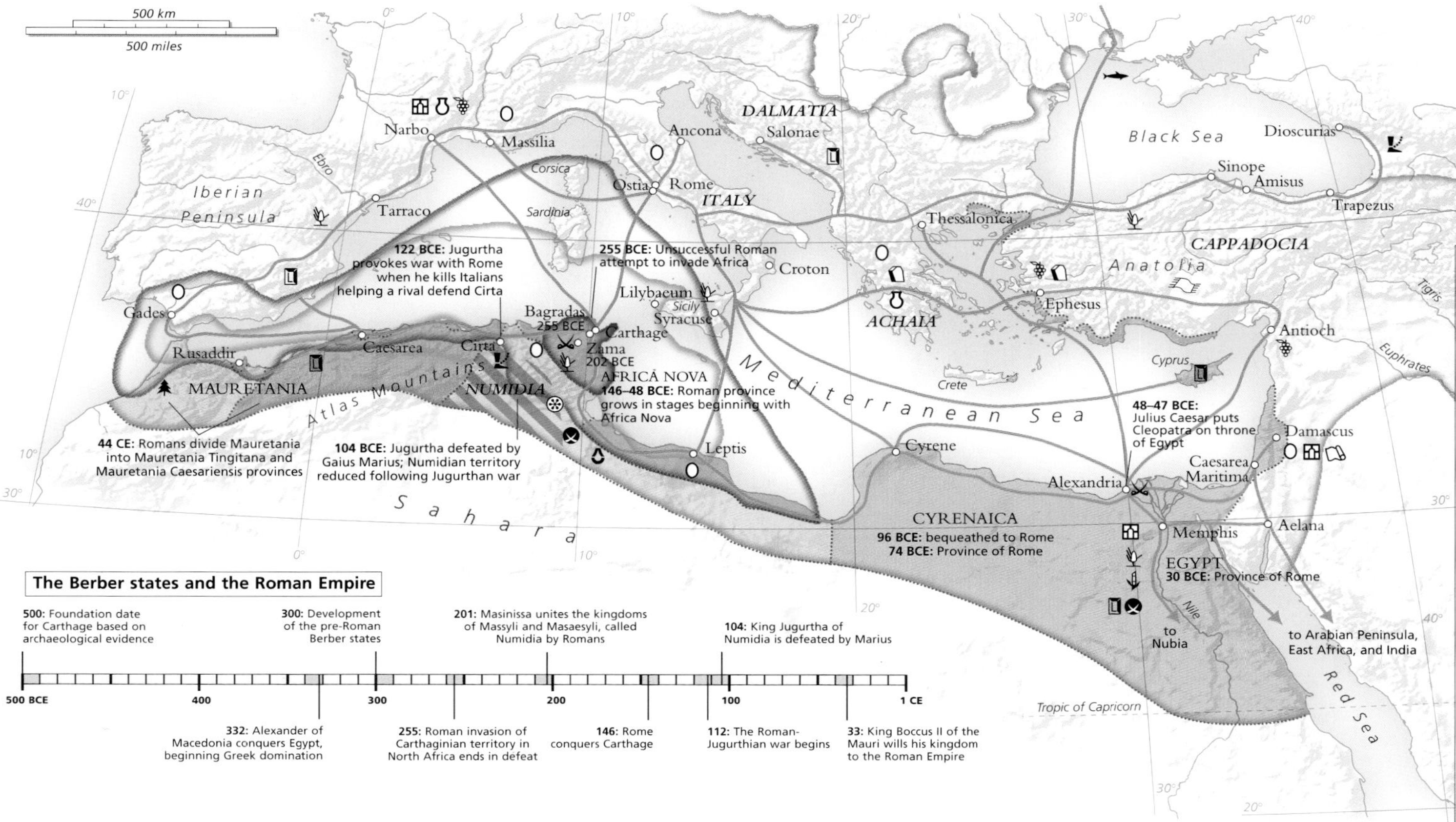

500 km
500 miles
Narbo
Massilia
Iberian Peninsula
Ebro
Tarraco
Corsica
Sardinia
Ostia
Rome
ITALY
Ancona
DALMATIA
Salonae
Black Sea
Dioscurias
Sinope
Amisus
Trapezus
Thessalonica
CAPPADOCIA
Anatolia
Ephesus
ACHAIA
Croton
Gades
Rusaddir
Caesarea
Cirta
MAURETANIA
NUMIDIA
Atlas Mountains
Bagradas 255 BCE
Carthage
Zama 202 BCE
Lilybaeum
Sicily
Syracuse
AFRICA NOVA
Leptis
Cyrene
Crete
Cyprus
Antioch
Euphrates
Tigris
Damascus
Caesarea Maritima
Alexandria
Memphis
Aelana
EGYPT
CYRENAICA
Mediterranean Sea
Sahara
Nile
Red Sea
Tropic of Capricorn
to Nubia
to Arabian Peninsula, East Africa, and India
122 BCE: Jugurtha provokes war with Rome when he kills Italians helping a rival defend Cirta
255 BCE: Unsuccessful Roman attempt to invade Africa
146–48 BCE: Roman province grows in stages beginning with Africa Nova
44 CE: Romans divide Mauretania into Mauretania Tingitana and Mauretania Caesariensis provinces
104 BCE: Jugurtha defeated by Gaius Marius; Numidian territory reduced following Jugurthan war
48–47 BCE: Julius Caesar puts Cleopatra on throne of Egypt
96 BCE: bequeathed to Rome
74 BCE: Province of Rome
30 BCE: Province of Rome

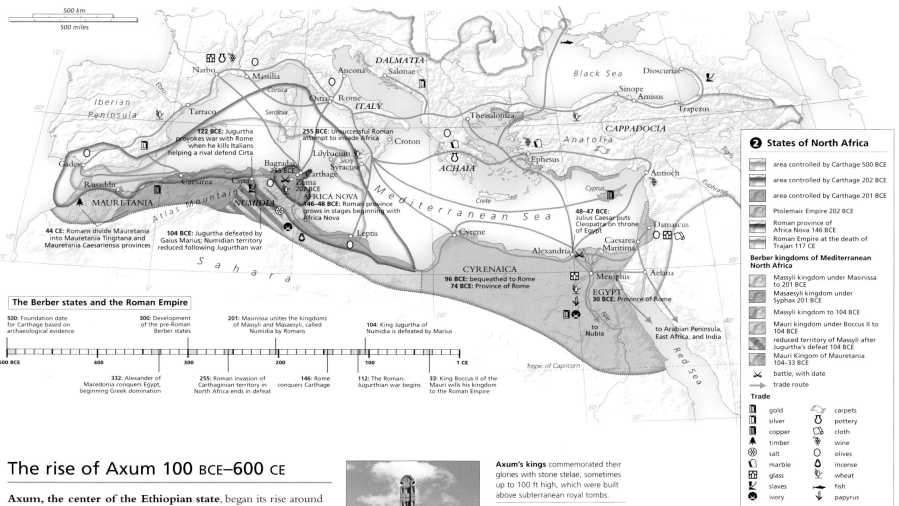

The Berber states and the Roman Empire

- 500 BCE: Foundation date for Carthage based on archaeological evidence
- 400
- 332: Alexander of Macedonia conquers Egypt, beginning Greek domination
- 300: Development of the pre-Roman Berber states
- 255: Roman invasion of Carthaginian territory in North Africa ends in defeat
- 201: Masinissa unites the kingdoms of Massyli and Masaesyli, called Numidia by Romans
- 146: Rome conquers Carthage
- 112: The Roman-Jugurthian war begins
- 104: King Jugurtha of Numidia is defeated by Marius
- 100
- 33: King Boccus II of the Mauri wills his kingdom to the Roman Empire
- 1 CE

2 States of North Africa

- area controlled by Carthage 500 BCE
- area controlled by Carthage 202 BCE
- area controlled by Carthage 201 BCE
- Ptolemaic Empire 202 BCE
- Roman province of Africa Nova 146 BCE
- Roman Empire at the death of Trajan 117 CE

Berber kingdoms of Mediterranean North Africa

- Massyli kingdom under Masinissa to 201 BCE
- Masaesyli kingdom under Syphax 201 BCE
- Massyli kingdom to 104 BCE
- Mauri kingdom under Boccus II to 104 BCE
- reduced territory of Massyli after Jugurtha's defeat 104 BCE
- Mauri Kingom of Mauretania 104–33 BCE
- battle, with date
- trade route

Trade

gold	carpets
silver	pottery
copper	cloth
timber	wine
salt	olives
marble	incense
glass	wheat
slaves	fish
ivory	papyrus

The rise of Axum 100 BCE–600 CE

Axum, the center of the Ethiopian state, began its rise around 100 BCE, becoming a major trading power by the end of the first century CE. The kingdom grew wealthy through its control of the incense-trading port of Adulis on the Red Sea *(see p.225)*. Axum provided Egypt, India, Persia, and Arabia with tortoiseshell, ivory, and rhinoceros horn. The kingdom reached its peak during the reign of King Ezana, who converted to Christianity c.350 CE. By 500 CE most of the country had adopted the new religion. In 525 CE Kaleb, one of Ezana's successors, conquered the southern part of the Arabian Peninsula, and Axum occupied this territory until 574 CE. With the spread of Islam, Axum lost its monopoly of the Red Sea to Muslim traders, and began to decline from around 600 CE.

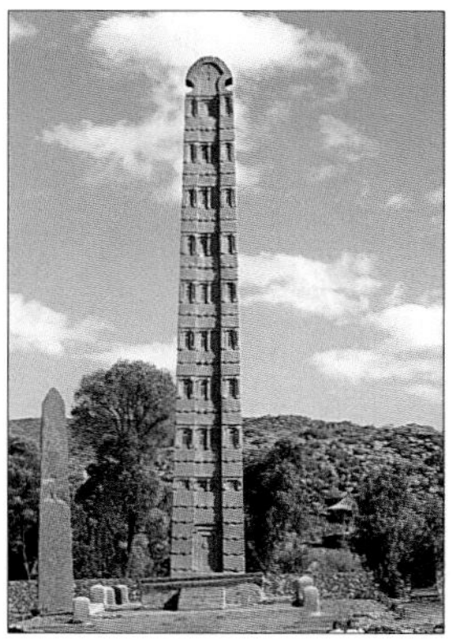

Axum's kings commemorated their glories with stone stelae, sometimes up to 100 ft high, which were built above subterranean royal tombs.

The rise and fall of kingdoms in northeast Africa

- 500 BCE: Foundation of Kingdom of Daamat, the first state of the Ethiopian Highlands
- 400 BCE
- 300 BCE: Capital of Napata moved to Meroe; the kingdom expands
- 200
- 100 BCE: Rise of Axum
- 1 CE
- 200
- 330 CE: Fall of Meroe to Axumites
- 350 CE: Conversion of Ezana of Axum to Christianity
- 400
- 525–574 CE: Axumite armies occupy southern Arabian Peninsula
- c.540 CE: Nubians convert to Christianity
- 600 CE

3 Northeast Africa 100 CE

- frankincense and myrrh
- gold
- ivory
- obsidian
- precious stones
- rhinoceros horn
- slaves
- tortoiseshell
- trade route

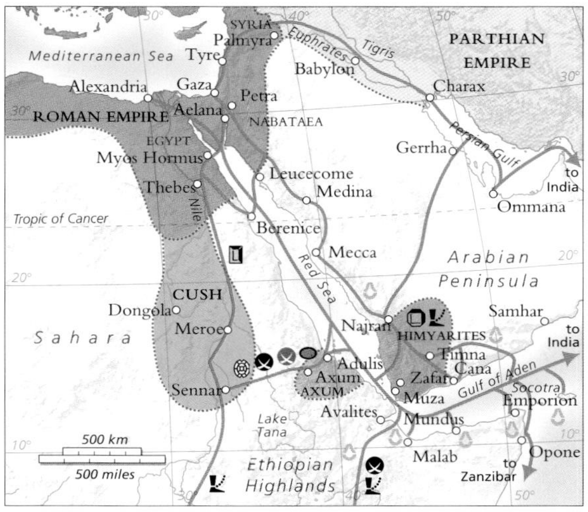

Mediterranean Sea
SYRIA
Palmyra
Tyre
Euphrates
Tigris
PARTHIAN EMPIRE
Babylon
Charax
Alexandria
Gaza
Petra
Aelana
ROMAN EMPIRE
NABATAEA
EGYPT
Myos Hormus
Gerrha
Persian Gulf
Leucecome
Medina
Thebes
Nile
to India
Ommana
Tropic of Cancer
Berenice
Mecca
Arabian Peninsula
Red Sea
CUSH
Dongola
Meroe
Sahara
Samhar
Najran
HIMYARITES
to India
Timna
Cana
Sennar
Adulis
Axum
AXUM
Zafar
Gulf of Aden
Socotra
Emporion
Avalites
Mundus
Lake Tana
Opone
Malab
Ethiopian Highlands
to Zanzibar
500 km
500 miles

4 Northeast Africa 350 CE

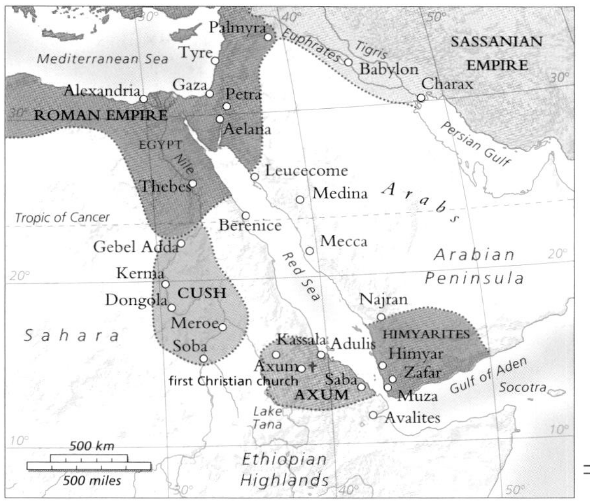

Mediterranean Sea
Palmyra
Tyre
Euphrates
Tigris
Babylon
SASSANIAN EMPIRE
Charax
Alexandria
Gaza
Petra
ROMAN EMPIRE
Aelana
EGYPT
Persian Gulf
Leucecome
Medina
Arabs
Thebes
Nile
Tropic of Cancer
Berenice
Gebel Adda
Mecca
Arabian Peninsula
Kerma
Dongola
CUSH
Red Sea
Najran
Meroe
Sahara
Soba
Kassala
Adulis
HIMYARITES
Himyar
Axum
Zafar
first Christian church
Saba
AXUM
Muza
Gulf of Aden
Socotra
Avalites
Lake Tana
Ethiopian Highlands
500 km
500 miles

5 Northeast Africa 500 CE

early Christian church 350 CE–600 CE

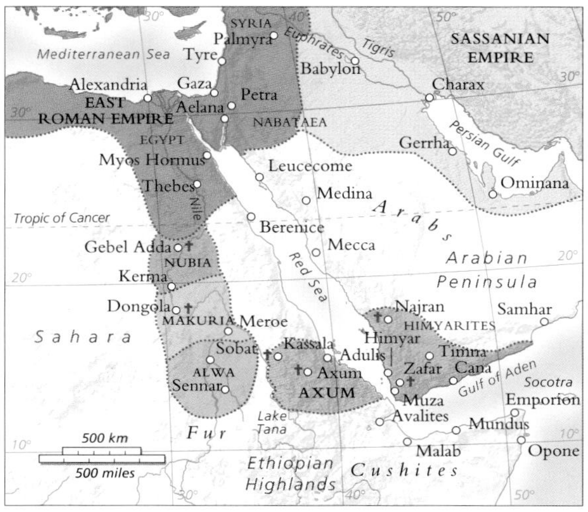

SYRIA
Palmyra
Mediterranean Sea
Tyre
Euphrates
Tigris
SASSANIAN EMPIRE
Babylon
Charax
Alexandria
Gaza
Petra
EAST ROMAN EMPIRE
Aelana
NABATAEA
EGYPT
Gerrha
Persian Gulf
Myos Hormus
Leucecome
Thebes
Ommana
Medina
Tropic of Cancer
Arabs
Berenice
Gebel Adda
Mecca
NUBIA
Kerma
Arabian Peninsula
Red Sea
Dongola
MAKURIA
Meroe
Najran
Samhar
HIMYARITES
Sahara
Soba
Kassala
Himyar
Timna
Adulis
Zafar
Cana
ALWA
Axum
Sennar
AXUM
Muza
Gulf of Aden
Socotra
Emporion
Avalites
Mundus
Fur
Lake Tana
Malab
Opone
Ethiopian Highlands
Cushites
500 km
500 miles

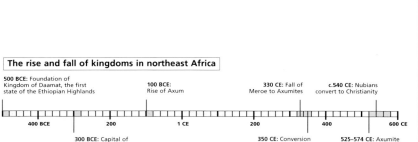

ISLAM AND NEW STATES IN AFRICA

Unearthed on the island of Pemba, these North African gold coins testify to Swahili trade with the Arab world.

FROM THE **10TH CENTURY, A SERIES** of empires arose in the sub-Saharan savannah. They attracted Muslim Arab traders who traveled south in search of salt, gold, and slaves. Through frequent contact, Islam gradually infiltrated the region by means of peaceful conversion. When the Muslim Berber Almoravids captured the capital of Ghana in 1076, causing the collapse of the empire, their conquest did little to advance the spread of Islam. Christian Ethiopia also withstood Muslim advances. However, Ghana's successors, Mali and Songhay, owed much of their wealth and civilization to the advent and adoption of Islam, as did the Kanem-Bornu Empire around Lake Chad, and, after the 15th century, the Hausa city-states. From the late 10th century, Arab merchant colonies were established in the coastal towns of East Africa, stimulating African trade with Arabia and India, and accelerating the southward spread of Islam.

African trade and the spread of Islam

Built in the 14th century, the great mosque at Jenne in Mali was constructed with sun-dried mud bricks.

Islamic expansion out of Arabia began in earnest following the death of the Prophet Muhammad in 632. By 640 Egypt had fallen into the hands of Muslim soldiers and settlers. From the 8th century, traders and clerics were the agents of Islam, spreading the religion along the commercial arteries of the Sahara which extended into West Africa, and up the Nile. By the 13th century the Saifawa kings of Kanem had adopted the faith. Islam had also traveled down the east coast of Africa, taken by seafaring Arabs who set up coastal trading centers. Trade between Arabs and Bantus necessitated a new language, so Swahili became the *lingua franca* of the east coast.

Carved by West African craftsmen, this 16th-century ivory horn *(above)* was produced for the European market. This is confirmed by its Portuguese-style inscriptions.

Dating from the 16th century, this blue and white Ming dynasty bowl *(left)* was found on the east coast of Africa, providing evidence of trade with China.

Islamic expansion in Africa from 600

- **632:** Death of Muhammad
- **635–40:** Conquest of Egypt by Arabs
- **c.800:** Emergence of trading towns on East African coast.
- **909:** Fatimid dynasty founded by Ubaydullah
- **1050:** King of Takrur converts to Islam
- **1270:** Beginning of Solomid dynasty in Ethiopia

| 600 | 700 | 800 | 900 | 1000 | 1100 | 1200 | 1300 |

- **625:** First Islamic Arab invasion of Makuria
- **680:** Arab armies reach Atlantic at Morocco
- **1076:** King of Ghana converts to Islam

① African trade and the spread of Islam 500–1500 ▶

- ------ frontiers 1500
- → Muslim trade routes
- limit of Muslim influence by 900
- limit of Muslim influence by 1100
- limit of Muslim influence by 1300
- limit of Muslim influence by 1500
- limit of Muslim influence in Spain 1492
- Christians c.1100
- Christians c.1500
- ◉ Portuguese possession in 1500

- copper
- gold
- dates
- fish
- flour
- ivory
- kola nuts
- leather
- porcelain
- perfume
- saffron
- salt
- silk
- slaves
- spice
- wax
- wool

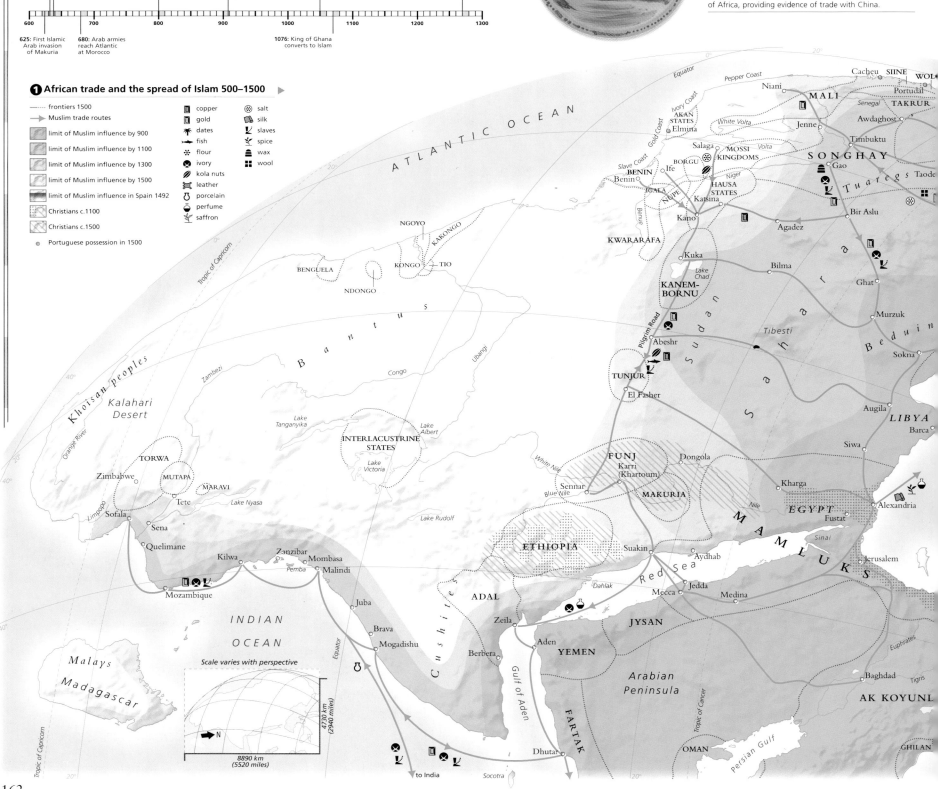

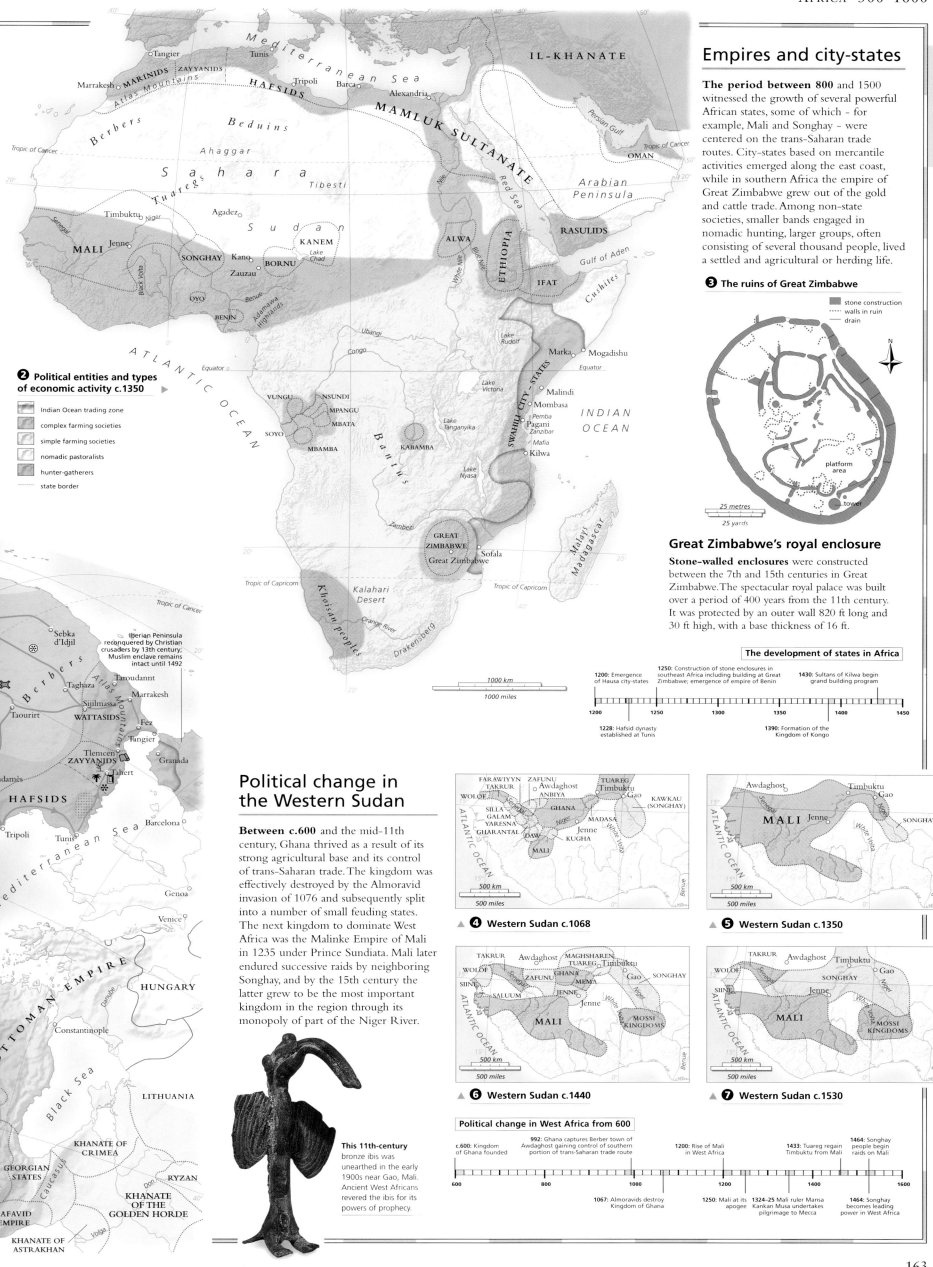

Empires and city-states

The period between 800 and 1500 witnessed the growth of several powerful African states, some of which - for example, Mali and Songhay - were centered on the trans-Saharan trade routes. City-states based on mercantile activities emerged along the east coast, while in southern Africa the empire of Great Zimbabwe grew out of the gold and cattle trade. Among non-state societies, smaller bands engaged in nomadic hunting, larger groups, often consisting of several thousand people, lived a settled and agricultural or herding life.

❸ The ruins of Great Zimbabwe

- ▮ stone construction
- ⋯ walls in ruin
- — drain

platform area

tower

25 metres
25 yards

Great Zimbabwe's royal enclosure

Stone-walled enclosures were constructed between the 7th and 15th centuries in Great Zimbabwe. The spectacular royal palace was built over a period of 400 years from the 11th century. It was protected by an outer wall 820 ft long and 30 ft high, with a base thickness of 16 ft.

The development of states in Africa

1200: Emergence of Hausa city-states	1250: Construction of stone enclosures in southeast Africa including building at Great Zimbabwe; emergence of empire of Benin			1430: Sultans of Kilwa begin grand building program	

| 1200 | 1250 | 1300 | 1350 | 1400 | 1450 |

1228: Hafsid dynasty established at Tunis

1390: Formation of the Kingdom of Kongo

❷ Political entities and types of economic activity c.1350 ▶

- ▮ Indian Ocean trading zone
- ▮ complex farming societies
- ▮ simple farming societies
- ▯ nomadic pastoralists
- ▮ hunter-gatherers
- ⋯ state border

Iberian Peninsula reconquered by Christian crusaders by 13th century; Muslim enclave remains intact until 1492

Political change in the Western Sudan

Between c.600 and the mid-11th century, Ghana thrived as a result of its strong agricultural base and its control of trans-Saharan trade. The kingdom was effectively destroyed by the Almoravid invasion of 1076 and subsequently split into a number of small feuding states. The next kingdom to dominate West Africa was the Malinke Empire of Mali in 1235 under Prince Sundiata. Mali later endured successive raids by neighboring Songhay, and by the 15th century the latter grew to be the most important kingdom in the region through its monopoly of part of the Niger River.

This 11th-century bronze ibis was unearthed in the early 1900s near Gao, Mali. Ancient West Africans revered the ibis for its powers of prophecy.

❹ Western Sudan c.1068

500 km
500 miles

❺ Western Sudan c.1350

500 km
500 miles

❻ Western Sudan c.1440

500 km
500 miles

❼ Western Sudan c.1530

500 km
500 miles

Political change in West Africa from 600

c.600: Kingdom of Ghana founded	992: Ghana captures Berber town of Awdaghost gaining control of southern portion of trans-Saharan trade route		1200: Rise of Mali in West Africa	1433: Tuareg regain Timbuktu from Mali	1464: Songhay people begin raids on Mali

| 600 | 800 | 1000 | 1200 | 1400 | 1600 |

1067: Almoravids destroy Kingdom of Ghana

1250: Mali at its apogee

1324–25 Mali ruler Mansa Kankan Musa undertakes pilgrimage to Mecca

1464: Songhay becomes leading power in West Africa

1000 km
1000 miles

EARLY MODERN AFRICA

Asante's well-armed warriors made it the most powerful state on the Gold Coast.

AFTER THE PORTUGUESE had led European expansion into Africa in the 15th century, a few colonies were established – in Angola, along the Zambezi Valley, and in the region of the Cape of Good Hope – but for the most part, African rulers contained and controlled the activities of the newcomers. In parts of West Africa they allowed Europeans to establish coastal forts and trading posts. With this new presence came increased opportunities for external trade, principally in gold, ivory, and slaves. After 1700, however, the importance of all other goods was totally eclipsed by the value of the Atlantic slave trade.

The 16th century saw the Ottoman Empire advance across North Africa as far as the Atlas Mountains. To the south, the great empire of Songhay yielded to Moroccan invaders in 1591, though the cycle of empires continued in West Africa with Great Fulo. In the early 18th century powerful coastal kingdoms arose in Asante and Dahomey, while Rozwi replaced Mwenemutapa in southeast Africa.

Southern and East Africa

The Portuguese presence in the region was challenged in the 17th century by the Rozwi empire, which drove them from the highlands of Zimbabwe, while Omani fleets captured many of their coastal forts in East Africa. Portugal was left with the semi-independent *prazos* (estates) of the Zambezi valley and the coastal towns of Sofala, Mozambique, and Inhambane. In 1652 the Dutch East India Company founded its colony at Cape Town. Rapid expansion in the 18th century brought Dutch settlers into conflict with the many small states of the Nguni region.

Fort Jesus, built in 1593 to protect Portuguese trading interests in Mombasa, fell to the Omanis in 1698.

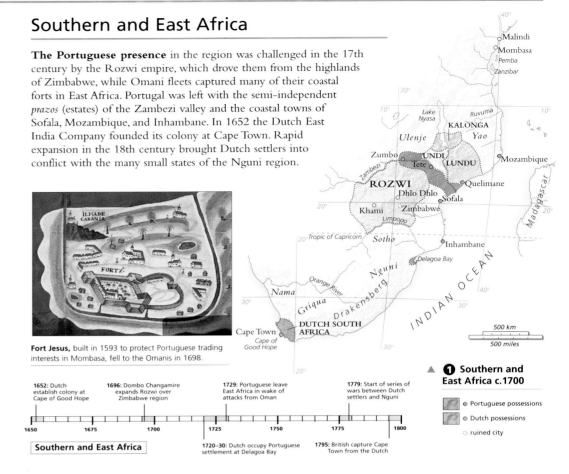

① Southern and East Africa c.1700

- Portuguese possessions
- Dutch possessions
- ruined city

1652: Dutch establish colony at Cape of Good Hope
1696: Dombo Changamire expands Rozwi over Zimbabwe region
1729: Portuguese leave East Africa in wake of attacks from Oman
1779: Start of series of wars between Dutch settlers and Nguni

1650 — 1675 — 1700 — 1725 — 1750 — 1775 — 1800

Southern and East Africa

1720–30: Dutch occupy Portuguese settlement at Delagoa Bay
1795: British capture Cape Town from the Dutch

The Fulbe, who lived by raising cattle for their neighbors, were found throughout much of West Africa. This 1730 engraving shows a Fulbe town on the Gambia River with a plantation and a corral for livestock.

African political development

In the 17th century, much of sub-Saharan Africa consisted of many small, self-governing units, typically about 30 miles across. In West Africa some 70% of the population probably lived in these "ministates." Boundaries remained stable for long periods, the people choosing their leaders on the basis of heredity, election, or other local customs. There were extensive empires such as Songhay and Mali, but these lay in the sparsely populated region now known as the Sahel. These and the other larger states, which ruled the remainder of the population, usually grew by incorporating smaller units, although they continued to use the local polities to enforce the law and raise tribute. Taxation took the form of a head or house tax. There was no concept of land ownership; it could not be bought or sold. Land was regarded as belonging to whoever farmed it. Slave ownership, on the other hand, was an important measure of personal wealth.

The formidable Queen Njinga ruled the kingdom of Ndongo from 1624 to 1663. She fought the Portuguese to a standstill.

② States of West and Central Africa 1625

- Portuguese possessions
- Dutch settlement

1624: Start of reign of Queen Njinga of Ndongo
1665: Civil war breaks out in Kongo, seriously weakening the kingdom
1701: Start of Asante's rise to prominence under Osei Tutu
1727: Dahomey's troops capture Whydah
1776: Abd al-Kadir leads Muslims in holy war along the Senegal River

1600 — 1625 — 1650 — 1675 — 1700 — 1725 — 1750 — 1775 — 1800

1591: Moroccan invaders destroy Songhay Empire
1637: Dutch take Portuguese fort of Elmina
c.1660: Collapse of Mali Empire
c.1730: Emergence of Fulbe confederation of Futa Jallon

West and Central Africa

The struggle for the Horn of Africa

Ethiopia's domination of the region came to an end in the 16th century. The Christian empire's expansion into Muslim lands to the south had often involved forced conversion and the destruction of Islamic literature and places of worship. In 1529 a dynamic imam from Adal, Ahmad Grañ, proclaimed a holy war against Ethiopia, winning many striking victories. In 1540 the Ethiopians sought aid from Portugal and Grañ was killed in battle in 1543. This ultimately inconclusive war laid waste the region, which allowed the Oromo to invade from the south. Organized in many independent mobile bands, they took over both Christian and Muslim lands and founded new kingdoms of their own. Many Oromo embraced Islam and some fought as mercenaries in civil wars in Ethiopia. The fortunes of the Ethiopian empire revived somewhat in the Gondar period in the 17th century, but its lands were much reduced.

1529: Ahmad Grañ leads *jihad* against Ethiopia	**1540:** Portuguese come to the aid of Ethiopia	**1597:** Start of period of civil war	**1636:** King Fasiladas founds permanent capital at Gondar	**1682:** Accession of Iyasu I, last great king of Gondar period

The decline of Ethiopia

1543: Death of Ahmad Grañ, shot by a Portuguese musketeer
1590: Oromo bands begin occupation of southern Ethiopia
1632: End of civil wars. Jesuit missionaries expelled from Ethiopia

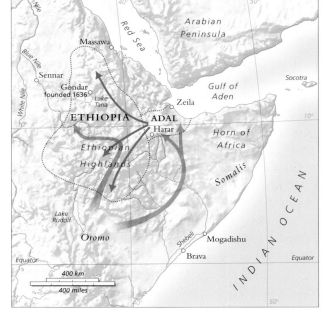

→ Jihad of Ahmad Grañ 1529–43
⇒ Oromo expansion 1550–1700
········ approximate state border 1500

Ethiopian King Fasiladas built the city of Gondar and this magnificent castle in 1636. Before his reign, the rulers of Ethiopia had never had a fixed residence, instead setting up a tented court for periods of six months to a year, then moving on to another part of the kingdom.

4 The African slave trade c.1750 ▶

Ottoman Empire
○ Portuguese possessions
○ Dutch possessions
○ French settlement
○ British settlement

Principal slave routes
⇒ Arab routes
⇒ British routes
⇒ Danish routes
⇒ Dutch routes
⇒ French routes
⇒ Moroccan routes
⇒ Portuguese routes

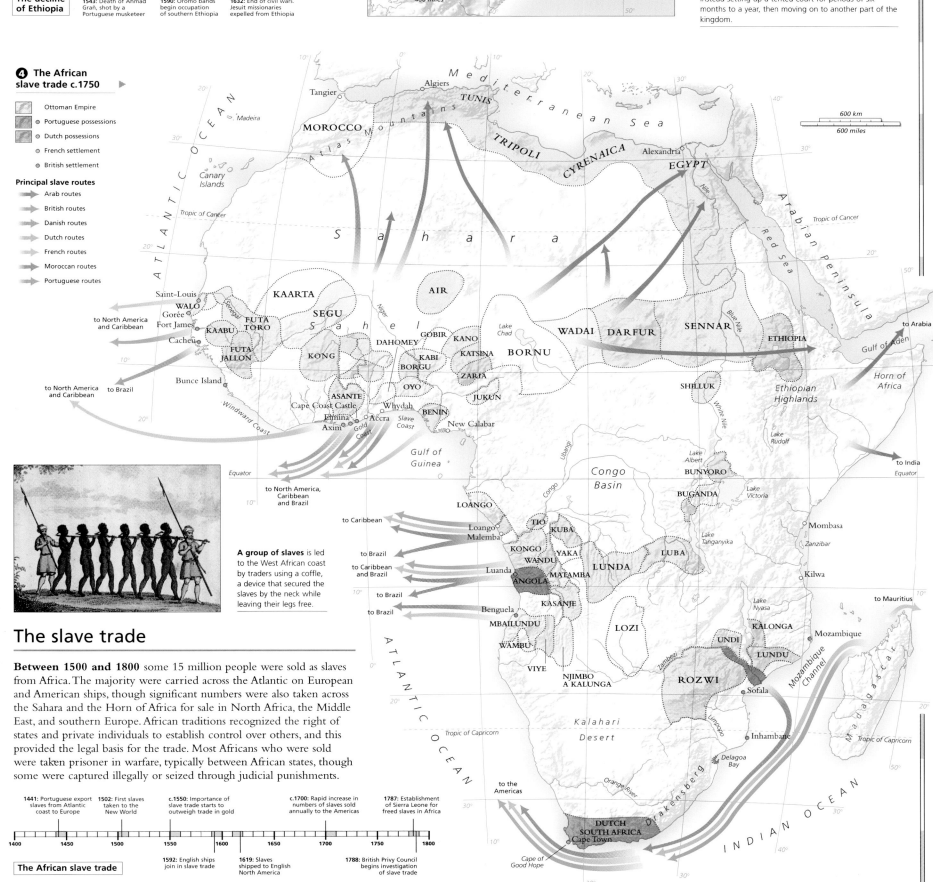

A group of slaves is led to the West African coast by traders using a coffle, a device that secured the slaves by the neck while leaving their legs free.

The slave trade

Between 1500 and 1800 some 15 million people were sold as slaves from Africa. The majority were carried across the Atlantic on European and American ships, though significant numbers were also taken across the Sahara and the Horn of Africa for sale in North Africa, the Middle East, and southern Europe. African traditions recognized the right of states and private individuals to establish control over others, and this provided the legal basis for the trade. Most Africans who were sold were taken prisoner in warfare, typically between African states, though some were captured illegally or seized through judicial punishments.

1441: Portuguese export slaves from Atlantic coast to Europe	**1502:** First slaves taken to the New World	**c.1550:** Importance of slave trade starts to outweigh trade in gold	**c.1700:** Rapid increase in numbers of slaves sold annually to the Americas	**1787:** Establishment of Sierra Leone for freed slaves in Africa

The African slave trade

1592: English ships join in slave trade
1619: Slaves shipped to English North America
1788: British Privy Council begins investigation of slave trade

THE COLONIZATION OF AFRICA

Cecil Rhodes, the embodiment of colonialism, planned to extend British rule in Africa from Cairo to Cape Town.

THE 19TH CENTURY was a period of revolutionary change in Africa. The states of West Africa were convulsed by a series of reformist Islamic *jihads*, while in the south the rise of Zulu militarism had catastrophic consequences for neighboring peoples. By the mid-19th century Africa was also undergoing a commercial revolution. Europeans could now offer high-quality machined goods in large quantities. As a result, Africa was condemned to the role of producer of primary goods. By the end of the century, many African kingdoms and clan-based communities were being replaced by states organized along indigenous lines. However, this process was forestalled by the decision of the major European powers to carve up the continent between them.

Commerce in the 19th century

The Arab slave trader Tibbu Tib organized his own state and security system in 1875 with the help of armed followers.

The development of new export goods in Europe had social implications for Africa. Reduced shipping costs brought about by the introduction of the steamship meant that European textile and metal goods arrived in force. The resultant decline in local industries was accompanied by a growth in the internal slave trade. The substantial carrying trade, especially the porterage trade of East and Central Africa, was run by small-scale entrepreneurs. While such ventures did not bring large profit, those involved enjoyed new and elevated social positions. Often the carrying trade was organized from a particular region, giving it an ethnic character. Enterprising African traders took advantage of the expanding economy to gain political power – for example, the copper trader Msiri won himself a kingdom.

Commercial Africa from 1815

1816: Wool mills, flax mills, sugar refineries, indigo factories, and glassworks established in Egypt	**c.1850:** Atlantic slave trade, including clandestine operations, begins to die out	**1875:** Tibbu Tib establishes trading principality

1815 1825 1835 1845 1855 1865 1875

1830: 20,000 slaves exported from central African ports to Brazil

1866: Copper trader Msiri establishes trading principality

❶ Commercial and political Africa c.1830

- cloves
- cocoa
- coffee
- copper
- cotton
- diamonds
- gold
- gum arabic
- honey and wax
- ivory
- olives
- palm products
- peanuts
- rubber
- slaves/migrant workers
- wheat
- wine
- trade route

- British possession
- French possession
- Ottoman territory
- Portuguese possession
- Spanish possession
- commercial group

Zulu and Afrikaner expansion

Under the leadership of Shaka, the Zulu were organized into a highly militarized kingdom. They conquered neighboring Nguni tribes and set off a series of wars which depopulated large parts of the southern interior, leaving it vulnerable to Afrikaner expansion. Afrikaners left Cape Colony between 1835 and the 1840s in search of pastureland and to escape from unwelcome British rule. They successfully defeated powerful military kingdoms as they progressed northward.

British reforms, such as the abolition of slavery, caused the exodus of many Boers from Cape Colony. They undertook the "Great Trek" in ox-drawn wagons.

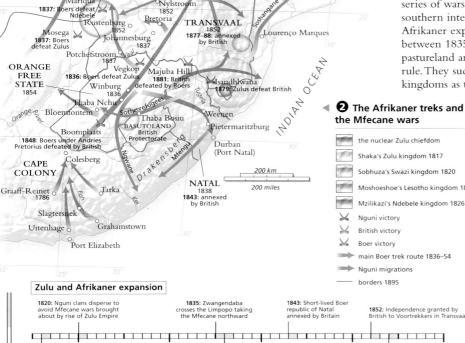

❷ The Afrikaner treks and the Mfecane wars

- the nuclear Zulu chiefdom
- Shaka's Zulu kingdom 1817
- Sobhuza's Swazi kingdom 1820
- Moshoeshoe's Lesotho kingdom 1824
- Mzilikazi's Ndebele kingdom 1826
- Nguni victory
- British victory
- Boer victory
- main Boer trek route 1836–54
- Nguni migrations
- borders 1895

Shaka armed the Zulu with long-bladed stabbing *assegais*, which forced them to fight at close quarters. Shield markings and headdress distinguished different regiments.

Zulu and Afrikaner expansion

1820: Nguni clans disperse to avoid Mfecane wars brought about by rise of Zulu Empire	**1835:** Zwangendaba crosses the Limpopo taking the Mfecane northward	**1843:** Short-lived Boer republic of Natal annexed by Britain	**1852:** Independence granted by British to Voortrekkers in Transvaal

1820 1830 1840 1850 1860

1816: Shaka becomes leader of the Zulu, a clan of the Nguni

1836: Start of the Great Trek

1854: Boers found the Orange Free State

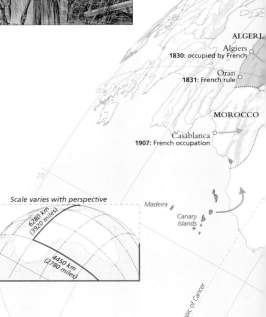

1830: occupied by French

1831: French rule

1907: French occupation

Scale varies with perspective

Islamic wars in western Africa

1807: Hausa kings replaced by Fulani emirs

1820: Usuman dan Fodio establishes Sokoto Fulani Kingdom

1852: 'Umar Tal conquers the Senegal valley

1861: 'Umar Tal's forces conquer Segu

1800 | 1810 | 1820 | 1830 | 1840 | 1850 | 1860 | 1870

1804: Jihad of Usuman dan Fodio

1816: Inspired by Usuman dan Fodio, Amadu Lobbo launches jihad in Masina

1863: Timbuktu falls to 'Umar Tal; he founds Tukulor Empire

1864: 'Umar Tal is killed attempting to suppress Fulani rebellion

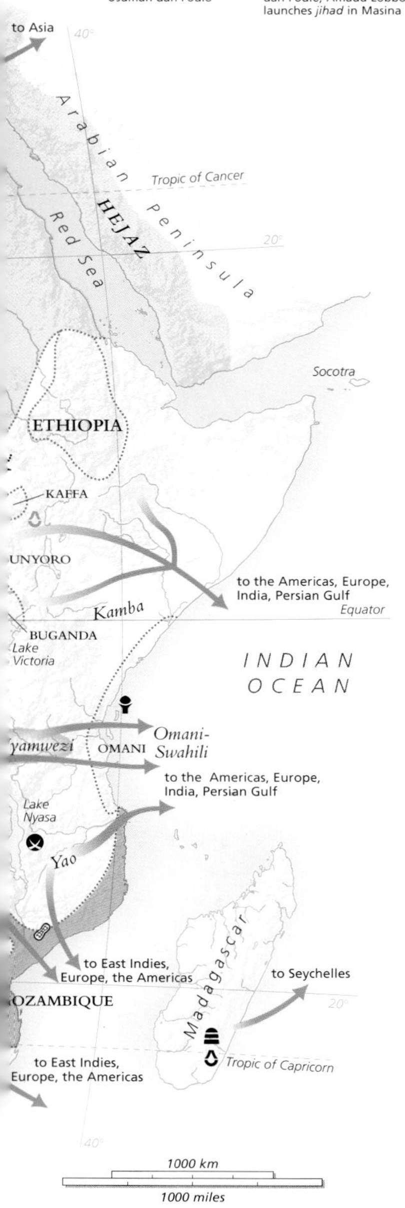

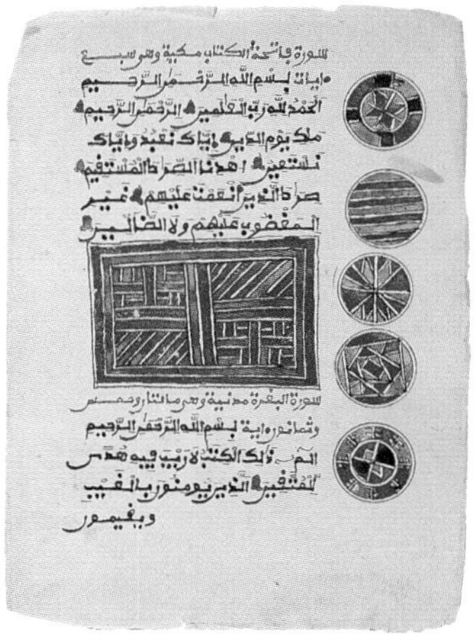

The text of this richly decorated 19th-century Koran is written in West African Sudani script. The large rectangular design marks the end of a chapter.

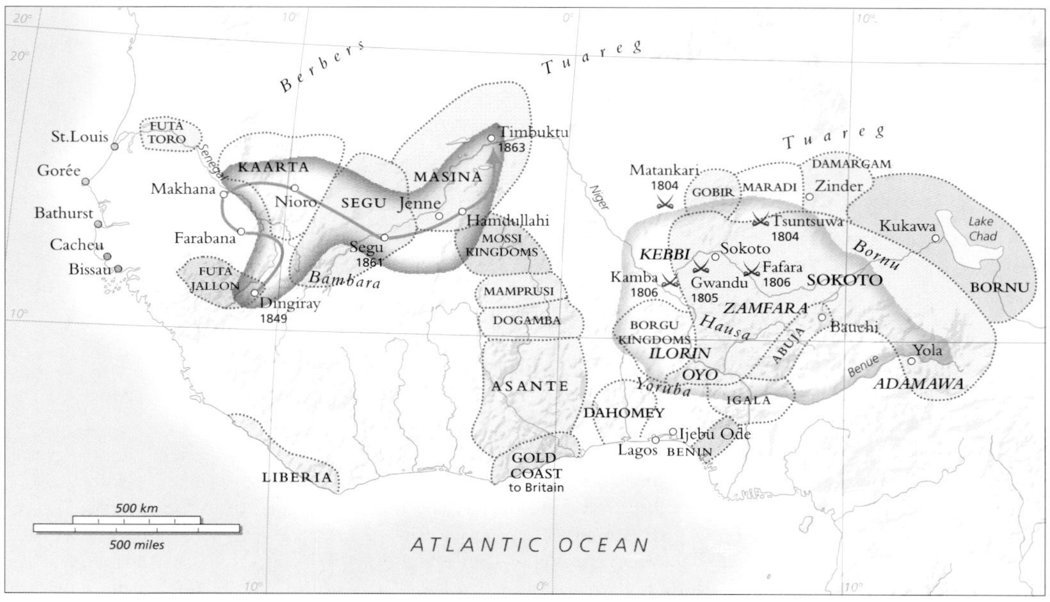

Islamic reform in West Africa

The jihads of West Africa were a source of major turmoil in the 19th century. The idea that reformers could overthrow governments they thought were unjust was deeply rooted in the region, and dated back to the 11th century Almoravid movement. Holy men challenged rulers, often because of their tyranny and corruption, and demanded change. Social problems also promoted reform, for example, Fula herdsmen often backed reformers against those who taxed and mistreated them. In other cases, it was humble peasants or slaves who converted to Islam. Tukulor cleric Usuman dan Fodio's jihad in Hausaland in 1804, led to the establishment of the islamic Sokoto Fulani Kingdom in 1820. Fulani cleric, al-Hajj 'Umar Tal set about reforming the Segu region in 1851 and by 1863 had founded the Tukulor Empire.

❸ 19th-century West African jihads ▶

- Sokoto Fulani Kingdom c.1820
- Tukulor Empire c.1864
- ⊙ British possession
- ⊙ French possession
- ⊙ Portuguese possesssion
- → jihad route of al-Hajj 'Umar Tal
- ⋯ borders c.1850
- ✕ conflict

500 km
500 miles

The conquest of the interior

The years after 1885 saw a race to complete the conquest of the African interior (see p.96). International rivalries between European powers, coupled with local merchant competition and the popularity of African conquest in the home arena, ensured European governmental interest in the continent. In many cases, initial conquests were funded by commercial interests, such as Cecil Rhodes' De Beers Consolidated Mines company. Most of the fighting personnel were Africans, hired mercenaries, or militarily trained slaves. The use of commercial contacts with African traders and the exploitation of local rivalries were as effective as brute force and the machine gun.

The conquest of Africa from 1880

1883: France begins its conquest of Madagascar

1884: Berlin Conference on Africa; Samory Touré proclaims his Islamic theocracy

1894: Britain occupies Buganda

1896: France takes Madagascar

1900-01: Britain annexes Asante

1908: Belgium takes over Congo Free State

1880 | 1890 | 1900 | 1910

1882: Britain occupies Egypt; Congo Free State formed by King Leopold of Belgium

1889: Italy establishes its first colony in Eritrea

1892: France destroys the Tukulor Empire

1904: French create federation of French West Africa

❹ European penetration of Africa ▼

Colonial territory c.1880
- Ottoman suzerainty
- British
- Portuguese
- French
- Spanish
- Boer Republics
- frontier of Christian missionary activities c.1880

European routes of expansion
- → Belgian
- → British
- → French
- → German
- → Italian
- → Portuguese
- → Spanish
- → main lines of missionary advance
- 1888 foundation date of colonial settlement

Colonial settlements
- ⊙ Belgian
- ⊙ Boer
- ⊙ British
- ⊙ French
- ⊙ German
- ⊙ Italian
- ⊙ Portuguese
- ○ other settlement

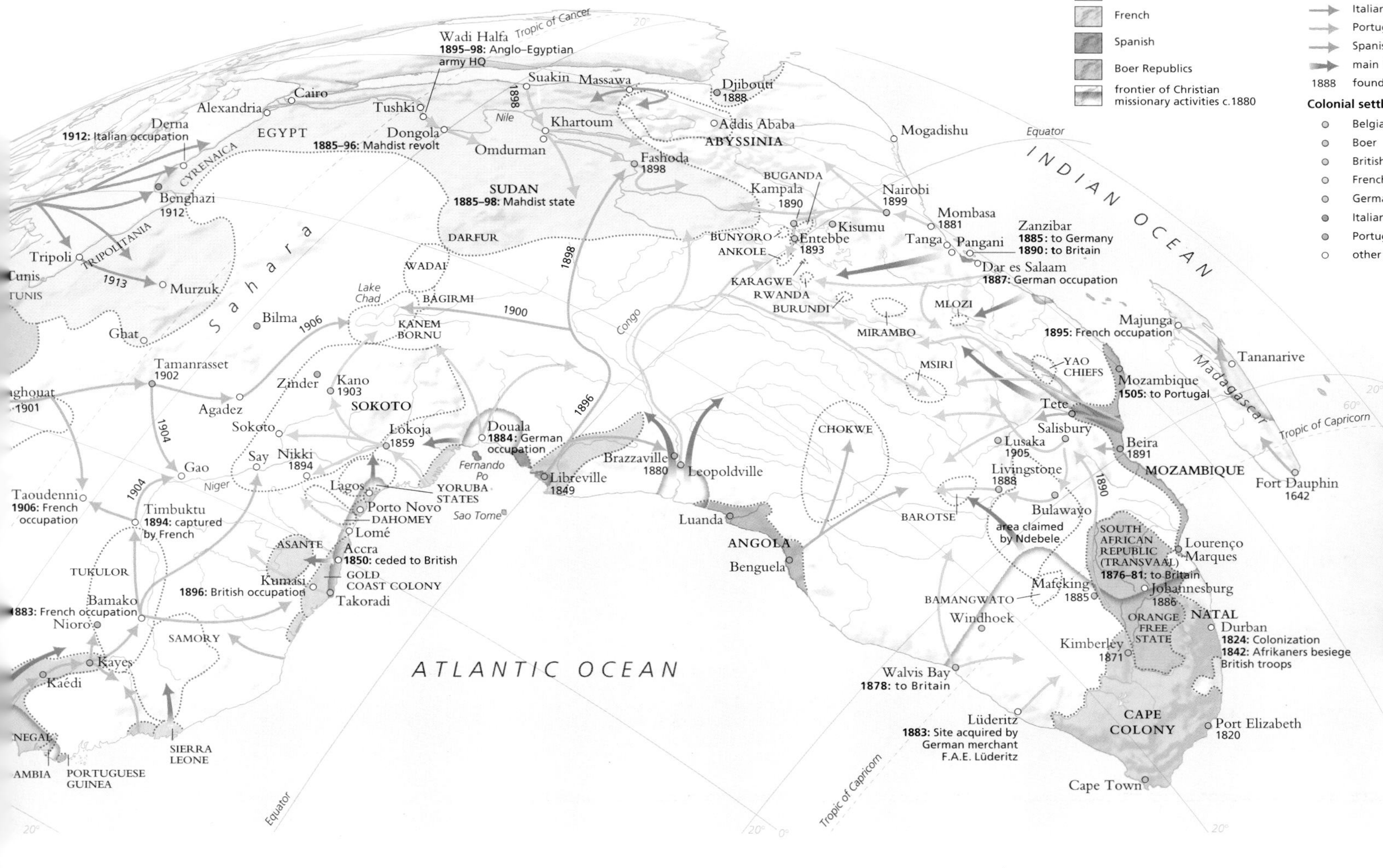

Armed and trained by France, these African soldiers, known as the Senegalese Rifles, helped France win territory in Africa.

POST-COLONIAL AFRICA

Julius Nyerere led the fight for independence in Tanganyika.

INDEPENDENT AFRICAN STATES, with few exceptions, were territorially identical to the European colonies they replaced. Most African countries gained independence between 1956 to 1968 and in many cases hasty attempts were made to set up European-style forms of government. However, leaders often became dictators, or the army seized power; many governments were corrupt and a number of countries were devastated by war. Moves were made towards multiparty democracy, most notably in South Africa, where the system of apartheid was dismantled in 1990.

African independence

After World War II the colonial powers in Africa faced demands for self-determination, and most countries gained independence around 1960. In the face of widespread opposition, Portugal clung on to its territories through the 1960s. This resulted in long and bloody wars in Angola, Guinea-Bissau, and Mozambique. There were also protracted struggles for majority rule in the former British colonies of Zimbabwe and South Africa. The presidential election victory of Nelson Mandela in 1994 marked the end of white minority rule in South Africa.

The national flag is raised in Ghana during an independence ceremony. The country was declared a republic on July 1, 1960, with Dr. Kwame Nkrumah as the first president.

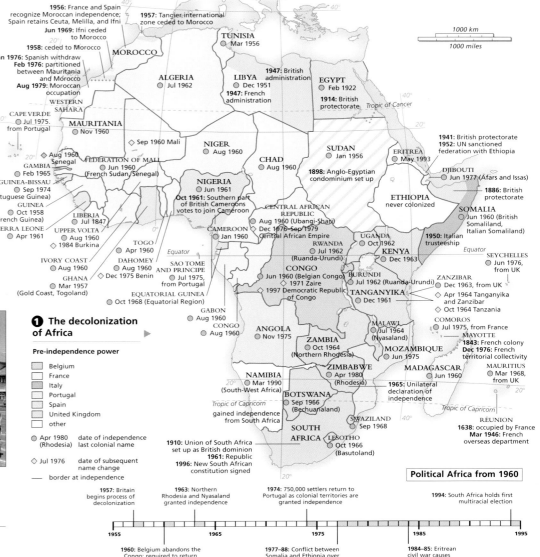

1 The decolonization of Africa

Pre-independence power

- Belgium
- France
- Italy
- Portugal
- Spain
- United Kingdom
- other

Apr 1980 (Rhodesia) — date of independence / last colonial name
Jul 1976 — date of subsequent name change
— border at independence

Political Africa from 1960

Timeline:

1957: Britain begins process of decolonization
1960: Belgium abandons the Congo; required to return to restore order weeks later
1963: Northern Rhodesia and Nyasaland granted independence
1974: 750,000 settlers return to Portugal as colonial territories are granted independence
1977–88: Conflict between Somalia and Ethiopia over claims to Ogaden region
1984–85: Eritrean civil war causes widespread famine
1994: South Africa holds first multiracial election

1955 · 1965 · 1975 · 1985 · 1995

The African economy

Industrial growth is government policy in a number of countries in Africa, and is seen as the way to progress economically. Countries with large manufacturing sectors include South Africa and oil-rich states such as Nigeria, Algeria, and Libya. Many other states rely on a single resource or cash crop for export income, leaving them vulnerable to market fluctuations.

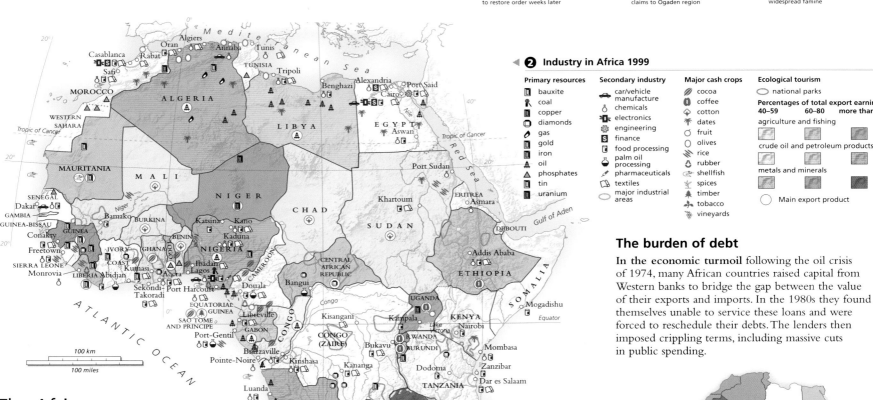

2 Industry in Africa 1999

Primary resources
- bauxite
- coal
- copper
- diamonds
- gas
- gold
- iron
- oil
- phosphates
- tin
- uranium

Secondary industry
- car/vehicle manufacture
- chemicals
- electronics
- engineering
- finance
- food processing
- palm oil processing
- pharmaceuticals
- textiles
- major industrial areas

Major cash crops
- cocoa
- coffee
- cotton
- dates
- fruit
- olives
- rice
- rubber
- shellfish
- spices
- timber
- tobacco
- vineyards

Ecological tourism
- national parks

Percentages of total export earnings
40–59 · 60–80 · more than 80
- agriculture and fishing
- crude oil and petroleum products
- metals and minerals

○ Main export product

The burden of debt

In the economic turmoil following the oil crisis of 1974, many African countries raised capital from Western banks to bridge the gap between the value of their exports and imports. In the 1980s they found themselves unable to service these loans and were forced to reschedule their debts. The lenders then imposed crippling terms, including massive cuts in public spending.

3 Debt as a percentage of GNP, 1999

- 0–24%
- 25–49%
- 50–99%
- 100–200%
- over 200%
- unknown

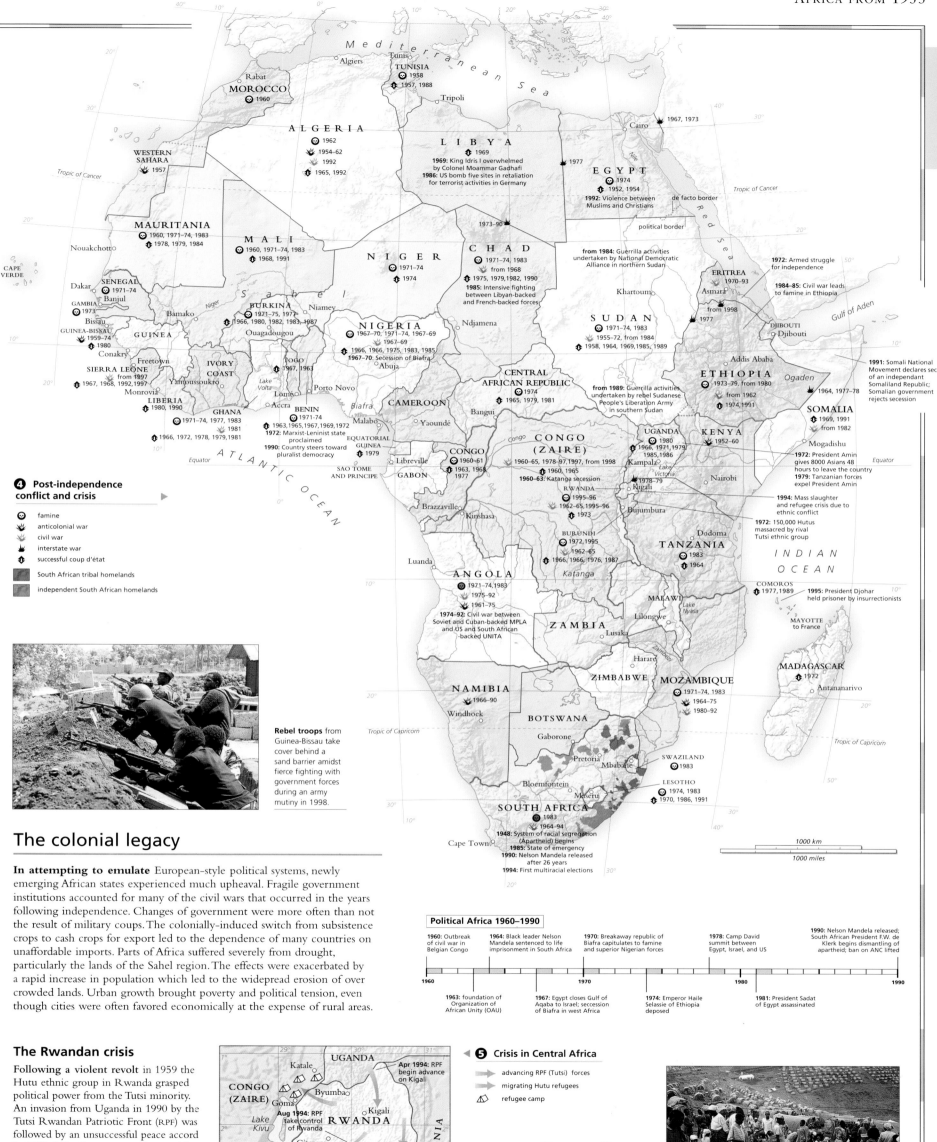

Post-independence conflict and crisis

- famine
- anticolonial war
- civil war
- interstate war
- successful coup d'état
- South African tribal homelands
- independent South African homelands

1969: King Idris I overwhelmed by Colonel Moammar Gadhafi
1986: US bomb five sites in retaliation for terrorist activities in Germany

1992: Violence between Muslims and Christians

from 1984: Guerrilla activities undertaken by National Democratic Alliance in northern Sudan

1972: Armed struggle for independence

1984–85: Civil war leads to famine in Ethiopia

1991: Somali National Movement declares secession of an independant Somaliland Republic; Somalian government rejects secession

1985: Intensive fighting between Libyan-backed and French-backed forces

1972: Marxist-Leninist state proclaimed
1990: Country steers toward pluralist democracy

1967–70: Secession of Biafra

from 1989: Guerrilla activities undertaken by rebel Sudanese People's Liberation Army in southern Sudan

1972: President Amin gives 8000 Asians 48 hours to leave the country
1979: Tanzanian forces expel President Amin

1994: Mass slaughter and refugee crisis due to ethnic conflict

1972: 150,000 Hutus massacred by rival Tutsi ethnic group

1960–63: Katanga secession

1995: President Djohar held prisoner by insurrectionists

1974–92: Civil war between Soviet and Cuban-backed MPLA and US and South African-backed UNITA

1948: System of racial segregation (Apartheid) begins
1985: State of emergency
1990: Nelson Mandela released after 26 years
1994: First multiracial elections

Rebel troops from Guinea-Bissau take cover behind a sand barrier amidst fierce fighting with government forces during an army mutiny in 1998.

The colonial legacy

In attempting to emulate European-style political systems, newly emerging African states experienced much upheaval. Fragile government institutions accounted for many of the civil wars that occurred in the years following independence. Changes of government were more often than not the result of military coups. The colonially-induced switch from subsistence crops to cash crops for export led to the dependence of many countries on unaffordable imports. Parts of Africa suffered severely from drought, particularly the lands of the Sahel region. The effects were exacerbated by a rapid increase in population which led to the widepread erosion of over crowded lands. Urban growth brought poverty and political tension, even though cities were often favored economically at the expense of rural areas.

Political Africa 1960–1990

1960: Outbreak of civil war in Belgian Congo

1964: Black leader Nelson Mandela sentenced to life imprisonment in South Africa

1970: Breakaway republic of Biafra capitulates to famine and superior Nigerian forces

1978: Camp David summit between Egypt, Israel, and US

1990: Nelson Mandela released; South African President F.W. de Klerk begins dismantling of apartheid; ban on ANC lifted

1963: foundation of Organization of African Unity (OAU)

1967: Egypt closes Gulf of Aqaba to Israel; secession of Biafra in west Africa

1974: Emperor Haile Selassie of Ethiopia deposed

1981: President Sadat of Egypt assassinated

The Rwandan crisis

Following a violent revolt in 1959 the Hutu ethnic group in Rwanda grasped political power from the Tutsi minority. An invasion from Uganda in 1990 by the Tutsi Rwandan Patriotic Front (RPF) was followed by an unsuccessful peace accord in 1992. A fragile peace was shattered by the death of President Hyabyarimana in 1994. Genocidal violence ensued and an estimated 500,000 Tutsi were massacred. Two million Hutus subsequently fled the country, seeking refuge in nearby states.

Apr 1994: RPF begin advance on Kigali

Aug 1994: RPF take control of Rwanda

Crisis in Central Africa

- advancing RPF (Tutsi) forces
- migrating Hutu refugees
- refugee camp

In 1994 over two million Rwandans, the majority of whom were Hutu, fled to refugee camps in neighboring countries. Many were forced to live in unsanitary conditions and outbreaks of cholera in crowded camps killed thousands.

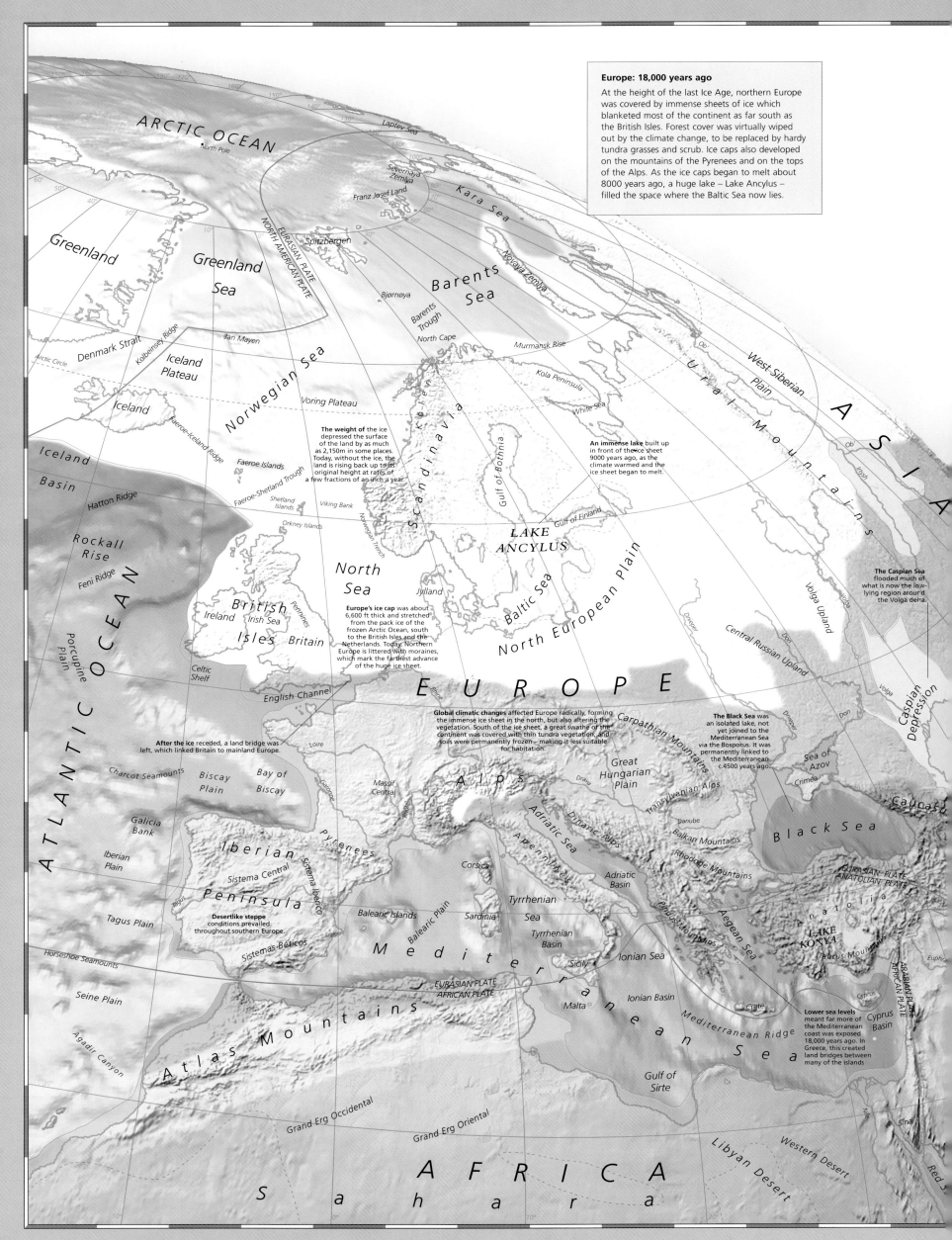

ARCTIC OCEAN

North Pole

Greenland

Greenland
Sea

Laptev Sea

Severnaya
Zemlya

Franz Josef Land

Kara Sea

ASIA

EURASIAN PLATE
NORTH AMERICAN PLATE

Spitzbergen

Novaya Zemlya

Barents
Sea

Bjørnøya

Barents
Trough

North Cape

Murmansk Rise

Ob

West Siberian
Plain

Irtysh

Ob

Ural Mountains

Denmark Strait

Arctic Circle

Kolbeinsey Ridge

Iceland
Plateau

Iceland

Faeroe-Iceland Ridge

Norwegian Sea

Voring Plateau

Kola Peninsula

White Sea

The weight of the ice
depressed the surface
of the land by as much
as 2,150m in some places.
Today, without the ice, the
land is rising back up to its
original height at rates of
a few fractions of an inch a year.

Gulf of Bothnia

An immense lake built up
in front of the ice sheet
9000 years ago, as the
climate warmed and the
ice sheet began to melt.

The Caspian Sea
flooded much of
what is now the low-
lying region around
the Volga delta.

Iceland
Basin

Hatton Ridge

Faeroe Islands

Faeroe-Shetland Trough

Shetland
Islands

Viking Bank

Scandinavia

Gulf of Finland

LAKE
ANCYLUS

Volga Upland

Volga

Rockall
Rise

Feni Ridge

Orkney Islands

Norwegian Trench

North
Sea

Jylland

Baltic Sea

Central Russian Upland

Dnieper

Caspian
Depression

ATLANTIC OCEAN

Porcupine
Plain

British
Isles

Ireland   Irish Sea

Pennines

Britain

Europe's ice cap was about
6,600 ft thick and stretched
from the pack ice of the
frozen Arctic Ocean, south
to the British Isles and the
Netherlands. Today, Northern
Europe is littered with moraines,
which mark the farthest advance
of the huge ice sheet.

North European Plain

Don

Volga

Celtic
Shelf

English Channel

Rhine

E U R O P E

Global climatic changes affected Europe radically, forming
the immense ice sheet in the north, but also altering the
vegetation. South of the ice sheet, a great swathe of the
continent was covered with thin tundra vegetation, and
soils were permanently frozen – making it less suitable
for habitation.

Carpathian Mountains

The Black Sea was
an isolated lake, not
yet joined to the
Mediterranean Sea
via the Bosporus. It was
permanently linked to
the Mediterranean
c.4500 years ago.

Sea of
Azov

Dnieper

Don

After the ice receded, a land bridge was
left, which linked Britain to mainland Europe.

Loire

Great
Hungarian
Plain

Crimea

Charcot Seamounts

Biscay
Plain

Bay of
Biscay

Garonne

Massif
Central

Rhone

A l p s

Drava

Danube

Transylvanian Alps

Caucasus

Black Sea

Galicia
Bank

Pyrenees

Adriatic Sea

Dinaric Alps

Balkan Mountains

EURASIAN PLATE
ANATOLIAN PLATE

Iberian
Plain

I b e r i a n

Ebro

Sistema Central

Sistema Ibérico

Corsica

Apennines

Adriatic
Basin

Rhodope Mountains

Aegean Sea

Anatolia

ARABIAN PLATE
AFRICAN PLATE

Tagus Plain

Tagus

P e n i n s u l a

Balearic Islands

Balearic Plain

Sardinia

Tyrrhenian
Sea

Pindus Mountains

LAKE
KONYA

Taurus Mountains

Euphra

Desertlike steppe
conditions prevailed
throughout southern Europe.

Sistemas Béticos

Tyrrhenian
Basin

Cyprus

Cyprus
Basin

Horseshoe Seamounts

M e d i t e r r a n e a n

Sicily

Ionian Sea

Crete

Seine Plain

Malta

Ionian Basin

M e d i t e r r a n e a n   S e a

Lower sea levels
meant far more of
the Mediterranean
coast was exposed
18,000 years ago. In
Greece, this created
land bridges between
many of the islands

Agadir Canyon

EURASIAN PLATE
AFRICAN PLATE

Mediterranean Ridge

Gulf of
Sirte

A t l a s   M o u n t a i n s

Grand Erg Occidental

Grand Erg Oriental

Libyan Desert

Western Desert

Sinai

Red S

A F R I C A

S a h a r a

Europe: 18,000 years ago

At the height of the last Ice Age, northern Europe
was covered by immense sheets of ice which
blanketed most of the continent as far south as
the British Isles. Forest cover was virtually wiped
out by the climate change, to be replaced by hardy
tundra grasses and scrub. Ice caps also developed
on the mountains of the Pyrenees and on the tops
of the Alps. As the ice caps began to melt about
8000 years ago, a huge lake – Lake Ancylus –
filled the space where the Baltic Sea now lies.

Vegetation type

- ice cap and glacier
- polar or alpine desert
- tundra
- semidesert or sparsely vegetated
- forest or open woodland
- temperate desert
- tropical desert
- desert
- coastline (present-day)
- coastline (18,000 years ago)

EUROPE
REGIONAL HISTORY

THE HISTORICAL LANDSCAPE

EUROPE, THE SECOND SMALLEST OF THE WORLD'S CONTINENTS, has a great diversity of topography, climate, and ecology, a rich pattern which contributed greatly to its inordinate influence on global history. Extensive oceanic and inland shorelines, abundantly fertile soils, and broadly temperate conditions provided innumerable heartlands for a wide array of cultures. Internecine rivalries created shifting patterns, themselves frequently overlaid by successive waves of migration and incursion. The shores of the Mediterranean provided a cradle for many powerful cultural groups, which formed myriad states and several empires until the 15th century, when the power base shifted to the emergent nations of the Atlantic coast. It was these aggressive, mercantile and pioneering maritime powers who vaulted Europe to a globally dominant position, through trade and colonialism, during the closing centuries of the 2nd millennium. As they collapsed, a seemingly ineradicable linguistic, economic, technological, and cultural imprint remained, which in the 20th century was widely adopted and adapted, creating an almost universal global culture.

During the Ice Age, the Alps were covered with extensive glacier systems that sculpted and carved the mountains into sharp pinnacles and peaks. The mountains provided a barrier between the cultures of the Mediterranean and those of Northern Europe.

The fertile plains of rivers such as the Danube provided the setting for early agricultural settlements, which spread north from the shores of the Aegean Sea from around 5000 BCE.

Europe's first cultures spread westward from Anatolia, reaching the fertile, often isolated coastal valleys around the Aegean between 7000 and 6000 BCE.

EUROPE
EXPLORATION AND MAPPING

The theodolite was first used in the 17th century. This model, dating from 1765 could measure both altitude and azimuth.

EUROPEANS LEARNED TO KNOW their lands by practical experience and scientific study. Trade and the acquisition of new land provided an impetus for travel and exploration. Phoenician traders moving west in the 9th century BCE, and the Greeks from the 8th century BCE explored the Mediterranean. They were followed by the Romans, whose road system eventually covered much of southern and western Europe. Long-range travel was next developed by the wide-ranging Scandinavians of the 9th and 10th centuries. The emphasis was on sea and river, not road transport. The Greeks were the earliest people to begin to codify their knowledge of Europe, and the sailors of the Mediterranean produced the most sophisticated charts and maps of Europe until the flowering of Dutch cartography in the 16th century, which laid the foundations for modern mapmaking.

The Vikings in the North Atlantic

The **extraordinary Viking voyages** of the 9th and 10th centuries were primarily for plunder – trade and the acquisition of new land came later. Sailing west from Norway into treacherous northern waters, the Vikings settled the Shetland islands and the Faeroes. Iceland was discovered in the mid-9th century, and despite the ice-logged winters, further travelers returned to colonize the island, founding settlements c.873, and establishing bases for voyages to Greenland and Labrador.

Viking ships were built with great care and attention to detail. The tiller (left) is carved in the shape of a snake, while the weather vane (below), made from polished bronze, is topped with a figure of a dog.

Mapping in the Classical era

This map reconstructs the Europe known to Pytheas. His journey was the first scientific exploration of northern Europe by Greeks. The map is based on Eratosthenes' three-continent (Europe, Africa, and Asia) world view. The Mediterranean familiar to the Greeks is accurately plotted; the northern topography is far more speculative.

The peoples of the Mediterranean made the earliest attempts at a survey of Europe. In 340 BCE, the Greek Pytheas traveled from Massalia to Britain, visiting the Orkneys and Shetlands; he later visited Norway and north Germany. The first attempts at scientific mapping were made in the Mediterranean: Eratosthenes successfully measured the diameter of the earth; Hipparchus suggested lines of latitude and longitude as reference points, and Ptolemy tried to show the surface of the earth using two conical projections, and provided points of reference for more than 8000 places.

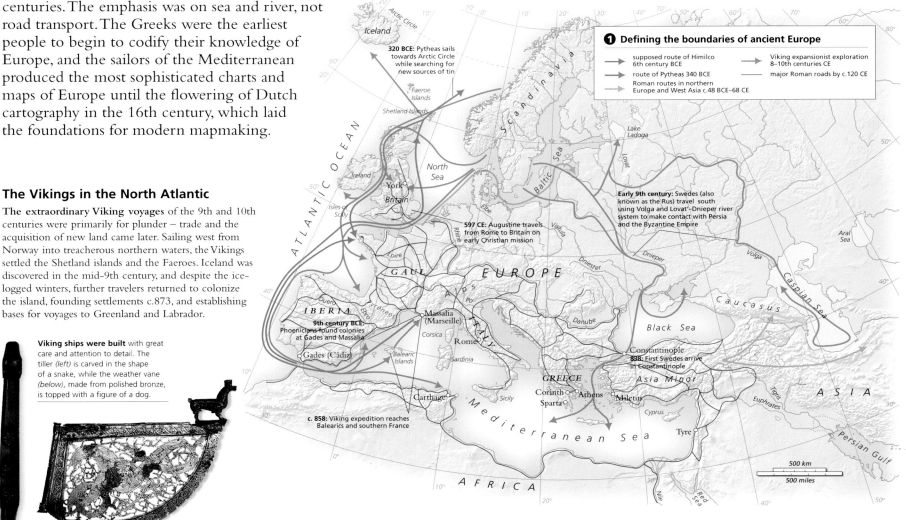

1 Defining the boundaries of ancient Europe

→ supposed route of Himilco 6th century BCE
→ route of Pytheas 340 BCE
→ Roman routes in northern Europe and West Asia c.48 BCE–68 CE
→ Viking expansionist exploration 8–10th centuries CE
— major Roman roads by c.120 CE

320 BCE: Pytheas sails towards Arctic Circle while searching for new sources of tin

Early 9th century: Swedes (also known as the Rus) travel south using Volga or Lovat'–Dnieper river system to make contact with Persia and the Byzantine Empire

597 CE: Augustine travels from Rome to Britain on early Christian mission

9th century BCE: Phoenicians found colonies at Gades and Massalia

838: First Swedes arrive in Constantinople

c. 858: Viking expedition reaches Balearics and southern France

500 km
500 miles

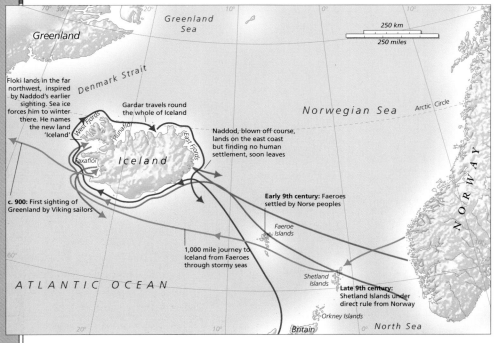

Greenland
Greenland Sea
250 km
250 miles

Floki lands in the far northwest, inspired by Naddod's earlier sighting. Sea ice forces him to winter there. He names the new land 'Iceland'

Gardar travels round the whole of Iceland

Naddod, blown off course, lands on the east coast but finding no human settlement, soon leaves

Iceland

c. 900: First sighting of Greenland by Viking sailors

Early 9th century: Faeroes settled by Norse peoples

1,000 mile journey to Iceland from Faeroes through stormy seas

Late 9th century: Shetland Islands under direct rule from Norway

ATLANTIC OCEAN

Orkney Islands

Britain

North Sea

2 The Viking discovery of Iceland

→ Gardar Svavarsson c. 860
→ Naddod c. 870
→ Floki Vilgerdarsson
→ other Viking explorers

The Peutinger Table, a strip map 23 ft long and 1 ft wide, showed roads in the Roman Empire – such as the Via Appia – with little reference to the surrounding countryside. It was probably first drawn in the 3rd century CE and was a useful tool for actually planning journeys. Some 5000 places are recorded, mostly in Europe.

The Vikings in the North Atlantic

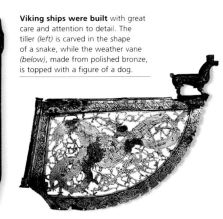

c.825: First settlement in the Faeroes

c.860: First trip round Iceland by Gardar Svavarsson

c.900: First sighting of Greenland by Viking seamen

750   800   850   900

795: First recorded Viking raid on isle of Iona

c.825: Irish monks probably first to discover Iceland

Late 860s: Brothers Ingolf and Hjerleif reconnoitre East Fjords

873: First permanent settlement started by Ingolf

Late 9th century: Shetlands come under direct Viking rule

Medieval mapping of Europe

Most of Europe was well known to travelers by the 11th century, but the accuracy with which it was mapped was extremely variable. The literate sailors of the Mediterranean were able to draw on the relatively sophisticated Portolan charts, which were made chiefly by Italian and Catalan navigators, but nothing comparable existed for the sailors of the north. Inland, largely imaginary wall maps represented Christian beliefs and the known world, with Jerusalem at the center of the earth, Europe at left, and Africa on the right. A second type of map was based on accumulated knowledge, and gave a recognizable, if distorted, picture of Europe. Examples include Gough's map, and the maps of Matthew Paris (1200–1259 CE). From the 15th century, Ptolemy's map of Europe *(see p.44)* was once again available and it was added to, and corrected in the light of new knowledge and re-published in the *Tabulae Modernae*. In 1425, Clavus, a Dane who had visited Iceland and Southern Greenland, added these, plus Norway, to the Ptolemaic base map.

The Hereford wall map *(left)* is perhaps the best known of the 600 or so "T-in-O maps" which are known to have survived. The T-shape of the Mediterranean Sea which divides the world into Europe, Africa and Asia is contained within a circle – the O.

Medieval mapping

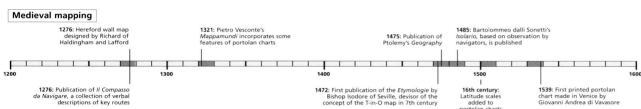

1276: Hereford wall map designed by Richard of Haldingham and Lafford

1321: Pietro Vesconte's *Mappamundi* incorporates some features of portolan charts

1475: Publication of Ptolemy's *Geography*

1485: Bartolommeo dalli Sonetti's *Isolario*, based on observation by navigators, is published

1276: Publication of *Il Compasso da Navigare*, a collection of verbal descriptions of key routes

1472: First publication of the *Etymologie* by Bishop Isodore of Seville, devisor of the concept of the T-in-O map in 7th century

16th century: Latitude scales added to portolan charts

1539: First printed portolan chart made in Venice by Giovanni Andrea di Vavasore

Portolan charts *(above)* were available to Mediterranean sailors from early Medieval times. They recorded the ports of the Mediterranean and Black Sea, giving landmarks, bearings, and distances, based on the Roman mile of 1000 paces.

The beginnings of modern cartography

In early modern Europe, increasing trade and a growing gentry class interested in their surroundings encouraged a new phase of mapmaking. Overseas territories and the possessions of the rich were mapped using surveying instruments such as the theodolite. Dutch cartographers made some of the most important innovations. Gerardus Mercator was the first to break from the Ptolemaic model. Mercator's projection rejected Ptolemy's conical model to show bearings with a scale identical in all directions. This made it particularly useful for navigators, and it is still widely used today. Another Dutchman, Willebrord Snell (Snellius), was the first to use triangulation to survey a large area. After carefully measuring a base line, he then employed trigonometry to calculate the distances to far off landmarks.

This map of Europe was produced by Mercator in 1554. It gives a detailed picture of settlement patterns, river networks, forest cover, and country boundaries, but some of the surrounding details - for example the proportions of Scandinavia - are far from accurate.

This detailed aerial view of Paris dates from 1576. It shows the original city wall, as well as building on the outskirts, agricultural areas – including windmills – and rough pasture on the edge of the city.

The Netherlands and the origins of modern cartography

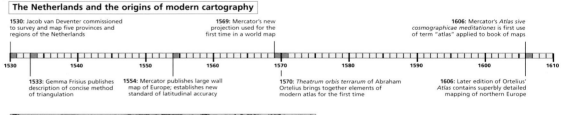

1530: Jacob van Deventer commissioned to survey and map five provinces and regions of the Netherlands

1569: Mercator's new projection used for the first time in a world map

1606: Mercator's *Atlas sive cosmographicae meditationes* is first use of term "atlas" applied to book of maps

1533: Gemma Frisius publishes description of concise method of triangulation

1554: Mercator publishes large wall map of Europe; establishes new standard of latitudinal accuracy

1570: *Theatrum orbis terrarum* of Abraham Ortelius brings together elements of modern atlas for the first time

1606: Later edition of Ortelius' *Atlas* contains superbly detailed mapping of northern Europe

Saxton's county map of England and Wales, published in 1579, shows the detail and accuracy which was being achieved by the 16th century. Other similar examples include Norden's county maps of 1593, and Ogilvie's road map published in *Britannia*.

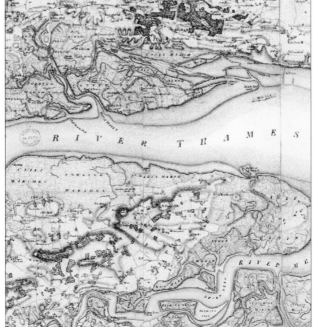

J.D. and C.F. Cassini continued Snellius' triangulation surveys in France. By 1744 all of France was covered by some 2000 triangles. The first sheets of a map of France on a scale of 1:86,400 were produced in 1756, but it was not until the Revolution that the last of the 182 sheets was published.

In England, fear of Napoleonic invasion and a need for detailed information about the land, led to a survey on a scale of two inches to the mile and publication on a scale of one inch to the mile. The first map of this series was sold as four sheets in 1801.

Surveyors from the Royal Engineers were responsible for making accurate maps of Britain and its Empire during the 19th century. Here they are shown undertaking a triangulation.

PREHISTORIC EUROPE

Mycenaean pottery, such as this goblet from Rhodes (c.1300 BCE), was traded throughout the eastern Mediterranean.

IN 7000 BCE, postglacial Europe, with its deciduous forests and increasingly temperate climate, was rich in natural resources and thinly populated by hunter-gatherers. By 1000 BCE, villages stretched from the Balkans to Scandinavia, and agriculture had reached even the marginal regions of the continent; there was a flourishing transcontinental traffic in salt, metals, and amber; and the first palace-based states had emerged on Crete and the Greek mainland. Although remains of settlements are rarely well preserved, a wide range of burials reveal, through grave goods as varied as woven textiles, ceramic vessels, and bronze axheads, an increasingly stratified society, in which individual possessions were a reflection of status.

The introduction of farming 7000–5000 BCE

The first potters of Central Europe used fired clay to make stylized human figures.

As agriculture spread from Anatolia into the Balkans and beyond, farming practices were adapted to more northerly latitudes, with an increased reliance on cattle and pigs and new, hardy strains of cereal. The mud-brick hill villages (tells) of the Middle East were replaced, in the thickly forested river valleys of Central Europe, by clusters of timber longhouses. The location of early farming communities can be charted by different pottery styles; incised Bandkeramik pottery is found from Hungary to the North Sea, while Cardial pottery, decorated with shell impressions, is found along the Mediterranean.

The spread of farming 7000–5000 BCE

c.7000: Farming spreads from Anatolia to southeastern Europe
c.6000: Farming starts to spread along the western coast of Mediterranean
c.5000: Agriculture well established in southern France and in the Netherlands

c.6500: Rising postglacial sea levels separate British Isles from the rest of the European continent
c.6000: First farming villages appear in southern Italy and Sicily
c.5400: Farming communities using Bandkeramik pottery in Central Europe

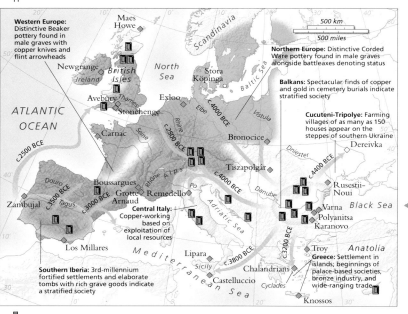

Timber longhouses, such as this example from Bylany in the Czech Republic, were built by the earliest farmers of Central Europe. The basic framework, made from plentiful timber supplies, was covered with wattle and daub. The buildings could be up to 150 ft long, and housed one or more families, as well as livestock and stores of food.

❶ The introduction of farming 7000–5000 BCE ▶

- spread of farming
- cultivated land by c.7000 BCE
- cultivated land by c.6000 BCE
- cultivated land by c.5000 BCE
- concentrations of Mesolithic settlements c.5000 BCE
- early farming settlement
- Balkan painted ware site
- Bandkeramik pottery site
- Cardial and incised pottery site

Europe in the Copper Age 4500–2500 BCE

This was an era of technological innovation and contact between communities. Both horses and wheeled vehicles spread eastward from the steppes, reaching western Europe by c.2500 BCE, while the introduction of the scratch plow increased productivity. Copper technology, which evolved in eastern Europe c.5000 BCE, spread throughout Europe over the next millennium. Finds of high prestige metalwork in some individual burials indicate that society was becoming more hierarchical, while distinctive pottery styles, known as Beaker Ware and Corded Ware, became widespread in central and western European burials, indicating the existence of a network of contact and exchange.

Marble figurines, made in the Cycladic Islands of Greece from c.2600 BCE, were placed in burials.

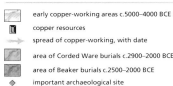

❷ Europe in the Copper Age 4500–2500 BCE

- early copper-working areas c.5000–4000 BCE
- copper resources
- spread of copper-working, with date
- area of Corded Ware burials c.2900–2000 BCE
- area of Beaker burials c.2500–2000 BCE
- important archaeological site

Europe in the Copper Age 4500–2500 BCE

c.4000: Farming villages of the Cucuteni-Tripolye group appear in southern Ukraine
c.3500: Stone circles and alignments, henges, and menhirs appear throughout northwestern Europe.
c.3000: Copper-working begins in southern France
c.2500: Copper-working reaches British Isles. Bell beaker pottery found in individual burials in western Europe

c.4000: Copper mines being exploited in Bulgaria and Yugoslavia
c.3500: First wheeled vehicles in Central Europe
c.2900: Appearance of Corded Ware pottery and stone battleaxes in burials in northern Europe

The stone alignments at Kermario in northwestern France date to c.3000 BCE. They were probably associated with processions and seasonal rituals.

Europe in the Bronze Age 2300–1500 BCE

The Bronze Age in Europe was a period of remarkable cultural and technological uniformity. Limited tin resources in western Europe, vital for bronze manufacture, were transported along long distance trade routes in exchange for other valued commodities – Baltic amber and salt. Access to these resources was a major factor in creating a distinct social elite, interred in large barrow burials, replete with a rich array of grave goods. By 1500 BCE, marginal land was being brought into cultivation to feed growing populations. These social and economic pressures led to increasing conflict, evident in the appearance of fortified settlements and the emergence of a warrior elite.

Many of the bronze artifacts made in Europe during the 2nd millennium BCE, such as this ritual bronze ax from Teteven in the Balkan Mountains, were status objects for the emerging warrior elite.

Scale varies with perspective

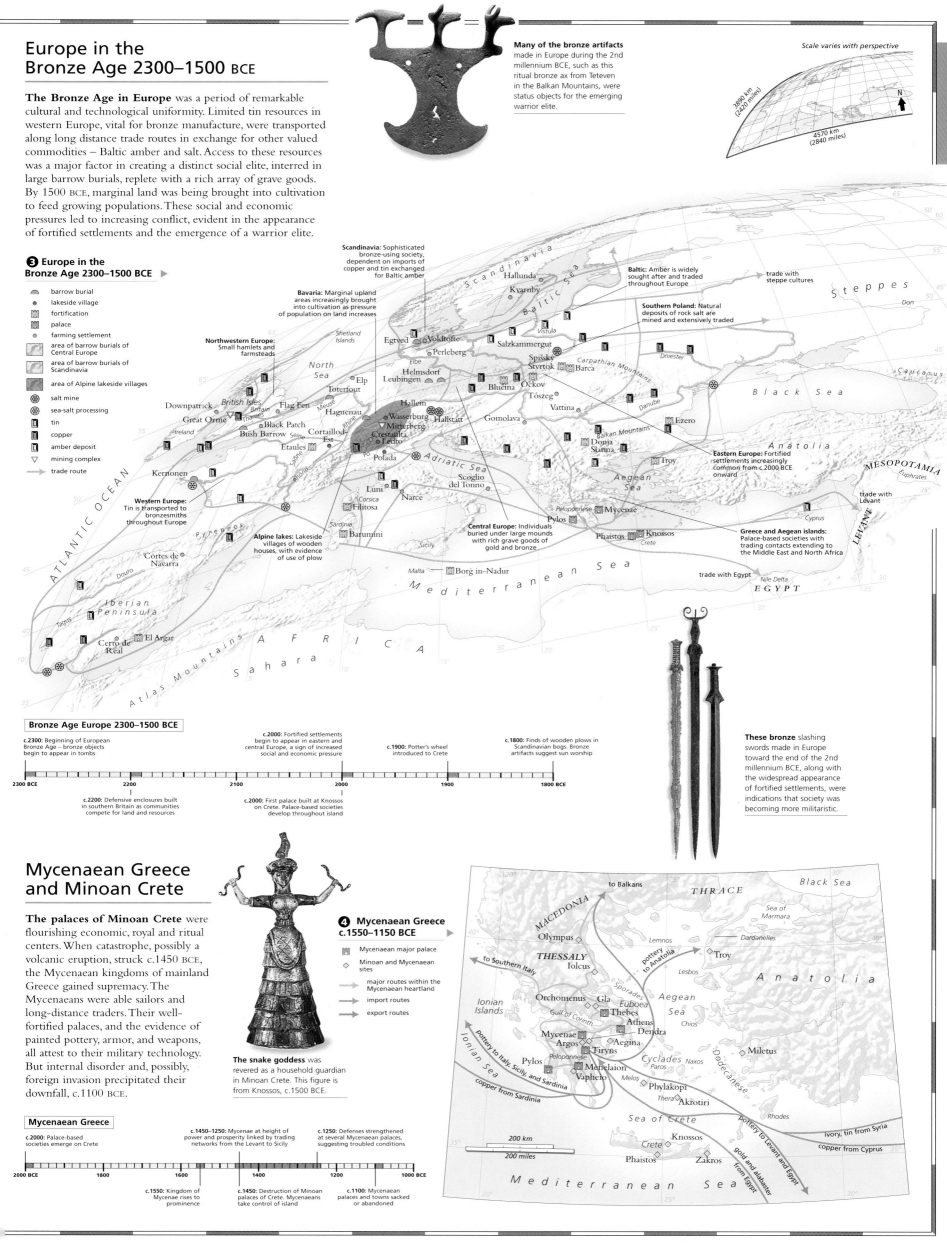

❸ Europe in the Bronze Age 2300–1500 BCE ▶

- barrow burial
- lakeside village
- fortification
- palace
- farming settlement
- area of barrow burials of Central Europe
- area of barrow burials of Scandinavia
- area of Alpine lakeside villages
- salt mine
- sea-salt processing
- tin
- copper
- amber deposit
- mining complex
- trade route

Scandinavia: Sophisticated bronze-using society, dependent on imports of copper and tin exchanged for Baltic amber

Bavaria: Marginal upland areas increasingly brought into cultivation as pressure of population on land increases

Baltic: Amber is widely sought after and traded throughout Europe

Southern Poland: Natural deposits of rock salt are mined and extensively traded

trade with steppe cultures

Northwestern Europe: Small hamlets and farmsteads

Western Europe: Tin is transported to bronzesmiths throughout Europe

Alpine lakes: Lakeside villages of wooden houses, with evidence of use of plow

Central Europe: Individuals buried under large mounds with rich grave goods of gold and bronze

Eastern Europe: Fortified settlements increasingly common from c.2000 BCE onward

Greece and Aegean islands: Palace-based societies with trading contacts extending to the Middle East and North Africa

trade with Levant

trade with Egypt

Map labels: Scandinavia, Hallunda, Kvarnby, Baltic Sea, Egtved, Voldtofte, Shetland Islands, North Sea, Elbe, Perleberg, Salzkammergut, Spišský Štvrtok, Barca, Vistula, Carpathian Mountains, Dniester, Don, Steppes, Caucasus, Black Sea, Anatolia, Mesopotamia, Euphrates, Helmsdorf, Leubingen, Bučina, Očkov, Tószeg, Vattina, Gomolava, Danube, Ezero, Troy, Donja Slatina, Aegean Sea, Balkan Mountains, Cyprus, Elp, Toterfout, Hallein, Wasserburg, Mitterberg, Hallstatt, Haguenau, Flag Fen, Meuse, Downpatrick, Great Orme, British Isles, Britain, Thames, Ireland, Black Patch, Bush Barrow, Cortaillod-Est, Etaules, Saône, Crestaulta, Ledro, Po, Polada, Adriatic Sea, Scoglio del Tonno, Kernonen, Rhône, Luni, Corsica, Filitosa, Narce, Peloponnese, Mycenae, Pylos, Phaistos, Knossos, Crete, Atlantic Ocean, Pyrenees, Sardinia, Barumini, Cortes de Navarra, Douro, Tagus, Iberian Peninsula, Cerro de Real, El Argar, Atlas Mountains, Sahara, Africa, Malta, Borg in-Nadur, Mediterranean Sea, Nile Delta, Egypt

Bronze Age Europe 2300–1500 BCE

c.2300: Beginning of European Bronze Age – bronze objects begin to appear in tombs

c.2200: Defensive enclosures built in southern Britain as communities compete for land and resources

c.2000: Fortified settlements begin to appear in eastern and central Europe, a sign of increased social and economic pressure

c.2000: First palace built at Knossos on Crete. Palace-based societies develop throughout island

c.1900: Potter's wheel introduced to Crete

c.1800: Finds of wooden plows in Scandinavian bogs. Bronze artifacts suggest sun worship

2300 BCE — 2200 — 2100 — 2000 — 1900 — 1800 BCE

These bronze slashing swords made in Europe toward the end of the 2nd millennium BCE, along with the widespread appearance of fortified settlements, were indications that society was becoming more militaristic.

Mycenaean Greece and Minoan Crete

The palaces of Minoan Crete were flourishing economic, royal and ritual centers. When catastrophe, possibly a volcanic eruption, struck c.1450 BCE, the Mycenaean kingdoms of mainland Greece gained supremacy. The Mycenaeans were able sailors and long-distance traders. Their well-fortified palaces, and the evidence of painted pottery, armor, and weapons, all attest to their military technology. But internal disorder and, possibly, foreign invasion precipitated their downfall, c.1100 BCE.

The snake goddess was revered as a household guardian in Minoan Crete. This figure is from Knossos, c.1500 BCE.

❹ Mycenaean Greece c.1550–1150 BCE ▶

- Mycenaean major palace
- Minoan and Mycenaean sites
- major routes within the Mycenaean heartland
- import routes
- export routes

Map labels: to Balkans, Thrace, Macedonia, Olympus, Thessaly, Iolcus, Lemnos, Dardanelles, Troy, Sea of Marmara, Black Sea, pottery to Anatolia, to Southern Italy, Ionian Islands, Orchomenus, Gla, Euboea, Thebes, Athens, Lesbos, Sporades, Chios, Aegean Sea, Anatolia, Mycenae, Argos, Tiryns, Aegina, Dendra, Cyclades, Naxos, Paros, Miletus, Dodecanese, pottery to Italy, Sicily, and Sardinia, Ionian Sea, Pylos, Menelaion, Vaphelo, Melos, Phylakopi, Thera, Akrotiri, Rhodes, pottery to Levant and Egypt, Sea of Crete, Knossos, ivory, tin from Syria, copper from Cyprus, Crete, Phaistos, Zakros, gold and alabaster from Egypt, copper from Sardinia, Gulf of Corinth, Peloponnese, Mediterranean Sea, 200 km, 200 miles

Mycenaean Greece

c.2000: Palace-based societies emerge on Crete

c.1550: Kingdom of Mycenae rises to prominence

c.1450–1250: Mycenae at height of power and prosperity linked by trading networks from the Levant to Sicily

c.1450: Destruction of Minoan palaces of Crete. Mycenaeans take control of island

c.1250: Defenses strengthened at several Mycenaean palaces, suggesting troubled conditions

c.1100: Mycenaean palaces and towns sacked or abandoned

2000 BCE — 1800 — 1600 — 1400 — 1200 — 1000 BCE

THE MEDITERRANEAN WORLD

This Phoenician carved ivory plaque was found at the Assyrian city of Nimrud.

BETWEEN 700 AND 300 BCE, the Mediterranean world shaped western civilization. The impact of Classical Greek ideas on art, architecture, literature, philosophy, science, and, through the revolutionary innovation of democratic government, on political institutions was profound and wide ranging. The conquests of Philip of Macedon and his son Alexander the Great *(see pp. 40–41)* took the fundamental features of Greek culture as far as the borders of India. Of other major civilizations, the Etruscans were undoubtedly influenced by the Greeks, both in the layout of their grid-plan cities and in their lifesize terra-cotta statues. The Phoenicians, an energetic, maritime people based in city-states in the Levant, took their culture, through trade and colonization, to the western shores of the Mediterranean.

The colonization of the Mediterranean

This magnificent Attic red-figure vase, which illustrates the Homeric myth of Odysseus and the Sirens, dates from c.490 BCE.

Both the Phoenicians and the Greeks became colonists during the 1st millennium BCE. The limited fertile terrain of the Greek homelands could not support the growing population, and many Greek cities sent colonists to western Anatolia, the Black Sea shores, Sicily and southern Italy, and even southern France, where Massalia (Marseille) was founded. The city of Miletus alone was responsible for establishing over 80 colonies. The Phoenicians set out in search of metals, initially setting up a colony in Cyprus to mine copper, and eventually founding Gades (Cadiz) because of nearby silver deposits. Their greatest colony was Carthage, which became a major power in its own right.

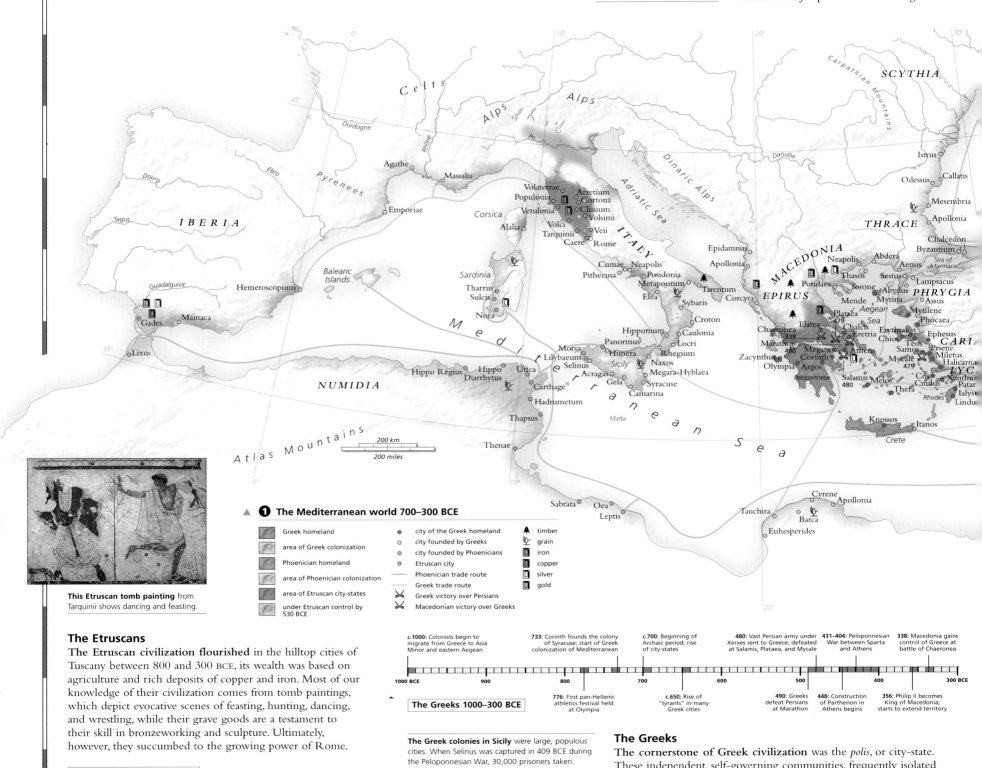

▲ **① The Mediterranean world 700–300 BCE**

Greek homeland	○ city of the Greek homeland	♠ timber
area of Greek colonization	○ city founded by Greeks	⚘ grain
Phoenician homeland	○ city founded by Phoenicians	▨ iron
area of Phoenician colonization	◉ Etruscan city	▨ copper
area of Etruscan city-states	— Phoenician trade route	▨ silver
under Etruscan control by 530 BCE	— Greek trade route	▨ gold
	⚔ Greek victory over Persians	
	⚔ Macedonian victory over Greeks	

This Etruscan tomb painting from Tarquinii shows dancing and feasting.

The Etruscans

The Etruscan civilization flourished in the hilltop cities of Tuscany between 800 and 300 BCE, its wealth was based on agriculture and rich deposits of copper and iron. Most of our knowledge of their civilization comes from tomb paintings, which depict evocative scenes of feasting, hunting, dancing, and wrestling, while their grave goods are a testament to their skill in bronzeworking and sculpture. Ultimately, however, they succumbed to the growing power of Rome.

The Etruscans 1000 BCE–1 CE

c.1000: Earliest villages on Palatine and nearby hills of Rome
c.616: Etruscan king Tarquin I rules Rome
509: Romans expel Etruscan king Tarquin II
396: Etruscan city of Veii taken by Rome
c.100: Language and culture of Etruscans in terminal decline

| 1000 BCE | 800 | 600 | 400 | 200 | 1 CE |

c.800: Emergence of Etruscan city states
c.690: Etruscan script developed from Greek
c.530: Etruscan influence at its height; extends as far south as Neapolis
250: Whole Italian peninsula under control of Rome

The Greeks 1000–300 BCE

c.1000: Colonists begin to migrate from Greece to Asia Minor and eastern Aegean
733: Corinth founds the colony of Syracuse; start of Greek colonization of Mediterranean
c.700: Beginning of Archaic period; rise of city-states
480: Vast Persian army under Xerxes sent to Greece; defeated at Salamis, Plataea, and Mycale
431–404: Peloponnesian War between Sparta and Athens
338: Macedonia gains control of Greece at battle of Chaeronea

| 1000 BCE | 900 | 800 | 700 | 600 | 500 | 400 | 300 BCE |

776: First pan-Hellenic athletics festival held at Olympia
c.650: Rise of "tyrants" in many Greek cities
490: Greeks defeat Persians at Marathon
448: Construction of Parthenon in Athens begins
356: Philip II becomes King of Macedonia; starts to extend territory

The Greek colonies in Sicily were large, populous cities. When Selinus was captured in 409 BCE during the Peloponnesian War, 30,000 prisoners taken. Its impressive ruins include six temples like this one, all dating from the 6th and 5th centuries BCE.

The Greeks

The cornerstone of Greek civilization was the *polis*, or city-state. These independent, self-governing communities, frequently isolated by Greece's rugged terrain, were based on walled cities, with outlying villages and farmland. Yet, despite the multiplicity of city-states, Greece was united by language, religion, and culture, reflected in harmonious architecture, sculpture, philosophy, and drama. Politically, the city-states swung between the extremes of oligarchy and democracy. While Athens was the birthplace of democracy, in Sparta a militaristic society was ruled by kings, supported by an underclass of serfs (*helots*).

The Phoenicians

A Semitic people whose home cities lay along a narrow strip of the eastern Mediterranean coast, the Phoenicians were the foremost traders and craftsmen of the Mediterranean, renowned for their skill in ivory carving, metalworking and glass manufacture. Perhaps their greatest legacy was their alphabetic writing system, which formed the basis of both the Greek and Roman scripts. The city of Carthage, founded as a colony, became a great power in its own right, leading a confederation of Phoenician cities which controlled southern Iberia, the western Mediterranean islands, and North Africa.

The limestone bust of "the Lady of Elche," from southern Iberia, shows the artistic influence of the Phoenician city of Carthage, which had close links with cities throughout the western Mediterranean.

The Phoenicians and the Carthaginians 1000–200 BCE

c. 1600: The Phoenicians begin to use the Canaanite script, the first alphabetic script

c. 1000: Phoenicians become main maritime power in Levant region

814: Traditional date for foundation of Carthage

264–241: First Punic War; Rome gains control of Carthaginian Sicily

c. 900: Phoenician ships sail westward in search of metals and found colonies near rich metal deposits

218–201: Second Punic War; Carthaginians invade Italy, but Rome eventually wins war to become regional superpower

| 1600 BCE | 1400 | 1200 | 1000 | 800 | 600 | 400 | 200 BCE |

The Athenian Empire

The city-states of Greece were united in their bid to repulse the Persians, which culminated in famous victories at Marathon (490) and Salamis (480). In 478, Athens emerged as the leader of a loose maritime confederation of eastern Aegean states, based on the tiny island of Delos. Membership of the Delian League involved participating in a common military policy, and contributing to a common treasury. Athens came increasingly to dominate the League, transferring funds to the city in 454, and ruthlessly crushing any attempts at revolt. Greatly enriched by League funds, Athens now entered its greatest period of power and prosperity. The League had, in effect, become an Athenian empire, much resented in many Greek cities.

The city of Athens claimed a special affinity with its patroness Athene, goddess of wisdom, war, and the arts and crafts.

❷ The Athenian Empire 454–428 BCE

Areas paying tribute to Athens: (number of tribute-paying states in brackets)

- Islands (29)
- Thrace (62)
- Hellespont (45)
- Ionia (35)
- Caria (81)
- Athenian homeland
- non-tribute paying areas belonging to Delian League
- states with tribute assessment of over 5 silver talents per annum (454–428 BCE)
- states with tribute assessment of 1–5 silver talents per annum (454–428 BCE)
- overseas dependencies of Athens
- states in revolt against Athens

The Peloponnesian War

Athens' high-handed imperialism made war with Sparta inevitable, and a system of alliances embroiled much of Greece in the conflict. The Athenians withstood Sparta's attacks on Attica by withdrawing to the safety of the city, preferring to do battle at sea. A truce was reached in 421 BCE, but when Athens unwisely sent an expedition to attack Syracuse, the Spartans captured the Athenian navy, presaging the end of the conflict. Greece was plunged into disarray until it was forcibly united by Philip of Macedon in 338 BCE.

❸ The Peloponnesian War 431–404 BCE

- Athenian Empire
- Athenian ally
- Sparta and allied states
- neutral territory
- Athenian victory
- Spartan victory

The fiercely patriotic, militaristic culture of Sparta is embodied in this small bronze of a soldier.

Athenian expedition to Sicily in 415 ends in Spartan victory at Syracuse, 413

416 BCE: taken by Athens

424 BCE: taken by Athens

❹ The city of Athens

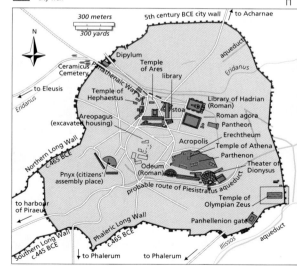

- remains from 6th–5th century BCE
- remains from 4th century BCE–2nd century CE
- road
- aqueduct
- city wall

Athens

The mid-5th century was Athens' golden age. Governed by the eminent statesman Pericles, and the home of such great intellectuals such as Plato, Sophocles, and Euripides, the city was dominated by the Parthenon temple, built of local marble by the sculptor Phidias, and approached by the monumental Propylea Gate. The Acropolis was the military and religious center of the city, while commercial and municipal life dominated the agora, or town square.

THE RISE OF ROME

The legionaries of Rome's citizen army were unmatched in discipline and skill.

ROME BEGAN THE 5TH CENTURY BCE as the most powerful city of the regional alliance known as the Latin League. By conquering the Etruscan city-state of Veii in 396 BCE, the Romans doubled their territory, and after the breakup of the Latin League in 338, they incorporated the whole Latin region. This gave them the manpower to defeat a coalition of Samnites, Etruscans, and Gauls in 295. When they faced the army of the Greek general Pyrrhus, they were able to sustain two crushing defeats before achieving victory in 275 BCE. With Italy now under its control, Rome turned its attention to foreign rivals. Following victory over Carthage in 202, it took less than a century to add North Africa, most of Iberia, southern Gaul, Macedon, Greece, and Asia Minor to its empire.

Rome and the Italian confederacy

Traditionally, this bronze bust of a stern Roman aristocrat has been identified as Lucius Junius Brutus, one of the founders of the Roman Republic in 509.

From the 5th to the 3rd century BCE, the city of Rome extended its area of domination to create a confederacy that united all Italy. Some cities were simply annexed and their inhabitants enjoyed the status of full Roman citizens, while others were granted a halfway form of citizenship that did not include the right to vote or hold office in Rome. Other peoples were considered "allies" and united to Rome by individual treaties. New towns known as "Latin colonies" extended the Roman presence throughout Italy, while "Roman colonies," where the inhabitants were full citizens, were established for defensive purposes, primarily along the Tyrrhenian coast. Beginning with the Via Appia in the 4th century BCE, the Romans built a road network that linked the whole peninsula.

Rome and its Latin allies c.495 BCE

Rome was the most powerful of the Latin city-states when the Republic was established in 509, though it controlled just 320 sq miles of territory.

The peoples of Italy in 500 BCE

Latin, the language Rome would spread throughout western Europe, was just one of many closely related Italic languages spoken by the tribes of central Italy. The most powerful peoples in the peninsula were the Greek colonists and the Etruscans, a sophisticated city-state people whose language suggests eastern Mediterranean origins. It had been the Etruscans' arrival in Rome in the 7th century BCE that transformed a cluster of small villages into a city.

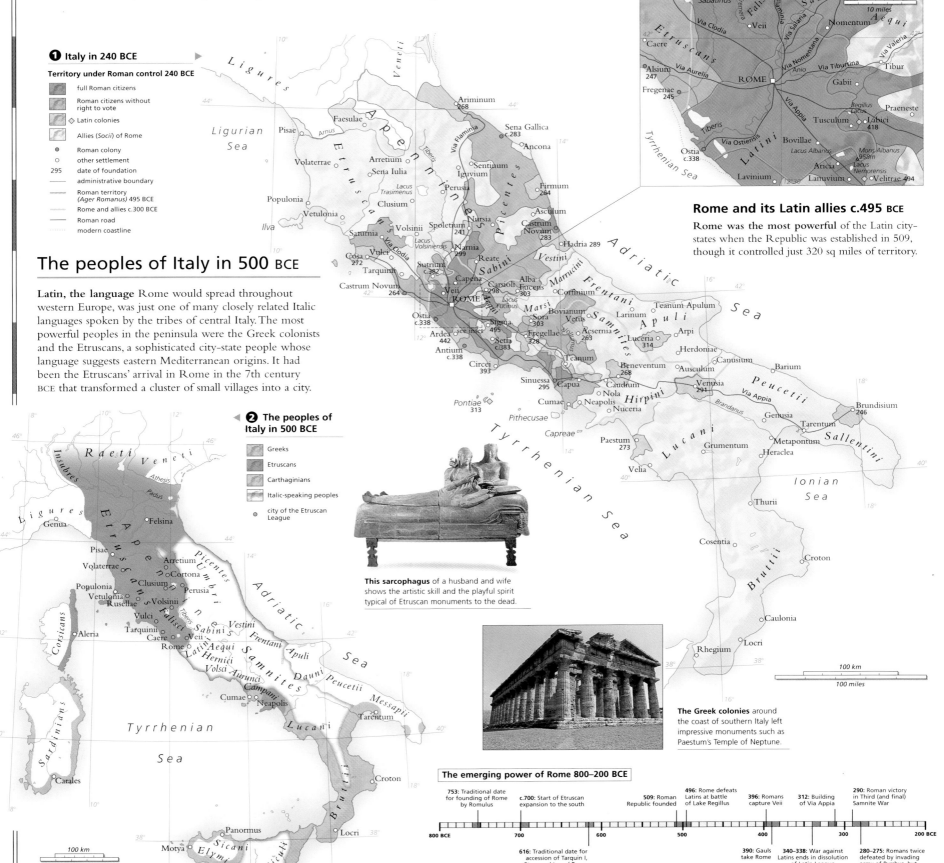

① Italy in 240 BCE

Territory under Roman control 240 BCE
- full Roman citizens
- Roman citizens without right to vote
- Latin colonies
- Allies (*Socii*) of Rome
- ● Roman colony
- ○ other settlement
- 295 date of foundation
- —— administrative boundary
- —— Roman territory (*Ager Romanus*) 495 BCE
- —— Rome and allies c.300 BCE
- —— Roman road
- ······ modern coastline

② The peoples of Italy in 500 BCE
- Greeks
- Etruscans
- Carthaginians
- Italic-speaking peoples
- ● city of the Etruscan League

This sarcophagus of a husband and wife shows the artistic skill and the playful spirit typical of Etruscan monuments to the dead.

The Greek colonies around the coast of southern Italy left impressive monuments such as Paestum's Temple of Neptune.

The emerging power of Rome 800–200 BCE

- **753:** Traditional date for founding of Rome by Romulus
- **c.700:** Start of Etruscan expansion to the south
- **509:** Roman Republic founded
- **496:** Rome defeats Latins at battle of Lake Regillus
- **396:** Romans capture Veii
- **312:** Building of Via Appia
- **290:** Roman victory in Third (and final) Samnite War
- **616:** Traditional date for accession of Tarquin I, Etruscan king of Rome
- **390:** Gauls take Rome
- **340–338:** War against Latins ends in dissolution of Latin League
- **280–275:** Romans twice defeated by invading army of Pyrrhus, but emerge victorious

Rome and Carthage: the Punic Wars

Founded by Phoenicians *(Punici)* in 814 BCE, Carthage grew to be the preeminent naval power in the western Mediterranean. Rome came into conflict with the Carthaginians in 264, the start of a series of three wars. In the first, the Romans pushed their enemies out of Sicily. Then, in 218, Rome forced a second war by opposing Carthaginian actions in Iberia. Despite many defeats at the hands of Hannibal, the Romans won this war and stripped Carthage of its navy. The final war (149–146) ended in the destruction of Carthage and the enslavement of its people.

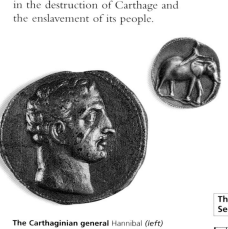

The Carthaginian general Hannibal *(left)* fought the Romans for 15 years in Italy. The smaller coin *(right)* shows an African elephant, used by the Carthaginians to strike terror into opposing armies.

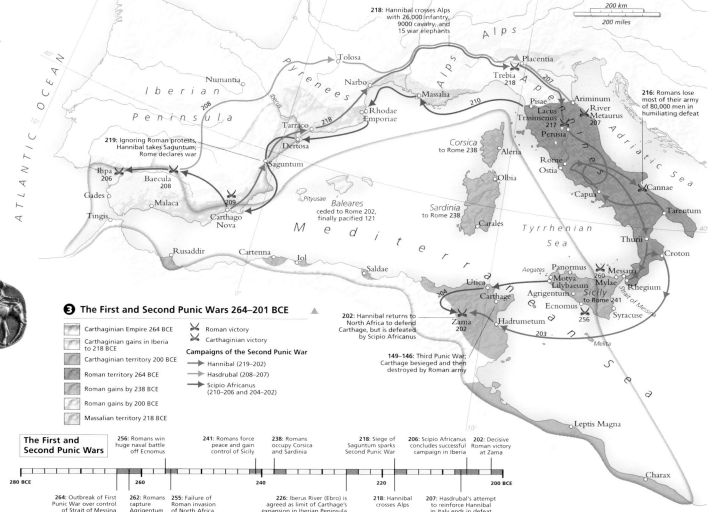

❸ The First and Second Punic Wars 264–201 BCE

- Carthaginian Empire 264 BCE
- Carthaginian gains in Iberia to 218 BCE
- Carthaginian territory 200 BCE
- Roman territory 264 BCE
- Roman gains by 238 BCE
- Roman gains by 200 BCE
- Massalian territory 218 BCE
- ✕ Roman victory
- ✕ Carthaginian victory

Campaigns of the Second Punic War
- → Hannibal (219–202)
- → Hasdrubal (208–207)
- → Scipio Africanus (210–206 and 204–202)

Map annotations:
- 218: Hannibal crosses Alps with 26,000 infantry, 9000 cavalry, and 15 war elephants
- 216: Romans lose most of their army in humiliating defeat
- 219: Ignoring Roman protests, Hannibal takes Saguntum; Rome declares war
- 202: Hannibal returns to North Africa to defend Carthage, but is defeated by Scipio Africanus
- 149–146: Third Punic War; Carthage besieged and then destroyed by Roman army

The First and Second Punic Wars (timeline)
- 280 BCE
- 264: Outbreak of First Punic War over control of Strait of Messina
- 262: Romans capture Agrigentum
- 256: Romans win huge naval battle off Ecnomus
- 255: Failure of Roman invasion of North Africa
- 260
- 241: Romans force peace and gain control of Sicily
- 240
- 238: Romans occupy Corsica and Sardinia
- 226: Iberus River (Ebro) is agreed as limit of Carthage's expansion in Iberian Peninsula
- 220
- 218: Siege of Saguntum sparks Second Punic War
- 218: Hannibal crosses Alps
- 206: Scipio Africanus concludes successful campaign in Iberia
- 207: Hasdrubal's attempt to reinforce Hannibal in Italy ends in defeat
- 202: Decisive Roman victory at Zama
- 200 BCE

The subjugation of Greece by Rome

In 200 BCE the major powers of the Greek world were Macedon and the Seleucid Empire. Two Greek federations had also emerged: the Aetolian League and the Achaean League, which included Corinth, largest of the mainland Greek cities. Other city-states, such as Athens and Sparta, maneuvered to maintain their independence, as did the Asian kingdom of Pergamum. Political tensions and appeals to Rome for help gave the Romans excuses for five major military interventions in the 2nd century. Macedon became a Roman province in 148; Greece succumbed in 146 after the Achaean War.

❹ Greece in 200 BCE

- Macedon
- ally of Macedon
- Aetolian League
- ally of Aetolian League
- Achaean League
- Seleucid Empire
- Ptolemaic Empire
- independent Greek states and cities
- Roman Empire
- ally of Rome
- ✕ Roman victory

Corinth was first an ally of Rome, then an enemy. It was razed to the ground in 146 by the Roman general Mummius. The ruins visible today *(left)* are of the later Roman city.

This fine mosaic of a lion hunt decorated the royal palace in the Macedonian capital of Pella. Even before annexing Macedon and Greece, Rome eagerly embraced Hellenistic culture and customs.

Rome's overseas provinces in 120 BCE

Following the defeat of Carthage in 202 BCE, Rome's empire expanded rapidly. Greece and the Greek states of Asia Minor were won through a combination of diplomacy and war, but long, costly campaigns were needed to subdue the tribes of the Iberian Peninsula. Carthage itself was added to the empire in 146. As the Romans extended their rule beyond Italy, they largely abandoned the principles of incorporation that they had applied in Italy and instead set up provinces. These were ruled by governors, who served short one- or two-year terms, maintained order, and oversaw the collection of taxes. Corruption and plundering by governors were common enough for a special permanent court to be set up to try such cases in 149.

Roman expansion 200–120 BCE (timeline)
- 200 BCE
- 200–196: Second Macedonian War
- 192–189: War with Seleucid king Antiochus; Roman victories at Thermopylae and Magnesia
- 180
- 172–167: Third Macedonian War
- 168: Romans crush Macedonians at Pydna
- 160
- 148: Roman victory in Fourth Macedonian War
- 146: Roman armies destroy conquered cities of Corinth and Carthage
- 140
- 139: Defeat of Lusitani
- 133: Romans take Iberian city of Numantia
- 133: Rome bequeathed province of Asia by king of Pergamum
- 120 BCE

❺ Roman conquests to 120 BCE

- Roman Empire c.200 BCE
- Roman gains by c.120 BCE
- Massalia and possessions
- independent Greek states and cities
- Ptolemaic Empire and possessions
- Seleucid Empire
- ASIA 133 Roman province and date of foundation
- *Volcae* 121 people and date of conquest by Rome

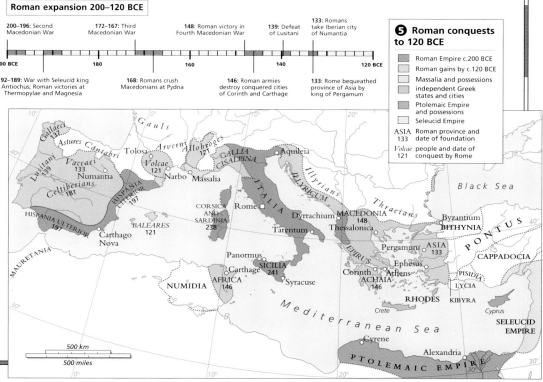

THE ROMAN EMPIRE

Constantine sealed the Empire's fate by moving the center of power to the east.

REPUBLICAN ROME asserted military control over most of the Mediterranean, but a century of internal political conflict and civil war prevented the development of an orderly imperial system. The first emperor, Augustus (27 BCE–14 CE), ended this period of disorder with his defeat of Mark Antony in 31 BCE and established the Principate – the military and political system that defended and governed the empire until the reforms of Diocletian and Constantine at the end of the 3rd century. At the height of its power in the 2nd century, Rome ruled over some 50 million people scattered in over 5000 administrative units. For the most part, subjects of the Empire accepted Roman rule, and, at least in the west, many adopted Roman culture and the Latin language. After 212 CE all free inhabitants of the Empire had the status of Roman citizens.

The Empire under Hadrian

The Empire reached its greatest extent early in the 2nd century under Trajan, who conquered Dacia, Arabia, Armenia, Assyria, and Mesopotamia. However, when Hadrian succeeded in 117 CE, he abandoned the last three provinces and adopted a defensive frontier strategy that would be followed by most of his successors. A professional army – under Hadrian it numbered just 300,000 – defended the frontiers and suppressed rebellions in trouble spots such as Britain and Judaea, while the navy kept the Mediterranean free of pirates. Fleets were also based on the Rhine and the Danube, which formed the northeastern frontier.

The Pont du Gard, part of the aqueduct that supplied Nemausus (Nîmes) in the south of France, is a fine example of the Romans' skill in civil engineering.

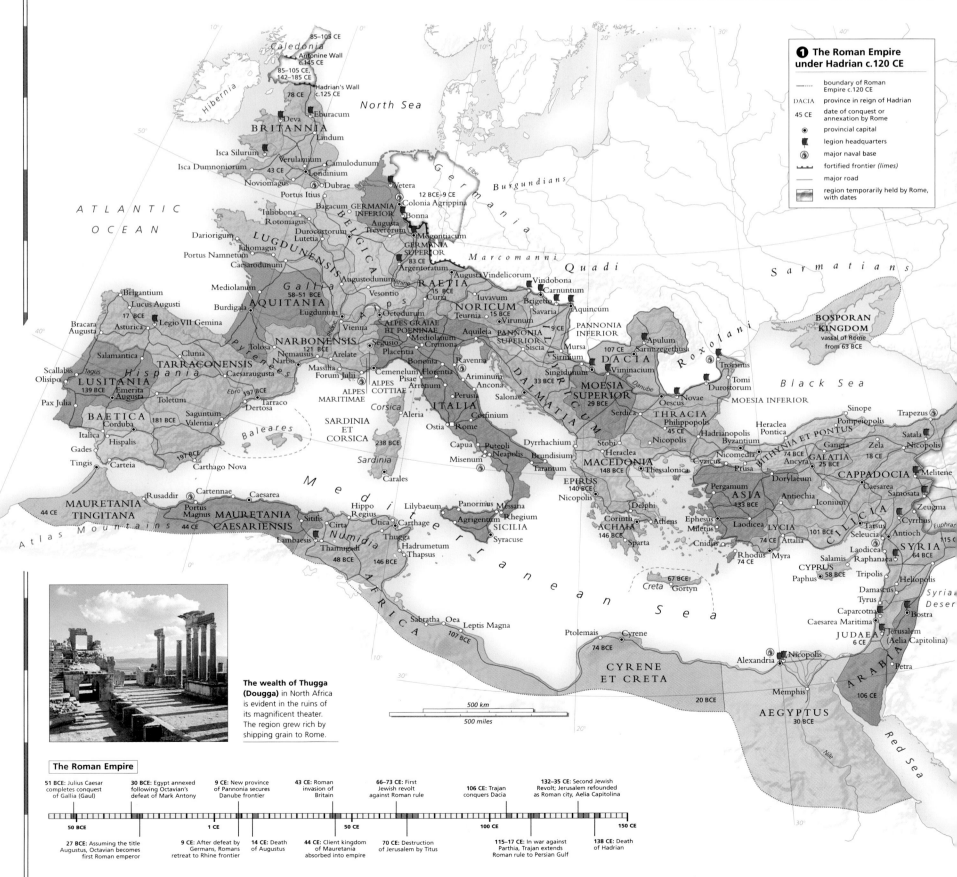

① **The Roman Empire under Hadrian c.120 CE**

- boundary of Roman Empire c.120 CE
- DACIA — province in reign of Hadrian
- 45 CE — date of conquest or annexation by Rome
- provincial capital
- legion headquarters
- major naval base
- fortified frontier (limes)
- major road
- region temporarily held by Rome, with dates

The wealth of Thugga (Dougga) in North Africa is evident in the ruins of its magnificent theater. The region grew rich by shipping grain to Rome.

500 km
500 miles

The Roman Empire

51 BCE: Julius Caesar completes conquest of Gallia (Gaul)

30 BCE: Egypt annexed following Octavian's defeat of Mark Antony

9 CE: New province of Pannonia secures Danube frontier

43 CE: Roman invasion of Britain

66–73 CE: First Jewish revolt against Roman rule

106 CE: Trajan conquers Dacia

132–35 CE: Second Jewish Revolt; Jerusalem refounded as Roman city, Aelia Capitolina

50 BCE	1 CE	50 CE	100 CE	150 CE

27 BCE: Assuming the title Augustus, Octavian becomes first Roman emperor

9 CE: After defeat by Germans, Romans retreat to Rhine frontier

14 CE: Death of Augustus

44 CE: Client kingdom of Mauretania absorbed into empire

70 CE: Destruction of Jerusalem by Titus

115–17 CE: In war against Parthia, Trajan extends Roman rule to Persian Gulf

138 CE: Death of Hadrian

The city of Rome

As the empire grew, so did Rome, reaching a population of about one million in the 2nd century CE. The city was sustained by food shipped up the Tiber from Ostia and aqueducts that delivered 100 gallons of water per head per day. Many Romans did not work, but were eligible for the *annona*, a free handout of grain. Following the example of Augustus, every emperor aimed to leave his mark on the city by building magnificent forums, palaces, theaters, arenas, and temples.

The Colosseum, completed in 80 CE, vied with the Circus Maximus racetrack as Rome's most popular stadium. It regularly attracted a full house of 50,000 to its gladiatorial and wild animal combats.

Earthenware amphorae were used to transport and store wine, olive oil, and fish sauce.

Supplying the city of Rome

Feeding the citizens of Rome required regular shipments of grain from Egypt and North Africa. These were landed at Ostia and Portus, a new port built by Trajan at the mouth of the Tiber, from where they were shipped on smaller galleys up river to the capital. Goods were carried by ship wherever possible, as this was much cheaper and faster than road transport. Rome imported food and raw materials from all over its empire. Marble for the pillars and statues that graced the city's temples and palaces often came from as far afield as Greece and Africa. Unusual imports included *garum*, a fermented fish sauce which the Romans used, much like ketchup, to add flavor to a wide variety of dishes, and murex, a shellfish that produced the purple dye used for imperial togas. To give an idea of the volume of goods imported to the city, Mons Testaceus, a large hill, 165 ft in height, was created in imperial times from the shards of broken amphorae from the rows of warehouses that lined the banks of the Tiber in the southwest of the city.

③ Supply routes to Rome

—	major shipping route	⚌	wool
	major grain-producing region		flax/linen
	wine		murex (purple dye)
	olive oil		marble
	garum (fish sauce)		timber
	honey		gold
	slaves		tin
	horses		copper

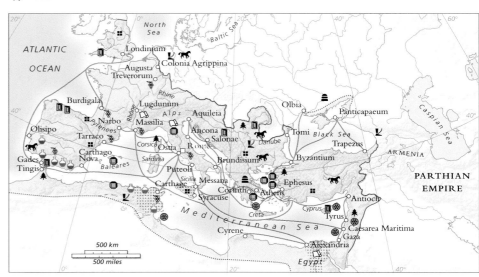

② Imperial Rome c.300 CE

	temple
	stadium or theater
	baths
	other important building
	built-up area within city wall
	city gate
—	aqueduct
⋯	city wall in Republican era 4th century BCE
	wall of Aurelian 271

This floor mosaic of Orpheus decorated a villa in Daphne, a wealthy suburb of Antioch, capital of the province of Syria.

The Tetrarchy of Diocletian and the final division of the Empire

In the 3rd century CE breakaway states such as the Kingdom of Palmyra threatened to destroy the Empire. To counter this, Diocletian (284–305) and Constantine (307–337) reorganized the structure of imperial administration. The existing provinces were divided into 100 smaller units, grouped in twelve larger regions called dioceses, each governed by a vicar. To share responsibility for defending the empire and to provide for an orderly succession, Diocletian established the joint rule of the Tetrarchy: two emperors with the title Augustus, one in the east, one in the west, each assisted by a junior emperor with the title of Caesar.

c.250: Period of civil wars and runaway inflation

270: Palmyra extends to Egypt

293: Diocletian establishes Tetrarchy and twelve dioceses

324: Constantine sole ruler

337: Constantine's death leads to fresh struggles over succession

395: Definitive division of empire into east and west on death of Theodosius

260: Gallic empire established by Postumus

273: Empire reunited by Aurelian

305: Abdication of Diocletian

312: Battle of Milvian Bridge, just north of Rome; Constantine defeats rival Maxentius

364: Rome loses war for control of Armenia to Sassanian Empire

The later Roman Empire 250–400 CE

④ The Roman Empire 240–395 CE

Parts of Empire ruled by:

	Diocletian
	Maximian
	Galerius
	Constantius
	boundary of Roman Empire 293 CE
PONTUS	diocese established by Diocletian 293 CE

○	principal residences of the tetrarchs
	Gallic Empire of Postumus 260–74 CE
	Kingdom of Palmyra 260–72 CE
	territory abandoned by Rome, with date
	division of Eastern and Western Empires 395 CE

The four tetrarchs ruled the Empire from 293 to 305. Similar forms of joint rule were tried during the 4th century until the Empire finally split in 395.

This gold coin shows the heads of Diocletian and Maximian, first co-rulers of the Roman Empire.

EUROPE AFTER THE FALL OF ROME

THE END OF THE WEST ROMAN EMPIRE in 476 did not signal an immediate descent into barbarism. The rulers of the new kingdoms maintained relations with the eastern emperor in Constantinople, and most pretended to govern on his behalf. In much of western Europe, Roman laws and institutions were retained and, sooner or later, the so-called "barbarians" all converted to Christianity. The East Roman (Byzantine) Empire continued to exert influence in the west. In the 6th century, Justinian, the most powerful emperor of the period, won back much of the West Roman Empire. But, after failing to halt the Lombard invasion of Italy in 568, the Byzantines were unable to reassert their authority. The eventual successors to the Romans in the west were the Franks and the papacy.

This glass drinking horn would have been used at feasts of the Lombard rulers of Italy.

The kingdoms of the new order

The last Roman emperor of authority in the west was Theodosius. On his death in 395, the empire was divided definitively in two. The 5th century saw the transfer of power in western Europe from the emperors to Germanic immigrants, for the most part groups recruited by the Romans to help them defend their lands *(see pp.52–53)*. Chief beneficiaries were the Goths. By 480 the Visigoths had established a large kingdom in Aquitaine and Iberia, with its capital at Toulouse. In 492 the Ostrogoths took Italy and the Dalmatian coast.

Christianity maintained a sense of continuity between the West Roman Empire and the kingdoms that replaced it. This late Roman sarcophagus is from Ravenna, capital of the Ostrogoths, successors to the Romans in Italy.

Classis was the port of Ravenna, capital of Ostrogothic and Byzantine Italy. This detail from a 6th-century mosaic shows the castle and ships riding at anchor in the harbor.

Europe in 500

The most powerful of the new kingdoms established in western Europe in 500 was that of Theodoric the Great, leader of the Ostrogoths. Though he ruled from Ravenna, the Senate still sat in Rome and relations between Romans and Goths were largely amicable. Royal marriages helped forge alliances with the Vandal and Visigothic kings in North Africa and Iberia. Theodoric hoped to create a power bloc to counter the might of the East Roman Empire, but after his death in 526 he was succeeded by his infant grandson, who died young, and the dynasty collapsed.

❶ The inheritors of the Roman Empire at 500

- Frankish expansion
- Ostrogothic expansion
- Byzantine reconquests
- Sassanian expansion

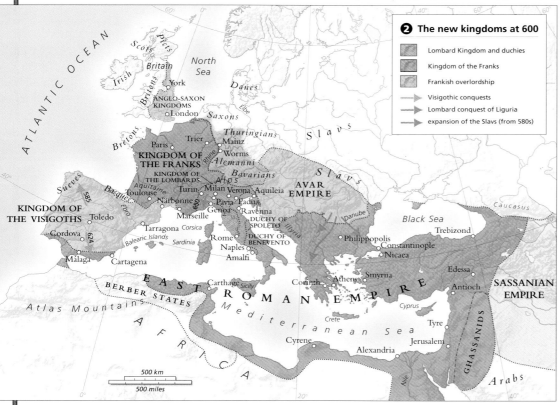

❷ The new kingdoms at 600

- Lombard Kingdom and duchies
- Kingdom of the Franks
- Frankish overlordship
- Visigothic conquests
- Lombard conquest of Liguria
- expansion of the Slavs (from 580s)

This Visigothic cross dates from the 6th century. Although Christian, the Visigoths were Arians (they denied the Trinity). This changed in 589, when King Reccared converted to the orthodox Catholicism of his Hispano-Roman subjects.

Europe in 600

The political map of Europe changed dramatically in the 6th century. In 600 the Visigoths still controlled the Iberian peninsula, but the Franks now ruled most of modern France. The East Roman Empire had reconquered North Africa, Italy, Illyria, and even part of southern Iberia. The destruction of the Roman heritage was far greater during the long war waged by the Byzantines against the Goths than during the previous century. Italy then fell prey to the Lombards (Langobardi), Germanic invaders from the northeast.

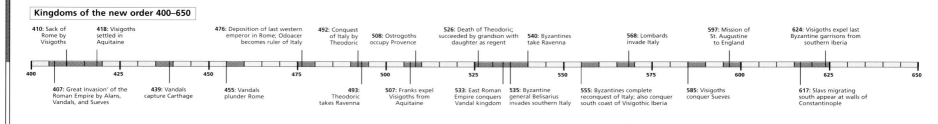

Kingdoms of the new order 400–650

410: Sack of Rome by Visigoths
418: Visigoths settled in Aquitaine
476: Deposition of last western emperor in Rome; Odoacer becomes ruler of Italy
492: Conquest of Italy by Theodoric
508: Ostrogoths occupy Provence
526: Death of Theodoric; succeeded by grandson with daughter as regent
540: Byzantines take Ravenna
568: Lombards invade Italy
597: Mission of St. Augustine to England
624: Visigoths expel last Byzantine garrisons from southern Iberia

407: 'Great Invasion' of the Roman Empire by Alans, Vandals, and Sueves
439: Vandals capture Carthage
455: Vandals plunder Rome
493: Theodoric takes Ravenna
507: Franks expel Visigoths from Aquitaine
533: East Roman Empire conquers Vandal kingdom
535: Byzantine general Belisarius invades southern Italy
555: Byzantines complete reconquest of Italy; also conquer south coast of Visigothic Iberia
585: Visigoths conquer Sueves
617: Slavs migrating south appear at walls of Constantinople

❸ Britain c.750

- Anglo-Saxon kingdoms
- Mercia and dependencies
- Celtic kingdoms
- Pictish kingdoms
- ⚔ battle
- ✝ important monastery

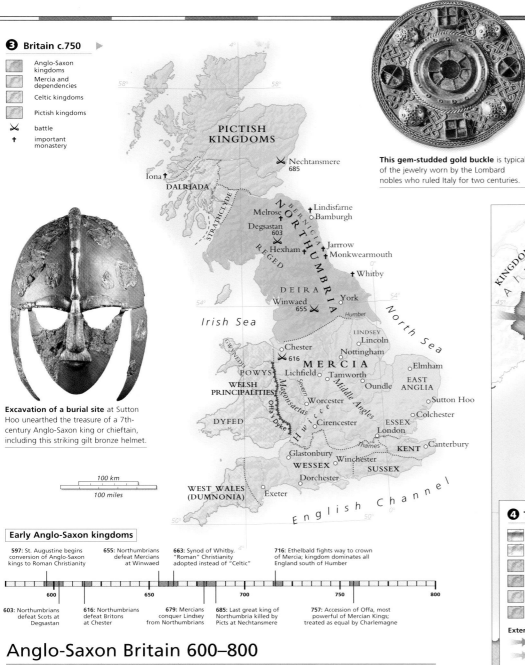

Excavation of a burial site at Sutton Hoo unearthed the treasure of a 7th-century Anglo-Saxon king or chieftain, including this striking gilt bronze helmet.

This gem-studded gold buckle is typical of the jewelry worn by the Lombard nobles who ruled Italy for two centuries.

Byzantine and Lombard Italy

After the expulsion of the Goths, control of Italy was contested by the Byzantines and the Lombards, the latter gradually winning more and more territory after their invasion of 568. Only rarely did the Lombard kings, based at Pavia, exercise authority over the southern dukedoms of Benevento and Spoleto. Similarly, representatives of Byzantium, including the pope, often acted independently according to their own interests. The Byzantines were ousted from Ravenna in 751, but Lombard rule there lasted only until 756. At the pope's request, Pépin, king of the Franks, invaded northern Italy and crushed the Lombards.

Following Lombard invasion of Italy in 568, their former territories are occupied by Avars and Slavs

❹ The struggle for Italy 565–750

- East Roman Empire 565
- Lombard territories 565
- under Lombard rule 590
- Lombard gains by 650
- Lombard gains by 744
- East Roman territory 744

External threats to Italy in the 7th century
- → Franks
- → Avars and Slavs

The struggle for Italy 550–750

568: Lombard invasion of Italy	**590–604:** Papacy of Gregory the Great, who negotiates with Lombards to save Rome	**653:** Conversion of Lombards to Christianity	**712:** Liutprand becomes Lombard king; tries to unite Italy	**751:** Lombards under Aistulf take Ravenna; end of Byzantine rule	**753–56:** Italy invaded by Pépin
554: Frankish invasion defeated; Italy under Byzantine control	**643:** Edict of Rothari: first book of Lombard law	**663:** Byzantine Emperor Constans II invades Italy and sacks Rome	**773–74:** Conquest of Lombards by Charlemagne; northern Italy comes under Frankish rule

Early Anglo-Saxon kingdoms

597: St. Augustine begins conversion of Anglo-Saxon kings to Roman Christianity	**655:** Northumbrians defeat Mercians at Winwaed	**663:** Synod of Whitby. "Roman" Christianity adopted instead of "Celtic"	**716:** Ethelbald fights way to crown of Mercia; kingdom dominates all England south of Humber
603: Northumbrians defeat Scots at Degsastan	**616:** Northumbrians defeat Britons at Chester	**679:** Mercians conquer Lindsey from Northumbrians	**685:** Last great king of Northumbria killed by Picts at Nechtansmere	**757:** Accession of Offa, most powerful of Mercian Kings; treated as equal by Charlemagne

Anglo-Saxon Britain 600–800

For the two centuries that followed the Roman withdrawal in 410, there are no accounts of events in Britain. The Celtic Britons fought each other, as well as Scottish invaders (from Ireland) and Angles, Saxons, and Jutes, who invaded across the North Sea from Denmark and north Germany. Around 600, following St Augustine's mission from Rome to convert the Anglo-Saxons, records appear of a number of kingdoms ruled by Anglo-Saxon kings (though some of these have British names). The west, notably Wales and West Wales (Dumnonia) remained in the hands of Celts. For most of the 7th century, the most powerful kingdom was Northumbria, whose kings briefly controlled much of Scotland. By 700, however, supremacy had passed to the midland kingdom of Mercia.

The early Frankish kingdoms 481–650

The only Germanic kingdom of any permanence established in this period was the Kingdom of the Franks, foundation of modern France. The first Frankish dynasty, the Merovingians, expanded from lands around Tournai under Clovis, who pushed southwest to the Loire, then defeated the Visigoths in Aquitaine. Clovis's sons destroyed the Burgundians and exercised control over several Germanic tribes to the east. When a powerful king such as Clovis died, his territories were divided between his heirs, provoking dynastic civil wars. The three major Frankish kingdoms were Neustria and Austrasia (together referred to as Francia), and Burgundy.

Dagobert I's throne is a powerful emblem of the continuity of the French kingdom, which lasted till the Revolution in 1790.

The early Frankish kingdoms 481–650

c.481: Accession of Clovis I	**c.497:** Clovis converts to Christianity	**558:** Chlothar I sole king of the Franks	**573:** Beginning of major civil wars between the Franks	**629:** Chlothar II dies; succeeded by son, Dagobert I,	**639:** Death of Dagobert; kingdom divided between two sons
507: Clovis defeats Visigoths at Vouillé	**511:** Death of Clovis; his kingdom divided between four sons	**561:** Death of Chlothar I; kingdom divided between his four sons	**613:** Chlothar II king of all Gaul; civil wars end

❺ The Kingdom of the Franks 486–537

- Frankish lands 486
- conquered by Clovis by 507
- conquered by 511
- Kingdom of Franks at the death of Clovis 511
- conquered by Clovis's sons 534
- conquered by Clovis's sons 537
- ⚔ battle

❻ Division of the Frankish kingdoms 561

- Charibert
- Sigebert
- Guntram
- Chilperic
- territory of Frankish overlordship
- ○ royal residence

THE HOLY ROMAN EMPIRE

This bronze statue of Charlemagne is an idealized 9th-century portrait, created after the Emperor's death.

THE FRANKISH KINGS Pepin and Charlemagne crushed the Lombards in Italy, granted lands to the pope, and extended the frontiers of Christian Europe. The coronation of Charlemagne as Holy Roman Emperor in 800 was an ambitious attempt by the papacy to recreate the central authority of imperial Rome. Yet by 843, the empire was divided. In the 10th century, a smaller Holy Roman Empire was established under the Saxon Ottonian dynasty. Otto I, who, like Charlemagne, was crowned in Rome, helped convert the Bohemians, Danes, and Poles to Christianity and stopped the advancing Magyars. Meanwhile, Viking raiders terrorized much of western Europe and in Russia, Swedish Vikings helped establish the new state of Kievan Rus.

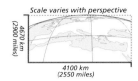

❶ The advance of Islam to 750

Umayyad Caliphate in 750 → Arab raid

Byzantine Empire in 750

Scale varies with perspective

4670 km (2900 miles)

4100 km (2550 miles)

The advance of Islam

In the 7th century, Arab armies carried Islam across the Middle East and North Africa, then, in 711, to the Iberian Peninsula. The Byzantine Empire suffered severe losses and Constantinople had to withstand determined sieges in 674 and 717. In the west, an Islamic invasion of France was turned back in 732 at Poitiers by Charles Martel, the grandfather of Charlemagne. This stemmed the Muslim advance, but Arab raids on all the Christian states of the Mediterranean continued.

The empire of Charlemagne

Charlemagne was both a warrior and a reformer. By 800, he had established Christian hegemony over much of western Europe, his conquest and conversion of Saxony and defeat of the Avars taking the eastern borders of his empire to the Slav world. "Marches," or buffer zones, protected the empire from the Slavs and from the Moorish Emirate of Cordova. The unity of western Christendom did not last: after the death of Louis the Pious in 840, the empire was divided between his three sons, and by 900 it had fragmented into smaller kingdoms. Local dukedoms and counties, the precursors of feudal domains, started to gain power at the expense of central authority.

Charlemagne's throne still stands in a vaulted chapel at Aachen (Aix-la-Chapelle), the most important of the emperor's many royal residences.

Pope Leo III crowned Charlemagne emperor in 800. This confirmed the Carolingians' right to their lands. When Charlemagne was born c.744, his father Pepin was not even king of the Franks, but mayor of the palace. He was elected king in 751.

❷ The empire of Charlemagne ▶

Frankish kingdom in 751	**Major campaigns**
conquest of Pepin	→ in reign of Pepin 751–68
conquest of Charlemagne	→ in reign of Charlemagne 768–814
regions recognizing Charlemagne as overlord, at least nominally	■ royal palace
states of the Church, part of Charlemagne's empire	
marches	
Byzantine possessions	

SAXONY 804 division of Charlemagne's empire, with date of final conquest

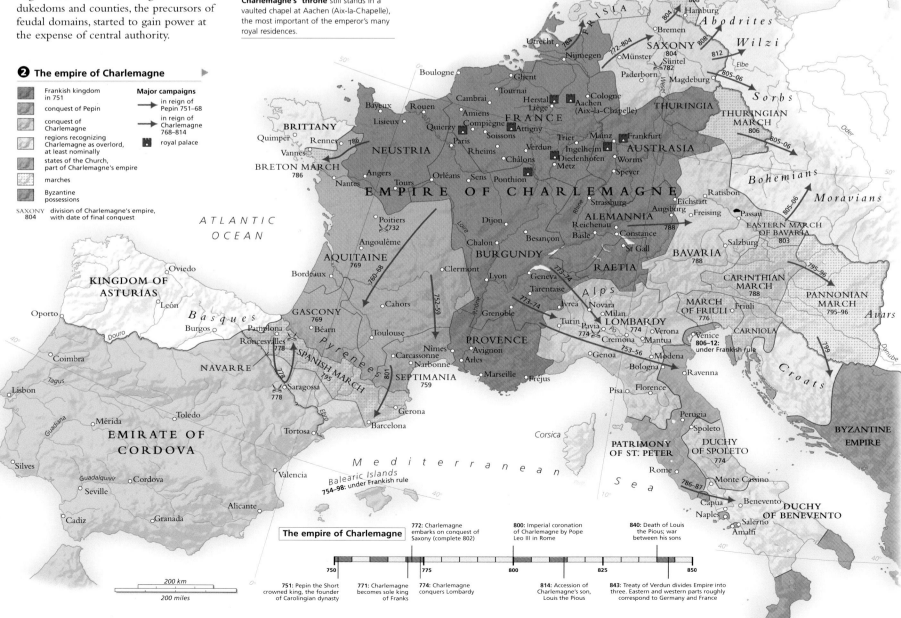

The empire of Charlemagne

751: Pepin the Short crowned king, the founder of Carolingian dynasty

771: Charlemagne becomes sole king of Franks

772: Charlemagne embarks on conquest of Saxony (complete 802)

774: Charlemagne conquers Lombardy

800: Imperial coronation of Charlemagne by Pope Leo III in Rome

814: Accession of Charlemagne's son, Louis the Pious

840: Death of Louis the Pious; war between his sons

843: Treaty of Verdun divides Empire into three. Eastern and western parts roughly correspond to Germany and France

200 km
200 miles

Europe 800–1000

The fragmentation of the Carolingian Empire led, by 900, to its division into eastern and western parts. In 919, the East Frankish crown passed to Henry I of Saxony, who established the Ottonian dynasty, which was to dominate Europe for the next two centuries. The decisive Ottonian defeat of the Magyars earned the respect of rival noblemen, and Otto I's conquest of Italy, and coronation as Holy Roman Emperor (962), legitimized his rule. Otto's successors reinforced their power in Germany by constant movement around their empire. They controlled bishoprics and churches, encouraged learning and literature, and presided over the formation of Christian states in Poland, Hungary, and Bohemia.

Carvings of Viking ships appear on a picture stone in Gotland, dating from the 8th century, just before the raids began. This scene shows the spirits of dead heroes.

The Vikings of Scandinavia

The Vikings earned a fearsome reputation when they began their raids on Europe in the late 8th century. Their leaders were probably warlords who had been displaced by more powerful kings. They targeted the wealth of towns, monasteries, and churches in England, Ireland, and France. By the late 9th century, they ruled kingdoms in England and Ireland, and the Duchy of Normandy in France. Once settled, they adopted Christianity and established commercial towns. The Swedish Vikings raided and traded along the rivers of Russia, making contact with the Byzantine Empire and the Islamic world, a rich source of silver. They founded a merchant town at Novgorod and won control of Kiev, which became capital of the extensive state of Kievan Rus.

Otto II, who reigned from 973 to 983, receives homage from the subject nations of his empire. Portraits of Holy Roman Emperors emulated those of the Byzantine emperors, who were portrayed as God's representatives on earth.

❸ Europe c.800–1000 ▶

- ----- frontiers c.1000
- Muslim lands
- Hungary
- Denmark
- Sweden
- Norway (under Danish rule)
- Byzantine Empire (under direct Byzantine rule)
- Byzantine dependencies (effectively independent)
- Holy Roman Empire

Viking settlement
- Danish
- Swedish
- Norwegian
- Danelaw 878–954

Expeditions and raids
- → Danish
- → Swedish
- → Norwegian
- ⟹ Magyar migration
- → Magyar raid
- → Muslim raid

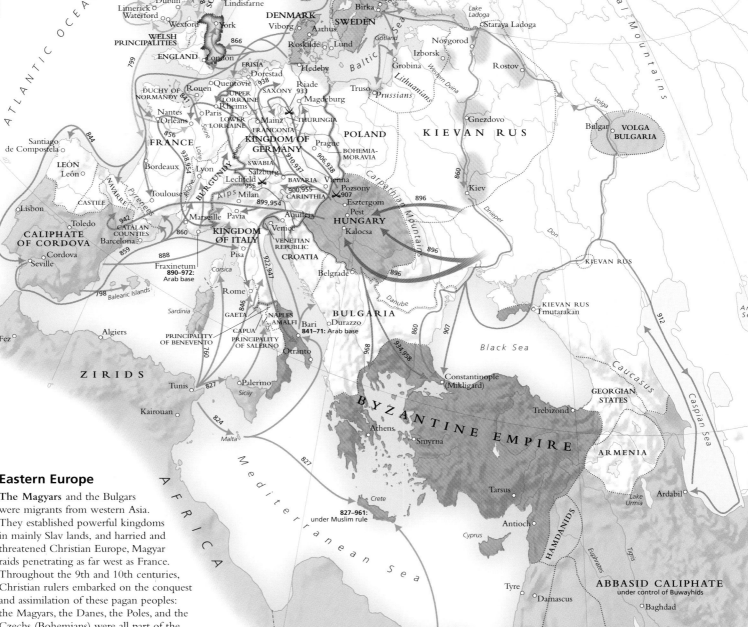

Stephen I of Hungary favored the Roman church over the Orthodox and in 1001 was recognized as king by the pope, who sent him a crown (above).

Eastern Europe

The Magyars and the Bulgars were migrants from western Asia. They established powerful kingdoms in mainly Slav lands, and harried and threatened Christian Europe, Magyar raids penetrating as far west as France. Throughout the 9th and 10th centuries, Christian rulers embarked on the conquest and assimilation of these pagan peoples: the Magyars, the Danes, the Poles, and the Czechs (Bohemians) were all part of the Catholic church by 1000, while the Byzantine Empire had crushed the Bulgars by 1018.

Europe 800–1000

790s: Beginnings of Viking raids on western Europe		
	841: Vikings establish settlement at Dublin	
		874: Viking "Great Army" creates kingdom of York

896: Magyars start to settle in Danube basin

911: Vikings found Duchy of Normandy

936: Henry is succeeded by his son, Otto I; Bohemians rebel (made tributary 950)

955: Otto defeats Magyars decisively at Lechfeld

980: Effective end of Viking dynasty at Dublin

1000: Poland joins Catholic church

1001: Coronation of Stephen I of Hungary

780 — 800 — 820 — 840 — 860 — 880 — 900 — 920 — 940 — 960 — 980 — 1000 — 1020

816: Byzantines make peace with Bulgars after prolonged military campaigns

844: Vikings raid as far as Toulouse

863: Saints Cyril and Methodius sent as missionaries to Moravia

919: Henry of Saxony elected king of eastern kingdom of the Franks (Germany)

933: Henry defeats Magyars at Riade

962: Otto I crowned Emperor by John XII; spends later years in Italy

980–83: Otto II campaigns against Arabs in Italy

990: Ottonian campaign against Bohemians

1018: Defeated Bulgars submit to Byzantine Empire

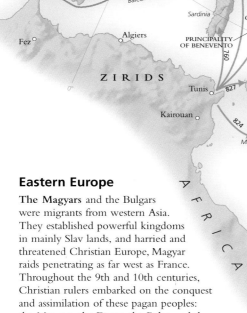

EUROPE IN THE AGE OF THE CRUSADES

Emperor Frederick Barbarossa is shown in Crusader dress. He drowned in 1190 on his way to the Third Crusade.

FOLLOWING THE SUCCESS of the First Crusade *(see pp. 64–65)*, the spirit of the venture captured the imagination of Christian Europe. Expeditions to subdue the pagans of the Baltic and campaigns against the Muslims in Iberia were undertaken with papal blessing. Ideals of chivalry inspired the new religious orders of warrior clerics established to protect pilgrims to the Holy Land, such as the Templars and Hospitallers. These organizations became immensely wealthy with hundreds of priories and estates in Europe. At the same time, it was a period of great intellectual excitement. The rediscovery of Classical texts inspired an interest in philosophy; universities were founded and new religious orders gave renewed energy to the Catholic Church.

The crusading ideal in Europe

The Knights Templar were so well rewarded for their services in the Holy Land that they became a powerful political force throughout Europe.

The ideal of Holy War which inspired the Crusaders to fight in the Iberian Peninsula and the Holy Land was used to justify other wars, conflicts, and even racist atrocities. In 1096, German mobs attacked and massacred as "unbelievers" the Jews in their own communities. Missionary efforts to convert the pagan peoples of Livonia, Lithuania, and Prussia became a crusade, preached by Pope Innocent III. One crusade was mounted against "heretics" within Christian Europe – the Cathars (Albigensians) of southern France. In 1212 a French shepherd boy even set out to lead a children's crusade to Jerusalem. Most of his followers got no further than Genoa and Marseille.

The crusading ideal

1118: Founder of Knights Templar granted site close to Solomon's temple in Jerusalem
1126: Hospitallers of St. John adopt a military role
1208: Crusade against Cathars, or Albigensians, in southern France
1283: Conquest of Prussia completed by Teutonic Knights
1312: Templar Order accused of heresy and suppressed by Pope

1050 — 1100 — 1150 — 1200 — 1250 — 1300 — 1350

1096: Attacks on Jewish communities by Crusaders and their supporters
1197: Order of Teutonic Knights established in the Holy Land
1233: Inquisition established in Toulouse
1306–10: Hospitallers conquer Rhodes, which becomes their base

❶ The crusading ideal in Europe 1100–1300

- predominantly pagan lands c.1100
- Muslim lands c.1180
- main Cathar region
- Waldensian strongholds
- → direction of Reconquest in Spain

Crusades in the Baltic
- → Danish expeditions
- → Swedish expeditions
- → direction of advance of Sword Brothers
- → direction of advance of Teutonic Knights

Other crusades
- → Albigensian Crusade 1209–13
- → Children's Crusade 1212
- ✦ massacre of Jews 1096
- ⊕ major Templar house 1300
- ⊕ headquarters of crusading orders in Spain
- — frontiers 1180
- Holy Roman Empire
- first state of Teutonic Knights 1211–15

The Norman conquest of England

The Duchy of Normandy was established in northern France by 911. In 1066, William, Duke of Normandy led an expedition to win the English throne from Harold, the last Anglo-Saxon king. Harold had seen off the threat of another claimant, Harald Hardrada of Norway, but, after a long march south, he was defeated by William at Hastings. Once England had been conquered, it was parceled out in fiefs amongst William's Norman knights.

❷ The Norman conquest of England 1066–1095

- → Harald Hardrada's route 1066
- → Harold's route 1066
- → William's route 1066
- William's possessions 1066
- conquered by 1070
- additional conquest by 1095
- area of uprising against Norman rule c.1070
- ✗ battle

The Norman conquest of England 1066

5 Jan: Death of Edward the Confessor, king of England; Harold assumes throne
Apr: Harold's fleet drives off Tostig; guards English Channel until September
25 Sep: Harold defeats his brother Tostig and Harald Hardrada at Stamford Bridge
14 Oct: Battle of Hastings; Harold defeated and killed
25 Dec: William crowned in London

Jan 1066 — Apr 1066 — Jul 1066 — Oct 1066 — Jan 1067

Apr: Raids along south coast of England by Harold's exiled brother Tostig
Aug–Sep: William assembles fleet and army at Dives-sur-Mer
28 Sep: William lands at Pevensey

William's success depended on a large fleet to ship men and horses across the English Channel, but the Normans had long abandoned the seagoing life of their Viking forebears. Yet they managed to build a fleet, depicted here in a scene from the Bayeux Tapestry, large enough to transport an army of perhaps 7000 men to England.

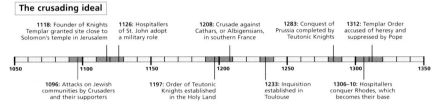

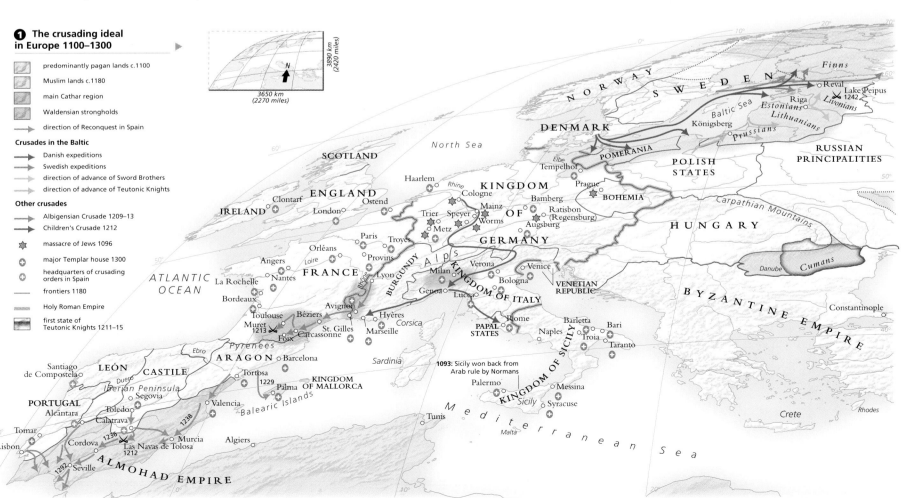

1093: Sicily won back from Arab rule by Normans

❸ The 12th-century renaissance in Europe ▶

- ■ university with date of foundation
- ▣ other important theological school
- Muslim lands reconquered by Christians 1030–1200
- Muslim lands reconquered by Christians 1200–1300
- ○ center of contact with Arab scholarship
- † major Cistercian house with date of foundation
- —— frontiers 1200
- Holy Roman Empire

(map labels)

NORWAY
SWEDEN
DENMARK
†Alvastra 1143
North Sea
Baltic Sea
SCOTLAND
IRELAND
†Mellifont 1142
†Newbattle 1140
†Melrose 1142
†Jervaulx 1150
Fountains 1132
†Rievaulx 1132
†Kirkstall 1147
WALES
ENGLAND
Oxford early 12th century
Cambridge 1209
London
Waverley 1128
Canterbury
Camp 1132
Cologne
KINGDOM OF GERMANY
†Wagrowiec 1143
POLAND
RUSSIAN PRINCIPALITIES
†Jedrzejów 1149
Prague 1348
Worms
Rhine
Elbe
c.1200: University of Paris has colleges for students from all over western Europe
Bec
Paris
Chartres
Rheims
Angers
Orléans c.1236
Meung
Tours
Clairvaux 1115
Ebrach 1127
†Pontigny 1114
Morimond 1115
†Lützel 1124
Eberbach 1135
†La Ferté 1113
Cîteaux 1098
1308: University of Lisbon transferred to Coimbra
FRANCE
Grenoble
Milan
Vicenza 1204
Padua (law) 1222
Heiligenkreuz 1137
HUNGARY
†Czikador 1142
Cahors 1332
Toulouse
†Morerula 1132
Avignon 1303
Piacenza 1248
Venice
Bologna (law) 1088
VENETIAN REPUBLIC
Arezzo 1215
LEÓN
León
NAVARRE
Pamplona
Béziers 1229
Montpellier (medicine) 12th century
Narbonne
Marseille
Genoa
Pisa
Perugia 1308
Assisi
Danube
SERBIA
BULGARIA
Coimbra
Alcobaça 1148
PORTUGAL
Salamanca 1218
Tarazona
Lérida 1300
ARAGON
Segovia
Lisbon 1290
CASTILE
Toledo
Barcelona
Siena 1246
Rome c.1140
1245
PAPAL STATES
Naples 1224
Salerno (medicine) since 9th century
BYZANTINE EMPIRE
Seville 1254
Cordova
Balearic Islands
Sardinia
Corsica
KINGDOM OF ITALY
KINGDOM OF SICILY
Palermo
Sicily
ALMOHAD EMPIRE
Mediterranean Sea

500 km
500 miles

The 12th-century renaissance

Christian idealism in this period was reflected in the growth of new monastic and teaching orders. The Cistercians, founded at Cîteaux in 1098, spread throughout Europe under the charismatic leadership of St. Bernard of Clairvaux. The early 13th century saw the even more rapid expansion of the orders founded by St. Francis of Assisi and St. Dominic. At the same time a renewed interest in scholarship led to the founding of new universities. The increased availability of the seminal texts of the ancient world, obtained through the medium of Arabic translations, was critically important for medieval scholars. By reconciling the science of Aristotle with Christian faith, St. Thomas Aquinas (d. 1274) gave Catholic theology an intellectual basis that lasted for centuries.

The Cistercians were founded in reaction to the idle life of monasteries financed by tithes. They worked their own land and were self-supporting, though they accepted gifts of marginal or recently conquered land. Their graceful architecture was plain and unadorned, as seen here in the refectory of Fountains Abbey in northern England.

The 12th-century renaissance

- **1098:** Foundation of new monastery at Cîteaux
- **1115:** Bernard founds Cistercian daughter house at Clairvaux
- **1126:** Birth of Muslim philosopher Averroes in Cordova
- **1158:** Frederick Barbarossa grants imperial protection to University of Bologna
- **1210:** St. Francis of Assisi gains papal recognition of his order of friars dedicated to poverty
- **1220:** First chapter of the Dominican order of friars
- **1249:** Foundation of Merton College, Oxford

(timeline: 1100 1150 1200 1250 1300)

The Angevin Empire

The laws of inheritance of feudal Europe enabled Henry II, Count of Anjou and King of England, to acquire lands that included England, Ireland, and most of western France. His marriage to Eleanor of Aquitaine meant that he ruled more of France than the French king, even though he was nominally the latter's vassal. He spent much of his reign defending his empire against Louis VII of France and the ambitions of his children. After his death in 1189, the Angevin empire soon disintegrated. In 1214, Philip II of France defeated Henry's son, John, ending English rule in Normandy. England, however, did keep western Aquitaine, and, in the 14th century, would renew its claims to France in the Hundred Years' War.

English possessions 1154–89

- **1152:** Henry marries Eleanor of Aquitaine
- **1154:** Succession of Henry II to English crown
- **1151:** Henry succeeds Geoffrey as Count of Anjou
- **1173–74:** Henry quells French-backed rebellion by his sons
- **1189:** Succession of Richard the Lionheart
- **1199:** Accession of John
- **1214:** Defeat of English and German allies at Bouvines

(timeline: 1140 1160 1180 1200 1220)

Henry II and Eleanor of Aquitaine had an intense, stormy relationship. She was imprisoned for intriguing against him on behalf of their eldest son Henry in 1173–74.

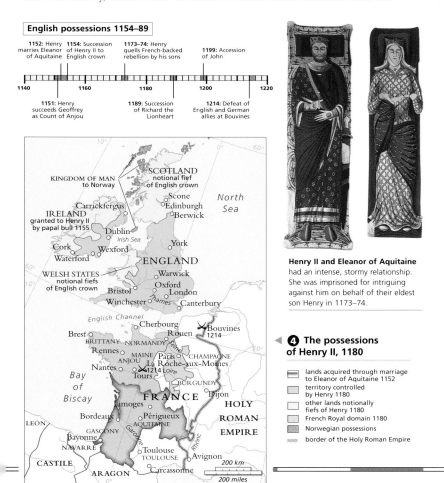

(map labels)

KINGDOM OF MAN to Norway
SCOTLAND notional fief of English crown
North Sea
IRELAND granted to Henry II by papal bull 1155
Carrickfergus
Scone
Edinburgh
Berwick
Dublin
Irish Sea
York
Cork
Waterford
Wexford
WELSH STATES notional fiefs of English crown
ENGLAND
Warwick
Oxford
London
Bristol
Winchester
Thames
Canterbury
English Channel
Cherbourg
Brest
BRITTANY
Rouen
Bouvines 1214
Rennes
NORMANDY
MAINE
Paris
CHAMPAGNE
La Roche-aux-Moines
Nantes
ANJOU
1214
Tours
Loire
Bay of Biscay
FRANCE
BURGUNDY
Dijon
HOLY ROMAN EMPIRE
Limoges
Bordeaux
GASCONY
PÉRIGORD
Périgueux
AQUITAINE
Bayonne
NAVARRE
CASTILE
LEÓN
TOULOUSE
Toulouse
Avignon
ARAGON
Carcassonne
Garonne

200 km
200 miles

❹ The possessions of Henry II, 1180

- lands acquired through marriage to Eleanor of Aquitaine 1152
- territory controlled by Henry 1180
- other lands notionally fiefs of Henry 1180
- French Royal domain 1180
- Norwegian possessions
- border of the Holy Roman Empire

Venice and the Latin Empire

As well as being the principal emporium for east-west trade, Venice also made money shipping Crusaders to the Ho;y Land. When the Fourth Crusade gathered in Venice in 1203, the leaders did not have enough money to pay. The Venetians diverted the fleet first to capture the Adriatic port of Zara, long coveted by Venice, then to Constantinople, where in 1204, the Crusaders sacked the city and installed their own emperor. The Empire was divided into Venetian colonies and Latin fiefs. There were now two empires in the east; the "Latin" empire, ruled from Constantinople, and a rump Byzantine Empire, ruled from Nicaea.

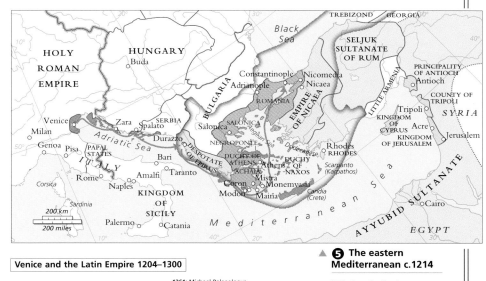

The Crusaders' motive for attacking Constantinople in 1203 was financial reward for restoring Alexius IV (son of deposed emperor Isaac Angelus) to the imperial throne. When the population rebelled and killed Alexius in 1204, the Crusaders took over the city for themselves.

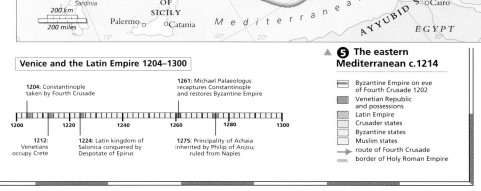

(map labels)

HOLY ROMAN EMPIRE
HUNGARY
Buda
Black Sea
TREBIZOND
GEORGIA
SELJUK SULTANATE OF RUM
PRINCIPALITY OF ANTIOCH
Constantinople
Nicomedia
Nicaea
Adrianople
BULGARIA
ROMANIA
EMPIRE OF NICAEA
Antioch
COUNTY OF TRIPOLI
Venice
Zara
SERBIA
Spalato
Milan
Genoa
Pisa
PAPAL STATES
Durazzo
Salonica
SALONICA
NEGROPONTE
Tripoli
LITTLE ARMENIA
KINGDOM OF CYPRUS
Acre
SYRIA
Adriatic Sea
Bari
DESPOTATE OF EPIRUS
DUCHY OF ATHENS
Athens
DUCHY OF NAXOS
Rhodes
RHODES
KINGDOM OF JERUSALEM
Jerusalem
ITALY
Rome
Amalfi
Taranto
ACHAIA
Coron
Mistra
Monemvasia
Scarpanto (Karpathos)
Corsica
Sardinia
Naples
KINGDOM OF SICILY
Modon
Maina
Candia (Crete)
Mediterranean Sea
Palermo
Catania
AYYUBID SULTANATE
EGYPT
Cairo

200 km
200 miles

Venice and the Latin Empire 1204–1300

- **1204:** Constantinople taken by Fourth Crusade
- **1212:** Venetians occupy Crete
- **1224:** Latin kingdom of Salonica conquered by Despotate of Epirus
- **1261:** Michael Palaeologus recaptures Constantinople and restores Byzantine Empire
- **1275:** Principality of Achaia inherited by Philip of Anjou; ruled from Naples

(timeline: 1200 1220 1240 1260 1280 1300)

❺ The eastern Mediterranean c.1214

- Byzantine Empire on eve of Fourth Crusade 1202
- Venetian Republic and possessions
- Latin Empire
- Crusader states
- Byzantine states
- Muslim states
- → route of Fourth Crusade
- border of Holy Roman Empire

EUROPE IN CRISIS

THE CONSOLIDATION of nation states on the eastern and western edges of Europe was matched, in the 13th century, by the decline of the Holy Roman Empire, its power depleted by long struggles with the papacy and the Italian city-states. In the east, raids by Mongols destroyed Kiev in 1240, and Russia, subject to Mongol overlords, developed in isolation until the 15th century. In the northeast, German colonization brought political and economic change, with a new trading axis around the Baltic Sea. During the 14th century, however, social unrest swept through Europe, compounded by famines, economic decline, dynastic wars, and the Black Death of 1347 *(see pp. 72–73)*, which wiped out a third of Europe's population in just two years.

This silver pfennig shows the Emperor Frederick II, whose claim to rule Italy alienated the popes.

The Empire and the papacy

Under the Hohenstaufen dynasty, the aspirations of the Holy Roman Emperors to universal authority were blocked by the papacy in central Italy, and the city-based communes of northern Italy. Emperor Frederick II (1211–50) clashed with Rome at a time when popes exercised great political power. After his death, the papacy gave the Kingdom of Sicily to Charles of Anjou, and Frederick's heirs were eliminated. Confronted with the growing power of France and England, the Empire lost any pretence to political supremacy in Europe; in Germany, a mosaic of clerical states, principalities, and free cities continued to undermine imperial authority.

Under Innocent III (1198–1216) the medieval papacy was at the height of its spiritual authority and temporal power.

England, Scotland, and Wales

After a century of peace along the Anglo-Scottish border, Edward I (1272–1307) set out to assert his overlordship over all the British Isles. In 1284 he annexed Wales, bestowing the title of Prince of Wales on his son, but Scotland proved more intractable; Edward's attempts to subdue the Scots were met with resistance led by Robert Bruce, the victor at Bannockburn (1314). Hoping to extend his domains, Bruce sent an expedition to Ireland in 1315. His brother Edward continued fighting there until his death in 1318. In 1328, after a devastating period of guerrilla warfare and border raiding, England acknowledged Scottish independence.

The Scottish king, Robert Bruce, pictured here with his second wife, was a noble of Norman descent like his English enemies.

England, Scotland, and Wales 1284–1337

1284: Edward I invades Wales	**1305:** Execution of William Wallace, Scottish nationalist leader	**1322:** Scottish barons assert independence in Declaration of Arbroath	**1329:** Death of Robert Bruce	**1337:** Start of Hundred Years' War; Scots ally with French against England

1280	1290	1300	1310	1320	1330	1340	1350

1296: Edward I invades Scotland	**1314:** English defeated at Bannockburn	**1318:** Edward Bruce killed in Ireland	**1328:** Scottish independence confirmed by Treaty of Northampton

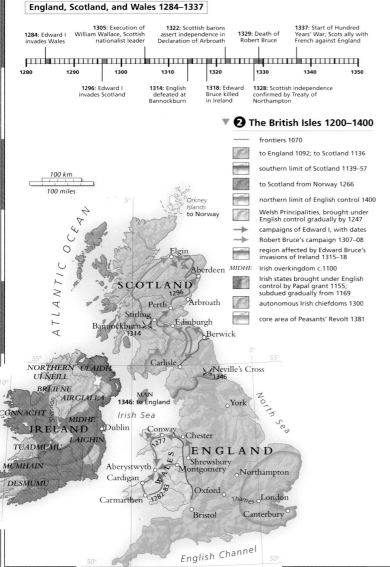

❷ The British Isles 1200–1400

- frontiers 1070
- to England 1092; to Scotland 1136
- southern limit of Scotland 1139–57
- to Scotland from Norway 1266
- northern limit of English control 1400
- Welsh Principalities, brought under English control gradually by 1247
- → campaigns of Edward I, with dates
- → Robert Bruce's campaign 1307–08
- → region affected by Edward Bruce's invasions of Ireland 1315–18
- *MIDHE* Irish overkingdom c.1100
- Irish states brought under English control by Papal grant 1155; subdued gradually from 1169
- autonomous Irish chiefdoms 1300
- core area of Peasants' Revolt 1381

100 km
100 miles

ATLANTIC OCEAN

Orkney Islands
to Norway

Elgin

Aberdeen

SCOTLAND
1296

Perth
Stirling
Bannockburn
1314
Edinburgh
Berwick

Arbroath

NORTHERN UI NEILL
UI NEILL
BREIFNE
AIRGIALLA
CONNACHT
MIDHE
IRELAND LAIGHIN
Dublin
TUADMUMU
MUMHAIN
DESMUMU

MAN
1346: to England
Irish Sea

Carlisle
Neville's Cross
1346
York
North Sea

Conway
Chester
WALES
ENGLAND
Shrewsbury
Aberystwyth
Montgomery
Northampton
Cardigan
Oxford
London
Carmarthen 1282–83
Thames
Bristol
Canterbury

English Channel

❶ The Empire of Frederick II

- frontier of Holy Roman Empire 1250
- Kingdom of Germany
- Kingdom of Italy
- under effective Hohenstaufen control 1250
- German lands largely under imperial or Hohenstaufen ownership
- Papal States 1178
- added by 1219
- added by 1278
- Venetian Republic and possessions
- ● member of Lombard League 1167
- frontiers 1250

DENMARK
Baltic Sea
North Sea
ENGLAND
FRISIA
Lübeck
Marienburg
Bremen
Stettin
POMERANIA
TEUTONIC ORDER
Utrecht
Elbe
SAXONY
Toruń
Antwerp
Dortmund
BRANDENBURG
Magdeburg
Poznań
Gniezno
LOWER LORRAINE
Aachen
Cologne
LUSATIA
POLISH PRINCIPALITIES
Rheims
Merseburg
THURINGIA
MEISSEN
Wrocław (Breslau)
Trier
Verdun
FRANCONIA
Eger
Prague
Metz
Nuremberg
Hagenau
KINGDOM OF BOHEMIA
Cracow
Troyes
UPPER LORRAINE
KINGDOM OF GERMANY
Danube
Ratisbon (Regensburg)
FRANCE
SWABIA
Ulm
Augsburg
BAVARIA
AUSTRIA
Citeaux
Basle
Constance
Salzburg
Melk
Vienna
Pozsony
Esztergom
Besançon
Zurich
TYROL
STYRIA
Graz
Buda
Székesfehérvár
KINGDOM OF ARLES
Lyon
Geneva
ALPS
CARINTHIA
FRIULI
HUNGARY
Pécs
Rhône
Como
Bergamo
Cortenuova 1237
VERONA
CARNIOLA
Legnano 1176
Novara
Brescia
Zágráb
Avignon
Vercelli
Milan
Piacenza
Mantua
VENETIAN REPUBLIC
Arles
Alessandria
KINGDOM OF
Cremona
Venice
Nice
LOMBARDY
ITALY
Reggio
Po
Parma
Modena Bologna
Ferrara
Danube
Genoa
Imola
Faenza
Rimini
San Marino
Zara
SERBIA
Pisa
TUSCANY
Florence
Ancona
Adriatic Sea
Ragusa
Siena
Perugia
Mediterranean Sea
Corsica
disputed between
Genoa and Pisa
Viterbo
Rome
Tagliacozzo 1268
BULGARIA
Dyrrhachium (Durazzo)
Gaeta
Capua
Benevento 1266
Bari
DESPOTATE OF EPIRUS
Naples
Amalfi
Otranto
KINGDOM OF SICILY 1194
Palermo
Messina
Syracuse

200 km
200 miles

The Hohenstaufens and the papacy

1167: Lombard League formed to oppose Emperor Frederick I Barbarossa in northern Italy	**1198:** Accession of Pope Innocent III	**1211:** Frederick II becomes Emperor	**1245:** Innocent IV excommunicates Frederick	**1268:** Charles of Anjou defeats Conradin, Frederick's grandson, at Tagliacozzo	**1282:** Sicilian Vespers; Charles of Anjou defeated by Aragonese	

1150	1170	1190	1210	1230	1250	1270	1290	1310

1194: Emperor Henry VI crowned King of Sicily	**1237:** Frederick II defeats Italian communes at Cortenuova	**1250:** Death of Frederick	**1305:** Pope Clement V takes up residency at Avignon, under French supervision	

Eastward expansion in the Baltic

A German-led wave of migration, from 1100–1350, transformed eastern and Baltic Europe. As peasants moved east in search of land and resources, German language and law became predominant; New towns were bound together in the Hanseatic League, a trading association with links from Muscovy to London. Crusades in the east were spearheaded by the Knights of the Teutonic Order, who began to wage war on the pagans of Prussia and Lithuania in 1226. They also took over the Sword Brothers' lands in Livonia. The Livonians and Prussians were subdued, but Lithuania expanded to the southeast to become a powerful state. It was united with Poland in 1386.

Marienburg was the headquarters of the Teutonic Knights from 1309. Part abbey, part fortress, it was built of brick like many of the castles erected by the crusading order in Prussia and Livonia.

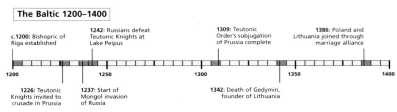

The Baltic 1200–1400

c.1200: Bishopric of Riga established	1242: Russians defeat Teutonic Knights at Lake Peipus
1226: Teutonic Knights invited to crusade in Prussia	1237: Start of Mongol invasion of Russia

1309: Teutonic Order's subjugation of Prussia complete

1342: Death of Gedymin, founder of Lithuania

1386: Poland and Lithuania joined through marriage alliance

▲ ❸ **The Baltic states 1100–1400**

frontier of Kievan Rus c.1100	under Danish control c.1225
Holy Roman Empire, 1100	eastern frontier of ethnic German settlement 1100
added to Holy Roman Empire by 1380	frontier of ethnic German settlement 1400
Sweden	possessions of the Hungarian Angevins
added to Sweden by 1323	○ member of Hanseatic League (not all shown)
→ main thrusts of Danish expansion	· · · · · frontiers 1380

Central and southeastern Europe

After the setbacks of the early 13th century, when eastern Europe was devastated by Mongol invasions, the consolidation of powerful new states began. In Bohemia, the imperial ambitions of Ottakar II (1253–78) briefly expanded his domain from Silesia to the Adriatic, but he came into conflict with Bohemian and German princes, and the Habsburgs were able to seize power in Austria on his death. Powerful monarchies were established in Lithuania under Gedymin (c.1315–42), in Poland under Casimir the Great (1333–70), and in Hungary under Louis the Great (1342–82). Bohemia under the Luxembourg dynasty remained an influential state, especially when the king was elected as the Emperor Charles IV. In the Balkans, Stefan Dušan (1331–55) forged for himself a substantial Serbian Empire, but it fell to the Ottomans in 1389.

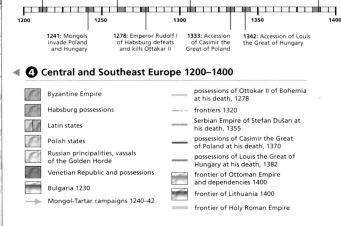

The Emperor Charles IV is shown with his Electors. His Golden Bull of 1356 set out clear rules for electing the emperor.

Central and southeastern Europe 1200–1400

1212: Golden Bull establishes Kingdom of Bohemia

1260: Ottakar II of Bohemia defeats Bela IV of Hungary

1306: Luxembourg dynasty acquires Bohemia

1389: Battle of Kosovo; Ottomans gain control of Balkans

1241: Mongols invade Poland and Hungary

1278: Emperor Rudolf I of Habsburg defeats and kills Ottokar II

1333: Accession of Casimir the Great of Poland

1342: Accession of Louis the Great of Hungary

◄ ❹ **Central and Southeast Europe 1200–1400**

Byzantine Empire	possessions of Ottokar II of Bohemia at his death, 1278
Habsburg possessions	frontiers 1320
Latin states	Serbian Empire of Stefan Dušan at his death, 1355
Polish states	possessions of Casimir the Great of Poland at his death, 1370
Russian principalities, vassals of the Golden Horde	possessions of Louis the Great of Hungary at his death, 1382
Venetian Republic and possessions	frontier of Ottoman Empire and dependencies 1400
Bulgaria 1230	frontier of Lithuania 1400
→ Mongol-Tartar campaigns 1240–42	frontier of Holy Roman Empire

TRADE IN MEDIEVAL EUROPE

The seal of Lübeck shows a cog, the ship used for large cargoes in northern Europe.

THE EXPLOSION IN EUROPE'S POPULATION, which nearly doubled between the 10th and 14th centuries, was caused by greatly increased agricultural productivity, enhanced by technological innovations, in particular the use of the iron plow, and large land clearance projects, which brought marginal land, such as marshes and forests, under cultivation. This demographic surge inevitably led to increased trading activity; merchants traversed the continent, using the trans-Alpine passes which provided arterial routes between Italy and the North and, from c.1300, new maritime routes which opened up the North and Baltic seas. Trade and commerce went hand in hand with urban development. Commercial wealth had a cultural impact; cities were enhanced with magnificent buildings and churches and, from c.1200, universities. As cities prospered, a new class, the bourgeoisie, emerged.

Medieval trade

From the 11th century the Alpine passes had linked the textile towns of Lombardy and manufacturing centers of the Po valley with northern Europe, rich in natural resources, such as timber, grain, wool, and metals. Merchants converged from all over Europe to trade at vast seasonal fairs. International bankers, such as the Florentine Peruzzi, facilitated payments and promoted business. Around 1300, the Genoese opened a new sea route to the North Sea through the Strait of Gibraltar; Bruges, at the end of the route, became a major city. In the Mediterranean, Genoa competed with Venice for the carrying trade. Venice controlled the valuable eastern routes, profiting from trade in silks, sugar, spices, and gemstones from India and East Asia. In northern Germany, an association of trading cities centered on Lübeck, the Hanseatic League, promoted monopolies and sought exclusive trading rights with towns in England, Scandinavia, and Flanders.

Italian towns

Northern Italy was well-endowed with populous, wealthy cities, such as Milan and Florence. The Italian cities did not develop under the direct rule of kings, emperors, or the nobility, and took advantage of this to assert their municipal rights, evolving their own constitutions, codes of law, and military forces, the "communal movement."

The textile industry flourished in Flanders and northern Italy. The horizontal loom (above) was introduced to Europe in the 11th century.

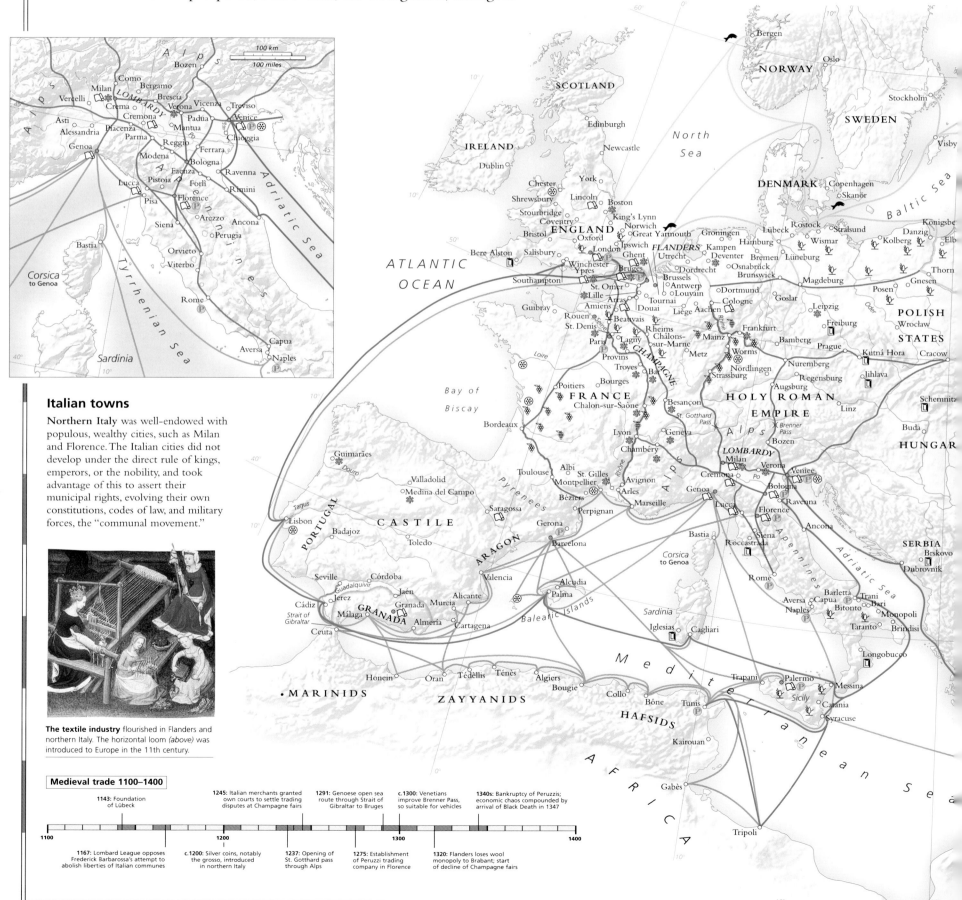

Medieval trade 1100–1400

1143: Foundation of Lübeck

1167: Lombard League opposes Frederick Barbarossa's attempt to abolish liberties of Italian communes

c.1200: Silver coins, notably the grosso, introduced in northern Italy

1237: Opening of St. Gotthard pass through Alps

1245: Italian merchants granted own courts to settle trading disputes at Champagne fairs

1275: Establishment of Peruzzi trading company in Florence

1291: Genoese open sea route through Strait of Gibraltar to Bruges

c.1300: Venetians improve Brenner Pass, so suitable for vehicles

1320: Flanders loses wool monopoly to Brabant; start of decline of Champagne fairs

1340s: Bankruptcy of Peruzzis; economic chaos compounded by arrival of Black Death in 1347

1100   1200   1300   1400

MONEY AND BANKING

Many gold and silver currencies circulated freely in Medieval Europe, irrespective of where they were minted, so money changing was inevitably an important profession. Traveling merchants left currency on deposit with money changers in exchange for a receipt, the first stage in the evolution of banking. By the 14th century the use of the bill of exchange, where one person instructs another to pay a sum of money to a third party, was widespread. The organization of bills of exchange was lucrative, and banking families, such as the Peruzzi and Bardi of Florence, became rich and powerful.

Venetian coinage included the silver grosso and the widely circulated gold ducat.

Medieval Italy gave the world the word "bank" from the *banco* (counter) where bankers transacted their business, as shown in this 14th-century illustration.

Medieval cities

Many of the cities of Medieval Europe owed their development to trade and commerce. The cities of northern Italy emerged from the 10th century onward, as entrepôts in the trade between Europe, Byzantium, and the Islamic world. In the 13th century, the demand for manufactured goods, such as glassware, textiles, and metalwork, led to the emergence of industrial centers, notably the Lombard textile towns and the wool centers of Flanders, such as Ghent, Bruges, and Ypres. By the mid-13th century, German expansion eastward had led to the growth of a thriving network of Baltic trading cities, including Lübeck, Hamburg, Danzig, and Riga.

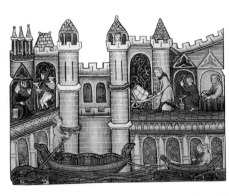

The Seine was vital to the economy of Paris. Boats of all sizes delivered goods along the river and the fortified bridges carried a constant flow of traders.

▼ ❷ **Paris c.1400**

- university and colleges
- other important building
- built-up area
- ✝ church
- city gate
- wall of Philip Augustus c.1200
- wall of Charles V 1357

Medieval Paris

From the 11th century, Paris benefited from the return of order and stability under the Capetian kings. Streets were paved, city walls enlarged and three "divisions" of the city emerged; the merchants were based on the right bank of the Seine, the university (recognized in 1200) on the left bank, with civic and religious institutions on the Île de la Cité. In the 14th century, however, the city stagnated under the dual blows of the Black Death (*see pp. 72–73*) and the Hundred Years' War; repeatedly fought over by the contending forces, it was beset by riots and civil disorder.

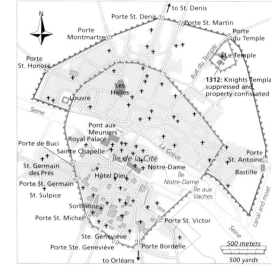

Medieval Paris

c.1200: Paris undergoes improvements; streets are paved	1257: Foundation of Sorbonne; it soon becomes most famous college of Paris University
1382: Tax riot is brutally suppressed; municipal government suspended	

1100 — 1200 — 1300 — 1400

1171: King Louis VII grants river-merchants' guild a monopoly of river trade

1220: Citizens of Paris granted right to collect import duty

1356: Provost of merchants, Étienne Marcel, takes over running of Paris and orders building of new city wall

Medieval Venice

Venice was perceived as the symbolic center of a liberal government and divinely ordered religious, civic, and commercial life. Its political focus was the Doge's Palace, residence of the elected Doge and center of government. Since the city's wealth depended on maritime trade, the government maintained a vast shipyard – the Darsena – to build galleys for war and for merchant ventures.

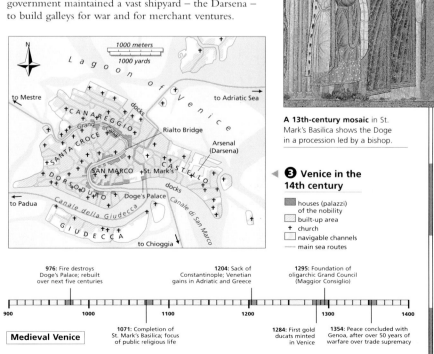

A 13th-century mosaic in St. Mark's Basilica shows the Doge in a procession led by a bishop.

◀ ❸ **Venice in the 14th century**

- houses (palazzi) of the nobility
- built-up area
- ✝ church
- navigable channels
- main sea routes

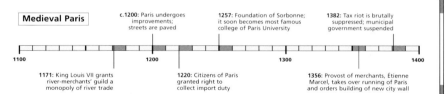

976: Fire destroys Doge's Palace; rebuilt over next five centuries

1204: Sack of Constantinople; Venetian gains in Adriatic and Greece

1295: Foundation of oligarchic Grand Council (Maggior Consiglio)

900 — 1000 — 1100 — 1200 — 1300 — 1400

Medieval Venice

1071: Completion of St. Mark's Basilica; focus of public religious life

1284: First gold ducats minted in Venice

1354: Peace concluded with Genoa, after over 50 years of warfare over trade supremacy

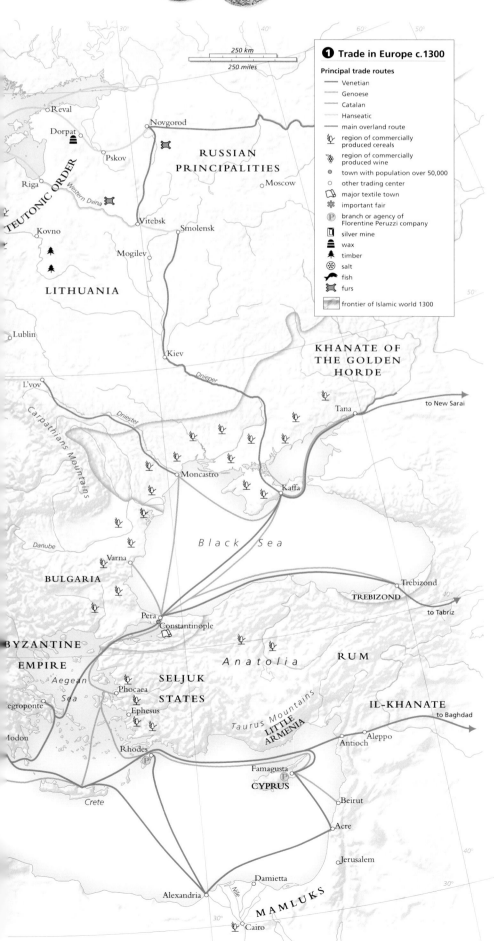

❶ **Trade in Europe c.1300**

Principal trade routes
- Venetian
- Genoese
- Catalan
- Hanseatic
- main overland route
- region of commercially produced cereals
- region of commercially produced wine
- ⊙ town with population over 50,000
- ○ other trading center
- major textile town
- ✱ important fair
- Ⓟ branch or agency of Florentine Peruzzi company
- silver mine
- wax
- timber
- salt
- fish
- furs
- frontier of Islamic world 1300

THE EMERGENCE OF MODERN STATES

Joan of Arc (1412–31) led the French to a famous victory against the English at Orléans in 1429 during the Hundred Years' War.

THE MAP OF EUROPE was redrawn throughout the 15th century as new nation-states appeared. France emerged, bruised but victorious, from the Hundred Years' War, soon to become the model of a modern nation state. Newly unified Spain vanquished the last Iberian outpost of Islam in 1492, emerging as a formidable power. The vast realm of Poland-Lithuania dominated Eastern Europe, while the Bohemians threw off imperial control. Feudal models of government were disappearing everywhere, and monarchies increasingly relied on the endorsement of the "estates," representative bodies of nobility, clergy, and the newly emerging bourgeoisie. Commercial centers such as the Netherlands and Italy saw a flowering of humanist philosophy, science, literature, and art, known as the Renaissance.

The Hundred Years' War

Over a century of intermittent conflict between France and England (1337–1453) was precipitated by the English kings' possessions in France and their claims to the French throne. Six major royal expeditions to France, starting with Edward III's landing in Antwerp in 1338 and ending with the death of Henry V in 1422, were interspersed with skirmishes and provincial campaigns led by independent war parties. After many setbacks, the triumphs of Joan of Arc (1429–30) led to a resurgence of French confidence and ultimately to English defeat.

The skill of 10,000 English longbowmen proved the deciding factor against the French cavalry at the battle of Crécy in 1346.

❷ The Hundred Years' War after 1400

- → campaign of Henry V, 1415
- → campaign of Henry V, 1421–22
- ▨ held by England or Burgundy, 1429
- → campaign of Earl of Salisbury autumn 1428
- ▨ possessions of House of Burgundy 1429
- → campaign of Joan of Arc 1429
- ▨ under Burgundian control by 1453
- ▨ added to France 1477
- ▨ added to France 1481
- ▨ acquired or occupied by France temporarily, with dates
- — frontiers 1493

1453: Calais is last English possession in France; held until 1558

May 1430: Joan of Arc captured by Burgundians

17 Jul 1429: Coronation of Charles VII

1422: Capture of Meaux secures northern France for Henry V

1428–29: Orléans besieged by English

❶ The Hundred Years' War to 1400

- ▨ limit of lands held by England 1300
- ▨ held by England at outbreak of war 1338
- ▨ added at Treaty of Brétigny 1360
- ▨ under English influence at outbreak of war
- ···· remained under English control 1380
- → campaign of Edward III, 1339–40
- → campaign of Edward III, 1342
- → campaign of Edward III, 1346
- → campaign of Black Prince, 1355
- → campaign of Black Prince, 1356
- → campaign of Edward III, 1359–60
- ▨ added to France gradually, 1301–16
- ▨ added to France 1349
- ▨ area of the *Jacquerie* 1358
- ▨ area affected by plundering of Great Companies 1360–66
- — frontiers 1380

The Hundred Years' War 1337–1453

1337: Philip VI of France confiscates Guyenne; Edward III claims kingdom of France
1356: English victory at Poitiers
1360: Treaty of Brétigny; peace lasts nine years, but bands of mercenaries, the Great Companies, ravage southeastern France
1420: Treaty of Troyes; Henry V marries Catherine of France
1435: Congress of Arras; Burgundy, an English ally, makes terms with France
1450: English lose Normandy

1346: English victory at Crécy
1358: *Jacquerie*: popular uprising against exploitation of countryside by soldiers
1396: 28-year truce agreed. Richard II marries Isabelle of France
1415: Henry V invades France; English victory at Agincourt
1429: Joan of Arc relieves Orléans
1453: English lose Guyenne

1300 — 1350 — 1400 — 1450

The *Reconquista*

The Christian reconquest of Moorish Spain began in earnest in the 11th century, led by the kingdoms of Navarre, Aragon, León-Castile, and Portugal. Despite strong Muslim counterattacks, the Christians had reconquered all but the small kingdom of Granada by 1260. León-Castile now dominated Iberia, and Aragon acquired extensive possessions in the western Mediterranean. These kingdoms, united by the marriage of Ferdinand II of Aragon and Isabella of Castile, embarked on a final crusade, and Granada fell in 1492.

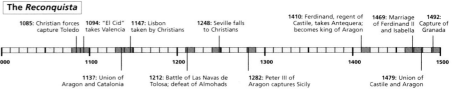

The Alhambra at Granada was built as a palace and fortress by the Moorish kings who ruled there until 1492. Following the expulsion of the Moors, much of the magnificent decoration was effaced or destroyed.

❸ The reconquest of Spain

- — limit of Umayyad Caliphate 732
- ▨ under Christian control by 1030
- → Almoravid campaigns 1080–1100
- ▨ lands controlled by El Cid 1092
- ▨ under Christian control by 1100
- — frontier of Almoravid Empire 1115
- ▨ under Christian control by 1180
- — frontier of Almohad Empire 1180
- ▨ under Christian control by 1280
- ▨ under Christian control by 1492
- — frontiers 1493
- ✕ Muslim victory with date
- ✕ Christian victory with date
- → major campaigns of reconquest with date

The *Reconquista*

1085: Christian forces capture Toledo
1094: "El Cid" takes Valencia
1147: Lisbon taken by Christians
1248: Seville falls to Christians
1410: Ferdinand, regent of Castile, takes Antequera; becomes king of Aragon
1469: Marriage of Ferdinand II and Isabella
1492: Capture of Granada

1000 — 1100 — 1200 — 1300 — 1400 — 1500

1137: Union of Aragon and Catalonia
1212: Battle of Las Navas de Tolosa; defeat of Almohads
1282: Peter III of Aragon captures Sicily
1479: Union of Castile and Aragon

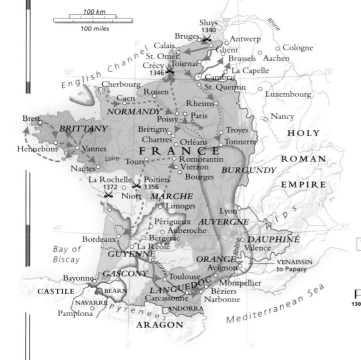

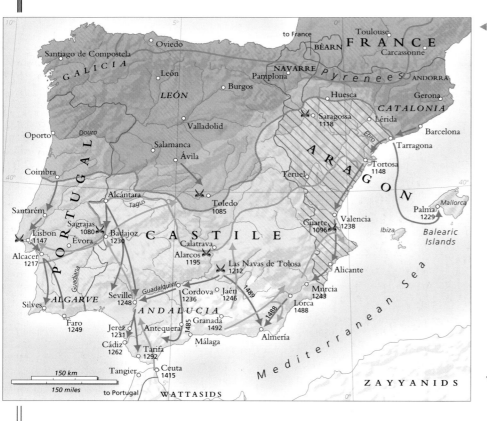

Central Europe in the 15th century

In Bohemia, the preachings of Jan Hus, which railed against the abuses of the clergy, were taken up by the Hussites, who called for a free Bohemia, and established a national Czech church. A new state in Bohemia was forged by Czech resistance to a series of bitter crusades launched by the Holy Roman Empire. The union of Poland and Lithuania in 1386 had created the largest realm in Christendom, its future secured by the defeat of the Teutonic Order in 1410. In the Holy Roman Empire, the Habsburgs sowed the seeds of future domination, acquiring by treaty, marriage, and conquest domains stretching from Austria and Styria to the Netherlands, and encompassing, from 1477, the lands of the Valois dukes of Burgundy.

The civil war initiated by the Hussites led to the deposing of Sigismund, king of Bohemia, who was forced to wage war on the Hussites on an almost annual basis until 1436. The picture *(left)* shows Hussite battle wagons drawn up in a defensive circle.

This coin was minted to honor Jan Hus, who was burned at the stake for heresy in 1415.

❹ Central Europe 1400–1500 ▶

	lost by Habsburgs during 14th and 15th centuries
	approximate extent of core Hussite area
	limit of area affected by Hussite campaigns 1425–34
→	campaign of János Hunyadi, 1443
	limit of direct Ottoman control, 1451
	Burgundian control 1477
	possessions of Matthias Corvinus of Hungary at his death 1490
	Jagiello possessions 1500
	Habsburg possessions 1500
	Papal States and notional dependencies 1500
	Venetian Republic 1500
- - -	frontiers 1500
⎯⎯	notional frontier of Holy Roman Empire 1500

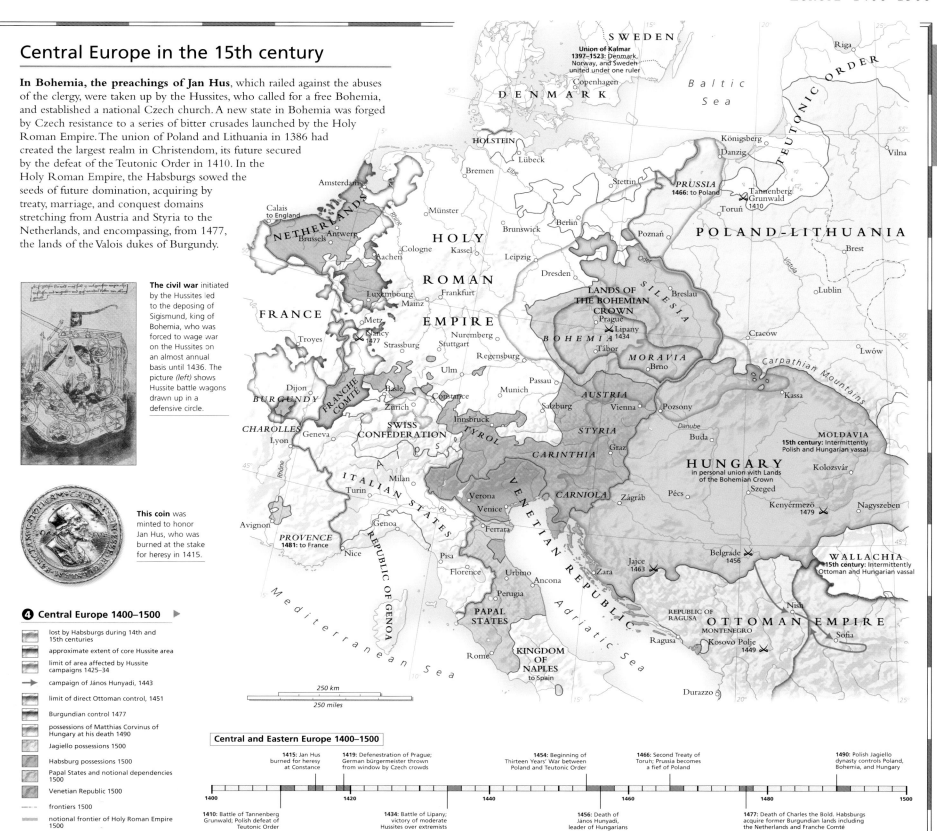

Central and Eastern Europe 1400–1500

1415: Jan Hus burned for heresy at Constance

1419: Defenestration of Prague; German bürgermeister thrown from window by Czech crowds

1454: Beginning of Thirteen Years' War between Poland and Teutonic Order

1466: Second Treaty of Toruń; Prussia becomes a fief of Poland

1490: Polish Jagiello dynasty controls Poland, Bohemia, and Hungary

1410: Battle of Tannenberg Grunwald; Polish defeat of Teutonic Order

1434: Battle of Lipany; victory of moderate Hussites over extremists

1456: Death of János Hunyadi, leader of Hungarians

1477: Death of Charles the Bold. Habsburgs acquire former Burgundian lands including the Netherlands and Franche Comté

The formation of Switzerland

The forest cantons of Switzerland were strategically placed to control vital Alpine passes, the route for pilgrims and merchants traveling between Italy and northern Europe. Increasingly, they resented attempts by their powerful neighbors to exert political control. In 1291, a union was formed by Uri, Schwyz, and Unterwalden, later joined by other cantons and cities, to defend a growing autonomy. The Swiss, in their conflicts with the Habsburgs and Burgundy, gained a formidable military reputation.

Victory in the Swabian War by 1499 brought *de facto* independence from the Empire. Membership of the Union continued to expand until the 16th century.

At the battle of Morgarten in 1315, a Swiss peasant army was able to defeat a Habsburg attack led by Leopold I of Austria and an army of knights.

The formation of Switzerland

1291: Union of Uri, Schwyz, and Unterwalden

1332: Luzern joins Union

1476: Battles of Grandson and Morat against Charles the Bold of Burgundy

1499: Swiss victory in Swabian War

1315: Battle of Morgarten; defeat of Habsburgs

1352: Berne joins Union

1386: Habsburg emperor, Leopold III defeated and killed at Sempach

1477: Battle of Nancy; Charles the Bold killed

❺ The growth of the Swiss Confederation

	first three cantons 1291
	added to Swiss Confederation by 1501
	added further by 1579
	frontier of Switzerland 1579
⎯⎯	frontiers 1815

The growth of Hungary

Following the ravages of the Mongol campaigns of 1241, which reduced the population in some areas by up to 60 percent, a succession of Angevin and German princes were elected to the Hungarian throne. The growing threat from the Ottomans, who had taken Constantinople in 1453, precipitated a revolt led by János Hunyadi. In 1458 he secured the throne for his son, Matthias Corvinus (1458–90), who subsequently achieved many notable military successes against the Ottoman Turks.

Matthias Corvinus brought many of the ideas of the Renaissance to the business of government, simplifying the administration and laws. However, his subjects bore a heavy tax burden, partly to finance his huge standing army, which was kept in readiness for campaigns against the Ottomans and other foreign adversaries.

THE AGE OF THE REFORMATION

Martin Luther's questioning of the doctrine and practice of Christianity led to the creation of the Protestant faith.

A SERIES OF PROFOUND CHANGES in theological doctrine and practice were to have violent political consequences in 16th-century Europe. The religious reformation, spearheaded by Martin Luther in 1517, divided much of the continent along religious lines, precipitating a series of wars which permanently sapped the strength of the Catholic Habsburg Empire. In northern Europe, new nations came to prominence; Sweden, Russia, and Denmark struggled for control of the Baltic, while in the Netherlands, a rising against the Catholic rule of Spain led to the independence of the Calvinist north. In the east, the expansion of the Ottoman Empire brought Christian Europe into conflict with Islam; the Turks exploited European disunity, penetrating as far as Vienna.

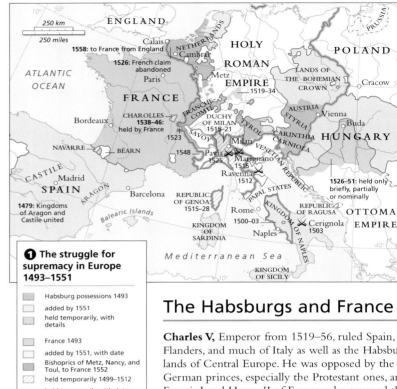

① The struggle for supremacy in Europe 1493–1551

- Habsburg possessions 1493
- added by 1551
- held temporarily, with details
- France 1493
- added by 1551, with date
- Bishoprics of Metz, Nancy, and Toul, to France 1552
- held temporarily 1499–1512
- held temporarily with date
- occupied by France 1536–39
- frontiers 1551
- frontier of Holy Roman Empire 1551

The Reformation

The spiritual complacency, material wealth, and abuses of power of the Roman Catholic church provoked a revolution in Christianity, inspired by the teachings of Martin Luther (1483–1546). His reformed theology, with its emphasis on study of the Bible, spread rapidly through northern Europe. Some opportunistic rulers, such as Henry VIII of England, embraced "Protestant" forms of religion in order to seize church lands. By 1570, Protestantism prevailed over much of central and northern Europe. In 1547, the Catholic Church summoned the Council of Trent, which reaffirmed fundamental doctrine, but condemned the worst clerical abuses.

St. Ignatius Loyola founded the Society of Jesus in 1534 to champion the Catholic Counter-Reformation. Highly-educated and assertively evangelical, the Jesuits took Catholic teachings to territory throughout the rapidly expanding Spanish Empire.

The Habsburg defeat of France at the battle of Pavia in 1525 is here commemorated in a contemporary tapestry. Even though Francis I of France was captured by the Spanish, the French finally abandoned their claim to Italy at the Treaty of Cateau-Cambrésis in 1559.

The Habsburgs and France

Charles V, Emperor from 1519–56, ruled Spain, Flanders, and much of Italy as well as the Habsburg lands of Central Europe. He was opposed by the German princes, especially the Protestant ones, and Francis I and Henry II of France, who pursued the claims of their predecessors to Italy. Constant wars wasted many lives and much money, but gained nothing. In 1556, Charles V abdicated, dividing his empire between his brother and his son.

French-Habsburg rivalry 1515-59

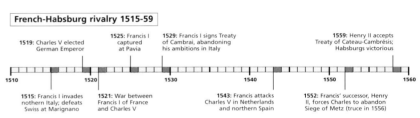

1519: Charles V elected German Emperor
1525: Francis I captured at Pavia
1529: Francis I signs Treaty of Cambrai, abandoning his ambitions in Italy
1559: Henry II accepts Treaty of Cateau-Cambrésis; Habsburgs victorious

1515: Francis I invades nothern Italy; defeats Swiss at Marignano
1521: War between Francis I of France and Charles V
1543: Francis attacks Charles V in Netherlands and northern Spain
1552: Francis' successor, Henry II, forces Charles to abandon Siege of Metz (truce in 1556)

The Reformation in Europe 1517–55

1529: At Diet of Speyer, Charles V attempts to reach compromise with Lutheran princes
1535: John Calvin formulates doctrine of predestination in Geneva
1545: Start of Council of Trent, which defines modern Catholicism

1517: Martin Luther posts 95 Theses condemning abuses of Catholic church at Wittenberg
1532: Henry VIII of England declares himself head of Church of England
1555: At Peace of Augsburg; Lutheran princes win right to choose their religion

② The religious map of Europe 1590 ▶

- almost exclusively Catholic, with just minimal Protestant presence in northern areas
- overwhelmingly Catholic, with appreciable Protestant minority
- Catholic majority, but with very strong Protestant minority
- exclusively or overwhelmingly Protestant, with only slight Catholic presence in places
- Protestant majority, with some Catholic presence
- mainly Catholic, with strong Greek Orthodox presence
- Greek Orthodox, with significant Muslim presence in some areas of the Balkans
- Muslim majority
- frontiers 1590
- frontier of Holy Roman Empire 1590
- *Calvinist* locally dominant Protestant denomination

Conflict in the Baltic 1500–1595

The collapse of the Union of Kalmar, which bound Sweden, Denmark, and Norway together, in 1523, precipitated a century of warfare around the Baltic Sea, bringing the growing power of Sweden into conflict with Russia and Denmark, which controlled the narrow outlet to the North Sea, vital for Swedish trade interests. The Reformation had led to the collapse of crusading orders such as the Teutonic Knights, opening up Livonia to the ambitions of Russia, Sweden, and Poland-Lithuania.

Ivan Vasilievich, Tsar of Russia from 1547 to 1584, was known as "the Terrible" for his drastic reforming of the hereditary aristocracy. Although his wars with Sweden and Poland were largely unsuccessful, he was able to expand the Russian Empire to include non-Slav states.

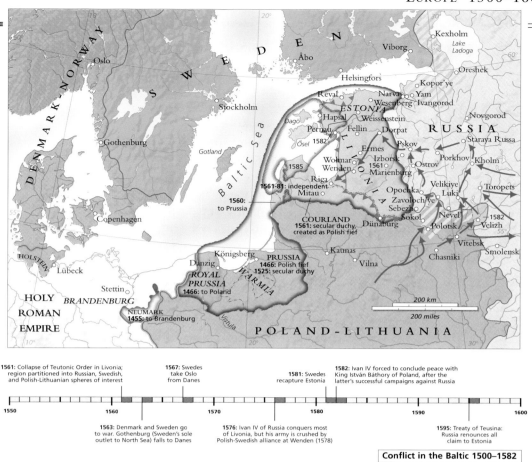

❸ **The Baltic in the 16th century** ▶

- area controlled by Teutonic Order 1450
- Poland-Lithuania and dependent territory 1558
- added to Poland by 1585, with date
- added to Sweden by 1583, with date
- to Sweden 1583–95
- Danish control 1558
- added to Denmark 1573
- possessions of Prince Magnus of Holstein 1564
- ▲▲ deepest advance of Russian forces into Livonia at various times during 1558–73
- to Russia 1563–70
- → campaigns of Polish King István Báthory 1579, 1580, 1581
- frontier of Holy Roman Empire
- frontiers 1595

1561: Collapse of Teutonic Order in Livonia; region partitioned into Russian, Swedish, and Polish-Lithuanian spheres of interest

1567: Swedes take Oslo from Danes

1581: Swedes recapture Estonia

1582: Ivan IV forced to conclude peace with King István Báthory of Poland, after the latter's successful campaigns against Russia

| 1550 | 1560 | 1570 | 1580 | 1590 | 1600 |

1563: Denmark and Sweden go to war. Gothenburg (Sweden's sole outlet to North Sea) falls to Danes

1576: Ivan IV of Russia conquers most of Livonia, but his army is crushed by Polish-Swedish alliance at Wenden (1578)

1595: Treaty of Teusina: Russia renounces all claim to Estonia

Conflict in the Baltic 1500–1582

The expansion of Ottoman power

By 1500, the Ottomans controlled the lands to the south and west of the Black Sea. With the accession of Suleyman I – "the Magnificent" – (1520–66), they turned their attention to Europe, increasing naval pressure on the eastern Mediterranean, and pushing northward into Moldavia, the Danube valley, and Hungary. In 1529, they were turned back after their unsuccessful siege of Vienna, but continued to maintain their pressure on the frontier of the Habsburg Empire, exploiting conflict in Europe by forming alliances with France against the Habsburgs, and gaining control of Transylvania in 1562.

This detail from an Italian manuscript records the victory of Habsburg forces over the Ottomans at the siege of Vienna in 1529. The illumination is one of a series entitled "Triumphs of Charles V."

◀ ❹ **The Ottoman frontier in 16th century**

- Ottoman Empire 1500
- added to Ottoman Empire by 1606, with dates
- Ottoman vassals 1606
- Habsburg possessions 1606
- temporary conquest by Ottoman Empire, with dates
- → Ottoman and Tartar attacks with dates
- frontiers 1606
- Holy Roman Empire

The expansion of Ottoman power 1453–1571

1484: Turks capture Akkerman at mouth of Dniester

1529: Unsuccessful Turkish siege of Vienna

1562: After inconclusive skirmishes, Ottomans gain Transylvania

| 1450 | 1500 | 1550 | 1600 |

1453: Constantinople falls to Ottomans

1526: Ottoman invasion of Hungary; Battle of Mohács

1547: Negotiated peace acknowledges Ottoman control of most of Hungary

1571: Naval battle of Lepanto; a decisive Christian victory

The Dutch Revolt

Philip II of Spain, a fierce champion of the Roman Catholic cause, was determined to suppress Calvinism in the Netherlands. He reacted harshly to demands by Dutch nobles for autonomy and religious freedom, and his reprisals, combined with onerous taxes, led to a general revolt under the leadership of William of Nassau, which the Spanish could not quell. In 1579, ten southern Catholic provinces were promised liberty; in reply, seven Calvinist northern provinces formed the Union of Utrecht. In a 1609 truce, their independence was conceded by Spain.

The Sea Beggars were Dutch rebels who took to the sea to combat the Spanish from foreign ports. In 1572, they mounted a successful attack on the fortress of Brill in southern Holland (above), encouraging Holland and Zeeland to join the revolt.

The Dutch Revolt 1565–1609

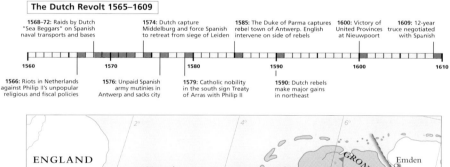

1568–72: Raids by Dutch "Sea Beggars" on Spanish naval transports and bases

1574: Dutch capture Middelburg and force Spanish to retreat from siege of Leiden

1585: The Duke of Parma captures rebel town of Antwerp. English intervene on side of rebels

1600: Victory of United Provinces at Nieuwpoort

1609: 12-year truce negotiated with Spanish

| 1560 | 1570 | 1580 | 1590 | 1600 | 1610 |

1566: Riots in Netherlands against Philip II's unpopular religious and fiscal policies

1576: Unpaid Spanish army mutinies in Antwerp and sacks city

1579: Catholic nobility in the south sign Treaty of Arras with Philip II

1590: Dutch rebels make major gains in northeast

❺ **The Dutch Revolt 1568–1609**

- frontier of Holy Roman Empire 1568
- Spanish Netherlands at outbreak of revolt 1568
- joined Union of Utrecht 1579 and 1581
- Union of Arras 1579
- ▲▲ limit of Spanish advance by 1589
- Netherlands in terms of 1609 truce
- ✕ Dutch victory
- ✕ Spanish victory

EARLY MODERN EUROPE

Cardinal Richelieu, was Louis XIII's chief minister and the architect of royal absolutism in France.

IN THE 17TH CENTURY, following years of destructive warfare, the modern European state system began to evolve. States were ruled centrally by autocratic (or absolutist) monarchs and bounded by clear, militarily secure frontiers. The Thirty Years' War laid waste large parts of central Europe, causing a decline in population from some 21 million in 1618 to 13 million in 1648. Under Louis XIV, France was involved in four costly wars, but emerged as the leading nation in Europe, eclipsing Spain, which entered a long period of decline. After a period of expansion under the Vasa kings, Sweden lost much of its Baltic empire by 1721. The Ottoman Turks struck once again at the heart of Europe, but were met by an increasingly powerful Austria, whose main rival in the region was Russia.

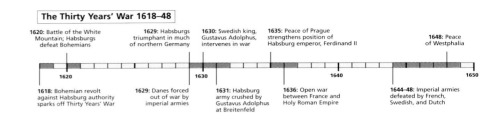

The Thirty Years' War 1618–48

- **1620:** Battle of the White Mountain; Habsburgs defeat Bohemians
- **1629:** Habsburgs triumphant in much of northern Germany
- **1630:** Swedish king, Gustavus Adolphus, intervenes in war
- **1635:** Peace of Prague strengthens position of Habsburg emperor, Ferdinand II
- **1648:** Peace of Westphalia
- **1618:** Bohemian revolt against Habsburg authority sparks off Thirty Years' War
- **1629:** Danes forced out of war by imperial armies
- **1631:** Habsburg army crushed by Gustavus Adolphus at Breitenfeld
- **1636:** Open war between France and Holy Roman Empire
- **1644–48:** Imperial armies defeated by French, Swedish, and Dutch

The Thirty Years' War

The Thirty Years' War provoked great advances in methods of mass destruction, and involved an unprecedented number of soldiers, over a million of whom died before it ceased. Much of Germany was devastated, towns were sacked, and their inhabitants raped and murdered.

The Thirty Years' War saw Protestant-Catholic rivalry and German constitutional issues subsumed in a wider European struggle. Habsburg attempts to control Bohemia and crush Protestantism coincided with the breakdown of constitutional mechanisms for resolving conflict in the Holy Roman Empire. Spain intervened to secure supply lines to the Netherlands; Danish and Swedish involvement followed as they competed for control of the Baltic. Fear of imperial absolutism, prompted by Austrian Habsburg victories in 1621 and 1634–35, led France to intervene in 1635 in support of Sweden. Prolonged negotiations from 1643 culminated in the Treaty of Westphalia, which fused attempts to secure peace in Europe with curbs on the emperor's authority in Germany.

① The Treaty of Westphalia, 1648

- Austrian Habsburg possessions
- Spanish Habsburg possessions
- Brandenburg possessions
- Danish possessions
- Swedish possessions
- Church lands
- ● electorate
- boundary of Holy Roman Empire, 1648
- - - frontiers 1648
- ⚔ major battle of Thirty Years' War

Political consolidation and resistance

European states were transformed in a process of internal political centralization and external consolidation. The legitimacy of these developments was often questioned, leading to civil wars and popular resistance. Foreign intervention turned local disputes into international conflicts, as in the Thirty Years' War. In western Europe, Spain's dominant position was broken by Portuguese and Dutch independence. The two rising powers in the region, France and England, developed in very different ways. In France, Louis XIV assumed absolute power, while in England, Charles I was arrested and executed for disregarding parliament, and although the English monarchy was restored, its powers were drastically curbed.

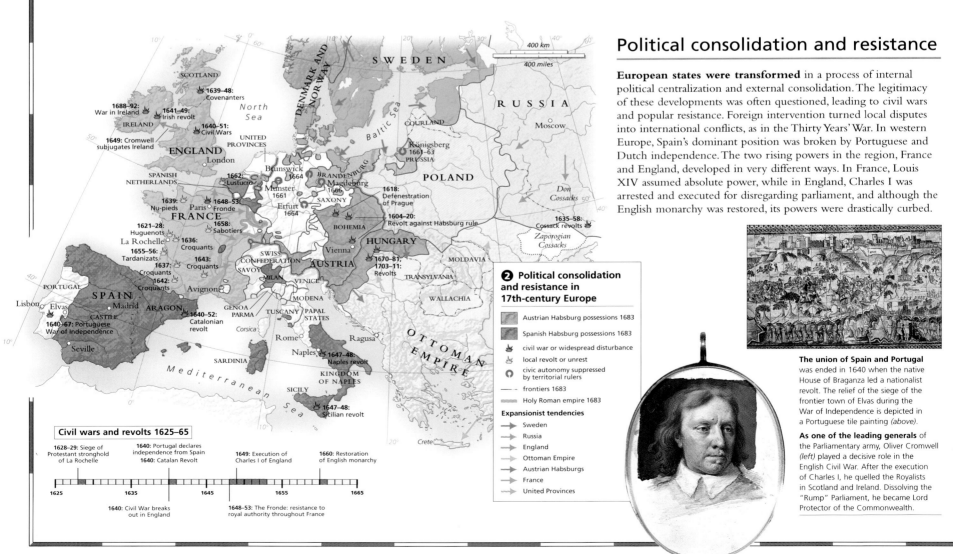

② Political consolidation and resistance in 17th-century Europe

- Austrian Habsburg possessions 1683
- Spanish Habsburg possessions 1683
- civil war or widespread disturbance
- local revolt or unrest
- civic autonomy suppressed by territorial rulers
- - - frontiers 1683
- Holy Roman empire 1683

Expansionist tendencies

- → Sweden
- → Russia
- → England
- → Ottoman Empire
- → Austrian Habsburgs
- → France
- → United Provinces

The union of Spain and Portugal was ended in 1640 when the native House of Braganza led a nationalist revolt. The relief of the siege of the frontier town of Elvas during the War of Independence is depicted in a Portuguese tile painting *(above)*.

As one of the leading generals of the Parliamentary army, Oliver Cromwell *(left)* played a decisive role in the English Civil War. After the execution of Charles I, he quelled the Royalists in Scotland and Ireland. Dissolving the "Rump" Parliament, he became Lord Protector of the Commonwealth.

Civil wars and revolts 1625–65

- **1628–29:** Siege of Protestant stronghold of La Rochelle
- **1640:** Portugal declares independence from Spain
- **1640:** Catalan Revolt
- **1649:** Execution of Charles I of England
- **1660:** Restoration of English monarchy
- **1640:** Civil War breaks out in England
- **1648–53:** The Fronde: resistance to royal authority throughout France

3 The Swedish Empire 1560–1721

- Sweden at the death of Gustavus Vasa 1560
- conquests by 1645
- conquests by 1658
- temporary Swedish acquisitions, with dates
- Russian gains from Sweden by treaty of Nystad, 1721
- → Swedish campaigns
- → Russians campaigns under Peter the Great
- trade routes
- frontiers, 1658

Habsburg–Ottoman conflict 1663–1718

In 1683 the Ottomans began their greatest onslaught on the Habsburg Empire by besieging Vienna with a huge army. Poland and the Papacy joined the German princes in an international relief effort which ended in Ottoman defeat.

In the mid-17th century, the Ottoman Empire resumed its expansion into southeastern Europe. Austrian attempts to challenge the Ottomans' control of Transylvania led to full-scale war in 1663. The Turkish advance on Vienna in 1664 was halted, but in 1683 the Turks besieged the city. The siege failed, and by 1687 the war had become a Habsburg war of conquest. The acquisition of Transylvania and Turkish Hungary transformed Austria into a great European power and loosened its traditional ties to the Holy Roman Empire.

1672: Greatest extent of Ottoman Empire
1699: Peace of Karlowitz confirms Austrian conquests
1716–18: Further Austrian victories, including capture of Belgrade
1664: Turkish advance on Vienna turned back at battle of St. Gotthard
1683: Siege of Vienna starts Great Turkish War

Habsburg-Ottoman wars 1663–1718

Sweden, Russia, and the Baltic

The 17th century witnessed the phenomenal growth of Sweden as an imperial power: by defeating regional rivals Denmark, Poland and Russia, it had by 1648 established a Baltic empire, the high point of which was reached during the reign of Charles X (1654–60). Lacking indigenous resources, however, Sweden's strength rested on its control of strategic harbors and customs points along the Baltic shore. Defense of these positions forced Sweden into a series of costly wars from 1655. After the Great Northern War, much of the empire was lost to the rising powers of Russia, Prussia, and Hanover.

Founded in 1703 by Peter the Great, St. Petersburg was modelled on European cities, its classical architecture and orderly street grid symbolizing the Tsar's westernizing policies.

The rise and fall of the Swedish Empire

1629: Sweden gains Livonia
1643: Sweden invades Denmark
1654: Start of reign of Charles X
1658: Peace of Roskilde; Denmark loses southern Sweden
1700: Great Northern War
1721: Peace of Nystad; Sweden cedes Ingria, Livonia, and Karelia to Russia
1632: Gustavus Adolphus dies at victorious battle of Lützen
1648: Substantial Swedish gains confirmed by Treaty of Westphalia
1675: Brandenburg defeats Sweden at Fehrbellin
1709: Charles XII's attempt to invade Russia halted at Poltava

The French state under Louis XIV, 1660–1715

Under Louis XIV, France pursued an expansionist, anti-Spanish policy. The expense of maintaining a large army and building a ring of frontier fortresses was met by administrative reforms, and tax collection in the provinces was overseen by royal officials *(intendants)*. In 1667–68 Louis' armies secured parts of the Spanish Netherlands. Although this provoked international opposition to French aggression, further gains were made in the Dutch War (1672–79). The occupation of various territories in 1679–84 (known as the *Réunions*) rationalized France's eastern frontier, but after defeat in the Nine Years' War (1688–97), most of these had to be given up. The War of the Spanish Succession (1701–14) brought France no further gains.

A ring of defensive fortresses was built by Vauban, a great military engineer, to secure French territory.

During his long reign, Louis XIV *(left)* established France as cultural and political leader of Europe.

The growth of France under Louis XIV

1667–68: France acquires parts of Flanders from Spain
1679–84: *Réunions*: annexation of territory west of the Rhine
1701–14: War of the Spanish Succession
1661: Louis XIV assumes personal rule
1672–79: Dutch War brings significant territorial gains
1688–97: Nine Years' War: Peace of Ryswick (Rijswijk) partially reverses the *Réunions*
1715: Death of Louis XIV

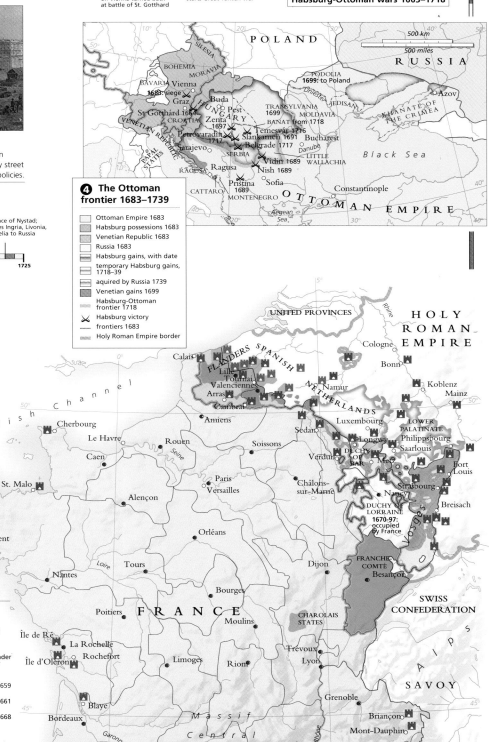
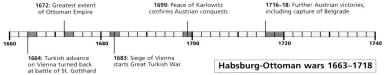

4 The Ottoman frontier 1683–1739

- Ottoman Empire 1683
- Habsburg possessions 1683
- Venetian Republic 1683
- Russia 1683
- Habsburg gains, with date
- temporary Habsburg gains, 1718–39
- aquired by Russia 1739
- Venetian gains 1699
- Habsburg-Ottoman frontier 1718
- ✕ Habsburg victory
- frontiers 1683
- Holy Roman Empire border

5 France 1648–1715

- France 1648
- frontier of Holy Roman Empire 1648
- French frontier 1713/14
- administrative regions under Louis XIV (intendances or généralités)
- French gains confirmed 1659
- French gains confirmed 1661
- French gains confirmed 1668
- French gains confirmed 1678–79
- areas temporarily annexed under the Réunions, 1684–97
- further French gains by 1697
- Vauban fortress
- fortified town
- barrier fortress
- administrative center

197

THE AGE OF ENLIGHTENMENT

Catherine the Great ruled the Russian Empire as an enlightened despot from 1762 to 1796.

THE 18TH CENTURY was a period of relative stability, when well-established monarchies ruled most of Europe and almost all the land was controlled by the nobility or the state. The Russian Empire and Prussia became leading powers. The rest of Germany remained a jigsaw of small states, as did Italy, while Poland was swallowed up by its powerful neighbors. Improved methods of cultivation fed Europe's escalating populations; towns and cities increased in size and number; trade and industry expanded to reach global markets; philosophy, science, and the arts flourished. Intellectual curiosity encouraged the radical political theories of the "Enlightenment," but alarmed reaction set in when the flag of liberty was raised in France in the last decade of the century. Though ultimately unsuccessful, the French Revolution would inspire many social and political reforms in the 19th century.

Cities and economic life 1700–1800

Despite the beginnings of industrialization in the 18th century, principally in textile production, in 1800 four out of five Europeans still depended on agriculture for their livelihood. The growing population – largely due to a fall in the death rate as a result of better health and hygiene – led to a rapid increase in the size of cities; in 1700 Europe had ten cities with over 100,000 inhabitants; by 1800 there were 17. At the same time, farmers adopted a more scientific approach to agriculture, introducing new, more productive crops and livestock. A general improvement in transportation by sea, road, river, and canal greatly stimulated trade throughout Europe and, as colonialism developed, with the rest of the world.

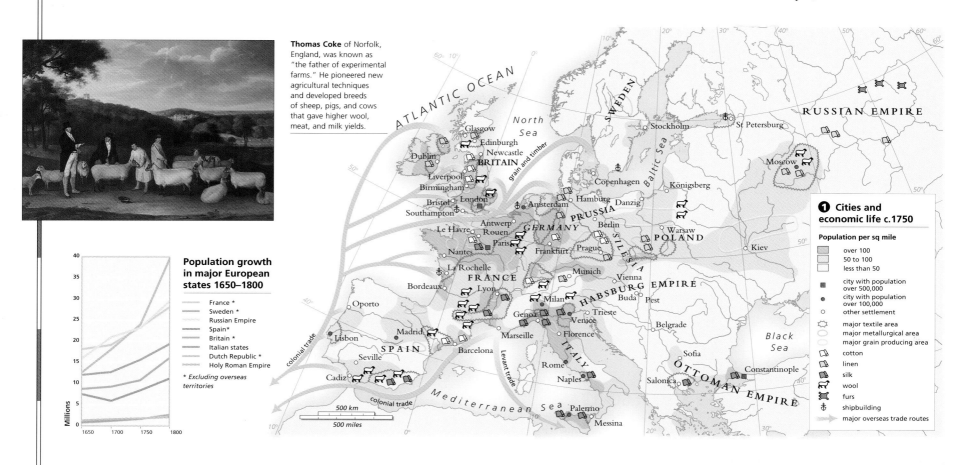

Thomas Coke of Norfolk, England, was known as "the father of experimental farms." He pioneered new agricultural techniques and developed breeds of sheep, pigs, and cows that gave higher wool, meat, and milk yields.

Population growth in major European states 1650–1800

- France *
- Sweden *
- Russian Empire
- Spain*
- Britain *
- Italian states
- Dutch Republic *
- Holy Roman Empire

* Excluding overseas territories

1 Cities and economic life c.1750

Population per sq mile
- over 100
- 50 to 100
- less than 50

- city with population over 500,000
- city with population over 100,000
- other settlement
- major textile area
- major metallurgical area
- major grain producing area
- cotton
- linen
- silk
- wool
- furs
- shipbuilding
- major overseas trade routes

The partitions of Poland

17th-century Poland was one of Europe's largest states, but suffered frequent territorial losses to its neighbors, especially Russia. The elective monarchy allowed foreign powers to interfere in Polish affairs, and in the late 18th century the Russians, the Habsburgs, and Prussia settled their differences at Poland's expense in three partitions which removed the country from the map.

2 The partitions of Poland 1772–95

- frontier of Poland in 1699

Partition of Poland in 1772
- to Prussia
- to Russian Empire
- to Habsburg Empire

Partition of Poland in 1793
- to Prussia
- to Russian Empire

Partition of Poland in 1795
- to Prussia
- to Russian Empire
- to Habsburg Empire
- frontiers in 1795

The decline of Poland 1550–1795

1569: Poland united with Lithuania
1660: East Prussia gains independence from Poland
1697: Start of rule by Electors of Saxony
1772: First partition of Poland
1795: Third partition

1629: Sweden acquires Livonia
1667: Russia acquires East Ukraine
1764: Russia secures Polish crown for Stanislas Poniatowski
1793: Second partition

THE ENLIGHTENMENT

The 18th-century "enlightened" writers, or *philosophes*, such as Voltaire and Diderot, appealed to human reason to challenge traditional assumptions about the Church, state, monarchy, education, and social institutions. "Man is born free, but everywhere he is in chains," wrote Jean-Jacques Rousseau in his *Social Contract* (1762), in which he sought to show how a democratic society could work.

Voltaire (1694–1778) used poetry, drama, and satire to express his political views, including his opposition to the Catholic Church. His radicalism often led to periods of exile from his native France.

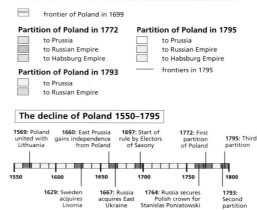

Published in 28 volumes from 1751–72, the *Encyclopédie* spread the philosophic and scientific ideas of the Enlightenment. It gave a comprehensive account of contemporary institutions and technologies, while fine engravings illustrated the work of all kinds of craftsmen, such as the instrument makers above.

The rise of Brandenburg Prussia

After the Peace of Westphalia in 1648, Germany consisted of some 300 small principalities, some Catholic, some Protestant. By the end of the 17th century Brandenburg was the dominant Protestant state. Frederick William (the "Great Elector"), gained full sovereignty in Prussia and created a powerful state with a huge standing army. With the accession of Frederick II (the "Great") in 1740, expansion continued, including the acquisition of Silesia from the Habsburg Empire. With additional territory from the partitions of Poland, by the end of the century Prussia had become one of Europe's Great Powers.

❸ The rise of Brandenburg Prussia 1648–1795

- Brandenburg in 1648
- acquisitions 1648–1707
- area held 1713–42
- acquisitions 1715–20
- acquisitions by Frederick the Great 1740–86
- temporary acquisitions by Frederick the Great 1740–86
- acquisitions from Poland 1793
- acquisitions from Poland 1795
- Habsburg possessions in 1795
- frontier of Holy Roman Empire, 1789

These splendidly uniformed cavalry officers are representative of the highly disciplined and efficient army which, by 1763, enabled Prussia to emerge as the dominant military force in 18th-century Europe.

The growth of Prussia in the 18th century

1713: Accession of Frederick William I, King of Prussia

1713: Treaty of Utrecht: Prussia gains Upper Gelderland and Neuchâtel

1715: Prussia takes Stralsund in Great North War against Sweden

1720: Treaty of Stockholm gives part of Western Pomerania to Prussia

1740: Accession of Frederick II (the "Great")

1740–48: War of the Austrian Succession

1742: Frederick completes rapid conquest of Silesia

1756–63: Seven Years' War: Prussia faces coalition of Austria, Russia, and France

1760: Austrian and Russian troops occupy Berlin, but Prussia survives

1763: Treaty of Hubertusburg allows Prussia to keep Silesia

1772: First partition of Poland; Prussian lands in the east now linked to Brandenburg

1786: Death of Frederick the Great

1793: Second partition of Poland

1795: Third partition of Poland

1700 · 1720 · 1740 · 1760 · 1780 · 1800

The French Revolution 1789–95

In May 1789, a political crisis forced Louis XVI to summon the Estates-General, a parliament of nobles, clergy, and commoners. The third estate (the commoners) demanded reform and declared itself a National Assembly. Noble and clerical privileges were abolished; provincial uprisings were directed against landowners, many of whom fled into exile. In 1792 the Revolution gathered momentum: Louis was imprisoned, the monarchy abolished, and France declared a republic. Mass conscription was introduced to meet the threat of invasion by Austria and Prussia and the king was executed. Power shifted to the radical Jacobins, who ruled by means of "the Terror," executing all "enemies of the people." Many regions opposed these excesses, notably the Vendée in the west, but resistance was crushed. In 1794 the Jacobins shared the fate of their victims. France, however, had been saved from invasion, and there followed a period of moderate rule – the Directory.

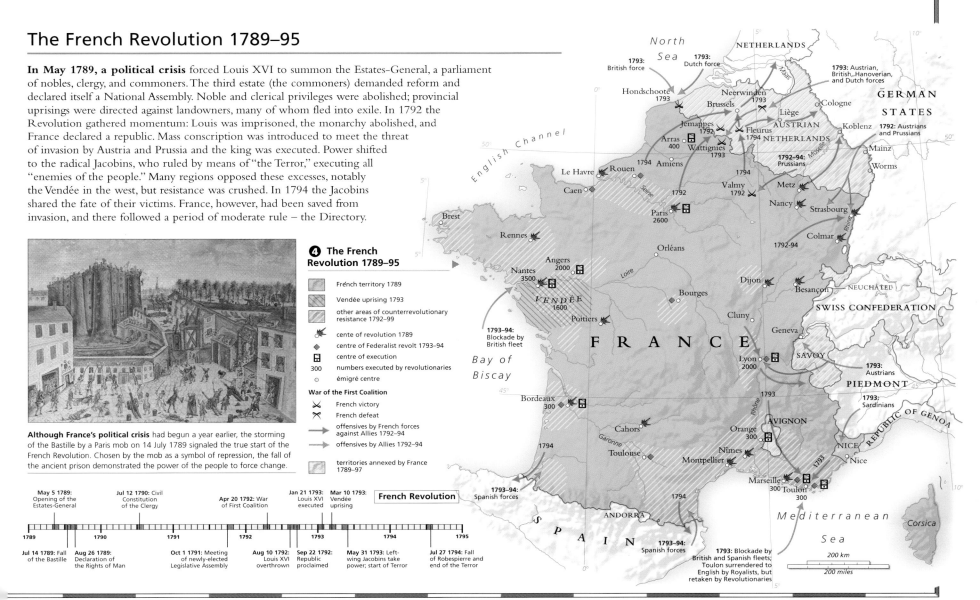

Although France's political crisis had begun a year earlier, the storming of the Bastille by a Paris mob on 14 July 1789 signaled the true start of the French Revolution. Chosen by the mob as a symbol of repression, the fall of the ancient prison demonstrated the power of the people to force change.

❹ The French Revolution 1789–95

- French territory 1789
- Vendée uprising 1793
- other areas of counterrevolutionary resistance 1792–99
- ✷ centre of revolution 1789
- ◆ centre of Federalist revolt 1793–94
- ⊞ centre of execution
- 300 numbers executed by revolutionaries
- ○ émigré centre

War of the First Coalition
- ◢ French victory
- ✕ French defeat
- → offensives by French forces against Allies 1792–94
- → offensives by Allies 1792–94
- territories annexed by France 1789–97

French Revolution

May 5 1789: Opening of the Estates-General

Jul 14 1789: Fall of the Bastille

Aug 26 1789: Declaration of the Rights of Man

Jul 12 1790: Civil Constitution of the Clergy

Oct 1 1791: Meeting of newly-elected Legislative Assembly

Apr 20 1792: War of First Coalition

Aug 10 1792: Louis XVI overthrown

Sep 22 1792: Republic proclaimed

Jan 21 1793: Louis XVI executed

Mar 10 1793: Vendée uprising

May 31 1793: Left-wing Jacobins take power; start of Terror

Jul 27 1794: Fall of Robespierre and end of the Terror

1789 · 1790 · 1791 · 1792 · 1793 · 1794 · 1795

NAPOLEONIC EUROPE

THE BRILLIANT REVOLUTIONARY GENERAL Napoleon Bonaparte returned from his Egyptian campaign in 1799 to stage a *coup d'état* which made him ruler of France as First Consul. During the Consulate he began reforms of the administration, the legal system, the Church, and education. In 1804, just over ten years after revolutionaries had executed Louis XVI, Napoleon took the title of emperor and began to create a dynasty, members of his family being given the crowns of conquered states.
His imperial ambitions were ultimately thwarted by Britain: its navy was used to blockade France and overrun French colonies, while a series of alliances completed an encirclement that contained and gradually reduced Napoleon's empire.

The Code Napoléon of 1804, the first modern law code, embraced many of the principles of the French Revolution.

The battle of Eylau in 1807 was fought in a blizzard, with the French heavily outnumbered and outgunned by the Russians. Though both sides claimed victory, the French lost more men. For the first time in his career, Napoleon had failed to win a major battle.

In this cartoon of 1812, Napoleon tries desperately to bridge the 2000 miles between Madrid and Moscow. The impossibility of personally masterminding both the Peninsular campaign in Spain and Portugal and the Russian campaign led to his downfall.

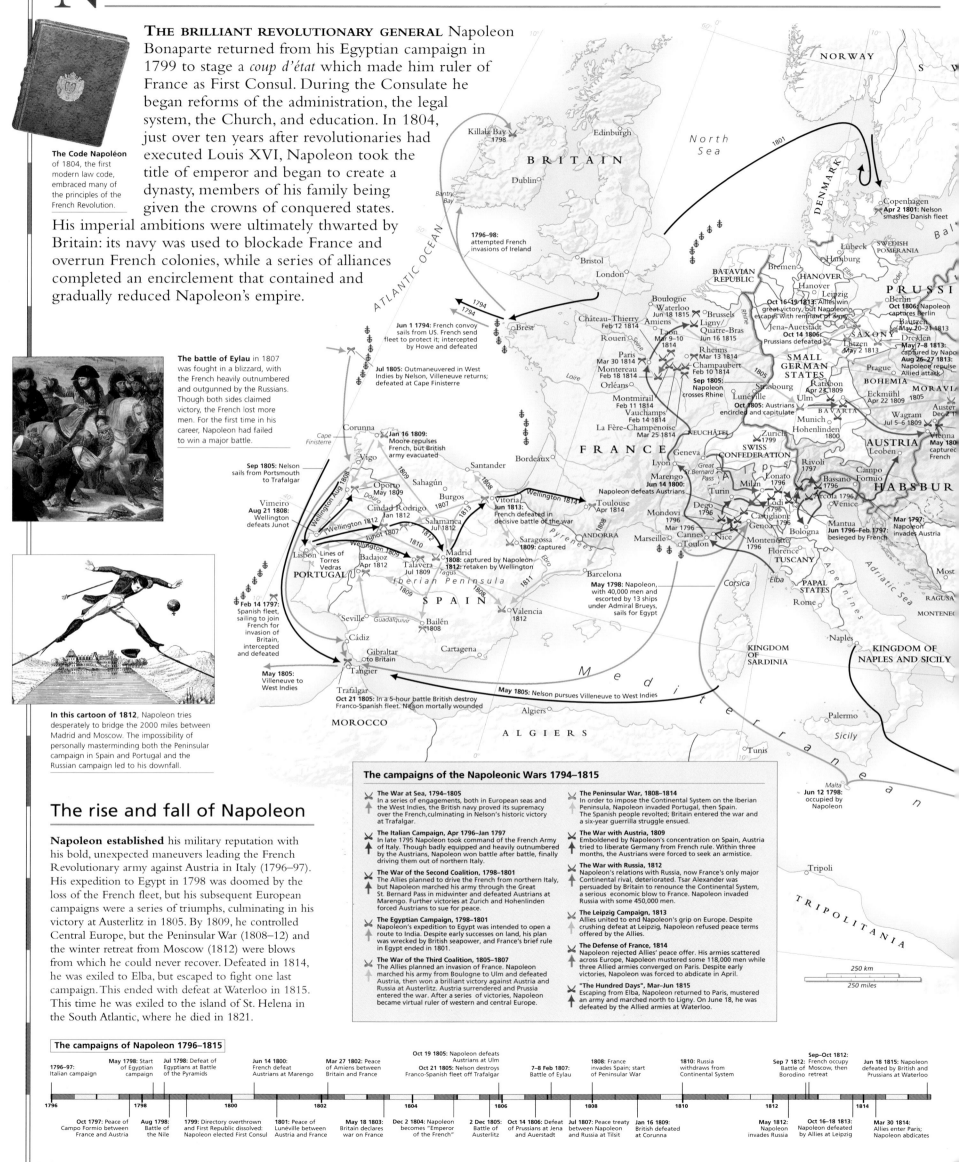

The rise and fall of Napoleon

Napoleon established his military reputation with his bold, unexpected maneuvers leading the French Revolutionary army against Austria in Italy (1796–97). His expedition to Egypt in 1798 was doomed by the loss of the French fleet, but his subsequent European campaigns were a series of triumphs, culminating in his victory at Austerlitz in 1805. By 1809, he controlled Central Europe, but the Peninsular War (1808–12) and the winter retreat from Moscow (1812) were blows from which he could never recover. Defeated in 1814, he was exiled to Elba, but escaped to fight one last campaign. This ended with defeat at Waterloo in 1815. This time he was exiled to the island of St. Helena in the South Atlantic, where he died in 1821.

The campaigns of the Napoleonic Wars 1794–1815

The War at Sea, 1794–1805
In a series of engagements, both in European seas and the West Indies, the British navy proved its supremacy over the French, culminating in Nelson's historic victory at Trafalgar.

The Italian Campaign, Apr 1796–Jan 1797
In late 1795 Napoleon took command of the French Army of Italy. Though badly equipped and heavily outnumbered by the Austrians, Napoleon won battle after battle, finally driving them out of northern Italy.

The War of the Second Coalition, 1798–1801
The Allies planned to drive the French from northern Italy, but Napoleon marched his army through the Great St. Bernard Pass in midwinter and defeated Austrians at Marengo. Further victories at Zurich and Hohenlinden forced Austrians to sue for peace.

The Egyptian Campaign, 1798–1801
Napoleon's expedition to Egypt was intended to open a route to India. Despite early successes on land, his plan was wrecked by British seapower, and France's brief rule in Egypt ended in 1801.

The War of the Third Coalition, 1805–1807
The Allies planned an invasion of France. Napoleon marched his army from Boulogne to Ulm and defeated Austria, then won a brilliant victory against Austria and Russia at Austerlitz. Austria surrendered and Prussia entered the war. After a series of victories, Napoleon became virtual ruler of western and central Europe.

The Peninsular War, 1808–1814
In order to impose the Continental System on the Iberian Peninsula, Napoleon invaded Portugal, then Spain. The Spanish people revolted; Britain entered the war and a six-year guerrilla struggle ensued.

The War with Austria, 1809
Emboldened by Napoleon's concentration on Spain, Austria tried to liberate Germany from French rule. Within three months, the Austrians were forced to seek an armistice.

The War with Russia, 1812
Napoleon's relations with Russia, now France's only major Continental rival, deteriorated. Tsar Alexander was persuaded by Britain to renounce the Continental System, a serious economic blow to France. Napoleon invaded Russia with some 450,000 men.

The Leipzig Campaign, 1813
Allies united to end Napoleon's grip on Europe. Despite crushing defeat at Leipzig, Napoleon refused peace terms offered by the Allies.

The Defense of France, 1814
Napoleon rejected Allies' peace offer. His armies scattered across Europe, Napoleon mustered some 118,000 men while three Allied armies converged on Paris. Despite early victories, Napoleon was forced to abdicate in April.

"The Hundred Days", Mar–Jun 1815
Escaping from Elba, Napoleon returned to Paris, mustered an army and marched north to Ligny. On June 18, he was defeated by the Allied armies at Waterloo.

The campaigns of Napoleon 1796–1815

- **1796–97:** Italian campaign
- **May 1798:** Start of Egyptian campaign
- **Jul 1798:** Defeat of Egyptians at Battle of the Pyramids
- **Jun 14 1800:** French defeat Austrians at Marengo
- **Mar 27 1802:** Peace of Amiens between Britain and France
- **Oct 19 1805:** Napoleon defeats Austrians at Ulm
- **Oct 21 1805:** Nelson destroys Franco-Spanish fleet off Trafalgar
- **7–8 Feb 1807:** Battle of Eylau
- **1808:** France invades Spain; start of Peninsular War
- **1810:** Russia withdraws from Continental System
- **Sep–Oct 1812:** French occupy Moscow, then retreat
- **Sep 7 1812:** Battle of Borodino
- **Jun 18 1815:** Napoleon defeated by British and Prussians at Waterloo

- **Oct 1797:** Peace of Campo Formio between France and Austria
- **Aug 1798:** Battle of the Nile
- **1799:** Directory overthrown and First Republic dissolved; Napoleon elected First Consul
- **1801:** Peace of Lunéville between Austria and France
- **May 18 1803:** Britain declares war on France
- **Dec 2 1804:** Napoleon becomes "Emperor of the French"
- **2 Dec 1805:** Battle of Austerlitz
- **Oct 14 1806:** Defeat of Prussians at Jena and Auerstadt
- **Jul 1807:** Peace treaty between Napoleon and Russia at Tilsit
- **Jan 16 1809:** British defeated at Corunna
- **May 1812:** Napoleon invades Russia
- **Oct 16–18 1813:** Napoleon defeated by Allies at Leipzig
- **Mar 30 1814:** Allies enter Paris; Napoleon abdicates

The Napoleonic Empire

Napoleon's empire grew in two stages. In the first (1800–07), his brilliant military victories established France as the dominant power in Europe. Lands that came under his rule before 1807 – France, the Low Countries, northern Italy, and western Germany – formed an "inner empire." Here, French institutions and the Napoleonic legal code took root, surviving the empire's fall in 1814–15. Those areas taken after 1807 – Spain, southern Italy, northern Germany, and Poland – felt the effects of Napoleonic rule less, and often fiercely rejected French influence.

On December 2, 1804, Napoleon crowned himself "Emperor of the French" in the Cathedral of Notre Dame, Paris, as recorded in this famous painting by Jacques-Louis David.

Map 1: The campaigns of Napoleon 1794–1815

Jul 1807: Treaty of Tilsit: ssia accepts humiliating terms. sia joins France against Britain

Sep 7 1812: Despite Napoleon becoming ill and handing over command in mid-battle, Russians defeated and lose some 50,000 men

Sep 14 1812: Napoleon enters Moscow with some 95,000 men. City set on fire by inhabitants. On Oct 19 Napoleon forced to abandon Moscow

left wing of army under Macdonald

Aug 17 1812: Russians, led by Kutuzov, escape Napoleon's trap and retreat toward Moscow

Jun 24 1812: Napoleon crosses the Neman

Nov 12 1812: French army, starved, frozen, and harried by regular and irregular Russian forces, continues retreat

Krasnov Nov 16–17

Dec 8 1812: Napoleon abandons army and returns to Paris to raise fresh troops

Nov 26–28 1812: Despite repulsing constant attacks by Russians, French cross frozen river on pontoon bridges. French lose over 30,000 men

Napoleon's main army Eylau 1807

Russian army abandons its pursuit; losses in the campaign, some 250,000

1805: Allies crushed; 27,000 men, French 9,000 ern-Essling 21–22 1809

The campaigns of Napoleon 1794–1815

- → British forces
- ✗ French victory (colored by campaign)
- ✗ French defeat (colored by campaign)
- ⚓ British blockade
- ▲ defensive lines
- Ⓒ French siege
- - - frontiers 1797
- Holy Roman Empire 1797

Ionian Islands **1797:** By Treaty of Campo Formio, islands taken from Venice by France in preparation for invasion of Egypt

1798: Sultan of Turkey declares holy war (jihad) on France; prepares to invade Egypt

British fleet under Nelson

Mar 1799: besieged by French, but Turks resist and in May Napoleon retreat to Egypt

Aug 1 1798: Battle of the Nile (Aboukir Bay): Nelson, with 13 ships, destroys French fleet

Apr 17 1799: French defeat Turks

Jul 21 1798: Napoleon defeats the Mamluks; captures Cairo

Napoleon's invasion of Egypt in July 1798 was intended to secure an overland route to India, but the destruction of his fleet by the British under Nelson at the battle of the Nile left the French forces stranded.

Map 2: The Empire of Napoleon by 1812

② The Empire of Napoleon by 1812 ▲

- French territory ruled directly from Paris 1812
- dependent state 1812
- British or British occupied territory
- 👑 state ruled by Napoleon or member of his family at some time between 1805–12

Opposition to Napoleon

Between 1793 and 1815 France fought all the major European powers, either singly or in coalitions. After his defeat of the Third Coalition in 1807, Napoleon ruled virtually the entire continent. Only Britain opposed him. To cripple the British economically, Napoleon tried to prevent all trade between continental Europe and Britain, but this blockade, known as the Continental System, proved difficult to enforce. Russian withdrawal from the system provoked the fatal march on Moscow of 1812, which was to lead to his downfall.

In July 1807, Napoleon met King Frederick William III and Queen Marie Louise of Prussia and Tsar Alexander I of Russia near Tilsit, Prussia, to discuss peace.

Mar 1808: National revolt against French invasion supported by Britain, which sends armies under Moore and Wellington

Map 3: Alliances in opposition to France 1792–1815

③ Alliances in opposition to France 1792–1815 ▶

Alliances against France in the Napoleonic Wars:
- ✗ wars of Second Coalition 1798–1800
- ✗ wars of Third Coalition 1805–07
- ✗ war with Austria 1809
- ✗ war with Russia 1812
- ✗ Wars of Liberation of France 1813–15

- France 1792
- annexed by France 1802
- satellites of France 1802
- Napoleon's Continental System
- Holy Roman Empire
- frontiers c.1802

THE GROWTH OF NATIONALISM

Otto von Bismarck, prime minister of Prussia 1862–1890, was chief architect of the unification of Germany.

TO RESTORE PEACE and stability after the turmoil of the Napoleonic Wars, the Congress of Vienna was convened in 1814. Attended by all the major European powers, but dominated by Austria, Britain, Russia, and Prussia, the Congress redrew the political map of Europe and restored many former ruling houses. The result was three decades of reactionary rule, during which nationalist and republican movements, inspired by the American and French models, challenged the status quo. In eastern Europe, Greece and the Balkan states took advantage of the weakness of the Ottoman Empire to gain independence. In the west, Italy and Germany finally achieved their dreams of unification. But traditional rivalry between royal houses was now replaced by rivalry between industrialized nation states – a rivalry which led, ultimately, to World War I.

Europe under the Vienna system

The Congress of Vienna met to share out the spoils of victory over Napoleon, though painful compromise was required to achieve a workable balance of power in Europe. Political stability was reestablished by restoring the hereditary monarchs overthrown by Napoleon. France, though deprived of all its conquests, once more had a Bourbon on the throne. But the restored monarchs ruled with too heavy a hand: liberal, republican, and nationalist revolts began to break out, reaching a crescendo in 1848 when the governments of France, Italy, and Austria were all shaken by insurrection.

The Congress of Vienna was attended by five monarchs and the heads of 216 princely families. It was dominated by the Austrian chancellor, Prince Metternich, seen here standing on the left at the signing of the final settlement.

Threats to the Vienna system 1814–50

- **1806:** Abolition of Holy Roman Empire
- **1814:** Napoleon abdicates; opening of Congress of Vienna
- **1815:** Napoleon escapes from exile, but is defeated at Waterloo; restoration of French monarchy
- **1820–23:** Revolts in Spain, Portugal, Naples, Sicily, Piedmont, and the Balkans
- **1821:** Start of Greek War of Independence which lasts until 1833
- **1830:** Revolution in Paris
- **1830–31:** Belgian War of Independence
- **1833–39:** First Carlist War in Spain
- **1848:** Second Republic in France with Louis-Napoleon as president
- **1848:** Revolutions throughout Europe

(timeline: 1800 – 1810 – 1820 – 1830 – 1840 – 1850)

① Europe after the Congress of Vienna 1815–52

MAIN MAP

- small German states
- areas in revolt against Louis-Napoleon in 1851
- German Confederation
- threat to Vienna System 1817–39
- revolution in 1848–49
- frontiers 1815

INSET: Belgian independence 1831–39

- United Netherlands 1815–31
- boundary of German Confederation 1815
- boundary of German Confederation 1839
- boundary between French and Flemish speakers

400 km
400 miles

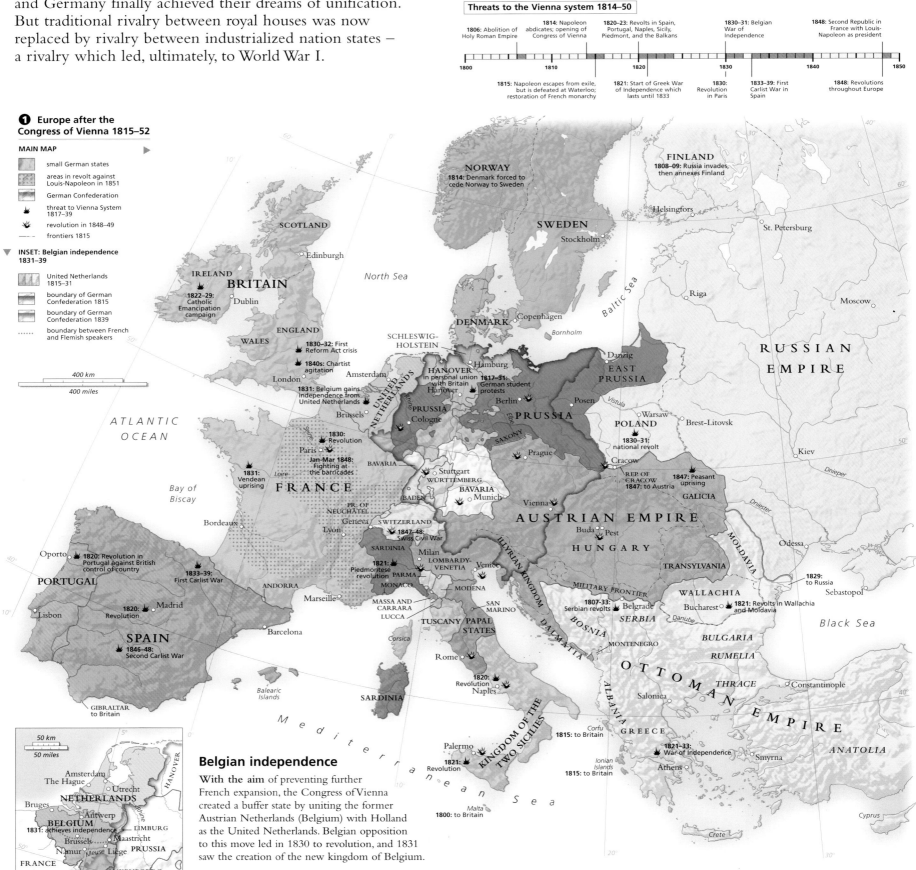

SCOTLAND
Edinburgh
IRELAND
BRITAIN
Dublin
1822–29: Catholic Emancipation campaign
ENGLAND
WALES
1830–32: First Reform Act crisis
1840s: Chartist agitation
London
North Sea
NORWAY
1814: Denmark forced to cede Norway to Sweden
SWEDEN
Stockholm
FINLAND
1808–09: Russia invades, then annexes Finland
Helsingfors
St. Petersburg
Riga
Moscow
RUSSIAN EMPIRE

ATLANTIC OCEAN

DENMARK
Copenhagen
Baltic Sea
Bornholm
Danzig
Hamburg
SCHLESWIG-HOLSTEIN
HANOVER in personal union with Britain
1817–31: German student protests
Amsterdam
UNITED NETHERLANDS
1831: Belgium gains independence from United Netherlands
Brussels
PRUSSIA
Cologne
Berlin
EAST PRUSSIA
Posen
Vistula
Warsaw
Brest-Litovsk
POLAND
1830–31: national revolt
SAXONY
Prague
Cracow
REP. OF CRACOW **1847:** to Austria
1847: Peasant uprising
GALICIA
Kiev
Dnieper

Bay of Biscay
1830: Revolution
Paris
Jan–Mar 1848: Fighting at the barricades
Loire
1831: Vendean uprising
FRANCE
BAVARIA
Stuttgart
WÜRTTEMBERG
Munich
BADEN
PR. OF NEUCHÂTEL
Geneva
SWITZERLAND
Lyon
1847–48: Swiss Civil War
Bordeaux
Vienna
AUSTRIAN EMPIRE
Buda Pest
HUNGARY
TRANSYLVANIA
MOLDAVIA
Odessa
Dniester
1829: to Russia
WALLACHIA
1821: Revolts in Wallachia and Moldavia
Sebastopol

Oporto
1820: Revolution in Portugal against British control of country
1833–39: First Carlist War
PORTUGAL
ANDORRA
Marseille
1820: Revolution
Madrid
Lisbon
SPAIN
Barcelona
1846–48: Second Carlist War
SARDINIA
Milan
LOMBARDY-VENETIA
1821: Piedmontese revolution
PARMA
MONACO
MASSA AND CARRARA
LUCCA
MODENA
SAN MARINO
Venice
ILLYRIAN KINGDOM
DALMATIA
BOSNIA
MILITARY FRONTIER
1807–33: Serbian revolts
Belgrade
SERBIA
Danube
Bucharest
MONTENEGRO
BULGARIA
RUMELIA
THRACE
Constantinople
Black Sea
ALBANIA
GREECE
1821–33: War of Independence
Salonica
OTTOMAN EMPIRE
Smyrna
ANATOLIA
Athens
Rome
TUSCANY PAPAL STATES
Corsica
1820: Revolution Naples
SARDINIA
1821: Revolution
Palermo
KINGDOM OF THE TWO SICILIES
Corfu **1815:** to Britain
Ionian Islands **1815:** to Britain
Balearic Islands
GIBRALTAR to Britain
Malta **1800:** to Britain
Crete
Cyprus
Mediterranean Sea

Belgian independence

With the aim of preventing further French expansion, the Congress of Vienna created a buffer state by uniting the former Austrian Netherlands (Belgium) with Holland as the United Netherlands. Belgian opposition to this move led in 1830 to revolution, and 1831 saw the creation of the new kingdom of Belgium.

50 km
50 miles

Amsterdam
The Hague
Utrecht
NETHERLANDS
Bruges
Antwerp
HANOVER
Rhine
BELGIUM
1831: achieves independence
Brussels
LIMBURG
Maastricht
Namur Liège
PRUSSIA
Meuse
FRANCE
1839: Eastern Luxembourg ruled by Dutch kings
1890: independent
LUXEMBOURG
Luxembourg

The unification of Germany

In 1815 Germany's states were reduced to a Confederation of 39 under Austrian leadership. These states were further united in 1834 by the formation of a customs union (Zollverein). In 1866 Bismarck, prime minister of Prussia, proposed a German Confederation which would exclude Austria. When Austria refused, Bismarck – bent on German unification – declared war on Austria. Following Austria's defeat, Bismarck established the North German Confederation. The German Empire, including Bavaria and other south German states, was created after Prussia's victory in the Franco-Prussian War in 1870.

Spiked helmets such as this one worn by a dragoon officer became emblems of German militarism.

In 1870, alarmed at the intentions of Prussia, Napoleon III declared war, but the French were defeated. Here, Napoleon surrenders to the Prussian king Wilhelm I.

The unification of Germany

1864: German-Danish War
1867: Prussia forms North German Confederation
1870: French defeated at Sedan
1871: Wilhelm I of Prussia proclaimed Emperor of Germany

1862: Bismarck prime minister of Prussia
1866: Austro-Prussian War
1870: Siege of Paris begins
1871: Germany adds Alsace-Lorraine to newly-created empire

(timeline: 1860 – 1865 – 1870 – 1875)

② The unification of Germany
- boundary of German Confederation of 1815
- Prussia in 1815
- Prussian gains by 1866
- other states in North German Confederation 1867
- other German states 1866
- Austro-Hungarian Empire 1867
- frontiers in 1866
- → attack on Denmark by Austro-Prussian forces 1864
- --→ Prussian armies in war with Austria 1866
- --→ Prussian invasion of France in Franco-Prussian War 1870–71
- boundary of German Empire 1871

The unification of Italy

The restoration of the old order in 1815 provoked a movement to liberate and unite Italy. In 1859 Cavour, prime minister of Sardinia-Piedmont, enlisted the help of French emperor Napoleon III to drive the Austrians out of Lombardy. In 1860 Sicily and Naples were conquered by Garibaldi and his 1000 "Redshirts," then handed over to Victor Emmanuel II of Sardinia, who became king of a united Italy in 1861. Rome was finally added to the new kingdom in 1870.

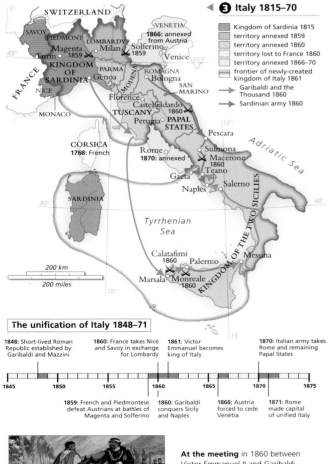

◀ ③ Italy 1815–70
- Kingdom of Sardinia 1815
- territory annexed 1859
- territory annexed 1860
- territory lost to France 1860
- territory annexed 1866–70
- frontier of newly-created kingdom of Italy 1861
- → Garibaldi and the Thousand 1860
- → Sardinian army 1860

The unification of Italy 1848–71

1848: Short-lived Roman Republic established by Garibaldi and Mazzini
1860: France takes Nice and Savoy in exchange for Lombardy
1861: Victor Emmanuel becomes king of Italy
1870: Italian army takes Rome and remaining Papal States

(timeline: 1845 – 1850 – 1855 – 1860 – 1865 – 1870 – 1875)

1859: French and Piedmontese defeat Austrians at battles of Magenta and Solferino
1860: Garibaldi conquers Sicily and Naples
1866: Austria forced to cede Venetia
1871: Rome made capital of unified Italy

At the meeting in 1860 between Victor Emmanuel II and Garibaldi at Teano, Garibaldi – a lifelong Republican – effectively presented the king with half of Italy.

Nationalism in the Balkans

Nationalism proved most volatile in the Balkans, where many subject peoples aspired to independence from the Ottomans. Initially only the Greeks were successful. Meanwhile, Austria and Russia vied to replace the Turks as the dominant power in the region. Russian expansionism provoked the Crimean War in 1854, when Russia was defeated by Britain, France, Austria, and Turkey, and the Russo-Turkish War of 1877–78. At the Congress of Berlin in 1878, Turkey was forced to abandon all claims to Montenegro, Romania, and Serbia. In 1912, intent on seizing the Ottomans' last remaining European territories, Serbia, Bulgaria, and Greece were victorious in the First Balkan War. Resentment over the division of the spoils sparked a new war, from which Serbia emerged triumphant, but the precarious situation would be a major cause of World War I.

In this cartoon of 1908, Ottoman sultan Abdul Hamid II sulks as more Balkan territory is whipped from under his feet by Austria and Bulgaria.

④ The Balkans and the Black Sea to 1913
- international boundaries 1913
- Ottoman Empire 1913
- Russian Empire 1913
- Austro-Hungarian Empire 1913
- Italy and possessions 1913
- Serbia 1833
- Serbian gain 1878
- Serbian gain 1913
- Greece 1830
- Greek gain 1864
- Greek gain 1881
- Greek gain 1913
- Romania 1861
- Romanian gain 1878
- Romanian gain 1913
- Bulgaria 1878
- Bulgarian gain 1885
- Bulgarian gain 1913
- Montenegro 1878
- Montenegrin gain 1913
- Albania 1913
- → Russian forces in Crimean War
- → Allied forces in Crimean War
- → Russian forces in 1877–78
- ✕ significant Ottoman defeat

The Balkans and the Black Sea 1850–1913

1854–56: Crimean War
1877–78: Russia, Serbia, and Montenegro at war with Turkey
1878: Congress of Berlin alters terms of San Stefano treaty; Bulgaria becomes autonomous principality within Ottoman Empire
1908: Bulgaria declares full independence
1913: Treaty of London confirms independent Albania

(timeline: 1850 – 1860 – 1870 – 1880 – 1890 – 1900 – 1910 – 1920)

1878: Treaty of San Stefano negotiated by Russia and Turkey
1885: Bulgaria granted Eastern Rumelia
1912: Serbia, Bulgaria, Greece, and Montenegro form Balkan League; First Balkan War
1913: Second Balkan War

THE INDUSTRIAL REVOLUTION

Matthew Boulton's metal works in Birmingham developed the steam engine for industrial use.

IN THE LATTER HALF of the 18th century, rapid technological, social, and economic changes began to transform Britain from an agrarian into a largely urban, industrial society. This process, which became known as the Industrial Revolution, spread to Europe in the course of the 19th century. The population of the continent doubled in this period and was fed by a similar growth in agricultural production. Changes included the use of new power sources such as coal and steam; new building materials, chiefly iron and steel; and technical innovations and improved systems of transportation. These developments led to large-scale production and the growth of the factory system.

Industrial chimneys dominate the Manchester skyline in this 19th-century engraving. Industry in Britain concentrated in cities where rich coal and iron deposits were in close proximity.

The move to the towns

Urban development was inextricably linked to the process of industrialization. The most marked 19th-century urban growth occurred in areas where labor-intensive, mechanized, and often factory-based industries were emerging. Rapid urbanization first occurred in Britain, where the urban population grew from 20% of the total population in 1800, to 41% in 1850. By the 1850s, many other European countries experienced urban growth at a rate comparable with that of Britain in the first half of the century.

The Industrial Revolution in Britain

A combination of geographical, political, and social factors ensured that Britain became the first industrial nation. The country possessed a number of natural ports facing the Atlantic, an established shipping trade, and a network of internal navigable waterways. It was richly endowed with coal and iron ore and could draw on a large market both at home and overseas. British colonies supplied raw materials and custom and an expanding population ensured buoyant demand at home. The textile industry in Britain was the first to benefit from new technical innovations which brought about greater production efficiency and output.

The replacement of water power with steam power greatly increased efficiency. Huge fly-wheels could drive machinery, such as that used here to make cable, at greater speeds.

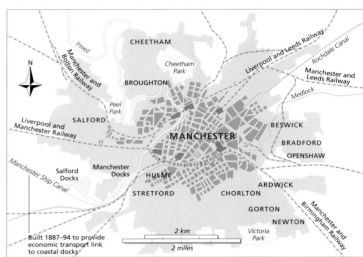

▲ ② The growth of Manchester 1840–1900

- railroad
- railroad station
- Manchester South junction viaduct
- park
- built-up area 1840
- growth of city 1840–1900

The advance of British technology from 1733

- **1733:** John Kay invents the flying shuttle
- **1765:** James Hargreaves invents "spinning jenny" which increases the output of spun cotton
- **1765:** James Watt builds improved steam engine with separate condenser
- **1785:** Power loom for cloth making revolutionizes weaving
- **1811–12:** Luddite rioters wreck new textile machinery in Derbyshire
- **1825:** First passenger steam railroad from Stockton to Darlington
- **1832:** Outbreak of cholera kills 31,000 people in Britain
- **1837:** First practical electric telegraph system produced by Cooke and Wheatstone
- **1838:** Launch of I.K. Brunel's *Great Western* steamship
- **1840:** Cheap postal system introduced; one penny per letter to anywhere in Britain
- **1842:** Lord Shaftesbury's Mines Act; underground employment of women and children prohibited

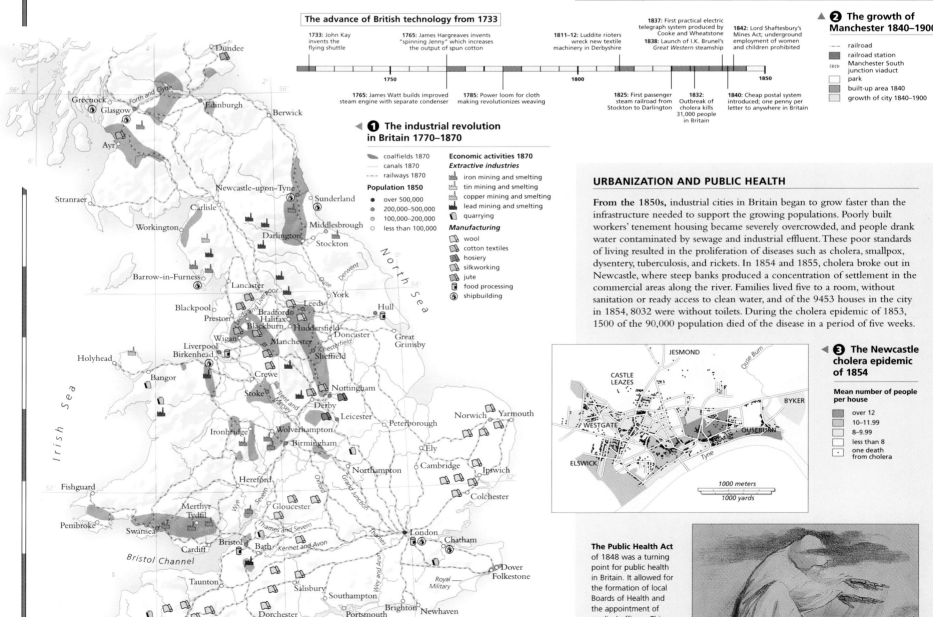

◀ ① The industrial revolution in Britain 1770–1870

- coalfields 1870
- canals 1870
- railways 1870

Population 1850
- ● over 500,000
- ● 200,000–500,000
- ◉ 100,000–200,000
- ○ less than 100,000

Economic activities 1870
Extractive industries
- iron mining and smelting
- tin mining and smelting
- copper mining and smelting
- lead mining and smelting
- quarrying

Manufacturing
- wool
- cotton textiles
- hosiery
- silkworking
- jute
- food processing
- shipbuilding

URBANIZATION AND PUBLIC HEALTH

From the 1850s, industrial cities in Britain began to grow faster than the infrastructure needed to support the growing populations. Poorly built workers' tenement housing became severely overcrowded, and people drank water contaminated by sewage and industrial effluent. These poor standards of living resulted in the proliferation of diseases such as cholera, smallpox, dysentery, tuberculosis, and rickets. In 1854 and 1855, cholera broke out in Newcastle, where steep banks produced a concentration of settlement in the commercial areas along the river. Families lived five to a room, without sanitation or ready access to clean water, and of the 9453 houses in the city in 1854, 8032 were without toilets. During the cholera epidemic of 1853, 1500 of the 90,000 population died of the disease in a period of five weeks.

◀ ③ The Newcastle cholera epidemic of 1854

Mean number of people per house
- over 12
- 10–11.99
- 8–9.99
- less than 8
- one death from cholera

The Public Health Act of 1848 was a turning point for public health in Britain. It allowed for the formation of local Boards of Health and the appointment of medical officers. This public health poster entitled *Cholera Tramples the Victor and the Vanquish'd Both,* warned people that no class was immune from the disease.

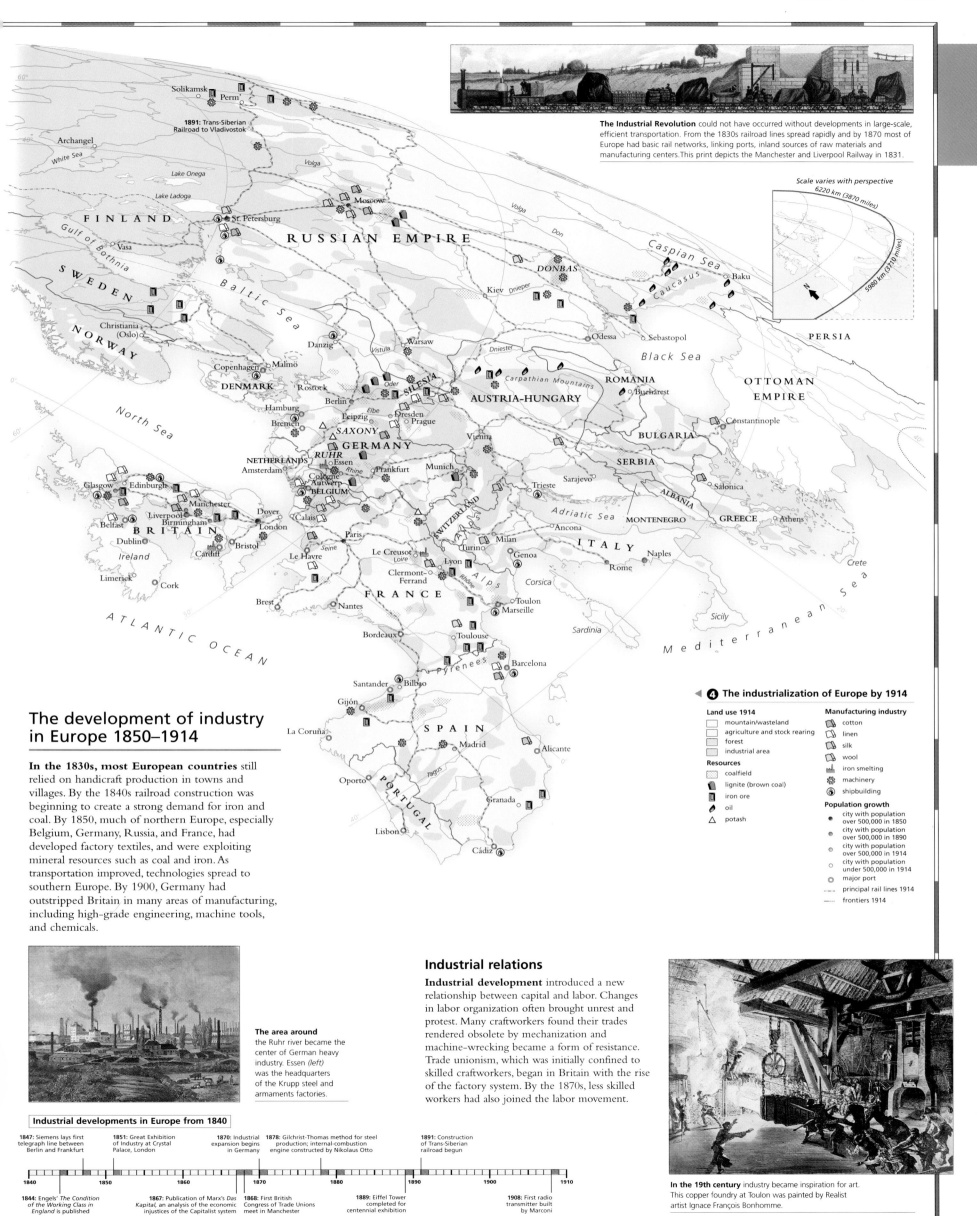

The Industrial Revolution could not have occurred without developments in large-scale, efficient transportation. From the 1830s railroad lines spread rapidly and by 1870 most of Europe had basic rail networks, linking ports, inland sources of raw materials and manufacturing centers. This print depicts the Manchester and Liverpool Railway in 1831.

Scale varies with perspective
6220 km (3870 miles)
5980 km (3710 miles)

N

The development of industry in Europe 1850–1914

In the 1830s, most European countries still relied on handicraft production in towns and villages. By the 1840s railroad construction was beginning to create a strong demand for iron and coal. By 1850, much of northern Europe, especially Belgium, Germany, Russia, and France, had developed factory textiles, and were exploiting mineral resources such as coal and iron. As transportation improved, technologies spread to southern Europe. By 1900, Germany had outstripped Britain in many areas of manufacturing, including high-grade engineering, machine tools, and chemicals.

4 The industrialization of Europe by 1914

Land use 1914
- mountain/wasteland
- agriculture and stock rearing
- forest
- industrial area

Resources
- coalfield
- lignite (brown coal)
- iron ore
- oil
- potash

Manufacturing industry
- cotton
- linen
- silk
- wool
- iron smelting
- machinery
- shipbuilding

Population growth
- city with population over 500,000 in 1850
- city with population over 500,000 in 1890
- city with population over 500,000 in 1914
- city with population under 500,000 in 1914
- major port
- principal rail lines 1914
- frontiers 1914

The area around the Ruhr river became the center of German heavy industry. Essen (left) was the headquarters of the Krupp steel and armaments factories.

Industrial relations

Industrial development introduced a new relationship between capital and labor. Changes in labor organization often brought unrest and protest. Many craftworkers found their trades rendered obsolete by mechanization and machine-wrecking became a form of resistance. Trade unionism, which was initially confined to skilled craftworkers, began in Britain with the rise of the factory system. By the 1870s, less skilled workers had also joined the labor movement.

In the 19th century industry became inspiration for art. This copper foundry at Toulon was painted by Realist artist Ignace François Bonhomme.

Industrial developments in Europe from 1840

1847: Siemens lays first telegraph line between Berlin and Frankfurt

1851: Great Exhibition of Industry at Crystal Palace, London

1870: Industrial expansion begins in Germany

1878: Gilchrist-Thomas method for steel production; internal-combustion engine constructed by Nikolaus Otto

1891: Construction of Trans-Siberian railroad begun

1840 1850 1860 1870 1880 1890 1900 1910

1844: Engels' *The Condition of the Working Class in England* is published

1867: Publication of Marx's *Das Kapital*, an analysis of the economic injustices of the Capitalist system

1868: First British Congress of Trade Unions meet in Manchester

1889: Eiffel Tower completed for centennial exhibition

1908: First radio transmitter built by Marconi

WORLD WAR I

Dynamic recruiting posters appealed directly to the patriotism of Europe's young men.

WORLD WAR I is one of history's watersheds. Austria-Hungary's attempt to assert its power developed into a protracted struggle that swept up most of Europe and the rest of the world in its train. The conflict mobilized 65 million troops, of whom nine million died and over one-third were wounded. Civilians also died – as a result of military action, starvation, and disease. The war was won by the Allied Powers, but at great cost. The German, Austro-Hungarian, Ottoman, and Russian empires were destroyed; European political and financial supremacy ended; and by 1918 the US had emerged as the greatest power in the world. The debt and disillusionment that followed paved the way for the revolutionary forces of the left and right that emerged in the 1930s in the wake of the Great Depression.

The start of World War I

World War I began in Europe in August 1914. A decade of increasingly severe political crises, combined with military and naval arms races among Europe's major powers, created an incendiary situation. The murder of Austrian Archduke Franz Ferdinand in Sarajevo in June 1914 proved the catalyst. Serbia, Montenegro, Russia, France, Belgium, and Britain (the Allied Powers) found themselves opposed to Austria-Hungary, Germany, and Turkey (the Central Powers). The Central powers were joined by Bulgaria in 1915, while the Allied powers gathered Italy by 1915 and Romania in 1916. In 1917, the US joined the war as an "associated power" on the Allied side.

❶ The balance of power in Europe, 1879–1918

◇ Austro–German alliance 1879–1918
◆ Three Emperors' alliance 1881–87
◆ Austro–Serbian alliance 1881–95
◇ Triple alliance 1882–1915
◇ Austro–German–Romanian alliance 1883–1916
◆ Reinsurance treaty 1887–90
◆ Franco–Russian alliance 1894–1917
◇ Russo–Bulgarian military convention 1902–13

Alliances on the eve of the war
☐ Allied Powers 1914
☐ Central Powers 1914
☐ neutral states 1914

War on the Western Front

By November 1914 the war on the Western Front had become largely static. A German offensive against Paris via Belgium was rapidly met by French and British forces, who forced them back to Flanders. For three years, the British and French armies, and the Germans at Verdun, undertook a series of futile and exceptionally costly offensives in which gains were generally no more than a few miles. The front was marked by long lines of trenches, from which the two sides sought to defend their positions. It was impossible for them to achieve any measure of surprise, or, with no room for maneuver, to shift their position at all.

For several years, the war in western Europe was fought along a barely shifting frontline, marked by a series of trenches. These British troops, from the Border Regiment are squatting in "funk holes" near Thiepval Wood during the battle of the Somme in 1916.

Tanks were first used at the end of the 1916 battle of the Somme and later during the Allied advance in the summer and autumn of 1918. Though they could cope with difficult terrain, the trench system provided considerable obstacles (left).

The Western Front

Aug 1914: Battle of the Frontiers | Oct 1914: The "race to the sea" | May 1916: Battle of Jutland in North Sea | Feb–Mar 1917: Germans withdraw to Hindenburg Line | Apr–May 1917: Allied offensives | Mar–Jul 1918: German offensives on Somme, Aisne, Noyon-Mondidier, and Champagne-Marne lines

1915 | 1916 | 1917 | 1917 | 1919

Sep 1914: Battle of the Marne; first battle of the Aisne | Feb–Dec 1916: Battle of Verdun | Jul–Nov 1916: Battle of the Somme | Apr 1917: US declares war on Central powers | Aug–Nov 1917: Third battle of Ypres | Jul–Oct 1918: Counteroffensives by Allies | Nov 1918: Armistice ends war on Western Front

❷ The Western Front 1914–16

The German offensive leads to stalemate

Facing a war on two fronts against enemies with larger armies, Germany sought to defeat France before Russia could fully mobilize. They planned to outflank the main French defenses by moving through Belgium and then through northern France to encircle France within six weeks. However, supply lines proved inadequate, and communications to, and between, the two main armies no better. The plan ignored British intervention, relying on the likelihood of French immobilization as the offensive progressed. French success at the battle of the Marne ended German hopes of a quick victory, and paved the way for the trench warfare that lasted until spring 1918.

Aircraft were used initially for reconnaissance and artillery spotting; later, in 1917–18 Germany and Britain used heavy bombers to destroy industrial and civilian targets.

Offensives and counteroffensives in 1918

When Russia withdrew in 1917, Germany needed to defeat Britain and France before US forces could be mustered in sufficient strength on the Western Front. The 1918 offensives were a strategic failure, sapping German resources and morale. The Allied Powers took advantage of their superior manpower and resources to counterattack successfully. With Germany's allies collapsing, its commanders were forced to seek the armistice that ended the war.

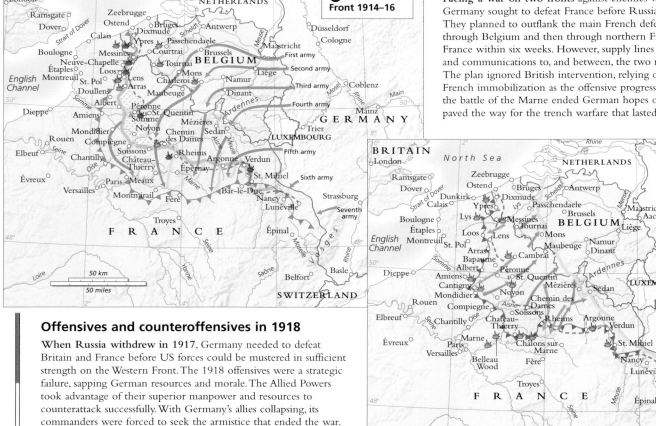

❸ The Western Front 1916–18

The Western Front 1914–1918

→ German invasion of France and Belgium, 1914
▲▲ farthest extent of German advance, 1914
⇒ German retreat
— line from end of 1914–Jul 1916
--- Hindenburg line
☐ gains by Allied powers 1916–17
⇨ Kaiserschlacht ("the Kaiser's battles") 1918
▲▲ German offensive Mar–Jul 1918
⇨ Allied counterattacks, 1918
— line at the Armistice Nov 11 1918

Major battles
⚔ 1914
⚔ 1915
⚔ 1916
⚔ 1917
⚔ 1918

War on the Eastern Front

There was far more movement on the Eastern Front than in the West, partly because of the much greater distances involved. Though the Russian army was generally superior to Austria-Hungary militarily, they were invariably defeated by the force of German arms. By the end of 1915, Russia had lost most of Poland, with more than two million troops taken prisoner. Inadequate military supplies and poor leadership produced a consequently high casualty rate: war-weariness and mutiny were key factors in bringing the Bolsheviks to power in 1917.

During the first German onslaught on the Eastern Front, casualty numbers were such that even churches were converted into makeshift field hospitals. The priest is giving a blessing to sick and wounded troops.

CASUALTIES OF WAR

The toll of military dead and wounded was appalling; of the millions mobilized on the Allied side, fewer than half escaped death or injury. The Central Powers' losses were even higher, particularly in Austria-Hungary. In total, nearly nine million men died in four years, with 23 million left physically or psychologically scarred. Civilians died too, from bombing raids, malnutrition, and disease.

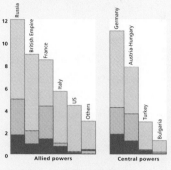

Military casualties (millions)

■ troops mobilized   ■ troops wounded
■ troops killed

The Eastern Front

The Eastern Front

Sep–Oct 1914: German operations in southwestern Poland
Feb 1915: Second Battle of Masurian Lakes
Jul–Sep 1915: Russian withdrawal
Aug–Sep 1916: Romanian offensive
Mar 1917: Russian Revolution
Jul 1917: Second Brusilov Offensive
Dec 1917: Russian armistice

1914   1915   1916   1917   1918

Aug 1914: Battle of Tannenberg
Sep 1914: First Battle of Masurian Lakes
Nov 1914: Battle of Lodz
May 1915: German breakthrough at Gorlice-Tarnow
Jun–Aug 1916: Brusilov Offensive by Russia
Sep–Dec 1916: Elimination of Romania
Jan 1918: Treaty of Brest-Litovsk allows Germany to occupy Ukraine and gain access to food supplies

4 The Eastern Front

→ Russian advances, 1914
▲▲ front line in 1914–15 (limit of Russian advance)
▲▲ limit of Austro-German advances, 1915–16
→ Brusilov offensives, 1916
→ Armistice line Dec 1917
→ German landings, 1917–18
▲▲ German offensives into Russia 1918
▲▲ German penetration into Russia by Jun 1918
▒ Area occupied by Central Powers under Treaty of Brest-Litovsk

Major battles:
⚜ 1914   ⚜ 1916
⚜ 1915   ⚜ 1917

War in the Balkans

Serbia survived three invasion attempts in 1914, but succumbed in 1915 to an Austro-German offensive supported by Bulgaria, which checked an Anglo-French attempt to support the Serbian army from Salonica. In 1916, having successfully contained Allied forces at Salonica and invaded Romania, Bulgarian armies were joined by Austro-German forces that captured Bucharest in December. The Bulgarians were able to defeat several Allied offensives in front of Salonica until September 1918 when a major offensive broke the Bulgarian front and morale. Forced to sue for an armistice, the Bulgarians saw their capital occupied by British forces, while French and Serbian forces liberated Belgrade on November 1.

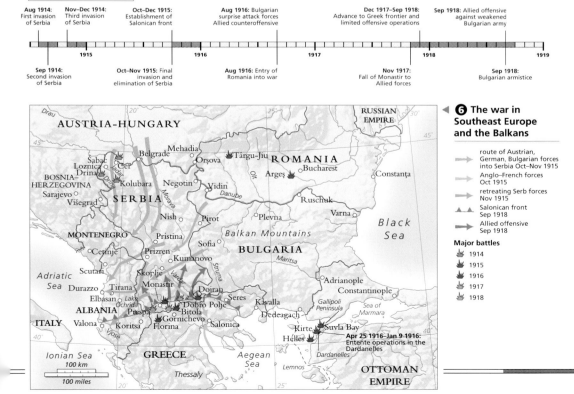

Lying in a key position at the head of the Gulf of Salonica, the port city of Salonica was a major focus for Allied operations in the Balkans during the First World War.

The war in the Balkans

Aug 1914: First invasion of Serbia
Nov–Dec 1914: Third invasion of Serbia
Oct–Dec 1915: Establishment of Salonican front
Aug 1916: Bulgarian surprise attack forces Allied counteroffensive
Dec 1917–Sep 1918: Advance to Greek frontier and limited offensive operations
Sep 1918: Allied offensive against weakened Bulgarian army

1915   1916   1917   1918   1919

Sep 1914: Second invasion of Serbia
Oct–Nov 1915: Final invasion and elimination of Serbia
Aug 1916: Entry of Romania into war
Nov 1917: Fall of Monastir to Allied forces
Sep 1918: Bulgarian armistice

6 The war in Southeast Europe and the Balkans

→ route of Austrian, German, Bulgarian forces into Serbia Oct–Nov 1915
→ Anglo-French forces Oct 1915
→ retreating Serb forces Nov 1915
▲▲ Salonican front Sep 1918
→ Allied offensive Sep 1918

Major battles
⚜ 1914
⚜ 1915
⚜ 1916
⚜ 1917
⚜ 1918

The Italian Front

Italy entered the war in 1915 in an opportunistic arrangement engineered by its leaders with the Allies to secure territory at the expense of Austria-Hungary. Fighting on the Italian Front was some of the most bitter of the war, with much of the fighting occurring in a series of battles close to the Isonzo River. The great battle of Caporetto in 1917 almost led to Italian defeat. Italy was more successful in subsequent fighting, but the terrible disillusionment after the war over the price paid for Italy's gains contributed heavily to the rise to power of Benito Mussolini and the Fascists.

Italian civilians suffered great privations during the years of warfare in the north of the country. Here, women – wheeling handcarts – and children flee following the 6th battle of the Isonzo.

5 The Italian Front 1915–1918

→ Italian offensives on the Isonzo River, 1915–17
→ Austro-German campaigns, 1917
▲▲ front line in Sep 1917
▲▲ front line Dec 1917–Oct 1918
→ Allied offensive, Oct 1918
→ Armistice line Nov 4 1918

Major battles
⚜ 1915
⚜ 1917
⚜ 1918

The war in Italy

Jun–Sep 1915: 1st and 2nd Battle of the Isonzo
Mar 1916: 5th Battle of the Isonzo
Aug–Sep 1916: 6th and 7th Battles of the Isonzo
May–Jun 1917: 10th Battle of the Isonzo
Oct–Nov 1917: Battle of Caporetto
Jun 1918: Battle of the Piave

1915   1916   1917   1918   1919

Oct–Nov 1915: 3rd and 4th Battles of the Isonzo
May–Jun 1916: Asiago Offensive by Austria
Oct–Nov 1916: 8th and 9th Battles of the Isonzo
Aug–Sep 1917: 11th Battle of the Isonzo
Nov 1918: Battle of Vittorio Veneto

EUROPE BETWEEN THE WARS

Vladimir Illich Lenin
was the architect of
the Bolshevik
Revolution.

AS WORLD WAR I drew to its close, the three great conservative empires of Europe – Russia, Austria-Hungary, and Germany – suffered cataclysmic change. Revolution in 1917 in Russia led to the seizure of power by Lenin and the Bolsheviks. After the end of the war, the victorious allies imposed peace treaties which dismembered Austria-Hungary and sliced territory from Germany – as well as imposing punitive financial penalties. New states sprang up right across Europe as nationalist aspirations coincided with the collapse of multinational empires.

Revolution and civil war in Russia

In 1917, Russia's Tsarist regime, ravaged by war and a failing economy, collapsed. The provisional government which replaced it failed to improve the economy, and in October 1917, the socialist Bolsheviks seized key installations in Petrograd and took control of a number of important towns. Civil war broke out as anti-Bolsheviks and pro-monarchists (the "Whites"), aided by troops from other European nations (the Entente powers), tried to overthrow them. However the well-organized Bolsheviks (the "Reds") held the heartland of Russia and by 1921 had defeated their weak, disunited opponents. Meanwhile, national groups on the periphery of Russia strove for independence. Finland, Estonia, Latvia, Lithuania, and Poland broke free and were able to remain so, but the independence of Armenia, Azerbaijan, and Georgia was short-lived. By 1924 the Bolsheviks were firmly in control and the Soviet Union came into being.

Europe after World War I

Following the end of World War I, Finland, Estonia, Latvia, and Lithuania gained independence from Russia; Czechoslovakia and Yugoslavia emerged from the wreckage of Austria-Hungary, while Poland reappeared as an independent state for the first time since its partition in 1794. In western Europe too, long-frustrated national discontent finally brought about the establishment of an independent Irish Free State in 1921. The birth of new states and changes in regime did not happen easily, and Finland and the new Irish state were both engulfed by civil war.

The immense reparations imposed on Germany by the Treaty of Versailles proved an impossible burden to a nation already crippled by the costs of the war. Hyperinflation during the 1920s so devalued the national currency that it became totally worthless. These children are using Deutschmarks as building blocks.

The aftermath of World War I

1919: Treaty of Versailles forces Germany to admit guilt for starting war and pay reparations to Allies	**1923:** Hyperinflation begins in Germany		**1924:** German reparations reduced by Dawes Plan
1919	**1921**	**1923**	**1925**
1920: League of Nations founded	**1921:** Birth of Irish Free State	**1923:** France occupies Ruhr region of Germany	**1925:** European boundaries stabilized by Treaty of Locarno

❶ Europe after World War I

European empires in 1914
German Empire	— frontiers 1923
Austro-Hungarian Empire	☐ new states
Russian Empire	

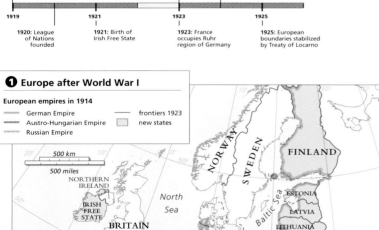

Scale varies with perspective

10,250 km (6370 miles)
6450 km (4010 miles)

The Russian Civil War

	Russian boundary after Treaty of Brest-Litovsk Mar 1918
→	Bolshevik forces
→	White Russian forces
→	Entente forces

▲ ❷ The Russian Revolution, the Russian Civil War, and the formation of the Soviet Union 1917–24

	the Russian Empire in 1914
	countries/republics which declared independence from Russia in 1917–18

The Bolshevik revolution
●	towns where Bolsheviks gained control 1917
◉	towns where Bolsheviks gained control 1918

The formation of the Soviet Union

★	republics temporarily independent from Russia 1917/18–21
	occupied by Japan 1918–22
	extent of Bolshevik territory in mid-1919
	Soviet Union by 1924
—	frontiers 1924
----	Trans-Siberian railroad

Revolution and civil war in Russia 1917–24

Mar 1917: Abdication of Tsar Nicholas II	**1918:** Start of civil war between Bolsheviks and White Russians **1918:** Treaty of Brest-Litovsk ends World War I in the east	**1920:** White Russia, Ukraine, and Caucasus Republics return to Russian control	**1922:** USSR (Union of Soviet Socialist Republics) is formed	
1917	**1919**	**1921**	**1923**	**1925**
Nov 1917: Bolsheviks begin to take control of European Russia	**1920:** Start of peasant revolts throughout Russia	**1921:** Russian civil war ends with Bolshevik victory. New economic policy encourages peasants to produce more food while modernization is taking place		**1924:** Lenin dies and is later succeeded by Josef Stalin

Economic crisis and political extremism

The US economic crisis of 1929 hit a Europe suffering from the aftermath of wartime dislocation. Industrial output and agricultural production fell sharply across the world, but the industrial nations were hardest hit. Farmers survived by retreating to subsistence production, but the collapse in industrial output brought unemployment on a massive scale. Without proper systems of social security to support the unemployed, poverty became widespread. The economic and social problems of the 1930s encouraged the growth of extreme political movements on both Left and Right, especially in Germany and Italy, where Fascism under Hitler and Mussolini became the defining political force.

In 1936 more than 200 men marched from Jarrow in northern England to London to draw attention to the plight of their town – formerly a center for shipbuilding – where male unemployment had reached more than 70%.

③ The Great Depression in Europe and the growth of political extremism

- Fascist regime
- Communist regime
- other dictatorship
- △ more than 20% unemployment by 1932
- ⚡ right-wing activity
- ⚔ strikes and riots during the 1930s
- 📉 60% decrease in industrial output since 1929 (1932 figures as a percentage of 1929)

The Great Depression in Europe

1929: Wall Street Crash precipitates worldwide depression	1931: European central banks collapse leading to further economic downturn	1933: Almost 25% of British workforce unemployed

1925   1927   1929   1931   1933   1935

1930: Almost 40% of German workforce unemployed

Revolution and nationalism in Europe

On achieving power in 1933, Hitler began a campaign to restore Germany to its position as a great international power. In 1936, German troops marched back into the Rhineland. The response from the western powers was weak, and in March 1938, Nazi Germany annexed Austria in the *Anschluss*. At Munich six months later, Britain and France allowed Germany to annex the Czech Sudetenland, signaling the breakup of the Czechoslovak state. Fascist Italy aped Hitler, conquering Ethiopia in 1935–36 and occupying Albania in 1939. Finally, bolstered by the Nazi–Soviet Pact Hitler ignored British and French protests to invade Poland in September 1939.

In March 1939 Nazi troops took control of the Czech lands and a puppet state was established in Slovakia. This photograph shows the entry of German troops into Prague, watched by wary Czech civilians.

⑤ Territorial expansion in Central Europe 1936–39

Territory taken over by Germany
- 1936
- 1938
- 1939

Territory taken over by Italy
- 1939

Territory taken over by Hungary
- 1938
- 1939

— frontiers 1936

◄ ④ The Spanish Civil War 1936–39

Land held by Nationalist forces
- Jul 1936
- Oct 1937
- Jul 1938
- Feb 1939

Land held by Republican forces
- Feb 1939
- — temporary independence, with dates

Many Spanish civilians were killed during the Civil War. This 1937 post card calls for aid for victims of air raids.

The Spanish Civil War

The Spanish elections of 1936 brought in the left-wing Popular Front government, precipitating a military revolt by conservative groups. A brutal civil war followed, with the right-wing Nationalists, led by General Franco and supported by Germany and Italy, triumphant against Republican groups.

The growth of nationalism in Europe

1931: Republican success in Spanish elections leads to flight of king	1934: Murder of Austrian Chancellor Dollfuss by Nazi supporters	1936: Germany reoccupies Rhineland	1938: Breakup of Czechoslovakia	
			1938: Germany occupies Austria (*Anschluss*)	1939: Signing of Nazi-Soviet Pact

1931   1933   1935   1937   1939

| | 1933: Hitler becomes Chancellor of Germany | 1936: Start of Spanish Civil War | 1938: Munich Agreement allows Germany to occupy Czech Sudetenland | 1939: German invasion of Poland |

WORLD WAR II IN EUROPE

Women were encouraged to join the war effort both as civilians and in the armed forces.

THE GREATEST WAR in Europe's history was initiated by a series of aggressive annexations and conquests by Hitler's Nazi Germany between 1939 and 1941. When the conflict ceased to be a series of campaigns and became a war, however, Germany was checked and then stripped of the initiative by an Allied force headed by two nations on the lateral extremes of Europe – Britain and the USSR – and from December 1941, a non-European nation, the US. Each of the latter proved more than Germany's equal in military and economic resources. The eventual Allied victory, following concerted assaults from the west, south, east, and the air, saved Europe from the scourge of Nazism but also completed Europe's devastation, bringing to an end 400 years of European global domination.

Following the Blitz (September 1940–May 1941) London became the first city in history to undergo ballistic missile attack from V1 flying bombs and V2 rockets (1944–45).

Blitzkrieg in Europe 1939–42

Between 1939 and 1941, lightning campaigns on land and in the air enabled Nazi Germany to conquer many of its weaker neighbors. In temporary alliance with the USSR, Germany annihilated Poland in the autumn of 1939. Denmark, Norway, Belgium, France, and the Netherlands were overrun in April–June 1940. Yugoslavia and Greece were occupied in April–May 1941, Britain was isolated, and Bulgaria, Romania, and Hungary brought under Nazi domination. Although a large contingent of German forces was committed to support Italy in North Africa, in June 1941 Hitler ordered a surprise attack on the USSR, hoping to destroy it in a single campaign. The attempt ended in failure because of the distances involved and unexpected Soviet resistance. In mid-winter 1941, the Nazi invasion forces were halted outside Moscow.

① Blitzkrieg in Europe 1939–42

- Axis territory Sep 1939
- German offensive, 1939–41
- Italian offensive, 1939–41
- airborne attacks
- cities severely bombed
- Axis conquests 1939
- Axis conquests 1940
- Axis conquests 1941
- Soviet conquests 1939–40
- Axis satellites
- Allied territories Dec 1941
- British retreats
- Allied offensive 1941
- neutral states

The Second World War 1939–42

Aug 1939: Germany and USSR sign non-aggression pact	**Apr 1940:** German invasion of Denmark and Norway
Jul–Oct 1940: Battle of Britain in skies over southern England	**Apr 1941:** German invasion of Yugoslavia and Greece
Dec 1941: Germany declares war on US	**Sep 1942:** Start of German siege of Stalingrad
Nov 1942: Germans occupy Vichy France	

Sep 1939: Germany and USSR invade Poland; France and Britain declare war on Germany

May–Jun 1940: Germany invades France, Netherlands, and Belgium

Oct 1940: Italy invades Albania and Greece

Jun 1941: Operation Barbarossa: German invasion of USSR

Nov 1941: USSR counterattacks against Germany

Oct–Nov 1942: UK defeats Germany at El Alamein

The Battle of the Atlantic

The battle over the supply of Europe was fought in the Atlantic. British destruction or containment of German surface warship raiders, following the sinking of the *Bismarck* in May 1941 and the blockade of supplies to "Fortress Europe," was followed by a German submarine (U-Boat) campaign against British shipping in western waters. Once the US entered the war in December 1941, U-boat attacks spread across the Atlantic. By summer 1943, US mass production of "Liberty" merchant ships, the use of the convoy system, increasing air cover, and the Allied interception of German radio traffic critically inhibited the effectiveness of the U-Boat "wolfpacks."

This Enigma encoding machine is being used by German naval personnel. By summer 1940, British counterintelligence experts had managed to crack the Enigma code, enabling them to interpret German radio traffic and disperse the intercepted messages (codenamed Ultra) throughout Allied High Command.

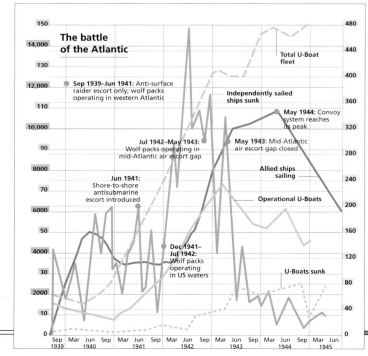

The battle of the Atlantic

- **Sep 1939–Jun 1941:** Anti-surface raider escort only; wolf packs operating in western Atlantic
- **Jul 1942–May 1943:** Wolf packs operating in mid-Atlantic air escort gap
- **Jun 1941:** Shore-to-shore antisubmarine escort introduced
- **Dec 1941–Jul 1942:** Wolf packs operating in US waters
- **Total U-Boat fleet**
- **Independently sailed ships sunk**
- **May 1944:** Convoy system reaches its peak
- **May 1943:** Mid-Atlantic air escort gap closed
- **Allied ships sailing**
- **Operational U-Boats**
- **U-Boats sunk**

② The Greater German Reich 1942

- Greater German Reich
- areas occupied by Germany and Finland
- Italy and areas occupied by Italy
- Axis satellites
- Allied territories
- neutral states

1940: Luxembourg absorbed into Germany

1941: to Romania

1941: returned to Romania

1941: returned to Romania

FRENCH NORTH AFRICA
500 km
500 miles

The Greater German Reich 1939–1943

The creation by the Nazis of a Greater German Reich encompassing their conquered and allied territories was based on five basic principles: pure "Aryan" regions were annexed or occupied and integrated into Germany under the aegis of the Gestapo secret police; noncorporated areas were placed under military control; puppet and satellite states were strictly controlled and exploited by coercion; the conquered areas of the East were ravaged and cleared for German settlement; and underlying all these policies a principle of ethnic cleansing, targeting Jews, Gypsies, political dissidents, and "social deviants," which began with imprisonment concentration camps or enslaved labour, but escalated by 1943 into a policy of systematic extermination.

③ The organization of persecution

- ▽ concentration camp
- ◇ extermination camp
- ■ site of mass killing
- ⊗ ghetto
- 8000 number of Jews killed

The Nazi impact on Europe

Nov 1938: *Kristallnacht:* coordinated Nazi attacks on Jews in Germany

Dec 1941: First death camp opened at Chelmno

Jan 1942: Plans for Final Solution agreed

Apr 1943: Jewish uprising in Warsaw

Jan 1945: Auschwitz liberated by Soviet Army

1939 · 1940 · 1941 · 1942 · 1943 · 1944 · 1945

Sep–Oct 1939: Invasion of Poland; mass murder of Jews; establishment of ghettoes

Jun 1941: Invasion of Russia; *Einsatzgruppen* murder squads active in Eastern Europe

Jul 1941: Hitler orders Final Solution (extermination of Europe's Jews)

mid-1942: Auschwitz death camp opened

Jul 1944: Majdanek camp liberated by Soviet Army

The Allied invasion of Europe 1943–45

A final German attempt to conquer the USSR brought their forces to Stalingrad by August 1942. The following winter saw their defeat there which, with Anglo-US victories in North Africa, brought the strategic initiative to the Allies. July 1943 witnessed Soviet victory at Kursk and Anglo-US landings in Sicily, initiating a Soviet onslaught in the East and the collapse of Italy. A sustained Anglo-US bombing offensive (from January 1943) and landings in southern France and Normandy meant, by summer 1944, that Germany was in retreat on all fronts. With its infrastructure, industry, capital, and leadership effectively destroyed, by May 1945 Germany was powerless to stop Soviet and Anglo-US forces finally meeting on the Elbe River and enforcing an unconditional surrender.

Jan 1943: Germans surrender at Stalingrad

Jun–Aug 1943: USSR defeats Germans in tank battle at Kursk

Jan 1944: End of 900-day siege of Leningrad

Jun 6 1944: D-Day: Allied forces land in Normandy

Oct–Nov 1944: Allies liberate Greece

Jan 1945: Soviet troops enter Budapest, Warsaw, and Auschwitz

May 1945: Germany surrenders

1943 · 1944 · 1945

Jul 1943: Allied forces land in Sicily

Sep–Oct 1943: Italian surrender to Allies; Germany occupies Rome and Milan. Italy declares war on Germany

Jul 1944: USSR enters Poland

Mar 1945: Allied forces cross Rhine

May 1945: Berlin surrenders to Soviet troops

World War II 1942–45

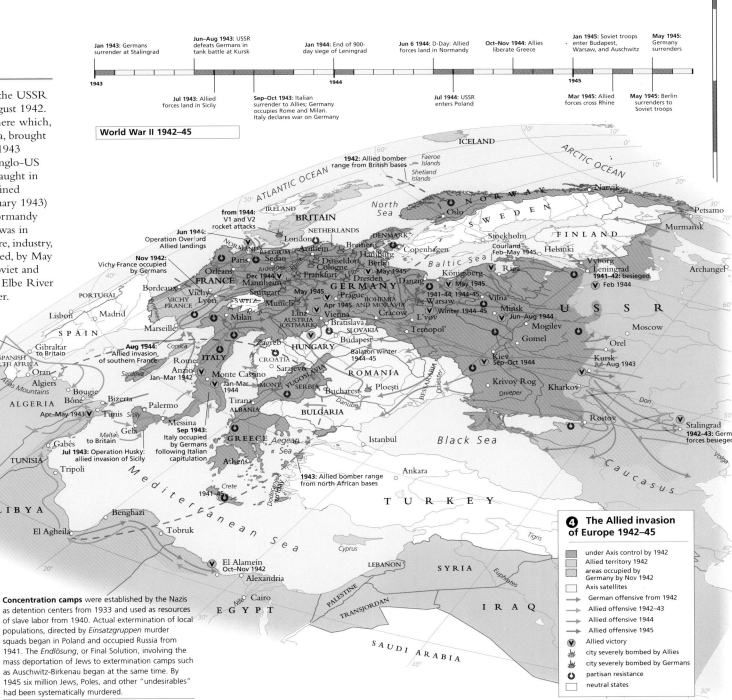

The Allied invasion of northern Europe began with Operation Overlord, the largest combined operation and successful shore-to-shore invasion in history; eight seaborne and airborne divisions established a beachhead in Normandy, on D-Day (June 6, 1944) supported by 6500 ships and 12,000 aircraft.

Concentration camps were established by the Nazis as detention centers from 1933 and used as resources of slave labor from 1940. Actual extermination of local populations, directed by *Einsatzgruppen* murder squads began in Poland and occupied Russia from 1941. The *Endlösung*, or Final Solution, involving the mass deportation of Jews to extermination camps such as Auschwitz-Birkenau began at the same time. By 1945 six million Jews, Poles, and other "undesirables" had been systematically murdered.

④ The Allied invasion of Europe 1942–45

- under Axis control by 1942
- Allied territory 1942
- areas occupied by Germany by Nov 1942
- Axis satellites
- → German offensive from 1942
- → Allied offensive 1942–43
- → Allied offensive 1944
- → Allied offensive 1945
- ▽ Allied victory
- city severely bombed by Allies
- city severely bombed by Germans
- partisan resistance
- neutral states

THE DIVISION OF POSTWAR EUROPE

AFTER WORLD WAR II, Europe was divided into the democratic West and Soviet-dominated Communist East. Germany, which by 1947 was partitioned along the same lines, played a pivotal role in the tensions between the two blocs. From 1945–52, millions of people were forcibly resettled, while many others fled persecution. The US, fearing that Communism would be an attractive alternative to postwar poverty and dislocation, financed the "Marshall Plan," an economic recovery programme for Europe. By 1948 a pro-Soviet bloc, bound by economic and military agreements, had been established in Eastern Europe. Attempts to challenge Soviet dominance in the Soviet bloc in the 1950s and 1960s were brutally suppressed.

Josef Stalin, leader of the Soviet Union 1929–53, headed a regime of terror and totalitarian rule.

The Allied occupation of postwar Germany

Following Germany's surrender in May 1945, the occupying powers – America, Britain, France and the USSR – divided Germany into four zones. Berlin, which lay within the Soviet zone, was similarly divided. In March 1948 the Western powers decided to unite their zones into a single economic unit. The USSR responded by launching a land blockade of Berlin in protest against the unification. The Western nations frustrated the blockade by airlifting essential supplies to their sectors of Berlin. The blockade was abandoned in 1949.

❶ The partition of Germany and Austria ▶

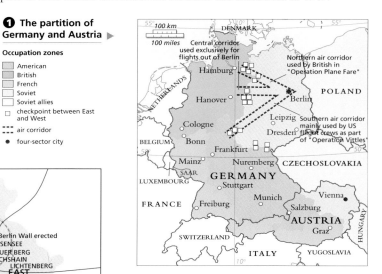

The occupation of Berlin

In accordance with agreements made at the Potsdam Conference in 1945, Berlin was partitioned in a similar way to Germany. Between 1949 and 1961, around 2.5 million East Germans fled from East to West Germany, including skilled workers and professionals. Their loss threatened to destroy the economic viability of the East German state. In response, East Germany built the Berlin Wall in 1961 to prevent migrations and possible economic catastrophe.

With Soviet consent, the East German authorities constructed the Berlin Wall in 1961. For 28 years the wall served to segregate East Germans from West Germany, becoming a potent symbol of the Cold War.

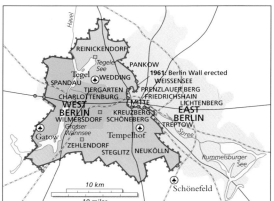

◀ ❷ The division of Berlin

Refugees and resettlement 1945–52

World War II left millions of Europeans displaced. In an attempt to reestablish ethnic and linguistic uniformity within political boundaries, more than 31 million people were resettled between 1945 and 1952. Under the Potsdam agreement, Cossacks and Russian prisoners of war were forcibly repatriated, often to death or imprisonment. Millions of Germans fled Eastern Europe ahead of the Red Army. Mutual transfers of peoples were organized to coincide with shifts in boundaries – for example between Poland and the Baltic republics, and between Hungary and Yugoslavia. Finns were displaced by the Soviet occupation of Karelia, and many Jewish Holocaust survivors fled to Palestine and the US.

These children were among millions forced to live in refugee camps while they waited to learn whether they could return to their former homes.

❸ Displaced peoples in East and Central Europe ▶

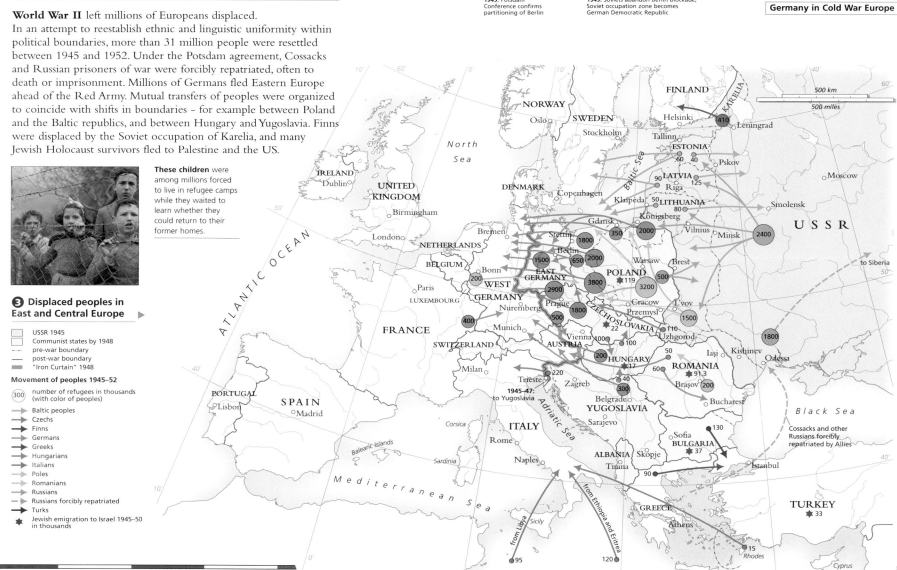

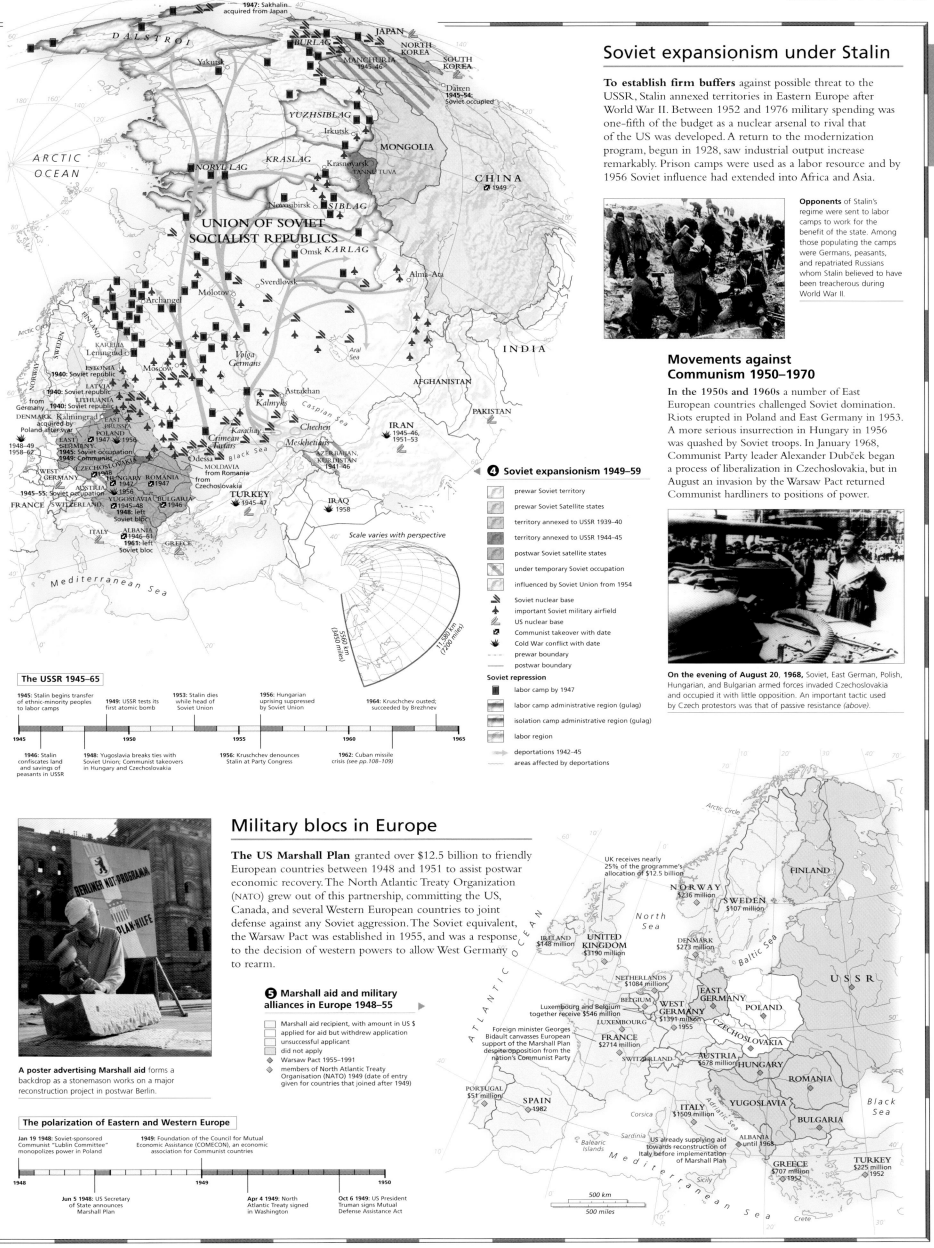

Soviet expansionism under Stalin

To establish firm buffers against possible threat to the USSR, Stalin annexed territories in Eastern Europe after World War II. Between 1952 and 1976 military spending was one-fifth of the budget as a nuclear arsenal to rival that of the US was developed. A return to the modernization program, begun in 1928, saw industrial output increase remarkably. Prison camps were used as a labor resource and by 1956 Soviet influence had extended into Africa and Asia.

Opponents of Stalin's regime were sent to labor camps to work for the benefit of the state. Among those populating the camps were Germans, peasants, and repatriated Russians whom Stalin believed to have been treacherous during World War II.

Movements against Communism 1950–1970

In the 1950s and 1960s a number of East European countries challenged Soviet domination. Riots erupted in Poland and East Germany in 1953. A more serious insurrection in Hungary in 1956 was quashed by Soviet troops. In January 1968, Communist Party leader Alexander Dubček began a process of liberalization in Czechoslovakia, but in August an invasion by the Warsaw Pact returned Communist hardliners to positions of power.

On the evening of August 20, 1968, Soviet, East German, Polish, Hungarian, and Bulgarian armed forces invaded Czechoslovakia and occupied it with little opposition. An important tactic used by Czech protestors was that of passive resistance (above).

4 Soviet expansionism 1949–59

- prewar Soviet territory
- prewar Soviet Satellite states
- territory annexed to USSR 1939–40
- territory annexed to USSR 1944–45
- postwar Soviet satellite states
- under temporary Soviet occupation
- influenced by Soviet Union from 1954
- Soviet nuclear base
- important Soviet military airfield
- US nuclear base
- Communist takeover with date
- Cold War conflict with date
- prewar boundary
- postwar boundary

Soviet repression
- labor camp by 1947
- labor camp administrative region (gulag)
- isolation camp administrative region (gulag)
- labor region
- deportations 1942–45
- areas affected by deportations

The USSR 1945–65

- **1945:** Stalin begins transfer of ethnic-minority peoples to labor camps
- **1946:** Stalin confiscates land and savings of peasants in USSR
- **1948:** Yugoslavia breaks ties with Soviet Union; Communist takeovers in Hungary and Czechoslovakia
- **1949:** USSR tests its first atomic bomb
- **1953:** Stalin dies while head of Soviet Union
- **1956:** Kruschchev denounces Stalin at Party Congress
- **1956:** Hungarian uprising suppressed by Soviet Union
- **1962:** Cuban missile crisis (see pp.108–109)
- **1964:** Kruschchev ousted; succeeded by Brezhnev

1945 — 1950 — 1955 — 1960 — 1965

Military blocs in Europe

The US Marshall Plan granted over $12.5 billion to friendly European countries between 1948 and 1951 to assist postwar economic recovery. The North Atlantic Treaty Organization (NATO) grew out of this partnership, committing the US, Canada, and several Western European countries to joint defense against any Soviet aggression. The Soviet equivalent, the Warsaw Pact was established in 1955, and was a response to the decision of western powers to allow West Germany to rearm.

A poster advertising Marshall aid forms a backdrop as a stonemason works on a major reconstruction project in postwar Berlin.

5 Marshall aid and military alliances in Europe 1948–55

- Marshall aid recipient, with amount in US $
- applied for aid but withdrew application
- unsuccessful applicant
- did not apply
- Warsaw Pact 1955–1991
- members of North Atlantic Treaty Organisation (NATO) 1949 (date of entry given for countries that joined after 1949)

The polarization of Eastern and Western Europe

- **Jan 19 1948:** Soviet-sponsored Communist "Lublin Committee" monopolizes power in Poland
- **Jun 5 1948:** US Secretary of State announces Marshall Plan
- **1949:** Foundation of the Council for Mutual Economic Assistance (COMECON), an economic association for Communist countries
- **Apr 4 1949:** North Atlantic Treaty signed in Washington
- **Oct 6 1949:** US President Truman signs Mutual Defense Assistance Act

1948 — 1949 — 1950

213

MODERN EUROPE

BETWEEN 1948 AND 1989, the ideological divide between Communist Eastern Europe and the West stood firm. Divisions within Europe were compounded by economic growth in the West and stagnation and decline in the East. In November 1989, the fall of the Berlin Wall signaled the end of the Cold War, and a rise of nationalism in Eastern Europe brought about the collapse of Communism and the Soviet bloc. A range of newly independent states were soon moving toward free elections, but political freedom had other, unforseen consequences. In 1991, historical ethnic tension fractured Yugoslavia. Conflict escalated into war in Bosnia in 1992, and bloody struggles in the Serbian province of Kosovo prompted NATO intervention in 1999.

In January 1999 the Euro was formally adopted as currency of the European Union.

The European Union

The European Economic Community (EEC) was established in 1957 to guarantee the economic success of its members, and to develop a political union of states in an attempt to alleviate the risk of another war. The success of the liberalized trade policies sponsored by the EEC from the 1960s brought about efforts for further integration. In December 1991, the Maastricht Treaty created the European Union (EU) and committed the members to the introduction of a single currency. From an initial six members in 1957, by 1999, the EU had 15 member states.

The European Union headquarters have been based in Brussels since 1957.

▲ **1** The growth of the European Union

- members of European Coal and Steel Community (ECSE), European Atomic Energy Community (EAEC) and European Economic Community (EEC) 1957
- EU original members 1957
- EU members by 1973
- EU members by 1986
- EU members by 1995
- applicants to EU (with date of application)
- members of Council for Mutual Economic Assistance (COMECON) 1949
- € members of the European Monetary Union Jan 1 1999

▲ **2** The collapse of Communism in Eastern Europe

- Soviet Union to 1991
- Soviet-dominated Eastern Europe to 1989
- German Democratic Republic (GDR), united with Federal Republic of Germany 1990
- Czechoslovakia to Dec 1992
- Yugoslavia to 1991
- other Communist state before 1991
- 1990 date of first free election

The disintegration of the Communist bloc

By the 1970s it became clear that Communist economic policies were failing the nations of Eastern Europe. Economic instability throughout the 1970s and 1980s brought much of the Eastern bloc to the point of bankruptcy. The Soviet leader, Gorbachev, abandoned the satellite states in an effort to save the economy of the USSR. Beginning with protests in East Germany in 1989 which brought down the Communist government, nation after nation asserted their independence in a series of massive popular demonstrations which swiftly ended more than 50 years of Soviet control in Eastern Europe.

The decline of the Russian economy from 1990 forced many people to work within the "informal economy" for income. This street vendor is selling toys from a makeshift stall.

The rise of nationalism

The wave of nationalism which began in the German Democratic Republic was repeated throughout Eastern Europe. The reunification of Germany in 1990 was followed by the collapse of the USSR and its division into 15 independent states. In 1993, Czechoslovakia split into two new republics: Slovakia and the Czech Republic. New governments were forced to implement strict economic measures to stem decline, and moderate socialism replaced Communism as the main political force in Eastern Europe.

In November 1989, these peaceful demonstrators in Prague united with other cities across Czechoslovakia in their protest against Communist rule to bring about the so-called "Velvet Revolution."

Conflict in Yugoslavia from 1991

Following the death of Communist premier Josip Broz (Tito) in 1980, the fragility of the multinational Federal People's Republic of Yugoslavia quickly became apparent. The election of Serbian leader Slobodan Milošević in 1987 brought an upsurge of Serb nationalism which struck fear in the multi-ethnic republics. In June 1991, the provinces of Slovenia and Croatia declared their independence. Serbian forces attacked both republics in an effort to compel their return to the federation. In January 1992, Serbs in Bosnia and Herzegovina began the persecution of Bosnia's Muslims – a policy which became known as "ethnic cleansing." Bitter fighting between Serbs, Muslims, and Croats ensued, and foreign intervention was required to bring the war to an end in 1995. In 1998, further persecution of non-Serb peoples – this time the ethnic Albanians of Kosovo – provoked NATO military intervention.

Bosnian Muslim refugees take up temporary residence on a basketball court as they flee Serbian forces at the height of the "ethnic cleansing" campaign in 1993.

❸ Conflict in former Yugoslavia 1990–99

The ethnic composition of Yugoslavia, 1991

- Albanian
- Bulgarian
- Croat
- Hungarian
- Macedonian
- Muslim
- Romanian
- Serb and Montenegrin
- Slovene
- Yugoslav regions
- (Nov 1992) date of secession from Federal Republic of Yugoslavia

The Croatian conflict

- Serb advances by Dec 1991
- Serb-controlled regions 1991–95/96
- Croat advances, autumn 1995

The Bosnian War

- secured by Yugoslav army and Bosnian Serb forces by Dec 1992
- area controlled by Bosnian Croat forces, Dec 1992
- attacking Serbs 1993
- attacking Bosnian Muslims 1993
- Autonomous Province of Western Bosnia Sep 1993–Aug 1994
- area remaining under control of breakaway Serbian forces, Oct 1995
- areas of combat between Croats and Bosnian Muslims
- Muslim secure zone

The Kosovan crisis

- Kosovo Liberation Army (KLA) stronghold
- Serb forces attacking KLA, 1999

The collapse of the Soviet Union

From 1985, Mikhail Gorbachev, leader of the Soviet Union, set about the political and economic reform of the Soviet system with his policies of *perestroika* (restructuring) and *glasnost* (openness). The Supreme Soviet Council was replaced with a Congress of People's deputies in 1988 and a 450-strong parliament was elected in 1989. In 1990 nationalist unrest grew out of economic decline. An attempted coup by hard-line Communists in 1991, quashed by Russian president Boris Yeltsin, brought an end to Communist rule and accelerated the disbandment of the USSR. Fifteen Soviet republics declared their independence to found the Commonwealth of Independent States (CIS) in 1991, later known as the Russian Federation.

War and ethnic tension in Yugoslavia from 1974

- **1974:** Revised Yugoslav constitution grants Kosovo autonomy
- **1987:** Slobodan Milošević rises to power in Yugoslavia
- **1989:** Fearing secession attempt Milošević strips Kosovo of autonomy it has enjoyed since 1974; tension between Serbs and ethnic Albanians escalates
- **1991:** Croatia, Slovenia, and Bosnia declare independence from Yugoslavia
- **1992:** All-out war in Bosnia
- **1995:** Peace agreement ends the Bosnian war
- **1998:** Milošević sends troops into areas controlled by Kosovo Liberation Army (KLA)
- **1999:** Peace talks collapse; NATO begins bombing campaign

Scale varies with perspective

12,320 km (7660 miles)
5560 km (3450 miles)

❹ The disintegration of the Soviet Union

- territory controlled by USSR in 1945
- Russian federation from 1991
- autonomous regions
- major concentration of minority Russians
- Commonwealth of Independent States 1991
- interstate conflict
- civil war
- ethnic conflict (with date)
- AD autonomous district

The decline of Communism in Europe

- **1986:** Gorbachev and US President Reagan meet at Reykjavik to discuss disarmament
- **1987:** Washington Arms Control Treaty decommissions one-fifth of Soviet arms
- **1988:** Gorbachev initiates *perestroika* and *glasnost*
- **1989:** Nationalist protests across Eastern Europe signal rejection of Communism
- **1990:** Reunification of Germany
- **1990–91:** Baltic republics declare independence; end of COMECON Jun 1991
- **1991:** Unsuccessful coup attempt in USSR; disintegration of Soviet Union
- **1992:** Civil war in Georgia, Bosnia-Herzegovina
- **1993:** Czech Republic and Slovakia become separate states
- **1994:** Russian troops invade Chechnya

Map labels (Soviet Union map):

- **1994:** Chechen declaration of independence provokes war with Russia
- **1989:** Kazakhs and Lezgians
- **1989–90:** Uzbeks and Meskhetians
- **1988:** Armenians and Azerbaijanis
- **1988** Nagorno-Karabakh to Azerbaijan
- **1989:** Kirghiz and Tajiks
- **1990:** Kirghiz and Uzbeks

WEST ASIA
REGIONAL HISTORY

THE HISTORICAL LANDSCAPE

A SEEMINGLY INHOSPITABLE REALM, arid, largely desert or mountainous plateau, West Asia lays claim to a panoply of grand names – the Garden of Eden, the Fertile Crescent, the Promised Land, the Cradle of Civilization, the Crossroads of History. Lying at the meeting point of the three Old World continents - Africa, Europe, and Asia - the region was blessed with the fertile soils, beneficent climate, and diverse demography to earn these titles. As such it remained the pivotal point of Old World, or Afro-Eurasian, culture, communications, trade, and – inevitably – warfare, until relatively recent times. In addition, possibly as a consequence of this geographic primacy, the region was also the birthplace of Judaism, Christianity, and Islam, which became three of the most widely observed world religions. Despite the attentions of European colonial powers, West Asia has upheld its inherent qualities and traditions; rivalries and divisions persist alongside ways of life and artistic traditions now centuries old, a cultural longevity sustained by religion on the one hand and, in the 20th century, by the region's control of the world's most valuable commodity – oil.

Most of West Asia is a combination of dry sandy deserts and mountainous plateaus that remain sparsely populated, or totally uninhabited even today.

The mountainous Iranian Plateau is cut off from the moist ocean air, and temperatures fluctuate greatly between night and day. Humans lived in the mountain fringes, but the plateau's interior remained empty of human settlement because of the cold, dry climate.

The banks of the Euphrates and Tigris rivers were where West Asia's first towns and cities were established. The fertile soils supported the world's first domesticated cereal crops from around 8000 BCE.

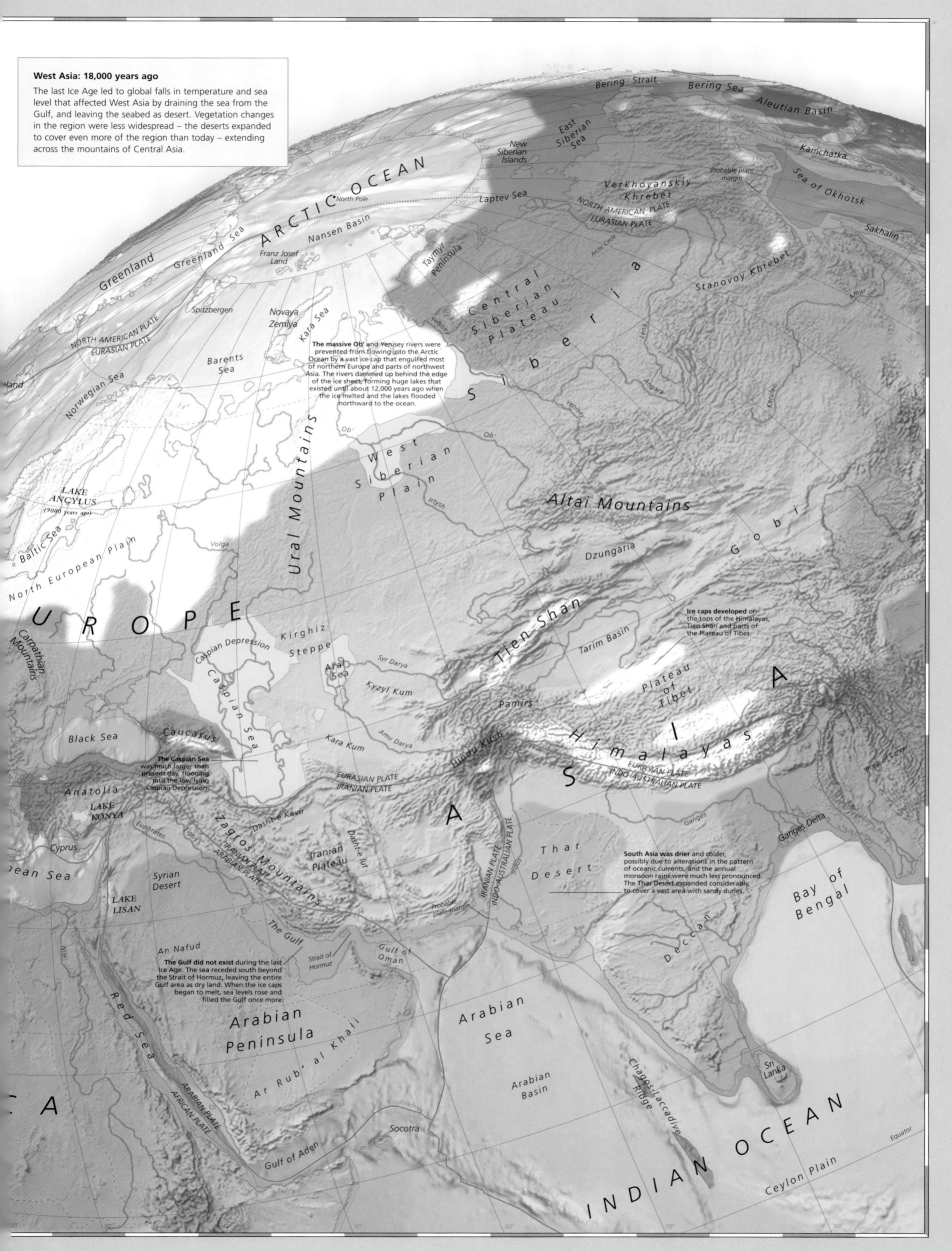

West Asia: 18,000 years ago

The last Ice Age led to global falls in temperature and sea level that affected West Asia by draining the sea from the Gulf, and leaving the seabed as desert. Vegetation changes in the region were less widespread – the deserts expanded to cover even more of the region than today – extending across the mountains of Central Asia.

ARCTIC OCEAN

North Pole

Bering Strait

Bering Sea

Aleutian Basin

East Siberian Sea

New Siberian Islands

Kamchatka

Sea of Okhotsk

Verkhoyanskiy Khrebet

NORTH AMERICAN PLATE
EURASIAN PLATE

Probable plate margin

Sakhalin

Greenland

Greenland Sea

Nansen Basin

Laptev Sea

Taymyr Peninsula

Central Siberian Plateau

Stanovoy Khrebet

Amur

Franz Josef Land

Spitzbergen

Novaya Zemlya

Kara Sea

Yenisey

S i b e r i a

Arctic Circle

Lena

Ket/Urtil

NORTH AMERICAN PLATE
EURASIAN PLATE

Norwegian Sea

Barents Sea

The massive Ob' and Yenisey rivers were prevented from flowing into the Arctic Ocean by a vast ice cap that engulfed most of northern Europe and parts of northwest Asia. The rivers dammed up behind the edge of the ice sheet, forming huge lakes that existed until about 12,000 years ago when the ice melted and the lakes flooded northward to the ocean.

Ob'

West Siberian Plain

Ob'

Angara

Yenisey

LAKE ANCYLUS
(9000 years ago)

Ural Mountains

Irtysh

Altai Mountains

G o b i

Baltic Sea

North European Plain

Volga

Dzungaria

Ice caps developed on the tops of the Himalayas, Tien Shan and parts of the Plateau of Tibet.

E U R O P E

Carpathian Mountains

Caspian Depression

Kirghiz Steppe

Syr Darya

Aral Sea

Kyzyl Kum

Tien Shan

Tarim Basin

Plateau of Tibet

A S I A

Caspian Sea

Pamirs

Black Sea

Caucasus

Kara Kum

Amu Darya

Hindu Kush

H i m a l a y a s

Tropic of Cancer

EURASIAN PLATE
INDO-AUSTRALIAN PLATE

The Caspian Sea was much larger than present day, flooding into the low-lying Caspian Depression.

EURASIAN PLATE
IRANIAN PLATE

Anatolia

LAKE KONYA

Dasht-e Kavir

Iranian Plateau

Dasht-e lut

A

Ganges

Ganges Delta

Cyprus

Euphrates

Tigris

Zagros Mountains

IRANIAN PLATE
ARABIAN PLATE

Thar Desert

IRANIAN PLATE
INDO-AUSTRALIAN PLATE

South Asia was drier and colder, possibly due to alterations in the pattern of oceanic currents, and the annual monsoon rains were much less pronounced. The Thar Desert expanded considerably, to cover a vast area with sandy dunes.

Bay of Bengal

...ean Sea

Syrian Desert

LAKE LISAN

Nile

An Nafud

Strait of Hormuz

Gulf of Oman

Deccan

Probable plate margin

The Gulf did not exist during the last Ice Age. The sea receded south beyond the Strait of Hormuz, leaving the entire Gulf area as dry land. When the ice caps began to melt, sea levels rose and filled the Gulf once more.

Red Sea

Arabian Peninsula

Ar Rub' al Khali

ARABIAN PLATE
AFRICAN PLATE

Arabian Sea

Arabian Basin

Chagos-Laccadive Ridge

Sri Lanka

...CA

Socotra

Gulf of Aden

INDIAN OCEAN

Ceylon Plain

Equator

WEST ASIA

EXPLORATION AND MAPPING

Invented by the Greeks, the astrolabe was developed by the Arabs into an indispensable tool of navigation.

SINCE THE EMERGENCE of city–states and trade, West Asia has formed the crossroads between Europe, Africa, and Asia. The Sumerians and Babylonians accumulated local geographical knowledge, but it was the Greeks, following the conquests of Alexander the Great, who began a systematic recording of the region's geography. The Romans built on the knowledge of the Greeks, as did the Arabs when, in the 7th century, Islam spread throughout West Asia. In the 13th century, when the Mongols controlled Central Asia, traffic between China and the West flourished, leaving the way open for the great journeys of Marco Polo and William of Rubruck. The region least well-known to outsiders, though its geography was well understood by its desert tribes, was Arabia, finally mapped in the 19th and 20th centuries.

The Greco-Roman view

Many merchants from Greek colonies in Asia Minor traded eastward to the Caspian Sea. Then, in the 4th century BCE, Alexander the Great led his army into West Asia, accompanied by a team of surveyors who recorded the route. Though none survive today, these records were a major source for subsequent geographers. Extending his quest for knowledge to the ocean, Alexander sent his admiral, Nearchus, to explore a route from the Indus to the Persian Gulf. The Greek merchant Hippalus was the first European sailor to recognize the regularity of the monsoon winds, harnessing them for his voyage to India. Arabia remained largely unknown, despite an exploratory expedition led by the Roman general Aelius Gallus.

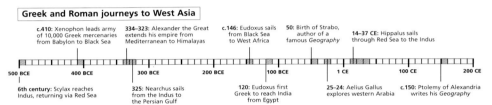

This reconstructed map shows the world known to the Greeks in 5th century BCE. It is based on descriptions in the *History* of Herodotus, who traveled in Europe, Egypt, and West Asia, and gathered additional information from people he met en route.

Greek and Roman journeys to West Asia

c.410: Xenophon leads army of 10,000 Greek mercenaries from Babylon to Black Sea
334–323: Alexander the Great extends his empire from Mediterranean to Himalayas
c.146: Eudoxus sails from Black Sea to West Africa
50: Birth of Strabo, author of a famous *Geography*
14–37 CE: Hippalus sails through Red Sea to the Indus

500 BCE · 400 BCE · 300 BCE · 200 BCE · 100 BCE · 1 CE · 100 CE · 200 CE

6th century: Scylax reaches Indus, returning via Red Sea
325: Nearchus sails from the Indus to the Persian Gulf
120: Eudoxus first Greek to reach India from Egypt
25–24: Aelius Gallus explores western Arabia
c.150: Ptolemy of Alexandria writes his *Geography*

Islamic travelers

Within a century of the death of Muhammad in 632, the Muslim world stretched from the Iberian Peninsula to the borders of Tang China. Building on knowledge acquired by earlier civilizations, in particular the Greeks, and incorporating information gathered by merchants, sailors, and other travelers, Arab geographers were able to create maps of the vast Islamic realms. By the 12th century they had an excellent understanding of West Asia, Europe, and North Africa. In 1325 Ibn Battuta *(see p.68)* began the first of the great journeys which were to take him to all corners of the Islamic world.

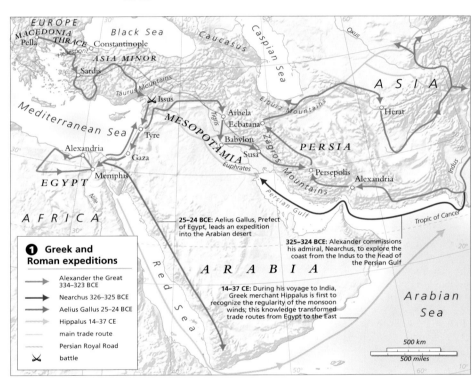

1 Greek and Roman expeditions

→ Alexander the Great 334–323 BCE
→ Nearchus 326–325 BCE
→ Aelius Gallus 25–24 BCE
→ Hippalus 14–37 CE
— main trade route
--- Persian Royal Road
⚔ battle

25–24 BCE: Aelius Gallus, Prefect of Egypt, leads an expedition into the Arabian desert

325–324 BCE: Alexander commissions his admiral, Nearchus, to explore the coast from the Indus to the head of the Persian Gulf

14–37 CE: During his voyage to India, Greek merchant Hippalus is first to recognize the regularity of the monsoon winds; this knowledge transformed trade routes from Egypt to the East

500 km
500 miles

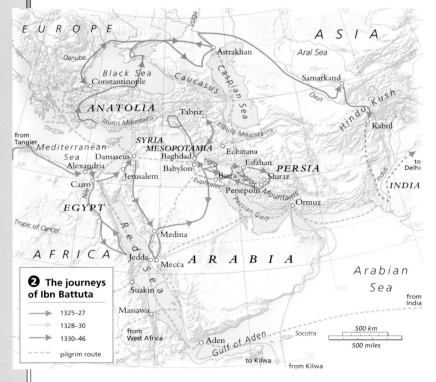

2 The journeys of Ibn Battuta

→ 1325–27
→ 1328–30
→ 1330–46
--- pilgrim route

500 km
500 miles

To a fanfare of trumpets, Muslims set out across the Arabian desert to make their pilgrimage to Mecca.

The Moroccan al-Idrisi was one of the most famous geographers of his day. The map shown here is a facsimile of the West Asian section of the beautiful world map he produced for Roger of Sicily c.1154. South is at the top, so the Mediterranean is on the right.

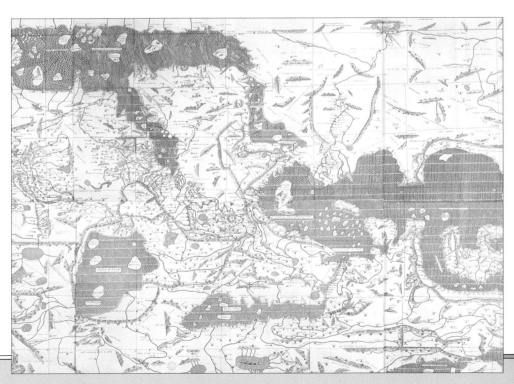

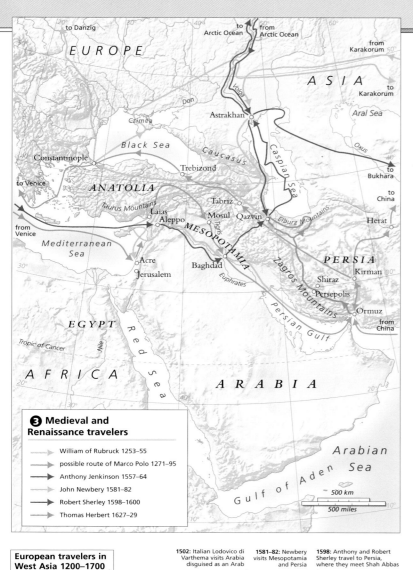

3 Medieval and Renaissance travelers

| William of Rubruck 1253–55 |
| possible route of Marco Polo 1271–95 |
| Anthony Jenkinson 1557–64 |
| John Newbery 1581–82 |
| Robert Sherley 1598–1600 |
| Thomas Herbert 1627–29 |

Medieval and Renaissance travelers from Europe

In the late 13th century, in the lull following the first Mongol invasions, Europeans began to venture east across Asia. Both William of Rubruck's mission to the Mongol Khan for Louis IX of France and Marco Polo's epic journeys yielded a wealth of geographical information. But with the rise to power of the Ottoman Turks, Central Asia's trade routes were once more closed to Europeans. Later explorers such as Sir Robert Sherley focused their attention on Persia, sworn enemy of the Turks.

European pilgrims visit the Holy Sepulchre in Jerusalem in this illustration from an illuminated manuscript of the travels of Marco Polo.

Juan de la Cosa's early 16th-century world map demonstrates how little Europeans of the period knew of West Asia to the east of the Holy Land. Inland from the Mediterranean coast, the cartographer compensated for lack of detail with an attractive illustration of the Three Kings on their journey to Bethlehem.

MAPS FOR PILGRIMS

The Holy Land has possibly been the subject of more maps than any other part of the world. To medieval Christians, the holy city of Jerusalem was the center of their world, a concept depicted by many medieval maps which show a circular walled city, instead of a rectangular one, to symbolize the perfection of the Heavenly Jerusalem. Pilgrims and crusaders traveling to the Holy Land carried with them maps which were little more than illustrated itineraries of the towns they would pass through on their journey through Europe.

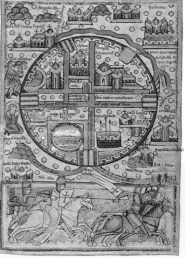

A 13th-century French map depicts the walled city of Jerusalem schematically, showing just the city's most important features, including the Holy Sepulchre and the Tower of David. Below, a crusader puts mounted Saracens to flight.

European travelers in West Asia 1200–1700

| 1200 | 1300 | 1400 | 1500 | 1600 | 1700 |

1502: Italian Lodovico di Varthema visits Arabia disguised as an Arab

1581–82: Newbery visits Mesopotamia and Persia

1598: Anthony and Robert Sherley travel to Persia, where they meet Shah Abbas

1253–55: William of Rubruck crosses Asia to Karakorum

1271–95: Marco Polo travels throughout Asia, returning by ship through Persian Gulf

1487–89: Portuguese Pero de Covilhã sails through Red Sea to India

1557–64: Jenkinson travels through Russia to Caspian Sea

1627: Herbert's travels in Persia

European travelers in Arabia

Although crisscrossed by Muslim pilgrim routes, maps of the interior of Arabia were rare until the 19th century. The region's hostile terrain and reputation for religious fanaticism remained considerable barriers to exploration by Europeans, despite the peninsula's wealth of valuable raw materials. Those that successfully penetrated Arabia did so armed with fluent Arabic and disguised as Muslims, particularly those who entered Islam's holy cities. The 19th century brought a rush of European explorers, especially the British, to Arabia. The last area to be explored was the Rub' al Khali (Empty Quarter), crossed first by Bertram Thomas in 1930–31 and explored more thoroughly by Wilfred Thesiger. The most detailed maps of the peninsula were made from the late 1920s following surveys by oil companies.

In 1762 a Danish surveyor, Carsten Niebuhr, took part in the first scientific expedition to the Arabian Peninsula. A team of Scandinavian and German experts recorded the flora and fauna of the Yemen and studied its peoples. Most of the party died, but Niebuhr survived and published an account of the expedition, *Descriptions of Arabia*, with several detailed maps of the region.

Non-Muslims entered Islam's holy cities at their peril. Richard Burton, seen here convincingly disguised as a Muslim pilgrim, visited both Mecca and Medina.

Europeans in the Arabian Peninsula 1800–1950

| 1800 | 1850 | 1900 | 1950 |

1812: Burckhardt discovers Petra, ancient capital of Nabataea

1853: Richard Burton visits Mecca and Medina in Arab disguise

1864: Guarmani travels through northern Nejd

1879: Wilfrid Scawen Blunt and his wife, Anne, travel to Nejd to buy horses

1930: Thomas first European to cross Empty Quarter

1946–48: Thesiger's double crossing of Empty Quarter

1814: Burckhardt visits Mecca

1818: Sadleir makes first east-west crossing

1862–63: Palgrave makes first west-east crossing through the Nafud

1876–78: Doughty's Arabian journeys

1888: Publication of Doughty's classic *Travels in Arabia Deserta*

1932: Philby crosses Empty Quarter

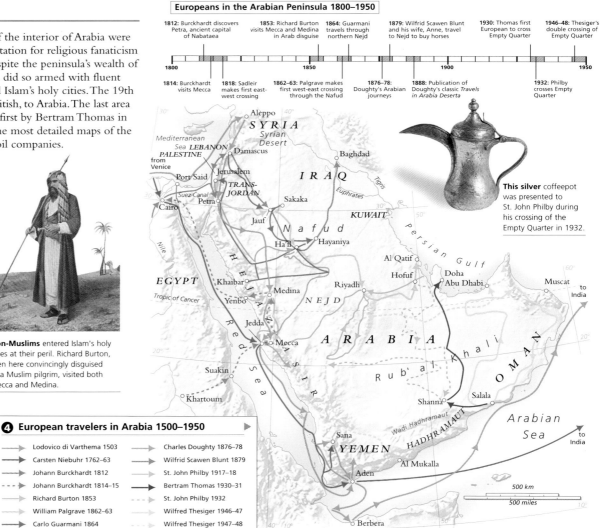

This silver coffeepot was presented to St. John Philby during his crossing of the Empty Quarter in 1932.

4 European travelers in Arabia 1500–1950

Lodovico di Varthema 1503	Charles Doughty 1876–78
Carsten Niebuhr 1762–63	Wilfrid Scawen Blunt 1879
Johann Burckhardt 1812	St. John Philby 1917–18
Johann Burckhardt 1814–15	Bertram Thomas 1930–31
Richard Burton 1853	St. John Philby 1932
William Palgrave 1862–63	Wilfred Thesiger 1946–47
Carlo Guarmani 1864	Wilfred Thesiger 1947–48

FROM VILLAGE TO EMPIRE

This inlaid chlorite vessel is decorated with a cat fighting a serpent. Made in southern Persia, it was found at Nippur in Mesopotamia.

THE "FERTILE CRESCENT" extends from the Persian Gulf along the flanks of the Zagros Mountains, then swings west across northern Mesopotamia and down the Mediterranean coast to Egypt. This region is traditionally seen as the cradle of civilization; here the first farming settlements were established, expanding into fortified walled towns. By 3500 BCE the first city-states, centres of production and trade *(see pp. 24–25)*, had grown up in Mesopotamia. In 2300 BCE, a number of these were united by Sargon of Akkad to form the first empire. Other empires followed: the empire of Ur, the first Assyrian Empire, the first Babylonian Empire. In the 2nd millennium BCE, a new center of power developed in Anatolia: the Hittite Empire, which battled with Egypt for control of the region.

The development of agriculture in the Fertile Crescent

Bounded by mountains to the north and east and desert to the south, the Fertile Crescent is relatively well-watered. Wild grains, such as einkorn wheat and barley, grew on the moist mountain uplands, also home to the ancestors of domestic sheep and goats. By 10,000 BCE, this combination of resources enabled local groups to establish the first settled agricultural communities; cereals were cultivated and stored, and animals domesticated.

Larger settlements, such as Jericho (8000 BCE) in the Jordan valley and Çatal Hüyük (7000 BCE) in Anatolia, became regional centers, surrounded by cultivable land and showing evidence of crafts and long-distance trade.

A number of skulls, with features modeled in gypsum and cowrie shells for eyes, were found beneath the floors of houses at Jericho.

The wall of a shrine at Çatal Hüyük was decorated with this painting of a stag's head, seen here in an artist's reconstruction. One of the oldest towns in the world, Çatal Hüyük had tightly-packed houses built of mud bricks with flat roofs.

❶ Early farming in southwest Asia 8000–5000 BCE ▷

Vegetation
- floodplain
- Mediterranean forest
- forest
- steppe
- semi-desert
- desert
- more than 250 mm mean annual rainfall

Areas of domestication of principal staple crops
- barley
- einkorn wheat
- emmer wheat
- present-day coastline/river
- ○ site of major farming settlement

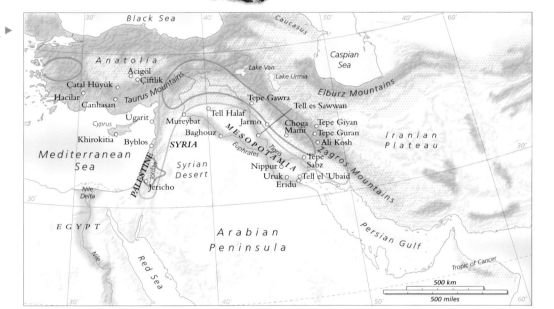

The first cities of West Asia

Farmers from northern and central Mesopotamia began to settle the alluvial plain of the Tigris and Euphrates around 6000 BCE. Irrigation enabled enough food to be produced to support large settled communities. In time, some settlements developed into cities. Each had at its heart a mud-brick temple raised on a high platform. These structures later became ziggurats like the one at Ur *(see pp. 24–25)*, one of the great Sumerian cities of the 3rd millennium BCE. While sharing a common culture, each city remained an independent city-state.

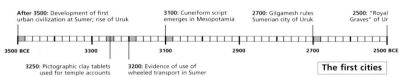

| After 3500: Development of first urban civilization at Sumer; rise of Uruk | 3100: Cuneiform script emerges in Mesopotamia | 2700: Gilgamesh rules Sumerian city of Uruk | 2500: "Royal Graves" of Ur |

| 3500 BCE | 3300 | 3100 | 2900 | 2700 | 2500 BCE |

3250: Pictographic clay tablets used for temple accounts
3200: Evidence of use of wheeled transport in Sumer

The first cities

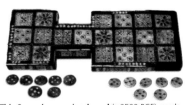

This Sumerian gaming-board (c.2500 BCE), made of wood and inlaid with shell, bone, and lapis lazuli, was found in the "Royal Graves" at Ur. Players cast dice or threw sticks before moving their counters, which were kept in a drawer set into the board.

The growth of Uruk

From 4000 BCE, Uruk expanded into one of the leading Sumerian cities. Its closely-packed mud-brick houses were enclosed by a 6 mile wall. Beyond the wall, crops such as barley, sesame, and onions grew in fields irrigated by a network of canals from the Euphrates. Two ceremonial complexes dominated the city; the Anu ziggurat and the Sanctuary of Eanna. The latter contained a columned hall 100 ft wide, the columns decorated with mosaics of colored stone cones set in mud plaster. Many of the works of art found at Uruk, Ur, and other Sumerian cities used materials such as alabaster, gemstones, and lapis lazuli, from as far afield as Central Asia and the Indus Valley.

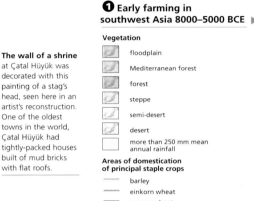

❷ The first cities c.4300–2300 BCE
- fertile area of early agriculture
- ziggurat or temple
- ○ city or important site
- irrigation and ancient water course
- present-day coastline/river
- trade route

200 km
200 miles

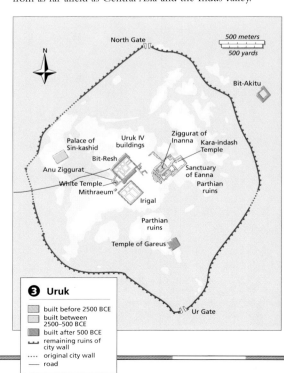

❸ Uruk
- built before 2500 BCE
- built between 2500–500 BCE
- built after 500 BCE
- remaining ruins of city wall
- original city wall
- road

500 meters
500 yards

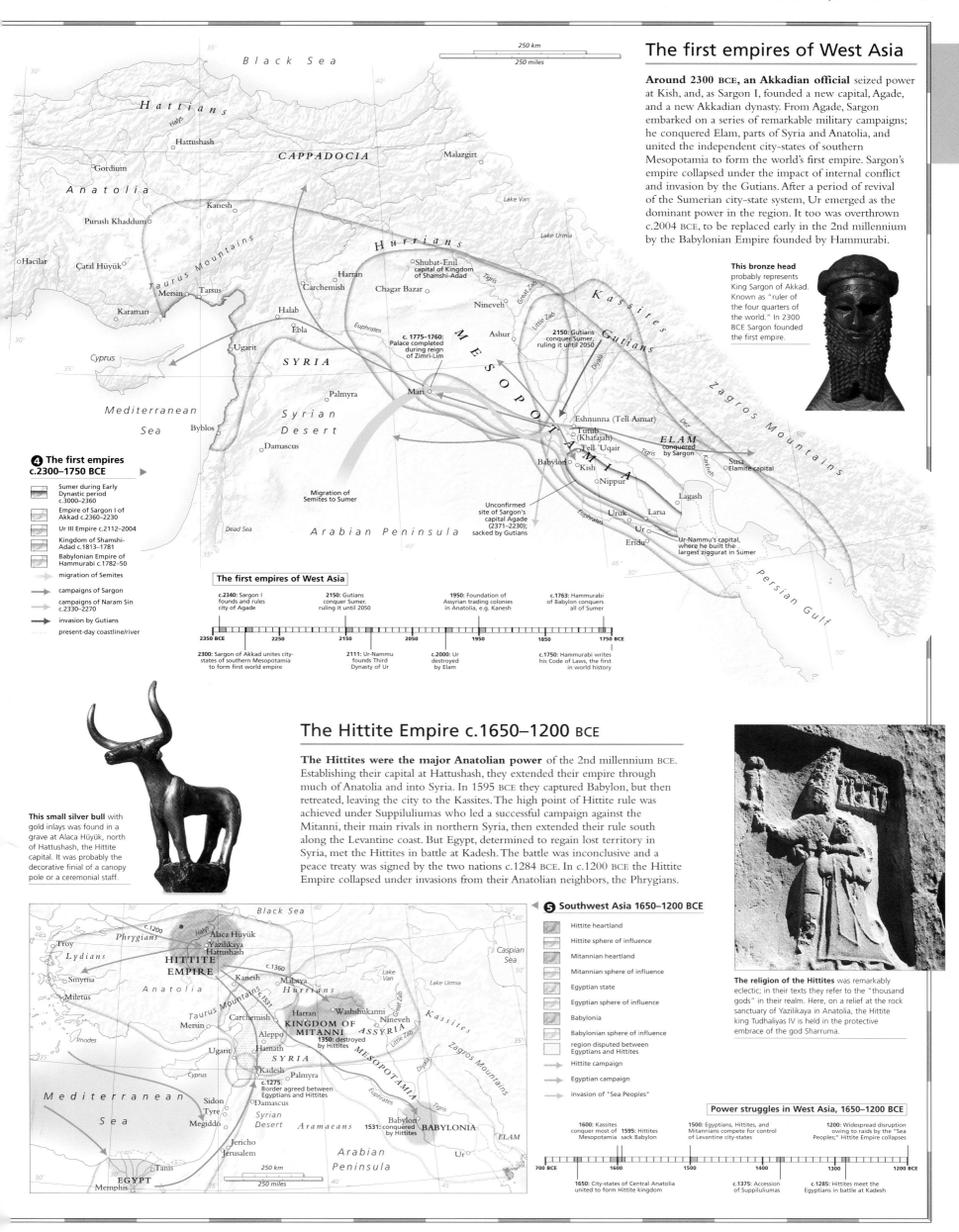

The first empires of West Asia

Around 2300 BCE, an Akkadian official seized power at Kish, and, as Sargon I, founded a new capital, Agade, and a new Akkadian dynasty. From Agade, Sargon embarked on a series of remarkable military campaigns; he conquered Elam, parts of Syria and Anatolia, and united the independent city-states of southern Mesopotamia to form the world's first empire. Sargon's empire collapsed under the impact of internal conflict and invasion by the Gutians. After a period of revival of the Sumerian city-state system, Ur emerged as the dominant power in the region. It too was overthrown c.2004 BCE, to be replaced early in the 2nd millennium by the Babylonian Empire founded by Hammurabi.

This bronze head probably represents King Sargon of Akkad. Known as "ruler of the four quarters of the world." In 2300 BCE Sargon founded the first empire.

④ The first empires c.2300–1750 BCE

- Sumer during Early Dynastic period c.3000–2360
- Empire of Sargon I of Akkad c.2360–2230
- Ur III Empire c.2112–2004
- Kingdom of Shamshi-Adad c.1813–1781
- Babylonian Empire of Hammurabi c.1782–50
- → migration of Semites
- → campaigns of Sargon
- → campaigns of Naram Sin c.2330–2270
- → invasion by Gutians
- ---- present-day coastline/river

The first empires of West Asia

c.2340: Sargon I founds and rules city of Agade	2150: Gutians conquer Sumer, ruling it until 2050	1950: Foundation of Assyrian trading colonies in Anatolia, e.g. Kanesh	c.1763: Hammurabi of Babylon conquers all of Sumer

| 2350 BCE | 2250 | 2150 | 2050 | 1950 | 1850 | 1750 BCE |

| 2300: Sargon of Akkad unites city-states of southern Mesopotamia to form first world empire | 2111: Ur-Nammu founds Third Dynasty of Ur | c.2000: Ur destroyed by Elam | c.1750: Hammurabi writes his Code of Laws, the first in world history |

The Hittite Empire c.1650–1200 BCE

The Hittites were the major Anatolian power of the 2nd millennium BCE. Establishing their capital at Hattushash, they extended their empire through much of Anatolia and into Syria. In 1595 BCE they captured Babylon, but then retreated, leaving the city to the Kassites. The high point of Hittite rule was achieved under Suppululiumas who led a successful campaign against the Mitanni, their main rivals in northern Syria, then extended their rule south along the Levantine coast. But Egypt, determined to regain lost territory in Syria, met the Hittites in battle at Kadesh. The battle was inconclusive and a peace treaty was signed by the two nations c.1284 BCE. In c.1200 BCE the Hittite Empire collapsed under invasions from their Anatolian neighbors, the Phrygians.

This small silver bull with gold inlays was found in a grave at Alaca Hüyük, north of Hattushash, the Hittite capital. It was probably the decorative finial of a canopy pole or a ceremonial staff.

The religion of the Hittites was remarkably eclectic; in their texts they refer to the "thousand gods" in their realm. Here, on a relief at the rock sanctuary of Yazilikaya in Anatolia, the Hittite king Tudhaliyas IV is held in the protective embrace of the god Sharruma.

⑤ Southwest Asia 1650–1200 BCE

- Hittite heartland
- Hittite sphere of influence
- Mitannian heartland
- Mitannian sphere of influence
- Egyptian state
- Egyptian sphere of influence
- Babylonia
- Babylonian sphere of influence
- region disputed between Egyptians and Hittites
- → Hittite campaign
- → Egyptian campaign
- → invasion of "Sea Peoples"

Power struggles in West Asia, 1650–1200 BCE

1600: Kassites conquer most of Mesopotamia	1595: Hittites sack Babylon	1500: Egyptians, Hittites, and Mitannians compete for control of Levantine city-states	1200: Widespread disruption owing to raids by the "Sea Peoples;" Hittite Empire collapses

| 700 BCE | 1600 | 1500 | 1400 | 1300 | 1200 BCE |

| 1650: City-states of Central Anatolia united to form Hittite kingdom | c.1375: Accession of Suppululiumas | c.1285: Hittites meet the Egyptians in battle at Kadesh |

221

EARLY EMPIRES OF WEST ASIA

The Ishtar Gate, the entrance to the great city of Babylon, was built by King Nebuchadnezzar II.

THE FIRST MILLENNIUM BCE saw a succession of powerful empires in West Asia. The first, established in the 10th century, was the Assyrian Empire. The Assyrians built their empire on the prowess of their armies and their administrative efficiency. After their overthrow by a Babylonian-Mede coalition in 612 BCE, Babylon became the dominant regional power, until it was overthrown in turn by the Persians. Founded by Cyrus the Great, the Persian Empire expanded to become the largest the world had yet seen, stretching from the Aegean to the Indus. While its empires rose and fell, West Asia was responsible for an invention of lasting value to the whole world. From its early beginnings in Mesopotamia, writing was developed into an alphabet by the Phoenicians, who carried it into the Mediterranean world, where it was adopted by the Greeks.

THE HISTORY AND LEGENDS OF MESOPOTAMIA

Much modern knowledge of the early history of West Asia is based on the libraries of clay tablets found at the palaces of the great rulers of Mesopotamia. The Royal Library of the Assyrian king Ashurbanipal at Nineveh yielded a spectacular find of some 20,000 clay tablets dealing with almost every aspect of life. One of the great literary compositions is the story of Gilgamesh, a legendary Sumerian king, based on an epic that dates back to the early 2nd millennium BCE. There is also an account of the creation, and another of a great deluge that covers the face of the earth with water. There are clear similarities between the account of the flood and the Biblical account of Noah's Flood in Genesis.

Gilgamesh was the legendary king of the Sumerian city-state of Uruk, and the hero of an epic in which he recounts his exploits during his search for immortality.

This ivory plaque was found at Megiddo, a small but important palace/fortress in northern Israel. It shows that Egyptian influence was still strong in the Levant.

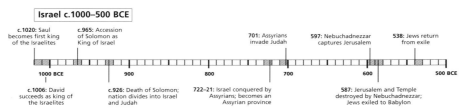

Israel c.1000–500 BCE

c.1020: Saul becomes first king of the Israelites
c.965: Accession of Solomon as King of Israel
701: Assyrians invade Judah
597: Nebuchadnezzar captures Jerusalem
538: Jews return from exile

c.1006: David succeeds as king of the Israelites
c.926: Death of Solomon; nation divides into Israel and Judah
722–21: Israel conquered by Assyrians; becomes an Assyrian province
587: Jerusalem and Temple destroyed by Nebuchadnezzar; Jews exiled to Babylon

Israel in the time of David

When David became as king of Israel c.1006 BCE, he moved the capital from Hebron to Jerusalem, establishing it as the political and religious center of the Israelites. By defeating the Philistines and extending Israelite rule in the region, David created a small empire. Under his successor, Solomon – builder of the Temple at Jerusalem – the nation prospered, but at his death in 926 BCE it divided into two kingdoms, Judah and Israel. In 721 BCE Israel was absorbed into the Assyrian Empire; Judah, having resisted repeated invasions, fell to Nebuchadnezzar of Babylon in 597 BCE. The city of Jerusalem was destroyed and the Jews forced into exile in Babylon for almost 50 years.

1 Palestine at the time of David c.1006–966 BCE ▶

- Judah and Israel
- conquered kingdom
- vassal
- boundary of David's empire
- boundary between kingdoms of Judah and Israel from 926

The Assyrian and Babylonian empires

950: Assyrian Empire founded
880: Nimrud becomes capital of Assyria
722: Accession of Sargon II; Israel absorbed into Assyria
689: Babylon destroyed by Assyrian king Sennacherib
612: Assyrian Empire falls; destruction of Nineveh
539: Conquest of Babylonia by Persian king, Cyrus II

900: Establishment of Kingdom of Urartu, which lasts till its destruction by Assyrians in 714
744: Accession of Tiglath-Pileser III
705: Capital of Assyria moves to Nineveh
669: Assyrian king Esarhaddon conquers north Egypt
605: Nebuchadnezzar II succeeds to throne of Babylon

The Assyrian and Babylonian empires c.950–600 BCE

The first Assyrian Empire was established early in the 2nd millennium BCE, but collapsed under attacks from Babylon and the Mitanni. Under a series of powerful and ruthless kings it was revived, reaching its apogee during the reigns of Tiglath-Pileser III, Sargon II, and Ashurbanipal. Babylon was reconquered, the Kingdom of Urartu defeated, and the empire extended to the Mediterranean and, briefly, into northern Egypt. These conquests were achieved by a well-equipped, well-disciplined army which made skilful use of cavalry. But in the mid-7th century BCE, attacks by Medes and Scythians,

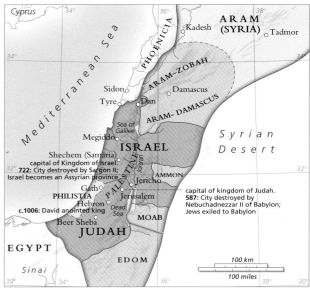

combined with a revolt in Babylonia, sent the empire into a terminal decline. In 625 BCE the Chaldeans took control of Babylon, and under Nebuchadnezzar II, the Babylonian Empire took over most of the former provinces of Assyria, including Syria and Palestine.

A relief from the Assyrian capital at Nineveh shows Assyrian soldiers using scaling ladders during King Ashurbanipal's siege of an Elamite city.

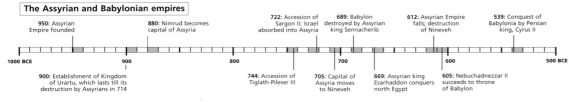

2 The Assyrian and Babylonian Empires 950–539 BCE

- under Ashur-dan II (934–912)
- added by death of Shalmaneser III (858–824)
- added by death of Sargon II (745–705)
- added by death of Ashurbanipal (668–626)
- New Babylonian Empire (625–539)
- present-day coastline/river

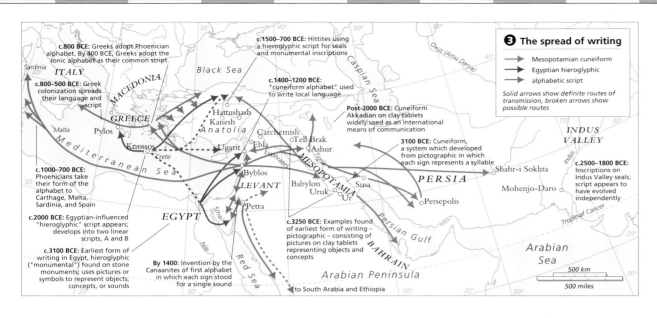

❸ The spread of writing

→ Mesopotamian cuneiform
→ Egyptian hieroglyphic
→ alphabetic script

Solid arrows show definite routes of transmission, broken arrows show possible routes

c.800 BCE: Greeks adopt Phoenician alphabet. By 400 BCE, Greeks adopt the Ionic alphabet as their common script.

c.800–500 BCE: Greek colonization spreads their language and script

c.1500–700 BCE: Hittites using a hieroglyphic script for seals and monumental inscriptions

c.1400–1200 BCE: "cuneiform alphabet" used to write local language

Post-2000 BCE: Cuneiform Akkadian on clay tablets widely used as an international means of communication

3100 BCE: Cuneiform, a system which developed from pictographic in which each sign represents a syllable

c.2500–1800 BCE: Inscriptions on Indus Valley seals; script appears to have evolved independently

c.1000–700 BCE: Phoenicians take their form of the alphabet to Carthage, Malta, Sardinia, and Spain

c.2000 BCE: Egyptian-influenced "hieroglyphic" script appears; develops into two linear scripts, A and B

c.3100 BCE: Earliest form of writing in Egypt, hieroglyphic ("monumental") found on stone monuments; uses pictures or symbols to represent objects, concepts, or sounds

c.3250 BCE: Examples found of earliest form of writing – pictographic – consisting of pictures on clay tablets representing objects and concepts

By 1400: Invention by the Canaanites of first alphabet in which each sign stood for a single sound

to South Arabia and Ethiopia

500 km
500 miles

The development of writing in West Asia

Pictographs – pictures which represented words – were the earliest form of writing, emerging in Mesopotamia in the 4th millennium BCE. In time, pictographs developed into the cuneiform script which was used to record several languages. The next step was taken by the Phoenicians: instead of using pictographs to represent words or ideas, they simplified writing into 22 different signs to represent the sounds of their speech. This alphabet is especially significant since it passed to the Greeks, then to the Romans, whose modified alphabet is still in use today.

The 7th-century BCE tablet *(right)* is an Assyrian account of the legend of the flood. The cuneiform (from the Latin, *cuneus*, a wedge) characters are made up of wedge-shaped impressions in soft clay.

The development of writing in West Asia

c.3250: First pictographic writing from Tell Brak, Mesopotamia

c.2500: Earliest syllabic script used in Sumerian literature

c.2000: Egyptian-influenced "hieroglyphic" script in Crete; develops into two linear scripts, A and B

c.1000–700: Phoenicians take alphabet to Carthage, Malta, Sardinia, and Spain

3500 BCE 3000 2500 2000 1500 1000 500 BCE

c.3100: Cuneiform writing emerges in Mesopotamia; hieroglyphic writing appears on Egyptian stone monuments

c.2500: Indus Valley civilization marks seals with inscriptions

c.1400: Development of first alphabets in Sinai and Levant

c.800: Greeks adopt Phoenician alphabet

The language on the 5th-century BCE cylinder seal *(left)* is Aramaic, which used the Phoenician-Hebrew alphabet. Aramaic became the administrative language of the Persian Empire and was thus in use from Anatolia to the Indus.

The first Persian Empire

Babylonian rule in Mesopotamia was ended by Cyrus the Great. Uniting the Medes and Persians, he founded the Persian Empire, naming it the Achaemenid Empire after an ancestor. Once in power, Cyrus defeated the Lydians, then unseated Nabonidas, King of Babylon. A tolerant ruler and magnanimous victor, Cyrus released the Jews from captivity in Babylon and authorized the rebuilding of the Temple in Jerusalem. Under Darius I ("the Great") and Xerxes I, the empire was extended, organized into 20 provinces ruled by satraps (governors), and a major road network constructed. But both rulers failed in their attempts to conquer Greece. Weakened from without by raiding nomads, and from within by ambitious satraps, the empire was defeated at Issus in 333 by Alexander the Great.

The simple but imposing tomb of Cyrus the Great at Pasargadae, where Cyrus built himself a permanent residence, commemorates an outstanding leader and founder of the Achaemenid Persian Empire.

The first Persian Empire

547–46: Cyrus defeats Croesus, King of the Lydians

530: Cyrus killed in battle against the nomads of Central Asia

521: Darius the Great ruler of Persian Empire

500: Building of the Persian Royal Road

486: Xerxes I becomes ruler of Persian Empire

545 BCE 535 525 515 505 495 485 475 BCE

c.550: Persian Empire established by Cyrus the Great

539: Conquest of Babylon by Cyrus

525: Cambyses II conquers Egypt and advances to Nubia and Libya

513: Darius invades Scythia

490: Persian invasion force defeated by Athenians at Marathon

480: Xerxes brings huge army to Greece, but is defeated at Salamis

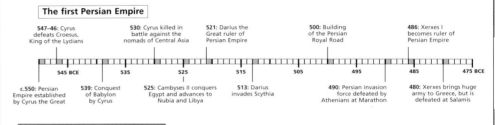

The great palace in Persepolis was begun in 518 BCE by Darius, but built mainly under Xerxes I. The wide staircase leading to the audience hall, or *apadana*, was decorated with carved reliefs of subject peoples bearing tribute.

❹ The Achaemenid Empire c.550–331 BCE

Persian homeland under Cyrus before 550 BCE
Kingdom of Medes, annexed 550 BCE
Kingdom of Lydians, annexed c.547 BCE
Kingdom of Babylonians, annexed 539 BCE
Kingdom of Egyptians, annexed 525 BCE
annexed by Darius I and Xerxes I

---- Persian Empire at greatest extent
—— Persian Royal Road
LYDIA Persian administrative district (satrapy) ruled by governor
→ major campaigns of Cyrus and Darius I
✕ battle with date

Wars with Greece 490–479 BCE
→ Persian campaigns against Greece
✕ Greek victory
✕ Persian victory
✕ indecisive battle
---- present-day river/coastline

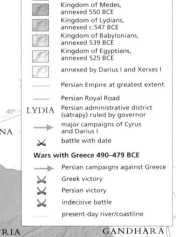

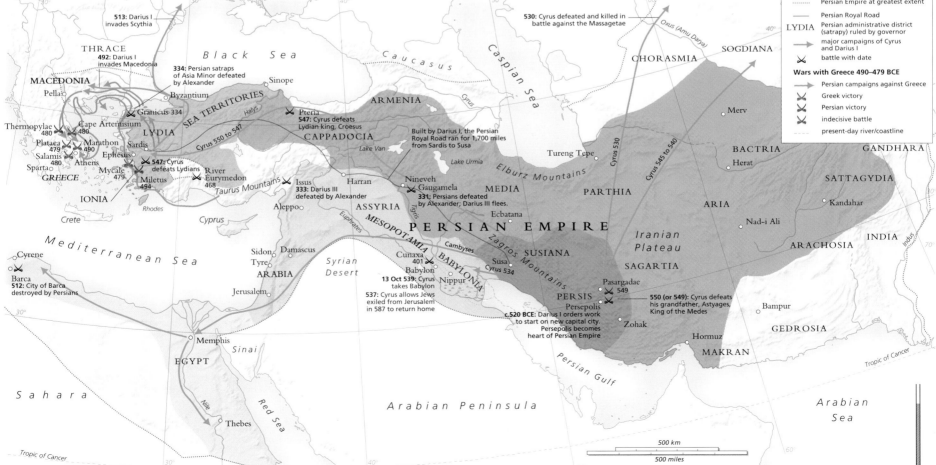

GREEK AND ROMAN EXPANSION

ALEXANDER THE GREAT'S CONQUESTS *(see pp. 40–41)* briefly united a vast tract of West Asia. Subsequently, empires competed and dynasties fell, but a widespread Hellenistic culture survived. In Persia and Mesopotamia, the Seleucids were ousted by the Parthians, who then clashed with an expansionist Rome. By 1 CE, Rome's empire formed a single vast trading area; its West Asian Greek-speaking provinces were the richest of all. A particularly valuable trade was in incense from southern Arabia. Unrest in the Roman Empire

This opalescent vase of molded glass was produced in Roman Syria in the 1st century CE.

was often religious. Rome suppressed two Jewish revolts, provoking a diaspora, but it was a new offshoot of Judaism, Christianity, that spread most effectively through the region *(see pp. 48–49)*. In the east, c.226 CE, the Sassanians succeeded the Parthians, establishing a new capital at Ctesiphon.

Seleucus I took the largest portion of Alexander's empire. His dynasty lasted until 129 BCE, most of his lands falling to Rome and the Parthians.

Alexander's successors

The death of Alexander was followed by a long struggle for his empire between his generals. With the elimination of three principal contenders – Antigonus at the battle of Ipsus, Lysimachus at Corupedium, Cassander through disease – three great monarchies were established: Macedonia under the Antigonids; Egypt under the Ptolemies; Mesopotamia and Persia under Seleucus I. During the reign of Antiochus III, the greatest of the Seleucids, the Seleucid Empire was extended, but his invasion of Greece in 192 BCE led to conflict with Rome and he was forced to make peace. Thereafter the Seleucid Empire declined.

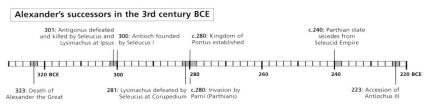

Alexander's successors in the 3rd century BCE

301: Antigonus defeated and killed by Seleucus and Lysimachus at Ipsus — 300: Antioch founded by Seleucus I — c.280: Kingdom of Pontus established — c.240: Parthian state secedes from Seleucid Empire

320 BCE — 300 — 280 — 260 — 240 — 220 BCE

323: Death of Alexander the Great — 281: Lysimachus defeated by Seleucus at Corupedium — c.280: Invasion by Parni (Parthians) — 223: Accession of Antiochus III

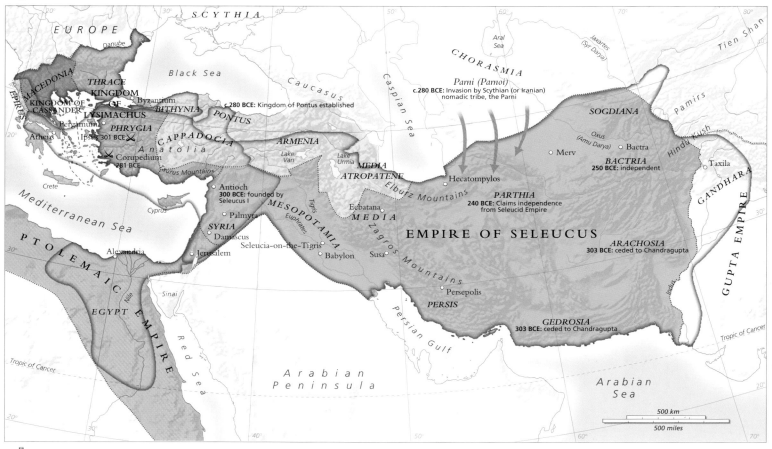

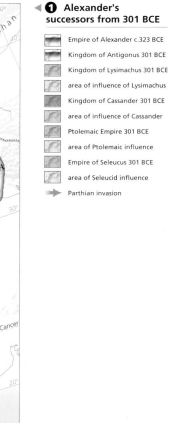

1 Alexander's successors from 301 BCE

- Empire of Alexander c.323 BCE
- Kingdom of Antigonus 301 BCE
- Kingdom of Lysimachus 301 BCE
- area of influence of Lysimachus
- Kingdom of Cassander 301 BCE
- area of influence of Cassander
- Ptolemaic Empire 301 BCE
- area of Ptolemaic influence
- Empire of Seleucus 301 BCE
- area of Seleucid influence
- → Parthian invasion

Parthia and Rome

The Parthians were renowned for their heavily armored cavalry and the skill of their mounted bowmen.

In about 240 BCE a Scythian people from the steppes of Turkmenistan broke away from Seleucid rule and established the Parthian state. A century later, under Mithridates I, they took Mesopotamia and founded a new capital at Ctesiphon. Roman expansion in the 1st century BCE brought conflict with Parthia; in 53 CE the Parthians defeated them at Carrhae. In the 2nd century CE, a weakened Parthia was invaded by Rome. Finally, 400 years of Parthian rule was ended by Ardashir, the first Sassanian ruler.

The Parthian Wars

53 BCE: Parthians defeat Romans at Carrhae — 114–117: Rome annexes Armenia and northern Mesopotamia — 165: Romans capture Dura Europos and sack Ctesiphon — 198: Northern Mesopotamia made Roman province

50 BCE — 1 — 50 CE — 100 — 150 — 200 — 250 CE

40 BCE: Parthians capture Jerusalem — 117: Death of Trajan; Rome gives up his conquests in Mesopotamia — 216: Romans invade Parthia and attack Arbela — 226: Parthia falls to Sassanians

2 Wars between Parthia and Rome 53 BCE–217 CE

- Roman Empire in early 2nd century CE
- Parthian Empire
- area disputed between Parthia and Rome
- → Roman campaign
- → Parthian campaign

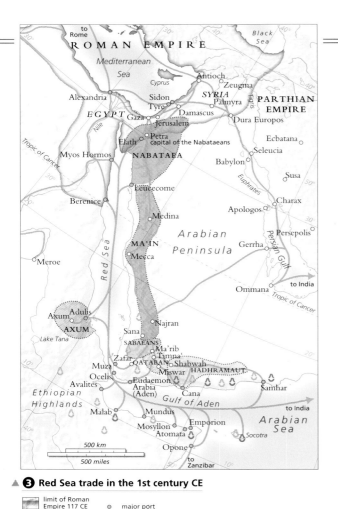

▲ ❸ Red Sea trade in the 1st century CE

limit of Roman Empire 117 CE	● major port
myrrh	→ trade route
frankincense	

Arabia's Red Sea trade

The aromatic gums frankincense and myrrh were prized commodities in the early civilizations of Egypt and West Asia. Both were widely used to make incense, perfumes, and cosmetics, while myrrh was also used for embalming. Mainly cultivated in southern Arabia, Ethiopia, and the island of Socotra, frankincense and myrrh were carried north by camel caravan to the cities of the eastern Mediterranean. Occupying a key point on this overland route, Petra, capital of the Nabataeans, became a wealthy city. As navigational skills improved and sailors learnt to harness the monsoon winds, frankincense and myrrh were increasingly transported by sea, thus benefiting those Arab states with major ports around the Gulf of Aden, such as Cana, Muza, and Eudaemon Arabia.

Incense consists of a mixture of gums and spices. The fragrant odor of burning incense was associated with religious rites and prayer throughout West Asia and the eastern Mediterranean, hence its great value. It was burned on small stone altars, such as this example from southern Arabia.

Roman Palestine

In 63 BCE Judaea was conquered by Rome, and it was in an atmosphere of anti-Roman protest by Jewish Zealots that Christianity developed in the 1st century CE. In 66 CE, discontent flared into open revolt, suppressed by a force of 60,000 men under Vespasian, and then by his son, Titus, who destroyed and looted the Jewish Temple in Jerusalem. Diehard Zealots took refuge on the rock fortress at Masada and, rather than submit to Rome, committed mass suicide. In 132 CE Bar Cochba led another revolt, which ended with the Roman destruction of Jerusalem.

After Christianity won acceptance under Constantine, many Roman artists turned from secular to sacred themes, such as the biblical scene depicted on this early Christian sarcophagus.

The Jewish diaspora 66–135 CE

The failed revolts of 66 and 132 CE precipitated a diaspora (Greek for "dispersion") of Jews from Palestine. Vast numbers were sold into slavery, became refugees in Galilee, or fled abroad, many to long-established centers in Babylonia and Mesopotamia. Jews were banished from Jerusalem, which was refounded as a Roman city (Aelia Capitolina). By the 2nd century CE Jews may have made up some 5–10% of the population of the Roman Empire; in some eastern cities, perhaps 25%. Remaining loyal to their faith, the exiled Jews continued to regard Judaea as their homeland.

A detail from the triumphal arch of Titus shows the great candlestick (menorah) and other treasures being looted from the Temple at Jerusalem by Roman soldiers.

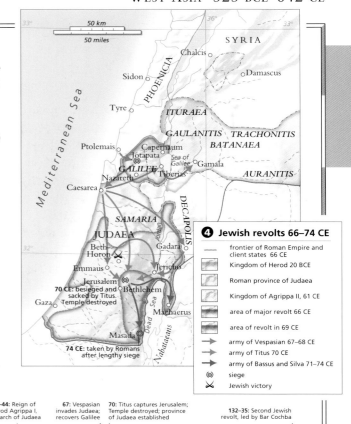

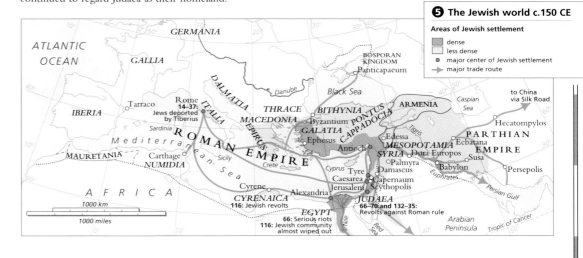

Sassanian Persia

Ardashir I rebelled against the Parthian king, Artabanus V, c.226 CE, and founded the Sassanian Empire He kept Ctesiphon as his capital and reintroduced Zoroastrianism as the state religion. The empire reached its peak of prosperity under Khosrau I. In the 7th century, his son, Khosrau II, invaded the Byzantine Empire, but was met by a successful counteroffensive. The weakened empire then fell to the Muslim Arabs.

A cameo depicts the capture of the Emperor Valerian by Shapur I, following the great Persian victory against the Romans near Edessa in 259 CE.

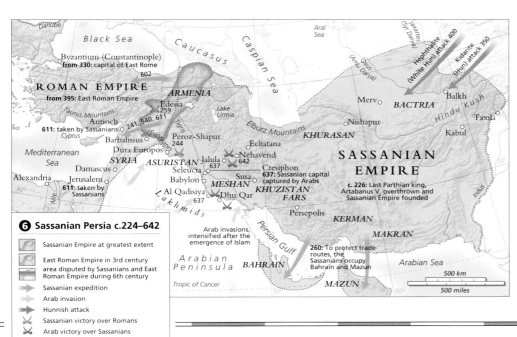

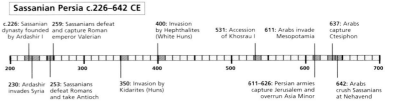

225

THE ADVENT OF ISLAM

This gold dinar shows Abd al-Malik, caliph from 685 to 705. He reorganized the army and the Islamic state.

IN 610, IN A CAVE south of Mecca, the Prophet Muhammad received the first of the messages from God which led him to found the Islamic faith. The clear, monotheistic message of Islam appealed to the Arabs, and within 30 years they had carried it to Persia and Palestine. The early Islamic empire was a single political entity, ruled by the caliph, or "successor" of Muhammad (see pp. 56–57). By 750 CE, Arab armies had carried Islam west to the Iberian Peninsula and east to Central Asia. The Abbasid Caliphate, with its capital usually at Baghdad, was founded in 750. It was an era of great prosperity, especially in the reign of Harun al-Rashid, but later caliphs lost all political power, ruling in name only over a steadily diminishing Caliphate.

Fine textiles decorated with the Cross and other Christian imagery were woven by Egypt's Copts under Byzantine and Islamic rule.

Religions in West Asia c.600

By 600 CE three major religions were firmly rooted in West Asia: Christianity, Judaism, and Zoroastrianism. Orthodox Christianity was the state religion of the Byzantine Empire; other Christian sects, such as the Nestorians, had strong followings in Mesopotamia and Persia. Jewish communities were scattered throughout the region. The most populous was probably in Babylonia, which was also the leading cultural center of the Jewish world. The Sassanian rulers of Persia tolerated Christians and Jews, although Zoroastrianism was the state religion. The Islamic invasion led to the emigration of many Zoroastrians, mainly to India.

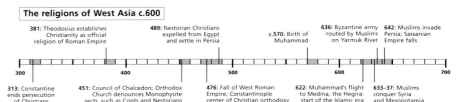

The religions of West Asia c.600

- 300
- 313: Constantine ends persecution of Christians
- 381: Theodosius establishes Christianity as official religion of Roman Empire
- 400
- 451: Council of Chalcedon; Orthodox Church denounces Monophysite sects, such as Copts and Nestorians
- 489: Nestorian Christians expelled from Egypt and settle in Persia
- 476: Fall of West Roman Empire; Constantinople center of Christian orthodoxy
- 500
- c.570: Birth of Muhammad
- 622: Muhammad's flight to Medina, the Hegira: start of the Islamic era
- 600
- 636: Byzantine army routed by Muslims on Yarmuk River
- 633–37: Muslims conquer Syria and Mesopotamia
- 642: Muslims invade Persia; Sassanian Empire falls
- 700

THE KORAN

The Koran (Qur'an) is the name given to the collected revelations transmitted to the Prophet Muhammad by the Archangel Gabriel, believed by Muslims to be the infallible word of Allah (God). Together, the revelations form the basis of Islam, the authority Muslims consult not only on questions of theological doctrine and ethics, but also on practical legal, political, and social matters. The Koranic revelations were committed to memory by the first disciples of the Prophet, and in 651 CE the first authorized Arabic text was prepared. The Koran is about the length of the New Testament of the Bible, and is divided into 114 *suras* or chapters as revealed to the Prophet at Mecca or Medina.

A fragment from a copy of the Koran (c.900) shows the beauty of Arabic calligraphy, regarded as the supreme art in the Islamic world. It is written in Kufic script, with the vowels indicated in red.

The spread of Islam

In 622 Muhammad and his followers, faced with hostility in Mecca, fled to Medina. In 630 he returned to Mecca with an army and took the city, thenceforth the religious center of Islam. At his death, he ruled almost half the Arabian Peninsula. His successors, who took the title "caliph" (successor or deputy), continued to spread his message through conquest: Syria, Mesopotamia, Persia, and Egypt were overrun by armies fired by the spirit of *jihad* (holy war). In 661 control of the Caliphate was gained by the Umayyad dynasty, who set up a new political capital at Damascus and extended the empire west to the Atlantic and east to the Indus.

Pilgrims in the ritual costume of two pieces of white cloth gather around the Ka'ba in the Great Mosque at Mecca.

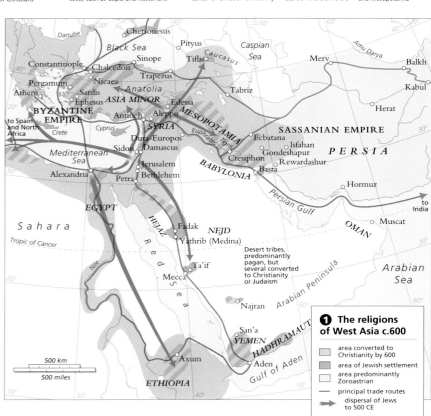

❶ The religions of West Asia c.600
- area converted to Christianity by 600
- area of Jewish settlement
- area predominantly Zoroastrian
- principal trade routes
- dispersal of Jews to 500 CE

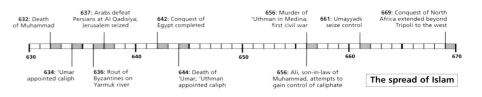

- 630
- 632: Death of Muhammad
- 634: 'Umar appointed caliph
- 636: Rout of Byzantines on Yarmuk river
- 637: Arabs defeat Persians at Al Qadisiya; Jerusalem seized
- 640
- 642: Conquest of Egypt completed
- 644: Death of 'Umar; 'Uthman appointed caliph
- 650
- 656: Murder of 'Uthman in Medina; first civil war
- 656: Ali, son-in-law of Muhammad, attempts to gain control of caliphate
- 660
- 661: Umayyads seize control
- 669: Conquest of North Africa extended beyond Tripoli to the west
- 670

The spread of Islam

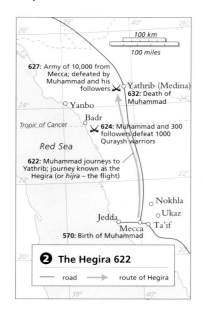

- 627: Army of 10,000 from Mecca; defeated by Muhammad and his followers
- 632: Death of Muhammad
- Yathrib (Medina)
- Yanbo
- Badr
- 624: Muhammad and 300 followers defeat 1000 Quraysh warriors
- Red Sea
- Tropic of Cancer
- 622: Muhammad journeys to Yathrib; journey known as the Hegira (or hijra – the flight)
- Nokhla
- Ukaz
- Jedda
- Mecca
- Ta'if
- 570: Birth of Muhammad

❷ The Hegira 622
- road
- route of Hegira

The Hegira (*hijra*)

Muhammad's flight from Mecca to Medina in 622 marks the start of the Islamic calendar. It was from Medina that Muhammad started to preach with success and spread the message of Islam. In recognition of this, the city's name was changed from Yathrib to Medina (the City), and it became the first political capital of the Islamic world. Mecca, however, had long been a holy city among the pagan tribes of the Arabian Peninsula and an important place of pilgrimage. Since it was also the birthplace of Muhammad and the site of his first revelations, it became the holiest city of Islam.

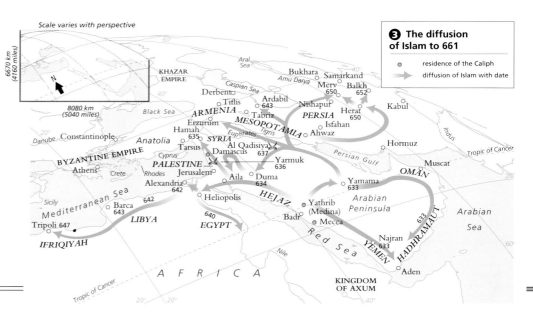

❸ The diffusion of Islam to 661
- residence of the Caliph
- diffusion of Islam with date

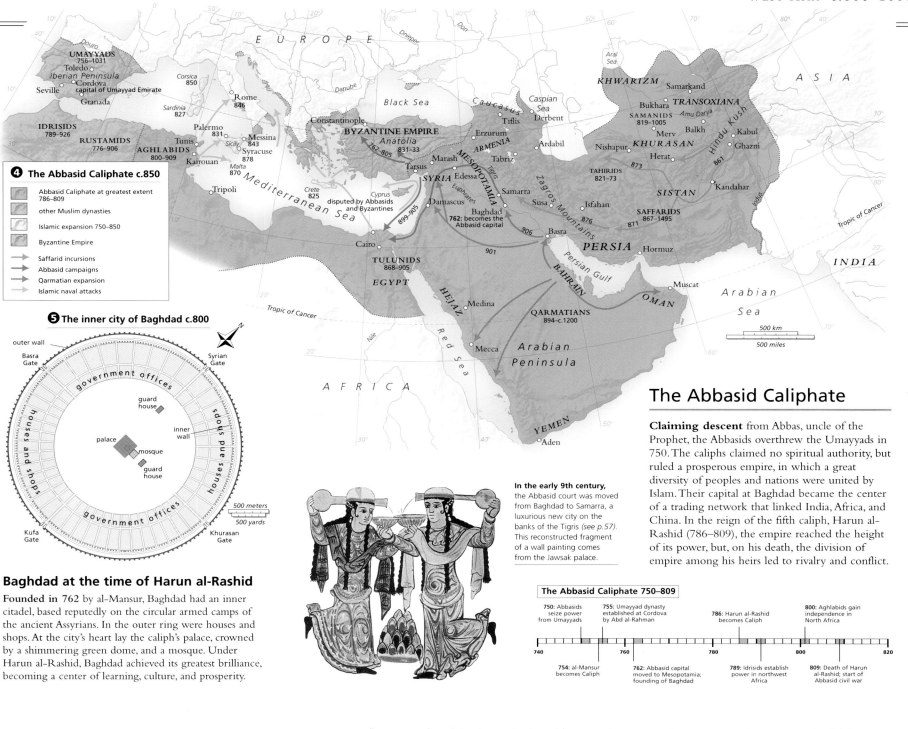

❹ The Abbasid Caliphate c.850

- Abbasid Caliphate at greatest extent 786–809
- other Muslim dynasties
- Islamic expansion 750–850
- Byzantine Empire
- → Saffarid incursions
- → Abbasid campaigns
- → Qarmatian expansion
- → Islamic naval attacks

❺ The inner city of Baghdad c.800

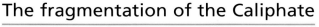

outer wall
Basra Gate
Syrian Gate
government offices
guard house
houses and shops
inner wall
palace
mosque
guard house
houses and shops
government offices
Kufa Gate
Khurasan Gate

500 meters
500 yards

Baghdad at the time of Harun al-Rashid

Founded in 762 by al-Mansur, Baghdad had an inner citadel, based reputedly on the circular armed camps of the ancient Assyrians. In the outer ring were houses and shops. At the city's heart lay the caliph's palace, crowned by a shimmering green dome, and a mosque. Under Harun al-Rashid, Baghdad achieved its greatest brilliance, becoming a center of learning, culture, and prosperity.

In the early 9th century, the Abbasid court was moved from Baghdad to Samarra, a luxurious new city on the banks of the Tigris (see p.57). This reconstructed fragment of a wall painting comes from the Jawsak palace.

The Abbasid Caliphate

Claiming descent from Abbas, uncle of the Prophet, the Abbasids overthrew the Umayyads in 750. The caliphs claimed no spiritual authority, but ruled a prosperous empire, in which a great diversity of peoples and nations were united by Islam. Their capital at Baghdad became the center of a trading network that linked India, Africa, and China. In the reign of the fifth caliph, Harun al-Rashid (786–809), the empire reached the height of its power, but, on his death, the division of empire among his heirs led to rivalry and conflict.

The Abbasid Caliphate 750–809

750: Abbasids seize power from Umayyads	755: Umayyad dynasty established at Cordova by Abd al-Rahman	786: Harun al-Rashid becomes Caliph	800: Aghlabids gain independence in North Africa

740 — 760 — 780 — 800 — 820

754: al-Mansur becomes Caliph	762: Abbasid capital moved to Mesopotamia; founding of Baghdad	789: Idrisids establish power in northwest Africa	809: Death of Harun al-Rashid; start of Abbasid civil war

The fragmentation of the Caliphate

Civil war on the death of Harun al-Rashid accelerated the Abbasids' loss of power, though they ruled in name until 1258. The lands of Islam, once ruled by a single caliph, fragmented into semiautonomous dynasties. Among these were the Fatimids of Egypt, the Samanids of Transoxiana, and the Ghaznavids of Afghanistan, who played a major role in the introduction of Islam to India. In 946, a Persian dynasty, the Buwayhids, invaded and occupied Baghdad. They became protectors of the Caliphate, an event that inspired a revival of Persian national identity.

All mosques share certain features, modeled on Muhammad's house at Medina. These include the *kibla*, the wall facing Mecca, the *minbar*, or pulpit, and the minaret – the tower from which the faithful are called to prayer. The minaret shown here is from the 9th-century mosque of Ibn Tulun at Cairo.

❻ The fragmentation of the Caliphate c.900–1030 ▶

- Abbasid Caliphate c.900
- residence of the Caliph c.900
- Byzantine Empire c.900
- → Samanid expansion in early 10th century
- → Ghaznavid expansion

Areas controlled in 1028 by
- Ghaznavids
- Fatimids
- Buwayhids

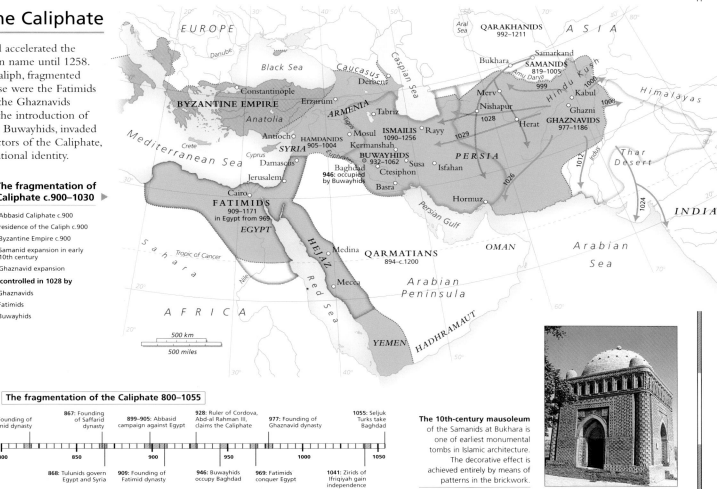

The 10th-century mausoleum of the Samanids at Bukhara is one of earliest monumental tombs in Islamic architecture. The decorative effect is achieved entirely by means of patterns in the brickwork.

The fragmentation of the Caliphate 800–1055

819: Founding of Samanid dynasty	867: Founding of Saffarid dynasty	899–905: Abbasid campaign against Egypt	928: Ruler of Cordova, Abd-al Rahman III, claims the Caliphate	977: Founding of Ghaznavid dynasty	1055: Seljuk Turks take Baghdad

800 — 850 — 900 — 950 — 1000 — 1050

868: Tulunids govern Egypt and Syria	909: Founding of Fatimid dynasty	946: Buwayhids occupy Baghdad	969: Fatimids conquer Egypt	1041: Zirids of Ifriqiyah gain independence

TURKISH AND MONGOL INVADERS

The Islamic warrior was armed with a long curved sword, often of highly-tempered steel and finely engraved.

IN THE 11TH CENTURY West Asia was invaded by the Seljuk Turks, nomads from Central Asia. Reuniting the central Abbasid lands, they emerged as the dominant power in Mesopotamia, Persia, and Anatolia. Their crushing victory at Manzikert in 1071 drove the Byzantines out of Asia Minor and provoked the Crusades. The Crusaders set out to regain the lands lost to Islam, but their capture of Jerusalem in 1099 was countered a century later by Saladin, who also became ruler of Egypt. In the mid-13th century, a new threat was presented by the Mongols, who conquered much of the region, but were halted by the Mamluks, who now ruled Egypt. In the late 14th century, Timur, the last Mongol conqueror, launched a series of campaigns which took him from Ankara to Delhi.

The Seljuk Turks and the Byzantines

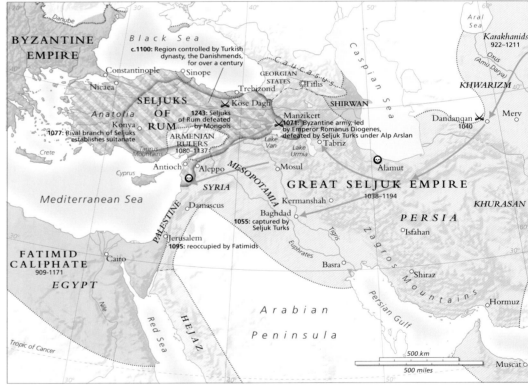

The Seljuks were great builders. Their architectural forms and intricate abstract designs had a lasting influence on Islamic art. This glazed tilework in Isfahan's Friday Mosque dates from the late 11th century.

In about 1040, a group of Turkish tribes swept out of the lands north of the Oxus. The Seljuks were the dominant clan. By 1055 they reached Baghdad, where they ruled in the name of the Abbasid caliph. Recent converts to Sunni Islam, the Seljuks planned to subdue all Shi'ites and infidels. Conquering Armenia, they then struck at the Byzantines in Asia Minor, defeating them at Manzikert in 1071. The seizure of Syria and much of Palestine from the Fatimids followed. After a period of civil war, the Seljuk Empire was split in two by the establishment in Anatolia of the independent Sultanate of Rum, with its capital at Konya. The Seljuks' control over their empire waned and they were crushed by the Mongols at Köse Dagh in 1243.

Saladin and the Ayyubid Sultanate

Saladin was a Kurdish general in the army of Nur al-Din, Zangid ruler of Mosul, who fought successfully against the Crusaders *(see pp. 64–65)* and his Muslim neighbors. Ousting the Fatimids from Egypt, he united Egypt and Syria under his rule. Hostilities with the Crusader states led in 1187 to Saladin's annihilation of Christian forces at Hattin and the capture of Jerusalem and Acre. This provoked the Third Crusade, in which the Crusaders recaptured most of the coastal plain of Palestine. The dynasty founded by Saladin, the Ayyubids, dominated the region until it fell to the Mamluks in 1250.

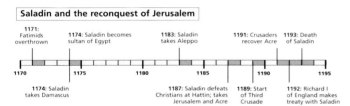

Saladin and the reconquest of Jerusalem

1171: Fatimids overthrown
1174: Saladin becomes sultan of Egypt
1183: Saladin takes Aleppo
1191: Crusaders recover Acre
1193: Death of Saladin

1170 — 1175 — 1180 — 1185 — 1190 — 1195

1174: Saladin takes Damascus
1187: Saladin defeats Christians at Hattin; takes Jerusalem and Acre
1189: Start of Third Crusade
1192: Richard I of England makes treaty with Saladin

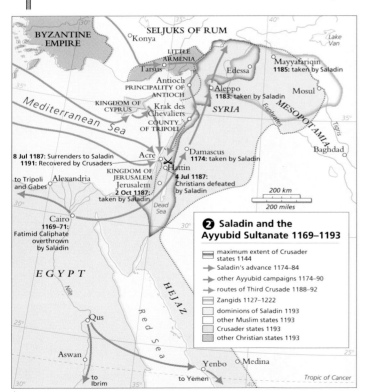

2 Saladin and the Ayyubid Sultanate 1169–1193

- maximum extent of Crusader states 1144
- Saladin's advance 1174–84
- other Ayyubid campaigns 1174–90
- routes of Third Crusade 1188–92
- Zangids 1127–1222
- dominions of Saladin 1193
- other Muslim states 1193
- Crusader states 1193
- other Christian states 1193

At the head of an army from Egypt, the Muslim leader Saladin (1138–1193) drove the Crusaders out of most of Palestine and Syria and recaptured Jerusalem, restoring the Dome of the Rock, one of Islam's oldest surviving shrines, to Muslim worship. Though a formidable leader, Saladin was recognized by the Crusaders as a chivalrous opponent.

The growth of the Great Seljuk Empire

c.1040: Seljuks conquer Afghanistan and eastern Persia
1069: Seljuks take Konya (Iconium)
1071: Alp Arslan, Seljuk leader defeats Byzantines at Manzikert
1084: Fall of Antioch to Seljuks
1092: Vizier Nizam al-Mulk murdered by Ismaili Assassin
1099: Crusaders recover Jerusalem

1040 — 1050 — 1060 — 1070 — 1080 — 1090 — 1100

1055: Seljuks established in Baghdad, ruling in the name of the Abbasid Caliph
1077: Province established in Anatolia with capital first at Nicaea and then Konya; dynasty comes to be known as the Seljuks of Rum (Rome)
1094: Seljuk dynasty of Syria founded with capital at Aleppo
1098: Crusaders recover Antioch

1 The Seljuk Turks and the Byzantine Empire from c.1025

- Byzantine frontier in Asia c.1025
- Byzantine Empire 1095
- Seljuk Empire c.1095
- Seljuk tributary states
- Byzantine territory overrun by Seljuks by 1095
- eastern frontier of area recovered by the Byzantine Empire by 1180
- other Muslim dynasty
- route of Seljuk invasion from Asia c.1038
- route of Byzantine army
- stronghold of the sect of the Assassins

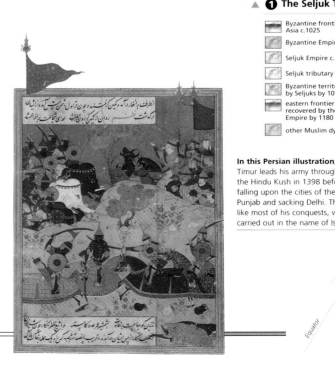

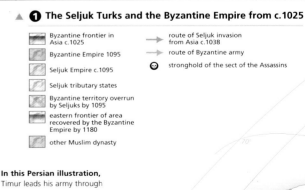

In this Persian illustration, Timur leads his army through the Hindu Kush in 1398 before falling upon the cities of the Punjab and sacking Delhi. This, like most of his conquests, was carried out in the name of Islam.

Mamluks and Mongols

The Mamluks, who seized power in Egypt in 1250, were chiefly Circassians from the Caucasus, captured in childhood and trained as slave bodyguards. Once in power, they extended their rule into Syria and built up a trading network in Africa and the Indian Ocean. Within five years of the Mamluks' rise to power, the Mongol Hülegü *(see pp.68–69)* led a powerful army into West Asia. After destroying Alamut, the stronghold of the Assassins (an Ismaili Shi'ite sect), Hülegü sacked Baghdad. The Mongol threat was averted by the death of the Mongol khan, Möngke which required Hülegü to withdraw his main army. Seizing their advantage, in 1260 the Mamluks marched north in the defence of Islam, and crushed the Mongol army at Ain Jalut.

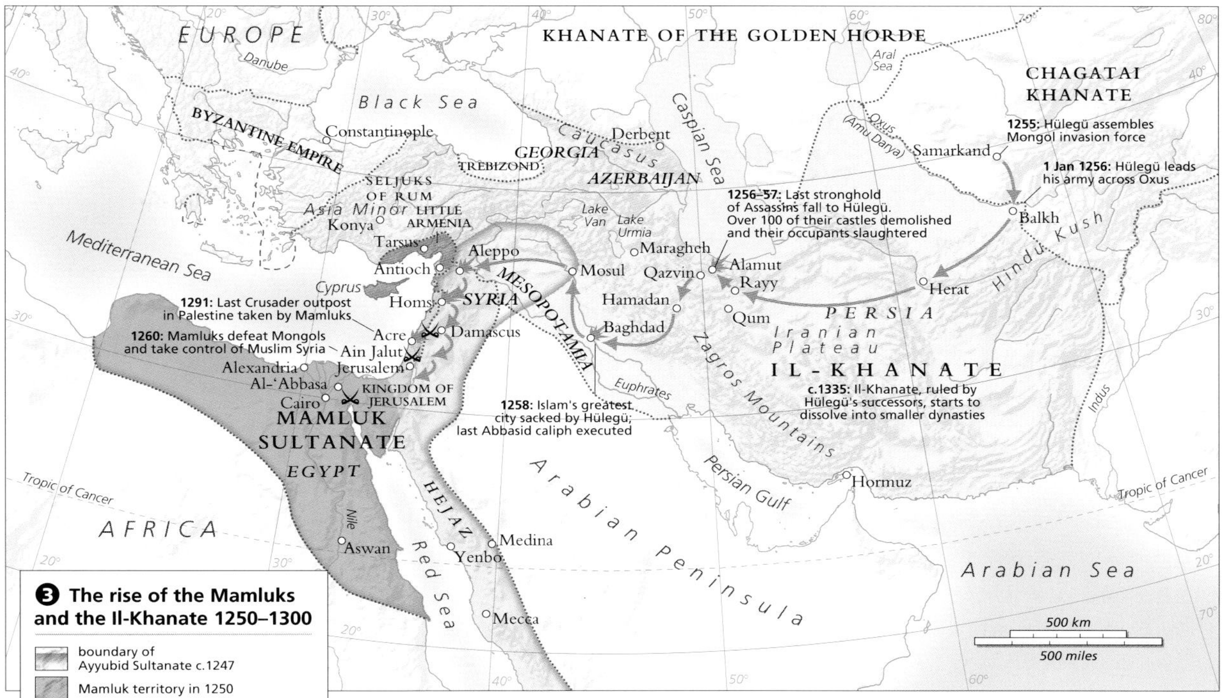
EUROPE
KHANATE OF THE GOLDEN HORDE
CHAGATAI KHANATE
Black Sea
BYZANTINE EMPIRE
Constantinople
TREBIZOND
GEORGIA
Derbent
AZERBAIJAN
Caspian Sea
Samarkand
1255: Hülegü assembles Mongol invasion force
1 Jan 1256: Hülegü leads his army across Oxus
SELJUKS OF RUM
Konya
LITTLE ARMENIA
Tarsus
Aleppo
Antioch
Cyprus
SYRIA
Homs
Damascus
Acre
Ain Jalut
Jerusalem
Alexandria
Al-'Abbasa
Cairo
KINGDOM OF JERUSALEM
MAMLUK SULTANATE
EGYPT
Mediterranean Sea
1291: Last Crusader outpost in Palestine taken by Mamluks
1260: Mamluks defeat Mongols and take control of Muslim Syria
1256–57: Last stronghold of Assassins fall to Hülegü. Over 100 of their castles demolished and their occupants slaughtered
Mosul
Maragheh
Qazvin
Alamut
Rayy
Hamadan
Baghdad
Qum
Balkh
Herat
Hindu Kush
PERSIA
Iranian Plateau
IL-KHANATE
c.1335: Il-Khanate, ruled by Hülegü's successors, starts to dissolve into smaller dynasties
MESOPOTAMIA
Zagros Mountains
1258: Islam's greatest city sacked by Hülegü; last Abbasid caliph executed
Persian Gulf
Hormuz
Tropic of Cancer
AFRICA
Aswan
Nile
HEJAZ
Medina
Yenbo
Red Sea
Mecca
Arabian Peninsula
Arabian Sea
500 km
500 miles

3 The rise of the Mamluks and the Il-Khanate 1250–1300

- boundary of Ayyubid Sultanate c.1247
- Mamluk territory in 1250
- annexed by Mamluks 1253
- annexed by Mamluks 1260
- Christian territory in the Levant conquered by Mamluks 1263–1291
- Christian territory after 1291
- Il-Khanate and vassals c.1259
- route of Mongol invasion under Hülegü
- sacked by Mongols

The Mamluk warrior was superbly trained, studying both the theory and practice of combat in military manuals, such as this one showing four cavalrymen exercising around a pool.

The Mongols and Mamluks in West Asia

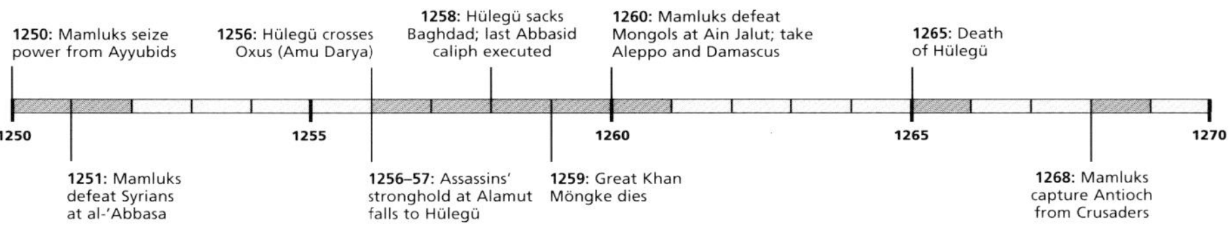
1250: Mamluks seize power from Ayyubids
1251: Mamluks defeat Syrians at al-'Abbasa
1256: Hülegü crosses Oxus (Amu Darya)
1256–57: Assassins' stronghold at Alamut falls to Hülegü
1258: Hülegü sacks Baghdad; last Abbasid caliph executed
1259: Great Khan Möngke dies
1260: Mamluks defeat Mongols at Ain Jalut; take Aleppo and Damascus
1265: Death of Hülegü
1268: Mamluks capture Antioch from Crusaders
1250
1255
1260
1265
1270

The Il-Khanate c.1260–1353

The first Il-Khan, Hülegü, entered a period of conflict with Berke, Khan of the Golden Horde. Berke, who had converted to Islam and allied himself with the Mamluks, resented Hülegü's new empire. By 1262 the situation had stabilized, and Hülegü settled on the well-watered plains of Azerbaijan and built a capital at Maragheh, from where he ruled the lands he had gained in Persia, Mesopotamia, Asia Minor, and the Caucasus. The Mongol dynasty established by Hülegü – the Il-Khanate – ruled Persia until 1353.

In 1258 the Mongols under Hülegü sacked the great city of Baghdad, the very heart of Arab civilization, and reputedly murdered 800,000 of its inhabitants. The last Abbasid caliph was captured, rolled in a carpet, and then trampled to death by galloping horses.

The dominions of Timur

Claiming descent from Genghis Khan, Timur the Lame became master of Transoxiana in 1369. Making Samarkand his capital, he embarked on a series of campaigns against Persia, the Golden Horde, the Sultanate of Delhi, the Mamluks, and the Ottomans. At Ankara in 1402, he defeated and captured the Ottoman Sultan Bayezid. In 35 years Timur created a vast empire; plans for invading China ceased with his death. Though his conquests struck fear into Muslim Asia, Timur's empire proved short-lived.

The campaigns of Timur 1379–1405

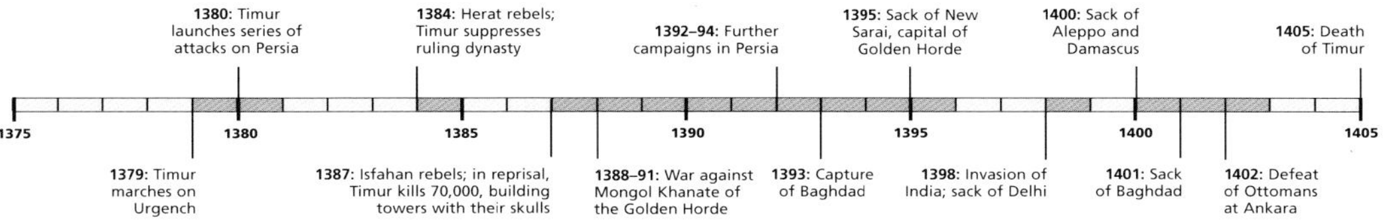
1379: Timur marches on Urgench
1380: Timur launches series of attacks on Persia
1384: Herat rebels; Timur suppresses ruling dynasty
1387: Isfahan rebels; in reprisal, Timur kills 70,000, building towers with their skulls
1388–91: War against Mongol Khanate of the Golden Horde
1392–94: Further campaigns in Persia
1393: Capture of Baghdad
1395: Sack of New Sarai, capital of Golden Horde
1398: Invasion of India; sack of Delhi
1400: Sack of Aleppo and Damascus
1401: Sack of Baghdad
1402: Defeat of Ottomans at Ankara
1405: Death of Timur
1375
1380
1385
1390
1395
1400
1405

Timur is buried beneath a slab of jade in the Gur-i Mir, Samarkand.

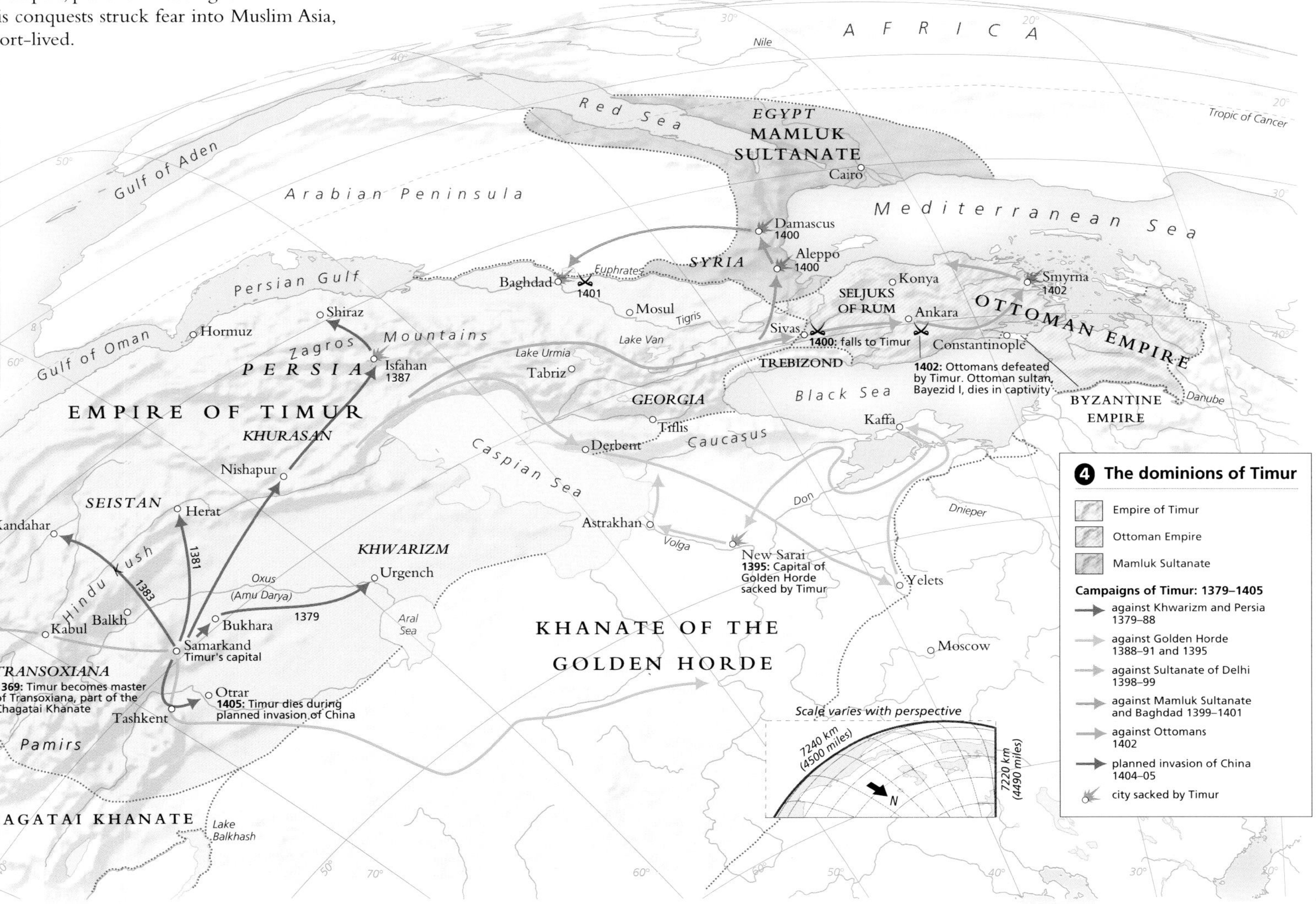
AFRICA
Nile
Tropic of Cancer
Red Sea
EGYPT
MAMLUK SULTANATE
Cairo
Gulf of Aden
Arabian Peninsula
Mediterranean Sea
Damascus 1400
Aleppo 1400
SYRIA
Euphrates
Baghdad
1401
Persian Gulf
Shiraz
Hormuz
Mosul
Tigris
Konya
SELJUKS OF RUM
Smyrna 1402
Ankara
OTTOMAN EMPIRE
Sivas
1400: falls to Timur
Constantinople
1402: Ottomans defeated by Timur. Ottoman sultan, Bayezid I, dies in captivity
Zagros Mountains
Lake Van
Gulf of Oman
PERSIA
Isfahan 1387
Lake Urmia
Tabriz
TREBIZOND
Black Sea
BYZANTINE EMPIRE
Danube
Arabian Sea
EMPIRE OF TIMUR
KHURASAN
GEORGIA
Tiflis
Kaffa
Derbent
Caucasus
Nishapur
Caspian Sea
Don
Dnieper
SEISTAN
Herat
1381
Kandahar
Hindu Kush
1383
Indus
Astrakhan
Volga
New Sarai
1395: Capital of Golden Horde sacked by Timur
Yelets
KHWARIZM
Urgench
Oxus (Amu Darya)
Bukhara
1379
Aral Sea
Balkh
Kabul
Multan
SULTANATE OF DELHI
1398: Timur invades India and sacks Delhi
PUNJAB
Samarkand
Timur's capital
TRANSOXIANA
1369: Timur becomes master of Transoxiana, part of the Chagatai Khanate
Otrar
1405: Timur dies during planned invasion of China
Tashkent
Delhi
Pamirs
Himalayas
KHANATE OF THE GOLDEN HORDE
Moscow
CHAGATAI KHANATE
Lake Balkhash
Scale varies with perspective
7240 km (4500 miles)
7220 km (4490 miles)
N

4 The dominions of Timur

- Empire of Timur
- Ottoman Empire
- Mamluk Sultanate

Campaigns of Timur: 1379–1405

- against Khwarizm and Persia 1379–88
- against Golden Horde 1388–91 and 1395
- against Sultanate of Delhi 1398–99
- against Mamluk Sultanate and Baghdad 1399–1401
- against Ottomans 1402
- planned invasion of China 1404–05
- city sacked by Timur

THE OTTOMAN EMPIRE

The conquests of Osman I (1299–1326) formed the nucleus of the Ottoman Empire.

THE OTTOMAN EMPIRE was one of the great world powers of the early modern age. At its height, the empire stretched from the Indian Ocean to Algiers, Hungary, and the Crimea. Constantinople, captured from the Byzantines in 1453 was a key center of power that had resisted non-Christian attack for 1000 years. Turkish expansion in the Balkans led to shifts in religious, ethnic, linguistic, and economic frontiers, which still have serious consequences in the modern world. The conquest of Egypt and Syria established a powerful presence in Africa and West Asia, although, in the east, the Ottomans faced powerful opposition from Safavid Persia, which flourished in the 16th and 17th centuries.

The rise of the Ottomans

The Ottoman state started as a small frontier principality dedicated to raids on Christian Byzantium. In the 14th century, led by a succession of warrior sultans, Osman I, Orkhan, and Murad I, the Ottomans began a series of rapid conquests. Sultans often waged war to obtain more land and money to reward their loyal troops. In an attempt to halt their progress, the threatened Christian states of the Balkans amassed an army, but were defeated at Kosovo in 1389. Sultan Bayezid I exploited this victory by annexing Bulgaria and invading Hungary, but expansion eastward was temporarily halted by Timur in 1402. Constantinople was finally taken by Mehmed II (the "Conqueror") in 1453.

The rise of the Ottomans 1300–1500

c.1300: Ottoman state founded by Osman | **1356:** Capture of Gallipoli; Ottomans advance into Europe | **1396:** Bayezid defeats Crusader army at Nicopolis | **1402:** Bayezid defeated by Timur at Ankara | **1453:** Turks take Constantinople

1326: Ottomans conquer Bursa | **1361:** Capture of Edirne (Adrianople) | **1389:** Serbs and Bosnians defeated at Kosovo | **1389:** Accession of Bayezid I | **1459:** Annexation of Serbia

1300 — 1350 — 1400 — 1450 — 1500

The Ottomans' rise to become a world power was based on their highly-trained army, seen here besieging Belgrade in 1456. The most feared troops were the janissaries, drawn from young slaves given in tribute and trained from childhood.

① Rise of the Ottoman Empire c.1300–1500

- nucleus of Ottoman Empire c.1300
- conquests of Osman I, c.1300–26
- conquests of Orkhan, 1326–62
- conquests of Murad I, 1362–89
- conquests of Bayezid I, 1389–1402
- Ottoman eastern frontier following Timur's invasion 1402
- Ottoman territory by 1451
- further Ottoman conquest by 1481
- vassal of Ottoman Empire by 1481
- under Venetian control c.1450
- Holy Roman Empire c.1480
- ---- frontiers in 1481
- ⚔ battle, with date
- ⟨⟩ siege, with date

1517: Selim I orders construction of Ottoman fleet at Suez; Portuguese attack on Jedda repulsed | **1538:** Ottomans subjugate Yemen and Aden and take occupy port of Basra on Persian Gulf | **1546:** Ottomans retake Basra after revolt | **1551–52:** Ottomans fail to oust Portuguese from Hormuz

1516–17: Ottomans conquer Syria, Egypt, the Hejaz, and Yemen | **1525:** Ottomans again defeat Portuguese fleet in Red Sea | **1538:** Failure of Ottoman blockade of Portuguese at Diu

1510 — 1520 — 1530 — 1540 — 1550 — 1560

Ottoman attempts to control trade in the Indian Ocean

Trade in the Indian Ocean

With their conquest in the early 16th century of Egypt, Mesopotamia, the Hejaz, and Yemen, the Ottomans gained control of trade through the Persian Gulf and the Red Sea. Ships carrying goods such as spices from India and the Moluccas and slaves from East Africa, docked at Aden and Jedda; from there they were transported overland to the markets of Cairo, Aleppo, Damascus, and north into Anatolia. Responding to persistent threats to their trade from the Portuguese, the Ottomans assembled fleets at Suez and Basra and made several attempts to oust the Portuguese from the region, but without lasting success.

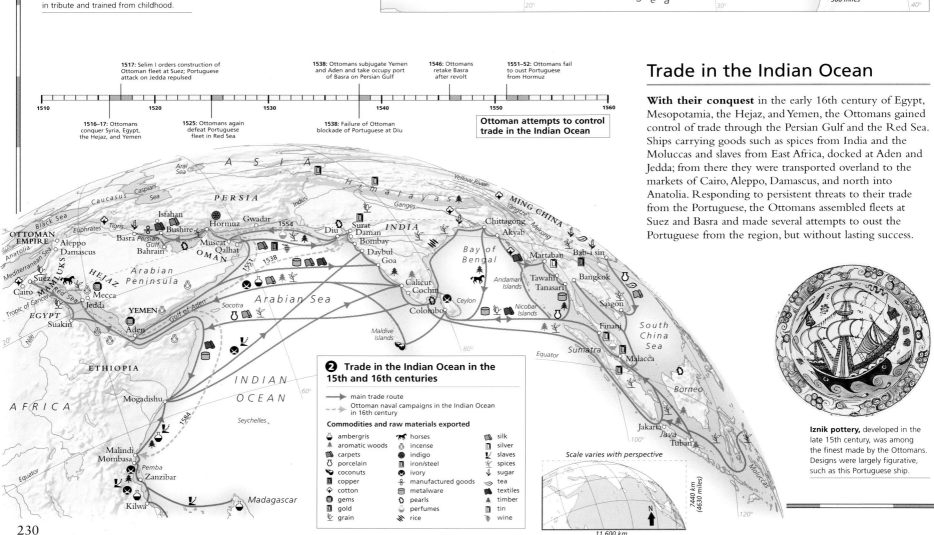

② Trade in the Indian Ocean in the 15th and 16th centuries

- → main trade route
- - - Ottoman naval campaigns in the Indian Ocean in 16th century

Commodities and raw materials exported

ambergris	horses	silk
aromatic woods	incense	silver
carpets	indigo	slaves
porcelain	iron/steel	spices
coconuts	ivory	sugar
copper	manufactured goods	tea
cotton	metalware	textiles
gems	pearls	timber
gold	perfumes	tin
grain	rice	wine

Scale varies with perspective

7440 km (4630 miles)

11,600 km (7210 miles)

Iznik pottery, developed in the late 15th century, was among the finest made by the Ottomans. Designs were largely figurative, such as this Portuguese ship.

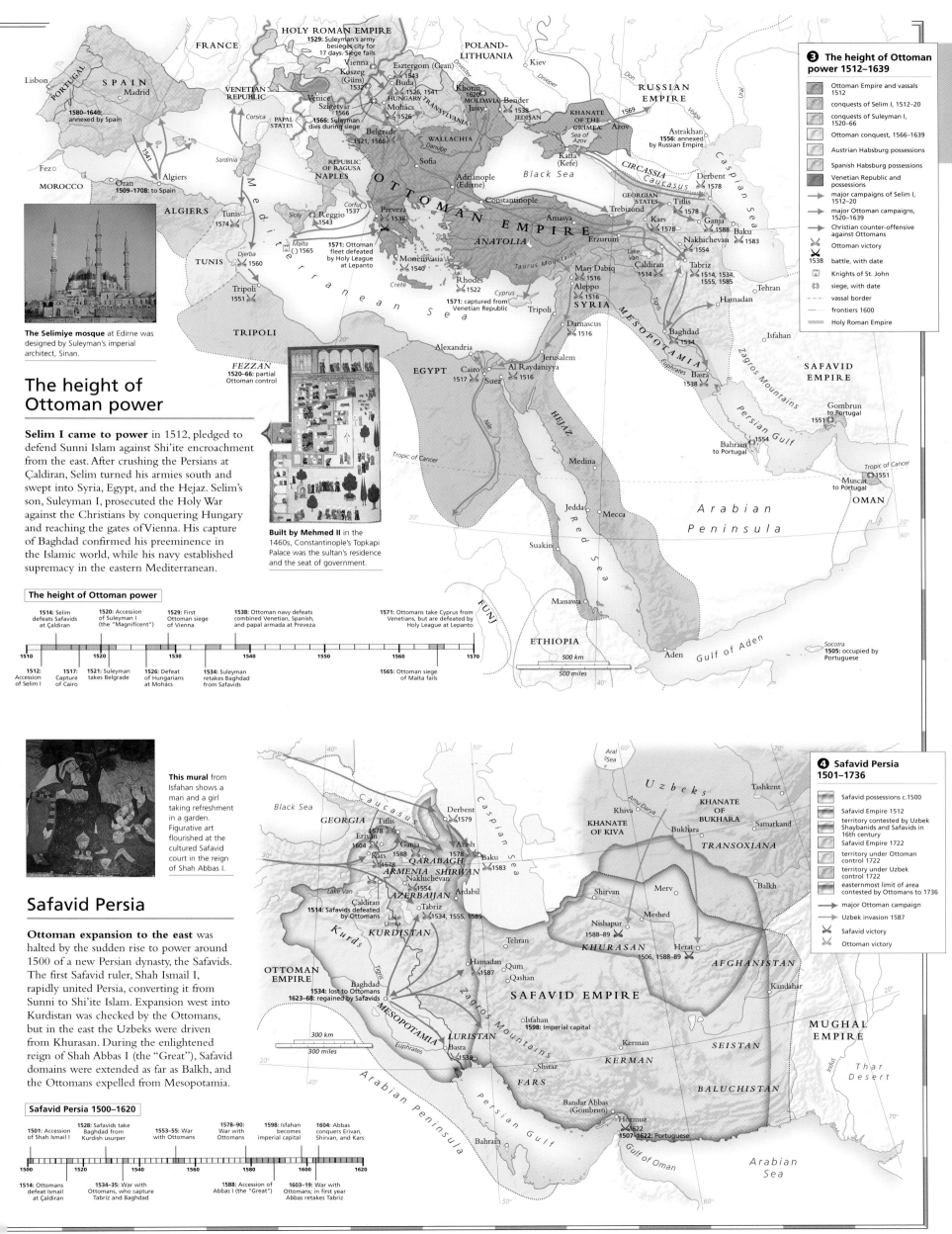

The height of Ottoman power

Selim I came to power in 1512, pledged to defend Sunni Islam against Shi'ite encroachment from the east. After crushing the Persians at Çaldiran, Selim turned his armies south and swept into Syria, Egypt, and the Hejaz. Selim's son, Suleyman I, prosecuted the Holy War against the Christians by conquering Hungary and reaching the gates of Vienna. His capture of Baghdad confirmed his preeminence in the Islamic world, while his navy established supremacy in the eastern Mediterranean.

The Selimiye mosque at Edirne was designed by Suleyman's imperial architect, Sinan.

Built by Mehmed II in the 1460s, Constantinople's Topkapi Palace was the sultan's residence and the seat of government.

❸ The height of Ottoman power 1512–1639

- Ottoman Empire and vassals 1512
- conquests of Selim I, 1512–20
- conquests of Suleyman I, 1520–66
- Ottoman conquest, 1566–1639
- Austrian Habsburg possessions
- Spanish Habsburg possessions
- Venetian Republic and possessions
- major campaigns of Selim I, 1512–20
- major Ottoman campaigns, 1520–1639
- Christian counter-offensive against Ottomans
- Ottoman victory
- 1538 battle, with date
- Knights of St. John
- siege, with date
- vassal border
- frontiers 1600
- Holy Roman Empire

The height of Ottoman power

- 1510
- **1512:** Accession of Selim I
- **1514:** Selim defeats Safavids at Çaldiran
- **1517:** Capture of Cairo
- 1520
- **1520:** Accession of Suleyman I (the "Magnificent")
- **1521:** Suleyman takes Belgrade
- **1526:** Defeat of Hungarians at Mohács
- 1530
- **1529:** First Ottoman siege of Vienna
- **1534:** Suleyman retakes Baghdad from Safavids
- 1540
- **1538:** Ottoman navy defeats combined Venetian, Spanish, and papal armada at Preveza
- 1550
- 1560
- **1565:** Ottoman siege of Malta fails
- **1571:** Ottomans take Cyprus from Venetians, but are defeated by Holy League at Lepanto
- 1570

Safavid Persia

Ottoman expansion to the east was halted by the sudden rise to power around 1500 of a new Persian dynasty, the Safavids. The first Safavid ruler, Shah Ismail I, rapidly united Persia, converting it from Sunni to Shi'ite Islam. Expansion west into Kurdistan was checked by the Ottomans, but in the east the Uzbeks were driven from Khurasan. During the enlightened reign of Shah Abbas I (the "Great"), Safavid domains were extended as far as Balkh, and the Ottomans expelled from Mesopotamia.

This mural from Isfahan shows a man and a girl taking refreshment in a garden. Figurative art flourished at the cultured Safavid court in the reign of Shah Abbas I.

❹ Safavid Persia 1501–1736

- Safavid possessions c.1500
- Safavid Empire 1512
- territory contested by Uzbek Shaybanids and Safavids in 16th century
- Safavid Empire 1722
- territory under Ottoman control 1722
- territory under Uzbek control 1722
- easternmost limit of area contested by Ottomans to 1736
- major Ottoman campaign
- Uzbek invasion 1587
- Safavid victory
- Ottoman victory

Safavid Persia 1500–1620

- 1500
- **1501:** Accession of Shah Ismail I
- **1514:** Ottomans defeat Ismail at Çaldiran
- 1520
- **1528:** Safavids take Baghdad from Kurdish usurper
- **1534–35:** War with Ottomans, who capture Tabriz and Baghdad
- 1540
- **1553–55:** War with Ottomans
- 1560
- **1578–90:** War with Ottomans
- **1588:** Accession of Abbas I (the "Great")
- 1580
- **1598:** Isfahan becomes imperial capital
- 1600
- **1603–19:** War with Ottomans; in first year Abbas retakes Tabriz
- **1604:** Abbas conquers Erivan, Shirvan, and Kars
- 1620

231

THE DECLINE OF THE OTTOMANS

Abdul Hamid II failed to modernize his empire and was deposed by the Young Turks in 1908.

AT THE HEIGHT OF ITS POWER in the 16th century, the Ottoman Empire stretched from the gates of Vienna to the Indian Ocean and from the Crimea to Algiers. By the end of the 18th century the empire was shrinking, its power eroded by a loss of internal authority and by the ambitions of the major European powers. Attempts to westernize and strengthen the empire foundered, and when the Turks entered World War I *(see pp.206–207)*, on the side of the Central Powers, they had lost all their territories in Africa, and most of them in Europe. Defeat in the war brought the empire to an end: British and French mandates were imposed in Mesopotamia and the Levant, and Saudi Arabia became independent. The Turks, however, established a new national identity for themselves by driving the Greeks from Anatolia and creating the modern republic of Turkey in 1923.

The empire in decline 1800–1913

By 1900 Turkey was attracting European tourists, seen here against the backdrop of Constantinople's domes and minarets. Many Turks now wore Western dress and had adopted Western habits.

Under pressure from the West, attempts were made to modernize the empire, notably in the period 1839–76. In 1908 a movement for more liberal government, led by the Young Turks, succeeded in deposing the sultan, Abdul Hamid II. The Ottomans' hold over the Balkans was broken by Greece gaining independence in 1830, followed by Serbia, Montenegro, and Romania in 1878, while Russia challenged Turkish control of the Black Sea. In Africa, the French seized Algeria and Tunisia, Britain occupied Egypt, and the Italians conquered Libya.

❶ The Ottoman Empire 1800–1913 ▶

- area lost by 1832
- area autonomous or under only nominal control by 1833
- area lost by 1882
- autonomous 1878; lost 1908
- area lost by 1913
- Ottoman Empire 1913

The Ottoman Empire 1815–1913

- **1830:** Algiers occupied by France
- **1840:** Empire under threat from Egypt; saved by British and Austrian intervention
- **1854–56:** Crimean War; French and British come to aid of Turks against Russia
- **1878:** Cyprus occupied by British
- **1881:** Tunisia occupied by French
- **1908:** Bosnia-Herzegovina annexed by Austro-Hungarian Empire
- **1912–13:** Balkan Wars

1815 · 1825 · 1835 · 1845 · 1855 · 1865 · 1875 · 1885 · 1895 · 1905 · 1915

- **1821–30:** Greek War of Independence
- **1839–61:** Sultan Abdul Majid I makes series of liberal *Tanzimat* decrees
- **1853:** Russians defeat Turkish navy at Sinop
- **1878:** Independence of Serbia, Montenegro, and Romania recognized at Berlin Congress
- **1882:** Egypt occupied by British
- **1908:** Bulgaria declares independence
- **1911:** Libya occupied by Italy

EGYPT AND THE SUEZ CANAL

An early sign of Ottoman decline was Muhammad Ali's establishment of a virtually independent Egypt after 1805. He and his successors encouraged European investment and in 1859 Egypt became the site of one of the century's greatest feats of engineering. The brainchild of a French diplomat, Ferdinand de Lesseps, who supervised its construction, the 105-mile Suez Canal linked the Mediterranean to the Red Sea. Cutting the sea journey from Britain to India by 6,000 miles, the canal opened in 1869 and became one of the world's most heavily used waterways. In 1875 Britain paid the bankrupt Khedive of Egypt four million pounds for a controlling interest in the canal, thus securing a lifeline to its empire in the east.

On the day after the opening ceremony in Port Said, 68 ships, headed by the *Aigle* with Empress Eugénie of France on board, sailed the length of the Suez Canal. This painting is from Eugénie's souvenir album of the event.

Emir Faisal, seen here with his bodyguard, united the Arabs and in 1916, together with Colonel T. E. Lawrence, led a successful revolt against the Turks. After the war Faisal became king of Iraq under the British mandate.

World War I

- **Feb 1915:** First Turkish attempt to capture Suez
- **Feb 1916:** Russians take Erzurum
- **Apr 1916:** British surrender at Kut al Amara
- **Mar 1917:** British take Baghdad
- **Oct 1918:** Turks surrender

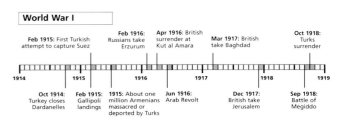

1914 · 1915 · 1916 · 1917 · 1918 · 1919

- **Oct 1914:** Turkey closes Dardanelles
- **Feb 1915:** Gallipoli landings
- **1915:** About one million Armenians massacred or deported by Turks
- **Jun 1916:** Arab Revolt
- **Dec 1917:** British take Jerusalem
- **Sep 1918:** Battle of Megiddo

The partition of the Ottoman Empire 1918–23

Following the Turkish surrender in 1918, Syria became a French mandate while Palestine, Iraq, and Transjordan became British mandates. By the Treaty of Sèvres (1920), Turkey was forced to give up all her non-Turkish lands; eastern Thrace and Smyrna were given to Greece. The Turkish sultan accepted the Treaty's conditions, but the Allies had underestimated the fervor of the Turkish Nationalists; led by Kemal Pasha, they launched an attack on the Greek invaders, driving them out of Anatolia. The present frontiers of Turkey were recognized by the Treaty of Lausanne in 1923. In the same year the last Ottoman sultan, Mehmed VI, was overthrown and Turkey became a republic.

In an attempt to cover the retreat of their own troops, a Greek cavalry detachment charges a Turkish force near Smyrna in 1922. Under the inspired leadership of Mustafa Kemal Pasha, Turkish Nationalists fought a fierce three-year campaign, eventually regaining eastern Thrace and Smyrna.

❸ Southwest Asia after the First World War

☐ British mandate	☐ area annexed by Turkey 1921
☐ French mandate	☐ area restored to Turkey by Treaty of Lausanne (1923)
☐ Turkey after Treaty of Sèvres (1920)	— international border 1926

Postwar Turkey

The Arabian Peninsula 1750–1950 (timeline)

May 1919: Greek forces land at Smyrna
Aug 1919: Kemal Pasha breaks away from authority of Istanbul government
Aug 1920: Treaty of Sèvres
Dec 1920: Armenia cedes half its territory to Turkey
1921: Turkish Nationalist government established in Ankara
Sep 1922: Turks recapture Smyrna
Jul 1923: Treaty of Lausanne recognizes Turkish sovereignty over Smyrna and eastern Thrace
Oct 1923: Turkish Republic proclaimed with Kemal Pasha as first president

The emergence of Saudi Arabia 1800–1932

The modern Saudi state has its origins in the 18th century when the Wahhabis – an orthodox sect attempting to preserve the "purity of Islam"– united the previously divided Arab tribes. Led by the Saud family, the Wahhabis raided into Mesopotamia, the Hejaz, and Syria, capturing Mecca in 1806. But in a series of campaigns (1812–18), the Wahhabis were crushed by armies from Egypt and Ottoman forces from the north. In 1902, Abd al-Aziz Ibn Saud led a Saudi resurgence. The Saud family gradually consolidated its power within the peninsula and, in 1932, the kingdom of Saudi Arabia was proclaimed.

Abd al-Aziz Ibn Saud regained his family's homelands around Riyadh, then founded a kingdom that he ruled until his death in 1953.

(timeline)
c.1750: Emergence of Wahhabi movement
1806: Wahhabis take Mecca
1812: Egyptian forces retake Mecca and Medina
c.1880: Birth of Abd al-Aziz Ibn Saud in Kuwait
1902: Ibn Saud reclaims his patrimony by capturing Riyadh
1932: Kingdom of Saudi Arabia proclaimed
1818: Wahhabi resistance crushed by Egyptian forces
1843: Fortunes of Saud family restored by Faisal
1887: Riyadh taken by Rashidis, who dominate Nejd
1926: Ibn Saud crowns himself King of the Hejaz and Sultan of Nejd
1938: First oil exported from Saudi

❹ The formation of Saudi Arabia

MAIN MAP: 1912–1932
☐ Ottoman Empire c.1912
☐ Saudi territory c.1912
☐ Saudi gains 1913
☐ Saudi gains 1920
☐ Saudi gains 1921–22
☐ Saudi gains 1924–25

INSET: 1800–1812
☐ Ottoman Empire c.1800
☐ Wahhabi territory c.1800
→ Wahhabi expansion in early 19th century
1805 date captured by Wahhabis

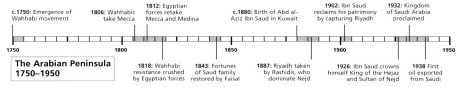

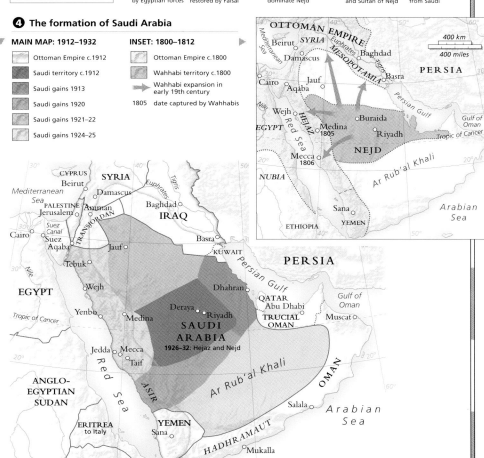

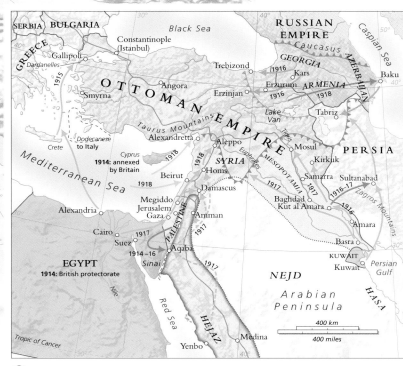

❷ The First World War in Southwest Asia

☐ Ottoman Empire 1914	▲▲▲ Russian/Turkish front 1917
☐ British Empire 1914	▲▲▲ Turkish lines at surrender, 1918
☐ Russian Empire 1914	→ Turkish forces
☐ area of Arab revolt (1916–18)	→ Allied forces
	---- Allied forces under Col T.E. Lawrence
	→ French forces
	→ Russian forces
	— rail line

British and Australian troops (left) land on the Gallipoli peninsula. They abandoned the offensive in January 1916, having lost over 250,000 men.

French General d'Esperey lands in Istanbul in 1919 to be greeted by British General Wilson (below). Behind Wilson stands Kemal Pasha (later known as Atatürk), who was to lead Turkey in its struggle to become a modern state.

World War I 1914–18

The Turks began the war well, pinning down an Allied force on the Gallipoli peninsula for nine months and halting the British in Mesopotamia. But they twice failed to take Suez, and in 1916 their Third Army was virtually destroyed by the Russians at Erzurum. The end came in 1918 when British forces, supported by Arab irregulars, drove north in a two-pronged attack, capturing Baghdad and Jerusalem, and eventually reaching Damascus.

MODERN WEST ASIA

Yasser Arafat, the chairman of the PLO since 1969, led the fight for recognition of Palestinian rights.

THE HISTORY OF WEST ASIA after World War II was dominated by two factors: oil, and the creation of the state of Israel. The discovery of huge reserves of oil throughout the Gulf region had an enormous impact on the economies and political status of all the states concerned. The UN decision of 1947 to partition Palestine into two states to form a Jewish homeland sparked the Arab-Israeli conflicts, which continue to this day. Israel has been recognized by the PLO and by its neighbors Egypt and Jordan, but not by states such as Syria and Iraq, while southern Lebanon remains a battleground between Israel and Arab guerrilla forces. A further threat to the region's stability is the resurgence of Islam: fundamentalist principles inspire many groups opposed to Israel and to the influence of the US and the West.

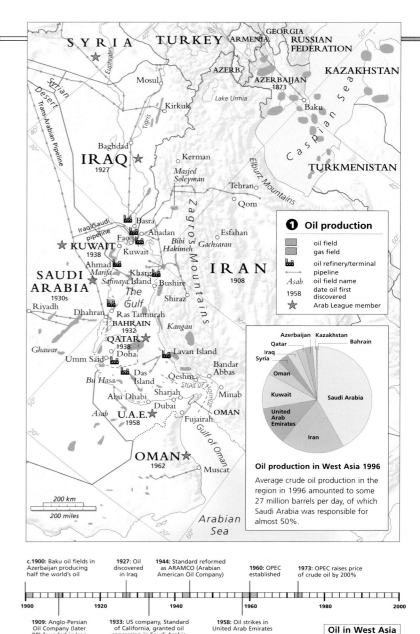

① Oil production

- oil field
- gas field
- oil refinery/terminal
- pipeline
- *Asab* oil field name
- 1958 date oil first discovered
- ★ Arab League member

Oil production in West Asia 1996

Average crude oil production in the region in 1996 amounted to some 27 million barrels per day, of which Saudi Arabia was responsible for almost 50%.

Oil production in the Gulf

The Gulf remains the world's most valuable and heavily exploited region of oil and natural gas production. As producers of 35% of the world's oil requirements by 1993, the Gulf states were able to exert powerful influence on the world's economies; increases in the price of crude oil, such as that imposed by OPEC (the Organization of Petroleum Exporting Countries) in 1973–74, had worldwide repercussions and regional conflicts that disrupt oil supplies were a cause for worldwide concern. In the 1990s, new oilfields in the Caspian Sea region north of the Gulf attracted substantial foreign investment.

The kingdom of Saudi Arabia contains an estimated 25.9% of the world's known oil reserves, 3.7% of its gas reserves, and is the world's leading oil exporter.

c.1900: Baku oil fields in Azerbaijan producing half the world's oil	1927: Oil discovered in Iraq	1944: Standard reformed as ARAMCO (Arabian American Oil Company)	1960: OPEC established	1973: OPEC raises price of crude oil by 200%	
1909: Anglo-Persian Oil Company (later BP) founded in Iran	1933: US company, Standard of California, granted oil concession in Saudi Arabia	1958: Oil strikes in United Arab Emirates			**Oil in West Asia**

1900 · 1920 · 1940 · 1960 · 1980 · 2000

Arab-Israeli wars

The state of Israel was established in May 1948. The next day five Arab armies invaded; Israel survived, but its refusal to acknowledge Palestinian claims, and the refusal of Arab states to recognize Israel, led to a succession of wars in which the Arabs were defeated and Israel occupied more territories. Disputes over these territories, and the Palestinian problem, continue to destabilize the region, despite an Egyptian-Israeli peace treaty in 1979. In 1993 Israel and the PLO signed an agreement in Oslo. Israel promised to give up land for peace, but putting this into practice is a long and difficult task.

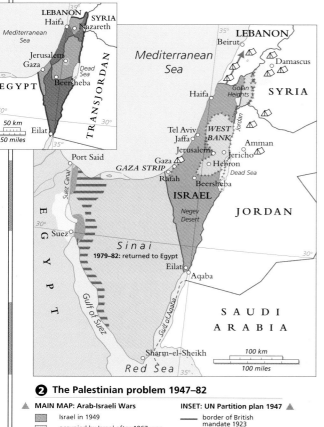

② The Palestinian problem 1947–82

▲ MAIN MAP: Arab-Israeli Wars
- Israel in 1949
- occupied by Israel after 1967 war
- occupied by Israel after 1973 war
- occupied by Israel after 1967 war reoccupied by Egypt after 1973 war
- demilitarized zone held by UN after Israel-Syria agreement, 1974, and 2nd Sinai agreement, 1975
- → route of Israel's invasion of Lebanon 1982
- ⌂ Palestinian refugee camps 1982
- +++++ disputed border

INSET: UN Partition plan 1947 ▲
- border of British mandate 1923
- proposed Arab State
- proposed Jewish State
- proposed international zone

Arab-Israeli Wars

1956: Suez crisis; Israel, France, and Britain invade Egypt	1967: Six Day War; Israel takes Sinai, Gaza, Golan Heights, West Bank, and Jerusalem	1979: Egypt and Israel sign peace treaty based on Camp David accords	
1947: UN partition of Palestine	1948: Invading Arab armies repulsed; some 725,000 Arabs flee Palestine	1973: Yom Kippur War	1982: Israel invades Lebanon

1940 · 1950 · 1960 · 1970 · 1980 · 1990

Israeli trucks transport Egyptian prisoners from the battlefield in the Six Day War of 1967. In one of modern history's most efficient military operations, Israel defeated the combined forces of Egypt, Jordan, and Syria in six days. Launching a lightning air strike, Israel destroyed the Arab air forces, while its tanks swept into Sinai.

Jewish and Palestinian Migrations

③ Migration 1947–96

▲ SMALL MAP: Palestinian emigration
→ 1947–48

▼ LARGE MAP: Jewish migration to Israel
→ 1948–71
→ 1972–96

Jewish immigration to Palestine from Europe increased sharply in the 1930s and 1940s as a result of persecution and the Holocaust. While the Jews accepted the UN partition plan, the Arabs declined it; in the subsequent civil war and Israel's 1948–49 war against the invading Arab states, tens of thousands of Palestinians fled their homes and became refugees (*left*). Since 1948 Israel has absorbed even greater numbers of immigrants (*below*).

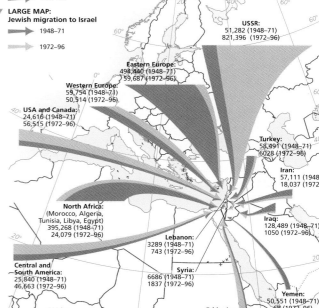

USSR: 51,282 (1948–71) 821,396 (1972–96)

Eastern Europe: 494,440 (1948–71) 59,687 (1972–96)

Western Europe: 59,754 (1948–71) 50,514 (1972–96)

USA and Canada: 24,616 (1948–71) 56,515 (1972–96)

Turkey: 58,491 (1948–71) 6028 (1972–96)

Iran: 57,111 (1948–71) 18,037 (1972–96)

North Africa: (Morocco, Algeria, Tunisia, Libya, Egypt) 395,268 (1948–71) 24,079 (1972–96)

Iraq: 128,489 (1948–71) 1050 (1972–96)

Lebanon: 3289 (1948–71) 743 (1972–96)

Central and South America: 25,840 (1948–71) 46,663 (1972–96)

Syria: 6686 (1948–71) 1837 (1972–96)

Yemen: 50,551 (1948–71) 68 (1972–96)

Ethiopia: 167 (1948–71) 49,862 (1972–1996)

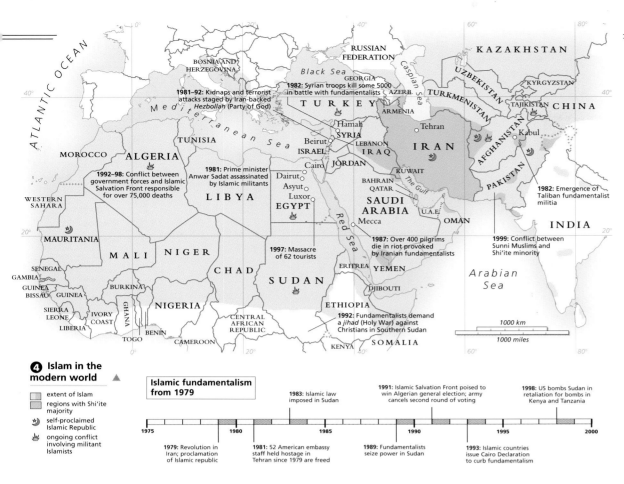

④ Islam in the modern world ▲

- ☐ extent of Islam
- ☐ regions with Shi'ite majority
- ☪ self-proclaimed Islamic Republic
- ⚔ ongoing conflict involving militant Islamists

Islamic fundamentalism

The current resurgence of Islam was inspired by Ayatollah Khomeini, ruler of the new Islamic Republic of Iran, who proclaimed a form of government in which the state is a religious institution and is ruled accordingly. Islamic fundamentalist movements seek to preserve the basic elements ("fundamentals") of the Sharia or Islamic law, and to oppose liberalism. The numerous manifestations of this resurgence – especially in the Sudan, Egypt, Algeria, and Afghanistan – have caused concern in the West and the former Soviet Union that Islamic fundamentalism might threaten the world's economic and political status quo.

Amid scenes of uncontrollable grief, Ayatollah Khomeini, Iran's leader and symbol of the Iranian revolution, is escorted to his grave by mourners in June 1989.

Islamic fundamentalism from 1979

1983: Islamic law imposed in Sudan

1991: Islamic Salvation Front poised to win Algerian general election; army cancels second round of voting

1998: US bombs Sudan in retaliation for bombs in Kenya and Tanzania

1975 — 1980 — 1985 — 1990 — 1995 — 2000

1979: Revolution in Iran; proclamation of Islamic republic

1981: 52 American embassy staff held hostage in Tehran since 1979 are freed

1989: Fundamentalists seize power in Sudan

1993: Islamic countries issue Cairo Declaration to curb fundamentalism

Conflict in the Gulf

The resurgence of Shi'ite Islam in Iran and a dispute over territory led Saddam Hussein, ruler of predominantly Sunni Iraq, to invade his neighbor in 1980. The bloody but inconclusive Iran-Iraq War lasted until 1988, when the UN brokered a cease-fire, making it the 20th century's longest conventional war. In 1990, with the intention of gaining control of Kuwait's oil reserves to rebuild his war machine, Saddam invaded Kuwait. The UN condemned the move, demanding Iraq's withdrawal. Iraq failed to comply and in January 1991 a US-led coalition of 29 states launched air and ground attacks. Kuwait was liberated and the defeated Iraqis subjected to harsh economic sanctions, but continued US–Iraqi hostility could plunge the region into another war.

Thousands of huge posters depicting Saddam Hussein in a warlike posture have been erected throughout Iraq. Behind the gun-toting president, his victorious armies can be seen in action.

The plight of the Kurds

Kurdish territories overlap large areas of Turkey, Iran, and Iraq. As a result of Kurdish insurgents allying with Iran during the Iran-Iraq War, in 1988 Saddam Hussein unleashed a campaign of vengeance against them involving the use of chemical weapons. Following Iraq's defeat in the Gulf War, a Kurdish rebellion erupted in northern Iraq which was brutally suppressed by Saddam. Over one million Kurds fled into Turkey and Iran. In May 1992 the Kurds elected their own government and became a semiindependent political entity.

Kurdish refugees flee across the mountains to Turkey in 1991 in the wake of Saddam Hussein's chemical attacks on their communities in northern Iraq.

Oil pollution

The Gulf wars left a terrible legacy of oil pollution. As Iraq's forces withdrew from Kuwait in 1991, they set on fire almost all of the country's 950 oil wells. The subsequent conflagration left a dense pall of black smoke over the entire region and an oil slick covering huge areas of the Gulf. Many of the blazing wells continued to burn for months.

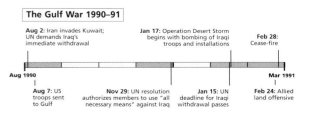

Pictures of seabirds like this cormorant, helpless in the face of the tide of oil released into the Gulf, became powerful emblems of the ecological damage caused by the Gulf War.

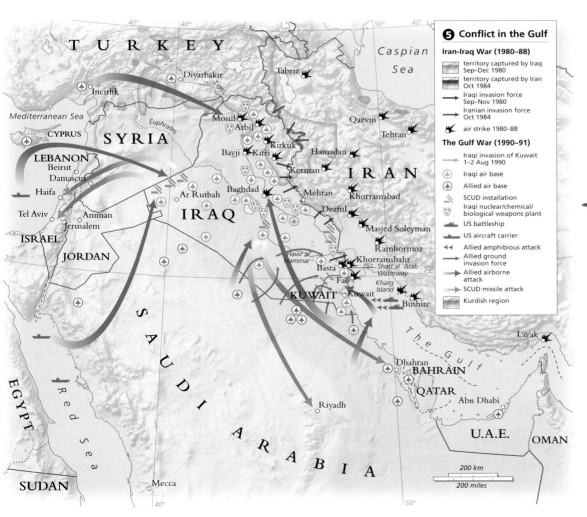

⑤ Conflict in the Gulf

Iran-Iraq War (1980–88)
- ☐ territory captured by Iraq Sep–Dec 1980
- ☐ territory captured by Iran Oct 1984
- → Iraqi invasion force Sep–Nov 1980
- → Iranian invasion force Oct 1984
- ✈ air strike 1980–88

The Gulf War (1990–91)
- → Iraqi invasion of Kuwait 1–2 Aug 1990
- Iraqi air base
- Allied air base
- SCUD installation
- Iraqi nuclear/chemical/ biological weapons plant
- US battleship
- US aircraft carrier
- Allied amphibious attack
- Allied ground invasion force
- Allied airborne attack
- SCUD missile attack
- ☐ Kurdish region

The Gulf War 1990–91

Aug 2: Iraq invades Kuwait; UN demands Iraq's immediate withdrawal

Jan 17: Operation Desert Storm begins with bombing of Iraqi troops and installations

Feb 28: Cease-fire

Aug 1990 — Mar 1991

Aug 7: US troops sent to Gulf

Nov 29: UN resolution authorizes members to use "all necessary means" against Iraq

Jan 15: UN deadline for Iraqi withdrawal passes

Feb 24: Allied land offensive

SOUTH AND SOUTHEAST ASIA
REGIONAL HISTORY

THE HISTORICAL LANDSCAPE

LYING LARGELY BETWEEN THE TROPICS, this region enjoys a complex geography incorporating the world's greatest mountains, some of the world's largest river systems and tropical rain forests, and the globe's most extensive archipelago. During the last Ice Age, lower sea levels rendered the shallow seas surrounding Southeast Asia into dry land, allowing humans to migrate from the Asian mainland through the islands of Southeast Asia. The Indian subcontinent was home to some of the world's earliest civilizations, founded on the banks of the Indus and Ganges rivers. Historically, the sheer size of the Indian subcontinent and variety of its peoples have attracted and resisted political unity in equal parts, and Hinduism, Buddhism, and Islam have provided the inspiration for remarkable eras of cultural, economic, and political efflorescence. The region is well-endowed with valuable natural resources and has attracted and fostered trade since the earliest times. Only in the recent centuries of colonial rivalry, have concerns about self-determination been overtaken by the need to meet the demands of soaring population growth.

The Thar Desert in western India is a small remnant of the larger Great Indian Sand Desert, that covered much of western India at the end of the last Ice Age.

The Mekong is one of many great rivers which radiate south and east from the Plateau of Tibet. The fluvial soils that accumulate around the lower reaches of these rivers are exceptionally fertile, and have long been utilized by humans for agriculture – especially the cultivation of rice.

The Himalayas have always been a barrier to human migration between South and East Asia. The first settlers entered southern Asia by passes that still provide the only means of traversing the mountains.

The Indus River flows from the Himalayas, through mountain meadows and down across fertile plains to the sea. The Indus Valley civilizations were the most sophisticated early societies in southern Asia.

South and Southeast Asia: 18,000 years ago

Climatic changes and a global fall in sea level affected South and Southeastern Asia. The drop in sea levels turned much of the continental shelf surrounding the islands of Southeast Asia into dry land, forming a wide land bridge that encompassed Java, Sumatra, and Borneo. Rain forests covered a much smaller area, and many forested zones became grasslands and scrub. In India, sand dunes in the Thar Desert expanded to occupy a much larger area than today.

Central
Siberian
Plateau

Arctic Circle

Ural Mountains

West
Siberian
Plain

S i b e r i a

Sea of Okhotsk

Kamchatka

NORTH AMERICAN PLATE

EURASIAN PLATE

Aral
Sea

Altai Mountains

Dzungaria

Great Khingan Range

Manchurian
Plain

Amur

Sakhalin

Kurile Islands

Kurile Trench

Tien Shan

Gobi

A S I A

Hokkaido

Tarim
Basin

Qilian Shan

Yellow River

Ordos
Desert

Yellow River

Bo Hai

Sea of Japan

Korea

Honshu

Kunlun Mountains

Plateau
of Tibet

Qin Ling

Great Plain
of China

Yangtze

Yellow
Sea

Japan Trench

Himalayas

Red
Basin

Nan Ling

East China
Sea

Ryukyu Islands

EURASIAN PLATE

PHILIPPINE PLATE

PACIFIC PLATE

Tropic of Cancer

Ganges

Brahmaputra

Patkai Range

Irrawaddy

Xi Jiang

Altao Shan

Taiwan

PHILIPPINE PLATE

Eastern Ghats

Arakan Yoma

Salween

Mekong

Gulf of
Tongking

Hainan

P A C I F I C

O C E A N

Bay of
Bengal

Colder, drier climates affected the vegetation of Southeast Asia. The rain forests that grew to blanket much of the area, covered much smaller portions of the continent.

South
China
Sea

Luzon

Philippine
Basin

Philippine Trench

Andaman
Islands

Isthmus of Kra

South China Basin

Palawan

Yap Trench

Andaman
Sea

Gulf of
Thailand

Sulu
Sea

Mindanao

Sri Lanka

Sri Lanka and India were linked by dry land at the end of the last Ice Age. Rising sea levels flooded the link between them, and made Sri Lanka an island, although even today the two are only separated by a narrow expanse of shallow sea.

Nicobar
Islands

Malay Peninsula

18,000 years ago, many of the shallow seas surrounding maritime Southeast Asia were dry land. The Sunda Shelf was a low-lying, thickly forested plain, and many of the East Indian islands were joined together as a long peninsula which stretched eastward to Australia.

Celebes
Sea

Halmahera

EURASIAN PLATE

Strait of Malacca

Sunda
Shelf

Borneo

Celebes

Seram

PACIFIC PLATE

Equator

Ninetyeast Ridge

INDO-AUSTRALIAN PLATE

S U N D A

The Sunda Shelf was dissected by a complex river system; all of these ancient rivers were drowned when sea levels rose.

Makassar Strait

INDO-AUSTRALIAN PLATE

New
Guinea

Ceylon Plain

Cocos
Basin

Sumatra

E a s t   I n d i e s

Banda
Sea

Molluccas

Java Trench

Java

Bali

Flores

Timor

Arafura Sea

O C E A N

237

SOUTH AND SOUTHEAST ASIA
EXPLORATION AND MAPPING

THE RELIGIONS OF SOUTH ASIA all have a long tradition of cosmography, though surviving maps are of relatively recent date. While some early maps may have related to secular themes, most would have been associated with religion and the place of humankind in a greater universe, reflecting the sacred geography of the Hindu, Jain, and Buddhist traditions. Despite the sophistication of Indian science and the great distances traveled by Indian – especially Buddhist – missionaries and merchants, there is little evidence of conventional geographical mapping until well after the establishment of Islam in the region. Following the establishment of the Portuguese in western India after 1498, European colonists, with competing territorial claims, spurred on the Western mapping of South and Southeast Asia. Commercial, economic, and military motives, combined with a zeal for knowledge, led to the British Survey of India from 1767, an epic project to map and define their eastern empire.

This 18th-century Hindu globe shows the heavens (in the top half) and the earthly realm (below).

The cosmographic tradition

A Jain diagram of the universe shows Mount Meru surrounded by concentric circles representing different continents and oceans.

The cosmographic conceptions of Hinduism, Buddhism, and Jainism, which attempted to locate the sacred places of this world in an imagined universe, were remarkably complex. Within each of them, Jambudvipa – the world inhabited by humans – formed only a very small part. In all cultures of Asia there is a strong belief that the fortunes of humans are affected by extraterrestrial forces whose influence can be foretold, in part, through astrology, with which astronomy was closely associated. Thus, mapping the heavens (on an astrolabe or other astronomical instruments) was a much more important concern than the geographic mapping of topography.

The lotus flower, redrawn here by Francis Wilford in 1805, was for Buddhists a symbol of the universe.

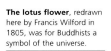

Indigenous mapping of South and Southeast Asia

Scarcely any surviving indigenous maps of the region are earlier than the 16th century. Maps were drawn for a variety of reasons: to provide information for the military; to illustrate itineraries or journeys; to legitimize territorial possessions. Maritime navigation charts from Gujarat date to the 17th century. Yet few surviving maps are strictly geographical, and virtually none are drawn to a fixed scale. Cosmographic views were sometimes combined with geographical knowledge of the known world.

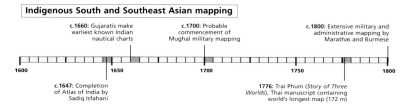

Indigenous South and Southeast Asian mapping

c.1660: Gujaratis make earliest known Indian nautical charts

c.1700: Probable commencement of Mughal military mapping

c.1800: Extensive military and administrative mapping by Marathas and Burmese

1600   1650   1700   1750   1800

c.1647: Completion of Atlas of India by Sadiq Isfahani

1776: Trai Phum (Story of Three Worlds), Thai manuscript containing world's longest map (172 m)

The astronomical observatory at Jaipur was one of five built by the Rajput king Sawai Jai Singh between 1722 and 1739. It contained remarkably accurate masonry instruments.

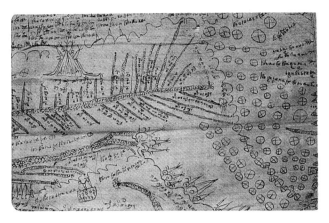

The sacred map of the Sundanese chiefdom of Timbanganten in western Java (left) was drawn in the late 16th century. It is still venerated by local villagers for its protective powers against the volcano clearly depicted on the left of the map.

The Mughal Emperor Jahangir is shown embracing Shah Abbas of Persia on a geographic globe, based on an Elizabethan model brought to the court by the first English ambassador in 1615 (right).

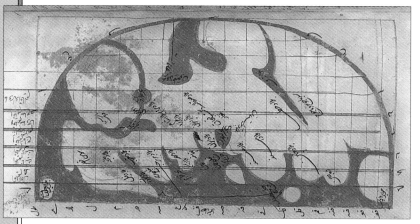

An encyclopedic work in Persian by Sadiq Isfahani of Jaunpur in northern India was finished in 1647. The section on travel contains a map (left) of the "inhabited quarter" (Africa and Eurasia), drawn in the traditional style of Islamic cosmography.

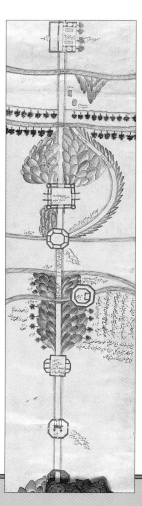

The detail (right) is from a Mughal map showing the route from Delhi to Kandahar by means of a system of straight lines and nodal points.

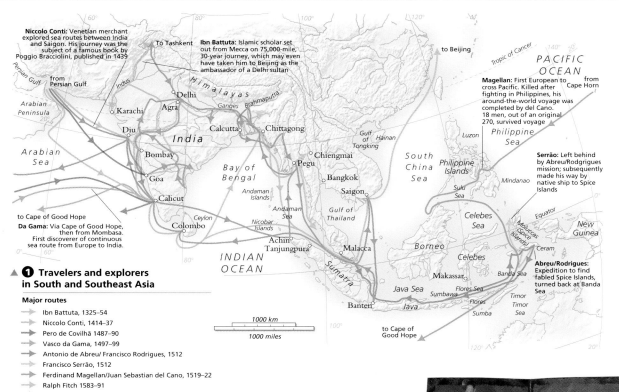

Niccolo Conti: Venetian merchant explored sea routes between India and Saigon. His journey was the subject of a famous book by Poggio Bracciolini, published in 1439

Ibn Battuta: Islamic scholar set out from Mecca on 75,000-mile, 30-year journey, which may even have taken him to Beijing as the ambassador of a Delhi sultan

Magellan: First European to cross Pacific. Killed after fighting in Philippines, his around-the-world voyage was completed by del Cano. 18 men, out of an original 270, survived voyage

Serrão: Left behind by Abreu/Rodrigues mission; subsequently made his way by native ship to Spice Islands

Abreu/Rodrigues: Expedition to find fabled Spice Islands, turned back at Banda Sea

Da Gama: Via Cape of Good Hope, then from Mombasa. First discoverer of continuous sea route from Europe to India.

1000 km
1000 miles

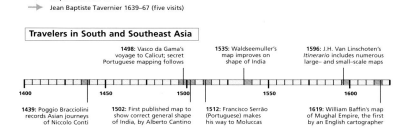

① Travelers and explorers in South and Southeast Asia

Major routes

→ Ibn Battuta, 1325–54
→ Niccolo Conti, 1414–37
→ Pero de Covilhã 1487–90
→ Vasco da Gama, 1497–99
→ Antonio de Abreu/ Francisco Rodrigues, 1512
→ Francisco Serrão, 1512
→ Ferdinand Magellan/Juan Sebastian del Cano, 1519–22
→ Ralph Fitch 1583–91
→ Jean Baptiste Tavernier 1639–67 (five visits)

Travelers in South and Southeast Asia

1498: Vasco da Gama's voyage to Calicut; secret Portuguese mapping follows

1535: Waldseemuller's map improves on shape of India

1596: J.H. Van Linschoten's *Itinerario* includes numerous large- and small-scale maps

1400 — 1450 — 1500 — 1550 — 1600

1439: Poggio Bracciolini records Asian journeys of Niccolo Conti

1502: First published map to show correct general shape of India, by Alberto Cantino

1512: Francisco Serrão (Portuguese) makes his way to Moluccas

1619: William Baffin's map of Mughal Empire, the first by an English cartographer

Travelers in South and Southeast Asia

The most celebrated medieval traveler in the region was Ibn Battuta of Tangier in the 14th century, even if his claim to have journeyed as far China may not be true. A century later Vasco da Gama was piloted across the Indian Ocean by a Gujarati Muslim. An even more southerly route opened up the richest prize of Southeast Asia – the fabled Spice Islands, subject of a Portuguese monopoly from 1512. In the 1590s the Dutch began to probe the southern Indian Ocean, using Mauritius as a staging-point.

This map of India and Ceylon dating from 1596 appears in Jan Huygen van Linschoten's *Itinerario*, a work instrumental in encouraging Dutch and English trade with India.

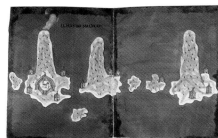

A Portuguese map of the Moluccas (1646) shows major settlements, volcanoes, and types of vegetation on the islands *(left)*.

This 17th-century French map shows the Kingdom of Siam, the Malay Peninsula, Sumatra, and Java, including political boundaries and areas of influence *(right)*.

The Survey of India

Although European mapping of India began in the wake of Vasco da Gama's 1498 landfall, it was not until after James Rennell's 1767 appointment as the first Surveyor General of the newly acquired province of Bengal that the British began to survey and map the country systematically. Initially, maps were based on observation, reports, and intelligence. From the late 18th century, British Army officers, such as Colin Mackenzie and William Lambton, began formal trigonometrical surveys. Sir George Everest, Lambton's successor, planned a vast network of triangulations, operated by a huge staff. He was careful to placate local princes, who feared that land surveys would infringe on their already eroded sovereignty.

James Rennell, surveyor of Bengal and Bihar, published this map in 1782, four years after his return to England. The cartouche depicts Britannia receiving the sacred scriptures of India from a Brahmin.

George Everest planned his trigonometrical triangulations on a grid overlying the entire subcontinent. His predecessor, William Lambton laid down the central north-south axis.

The Indian Atlas of J. & C. Walker was commissioned by the East India Company in 1823. It was produced at a scale of four miles to one inch.

The Survey of India

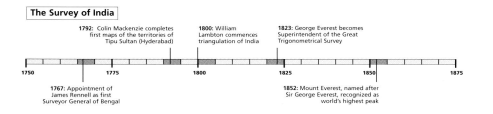

1792: Colin Mackenzie completes first maps of the territories of Tipu Sultan (Hyderabad)

1800: William Lambton commences triangulation of India

1823: George Everest becomes Superintendent of the Great Trigonometrical Survey

1750 — 1775 — 1800 — 1825 — 1850 — 1875

1767: Appointment of James Rennell as first Surveyor General of Bengal

1852: Mount Everest, named after Sir George Everest, recognized as world's highest peak

The scientific exploration of Southeast Asia

In 1854, the British naturalist Alfred Wallace set out for Singapore, and spent the next eight years traveling around the islands of the East Indies and New Guinea. He observed and collected a vast number of animal species, many previously unknown to western science. Most importantly, he observed a dramatic change in fauna at the center of the region; the eastern species are distinctly Australian, the western, Asian. He argued that the eastern part of the archipelago was therefore once part of a Pacific continent. The boundary between the two faunal regions came to be called the Wallace Line.

Alfred Wallace's account of his Southeast Asian travels, published in 1869, contains many fine illustrations of the species encountered on his journey, such as this black cockatoo from the Aru Islands.

The series of maps published in Alfred Wallace's account of his journey to Southeast Asia show, in great detail, the terrain which he explored. This map, of Ceram in the Moluccas, shows the region where he encountered and carefully observed many different types of birds of paradise, and first began to devise his theories about species evolution.

▼ ② The scientific journeys of Alfred Wallace in Southeast Asia

→ journeys of Alfred Wallace, 1854–62
--- Wallace "line"
- - - inferred ancient coastline
▢ eastern limit of transitional faunal zone

500 km
500 miles

EARLY CIVILIZATIONS OF SOUTH ASIA

This perforated pot from Mohenjo-Daro was used for carrying perfume.

COPPER AND BRONZE technology, reaching South and Southeast Asia during the 5th to 3rd millennia BCE, may have encouraged the development of urban civilizations in the Indus Valley in the mid–3rd millennium BCE. The cities of the Indus established trading links which extended to Mesopotamia. The cities' demise c.1500 BCE may have been caused by Sanskrit-speaking Aryan invaders, whose influence spread across India over the next thousand years. In the 5th century BCE, the region of Magadha gained ascendancy over the small states of the Ganges plain. Chandragupta Maurya established a vigorous new dynasty with its capital at Pataliputra in 321 BCE, which reached its apogee in the following century in the reign of Ashoka. In Southeast Asia, Sanskrit inscriptions from c.400 BCE are evidence of early Indian influence in the region.

The development of Harappan culture

This bust of a bearded man from Mohenjo-Daro c.2100 BCE, possibly represents a priest-king.

Harappan culture arose from agricultural and pastoral cultures in the hills of nearby Baluchistan during the late 4th millennium BCE and expanded from its core area on the Indus valley as far east as the Ganges River and south to present-day Maharashtra. Indus civilization is marked by regularly laid-out cities, built of baked brick, and dominated by imposing citadels, which contained religious, ceremonial and administrative buildings. Many of the streets of the residential areas had brick-roofed drains with regular inspection holes. Weights, measures, and bricks were all standardized, indicating a high level of cultural uniformity. The demise of Indus civilization may have been caused by invasion or by environmental change which disrupted the delicate balance between the cities and their agricultural base.

Pre-Mauryan cultures in South Asia

c.2500: Harappan Bronze Age civilization centered on Indus Valley until c.1500 BCE	**c.1500:** Vedic Aryans begin to spread over much of northwest and north of Indian subcontinent	**c.1000:** Iron technology starts to diffuse over much of India	**Late 6th-early 5th century:** Emergence of Buddhism and Hinduism
2500 BCE	2000	1500	1000	500 BCE

c.1000: Aryans begin shift from pastoral to agricultural lifestyle and establish a number of small states

Mid-6th century: Magadha emerges as preeminent state in India

---

❶ The citadel at Mohenjo-Daro

college
stupa
great bath
granary

N

200 meters
200 yards

❷ The development of Harappan culture, late 4th–early 2nd millennium BCE ▶

Baluchistan hill cultures

▦ hill cultures of Baluchistan, late 4th–late 3rd millennium BCE

◆ major site

◇ other site (selected)

Harappan cultures

▦ area of early Harappan culture, mid- to late 3rd millennium BCE

▦ limit of mature Harappan culture, to mid-2nd millennium BCE

◆ major site

◇ other site

▦ major clusters of urban sites

◇ other important contemporary site

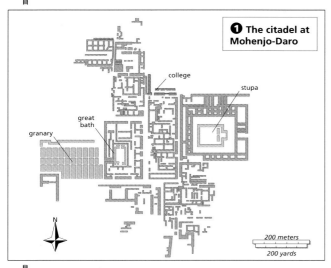

Bronze tools and weapons from Mohenjo-Daro reveal the city's high level of technological sophistication.

Mohenjo-Daro

This ancient city, along with Harappa, was one of the two greatest urban centers of Harappan civilization. With an area of 150 acres, the city's population may have been as high as 50,000. The houses of the lower town were divided into nine blocks by regular streets. The city was a major center of both trade and manufacture.

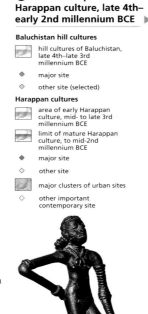

Stylish Harappan bronzes include this elegant dancer.

The Bronze Age in Southeast Asia to 1000 BCE

Archaeologists have unearthed numerous and diverse bronzes from Southeast Asia, some possibly dating as far back as 2000 BCE. However, the associated level of civilization prior to the diffusion of Indian and Chinese influences is only vaguely understood. Certainly, the presence of bronze artefacts in some of the burials of the period, notably at Non Nok Tha and Ban Chiang in Thailand, indicates that society was becoming increasingly stratified. Sophisticated techniques, such as lost-wax casting and closed molds, were used, and earthenware crucibles found near the burials suggest that the craftsmanship was local.

◀ ❸ Bronze Age Southeast Asia from c.1500 BCE

◇ major Bronze Age site

◉ find of Dong Son-type drum

This pottery urn mounted on four supporting legs was made in Thailand c.3000–2000 BCE.

Bronze Dong Son drums, such as this one from Vietnam, c.500 BCE have been found throughout the region.

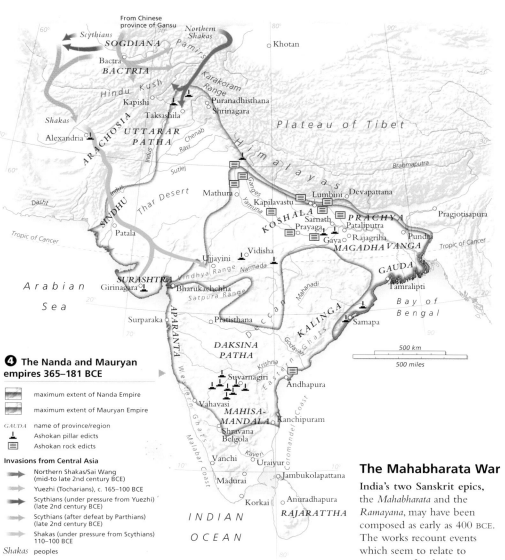

❹ The Nanda and Mauryan empires 365–181 BCE

	maximum extent of Nanda Empire
	maximum extent of Mauryan Empire
GAUDA	name of province/region
⊥	Ashokan pillar edicts
▣	Ashokan rock edicts

Invasions from Central Asia

→	Northern Shakas/Sai Wang (mid-to late 2nd century BCE)
→	Yuezhi (Tocharians), c. 165–100 BCE
→	Scythians (under pressure from Yuezhi) (late 2nd century BCE)
→	Scythians (after defeat by Parthians) (late 2nd century BCE)
→	Shakas (under pressure from Scythians) 110–100 BCE

Shakas peoples

The central narrative of the *Mahabharata* tells the story of the struggle for supremacy between two groups of cousins – the Kauravas and the Pandavas. This manuscript illustration shows a chariot battle between the two forces.

The Nanda and Mauryan empires c.365–181 BCE

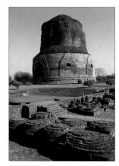

A Buddhist stupa still stands at Sarnath, a Mauryan city on the northern Ganges plain.

By c.600 BCE, the Ganges plain was dominated by 16 distinct political units which, over the next century, all came under the control of the state of Magadha. By the time of the Nanda dynasty (c.365–321 BCE) the extent of the Magadhan Empire was already substantial. The succeeding Mauryan Empire (321–181 BCE), however, was the first to achieve pan-Indian status and its political and cultural influence extended well beyond the subcontinent. When the Mauryan leader Ashoka converted to Buddhism (c.260 BCE), he foreswore war. Following the decline of the empire, northwest India suffered a series of invasions by peoples from northeast Asia, propelled into migration by the expansion of Han China.

The Mauryan Empire and successor states in South Asia

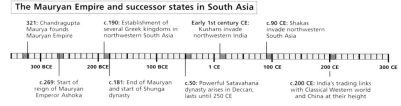

321: Chandragupta Maurya founds Mauryan Empire

c.190: Establishment of several Greek kingdoms in northwestern South Asia

Early 1st century CE: Kushans invade northwestern India

c.90 CE: Shakas invade northwestern South Asia

c.269: Start of reign of Mauryan Emperor Ashoka

c.181: End of Mauryan and start of Shunga dynasty

c.50: Powerful Satavahana dynasty arises in Deccan, lasts until 250 CE

c.200 CE: India's trading links with Classical Western world and China at their height

300 BCE — 200 BCE — 100 BCE — 1 CE — 100 CE — 200 CE — 300 CE

The Mahabharata War

India's two Sanskrit epics, the *Mahabharata* and the *Ramayana*, may have been composed as early as 400 BCE. The works recount events which seem to relate to a great war fought in northwestern India several centuries earlier. The later magnification of this conflict into a pan-Indian struggle is probably the result of post-Mauryan mythology. The peoples identified in this map are among those who came within the ambit of expanding Mauryan power.

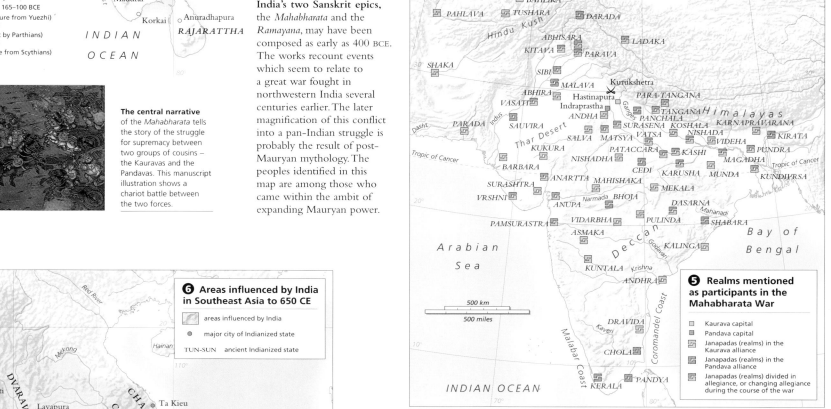

❺ Realms mentioned as participants in the Mahabharata War

▫	Kaurava capital
▪	Pandava capital
⊞	Janapadas (realms) in the Kaurava alliance
⊞	Janapadas (realms) in the Pandava alliance
⊞	Janapadas (realms) divided in allegiance, or changing allegiance during the course of the war

❻ Areas influenced by India in Southeast Asia to 650 CE

	areas influenced by India
●	major city of Indianized state
TUN-SUN	ancient Indianized state

Indian influence in Southeast Asia to 650 CE

To ancient Indians Southeast Asia was known as *Suvarnadvipa*, the continent of gold. The number of Indians who traded and migrated there was not great, but their influence was profound. Brahmin, the high-caste priests of Hindu India, acted as ritual specialists, while other advisers attended numerous royal courts. Although indigenous cultures revered Indian traditions, art, and music, they also marked Hinduism and Buddhism with a distinctive local character.

A bronze statue of the Hindu deity, Vishnu from Thailand (7th century CE) reflects the impact of Indian civilization on Southeast Asia.

Early Southeast Asian civilizations

111: Chinese Han Empire conquers and incorporates northern Vietnam

1st century CE: Buddhism starts to spread to many coastal localities of mainland Southeast Asia

c.192: Establishment of Lin-yi/ Champa, longest-lived Hinduized state of Southeast Asia

6th century: Rise of Indianized Mon state of Dvaravati in what is now Thailand

300 BCE — 150 — 1 CE — 150 — 300 — 450 — 600 CE

257: State of Au Lac established in Red River basin; succeeded by Nam Viet in 207

1st century CE: Funan, precursor of Cambodia, arises as first Hinduized state of Southeast Asia

c.550: Khmer state of Chenla overthrows its former suzerain, Funan

THE RELIGIONS OF SOUTHERN ASIA

This relief of the Buddha is in the Gandhara style, inspired by Greco-Roman sculpture.

THE HISTORY OF SOUTH AND SOUTHEAST ASIA is inextricably linked to the diffusion and development of religions, and the interaction between different systems of belief. Indeed, the identity of most of the region's populations has long been defined by religion. India was the cultural birthplace of both Hinduism and Buddhism, as well as other less widespread faiths, such as Jainism and Sikhism. Buddhism once enjoyed substantial political patronage from Indian rulers, but ultimately failed to become established among the masses. The resurgence of Hinduism in the course of the 1st millennium CE and the spread of Islam in the 8th–13th centuries also contributed to the demise of Buddhism in the land of its birth. Many imported faiths, including Buddhism, Hinduism, Islam, and, most recently, Christianity, have planted roots in the receptive soil of various parts of Southeast Asia.

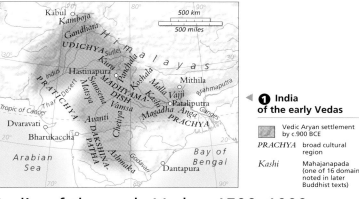

◀ **❶ India** of the early Vedas

░ Vedic Aryan settlement by c.900 BCE
PRACHYA broad cultural region
Kashi Mahajanapada (one of 16 domains noted in later Buddhist texts)

India of the early Vedas, 1500–1000 BCE

The *Rig Veda* (completed c.900 BCE) is the great literary monument left by the early Aryan settlers of northern India. This collection of sacred hymns traces the development of religious ideas as they were passed down orally from generation to generation. They depict the Aryans as chariot-driving warriors, formerly nomadic pastoralists, gradually adapting to a settled way of life. Later Buddhist texts abound in geographic references and mention the 16 great domains of north and central India – the *Mahajanapadas*.

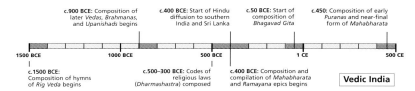

India of the Puranas

During the 1st millennium BCE, as the Aryan tribes coalesced into small kingdoms and republics, their religion became more comparable to the current form of Hinduism. As non-Aryan peoples were conquered and absorbed, a caste-based social order dominated by a Brahman priesthood, who oversaw increasingly elaborate rituals, and by a warrior caste (*Kshatriyas*) emerged. At first conquered peoples formed the lower strata of society. The expansion of Hindu culture can be traced through sacred texts; the collection of encyclopedic works – known as the *Puranas* – are rich in geographic content. They divide India up into a series of states or realms known as *janapadas*.

This bronze figure of Shiva, dating from the 11th century CE, depicts him as Lord of the Dance. He is surrounded by a circle of fire, which symbolizes both death and rebirth.

The hearth of Buddhism and Jainism

Buddhism and Jainism arose in the Gangetic Plain during the 6th century BCE, partly in reaction to the ritual excesses and social inequalities within Brahmanism. Both faiths stress *ahisma* (nonviolence), nonattachment to worldly possessions, and religious meditation. Both diffused widely and enjoyed the patronage of numerous political rulers prior to the advent of Islam in northern India, although the number of followers, especially of Jainism, may not have been great.

India's largest collection of Buddhist monuments is found at Sanchi in Central India. They were built from the 3rd century BCE to the 11th century CE.

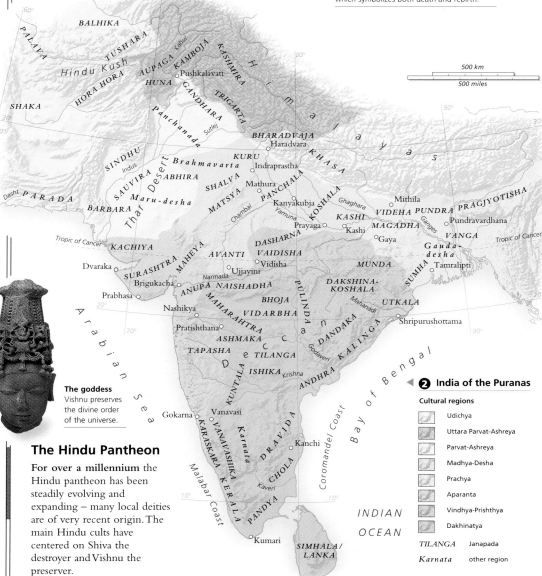

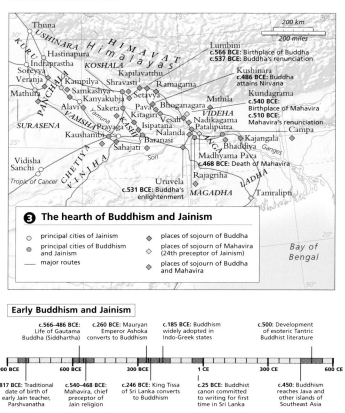

❷ India of the Puranas

Cultural regions
- Udichya
- Uttara Parvat-Ashreya
- Parvat-Ashreya
- Madhya-Desha
- Prachya
- Aparanta
- Vindhya-Prishtha
- Dakhinatya

TILANGA Janapada
Karnata other region

❸ The hearth of Buddhism and Jainism

○ principal cities of Jainism
◉ principal cities of Buddhism and Jainism
— major routes
◆ places of sojourn of Buddha
◇ places of sojourn of Mahavira (24th preceptor of Jainism)
◆ places of sojourn of Buddha and Mahavira

The Hindu Pantheon

For over a millennium the Hindu pantheon has been steadily evolving and expanding – many local deities are of very recent origin. The main Hindu cults have centered on Shiva the destroyer and Vishnu the preserver.

The goddess Vishnu preserves the divine order of the universe.

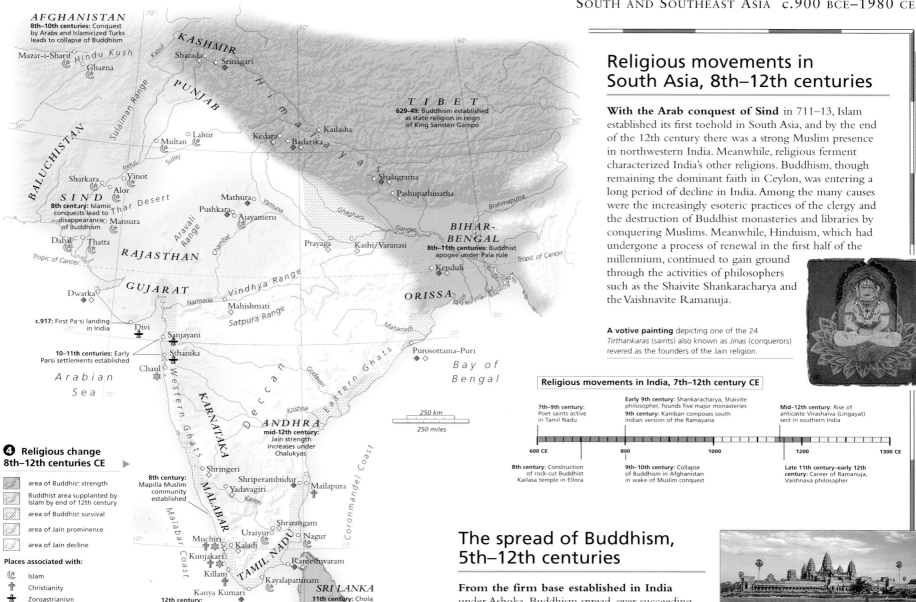

area of Buddhist strength
Buddhist area supplanted by Islam by end of 12th century
area of Buddhist survival
area of Jain prominence
area of Jain decline

Places associated with:
☪ Islam
✝ Christianity
卐 Zoroastrianism
✡ Judaism
◆ Hindu Shaivite philosopher Shankaracharya (788–820)
◇ Hindu Vaishnava philosopher Ramanuja (11th century)

Religious movements in South Asia, 8th–12th centuries

With the Arab conquest of Sind in 711–13, Islam established its first toehold in South Asia, and by the end of the 12th century there was a strong Muslim presence in northwestern India. Meanwhile, religious ferment characterized India's other religions. Buddhism, though remaining the dominant faith in Ceylon, was entering a long period of decline in India. Among the many causes were the increasingly esoteric practices of the clergy and the destruction of Buddhist monasteries and libraries by conquering Muslims. Meanwhile, Hinduism, which had undergone a process of renewal in the first half of the millennium, continued to gain ground through the activities of philosophers such as the Shaivite Shankaracharya and the Vaishnavite Ramanuja.

A votive painting depicting one of the 24 Tirthankaras (saints) also known as Jinas (conquerors) revered as the founders of the Jain religion.

Religious movements in India, 7th–12th century CE

7th–9th century: Poet saints active in Tamil Nadu | Early 9th century: Shankaracharya, Shaivite philosopher, founds five major monasteries | 9th century: Kamban composes south Indian version of the Ramayana | Mid-12th century: Rise of anticaste Virashaiva (Lingayat) sect in southern India
8th century: Construction of rock-cut Buddhist Kailasa temple in Ellora | 9th–10th century: Collapse of Buddhism in Afghanistan in wake of Muslim conquest | Late 11th century–early 12th century: Career of Ramanuja, Vaishnava philosopher

The spread of Buddhism, 5th–12th centuries

From the firm base established in India under Ashoka, Buddhism spread, over succeeding centuries, to neighboring and distant lands. By the 5th century CE it had taken root in many parts of Southeast Asia, frequently in conjunction with Hinduism and sponsored by increasingly Indianized states. The Mahayana and Theravada schools were both initially well represented; new contacts coming from Ceylon in the 12th century led to the increasing dominance of the latter.

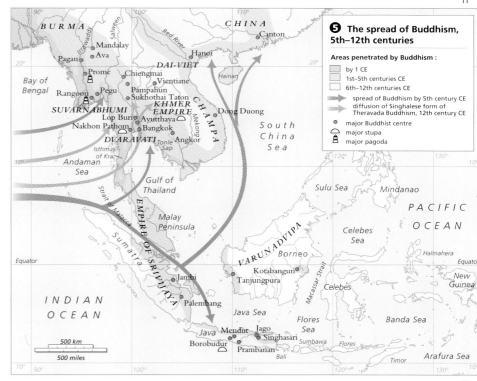

The great temple complex of Angkor Wat in Cambodia was built by the Khmer ruler, Suryavarman II (1113–50) as a monument to his own divinity as the embodiment of Lord Vishnu.

⑤ The spread of Buddhism, 5th–12th centuries

Areas penetrated by Buddhism:
by 1 CE
1st–5th centuries CE
6th–11th centuries CE
→ spread of Buddhism by 5th century CE
→ diffusion of Singhalese form of Theravada Buddhism, 12th century
● major Buddhist centre
⌂ major stupa
⌂ major pagoda

The spread of Islam in Southeast Asia

Indian Muslim traders settled in the mercantile centers of Southeast Asia as early as the 10th century, but it was only after the conversion to Islam of the ruler of the powerful Sumatran state of Achin that the mainly peaceful process of Islamization began in earnest. In rapid succession, the princes of other small trading states also embraced the new faith. From their coastal capitals, Islam gradually penetrated inland, a process still underway in parts of present-day Indonesia.

A Dutch engraving of 1596 shows an envoy from Mecca meeting the governor of Bantam in west Java, an example of the East Indies' strong links with the Muslim world.

The diffusion of Islam in South and Southeast Asia

711–12: Arab conquest of Sind introduces Islam to South Asia | c.1000: Mahmud of Ghazna conquers northwest India | 1295: Conversion of Sultan of Achin to Islam, which spreads over much of the East Indies
c.750: Muslim merchants establish Islam in Kerala, southwest India | c.1200: Muslim Sufi saint, Mu'in al-Din Chishti, founds first Sufi order in subcontinent

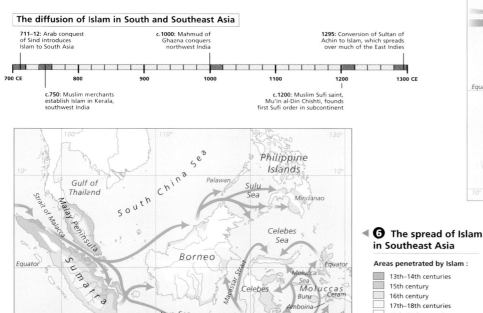

⑥ The spread of Islam in Southeast Asia

Areas penetrated by Islam:
13th–14th centuries
15th century
16th century
17th–18th centuries
19th–20th centuries
→ spread of Islam

The Buddhist stupa at Borobudur, Java, symbolizes via its structure, the Buddhist transition from reality at its base – for example in this panel showing sailing vessels – to the achievement of spiritual enlightenment at the summit.

STATES AND EMPIRES 300–1525

Bajang Ratu was the capital of the Majapahit kingdom in Central Java.

SOUTH ASIA WAS ruled by a great diversity of regional powers for much of this period. However, in the 4th century CE, the Gupta dynasty succeeded in uniting much of the Indian subcontinent. The next 200 years are often described as a "golden age" of Indian civilization. It was not until the 13th century that so much of India again came under the control of a single state, the Delhi Sultanate. The Turkish dynasties that ruled the Sultanate were unable to maintain effective control over so vast an area, and its power declined in the 14th century. Southeast Asia also witnessed the rise and fall of numerous states. Kambujadesha, with its magnificent capital at Angkor, dominated the mainland, while the two greatest states of the Indonesian archipelago were Srivijaya and, later, Majapahit.

Medieval states 550–1206

This rock carving depicts a scene from the epic poem *Mahabharata*.

The multiplicity of regional powers that dominated India during this period all developed distinctive cultural styles, whose legacy survives in architecture, literature, and tradition. Some of them achieved, for brief periods, quasi-imperial status. The struggle for control of the Ganges plain was dominated by three major states: the Gurjara-Pratiharas, the Palas, and the Rashtrakutas. In the south, two major powers emerged; the Chalukyas in the west, and the Tamil Cholas in the east. Under Rajaraja (985–1014), the Cholas conquered much of southern India and Ceylon, their rule extending to the Malay Peninsula.

Medieval states

320: Chandra Gupta I founds Gupta Empire; India's "golden age"
c.495: Huna invasions weaken Guptas in northern India
c.880: Gurjara-Pratiharas rule over virtually the whole of northern India
c.1025: Apogee of Tamil Chola dynasty

| 300 | 500 | 700 | 900 | 1100 |

c.540: King Harsha restores mighty Hindu state in Kanyakubja, northern India
c.750: Apogee of Pala dynasty, the last major Buddhist state in South Asia
c.825: Rashtrakuta dynasty rules over south India and Sri Lanka

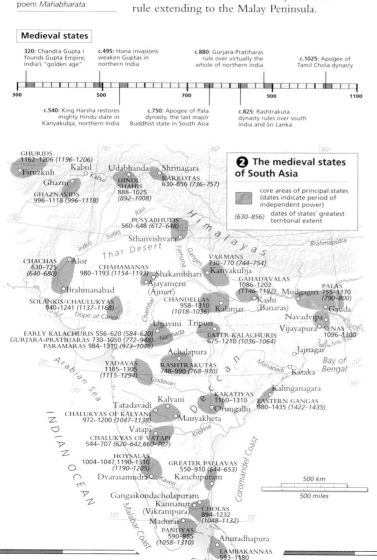

② The medieval states of South Asia

- core areas of principal states (dates indicate period of independent power)
- (630–856) dates of states' greatest territorial extent

The imperial Guptas c.300–550

This wall painting depicting a scene from the life of the Buddha is from the spectacular cave sanctuaries at Ajanta, central India.

The authority of the Guptas extended over many conquered states whose rulers remained on their thrones in a tributary relationship to the Gupta sovereign. They held sway over other regional powers by virtue of diplomacy and marital alliances. Peace, prosperity, scholarly debate, and religious tolerance all encouraged a florescence of Indian art – in particular, in sculpture, painting, poetry, and drama. But Gupta rule was shattered by the invasion of Hunas (Hephthalites), nomads from Central Asia, in the 6th century.

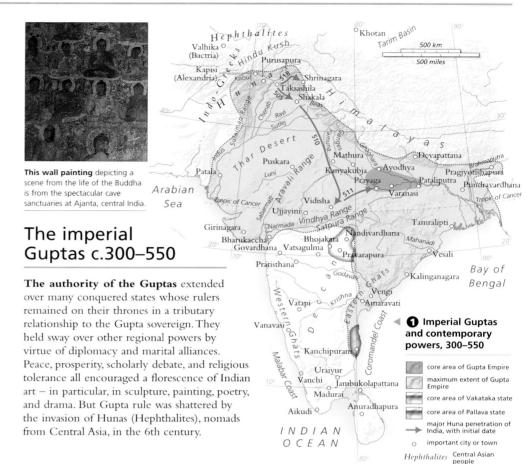

① Imperial Guptas and contemporary powers, 300–550

- core area of Gupta Empire
- maximum extent of Gupta Empire
- core area of Vakataka state
- core area of Pallava state
- major Huna penetration of India, with initial date
- important city or town
- *Hephthalites* Central Asian people

The Brihadeshwana temple at Thanjavur (Tanjore) is one of several fine Dravidian temples in the city, dating from the 11th century when it was the capital of the Chola kingdom.

The Delhi Sultanate 1206–1526

The invasion of Mahmud of Ghazna in the 11th century, highlighted India's political and military vulnerability, and subsequent invasions by Turkish peoples from Central Asia led to the establishment of the Mamluk dynasty of the Delhi Sultanate in 1206. The territory controlled by the five successive dynasties that ruled the Sultanate fluctuated greatly, reaching its greatest extent under the Tughluqs. Administrative inefficiency and an ill-advised attempt to move the capital south to Daulatabad hastened the Sultanate's decline, and much of India fragmented once again into warring kingdoms.

The Delhi Sultanate

c.1025: Conquest of Punjab by Ghaznavids
1192–93: Afghan Ghurids defeat Rajputs and seize Delhi and much of northern India
1206: Breakaway Mamluk (Slave) dynasty, under Aibak, establishes Delhi Sultanate
1398: Sack of Delhi by Timur (Tamerlane) leads to fall of Tughluq dynasty

| 1000 | 1100 | 1200 | 1300 | 1400 |

1336: Rebellion against Tughluq marks beginning of Vijayanagara Empire
1345: Hasan Gangu, governor of Tughluq Deccani domains, revolts and founds Bahmani kingdom

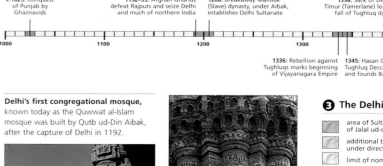

Delhi's first congregational mosque, known today as the Quwwat al-Islam mosque was built by Qutb ud-Din Aibak, after the capture of Delhi in 1192.

The ornate sandstone pillar of Delhi's Qutb Minar, built c.1200, is adorned with Arabic calligraphy.

③ The Delhi Sultanate

- area of Sultanate at accession of Jalal ud-din Khalji, 1290
- additional territory at some time under direct Khalji administration
- limit of nominal Khalji vassals
- possible route of Khalji raids against Mongols
- extent of Sultanate at accession of Ghiyas ud-din Tughluq, 1320
- maximum extent of Sultanate under direct Tughluq administration
- limit of nominal Tughluq vassals
- *Ahoms* peoples and dynasties
- *SIND* cultural region

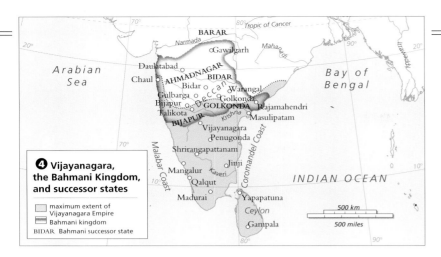

❹ Vijayanagara, the Bahmani Kingdom, and successor states

- maximum extent of Vijayanagara Empire
- Bahmani kingdom
- **BIDAR** Bahmani successor state

The Vijayanagara Empire 1335–1570

The decline of the Delhi Sultanate led to the breakaway of the Muslim-controlled areas of the Deccan and the creation, in 1347, of the Bahmani Kingdom. To the south, in the Krishna valley, the powerful new Hindu kingdom of Vijayanagara was firmly established by 1345. Its splendid capital, Vijayanagara (modern Hampi), was a magnificent temple city, with massive fortifications and a royal palace. Vijayanagara successfully withstood repeated attempts by the Bahmani Kingdom to expand southward. The Bahmani Kingdom divided into five sultanates in 1518, and Vijayanagara finally succumbed in 1570, after a disastrous defeat at Talikota in 1564.

The royal capital of Vijayanagara ("city of victory"), founded in the mid-14th century, was destroyed by invaders from the Deccani sultanates in 1565.

Major states of Southeast Asia 650–1250

The major states of mainland Southeast Asia, although extensive, were loosely controlled and included substantial tribal populations. Their civilizations were clearly Indianized, but this influence generally diminished with distance from their core regions. The Khmer state of Kambujadesha, with its impressive capital at Angkor, dominated the mainland. In the East Indies, the leading states were bound together largely by commercial ties. The maritime empire of Srivijaya, with its capital at Palembang in Sumatra, controlled international trade through the straits of Malacca and Sunda.

This carved relief from the 13th-century temple complex at Angkor Thom, part of the Khmer capital of Angkor, shows mounted soldiers accompanying a war elephant being transported in a cart pulled by donkeys.

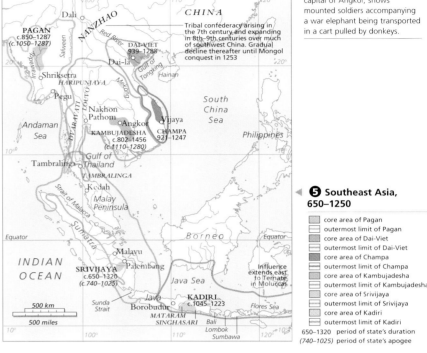

◄ ❺ Southeast Asia, 650–1250

- core area of Pagan
- outermost limit of Pagan
- core area of Dai-Viet
- outermost limit of Dai-Viet
- core area of Champa
- outermost limit of Champa
- core area of Kambujadesha
- outermost limit of Kambujadesha
- core area of Srivijaya
- outermost limit of Srivijaya
- core area of Kadiri
- outermost limit of Kadiri

650–1320 period of state's duration
(740–1025) period of state's apogee

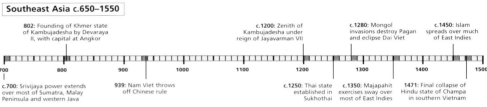

Southeast Asia c.650–1550

- **802:** Founding of Khmer state of Kambujadesha by Devaraya II, with capital at Angkor
- **c.1200:** Zenith of Kambujadesha under reign of Jayavarman VII
- **c.1280:** Mongol invasions destroy Pagan and eclipse Dai Viet
- **c.1450:** Islam spreads over much of East Indies
- **c.700:** Srivijaya power extends over most of Sumatra, Malay Peninsula and western Java
- **939:** Nam Viet throws off Chinese rule
- **c.1250:** Thai state established in Sukhothai
- **c.1350:** Majapahit exercises sway over most of East Indies
- **1471:** Final collapse of Hindu state of Champa in southern Vietnam

Major states of Southeast Asia 1250–1550

During this period there was a marked increase in the number of medium-sized contenders for power throughout the region. The decline of Kambujadesha was matched by the rise of several ethnically Thai states and the destruction of the long-lived state of Champa by the sinicized kingdom of Dai-Viet. In the East Indies, dominance passed from Srivijaya to Majapahit which, in the 14th century, established the most extensive commercial empire that the area was to see in precolonial times.

▼ ❻ Southeast Asia, 1250–1550

Outer limits of areas at some time subject to the following major states:

- Toungoo
- Ava
- Pegu
- Sukhothai
- Ayuthia
- Kambuja
- Champa
- Dai-Viet
- Singhasari
- Melaka
- Majapahit
- **BALI** other states

A bronze water vessel in the shape of a duck, from Thailand, demonstrates the technological refinement of the metal-workers of Southeast Asia.

The Garai Cham tower from the city of Phan Rang, in the Hindu-Buddhist kingdom of Champa, which flourished in southern Vietnam (7th–12th centuries), but was absorbed by Dai-Viet in 1471.

MUGHALS, MARATHAS, EUROPEANS

Shah Jahan (1627–58) was one of the greatest of the Mughal emperors.

THE CONQUEST OF NORTHERN INDIA in 1526 by the Muslim Mughal chief, Babur, was to usher in a new era, marked by orderly government, economic prosperity, and great achievements in the arts, notably architecture, miniature painting, and literature. When, after the stern rule of Aurangzeb, the empire fell into disarray, the Hindu Marathas expanded rapidly from their Deccan base and dominated Indian affairs until their defeat by the British early in the 19th century. Vasco da Gama's voyage to India in 1498 opened up new trade routes, enabling European powers to establish commercial toeholds; spices, textiles, and jewels were soon being exported to western markets.

The Mughals, 1526–1857

In 1526 the Mughals, led by Babur, a descendant of Timur *(see p.229)*, swept across much of northern India. His successor, Humayun, expelled by the governor of Bihar in 1539, returned in 1555 to establish a long-lived dynasty and an expansionist empire. The reign of Akbar (1556–1605) was a time of cultural florescence and religious tolerance. Later in the 17th century, Aurangzeb's long and harsh rule led to revolt. Many provinces seceded, and the rise of the Maratha confederacy from 1646 eventually reduced the Mughals to puppet rulers.

This miniature shows Shah Jahan with his four sons. His third son, Aurangzeb, deposed him in 1658.

The tomb of Sheikh Salim lies in the Great Mosque at Fatehpur Sikri. Construction of the spectacular red limestone city began in the 1570s in the reign of Akbar.

Emperor Shah Jahan built the Taj Mahal c.1654 as a mausoleum for his beloved wife, Mumtaz. This exquisite structure of white marble is one of the masterpieces of Mughal architecture.

The Mughal Empire

- 1526: Babur conquers Delhi and founds Mughal Empire
- 1556–1605: Reign of Akbar marked by territorial expansion and cordial Hindu-Muslim relations
- 1658–1707: Empire reaches maximum extent during reign of Aurangzeb
- 1724: Independent rule over Deccan by Nizam of Hyderabad hastens disintegration of empire
- 1739: Sack of Delhi by Persians and Afghans under Nadir Shah
- 1788: Mughal emperors become puppets of Marathas
- 1803: British occupy Delhi
- 1857: Last Mughal Emperor, the puppet Bahadur Shah II, dethroned and exiled by British

1500 | 1600 | 1700 | 1800 | 1900

Nadir Shah of Persia is shown sacking Delhi in 1739. His invasion, and the growing power of the Marathas, led to the downfall of the Mughals.

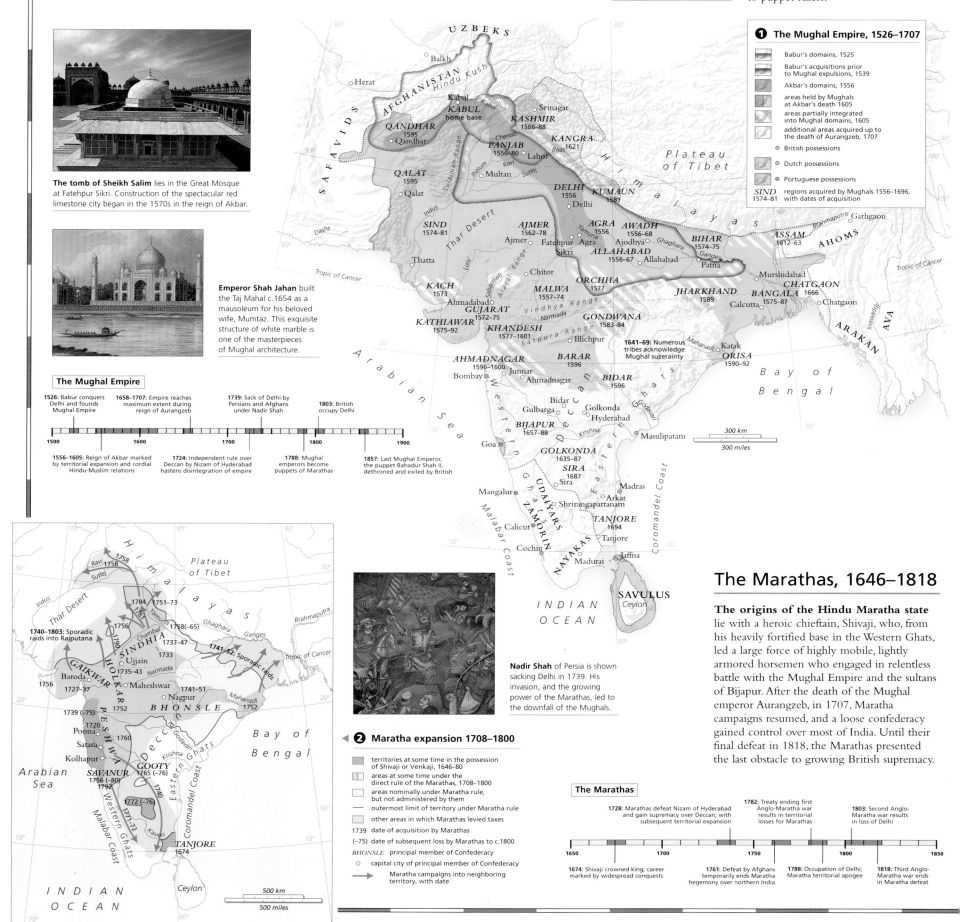

① The Mughal Empire, 1526–1707

- Babur's domains, 1525
- Babur's acquisitions prior to Mughal expulsions, 1539
- Akbar's domains, 1556
- areas held by Mughals at Akbar's death 1605
- areas partially integrated into Mughal domains, 1605
- additional areas acquired up to the death of Aurangzeb, 1707
- British possessions
- Dutch possessions
- Portuguese possessions
- SIND 1574–81 regions acquired by Mughals 1556–1696, with dates of acquisition

② Maratha expansion 1708–1800

- territories at some time in the possession of Shivaji or Venkaji, 1646–80
- areas at some time under the direct rule of the Marathas, 1708–1800
- areas nominally under Maratha rule, but not administered by them
- — outermost limit of territory under Maratha rule
- other areas in which Marathas levied taxes
- 1739 date of acquisition by Marathas
- (–75) date of subsequent loss by Marathas to c.1800
- BHONSLE principal member of Confederacy
- ○ capital city of principal member of Confederacy
- → Maratha campaigns into neighboring territory, with date

The Marathas, 1646–1818

The origins of the Hindu Maratha state lie with a heroic chieftain, Shivaji, who, from his heavily fortified base in the Western Ghats, led a large force of highly mobile, lightly armored horsemen who engaged in relentless battle with the Mughal Empire and the sultans of Bijapur. After the death of the Mughal emperor Aurangzeb, in 1707, Maratha campaigns resumed, and a loose confederacy gained control over most of India. Until their final defeat in 1818, the Marathas presented the last obstacle to growing British supremacy.

The Marathas

- 1674: Shivaji crowned king; career marked by widespread conquests
- 1728: Marathas defeat Nizam of Hyderabad and gain supremacy over Deccan; with subsequent territorial expansion
- 1761: Defeat by Afghans temporarily ends Maratha hegemony over northern India
- 1782: Treaty ending first Anglo-Maratha war results in territorial losses for Marathas
- 1788: Occupation of Delhi; Maratha territorial apogee
- 1803: Second Anglo-Maratha war results in loss of Delhi
- 1818: Third Anglo-Maratha war ends in Maratha defeat

1650 | 1700 | 1750 | 1800 | 1850

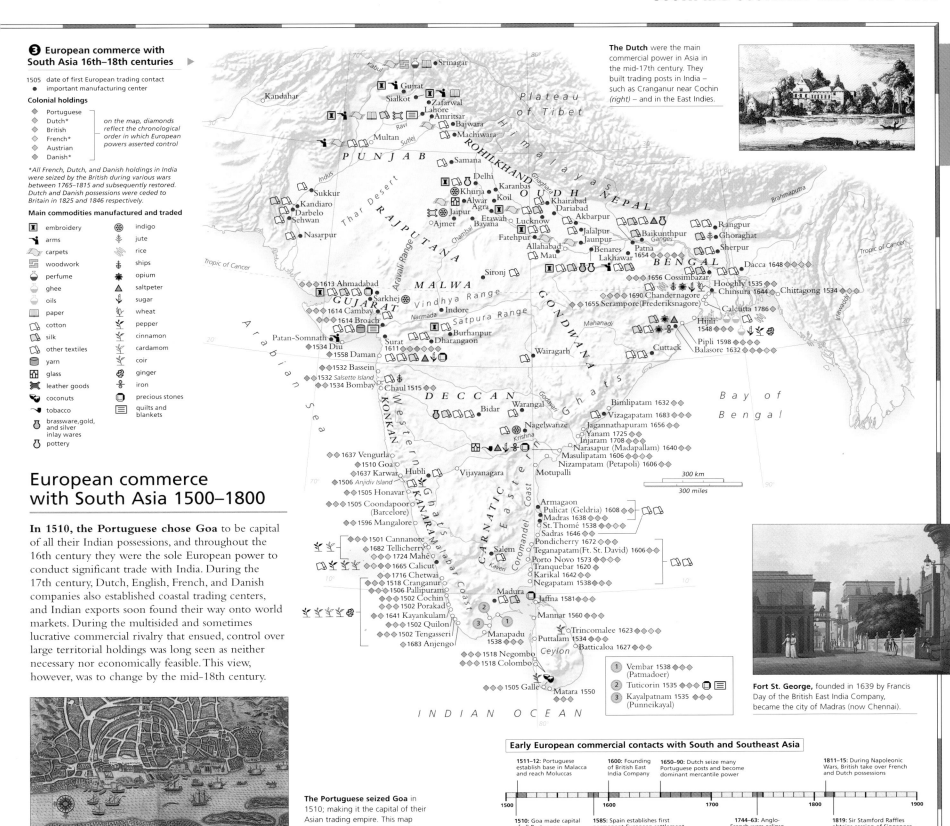

❸ European commerce with South Asia 16th–18th centuries ▶

1505 date of first European trading contact
● important manufacturing center

Colonial holdings
◇ Portuguese
◇ Dutch*
◇ British
◇ French*
◇ Austrian
◇ Danish*

on the map, diamonds reflect the chronological order in which European powers asserted control

All French, Dutch, and Danish holdings in India were seized by the British during various wars between 1765–1815 and subsequently restored. Dutch and Danish possessions were ceded to Britain in 1825 and 1846 respectively.

Main commodities manufactured and traded

embroidery	indigo		
arms	jute		
carpets	rice		
woodwork	ships		
perfume	opium		
ghee	saltpeter		
oils	sugar		
paper	wheat		
cotton	pepper		
silk	cinnamon		
other textiles	cardamom		
yarn	coir		
glass	ginger		
leather goods	iron		
coconuts	precious stones		
tobacco	quilts and blankets		
brassware, gold, and silver inlay wares			
pottery			

The Dutch were the main commercial power in Asia in the mid-17th century. They built trading posts in India – such as Cranganur near Cochin (right) – and in the East Indies.

European commerce with South Asia 1500–1800

In 1510, the Portuguese chose Goa to be capital of all their Indian possessions, and throughout the 16th century they were the sole European power to conduct significant trade with India. During the 17th century, Dutch, English, French, and Danish companies also established coastal trading centers, and Indian exports soon found their way onto world markets. During the multisided and sometimes lucrative commercial rivalry that ensued, control over large territorial holdings was long seen as neither necessary nor economically feasible. This view, however, was to change by the mid-18th century.

The Portuguese seized Goa in 1510; making it the capital of their Asian trading empire. This map of the city was engraved c.1600.

Fort St. George, founded in 1639 by Francis Day of the British East India Company, became the city of Madras (now Chennai).

Early European commercial contacts with South and Southeast Asia

1511–12: Portuguese establish base in Malacca and reach Moluccas

1600: Founding of British East India Company

1650–90: Dutch seize many Portuguese posts and become dominant mercantile power

1811–15: During Napoleonic Wars, British take over French and Dutch possessions

1510: Goa made capital of all Portuguese possessions in Asia

1585: Spain establishes first permanent European settlement at Cebu, in Philippines

1744–63: Anglo-French wars eclipse French power in Asia

1819: Sir Stamford Raffles obtains cession of Singapore for British East India Company

❹ South East Asian contacts with Europe c.1550–1800

European territories in 1800
▪ Portuguese
▪ Dutch acquisition/trade area
▪ Spanish acquisition/trade area
▪ British

Acquired by European powers, with date
◇ Portuguese
◇ Dutch
◇ Spanish
◇ British
◇ Danish
◇ French

1521 dates indicate year of occupation
BALI trade domains of Southeast Asia in late 17th century

European and Southeast Asian contacts 1500–1800

The commercial penetration of Southeast Asia by Europeans began shortly after the Portuguese arrival in India. The Spanish established links with the Philippines after Magellan's discovery of the islands in 1521 during the first circumnavigation of the globe. Dutch and British trade in the region did not begin until the 17th century. As in India, the European powers established "factories," often fortified, at many points along the coast. They cooperated with local magnates, both indigenous and Chinese, who had already carved out trading domains.

The Moluccan island of Ambon (right) was reached by the Portuguese in 1512. They were ousted by the Dutch in 1605. This 17th-century engraving shows Dutch East India Company ships sailing near the island.

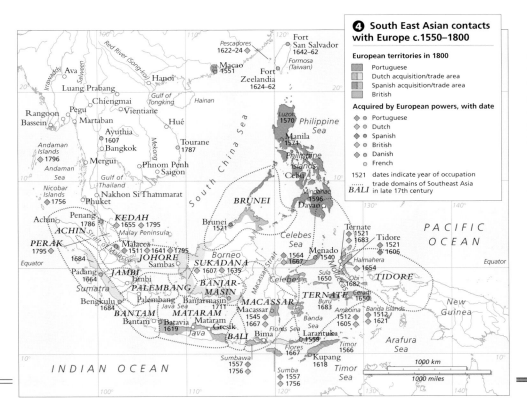

THE AGE OF COLONIAL EXPANSION

Sir Stamford Raffles refounded the port city of Singapore in 1819.

BETWEEN 1765 AND 1914 the European powers completed their conquest and annexation of most of South and Southeast Asia. Nepal and Afghanistan were greatly reduced in size and made protectorates of Britain, while Siam, though shorn of most of its outer territories, maintained its independence, acting as a buffer between the British and the French. There were many reasons for European conquest, including commercial disputes, the desire to control resources, diplomatic entanglements, and strategic considerations. All were the inevitable result of interaction between nations with vastly differing military and naval resources in an age of imperial expansion.

Major indigenous powers confronting British and French colonizers

1749: Mysore starts to become major power in southern India
1754: Powerful Burmese dynasty established on capture of Ava by Alaungpaya
1802: With French aid, Nguyen Anh unites and becomes emperor of Vietnam
1857–59: Revolt ("Mutiny") attempts to oust British from India

c.1720: Marathas start to expand over most of India
1757: Expansion of Gurkha (Nepali) domains over much of Himalayas
1782: Siam reaches territorial apogee under Rama I
1785: Burmese invasion of Siam and counterinvasion by Siam of Burma
1839–42: Afghans under Dost Mohammed defeat British in First Afghan War

Warren Hastings, the first British governor-general of India (1774–85), is shown here dining with Indian princes. He was forced to confront both the Marathas and Mysore during the first phase of British expansion in India.

Indigenous powers and colonization

Even after the collapse of the Mughal Empire in 1761, significant states stood in the path of Western colonial expansion in both India and Southeast Asia. In India, the foremost power was the Maratha Confederacy, while in Southeast Asia, Burma, Siam, and Vietnam expanded in size and strength. At the dawn of the 19th century no large states remained over most of the East Indies, but Dutch commercial dominance was not yet reflected in territorial holdings.

British control in South Asia 1757–1914

Britain's imperial ventures in India began with the commercial activities of the East India Company. In 1757, the victory of Robert Clive at Plassey over a French and Mughal force and the acquisition of the right to collect taxes in Bengal began an era of territorial expansion which ended with British claims to the Northeast Frontier Agency in 1914. With a pivotal role in the British Empire, India became enmeshed in European rivalries; from 1848, colonial acquisitions along the periphery of the subcontinent had greater strategic than economic impact.

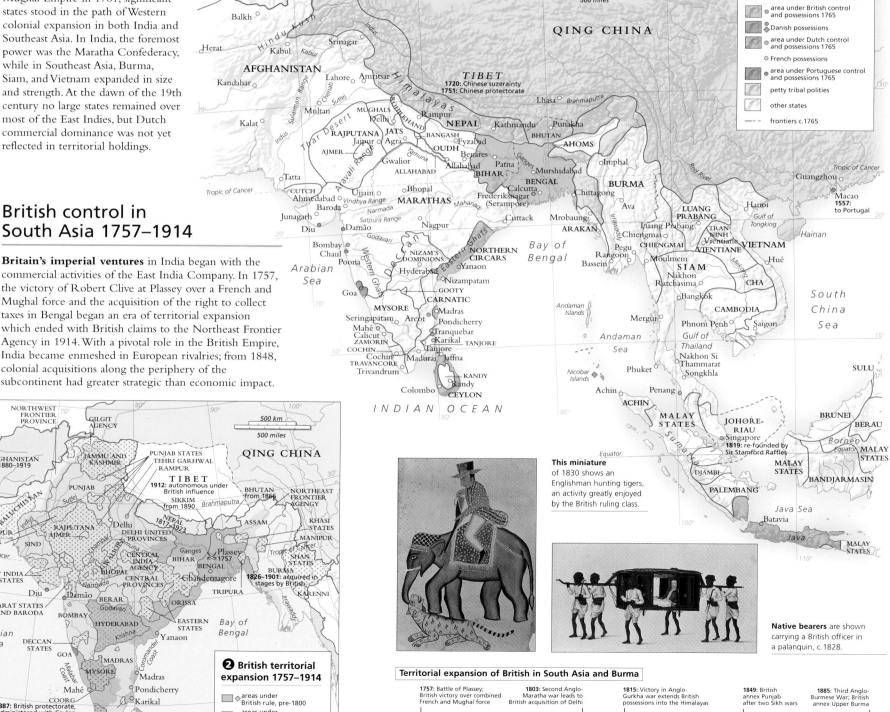

① South and Southeast Asia 1765

- area under British control and possessions 1765
- Danish possessions
- area under Dutch control and possessions 1765
- French possessions
- area under Portuguese control and possessions 1765
- petty tribal polities
- other states
- frontiers c.1765

This miniature of 1830 shows an Englishman hunting tigers, an activity greatly enjoyed by the British ruling class.

Native bearers are shown carrying a British officer in a palanquin, c.1828.

② British territorial expansion 1757–1914

- areas under British rule, pre-1800
- areas under British rule, 1800–50
- areas under British rule, post-1850
- Muslim princely state
- non-Muslim princely state
- British protectorate, with dates
- Portuguese colony
- French colony

1887: British protectorate, administered with Ceylon

1798: made crown colony separate from India

Territorial expansion of British in South Asia and Burma

1757: Battle of Plassey; British victory over combined French and Mughal force
1803: Second Anglo-Maratha war leads to British acquisition of Delhi
1815: Victory in Anglo-Gurkha war extends British possessions into the Himalayas
1849: British annex Punjab after two Sikh wars
1885: Third Anglo-Burmese War; British annex Upper Burma

1799: British-led coalition defeats and partitions Mysore; British obtain the Carnatic coast
1815: British annex Ceylonese kingdom of Kandy
1826: First Anglo-Burmese War; British acquire coastal areas
1852: Second Anglo-Burmese War; British occupy Lower Burma

The Revolt of 1857–59

Much more than a mutiny, the revolt of 1857–59 involved not merely the defection of large sections of the British Indian army, but also a series of peasant insurrections, led either by local rulers or *zamindars* (great landlords), aimed at throwing off the imperial yoke. The revolt failed because of its lack of a coordinated command structure and British superiority in military intelligence, organization, and logistics.

British troops are shown rushing to quell the revolt at Umballa in 1859. The reforms made after the Revolt helped secure the British presence in India for another 90 years.

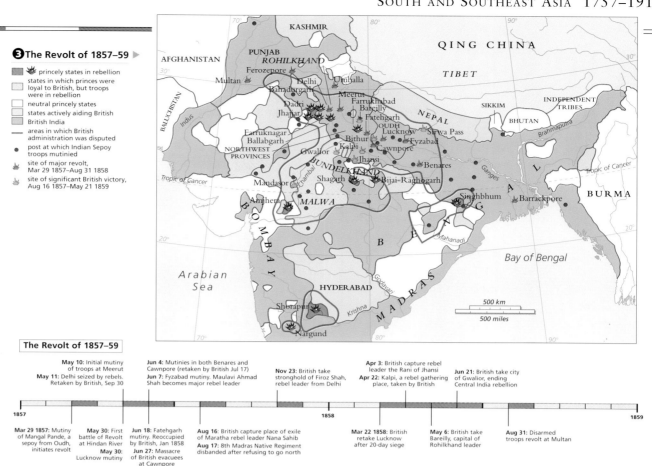

❸ **The Revolt of 1857–59** ▶

- ▨ princely states in rebellion
- ☐ states in which princes were loyal to British, but troops were in rebellion
- ☐ neutral princely states
- ▨ states actively aiding British British India
- — areas in which British administration was disputed
- ● post at which Indian Sepoy troops mutinied
- ⚜ site of major revolt, Mar 29 1857–Aug 31 1858
- ⚜ site of significant British victory, Aug 16 1857–May 21 1859

The Revolt of 1857–59

May 10: Initial mutiny of troops at Meerut	**Jun 4:** Mutinies in both Benares and Cawnpore (retaken by British Jul 17)
May 11: Delhi seized by rebels. Retaken by British, Sep 30	**Jun 7:** Fyzabad mutiny. Maulavi Ahmad Shah becomes major rebel leader

Nov 23: British take stronghold of Firoz Shah, rebel leader from Delhi

Apr 3: British capture rebel leader the Rani of Jhansi
Apr 22: Kalpi, a rebel gathering place, taken by British

Jun 21: British take city of Gwalior, ending Central India rebellion

1857 — 1858 — 1859

Mar 29 1857: Mutiny of Mangal Pande, a sepoy from Oudh, initiates revolt

May 30: First battle of Revolt at Hindan River
May 30: Lucknow mutiny

Jun 18: Fatehgarh mutiny. Reoccupied by British, Jan 1858
Jun 27: Massacre of British evacuees at Cawnpore

Aug 16: British capture place of exile of Maratha rebel leader Nana Sahib
Aug 17: 8th Madras Native Regiment disbanded after refusing to go north

Mar 22 1858: British retake Lucknow after 20-day siege

May 6: British take Bareilly, capital of Rohilkhand leader

Aug 31: Disarmed troops revolt at Multan

❹ **The economy of India and Ceylon, 1857** ▶

Agriculture
- mainly peasant agriculture
- scattered cultivation, hunting and gathering, and limited pastoralism
- predominantly pastoralism, with scattered pockets of agriculture
- forested areas

Industry
- coal-mining areas
- sites of extraction of other minerals

Manufacturing centers
- metalworking
- arms
- ship building
- textiles
- glazed pottery, tiles, and ceramics
- woodworking and furniture making
- jewelry
- ivory carving

Transportation
- — important road
- --- railroad
- --- railroad under construction

Population
- ● city with population of over 500,000
- ● city with population of 100,000–500,000
- ● city with population of 50,000–100,000
- ○ important city with population of less than 50,000

Principal types of agricultural produce

areca		pepper	
cacao		potato	
cinnamon		rape	
coconuts		salt	
coffee		sandalwood	
cotton		sesame	
dates		spices	
fruits		sugar	
indigo		sunflower	
jute		tea	
mustard		teak	
opium		tobacco	
palm sugar			

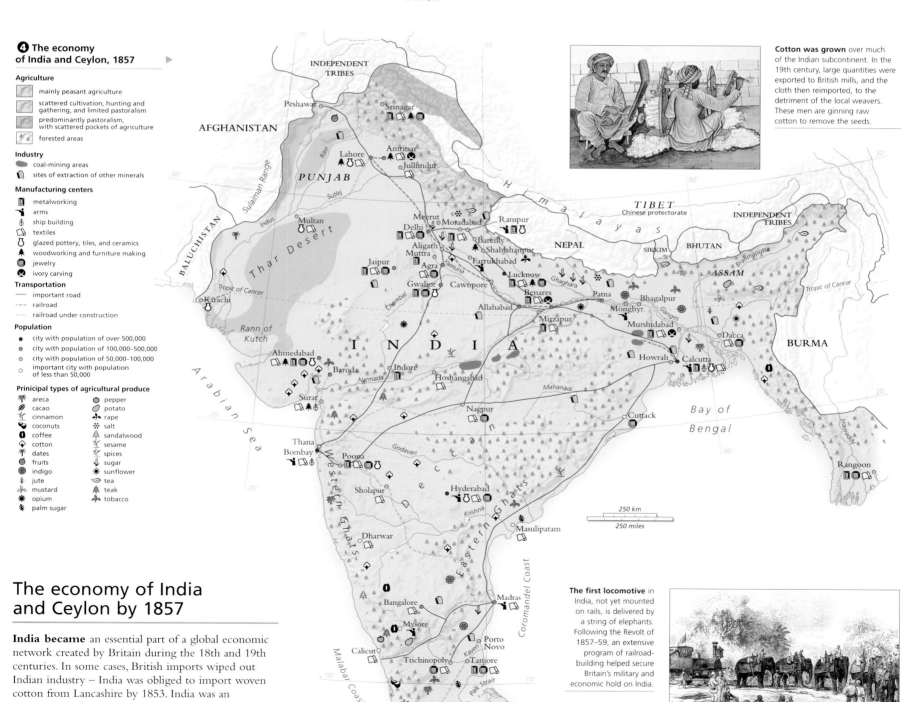

Cotton was grown over much of the Indian subcontinent. In the 19th century, large quantities were exported to British mills, and the cloth then reimported, to the detriment of the local weavers. These men are ginning raw cotton to remove the seeds.

The first locomotive in India, not yet mounted on rails, is delivered by a string of elephants. Following the Revolt of 1857–59, an extensive program of railroad-building helped secure Britain's military and economic hold on India.

The economy of India and Ceylon by 1857

India became an essential part of a global economic network created by Britain during the 18th and 19th centuries. In some cases, British imports wiped out Indian industry – India was obliged to import woven cotton from Lancashire by 1853. India was an overwhelmingly peasant society in 1857, but railroads, canals, plantations, mines, small-scale factories, and the growth of busy port cities and administrative centres were transforming its economic landscape.

THE COLONIAL APOGEE AND DEMISE

M.K. Gandhi (1869–1948), was the hero of India's independence movement.

TWO NEW COLONIAL POWERS, the US and Japan, entered Southeast Asia at the beginning of the 20th century. The Philippines were annexed by the US following the Spanish-American War of 1898; the Japanese took over the German Pacific island colonies north of the equator in 1919 and acquired virtually the whole of Southeast Asia by force in World War II. Though the early 20th century can be seen as the apogee of colonialism in the region, especially in British India, there was already strong opposition to foreign rule. The Indian National Congress, founded in 1885, initially sought reforms, but by the 1930s demanded complete independence. In the Philippines, a revolutionary independence movement was well established when the Americans took over. But while India's freedom struggle was, on the whole, peaceful, the struggle in most of Southeast Asia was bloody, nowhere more so than in Vietnam.

The partition and reunification of Bengal 1905–12

Lord Curzon's 1905 partition of India's most populous province, Bengal, was fiercely opposed on many grounds by both Hindus and Muslims. Some upper-class Hindus, for example, feared that the creation of East Bengal and Assam, a Muslim-majority province, would restrict their access to government employment. The Muslim League, formed in 1906, urged that legislation should provide for separate electorates for Muslim minorities, to guarantee their representation in Hindu-majority areas. In 1912, the Bengali-speaking areas of the old province were reunited.

▼ ❷ **The partition and reunification of Bengal, 1905–12**

— national border
— provincial boundary
⋯⋯ provincial boundary prior to 1905
— line of 1905 partition

▦ Muslim majority area
▨ British districts
☐ native states and protectorates
▦ frontier area

The independence struggle 1879–1947

Indian nationalist movements took many forms in the course of the long struggle for independence. The Indian National Congress, originally an organization of the Western-educated elite, became a mass popular movement after the return to India in 1915 of the charismatic Mohandas K. Gandhi. By the 1930s, cautious calls for self-rule had become unequivocal demands for independence.

British officers serving in India led lives of conspicuous ease, their lifestyles supported by domestic staff, as this photograph of a servant giving a pedicure shows.

The freedom movement in India

1885: Founding of the Indian National Congress

1906: Foundation of Muslim League

1920: Start of civil disobedience campaigns by M. K. Gandhi in support of independence struggle

1918: Indian contribution to World War I earns it membership in League of Nations

1937: Burma is separated from India and made crown colony

1939: Congress ministries resign because India given no voice in respect to participation in World War II

1945: India becomes UN charter member

1947: New independent dominions of India and Pakistan are born

1948: Burma and Ceylon become independent; former withdraws from Commonwealth

1890 1900 1910 1920 1930 1940 1950

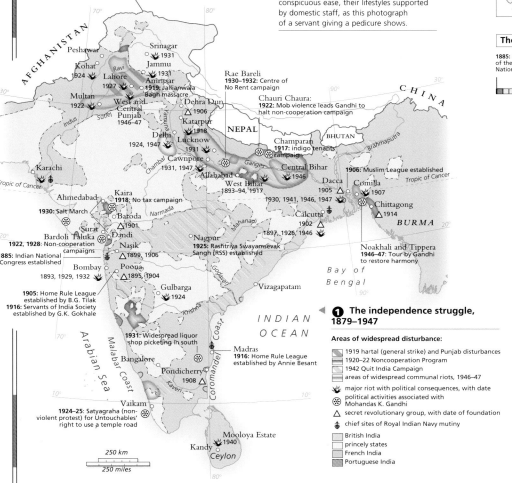

▲ ❶ **The independence struggle, 1879–1947**

Areas of widespread disturbance:

▨ 1919 hartal (general strike) and Punjab disturbances
☐ 1920–22 Noncooperation Program
☐ 1942 Quit India Campaign
☐ areas of widespread communal riots, 1946–47
☙ major riot with political consequences, with date
⊙ political activities associated with Mohandas K. Gandhi
△ secret revolutionary group, with date of foundation
⚓ chief sites of Royal Indian Navy mutiny

☐ British India
☐ princely states
☐ French India
☐ Portuguese India

World War II in South and Southeast Asia

The Japanese swiftly overran Southeast Asia, occupying the whole region by March 1942. The Allied counteroffensive consisted of US advances across the western Pacific from 1943, and the advance of British and Indian troops through Burma from 1944. But Japanese occupation had unleashed a tide of nationalism which was to have a grave impact on the postwar maintenance of the status quo, leading to the creation of new nations and the end of the European empires.

These Japanese prisoners of war were taken after the capture of Guadalcanal in 1942 – a key campaign in the US amphibious offensive.

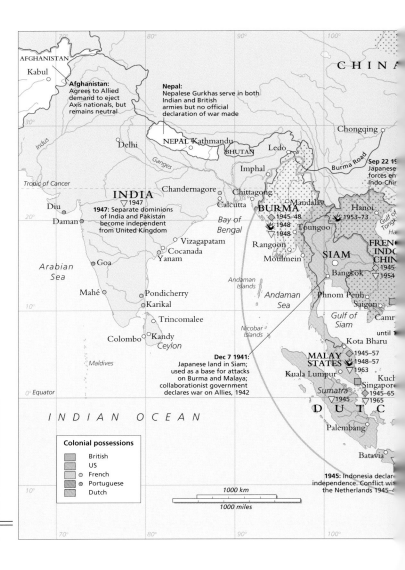

Colonial possessions

☐ British
☐ US
⊙ French
⊙ Portuguese
☐ Dutch

Political changes in Southeast Asia

1945: Sukarno and Ho Chi Minh declare independence for Indonesia and Vietnam respectively

1954: Geneva accords allow separate governments in North and South Vietnam

1957: Malaya granted independence, despite ongoing Communist insurrection

1963: Federation of Malaysia incorporates Singapore, Sarawak, and Sabah, along with Malaya

1975: Communist regimes come to power in South Vietnam, Laos, and Cambodia

1946: Philippines obtain their independence

1954: Sukarno abrogates union with Dutch and declares unitary state of Indonesia

1964: Gulf of Tonkin resolution authorizes US air strikes against North Vietnam and Viet Cong; war soon spreads to Laos and Cambodia

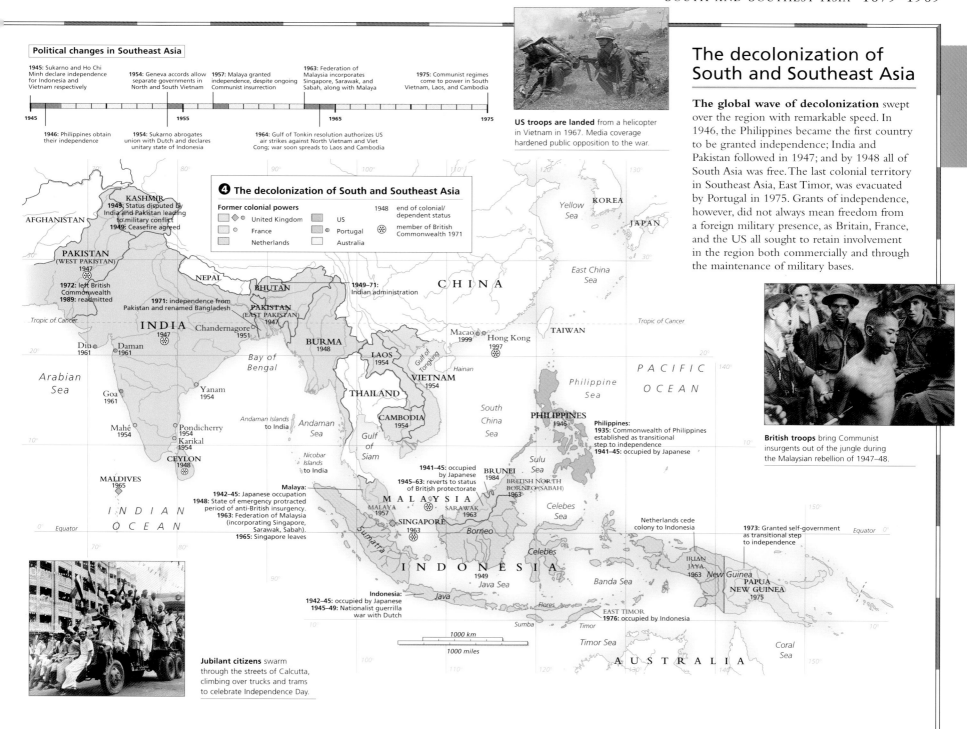

④ The decolonization of South and Southeast Asia

US troops are landed from a helicopter in Vietnam in 1967. Media coverage hardened public opposition to the war.

The decolonization of South and Southeast Asia

The global wave of decolonization swept over the region with remarkable speed. In 1946, the Philippines became the first country to be granted independence; India and Pakistan followed in 1947; and by 1948 all of South Asia was free. The last colonial territory in Southeast Asia, East Timor, was evacuated by Portugal in 1975. Grants of independence, however, did not always mean freedom from a foreign military presence, as Britain, France, and the US all sought to retain involvement in the region both commercially and through the maintenance of military bases.

British troops bring Communist insurgents out of the jungle during the Malaysian rebellion of 1947–48.

Jubilant citizens swarm through the streets of Calcutta, climbing over trucks and trams to celebrate Independence Day.

The impact of the Cold War 1946–89

The Vietnam War, the most violent and protracted conflict in Southeast Asia in the 20th century, was, in many ways, a proxy struggle for the US, China, and the USSR within the global context of the Cold War. Although Vietnam's independence was proclaimed at the end of World War II, it took three decades of bloody struggle – affecting both Vietnam and the neighboring states of Laos and Cambodia – before the French, and then the Americans who replaced them, were evicted from French Indochina.

⑤ The Vietnam War ▶

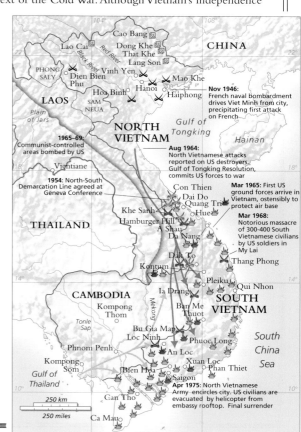

MODERN SOUTH AND SOUTHEAST ASIA

Jawaharlal Nehru, his daughter Indira Gandhi, and grandson Rajiv Gandhi (above) all served as Indian prime ministers.

IN MOST OF THE COUNTRIES of the region, securing independence failed to usher in an era of political peace and stability. The ethnic, religious, and linguistic heterogeneity of their populations quickly led to demands for readjustment of the political map and, in many instances, to secessionist movements and wars for independence. Notwithstanding all these internal and external stresses, most of the countries in South and Southeast Asia took great strides on the path of economic, social, and cultural development under a variety of political systems and economic philosophies. Life expectancy, levels of literacy, and per capita material consumption, especially for the growing middle and upper classes, were far higher than they were during the colonial era, and the economic infrastructure greatly expanded, with the development of a varied commercial base.

South Asia from 1948

In creating Pakistan, the 1947 partition of India established a political entity which could not withstand the many subsequent stresses between its two distant wings. In 1971 Pakistan was split between its eastern and western halves, and the new state of Bangladesh was formed. There were also a series of international disputes over areas whose borders were not adequately defined during the colonial era or, in the still-unresolved case of Kashmir, over an area whose future was left undecided when the British left India.

❷ Jammu and Kashmir

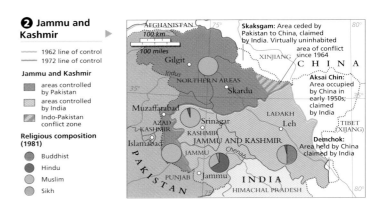

1962 line of control
1972 line of control

Jammu and Kashmir
◻ areas controlled by Pakistan
◻ areas controlled by India
▨ Indo-Pakistan conflict zone

Religious composition (1981)
● Buddhist
● Hindu
○ Muslim
● Sikh

Skaksgam: Area ceded by Pakistan to China, claimed by India. Virtually uninhabited area of conflict since 1964

Aksai Chin: Area occupied by China in early 1950s; claimed by India

Demchok: Area held by China claimed by India

Conflict over Jammu and Kashmir

India and Pakistan have contested possession of the Muslim-majority state of Kashmir since 1947, when the Hindu maharajah acceded to India, and fought wars over the territory in 1947–48 and 1965. Since 1989, there has been an independence movement in the Indian-held portion of the state, although India insists this is the handiwork of terrorists aided by Pakistan.

Territorial changes since 1947

The urgent task of integrating more than 600 largely autonomous princely states into the new Indian union was accomplished by 1950. But demands for more linguistically homogeneous states soon surfaced. The partition of the multilingual state of Madras in 1954 was the first in a long series of changes, including the creation of a number of tribal states, that have altered India's political map.

In 1984 the Indian army attacked Sikh militants who were occupying the Golden Temple of Amritsar, the Sikhs' holiest shrine.

Territorial conflicts in South Asia

1947: Start of Indo-Pakistani War fought over Jammu and Kashmir; UN ceasefire line agreed in 1949

1962: India set back in brief Sino-Indian border war after years of intermittent clashes

1971: Successful rebellion leads to creation of Bangladesh. Third Indo-Pakistani war as India intervenes in Bangladesh freedom struggle

1950   1960   1970   1980   1990

1955: Afghan government supports movement for separation of Pakhtunistan from Pakistan

1965: Second inconclusive Indo-Pakistani war over Jammu and Kashmir

1989: Start of violent insurrection against Indian rule in Jammu and Kashmir

The birth of Bangladesh

The two sectors of Pakistan had little in common apart from their Muslim faith, and the stresses on federalism and parliamentary democracy in the union caused its rupture. The Bangladeshi independence struggle was led by the Awami League, with active military support from India.

❸ The birth of Bangladesh

▽ site of violent clash between Bengalis and Pakistan army, Mar 1–2 1971
△ site of Pakistan army "crackdown" Mar 25–26 1971
◇ site of major act of sabotage by Mukti Bahini guerrillas (Bengal Liberation Army)
◻ area of marked guerrilla activity
◻ site of Indo-Pakistani border incident
→ refugees fleeing Bangladesh (with number of refugees)

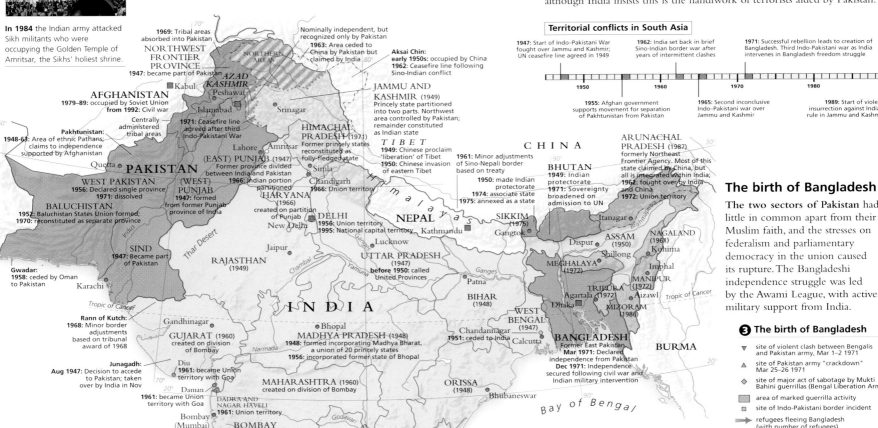

❶ The formation of contemporary South Asia, 1947–99

Boundaries in 1975
— agreed or de facto international boundaries, demarcated
--- extent of international territorial claim
···· line of control in Kashmir
— state or province after 1975

Territories
▨ Union territories created after 1956, now fully-fledged states
▨ East and West Pakistan 1967
▨ Area disputed between India and Pakistan
▨ former protectorate
▨ former French colonial possessions
▨ former Portuguese colonial possessions
▨ contemporary Indian state, with date of formation
■ national capital
● state capital
(1947) achievement of statehood

1969: Tribal areas absorbed into Pakistan

Nominally independent, but recognized only by Pakistan

NORTHWEST FRONTIER PROVINCE
1947: became part of Pakistan

NORTHERN AREAS

1963: Area ceded to China by Pakistan but claimed by India

Aksai Chin: early 1950s: occupied by China
1962: Ceasefire line following Sino-Indian conflict

AZAD KASHMIR

AFGHANISTAN
1979–88: occupied by Soviet Union from 1992: Civil war

Kabul   Peshawar

Islamabad

Srinagar

JAMMU AND KASHMIR (1949)
Princely state partitioned into two parts. Northwest area controlled by Pakistan; remainder constituted as Indian state

1971: Ceasefire line agreed after third Indo-Pakistani War

TIBET
1949: Chinese proclaim 'liberation' of Tibet
1950: Chinese invasion of eastern Tibet

1961: Minor adjustments of Sino-Nepali border based on treaty

Pakhtunistan:
1948-63: Area of ethnic Pathans; claims to independence supported by Afghanistan

Centrally administered tribal areas

HIMACHAL PRADESH (1971)
Former princely states reconstituted as fully-fledged state

CHINA

ARUNACHAL PRADESH (1987)
formerly Northeast Frontier Agency. Most of this state claimed by China, but all is integrated within India; 1962: fought over by India and China
1972: Union territory

Quetta

PAKISTAN

Lahore   Amritsar

(EAST) PUNJAB (1947)
Former province divided between India and Pakistan
1966: Indian portion partitioned

Simla

Chandigarh
1966: Union territory

HARYANA (1966)
created on partition of Punjab

BHUTAN
1949: Indian protectorate
1971: Sovereignty broadened on admission to UN

1950: made Indian protectorate
1974: associate state
1975: annexed as a state

WEST PAKISTAN
1956: Declared single province
1971: dissolved

(WEST) PUNJAB (1947)
1947: formed from former Punjab province of India

DELHI
1956: Union territory
1995: National capital territory

New Delhi

NEPAL

Kathmandu

SIKKIM (1975)
Gangtok

ASSAM (1950)
Dispur

NAGALAND (1961)
Kohima

BALUCHISTAN
1952: Baluchistan States Union formed; 1970: reconstituted as separate province

Lucknow

UTTAR PRADESH (1947)
before 1950: called United Provinces

MEGHALAYA (1972)
Shillong

Imphal

MANIPUR (1972)

Gwadar:
1958: ceded by Oman to Pakistan

Karachi

SIND
1947: Became part of Pakistan

Jaipur

RAJASTHAN (1949)

Patna

BIHAR (1948)

TRIPURA (1972)
Agartala

Aizawl

MIZORAM (1986)

Rann of Kutch:
1968: Minor border adjustments based on tribunal award of 1968

Gandhinagar

INDIA

Bhopal

MADHYA PRADESH (1948)
1948: formed incorporating Madhya Bharat, a union of 20 princely states
1956: incorporated former state of Bhopal

WEST BENGAL (1947)

Chandannagar
1951: ceded to India

Calcutta

BANGLADESH
Former East Pakistan
Mar 1971: Declared independence from Pakistan
Dec 1971: Independence secured following civil war and Indian military intervention

BURMA

Dhaka

Junagadh:
Aug 1947: Decision to accede to Pakistan; taken over by India in Nov

GUJARAT (1960)
created on division of Bombay

Diu
1961: became Union territory with Goa

Daman

Narmada

MAHARASHTRA (1960)
created on division of Bombay

ORISSA (1948)

Bhubaneswar

Bay of Bengal

DADRA AND NAGAR HAVELI
1961: Union territory

Bombay (Mumbai)

BOMBAY
1956: incorporated part of former state of Hyderabad
1960: divided into Gujarat and Maharashtra

Hyderabad

200 km
200 miles

GOA (1987)
1961: annexed by India
Panaji

ANDHRA PRADESH (1953)
1953: separation from Madras;
1956: incorporated part of former state of Hyderabad

Yanam
1955: ceded to India

KARNATAKA (1947)
1947-73 called Mysore
1953: boundaries altered
1956: part of former state of Hyderabad was incorporated

Bangalore

Arabian Sea

Mahe
1955: ceded to India

Malabar Coast

Madras (Chennai)

Coromandel Coast

Pondicherry
1955: ceded to India

TAMIL NADU (1956)
1947-69: called Madras

Karikal
1955: ceded to India

KERALA (1956)
1949: Travancore and Cochin state formed
1956: incorporated former state of Travancore and Cochin

Palk Strait:
Indo-Sri Lankan accord on division of water and islands

Trivandrum

INDIAN OCEAN

Colombo

SRI LANKA (CEYLON)
1947: dominion status
1948: full independence

In 1949 refugees were driven from their homes by Indo-Pakistani border clashes in Kashmir.

❸ [Bangladesh refugee map]

NEPAL
Pachingarh
Rangpur 675,000
Saidpur
Dinajpur
Hilli
Balurghat

ASSAM 375,000
NAGALAND
Atgram
MEGHALAYA
Sylhet
Karimganj
Rahanagar
MANIPUR 1.8 million
TRIPURA
Akhaura
Agartala
Kamalpur
Comilla
MIZORAM

BIHAR 25,000
Shikarpur
Meherpur
Jibannagar
Chugacha
Jessore
Boyra

BANGLADESH
Jaydebpur
Dhaka
Jibannagar
6.4 million

WEST BENGAL
Khulna
Chalna
Chittagong

Nov 1970: Area seriously devastated by cyclone. Inadequate government response provokes eastern opposition to martial law regime imposed from West Pakistan

Madhya Pradesh (off map) 125,000

Bay of Bengal

100 km
100 miles

BURMA

Secessionist movements and regional cooperation

The post-independence era in South and Southeast Asia has been characterized by a multitude of internal movements among subnational groups who have called for greater recognition, autonomy, and even independence. These have been treated with varying degrees of tolerance by the national governments. At the same time, the nations of South and Southeast Asia have embarked upon endeavours to bring about greater supranational and extra-regional cooperation. The latter efforts have been, in varying degrees, military, political, and economic in nature.

The Communist Khmer Rouge operated from a rural power base.

Cambodia

From 1975, the Communist Khmer Rouge conducted a social program in Cambodia which led to the deaths of over a million people, and the forced "reeducation" of millions more. The Vietnamese invaded in 1979 and withdrew in 1989. In 1993, the Khmer Rouge refused to take part in UN-sponsored elections.

Indonesian army troops are seen looting rice in from paddy fields in East Timor, where repression of prosecessionists has been particularly brutal.

East Timor

Originally a Portuguese colony, East Timor was invaded by Indonesia in 1975. The secessionist FRETILIN (East Timor Revolutionary Liberation Front) continues to resist Indonesian occupation. East Timor's incorporation as a province of Indonesia is not recognized by the UN.

The Tamil Tigers have been fighting for Tamil independence from the rest of Sri Lanka since the early 1980s. They remain the most feared militant group.

Sri Lanka

Since Sri Lanka gained independence in 1948, relations have deteriorated between the Sinhalese-speaking, mainly Buddhist, majority and the mainly Hindu Tamils, the island's principal minority. A bloody secessionist war began in 1984.

Map annotations

Afghanistan: Complete civil war since 1992; ethnic divisons between majority Pathans and minority tribes lie behind much of the conflict

Bhutan: Ethnic tension between indigenous Drupka people and Nepali immigrants in the south

Burma: Numerous dissident minorities in rebellion. Ethnic rebel groups (Karens) have joined forces with political groups to end military rule and bring in the democratic government which was legally elected in 1990.

Laos: Small pockets of resistance by Hmong (mountain tribes) to Communist government since 1975

Vietnam: Mountain minorities (Montagnards) and Chinese ethnic groups regarded with suspicion by Communist government

Cambodia: Following withdrawal of Vietnamese troops in 1989, Khmer Rouge resumed armed struggle in central and western Cambodia, provoking government counter-offensives

Pakistan: Non-Punjabi minority secessionist movements

India: Internal riots and uprisings since the 1950s have been directed at reorganizing state boundaries mainly on linguistic grounds. Most civil disorder is confined to the larger cities. Tribal conflict in the northeast and secessionist movements in Kashmir are ongoing

Bangladesh: Tribes are demanding autonomy in the Chittagong Hills

Thailand: Secessionist movement amongst Muslim Malays

Sri Lanka: Ongoing conflict between majority Sinhalese government and Tamil minority who are fighting for an independent state, Tamil Eelam

Achin: Aceh people of northern Sumatra in conflict with Indonesian government

Malaysia: Malay/Chinese immigrant tension stimulated by positive discrimination laws introduced in 1970

Singapore: Multiparty democracy in name only; opposition faces severe restrictions

Philippines: Communist and Muslim separatists have been fighting government for over 25 years

Brunei: Ruled by Sultan's decree following a failed rebellion in 1962

Indonesia: Java-dominated government suppresses local culture and politics, leading to secessionist movements. Conflict with ethnic Chinese

Irian Jaya: Free Papua movement seeking autonomy from Indonesia. Outbreaks of violence in 1977, 1978 and 1981

East Timor: Repression and persecution by Indonesian government since declaration of independence in 1985

④ Secessionist movements and regional cooperation

- secessionist movements
- violent protests against existing borders on linguistic grounds
- tribal/ethnic minority conflict with ruling power
- conflict between indigenous groups
- other violent uprisings

Membership of Asian Regional Movements:

ADB	Asian Development Bank, est. 1966
APEC	Asia-Pacific Economic Cooperation, est. 1989
ASEAN	Association for Southeast Asian Nations, est. 1967
CP	Colombo Plan, est. 1951
ESCAP	Economic and Social Commission for Asia and Pacific, est. 1947
SAARC	South Asian Association for Regional Cooperation, est. 1985

Secessionist movements and political coups

1955: Naga uprising in northeastern India, the first of numerous tribal insurrections

1965: Failed Marxist coup and military countercoup in Indonesia ends Sukarno regime

1975: Khmer Rouge take over Cambodia; impose regime of extreme terror

1981: Start of Sikh struggle for independent state of Khalistan in Indian Punjab

1958: Abortive secessionist uprisings in Baluchistan, Pakistan

1962: Military take over rule of Burma

1972: Ferdinand Marcos declares martial law in Philippines

1979: Deposition of monarchy in Afghanistan; Soviet invasion and civil war

1982: Start of struggle in Sri Lanka for independent state of Tamil Eelam

1955 — 1965 — 1975 — 1985

The urbanization of South and Southeast Asia

The development of South and Southeast Asia is reflected dramatically in its burgeoning cities, some of which, notably Bombay (Mumbai), are among the largest in the world. Of the roughly 1.8 billion people now inhabiting the region about 500 million live in urban areas. However, growing populations, the majority still dependent on agriculture and living in densely settled areas such as the great river valleys of the Ganges, Indus, and Mekong, place an increasing burden on fragile ecosystems, with potentially disastrous consequences for the environment.

Poverty drives many of India's rural poor to the increasingly overcrowded cities.

The modern financial centre of Singapore towers over the harbor, a reminder of the island state's origins as a strategic trading settlement.

⑤ The urbanization of South and Southeast Asia, 1993

Urban centers (populations in 1993)

- over 16 million
- 8–16 million
- 4–8 million
- 2–4 million
- under 2 million
- capital city

Population density per square kilometer

- 300–1000
- 100–299
- 50–99
- 10–49

The urban/rural divide

- urban population
- rural population

NORTH AND EAST ASIA
REGIONAL HISTORY

Vegetation type

ice cap and glacier
polar or alpine desert
tundra
semidesert or sparsely vegetated
grassland
forest or open woodland
tropical rain forest
temperate desert
tropical desert
desert
coastline (present-day)
coastline (18,000 years ago)

THE HISTORICAL LANDSCAPE

THE FRAGMENTED GEOGRAPHY of this, the world's largest uninterrupted land mass, has produced a wide variety of historical scenarios. The mountainous massifs at its heart – the Plateau of Tibet, the Altai, Tien Shan, and Pamir ranges – enclose the arid Takla Makan, Gobi, and Ordos deserts, which together comprise a hostile and sparsely inhabited realm. Stretching in a wide arc around this region are the massive steppes, long home to pastoral nomads whose turbulent history was punctuated by sorties against their sedentary neighbors and, occasionally, violent irruptions which impelled their skilled and fast-moving horsemen across Eurasia. Broad rivers flow north across Siberia to the Arctic, and west to inland deltas and landlocked seas such as the Aral and Caspian. To the east, the fertile floodplains of the Yellow River and the Yangtze were the focus of the world's oldest surviving civilization, that of China, an enormous demographic and cultural fulcrum which dominates East Asia, and whose influence has been cast far across the peninsulas and archipelagos of the Pacific Rim.

Japan was settled by hunter-gatherers about 30,000 years ago. At the the time of the last Ice Age, most of the Japanese islands were densely forested, with settlement only in the coastal regions.

The Yellow River flows down to the plains of eastern China across a plateau of fertile *loess* – fine silty soils created by the erosion of glacial material. The river cuts down through the soft sediments, washing them downstream and depositing them on the Great Plain of China, resulting in exceptionally fertile soils, suitable for a wide range of crops.

Siberia was a cold, frozen region at the time of the last Ice Age, sparsely inhabited by hunter-gatherers. Unlike northern Europe and North America, Siberia was not covered by an ice cap because of the lack of moisture across the region. The extreme cold preserved the remains of creatures such as mammoths, along with evidence of the shelters built by the people who hunted them.

North and East Asia: 18,000 years ago

North Asia was relatively ice-free during the last Ice Age, except for the extension of the European ice sheet to the east of the Ural Mountains, covering only a small part of the West Siberian Plain. The climate, however, was still bitterly cold, far colder than it is today. Extreme temperatures in southern Siberia limited vegetation to scrubby tundra plants across most of North Asia. Along the Ob' and Yenisey rivers, two large lakes were formed where the rivers dammed up behind the edge of the European ice sheet.

NORTH AND EAST ASIA
EXPLORATION AND MAPPING

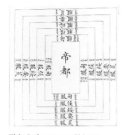

This 3rd-century Chinese view of the world placed the imperial capital at the center of a grid, with outlying areas organized in a regular, diminishing hierarchy.

THE GROWTH OF KNOWLEDGE of Central Asia was very gradual. Mountain barriers, extensive deserts, and climatic extremes hemmed in and defined the cultures of the region. The rulers of both China and India rarely looked beyond their frontiers, while remote states such as Tibet and Japan actively shunned external contact. In the Classical and Medieval eras perilous trade routes provided limited passage for missionaries and entrepreneurs, supplanted in the 16th century by the growth of maritime trade and European colonialists. In the 19th-century imperial European powers vied for control of Asia's land and wealth, a struggle echoed today as rich mineral resources attract increasing attention.

The early mapping of Japan

Following the introduction of Chinese administrative ideas during the 7th century CE, the southern Japanese islands were divided into 68 provinces. The limited size of the state made it possible to conduct surveys of land and population in order to raise taxes; the first maps were of individual estates, but with the creation of centralized government in 710, the Buddhist priest Gyogi began to draw up national diagrams featuring the provinces. Gyogi-style maps typically show south at the top, and often include fantastical lands.

A Gyogi-style map of Honshu from 1305, orientated with south at the top, naming and listing the 68 Japanese provinces.

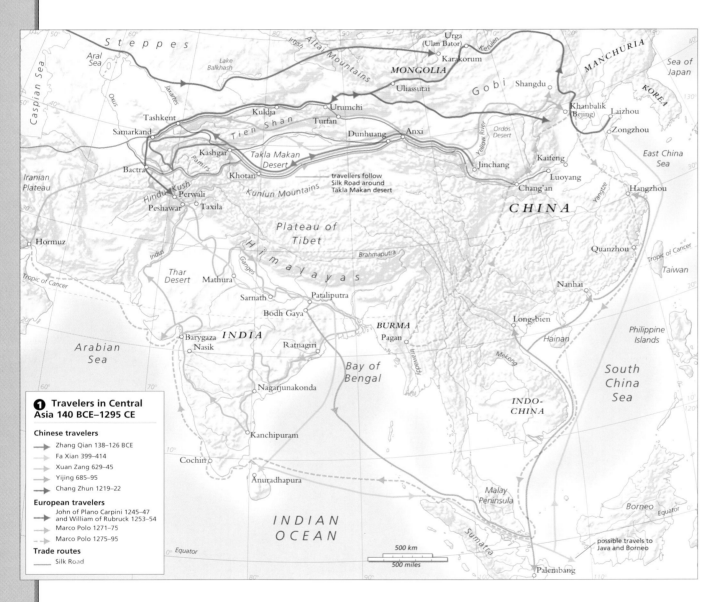

① Travelers in Central Asia 140 BCE–1295 CE

Chinese travelers
- → Zhang Qian 138–126 BCE
- → Fa Xian 399–414
- → Xuan Zang 629–45
- → Yijing 685–95
- → Chang Zhun 1219–22

European travelers
- → John of Plano Carpini 1245–47 and William of Rubruck 1253–54
- → Marco Polo 1271–75
- → Marco Polo 1275–95

Trade routes
- —— Silk Road

500 km
500 miles

Mapping was an essential tool in administering the vast Chinese empire. Here a cartographer presents a Tang emperor with a map of his domains.

The conquest of Central Asia by the Mongols in the 13th century re-opened the Silk Road for trans-Asian trade. This Persian painting shows some Chinese merchant traders.

Travelers in Central Asia

The first recorded travelers in Central Asia were diplomatic missions, such as Zang Qian, or Chinese Buddhist priests on pilgrimage to India, such as Fa Xian and Xuan Zang. Over 1000 years later the "Mongol Peace" encouraged further missions (Chang Zhun), while the secure trading routes drew Christian missionaries and traders such as Marco Polo to the east. Their extensive accounts contributed greatly to knowledge of the region.

A 17th-century European copy of a Chinese map by Zhu Siben, a leading 14th-century Chinese cartographer. It is notable for the details of coastline and drainage – knowledge of river systems was regarded as a vital means of controlling China; the use of a grid to establish a projection was a Chinese invention.

c.1000 BCE: Western Zhou sponsor exploration and recording of China's geography

2 CE: First census of Chinese population

607: First record of Japanese diplomatic mission to China

751: Arabs reach Central Asia, and defeat Tang

c.1220: Zhao Rugua publishes account of travels in Southeast Asia

1000 BCE   500 BCE   1 CE   500 CE   1000 CE

Early knowledge of Asia

1st century BCE: Silk Road opens linking southwest Asia and China

c.250: Lodestone compass used in China

c.900: First maps of Japan, showing provinces

1206: Mongols begin conquest of Central Asia

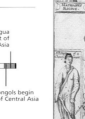

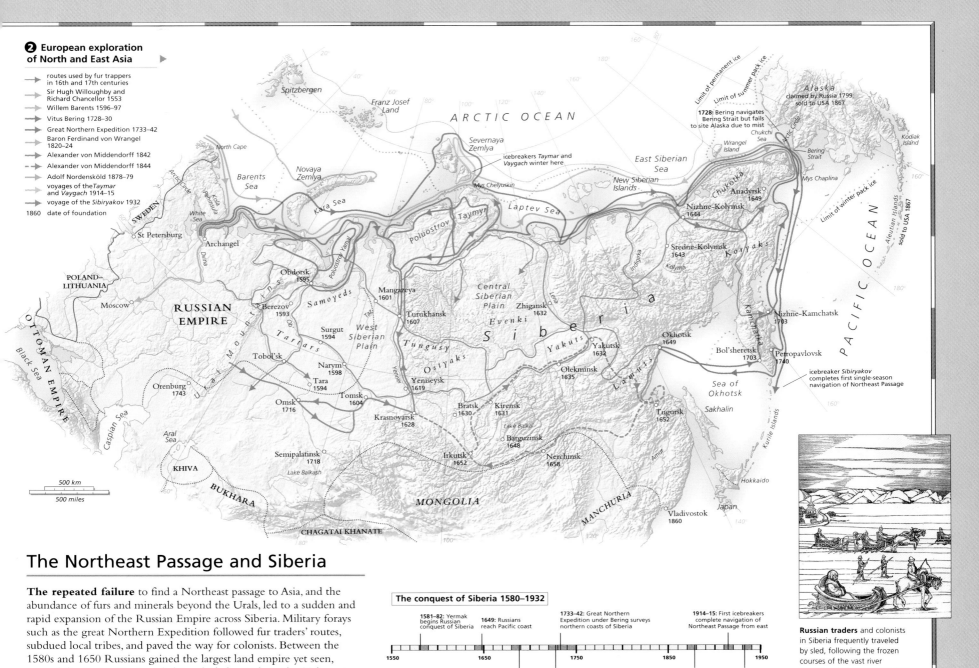

② European exploration of North and East Asia ▶

→ routes used by fur trappers in 16th and 17th centuries
→ Sir Hugh Willoughby and Richard Chancellor 1553
→ Willem Barents 1596–97
→ Vitus Bering 1728–30
→ Great Northern Expedition 1733–42
→ Baron Ferdinand von Wrangel 1820–24
→ Alexander von Middendorff 1842
→ Alexander von Middendorff 1844
→ Adolf Nordensköld 1878–79
→ voyages of the *Taymar* and *Vaygach* 1914–15
→ voyage of the *Sibiryakov* 1932
1860 date of foundation

icebreaker *Sibiryakov* completes first single-season navigation of Northeast Passage

The Northeast Passage and Siberia

The repeated failure to find a Northeast passage to Asia, and the abundance of furs and minerals beyond the Urals, led to a sudden and rapid expansion of the Russian Empire across Siberia. Military forays such as the great Northern Expedition followed fur traders' routes, subdued local tribes, and paved the way for colonists. Between the 1580s and 1650 Russians gained the largest land empire yet seen, crossed the Bering Strait, and claimed Alaska. Only in the 20th century did icebreakers open the maritime route across the Arctic Ocean.

The conquest of Siberia 1580–1932

1581–82: Yermak begins Russian conquest of Siberia
1649: Russians reach Pacific coast
1733–42: Great Northern Expedition under Bering surveys northern coasts of Siberia
1914–15: First icebreakers complete navigation of Northeast Passage from east

1689: Treaty of Nerchinsk agrees Russian and Chinese spheres of influence in east Asia
1728: Vitus Bering navigates Bering Strait
1878–79: Nordensköld completes first navigation of Northeast Passage from west
1932: First single-season traverse of Northeast Passage by icebreaker *Sibiryakov*

1550 … 1650 … 1750 … 1850 … 1950

Russian traders and colonists in Siberia frequently traveled by sled, following the frozen courses of the vast river systems, which in summer they traversed by boat portage.

Nominally under Chinese control during the 19th century, in effect Tibet remained independent, closed to the outside world. This 18th-century Tibetan painting maps the splendor of the Dalai Lama's Potala palace in Lhasa.

Both Russia and Britain regarded accurate mapping (below) as essential to imperial control. The maps of Nepal and Tibet produced covertly by local "pundits," provided essential intelligence for Anglo-Indian imperialists.

On the roof of the world

As the imperial world map was filled in during the 19th century, so the most remote regions of Central Asia began to be explored and claimed. Jesuit missionaries and diplomatic missions (frequently backed by force) had limited success in penetrating the fastnesses of Tibet. In India, the British recruited local guides as secret agents (pundits) to conduct clandestine surveys. Only during the last century did scientists (often Russian) such as Przhevalsky and Roerich explore the plateaux and mountains in any detail.

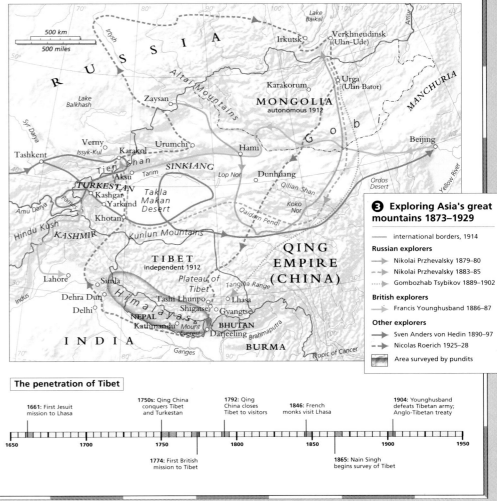

③ Exploring Asia's great mountains 1873–1929

— international borders, 1914

Russian explorers
—— Nikolai Przhevalsky 1879–80
--- Nikolai Przhevalsky 1883–85
···· Gombozhab Tsybikov 1889–1902

British explorers
—— Francis Younghusband 1886–87

Other explorers
→ Sven Anders von Hedin 1890–97
→ Nicolas Roerich 1925–28
▨ Area surveyed by pundits

The penetration of Tibet

1661: First Jesuit mission to Lhasa
1750s: Qing China conquers Tibet and Turkestan
1792: Qing China closes Tibet to visitors
1846: French monks visit Lhasa
1904: Younghusband defeats Tibetan army; Anglo-Tibetan treaty

1774: First British mission to Tibet
1865: Nain Singh begins survey of Tibet

1650 … 1700 … 1750 … 1800 … 1850 … 1900 … 1950

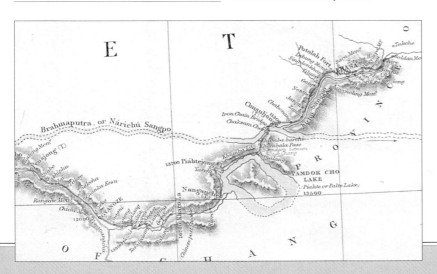

THE FIRST EAST ASIAN CIVILIZATIONS

Some of the earliest Chinese script is preserved on oracle bones from the Shang period c.1400 BCE.

THE EMERGENCE OF ORGANIZED CULTURES in East Asia took a variety of forms. The fertile soils of the Yellow River Basin and the Yangtze Valley provided the potential for the development of the first agricultural communities in the region 8000 years ago. Pottery working with kilns and bronze technology developed, accompanied by the first Chinese states and empires; the region remains to this day the heartland of China's culture and population. In Japan, the abundance of natural resources, especially fish and seafood, meant that hunter-gathering persisted, alongside features normally associated with sedentary agriculture – the world's earliest pottery is found here. Across the steppe grasslands of Central Asia, dominated by seasonal migration in search of pasture, communities developed a mobile culture now revealed through elaborate burials and decorated grave goods.

The agricultural revolution in Central and East Asia from c.10,000 BCE

The hardy yak provided abundant meat, furs for clothing and tents, and dairy products for the nomadic pastoralists of Central Asia.

A wide range of crops and plants was domesticated across East Asia from c.10,000 BCE. The pig was the most widely domesticated animal, and varieties of cattle such as oxen, yak, and banteng supported migratory herders. It was the domestication of staple crops such as millet and rice that provided the basis for population growth and, later, the first Chinese cities and states. Rice was cultivated in the Yangtze Valley around 6000 BCE, reaching Korea some 4000 years later and Japan in the 1st millennium BCE. In the Yellow River Valley of northern China, millet was domesticated.

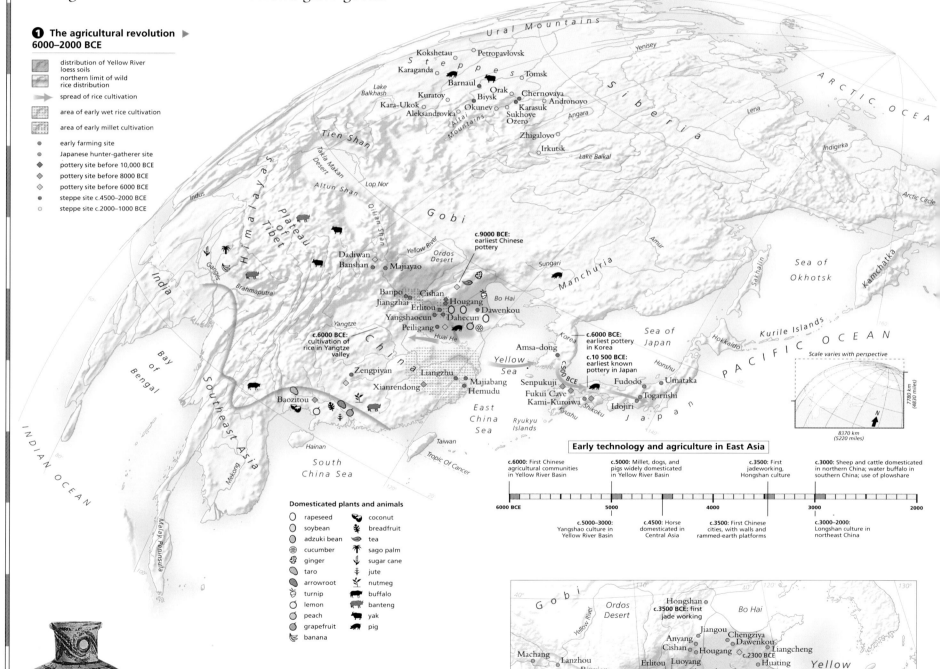

① The agricultural revolution 6000–2000 BCE

- distribution of Yellow River loess soils
- northern limit of wild rice distribution
- → spread of rice cultivation
- area of early wet rice cultivation
- area of early millet cultivation
- • early farming site
- • Japanese hunter-gatherer site
- ♦ pottery site before 10,000 BCE
- ◇ pottery site before 8000 BCE
- ◇ pottery site before 6000 BCE
- • steppe site c.4500–2000 BCE
- ○ steppe site c.2000–1000 BCE

Domesticated plants and animals

○	rapeseed		coconut
○	soybean		breadfruit
○	adzuki bean		tea
⊛	cucumber		sago palm
○	ginger		sugar cane
○	taro		jute
○	arrowroot		nutmeg
○	turnip		buffalo
○	lemon		banteng
○	peach		yak
○	grapefruit		pig
○	banana		

Early technology and agriculture in East Asia

6000 BCE	5000	4000	3000	2000
c.6000: First Chinese agricultural communities in Yellow River Basin	**c.5000:** Millet, dogs, and pigs widely domesticated in Yellow River Basin	**c.3500:** First jadeworking, Hongshan culture	**c.3000:** Sheep and cattle domesticated in northern China; water buffalo in southern China; use of plowshare	
c.5000–3000: Yangshao culture in Yellow River Basin	**c.4500:** Horse domesticated in Central Asia	**c.3500:** First Chinese cities, with walls and rammed-earth platforms	**c.3000–2000:** Longshan culture in northeast China	

Scale varies with perspective

Neolithic China c.4000–2000 BCE

The geometric decoration of Yangshao pottery probably had a ritualistic significance.

The early agricultural communities in the Yellow River Basin developed common cultural characteristics known to us through settlement patterns, burial practices and pottery. The Yangshao was the first identifiable culture, producing distinctive decorated pottery vessels. By about 3000 BCE this was replaced by the more prosperous and sophisticated Longshan culture, which spread throughout the basin and the coastal plain. Technological advances occurred in pottery, copperworking was introduced, the plowshare was in use, and by 2700 BCE silk weaving had begun.

② Neolithic China

- area of Yangshao culture
- area of Longshan culture by c.2500 BCE
- • major neolithic site
- ◇ site with pottery kilns from c.4000 BCE

c.3500 BCE: first jade working

c.2300 BCE

c.1500 BCE: earliest evidence of glazed pottery

c.5000 BCE: early lacquer working

200 km
200 miles

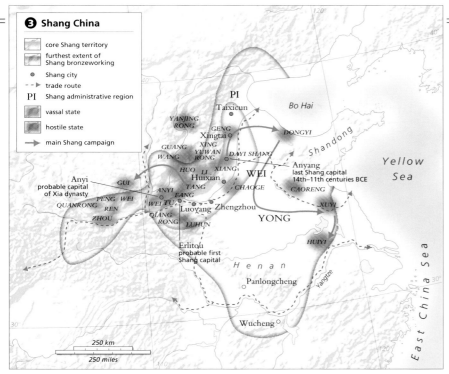

❸ Shang China

- ▨ core Shang territory
- ▨ furthest extent of Shang bronzeworking
- ● Shang city
- - -▶ trade route
- **PI** Shang administrative region
- ▨ vassal state
- ▨ hostile state
- ➜ main Shang campaign

Shang China 1800–1027 BCE

In about 1800 BCE, the nucleus of the first Chinese state emerged in the Yellow River Valley of northern China. The Shang state was feudal, with its core territory under the direct control of the kings, but outlying areas less securely attached. The Shang kings used ancestor worship and divination to confirm their dynastic status. Their successive capitals were mainly ritual centers with palace complexes and elaborate royal burial places. The Shang were skilled in writing, and were exponents of martial conquest, divination, and human sacrifice. Bronzeworking (often for military purposes), stonecarving, and potterymaking, were harnessed to religion and the state.

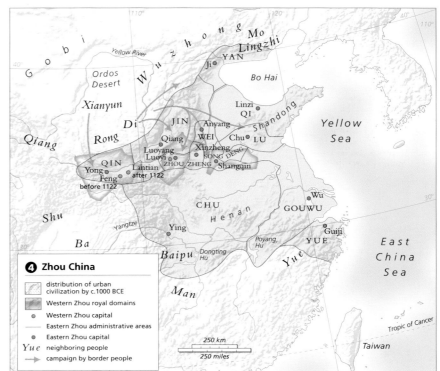

Although the Shang used bronze widely for everyday objects and armaments, they produced sophisticated vessels – often in the shape of animals – for specific ritualistic and sacrificial functions.

Timeline (Shang China):
- c.2000: Xia dynasty, probable forerunners of the Shang, established
- c.1800: Beginnings of Shang state
- 1400: Anyang becomes Shang capital
- 1027: Western Zhou dynasty supplants Shang
- c.1700: First bronze vessels cast
- c.1400: Earliest evidence of Chinese writing on oracle bones
- c.1200: Wheeled chariots spread to China from Central Asia

2000 BCE — 1800 — 1600 — 1400 — 1200 — 1000 BCE

Shang China

Zhou China 1027–403 BCE

The 11th century BCE saw political control wrested from the Shang by the Zhou (Chou), based west of the Shang capital. Under the Western Zhou greater political unity developed, the royal family assigning territories to their vassals to create a proto-feudal state. Human sacrifice declined, defensive walls began to be built, and the first literary records of Chinese history emerged. Constant rivalry and dissent gradually eroded centralized power, and from 770 BCE a new capital was established at Luoyang under the Eastern Zhou. A looser political federation came about, bound together by the need for defense against hostile neighbors, and by common cultural values reflected in the use of coinage, in richly decorated tombs, and in the writings of Confucius.

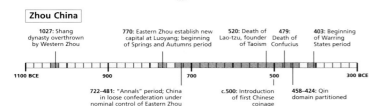

The first Chinese coins came into use around 500 BCE, and were normally cast in bronze in the form of tools.

Zhou China

Timeline (Zhou China):
- 1027: Shang dynasty overthrown by Western Zhou
- 770: Eastern Zhou establish new capital at Luoyang; beginning of Springs and Autumns period
- 520: Death of Lao-tzu, founder of Taoism
- 479: Death of Confucius
- 403: Beginning of Warring States period
- 722–481: "Annals" period; China in loose confederation under nominal control of Eastern Zhou
- c.500: Introduction of first Chinese coinage
- 458–424: Qin domain partitioned

1100 BCE — 900 — 700 — 500 — 300 BCE

❹ Zhou China

- ▨ distribution of urban civilization by c.1000 BCE
- ▨ Western Zhou royal domains
- ● Western Zhou capital
- — Eastern Zhou administrative areas
- ● Eastern Zhou capital
- *Yue* neighboring people
- ➜ campaign by border people

Qin China 221–206 BCE

The Zhou confederation eventually collapsed into bitter civil war. The Warring States period (403–221 BCE) was gradually brought to an end by the Qin dynasty, who created by alliance, diplomacy, and conquest, the first unified Chinese empire. A series of ruthless campaigns by Shi Huangdi (the First Emperor) extended Qin domains far to the north and to the south beyond the Yangtze valley to the borders of modern Vietnam; in their wake, a process of centralization and standardization was introduced to minimize regional differences and tribal dissent. The area of the Chinese state was effectively tripled in 16 years, while the constant threat to the northern borders by nomadic steppe peoples such as the Xiongnu led to the construction of the first Great Wall.

Timeline (Qin China):
- 247: King Zheng (later Shi Huangdi) becomes ruler of Qin domain
- 230: Campaigns of Shi Huangdi begin
- 221: Qin Empire established, organized into 36 commanderies
- 214: Slave labor used to link ramparts to form Great Wall
- 210: Death of Shi Huangdi, entombed with vast terra-cotta army
- 221–207: General disarmament, standardization of weights, measures, and axle widths to facilitate commerce
- 213: Proscription of nonscientific books; standardization and simplification of Chinese script
- 206: Beginning of Han dynasty

250 BCE — 240 — 230 — 220 — 210 — 200 BCE

Qin China

Thousands of life-size terra-cotta soldiers and horses were buried near Shi Huangdi's tomb outside Xianyang, a testament to his military might and concern for his destiny in the afterlife.

❺ Qin China

- ▨ original Qin territory c.350 BCE
- ▨ Qin expansion by 288 BCE
- ▨ Qin expansion by 220 BCE
- **HAN 230** Qin acquisition with date
- ▨ areas under Qin control after unification
- ● Qin state capitals and administrative center
- ▨▨▨ defensive wall
- *Yue* people

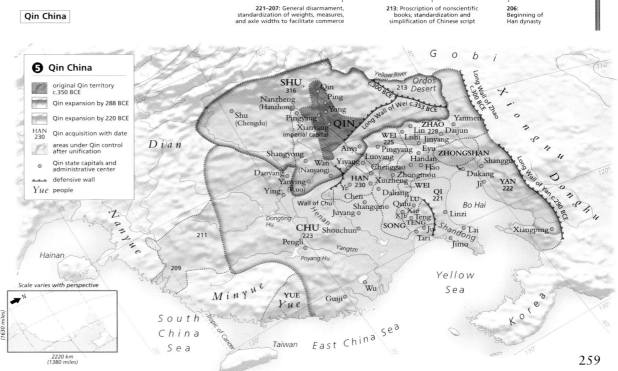

THE HAN AND THE GREAT MIGRATIONS

A **ceremonial bronze** bridle from the Han period reflects the importance of Chinese cavalry skills.

THE UNIFICATION OF CHINA under an authoritarian centralized regime by the Qin in 221 BCE paved the way for the Han, who assumed control in 206 BCE. The Han consolidated Chinese control of the south, pushing indigenous populations into more marginal areas, as well as expanding far into Central Asia along the Silk Road. In doing so, the Han established a domain by far the greatest the world had ever seen, and provided a template for Chinese territorial aspirations for the next two millennia. Largely self-sufficient, the Han nevertheless benefited from trans-Asian trade *(see pp. 44–45)*, but were constantly troubled by the steppe peoples, especially the Xiongnu, mounted pastoralists who harassed their northern borders.

Han China 206 BCE–220 CE

Tomb pottery from the Han period often celebrates daily life, as in this model of a farm building, complete with sheep and donkey.

The Han, who ruled China for over 400 years (apart from a brief interregnum under Wang Mang from 9–25 CE), established China as the most dominant cultural, political, and economic force in Asia. They constructed a new Great Wall to protect their northern borders, and established military garrisons from Korea in the east to Champa (Vietnam) in the south and Ferghana in the west to protect their expanding empire. Trade – along the great trans-Eurasian land routes and by sea – flourished; Buddhism entered China during this period (although the Han bureaucracy was structured on Confucian principles); and by 2 CE the first imperial census revealed a Chinese population of over 57 million, living mainly in the river valleys of the north.

The Han dynasty

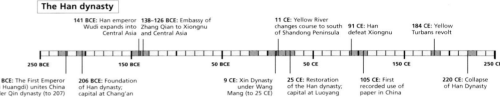

141 BCE: Han emperor Wudi expands into Central Asia	11 CE: Yellow River changes course to south of Shandong Peninsula
138–126 BCE: Embassy of Zhang Qian to Xiongnu and Central Asia	91 CE: Han defeat Xiongnu
	184 CE: Yellow Turbans revolt

250 BCE — 150 BCE — 50 BCE — 50 CE — 150 CE — 250 CE

221 BCE: The First Emperor (Shi Huangdi) unites China under Qin dynasty (to 207)
206 BCE: Foundation of Han dynasty; capital at Chang'an
9 CE: Xin Dynasty under Wang Mang (to 25 CE)
25 CE: Restoration of the Han dynasty; capital at Luoyang
105 CE: First recorded use of paper in China
220 CE: Collapse of Han Dynasty

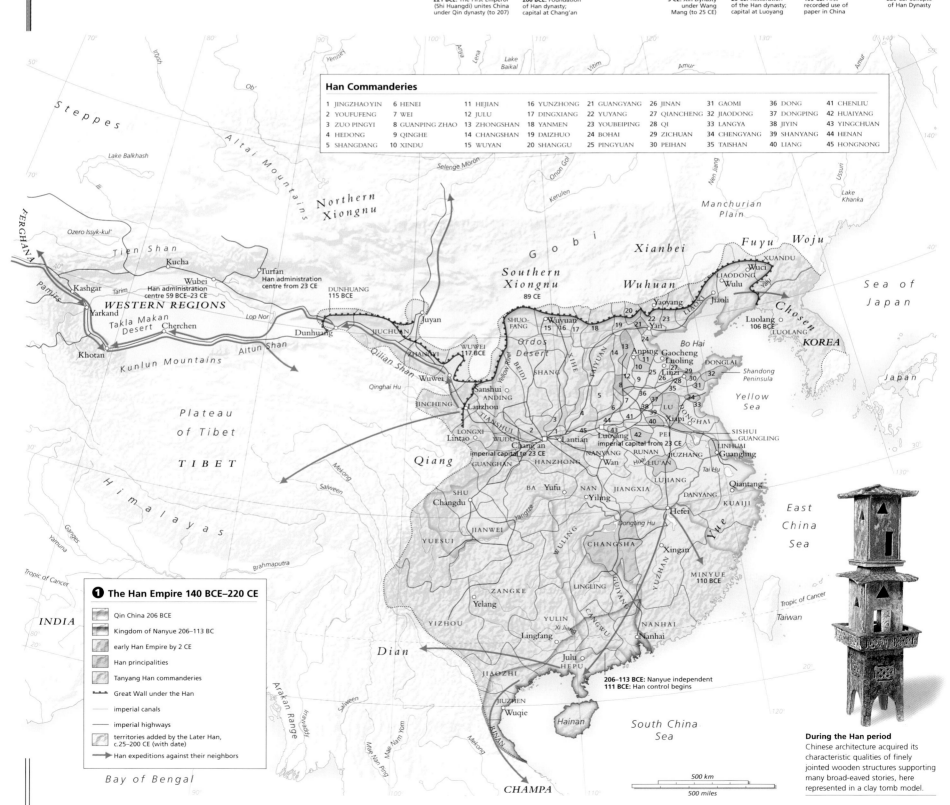

Han Commanderies

1 JINGZHAO YIN	6 HENEI	11 HEJIAN	16 YUNZHONG	21 GUANGYANG	26 JINAN	31 GAOMI	36 DONG	41 CHENLIU
2 YOUFUFENG	7 WEI	12 JULU	17 DINGXIANG	22 YUYANG	27 QIANCHENG	32 JIAODONG	37 DONGPING	42 HUAIYANG
3 ZUO PINGYI	8 GUANPING ZHAO	13 ZHONGSHAN	18 YANMEN	23 YOUBEIPING	28 QI	33 LANGYA	38 JIYIN	43 YINGCHUAN
4 HEDONG	9 QINGHE	14 CHANGSHAN	19 DAIZHUO	24 BOHAI	29 ZICHUAN	34 CHENGYANG	39 SHANYANG	44 HENAN
5 SHANGDANG	10 XINDU	15 WUYAN	20 SHANGGU	25 PINGYUAN	30 PEIHAN	35 TAISHAN	40 LIANG	45 HONGNONG

❶ The Han Empire 140 BCE–220 CE

- Qin China 206 BCE
- Kingdom of Nanyue 206–113 BC
- early Han Empire by 2 CE
- Han principalities
- Tanyang Han commanderies
- Great Wall under the Han
- imperial canals
- imperial highways
- territories added by the Later Han, c.25–200 CE (with date)
- Han expeditions against their neighbors

During the Han period
Chinese architecture acquired its characteristic qualities of finely jointed wooden structures supporting many broad-eaved stories, here represented in a clay tomb model.

500 km
500 miles

The fragmentation of China 220–589 CE

The threat posed by the steppe warriors' extraordinary horsemanship is illustrated in this relief tile from Sichuan. The mounted archer is performing a "Parthian" shot at full gallop, in full control of both his weapon and his speeding horse.

A series of revolts, the inability to collect taxes from northern vassals, and an increasing reliance on mercenaries recruited from steppe tribes led to the collapse of the Han dynasty and a prolonged period of turmoil in China. The north fell prey to a succession of non-Chinese peoples, the most notable being the Turkic Toba (or Northern) Wei, while the Chinese aristocracy withdrew to the south. During this period the collapse of Chinese institutions saw a decline in respect for Confucian values and the growth of Taoist cults and Buddhism.

Maps

❷ The Three Kingdoms c.250 CE ▲

Labels: Gobi, Xiongnu, Wuhuan, Di, Xianbei, Yellow River, Bo Hai, WEI 220–640 CE, Chang'an, Luoyang, Yellow Sea, Qiang, Jiankang, Chengdu, SHU 221–263 CE, WU 222–277 CE, Taiwan, Tropic of Cancer, South China Sea, Hainan, 500 km, 500 miles

❺ China c.560 CE ▲

Labels: Gobi, Eastern Turks, Western Turks, Yellow River, Bo Hai, NORTHERN QI, Ye, Yellow Sea, Chang'an, NORTHERN ZHOU, 573: controlled by Chen, Jiankang, CHEN, Yangtze, Taiwan, Tropic of Cancer, South China Sea, Hainan, 500 km, 500 miles

❸ The later Sixteen Kingdoms period c.400 CE ▲

Labels: NORTHERN LIANG, Gobi, NORTHERN YAN, Lungcheng, Dunhuang, Zhangye, Pingcheng, Bo Hai, Wuwei, WEI, SOUTHERN YAN, WESTERN LIANG, XIA, Chang'an, Luoyang, Yellow River, Yellow Sea, SOUTHERN LIANG, Guangu, Jiankang, Yangtze, EASTERN JIN, Tropic of Cancer, South China Sea, Hainan, Taiwan, 500 km, 500 miles

❹ The Toba Wei c.440–500 CE ▲

Labels: Gobi, Shengle first Wei capital, Ruanruan, Western Turks, Yellow River, Pingcheng second Wei capital, Bo Hai, Tuyuhun, TOBA (NORTHERN) WEI, Yang, Luoyang, Yellow Sea, Jiankang, Qiang, Yangtze, LIU SONG 420–478 CE, SOUTHERN QI 479–501 CE, LIANG 502–556 CE, Taiwan, Tropic of Cancer, South China Sea, Hainan, 500 km, 500 miles

Imperial Toba Wei pastures   Toba Wei conquests c.500 BCE

The fragmentation of China (timeline)

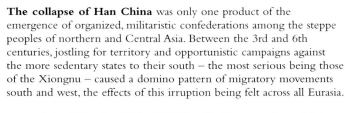

220: Emergence of Three Kingdoms
280: Western Jin conquer southern China
439: Northern (Toba) Wei dominate northern China (to 534)
524: Invasion of Wei by Ruanruan and Turks
557: Beginning of Northern Zhou dynasty (to 581)

265: Western Jin take over Wei state
304: Sixteen Kingdoms period (to 439)
490: Northern Wei rebuild Luoyang
552: Northern Qi dynasty (to 577)
581: China reunited under Sui dynasty (to 617)

(Timeline marks: 200, 300, 400, 500, 600)

The steppe kingdoms of Central Asia

The collapse of Han China was only one product of the emergence of organized, militaristic confederations among the steppe peoples of northern and Central Asia. Between the 3rd and 6th centuries, jostling for territory and opportunistic campaigns against the more sedentary states to their south – the most serious being those of the Xiongnu – caused a domino pattern of migratory movements south and west, the effects of this irruption being felt across all Eurasia.

The Xiongnu owed much of their military success to their understanding of cavalry tactics. In addition to the fast, lightly armored skirmishers associated with steppe peoples, they maintained a heavy cavalry (*left*) capable of breaking through massed infantry.

▼ ❻ The steppe kingdoms of Central Asia

- area occupied by nomadic agriculturalists
- Xiongnu homeland
- Han Empire at greatest extent c.200 CE
- Gupta Empire at greatest extent c.400 CE
- Sassanian Persia c.250 CE
- Kushan Empire c.275 CE
- Toba Wei c.500 CE
- Eastern Turks c.600 CE
- Western Turks c.600 CE
- Silk Road

Major movements of steppe peoples:
- 1st–3rd century CE
- 300–350
- 350–500
- after 500

This iron Bactrian plaque plated in sheet gold with turquoise gems, and depicting a horseman, is typical of the intricate but very portable art of the steppe peoples.

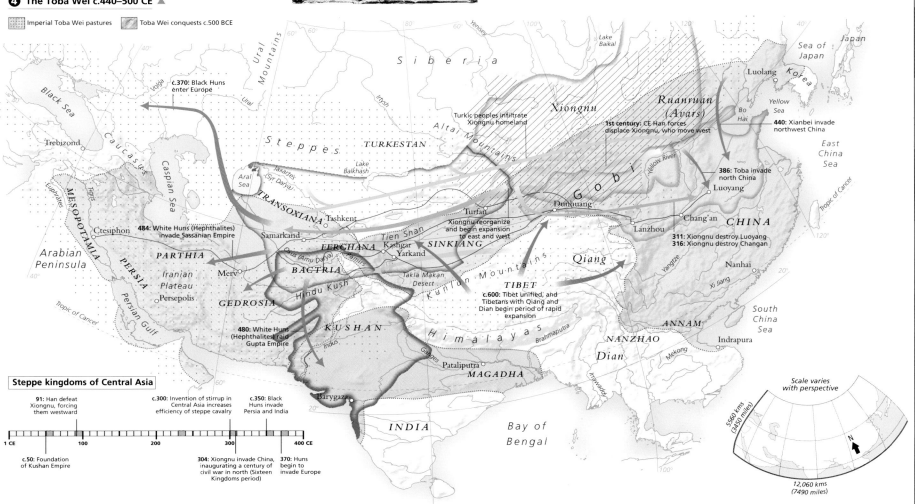

Map labels: Siberia, Ural Mountains, Lake Baikal, Yenisei, Irtysh, Sea of Japan, Japan, c.370: Black Huns enter Europe, Volga, Black Sea, Ural, Turkic peoples infiltrate Xiongnu homeland, Xiongnu, Ruanruan (Avars), Luolang, Korea, Yellow Sea, Bo Hai, 440: Xianbei invade northwest China, Trebizond, Caucasus, Steppes, TURKESTAN, Altai Mountains, 1st century: CE Han forces displace Xiongnu, who move west, East China Sea, Caspian Sea, Lake Balkhash, Jaxartes (Syr Darya), Aral Sea, Turfan: Xiongnu reorganize and begin expansion to east and west, Gobi, Dunhuang, Yellow River, 386: Toba invade north China, Luoyang, 484: White Huns (Hephthalites) invade Sassanian Empire, TRANSOXIANA, Tashkent, Tien Shan, Chang'an, CHINA, Lanzhou, 311: Xiongnu destroy Luoyang, 316: Xiongnu destroy Changan, Ctesiphon, Samarkand, FERGHANA, Kashgar, SINKIANG, Oxus (Amu Darya), Yarkand, Tarim, Qiang, Nanhai, MESOPOTAMIA, PARTHIA, BACTRIA, Merv, Takla Makan Desert, Kunlun Mountains, Xi Jiang, Arabian Peninsula, Iranian Plateau, PERSIA, Hindu Kush, TIBET, c.600: Tibet unified, and Tibetans with Qiang and Dian begin period of rapid expansion, Tropic of Cancer, Persepolis, GEDROSIA, Himalayas, Brahmaputra, ANNAM, Indrapura, Persian Gulf, KUSHAN, 480: White Huns (Hephthalites) raid Gupta Empire, Indus, Ganges, NANZHAO, Dian, Mekong, South China Sea, Pataliputra, MAGADHA, Irrawaddy, Barygaza, INDIA, Bay of Bengal, Scale varies with perspective, 5560 kms (3450 miles), 12,060 kms (7490 miles), N

Steppe kingdoms of Central Asia (timeline)

91: Han defeat Xiongnu, forcing them westward
c.300: Invention of stirrup in Central Asia increases efficiency of steppe cavalry
c.350: Black Huns invade Persia and India

c.50: Foundation of Kushan Empire
304: Xiongnu invade China, inaugurating a century of civil war in north (Sixteen Kingdoms period)
370: Huns begin to invade Europe

(Timeline marks: 1 CE, 100, 200, 300, 400 CE)

EARLY MEDIEVAL EAST ASIA

THE TANG BROUGHT CHINA under a unified administration in 618, and rapidly extended its domains far into Central Asia, briefly achieving by 742 a territorial extent and era of stable growth comparable to that of their Han forebears. The influence of Chinese culture also spread during this period, which in turn saw the establishment of similarly organized states around their frontiers on all sides. Chinese forces were defeated in 751 by Arab armies on the Talas River, which inaugurated a process of Islamicization in Central Asia and loosened Tang control in the region. But China's greatest threats continued to lie to the north, where coalitions of steppe peoples began to establish expansionist regimes, eager to control the Chinese heartland.

This porcelain incense burner in the shape of a duck dates from the Song period. Song pottery was widely traded.

Tang China

Tang China was unified under a centralized government, political and commercial integration established by a network of highways and canals centered on the capital Chang'an. The Yangtze Valley became an increasingly important economic region, while commerce focused on the coastal plain. The stability and prosperity of Tang China attracted both emulation and envy among its neighbors. But the Tang dynasty was fatally weakened by peasant revolts from the 870s and the empire eventually fragmented into local regimes which vied for power for over a century.

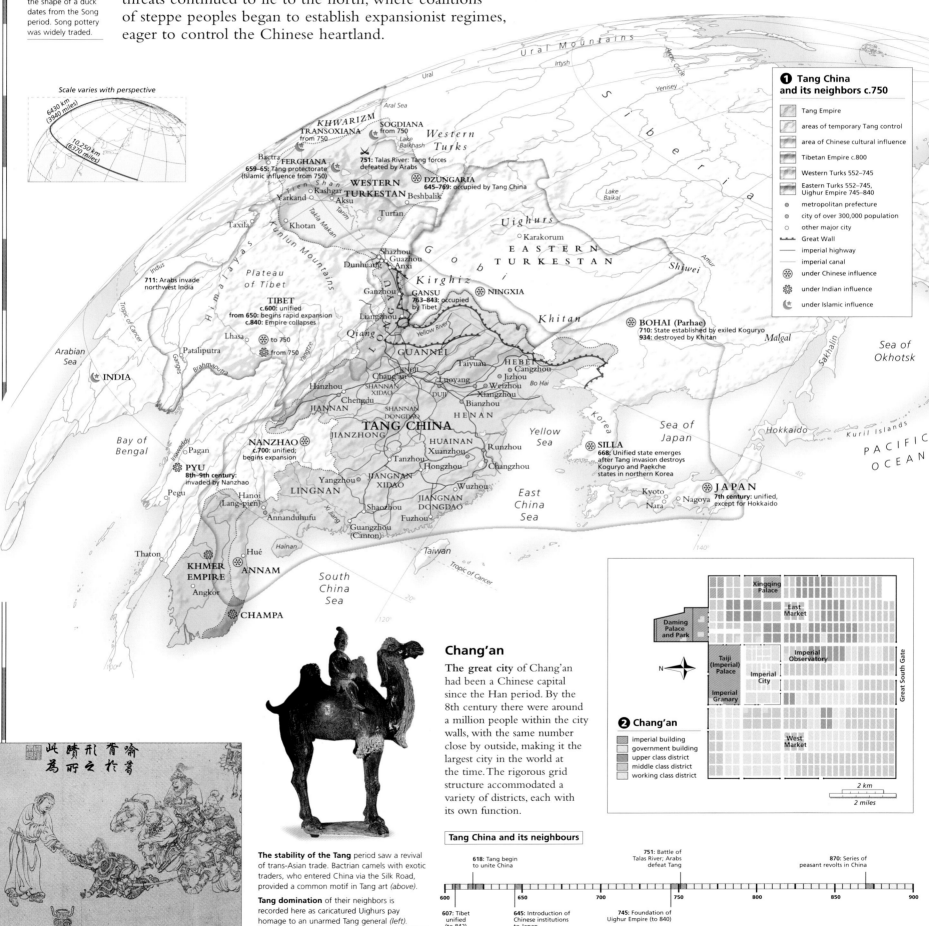

1 Tang China and its neighbors c.750

- Tang Empire
- areas of temporary Tang control
- area of Chinese cultural influence
- Tibetan Empire c.800
- Western Turks 552–745
- Eastern Turks 552–745, Uighur Empire 745–840
- ● metropolitan prefecture
- ● city of over 300,000 population
- ○ other major city
- Great Wall
- imperial highway
- imperial canal
- ✿ under Chinese influence
- ✿ under Indian influence
- ☾ under Islamic influence

Scale varies with perspective

6430 km (3940 miles)
10 250 km (6370 miles)

KHWARIZM
TRANSOXIANA from 750
SOGDIANA from 750
Bactra
FERGHANA 659–65: Tang protectorate (Islamic influence from 750)
751: Talas River: Tang forces defeated by Arabs
645–769: occupied by Tang China
DZUNGARIA
Yarkand   Kashgar   Aksu
Taxila   Khotan   Turfan
WESTERN TURKESTAN   Beshbalik
Western Turks
Lake Balkhash
Aral Sea
Ural
Western Turks

711: Arabs invade northwest India

TIBET c.600: unified from 650: begins rapid expansion c.840: Empire collapses
Lhasa
Shazhou   Guazhou   Anxi
Dunhuang
GANSU 763–843: occupied by Tibet
Ganzhou   **NINGXIA**
Liangzhou
Qiang
Kirghiz
Gobi
EASTERN TURKESTAN
Karakorum
Uighurs
Shiwei
Amur
Khitan
BOHAI (Parhae) 710: State established by exiled Koguryo 934: destroyed by Khitan
Malgal

Plateau of Tibet
Kunlun Mountains
Himalayas
Indus
Ganges   *Brahmaputra*
Pataliputra
INDIA
✿ to 750
✿ from 750
Yellow River

GUANNEI
Taiyuan   **HEBEI**   Cangzhou
Chang'an   Luoyang   Jizhou
Weizhou   Xiangzhou
SHANNAN XIDAO   **DUJI**   Bianzhou
Chengdu   **SHANNAN DONGDAO**   **HENAN**
JIANNAN
TANG CHINA
JIANZHONG   **HUAINAN**
NANZHAO c.700: unified; begins expansion
Xuanzhou
Tanzhou   Runzhou
Sea of Japan
SILLA 668: Unified state emerges after Tang invasion destroys Koguryo and Paekche states in northern Korea
Hokkaido
Kuril Islands
PACIFIC OCEAN
Sea of Okhotsk
Sakhalin
Korea
Yellow Sea
Bo Hai

PYU 8th–9th century: invaded by Nanzhao
Pegu
Pagan
Hanoi (Lang-pien)
LINGNAN
Yangzhou   **JIANGNAN XIDAO**
Hongzhou   Changzhou
Shaozhou   **JIANGNAN DONGDAO**
Wuzhou
Fuzhou
Guangzhou (Canton)
East China Sea
Kyoto   Nagoya
Nara
JAPAN 7th century: unified, except for Hokkaido

Annanduhufu
Hué
KHMER EMPIRE
Angkor
Thaton
ANNAN
Xi Jiang
Hainan
CHAMPA
South China Sea
Taiwan
Tropic of Cancer

Bay of Bengal
Arabian Sea
Irrawaddy

Chang'an

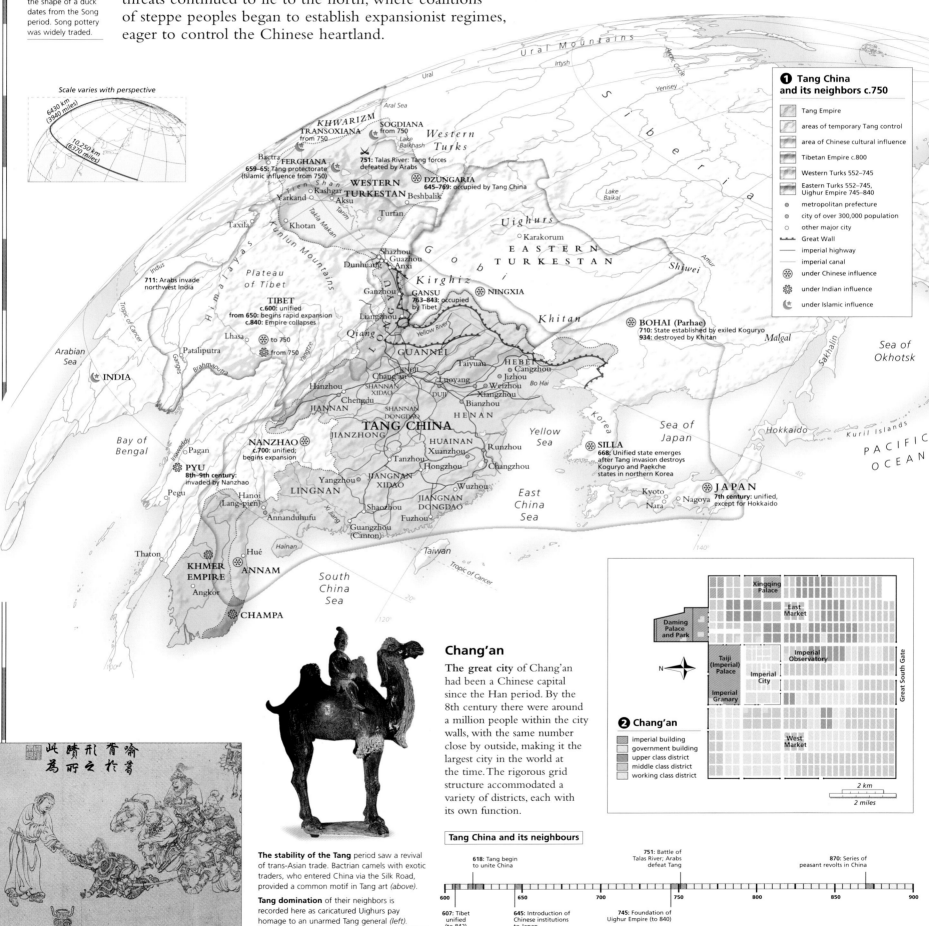

The great city of Chang'an had been a Chinese capital since the Han period. By the 8th century there were around a million people within the city walls, with the same number close by outside, making it the largest city in the world at the time. The rigorous grid structure accommodated a variety of districts, each with its own function.

Xingqing Palace
Daming Palace and Park
East Market
Taiji (Imperial) Palace
Imperial Observatory
Imperial City
Imperial Granary
N
West Market
Great South Gate

2 Chang'an
- imperial building
- government building
- upper class district
- middle class district
- working class district

2 km
2 miles

The stability of the Tang period saw a revival of trans-Asian trade. Bactrian camels with exotic traders, who entered China via the Silk Road, provided a common motif in Tang art (*above*).

Tang domination of their neighbors is recorded here as caricatured Uighurs pay homage to an unarmed Tang general (*left*).

Tang China and its neighbours

618: Tang begin to unite China		751: Battle of Talas River; Arabs defeat Tang	870: Series of peasant revolts in China

600 — 650 — 700 — 750 — 800 — 850 — 900

607: Tibet unified (to 842)
645: Introduction of Chinese institutions to Japan
745: Foundation of Uighur Empire (to 840)

Song China

The anarchy which followed the fragmentation of the Tang Empire was followed by the period known as the Five Dynasties and Ten Kingdoms, when China was broken up into as many as ten states. The Song arose in northern China in 960, expanding to form a Chinese empire by 979, although they lost control of the north to the Khitans, who established the Liao Empire in Manchuria, balanced to the west by another steppe empire, the Tangut Xixia Empire. The Jurchen, vassals of the Liao, established the Jin state, which seized the Song capital of Kaifeng, restricting Song rule to the south. The Song period was nevertheless one of great prosperity.

The growth in trade under the Tang and Song brought a need for currency. The mercantile practice of issuing paper receipts in place of weighty bullion transactions was adopted by the government in the 1120s, resulting in the world's first paper money; this printed banknote dates from 1287.

❸ The Five Dynasties 881–979 ▲

- ☐ Chinese states
- ☐ states occupied by non-Chinese peoples

❺ The Southern Song 1127–1234

- ☐ capital city
- ☐ Song empire
- ☐ other states/empires

❹ Song China 960–1127 ▲

- imperial canal
- imperial highway
- ☐ national capital
- ◉ provincial capital

Fine porcelain and stoneware was produced in a range of regional centers in Song China, where mass-production techniques developed to meet international demands.

POPULATION CHANGE IN CHINA

A shift in Chinese population distribution had occurred by the Song period; the Yellow River remained heavily populated, while the area south of Yangtze Basin became agricultural.

742

❻ Chinese population

- high density
- ☐ low density

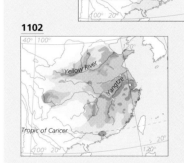

1102

916: Foundation of Khitan Empire

947: Khitans invade northern China, establishing Liao Dynasty at Beijing

1035: Foundation of Xixia Empire

1126: Jin take control of northern China

900 — 950 — 1000 — 1050 — 1100 — 1150 — 1200

907: Beginning of Five Dynasties and Ten Kingdoms period (to 960)

939: Annam independent

974: Song dynasty unites China

| Song China |

The Yuan (Mongol) invasion

The Mongol conquest of Jin in 1234 occasioned enormous violence and destruction. But the Mongols rapidly adopted Chinese customs and institutions (see pp. 68–69), and the eventual conquest of the Song south in 1278 was less brutal. Subsequent campaigns brought outlying areas under temporary Mongol control, and expanded Chinese administration far to the southwest, but the Mongols only exercised temporary control over Tibet and Southeast Asia.

This illustration from an early military manual shows a portable scaling ladder used in siege warfare. Other innovations of this period included the catapult.

The Japanese defeat of Kublai's armies in 1274 (30,000 troops) and 1281 (140,000 troops), the largest amphibious invasion forces of premodern times, were recorded in an illustrated scroll in the 1290s (left).

❼ The Mongol (Yuan) period c.1300

- ☐ southern extent of Mongol conquest to 1279
- ☐ Mongol conquest 1280–1368
- ☐ imperial capital
- ◉ provincial capital
- GANSU   Yuan province
- ☐ area of loose or temporary Mongol control

| The Yuan Dynasty |

1264: Foundation of Yuan dynasty by Kublai Khan

1281: Second attempted invasion of Japan

1287: Expedition to Pagan

1292: Expedition to Java

1230 — 1250 — 1270 — 1290 — 1310

1234: Mongols invade Jin Empire

1274: First attempted invasion of Japan

1279: Yuan take over Southern Song

1283: Expeditions against Annam and Champa

THE FIRST STATES IN JAPAN AND KOREA

DURING THE FIRST CENTURIES CE a group of powerful states developed to the east of China. Yamato, centered on what was to became the traditional heartland of Japan, grew to dominate the southern Japanese islands, while Korea saw the development of three states – Paekche, Silla, and Koguryo. Both areas came under the influence of Buddhism and of Chinese culture and politics during the 5th and 6th centuries. The various states of Korea would continue to be regarded by the Chinese as vassals, but Japan affirmed its independent status, maintaining an imperial court, albeit dominated by a succession of warrior lords.

Dotaku ceremonial bells, c.100 BCE, are typical of early Japanese bronze casting.

State formation in Japan and Korea

Japanese haniwa warrior figures, placed on tombs, reflect the martial qualities of Japan in the 5th and 6th centuries CE.

The basis for state formation in East Asia was the agricultural surplus provided by the spread of rice cultivation, associated with Yayoi culture in Japan. In southeast Japan, the Yamato state began to expand from about 500 CE, and in doing so provoked neighboring cultures such as Kibi and Izumo, to become more politically organized in defense of their territory. In Korea, partly occupied by Han China in the 1st century BCE, the states of Koguryo, Paekche, and Silla emerged, Silla growing to dominate the peninsula by the end of the 7th century. Yamato came under increasing Chinese influence and the introduction of Buddhism in the mid-6th century began a transformation of Japanese society.

The first states

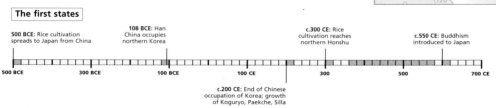

500 BCE: Rice cultivation spreads to Japan from China

108 BCE: Han China occupies northern Korea

c.300 CE: Rice cultivation reaches northern Honshu

c.550 CE: Buddhism introduced to Japan

c.200 CE: End of Chinese occupation of Korea; growth of Koguryo, Paekche, Silla

▲ **❶ State formation in Korea and Japan 100 BCE–650 CE**

- spread of Yayoi culture to 100 BCE
- 100 BCE–100 CE
- after 100 CE
- Han Empire c.108 BCE
- SILLA early states emerging c.100–650 CE
- expansion of Yamato state
- expansion of Silla state
- state capital

◀ **❷ The first empires c.300–900 CE**

YANGJU administrative divisions of Silla

- extent of Paekche to 660
- furthest southern extent of Chinese (Han and Wei) control in Korea
- extent of Silla power 670–935
- extent of Nara state by 600
- trade route

Phases of Japanese settlement and expansion

- by mid–8th century
- by late 8th century
- by early 9th century
- by mid–9th century

The first empires c.600–900 CE

Early imperial ambitions from about 500 CE focused on the Korean Peninsula. The Japanese Yamato state had exercised some influence in the south, and formed an alliance with Paekche against Silla. Tang China, which regarded all these states as effectively vassals, provided Silla with forces to overwhelm Paekche and the northern mountain state of Koguryo in the 660s. Thereafter, Japan withdrew and began to establish formal diplomatic relations with China, while the defeated Koguryo retreated north to establish an empire in Manchuria – Pohai which was similarly based on the Chinese model.

This Shinto shrine at Hakata in Kyushu is typical of traditional Japanese religion. Shinto observes the *kami*, the combined forces of nature and ancestral spirits. Shrines are often located on rocks, islands, and waterfalls, and include a *torii* or sacred gateway, significant features being linked by a straw rope replaced each year.

The struggle for Korea

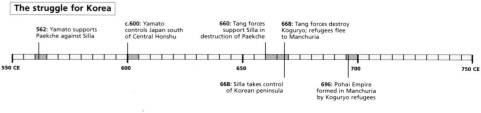

562: Yamato supports Paekche against Silla

c.600: Yamato controls Japan south of Central Honshu

660: Tang forces support Silla in destruction of Paekche

668: Tang forces destroy Koguryo; refugees flee to Manchuria

668: Silla takes control of Korean peninsula

696: Pohai Empire formed in Manchuria by Koguryo refugees

The Taika Reform and the Ritsuryo state

From the 6th century, the increasing influence of Chinese institutions and of Buddhism began to transform Japan from a clan-based society into an imperial state. Under Prince Shotoku a new imperial structure was introduced (based on Chinese criminal (*ritsu*) and civil (*ryu*) law). Provinces were linked by highways and there was a centralized tax system. New capitals were built at Fujiwara then Heijo-kyo, and Buddhism formalized as a state religion alongside traditional Shinto. By the 10th century the provincial governors, tasked with quelling regional rebellion, were also involved in internecine warfare, conflict which also drew in other groups such as the substantial armies of warrior priests maintained by Buddhist temples.

❸ **Japan under the Nara Ritsuryo state** ▶

- district boundaries after Taika Reform (646)
- ○ provincial center
- highway
- seaway
- ▲ sacred Buddhist mountain

The rise of the warrior lords

- **645:** Taika Reform under Prince Shotoku
- **794–1185 CE:** Heian Period; transition from Chinese influence to warrior lords
- **c.1160:** Taira clan gain political control
- **710–784:** Nara Period. Establishment of new capital, imperial court, and Japanese Buddhism
- **858–1160:** Ascendancy of the Fujiwara clan
- **1051–1087:** Minamoto clan gain control of north and east Honshu

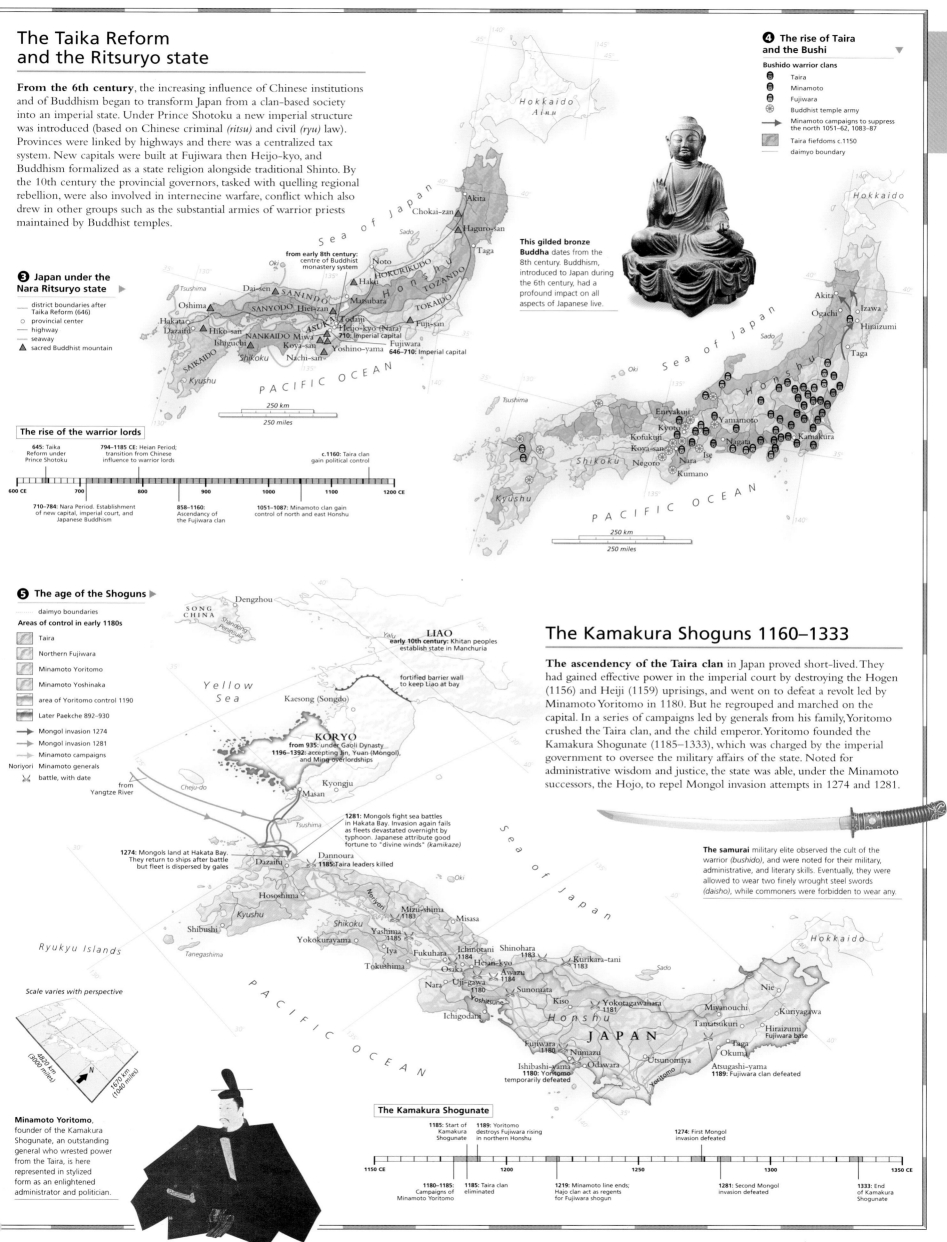

This gilded bronze Buddha dates from the 8th century. Buddhism, introduced to Japan during the 6th century, had a profound impact on all aspects of Japanese live.

❹ **The rise of Taira and the Bushi** ▼

Bushido warrior clans
- Taira
- Minamoto
- Fujiwara
- Buddhist temple army
- ➔ Minamoto campaigns to suppress the north 1051–62, 1083–87
- Taira fiefdoms c.1150
- daimyo boundary

The Kamakura Shoguns 1160–1333

The ascendency of the Taira clan in Japan proved short-lived. They had gained effective power in the imperial court by destroying the Hogen (1156) and Heiji (1159) uprisings, and went on to defeat a revolt led by Minamoto Yoritomo in 1180. But he regrouped and marched on the capital. In a series of campaigns led by generals from his family, Yoritomo crushed the Taira clan, and the child emperor. Yoritomo founded the Kamakura Shogunate (1185–1333), which was charged by the imperial government to oversee the military affairs of the state. Noted for administrative wisdom and justice, the state was able, under the Minamoto successors, the Hojo, to repel Mongol invasion attempts in 1274 and 1281.

The samurai military elite observed the cult of the warrior (*bushido*), and were noted for their military, administrative, and literary skills. Eventually, they were allowed to wear two finely wrought steel swords (*daisho*), while commoners were forbidden to wear any.

❺ **The age of the Shoguns** ▶

- daimyo boundaries
- **Areas of control in early 1180s**
- Taira
- Northern Fujiwara
- Minamoto Yoritomo
- Minamoto Yoshinaka
- area of Yoritomo control 1190
- Later Paekche 892–930
- ➔ Mongol invasion 1274
- ➔ Mongol invasion 1281
- ➔ Minamoto campaigns
- Noriyori Minamoto generals
- ⚔ battle, with date

Minamoto Yoritomo, founder of the Kamakura Shogunate, an outstanding general who wrested power from the Taira, is here represented in stylized form as an enlightened administrator and politician.

The Kamakura Shogunate

- **1185:** Start of Kamakura Shogunate
- **1189:** Yoritomo destroys Fujiwara rising in northern Honshu
- **1274:** First Mongol invasion defeated
- **1180–1185:** Campaigns of Minamoto Yoritomo
- **1185:** Taira clan eliminated
- **1219:** Minamoto line ends; Hajo clan act as regents for Fujiwara shogun
- **1281:** Second Mongol invasion defeated
- **1333:** End of Kamakura Shogunate

EAST ASIA AND THE MING

Zhu Yuanzhang, founder of the Ming Dynasty, ousted the Mongols to become emperor.

WITH THE ESTABLISHMENT of the Ming by Zhu Yuanzhang in 1368, China came under the unified control of a native dynasty for the first time in over 400 years. After an initial phase of expansionism and international diplomacy, most notably the missions of the great admiral Zheng He, the haughty and aristocratic Ming rulers became passive, inward-looking, and dominated by eunuch bureaucrats. Nevertheless, Ming China prospered greatly from the creation (largely by Europeans) of a global trading network, and the population boomed to some 150 million by 1600. Ming consolidation was emulated by their neighbors, with the growth of wealthy trading states across Central Asia, and the reunification of Japan under the Ashikaga Shogunate and their successors.

China under the Ming dynasty

The Great Wall had its origins in the Qin dynasty (221 BCE) but it was the Ming who, after ejecting the Mongol (Yuan) dynasty, rebuilt it and extended it in its current form.

The Ming arose from the increasing chaos which attended the decline of the Mongol Yuan dynasty. One rebel leader, Zhu Yuanzhang (or Taizu) eventually overcame his rivals and established a capital at Nanjing in 1356, and within 12 years had ousted the remaining Mongols. An initially aggressive foreign policy led to the reincorporation of the southwest and campaigns in Annam and Mongolia, but by the mid-15th century the empire became increasingly defensive and factionalized. However, the Chinese infrastructure grew under imperial patronage, and the impact of trade led to the growth of great industrial centers – including Yangzhou and Nanjing – at the mouth of the Yangtze, linked to Beijing by the Grand Canal. The unwieldy Ming bureaucracy was to prove incapable of responding swiftly to change.

Under Taizu's son, Chengzu, Ming expansionism reached its apogee with the voyages of Zheng He to Southeast Asia and the Indian Ocean. Conceived on a grand scale (the fourth voyage, 1413–15, involved over 60 large vessels and 28,000 men), these missions were designed to exact tribute to the Ming court. This silk painting records a giraffe brought back from Africa on the seventh voyage (1431–33).

Revolts under the Ming

The ineffective government of the Ming was beset by internal dissent, often arising from crop failures and floods, exacerbated by resistance to taxation and the pressures of rapid urban growth and inflation. Rebellions in the 1440s led to over a million deaths, but two major revolts in the 1640s directly challenged Ming authority. When Li Zicheng's rebel forces took Beijing in 1644, the last Ming emperor committed suicide.

❷ Revolts under the Ming

- Ming China
- widespread agrarian unrest 1626–41
- area controlled by Zhang Xianzhong 1641–44
- area controlled by Zhang Xianzhong 1644–47
- area controlled by Li Zicheng 1641–45
- urban riots

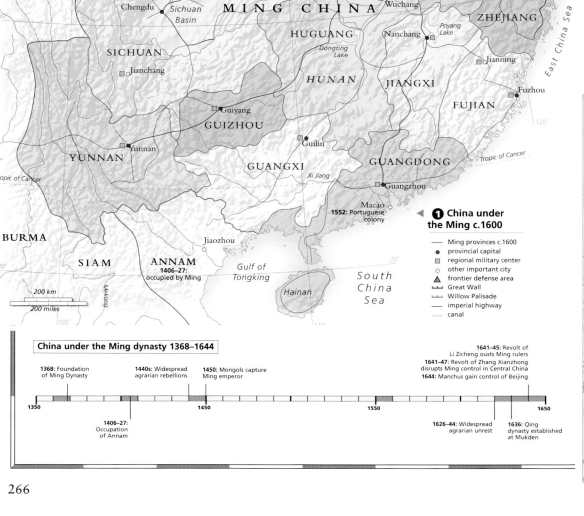

❶ China under the Ming c.1600

- Ming provinces c.1600
- provincial capital
- regional military center
- other important city
- frontier defense area
- Great Wall
- Willow Palisade
- imperial highway
- canal

China under the Ming dynasty 1368–1644

- **1368:** Foundation of Ming Dynasty
- **1440s:** Widespread agrarian rebellions
- **1450:** Mongols capture Ming emperor
- **1406–27:** Occupation of Annam
- **1626–44:** Widespread agrarian unrest
- **1641–45:** Revolt of Li Zicheng ousts Ming rulers
- **1641–47:** Revolt of Zhang Xianzhong disrupts Ming control in Central China
- **1644:** Manchus gain control of Beijing
- **1636:** Qing dynasty established at Mukden

1350 | 1450 | 1550 | 1650

The states of Central Asia

By the mid-16th century, a range of largely Islamic states had evolved across Central Asia, thriving on control of the revitalized east-west trade that had emerged under the so-called "Mongol Peace." Some of these were devolved successor states to the brief era of Mongol dominance but others, such as the Uzbek Empire, were of Turkic origin. Although rulers constantly vied for territorial control, the region enjoyed an era of cultural wealth and continuity, thriving on the periphery of, and exhange between, older and more stable civilizations.

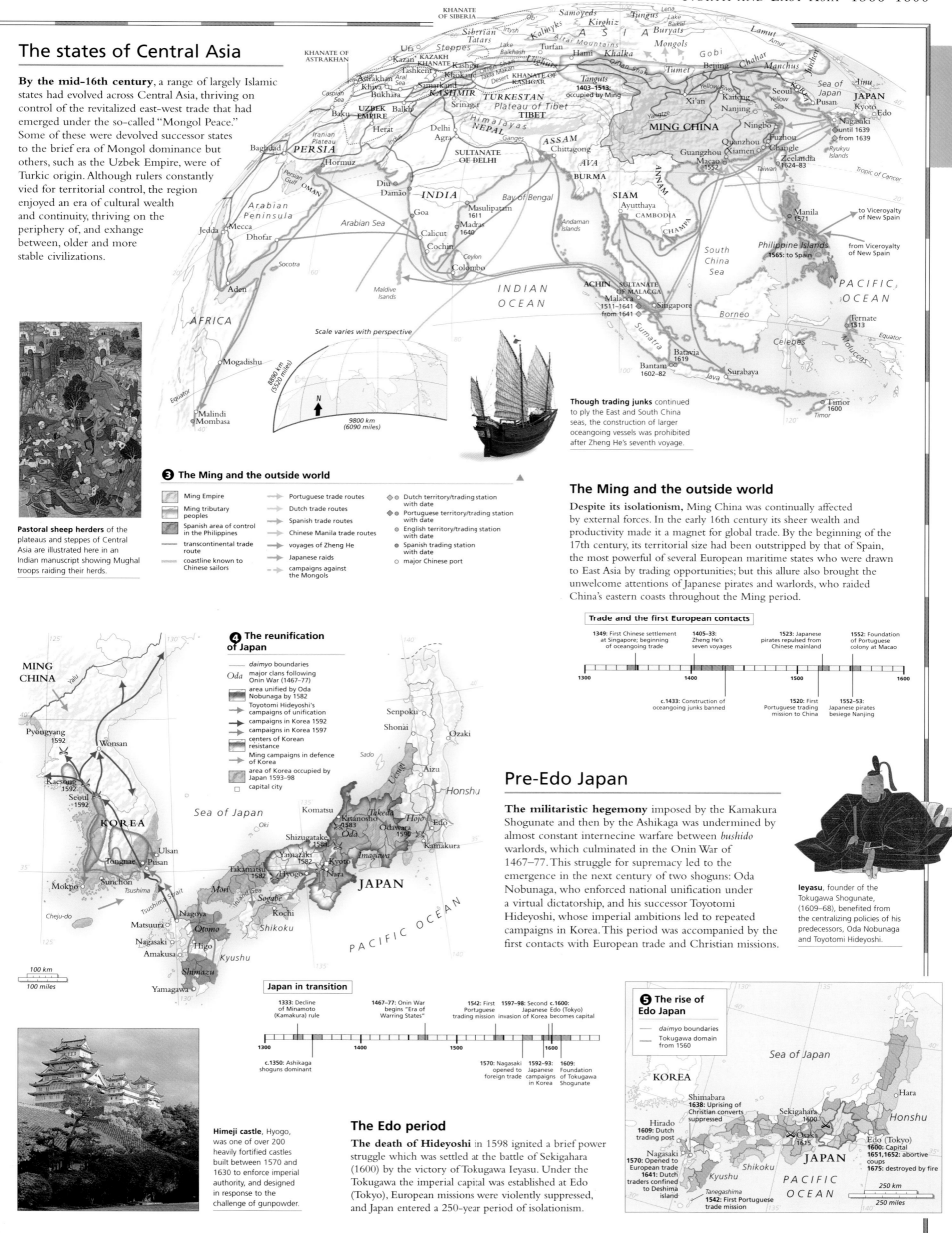

Pastoral sheep herders of the plateaus and steppes of Central Asia are illustrated here in an Indian manuscript showing Mughal troops raiding their herds.

Though trading junks continued to ply the East and South China seas, the construction of larger oceangoing vessels was prohibited after Zheng He's seventh voyage.

❸ The Ming and the outside world

- Ming Empire
- Ming tributary peoples
- Spanish area of control in the Philippines
- transcontinental trade route
- coastline known to Chinese sailors
- Portuguese trade routes
- Dutch trade routes
- Spanish trade routes
- Chinese Manila trade routes
- voyages of Zheng He
- Japanese raids
- campaigns against the Mongols
- Dutch territory/trading station with date
- Portuguese territory/trading station with date
- English territory/trading station with date
- Spanish trading station with date
- major Chinese port

The Ming and the outside world

Despite its isolationism, Ming China was continually affected by external forces. In the early 16th century its sheer wealth and productivity made it a magnet for global trade. By the beginning of the 17th century, its territorial size had been outstripped by that of Spain, the most powerful of several European maritime states who were drawn to East Asia by trading opportunities; but this allure also brought the unwelcome attentions of Japanese pirates and warlords, who raided China's eastern coasts throughout the Ming period.

Trade and the first European contacts

1349: First Chinese settlement at Singapore; beginning of oceangoing trade	**1405–33:** Zheng He's seven voyages	**1523:** Japanese pirates repulsed from Chinese mainland	**1552:** Foundation of Portuguese colony at Macao
1300	1400	1500	1600
c.1433: Construction of oceangoing junks banned		**1520:** First Portuguese trading mission to China	**1552–53:** Japanese pirates besiege Nanjing

❹ The reunification of Japan

- daimyo boundaries
- *Oda* major clans following Onin War (1467–77)
- area unified by Oda Nobunaga by 1582
- Toyotomi Hideyoshi's campaigns of unification
- campaigns in Korea 1592
- campaigns in Korea 1597
- centers of Korean resistance
- Ming campaigns in defence of Korea
- area of Korea occupied by Japan 1593–98
- capital city

Pre-Edo Japan

The militaristic hegemony imposed by the Kamakura Shogunate and then by the Ashikaga was undermined by almost constant internecine warfare between *bushido* warlords, which culminated in the Onin War of 1467–77. This struggle for supremacy led to the emergence in the next century of two shoguns: Oda Nobunaga, who enforced national unification under a virtual dictatorship, and his successor Toyotomi Hideyoshi, whose imperial ambitions led to repeated campaigns in Korea. This period was accompanied by the first contacts with European trade and Christian missions.

Ieyasu, founder of the Tokugawa Shogunate, (1609–68), benefited from the centralizing policies of his predecessors, Oda Nobunaga and Toyotomi Hideyoshi.

Japan in transition

1333: Decline of Minamoto (Kamakura) rule	**1467–77:** Onin War begins "Era of Warring States"	**1542:** First Portuguese trading mission	**1597–98:** Second Japanese invasion of Korea	**c.1600:** Edo (Tokyo) becomes capital
1300	1400	1500	1600	
c.1350: Ashikaga shoguns dominant		**1570:** Nagasaki opened to foreign trade	**1592–93:** Japanese campaigns in Korea	**1609:** Foundation of Tokugawa Shogunate

Himeji castle, Hyogo, was one of over 200 heavily fortified castles built between 1570 and 1630 to enforce imperial authority, and designed in response to the challenge of gunpowder.

The Edo period

The death of Hideyoshi in 1598 ignited a brief power struggle which was settled at the battle of Sekigahara (1600) by the victory of Tokugawa Ieyasu. Under the Tokugawa the imperial capital was established at Edo (Tokyo), European missions were violently suppressed, and Japan entered a 250-year period of isolationism.

❺ The rise of Edo Japan

- daimyo boundaries
- Tokugawa domain from 1560

1638: Uprising of Christian converts suppressed

1609: Dutch trading post

1570: Opened to European trade

1641: Dutch traders confined to Deshima island

1542: First Portuguese trade mission

1600: Capital
1651, 1652: abortive coups
1675: destroyed by fire

THE ERA OF THE QING EMPIRE

Qing China produced porcelain, jade, intaglio, carpets, and silk goods specifically for Western markets.

THE MANCHUS had already built a state along Chinese lines in southern Manchuria, based at Mukden, and were poised to take advantage of the Ming collapse in 1644. They swiftly suppressed the rebels and by the end of the 17th century had reduced Ming resistance in the south. The 18th century was a stable period of expansion and prosperity, as the Manchu, or Qing dynasty, adopted Chinese ways. Successive campaigns established an enormous empire and an array of tributary states, while regional uprisings were ruthlessly crushed. But by the 19th century the pressures of European imperial expansion and internal dissent on an unprecedented scale brought regression, isolationism, resistance to reform, and political decay.

China under the Qing

The military expansion of the Qing Empire continued throughout the 17th and 18th centuries, provoked in part by the threat of Russian, British, and French moves into Asia. Only part of the vast Qing realms were directly governed by the Manchus or settled by the Chinese, but were secured through military garrisons. The cost of this expansion was huge, and was funded by trade, largely paid for in bullion. In the 19th century, as the Qing economy faltered under pressure from European manipulation, so did the Manchu ability to administer their domains.

The Manchu rulers of the Qing Dynasty rapidly adopted the courtly manners, customs, and aristocratic aloofness of their Ming forebears. Here Kangxi (r.1662–1722) is portrayed in formal imperial splendor.

The expansion of Qing China

- 1636: Manchus establish Qing imperial rule at Mukden
- 1644: Qing forces enter Beijing
- 1683: Conquest of Taiwan
- 1689: Treaty of Nerchinsk; acquisition of Amur and Ussuri regions from Russia
- 1696–97: Suppression of Mongolia
- 1720: Formal control of Xinjiang established
- 1751: Invasion of Tibet
- 1758–59: Campaigns against Kalmyks
- 1765–69: Attempted invasion of Burma; establishment of suzerainty
- 1788: Attempted invasion of Annam
- 1792: Invasion of Nepal

(timeline: 1600 — 1700 — 1800)

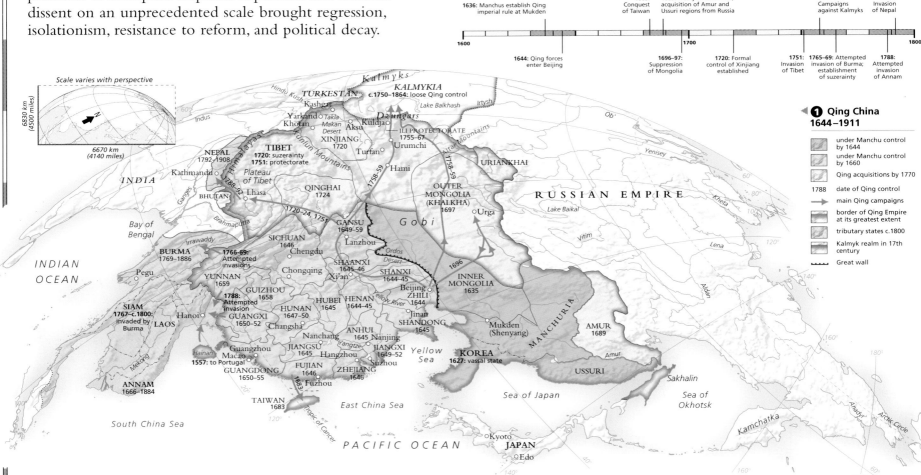

① Qing China 1644–1911

- under Manchu control by 1644
- under Manchu control by 1660
- Qing acquisitions by 1770
- 1788 date of Qing control
- main Qing campaigns
- border of Qing Empire at its greatest extent
- tributary states c.1800
- Kalmyk realm in 17th century
- Great wall

The decline of the Qing

The Manchus successfully suppressed a major rebellion by Ming supporters in southern China, largely by reduction and coercion, early in their reign. Subsequent revolts took a variety of forms: tribal uprisings, Muslim *jihads,* and millenarian sects. In most instances these were provoked by population pressures and economic distress. The great Taiping and Nian peasant rebellions in the mid-19th century left some 25 million dead, and although they vitally threatened Qing stability they were ultimately unsuccessful. The former, led by a Christian visionary, invoked tacit support among the hawkish European powers. In contrast, the populist Boxer rebellion was explicitly anti-European and enjoyed covert support from the Qing rulers.

The Taiping rebellion began in southern China in 1850; by 1853 the rebel armies had moved north to establish a base at Nanjing (*above*). From here they courted foreign powers based at Shanghai, to threaten the Qing in Beijing.

Revolts against the Qing

- 1674: Start of pro-Ming revolts in southern China; finally suppressed 1683
- 1850: Start of Taiping rebellion; widespread uprising in southern China; ends 1863
- 1853: Nian peasant rebellion around Kaifeng; ends 1868
- 1855: *Jihad* of Yunnan Muslims; ends 1873
- 1863: Start of Northwest uprising; largest Muslim *jihad;* ends 1873
- 1900–01: Boxer rebellion; popular anti-Western rebellion

(timeline: 1700 — 1800 — 1900)

② Revolts under the Qing Empire

- area of Three Feudatories and other pro-Ming rebellions, 1674–83
- Qing Empire
- tribal risings
- Muslim revolts
- area of Northwestern Muslim rising 1863–73
- sectarian uprising
- area controlled by Taiping rebels 1853–63
- Taiping rebellion
- area of Nian rebellion 1853–68
- Nian rebellion
- area of Boxer uprising 1900–01
- Guizhou Muslim uprising 1854–72
- frontier of Qing Empire 1850

Russian expansion in North Asia 1600–1914

The Russian march across Siberia, in the wake of fur trappers, involved physical hardship but provoked little resistance from native peoples. The expansion to the south and east was more hard-fought, against the Kazakhs and Turkic peoples of Central Asia, but western military techniques prevailed. Further east, the conquest of the Amur and Ussuri regions from Qing China gave Russia access to the Pacific. With the bolition of serfdom in 1861, a wave of Russian migrants swept east. Russian progress resulted in an Anglo-Japanese alliance (1902), and was only finally halted by the Russo-Japanese War of 1904–05 *(see page 270).*

The Trans-Siberian Railway, covering 4,500 miles between Moscow and Vladivostok, was designed to bind Russia's Asian provinces together and to reinforce its presence in the Pacific.

3 Russian expansion in Asia 1600–1914

Russian Empire c.1600	acquisitions 1877–1914	1788 date of foundation or acquisition
acquisitions 1600–1725	temporary acquisition, with dates	Trans-Siberian Railway, built 1891–1917
acquisitions 1726–1855	Russian sphere of influence, 1914	borders 1914
acquisitions 1856–76		

The growth of Russia in Asia

1697: Start of conquest of Kamchatka; completed in 1732 it gives Russian control of Siberia	**1858–60:** Russia regains control of Amur-Ussuri region **1860:** Foundation of Vladivostok
1689: Treaty of Nerchinsk settles territorial dispute with Qing China	**1868–70:** Suppression of Muslim states of Bukhara and Samarkand
1730–34: Suppression of Khazaks	**1900–05:** Occupation of Manchuria

1700 · 1750 · 1800 · 1850 · 1900

1864: Establishment of control in Kalmykia (Semipalatinsk)

1891: Construction of Trans-Siberian Railway started; completed 1917

1904–05: Russo-Japanese war halts Russian expansion

Foreign imperialism in East Asia

The rapidly expanded Qing economy of the 18th century made it prey to foreign ambitions. The dynasty's failure to halt the highly profitable illegal British trade in opium in 1839–42 revealed its weaknesses. Hong Kong was the first of many territorial and trading concessions which gave not only the Europeans but the Russians and Japanese valuable toeholds in the Middle Kingdom. Qing complacency, resistance to modernization, and their inability to counter growing internal dissent played into their adversaries' hands. By the end of the 19th century, despite belated attempts to reform, the Qing were a power in name only.

Foreign incursions into China

1841: Foundation of British colony at Hong Kong	**1860:** Anglo-French forces occupy Beijing forcing further cessions	**1904–05:** Russo-Japanese war; Russian occupied territories taken over by Japan

1840 · 1850 · 1860 · 1870 · 1880 · 1890 · 1900

1840–42: Opium War; British attacks force trading concessions

1858–60: Loss of Amur-Ussuri region to Russia

1898–1905: Port Arthur leased to Russia

1900–05: Russian occupation of Manchuria

4 Foreign imperialism in East Asia, 1840–1910

Area of control	Area of influence
Russian	Russian
Japanese	Japanese
French	French
British	British
Dutch	German
American	
Portuguese	

1893 date of acquisition by foreign power

Leased territory	Treaty ports
Japanese	Japanese
French	French
British	British
Portuguese	American
German	open port

Qing Empire at its greatest extent c.1850

Foreign attacks on China

→ British (Opium War 1840–42)

→ Anglo-French campaigns 1858–60

→ French 1883–85

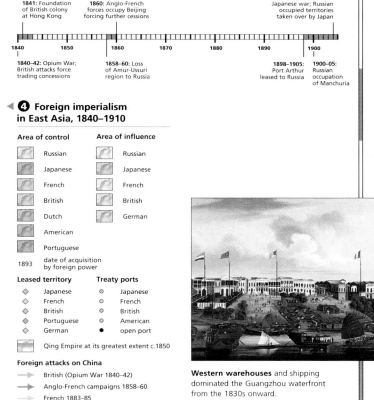

Western warehouses and shipping dominated the Guangzhou waterfront from the 1830s onward.

269

THE MODERNIZATION OF EAST ASIA

Jiang Jieshi (Chiang Kai-shek) assumed control of the Chinese Nationalist Party in 1925.

BOTH JAPAN AND CHINA entered the 19th century under feudal, courtly, isolationist, and reactionary regimes which had held power since the 17th century. By 1900 their development stood in stark contrast. Japan under the Tokugawa Shogunate was a prosperous, sophisticated society, socially developed, universally literate, and ready for modernization. When this came – through international trade pressure – Japan adopted the role of a progressive industrialized state, keen to dominate East Asian affairs. It was aided by the Qing dynasty's rejection of external pressures and internal demands for reform in China. The end of the Qing dynasty coincided with Japanese territorial aspirations, widespread factionalism among reforming groups in China itself, and the rise of Communism in its largest neighbor, Russia.

Japanese modernization 1868–1919

When US Commodore Perry's fleet entered Tokyo Bay in 1853 to demand international trading rights with Japan, the 200-year policy of isolationism under the Tokugawa Shogunate (Bakufu) effectively ended. Reformist forces based in the south conducted a campaign (the Boshin War 1868–69) which restored the Meiji ("enlightened rule") emperor, and inaugurated political, social, and economic reform. The nation was divided into prefectures, and a centralized bureaucracy introduced a new constitution, the construction of a railroad system, and the creation of modern industries, such as shipbuilding.

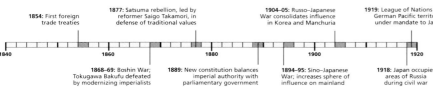

The modernization of Japan

- **1854:** First foreign trade treaties
- **1868–69:** Boshin War; Tokugawa Bakufu defeated by modernizing imperialists
- **1877:** Satsuma rebellion, led by reformer Saigo Takamori, in defense of traditional values
- **1889:** New constitution balances imperial authority with parliamentary government
- **1904–05:** Russo-Japanese War consolidates influence in Korea and Manchuria
- **1894–95:** Sino-Japanese War; increases sphere of influence on mainland
- **1919:** League of Nations accords German Pacific territories under mandate to Japan
- **1918:** Japan occupies areas of Russia during civil war

Visitors to Japan were confined to Nagasaki for almost 400 years. In 1853, when Commodore Perry took warships into Tokyo Bay to enforce US trading treaties with Japan, the confrontation between Japan and the West reached crisis point.

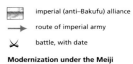

◀ ❶ Japanese modernization 1868–1918

Boshin War 1868–69
- imperial (anti-Bakufu) alliance
- route of imperial army
- battle, with date

Modernization under the Meiji
- KOCHI — prefectures established 1871
- main industrial areas by 1918
- railroads built 1868–1918

Traditional industries
- ceramics
- textiles
- silk

Industries developed after 1868
- manufacturing
- machine-building
- shipbuilding
- chemicals
- city of over 500,000 in 1918
- city of over 100,000 in 1918
- other major city

Japanese expansion 1868–1936

The entry of Japan onto the world's stage in 1868 was accompanied by an active policy of territorial expansion to support its rapidly expanding economy. Supported by the US (its principal trading partner by 1918), Japan claimed neighboring islands and gained territory as a result of wars against China (1894–95) and Russia (1904–05) – leading to the annexation of Formosa and Korea. Japan's firm commitment to the Allies during World War I (1914–18) gave her lands in the Pacific, and she rapidly gained other substantial footholds on mainland Asia.

After the Meiji revolution Japanese transportation modernized rapidly; steamships, railroads, and later automobiles were introduced.

▲ ❸ The Sino-Japanese War 1894–95
- area of Tonghak rebellion
- Japanese advance
- Japanese victory
- area leased to Japan 1895

The Sino-Japanese War 1894–95

Upon the outbreak of a populist, quasi-religious nationalist rebellion, the Tonghak Revolt (1894), the Korean court appealed to both Qing China and Japan for support. The Japanese forces compromised the Korean royal family, and open conflict with China erupted; the modern equipment and tactics employed by the Japanese forced Qing forces back to the Liaodong Peninsula, which with Taiwan was ceded to the victors, and Korea entered the Japanese sphere of influence.

The Russo-Japanese War 1904–05

Territorial rivalry and mutual animosity between Russia and Japan, already overheated by Russia's adventurist occupation of Manchuria in 1897, came to a head when Japanese vessels bombarded Russian ships at Port Arthur in 1904. The Japanese moved rapidly to secure a series of successes in southern Manchuria, exploiting their effective control of Korea, and victory was sealed when the Russian Baltic Fleet was savaged by Japanese ships in the Tsushima Strait (1905).

▼ ❹ The Russo-Japanese War 1904–05
- Qing China
- to Russia 1897, to Japan 1905
- area leased to Japan 1895
- Japanese advances 1904–05
- route of Russian Baltic fleet
- Japanese victory, with date

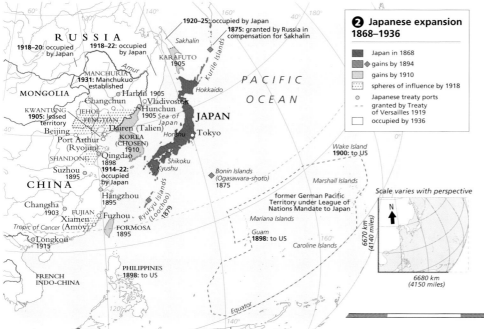

❷ Japanese expansion 1868–1936
- Japan in 1868
- gains by 1894
- gains by 1910
- spheres of influence by 1918
- Japanese treaty ports
- granted by Treaty of Versailles 1919
- occupied by 1936

National victories against China and Russia in the 1890s were celebrated in a dynamic manner by Japanese artists whose style influenced the development of 20th-century graphic art.

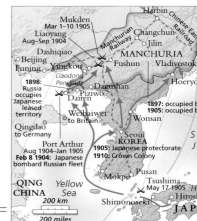

The Chinese Revolution of 1911

After a century of almost continual internal dissent, and some ten attempted revolutions since 1890, the Qing dynasty finally recognized the need for reform in 1911. An almost spontaneous eruption of revolt across China (orchestrated by telegraph) led within five months to the abdication of the boy emperor in favour of a reformist Qing general, Yuan Shikai. Meanwhile, the leader of the Nationalist uprising, Sun Zhongshan, proclaimed a republican constitution in Nanjing. The fragile situation, with Yuan rapidly adopting dictatorial measures, began to collapse into bitter regional strife.

The Dowager Empress Cixi, was photographed in regal splendor as the Qing dynasty drew to its close. Her regency between 1861 and 1908 represented the last bastion of Qing conservatism in the face of reform and modernization.

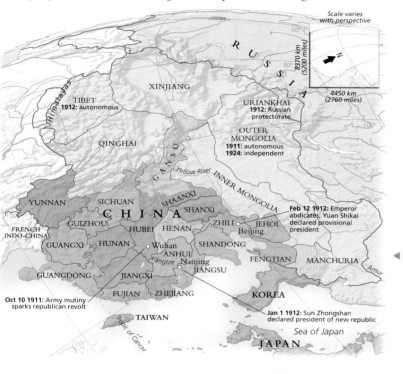

Scale varies with perspective

8370 km (5200 miles)
4450 km (2760 miles)

⑤ The Chinese Revolution 1911

- joined revolt Oct 1911
- joined revolt Nov 1911
- joined revolt after Nov 1911
- rest of Qing Empire
- occupied by Japan

Revolution in China 1911–28

Oct 16 1911: Mutiny by reformist army officers sparks nationwide revolt
1913: Parliamentary elections; Nationalists win over 50% of seats. Yuan refuses to endorse constitution
May 4 1919: Movement revives Nationalist cause, provoked by international support for Japan's claims in mainland China
1926–28: Nationalist Northern Expedition unites Chinese heartland
1927–28: Nationalist purge of Communist allies

Jan 1912: Sun Zhongshan declares republican constitution in Nanjing
Feb 1912: Abdication of last Qing emperor; Yuan Shikai assumes power as president
1915: Yuan announces plans to become emperor
1925: Sun Zhongshan dies, succeeded by Jiang Jieshi

1910 1915 1920 1925 1930

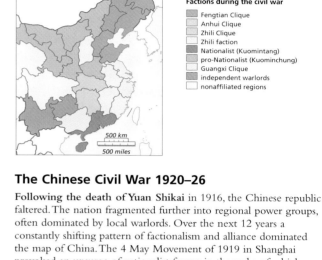

1920 · 1924 · 1926

500 km / 500 miles

⑥ The Chinese Civil War 1920–26

Factions during the civil war
- Fengtian Clique
- Anhui Clique
- Zhili Clique
- Zhili faction
- Nationalist (Kuomintang)
- pro-Nationalist (Kuominchung)
- Guangxi Clique
- independent warlords
- nonaffiliated regions

The Chinese Civil War 1920–26

Following the death of Yuan Shikai in 1916, the Chinese republic faltered. The nation fragmented further into regional power groups, often dominated by local warlords. Over the next 12 years a constantly shifting pattern of factionalism and alliance dominated the map of China. The 4 May Movement of 1919 in Shanghai provoked an upsurge of nationalist fervor, in the wake of which the Chinese Communist Party was formed (1921); Sun Zhongshan's Nationalists (Kuomintang) formed an alliance with the Communists, and began a campaign of unification which culminated in the Northern Expedition of 1926–28. This was led by Sun's successor, Moscow-trained Jiang Jieshi (Chiang Kai-shek), who then inaugurated a bloody purge of the Communists.

▲ ⑦ Nationalist China

- under direct control of Nationalist government at Nanjing 1928
- Nanjing control 1929–34
- Nanjing control 1935–37
- Japanese sphere of influence by 1935
- route of Northern Expedition
- pro-Nationalist forces

The Red Flag over Asia

In the wake of the Civil War (1918–21), the Russian Bolsheviks moved swiftly to consolidate their control of Asian areas of Russia. They harnessed technology and modernism with propaganda techniques to achieve the socialist revolution. Communist republics had been set up in the Far East, at Tannu-Tuva, and in Central Asia. These were gradually coerced into merging with the Soviet Union, while military support was provided to oust Chinese troops from Mongolia. The active export of Bolshevik Communism (Comintern) continued in various forms, notably in China and India.

Bolshevik "Agitation-Instruction" trains decorated with revolutionary themes traveled to every corner of the USSR to spread the gospel of Communism.

The spread of Communism in Asia

1917: Bolshevik revolution in Russia
May 4 1919: Movement in China, resurgence of Nationalism
1921: Chinese Communist Party founded
1925: Asiatic borders of USSR consolidated
1927–28: Chinese Nationalists purge Communists

1918–22: Civil war and foreign intervention in Russia
1919: Third International (Comintern); Bolsheviks commit to international revolution
1924: Death of Lenin
1926: Jiang Jieshi leads Nationalist campaign to unify China

1915 1920 1925 1930

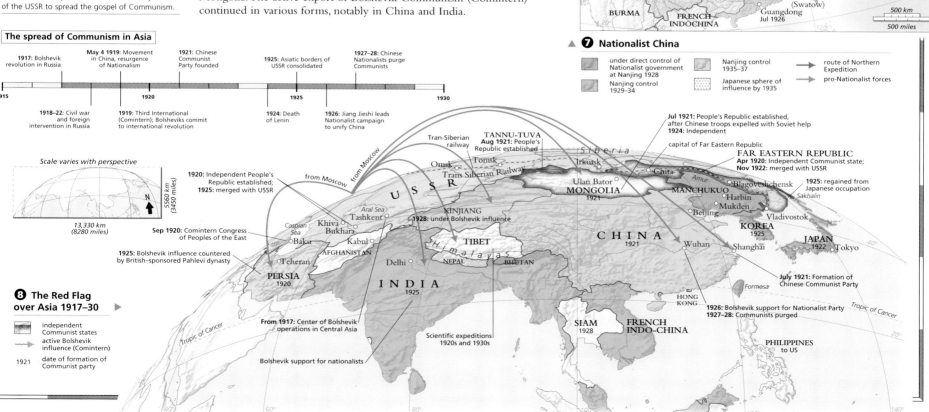

Scale varies with perspective

5560 km (3450 miles)
13,330 km (8280 miles)

⑧ The Red Flag over Asia 1917–30 ▶

- independent Communist states
- active Bolshevik influence (Comintern)
- 1921 date of formation of Communist party

THE WAR IN THE PACIFIC

Japanese expansionism in Manchuria and Jehol accelerated in 1937 with a full-scale invasion of China.

FOLLOWING WORLD WAR I, Japan was accorded an extended sphere of territorial control in the Pacific. The Chinese Civil War enabled Japan to extend its territorial ambitions on the East Asian mainland, culminating in outright warfare in China by 1937. But international sanctions, designed to limit Japan's aspirations resulted, by 1940, in a political standoff. Next year, Japan went to war, calculating its chances on the basis of its rapid industrial development, the colonial powers' involvement in Hitler's war in Europe, and the bounty which would accrue from the establishment of an anti-Western "Greater East Asia Co-Prosperity Sphere." By June 1942 Japan was trying to maintain a front line over 22,000 miles in extent – inevitably, it proved indefensible.

The Japanese offensive 1941–42

Almost simultaneous preemptive strikes in December 1941 against the US naval base at Pearl Harbor, Hawaii, the US-controlled Philippines, the Dutch East Indies, and the British Malayan states created at a stroke and for a brief

The Japanese army's comprehensive training in military techniques such as jungle warfare and amphibious assaults proved an essential element in their initial successes in China and tropical Southeast Asia.

historical moment, the largest contiguous empire the world has ever seen. Campaigns in New Guinea, the Solomons, and Burma extended it even further. The combination of surprise (Japan attacked before declaring war), detailed strategic planning, the use of innovative aggressive methods (amphibious landings, aircraft carriers, tactical bombing, jungle tactics), and a disregard for the "acceptable" rules of warfare proved initially irresistible.

The surprise Japanese bombing raid on the US naval base at Pearl Harbor on December 7, 1941, was designed, at least temporarily, to destroy US sea power in the Pacific. Only 18 of the 94 warships at anchor were actually put out of action, but as a result, the US was drawn into war against Japan and its Axis allies.

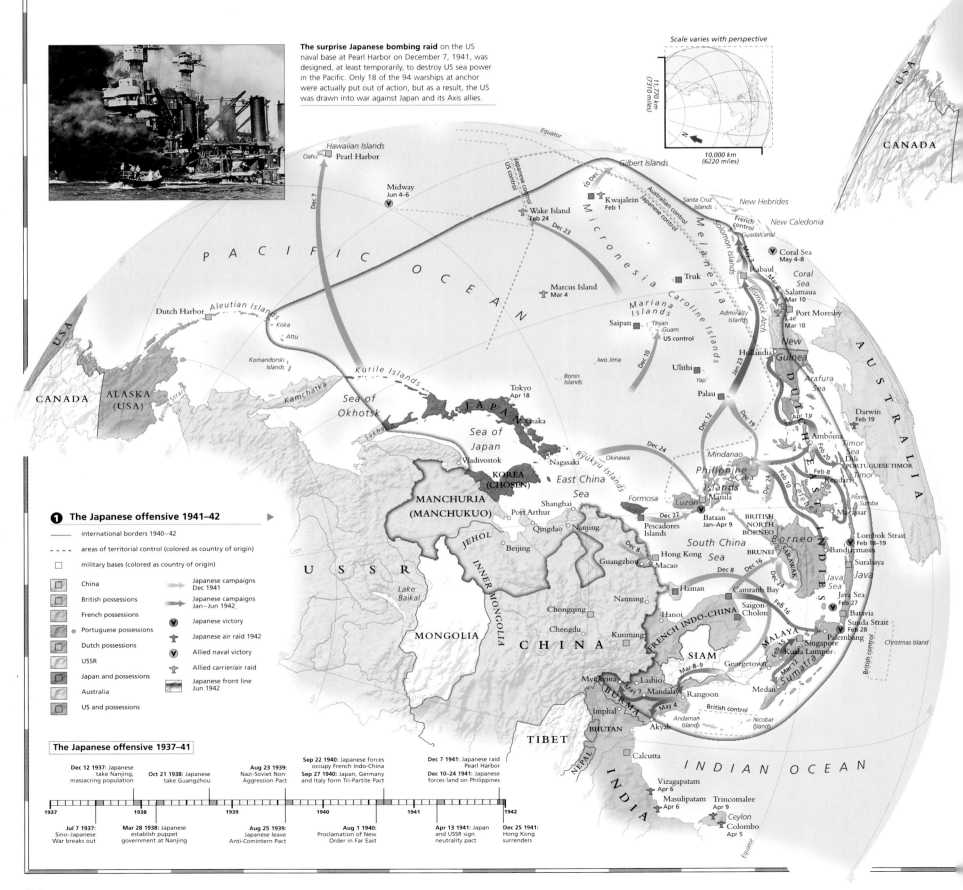

① The Japanese offensive 1941–42

- —— international borders 1940–42
- - - - areas of territorial control (colored as country of origin)
- ☐ military bases (colored as country of origin)

China	➡ Japanese campaigns Dec 1941
British possessions	➡ Japanese campaigns Jan–Jun 1942
French possessions	▼ Japanese victory
Portuguese possessions	⚓ Japanese air raid 1942
Dutch possessions	▼ Allied naval victory
USSR	⚓ Allied carrier/air raid
Japan and possessions	Japanese front line Jun 1942
Australia	
US and possessions	

The Japanese offensive 1937–41

Dec 12 1937: Japanese take Nanjing, massacring population

Oct 21 1938: Japanese take Guangzhou

Aug 23 1939: Nazi-Soviet Non-Aggression Pact

Sep 22 1940: Japanese forces occupy French Indo-China
Sep 27 1940: Japan, Germany and Italy form Tri-Partite Pact

Dec 7 1941: Japanese raid Pearl Harbor
Dec 10–24 1941: Japanese forces land on Philippines

Jul 7 1937: Sino–Japanese War breaks out

Mar 28 1938: Japanese establish puppet government at Nanjing

Aug 25 1939: Japanese leave Anti-Comintern Pact

Aug 1 1940: Proclamation of New Order in Far East

Apr 13 1941: Japan and USSR sign neutrality pact

Dec 25 1941: Hong Kong surrenders

The Allied counteroffensive 1942–45

In mid-1942 the Allied defeat of naval forces in the Coral Sea and at Midway halted the Japanese advance. Over the next year, bitter campaigns on and around Guadalcanal in the Solomons proved a turning point. American industrial mobilization on a massive scale fed a selective island-hopping campaign designed to disrupt the internal communications of the Japanese empire and to bring air power within striking distance of the Japanese home islands. Japanese resistance was so fierce that it took the US explosion of two newly developed atomic bombs over Japan, which was followed by a Soviet land campaign in Manchuria, to force a surrender.

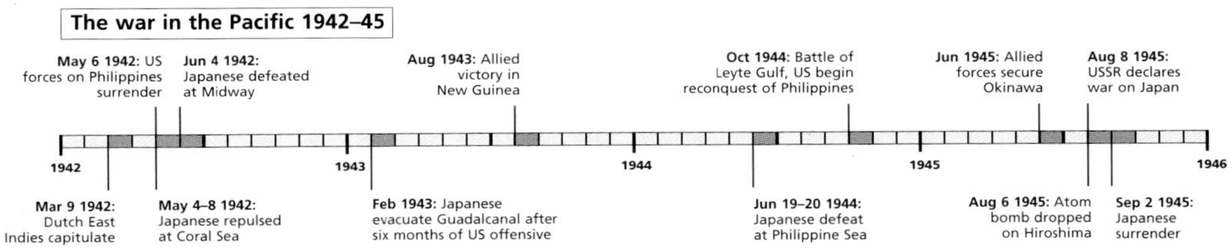

The war in the Pacific 1942–45

May 6 1942: US forces on Philippines surrender
Jun 4 1942: Japanese defeated at Midway
Aug 1943: Allied victory in New Guinea
Oct 1944: Battle of Leyte Gulf, US begin reconquest of Philippines
Jun 1945: Allied forces secure Okinawa
Aug 8 1945: USSR declares war on Japan

1942 — 1943 — 1944 — 1945 — 1946

Mar 9 1942: Dutch East Indies capitulate
May 4–8 1942: Japanese repulsed at Coral Sea
Feb 1943: Japanese evacuate Guadalcanal after six months of US offensive
Jun 19–20 1944: Japanese defeat at Philippine Sea
Aug 6 1945: Atom bomb dropped on Hiroshima
Sep 2 1945: Japanese surrender

The US refinement of amphibious operations, landing large forces supported by naval bombardment and carrier-borne air power, was a key element in their reconquest of the Pacific.

Scale varies with perspective

11,770 km (7310 miles)

10,000 km (6220 miles)

❷ The Allied counteroffensive 1942–45

- ➤ Japanese offensives
- ➤ Allied offensives 1943
- ➤ Allied offensives 1944
- ➤ Allied offensives 1945
- Japanese front line Jun 1942
- Japanese front line Sep 1944
- Japanese front line Aug 1945
- ◻ Chinese military base
- ◻ British military base
- ◻ US military base
- Ⓥ Allied naval victory
- Allied amphibious assault
- Japanese base isolated by Allies
- Japanese air/naval base taken by Allies

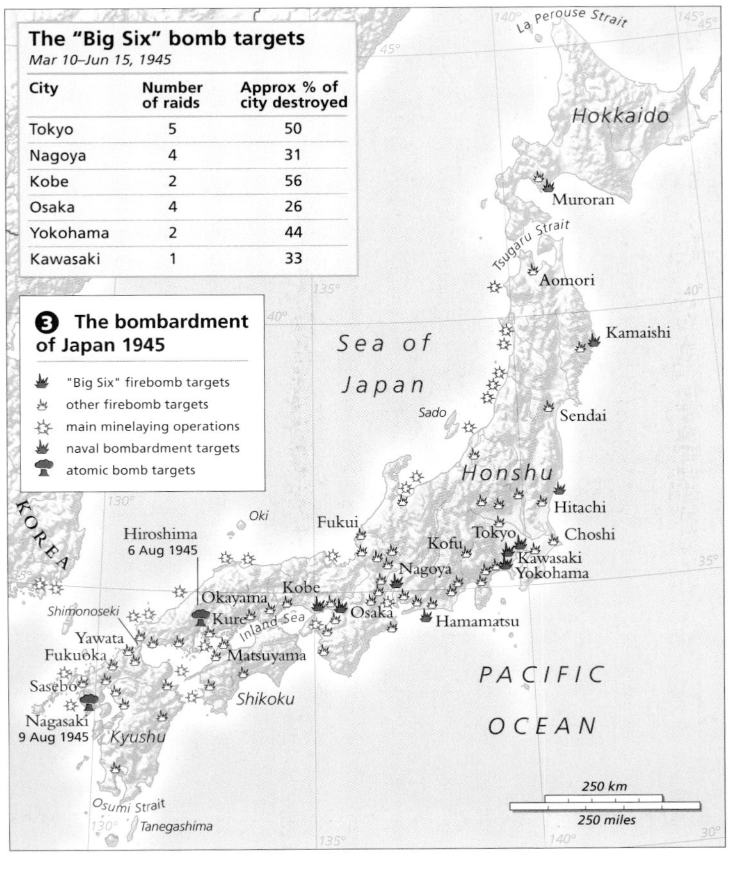

The "Big Six" bomb targets
Mar 10–Jun 15, 1945

City	Number of raids	Approx % of city destroyed
Tokyo	5	50
Nagoya	4	31
Kobe	2	56
Osaka	4	26
Yokohama	2	44
Kawasaki	1	33

❸ The bombardment of Japan 1945

- ⚲ "Big Six" firebomb targets
- ⚘ other firebomb targets
- ⚵ main minelaying operations
- ⚴ naval bombardment targets
- ⚛ atomic bomb targets

The bombardment of Japan

The Allied air assault began in June 1944 with raids from Chengdu in China. With the capture of the Marianas, Iwo Jima, and Okinawa, greater air power could be brought to bear, bombing cities and sowing mines in Japan's home waters. Complemented by carrier-supported raids from March 1945, which inaugurated the "Big Six" firebomb raids against key cities, over 50 other cities were attacked; merchant shipping was reduced by over 80%, over half of Japan's urban area was devastated, one-third of all buildings destroyed, and 13 million people made homeless. It culminated in the atomic bomb attacks against Hiroshima and Nagasaki, killing over 150,000 people.

As the Allied forces closed in on the home islands, Japanese resistance became more tenacious. Volunteer squadrons of suicide (kamikaze) fighter-bomber pilots were recruited to attack the Allied fleet.

COMMUNISM AND CAPITALISM

A high-speed train passing Mount Fuji exemplifies Japan's rapid development as one of the world's leading economies

THE HISTORY OF EAST ASIA from 1945 was dominated by the contrasting ideologies of Communism and capitalism. In China, where the population increased by one-third to 880 million between 1950 and 1970, Mao Zedong and his successors sought a social revolution through centralization, collectivization, and the ruthless elimination of dissent. Japan, rebuilt and supported by its Western conquerors, enjoyed an unprecedented economic boom. Spurred by the Japanese example, and supported by the US in an attempt to contain the spread of Communism, this success spread around the Pacific Rim. In Central Asia, the collapse of the Soviet Union in 1990 saw Islam revitalized, accompanied by a resurgence of traditional ethnic rivalries.

Mao Zedong's vision of a Communist revolution in China was underpinned by the mobilization of the masses down to a family level, spread by his writings, mass education, and by propaganda (above).

The Communist revolution in China 1927–49

Following the schism with the Nationalists in 1927, the Communists withdrew to isolated mountain bases. In 1934, Mao Zedong led the Communists north (the Long March) to Yenan. During the war against Japan, Communist guerrilla groups operated extensively within occupied territory and organized popular resistance, while the Nationalists withdrew to Chongqing in the remote southwest. Upon the Japanese surrender, Soviet forces occupied Manchuria, giving the Communists a further advantage, and they rapidly gained control of the cultural and industrial heartland of the northeast. By 1948 open warfare had broken out, but with the collapse of their forces north of the Yangtze, the Nationalists withdrew to Taiwan. The People's Republic of China was established in 1949.

China under the Communists

The victorious Chinese Communists were confronted by the immediate need to implement socialist reforms, to create a centralized, Party-led, political and economic infrastructure, and to modernize industry, after almost 40 years of turmoil. Mao Zedong used propaganda and coercion to mobilize the peasants through collectivization of agriculture and mass labor projects. Energy-producing programs increased coal and oil output, and hydroelectric and nuclear plants were constructed. The Great Leap Forward attempted to divert labor from agriculture toward industry, but resulted in famine and 30 million deaths. Ideological purges continued, notably during the Cultural Revolution (1966). After Mao's death in 1976, China began tentative liberalization although this faltered with the massacre of pro-democracy protestors in 1989.

The Great Leap Forward (1957–58) redirected peasant labor to massive public works projects to transform China from an agricultural to an industrial economy. The nation's agricultural capacity was drastically reduced, causing widespread famine in the 1960s.

China under Communist rule

1950–56: Land reform and collectivization of agriculture; millions of landowners executed

1957–59: Great Leap Forward; attempt to increase productivity and boost industry

1959: Start of Three Hard Years; widespread famine

1966: Cultural Revolution; massive purge, formation of revolutionary Red Guard

1968: Red Guards disbanded

1976: Death of Mao Zedong

1978: Beginnings of economic liberalization under Deng Xiaoping

1989: Suppression of pro-democracy movement

1950 1960 1970 1980 1990

❶ The Communist Revolution in China

⬭ Communist centers 1934

➡ Long March Oct 1934–Oct 1935

▨ area under Japanese control 1944

▨ area under Communist (PLA) control 1946

▨ area under Communist (PLA) control by mid-1949

— area of Communist guerrilla operations 1944–49

⤫ battle

➜ principal Communist campaigns

○ city with date of Communist control

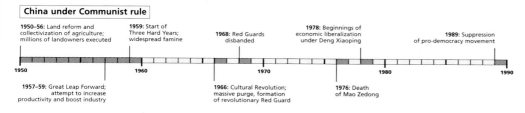

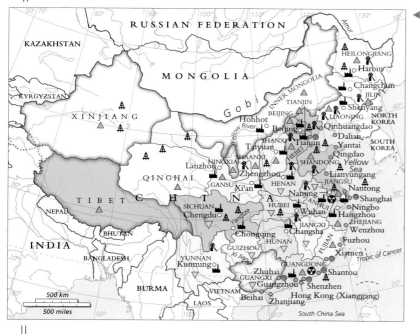

❷ Chinese economic development from 1950

▨ boundary of Autonomous Regions

Percentage population growth 1950–90

▨ over 100%
▨ 75–100%
▨ 55–75%
▨ less than 55%

Economic development under Mao Zedong

⛏ oilfield
⛏ coalfield
☢ nuclear plant
▪ industrial center

Economic development since 1980

● Special Economic Zone
○ open port
△ average income more than 80% of national average, 1990s
▽ average income less than 80% of national average, 1990s

The Long March of 1934–35 strategically relocated and united the forces of the Communist party. The 8000 or so survivors of the campaign later became the core of the party, although it was only following a bitter power struggle that Mao Zedong, seen here addressing his troops, became supreme leader.

The Communist Revolution

Oct 1934–Oct 1935: Long March unites Communists

1927: Split between Nationalists and Communists

1937: Sino-Japanese war breaks out

1945: Japanese surrender in Second World War

1946–49: Civil war between Nationalists and Communists

1949: Republic of China set up in Taiwan

1949: People's Republic of China established

1925 1930 1935 1940 1945 1950

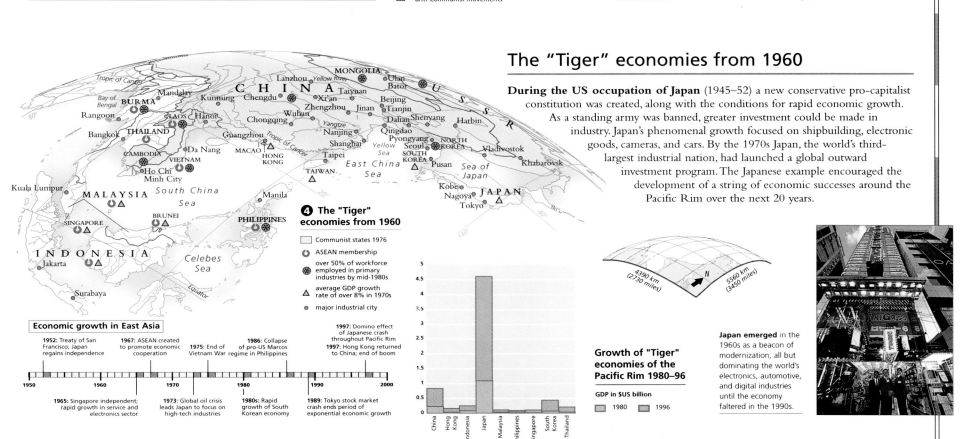

Chinese expansionism from 1949

The cooling of relations between the West and the Communist bloc was further chilled by China's involvement in the Korean War, its covert support for Communist guerrillas elsewhere, and by its ideological split with the Soviet Union in 1960, sparked by the Amur-Ussuri border dispute. Chinese isolationism was balanced by an aggressive internal and foreign policy. Tibet was invaded and occupied, and the divine ruler, the Dalai Lama, exiled in 1959. It was formally absorbed as an Autonomous Region of China in 1965. Border disputes brought a brief war with India in 1962, and a temporary invasion of North Vietnam in 1979. Irredentist Taiwan remained a thorn in China's side, while the need to control potential oil and gas deposits saw China defending remote claims in the South China Sea.

The invasion of Tibet in 1950 was the most significant incident of Chinese expansionism since the Communist Revolution. Traditional ways of life and beliefs were suppressed and, following a revolt in 1959, Tibet's spiritual and political leader, the Dalai Lama, was forced into exile.

❸ **Chinese expansion from 1949**

- ☐ Chinese provinces
- ☐ Autonomous Regions (Zizhiqu)
- ⚔ territorial/border dispute
- → Chinese invasion
- ★ Chinese support for Communist insurgents
- ⚒ Soviet support for Communists after 1960
- 🏛 suppression of anti-Communist movements

The expansion of China, 1950–1980

1950: Chinese invasion of Tibet	1960: Amur-Ussuri border dispute; ideological split with USSR	1962: Sino-Indian War over border claim at Arunachal Pradesh; rectification of border claims with Pakistan, Nepal, and Burma	1979: US severs relations with Taiwan in return for detente with China

1950 — 1955 — 1960 — 1965 — 1970 — 1975 — 1980

- 1950: Chinese troops invade Korea
- 1959: Tibetan rebellion crushed, religious institutions banned
- 1971: China admitted to United Nations; Taiwan expelled
- 1979: Invasion of North Vietnam

The "Tiger" economies from 1960

During the US occupation of Japan (1945–52) a new conservative pro-capitalist constitution was created, along with the conditions for rapid economic growth. As a standing army was banned, greater investment could be made in industry. Japan's phenomenal growth focused on shipbuilding, electronic goods, cameras, and cars. By the 1970s Japan, the world's third-largest industrial nation, had launched a global outward investment program. The Japanese example encouraged the development of a string of economic successes around the Pacific Rim over the next 20 years.

❹ **The "Tiger" economies from 1960**

- ☐ Communist states 1976
- ⚙ ASEAN membership
- ⚙ over 50% of workforce employed in primary industries by mid-1980s
- △ average GDP growth rate of over 8% in 1970s
- ● major industrial city

Growth of "Tiger" economies of the Pacific Rim 1980–96

GDP in $US billion
- ☐ 1980
- ☐ 1996

(bar chart: China, Hong Kong, Indonesia, Japan, Malaysia, Philippines, Singapore, South Korea, Thailand)

Japan emerged in the 1960s as a beacon of modernization, all but dominating the world's electronics, automotive, and digital industries until the economy faltered in the 1990s.

Economic growth in East Asia

1952: Treaty of San Francisco; Japan regains independence	1967: ASEAN created to promote economic cooperation	1975: End of pro-US Marcos regime in Philippines	1986: Collapse of pro-US Marcos regime in Philippines	1997: Domino effect of Japanese crash throughout Pacific Rim
				1997: Hong Kong returned to China; end of boom

1950 — 1960 — 1970 — 1980 — 1990 — 2000

- 1965: Singapore independent; rapid growth in service and electronics sector
- 1973: Global oil crisis leads Japan to focus on high-tech industries
- 1980s: Rapid growth of South Korean economy
- 1989: Tokyo stock market crash ends period of exponential economic growth

Islam and nationalism in Central Asia

Islam in Central Asia survived suppression and political change, to reemerge as a vital force in the region's politics. Signalled by the *mujahedin* rebellion in Afghanistan (from 1973), and the establishment of an Islamic Republic in Iran in 1979, the revival progressed with the *mujahedin* defeat of a Soviet invasion (1979–89), and the collapse of the USSR in 1990. Ethnic rivalry flared up across the new republics, with persistent tensions between Shia and Sunni Muslims, notably in the 1995 military offensive in Afghanistan by the mainly Sunni Taliban.

The Islamic states of Central Asia inherited widespread environmental damage, especially in Kazakhstan, where the Soviet nuclear testing and space center at Baykonur (above) was based.

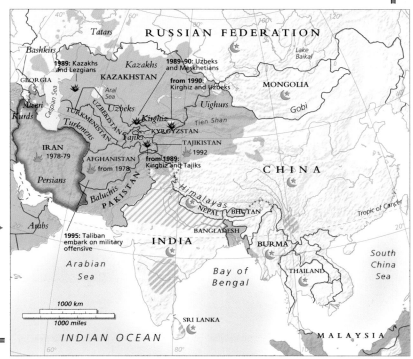

❺ **Islam and nationalism in Asia** ▶

- ☐ predominantly Muslim populations
- ☐ Muslim minorities
- ☐ Shia majority
- ⚔ ethnic conflict
- ⚒ Islamic revolution/civil war

North and Central Asia since 1970

1973: Mujahedin rebellion in Afghanistan	1979: Soviet invasion of Afghanistan	1990–91: Collapse of USSR; creation of Central Asian republics	1995: Taliban militia reignites Afghan civil war	

1970 — 1975 — 1980 — 1985 — 1990 — 1995

- 1979: Islamic revolution in Iran
- 1989: Soviet troops withdraw from Afghanistan

AUSTRALASIA AND OCEANIA
REGIONAL HISTORY

THE HISTORICAL LANDSCAPE

THE INSULAR CONTINENT OF AUSTRALIA and the myriad island groups of Melanesia, Micronesia, and Polynesia, strewn across the Pacific Ocean, share the most unlikely chapter in world history. Australia and New Guinea were first colonized some 60,000 years ago by migrants crossing the Southeast Asian landbridge, who completed their journey by boat – the world's first navigators. As sea levels rose after the last Ice Age, they became divided and isolated, maintaining simple, sustainable lifestyles in remote communities until European contact in the 18th century when their vulnerability was fatally exposed. The settlement of the Pacific islands, beginning some 30,000 years ago, again depended on navigational skills, and developed from about 1500 BCE into a process of active colonization. By 1000 CE, Polynesians were the most widely distributed ethnic group on the face of the earth, with settlements from New Zealand to Hawaii. The region was the penultimate target of European imperialists, leaving only the barren tracts of the Arctic ice cap and continental Antarctica as the final, ephemeral prizes in Europe's race for global domination – a race of heroic futility played out across the opening years of the 20th century.

Initially settlements were concentrated around the coasts; then, as the population grew, people moved inland to colonize the flat glacial plains of the interior.

Australia's deserts were more extensive during the last Ice Age. As the land bridge between Australia and New Guinea was flooded, settlers retreated south into the desert margins of Australia.

Most Pacific islands are volcanic, formed by eruptions on the sea floor which accumulate a cone of volcanic material, eventually rising above the ocean surface. As the volcano becomes extinct, coral reefs grow around the island's fringes. Humans first sailed to the Pacific islands from New Guinea and the Solomon Islands, reaching Fiji by 1500 BCE.

Vegetation type

	ice cap and glacier
	tundra
	semidesert or sparsely vegetated
	grassland
	forest or open woodland
	tropical rain forest
	tropical desert
	desert
	coastline (present-day)
	coastline (18,000 years ago)

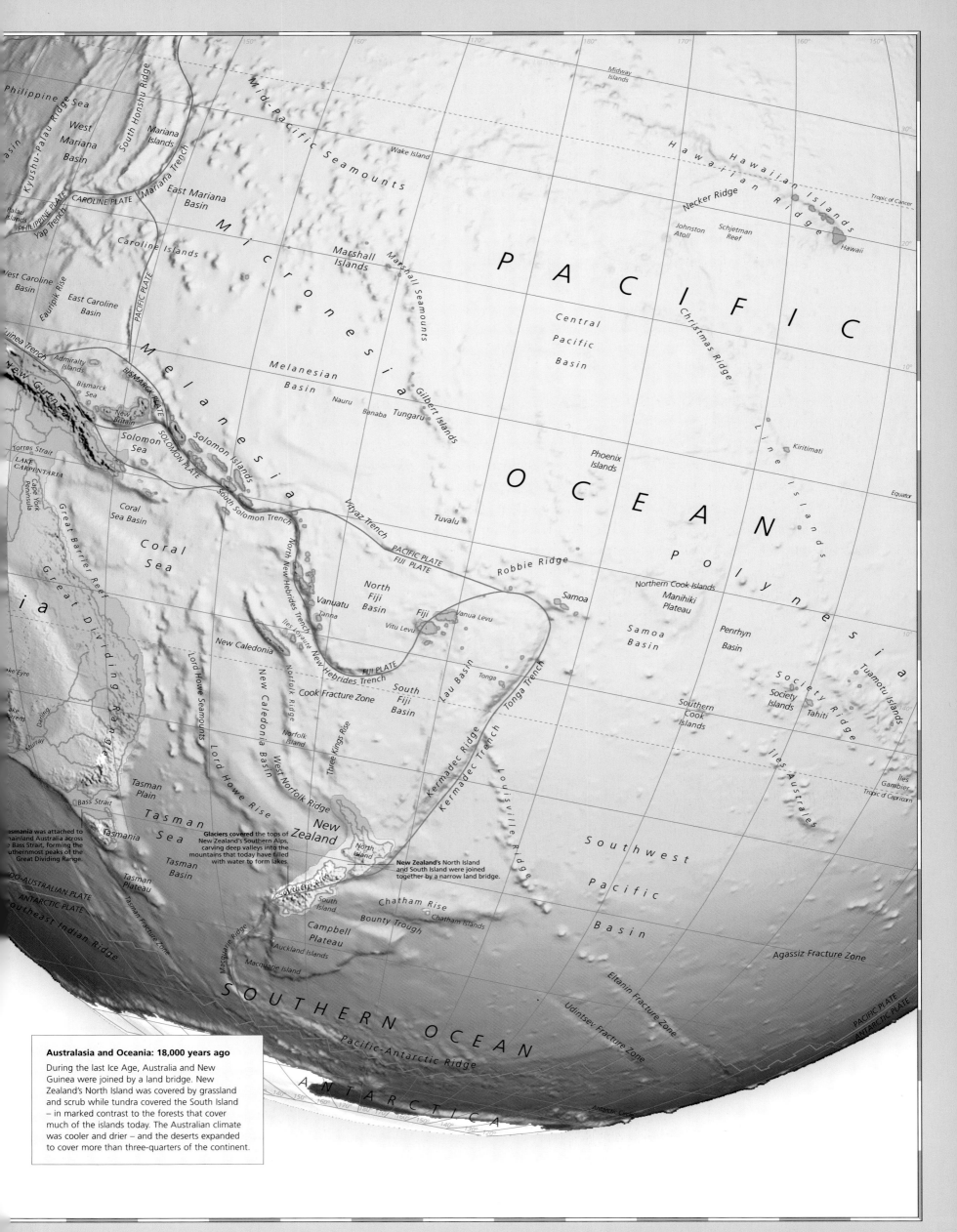

PACIFIC OCEAN

SOUTHERN OCEAN

ANTARCTICA

Australasia and Oceania: 18,000 years ago

During the last Ice Age, Australia and New Guinea were joined by a land bridge. New Zealand's North Island was covered by grassland and scrub while tundra covered the South Island – in marked contrast to the forests that cover much of the islands today. The Australian climate was cooler and drier – and the deserts expanded to cover more than three-quarters of the continent.

Glaciers covered the tops of New Zealand's Southern Alps, carving deep valleys into the mountains that today have filled with water to form lakes.

New Zealand's North Island and South Island were joined together by a narrow land bridge.

Tasmania was attached to mainland Australia across the Bass Strait, forming the southernmost peaks of the Great Dividing Range.

277

AUSTRALASIA AND OCEANIA
EXPLORATION AND MAPPING

Abel Tasman reached Tasmania and New Zealand in 1642 in his search for a great southern continent.

ALMOST ALL THE PACIFIC ISLANDS had been discovered and, when habitable, settled by Polynesian voyagers some 500 years before European explorers ventured into the ocean. After Magellan's pioneering crossing of 1521, it took three centuries to chart the whole Pacific. The continent of Australia presented even greater problems. Ever since Classical times, European world maps had included a vast southern continent, *Terra Australis Incognita*. It was not until James Cook's voyages in the 18th century that the true extent of Australia was established. New Guinea's mountainous interior was not explored by Europeans until the 20th century.

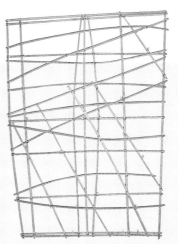

STICK CHARTS OF THE MARSHALL ISLANDS

The Melanesian and Polynesian peoples who have been sailing the Pacific for four millennia have built up a vast store of knowledge of its islands, winds, and currents. The inhabitants of the Marshall Islands make charts of sticks and shells. Some are actual maps of surrounding islands and are carried aboard their canoes. Others are teaching aids. The *mattang*, for example, is not a map as such; it demonstrates the way islands affect patterns in the ocean's swell, an invaluable means of detecting the presence of low-lying atolls.

This typical *mattang* chart is made of the midribs of coconut fronds. Shells mark the location of islands and the sticks show variations in ocean swell.

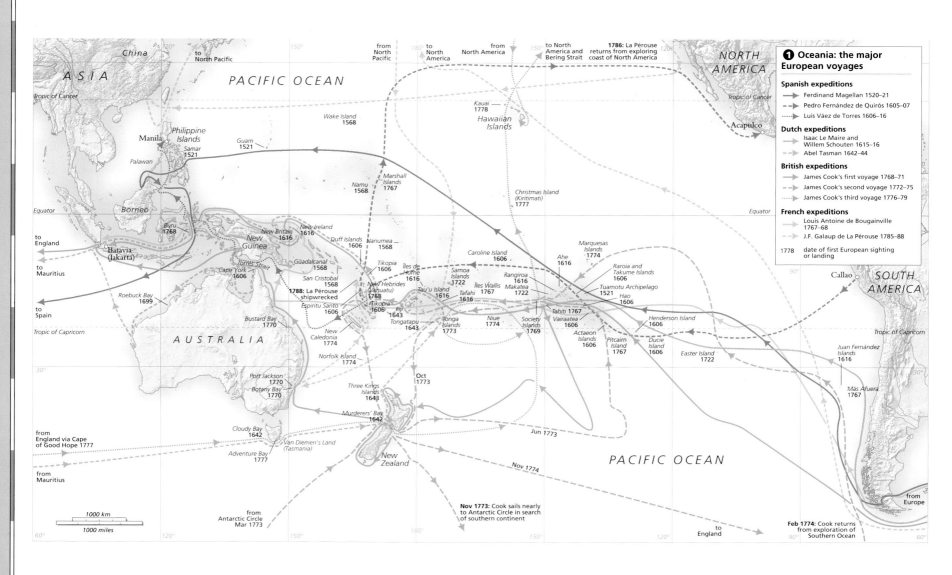

❶ Oceania: the major European voyages

Spanish expeditions
- Ferdinand Magellan 1520–21
- Pedro Fernández de Quirós 1605–07
- Luis Váez de Torres 1606–16

Dutch expeditions
- Isaac Le Maire and Willem Schouten 1615–16
- Abel Tasman 1642–44

British expeditions
- James Cook's first voyage 1768–71
- James Cook's second voyage 1772–75
- James Cook's third voyage 1776–79

French expeditions
- Louis Antoine de Bougainville 1767–68
- J.F. Galaup de La Pérouse 1785–88

1778 date of first European sighting or landing

European voyages of discovery

In the 16th century the Spanish sailed into the Pacific out of curiosity and greed, seeking routes to the riches of China and the "Spice Islands." At first they did not intrude too greatly on the life of the islands, using them as stopovers to pick up food and water. In Australasia the Dutch led the way, but, seeing no potential profit in Australia or New Zealand, left them alone. Things changed in the 18th century when the French and the British were competing for domination of the globe. The three voyages of Captain James Cook transformed Europe's understanding of Oceania, and it was in part the popularity of accounts of Cook's voyages that spurred European and American exploitation and colonization of the region in the 19th century.

Dutch mariners provided the data for this 1593 map. It gives a reasonably accurate picture of the Solomon Islands and part of the north coast of New Guinea, but the shape and extent of Australia are still a mystery. Here, it is at least divided from New Guinea by a strait – many later maps show the two islands attached.

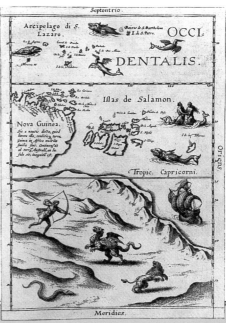

The Resolution, James Cook's ship on his epic second voyage of 1772–75, was originally built to carry coal.

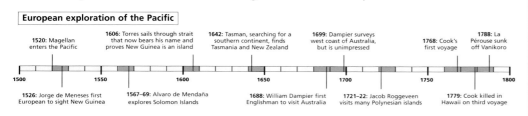

European exploration of the Pacific

- **1520:** Magellan enters the Pacific
- **1526:** Jorge de Meneses first European to sight New Guinea
- **1567–69:** Alvaro de Mendaña explores Solomon Islands
- **1606:** Torres sails through strait that now bears his name and proves New Guinea is an island
- **1642:** Tasman, searching for a southern continent, finds Tasmania and New Zealand
- **1688:** William Dampier first Englishman to visit Australia
- **1699:** Dampier surveys west coast of Australia, but is unimpressed
- **1721–22:** Jacob Roggeveen visits many Polynesian islands
- **1768:** Cook's first voyage
- **1779:** Cook killed in Hawaii on third voyage
- **1788:** La Pérouse sunk off Vanikoro

Burke and Wills set off in 1860 to cross Australia from south to north in a fanfare of publicity. Their confidence was misplaced; Aboriginals they encountered helped them find food and water, but eventually they died of hunger.

❷ Exploration in Australia and New Guinea 1798–1928 ▶

→ George Bass and Matthew Flinders 1798–99
→ Matthew Flinders 1802–03
→ Charles Sturt 1828–46
→ Thomas Mitchell 1836–46
→ Edward Eyre 1839–41
→ Ludwig Leichhardt 1844–45
→ Edmund Kennedy 1848
→ Robert Burke and William Wills 1860–61
→ John Stuart 1861–62
→ Peter Warburton 1872–73
→ John Forrest 1874
→ Ernest Giles 1875–76
→ Luigi Maria d'Albertis 1876
→ Alexander Forrest 1879
→ Charles Karius 1927–28

Exploring Australia and New Guinea

1802–03: Flinders circumnavigates Australia	**1829–30:** Sturt's journeys pave way for founding of colony of South Australia in 1836	**1875:** D'Albertis makes first of three trips up Fly River	**1927–28:** Karius expedition crosses New Guinea from south to north

1800 — 1825 — 1850 — 1875 — 1900 — 1925 — 1950

1813: Route found across Blue Mountains **1841:** Eyre is first European to cross Nullarbor Plain **1879:** Forrest explores from Port Hedland across Kimberley Plateau

Australia and New Guinea: explorers of the interior

Australia never aroused the curiosity of the Dutch who knew only the hostile west coast. The British, who settled in the more temperate southeast, were gradually drawn to the interior, first by the lure of gold and the search for grazing land, later by curiosity about the vast deserts of the interior. Expeditions such as those of Burke and Leichhardt used imported camels. New Guinea was even more unwelcoming to intruders with its mountains and dense rain forest. Most 19th-century explorers of the island followed the courses of rivers, while parts of the highlands remained inaccessible until the age of the airplane.

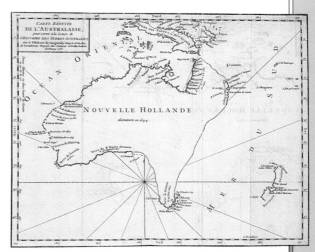

James Cook took a copy of this French map of 1756 with him on his voyage of 1768–71. The west coast of Australia is well charted because Dutch ships bound for the East Indies were often blown ashore there. The east was unexplored until Cook himself charted it and the fact that Tasmania was an island was established by Flinders and Bass in 1798–99.

Sealers, whalers, and traders

The first outsiders to have a significant impact in the Pacific were American sealers in the late 18th century. Traders soon followed to supply their sailing ships, establishing stations throughout the Pacific. By the 1820s, with Atlantic whale stocks depleted, whalers were also starting to arrive in large numbers, with calamitous results: introduced diseases caused the destruction of entire island societies. In the 1860s came a further threat – "blackbirders," slave raiders operating initially out of Peru, later carrying off the young males of many islands to work in the canefields of Queensland, Australia.

Sperm whales were the chief quarry of Pacific whalers, due to the growing market for their oil, used in industrialized Europe and the US for lubricating machinery.

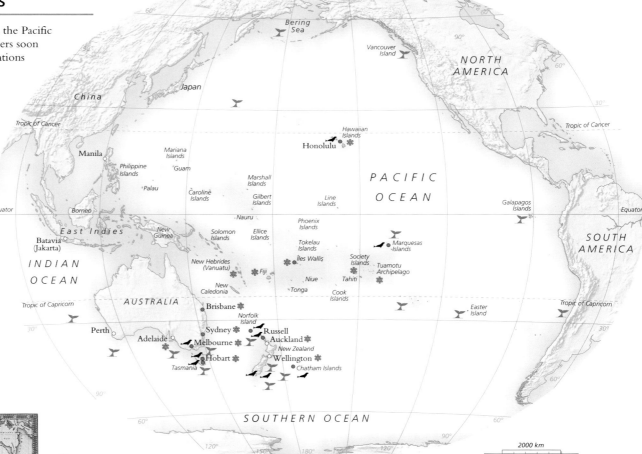

❸ Europeans and Americans in the Pacific 1800–50 ▲

- ⚓ major whaling ground
- 🐋 whaling station
- ⚓ sealing station
- ✳ trading station

Knowledge of the Pacific expanded rapidly with the arrival of American and European whaling ships in the 19th century. By 1837, when this map was published, the picture was almost complete.

Exploitation of the Pacific 1800–1850

1800: Tahiti starts supplying Port Jackson (Sydney) with pigs	**1820:** American whalers based on Îles Wallis	**c.1825:** Whaling and sealing stations on east coast of New Zealand	**c.1840:** Copra becomes mainstay of trade on Society Islands	**1849:** US alone has 760 whaling ships operating in Pacific

1800 — 1810 — 1820 — 1830 — 1840 — 1850

1804: Sandalwood traders arrive in Fiji **1825:** Solomon Islands attract traders in turtleshell and mother-of-pearl **1841:** At least 35 whaling stations in Tasmania

PREHISTORIC OCEANIA

This fine carving from Rurutu in the Austral Islands shows the local god A'a.

DURING THE ICE AGES, Australia, New Guinea, and Tasmania were linked by land bridges to form the continent of Sahul. The first people to inhabit the region were Australoids, ancestors of today's Papuans and Australia's Aborigines, who may have reached Sahul as early as 60,000 years ago. The next significant wave of immigrants did not come until 6000 BCE, when Austronesian people fanned out through the Philippines and the East Indies. They mixed with the resident Australoids to produce the heterogeneous population of Melanesia. Around 1500 BCE the Austronesians, the greatest seafarers of prehistory, reached Fiji, and soon after that Samoa, starting point for later Polynesian expansion to the eastern Pacific and the eventual settlement of islands as far apart as Hawaii and New Zealand.

THE DREAMTIME

Australian Aboriginal cultures vary greatly; however, nearly all share the concept of "dreamtime" – the time of creation. Aboriginal lore maintains that, before creation, basic matter existed, but then the spirits of dreaming imbued the world with physical features and spiritual substance. The landscape can be read as a complex system of signs revealing the truth of these ancestral spirits.

The spirit figure in this rock painting in Kakadu National Park is Barrginj, wife of Lightning Man.

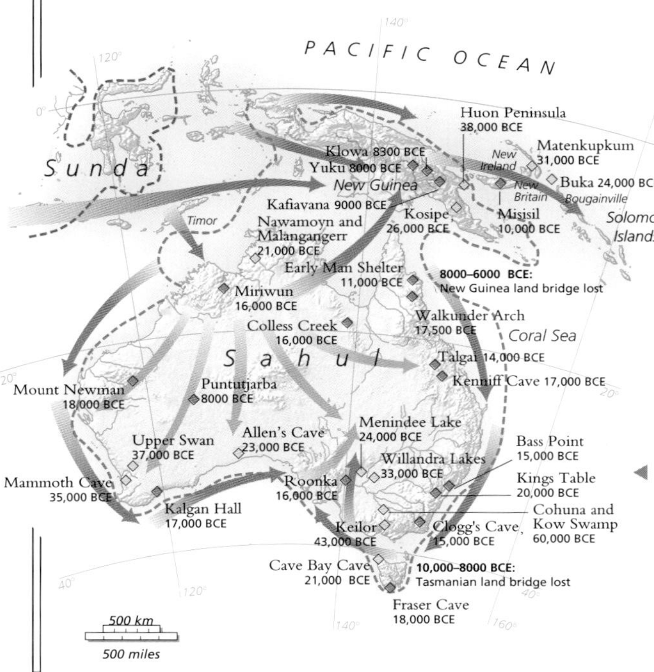

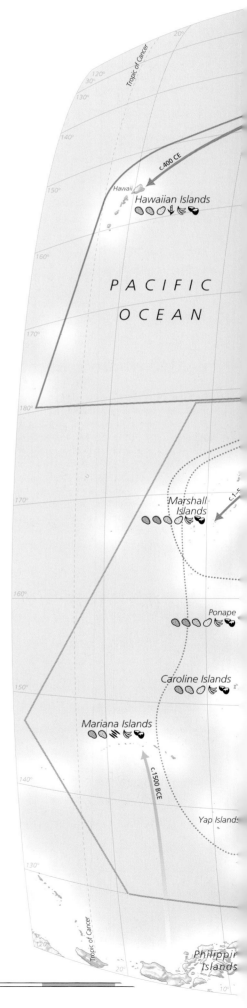

The settlement of Australia, Tasmania, and New Guinea

No one knows exactly when or by what route the first settlers reached Australia and New Guinea. What is certain is that they would have had to cross a stretch of open sea. In the case of Australia, this was probably from the island of Timor, 45 miles from the mainland, when sea level was at its lowest. Although Australia enjoyed a better climate with higher rainfall than today, settlement would have been largely near the coast. Valuable archaeological evidence was lost when sea levels rose again at the end of the last Ice Age. At this point the Tasmanians, who may have been an early wave of immigrants, were cut off from the mainland.

❶ The settlement of Australia, Tasmania, and New Guinea

Archaeological sites with approximate date of earliest human presence
◇ pre 20,000 BCE
◆ post 20,000 BCE
➡ probable migration routes
➡ possible migration routes
--- maximum extent of Sahul landmass c.16,000 BCE
--- maximum extent of Sunda landmass c.16,000 BCE

Map labels: Huon Peninsula 38,000 BCE; Klowa 8300 BCE; Yuku 8000 BCE; Matenkupkum 31,000 BCE; Kafiavana 9000 BCE; Kosipe 26,000 BCE; Misisil 10,000 BCE; Buka 24,000 BCE; Bougainville; Solomon Islands; Nawamoyn and Malangangerr 21,000 BCE; Early Man Shelter 11,000 BCE; 8000–6000 BCE: New Guinea land bridge lost; Miriwun 16,000 BCE; Walkunder Arch 17,500 BCE; Coral Sea; Colless Creek 16,000 BCE; Talgai 14,000 BCE; Kenniff Cave 17,000 BCE; Mount Newman 18,000 BCE; Puntutjarba 8000 BCE; Menindee Lake 24,000 BCE; Bass Point 15,000 BCE; Upper Swan 37,000 BCE; Allen's Cave 23,000 BCE; Willandra Lakes 33,000 BCE; Kings Table 20,000 BCE; Mammoth Cave 35,000 BCE; Roonka 16,000 BCE; Cohuna and Kow Swamp 60,000 BCE; Kalgan Hall 17,000 BCE; Keilor 43,000 BCE; Clogg's Cave 15,000 BCE; Cave Bay Cave 21,000 BCE; 10,000–8000 BCE: Tasmanian land bridge lost; Fraser Cave 18,000 BCE; PACIFIC OCEAN; Sunda; New Guinea; Timor; Sahul; 500 km; 500 miles

The settlement of Australia and New Guinea

60,000: Possible date of partial male skeleton found at Kow Swamp on Murray River

40,000: Australoids start voyaging out toward Solomon Islands

30,000: Careful burial of male body near Lake Mungo, one of the Willandra Lakes sites

10,000: First human-like figures in Australian rock art

c.8000–6000: Rising sea level covers New Guinea land bridge

38,000: Campfire site on New Guinea's Huon Peninsula

18,000: Fraser Cave on southern tip of Tasmania occupied

c.10,000: Land bridge connecting Australia and Tasmania starts to disappear

[Timeline: 60,000 BCE — 50,000 — 40,000 — 30,000 — 20,000 — 10,000 — 1 CE]

Within their home range, most Aborigines led a largely nomadic life, following the food supply according to the seasons. The men were armed with spears for hunting, as in this rock painting; the women carried digging sticks and baskets.

Prehistoric agricultural development on New Guinea

The Australoids of Sahul were hunter-gatherers. However, as early as 10,000 BCE, New Guineans began clearing dense forests, placing them among the world's first crop gardeners. Remains of pigs and dogs dating from 4000–3000 BCE suggest these were brought to New Guinea by Austronesian immigrants, who also introduced techniques of taro cultivation and swamp drainage and management. These soon spread from coastal regions to the Western Highlands. The inhabitants of the Eastern Highlands, however, grew a different staple rootcrop, *Pueraria lobata*, while continuing to hunt and gather.

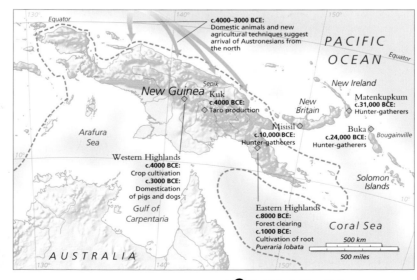

Map labels: c.4000–3000 BCE: Domestic animals and new agricultural techniques suggest arrival of Austronesians from the north; PACIFIC OCEAN; Equator; New Guinea; Sepik; Kuk c.4000 BCE: Taro production; New Ireland; New Britain; Matenkupkum c.31,000 BCE: Hunter-gatherers; Arafura Sea; Misisil c.10,000 BCE: Hunter-gatherers; Buka c.24,000 BCE: Hunter-gatherers; Bougainville; Western Highlands c.4000 BCE: Crop cultivation c.3000 BCE: Domestication of pigs and dogs; Gulf of Carpentaria; Solomon Islands; Eastern Highlands c.8000 BCE: Forest clearing c.1000 BCE: Cultivation of root Pueraria lobata; Coral Sea; AUSTRALIA; 500 km; 500 miles

▲ ❷ Prehistoric New Guinea
➡ possible routes of Austronesians
--- maximum extent of Sahul landmass c.16,000 BCE
◇ archaeological site

Horticulture in New Guinea has changed little over 10,000 years. Yams, introduced from Asia by Austronesian peoples in about 4000 BCE, became a staple throughout the Pacific.

Map labels (right map): Tropic of Cancer; Hawaiian Islands; c.400 CE; PACIFIC OCEAN; Marshall Islands; Ponape; Caroline Islands; Mariana Islands; Yap Islands; c.1500 BCE; Philippine Islands

The peopling of the Pacific

Settlement of the Pacific was accomplished in two epic series of migrations. From about 2000 BCE Austronesian peoples settled Melanesia, sailing from the Philippines, the Bismarck Archipelago, the Solomons, and ultimately Fiji. Their spread can be charted by their distinctive Lapita pottery. The Fiji-Tonga-Samoa crescent was the cradle of a new, equally dynamic culture: the Polynesians. A major migration, probably from Samoa, to the Marquesas, was the springboard that launched the Polynesians to the remaining far-flung islands of the Pacific, from New Zealand in the south to Hawaii in the north and Rapa Nui (Easter Island) in the east.

Prehistoric migrations in the Pacific

c.6000: Migrations from Southeast Asia give rise to Austronesian culture

c.4000: Austronesians reach southwestern Pacific islands

2000: Austronesians settle New Caledonia

c.1000: Emergence of archaic Polynesian society in Fiji, Tonga, and Samoa

1000 CE: Almost all Pacific islands inhabited

6000 BCE | 5000 BCE | 4000 BCE | 3000 BCE | 2000 BCE | 1000 BCE | 1 CE | 1000 CE

1600: Earliest datable Lapita pottery from Bismarck Archipelago

c.200: Migration of Samoans to the Marquesas

c.300 CE: Rapa Nui (Easter Island) settled

Many deities with a clear common ancestry appear in slightly different forms throughout Polynesia. This wooden carving of the war-god Ku was made in Hawaii in the early 19th century.

The boats used by the Polynesians for their great migrations were double-hulled canoes like this modern reconstruction. As well as staple crops, they took with them pigs, chickens, and dogs.

This ornate carved head of a Maori war canoe was recorded by a 19th-century illustrator. In cool, temperate New Zealand, the Maori way of life was very different from that of societies on smaller, warmer islands to the north, but in their arts and beliefs the Maori still display many aspects of their Polynesian roots.

Scale varies with perspective

11,580 km (7200 miles)

8890 km (5520 miles)

N

Rapa Nui (Easter Island)

Rapa Nui's history reflects its geographical isolation. Settled around 300 CE, it once supported a population of perhaps 7000. The society that erected the famous giant statues started to collapse around 1680. The once palm-covered island was by then denuded of trees. With no wood for boats and therefore no fish, islanders fought for control of the scarce food resources: chickens, bananas, sweet potatoes, and yams. Another catastrophe came in 1862 when some 1300 islanders, one-third of the population, were carried off by Peruvian slavers.

Rapa Nui's statues were made to stand on stone platforms, altars sacred to the island's various clans. Many had topknots of red tufa. These examples were left near the quarry, when the society collapsed in the 17th century.

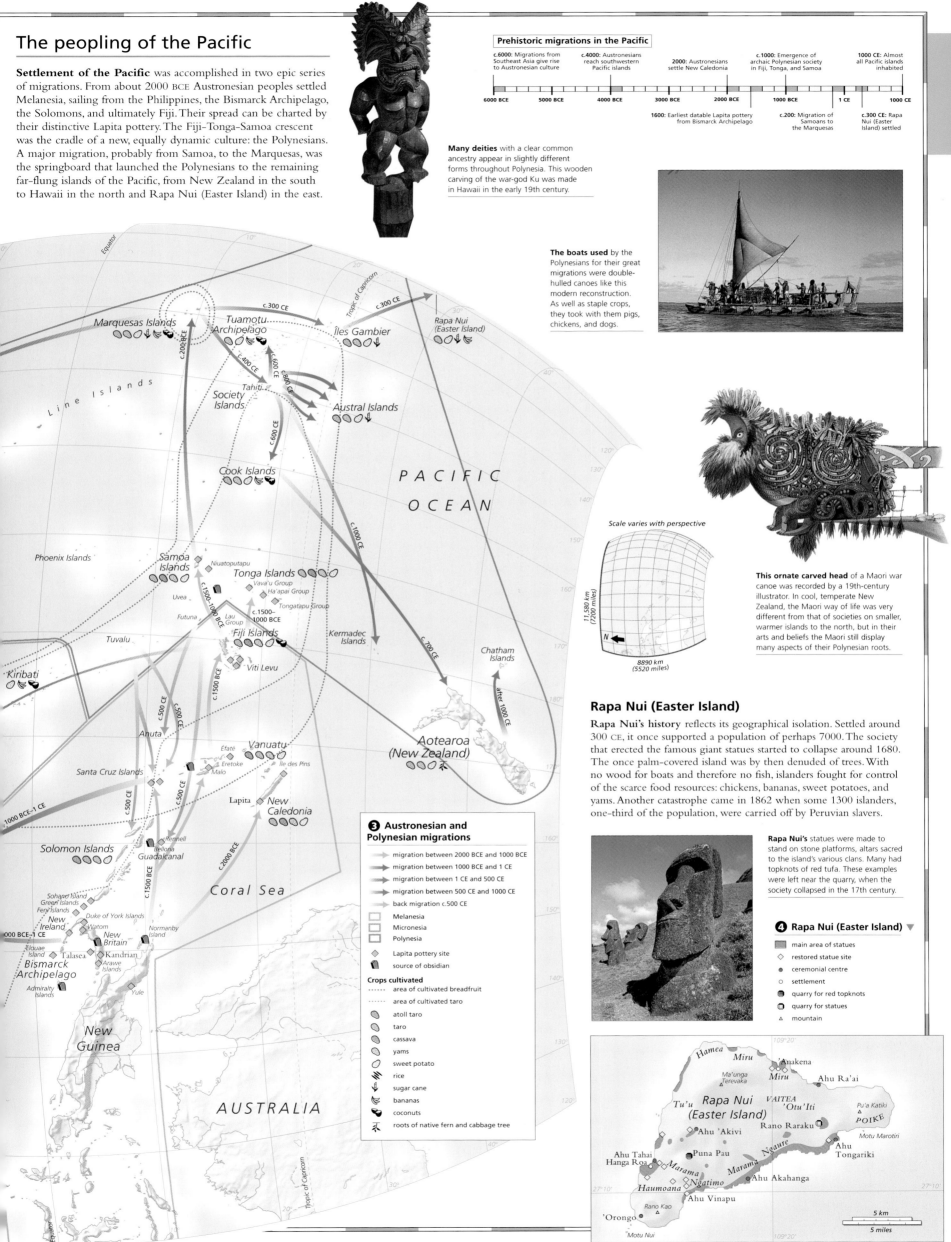

❸ Austronesian and Polynesian migrations

→ migration between 2000 BCE and 1000 BCE
→ migration between 1000 BCE and 1 CE
→ migration between 1 CE and 500 CE
→ migration between 500 CE and 1000 CE
→ back migration c.500 CE

☐ Melanesia
☐ Micronesia
☐ Polynesia

◆ Lapita pottery site
◆ source of obsidian

Crops cultivated

····· area of cultivated breadfruit
····· area of cultivated taro
◯ atoll taro
◯ taro
◯ cassava
◯ yams
◯ sweet potato
≈ rice
↓ sugar cane
🍌 bananas
🥥 coconuts
🌿 roots of native fern and cabbage tree

❹ Rapa Nui (Easter Island) ▼

☐ main area of statues
◇ restored statue site
● ceremonial centre
○ settlement
⬡ quarry for red topknots
⬡ quarry for statues
△ mountain

PACIFIC OCEAN

Equator

Line Islands

Marquesas Islands

Tuamotu Archipelago

Îles Gambier

Rapa Nui (Easter Island)

c.300 CE
c.300 CE
c.200 BCE
c.400 CE
c.600 CE
c.800 CE

Tahiti
Society Islands

Austral Islands

c.600 CE

Cook Islands

Phoenix Islands

Samoa Islands

Niuatoputapu

Tonga Islands

Vava'u Group
Ha'apai Group
Tongatapu Group

Uvea
Futuna
Lau Group

c.1500–1000 BCE
c.1500–1000 BCE

Fiji Islands

Viti Levu

Kermadec Islands

Chatham Islands

after 1000 CE

c.1000 CE

c.700 CE

Kiribati

Tuvalu

Anuta

Vanuatu

Éfaté
Eretoke
Malo
Île des Pins

Aotearoa (New Zealand)

Santa Cruz Islands

Lapita

New Caledonia

c.500 CE
c.500 CE
c.500 CE
c.500 CE
c.1500 BCE
c.1500 BCE
c.2000 BCE

Coral Sea

Solomon Islands

Rennell
Bellona
Guadalcanal

1000 BCE–1 CE

Sohano Island
Green Islands
Feni Islands
New Ireland
Duke of York Islands
Watom
New Britain

Normanby Island

1000 BCE–1 CE
Éloaue Island
Talasea
Kandrian
Arawe Islands

Bismarck Archipelago

Admiralty Islands

Yule

New Guinea

AUSTRALIA

Tropic of Capricorn

Hamea
Miru
Miru
'Anakena
Ma'unga Terevaka
Ahu Ra'ai

Tu'u
Rapa Nui (Easter Island)
VAITEA
'Otu'Iti
Pu'a Katiki
POIKE

Ahu 'Akivi
Rano Raraku
Motu Marotiri

Ahu Tahai
Hanga Roa
Puna Pau
Marama
Ngatimo
Ngaure
Ahu Tongariki
Ahu Akahanga

Haumoana
Ahu Vinapu

'Orongo
Rano Kao

Motu Nui

5 km
5 miles

THE COLONIZATION OF AUSTRALASIA

Australian convicts working in road gangs wore distinctive dress and were chained.

THE BRITISH COLONIES in Australia and New Zealand rank with the US as the most successful transplantations of European culture to another continent. Neither colony had auspicious beginnings: Australia was where Britain transported its unwanted criminals; New Zealand was a convenient base for sealers and whalers in search of quick profits. In time, both started to attract emigrants from Europe in their tens of thousands. As in the US, the colonists simply drove out the native peoples by any means available. The Aborigines of Australia and the Maori of New Zealand were treated as obstacles to the progress of settlers who wanted to raise familiar European crops and livestock on their lands. In Tasmania, settlers wiped out the entire population in the space of 70 years.

THE FIRST FLEET AND BOTANY BAY

In January 1788, to the astonishment of the local Aborigines, a fleet of 11 British ships sailed into Botany Bay. On board were 778 convicts and their jailers. After his visit in 1770, Captain Cook had described Botany Bay as well-watered and fertile, but this proved untrue and the convicts were moved to Port Jackson, a natural harbor to the north. The penal settlement at Port Jackson grew to become Australia's largest city – Sydney. However, it was the name Botany Bay that stuck in the British imagination as the time-honored destination for transported convicts.

A detachment of ships from the First Fleet sails to join the others anchored in Botany Bay.

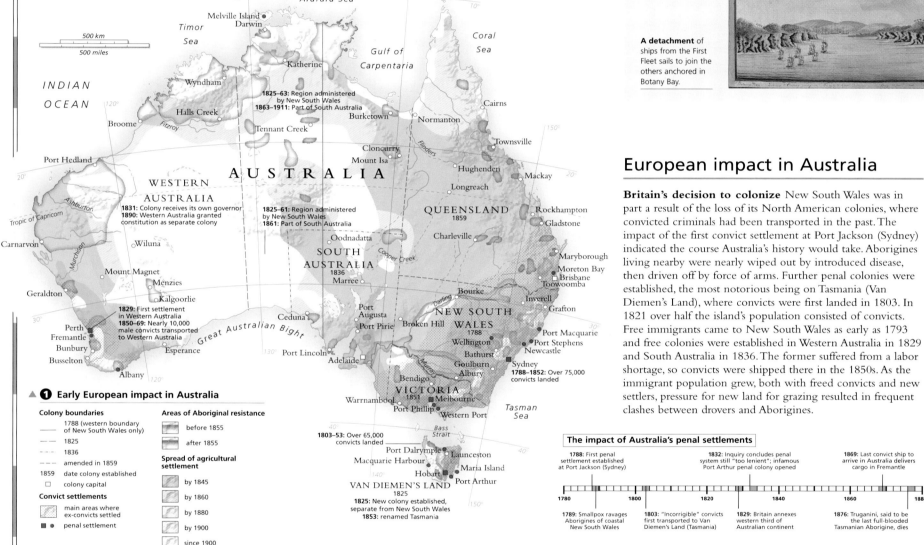

① Early European impact in Australia

Colony boundaries
- 1788 (western boundary of New South Wales only)
- 1825
- 1836
- amended in 1859
- 1859 date colony established
- □ colony capital

Convict settlements
- main areas where ex-convicts settled
- ■ ● penal settlement

Areas of Aboriginal resistance
- before 1855
- after 1855

Spread of agricultural settlement
- by 1845
- by 1860
- by 1880
- by 1900
- since 1900
- area unsuitable for agriculture

European impact in Australia

Britain's decision to colonize New South Wales was in part a result of the loss of its North American colonies, where convicted criminals had been transported in the past. The impact of the first convict settlement at Port Jackson (Sydney) indicated the course Australia's history would take. Aborigines living nearby were nearly wiped out by introduced disease, then driven off by force of arms. Further penal colonies were established, the most notorious being on Tasmania (Van Diemen's Land), where convicts were first landed in 1803. In 1821 over half the island's population consisted of convicts. Free immigrants came to New South Wales as early as 1793 and free colonies were established in Western Australia in 1829 and South Australia in 1836. The former suffered from a labor shortage, so convicts were shipped there in the 1850s. As the immigrant population grew, both with freed convicts and new settlers, pressure for new land for grazing resulted in frequent clashes between drovers and Aborigines.

The impact of Australia's penal settlements

1788: First penal settlement established at Port Jackson (Sydney)		**1832:** Inquiry concludes penal system still "too lenient"; infamous Port Arthur penal colony opened		**1869:** Last convict ship to arrive in Australia delivers cargo in Fremantle

| 1780 | 1800 | 1820 | 1840 | 1860 | 1880 |

| **1789:** Smallpox ravages Aborigines of coastal New South Wales | **1803:** "Incorrigible" convicts first transported to Van Diemen's Land (Tasmania) | **1829:** Britain annexes western third of Australian continent | **1876:** Truganini, said to be the last full-blooded Tasmanian Aborigine, dies |

The lure of gold

The event that accelerated the growth of the Australian colonies was the discovery of gold in New South Wales and Victoria in 1851. The richest finds were at Bendigo and Ballarat, and in the 1850s more than 1000 tons of gold were dug up in Victoria. In a gold rush to rival that of California in 1849, the population of Australia trebled in less than a decade. A later gold rush occurred in the 1890s when gold was discovered at Kalgoorlie in the remote deserts of Western Australia.

Gold rushes in Australia 1851–1900

1851: First gold strike at Bathurst, New South Wales	**1861:** At Lambing Flat, white miners burn camps of 3000 Chinese miners	**c.1890:** Gold discovered at Kalgoorlie, Western Australia	

| 1850 | 1860 | 1870 | 1880 | 1890 | 1900 |

| **1854–55:** Eureka uprising by Ballarat miners; police kill 45. In following year New South Wales and Victoria granted parliaments | **1890:** Western Australia last state to be granted self-government |

Population growth in Victoria and New South Wales 1851–91
- Victoria
- New South Wales

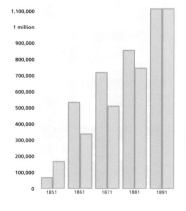

Miners pump water for gold-panning on a claim near Bathurst. Many who arrived in Australia in the 1850s were experienced prospectors from the California gold rush.

② Australian goldfields 1850–90

Discovery of goldfields
- 1850–60
- 1860–70
- 1870–90

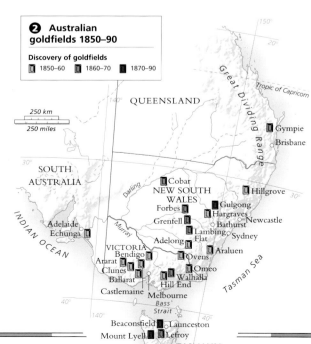

Federation Australia

The Commonwealth of Australia was established in 1901 after referendums in the six states had voted for a federation. Throughout the 20th century, traditional agriculture and stock-rearing met problems through lack of water, and disasters such as a plague of introduced rabbits. After World War II, however, the country enjoyed a period of prosperity with the discovery of valuable mineral reserves and immigration was encouraged. In the late 1980s the Aboriginal population found a new political consciousness and began to lodge claims to traditional tribal lands.

Aboriginal protesters at the Australian bicentennial celebrations of 1988 display the Aboriginal flag to draw attention to two centuries of neglect and marginalization.

Federation Australia 1901–99

1901: Australia becomes self-governing federation within British Empire
1930s: Australia hit hard by global depression
1948: White immigration, especially from UK, becomes postwar policy
1975: Restrictions imposed on immigration
1988: Bicentennial celebrations occasion Aboriginal protests

| 1900 | 1920 | 1940 | 1960 | 1980 | 2000 |

1914–18: Over 60,000 Australian troops lose lives in First World War
1942: Australia under threat of invasion as Japanese bomb Darwin
1972: Labour government of Gough Whitlam challenges paternalistic attitude of UK to Australia

▲ ❸ **Federal Australia from 1901**

Land use
- arable land
- rough grazing
- forest and woodland
- desert
- mountain region
- major areas subject to Aboriginal title claims 1997
- state boundary
- ● state capital

Mineral resources
- coal
- oil
- gas
- iron
- lead and zinc
- bauxite/aluminium
- uranium
- gold
- precious stones

Europe encounters New Zealand

The first European settlements in New Zealand were sealing and whaling stations, set up around 1800. At first they enjoyed good relations with the local Maori, who were eager to trade so they could get hold of metal axes and muskets. The results were disastrous: intertribal warfare took on a totally new character, tribes with muskets being able to massacre those without, and migrations spread the conflict throughout both islands. It was against this background that the New Zealand Company was set up to encourage British immigrants with assisted passages.

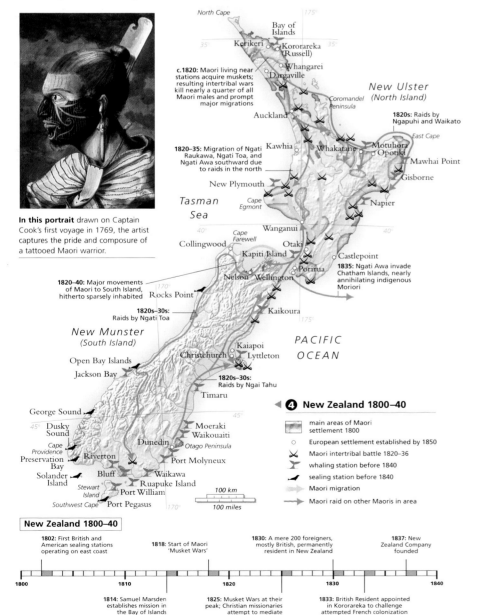

In this portrait drawn on Captain Cook's first voyage in 1769, the artist captures the pride and composure of a tattooed Maori warrior.

◀ ❹ **New Zealand 1800–40**

- main areas of Maori settlement 1800
- ○ European settlement established by 1850
- Maori intertribal battle 1820–36
- whaling station before 1840
- sealing station before 1840
- Maori migration
- Maori raid on other Maoris in area

New Zealand 1800–40

1802: First British and American sealing stations operating on east coast
1818: Start of Maori 'Musket Wars'
1830: A mere 200 foreigners, mostly British, permanently resident in New Zealand
1837: New Zealand Company founded

| 1800 | 1810 | 1820 | 1830 | 1840 |

1814: Samuel Marsden establishes mission in the Bay of Islands
1825: Musket Wars at their peak; Christian missionaries attempt to mediate
1833: British Resident appointed in Kororareka to challenge attempted French colonization

New Zealand becomes British

The Treaty of Waitangi, signed in 1840 by over 500 Maori chiefs, gave sovereignty over New Zealand to Britain, while guaranteeing Maori ownership of the land. In practice, the Crown – and later private individuals – purchased the land for trifling sums. In response to this, the Maori fought long, bloody wars against the intruders. Unlike Australia's Aborigines, who used hit-and-run tactics, the Maori waged sustained battles from fortified stockades and earthworks. After their defeat, they were reduced to marginal existence. Only in the 1990s did the Maori, some 15% of the population, start to receive substantial compensation for the wrongs of Waitangi.

New Zealand 1840–70

1840: Treaty of Waitangi
1845–46: Northern War, started by Ngapuhi chiefs deprived of trade when capital moved from Russell to Auckland
1860: Settler population over 100,000; Europeans outnumber Maori
1861: Gold discovered in Otago province
1870: Maori resistance effectively crushed

| 1840 | 1850 | 1860 | 1870 |

1841: New Zealand becomes a separate Crown Colony
1852: Constitution Act divides New Zealand into six provinces
1858: King Movement demands Maori state and opposes further land sales
1862: Second Maori War
c.1865: Some 14,000 British troops deployed in New Zealand

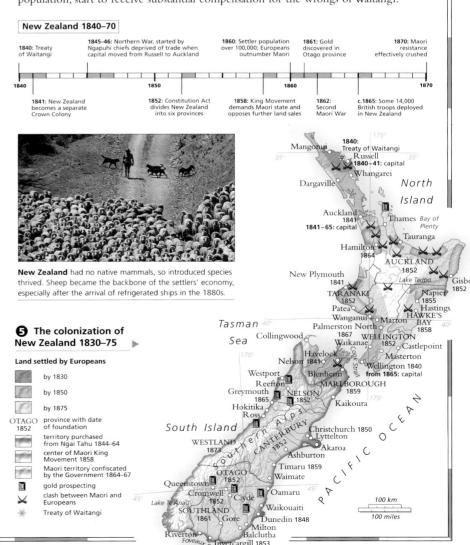

New Zealand had no native mammals, so introduced species thrived. Sheep became the backbone of the settlers' economy, especially after the arrival of refrigerated ships in the 1880s.

❺ **The colonization of New Zealand 1830–75** ▶

Land settled by Europeans
- by 1830
- by 1850
- by 1875
- OTAGO 1852 province with date of foundation
- territory purchased from Ngai Tahu 1844–64
- center of Maori King Movement 1858
- Maori territory confiscated by the Government 1864–67
- gold prospecting
- clash between Maori and Europeans
- Treaty of Waitangi

THE COLONIZATION OF THE PACIFIC

A Hawaiian surfer typifies the modern image of the Pacific as a vast playground for leisure pursuits.

THE 19TH CENTURY WITNESSED the near annihilation of many Pacific island societies. Firearms made intertribal warfare more lethal, but many more deaths were caused by alien diseases, especially measles and influenza. Killings by colonial powers as they asserted their authority, and "blackbirding" (slave-raiding for laborers in the sugarcane fields of Queensland and elsewhere) also contributed to the rapid depopulation of the islands. Many demoralized communities experienced an alarming fall in birth rate. However, subsequent repopulation by immigrant Europeans, Indians, Chinese, Japanese, North and South Americans rebuilt many island societies with new forms of trade, culture, and administration. European and American governments put in place political structures that, over time, enabled remnant Pacific peoples to survive as a host of new nations, territories and federations. Many of these now seek a wider forum. In the 1990s governments started to make calls for a "United States of the Pacific."

MISSIONARIES IN THE SOUTH SEAS

Throughout most of the Pacific, a region that had hitherto known only nature and ancestor worship, ancient values and practices were swept away by the arrival of Christianity. In the 17th century the Spanish founded missions in Micronesia, but by the mid-19th century Roman Catholic, Anglican, and Methodist missions were operating across Polynesia. Often the islanders' first contact with European customs, the missions paved the way for the wholesale Europeanization of Pacific cultures. Today a conservative, communal Christianity is the dominant feature of many Pacific island communities.

The high priest of Tahitian ruler Pomare II kneels before representatives of the London Missionary Society. The conversion of Pomare, who took control of Tahiti in 1815, was seen as a triumph for the society.

Imperialism in the Pacific

The expense of administering far-flung islands in the Pacific did not always appeal to the great 19th-century colonial powers. As a rule, they preferred to promise friendly rulers the status of protectorate. Toward the end of the century, however, colonial rivalry, especially between the French, Germans, and British led to the formal annexation of many territories. In larger territories, such as Fiji and Hawaii, where there was the possibility of establishing plantations, annexation was followed by the importation of large numbers of migrant workers.

❶ Imperialism in the Pacific ▶

Period of first European contact
- 16th century
- 17th century
- 18th century

European and US trading posts
- ✳ by 1700
- ✴ by 1850

Protectorates and colonies
- ○ protectorate with date established
- ◇ colony with date established
- ◇ Australian
- ◉◇ British
- ◇ Chilean
- ◇ Dutch
- ○◇ French
- ○◇ German
- ◇ Japanese
- ◆ NZ
- ◇ Spanish
- ○◇ US
- ── Australian mandate 1920
- ── frontiers 1900

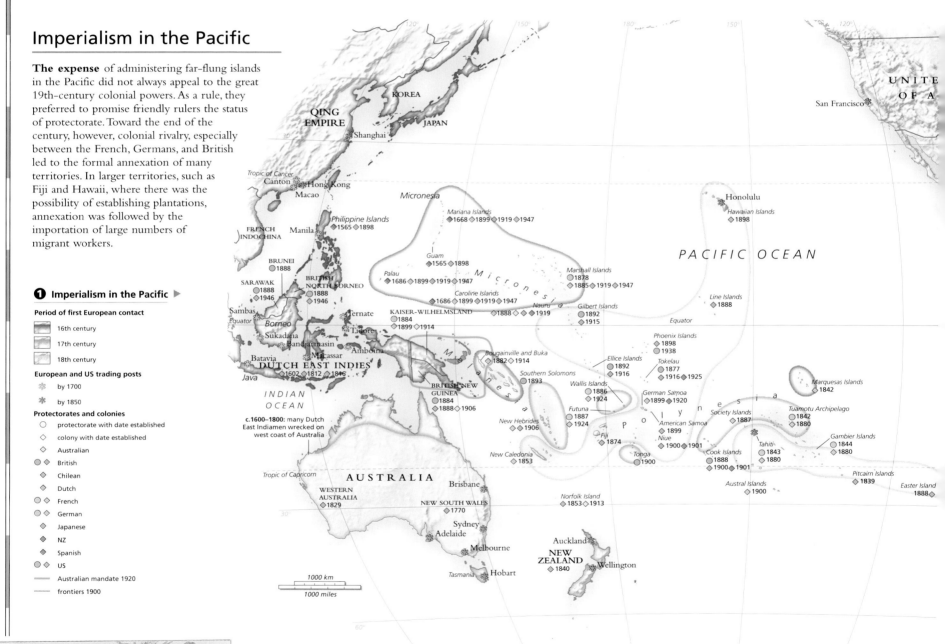

This pictorial proclamation, issued in Australia in 1829, aimed to show the fairness of British justice. If an Aborigine killed a European, he would be hanged; if a European killed an Aborigine, he would suffer the same fate. In practice, this ideal was very rarely implemented in any of the European colonies in the Pacific.

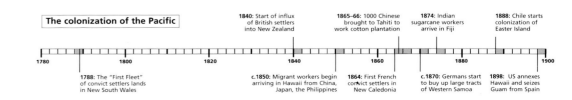

The colonization of the Pacific

- **1840:** Start of influx of British settlers into New Zealand
- **1865–66:** 1000 Chinese brought to Tahiti to work cotton plantation
- **1874:** Indian sugarcane workers arrive in Fiji
- **1888:** Chile starts colonization of Easter Island
- **1788:** The "First Fleet" of convict settlers lands in New South Wales
- **c.1850:** Migrant workers begin arriving in Hawaii from China, Japan, the Philippines
- **1864:** First French convict settlers in New Caledonia
- **c.1870:** Germans start to buy up large tracts of Western Samoa
- **1898:** US annexes Hawaii and seizes Guam from Spain

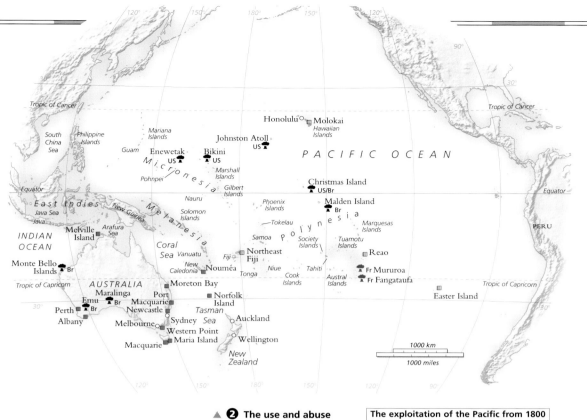

The abuse of Pacific resources

From the late 18th century, with Britain's decision to use Australia as a penal colony, European and American contacts with the Pacific produced a continuous catalog of violation and abuse. In the 19th century, the islands' isolation suggested their use as penal and leper colonies. In more recent times, their remoteness was exploited for experiments with weapons that could not be tested elsewhere. US nuclear tests in the Marshall Islands robbed islanders of a homeland for at least 50 years, while the French destroyed the islands of Mururoa and Fangataufa in the Tuamotus. Phosphate mining on Nauru created a moonscape that will take centuries to heal.

A nuclear bomb of 13 kilotons was detonated at ground level on Enewetak atoll in the Marshall Islands in 1956 as part of the US weapon-testing program.

❷ The use and abuse of Pacific resources

19th century
■ penal center
□ leper colony

20th century
☢ nuclear test site 1946–63
☢ nuclear test site 1966–90

The exploitation of the Pacific from 1800

1814: In ten years Australian cutters have denuded Fiji of sandalwood reserves
1862–63: Thousands of islanders "blackbirded" to Peru
1895: More than 50,000 Melanesians indentured to Australia's canefields
1912: Start of phosphate mining on Nauru
1966: France begins testing nuclear bombs in the Tuamotu Islands
1996: France halts nuclear testing in the Pacific

1815: First kauri gum exported from New Zealand to Sydney
c.1850: Copra becomes mainstay of Society Islands' economy
1870: First shipload of lepers transported to Kalaupapa Peninsula, Molokai, Hawaii
c.1890: Kauri gum, for varnish, becomes New Zealand's chief export
1946: US begins nuclear tests at Enewetak and Bikini atolls in Micronesia
1985: South Pacific Forum declares nuclear-free Pacific; US and France reject this

1800 1850 1900 1950 2000

Decolonization and nationhood

Australia achieved nationhood on January 1, 1901, New Zealand six years later. However, in both countries the native peoples had been dispossessed by colonists. It was many years before colonized Pacific peoples were deemed to have reached political majority. World War II loosened colonial ties and encouraged a sense of national identity. In 1962 Western Samoa became the first indigenous Pacific state to achieve full nationhood. Within 18 years, eight others had followed. Today, a wide variety of political systems and free associations with former colonial powers coexist – from Tonga's independent monarchy to Hawaii's US statehood.

Western Samoa became fully independent from New Zealand in 1962. The capital Apia, with its post office and town clock, still has the look of a colonial town. Ties with New Zealand remain strong: the rising population and a shortage of jobs compel many islanders to migrate there in search of work.

1945: War in Pacific ends
1951: ANZUS security pact between Australia, New Zealand, and US
1971: First South Pacific Forum, annual meeting of heads of government
1987: Two military-led coups disrupt Fijian democracy
1998: End of bloody civil war in Bougainville

1940 1950 1960 1970 1980 1990 2000

1962: Western Samoa gains independence
1983: Federated States of Micronesia and Marshall Islands enter free association with US
1997: First settlements in New Zealand's review of 1840 Treaty of Waitangi

The Pacific from 1945

❸ Decolonization and nationhood ▶

○ independent from (with date)
◇ dependency of
◐ Australia
◓ France
◑ Netherlands
◒ New Zealand
◑ UK
◓ US
☢ conflict since 1980

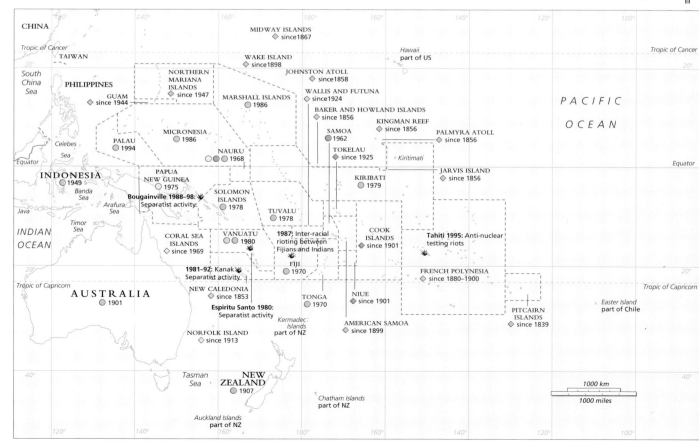

THE ARCTIC AND ANTARCTICA

EXPLORATION AND MAPPING

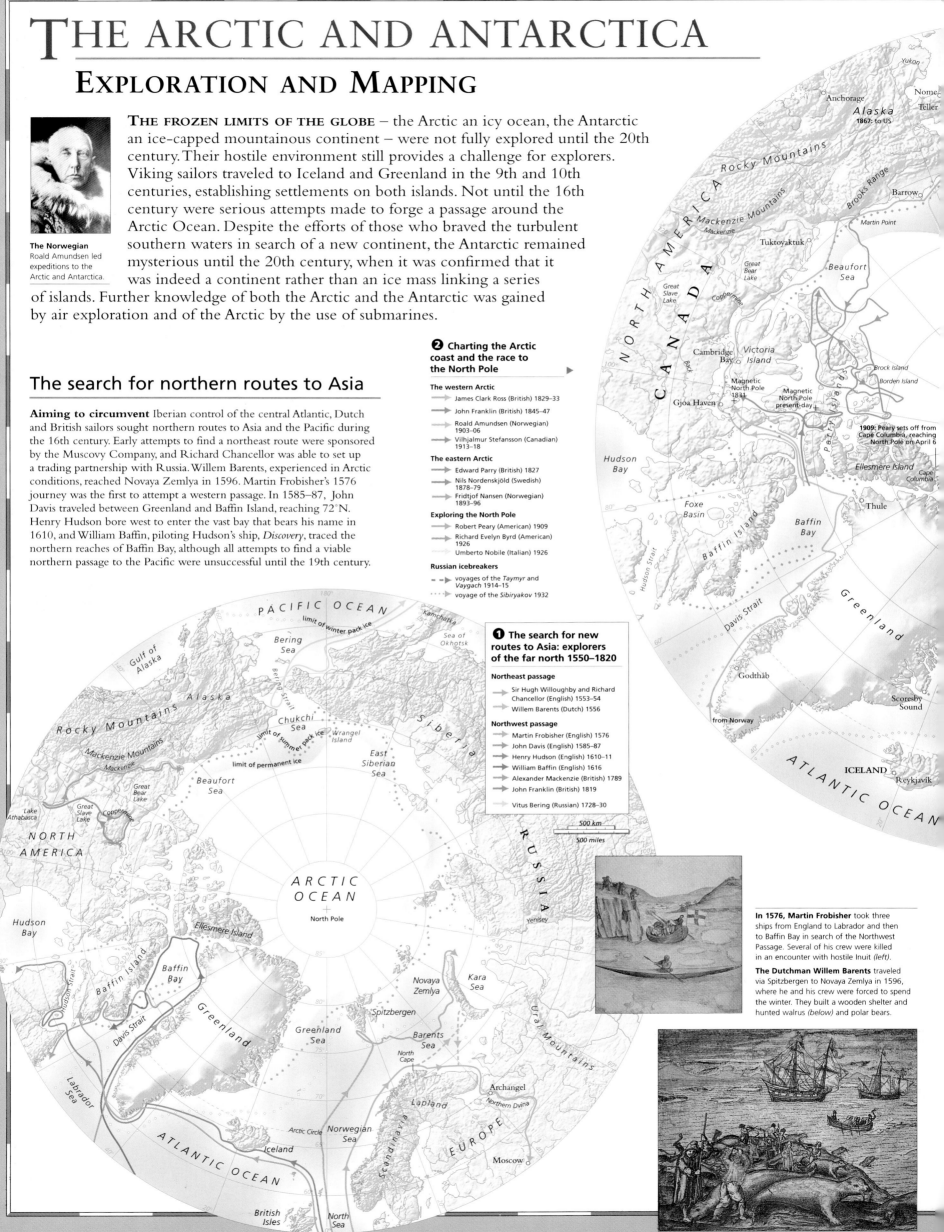

The Norwegian Roald Amundsen led expeditions to the Arctic and Antarctica.

THE FROZEN LIMITS OF THE GLOBE – the Arctic an icy ocean, the Antarctic an ice-capped mountainous continent – were not fully explored until the 20th century. Their hostile environment still provides a challenge for explorers. Viking sailors traveled to Iceland and Greenland in the 9th and 10th centuries, establishing settlements on both islands. Not until the 16th century were serious attempts made to forge a passage around the Arctic Ocean. Despite the efforts of those who braved the turbulent southern waters in search of a new continent, the Antarctic remained mysterious until the 20th century, when it was confirmed that it was indeed a continent rather than an ice mass linking a series of islands. Further knowledge of both the Arctic and the Antarctic was gained by air exploration and of the Arctic by the use of submarines.

The search for northern routes to Asia

Aiming to circumvent Iberian control of the central Atlantic, Dutch and British sailors sought northern routes to Asia and the Pacific during the 16th century. Early attempts to find a northeast route were sponsored by the Muscovy Company, and Richard Chancellor was able to set up a trading partnership with Russia. Willem Barents, experienced in Arctic conditions, reached Novaya Zemlya in 1596. Martin Frobisher's 1576 journey was the first to attempt a western passage. In 1585–87, John Davis traveled between Greenland and Baffin Island, reaching 72°N. Henry Hudson bore west to enter the vast bay that bears his name in 1610, and William Baffin, piloting Hudson's ship, *Discovery*, traced the northern reaches of Baffin Bay, although all attempts to find a viable northern passage to the Pacific were unsuccessful until the 19th century.

❷ Charting the Arctic coast and the race to the North Pole ▶

The western Arctic

→ James Clark Ross (British) 1829–33
→ John Franklin (British) 1845–47
→ Roald Amundsen (Norwegian) 1903–06
→ Vilhjalmur Stefansson (Canadian) 1913–18

The eastern Arctic

→ Edward Parry (British) 1827
→ Nils Nordenskjöld (Swedish) 1878–79
→ Fridtjof Nansen (Norwegian) 1893–96

Exploring the North Pole

→ Robert Peary (American) 1909
→ Richard Evelyn Byrd (American) 1926
→ Umberto Nobile (Italian) 1926

Russian icebreakers

- - - voyages of the *Taymyr* and *Vaygach* 1914–15
········ voyage of the *Sibiryakov* 1932

❶ The search for new routes to Asia: explorers of the far north 1550–1820

Northeast passage

→ Sir Hugh Willoughby and Richard Chancellor (English) 1553–54
→ Willem Barents (Dutch) 1556

Northwest passage

→ Martin Frobisher (English) 1576
→ John Davis (English) 1585–87
→ Henry Hudson (English) 1610–11
→ William Baffin (English) 1616
→ Alexander Mackenzie (British) 1789
→ John Franklin (British) 1819
→ Vitus Bering (Russian) 1728–30

500 km
500 miles

1909: Peary sets off from Cape Columbia, reaching North Pole on April 6

In 1576, Martin Frobisher took three ships from England to Labrador and then to Baffin Bay in search of the Northwest Passage. Several of his crew were killed in an encounter with hostile Inuit (*left*).

The Dutchman Willem Barents traveled via Spitzbergen to Novaya Zemlya in 1596, where he and his crew were forced to spend the winter. They built a wooden shelter and hunted walrus (*below*) and polar bears.

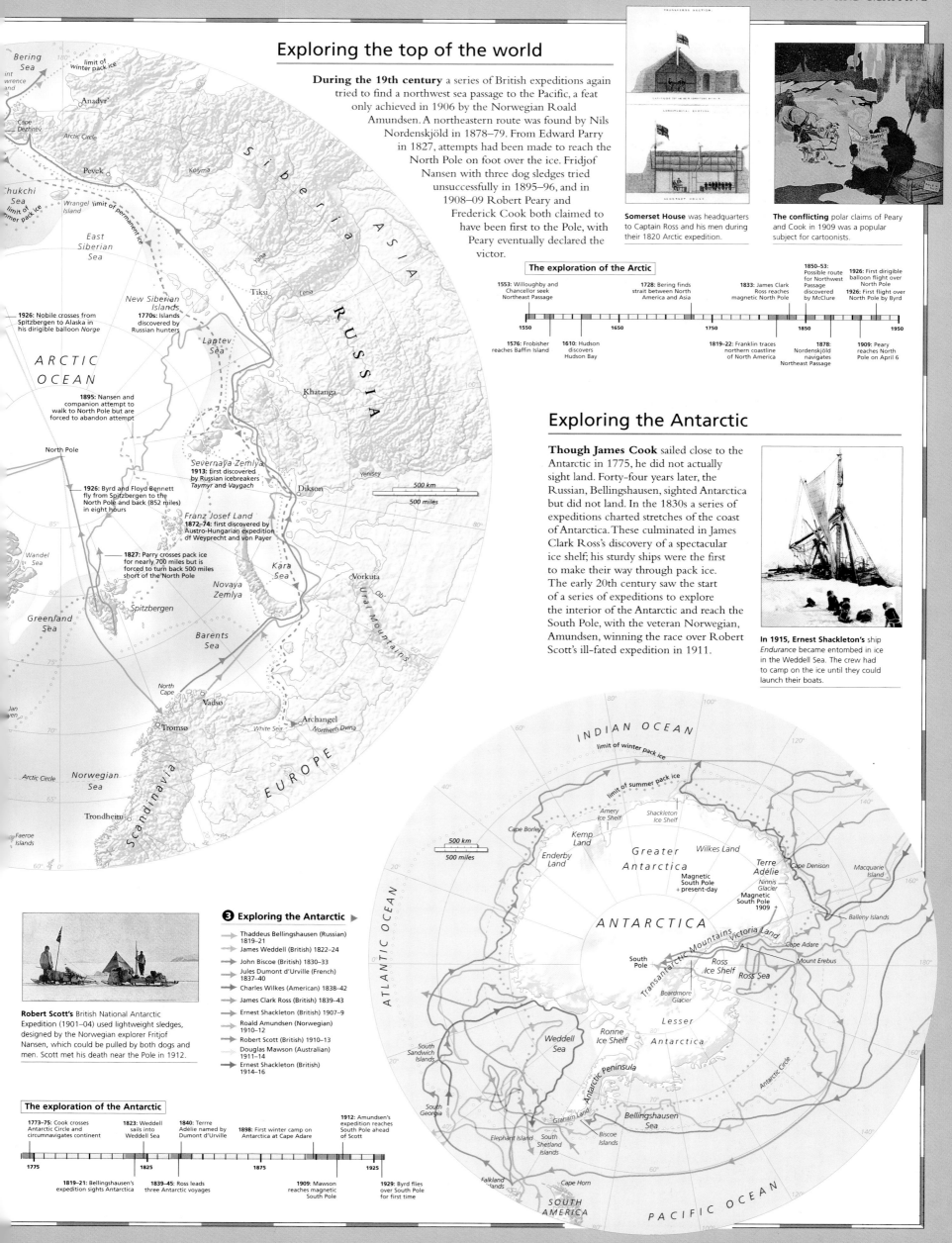

Exploring the top of the world

During the 19th century a series of British expeditions again tried to find a northwest sea passage to the Pacific, a feat only achieved in 1906 by the Norwegian Roald Amundsen. A northeastern route was found by Nils Nordenskjöld in 1878–79. From Edward Parry in 1827, attempts had been made to reach the North Pole on foot over the ice. Fridjof Nansen with three dog sledges tried unsuccessfully in 1895–96, and in 1908–09 Robert Peary and Frederick Cook both claimed to have been first to the Pole, with Peary eventually declared the victor.

Somerset House was headquarters to Captain Ross and his men during their 1820 Arctic expedition.

The conflicting polar claims of Peary and Cook in 1909 was a popular subject for cartoonists.

The exploration of the Arctic

1553: Willoughby and Chancellor seek Northeast Passage
1728: Bering finds strait between North America and Asia
1833: James Clark Ross reaches magnetic North Pole
1850–53: Possible route for Northwest Passage discovered by McClure
1926: First dirigible balloon flight over North Pole
1926: First flight over North Pole by Byrd

1550 1650 1750 1850 1950

1576: Frobisher reaches Baffin Island
1610: Hudson discovers Hudson Bay
1819–22: Franklin traces northern coastline of North America
1878: Nordenskjöld navigates Northeast Passage
1909: Peary reaches North Pole on April 6

1926: Nobile crosses from Spitzbergen to Alaska in his dirigible balloon *Norge*

1770s: Islands discovered by Russian hunters

1895: Nansen and companion attempt to walk to North Pole but are forced to abandon attempt

1913: first discovered by Russian icebreakers *Taymyr* and *Vaygach*

1926: Byrd and Floyd Bennett fly from Spitzbergen to the North Pole and back (852 miles) in eight hours

1872–74: first discovered by Austro-Hungarian expedition of Weyprecht and von Payer

1827: Parry crosses pack ice for nearly 700 miles but is forced to turn back 500 miles short of the North Pole

500 km
500 miles

Exploring the Antarctic

Though James Cook sailed close to the Antarctic in 1775, he did not actually sight land. Forty-four years later, the Russian, Bellingshausen, sighted Antarctica but did not land. In the 1830s a series of expeditions charted stretches of the coast of Antarctica. These culminated in James Clark Ross's discovery of a spectacular ice shelf; his sturdy ships were the first to make their way through pack ice. The early 20th century saw the start of a series of expeditions to explore the interior of the Antarctic and reach the South Pole, with the veteran Norwegian, Amundsen, winning the race over Robert Scott's ill-fated expedition in 1911.

In 1915, Ernest Shackleton's ship *Endurance* became entombed in ice in the Weddell Sea. The crew had to camp on the ice until they could launch their boats.

Robert Scott's British National Antarctic Expedition (1901–04) used lightweight sledges, designed by the Norwegian explorer Fritjof Nansen, which could be pulled by both dogs and men. Scott met his death near the Pole in 1912.

❸ Exploring the Antarctic ▶

Thaddeus Bellingshausen (Russian) 1819–21
James Weddell (British) 1822–24
John Biscoe (British) 1830–33
Jules Dumont d'Urville (French) 1837–40
Charles Wilkes (American) 1838–42
James Clark Ross (British) 1839–43
Ernest Shackleton (British) 1907–9
Roald Amundsen (Norwegian) 1910–12
Robert Scott (British) 1910–13
Douglas Mawson (Australian) 1911–14
Ernest Shackleton (British) 1914–16

The exploration of the Antarctic

1773–75: Cook crosses Antarctic Circle and circumnavigates continent
1823: Weddell sails into Weddell Sea
1840: Terrre Adélie named by Dumont d'Urville
1898: First winter camp on Antarctica at Cape Adare
1912: Amundsen's expedition reaches South Pole ahead of Scott

1775 1825 1875 1925

1819–21: Bellingshausen's expedition sights Antarctica
1839–45: Ross leads three Antarctic voyages
1909: Mawson reaches magnetic South Pole
1929: Byrd flies over South Pole for first time

KEY TO MAP FEATURES

PHYSICAL FEATURES

coastline	
ancient coastline	
major river	
minor river	
major seasonal river	

ancient river course	
canal	
aqueduct	
dam	
spring / well / waterhole / oasis	

perennial lake	
seasonal lake	
perennial salt lake	
ancient lake	
marsh / salt marsh	

ice cap / sheet	
ice shelf	
glacier	
summer pack ice limit	
winter pack ice limit	

elevation above sea level (mountain height)	
volcano	
pass	

GRATICULE FEATURES

Equator	
lines of latitude / longitude	
tropics / polar circles	
degrees of longitude / latitude	45°

BORDERS

international border		maritime border	
undefined border		internal border	
vassal state border			
disputed border			

COMMUNICATIONS

major road	
minor road	
major railroad	
railroad under construction	

SETTLEMENT / POSSESSION

o	settlement symbol
◇	colonial possession

TYPOGRAPHIC KEY

REGIONS

state / political region...**LAOS**

administrative region within a state.... HENAN

cultural / undefined region / group............... *FERGHANA*

SETTLEMENTS

settlement / symbol location / definition............Farnham

PHYSICAL FEATURES

continent / ocean............. AFRICA

INDIAN OCEAN

landscape features........*Mekong*

Lake Rudolf

Tien Shan

Sahara

MISCELLANEOUS

tropics / polar circles.................... *Antarctic Circle*

people / cultural group.. *Samoyeds*

annotation...................... 1914: British protectorate

POLITICAL COLOR GUIDE

China	Italy	Spain (Aragon)	New Zealand		Buddhism
Persia / Iran	Ottoman / Turkey	Portugal	Australia		Islam
Rome	England / Britain / UK	Netherlands	Belgium		Hinduism
Japan	France	Germany	other state / cultural region		Confucianism / Taoism
Norway	Denmark	Russia			Christianity
USA	Spain (Castile)	India			Roman Catholic
					Judaism
					other religion

RELIGION COLOUR GUIDE

Buddhism
Islam
Hinduism
Confucianism / Taoism
Christianity
Roman Catholic
Judaism
other religion

(NB. the colors which identify political regions have, as far as possible, been used consistently throughout the atlas. Any variations are clearly identified in the individual map keys)

GUIDE TO MAP INTERPRETATION

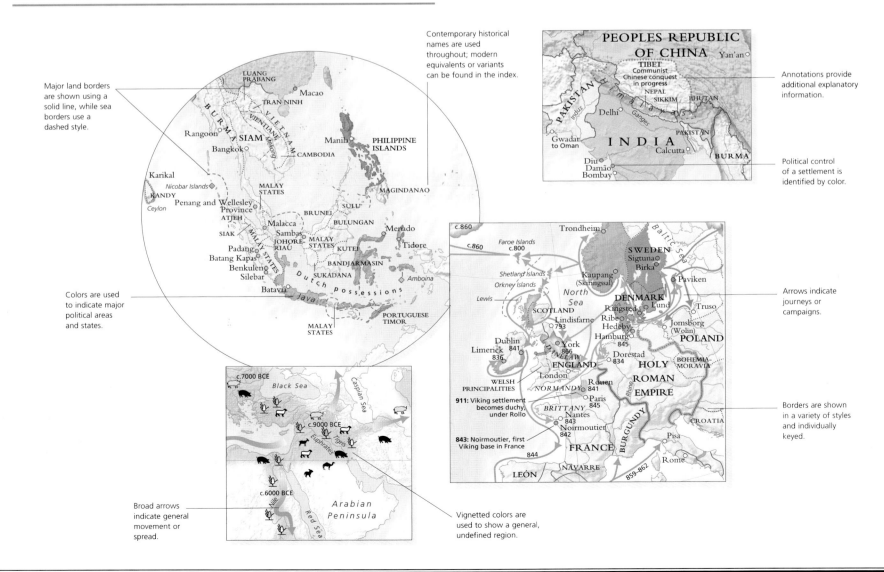

Contemporary historical names are used throughout; modern equivalents or variants can be found in the index.

Annotations provide additional explanatory information.

Political control of a settlement is identified by color.

Major land borders are shown using a solid line, while sea borders use a dashed style.

Colors are used to indicate major political areas and states.

Arrows indicate journeys or campaigns.

Broad arrows indicate general movement or spread.

Vignetted colors are used to show a general, undefined region.

Borders are shown in a variety of styles and individually keyed.

SUBJECT INDEX AND GLOSSARY

In addition to acting as a page reference guide to the people, events, and themes referred to in the Atlas, the Subject Index and Glossary is intended to provide supplementary information and explanation of those features which appear in the Atlas.

Page references are indicated using the following symbols:

✤ text reference   ● timeline reference

◆ map reference, indicating page number and map number;

❑ picture/caption reference.

Dates in the Atlas are expressed in the following way:

BP Before Present. Generally used for dates more than 10,000 years ago.

BCE Before Common Era (indicating number of years before the supposed year of Christ's birth).

CE Common Era (indicating number of years since the supposed year of Christ's birth).

Key to index: ✤ text   ❑ picture   var. variant name   f/n full name   r. ruled   WW I World War I
● timeline   ◆ map   aka also known as   prev. previously known as   ✕ battle   WW II World War II

289

B

SUBJECT INDEX AND GLOSSARY: **Edward III – Federal Bureau of Investigation**

to defeat de Montfort at the battle of Evesham (1265). Constant campaigning led to the annexation of north and west Wales, and much of the rest of his reign was spent attempting to unite England and Scotland against fierce Scottish opposition. Though he defeated William Wallace's armies at Falkirk in 1298, he was unable to control Scotland and died at Carlisle on the way to confront the newly crowned Robert the Bruce. His reorganization of both local and central government and judicial reforms won him comparisons with the emperor Justinian.
campaigns ✤188, ◆188 (2)
Edward III (1312–77) King of England (r.1327–77). Son of Edward II, in 1330 he overthrew his French mother, Isabella, who had governed during his minority. In the early years of his reign he became involved in wars with Scotland. In 1337 his claim to the French throne provoked the Hundred Years' War, during which he fought in the battle of Crécy and at the siege of Calais.
campaigns ✤192, ◆192 (1)
Edward, Prince of Wales (*aka* the Black Prince) (1330–76). The son of Edward III, he was an outstanding English military commander in the Hundred Years' War, fighting with distinction at Crécy and winning a great victory at Poitiers (1356). Said to have gained his title because he appeared in battle wearing black armor. ◆192 (1)
Edward the Confessor (c.1003–66). King of England (r.1042–66). Edward is remembered for his piety – he was canonized in 1611 – and as founder of Westminster Abbey in London. His reign, however, was marked by feuds that would erupt on his death into a battle for succession to the throne between Harold, son of Earl Godwin of Wessex, and William of Normandy. ✤186●
EEC European Economic Community
created (1957) ✤106●
See also European Union
Egypt
ancient Egypt
✤159●, ◆159 (1) (2) (3)
BCE ✤30, ✤31●, ✤34–5
See also Fatimid dynasty; Pharaonic Egypt; Ptolemaic dynasty; Saite dynasty
foreign affairs
Camp David Summit (1978) ✤169●
invades Sudan (1820) ✤90
Six Day War (1967) ✤107●
growth, early history (c.5000–3000) ✤159, ✤159●, ◆159 (2) (3) (4) (5)
home affairs
agricultural wealth (BCE) ✤27●, ✤158
cult centers (BCE) ◆37 (3)
Hittite and Mitanni conflict (1500) ✤27●
invasions (BCE) ✤35●, ✤38
Mamluk takeover (1250) ✤67●
Mamluks conquered by Ottomans (1517) ✤79●
New Kingdom ✤26, ✤26–7
occupied by British ✤95●, ✤167●, ✤232
occupied by Napoleon Bonaparte (1798) ✤87●
Roman province ✤42, ✤46
ruled by Hyksos (1633 BCE) ✤27●
innovations
mummification ❑31
papyrus ❑30
pyramids ❑22
Roman mummy case ❑47
religion
BCE state religion ◆36 (1)
Christian converts ✤46, ✤50
Islamic fundamentalism ✤235
Jewish exodus (c.1200 BCE) ✤31
sun worship (1350 BCE) ✤27●
trade and industry
factories and refineries (1816) ✤166●
Nile–Red Sea canal (500 BCE) ✤35●
Egyptian-Israeli peace treaty (*var.* Camp David Agreement) (1979). Egypt became the first Arab state to recognize Israel. The lands in the Sinai occupied by Israel since 1967 were returned to Egypt. ✤138●, ✤169●, ✤234
einkorn Wheat (ancestor of modern wheat) ❑21
Einsatzgruppen German or Axis security police, controlled by SS, operating as extermination squads in eastern Europe in the wake of conventional armed forces. ✤211●
Eisenhower Doctrine (1957). US foreign-policy declaration by President Eisenhower which promised aid to any Middle Eastern country in combating aggression from Communist countries. Like the Truman Doctrine, it aimed at total resistance to any extension of Soviet influence. ✤138●
Eisenhower, Dwight David (1890–1969) US general and 34th president of the US (Republican 1952–60). During WW II he commanded US forces in N. Africa and Operation Overlord. In 1944 he became Supreme Commander of the Allied forces. After the war he was Supreme Commander of NATO land forces until his election as US President in 1952. He oversaw the end of the Korean War (1953) and the setting up of SEATO, and his presidency witnessed the emergence of the civil rights movement. He was re-elected in 1956. ✤139●
El Alamein ⚔ of WW II (Oct–Nov 1942). Marked the beginning of the Allied conquest of N. Africa by British and Commonwealth forces. ◆210 (1)
El-Armarna (*var.* Akhetaton).
plan of city ✤29, ◆29 (5)
plaster fragment from Great Palace ❑29
See also Akhenaton
El Dorado Myth among Spanish *conquistadores* in S. America of a golden man or a golden country.
search for ✤146, ❑149
El Mirador Maya city complex ✤46, ✤121●
El Salvador, civil war (1979–1991). Civil war between the US-backed right-wing government and left-wing FMLN guerrillas (named after Farabundo Martí, the leader of a popular insurrection in 1932). The war ended with a UN-brokered peace agreement.
civil war ends (1991) ✤110●
US intervention ◆139 (5)
Elam State of S.W. Mesopotamia. The Elamites made Susa their capital and flourished in the 13th century BCE, when their empire stretched from Babylon to Persepolis. They gained control of the great Sumerian city of Ur c.2000 BCE. ◆26–7, ◆222 (2)
Assyrian siege of Elamite city ❑222
Eleanor of Aquitaine (c.1122–1204). Married first to Louis VII of France, Eleanor became the wife of Henry II of England, when that marriage was annulled. Active in the management of her own lands in political life, Eleanor supported her sons, Richard and John, in a rebellion against their father and was imprisoned for 15 years. Later she acted as regent for Richard I while he was crusading abroad, and led an army to crush a rebellion in Anjou against her son John in 1200. ❑187
electrostatics Development of ✤80
electrum Early use of ✤35
Elizabeth I (1533–1603) Queen of England (1558–1603). Daughter of Henry VIII and Anne Boleyn, she ascended the throne on the death of her half-sister Mary I. She established the Church of England and put an end to Catholic plots, notably by executing Mary, Queen of Scots (1587) and defeating the Spanish Armada (1588). An intelligent and industrious monarch, under her rule the nation achieved prestige, stability, and prosperity, and a great flourishing of the arts.
Elmina (*var.* São Jorge da Mina)
founded by Portuguese (1482) ✤75●, ✤156●
taken by Dutch (1637) ✤164●
trading post ✤78
Elvas Relief of siege ❑196
Emancipation Proclamation US President Abraham Lincoln's announcement of Sep 22, 1862, that all slaves in rebellion against the Confederate states were free from the start of 1863. The Civil War thus became a fight against slavery, and the Union was able to recruit thousands of black troops to its cause. ✤130–131
Emory, Lt. William 19th-century explorer of the western US.
expedition (1846) ◆119 (3)
Empire of the Khwarizm Shah *see* Khwarizm Empire
Empty Quarter *see* Rub' al Khali.
Encyclopédie *see* Diderot
Endara, Guillermo President of Panama ✤139
Endeavour Captain Cook's ship ✤87
Endlösing *see* Final Solution.
England
Scotland and Wales (1284–1337) ✤188●
See also Britain
English Civil War (*aka* the Great Rebellion) (1640–51). Fighting in the British Isles between Parliamentarians and supporters of the monarchy. It was precipitated by the Bishops' War (1639, 1640) with Scotland. The civil war caused comparatively little loss of life or destruction of property, but led to the execution of King Charles I and his replacement by the Protectorate of Oliver Cromwell. ✤196●, ◆196 (2)
English East India Company The "Governor and Company of Merchants of London trading into the East Indies" was founded in 1600 by Queen Elizabeth I. Initially, British expeditions to the East were confronted by the Portuguese, but the building of a factory at Surat (1612) began the British settlement of India. The company gained concessions under the Mughals, and won control of Bengal in 1757. But its political activities were gradually curtailed and, after the Mutiny of 1857, it ceased to be the British government's agency in India. It was dissolved in 1873. ✤79●, ✤91●, ✤95, ✤248, ❑239, ◆247 (3), ❑247
coastal trading posts (17th century) ✤83●
military campaigns (17th century) ✤87
Enigma Code name for German telecommunications encryption during WW II. *See also* Ultra. ❑210
Enlil Chief deity of the Sumerian pantheon, Enlil embodied energy and force. His Akkadian counterpart, Bel, was the Mesopotamian god of the atmosphere. ✤28
ensete African relative of the banana. ◆21 (2), ◆158 (1)
Entente forces Collective name given to the European nations in alliance against Germany, Austria-Hungary, and their allies (the Central Powers) during WW I. Also used to denote the foreign powers in alliance against the Bolsheviks during the Russian Civil War. *See also* Allied forces. ✤206–7, ◆206–7 (1)–(6), ◆208 (2)
entrepôt A port to which goods are brought for import, export, and distribution. ✤45
environment
different ways of life (BCE) ✤16, ◆16 (1)
survival strategies (BCE) ✤16
Eratosthenes of Cyrene (c.276–194 BCE). Greek geographer, astronomer, and mathematician. Among a range of achievements he measured the circumference of the earth and invented a system for identifying prime numbers, as well as writing on geography, literary criticism, and chronology. ✤172
Erik the Red 10th-century Norwegian navigator and explorer. Having sighted Greenland in about 983, he returned to Iceland to persuade Viking settlers to follow him. He set out in 986 with 25 ships and founded two settlements. The early settlers of Greenland followed an Icelandic model of government; Erik the Red acted as the "Law Speaker." At its peak, the Norse population of Greenland numbered c.4,000. ✤60●
Eriksson, Leif ("the Lucky") (b.c.970) Viking explorer. He may have been first European to land in N. America. In search of grazing and timber he founded settlements in Greenland, and was later based in l'Anse-aux-Meadows in present-day Newfoundland. ✤62●, ◆118 (1)
Eriksson, Thorvald Viking explorer of N. America (1003) and brother of Leif Eriksson. ◆118 (1)
Eritrea
civil war (1984–85) ✤168●
Italian colony (1889) ✤167●
Eritou Founded (1900 BCE) ✤27●
Eskimo *see* Aleut; Inuit
Esperey, General d' lands in Istanbul ❑233
Esquival, Juan de 16th-century Spanish explorer of N. America. ✤125, ◆125 (4)
Essequibo First Dutch settlements ✤149●
Estado Novo *see* New State
Ethelbald Anglo-Saxon Mercian king ✤183●
Ethiopia (*var.* Abyssinia)
Arab trading in Highlands (c.1000) ✤61●
aromatic gum trade (1st century CE) ✤225, ◆225 (3)
Christian kingdom expands ✤67●
death of Amde Sion (1344) ✤71●
decline of ✤165●
famine (1987) ✤111●
Italian invasion (1935) ✤103●
Jesuits expelled (1632) ✤165●
Ogaden region conflict (1960) ✤168●
revival of Red Sea trade ✤62
Soviet anti-Western support ✤109
struggle for the Horn of Africa ✤165, ◆165 (3)
toured by James Bruce (1768–73) ✤157
Zagwe dynasty church ❑62
Etowah Mississippian cultural site ✤123
Etruscans Ancient people who flourished in west and central Italy from the 8th century BCE. At their height they ruled in Rome. The last Etruscan king, Tarquin II, was overthrown in 509 BCE, and in 283 BCE they succumbed completely to the Romans, but their cultural influence endured; skilled engineers and urban planners, they were also accomplished metal workers and traded with Greece.
1000 BCE–1 CE ✤176●
city-states (BCE) ✤31●
Mediterranean world (700–300 BCE) ◆176 (1)
peoples of Italy (500 BCE) ✤178, ◆178 (2)
Rome expels overlords (510 BCE) 34●
sarcophagus ❑178
state religion (BCE) ◆36 (1)
tomb frescoes ❑34, ❑176
Etymologie (Isodore of Seville) ✤173●
EU *see* European Union
Eudoxus of Cyzicus (b.c.135 BCE). Greek explorer, who twice made trading journeys to India on behalf of the Ptolemaic kings of Egypt.
sails from Black Sea to W. Africa (c.146 BCE) ✤218●
sails from India to Egypt (120 BCE) ✤218●
Eugénie, Empress (1826–1920) Empress of France. Born in Spain, she was courted by the French emperor, Napoleon III. After his deposition in 1871, she fled to England, where he joined her after a period of imprisonment in Germany. ❑232
eunuchs in China ✤47
Euphrates Babylonian map ❑34
Eurasia Geopolitical term for combined continents of Europe and Asia, historically often including Egypt and Greco-Roman tracts of N. Africa.
✤16●, ✤30–1, ◆44–5 (c.1300) ◆68 (2)
map by Ptolemy ❑44
Euripides (484–406 BCE). Athenian tragic dramatist, originally an artist, who took up literature and wrote 80 dramas, 19 of which survive. ✤177
Europe 170–215
800–1000 ◆185 (3)
Ages
Crusades ✤186–6, ◆186–7 (1) (2) (3) (4) (5)
Enlightenment ✤198–9
Reformation ✤194–5, ✤194●
BCE
✤15, ✤15●, ✤18, ✤31●, ✤38
introduction of farming (7000–5000 BCE) ✤174, 174●, ◆174 (1)
Copper Age (4500–2500 BCE) ✤174, ✤174●, ◆174 (2)
Bronze Age (2300–1500 BCE) ✤175, ✤175●, ◆175 (3)
historical landscape ✤171, ◆170–1
prehistoric ✤174–5
Central and southeastern (1200–1400) ✤189, ✤189●, ◆189 (4)
conflict
1743–63 ✤88●
caused by land settlement (1250 BCE) ✤27
Congress of Vienna (1815) ✤202, ✤202●, ◆202 (1)
in crisis ✤188–9
devolution ✤112, ❑112, ◆112 (2)
division of postwar Europe ✤212–13, ◆212 (1) (2)
empires ✤88, ◆88 (1)
Europe between the wars ✤208–9, ◆208 (1) (2) (4)
Hundred Years' War ✤70●, ✤75●, ✤187, ✤191, ✤192, ✤192●, ◆192 (1) (2)
political consolidation and resistance in the 17th-century ✤196, ✤196●, ◆196 (2)
revolutionary period (1830–48) ✤90
Thirty Years' War (1618–48) ✤82, ✤196, ✤196●, ❑196, ◆196 (1)
World Wars *see* Wars, World War I; World War II
expansion
colonizing voyages (1492–1597) ◆80–1 (1)
in S. and S.E. Asia ✤248–9, ◆248 (1) (2)
new era of prosperity ✤62, ✤62●
territorial ◆77 (5)
the Mediterranean world c.500 BCE ✤176–7
migrations and invasions (350–500 CE) ◆53 (2)
nation states ✤192–3
evolution of state system (17th century) ✤196–7
growth of nationalism ✤202–3, ✤209, ✤209●, ❑214
struggle for supremacy ✤194, ◆194 (1)
population ✤94, ✤198
religion, Protestant Reformation ✤78, ✤82
renaissance
(12th century) ✤187, ✤187●, ◆187 (3)
(15th century) ✤75, ✤192
Roman Empire ✤182–3, ◆182 (1)
trade and industry
Asian commercial contacts ✤247, ✤247●, ◆247 (3) (4)
development (1850–1914) ✤205, ✤205●, ❑205, ◆205 (4)
medieval ◆190–1, ◆190–1 (1)
See also individual countries
European Atomic Energy Community (EURATOM). International organization founded in 1957 by the Treaty of Rome to promote and develop the peaceful use of atomic energy in Europe. ✤214
European Coal and Steel Community (ECSC). Body established in 1952 to coordinate the production of coal and steel in France, Italy, W. Germany, and the Benelux countries. ✤214
European Economic Community (EEC) see European Union.
European Recovery Program *see* Marshall Plan
European Union (EU) Organization formed (1993) to integrate the economies of 15 member states and promote cooperation and coordination of policies. It originated in Treaty of Rome (1957) and the formation of the EEC (France, Germany, Italy, Belgium, Netherlands), admitting UK, Irish Republic, Spain, Portugal, Denmark, Greece in 1972 (EC), the organization developed in 1990s toward greater and fuller integration. ✤108, ✤214, ◆214 (1)
created (1957) ✤106●, ✤214, ❑214
European Union Treaty *see* Maastrict Treaty
EURATOM *see* European Atomic Energy Community
Eutaw Springs ⚔ of American Revolutionary War (Sep 8, 1781). British victory. ◆127 (3)
Everest, Sir George (1790–1866). Army officer with the British East India Company who instituted the great Trigonometrical Survey of India. From 1823 he was responsible for triangulating the entire subcontinent, and was renowned for his efficiency. Mount Everest was named after him. ✤239, ✤239●, ❑239
evolution
development of modern humans ✤14–15, ◆14–15, ❑14–15
Scopes "Monkey Trial" (1925) ✤135
exploration and mapping
places
Africa, ✤156–7, ◆156 (1) (2) (3), ◆157 (4) (5)
America
N. America ◆118 (1) (2) (3)
S. America ◆142 (1) (2) (3)
Arctic, race to the N. Pole ✤286, ◆286 (2)
Asia, W. Asia ◆218–19 (1) (2) (3) (4)
Europe, expansion ◆80–1 (1), ◆142 (1)
Pacific, ✤278●, ✤279, ❑279, ◆279 (3)
South and S.E. Asia ✤238–9, ❑239, ❑247, ◆239 (1) (2)
travelers, European voyages ✤239, ✤278, ◆239 (1)
atlas
Atlas Contractus ❑119
Catalan ❑68, ❑70, ❑71
cartography ✤173, ❑173
geological, 19th-century maps ❑91
globes ❑55, ❑62, ❑75, ❑238
places
Africa
(1808), ❑157
Babylonian map (c.600 BCE) ❑34
Europeans in Arabia ◆219 (4)
The Nile in Flood (Roman mosaic) ❑47
America
Central America and the Caribbean (16th century) ❑79
Civil War ❑94
Antarctic exploration ✤287●, ◆287 (3)
Arctic
charting the coast ✤286, ◆286 (2)
exploration ✤287●
Asia
city of Nippur ❑28
new routes ✤286, ◆286 (1)
N. and E. ✤256–7
eastern hemisphere by Joan Blaeu ❑83
Eurasia (Ptolemy) ❑44
Europe
Classical era ❑172
defining ancient boundaries ◆172 (1)
Greek and Roman expeditions ◆218 (1)
Greek world (500 BCE) ❑218
medieval mapping ✤173, ✤173●, ❑173
new map (1815) ✤90●
Peutinger Table ❑172
Spanish colonization ✤125, ◆125 (4)
Mediterranean, mosaic map of Jerusalem ❑51
New Zealand, Captain Cook's ❑87
Oceania
◆77 (7), ◆278 (1)
explorers ✤60–1
Indian Ocean ◆61 (3)
Pacific
Marshall Islands ❑278
Polynesian migrations ◆60 (2)
Solomon Islands (1593) ❑278
world
Magellan's circumnavigation ❑80
medieval *mappamundi* ❑66
New World by Ortelius ✤79
road maps ❑99
schematic maps ❑102
technology
printing ✤94
remote-sensed mapping ❑110
travelers, medieval and Renaissance ◆218 (3)
Viking world (c.1000) ◆60–1 (1)
See also cartography; names of explorers and travelers
Eylau ⚔ of Napoleonic Wars – the War of the 3rd Coalition (1807). French victory. ◆200 (1)
Eyre, Edward (1815–1901). British-born explorer of Australia. Eyre's journeys were inspired by the search for new pasturelands for cattle. His greatest journey was his crossing of the Nullarbor Plain in 1840–41. It would have failed without the local Aborigines who helped the expedition find water. ◆279 (2)
Ezana Axumite king (c.350) ✤50●

F

Fa Xian (*var.* Fa Hsien) (*fl.* c.400 CE). Chinese Buddhist monk and traveler. Made the first recorded journey overland from China to India and back by sea between 399 and 414 CE. The purpose of his travels was the gathering of religious texts, but his experiences greatly enriched Chinese geography. ✤49●, ◆256 (1)
Faeroe Islands
Settled by Vikings ✤172
Fa Hsien *see* Fa Xian
Faisal I (*var.* Feisal) (1885–1933). Joined T.E. Lawrence in Arab Revolt (1916–18) against Turkey during WW I. Became King of Iraq (1921–33). In 1930 he negotiated a treaty with the British, who held mandate in Iraq, that gave Iraq independence. ❑232
See also Lawrence, T.E.
Falklands War Conflict (1982) between Argentina and the UK. ✤110●, ◆152 (1)
Fallam, Robert 17th-century explorer of eastern N. America. Accompanied Thomas Batts in 1671 in search of a mythical South Sea. ◆119 (2)
Fallen Timbers ⚔ (Aug 20, 1794). US victory over the Northwest Indian Confederation which enabled the extension of white settlement of their former territory, particularly in Ohio. ✤128–129 (2)
farming
18th-century Europe ✤198
Cucuteni-Tripolye villages (c.4000 BCE) ✤174
development of communities (BCE) ✤22
early N. American ✤120, ◆121 (1)
early S. American ✤144, ◆147 (2)
early spread of (7000–5000 BCE) ✤174●
early village plan ❑18
horticulture villages (BCE) ✤34●
introduction to Europe (7000–5000 BCE) ✤174, ◆174 (1)
major cash crops (1870–1910) ◆92 (1)
permanent shelter ❑21
refrigerated shipping (1880s) ✤92●
societies (c.1350) ◆162 (1)
technology opens markets (1870–1910) ◆92 (1)
timber longhouse ❑174
tools (BCE) ✤16●, ✤22, ✤34, ✤258●
See also agriculture; animal and plant domestication
Fashoda ⚔ (1898). British and French clash in N. Africa ✤95
Fasiladas, King (d.1667) Ethiopian emperor (r.1632–67). Severed links between his country and Europe, instigating a policy of isolation that lasted for more than two centuries. ✤165
Fatimid dynasty (909–1171). A Muslim dynasty, founded in Tunisia, N. Africa, the Fatimids claimed descent from Fatima, Muhammad's daughter. In 969 the fourth Fatimid Caliph, Muizz, conquered Egypt and established his capital at Cairo, from where the Fatimids ruled until the 12th century. ✤58, ✤227, ◆227 (6)
Caliphate (1144) ◆65 (3)
control Egypt (969) ✤58●
dynasty (969–1171) ✤58●, ✤63●, ✤162●
expel Aghlabids (909) ✤58●
lose control of Ifriqiya (1048) ✤63●
Fazzan *see* Garamantes
Federal Bureau of Investigation (FBI). US government agency first established in 1908. Deals with matters of internal security, counterintelligence and federal law-enforcement. ✤135●

Key to index: ✣ text ❑ picture *var.* variant name *f/n* full name *r.* ruled WW I World War I
● timeline ◆ map *aka* also known as *prev.* previously known as ⚔ battle WW II World War II

SUBJECT INDEX AND GLOSSARY: *Kristallnacht* – Luxembourg dynasty

Kristallnacht (*var. Eng.* "The night of the broken glass") (Nov 9, 1938). 91 Jews were killed and many synagogues burned down in coordinated attacks by Nazis against Jews and Jewish property in Germany and Austria. ✣211
K'ung-fu-tzu *see* Confucius
Ku Klux Klan Extreme right-wing organization, founded in the southern US after the American Civil War to oppose the new rights granted to Blacks. Though the original Klan was outlawed in 1871, a new version appeared about 1915, reaching the height of its membership during the 1920s and carrying out acts of terrorism and murder against other minority groups including Jews, Catholics, and immigrants. ✣135, ❑135, ◆135 (6)
Kublai Khan (*var.* Kubilai Khan) (1215–94) Great Khan of the Mongols from 1260. Founder of the Yuan dynasty which united China, and first foreigner ever to rule a united China.
- (d.1294) ✣67●, ✣69●
- defeated by Japanese (1274) ❑263
- elected Great Khan (1264) ✣67●
- ends civil war (1264) ✣68●
- founds Khanbaliq (Beijing) (1266) ✣68●, ❑69
- Mongol campaigns (1260–94) ◆68–9 (1)
- Song Empire campaign (1260–79) ✣67

Kuomintang (*var.* Guomindang) Chinese Nationalist Party. Political party that ruled China from 1928 until the Communist victory in 1949. ✣271
Kurds Sunni Muslim people, numbering some 9–10 million, who occupy a mountainous region divided between Turkey, Iran, Iraq and Syria which the Kurds themselves call Kurdistan. They are politically oppressed in Turkey, and subject to religious persecution in Iraq. In 1988 the support given by Kurdish insurgents to Iran during the Iran-Iraq war led to the use of chemical weapons against them by Saddam Hussein. When Iraq was defeated in the Gulf War, the Kurds staged a revolt in northern Iraq. ✣235, ◆235 (5)
Kursk ⚔ of WW II (Jul–Aug 1943). Major tank engagement in which Soviet forces destroyed much of Germany's armored capacity in Russia; largest tank battle in history. ◆211 (4)
Kushan Empire (*var.* Kushana). State of south Central Asia created in 1st century CE, capital Peshawar, which grew to straddle the Hindu Kush and the Pamirs, incorporating Punjab, Afghanistan, and Sogdiana. The founder of the second Kushana dynasty, Kanishka (r.c.78–96 CE), adopted Buddhism and aided its dissemination along the Silk Road to China. ◆44–5, ◆46–7, ✣47●
Kushana *see* Kushan Empire
Kutuzov, Mikhail Ilarionovich (1745–1813) Russian soldier. Commander-in-Chief of the Russian forces which defeated Napoleon at Borodino (1812) and pursued the French army during its retreat from Moscow. ◆200 (1)
Kyoho Era begins in Japan (1716) ✣87●
Kyoto Japanese capital (794) ✣59●, ◆265 (4)

L

l'Olonnois, François 17th-century French privateer in the Caribbean. ◆85 (2)
La Florida Ceremonial center built (c.1800 BCE) ✣26
La Pérouse, J.F. Galaup de (1741–88). French explorer of Oceania, whose epic voyage around the Pacific ended in shipwreck off the Santa Cruz Islands. ◆278 (1)
La Rochelle Siege (1628–29) ✣196●
La Salle, René-Robert Cavelier Sieur de (1643–87) French explorer of N. America. Between 1679 and 1681 he explored the Great Lakes before traveling the length of the Mississippi and reaching its mouth in 1682. He took over the Mississippi Valley for France, naming the region Louisiana. ◆119 (2)
La Venta Olmec center (BCE) ✣30, ✣34
lacquerwork An ancient Chinese invention, this is a hard waterproof substance made from the resin of the *rhus vernicifera* tree. It can be colored, polished, and carved, and is used for many decorative purposes. ✣35●, ✣44
Lake Regillus ⚔ of (496 BCE). Roman victory over an alliance of surrounding Latin cities. The battle ensured Rome's dominance over neighboring cities. ✣178●, ◆178 (1 inset)
Lalibela St. George's church ❑62
Lambton, William Survey of India ✣239, ✣239●, ❑239
Lancashire Cotton towns ◆93 (4)
land drainage *see* irrigation
Lander, Richard (1804–34). British explorer of W. Africa who traced the course of the lower Niger River to its delta. ◆157 (4)
Langobardi *see* Lombards
Lao Tzu *see* Laozi
Laos
- Burmese invasion ✣79
- independence (1954) ✣107●, ◆251 (4)
- Vietnam War ◆251 (5)

Laozi (*var.* Lao Tzu). 6th-century BCE Chinese philosopher and sage. Regarded as the inspiration for Taoism and for one of its principal works, the Tao-te Ching, compiled c.300 years after his death. This teaches self-sufficiency, simplicity, respect for nature and ancestors. ✣35●, ✣37, ✣259●
lapis lazuli Deep blue stone, a silicate of sodium and aluminum. Found in metamorphosed limestones, in ancient times it was used as the source of a blue pigment.
- royal standard of Ur ❑23
- trade (c.2500 BCE) ✣24●, ✣25, ◆24–5 (2)

Lapita Austronesian speakers, ancestors of modern Polynesians. Their distinctive style of pottery provides evidence for their migrations in the western Pacific. Remains of their pottery have been found in the Bismarck Archipelago, Fiji, Samoa, and New Caledonia, all dating from the first millennium BCE. ◆281 (3), ✣281●
- colonizers of Pacific Ocean (c.1500 BCE) ✣27, ✣60●
- pottery ❑27

Lascaux Cave paintings (17,000 BP) ✣17●, ◆17 (3)
Lashio ⚔ of WW II (Apr 1942) marking Japanese control of central Burma. ✣104, ◆104 (2)
Las Navas de Tolosa ⚔ of Reconquest of Spain (1212). Defeat of Almohads. ◆186 (1)
Later Han *see* Han dynasty.
Latin colony Dependency of ancient Rome in Italy, where inhabitants had limited rights compared to full Roman citizens. ✣178, ◆178 (1)
Latin League Confederacy of small city-states established in the 5th century BCE. The supremacy of Rome gradually made the principles of the league obsolete and it was formally abandoned in 338. ✣178
Latins People of central Italy whose lands were annexed by Rome in the 4th century BCE. Their language was carried by the Romans throughout their empire. ✣178●
Lausanne, Treaty of (1922–23). Peace treaty between WW I Allies and Turkey resolving problems caused by Treaty of Sèvres, which had been rejected by the new Turkish government led by Atatürk. Turkey recovered eastern Thrace, and the Dardanelles were opened to all shipping. ◆233 (3)
See also Sèvres, Treaty of
Lawrence, Thomas Edward (*aka* "Lawrence of Arabia") (1888–1935) British scholar, soldier, and author. In 1916 he joined the Arab Revolt against the Turks led by Emir Faisal, and participated in the capture of Damascus (1918). He was an adviser to Faisal at the Paris Peace Conference, but later withdrew from public life. His account of the Arab Revolt, *Seven Pillars of Wisdom* (1926), has become one of the classics of English literature. ✣❑232, ◆233 (2)
Léry, Chaussegros de 18th-century French explorer of N. America
- expedition (1729) ✣119●, ◆119 (2)

Le Maire, Jacob (d.1616) Dutch explorer. Commander of voyage around Cape Horn and across the Pacific in 1615–16 with Willem Schouten as pilot. The expedition failed in its aim of finding a practicable route to the Indies in order to break the Dutch East India Company's monopoly of the spice trade. Le Maire died in the Indian Ocean on the homeward journey. ◆278 (1)
lead First use ✣18–19
League of Nations Established by the Allied Powers at the Paris Peace Conference (1919) after WW I, the league aimed, by arms reduction, international arbitration, and diplomacy, to reduce the threat of further conflict. The league was weakened from the outset by the refusal of US Congress to ratify the Treaty of Versailles; and during the 1930s it proved unable to contain the expansionism of Germany, Japan, and Italy. It was replaced in 1946 by the United Nations.
- created (1920) ✣98●
- proved ineffective ✣102

Lebanon Israel invades (1982) ✣234●, ◆234 (2)
Lechfeld ⚔ (955). Magyars defeated by Otto I. ◆185 (3)
Leeuwenhoek, Anton van Maker of optical instruments ✣83
Leipzig ⚔ of Napoleonic Wars (14–16 Oct 1813). Allies won great victory over Napoleon but he was able to escape with a remnant of his army. ◆200 (1)
Legnano ⚔ (1176). Defeat of Frederick Barbarossa by Lombard League. ◆188 (1)
Leichhardt, Ludwig (1813–48) Prussian-born explorer of the Australian interior. His party vanished without trace on his attempt to cross Australia from east to west in 1848. ◆279 (2)
Lenin, Vladimir Ilyich (*prev.* Ulyanov) (1870–1924) Russian revolutionary leader. The architect of the Bolshevik revolution in Russia, Lenin advocated the creation of a core of professional activists to spearhead a Marxist revolution. In Oct 1917, following the deposing of Tsar Nicholas II, Lenin's Bolsheviks overthrew the provisional government to inaugurate the "dictatorship of the proletariat." ❑208, ✣208
Leningrad (*hist.* and *mod.* St. Petersburg, *temp.* Petrograd, 1914–23, *var. Rus.* Sankt-Peterburg). City and port of western Russia, founded by Peter the Great; ⚔ of WW II, Soviets besieged by Germans 1941–43. ◆210 (1), ✣211●
Leo I, Pope (*aka* St. Leo I, Leo the Great) (d.461) (r.460–61).
- saves Rome from Huns ✣53

Leo III, Pope (r.795–816). Leo called on Charlemagne to secure his papal throne and in return created him Holy Roman Emperor, thus beginning the medieval interdependence and rivalry between popes and emperors. ❑184
Leopold II (1835–1909). The second king of the Belgians (r.1865–1909). He was the prime mover behind the establishment of the Congo Free State, which gradually became his own private African business venture. The administration of the state was severely criticized for the brutal methods used to force native people to pick rubber. In 1908 Leopold handed the Congo over to the Belgian government and it was then administered as a colony. ✣167●, ◆195 (4)
Lepanto ⚔ of (1571) Decisive naval engagement at which the Ottoman fleet was destroyed by the Venetian-led Holy League. ✣79, ✣195●
Lepenski Vir Important early European settlement c.6000 BCE. ❑18
Léry, Chaussegros de 18th-century French explorer of North America. In his capacity as Chief Engineer of Canada, de Léry conducted a thorough survey of the upper Ohio River in 1729 ◆119 (2)
Lesotho Kingdom (1824) ◆166 (2)
Lesseps, Ferdinand, Vicomte de (1805–94) French diplomat and engineer. In 1854 he began to plan the Suez Canal, supervising its construction until its opening in 1869. In 1881 work began on his plan for a Panama Canal, but this had to be abandoned in 1888 and was not completed until 1914. *See also* Suez Canal. ✣232
Lewis, Meriwether (1774–1809) US explorer. With Clark, led the famous expedition (1803–06) sponsored by President Jefferson to explore the land acquired in the Louisiana Purchase and find a land route to the Pacific.
- Columbia River map ❑119
- portrait ❑118
- US expedition (1805–07) ◆119 (3)

Lewis Outer Hebrides, chesspieces (12th century) ❑60
Lexington ⚔ of American Revolutionary War (Apr 19, 1775). British victory. ◆127 (3)
Leyte Gulf Naval ⚔ of WW II (Oct 1944). Major US victory over Japan, facilitating US invasion of Philippines. ✣105, ◆273 (2)
Lhasa
- Dalai Lama's Potala palace ❑257
- first Jesuit mission (1661) ✣257●
- visit by French monks (1846) ✣257●

Li dynasty *see* Yi dynasty
Li Tzu-cheng *see* Li Zicheng.
Li Zicheng (*var.* Li Tzu-cheng) (c.1605–45) Chinese rebel leader whose entry in 1644 into Beijing precipitated the suicide of the last Ming emperor. ❑266●**Liao** *see* Khitans
Liao Empire Extensive state established by the nomadic Khitan people in Manchuria, Mongolia, and northeastern China in the early 10th century. The empire coexisted with the Chinese Song dynasty, but, in 1125, fell to the Jurchen people, who founded the Jin dynasty of northern China. ◆263 (3) (4)
- founded by Khitans ✣263
- defeated by Manchurian Jin (1125) ✣63●
- Song China subject state (1005) ✣63●

Liberia Founded by freed slaves (1822) ✣91●
Libya 168–9
- bombed by US (1986) ✣111●
- conquered by Italy ✣232
- industrial growth ✣168, ◆168 (2)
- modern political development ◆169 (4)

Liegnitz ⚔ (1241). Polish army defeated by Mongols. ◆189 (3)
Liguria Lombard conquest (600 CE) ◆182 (2)
Lima
- founded (1535) ✣148●
- center of Spanish Empire in S. America ✣81
- cultural region ◆145 (4)

limes Defensive lines built by the Romans to protect the borders of their empire. The *limes* could consist of a continuous wall, as in northern Britain and parts of the German frontier, or a string of isolated forts, as in Syria. ◆180 (1)
Limited War Doctrine Strategic policy of limited military commitment and geographic containment, developed by the Western Allies during the Korean War, in an attempt to contain the spread of Cold War confrontations into intercontinental conflict. ✣109
Lincoln, Abraham (1809–65) 16th president of the US (Republican, 1861–65). The setting up of the Republican party in 1856, to oppose the extension of slavery in the US, brought Abraham Lincoln, a self-educated lawyer who had sat in Congress since 1846, to national prominence. In 1860 he won a comfortable majority in the presidential election but was unable to prevent the secession of seven of the Southern states from the Union, and the resultant Civil War between the Union and Confederate states. While defining the preservation of the Union as the primary issue of the war, most famously in the Gettysburg Address of 1863, his Emancipation Proclamation of the same year freed the slaves in the Southern states. Reelected for a second term in 1865, he was assassinated barely a month after his inaugural address.
- assassination ✣131●
- Emancipation Proclamation ✣130, ✣131●
- portrait ❑130

Linear A *see* Minoans
Linschoten, J. H. Van Late 16th-century Dutch cartographer. ✣239●, ❑239
Lisbon
- expedition sent to Brazil (1502) ✣149●
- Moors lose to Crusaders (1147) ✣62●, ◆64 (1)
- in Spanish Empire ✣81

Lithuania
- expansion ✣189, ◆189 (4)
- joined with Poland (1386) ✣189●

Little Bighorn ⚔ (1876). American forces, led by General Custer, destroyed by Sioux and Cheyenne. ◆128–9 (2)
Livingstone, David (1813–73). Scottish missionary who, during his three visits to Africa in the period 1841–73, undertook journeys of exploration throughout the southern half of the continent. He was the first European to reach Lake Ngami in 1849 and the first to see the Victoria Falls in 1855. Appalled by the treatment of African slaves, he dedicated much of his life to fighting the trade, clashing frequently with the Boers and Portuguese. Between 1866 and 1871 no news was heard of Livingstone until he was tracked down by Henry Morton Stanley, who had been sent by a New York newspaper to find him.
- explorer of Africa ◆157 (4)

Livonian Order *see* Sword Brothers ✣189
Llanos de Mojos Drainage earthworks ✣145
Lübeck Seal ❑190
Lodi ⚔ of Napoleon's Italian campaign (1896). French victory. ◆200 (1)
Lodi, Peace of (1454) Ended wars in Italy between Milan, Venice, Florence, and the Papal States. ✣75●
Lodz ⚔ of WW I (11–25 Nov 1914). German occupation followed Russian defeat ✣206●, ◆206 (4)
Lollards Reforming religious group, influential in Europe during the 14th–15th centuries, famous for their attacks on church corruption and emphasis on the Biblical scriptures. ✣70
Lombard League Alliance of cities of northern Italy formed in 1167 to oppose the German Emperor Frederick I (Barbarossa). 188●, ◆188 (1), ✣190●
Lombards (*var.* Langobardi). Germanic people settled along the Danube in the 5th century. In 568 they invaded northern Italy, swiftly overrunning the region now known as Lombardy and establishing two southern duchies, Benevento and Spoleto. They never controlled the whole of Italy and conflict with the Byzantine Empire and the Papacy continued for 200 years, until their defeat by Charlemagne in 774.
- capture Ravenna (752) ✣58●
- defeated by Charlemagne (774) ✣58●
- gem-studded gold buckle ❑183
- glass drinking horn ❑182
- kingdom and duchies (600 CE) ◆182 (2)
- struggle for Italy ✣184, ✣184●, ◆183 (4)

London
- reconquered by Alfred the Great (885) ✣58●
- Underground ✣92●, ❑102

Long Island ⚔ of American Revolutionary War (Aug 27, 1776). British victory. ◆127 (3)
Long, Major Stephen H. (1784–1864) US army engineer and explorer. Led expeditions along the Missouri (1819–20) and the Platte and South Platte rivers in the Rocky Mountains, south to the Red River (1821). Produced a map which named the region as the Great American Desert. Later explored the 49th parallel. ◆119 (3)
Long March (Oct 1934–Oct 1935). Withdrawal of the Communist forces during the Chinese Civil War from their bases in southern China to the northwest, led by Mao Zedong. ✣274●, ❑274, ◆274 (1)
Longmen nr Luoyang, Chinese Buddhist cave-temple ❑51
Longshan culture Named after Long Shan (Dragon Mountain) in northeast China's Shandong province. This Neolithic culture developed from the Yangshao culture as bronze was coming into use, and flourished between c.3000–1700 BCE in the Yellow River valley. Their economy was based on millet, pigs, cows, and goats, and is characterized by polished stone tools and distinctive pottery, the first in the Far East made on a fast wheel, and kiln – fired to a uniform black color. ✣258●, ❑23, ◆258 (2)
López de Cárdenas, Garcia 16th-century Spanish explorer of the Americas, a member of Coronado's expedition north from Mexico in 1540–42. ◆118 (1)
Lord Curzon (*f/n* George Nathanial Curzon, Marquis of Kedleston) (1898–1905) Viceroy of India (1898–1905). An energetic reformer of the civil service, education system, and police force, he created the new Northwest Frontier Province (1898) and partitioned the province of Bengal (1905). ✣250
Los Angeles
- ethnic distribution (1960–90) ✣137, ◆137 (6)
- Hollywood film studios (1919) ✣135, ❑135
- race riots (1940s) ✣135●
- Watts Riots (1965) ✣137●

Louis I (*aka* Louis the Great) (1326–82). King of Hungary. A member of the Anjou dynasty that became kings of Naples in the 13th century, Louis frequently intervened in Neapolitan politics after the murder of his brother, the Queen's consort, in 1345. He also fought three wars with Venice for control of the Dalmatian coast. In 1370 he inherited the crown of Poland, but could not really impose his authority there. ✣189, ◆189 (4)
Louis the Pious (778–840) Frankish king, son of Charlemagne. Crowned by his father in 813, Louis attempted to hold the Carolingian Empire together, but the last decade of his reign was marked by civil wars between him and his four sons. ✣184, ✣184●
Louis VII (1120–80) King of France. In 1152 Louis divorced Eleanor of Aquitaine, who then married Henry of Anjou, who became king of England as Henry II in 1154. This weakened the position of the French crown, as large tracts of France came under English control. ✣187
- Crusade route (1147–49) ◆64–5 (2)
- trade monopoly ✣191●

Louis IX (*aka* St. Louis) (1214–70). King of France. Famed for his piety, for which he was canonized in 1297, Louis was also an enthusiastic crusader and organized and led two crusades. On the first in 1248, he was captured and ransomed in Egypt. On the second in 1270, he died while besieging Tunis. ✣64, ✣66●, ◆64–5 (2)
- initiated W. Asia exploration ✣219
- coffin returned to France ❑64

Louis XIV (*aka* "the Sun King") (1638–1715) King of France (r.1643–1715). Effective ruler after 1661, he established an absolute monarchy. For the next 50 years he was the most powerful monarch in Europe, but his ambition to establish French supremacy in Europe led to numerous wars, especially with Spain, Holland, and England. His attempt to forge a union between France and Spain led to the War of the Spanish Succession (1701–14), which left France virtually bankrupt. His long reign was marked by a flourishing of the French arts, symbolized by the Palace of Versailles.
- France under Louis XIV ✣197, ✣197●, ◆197 (5)
- king of France (1643–1715) ✣86●, ✣196
- portrait ❑82, ❑197

Louis XVI (1754–93) King of France. In 1788 Louis' financial problems forced him to summon the Estates-General (the French parliament that had not met since 1614). This became the National Assembly and precipitated the French Revolution. Louis became virtually a prisoner of the state. His unsuccessful attempt to flee France in 1791 led to his trial the following year and in 1793 he was guillotined for treason.
- French Revolution ✣82, ✣86, ✣90, ✣199, ❑199, ◆199 (4)
- guillotined (1793) ❑86

Louis-Napoleon *see* Napoleon III
Louis Philippe (1773–1850) King of France (r.1830–48). Son of the Duke of Orléans, cousin of Louis XVI, Louis Philippe, like his father, who was known as Philippe Égalité, at first supported the Revolution. But after Louis Philippe fled the country, his father was executed in 1793. Louis Philippe was invited to become king in 1830 after the July Revolution of that year, but abdicated during the 1848 Revolution and died in exile in England. ✣90
Louisiana Purchase French territory added to the US in 1803 following its purchase from France for less than 3 cents an acre by Thomas Jefferson. It more than doubled the area of the US at the time, adding more than 828,000 sq miles (2,144,520 sq km) of territory. ◆129 (1), ✣128
- exploration by Lewis and Clarke (1805–06) ✣119●
- sale of French territory (1803) ✣90●

Lovelock Cave Duck decoys (c.1500 BCE) ❑26
Lower Moesia Visigoth settlement area ✣53
Lucius Tarquinius Priscus *see* Tarquin I
Lucius Tarquinius Superbus *see* Tarquin II
Luddite riots Protests by English textile workers, chiefly in the Midlands, alarmed at the introduction of industrial machinery and fearful of job losses. The first such riots, accompanied by widespread machine-wrecking, occurred in 1811 ✣204●
Ludwig, Daniel Keith (1897–1992). American entrepreneur who began a billion-dollar development of the Jari River valley in Brazil, but in 1982 he abandoned the costly project, which had led to the destruction of large tracts of tropical rain forest. ✣153●
Luoyang
- conquered by Qin (256 BCE) ✣39
- northern Wei capital (c.490) ✣51●

Luther, Martin (1483–1546). German scholar and priest whose questioning of certain church practices led to the Protestant Reformation. He first clashed with the Catholic authorities in 1517 after his *95 Theses*, attacking the sale of indulgences, denied that the pope and clergy could forgive sins. He inspired a movement that revolutionized religious thought, incidentally provoking much social and political upheaval in northern Europe. ✣78●, ✣194, ✣194●
Luxembourg dynasty The counts of Luxembourg were a powerful dynasty in the late Middle Ages. They were also kings of Bohemia and four of their number were elected emperor, the most famous being Charles IV.
- possessions ◆70–1, ✣189, ◆189 (4), ◆194 (2)
- creation of modern duchy ✣202, ◆202 (1 inset)

Key to index: ✣ text ● timeline ❑ picture ◆ map *var.* variant name *aka* also known as *f/n* full name *prev.* previously known as r. ruled ⚔ battle WW I World War I WW II World War II

SUBJECT INDEX AND GLOSSARY: **Nicaragua, civil war – Pacific Ocean**

Nicaragua, civil war (1978–89). After 40 years of dictatorship, a revolution in 1978 by the left-wing Sandinistas, who drew on the support of a rural peasant base, began 11 years of civil war. Despite losing the first free elections of 1990, the Sandinistas remain a potent force in the country, increasingly threatening the stability of the government.
civil war (1979) ✣110●
US intervention ✣139●, ◆139 (5)
Niebuhr, Carsten (1733–1815). German-born surveyor who took part in an international scientific expedition in 1761, financed by the King of Denmark, to explore the Arabian Peninsula. Niebuhr was the only survivor. His systematic accounts of the expedition, containing maps and illustrations, were published in 1772 and 1774. ◆219 (4)
Nieuwpoort ⚔ of Dutch Revolt (1600). Dutch victory over Spain. ◆195 (5)
Niger Basin, Arabic and Portuguese views ◆156 (1) (2)
Niger Delta
Nok culture (BCE) ✣38
Oyo main tribe (1747) ✣87●
Nigeria
independence ◆169 (1)
industrial growth ✣168, ◆168 (2)
secession of Biafra and civil war (1967–70) ✣107●, ◆169 (4), ✣169●
Nimrud
(BCE) ✣31, ✣35●
Phoenician carved plaque ❑176
Ninety-five Theses (1517). Document demanding ecclesiastical reforms, especially with regard to the sale of indulgences, nailed to a church door in Wittenberg by Martin Luther. ✣95●
See also Martin Luther.
Nineveh (BCE) ✣31, ✣35●
Niño, Andreas 16th-century Spanish explorer of Central America. ✣125, ◆125 (4)
Nippur Plan of city (BCE) ✣28, ❑28, ◆28 (2)
Nirvana *see* Buddhism.
Nisa Parthian capital ✣43
Nixon, Richard Milhous (1913–94) 37th president of the US. (Republican, 1969–74). Came to political prominence as a member of HUAC (the House Committee on Un-American Activities) investigating the Alger Hiss case. He served as vice president under Dwight D. Eisenhower from 1952–59, but lost the 1960 presidential election to John F. Kennedy. He was eventually elected president in 1968 and won a second term in 1972 by a narrow margin. Nixon's term of office saw the invasion of Cambodia in 1970, the ending of the Vietnam War, the initiation of arms limitation talks with the Soviet Union and the reestablishment of US relations with China. His involvement in the Watergate scandal led to his resignation in 1974, although he was granted a full pardon by his successor, Gerald Ford. ✣139●
Njinga Queen of the Ndongo kingdom in southwest Africa (r.1624–63). She resisted Portuguese attempts to expand their control of the Angola region. ❑164
Nkrumah, Dr. Kwame (1909–72). Ghanaian nationalist leader who led the Gold Coast's drive for independence from Britain and presided over its emergence as the new nation of Ghana. He headed the country from independence in 1957 until he was overthrown by a coup in 1966. ✣168
Nobile, Umberto (1885–1978) Italian aviator. Crossed the N. Pole in his dirigible balloon in 1926, along with Amundsen and 14 others. A second expedition ended in disaster with the loss of seven lives. ◆286–7 (2)
Noin Ula Burial site (BCE) ✣39●
Nok culture *var.* Nok figurine culture. Ancient Iron Age culture that existed on the Benue plateau of Nigeria between about 500 BCE and 200 CE. They produced the earliest known ironworking south of the Sahara, and distinctive terra-cotta figurines. ✣160, ❑38, ◆160 (1)
Nok figurine culture *see* Nok culture
Norden's county maps ✣173
Nordenskjöld, Baron Nils Adolf Erik (1832–1901) Swedish explorer and scientist. Made several expeditions to Spitzbergen. In 1870 led expedition to explore Greenland ice cap. In 1878–79, he sailed through the Northeast Passage on the ship *Vega*. ◆286–7 (2)
Noriega, General Manuel Antonio Morena (1940–) Panamanian politician and soldier. As commander of the National Guard and *de facto* ruler of Panama (1982–89), Noriega enjoyed US support until 1987. In 1988 he was indicted by a US grand jury on charges of drug trafficking, and in 1989 he was arrested during a US military operation in Panama, and deported to the US. ❑139
Normans Name given to the Vikings, chiefly of Danish origin, who, under their leader Rollo, settled in northern France from the early 10th century. Originally the word meant Northmen or Norsemen. The Viking settlers of Normandy soon became French speakers, well integrated with the local population, but their adventurous spirit showed itself in the 11th century in their conquests of England and of Southern Italy and Sicily.
conquest of England (1066) ✣62●, ✣186, ✣186●, ❑186, ◆186 (2)
of Sicily (1091) ✣62●
Normandy Landings (*var.* D-Day, *Operation Overlord*) ⚔ of WW II (Jun–Jul 1944). Allied combined operation, the largest amphibious landing in history, which initiated the Allied invasion of Nazi Europe. ✣105, ✣105●, ◆105 (3), ◆211 (4)
Normandy
Duchy founded by Vikings (911) ✣185●, ◆185 (3)
Norsemen *see* Vikings
North Africa 158–169
Berber states ✣161, ◆161 (2)
colonized by Vandals ✣52–3, ◆52 (1) (2)
Fatimid rulers ✣58
reconquered by Justinian ✣54
Roman amphitheater ❑161
Roman Empire ✣42
spread of Islam ◆56 (1), ✣86, ✣111
North America 116–139
1865–1920 ✣132–3
Anglo-French conflict ✣126–7, ◆127 (2)
big game hunting (BCE) ✣18
boom and bust (1914–41) ✣134–5
California Gold Rush (1849) ✣90●, ✣93
cemetery (BCE) ✣18●
cities and empires ✣122–3
colonization ✣86, ◆126 (1)
cultures
Adena (1000 BCE) ✣30
Anasazi ✣58, ✣62●
Aztec ✣66, ✣74, ✣78, ◆124 (1) (2) (3)
Hopewell (BCE) ✣38●, ✣46●, ✣120, ✣123, ◆36 (1)
Maya ✣46●, ✣50, ✣54, ✣58●, ✣66●, ✣124
Mogollon ✣58
Olmec (BCE) ✣30●, ✣34
decline of the Democratic South ✣139
early peoples ✣120–1, ◆121 (4)
early subsistence and agriculture ✣26, ✣90, ◆120 (1)
eastern interior ✣119, ◆119 (2)
expansion ✣82, ✣90, ✣128, ◆128 (2)
exploration and mapping ✣60●, ✣118, ◆118–19 (1) (2) (3)
historical landscape ✣116–17
indigenous people ✣90, ✣118, ✣123, ✣126, ✣128–9
population changes ✣126
seizing of the West ✣128, ✣128●, ◆128–9 (2)
settlement and conflict ✣126–7, ✣128–9, ✣136–7, ◆128 (2)
settlers populate the West ❑94, ❑128
societies in transition ✣136–7
Spanish exploration and colonization ✣125●, ◆125 (4)
struggle for nationhood ✣128, ✣128●, ◆128–9 (2)
wagon trails ◆128 (2)
wildlife ❑118
North American Free Trade Agreement (NAFTA). Agreement between the US, Canada, and Mexico to remove trade barriers between the three nations for a ten-year period. It came into force in Jan 1994. ✣136●
See also USA, Canada
North Atlantic Treaty Organization (NATO). Established in 1949 as security coalition among Western Allies, dominated by US. Frequently deployed troops from member states as peacekeeping forces, but played a large role in Gulf War (1991) and Yugoslav conflict (1999).
created 1949 ✣108, ✣109●, ✣213
Cold War alliances ✣109, ✣138, ◆108–9 (1)
conventional arms limitation (1990) ✣109●
US collective defense treaties (1983) ◆138 (1)
Warsaw Pact (1955) ✣106●, ✣108, ◆108 (3)
North Korea *see* Korea
North Vietnam *see* Vietnam
Northeast Passage Maritime route along the northern coast of Europe and Asia between the Atlantic and Pacific oceans, not fully navigated until 20th century. ◆257 (2)
search for routes to Asia (1550–1820) ✣80●, ✣257●, ✣286, ◆286 (1)
Northern Chou *see* Northern Zhou
Northern Expedition (1926–28) An attempt by the Kuomintang (Guomindang) to unify China, led by Jiang Jieshi (Chiang Kai-shek). ✣271●
Northern Song *see* Song dynasty.
Northern Wei *see* Toba Wei.
Northern Zhou (var. Northern Chou) Ruling dynasty of northern China (557–581) that overthrew the Northern Qi. ✣261●, ◆261 (5)
Norway
800–1000 ◆185 (3)
foreign affairs
possessions
1925 ◆98–9
1950 ◆102–3
1975 ◆106–7
accession of Canute (1016) ✣62●
Norwegians settle in Scotland (c.900 CE) ✣60●
WW II, mobilization and casualty figures ✣105
Union of Kalmar (1397) ✣70●
Novgorod
founded by Rurik the Viking (862 CE) ✣60●, ✣185
granted independence (1136) ✣62●
NRA *see* National Recovery Administration
Nubia The name given by the Egyptians to the area extending from the First Cataract of the Nile south to the Sudan. Its capital was first at Napata then at Meroë. In the 2nd millennium BCE the Nubians were under Egyptian rule, but themselves ruled Egypt in the 1st millennium, making Napata briefly the center of the ancient world. Egypt's 25th dynasty, 751–668 BCE, came from Cush and 300 of their pyramids remain.
BCE ✣30, ✣31●, ✣34
confederacy of chiefdoms ✣159 (3)
Coptic Christianity ✣58
gold deposits (BCE) ✣26
Nubt Confederacy (BCE) ◆159 (2)
Nuclear Age General term for the period since the end of WW II when nuclear fission technology, used for power generation and weapons of mass destruction, was developed by a coterie of powerful nations.
bombing of Japan ✣104, ✣273, ◆273 (3)
Pacific test sites ❑285, ◆285 (2)
numerical systems
evolution ✣33, ◆33 (2)
See also mathematics
Numidia Roman province north of the Sahara in N. Africa.
Berber state ◆161 (2)
Christian converts (c.150 CE) ✣47●
Roman control ✣46
under Masinissa (c.210 BCE) ◆42–3
Nur al-Din (d.1174). Turkish leader of Muslim resistance to the crusader states from his territories in Syria. He sent his general Saladin to Egypt, where he brought the Fatimid Caliphate to an end in 1169. ✣65●
Nyasa, Lake Reached by Livingstone (1859) ✣157●, ◆168 (1)
Nyasaland (now Malawi). Granted independence (1963) ✣168●
Nyerere, Julius (1922–) The first prime minister of independent Tanganyika (1961), who became the first president of the new state of Tanzania (1964). Nyerere was also the major force behind the Organization of African Unity (OAU). ❑168

O

O'Higgins, Bernardo (1778–1842) Liberator of Chile. Son of an Irish-born soldier who emigrated to Chile, O'Higgins rose to be leader of the patriotic forces that fought for liberation from Spain from 1810. Defeated and driven from Chile in 1814, he received support from the newly independent Republic of Río de la Plata, crossed the Andes with José de San Martín, and won the decisive battle of Chacabuco in 1817. He became the first president of Chile, but his authoritarian rule was unpopular and he was driven from office in 1823. He died in exile in Peru. ◆150 (1)
Oaxaca Region of southern Mexico which was the site for the some of the earliest civilizations of Central America including the Olmec. ◆36 (1), ✣121
Ocampo, Sebastián de Early 16th-century Spanish conquistador, leader of expedition from Hispaniola to Cuba. ✣125, ◆125 (4)
Occaneechee Path Exploration (1673) ✣119●
Oceania General geographic term for the island groups of the Pacific Ocean, sometimes including Australia and New Zealand. 276–285
✣55, ✣91●
Austronesian and Polynesian migrations ◆280–1 (3)
and Australasia, historical landscape ✣276–7, ◆276–7
exploration and mapping ✣278–9, ◆278–9 (1) (3)
peopling the Pacific ◆280–1 (3)
prehistoric ✣15, ◆280–1
Octavian *see* Augustus Caesar
Oda Nobunaga (1534–82) Provincial leader who initiated the unification of Japan (r.1568–82). ✣266, ◆266 (4)
Odoacer 5th-century barbarian chieftain, who in 476 deposed the last Roman emperor, Romulus Augustulus, to become ruler of Italy with his capital at Ravenna. He was killed in 493 after surrendering to Theodoric.
rules Italy (476) ✣182●
defeated by Ostrogoths (492) ✣53●
Offa (r.757–96). King of Mercia, which during Offa's reign became the most powerful of the Anglo-Saxon kingdoms of Britain. 183●
Offa's Dike Rampart and ditch built c.785 by Offa of Mercia to define the border between the English and the Welsh. ◆183 (3)
Ogedei *see* Ögödei
Ogilvie's road maps ✣173
Ögödei (var. Ogedei) (d.1241). Mongol leader, son of Genghis Khan, who led successful campaigns against the Khwarizm Shah and the Jin of northern China. He was elected Great Khan in 1229.
elected Great Khan (1229) ✣69●
Mongol campaigns (1229–41) ◆68–9 (1)
Ohio
Kent State University protest (1970) ✣137●, ◆137 (7)
migration (1917–20) ✣134
Ohio River
Adena culture (1000 BCE) ✣30
first proper survey (1729) ✣119●
oil
crisis causes inflation (1973) ✣106●
exploitation ✣107, ✣138
OPEC founded ✣107●
pollution ❑235
production in Gulf region ◆234 (1)
Oirats Nomad raids on China ✣75
Okinawa ⚔ of WW II (Mar–Jun 1945). Major US amphibious assault which, with Iwo Jima, secured an island base for strategic bombing campaign against Japan. ◆272 (1), ◆273 (2)
Old Kingdom (2575–2134 BCE). Period of Egyptian history encompassing the 4th to the 8th Dynasties which was especially notable for the building of the pyramids. ◆36 (1), ✣159●, ◆159 (3)
Old World General geographic term for Africa and Eurasia, prior to European discovery of Americas and Australasia.
Olid, Cristóbal de Early 16th-century Spanish *conquistador*, leader of expedition from Mexico to Honduras. ✣125, ◆125 (4)
oligarchy In the ancient Greek city-states an oligarchy was in place when power was in the hands of a minority of male citizens, as contrasted with democracy when power was held by the majority. ✣176
Olmec culture Elaborate Central American native culture based on the Mexican Gulf coast, which flourished between 1200 and 600 BCE. The Olmecs influenced the rise and development of other great civilizations and are credited with having the first planned religious centers, with monumental sculptures and temples, and with devising the 260-day Mesoamerican calendar.
civilization (1200 BCE) ✣30●, ✣34, ❑30, ◆121 (2)
heartlands ◆121 (3)
jade ceremonial adze ❑121
state religion (BCE) ◆36 (1)
Olustee ⚔ of American Civil War (Feb 20, 1864). Union victory. ◆131 (7)
Olympia Athletics festival (776 BCE) ✣31●
Olympic Games Revived (1896) ✣94●
Omagua People of the Upper Amazon region of S. America. ✣147, ◆147 (2)
Omani Arabs
attack Portuguese in E. Africa (1729) ✣164●
capture Mombasa (1698) ✣83●
Oñate, Cristóbal de 16th-century Spanish explorer, leader of an expedition from Mexico to New Mexico and Arizona. ✣125, ◆125 (4)
Oñate, Juan de (c.1550–1630) Spanish *conquistador*. Led colonizing expedition into New Mexico in 1598 establishing settlements north of the Rio Grande. Reached mouth of Colorado River in 1605. Governor of New Mexico from 1605–08. ✣125, ◆125 (4)
Onin War (1467–77). Struggle between Japanese warlords. ✣267●, ◆267 (4)
OPEC *see* Organization of Petroleum Exporting Countries
Operation Market Garden *see* Arnhem
Operation Overlord *see* D-Day, Normandy Landings
Opium Wars Confrontations (1839–42) (1850–60) arising from Chinese (Qing) attempts to limit the profitable British opium trade in south and east China. British naval forces attacked or blockaded several Chinese ports (Guangzhou, Xiamen, Fuzhou, Ningbo, Tianjin, Shanghai) wresting the first of many territorial trading cessions (Treaty Ports) in the peace settlement, the Treaty of Nanjing (1842). ✣91●, ✣269●, ◆269 (4)
optical instruments Newton's reflecting telescope ❑83
oracles
bones for divination ✣27●
Shang dynasty interpretations ❑32
Orange Free State founded (1854) ✣166●
Orange River, reached by Dutch settlers (1720) ✣87●
Orbigny, Alcide Dessalines d' (1802–57). French paleontologist, who spent eight years (1826–34) traveling in South America, producing a 10-volume account of his travels and the first detailed map of the whole continent. His observations on fossils in sedimentary rocks gave rise to the science of micropaleontology. ✣143
Orellana, Francisco de (c.1490–1546) Spanish *conquistador*. Orellana was a member of an expedition to the eastern slopes of the Andes led by Gonzalo Pizarro, brother of Francisco. He and companions became separated from the main party and sailed the length of the Amazon. ✣142●, ◆142 (1)
Organization of African Unity (OAU). Founded (1963). ✣169●
Organization of Petroleum Exporting Countries (OPEC). International organization seeking to regulate the price of oil. Founded in 1960, it consists of thirteen oil-producing countries which include Saudi Arabia, Iran, Iraq, Kuwait, Venezuela, Libya, and Algeria.
founded ✣107●, ✣234
restricts supplies (1973) ✣107●
Orinoco Raleigh's expeditions ✣149
Oriskany ⚔ of American Revolutionary War (Aug 6, 1777). American victory. ◆127 (3)
Orléans Siege (1429). Turning point in Hundred Years' War. The city, under siege from the English, was relieved by the French, inspired by Joan of Arc. ✣75●, ✣192, ✣192●
Oromo People of East Africa who migrated north into Ethiopia in large numbers in the 16th and 17th centuries. ✣165, ◆165 (3)
Orozco, Francisco 16th-century Spanish explorer of N. America.
colonizing expedition (1521) ✣125, ◆125 (4)
Orozco, Pascual Mexican revolutionary leader ✣133
Ortelius, Abraham (1527–98) Dutch cartographer and publisher. Publisher of the first "modern" atlas, the *Theatrum Orbis Terrarum* in 1670. ✣79, ✣173●
Osaka Emergence of Yamato state (c.300) ✣51●
Osei Tutu (d. 1712). Founder and first ruler of the Asante nation. ✣164●
Osman I (c.1258–1324) Founder of the Ottoman dynasty, which grew powerful in the regions of northwest Anatolia bordering Byzantium. By the time of his death the Ottomans controlled most of Bithynia. ✣67●, ❑230
Ostrogoths The "Eastern Goths" first emerged as a threat to Rome in 453, after the death of Attila and the dispersal of the Huns. Under their leader, Theodoric the Great, they conquered Italy in 493, establishing a kingdom that lasted until 553. ✣182
See also Goths.
Otto I (*aka* Otto the Great) (912–73). He was elected king of the Germans in 936 and crowned emperor in 962. His defeat of the Magyars at Lechfeld in 955 put an end to their raids on western Europe. Made Germany the most powerful political entity in western Europe.
defeats Magyars (955) ✣58●, ✣185
Holy Roman Emperor ✣58, ✣185, ✣185●
Otto II (955–83) Holy Roman Emperor. Joint emperor with his father Otto I from 967.
Italian campaign ✣185●
portrait ❑185
Ottokar II (1230–78). King of Bohemia, who extended Bohemian rule almost to the Adriatic. He was defeated by the Emperor Rudolf of Habsburg at the battle of Marchfeld. ✣189●, ◆189 (4)
Ottoman Empire Islamic empire established in Anatolia in the late 13th century by Turkish tribes. It rapidly spread into Europe, reaching its peak in the 16th century when it stretched from the Persian Gulf to Morocco in the south, and from the Crimea to the gates of Vienna in the north. After the unsuccessful siege of Vienna (1683), the empire began a protracted decline, collapsing altogether when Turkey was defeated in WW I. 230–233
1200–1400 ◆189 (4)
1300–1500 ◆230 (1)
1400 ◆70–1, ◆229 (4)
1500 ◆74–5, ◆193 (4)
1512–1639 ◆231 (3)
1600 ◆78–9
1700 ◆82–3
1800 ◆86–7
1800–1913 ✣232, ✣232●, ◆167 (4), ◆232–3 (1)
1850 ◆90–1
1900 ◆94–5, ◆166 (1)
founded (1299) ✣67●, ✣230
Bursa becomes capital (1326) ✣71●
decline and collapse ✣86●, ✣98, 232
partition (1918–23) ✣233
defeats
by Timur (1402) ✣95●
European lands lost (1912–13) ✣99●
⚔ Lepanto (1571) ✣79, ✣231●
Safavid Persia (1501–1736) ✣231, ◆231 (4)
siege of Vienna (1683) ✣82●, ✣195
expansion
rise of the empire ✣230, ✣230●, ◆230 (1)
consolidation and resistance (17th century) ✣196, ✣196●, ◆196 (2)
frontier (16th century) ◆195 (4)
height of power (1512–1639) ✣231, ✣231●, ◆231 (3)
Mamluks conquered in Egypt (1517) ✣79●
naval campaigns (15th–16th century) ◆230 (2)
of power (1453–1571) ✣194, ✣194●
seizes Anatolia ✣71
southeastern Europe (1354) ✣71●
Trebizond (1461) ✣75●
WW I ✣99●
Habsburg conflict (1663–171) ✣197, ◆197 (4)
Indian Ocean trade ✣230, ◆230 (2)
Janissary corps (c.1380) ✣71●, ❑230
sultan deposed (1908) ✣99●
See also Balkans; Turkey
Ottonian dynasty Saxon dynasty, named after Otto I, Holy Roman Emperors in the 10th and 11th centuries. ✣185, ✣185●
Oudney, Walter (d.1824) British naval officer and explorer. He accompanied Denham and Clapperton across the Sahara to Lake Chad in 1822, but died during the journey. ◆157 (4)
Oyo West African state that dominated the region between the Volta and the Niger in the 18th century.
main power in Niger Delta (1747) ✣87●
slave trade ✣82
state established (c.1500) ✣79●

P

Pachacuti Inca (*var.* Pachacutec) The ruler in whose reign (1438–71) the Inca Empire expanded from its heartlands around Cuzco to dominate the Andean region as far north as Quito. ✣74●, ◆147 (3)
Pacific Ocean
colonization
(19th century) ✣284–5, ✣284●
c.1500 ✣27, ◆26–7
decolonization and nationhood ✣285, ◆285 (3)
imperialism ◆284 (1)
Japan takes German colonies (1914) ✣99
Japanese naval power limited (1922) ✣99●
missionaries in the South Seas ✣284, ❑284
Polynesian ✣55
reached by Russians (1649) ✣257●
use and abuse of resources ◆185 (2)
migrations
Austronesian and Polynesian ✣281, ◆280–1 (3)
importation of migrant workers ✣284

308

Key to index: ✣ text ● timeline ❑ picture ◆ map *var.* variant name *aka* also known as *f/n* full name *prev.* previously known as r. ruled ⚔ battle WW I World War I WW II World War II

in disaster and Raleigh was executed on his return to England. ✤149
Ramayana Classical Sanskrit epic of India relating the adventures of Rama, probably composed in the 3rd century BCE. Based on numerous legends, the epic was revised and set down in its best known form by the poet Tulsi Das (1532–1623). ✤241, ◆36 (2)
Rameses III (*var.* Ramesses) (r.c.1184–53 BCE) Second king of the 20th dynasty of Egypt. Went to war with the Philistines and the "Sea Peoples." ✤31●
Ramesses *see* Rameses III
Rangoon Founded (1755) ✤87●
Rapa Nui (*var.* Easter Island)
colonized by Chile ✤284●
settled by Polynesians ✤55●, ✤60, ✤281, ◆281 (4)
temple platforms ✤60●, ❑281
Rashtrakutas A powerful kingdom established in 753 CE in the northern Deccan. At its peak, Rashtrakuta control extended from southern Gujarat to Tanjore. ✤244●, ◆244 (2)
Ravenna Capital of Italy under the Ostrogoths and Byzantines.
captured by Lombards (752) ✤58●
captured by Ostrogoths (492) ✤53, ✤182
detail from mosaic (6th century) ❑182
sarcophagus ❑182
Raymond of Toulouse Crusade route (1096–99) ◆64–5 (2)
Reagan, Ronald Wilson (1911–). 40th president of the United States (Republican, 1981–89). A former movie actor, as president of the Screen Actors' Guild Reagan cooperated with efforts to combat alleged Communist influences in the American film industry. He was governor of California from 1967–74. In 1980 he won the presidential election in a landslide victory. During his tenure he greatly increased military spending while reducing taxes and cutting back on general government expenditure. He introduced the controversial SDI (Strategic Defense Initiative) and signed the INF treaty with the Soviet Union, which limited intermediate range missiles. His administration was damaged by revelations that profits from arms deals with Iran had been used to support the Contra rebels against the Sandinista government of Nicaragua. ✤139, ✤139●
Recife Taken by Portuguese (1654) ✤149●
Reconquest of Spain (*var. Sp.* Reconquista). The reconquest of Muslim Spain by the Christian states, from the 11th to the 15th century. ✤192, ✤192●, ◆186 (1), ◆192 (3)
Reconquista *see* Reconquest of Spain
Reconstruction (1865–77). Period following the US Civil War in which the southern states were controlled by the Federal government and social legislation including the granting of new rights to Blacks was introduced. But a new Republican government returned power to white leaders who reintroduced segregation in the South. ✤132
Recuay Cultural region ◆145 (4)
Red River Indian War (1874–75). Major uprising by members of the Arapaho, Cheyenne, Comanche, Kiowa, and Kataka tribes from reservations in Oklahoma and Texas against white settlers in the area. US forces led by General William Sherman were forced to fight 14 battles against the natives in the Red River Valley, before their eventual surrender. ✤128–9●, ◆128–9
Red Scare Name given to the fear of Communist subversion in the US which arose in the late 1940s, leading to the setting up of schemes such as the Federal Employee Loyalty Program, and Senator Joseph McCarthy's list of government employees whom he claimed had Soviet sympathies. The scare led to a significant degree of persecution of those suspected of Communist sympathies, and many people – especially in the government, schools, universities, and the mass media – found themselves unable to work because of their suspected beliefs. ✤135●
Red Sea trade (1st century CE) ✤225, ◆225 (3)
reducciones Jesuit frontier settlements in Spanish S. America ✤143, ◆143 (2)
Reformation Religious reformation of the 16th century which took place in the Roman Catholic church, led by Martin Luther and John Calvin. The Reformation had long-term political, economic, and social effects, and laid the groundwork for the foundation of Protestantism. ✤194–5, ✤195●
refrigeration First commercial units (1856) ✤92●
refugees and resettlement ✤212, ◆212 (3)
Reiss, Wilhelm 19th-century German explorer of S. America, who scaled the volcano Cotopaxi in 1872. ✤143●
religion
Buddhism (to 400 CE) ◆49 (3)
characteristics ◆36 (1)
development of organized ✤36–7
global ✤48–9
Mediterranean cults ◆37 (3)
Mithraism, Judaism, and Christianity (to 600 BCE) ◆48 (1)
old world ✤49, ◆49 (4)
South Asian ◆36 (2)
state ◆36 (1)
Taoism and Confucianism ◆37 (4)
Remojadas Early Mexican civilization (c.600–900 CE) ◆122 (1)
Renaissance (*var.* Renascence, c.1300–1550). Period of cultural, economic, and political efflorescence in medieval Europe, characterized by the rediscovery of classical Greek and Roman culture, which found expression, initially in Italy, in the growth of humanist studies and writing, and in a revitalization of architecture, painting, sculpture, and the arts in general.
comes into being ✤75
in Europe (12th century) ✤187, ✤187●, ◆187 (3)
travelers in W. Asia ◆219 (3)
Renascence *see* Renaissance
Rennell, James (1742–1830). British naval officer who became the surveyor-general of Bengal in 1764. He was responsible for the first consistent mapping of the Indian subcontinent, the Survey of India. ✤239●, ❑239
Republican Party One of the two major political parties of the US. Formed in 1854 to support anti-slavery policies prior to the Civil War, Abraham Lincoln was its first president. Today, it favors limited government and interventionist foreign policy and is generally considered to be more right-wing than the Democratic Party. ✤130–1, ◆135 (5), ◆139 (4)
Réunions Lands occupied by France during the reign of Louis XIV following the decisions of a special court convened for the purpose, the Chambre des Réunions. Important annexations included Luxembourg (1679) and Strasbourg (1684). Most of the territories had to be returned by the Treaty of Ryswijk (1697). ✤197●, ◆197 (5)
revolts
against rule of Louis-Napoleon ✤202, ✤202●
Boxer rebellion (1898) ✤95, ◆97, ❑97, ◆268 (2)
Dutch (1568–1609) ✤195, ✤195●, ◆195 (5)
English Peasants' (1381) ✤70●, ◆188 (2)
European students (1968) ✤106●
following Black Death ✤70
fragmentation of China (220–589) ✤261
Hungarian Hunyadi ✤193●
Indian Mutiny ✤95●, ✤249, ✤249●, ◆249 (3)
movements against colonial rule (1880–1920) ✤97, ◆97 (4)
Taiping rebellion (1850–64) ✤95●, ❑268
Warsaw Pact crushes Hungarian (1956) ✤106●
Yellow Turbans (147 CE) ✤47●
revolutions
American (1775) ✤86, ✤126–7, ◆127 (3)
Chinese (1911) ✤271, ◆271 (5)
Cuban ✤152
economic ✤92–3
era of revolution 1768–1868 ✤89, ✤89●, ◆88–9 (2)
in Europe ✤90●, ✤202●, ✤209
factors leading to industrial ✤86
French ✤82, ✤86, ✤90, ✤199, ❑199, ◆199 (4)
impact of industrial ✤92, ◆92 (1)
inventions and world economy (1835–95) ✤92●
Liberty on the Barricades (painting) ❑89
political crackdowns ✤100●
Russian (1905, 1917) ✤98●, ✤99●, ✤208, ◆208 (2)
See also industrial revolution
Rhodes, Cecil (1853–1902). Financier, statesman, and empire builder of British South Africa. He was prime minister of Cape Colony (1890–96) and founder of the diamond mining company De Beers Consolidated Mines Limited (1888).
De Beers Consolidated Mines ✤167
Hospitallers headquarters (1310) ✤64●
portrait ❑166
Rhodesia ◆168 (1)
Northern Rhodesia granted independence (1963) ✤168●
See also Zimbabwe
Ri dynasty *see* Yi dynasty
Ricci, Matteo (1552–1610) Italian Jesuit missionary and cartographer. Joined Jesuit mission in Macao in 1582, and then established mission on Chinese territory, eventually settling in Beijing in 1601. His maps and other data gave the Western world unprecedented access to information about China. ✤80
Richard I of England (*aka* Richard the Lion-Heart, Lion-Hearted, *Fr.* Richard Coeur de Lion) (1157–1199). Duke of Aquitaine from 1168 and of Poitiers from 1172 and king of England, duke of Normandy, and count of Anjou (r.1189–99). His prowess in the Third Crusade (1189–92) made him a popular king in his own time.
Crusade route (1189–92) ◆64–5 (2)
jousts with Saladin ❑64
succession (1189) ✤187●
Richard II (1367–1400) King of England (r.1377–99). Son of Edward the Black Prince. Deposed in 1399 by his cousin, Henry of Lancaster, later crowned Henry IV. He died in prison, possibly murdered. ✤192●
Richelieu, Cardinal Chief minister of Louis XIII with whom he collaborated to make France a leading European power. ❑196
Riel Rebellions (1869) (1885). Rebellions by the Metis (mixed race descendants of the Cree tribes and French fur traders) and their native allies against incursions of European settlers into their lands. ◆129 (2)
Rig Veda Completed c.900 BCE, this is the great literary monument of Aryan settlers of the Punjab. A collection of sacred hymns, it traces the religious development of Aryan India and depicts the Aryan settlers as chariot-driving warriors who gradually adapt to a more sedentary life. It is rich in geographical references. ✤36, ✤242, 242●, ◆242 (1)
Rio de Janeiro
Brazilian capital (1763) ✤149●
Carnival dancers ❑112
France Antarctique colony (1555) ✤149●
Río de la Plata Viceroyalty established (1776) ✤148●
Ripon Falls Source of Nile ✤157
roads
maps ❑99
Ogilvie's maps ✤173
Peutinger Table ❑172
Roman (by c.120 CE) ◆172 (1)
Robert I "the Bruce" (1274–1329) King of Scotland (r.1306–29). Crowned in 1306 in defiance of King Edward I of England. Decisively defeated the English at the battle of Bannockburn (1314). English acknowledgment of Scottish independence and Robert's right to the throne came in 1328.
victor at Bannockburn ✤188●, ❑188, ◆188 (2)
Robert of Normandy (c.1054–1134) Duke of Normandy (r.1087–1106). Eldest son of King William I of England. Inherited Normandy upon the death of his father, while his brother William inherited the throne of England. Took part in the First Crusade (1096–1100).
Crusade route (1096–99) ◆64–5 (2)
Robespierre, Maximilien François Marie-Isidore de (1758–94). French revolutionary and Jacobin leader who played a key role in the overthrow of the moderate Girondins. A member of the Committee of Public Safety which instituted the Reign of Terror (1793–4). Overthrown by the Convention, he was tried and guillotined. ✤199●
See also French Revolution, Jacobins, Terror, Reign of
rock art The oldest known art form, dating back to c.30,000 BCE in Western Europe, usually depicting hunting scenes and found in caves or, commonly in African examples, rock shelters and exposed rock faces. The images are either painted or etched into the rock surface, and are not purely decorative: some occur in recesses so difficult to access that they are thought to have played a part in ritual activities. Rock art is more abundant in the Saharan region than anywhere else in the world. ✤17●, ◆17 (3) (5)
Roerich, Nicolas (1874–1947) Russian traveler and painter in Central Asia. ◆257 (3)
Roger II of Sicily (1095–1154) (r.1101–54) First Norman king of Sicily, whose court at Palermo was one of the most magnificent in Europe, a meeting place for Christian and Arab scholars. Commissioned the *Book of Roger*, a medieval book of maps. ◆62, ✤218
Roggeveen, Jacob (1659–1729). Dutch explorer. His voyage across the Pacific in 1722 established the first European contact with a number of islands, including Rapa Nui (Easter Island) and Samoa. ✤278●
Roman Catholicism *see* Catholicism
Roman Empire The largest empire ever established in Europe, stretching from northern Britain to Egypt. From its apogee in the 2nd century CE, the empire became increasingly difficult to govern, and in 395 it was divided into two. The Western Empire fell in 476, but the East Roman (or Byzantine) Empire, with its capital at Constantinople, survived until 1453. ◆42–3, ◆46–7, ◆50–1, ◆52–3, ◆54–5
51 BCE to 138 CE ✤180●
c.117 CE at the death of Trajan ◆161 (2)
c.120 CE under Hadrian ◆180 (1)
240–395 CE ✤181, ◆181 (4)
250–400 CE ✤180●
476 CE end of the Empire ✤182
Attila the Hun defeated (451) ✤50●
and Carthage: the Punic Wars ✤42, ✤179, ◆179 (3)
conflict with Sassanian ✤50
conquests (to 120 BCE) ✤179, ◆179 (5)
depictions
exotic animal combat ❑44
maritime trade ❑44
mummy case ❑47
The Nile in Flood mosaic ✤47
Europe after the fall ✤182, ◆182 (1)
expansion program ✤42, ✤179●, ✤224–5, ◆224 (2)
exploration and mapping ✤42, ✤47, ◆218 (1)
Africa (c.150) ◆156 (3)
boundaries of ancient Europe ◆172 (1)
Hadrian's defensive strategy ✤180
Italian confederacy (264 BCE) ✤38●
mythological pantheon ✤37
overseas provinces (120 BCE) ✤179
Palatine Hill village (BCE) ✤31●
subjugation of Greece ✤179, ◆179 (4)
territory (240 BCE) ◆178 (1)
Tetrarchy of Diocletian ✤50, ✤181, ❑181, ◆181 (4)
trade, classical world ◆44–5
Western Empire collapses (476) ✤50●
See also Rome
Romania
end of Communism (1989) ✤110●
granted independence ✤232
See also Balkans, nationalism; Wars, World War I; World War II
Rome Rome began as a small city-state which, through military might combined with skillful use of threats and alliances, conquered first the Italian Peninsula, then, by the 1st century BCE, the entire Mediterranean world. The city of Rome's importance declined from the 4th century CE. From the 7th century, it regained prestige as the seat of the pope and headquarters of the Roman Catholic Church. It was ruled by the papacy until it became the capital of the newly united kingdom of Italy in 1871.
earthenware amphora ❑181
Imperial Rome (c.300 CE) ✤181, ◆181 (2)
legionary ❑178
politics
capital of united Italy (1871) ✤94●
and the Italian Confederacy ✤178
and Latin allies (c.495 BCE) ✤178
ruins of Colosseum ❑181
sacked by Vandals (455) ✤52●
sacked by Visigoths (410) ✤53●, ✤182●
saved from Huns ✤53
saved from Lombards ✤183●
supply routes ✤181, ◆181 (3)
See also Roman Empire.
Rome, Treaty of *see* European Union
Romulus Augustus Roman Emperor, deposed (476) ✤50●
Roosevelt, Franklin Delano (*aka* FDR) (1882–1945) 32nd president of the US (Democrat, 1932–45). Roosevelt became president in 1932, on the cusp of the worst years of the Great Depression. He immediately launched a series of reforms collectively known as the "New Deal" to combat the depression; these included the abandonment of the gold standard and agricultural price support, as well as programs such as the Works Progress Administration, aimed at providing work for the unemployed, and the creation of a Social Security Act. His "common touch" and immense personal popularity saw him elected for an unprecedented four terms. Though initially opposed to involvement in conflict in Europe, by the outbreak of WW II, he broke with neutrality to support the Allied position, bringing the US fully into the war following the bombing of Pearl Harbor in Dec 1941.
American President (1932–45) ✤134, ✤139
New Deal
✤102, ✤134, ✤134●, ✤135
FDR effect ✤135
NRA recovery program ❑134
WPA (Works Progress Administration) ❑134
portrait ❑135
World War II
Casablanca conference (1943) ✤104●
Tehran conference ✤105●
Yalta "Big Three" conference (1945) ❑105
Roosevelt, Theodore (Teddy) (1858–1919) 26th president of the US (Republican, 1901–09). After commanding the "Roughriders" in the Spanish-American War (1898), Roosevelt returned as governor of New York from 1898–1900, and was subsequently elected vice president. He became president following the assassination of William McKinley. He initiated the building of the Panama Canal, strengthened the US navy, and won the Nobel Peace Prize in 1906 for his part in ending the Russo-Japanese war. He formed a "progressive" movement in the Republican party but was defeated on the Progressive ticket in the elections of 1910.
US President 1901–09 ✤132
era of economic boom ❑132
Rosas, Juan Manuel de (1793–1877) Argentinian dictator. Although his official title was only governor of Buenos Aires province, Rosas was the effective ruler of Argentina from 1829–52. He owed his position to his loyal force of gauchos, and his wars of conquest against the Patagonian native tribes. ❑151
Rosebloom, Johannes 17th-century explorer in N. America. Employed by Governor Thomas Dongan to discover new routes for the fur trade. Reached Michilimackinac between Lakes Huron and Michigan in 1685 after traveling for three months. ◆119 (2)
Rosenberg, Ethel and Julius (1915–53), (1918–53). American Communists and part of a transatlantic spy ring. Convicted of passing on atomic secrets to the Soviet Union and executed. They were the first US citizens to be executed for espionage. ❑108
Rosetta stone Basalt slab inscribed by priests of Ptolemy V of Egypt in hieroglyphic, demotic, and Greek. Found near the city of Rosetta in Egypt in 1799 and taken by the British in 1801; now in the British Museum in London. Served as the key to understanding Egyptian hieroglyphics. ❑42
Ross, Sir James Clark (1800–62) British naval officer and explorer of the poles. Accompanied both Edward Parry and his uncle John Ross on expeditions in the Arctic. In 1839–43 he led the navy's first major Antarctic expedition. He discovered the Ross Sea, the Ross Ice Shelf, Ross Island, and Victoria Land.
Antarctic exploration (1839–43) ◆287 (3)
Arctic explorer (1829–33) ❑287, ◆286–7 (2)
Rotz, John Early map of S. America (1542) ❑142
Rousseau, Jean Jacques (1712–78) French philosopher and writer. Believed in the original goodness of human nature and that it was society that created inequality and misery. His most famous work, *Du Contrat Social* (1762), profoundly influenced French revolutionary thought. ✤198
Royal Road Road constructed under the Persian Achaemenid Empire in the 6th century BCE from Susa, the ancient capital of Persia, to Sardis, on the Aegean Sea.
construction ✤35, ✤223●, ◆223 (4)
Rozwi Empire Empire of southern Africa (c.1684–early 19th-century)
challenges Portuguese (17th century) ✤164
replaces Mwenemutapa ✤164
Ruanruan (*var.* Juan-juan, Avars). Nomadic steppe peoples whose expulsion from Mongolia by the Blue (Celestial) Turks in the 4th century CE impelled them westward, entering Europe in the mid-6th century. *See also* Avars. ✤261●, ◆261 (4)
Rub' al Khali (*var.* the "Empty Quarter"). Area of waterless desert covering some 3,000,000 sq miles (777,000 sq km) of the southern Arabian Peninsula.
19th- and 20th-century explorers ✤219●
Rudolf I (1218–91) Count of Habsburg and Holy Roman Emperor. The first Habsburg to be elected Emperor, Rudolf secured Austria as the center of the Habsburg domains through his defeat of Ottokar II of Bohemia in 1278. ✤189●
Rukh (1377–1447). Mongol shah, son of Timur ✤75
Rum Seljuk Sultanate in Anatolia in the 12th and 13th centuries, with its capital at Konya (Iconium). Its name is derived from Rome, because its lands had been captured from the Byzantine (East Roman) Empire. ◆65 (1) (2), ✤228
Rurik the Viking (r.c.862–79). Semi-legendary Swedish ruler of the merchant town of Novgorod, seen as the founder of the Russian state (named after "Rus," the Finnish word for Swede). ✤60●
Russia State originating in rise of Muscovy in 16th century under Ivan IV, who defeated the Tatars and united neighboring principalities, proclaiming himself Tsar. Consolidated power in eastern Europe and expanded beyond Urals in 17th century (notably under Peter the Great), to dominate northern and central Asia by 18th century. Tsarist rule toppled by Bolshevik (Communist) revolution in 1917.
194–215, 257–273
See also USSR
foreign affairs
Alaskan expeditions (1816–65) ◆119 (3)
Balkan nationalism ✤203, ◆203 (4)
Baltic states, conflict ✤195, ✤195●, ✤197, ◆195 (3), ◆197 (3)
Bering Strait-Alaska exploration (16th–17th century) ✤257
claim on N. America (1821) ◆128 (2)
conquers and annexes Crimea (1783) ✤86●
Crimean War (1854) ✤94, ✤203
Empire *see below*
France, opposition alliances (1792–1815) ✤90●, ✤201, ◆201 (3)
neutrality pact with Japan (1939) ✤103●
Treaty of Nerchinsk with China (1689) ✤83●, ✤257●
Turkey and the Black Sea ✤203, ✤232, ◆203 (4)
withdraws from Amur basin (1689) ✤83●
World War I *see* Wars, World War I
World War II see Wars, World War II
Golden Horde vassals (1200–1400) ◆189 (4)
home affairs
Bolshevik Revolution (1917) ✤98●
Mongol conquest begins (1237) ✤66●
Mongol raids (1222) ◆68
population growth (1650–1800) ❑198
revolutions (1905, 1917) ✤98●, ✤99●, ✤208, ◆208 (2)
serfdom abolished (1861) ✤94●, ✤269
trade and industry, Japanese commercial talks (1804) ✤91●
Russian Empire ✤195, ✤208
1800 ◆86–7
1850 ◆90–1
1900 ◆94–5
expansion ✤78, ✤82, ✤257, ✤269, ✤269●, ◆269 (3)
European, consolidation and resistance (17th century) ✤196, ✤196●, ◆196 (2)
Russian Revolution (1917). Revolution which saw the overthrow of Tsar Nicholas II by the Communist Bolsheviks, who took over the Winter Palace and swiftly established strongholds in towns throughout European Russia. In 1918, a new constitution was declared, which established the Union of Soviet Socialist Republics (USSR or Soviet Union). ✤208●, ◆208 (2)
Russo-Japanese War (1904–05) War caused by territorial disputes between Japan and Russia. Culminated in Japanese victory over the Russian Baltic Fleet in the Tsushima Strait. ✤99, ✤270, ◆270 (4)
Ruth, Babe (*aka* George Herman Ruth) (1895–1948) US baseball player. Played for Boston Red Sox, New York Yankees, and Boston Braves. Famous for his 714 home runs and 10 World Series, he is still considered to be baseball's greatest all-rounder. ❑135
Rwanda
crisis ✤169, ❑169, ◆169 (5)
interethnic warfare ✤111, ✤111●
Hutu massacre (1994) ✤111●

Key to index: ✛ text ❏ picture *var.* variant name *fln* full name *r.* ruled WW I World War I
● timeline ◆ map *aka* also known as *prev.* previously known as ⚔ battle WW II World War II

V

INDEX–GAZETTEER

Glossary of Abbreviations

This glossary provides a comprehensive guide to the abbreviations used in this Atlas, in the Subject Index and Glossary, and in the Index-Gazetteer.

A

abbrev. abbreviated
Afr. Afrikaans
aka also known as
Alb. Albanian
Amh. Amharic
anc. ancient
approx. approximately
Ar. Arabic
Arm. Armenian
ASEAN Association of South East Asian Nations
ASSR Autonomous Soviet Socialist Republic
Aust. Australian
Az. Azerbaijani
Azerb. Azerbaijan

B

Basq. Basque
BCE before Common Era
Bel. Belarussian
Ben. Bengali
Ber. Berber
B-H Bosnia-Herzegovina
Bibl. Biblical
bn billion (one thousand million)
BP British Petroleum
Bret. Breton
Brit. British
Bul. Bulgarian
Bur. Burmese

C

C central
C. Cape
Cam. Cambodian
Cant. Cantonese
CAR Central African Republic
Cast. Castilian
Cat. Catalan
Chin. Chinese
CIS Commonwealth of Independent States
Cro. Croat
Cz. Czech
Czech Rep. Czech Republic

D

Dan. Danish
Div. Divehi
Dom. Rep. Dominican Republic
Dut. Dutch

E

E. east
EC see EU
EEC see EU
ECU European Currency Unit
EMS European Monetary System
Eng. English
est estimated
Est. Estonian
EU European Union (previously European Community [EC], European Economic Community [EEC])

F

Faer. Faeroese
Fij. Fijian
Fin. Finnish
fl. Floruit
Fln. full name
Fr. French
Fris. Frisian
ft foot/feet
FYROM Former Yugoslav Republic of Macedonia

G

Gael. Gaelic
Gal. Galician
GDP Gross Domestic Product (the total value of goods and services produced by a country excluding income from foreign countries)
Geor. Georgian
Ger. German
Gk Greek
GNP Gross National Product (the total value of goods and services produced by a country)

H

Heb. Hebrew
HEP hydro-electric power
Hind. Hindi
hist. historical
Hung. Hungarian

I

I. Island
Icel. Icelandic
In. Inuit (Eskimo)
Ind. Indonesian
Intl International
Ir. Irish
Is Islands
It. Italian

J

Jap. Japanese

K

Kaz. Kazakh
Kir. Kirghiz
km kilometer(s)
km² square kilometer (singular)
Kor. Korean
Kurd. Kurdish

L

L. Lake
Lao. Laotian
Lapp. Lappish
Lat. Latin
Latv. Latvian
Liech. Liechtenstein
Lith. Lithuanian
Lux. Luxembourg

M

m million/meter(s)
Mac. Macedonian
Maced. Macedonia
Mal. Malay
Malg. Malagasy
Malt. Maltese
mi. mile(s)
mod. modern
Mong. Mongolian
Mt. Mountain
Mts Mountains

N

N. north
NAFTA North American Free Trade Agreement
Nep. Nepali
Neth. Netherlands
Nic. Nicaraguan
Nor. Norwegian
NZ New Zealand

O

off. officially/ official name

P

Pash. Pashtu
PNG Papua New Guinea
Pol. Polish
Poly. Polynesian
Port. Portuguese
prev. previously known as

R

r. ruled
Rep. Republic
Res. Reservoir
Rmsch Romansch
Rom. Romanian
Rus. Russian
Russ. Fed. Russian Federation

S

S. south
SCr. Serbo-Croatian
Sinh. Sinhala
Slvk. Slovak
Slvn. Slovene
Som. Somali
Sp. Spanish
St., St Saint
Strs Straits
Swa. Swahili
Swe. Swedish
Switz. Switzerland

T

Taj. Tajik
Th. Thai
Thai. Thailand
Tib. Tibetan
Turk. Turkish
Turkm. Turkmenistan

U

UAE United Arab Emirates
Uigh. Uighur
UK United Kingdom
Ukr. Ukrainian
UN United Nations
Urd. Urdu
US/USA United States of America
USSR Union of Soviet Socialist Republics
Uzb. Uzbek

V

var. variant
Vtn. Vietnamese

W

W. west
Wel. Welsh
WWI World War I
WWII World War II

Y

Yugo. Yugoslavia

This index lists all the place names and features shown on the maps in this Atlas.

Place name spelling

The policy followed throughout the Atlas is to use the contemporary historical name or spelling appropriate for the period or theme of the map. English conventional names, where they exist, have been used for international features e.g. oceans and country names.

All European language spellings use full diacritics, but no diacritics have been used for transliterated spellings (e.g. from Chinese or Cyrillic).

In translating Chinese names, the Pinyin system has been used throughout the Atlas, although alternative spelling systems have been cross-referred.

In spelling pre-Columbian Central and South American names, the later addition of Spanish accents has been avoided.

The index also contains commonly found alternative names and variant spellings, which are fully cross-referenced.

Index structure

All main entry names are those of settlements unless otherwise indicated by the use of italicized definitions.

In order to avoid unnecessary repetition, the names of frequently recurring states on the World Era Overview maps have been omitted. Those places which *only* appear on the World Era Overview maps have been included.

A

Aachen *anc.* Aquae Grani, Aquisgranum; *Dut.* Aken, *Fr.* Aix-la-Chapelle Central Europe (Germany) early modern states *193* (4) economy *190* (1) Franks *184* (2) medieval states *188* (1), (2) Reformation *195* (5) WWI *206* (3)
Aarhus *var.* Århus Scandinavia (Denmark) medieval states *185* (3)
Abadan *oil terminal* Southwest Asia (Iran) economy *234* (1)
Abai *see* Blue Nile
Abaj Takalik Central America (Mexico) first civilizations *121* (2)
Abancay South America (Peru) Incas *147* (3)
Abariringa *see* Canton Island
Abay Wenz *see* Blue Nile
Abbasid Caliphate *state* Southwest Asia early Islam *57* (2) medieval states *185* (3) Mongols *68–69* (1)
Abbeville France medieval states *192* (2)
Abdera Greece ancient Greece *177* (3) first civilizations *177* (1)
Abdera *settlement/state* Greece ancient Greece *177* (2)
Abéché *see* Abeshr
Abenaki *people* North America colonization *126* (1)
Abensberg *battle* Central Europe (Germany) Napoleon *200–201* (1)
Aberbrothock *see* Arbroath
Aberdeen *anc.* Devana British Isles (United Kingdom) medieval states *188* (2)
Abergwaun *see* Fishguard
Abertawe *see* Swansea
Aberteifi *see* Cardigan
Aberystwyth British Isles (Wales) medieval states *188* (2)
Abeshr *mod.* Abéché Central Africa (Chad) Islam *163* (1)
Abhiras *dynasty* South Asia first empires *241* (5) world religions *242* (2)
Abhisara *state* South Asia first empires *241* (5)
Abidjan West Africa (Ivory Coast) economy *168* (2)
Abina South Asia (India) medieval voyages *61* (3)
Abitibi *people* North America cultural groups *123* (3)
Abkhazia *region* Southwest Asia Soviet Union *214–215* (4)
Åbo Scandinavia (Finland) early modern states *195* (3) medieval states *189* (3)
Åbo *see* Surabaya
Abodrites *people* Central Europe Franks *184* (2)
Aboriginal Hunter-Gatherers of Australia *people* Australia the world in 2500 BCE *22–23* *see also* Australian Aborigines
Abu Dhabi *var.* Abū Ẓabī; *Ar.* Abū Ẓaby Southwest Asia (United Arab Emirates) 20th-century politics *233* (4) economy *234* (1) exploration *219* (4)
Abu Dulaf *congregational mosque* Southwest Asia (Iraq) early Islam *57* (3)
Abu Hurayrah *see* Abu Hureyra
Abu Hureyra *var.* Abu Hurayrah Southwest Asia (Syria) the world in 5000 BCE *18–19*
Abuja *state* West Africa the world in 1850 *90–91*
Abu Rawash Egypt ancient Egypt *159* (3)
Abu Salabikh Southwest Asia (Iraq) first cities *220* (2)
Abu Simbel *early food production site* Egypt early agriculture *158* (1)
Abusir Egypt ancient Egypt *159* (2), (3)
Abū Ẓabī *see* Abu Dhabi
Abū Ẓaby *see* Abu Dhabi
Abydos *var.* Abydus Egypt ancient Egypt *159* (2), (3), (4), (5) first cities *28–29* (1) first civilizations *24* (2)
Abydos *var.* Abydus *settlement/state* Southwest Asia (Turkey) ancient Greece *177* (2) first civilizations *177* (1)
Abydus *see* Abydos
Abyssinia *mod.* Ethiopia *state* East Africa 20th-century politics *233* (4) European imperialism *96* (1), *97* (4) trade *165* (3), *167* (1) WWII *104* (2) *see also* Ethiopia
Acachinamco Central America (Mexico) Aztecs *124* (3)
Acadia *mod.* Nova Scotia *region* North America the world in 1700 *82–83* *see also* Nova Scotia
Acalbixca Central America (Mexico) Aztecs *124* (2)
Acanceh Central America (Mexico) first civilizations *123* (2)
Acanthus *settlement/state* Greece ancient Greece *177* (2), (3)
Acapulco *var.* Acapulco de Juárez Central America (Mexico) European expansion *80–81* (1), *81* (3), *84–85* (1) exploration *143* (3) first civilizations *122* (1) US economy *136* (2)
Acapulco de Juárez *see* Acapulco
Acarí South America (Peru) Incas *147* (3)
Acarnania *state* Greece ancient Greece *179* (4)
Acatitla Central America (Mexico) Aztecs *124* (3)
Acatlan Central America (Mexico) first civilizations *122* (1)
Acayocan Central America (Mexico) Aztecs *124* (3)
Accho *see* Acco, Acre
Acco *mod.* 'Akko; *Bibl.* Accho, Ptolemaïs; *Eng.* Acre, *Fr.* Saint-Jean-d'Acre Southwest Asia (Israel) ancient Egypt *159* (5) *see also* Acre
Accra *var.* Fort James West Africa (Ghana) colonization *167* (4) economy *168* (2) empire and revolution *88* (1) slave trade *165* (4) trade *164* (2)
Acemhüyük Southwest Asia (Turkey) first cities *28–29* (1)
Achaea *see* Achaia
Achaean League *var.* Principality of Achaia *state* Greece the world in 250 BCE *38–39* *see also* Achaia
Achaia *var.* Achaea Greece ancient Greece *177* (3)
Achaia, Principality of *see* Achaean League
Achalapura South Asia (India) early medieval states *244* (2)
Acheh *see* Achin
Achin *var.* Acheh, Atchin, Atjeh; *mod.* Aceh Maritime Southeast Asia (Indonesia) colonialism *247* (4) early medieval states *245* (6) Soviet Union *214–215* (4)
Achin *mod.* Aceh; *prev.* Acheh, Atjeh *region/state* Maritime Southeast Asia colonialism *247* (4) early medieval states *245* (6) European imperialism *97* (3) postwar politics *253* (4) trade *267* (3)
Acigöl Southwest Asia (Turkey) early agriculture *220* (1)
Acolapissa *people* North America colonization *126* (1)
Acolhuacan *state* Central America Aztecs *124* (1)
Acolman Central America (Mexico) Aztecs *124* (2)
Acoma *people* North America colonization *126* (1)
Açores *see* Azores
Açores, Arquipélago dos *see* Azores
Açores, Ilhas dos *see* Azores
Acragas Italy first civilizations *177* (1)
Acre *mod.* 'Akko; *prev.* Acco; *Bibl.* Accho, Ptolemaïs; *Fr.* Saint-Jean-d'Acre Southwest Asia (Israel) crusades *228* (2), *65* (3) economy *190* (1) exploration *219* (3) medieval states *187* (5) Mongols *229* (3), *68* (2) Napoleon *200–201* (1) *see also* Acco
Acre *state* South America empire and revolution *151* (3)
Acropolis *temple* Greece ancient Greece *177* (4)
Acrothooi *state* Greece ancient Greece *177* (2)
Actaeon Islands *island group* Pacific Ocean exploration *278* (1)
Actium *Gk.* Aktion Greece the world in 1 CE *42–43*
Acton *battle* North America (USA) the growth of the US *129* (2)
Adab Southwest Asia (Iraq) first cities *220* (2) first civilizations *24* (3)
Adal *state* East Africa Islam *163* (1) trade *165* (3)
Adalia *mod.* Antalya; *prev.* Attalia; *anc.* Attaleia Southwest Asia (Turkey) 20th-century politics *233* (3) crusades *65* (3), *64–65* (2) *see also* Attalia
Adamawa *region* West Africa Islam *167* (3)
Adamawa Highlands *Mountain range* West Africa economy *163* (2)
Adamello *mountain* Italy WWI *207* (5)
Adamstown Pacific Ocean (Pitcairn Islands) decolonization *285* (3)
'Adan *see* Aden, Eudaemon Arabia
Adana *var.* Seyhan Southwest Asia (Turkey) 20th-century politics *233* (3) early Islam *56–57* (1) Ottomans *230* (1)
Adare, Cape *headland* Antarctica Antarctic Exploration *287* (3)
Ad Dawḩah *see* Doha
Addis Ababa *Amh.* Ādīs Ābeba East Africa (Ethiopia) colonization *167* (4) economy *168* (2)
Adelaide Australia colonization *282* (1), (2), *283* (3), *284–285* (1) exploration *279* (2), (3) imperial global economy *92* (1) prehistoric culture *17* (5)
Adélie, Terre *physical region* Antarctica Antarctic Exploration *287* (3)
Adelong *goldfield* Australia colonization *282* (2)
Aden *var.* Eudaemon Arabia; *Ar.* 'Adan, *Chin.* A-tan Southwest Asia (Yemen) ancient trade *44–45* (1) biological diffusion *72–73* (1) early Islam *56–57* (1), *57* (2) European expansion *84–85* (1) exploration *156* (3), *219* (4) imperial global economy *92* (1) Islam *163* (1), *226* (2), *227* (4) medieval voyages *61* (3) Mongols *68* (2) Ottomans *231* (3) trade *230* (2), *267* (3) 20th-century politics *233* (4) *see also* Eudaemon Arabia
Adena North America (USA) first religions *36* (1)
Adena *burial mound* North America (USA) first civilizations *121* (4)
Adena/Hopewell Culture *people* North America the world in 250 BCE *38–39* the world in 1 CE *42–43*
Adena Park *burial mound* North America (USA) first civilizations *121* (4)
Aden, Gulf of *var.* Badyarada 'Adméd *gulf* Southwest Asia early agriculture *158* (1) early cultures *161* (3), (4), (5) early trade *225* (3) economy *163* (2), (3) exploration *218* (2) Islam *163* (1) Ottomans *231* (3) slave trade *165* (4) Timur *229* (4) trade *165* (3), *230* (2) 20th-century politics *233* (4)
Aden Protectorate *colonial possession/state* Southwest Asia 20th-century politics *233* (4) Cold War *109* (1) WWII *104* (1)
Adige *Ger.* Etsch *river* Italy WWI *207* (5)
Ādīs Ābeba *see* Addis Ababa
Admiralty Island *island* North America exploration *278* (1)
Admiralty Islands *island group* Pacific Ocean early cultures *280–281* (3) medieval voyages *60* (2) WWII *272* (1), *273* (2)
Adobe Walls *battle* North America (USA) the growth of the US *129* (2)
Adrar Bous West Africa (Niger) early agriculture *158* (1)
Adrar Tioueïne North Africa (Algeria) early agriculture *158* (1)
Adria *see* Hadria
Adrianople *mod.* Edirne; *anc.* Adrianopolis, Hadrianopolis *Christian archbishopric/settlement* Southwest Asia (Turkey) crusades *64–65* (2) medieval states *187* (5), *189* (4) Ottomans *195* (4), *230* (1), *231* (3) Reformation *194* (2) world religions *48* (1) WWI *207* (6) *see also* Adrianopolis, Edirne, Hadrianopolis
Adrianopolis *Eng.* Adrianople, *Turk.* Edirne Southwest Asia (Turkey) ancient Rome *182* (1) *see also* Adrianople, Edirne
Adrianopolis *battle* Southwest Asia (Turkey) great migrations *52–53* (1)
Adriatic Sea *sea* Southeast Europe ancient Rome *179* (3) Bronze Age *175* (3) Copper Age *174* (2) early agriculture *174* (1) early modern states *193* (4) early states *178* (1), (2) economy *190* (1) empire and revolution *202* (3) first civilizations *177* (1) interwar *209* (3), (5) medieval states *183* (4), *187* (5), *188* (1), *189* (4) Ottomans *230* (1) postwar economy *213* (5), *214* (2), *215* (3) postwar politics *212* (3) Reformation *194* (2) WWI *207* (5), (6)
Adulis *settlement/state* East Africa (Eritrea) ancient trade *44* (2), *44–45* (1) early cultures *160* (1), *161* (3), (4), (5) early trade *225* (3)
Adventure Bay *bay* Australia exploration *278* (1)
Adwuku West Africa (Ghana) early agriculture *158* (1)
Adygeya *region* Eastern Europe Soviet Union *214–215* (4)
Aegae Greece Hellenistic world *40–41* (1)
Aegates *mod.* Isole Egadi *island group* Italy ancient Rome *179* (3)
Aegean Sea *Gk.* Aigaíon Pélagos, Aigaío Pélagos, *Turk.* Ege Denizi *sea* Greece ancient Greece *177* (2), (3), *179* (4) Bronze Age *175* (3) early agriculture *174* (1) economy *190* (1) first civilizations *175* (4), *177* (1) medieval states *187* (5), *189* (4) Ottomans *197* (4), *230* (1) Reformation *194* (2) WWI *207* (6) WWII *210* (1), *211* (4) 20th-century politics *233* (3)
Aegina *var.* Aíyina, Egina *settlement/state* Greece ancient Greece *177* (2) first civilizations *175* (4)
Aegospotami *battle* Southwest Asia (Turkey) ancient Greece *177* (3)
Aegyptus *province* North Africa ancient Rome *180–181* (1) ancient trade *44* (2)
Aelana Southwest Asia (Jordan) early cultures *161* (2), (3), (4), (5)
Aelaniticus, Sinus *see* Aqaba, Gulf of
Aelia Capitolina *see* Jerusalem
Aemona *see* Ljubljana
Aenea Greece ancient Greece *177* (2)
Aenus Greece first civilizations *177* (1)
Aenus *state* Greece ancient Greece *177* (2)
Aequi *people* Italy early states *178* (1), (2)
Aesernia *mod.* Isernia Italy early states *178* (1)
Aethiopia *region* East Africa ancient trade *44* (2)
Aetolia *region* Greece Hellenistic world *40–41* (1)
Afalou Bou Rhummel North Africa (Algeria) the world in 10,000 BCE *14–15*
Afars and Issas, French Territory of the *mod.* Djibouti; *prev.* French Somaliland *state* East Africa the world in 1975 *106–107* *see also* Djibouti, French Somaliland
Afghanistan *region/state* Central Asia Cold War *109* (1) colonialism *248* (1), (2), *269* (3), (4) Communism *271* (8) decolonization *250* (1), *251* (4) economy *249* (4) empire and revolution *249* (3) historical geography *275* (5) Islam *227* (4) medieval Persia *231* (4) Ottomans *232–233* (1) postwar economy *253* (5) postwar politics *252* (1), *253* (4) Soviet Union *208* (2), *213* (4) the world in 1950 *102–103* the modern world *113* (3), (4) US superpower *138* (1) world religions *226* (1), *243* (4) WWII *251* (3) 20th century *234* (2)
Afikpo *early food production site* West Africa (Nigeria) early agriculture *158* (1)
Africa *continent* *154-169* **Africa, Exarchate of** *state* North Africa medieval states *183* (4)
Africa, Horn of *physical region* East Africa European expansion *84–85* (1) slave trade *165* (4) trade *165* (3)
Africa Nova *province* North Africa early cultures *161* (2)
Afuddo *mod.* Nimule East Africa (Sudan) exploration *157* (4), (5)
Afyeh *early food production site* Egypt early agriculture *158* (1)
Agadès *see* Agadez
Agadez *prev.* Agadès West Africa (Niger) colonization *167* (4) early agriculture *158* (1) economy *163* (2) exploration *157* (4) Islam *163* (1)
Agadir North Africa (Morocco) exploration *157* (4)
Agana Pacific Ocean (Guam) decolonization *285* (3)
Agartala South Asia (India) postwar politics *252* (1), (3)
Agatha *see* Agathe
Agathe *var.* Agatha; *mod.* Agde France first civilizations *177* (1)
Agde *see* Agathe
Agendicum *see* Sens
Aggassiz, Lake *lake* North America the world in 10,000 BCE *14–15*
Aghlabids *dynasty* North Africa early Islam *57* (2) Islam *227* (4)
Agincourt *battle* France medieval states *192* (2)
Aginsky Buryat Ad *autonomous region* Siberia (Russian Federation) Soviet Union *214–215* (4)
Agordat *early food site* East Africa (Eritrea) early agriculture *158* (1)
Agra South Asia (India) colonialism *248* (1) early medieval states *244–245* (3) economy *249* (4) Mughal Empire *246* (1) postwar economy *253* (5) trade *267* (3)
Agra *state* South Asia Mughal Empire *246* (1)
Agra and Oudh, United Provinces of *see* Uttar Pradesh
Agram *see* Zagreb, Zágráb
Agri Decumates *region* Central Europe ancient Rome *181* (4)
Agrigento *see* Agrigentum
Agrigentum *mod.* Agrigento Italy ancient Rome *179* (3), *180–181* (1) first religions *37* (3)
Aguada South America (Colombia) early cultures *146* (1)
Aguascalientes Central America (Mexico) Mexican Revolution *133* (3)
Agulhas, Cape *Afr.* Kaap Agulhas *headland* South Africa European imperialism *96* (2)
Agulhas, Kaap *see* Agulhas, Cape
Ahaggar *mountain range* North Africa ancient trade *44–45* (1) early cultures *160* (1) economy *163* (2) first humans *13* (2) historical geography *154–155* (1)
Ahe *island* Pacific Ocean exploration *278* (1)
Ahicchatra *religious site* South Asia (India) first religions *36* (2)
Ah Kin Chel *state* Central America Aztecs *124* (1)
Ahmad *oil terminal* Southwest Asia (Kuwait) economy *234* (1)
Ahmadābād *see* Ahmadabad
Ahmadnagar *var.* Ahmednagar South Asia (India) Mughal Empire *246* (1)
Ahmadnagar *state* South Asia early medieval states *245* (4) Mughal Empire *246* (1)
Ahmedabad *var.* Ahmadābād South Asia (India) colonialism *247* (3), *248* (1) decolonization *250* (1) economy *249* (4) imperial global economy *93* (5) postwar economy *253* (5)
Ahmednagar *see* Ahmadnagar
Ahoms *dynasty* South Asia early medieval states *244–245* (3) Mughal Empire *246* (1)
Ahtena *people* North America cultural groups *123* (3)
Ahteut North America (USA) cultural groups *123* (3)
Ahu Akahanga *archaeological site* Pacific Ocean (Eastern Island) early cultures *281* (4)
Ahu 'Akivi *archaeological site* Pacific Ocean (Eastern Island) early cultures *281* (4)
Ahuehuetlan Central America (Mexico) Aztecs *124* (3)
Ahuilizapan Central America (Mexico) colonization *125* (5)
Ahu Ra'ai *archaeological site* Pacific Ocean (Eastern Island) early cultures *281* (4)
Ahu Tongariki *archaeological site* Pacific Ocean (Eastern Island) early cultures *281* (4)
Ahu Vinapu *archaeological site* South America (Chile) early cultures *281* (4)
Aichi *var.* Aiti *prefecture* Japan economy *270* (1)
Aigaíon Pélagos *see* Aegean Sea
Aigaío Pélagos *see* Aegean Sea
Aigues-Mortes France crusades *64–65* (2)
Aigun *see* Aihun
Aihun *var.* Aigun East Asia (China) colonialism *269* (4)
Ai Khanoum *see* Alexandria ad Oxum
Aikudi South Asia (India) early medieval states *244* (1)
Aila *var.* Elath; *mod.* Eilat, Elat Southwest Asia (Israel) medieval voyages *61* (3) *see also* Eilat, Elath
Ailah Southwest Asia (Israel) crusades *65* (3)
Ain Jalut *battle* Southwest Asia (Israel) Mongols *229* (3), *68–69* (1)
Ainu *people* Japan early modern states *265* (5) medieval states *262–263* (1), (2), *265* (3) trade *267* (3)
Air *state* West Africa slave trade *165* (4)
Airgialla *state* British Isles medieval states *188* (2)
Ais *people* North America colonization *125* (4), *126* (1)
Aisne *river* France WWI *206* (2), (3)
Aiti *see* Aichi
Aix-en-Provence France early modern states *197* (5)
Aix-la-Chapelle *see* Aachen
Aíyina *see* Aegina
Aizawl South Asia (India) postwar politics *252* (1)
Aizu Japan early modern states *267* (4)
Ajanta *Buddhist center/settlement* South Asia (India) first religions *36* (2) world religions *49* (3)
Ajayameru *var.* Ajmer, Ajmere South Asia (India) early medieval states *244* (2) world religions *243* (4) *see also* Ajmer
Ajdabiya North Africa (Libya) early Islam *56–57* (1)
Ajman Southwest Asia (United Arab Emirates) first civilizations *24* (3)
Ajmer *var.* Ajayameru, Ajmere South Asia (India) colonialism *247* (3) Mughal Empire *246* (1) *see also* Ajayameru
Ajmer *var.* Ajmere *state* South Asia colonialism *248* (2) Mughal Empire *246* (1)
Ajmere *see* Ajmer, Ajayameru
Ajnadain Southwest Asia (Israel) Islam *226* (2)
Ajnadain *battle* Southwest Asia (Israel) early Islam *56–57* (1)
Ajodhya South Asia (India) Mughal Empire *246* (1)
Akaba *see* Aelana, Aqaba
Akamagaseki *see* Shimonoseki
Akan States *state* West Africa Islam *163* (1) trade *164* (2)
Akaroa New Zealand colonization *283* (5)
Akbarpur South Asia (India) colonialism *247* (3)
Aken *see* Aachen
Akermanceaster *see* Bath
Akhaura South Asia (Bangladesh) postwar politics *252* (3)
Akhenaten Egypt ancient Egypt *159* (5)
Akhetaten *var.* Tell el-Amarna Egypt ancient Egypt *159* (5)
Akhisar *see* Thyatira
Akhmim *var.* Ipu Egypt ancient Egypt *159* (5)
Akira *early food production site* East Africa (Kenya) early agriculture *158* (1)
Akita Japan economy *270* (1) medieval states *264* (2), *265* (3), (4)
Akita *prefecture* Japan economy *270* (1)
Akjoujt *prev.* Fort-Repoux West Africa (Mauritania) early agriculture *158* (1)
Akkad Southwest Asia (Iraq) the world in 1250 BCE *26–27*
Akkad *state* Southwest Asia first civilizations *221* (4)
Akkerman Eastern Europe (Ukraine) Ottomans *195* (4)
'Akko *see* Acco, Acre

INDEX-GAZETTEER: **Aquisgranum – Bactria**

ancient Rome 180–181 (1) see also Buda, Budapest
Aquisgranum see Aachen
Aquitaine mod. Guyenne; anc. Aquitania region France Franks 183 (6), 184 (2) medieval states 187 (4) see also Aquitania, Guyenne
Aquitania province France ancient Rome 180–181 (1)
Arabia region Southwest Asia ancient Persia 223 (4) ancient Rome 180–181 (1) ancient trade 44 (2) crusades 65 (1) exploration 156 (3), 157 (4), 218 (1), (2), 219 (3), (4), 239 (1) Islam 226 (2), 227 (4), (5) medieval voyages 61 (3) Mongols 68 (2) the modern world 113 (4) world religions 226 (1)
Arabian Desert var. Aş flairá' ash Sharqíyah; Eng. Eastern Desert desert Egypt ancient Egypt 159 (2), (3), (5) early agriculture 220 (1) early trade 225 (3) first cities 220 (2) first civilizations 221 (4) see also Eastern Desert
Arabian Peninsula physical region Southwest Asia ancient Egypt 159 (5) ancient Persia 223 (4) biological diffusion 72–73 (1) early agriculture 20–21 (2) early cultures 160 (1), 161 (3) early Islam 57 (2) early systems 223 (3) economy 163 (2) first civilizations 222 (2) Hellenistic world 41 (2) imperial global economy 92 (1) Islam 163 (1) medieval Persia 231 (4) medieval states 261 (6) Ottomans 231 (3), 232–233 (1) prehistoric culture 16 (1) slave trade 165 (4) trade 165 (3), 230 (2), 267 (3) world religions 49 (4) WWI 233 (2)
Arabian Sea var. Sinus Arabicus sea Indian Ocean ancient Persia 225 (6) ancient trade 44–45 (1) biological diffusion 72–73 (1) colonialism 247 (3), 248 (1), (2) decolonization 251 (4) early agriculture 20–21 (2) early Islam 57 (2) early medieval states 244 (1), 244–245 (3) early religions 48 (2) early trade 225 (3) economy 249 (4) empire and revolution 249 (3), 88–89 (2) exploration 156 (3), 218 (1), (2), 219 (4), 239 (1) first cities 28–29 (1) first civilizations 24 (2), 25 (3) first religions 36 (2) Hellenistic world 224 (1) historical geography 236–237 (1), 275 (5) Islam 227 (4) Marathas 246 (2) medieval states 261 (6) medieval voyages 61 (3) Mongols 229 (3), 68–69 (1) postwar economy 253 (5) postwar politics 252 (1) Timur 229 (4) trade 230 (2) world religions 243 (4), 49 (3) WWII 251 (3) see also Arabicus, Sinus
Arabicus, Sinus sea Indian Ocean ancient trade 44 (2)
'Arab, Khalīj al see Persian Gulf
Arabs people North Africa ancient Rome 181 (4), 182 (1) ancient trade 44–45 (1) historical geography 275 (5) medieval states 182 (2) Ottomans 232–233 (1)
Aracaju South America (Brazil) politics 152 (1)
Arachosia region South Asia ancient Persia 223 (4) first empires 241 (4) Hellenistic world 224 (1)
Aradus Fr. Rouad; Bibl. Arvad; later Arwad Southwest Asia (Lebanon) first civilizations 177 (1) Hellenistic world 40–41 (1)
Arafura Sea Ind. Laut Arafuru sea Southeast Asia Bronze Age 240 (3) colonization 282 (1), 283 (3) European imperialism 97 (3) exploration 279 (2) Islam 243 (6) world religions 243 (5) WWII 272 (1), 273 (2)
Arafuru, Laut see Arafura Sea
Arago archaeological site Iberian Peninsula (France) first humans 13 (2)
Aragon Sp. Aragón state Iberian Peninsula crusades 186 (1), 64–65 (2) early modern states 194 (1) Islam 192 (3) medieval states 187 (3), (4), 192 (1), (2) Reformation 196 (2)
Araguaia var. Araguaya, Río Araguaia river South America colonization 149 (3) early cultures 144 (1), 145 (2) environment 153 (4)
Araguaia, Río see Araguaia
Araguaya see Araguaia
Arakan prev. Candra state Mainland Southeast Asia colonialism 269 (4) early medieval states 245 (6) Mughal Empire 246 (1) see also Candra
Araks var. Aras Nehri river Southwest Asia first civilizations 24 (2), 25 (3)
Aral Sea Kaz. Aral Tengizi, Rus. Aral'skoye More, Uzb. Orol Dengizi inland sea Central Asia ancient Persia 225 (6) ancient trade 44–45 (1) colonialism 269 (3) Communism 271 (8) early Islam 56–57 (1), 57 (2) exploration 172 (1), 218 (2), 219 (3), 256 (1) first humans 13 (2) global knowledge 76–77 (1) Hellenistic world 224 (1) historical geography 275 (5) Islam 226 (2), 227 (4) medieval states 261 (6), 262–263 (1) Mongols 68 (2), 68–69 (1) Ottomans 232–233 (1) Seljuks 228 (1) Soviet Union 208 (2), 213 (4) Timur 229 (4) trade 230 (2), 267 (3) world religions 226 (1), 49 (3), (4)
Aral'skoye More see Aral Sea
Aral Tengizi see Aral Sea
Araluen goldfield Australia colonization 282 (2)
Aram var. Syria state Southwest Asia first civilizations 222 (1) see also Syria
Aramaeans people Southwest Asia first civilizations 221 (5)
Aram-Damascus state Southwest Asia first civilizations 222 (1)
Aramis hominid site Central Africa (Chad) first humans 12 (1)
Aram-Zobah state Southwest Asia first civilizations 222 (1)
Araouane Lake lake West Africa historical geography 154–155 (1)
Ara Pacis building Italy ancient Rome 181 (2)
Arapaho people North America colonization 126 (1)
Araquinoid people South America the world in 500 CE 50–51 the world in 1000 58–59 the world in 1300 66–67
Ararat goldfield Australia colonization 282 (2)
Arash battle Southwest Asia (Azerbaijan) medieval Persia 231 (4)
Aras Nehri see Araks
Araucanians people South America early cultures 147 (2)
Arausio mod. Orange church council France world religions 48 (1) see also Orange
Aravaipa Apache people North America colonization 125 (4)
Aravali Range mountain range South Asia colonialism 247 (3), 248 (1) early medieval states 244 (1), 244–245 (3) first cities 240 (2) Mughal Empire 246 (1) world religions 243 (4)
Arawak people West Indies colonization 125 (4)
Arawe Islands island group New Guinea early cultures 280–281 (3) medieval voyages 60 (2)
Araxes river Southwest Asia Hellenistic world 40–41 (1)
Arbela var. Erbil, Irbīl; mod. Arbīl; Kurd. Hawlēr Christian archbishopric/settlement Southwest Asia (Iraq) exploration 218 (1) Hellenistic world 40–41 (1) world religions 48 (1) see also Arbil
Arbela battle Southwest Asia (Turkey) ancient Rome 224 (2)
Arbil Southwest Asia (Iraq) 20th-century politics 235 (5)
Arbroath anc. Aberbrothock British Isles (United Kingdom) medieval states 188 (2)
Archangel Rus. Arkhangel'sk Eastern Europe (Russian Federation) economy 205 (4) European expansion 80–81 (1) exploration 257 (2), 286 (1), 287 (2) Soviet Union 208 (2), 213 (4) WWII 210 (1), 211 (4) see also Arkhangel'sk
Arcola battle Italy Napoleon 200–201 (1)
Arcot South Asia (India) colonialism 248 (1)
Arctic region North America early agriculture 120 (1) exploration 286-287
Arctic hunter-gatherers people Eastern Europe/Siberia/North America the world in 1250 BCE 26–27
Arctic Ocean ocean biological diffusion 73 (2) cultural groups 123 (3) early agriculture 120 (1) empire and revolution 88 (1), 88–89 (2) European expansion 80–81 (1), 81 (2) exploration 257 (2), 286 (1), 287 (2) first humans 13 (2) global immigration 100 (1) medieval states 185 (3), 262–263 (1) Soviet Union 208 (2), 213 (4) the growth of the US 129 (2), 132 (1), 133 (4) US superpower 138 (1) WWII 104 (1), (2), 105 (3), 211 (4) Cold War 109 (1) colonialism 269 (3)
Arcy-sur-Cure archaeological site France prehistoric culture 17 (3)
Ardabil Southwest Asia (Iran) early Islam 56–57 (1) Islam 226 (2), 227 (4) medieval Persia 231 (4) medieval states 185 (3)
Ardea Italy early states 178 (1)
Ardeal see Transylvania
Ardennes battle Low Countries (Belgium) WWII 105 (3)
Ardennes physical region Low Countries (Belgium) WWI 206 (2), (3) WWII 211 (4)
Ardwick British Isles economy 204 (2)
Arelas see Arelate, Arles
Arelate mod. Arles Christian archbishopric/settlement France ancient Rome 180–181 (1) world religions 48 (1) see also Arles
Arene Candide Italy early agriculture 174 (1)
Areopagus building Greece ancient Greece 177 (4)
Arequipa South America (Peru) colonization 148 (2) empire and revolution 151 (3) environment 153 (4) politics 151 (4)
Ares, Temple of temple Greece ancient Greece 177 (4)
Arezzo anc. Arretium settlement/university Italy economy 190 (1) medieval states 187 (3) see also Arretium
Argentina prev. Argentine Confederation state South America empire and revolution 151 (3) environment 153 (4) global immigration 100 (1), 101 (2) imperial global economy 92 (1) narcotics 153 (5) politics 151 (4), 152 (1), (2) the growth of the US 133 (4) the modern world 112 (1), 113 (4) US superpower 138 (1) WWII 105 (3) Cold War 109 (1) economy 153 (3) see also Argentine Confederation
Argentine Confederation mod. Argentina state South America the world in 1850 90–91 see also Argentina
Argentoratum mod. Strasbourg legion headquarters/mithraic site France ancient Rome 180–181 (1) world religions 48 (1) see alsoStrasbourg, Strassburg
Argeş battle Southeast Europe (Romania) WWI 207 (6)
Argesh Southeast Europe (Romania) Ottomans 230 (1)
Argilus state Greece ancient Greece 177 (2)
Arginusae Insulae see Arginusae Islands
Arginusae Islands Lat. Arginusae Insulae battle Greece ancient Greece 177 (3)
Argissa Greece early agriculture 174 (1)
Argonne France WWI 206 (2), (3)
Argos Greece ancient Greece 177 (3), 179 (4) first civilizations 175 (4), 177 (1)
Arguin West Africa (Mauritania) European expansion 84–85 (1)
Arguin Island island West Indies the world in 1500 74–75 the world in 1600 78–79 the world in 1700 82–83 the world in 1800 86–87 the world in 1850 90–91
Århus see Aarhus
Aria province/region Central Asia ancient Persia 223 (4) ancient trade 44 (2) Hellenistic world 40–41 (1)
Aria see Alexandria Areion, Herat
Arica prev. San Marcos de Arica South America (Chile) colonization 148 (2) empire and revolution 150 (1), 151 (3) environment 153 (4) European expansion 81 (3) politics 151 (4)
Arica battle South America (Chile) politics 151 (4)
Aricara battle North America (USA) the growth of the US 129 (2)
Aricia Italy early states 178 (1)
Arīḩā see Jericho
Arikara people North America colonization 126 (1)
Ariminum mod. Rimini Italy ancient Rome 179 (3), 180–181 (1) early states 178 (1), (2) world religions 48 (1) see also Rimini
Arisbe settlement/state Southwest Asia (Turkey) ancient Greece 177 (2)
Aristé people South America the world in 1300 66–67
Arizona region/state North America Mexican Revolution 133 (3) the growth of the US 129 (1) US economy 134 (2)
Arizpe fort Central America (Mexico) colonization 125 (4)
Arkansas region North America imperial global economy 93 (5) the growth of the US 129 (1) US Civil War 130 (2), 130 (3), (4), (5), 131 (6), (7) US economy 134 (2), 139 (3) US society 137 (6) US superpower 139 (5)
Arkansas river North America colonization 125 (4), 126 (1) cultural groups 122 (5) exploration 118 (1), 119 (2) first civilizations 121 (4) the growth of the US 129 (2) US Civil War 131 (6)
Arkat mod. Arcot South Asia (India) Mughal Empire 246 (1) see also Arcot
Arkhangel'sk Eng. Archangel Eastern Europe (Russian Federation) Cold War 108 (3) Soviet Union 214–215 (4) see also Archangel
Arles var. Arles-sur-Rhône; anc. Arelas, Arelate France economy 190 (1) Franks 183 (5), (6), 184 (2) medieval states 188 (1) see also Arelate
Arles, Kingdom of state Central Europe/France medieval states 188 (1)
Arles-sur-Rhône see Arelate, Arles
Arlit West Africa (Niger) early agriculture 158 (1)
Armagaon South Asia (India) colonialism 247 (3)
Armagnac region France medieval states 192 (2)
Armant anc. Hermonthis Egypt ancient Egypt 159 (2), (4), (5)
Armenia prev. Armenian Soviet Socialist Republic; anc. Urartu; Arm. Hayastan region/state Southwest Asia ancient Persia 223 (4), 225 (6) ancient Rome 180–181 (1), 181 (3), (4), 224 (2), 225 (5) ancient trade 44 (2), 44–45 (1) crusades 65 (3) early Islam 56–57 (1) economy 234 (1) Hellenistic world 224 (1) Islam 226 (2), 227 (4), (5), 235 (4) medieval Persia 231 (4) medieval states 185 (3), 187 (5) Ottomans 232–233 (1) postwar economy 214 (2) Soviet Union 208 (2), 214–215 (4) world religions 226 (1) WWI 233 (2) 20th-century politics 233 (3) see also Armenian Soviet Socialist republic, Urartu
Armenian Rulers state Southwest Asia Seljuks 228 (1)
Armenians people Southwest Asia Ottomans 232–233 (1)
Armenian Soviet Socialist Republic state Southwest Asia 20th-century politics 233 (3)
Armstrong region North America first civilizations 121 (4)
Arnhem Low Countries (Netherlands) WWII 211 (4)
Arno see Arnus
Arnus mod. Arno river Italy early states 178 (1)
Aromata East Africa (Somalia) ancient trade 44–45 (1)
Arpi Italy early states 178 (1)
Arras anc. Nemetocenna France early modern states 197 (5) economy 190 (1) empire and revolution 199 (4) medieval states 192 (2) Reformation 195 (5) WWI 206 (2), (3)
Arretium mod. Arezzo Italy ancient Rome 180–181 (1) early states 178 (1), (2) first civilizations 177 (1) see also Arezzo
Arriaca see Guadalajara
Ar Riyāḑ see Riyadh
Arroyo Sonso archaeological site Central America (Mexico) first civilizations 121 (3)
Ar Rub 'al Khali Eng. Empty Quarter, Great Sandy Desert desert southwest Asia exploration 219 (4) historical geography 170–171 (1) 20th-century politics 233 (4)
Ar Rutbah var. Rutba Southwest Asia (Iraq) 20th-century politics 235 (5)
Arsenal var. Darsena building Italy economy 191 (3)
Arsur battle Southwest Asia (Israel) crusades 65 (3)
Arta anc. Ambracia Greece medieval states 189 (4) see also Ambracia
Artacoana Central Asia (Afghanistan) Hellenistic world 40–41 (1)
Artashat Christian patriarchate Southwest Asia (Armenia) world religions 48 (1)
Artemita Southwest Asia (Iraq) Hellenistic world 41 (2)
Artois region France medieval states 192 (2) Reformation 195 (5)
Arua people South America the world in 1400 70–71
Aruaki people South America early cultures 147 (2)
Aruba island West Indies the world in 1800 86–87 the world in 1850 90–91 the modern world 110–111
Aru Islands island Maritime Southeast Asia exploration 239 (2)
Arumvale Australia the World in 10,000 BCE 14–15
Arunachal Pradesh prev. North East Frontier Agency region South Asia postwar economy 275 (3) postwar politics 252 (1)
Arvac people South America the world in 1500 74–75 the world in 1600 78–79 the world in 1700 82–83
Arvad see Aradus
Arvand Rūd see Shatt al 'Arab Waterway
Arverni people France ancient Rome 179 (5)
Arwad see Aradus
Aryan people South Asia ancient India 242 (1)
Asab Ar. Al 'Aşab oil field Southwest Asia economy 234 (1)
Asabon Southwest Asia (Oman) ancient trade 44–45 (1)
Asahikawa Japan economy 270 (1)
Asaku Japan medieval states 264 (1)
Asante var. Ashanti state West Africa colonization 167 (4) slave trade 165 (4) trade 167 (1)
Ascalon mod. Ashqelon Southwest Asia (Israel) ancient Egypt 159 (5) crusades 64–65 (2), 65 (3)
Ascension island Atlantic Ocean exploration 156 (3)
Ascensión Central America (Mexico) Mexican Revolution 133 (3)
Ascension Island see Pohnpei, Ponape
Ascoli Satriano see Asculum
Asculum mod. Ascoli Satriano Italy early states 178 (1)
Asejire West Africa (Nigeria) early agriculture 158 (1)
Ashanti see Asante
A Shau battle Mainland Southeast Asia (Vietnam) postwar politics 251 (5)
Ashburton New Zealand colonization 283 (5)
Ashburton River river Australia prehistoric culture 17 (5) colonization 282 (1) exploration 279 (2)
Ashgabat prev. Poltoratsk, earlier Ashkhabad Central Asia (Turkmenistan) Soviet Union 214–215 (4) see also shkhabad
Ashkhabad mod. Ashgabat; prev. Poltoratsk Central Asia (Turkmenistan) colonialism 269 (3) see also Ashgabat
Ashmaka region South Asia ancient India 242 (1) world religions 242 (2)
Ashmore and Cartier Islands colonial possession Indian Ocean global immigration 100 (1)
Ashqelon see Ascalon
Ash Shām see Damascus
Ash Shāriqah see Sharjah
ash Sharqīyah, Aş Şaḩrā' see Arabian Desert, Eastern Desert
Ashur Southwest Asia (Iraq) early systems 223 (3) first cities 220 (2) first civilizations 221 (4), 222 (2), 25 (3)
Asia continent 216-255 ancient trade 44–45 (1) biological diffusion 73 (3) crusades 65 (1) early agriculture 20–21 (2) early Islam 56–57 (1), 57 (2) early systems 32 (1), 33 (2), (3) empire and revolution 88 (1) European expansion 80–81 (1), 81 (2), (3) European imperialism 96 (1) exploration 156 (3), 172 (1), (2), 219 (3), 287 (2) first humans 13 (2) first religions 36 (1) global immigration 100 (1), 101 (3) historical geography 154–155 (1) imperial global economy 93 (2) Ottomans 232–233 (1) trade 230 (2), 267 (3) world religions 49 (4)
Asia province Southwest Asia ancient Rome 179 (5), 180–181 (1)
Asiago Italy WWI 207 (5)
Asia Minor region Southwest Asia ancient Rome 224 (2) ancient trade 44–45 (1) biological diffusion 72–73 (1) crusades 65 (1) early systems 223 (3) exploration 172 (1) Islam 226 (2), 227 (5) Ottomans 231 (3) world religions 226 (1), 49 (4)
Asiana province Southwest Asia ancient Rome 181 (4)
Asir state Southwest Asia the world in 1925 98–99
Asir Ar. 'Asīr mountain range Southwest Asia 20th-century politics 233 (4) exploration 219 (4)
Asmaka region/state South Asia first empires 241 (5) first religions 36 (2)
Asmara East Africa (Eritrea) economy 168 (2) politics 169 (4)
Aspadana see Isfahan
Aspern-Essling battle Central Europe (Germany) Napoleon 200–201 (1)
Aspero early ceremonial center/settlement South America (Peru) early cultures 144 (1)
Asphaltites, Lacus see Dead Sea
Aspinwall see Colón
Assam region/state South Asia colonialism 248 (2), 269 (4) decolonization 250 (2) early modern states 266 (1) economy 249 (4) Mughal Empire 246 (1) postwar politics 252 (1), (3), 253 (4)
Assamese States state South Asia the world in 1500 74–75 the world in 1600 78–79
Assassins people Southwest Asia crusades 65 (3)
Assiniboin people North America colonization 126 (1)
Assinie West Africa (Ivory Coast) the world in 1700 82–83
Assiout see Asyut
Assisi Italy medieval states 187 (3)
Assiut see Asyut
Asslou see Bir Aslu
Assos settlement/state Southwest Asia (Turkey) ancient Greece 177 (2)
Assouan see Aswân, Qus, Syene
Assuan see Aswân, Qus, Syene
Assus Southwest Asia (Turkey) first civilizations 177 (1)
As Suways see Suez
Assyria province Southwest Asia ancient Persia 223 (4)
Asta Colonia see Asti
Astacus settlement/state Southwest Asia (Turkey) ancient Greece 177 (2)
Astana Buddhist center East Asia (China) world religions 49 (3)
Asta Pompeia see Asti
Asti anc. Asta Colonia, Asta Pompeia, Hasta Colonia, Hasta Pompeia Italy economy 190 (1), 190–191
Astrakhan Eastern Europe (Russian Federation) colonialism 269 (3) exploration 219 (3) Ottomans 231 (3) Soviet Union 208 (2), 213 (4) Timur 229 (4) trade 267 (3)
Astrakhan, Khanate of state Central Asia/Eastern Europe Islam 163 (1) trade 267 (3)
Astures people Iberian Peninsula ancient Rome 179 (5)
Asturias state Iberian Peninsula Franks 184 (2) Islam 184 (1)
Asturias see Oviedo
Asturica Iberian Peninsula (Spain) ancient Rome 180–181 (1)
Astypalaea settlement/state Greece ancient Greece 177 (2)
Asuka Japan medieval states 264 (2)
Asuka region Japan medieval states 265 (3)
Asunción South America (Paraguay) colonization 148 (2) empire and revolution 150 (1) environment 153 (4) exploration 143 (2) politics 152 (1), (2)
Asuncion Mita Central America (Mexico) first civilizations 123 (2)
Asuristan state Southwest Asia ancient Persia 225 (6)
Aswân var. Assouan, Assuan, Qus; anc. Syene Egypt crusades 228 (2) early Islam 56–57 (1) economy 168 (2) Mongols 229 (3) see also Qus, Syene
Asyut var. Assiout, Assiut, Sauty, Siut; anc. Lycopolis Egypt ancient Egypt 159 (3), (4), (5) exploration 157 (5) first cities 28–29 (1) Islam 235 (4) see also Sauty
Atacama region/state South America politics 151 (4) the world in 250 BCE 38–39
Atacama people South America early cultures 147 (2)
Atacama Desert Eng. Desierto de Atacama desert South America early cultures 144 (1), 145 (2) empire and revolution 150 (1), 151 (3) Incas 147 (3) politics 151 (4)
Atacama, Desierto de see Atacama Desert
Atacama, San Pedro de South America (Chile) early cultures 146 (1)
Atakapa people Central America colonization 125 (4), 126 (1)
A-tan see Aden, Eudaemon Arabia
Atapuerca archaeological site Iberian Peninsula (Spain) first humans 13 (2)
Atarco South America (Peru) early cultures 146 (1)
Atazta Central America (Mexico) first civilizations 122 (1)
Atbara var. 'Aţbārah East Africa (Sudan) exploration 157 (5)
Atbara var. Nahr 'Aţbārah river East Africa exploration 157 (5)
'Aţbārah see Atbara
'Aţbarah, Nahr see Atbara
Atchin see Aceh, Achin
Aten Temple var. Aton building Egypt first cities 29 (5)
Atepehuacan Central America (Mexico) Aztecs 124 (3)
Atepetla Central America (Mexico) Aztecs 124 (3)
Atgram South Asia (Bangladesh) postwar politics 252 (3)
Athabasca var. Athabaska river North America the growth of the US 129 (2)
Athabasca, Lake lake North America colonization 126 (1) early agriculture 120 (1) exploration 119 (3), 286 (1) the growth of the US 129 (2)
Athabaska see Athabasca
Athenae see Athens
Athena, Temple of temple Greece ancient Greece 177 (4)
Athens prev. Athínai, anc. Athenae; Gk. Athína Greece ancient Greece 177 (3), 179 (4) ancient Persia 223 (4) ancient Rome 179 (5), 180–181 (1), 181 (3), (4), 182 (1) biological diffusion 72–73 (1) Cold War 108 (3) early systems 32 (1), 33 (2), (3) economy 205 (4) empire and revolution 202 (1) exploration 172 (1) first cities 28–29 (1) first civilizations 175 (4), 177 (1) first religions 36 (1) great migrations 52–53 (1) Hellenistic world 224 (1) interwar 209 (3) Islam 226 (2) medieval states 182 (2), 185 (3), 187 (5), 189 (4) Napoleon 200–201 (1), 201 (2), (3) Ottomans 202 (4), 230 (1) postwar politics 212 (3) world religions 48 (1) WWII 210 (1), 211 (2), (4)
Athens state Greece medieval states 187 (5), 189 (4)
Athesis river Italy early states 178 (2)
Athína see Athens
Athínai see Athens
Athr Southwest Asia (Saudi Arabia) early Islam 56–57 (1) medieval voyages 61 (3)
Athribis Egypt first cities 28–29 (1)
Atico South America (Peru) Incas 147 (3)
Atitlan, Lago de lake Central America first civilizations 123 (2)
Atjeh see Achin
Atlacomulco Central America (Mexico) first civilizations 122 (1)
Atlacuihuayan Central America (Mexico) Aztecs 124 (2), (3)
Atlan state Central America Aztecs 124 (1)
Atlanta North America (USA) the growth of the US 129 (2), 132 (1) US Civil War 130 (5), 131 (7) US economy 134 (1) US politics 135 (6) US society 137 (6)
Atlanta battle North America (USA) US Civil War 131 (7)
Atlantic and Pacific Railroad railroad North America the growth of the US 129 (2)
Atlantic Ocean Port. Oceano Atlântico ocean ancient trade 44–45 (1) biological diffusion 72–73 (1), 73 (2), (3) colonization 125 (4), 126 (1), 148 (2), 149 (3), (4) empire and revolution 127 (2), (3), 150 (1), 151 (3), 202 (1), 88–89 (2) environment 153 (4) European expansion 80–81 (1), 81 (2), (3), 84–85 (1), 85 (2) European imperialism 96 (1), (2), 97 (4) exploration 118 (1), 119 (2), (3), 142 (1), 143 (2), (3), 156 (1), (2), (3), 172 (1), (2), 286 (1), 287 (2) global immigration 100 (1), 101 (2), (3) global knowledge 76 (1), (2), 76–77 (1), 77 (5) great migrations 52–53 (1), 53 (2) imperial global economy 92 (1), 93 (2) interwar 209 (3) medieval voyages 60–61 (1) politics 152 (1) postwar economy 213 (5) post-war politics 212 (3) slave trade 165 (4) the growth of the US 129 (2), 132 (1), 133 (4) the world in 1300 66–67 trade 163 (4), (5), (6), (7), 164 (2), 167 (1) US Civil War 131 (6), (7) US economy 138 (2) US superpower 138 (1) WWI 208 (1) WWII 104 (1), (2), 105 (3), (4), 210 (1), 211 (2), (4) see also Occidental, Oceanus
Atlapulco Central America (Mexico) Aztecs 124 (2)
Atlas Mountains mountain range North Africa ancient Rome 180–181 (1) ancient trade 44–45 (1) biological diffusion 72–73 (1) Bronze Age 175 (3) crusades 64–65 (2) early agriculture 174 (1) early cultures 160 (1), 161 (2) early Islam 56–57 (1), 57 (2) economy 163 (2) global knowledge 76–77 (1) Islam 163 (1) medieval states 182 (2) Ottomans 232–233 (1) slave trade 165 (4) WWII 210 (1), 211 (4)
Atlatonco Central America (Mexico) Aztecs 124 (2)
Atlazolpa Central America (Mexico) Aztecs 124 (3)
Atlixio Central America (Mexico) colonization 125 (5)
Atomata major port/settlement East Africa (Somalia) early trade 225 (3)
Aton see Aten Temple
Atontonilco state Central America Aztecs 124 (1)
Atoyac Central America (Mexico) Aztecs 124 (3)
Atoyac river North America colonization 125 (5)
Atsugashi-yama battle Japan early modern states 265 (5)
Attaleia see Adalia, Attalia
Attalia later Adalia; mod. Antalya; anc. Attaleia Southwest Asia (Turkey) ancient Rome 180–181 (1) Hellenistic world 41 (2) see also Adalia
Attica region Greece ancient Greece 177 (2)
Attigny France Franks 184 (2)
Attikamek people North America colonization 126 (1)
Attu island North America WWII 272 (1), 273 (2)
Atwetwebooso archaeological site West Africa (Ghana) early cultures 160 (1)
Atzacualco Central America (Mexico) Aztecs 124 (3)
Atzalan North America (USA) cultural groups 122 (5)
Atzcapotzalco see Azcapotzalco
Auberoche France medieval states 192 (1)
Auch France early modern states 197 (5)
Auckland New Zealand colonization 283 (4), (5), 284–285 (1) decolonization 285 (3) environmentalism 285 (2) exploration 279 (3)
Auckland region New Zealand colonization 283 (5)
Auckland Islands island group New Zealand decolonization 285 (3) exploration 276–277 (1)
Auerstedt see Jena Auerstädt
Augila var. Awjilah North Africa (Libya) Islam 163 (1)
Augsbourg see Augsburg
Augsburg anc. Augusta Vindelicorum; Fr. Augsbourg Central Europe (Germany) biological diffusion 72–73 (1) crusades 186 (1) economy 190 (1) Franks 184 (2) medieval states 188 (1) Reformation 194 (2) see also Augusta Vindelicorum
Augusta North America (USA) empire and revolution 127 (3) the growth of the US 129 (2) US Civil War 131 (7)
Augusta battle North America (USA) empire and revolution 127 (3)
Augusta see London, Londinium
Augusta Suessionum see Soissons
Augusta Taurinorum mod. Torino; Eng. Turin Italy great migrations 52–53 (1)
Augusta Treverorum mod. Trier, Eng. Treves, Fr. Trèves Central Europe (Germany) ancient Rome 180–181 (1), 181 (3), (4) ancient trade 44 (2), 44–45 (1) great migrations 52–53 (1) world religions 48 (1) see also Trier
Augusta Vangionum see Worms
Augusta Vindelicorum mod. Augsburg Central Europe (Germany) ancient Rome 180–181 (1) see also Augsburg
Augustobona Tricassium see Troyes
Augustodunum mod. Autun France ancient Rome 180–181 (1)
Augustodurum see Bayeux
Augustoritum Lemovicensium see Limoges
Augustus, Mausoleum of building Italy ancient Rome 181 (2)
Aupaga region South Asia world religions 242 (2)
Auraitis cultural region Southwest Asia ancient Rome 225 (4)
Aurelianum see Orléans
Aurelia, Via road Italy ancient Rome 181 (2) early states 178 (1)
Aurunci people Italy early states 178 (2)
Auschwitz-Birkenau concentration camp Central Europe WWII 211 (3)
Ausculum Italy early states 178 (1)
Aussa state East Africa the world in 1600 78–79
Austerlitz Central Europe (Austria) Napolean 200-201 the world in 1850 90–91
Austin North America (USA) the growth of the US 129 (2), 132 (1)
Australia prev. Australian Colonies, New Holland state Australia early agriculture 20–21 (2) early cultures 280–281 (3) environmentalism 285 (2) European expansion 80–81 (1) exploration 276–277 (1), 279 (2), (3) first humans 13 (2) global immigration 100 (1), 101 (3) historical geography 254–255 (1) imperial global economy 92 (1), 93 (2) medieval voyages 60 (2) the growth of the US 133 (4) US economy 138 (2) US superpower 138 (1) WWII 104 (1), 105 (4), 251 (3), 272 (1), 273 (2) Cold War 109 (1) colonization 282 (1) decolonization 251 (4), 285 (3) see also Australian Colonies
Australian Aborigines people Australia the world in 750 BCE 30–31 passim
Australian Colonies mod. Australia; prev. New Holland colonial possession Australia the world in 1850 90–91 the world in 1900 94–95 see also Australia
Austral Islands island group Pacific Ocean colonization 284–285 (1) early cultures 280–281 (3) environmentalism 285 (2) exploration 279 (3) medieval voyages 60 (2)
Austrasia region Central Europe Franks 183 (6), 184 (2)
Austria Ger. Österreich region/state Central Europe early modern states 193 (4), (5), 194 (1) empire and revolution 198 (2), 199 (3), 202 (2) interwar 209 (3), (5) medieval states 183 (4), 188 (1), 189 (4) Napoleon 200–201 (1) postwar economy 213 (5), 214 (1), (2), 215 (3) postwar politics 212 (1), (3) Reformation 196 (1), (2) Soviet Union 213 (4) the modern world 112 (2), 113 (3) WWI 208 (1) WWII 210 (1), 211 (2), (3), (4) Cold War 108 (3)
Austria-Hungary state Central Europe economy 205 (4) global immigration 100 (1) imperial global economy 92 (1) WWI 207 (6)
Austrian Empire state Central Europe/Eastern Europe empire and revolution 202 (1) Napoleon 201 (2) Ottomans 232–233 (1)
Austrian Habsburg Possessions state Central Europe Reformation 194 (2)
Austrian Netherlands vassal state Low Countries empire and revolution 199 (3), (4)
Austro-Hungarian Empire state Central Europe empire and revolution 202 (3) Ottomans 202 (4) WWI 207 (4), (5) early 20th century 206 (1)
Autun see Augustodunum
Auvergne region France Franks 183 (6) medieval states 192 (1)
Ava Mainland Southeast Asia (Burma) colonialism 247 (4), 248 (1) early medieval states 245 (6) world religions 243 (5)
Ava region/state Mainland Southeast Asia Mughal Empire 246 (1) trade 267 (3)
Avalites East Africa (Djibouti) ancient trade 44–45 (1) early cultures 161 (3), (4), (5) early trade 225 (3)
Avanti South Asia (India) early religions 48 (2)
Avanti region/state South Asia ancient India 242 (1) early religions 48 (2) first religions 36 (2) world religions 242 (2)
Avar Empire state Central Europe early Islam 56–57 (1) medieval states 182 (2)
Avaricum see Bourges
Avaris Egypt ancient Egypt 159 (4)
Avars people Eastern Europe Franks 184 (2) medieval states 182 (2)
Avarua Pacific Ocean (Cook Islands) decolonization 285 (3)
Avebury archaeological site British Isles (United Kingdom) Copper Age 174 (2)
Avenio see Avignon
Aventine Hill Lat. Mons Aventinus hill Italy ancient Rome 181 (2)
Aventinus, Mons see Aventine Hill
Aversa Italy economy 190 (1)
Avignon anc. Avenio settlement/university France crusades 186 (1) early modern states 193 (4), 197 (5) economy 190 (1) Franks 183 (5), 184 (2) medieval states 187 (3), (4), 88 (1), (2) Reformation 194 (2)
Avignon anc. Avenio state France empire and revolution 199 (4)
Awadh state South Asia Mughal Empire 246 (1)
Awazu battle Japan early modern states 265 (5)
Awdaghost West Africa (Mauritania) Islam 163 (1) trade 163 (4), (5), (6), (7)
Awjilah see Augila
Axim West Africa (Ghana) exploration 156 (3) slave trade 165 (4) trade 164 (2)
Axiós see Vardar
Axocopan state Central America Aztecs 124 (1)
Axotla Central America (Mexico) Aztecs 124 (3)
Axum East Africa (Ethiopia) ancient trade 44–45 (1) early cultures 160 (1), 161 (3), (4), (5) early trade 225 (3) world religions 49 (4)
Axum state East Africa ancient trade 44–45 (1) early cultures 160 (1), 161 (3), (4), (5) Islam 226 (2) world religions 226 (1), 49 (4)
Ayacucho South America (Peru) Incas 148 (1) narcotics 153 (5)
Ayacucho battle South America (Peru) empire and revolution 150 (1), 88–89 (2)
Ayacucho Valley South America (Peru) the world in 5000 BCE 18–19
Ayas see Laias
Ayaviri South America (Peru) Incas 147 (3)
Aydhab Egypt biological diffusion 72–73 (1) Islam 163 (1)
Ayeyarwady see Irrawaddy
Ayodhya South Asia (India) early medieval states 244 (1) early religions 48 (2) first religions 36 (2) Mughal Empire 246 (1)
Ayotzinco Central America (Mexico) colonization 125 (5)
Ayr British Isles (United Kingdom) economy 204 (1)
Ayuthia see Ayutthaya
Ayutla Central America (Mexico) Aztecs 124 (1)
Ayutthaya var. Ayuthia, Phra Nakhon Si Ayutthaya settlement/temple Mainland Southeast Asia (Thailand) early medieval states 245 (6) Marathas 246 (2) trade 267 (3) world religions 243 (5)
Ayyubid Sultanate state Egypt/North Africa/Southwest Asia crusades 65 (3) medieval states 187 (5) Mongols 68–69 (1)
Azad Kashmir region South Asia postwar politics 252 (1), (2)
Azak see Azov
Azärbaycan see Azerbaijan
Azcapotzalco var. Atzcapotzalco Central America (Mexico) Aztecs 124 (2), (3) first civilizations 122 (1)
Azerbaijan Az. Azärbaycan region Central Asia economy 234 (1) Islam 227 (4) medieval Persia 231 (4) postwar economy 214 (2) Soviet Union 208 (2), 213 (4) the modern world 113 (3) WWI 233 (2)
Azerbaijani Republic see Azerbaijan
Azeri people Southwest Asia Islam 275 (5)
Azimabad see Patna
Azores Port. Açores, Ilhas dos Açores, Arquipélago dos Açores island group Atlantic Ocean Cold War 109 (1) European expansion 80–81 (1) US superpower 138 (1) WWII 104 (2)
Azov Turk. Azak Eastern Europe (Ukraine) Ottomans 197 (4), 231 (3)
Azov, Sea of sea Eastern Europe Ottomans 202 (4), 230 (1), 231 (3) WWI 207 (4)
Azraq, Bahr El see Blue Nile
Aztec Empire state Central America the world in 1500 74–75 , 76 (2), 124-125
Aztecs people Central America colonization 126 (1)
'Azza see Gaza
Az Zāb al Kabīr see Great Zab
Aẓ Ẓahran see Dhahran

B

Ba var. Pa province/region East Asia first religions 37 (4) first states 260 (1)
Ba people East Asia first cities 259 (4)
Ba see Pegu
Baalbek var. Ba'labakk; anc. Heliopolis Lebanon Southwest Asia (Lebanon) crusades 65 (3) first religions 37 (3) see also Heliopolis
Bab-i Sin East Asia (China) trade 230 (2)
Babi Yar massacre Eastern Europe WWII 211 (3)
Babylon Southwest Asia (Iraq) ancient Persia 223 (4), 225 (6) ancient Rome 224 (2), 225 (5) ancient trade 44 (2), 44–45 (1) early cultures 161 (3), (4), (5) early medieval states 244 (1) early systems 223 (3) early trade 225 (3) exploration 218 (1), (2) first civilizations 221 (4), (5), 222 (2) Hellenistic world 40–41 (1), 41 (2)
Babylonia province Southwest Asia ancient Persia 223 (4) first civilizations 221 (5), 222 (2) Hellenistic world 40–41 (1), 41 (2)
Bachíniva Central America (Mexico) Mexican Revolution 133 (3)
Back river North America exploration 287 (2)
Bactra var. Valhika, Zariaspa; mod. Balkh Buddhist center/settlement Central Asia (Afghanistan) ancient Persia 223 (4) ancient trade 44 (2), 44–45 (1) exploration 256 (1) first empires 241 (4) Hellenistic world 224 (1) medieval states 262–263 (1) world religions 49 (3), (4) see also Balkh, Valhika
Bactria region/state Central Asia ancient Persia 223 (4), 225 (6) ancient Rome 224 (2) ancient trade 44 (2), 44–45 (1) first empires 241 (4) Hellenistic world 224 (1)

INDEX-GAZETTEER: **Celebes Sea – Cold Harbor**

trade 267 (3) world religions 243 (5), 49 (4) WWII 251 (3), 272 (1), 273 (2)
Celebes Sea Ind. Laut Sulawesi sea Maritime Southeast Asia Bronze Age 240 (3) colonialism 247 (4) decolonization 251 (4) early medieval states 245 (6) European imperialism 97 (3) exploration 239 (1), (2) Islam 243 (6) postwar economy 253 (5) postwar politics 253 (4) world religions 243 (5)
Celenderis Southwest Asia (Turkey) first civilizations 177 (1)
Celestial Empire see China, Han Empire
Celtiberi see Celtiberians
Celtiberians Lat. Celtiberi people Iberian Peninsula ancient Rome 179 (5)
Celtic peoples people British Isles/France/Germany the world in 250 BCE 38–39 the world in 500CE 50–51
Celts people Western Europe ancient trade 44–45 (1) early systems 33 (3) first civilizations 177 (1) great migrations 53 (2) the world in 500 BCE 34–35
Cemenelium see Cemenelum
Cemenelum var. Cemenelium Italy ancient Rome 180–181 (1)
Cempoala Central America (Mexico) first civilizations 122 (1)
Cempohuallan Central America (Mexico) colonization 125 (5)
Central African Empire see Central African Republic
Central African Republic abbrev. CAR; prev. Central African Empire, Ubangi-Shari, Oubangui-Chari state Central Africa Cold War 109 (1) decolonization 168 (1) economy 168 (2), (3) Islam 235 (4) the modern world 112 (1), 113 (3) see also Ubangi-Shari
Central America region Central America first religions 36 (1) US economy 138 (2)
Central America, United Provinces of state Central America empire and revolution 88–89 (2)
Central Asia region Asia biological diffusion 73 (2)
Central Bihar region South Asia decolonization 250 (1)
Central India Agency state South Asia colonialism 248 (2)
Central Makran Range mountain range South Asia first cities 240 (2)
Central Overland Route wagon train route North America the growth of the US 129 (2)
Central Pacific Railroad railway North America global immigration 100 (1) the growth of the US 129 (2)
Central Provinces state South Asia colonialism 248 (2)
Central Siberian Plain plain Siberia exploration 257 (2)
Central Western Queensland archaeological site Australia prehistoric culture 17 (5)
Cephalonia island Greece ancient Greece 177 (3), 179 (4) Ottomans 230 (1)
Cer battle Southeast Europe (Yugoslavia) WWI 207 (6)
Ceram var. Serang, Pulau Seram, Seram island Maritime Southeast Asia colonialism 247 (4) early medieval states 245 (6) exploration 239 (1), (2) Islam 243 (6)
Ceramicus Cemetery Gr. Kerameikos Cemetery cemetery Greece ancient Greece 177 (4)
Ceram Sea var. Seram Sea; Ind. Laut Seram sea Maritime Southeast Asia early medieval states 245 (6) exploration 239 (2)
Ceras state South Asia Mongols 68–69 (1)
Cerdaña see Cerdagne
Ceres Sea sea Indian Ocean Islam 243 (6)
Ceribon see Cheribon
Cerignola battle Italy early modern states 194 (1)
Cerrillos South America (Peru) early cultures 145 (4)
Cerro Iberian Peninsula (Spain) Bronze Age 175 (3)
Cerro de la Bomba Central America (Mexico) first civilizations 121 (2)
Cerro de las Mesas region/settlement Central America first civilizations 121 (2), 122 (1)
Cerro Gordo Central America (Mexico) the growth of the US 129 (2)
Cerros Central America (Mexico) first civilizations 123 (2)
Cerro Sechín early ceremonial center South America (Peru) early cultures 144 (1), 145 (3)
Cerro Vicús South America (Peru) early cultures 145 (4)
Cerveteri see Caere
Cēsis see Wenden
Česká Republika see Czech Republic
Cetinje Southeast Europe (Yugoslavia) WWI 207 (6)
Ceuta var. Sebta North Africa (Spain/Morocco) biological diffusion 72–73 (1) economy 190 (1) Islam 192 (3)
Cévennes mountain range France early modern states 197 (5)
Ceylon var. Saylan, Sarandib; mod. Sri Lanka; Chin. Hsi-lan; anc. Taprobane, Simhala, Sinhala, Lambakannas, Lanka region/state/island South Asia biological diffusion 72–73 (1) colonialism 247 (3), 248 (1), (2) decolonization 250 (1), 251 (4) economy 249 (4) European expansion 84–85 (1) exploration 239 (1) global immigration 100 (1) Marathas 246 (2) Mongols 68 (2) Mughal Empire 246 (1) trade 230 (2), 267 (3) WWII 251 (3), 272 (1), 273 (2) see also Lambakannas, Lanka, Simhala, Sri Lanka, Taprobana
Ceyre to the Caribs see Marie Galante
Chacabuco battle South America (Chile) empire and revolution 150 (1), 88–89 (2)
Chacalapan see Chicolapan
Chachalacas Central America (Mexico) first civilizations 122 (1)
Chachas state South Asia early medieval states 244 (2)
Chaco region South America colonization 148 (2) exploration 143 (2)
Chaco Canyon archaeological site/settlement North America (USA) cultural groups 123 (4)
Chad Fr. Tchad state Central Africa decolonization 168 (1) economy 168 (2), (3) Islam 235 (4) the modern world 112 (1), 113 (3), (4)
Chadians people Central Africa/West Africa ancient trade 44–45 (1) early cultures 160 (1)
Chad, Lake Fr. Lac Tchad lake Central Africa ancient trade 44–45 (1) early cultures 160 (1) economy 163 (2)
European imperialism 96 (1) exploration 157 (4) first humans 12 (1), 13 (2) historical geography 154–155 (1) Islam 163 (1), 167 (3) slave trade 165 (4)
Chagai Hills mountain range South Asia first cities 240 (2)
Chagar Bazar Southwest Asia (Syria) first civilizations 221 (4)
Chagatai Khanate var. Khanate of Kashgar, Chagatayids state/region Central Asia/East Asia biological diffusion 72–73 (1) Mongols 229 (3), 68 (2) Timur 229 (4)
Chagatais people South Asia early medieval states 244–245 (3)
Chagatayids see Chagatai Khanate
Chagos Archipelago var. Chagos Islands; mod. British Indian Ocean Territory island group Indian Ocean the world in 1850 90–91 the world in 1900 94–95 the world in 1925 98–99 the world in 1950 102–103 see also British Indian Ocean Territory
Chagos Islands see British Indian Ocean Territory, Chagos Archipelago
Chahamanas state South Asia early medieval states 244 (2)
Chahar region East Asia postwar politics 271 (7)
Chahar people East Asia trade 267 (3)
Chakan state Central America Aztecs 124 (1)
Chakchiuma people Central America colonization 125 (4)
Chalandriani archaeological site Greece Copper Age 174 (2)
Chalcatzinco Central America (Mexico) first civilizations 121 (2), 122 (1)
Chalcedon Southwest Asia (Turkey) first civilizations 177 (1) world religions 226 (1)
Chalcedon state Greece ancient Greece 177 (2)
Chalchuapa Central America (El Salvador) first civilizations 121 (2)
Chalcis Southwest Asia (Syria) ancient Rome 225 (4)
Chalcis mod. Chalkída; var. Halkida; prev. Khalkís settlement/state Greece ancient Greece 177 (2), (3), 179 (4) first civilizations 177 (1)
Chalco Central America (Mexico) Aztecs 124 (2)
Chalco state Central America Aztecs 124 (1)
Chalco, Lake lake Central America Aztecs 124 (2)
Chaldiran see Çaldiran
Chalkída see Chalcis
Chalma Central America (Mexico) Aztecs 124 (3)
Chalna var. Pankhali South Asia (Bangladesh) postwar politics 252 (3)
Chalon France Franks 183 (5), (6), 184 (2)
Châlons France Franks 184 (2)
Châlons-sur-Marne France early modern states 197 (5) economy 190 (1) WWI 206 (3)
Chalon-sur-Saône anc. Cabillonum France economy 190 (1)
Chaluka North America (USA) cultural groups 123 (3)
Chalukyas people/state South Asia world religions 243 (4)
Chama Central America (Mexico) first civilizations 123 (2)
Chambal river South Asia colonialism 247 (3), 248 (2) decolonization 250 (1) early medieval states 244 (2), 244–245 (3) economy 249 (4) Marathas 246 (2) postwar politics 252 (1) world religions 242 (2), 243 (4)
Chambéry anc. Camberia France economy 190 (1)
Champa South Asia (India) early religions 48 (2)
Champa region/state Mainland Southeast Asia ancient India 241 (6) biological diffusion 72–73 (1) early medieval states 245 (5) first states 260 (1) medieval states 261 (6), 262–263 (1), 263 (6) Mongols 68–69 (1) trade 67 (3) world religions 243 (5), 49 (4)
Champagne region France economy 190 (1) medieval states 187 (4)
Champaran region South Asia decolonization 250 (1)
Champaubert battle France Napoleon 200–201 (1)
Champlain, Lake lake North America colonization 126 (1) empire and revolution 127 (2) exploration 119 (2)
Champutun state Central America Aztecs 124 (1)
Chams people Mainland Southeast Asia ancient trade 44–45 (1)
Chanca people South America early cultures 147 (2)
Chancay South America (Peru) early cultures 146 (1)
Chance North America (USA) cultural groups 122 (5)
Chancellorsville North America (USA) US Civil War 131 (6)
Chan Chan South America (Peru) early cultures 146 (1) Incas 147 (3)
Chandannagar prev. Chandernagore South Asia (India) postwar politics 252 (1) see also Chandernagore
Chandellas state South Asia early medieval states 244 (2)
Chandernagore colonial possession/settlement South Asia colonialism 247 (3), 248 (2), 269 (4) decolonization 251 (4) empire and revolution 88 (1) WWII 251 (3)
Chandigarh South Asia (India) postwar politics 252 (1)
Chandra state Mainland Southeast Asia ancient India 241 (6)
Chandragupta, Empire of state South Asia Hellenistic world 224 (1)
Chang'an var. Ch'ang-an East Asia (China) ancient trade 44–45 (1) exploration 256 (1) first religions 37 (4) first states 260 (1), 261 (2), (3) medieval states 261 (5), (6), 262–263 (1) world religions 49 (3), (4) see also Xi'an
Changbai East Asia (China) Cold War 109 (4)
Changchou see Changzhou
Changchun var. Ch'ang-ch'un; prev. Hsinking East Asia (China) imperialism 270 (2) Russo-Japanese War 270 (4)
Changchun battle East Asia (China) economy 274 (1) postwar politics 274 (2)
Changde East Asia (China) medieval states 263 (6)
Chang Jiang see Yangtze
Changle East Asia (China) trade 267 (3)
Changsha var. Ch'angsha, Ch'ang-sha East Asia (China) biological diffusion 72–73 (1) colonialism 269 (4) early modern states 268 (1) economy 274 (1) imperialism 270 (2) postwar politics 271 (7), 274 (2) world religions 49 (3) WWII 251 (3)
Changsha province East Asia first states 260 (1)
Changwu archaeological site East Asia (China) first humans 13 (2)
Changyang archaeological site East Asia (China) first humans 13 (2)
Changzhou var. Changchou East Asia (China) medieval states 262–263 (1)
Chanhu-Daro archaeological site/settlement South Asia (Pakistan) first cities 240 (2) first civilizations 24 (2)
Channel Islands Fr. Îles Normandes island group English Channel medieval states 186 (2)
Chantilly France WWI 206 (2), (3)
Chao see Zhao
Ch'ao-an see Chaozhou
Chaochow see Chaozhou
Chaoge vassal state East Asia first cities 259 (3)
Chaozhou var. Ch'ao-an; prev. Chaochow East Asia (China) medieval states 263 (5)
Chaplina, Mys Eng. Cape Chaplino headland Siberia exploration 257 (2)
Chaplino, Cape see Chaplina, Mys
Chapultepec Central America (Mexico) Aztecs 124 (2), (3) colonization 125 (5) first civilizations 122 (1)
Charax Southwest Asia (Iraq) ancient trade 44–45 (1) early cultures 161 (3), (4), (5) early trade 225 (3) Hellenistic world 41 (2)
Charay North Africa (Libya) ancient Rome 179 (3)
Charcas, Presidencia of region South America colonization 148 (2)
Charlemagne, Empire of state France Franks 184 (2)
Charleroi Low Countries (Belgium) WWI 206 (2), (3)
Charleston North America (USA) colonization 126 (1) empire and revolution 127 (3) European expansion 84–85 (1) imperial global economy 93 (5) the growth of the US 129 (2), 132 (1) US Civil War 130 (5), 131 (6), (7) US society 137 (6)
Charleston battle North America (USA) empire and revolution 127 (3)
Charleville Australia colonization 282 (1)
Charlotte North America (USA) empire and revolution 127 (3)
Charlottenburg Central Europe (Germany) postwar politics 212 (2)
Charlottesville North America (USA) empire and revolution 127 (3)
Charlottetown North America (Canada) the growth of the US 129 (2), 132 (1)
Charolais States state France early modern states 197 (5)
Charolles state France early modern states 194 (1)
Charsadda South Asia (Pakistan) first religions 36 (2) Hellenistic world 41 (2)
Chartres France medieval states 187 (3)
Chasniki Eastern Europe (Belorussia) early modern states 195 (3)
Château-Thierry France WWI 206 (2), (3)
Château-Thierry battle France Napoleon 200–201 (1)
Chatgaon mod. Chittagong; var. Ch¯attag¯am South Asia (Bangladesh) early medieval states 244–245 (3) Mughal Empire 246 (1) see also Chittagong
Chatgaon state South Asia Mughal Empire 246 (1)
Chatham British Isles (United Kingdom) economy 204 (1)
Chatham Islands island group Pacific Ocean decolonization 285 (3) early cultures 280–281 (3) medieval voyages 60 (2)
Chatot people Central America colonization 125 (4)
Chāttagām see Chatgaon, Chittagong
Chattahooochee river North America cultural groups 122 (5) US Civil War 131 (6)
Chattanooga North America (USA) US Civil War 131 (6), (7)
Chaul South Asia (India) colonialism 247 (3) early medieval states 245 (4) world religions 243 (4)
Chaulukyas dynasty South Asia Mongols 68–69 (1)
Chauri Chaura South Asia (India) decolonization 250 (1)
Chauvet archaeological site France prehistoric culture 17 (2)
Chavín state South America first religions 36 (1)
Chavín de Huantar early ceremonial center South America (Peru) early cultures 144 (1), 145 (3), (4) first religions 36 (1)
Chawasha people Central America colonization 125 (4)
Cheb see Eger
Chechen people Southwest Asia Soviet Union 213 (4)
Che-chiang see Zhejiang
Chechnya region Eastern Europe Soviet Union 214–215 (4)
Chedi var. Cedi region/state South Asia first empires 241 (5) first religions 36 (2)
Cheetham British Isles (United Kingdom) economy 204 (2)
Chefoo see Zhifu
Cheju-do prev. Quelpart; Jap. Saishū island East Asia Cold War 109 (4) early modern states 265 (5), 267 (4) medieval states 264 (1), (2) see also Quelpart
Chekiang see Zhejiang
Chełmno concentration camp Central Europe WWII 211 (3)
Chełmno see Kulm
Chelyabinsk Eastern Europe (Russian Federation) Soviet Union 214–215 (4)
Chelyuskin, Cape see Chelyuskin, Mys
Chelyuskin, Mys Eng. Cape Chelyuskin headland Siberia exploration 257 (2)
Chemin des Dames France WWI 206 (2), (3)
Chemulpo see Inchon
Chen East Asia (China) first cities 259 (5) first religions 37 (4)
Chen state East Asia medieval states 261 (5)
Chenab river South Asia colonialism 248 (1) early medieval states 244 (1) first cities 240 (2) Mughal Empire 246 (1) postwar politics 252 (2)
Ch'eng-chou, Chengchow see Zhengzhou
Chengdu var. Chengtu, Ch'eng-tu; prev. Shu East Asia (China) ancient trade 44–45 (1) biological diffusion 72–73 (1) colonialism 269 (4) early modern states 266 (1), (2), 268 (1) first states 260 (1), 261 (2) Islam 275 (4) medieval states 262–263 (1), 263 (3), (4), (5), (6) Mongols 68–69 (1) postwar economy 275 (3) postwar politics 274 (2) world religions 49 (3) WWII 272 (1), 273 (2)
Chenggao East Asia (China) first cities 259 (5)
Chenghsien see Zhengzhou
Chengtian rebellion East Asia early modern states 266 (2)
Ch'eng-tu, Chengtu see Chengdu
Chengziya archaeological site/settlement East Asia (China) early agriculture 258 (2)
Chenkiang see Zhenjiang
Chenla mod. Cambodia; prev. Funan, later Khmer, Kambujadesha state Mainland Southeast Asia ancient India 241 (6) world religions 49 (4) see also Cambodia, Funan, Kambujadesha, Khmer
Chenla and Empire of Funan see Chenla
Chennai see Madras
Cheraw North America (USA) empire and revolution 127 (3)
Cheraw people North America colonization 125 (4)
Cherbourg anc. Carusbur France early modern states 197 (5) medieval states 187 (4), 192 (1), (2) WWII 210 (1)
Cherchell see Caesarea, Iol
Cherchen Chin. Qiemo East Asia (China) biological diffusion 72–73 (1) first states 260 (1)
Cheribon mod. Ceribon; Dut. Tjeribon state Maritime Southeast Asia the world in 1600 78–79
Cherkess see Circassians
Chernigov Ukr. Chernihiv Eastern Europe (Ukraine) Mongols 68–69 (1)
Chernihiv see Chernigov
Chernobyl Eastern Europe (Ukraine) Soviet Union 214–215 (4)
Chernomen var. Maritsa battle Greece medieval states 189 (4)
Cherno More see Black Sea
Chernovaya archaeological site/settlement Siberia (Russian Federation) early agriculture 258 (1)
Chernoye More see Black Sea
Cherokee people North America colonization 125 (4), 126 (1)
Cherry Island see Anuta
Cherry Valley North America (USA) empire and revolution 127 (3)
Chersonesus state Greece ancient Greece 177 (2)
Chesapeake Bay inlet North America empire and revolution 127 (2), (3)
Cheshire region British Isles imperial global economy 93 (4)
Chesowanja archaeological site East Africa (Kenya) first humans 12 (1)
Chester hist. Legaceaster, Lat. Deva, Devana Castra; Wel. Caerleon British Isles (United Kingdom) economy 190 (1) medieval states 183 (3), 188 (2) see also Deva
Chester battle British Isles (United Kingdom) medieval states 183 (3)
Chesterfield canal British Isles economy 204 (1)
Chetiya region South Asia ancient India 242 (1) world religions 242 (3)
Chetwai South Asia (India) colonialism 247 (3)
Chevdar Southeast Europe (Bulgaria) early agriculture 174 (1)
Cheyenne North America (USA) the growth of the US 129 (2)
Cheyenne people North America colonization 126 (1)
Ch'i see Qi, Qi Empire
Chiaha people North America colonization 125 (4)
Chiang-hsi see Jiangxi
Chiang-ling see Jiangling
Chiang Mai see Chiengmai
Chiangnan Hsitao see Jiangnan Xidao
Chiang-su see Jiangsu
Chian-ning see Nanjing
Chiapa de Corzo Central America (Mexico) first civilizations 121 (2), 122 (1), 123 (2)
Chiapas state Central America Mexican Revolution 133 (3) the growth of the US 129 (2)
Chiauhtla Central America (Mexico) Aztecs 124 (2)
Chiba var. Tiba prefecture Japan economy 270 (1)
Chibcha people/state South America early cultures 147 (2)
Chibcha (Muisca) Chiefdoms state South America early cultures 146 (1)
Chicago North America (USA) exploration 119 (3) imperial global economy 92 (1) the growth of the US 129 (2), 132 (1) the modern world 113 (4) US Civil War 130 (5) US economy 134 (1), (3), 136 (2) US politics 135 (6)
Chicama archaeological site South America (Peru) early cultures 145 (3)
Chichén Itzá Central America (Mexico) Aztecs 124 (1) first civilizations 123 (2) first religions 36 (1)
Chichou see Jizhou
Chickamauga North America (USA) US Civil War 131 (7)
Chickamauga var. Chickamanga Creek battle North America (USA) US Civil War 131 (7)
Chickasaw people North America colonization 125 (4), 126 (1)
Chiclayo South America (Peru) environment 153 (4) narcotics 153 (5)
Chicolapan var. Chacalapan Central America (Mexico) Aztecs 124 (2)
Chiconauhtla Central America (Mexico) Aztecs 124 (2)
Chien-Chung see Jianzhong
Chiengmai var. Chiangmai, Kiangmai; mod. Chiang Mai Mainland Southeast Asia (Thailand) colonialism 247 (4), 248 (1) exploration 239 (1) world religions 243 (5)
Chiengmai var. Chiangmai, Kiangmai; mod. Chiang Mai state Mainland Southeast Asia the world in 1300 66–67 the world in 1400 70–71 the world in 1500 74–75 the world in 1700 82–83
Chien-k'ang see Jiankang
Chiennan see Jiannan
Chien-yeh see Jianye, Nanjing
Chihli see Zhili
Chihuahua Central America (Mexico) Mexican Revolution 133 (3)
Chihuahua state Central America Mexican Revolution 133 (3) the growth of the US 129 (2)
Chihuahua battle Central America (Mexico) the growth of the US 129 (2)
Chihuahua Desert desert North America/Central America cultural groups 123 (4)
Chikinchel state Central America Aztecs 124 (1)
Chilca South America (Peru) the world in 2500 BCE 22–23
Chilcotin people North America cultural groups 123 (3)
Children's Crusade crusade Central Europe crusades 186 (1)
Chile state South America economy 153 (3) empire and revolution 150 (1), 151 (3), 88–89 (2) environment 153 (4) global immigration 100 (1), 101 (2) imperial global economy 92 (1) narcotics 153 (5) politics 151 (4), 152 (1) the growth of the US 133 (4) the modern world 112 (1), 113 (4) US superpower 138 (1) WWII 105 (3) Cold War 109 (1)
Chile, Captaincy-General and Presidencia of region South America colonization 148 (2)
Chilecito South America (Argentina) empire and revolution 151 (3) Incas 147 (3)
Chi-lin see Jilin, Kirin
Chillon river South America early cultures 145 (3)
Chiloé, Isla de var. Isla Grande de Chiloé island South America European expansion 80–81 (1) exploration 143 (3)
Chimalhuacan Central America (Mexico) Aztecs 124 (2)
Chimbote South America (Peru) environment 153 (4)
Chimú people/state South America early cultures 147 (2)
Chin state East Asia medieval states 263 (3)
China var. People's Republic of China; prev. Cathay, Sinae, Qing Empire region/state East Asia ancient trade 44–45 (1) biological diffusion 72–73 (1) Chinese revolution 271 (5) early medieval states 245 (5) early systems 32 (1), 33 (2), (3) economy 274 (1) empire and revolution 88 (1) European expansion 84–85 (1) exploration 257 (3) first humans 13 (2) first religions 36 (1), 37 (4) global immigration 100 (1), 101 (2), (3) global knowledge 77 (6) imperial global economy 92 (1) imperialism 270 (2) Islam 235 (4) medieval states 261 (6), 264 (2) medieval voyages 61 (3) Mongols 68 (2) postwar economy 253 (5), 275 (3) postwar politics 251 (5), 252 (1), 253 (4), 274 (2) Soviet Union 208 (2), 213 (4) the growth of the US 133 (4) the modern world 113 (3), (4) world religions 243 (5), 49 (3), (4) WWII 104 (2), 105 (4), 251 (3), 272 (1), 273 (2) Cold War 109 (1), (4) colonization 284–285 (1) Communism 271 (8) decolonization 250 (1), 251 (4), 285 (3) see also Cathay, Qing Empire, Sinae
Chi-nan see Jinan
China, People's Republic of see China
China, Republic of var. Formosa, Formo'sa; mod. Taiwan state East Asia the world in 1950 102–103 see also Taiwan
Chincha, Islas de island group South America empire and revolution 151 (3)
Chin-ch'ang see Jinchang
Chin-ch'uan see Jinchuan
Chindaka-Nagas dynasty South Asia Mongols 68–69 (1)
Chingchi see Jingji
Ch'ing Hai see Qinghai, Hu
Chinghai see Qinghai
Ching-nan state East Asia medieval states 263 (3)
Ch'ing-tao see Qingdao, Tsingtao
Chinkiang see Zhenjiang
Chinkultic Central America (Mexico) first civilizations 123 (2)
Chinmen Tao see Quemoy
Chinnereth see Galilee, Sea of
Chinon France medieval states 192 (2)
Chinsura prev. Chunchura South Asia (India) colonialism 247 (3)
Chin-t'ien see Jintian
Chinwangtao see Qinhuangdao
Chioggia anc. Fossa Claudia Italy economy 190 (1)
Chios var. Hios, Khíos; It. Scio, Turk. Sakiz-Adasi settlement/island Greece ancient Greece 177 (2), (3), 179 (4) first civilizations 175 (4), 177 (1)
Chipata Southern Africa (Malawi) early cultures 160 (1)
Chipewyan people North America colonization 126 (1) cultural groups 123 (3)
Chippewa, Lake lake North America the world in 10,000 BCE 14–15
Chiquihuitillo Central America (Mexico) first civilizations 122 (1)
Chiquito people South America early cultures 147 (2)
Chiquitos region South America colonization 148 (2) exploration 143 (2)
Chiquitoy South America (Peru) Incas 147 (3)
Chirand South Asia (India) the world in 2500 BCE 22–23
Chire see Shire
Chiricahua Apache people North America colonization 125 (4)
Chiripa archaeological site South America (Bolivia) early cultures 144 (1)
Chishima-rettō see Kurile Islands
Chisholm Trail wagon train route North America the growth of the US 129 (2)
Chita Siberia (Russian Federation) colonialism 269 (3) Communism 271 (8) Soviet Union 208 (2)
Chitambo East Africa (Zambia) exploration 157 (4)
Chitato Southern Africa (Angola) Cold War 109 (5)
Chitimacha people Central America/North America colonization 125 (4), 126 (1)
Chitor South Asia (India) early medieval states 244–245 (3) Mughal Empire 246 (1)
Chittagong prev. Chatgaon; Ben. Chāttagām South Asia (Bangladesh) biological diffusion 72–73 (1) colonialism 247 (3), 248 (1) decolonization 250 (1) exploration 239 (1) postwar economy 253 (5) postwar politics 252 (3) trade 230 (2), 267 (3) WWII 251 (3) see also Chatgaon
Chittagong Hills region South Asia postwar politics 253 (4)
Chiusi see Clusium
Chkalov see Orenburg
Chocola Central America (Mexico) first civilizations 123 (2)
Choctaw people North America colonization 125 (4), 126 (1)
Chocuan state Central America Aztecs 124 (1)
Choga Mami Southwest Asia (Iraq) early agriculture 220 (1)
Choga Mish Southwest Asia (Iran) first cities 220 (2)
Chogwe East Africa (Tanzania) exploration 157 (4)
Chokai-zan mountain Japan medieval states 265 (3)
Chokwe var. Cokwe people/state Central Africa/Southern Africa colonization 167 (4) trade 167 (1)
Cholas region/state South Asia ancient trade 44–45 (1) early medieval states 244 (2) Mongols 68–69 (1) world religions 242 (2)
Cholm see Kholm
Cholollan Central America (Mexico) colonization 125 (5)
Cholula Central America (Mexico) first civilizations 122 (1)
Chondwe archaeological site Southern Africa (Zambia) early cultures 160 (1)
Chongjin East Asia (North Korea) Cold War 109 (4)
Chongoyapa archaeological site South America (Peru) early cultures 145 (3)
Chongqing var. Ch'ung-ch'ing, Chungking, Pahsien, Yuzhou East Asia (China) biological diffusion 72–73 (1) colonialism 269 (4) early modern states 266 (2), 268 (1) economy 274 (1) Islam 275 (4) medieval states 263 (6) postwar politics 271 (7), 274 (2) WWII 251 (3), 272 (1), 273 (2)
Chonju region East Asia medieval states 264 (2)
Chonos Archipelago island group South America exploration 143 (3)
Chopani-Mando South Asia (India) the world in 5000 BCE 18–19
Chorasmia province Central Asia ancient Persia 223 (4)
Chorlton British Isles (United Kingdom) economy 204 (2)
Chorne More see Black Sea
Chorrera archaeological site/settlement South America (Ecuador) early cultures 144 (1)
Chosan East Asia (North Korea) Cold War 109 (4)
Chōsen see Choson, Korea, Koryo, Silla
Chōsen-kaikyō see Korea Strait
Choshi Jap. Chōshi bomb target Japan Communism 273 (3)
Choson var. Chosen; later Silla; mod. Korea; Koryo state East Asia the world in 250 BCE 38–39 see also Korea, Silla, Koryo
Chotuna South America (Peru) early cultures 146 (1)
Christchurch New Zealand colonization 283 (4), (5) decolonization 285 (3)
Christiania var. Kristiania, mod. Oslo Scandinavia (Norway) early modern states 197 (3) economy 205 (4) see also Oslo
Christmas Island colonial possession/state Indian Ocean the world in 1975 106–107 the modern world 110–111
Christmas Island mod. Kiritimati island/nuclear test Pacific Ocean environmentalism 285 (2) WWII 272 (1), 273 (2) see also Kiritimati
Chryse Chersonesus region Greece ancient trade 44 (2)
Chu region/state East Asia first cities 259 (4), (5) first religions 37 (4) medieval states 263 (3)
Chubut river South America empire and revolution 151 (3) environment 153 (4)
Chubut see Rawson
Chucalissa North America (USA) cultural groups 122 (5)
Chucuito South America (Peru) early cultures 146 (1) Incas 147 (3)
Chudskoye Ozero see Peipus, Lake
Chu-fu see Zhufu
Chugacha South Asia (Bangladesh) postwar politics 252 (3)
Chukchi people Siberia the world in 1700 82–83 the world in 1800 86–87
Chukchi Sea sea Arctic Ocean exploration 257 (2), 286 (1), 287 (2)
Chukotka region Siberia exploration 257 (2)
Chukumuk Central America (Mexico) first civilizations 123 (2)
Chu-lu see Zhulu
Chunchura see Chinsura
Ch'ung-ch'ing, Chungking see Chongqing
Chung nan Shan see Zhongnan Shan
Chung t'iao Shan see Zhongtiao Shan
Chupicuaro Central America (Mexico) first civilizations 121 (2)
Chuquiabo South America (Bolivia) Incas 147 (3)
Chuquibamba South America (Peru) early cultures 146 (1)
Chuquicamata South America (Chile) environment 153 (4)
Chuquisaca var. La Plata; mod. Sucre South America (Bolivia) empire and revolution 150 (1) see also Sucre
Chur anc. Curia, Curia Rhaetorum; Fr. Coire, It. Coira, Rmsch. Cuera, Quera Central Europe (Switzerland) early modern states 193 (5) see also Curia
Churchill River river North America colonization 126 (1) the growth of the US 129 (2)
Chustenahlah battle North America (USA) the growth of the US 129 (2)
Chuuk var. Hogoley Islands; prev. Truk Islands island group Pacific Ocean environmentalism 285 (2) see also Truk
Chu, Wall of wall East Asia (China) first cities 259 (5)
Ciboney people West Indies colonization 125 (4)
Ciénaga de Oro South America (Colombia) early cultures 146 (1)
Çiftlik Southwest Asia (Turkey) early agriculture 220 (1)
Cihuatlan state Central America Aztecs 124 (1)
Cilicia region Southwest Asia ancient Rome 180–181 (1) crusades 65 (3) first civilizations 222 (2) Hellenistic world 40–41 (1)
Cimmerians people Southwest Asia the world in 750 BCE 30–31
Cina Selatan, Laut see South China Sea
Cincinnati North America (USA) the growth of the US 129 (2), 132 (1) US Civil War 131 (6), (7) US economy 134 (1), (3) US politics 135 (6)
Cipangu var. Japan island group Japan global knowledge 76 (9) see also Japan
Circassia region Eastern Europe Ottomans 231 (3)
Circassians var. Cherkess people Eastern Europe Mongols 68–69 (1) Ottomans 232–233 (1)
Circei mod. San Felice Circco Italy early states 178 (1)
Circeo archaeological site Italy first humans 13 (2)
Circum-Caribbean region/physical region West Indies early agriculture 120 (1) early cultures 144 (1)
Circus Maximus building Italy ancient Rome 181 (2)
Cirencester anc. Corinium, Corinium Dobunorum British Isles (United Kingdom) medieval states 183 (3)
Cirta North Africa (Algeria) ancient Rome 180–181 (1) early cultures 161 (2)
Cisalpine Republic state Italy the world in 1800 86–87
Cishan archaeological site/settlement East Asia early agriculture 258 (1), (2)
Cîteaux major cistercian house/settlement France medieval states 187 (3), 188 (1)
Citlaltepec Central America (Mexico) Aztecs 124 (2)
Ciudad Bolívar prev. Angostura South America (Venezuela) empire and revolution 151 (3) see also Angostura
Ciudad del Este prev. Presidente Stroessner, Puerto Presidente Stroessner South America (Paraguay) environment 153 (4)
Ciudad de México see Mexico, Mexico City, Tenochtitlan
Ciudad de Panamá see Panamá, Panamá City
Ciudad Guayana South America (Venezuela) environment 153 (4)
Ciudad Juárez Central America (Mexico) Mexican Revolution 133 (3)
Ciudad Madero Central America (Mexico) Mexican Revolution 133 (3)
Ciudad Real South America (Paraguay) colonization 148 (2)
Ciudad Rodrigo battle Iberian Peninsula (Spain) Napoleon 200–201 (1)
Ciudad Trujillo see Santo Domingo
Cividale Italy WWI 207 (5)
Civitas Nemetum see Speyer
Clairvaux major cistercian house France medieval states 187 (3)
Clasons Point North America (USA) cultural groups 122 (5)
Claudia, Aqua aqueduct Italy ancient Rome 181 (2)
Claudius, Temple of building Italy ancient Rome 181 (2)
Clausentum see Southampton
Clazomenae settlement/state Southwest Asia (Turkey) ancient Greece 177 (2) first civilizations 177 (1)
Clearwater battle North America (USA) the growth of the US 129 (2)
Clemsons Island North America (USA) cultural groups 122 (5)
Cleonae state Greece ancient Greece 177 (2)
Clermont France crusades 64–65 (2) Franks 183 (5), (6), 184 (2)
Clermont-Ferrand France economy 205 (4)
Cleveland North America (USA) the growth of the US 129 (2), 132 (1) US economy 134 (1), (3)
Cleves Ger. Kleve region Central Europe empire and revolution 199 (3)
Clipperton Island colonial possession/state/island Pacific Ocean the world in 1950 102–103 the world in 1975 106–107 the modern world 110–111
Clodia, Via road Italy early states 178 (1)
Clodia, Via road Italy early states 178 (1)
Clogg's Cave Australia exploration 280 (1)
Cloncurry Australia colonization 282 (1)
Clontarf British Isles (Ireland) crusades 186 (1)
Cloudy Bay bay New Zealand exploration 278 (1)
Clovis North America (USA) the world in 10,000 BCE 14–15
Clunes goldfield Australia colonization 282 (2)
Clunia Iberian Peninsula (Spain) ancient Rome 180–181 (1)
Cluny France empire and revolution 199 (4)
Clusium mod. Chiusi Italy early states 178 (1), (2) first civilizations 177 (1)
Clyde New Zealand colonization 283 (5)
Cnidus Southwest Asia (Turkey) ancient Greece 177 (3) ancient Rome 180–181 (1) first civilizations 177 (1) Hellenistic world 40–41 (1), 41 (2)
Cnidus state Greece ancient Greece 177 (2)
Cnossus see Knossos
Coahuila state Central America Mexican Revolution 133 (3) the growth of the US 129 (2)
Coahuiltec people Central America/North America colonization 125 (4), 126 (1)
Coast Mountains Fr. Chaîne Côtière mountain range North America the growth of the US 129 (2)
Coatepec Central America (Mexico) Aztecs 124 (2)
Coatlayauhcan Central America (Mexico) Aztecs 124 (3)
Coatlinchan Central America (Mexico) Aztecs 124 (2)
Coatzacoalcos river Central America first civilizations 121 (3)
Coba Central America (Mexico) first civilizations 123 (2)
Cobar goldfield Australia colonization 282 (2)
Coblenz Central Europe (Germany) WWI 206 (2), (3)
Cocanada South Asia (India) WWII 251 (3)
Cochabamba prev. Oropeza South America (Bolivia) Incas 147 (3) narcotics 153 (5)
Cochimi people Central America colonization 125 (4)
Cochin var. Kochi; early Chin. Ko-chih South Asia (India) colonialism 247 (3), 248 (1) Mughal Empire 246 (1) postwar economy 253 (5) trade 230 (2), 267 (3)
Cochin China colonial possession/state Mainland Southeast Asia colonialism 269 (4) European imperialism 97 (3)
Cochinos, Bahía de see Pigs, Bay of
Coco people Central America colonization 125 (4)
Cocopa people Central America colonization 125 (4), 126 (1)
Cocos Islands colonial possession/island group Indian Ocean the world in 1900 94–95 the world in 1925 98–99 the world in 1950 102–103 the world in 1975 106–107 the modern world 110–111
Cod, Cape headland North America empire and revolution 127 (2)
Cognac anc. Compniacum France Reformation 194 (2)
Cohuna and Kow Swamp Australia exploration 280 (1)
Coimbatore South Asia (India) postwar economy 253 (5)
Coimbra anc. Conimbria, Conimbriga settlement Iberian Peninsula (Portugal) Franks 184 (2) Islam 192 (3) medieval states 187 (3)
Coira see Chur, Curia
Coire see Chur, Curia
Coixtlahuacan state Central America Aztecs 124 (1)
Cokwe see Chokwe
Cola state South Asia first empires 241 (5)
Colas see Cholas
Colchester hist. Colneceaste; anc. Camulodunum British Isles (United Kingdom) economy 204 (1) medieval states 183 (3) see also Camulodunum
Colchi South Asia (India) ancient trade 44–45 (1)
Colchis region Eastern Europe Hellenistic world 40–41 (1)
Cold Harbor battle North America (USA) US Civil War 131 (7)

D

INDEX-GAZETTEER: **Dapenkeng – Éfaté**

medieval states 189 (3), (4) Napoleon 200–201 (1) WWI 207 (4) WWII 210 (1), 211 (4)
Dapenkeng archaeological site East Asia early agriculture 258 (1)
Darada state South Asia first empires 241 (5)
Daradus river West Africa (Senegal) ancient trade 44 (2)
Dara-i-Kur Central Asia (Uzbekistan) the world in 2500 BCE 22–23
Darbelo South Asia (Pakistan) colonialism 247 (3)
Dardanelles var. Hellespont; Turk. Çanakkale Boğazı sea waterway Southwest Asia (Greece) first civilizations 175 (4) WWI 207 (6), 233 (2)
Dar-el-Beida see Casablanca
Dar es Salaam East Africa (Tanzania) colonization 167 (4) economy 168 (2) exploration 156 (3), 157 (4), (5)
Dar es-Soltan archaeological site North Africa (Morocco) first humans 13 (2)
Darfur state East Africa colonization 167 (4) slave trade 165 (4) trade 167 (1)
Dargaville New Zealand colonization 283 (4), (5)
Dariabad South Asia (India) colonialism 247 (3)
Darién, Golfo del see Darien, Gulf of
Darien, Gulf of Sp. Golfo del Darién gulf South America colonization 148 (2) Incas 148 (1)
Darien, Isthmus of see Panama, Isthmus of
Dariorigum France ancient Rome 180–181 (1)
Dar'īyah see Deraya
Darjeeling South Asia (India) exploration 257 (3)
Darling river Australia colonization 282 (1), (2), 283 (3) early agriculture 20–21 (2) exploration 279 (2) prehistoric culture 17 (5)
Darlington British Isles (United Kingdom) economy 204 (1)
Darsena see Arsenal
Dar Tichit West Africa (Mauritania) early agriculture 158 (1)
Darwin prev. Palmerston, Port Darwin Australia colonization 282 (1), 283 (3), 284–285 environmentalism 285 (2) exploration 279 (2) prehistoric culture 17 (5) WWII 251 (3), 272 (1)
Dās island Southwest Asia economy 234 (1)
Dasapura South Asia (India) early religions 48 (2)
Dasharna region/state South Asia first empires 241 (5) world religions 242 (2)
Dashhowuz see Dashkhovuz
Dashiqiao var. Tashihkiao East Asia (China) Russo-Japanese War 270 (4)
Dashkhovuz prev. Tashauz; Turkm. Dashhowuz Central Asia (Turkmenistan) Soviet Union 214–215 (4)
Dasht river South Asia first cities 240 (2) first civilizations 24 (2), 25 (3) first empires 241 (4), (5) Mughal Empire 246 (1) world religions 242 (2)
Dating East Asia (China) medieval states 263 (5)
Datong East Asia (China) medieval states 263 (4)
Datong East Asia (China) early modern states 266 (1) medieval states 263 (5) world religions 49 (3)
Daugava see Western Dvina
Daugavpils see Dünaburg
Daulatabad South Asia (India) early medieval states 245 (4)
Dauni people Italy early states 178 (2)
Dauphiné region France medieval states 192 (1), (2)
Davao off. Davao City Philippines colonialism 247 (4)
Davao City see Davao
Davis Strait sea waterway North America exploration 286 (1), 287 (2) the growth of the US 129 (2)
Daw state West Africa trade 163 (4)
Dawaro state East Africa the world in 1200 62–63 the world in 1300 66–67
Dawenkou archaeological site East Asia early agriculture 258 (1), (2)
Dawson see Dawson City
Dawson City mod. Dawson North America (Canada) imperial global economy 93 (3)
Dawston see Degsastan
Daybul var. Daibol South Asia (India) medieval voyages 61 (3) trade 230 (2)
Daybul see Daibul
Dayi Shang vassal state East Asia first cities 259 (3)
Dayton North America (USA) US politics 135 (6)
Da Yunhe see Grand Canal
Dazaifu Japan early modern states 265 (5) medieval states 264 (2), 265 (3)
Dazhangheguo state East Asia medieval states 263 (3)
DDR see German Democratic Republic
Dead Sea var. Bahret Lut, Lacus Asphaltites; Ar. Al Baḥr al Mayyit, Baḥrat Lūt, Heb. Yam HaMelaḥ salt lake Southwest Asia 20th century 234 (2) 20th-century politics 233 (3) ancient Rome 225 (4) crusades 65 (3) first civilizations 221 (4), 222 (1)
De Blicquy North America (Canada) cultural groups 123 (3)
Debrecen prev. Debreczen; Ger. Debreczin, Rom. Debreţin Central Europe (Hungary) Reformation 194 (2)
Debreczen, Debreczin see Debrecen
Debreţin see Debrecen
Decapolis state Southwest Asia ancient Rome 225 (4)
Deccan plateau/region South Asia colonialism 247 (3), 248 (1) early medieval states 244 (1), (2), 244–245 (3) economy 249 (4) first empires 241 (4), (5) first religions 36 (2) imperial global economy 93 (5) Marathas 246 (2) Mughal Empire 246 (1) postwar politics 252 (1) world religions 242 (2), 243 (4)
Deccan States state South Asia colonialism 248 (2)
Dedeagach mod. Alexandroupolis Greece WWI 207 (6)
Dego battle Italy Napoleon 200–201 (1)
Degsastan var. Dawston battle British Isles (United Kingdom) medieval states 183 (3)
Dehli see Delhi, Indraprastha
Dehra Dun South Asia (India) decolonization 250 (1) exploration 257 (3)
Deira region British Isles medieval states 183 (3)
Deir el-Bahri Egypt ancient Egypt 159 (4)
Deir el-Balah Southwest Asia (Israel) ancient Egypt 159 (5)
Deir el-Bersha Egypt ancient Egypt 159 (4)
Deir el-Gabrawi Egypt ancient Egypt 159 (3)
Delagoa Bay var. Baía de Lourenço Marques bay Southern Africa slave trade 165 (4)
Delaware state North America empire and revolution 127 (2), (3) the growth of the US 129 (1) US Civil War 130 (2), (3), (4), (5), 131 (6), (7) US economy 134 (2)
Delaware people North America colonization 126 (1)
Delgado, Cape headland Southern Africa exploration 156 (3)
Delhi var. Dehli, Hind. Dilli; prev. Indraprastha; hist. Shahjahanabad South Asia (India) biological diffusion 72–73 (1) colonialism 247 (3), 248 (1), 269 (4) Communism 271 (8) decolonization 250 (1) early medieval states 244–245 (3) economy 249 (4) empire and revolution 249 (3) exploration 239 (1), 257 (3) global immigration 101 (3) imperial global economy 92 (1), 93 (5) Mongols 68 (2) Mughal Empire 246 (1) postwar economy 253 (5) Timur 229 (4) trade 267 (3) US superpower 138 (1) WWII 251 (3) see also Indraprastha
Delhi region South Asia postwar politics 252 (1)
Delhi, Sultanate of state South Asia Mongols 68–69 (1) Mughal Empire 246 (1) Timur 229 (4)
Delhi United Provinces state South Asia colonialism 248 (2)
Delium battle Greece ancient Greece 177 (3)
Delos Greece ancient Greece 179 (4)
Delphi religious site/settlement Greece ancient Greece 177 (3), 179 (4) ancient Rome 180–181 (1) first religions 36 (1), 37 (3)
Demchok var. Dêmqog region South Asia postwar politics 252 (1)
Demerara colonial possession South America colonization 149 (4)
Demetrias Greece Hellenistic world 41 (2)
Demnat North Africa (Morocco) exploration 157 (4)
Demotika state Southeast Europe WWII 211 (2)
Dêmqog see Demchok
Dendra Greece first civilizations 175 (4)
Deng state East Asia first cities 259 (4)
Dengchong East Asia (China) medieval states 263 (6)
Dengkil archaeological site Mainland Southeast Asia (Malaysia) Bronze Age 240 (3)
Dengyue var. Tengchung East Asia (China) colonialism 269 (4)
Dengzhou var. Teng-chou East Asia (China) early modern states 265 (5), 266 (1) medieval states 264 (2) Mongols 68–69 (1)
Denison, Cape headland Antarctica Antarctic Exploration 287 (3)
Denjong see Sikkim
Denkyera state West Africa the world in 1700 82–83
Denmark anc. Hafnia; Dan. Danmark; state Scandinavia crusades 186 (1), 64–65 (2) early modern states 193 (4), 197 (3) economy 190 (1), 205 (4) empire and revolution 199 (3), 202 (1), (2) European expansion 84–85 (1) interwar 209 (3), (5) medieval states 185 (3), 188 (1), 189 (3), (4) medieval voyages 60–61 (1) Mongols 68–69 (1) Napoleon 200–201 (1), 201 (2) postwar economy 213 (5), 214 (1), (2) postwar politics 212 (1), (3) Reformation 196 (1) Soviet Union 213 (4) the modern world 112 (2) US superpower 138 (1) WWII 210 (1), 211 (2), (4) Cold War 108 (3), 109 (1) early 20th century 206 (1)
Denmark-Norway state Scandinavia early modern states 195 (3) Reformation 194 (2)
Denmark Strait var. Danmarksstraedet sea waterway Atlantic Ocean exploration 172 (2)
Denver North America (USA) the growth of the US 129 (2), 132 (1) US economy 134 (1), 136 (2) US politics 135 (6)
Depford Culture people North America the world in 250 BCE 38–39
Deraya Ar. Dar'īyah Southwest Asia (Saudi Arabia) 20th-century politics 233 (4)
Derbend see Derbent
Derbent Eastern Europe (Russian Federation) Islam 226 (2), 227 (4), (5) medieval Persia 231 (4) Mongols 229 (3), 68–69 (1) Ottomans 231 (3) Timur 229 (4)
Derby British Isles (United Kingdom) economy 204 (1)
Derbyshire region British Isles imperial global economy 93 (4)
Dereivka archaeological site Eastern Europe (Ukraine) Copper Age 174 (2)
Derna North Africa (Libya) colonization 167 (4)
Dertosa mod. Tortosa Iberian Peninsula (Spain) ancient Rome 179 (3), 180–181 (1) see also Tortosa
Derwent river British Isles economy 204 (1)
Desalpur archaeological site South Asia (India) first cities 240 (2)
Deseado river South America colonization 148 (2)
Desert Gatherers people North America the world in 250 CE 46–47 passim.
Des Moines North America (USA) the growth of the US 129 (2)
Desmumu state British Isles medieval states 188 (2)
Desna river Eastern Europe WWI 207 (4)
Desterro mod. Florianópolis South America (Brazil) colonization 149 (3), (4)
Detroit prev. Fort Pontchartrain North America (USA) colonization 126 (1) the growth of the US 129 (2), 132 (1) US economy 134 (1), (3) US politics 135 (6)
Deutschland see Germany
Deutsch-Südwestafrika see Southwest Africa, German Southwest Africa
Deva var. Legaceaster, Devana Castra; mod. Chester; Wel. Caerleon; legion headquarters/mithraic site British Isles (United Kingdom) ancient Rome 180–181 (1) world religions 48 (1) see also Chester
Devagiri South Asia (India) early religions 48 (2)
Devagiri region South Asia early medieval states 244–245 (3)
Devana see Aberdeen
Devana Castra see Chester, Deva
Devapattana South Asia (Nepal) early medieval states 244 (1) first empires 241 (4)
Deventer Low Countries (Netherlands) economy 190 (1)
Devils Lake burial mound North America (USA) first civilizations 121 (4)
Dez river Southwest Asia first cities 220 (2) first civilizations 221 (4)
Dezful Southwest Asia (Iran) 20th-century politics 235 (5)
Dezhnev, Cape headland Siberia exploration 287 (2)
Dhahran Ar. Az̧ Z̧ahran Southwest Asia (Saudi Arabia) 20th-century politics 233 (4), 235 (5) economy 234 (1) US superpower 138 (1)
Dhaka prev. Dacca South Asia (Bangladesh) postwar economy 253 (5) postwar politics 252 (1), (3) see also Dacca
Dhanbad South Asia (India) postwar economy 253 (5)
Dharangaon South Asia (India) colonialism 247 (3)
Dharwar South Asia (India) economy 249 (4)
Dhlo Dhlo Southern Africa (Zimbabwe) trade 164 (1)
Dhodhekánisos see Dodecanese
Dhofar Southwest Asia (Yemen) trade 267 (3)
Dholavira archaeological site South Asia (Pakistan) first cities 240 (2)
Dhualdadr see Dulkadir
Dhu Qar Southwest Asia (Iraq) ancient Persia 225 (6)
Di people East Asia first cities 259 (4) first states 261 (2)
Diamantina South America (Brazil) colonization 149 (3) empire and revolution 151 (3)
Dian people/state East Asia/Mainland Southeast Asia first cities 259 (5) first states 260 (1) medieval states 261 (6)
Dias Point see Volta, Cape da
Dibio see Dijon
Dickson North America (USA) cultural groups 122 (5)
Dicle see Tigris
Didyma religious site Southwest Asia (Turkey) first religions 37 (3)
Diedenhofen var. Thionville France Franks 184 (2)
Diegueño people North America colonization 125 (4)
Die Kelders archaeological site Southern Africa (South Africa) early cultures 160 (1) first humans 13 (2)
Dien Bien Phu battle Mainland Southeast Asia (Vietnam) postwar politics 251 (5)
Dieppe France WWI 206 (2), (3)
Dieu, Hôtel building France economy 191 (2)
Dihang see Brahmaputra
Dijlah see Tigris
Dijon anc. Dibio France early modern states 193 (4), 197 (5) empire and revolution 199 (4) Franks 184 (2) medieval states 187 (4), 192 (2)
Dikbosch archaeological site Southern Africa (South Africa) early cultures 160 (1)
Dikson Siberia (Russian Federation) exploration 287 (2)
Dikwa West Africa (Nigeria) exploration 157 (4)
Dili var. Dilli, Dilly Maritime Southeast Asia (Indonesia) WWII 272 (1), 273 (2)
Dilli, Dilly see Dili
Dilli see Delhi, Indraprastha
Dilmun Arabian Peninsula first civilizations 24 (2), 25 (3)
Dimashq see Damascus
Dinajpur South Asia (Bangladesh) postwar politics 252 (3)
Dinant Low Countries (Belgium) WWI 206 (2), (3)
Dingcun archaeological site East Asia (China) first humans 13 (2)
Dingiray West Africa (Guinea) Islam 167 (3)
Dingliao military base /rebellion East Asia early modern states 266 (1), (2)
Diocaesarea Christian archbishopric Southwest Asia (Syria) world religions 48 (1)
Diocletian, Baths of Lat. Thermae Diocletiani building (Italy) ancient Rome 181 (2)
Diocletiani, Thermae see Diocletian, Baths of
Dion state Greece ancient Greece 177 (2)
Dionysus, Theatre of building Greece ancient Greece 177 (4)
Dioscurias Southwest Asia (Georgia) early cultures 161 (2) first civilizations 177 (1)
Diospolis Magna see Thebes
Dipylon see Dipylum
Dipylum var. Dipylon building Greece ancient Greece 177 (4)
Dire Dawa archaeological site East Africa (Ethiopia) first humans 13 (2)
Dishasha Egypt ancient Egypt 159 (3)
Dispur South Asia (India) postwar politics 252 (1)
Diu South Asia (India) colonialism 247 (3), 248 (1), 269 (4) decolonization 251 (4) empire and revolution 88–89 (2) exploration 239 (1) postwar politics 252 (1) trade 230 (2), 67 (3) WWII 251 (3)
Divi mod. Diu South Asia (India) world religions 243 (4) see also Diu
Divodurum Mediomatricum see Metz
Divostin Southeast Europe (Yugoslavia) early agriculture 174 (1)
Dixmude Low Countries (Belgium) WWI 206 (2), (3)
Diyala var. Rudkhaneh-ye Sīrvān, Sirwan, Diyālā, Nahr river Southwest Asia first cities 220 (2) first civilizations 221 (4), (5)
Diyarbakir Southwest Asia (Turkey) 20th-century politics 235 (5)
Djailolo see Halmahera
Djakarta see Batavia, Jakarta
Djambi see Jambi
Djawa see Java
Djenné see Jenne
Djerba island North Africa Ottomans 231 (3)
Djibouti East Africa (Djibouti) colonization 167 (4) European imperialism 96 (1)
Djibouti var. Jibuti; prev. French Somaliland, French Territory of the Afars and Issas; Fr. Côte Française des Somlis state East Africa decolonization 168 (1) economy 168 (2) Islam 235 (4) the modern world 112 (1), 113 (3) see also French Somaliland, French Territory of the Afars and Issas
Dnepr see Dnieper
Dnepropetrovsk see Dnipropetrovs'k, Yekaterinoslav
Dnestr see Dniester
Dnieper Bel. Dnyapro, Rus. Dnepr, Ukr. Dnipro river Eastern Europe ancient trade 44–45 (1) biological diffusion 72–73 (1) crusades 64–65 (2) early Islam 56–57 (1) economy 190 (1) empire and revolution 198 (2), 202 (1) exploration 172 (1) first humans 13 (2) Islam 227 (4) medieval states 185 (3) medieval voyages 60–61 (1) Mongols 68–69 (1) Napoleon 200–201 (1) Ottomans 202 (4), 230 (1), 231 (3), 232–233 (1) prehistoric culture 17 (4) Timur 229 (4) WWI 207 (4) WWII 210 (1), 211 (4)
Dniester anc. Tyras; Rom. Nistru, Rus. Dnestr, Ukr. Dnister river Eastern Europe Bronze Age 175 (3) Copper Age 174 (2) crusades 64–65 (2) early agriculture 174 (1) economy 190 (1), 205 (4) empire and revolution 198 (2), 202 (1) exploration 172 (1) great migrations 52–53 (1), 53 (2) medieval states 189 (4) Mongols 68–69 (1) Napoleon 200–201 (1) Ottomans 197 (4), 230 (1), 231 (3) WWI 207 (4) WWII 210 (1), 211 (4)
Dnipro see Dnieper
Dnipropetrovs'k var. Yekaterinoslav; Rus. Dnepropetrovsk Eastern Europe (Ukraine) Soviet Union 214–215 (4) see also Yekaterinoslav
Dnister see Dniester
Dnyapro see Dnieper
Doboj Southeast Europe (Bosnia and Herzegovina) postwar economy 215 (3)
Dobro Polje battle Southeast Europe (FYR Macedonia) WWI 207 (6)
Dobruja region/vassal state Southeast Europe Ottomans 202 (4), 230 (1)
Dodecanese var. Dodecanese Islands, Nóties Sporádes; prev. Dhodhekánisos state/island group Greece ancient Greece 177 (2), (3) first civilizations 175 (4) medieval states 187 (5) Ottomans 202 (4), 232–233 (1) WWI 210 (1), 233 (2) WWII 211 (2), (4) 20th-century politics 233 (3)
Dodecanese Islands see Dodecanese
Do Dimmi West Africa (Niger) early agriculture 158 (1)
Dodoma East Africa (Tanzania) economy 168 (2) exploration 157 (5)
Dodona religious site Greece first religions 37 (3)
Doge's Palace building Italy economy 191 (3)
Dogrib people North America cultural groups 123 (3)
Doha Southwest Asia (Qatar) economy 234 (1) exploration 219 (4)
Dojran battle Southeast Europe (FYR Macedonia) WWI 207 (6)
Dolní Věstonice archaeological site/settlement Central Europe (Poland) prehistoric culture 17 (4)
Dolomites var. Dolomiti; It. Dolomitiche, Alpi mountain range Italy WWI 207 (5)
Dolomiti, Dolomitiche, Alpi see Dolomites
Dominica colonial possession/state/island West Indies empire and revolution 150 (1) European expansion 85 (2) the growth of the US 129 (2) the modern world 112 (1) US economy 136 (2) US politics 139 (4)
Dominican Republic state West Indies Cold War 108 (2), 109 (1) the growth of the US 129 (2), 133 (4) the world in 1850 90–91 the world in 1900 94–95 the world in 1925 98–99 the world in 1950 102–103 the world in 1975 106–107 the modern world 110–111 , 112 (1), 113 (4) US economy 136 (2) US politics 139 (4) US superpower 138 (1) WWII 104 (1)
Domitian, Stadium of building Italy ancient Rome 181 (2)
Domrémy France medieval states 192 (2)
Don anc. Tanais river Eastern Europe ancient trade 44–45 (1) biological diffusion 72–73 (1) Bronze Age 175 (3) early agriculture 174 (1) early Islam 56–57 (1) economy 205 (4) first humans 13 (2) great migrations 52–53 (1) Islam 163 (1), 227 (4) medieval states 185 (3) Mongols 68–69 (1) Napoleon 200–201 (1) Ottomans 230 (1), 231 (3), 232–233 (1) prehistoric culture 17 (4) Timur 229 (4) WWI 207 (4) WWII 210 (1), 211 (4)
Donau see Danube
Donbas region Eastern Europe economy 205 (4)
Doncaster anc. Danum British Isles (United Kingdom) economy 204 (1)
Don Cossacks people Eastern Europe/Siberia Reformation 196 (2)
Donets river Eastern Europe WWI 207 (4)
Donets'k Eastern Europe (Ukraine) Soviet Union 214–215 (4)
Dong Ap Bia see Hamburger Hill
Dong Dau Mainland Southeast Asia (Vietnam) the world in 2500 BCE 22–23
Dong Duong Mainland Southeast Asia (Vietnam) world religions 243 (5), 49 (4)
Dong Hai see East China Sea
Donghu state East Asia first cities 259 (5)
Dong Khe fort Mainland Southeast Asia postwar politics 251 (5)
Dongola var. Donqola, Dunqulah East Africa (Sudan) ancient trade 44–45 (1) colonization 167 (4) early cultures 161 (3), (4), (5) Islam 163 (1)
Dong Son archaeological site/settlement Mainland Southeast Asia (Thailand) Bronze Age 240 (3)
Dongting Hu lake East Asia early modern states 266 (1) first cities 259 (4), (5) first states 260 (1)
Dongyi state East Asia first cities 259 (3)
Donja Slatina fort Southeast Europe (Yugoslavia) Bronze Age 175 (3)
Donqola see Dongola
Doornik see Tournai
Dorchester anc. Durnovaria British Isles (United Kingdom) economy 204 (1) medieval states 183 (3)
Dordogne river France first civilizations 177 (1)
Dordrecht var. Dordt, Dort Low Countries (Netherlands) economy 190 (1)
Dordt see Dordrecht
Dorestad Low Countries (Netherlands) medieval states 185 (3) medieval voyages 60–61 (1)
Dori West Africa (Burkina) exploration 157 (4)
Dornach battle Central Europe (Switzerland) early modern states 193 (5)
Dorpat Eastern Europe (Estonia) early modern states 195 (3) economy 190 (1) medieval states 189 (3)
Dorsoduro Italy economy 191 (3)
Dort see Dordrecht
Dortmund Central Europe (Germany) economy 190 (1) medieval states 188 (1)
Dorylaeum Southwest Asia (Turkey) ancient Rome 180–181 (1)
Dorylaeum battle Southwest Asia (Turkey) crusades 64–65 (2)
Dospad Dagh see Rhodope Mountains
Douai anc. Duacum; prev. Douay France economy 190 (1)
Douala var. Duala Central Africa (Cameroon) colonization 167 (4) economy 168 (2)
Douanas river Mainland Southeast Asia ancient trade 44 (2)
Douay see Douai
Doullens France WWI 206 (2)
Douro Sp. Duero river Iberian Peninsula Bronze Age 175 (3) Copper Age 174 (2) crusades 64–65 (2) early agriculture 174 (1) economy 190 (1) first civilizations 177 (1) great migrations 52–53 (1), 53 (2) see also Duero
Dove Creek battle North America (USA) the growth of the US 129 (2)
Dover British Isles (United Kingdom) economy 204 (1), 205 (4) WWI 206 (2), (3)
Dover North America (USA) the growth of the US 129 (2)
Dover, Strait of var. Straits of Dover; Fr. Pas de Calais sea waterway Western Europe WWI 206 (2), (3)
Dover, Straits of see Dover, Strait of
Downpatrick Ir. Dún Pádraig British Isles (United Kingdom) Bronze Age 175 (3)
Drač see Durazzo
Draç see Durazzo
Drakensberg physical region Southern Africa economy 163 (2) first humans 12 (1) slave trade 165 (4) trade 164 (1)
Drancy ghetto France WWII 211 (3)
Drangiana region Central Asia Hellenistic world 40–41 (1)
Drapsaca Central Asia (Afghanistan) Hellenistic world 40–41 (1)
Drau var. Drava; Eng. Drave, Hung. Dráva river Southeast Europe WWI 207 (5), (6) see also Drava
Drava var. Drau; Eng. Drave, Hung. Dráva river Southeast Europe postwar economy 215 (3) see also Drau
Dráva, Drave see Drau, Drava
Dravida region/state South Asia early religions 48 (2) first empires 241 (5) world religions 242 (2)
Drenthe province Low Countries Reformation 195 (5)
Drepanum see Trapani
Dresden Central Europe (Germany) early modern states 193 (4) economy 205 (4) empire and revolution 199 (3) postwar politics 212 (1) Reformation 196 (1) WWII 211 (4)
Dresden battle Central Europe (Germany) Napoleon 200–201 (1)
Drina river Southeast Europe exploration 257 (2) postwar economy 215 (3) WWI 207 (6)
Drontheim see Trondheim
Druk-yul see Bhutan
Dry Creek archaeological site North America the world in 10,000 BCE 14–15
Duacum see Douai
Duala see Douala
Dubai Ar. Dubayy Southwest Asia (United Arab Emirates) economy 234 (1)
Dubayy see Dubai
Dublin British Isles (Ireland) biological diffusion 72–73 (1) economy 190 (1), 205 (4) empire and revolution 202 (1) interwar 209 (3) medieval states 185 (3), 186 (2), 187 (4), 188 (2) medieval voyages 60–61 (1) Napoleon 200–201 (1), 201 (2) postwar politics 212 (3) Reformation 194 (2) WWII 211 (2)
Dubrae var. Dubris; mod. Dover archaeological site British Isles (United Kingdom) ancient Rome 180–181 (1) see also Dover
Dubris see Dover, Dubrae
Dubrovnik It. Ragusa Southeast Europe (Croatia) postwar economy 215 (3) see also Ragusa
Ducie Island island Pacific Ocean exploration 278 (1)
Duero Port. Douro river Iberian Peninsula crusades 186 (1) early Islam 56–57 (1) exploration 172 (1) Franks 184 (2) interwar 209 (4) Islam 192 (3) Napoleon 200–201 (1) prehistoric culture 17 (3) see also Douro
Duff Islands island group Pacific Ocean exploration 278 (1)
Dufile East Africa (Uganda) exploration 157 (4)
Duinekerke see Dunkirk
Duji var. Tuchi province East Asia medieval states 262–263 (1)
Dukang East Asia (China) first cities 259 (5)
Duke of York Island island Pacific Ocean medieval voyages 60 (2)
Duke of York Islands island group Pacific Ocean early cultures 280–281 (3)
Dulkadir var. Dhualdadr state Southwest Asia the world in 1400 70–71 the world in 1500 74–75
Dumbarton British Isles (United Kingdom) medieval states 186 (2)
Dumyât see Damietta
Duna see Danube
Düna see Western Dvina
Dünaburg Eastern Europe (Latvia) early modern states 195 (3) medieval states 189 (3)
Dunaj see Danube, Vienna
Dunărea, Dunav see Danube
Dundee British Isles (United Kingdom) economy 204 (1)
Dunedin settlement/whaling station New Zealand colonization 283 (4), (5)
Dunholme see Durham
Dunhuang settlement East Asia (China) ancient trade 44–45 (1) exploration 256 (1), 257 (3) first states 260 (1), 261 (3) medieval states 261 (6), 262–263 (1), 263 (6) world religions 49 (3), (4)
Dunhuang province East Asia first states 260 (1)
Dunkerque see Dunkirk
Dunkirk prev. Dunquerque; Flem. Duinekerke, Fr. Dunkerque, France Reformation 195 (5) WWI 206 (3)
Dún Pádraig see Downpatrick
Dunquerque see Dunkirk
Dunqul Egypt ancient Egypt 159 (4)
Dunqulah see Dongola
Du Page County region North America
Dura Europos settlement Southwest Asia (Iraq) ancient Persia 225 (6) ancient Rome 180–181 (1), 224 (2), 225 (5) early trade 225 (3) Hellenistic world 41 (2) world religions 226 (1)
Durango Central America (Mexico) colonization 125 (4) Mexican Revolution 133 (3)
Durango state Central America Mexican Revolution 133 (3) the growth of the US 129 (2)
Durazzo anc. Dyrrachium; mod. Durrës, Dursi; SCr. Drač, Turk. Draç Southeast Europe (Albania) crusades 64–65 (2) early modern states 193 (4) medieval states 185 (3), 187 (5), 188 (1), 189 (4) Ottomans 230 (1) WWI 207 (6) see also Dyrrachium
Durban var. Port Natal Southern Africa (South Africa) colonization 166 (2), 167 (4) economy 168 (2) European imperialism 96 (2)
Durham prev. Dunholme British Isles (United Kingdom) medieval states 186 (2)
Dürnkrut battle Central Europe (Austria) medieval states 189 (4)
Durnovaria see Dorchester
Durocortorum France ancient Rome 180–181 (1), 181 (4)
Durostorum var. Silistria; mod. Silistra, legion headquarters Southeast Europe (Bulgaria) ancient Rome 180–181 (1) see also Silistria
Durovernum see Canterbury
Durrës see Durazzo
Durrës see Dyrrachium
Dursi see Durazzo
Dushanbe var. Dyushambe; prev. Stalinabad, Taj. Stalinobod Central Asia (Tajikistan) Soviet Union 214–215 (4)
Dusky Sound sealing station New Zealand colonization 283 (4)
Düsseldorf Central Europe (Germany) WWI 206 (2), (3) WWII 211 (4)
Dust Bowl drought North America US economy 134 (3)
Dutch Brazil colonial possession South America colonization 149 (4)
Dutch East Indies mod. Indonesia; prev. Netherlands East Indies colonial possession Maritime Southeast Asia colonialism 269 (4) colonization 284–285 (1) European imperialism 97 (3), (4) exploration 279 (3) empire and revolution 88–89 (2) global immigration 100 (1) the growth of the US 133 (4) WWII 104 (1), 251 (3), 272 (1), 273 (2) see also Indonesia
Dutch Guiana var. Netherlands Guiana; mod. Surinam, Suriname colonial possession/state South America Cold War 109 (1) WWII 104 (1) see also Surinam
Dutch Harbor military base North America (USA) WWII 104 (2), 272 (1), 273 (2)
Dutch Netherlands rebellion Low Countries empire and revolution 88–89 (2)
Dutch New Guinea colonial possession/state New Guinea Cold War 109 (1) European imperialism 97 (3)
Dutch Republic see Batavian Republic, Netherlands, United Provinces
Dutch South Africa colonial possession Southern Africa slave trade 165 (4) trade 164 (1)
Dutch West Indies see Netherlands Antilles
Dvaraka South Asia (India) world religions 242 (2)
Dvarasamudra South Asia (India) early medieval states 244 (2), 244–245 (3)
Dvaravati South Asia (India) ancient India 242 (1) early religions 48 (2)
Dvaravati region/state South Asia ancient India 241 (6) early medieval states 245 (5) world religions 243 (5), 49 (4)
Dvin Christian archbishopric Southwest Asia (Armenia) world religions 48 (1)
Dvina river Eastern Europe early modern states 197 (3) WWI 207 (4)
Dvinsk Eastern Europe (Latvia) WWI 207 (4)
Dvinsk see Dünaburg
Dwarka South Asia (India) early medieval states 244–245 (3) world religions 243 (4)
Dyfed region British Isles medieval states 183 (3)
Dyrrhachium mod. Durrës; It. Durazzo, SCr. Drač, Turk. Draç Southeast Europe (Albania) ancient Rome 179 (5), 180–181 (1) see also Durazzo
Dyushambe see Dushanbe
Dza Chu see Mekong
Dzhruchula archaeological site Eastern Europe (Russian Federation) first humans 13 (2)
Dzibilchaltún Central America (Mexico) first civilizations 121 (2)
Dzungaria region Central Asia ancient trade 44–45 (1) medieval states 262–263 (1)
Dzungars people/rebellion Central Asia early modern states 268 (1) empire and revolution 268 (2)
Dzungars, Khanate of the state East Asia
Dzvina see Western Dvina

E

Eagle Pass North America (USA) Mexican Revolution 133 (3)
Eagle Rock North America (USA) US economy 135 (4)
Eanna building Southwest Asia (Iraq) first cities 220 (3)
Early Kalachuris dynasty South Asia early medieval states 244 (2)
Early Man Shelter Australia exploration 280 (1)
Early Mississippian Culture people North America the world in 1000 58–59
East Anglia state British Isles medieval states 183 (3)
East Antarctica see Greater Antarctica
East Asia region East Asia biological diffusion 73 (2)
East Bengal and Assam region South Asia decolonization 250 (2)
East Berlin Central Europe (Germany) postwar politics 212 (2)
East Cape headland Australia colonization 283 (4)
East China Sea Chin. Dong Hai sea East Asia ancient trade 44–45 (1) biological diffusion 72–73 (1) decolonization 251 (4) early agriculture 20–21 (2), 258 (1), (2) early modern states 266 (1) economy 274 (1) first cities 259 (3), (4), (5) first states 260 (1) Islam 275 (4) medieval states 262–263 (1), 263 (6) Mongols 68 (2), 68–69 (1) postwar politics 271 (7) world religions 49 (3) WWII 272 (1), 273 (2)
Easter Island var. Isla de Pascua, Rapa Nui island Pacific Ocean colonization 284–285 (1) decolonization 285 (3) environmentalism 285 (3) exploration 278 (1), 279 (3) see also Rapa Nui
Eastern Chalukyas dynasty South Asia the world in 1000 58–59
Eastern Desert var. Aş Şaḩrā' ash Sharqīyah; Eng. Arabian Desert desert Egypt ancient Egypt 159 (5) see also Arabian Desert
Eastern Europe region Eastern Europe US economy 138 (2)
Eastern Gangas dynasty South Asia early medieval states 244 (2), 244–245 (3) Mongols 68–69 (1)
Eastern Ghats mountain range South Asia early medieval states 244 (1), 244–245 (3) economy 249 (4) first empires 241 (4) first religions 36 (2) Mughal Empire 246 (1) colonialism 247 (3), 248 (1)
Eastern Jin state East Asia first states 261 (3)
Eastern March region Eastern Europe Franks 184 (2)
Eastern Pomerania region Central Europe empire and revolution 199 (3)
Eastern Rumelia region Southeast Europe Ottomans 202 (4), 232–233 (1)
Eastern Sierra Madre see Sierra Madre Oriental
Eastern Solomons battle Pacific Ocean (Solomon Islands) WWII 273 (2)
Eastern States state South Asia colonialism 248 (2)
Eastern Thrace region Southwest Asia 20th-century politics 233 (3)
Eastern Turkestan state East Asia medieval states 262–263 (1)
Eastern Woodland Culture people North America the world in 500 CE 50–51 the world in 750 CE 54–55
East Fjords fjords Atlantic Ocean (Iceland) exploration 172 (2)
East Florida colonial possession North America empire and revolution 127 (3)
East Friesland see East Frisia
East Frisia var. East Friesland region Central Europe empire and revolution 199 (3)
East Germany state Central Europe Cold War 109 (1) postwar economy 213 (5) postwar politics 212 (3) Soviet Union 213 (4)
East Greenland Inuit people North America cultural groups 123 (3)
East Indies island group Maritime Southeast Asia ancient trade 44–45 (1) global knowledge 76–77 (1) medieval voyages 61 (3)
East Java Kingdom state Maritime Southeast Asia the world in 1000 58–59
East London prev. Emonti; Afr. Oos-Londen, Port Rex Southern Africa (South Africa) economy 168 (2) European imperialism 96 (2)
Eastmain North America (Canada) colonization 126 (1)
East Pakistan mod. Bangladesh state South Asia Cold War 109 (1) decolonization 251 (4) see also Bangladesh
East Prussia region Central Europe empire and revolution 198 (2), 199 (3), 202 (2) interwar 209 (3), (5) Soviet Union 213 (4) WWI 207 (4), 208 (1) WWII 210 (1)
East River river North America the growth of the US 132 (2)
East Roman Empire var. Byzantine Empire state Southeast Europe/Southwest Asia ancient Rome 182 (1) early cultures 160 (1), 161 (5) Franks 183 (6) medieval states 182 (2), 183 (4) see also Byzantine Empire
East Siberian Sea sea Arctic Ocean exploration 257 (2), 286 (1), 287 (2)
East Timor region Maritime Southeast Asia decolonization 251 (4)
East Ukraine region Eastern Europe empire and revolution 198 (2)
Ebbou archaeological site France prehistoric culture 17 (3)
Eberbach major cistercian house Central Europe medieval states 187 (3)
Ebla Southwest Asia (Syria) early systems 223 (3) first civilizations 221 (4), 24 (2)
Eblana see Dublin
Ebora see Évora
Eboracum see Eburacum, York
Ebrach major cistercian house Central Europe medieval states 187 (3)
Ebro Lat. Iberus river Iberian Peninsula ancient Rome 180–181 (1) crusades 186 (1) early cultures 161 (2) early Islam 56–57 (1) exploration 172 (1) first civilizations 177 (1) Franks 184 (2) interwar 209 (4) Islam 192 (3) medieval states 182 (2) Napoleon 200–201 (1) prehistoric culture 17 (3) see also Iberus
Eburacum var. Eboracum; mod. York legion headquarters/mithraic site/settlement British Isles (United Kingdom) ancient Rome 180–181 (1), 181 (4) world religions 48 (1) see also York
Ebusus see Ibiza
Ecab state Central America Aztecs 124 (1)
Ecatepe Central America (Mexico) Aztecs 124 (2)
Ecbatana mod. Hamadan Southwest Asia (Iran) ancient Persia 223 (4), 225 (6) ancient Rome 224 (2), 225 (5) ancient trade 44–45 (1) early trade 225 (3) exploration 218 (1) first civilizations 222 (2) Hellenistic world 224 (1) world religions 226 (1) see also Hamadan
Echunga goldfield Australia colonization 282 (2)
Eckmühl Central Europe (Germany) Napoleon 200–201 (1)
Ecuador state South America economy 153 (3) empire and revolution 150 (2), 151 (3) environment 153 (4) imperial global economy 92 (1) politics 152 (1) the growth of the US 133 (4) the modern world 112 (1), 113 (4) US superpower 138 (1) WWII 105 (3) Cold War 109 (1)
Edendale North America (USA) US economy 135 (4)
Edessa mod. Şanlıurfa, Urfa Christian archbishopric/settlement Southwest Asia (Turkey) ancient Rome 224 (2), 225 (5) crusades 228 (2), 65 (3) Hellenistic world 41 (2) Islam 227 (4) world religions 226 (1)ancient Persia 225 (6) crusades 64–65 (2)
Edessa, County of state Southwest Asia Crusades 65 (3)
Edfu var. Idfu Egypt ancient Egypt 159 (3) first cities 28–29 (1) first civilizations 24 (2)
Edinburgh British Isles (United Kingdom) biological diffusion 72–73 (1) economy 190 (1), 205 (4) empire and revolution 202 (1) medieval states 186 (2), 187 (4), 188 (1) Napoleon 200–201 (1), 201 (2) Reformation 194 (2)
Edirne Greece Ottomans 202 (4)
Edmonton North America (Canada) the growth of the US 129 (2), 132 (1) US economy 136 (2) US superpower 138 (1)
Edo mod. Tokyo, Tōkyō (Japan) early modern states 267 (4), 268 (1) economy 270 (1) trade 267 (3) see also Tokyo
Edom state Southwest Asia first civilizations 222 (1)
Edward, Lake var. Albert Edward Nyanza, Edward Nyanza, Lac Idi Amin, Lake Rutanzige lake East Africa exploration 157 (4) first humans 12 (1)
Edward Nyanza see Edward, Lake
Edward VII Land physical region Antarctica Antarctic Exploration 287 (3)
Edzna Central America (Mexico) first civilizations 123 (2)
Eems see Ems
Eesti see Estonia
Éfaté settlement/island Pacific Ocean (Vanuatu) early cultures 280–281 (3) environmentalism 285 (2) medieval voyages 60 (2)

INDEX-GAZETTEER: Efes – Fraser Cave

Efes see Ephesus
Eflâk see Wallachia
Egadi, Isole see Aegates
Egbaland state West Africa Islam 167 (3)
Ege Denizi see Aegean Sea
Eger mod. Cheb Central Europe (Czech Republic) medieval states 188 (1)
Egina see Aegina
Egmont, Cape headland New Zealand colonization 283 (4)
Egoli see Johannesburg
Egtved burial mound/settlement Scandinavia (Denmark) Bronze Age 175 (3)
Egypt prev. United Arab Republic; anc. Aegyptus region/state Egypt ancient Egypt 159 (4) ancient Persia 223 (4) ancient Rome 181 (4), 224 (2), 225 (5) ancient trade 44–45 (1) biological diffusion 72–73 (1) colonization 167 (4) crusades 65 (1), 228 (2), 65 (3) decolonization 168 (1) early 20th century 206 (1) early agriculture 220 (1) early cultures 161 (2), (3), (4), (5) early Islam 57 (2) early systems 223 (3), 32 (1), 33 (2), (3) early trade 225 (3) economy 168 (2), (3) European expansion 84–85 (1) European imperialism 96 (1), 97 (4) exploration 157 (5), 218 (1), (2), 219 (3), (4) first cities 220 (2) first civilizations 177 (1), 221 (5), 222 (1), (2) first religions 36 (1), 37 (3) Hellenistic world 224 (1), 41 (2) imperial global economy 92 (1) Islam 163 (1), 226 (2), 227 (4), (5), 235 (4) medieval states 187 (5) medieval voyages 61 (3) Mongols 229 (3), 68 (2) Napoleon 200–201 (1) Ottomans 231 (3), 232–233 (1) Seljuks 228 (1) slave trade 165 (4) the modern world 112 (1), 113 (3), (4) Timur 229 (4) trade 167 (1), 230 (2) US superpower 138 (1) world religions 226 (1), 49 (4) WWI 233 (2) WWII 104 (1), (2), 210 (1), 211 (4) 20th century 234 (2) 20th-century politics 233 (3), (4), 235 (5) see also Aegyptus
Egyptians people East Africa trade 167 (1)
Ehime prefecture Japan economy 270 (1)
Eichstätt Central Europe (Germany) Franks 184 (2)
Eight Trigrams Sect rebellion East Asia empire and revolution 268 (2)
Eilat var. Aila, Elat, Elath Southwest Asia (Israel) 20th century 234 (2) see also Aila, Elath
Éire see Hibernia, Ireland
Éireann, Muir see Irish Sea
Eivissa see Ibiza
Ekain archaeological site Iberian Peninsula (Spain) prehistoric culture 17 (3)
Ekapa see Cape Town
Ekven North America (USA) cultural groups 123 (3)
El Abra Cave archaeological site South America (Colombia) early cultures 144 (1)
El Agheila North Africa (Libya) WWII 210 (1), 211 (4)
Elaine incident North America (USA) US politics 135 (6)
El Alamein battle Egypt WWII 104 (2), 211 (4
Elam var. Susiana, Uvja; mod. Khūzestān, Khuzistan state Southwest Asia first civilizations 221 (4), (5), 222 (2)
El-Amarna Egypt first cities 28–29 (1), 29 (5)
Eland's Bay archaeological site Southern Africa (South Africa) early cultures 160 (1)
Elandslaagte battle Southern Africa (South Africa) European imperialism 96 (2)
El Argar fort Iberian Peninsula (Spain) Bronze Age 175 (3)
Elat see Aila, Eilat, Elath
Elatea Greece first civilizations 177 (1)
Elat, Gulf of see Aqaba, Gulf of
Elath var. Aila, Eilat; mod. Elat Southwest Asia (Israel) early trade 225 (3) see also Aila, Eilat
Elath see Aelana, Aqaba
Elba island Italy Napoleon 200–201 (1)
El-Ballas Egypt ancient Egypt 159 (2)
Elbasan var. Elbasani Southeast Europe (Albania) WWI 207 (6)
Elbasani see Elbasan
El Baul Central America (Mexico) first civilizations 123 (2)
Elbe Lat. Albis; Lat. Albis river Central Europe ancient Rome 180–181 (1) ancient trade 44–45 (1) Bronze Age 175 (3) Copper Age 174 (2) crusades 186 (1), 64–65 (2) early agriculture 174 (1) early modern states 193 (4) economy 205 (4) empire and revolution 199 (3), 202 (1), (2) exploration 172 (1) Franks 184 (2) great migrations 52–53 (1), 53 (2) interwar 209 (5) medieval states 182 (2), 187 (3), 188 (1), 189 (3), (4) Mongols 68–69 (1) Napoleon 200–201 (1), 201 (2), (3) prehistoric culture 17 (4) Reformation 196 (1) WWII 210 (1)
Elbeuf France WWI 206 (2), (3)
Elbing Central Europe (Poland) early modern states 197 (3) economy 190 (1) medieval states 189 (3)
El Bosque Central America (Nicaragua) the world in 10,000 BCE 14–15
Elburz Mountains Per. Reshteh-ye Kūhhā-ye Alborz mountain range Southwest Asia ancient Persia 223 (4), 225 (6) early agriculture 220 (1) economy 234 (1) exploration 218 (1), (2), 219 (3) first cities 28–29 (1) first civilizations 221 (4), 222 (2) Hellenistic world 224 (1) Mongols 68–69 (1) WWI 233 (2)
El Carmen South America (Argentina) exploration 143 (3)
El Castillo archaeological site Iberian Peninsula (Spain) prehistoric culture 17 (3)
El-Derr Egypt ancient Egypt 159 (5)
El Djazaïr see Algiers
Elea Italy first civilizations 177 (1)
Elefantes see Olifants
Elephanta Buddhist center South Asia (India) world religions 49 (3)
Elephantine Egypt ancient Egypt 159 (2), (3), (4), (5) early cultures 160 (1) first cities 28–29 (1) first civilizations 24 (2)
Elephant Island island Antarctica Antarctic Exploration 287 (3)
El Fasher var. Al Fāshir East Africa (Sudan) Islam 163 (1)
El Ferrol Iberian Peninsula (Spain) interwar 209 (4)
Elgin British Isles (United Kingdom) medieval states 188 (2)
El Gîza see Giza
El Guettar archaeological site North Africa (Tunisia) first humans 13 (2)
El Inga South America (Colombia) the world in 10,000 BCE 14–15
Elis state Greece ancient Greece 179 (4)
Élisabethville see Lubumbashi
El-Jadida see Mazagan
El Jobo Central America (Mexico) first civilizations 123 (2)
El-Kab Egypt ancient Egypt 159 (5) first civilizations 24 (2)
El Khartûm see Karri, Khartoum
El Khril North Africa (Morocco) early agriculture 158 (1)
El-Lahun Egypt ancient Egypt 159 (4)
Ellás see Greece, Hellas
Ellesmere Island island North America cultural groups 123 (3) exploration 286 (1), 287 (2) the growth of the US 129 (2)
Ellice Islands mod. Tuvalu island group Pacific Ocean colonization 284–285 (1) exploration 279 (3) see also Tuvalu
El-Lisht Egypt ancient Egypt 159 (4) first cities 28–29 (1)
Ellora Buddhist center South Asia (India) world religions 49 (3)
El Mesón archaeological site Central America (Mexico) first civilizations 121 (3)
Elmham British Isles (United Kingdom) medieval states 183 (3)
Elmina West Africa (Ghana) European expansion 84–85 (1) exploration 156 (3) Islam 163 (1) slave trade 165 (4) trade 164 (2)
El Mirador Central America (Mexico) first civilizations 123 (2)
El Morro archaeological site North America (USA) cultural groups 123 (4)
Elne see Illiberis
Eloaue Island island Melanesia medieval voyages 60 (2)
El Opeño Central America (Mexico) first civilizations 121 (2)
Elouae Islands island group Melanesia early cultures 280–281 (3)
Elp Low Countries (Netherlands) Bronze Age 175 (3)
El Paraíso early ceremonial center/settlement South America (Peru) early cultures 144 (1)
El Paso North America (USA) Mexican Revolution 133 (3) US economy 136 (2)
El Paso battle North America (USA) the growth of the US 129 (2)
El Paso del Norte North America (USA) colonization 125 (4)
El Purgatório South America (Peru) early cultures 146 (1)
El Qâhira see Cairo, Fustat
El Salvador prev. Salvador state Central America the growth of the US 129 (2) US economy 136 (2) US politics 139 (4) US superpower 138 (1) Cold War 108 (2), 109 (1) see also Salvador
Elsloo Low Countries (Netherlands) early agriculture 174 (1)
El Suweis see Suez
Elswick British Isles (United Kingdom) economy 204 (3)
El Tajin Central America (Mexico) first civilizations 122 (1)
El Teul Central America (Mexico) first civilizations 122 (1)
El Trapiche Central America (Mexico) first civilizations 121 (2)
Elvas Iberian Peninsula (Portugal) Reformation 196 (2)
El Viejon Central America (Mexico) first civilizations 121 (2)
Ely British Isles (United Kingdom) economy 204 (1) medieval states 186 (2)
Elymais state Southwest Asia ancient Rome 224 (2)
Elymi people Italy early states 178 (2)
Emden Central Europe (Germany) Reformation 195 (5)
Emerald Isle see Montserrat
Emerald Mound North America (USA) cultural groups 122 (5)
Emerita Augusta mod. Mérida Iberian Peninsula (Spain) ancient Rome 180–181 (1), 181 (4) world religions 48 (1) see also Mérida
Emesa religious site/settlement Southwest Asia (Syria) first religions 37 (3) Hellenistic world 40–41 (1)
Emilia region Italy medieval states 183 (4)
Emin mod. Niger river West Africa exploration 156 (2) see also Niger
Emmaus Southwest Asia (Syria) ancient Rome 225 (4)
Emona see Ljubljana
Emonti see East London
Emporiae mod. Ampurias Iberian Peninsula (Spain) ancient Rome 179 (3) first civilizations 177 (1)
Emporion East Africa (Somalia) ancient trade 44–45 (1) early cultures 161 (3), (5)
Emporium building Italy ancient Rome 181 (2)
Empty Quarter see Ar Rub 'al Khali
Ems Dut. Eems river Central Europe Reformation 195 (5)
Emu nuclear test Australia environmentalism 285 (2)
Emuckfaw battle North America (USA) the growth of the US 129 (2)
Encounter Bay inlet Australia exploration 279 (2)
Enderby Land physical region Antarctica Antarctic Exploration 287 (3)
Enewetak prev. Eniwetok nuclear test Pacific Ocean environmentalism 285 (2) see also Eniwetok
Engaruka archaeological site East Africa (Tanzania) early cultures 160 (1)
Engis Low Countries (Belgium) the world in 10,000 BCE 14–15
England Lat. Anglia state British Isles crusades 186 (1), 64–65 (2) early modern states 194 (1) economy 190 (1) empire and revolution 202 (1) European expansion 80–81 (1) medieval states 185 (3), 186 (2), 187 (3), (4), 188 (1), (2) medieval voyages 60–61 (1) Reformation 194 (2), 196 (1), (2)
Englewood North America (USA) cultural groups 122 (5)
English Channel sea waterway Western Europe early modern states 197 (5) economy 204 (1) empire and revolution 199 (4) medieval states 183 (3), 186 (2), 187 (4), 188 (2), 192 (1), (2) WWI 206 (2), (3)
Eniwetok island Pacific Ocean WWII 104 (1), 273 (2)
Enkomi Southwest Asia (Cyprus) ancient Egypt 159 (5)
Enlil, Temple of building Southwest Asia (Iraq) first cities 28 (2)
En Nazira see Nazareth
Eno people North America colonization 125 (4)
Enotachopco Creek battle North America (USA) the growth of the US 129 (2)
Enryakuji Buddhist temple army Japan medieval states 265 (4)
Entebbe East Africa (Uganda) colonization 167 (4)
Entrevaux France early modern states 197 (5)
Épernay France WWI 206 (2), (3)
Ephesos see Ephesus
Ephesus Southwest Asia (Turkey) ancient Greece 177 (3), 179 (4) ancient Persia 223 (4) ancient Rome 179 (5), 180–181 (1), 181 (3), (4), 182 (1), 225 (5) crusades 64–65 (2) early cultures 161 (2) economy 190 (1) first civilizations 177 (1) first religions 37 (3) Hellenistic world 40–41 (1) world religions 226 (1)
Ephesus state Greece ancient Greece 177 (2)
Ephthalites see Hephthalites, Empire of the
Epidamnus Southeast Europe (Albania) ancient Greece 179 (4) first civilizations 177 (1)
Epidaurus Greece ancient Greece 177 (3)
Épinal France WWI 206 (2), (3)
Epirus region Greece ancient Greece 177 (3), 179 (4) ancient Rome 179 (5), 180–181 (1), 225 (5) first civilizations 177 (1) Hellenistic world 224 (1) medieval states 189 (4) Mongols 68–69 (1)
Epirus, Despotate of state Southeast Europe medieval states 187 (5), 188 (1)
Epitoli see Pretoria
Equatorial Guinea var. Rio Muni; prev. Spanish Guinea state Central Africa decolonization 168 (1) economy 168 (2) the modern world 112 (1) see also Spanish Guinea
Erautini see Johannesburg
Erbil see Arbela
Erdély see Transylvania
Erebus, Mount mountain Antarctica Antarctic Exploration 287 (3)
Erech see Uruk
Erechtheum temple Greece ancient Greece 177 (4)
Eressus state Greece ancient Greece 177 (2)
Eretoka island Pacific Ocean early cultures 280–281 (3) medieval voyages 60 (2)
Eretria Greece ancient Greece 177 (3) first civilizations 177 (1)
Eretria state Greece ancient Greece 177 (2)
Erevan see Erivan, Yerevan
Erfurt rebellion/settlement Central Europe (Germany) early agriculture 174 (1) Reformation 196 (2)
Eridanos see Eridanus
Eridanus var. Eridanos river Greece ancient Greece 177 (4)
Eridu settlement/temple Southwest Asia (Iraq) early agriculture 220 (1) first cities 220 (2), 28–29 (1) first civilizations 221 (4)
Erie people North America colonization 126 (1)
Erie, Lake lake North America colonization 126 (1) cultural groups 122 (5) early agriculture 120 (1) empire and revolution 127 (2), (3) exploration 118 (1), 119 (2), (3) first civilizations 121 (4) the growth of the US 129 (2) US Civil War 131 (6), (7)
Eritrea colonial possession/state East Africa decolonization 168 (1) economy 168 (2), (3) European imperialism 96 (1) Islam 235 (4) the modern world 112 (1), 113 (3) WWI 104 (1) 20th-century politics 233 (4)
Erivan Southwest Asia (Azerbaijan) medieval Persia 231 (4)
Erligang archaeological site East Asia early agriculture 258 (2)
Erlitou archaeological site/settlement East Asia early agriculture 258 (1), (2) first cities 259 (3), 28–29 (1)
Ermeland see Warmia
Ermes Eastern Europe (Latvia) early modern states 195 (3)
Ertis see Irtysh
Erythrae settlement/state Southwest Asia (Turkey) ancient Greece 177 (2) first civilizations 177 (1)
Erzerum see Erzurum
Erzincan see Erzinjan
Erzinjan mod. Erzincan Southwest Asia (Turkey) WWI 233 (2)
Erzurum var. Erzerum; anc. Theodosiopolis Southwest Asia (Turkey) early Islam 56–57 (1) Islam 226 (2), 227 (4), (5) Ottomans 230 (1), 231 (3) WWI 233 (2)
Escalón Central America (Mexico) Mexican Revolution 133 (3)
Escaut see Scheldt
Eşfahān see Isfahan
Eshnunna settlement/temple Southwest Asia (Iraq) first cities 220 (2), 28–29 (1) first civilizations 221 (4), 24 (2), 25 (3)
Esh Shaheinab East Africa (Sudan) the world in 5000 BCE 18–19
Esh Sham see Damascus
Eskimo see Inuit
Esna var. Isna Egypt ancient Egypt 159 (4)
España see Spain
Esperance Australia colonization 282 (1), 283 (3) exploration 279 (2)
Espiríto Santo region South America colonization 149 (3)
Espiritu Santo settlement/island Pacific Ocean (Vanuatu) environmentalism 285 (2) exploration 278 (1) WWII 104 (2)
Esquiline Hill Lat. Mons Esquilinus hill Italy ancient Rome 181 (2)
Esquilinus, Mons see Esquiline Hill
Essaouira see Mogador
Esseg see Osijek
Essen var. Essen an der Ruhr Central Europe (Germany) economy 205 (4) WWII 210 (1), 211 (2), (3)
Essen an der Ruhr see Essen
Essequibo colonial possession South America colonization 149 (4)
Essex state British Isles medieval states 183 (3)
Es-Skhul archaeological site Southwest Asia (Israel) first humans 13 (2)
Estero Rabón archaeological site Central America (Mexico) first civilizations 121 (3)
Estland see Estonia
Estonia Est. Eesti, Ger. Estland, Latv. Igaunija region/state Eastern Europe early modern states 195 (3) interwar 209 (3) postwar economy 214 (1), (2) postwar politics 212 (3) Soviet Union 208 (2), 213 (4) the modern world 112 (2) WWI 207 (4), 208 (1) WWII 210 (1)
Estonians people Eastern Europe crusades 186 (1) Mongols 68–69 (1)
Eszék see Osijek
Esztergom anc. Strigonium; Ger. Gran battle/settlement Central Europe (Hungary) medieval states 185 (3), 188 (1), 189 (4) Mongols 68–69 (1) see also Gran
Étaples France WWI 206 (2), (3)
Etaules fort France Bronze Age 175 (3)
Etawah South Asia (India) colonialism 247 (3)
Ethiopia prev. Abyssinia state East Africa decolonization 168 (1) economy 163 (2), (3) European expansion 84–85 (1) exploration 157 (5) Islam 163 (1), 235 (4) medieval voyages 61 (3) slave trade 165 (4) the modern world 112 (1), 113 (3), (4) trade 230 (2) world religions 226 (1), 49 (4) 20th-century politics 233 (4) Cold War 109 (1) see also Abyssinia
Ethiopian Highlands var. Ethiopian Plateau plateau East Africa ancient trade 44–45 (1) early cultures 160 (1), 161 (3), (4), (5) early trade 225 (3) exploration 157 (5) first humans 12 (1), 13 (2) medieval voyages 61 (3) slave trade 165 (4) trade 165 (3)
Ethiopian Plateau see Ethiopian Highlands
Etowah North America (USA) cultural groups 122 (5)
Etowah battle North America (USA) the growth of the US 129 (2)
Etruscan Cities state Italy the world in 500 BCE 34–35
Etruscans people Italy early states 178 (1), (2) first religions 36 (1)
Etsch see Adige
Etzatlan Central America (Mexico) first civilizations 122 (1)
Euboea vassal state/island Greece ancient Greece 177 (2), (3), 179 (4) first civilizations 175 (4)
Eudaemon Arabia var. Aden; Ar. 'Adan, Chin. A-tan Southwest Asia (Yemen) early trade 225 (3) see also Aden
Euhesperides North Africa (Libya) first civilizations 177 (1)
Eupatoria Eastern Europe (Ukraine) Ottomans 202 (4)
Euphrates Ar. Al Furāt, Turk. Firat Nehri river Southwest Asia ancient Egypt 159 (5) ancient Persia 223 (4), 225 (6) ancient Rome 180–181 (1), 224 (2), 225 (5) ancient trade 44–45 (1) biological diffusion 72–73 (1), 73 (3) Bronze Age 175 (3) crusades 228 (2), 65 (3) early agriculture 174 (1), 20–21 (2), 220 (1) early cultures 161 (2), (3), (4), (5) early Islam 56–57 (1), 57 (2), (3) early systems 223 (3) early trade 225 (3) economy 234 (1) exploration 172 (1), (2), 219 (3), (4) first cities 220 (2), 28–29 (1) first civilizations 221 (4), (5), 222 (2), 25 (3) first humans 13 (2) first religions 36 (1) great migrations 52–53 (1) Hellenistic world 224 (1), 41 (2) Islam 163 (1), 226 (2), 227 (4), (5) medieval Persia 231 (4) medieval states 185 (3), 261 (6) Mongols 229 (3), 68–69 (1) Ottomans 230 (1), 231 (3), 232–233 (1) Seljuks 228 (1) Timur 229 (4) trade 230 (2) world religions 226 (1), 49 (4) WWI 233 (2) WWII 211 (4) 20th-century politics 233 (3), 235 (5)
Europa var. Europe continent ancient trade 44 (2) see also Europe
European Russia region Eastern Europe global immigration 100 (1)
Eurymedon, River battle Southwest Asia (Turkey) ancient Persia 223 (4)
Eusebia see Caesaria Cappadociae, Kayseri
Eutaw Springs battle North America (USA) empire and revolution 127 (3)
Euxine Sea see Black Sea
Euxinus, Pontus sea Asia/Europe ancient trade 44 (2)
Even see Lamut
Everest, Mount mountain East Asia exploration 257 (3)
Évora anc. Ebora; Lat. Liberalitas Julia Iberian Peninsula (Portugal) Islam 192 (3)
Évreux France WWI 206 (2), (3)
Évros see Maritsa
Exeter anc. Isca Dumnoniorum British Isles (United Kingdom) economy 204 (1) medieval states 183 (3), 186 (2) see also Isca Dumnoniorum
Exloo archaeological site/settlement Low Countries (Belgium) Copper Age 174 (2)
Eylau battle Central Europe (Poland) Napoleon 200–201 (1)
Eyre, Lake salt lake Australia exploration 276–277 (1)
Eyu East Asia (China) first cities 259 (5)
Ezero fort Southeast Europe (Bulgaria) Bronze Age 175 (3)

F

Fadak Southwest Asia (Saudi Arabia) world religions 226 (1)
Faenza anc. Faventia Italy economy 190 (1) medieval states 188 (1)
Faeroe Islands Dan. Færøerne, Faer. Føroyar colonial possession/island group Atlantic Ocean exploration 172 (1), (2) historical geography 170–171 (1) medieval states 185 (3) medieval voyages 60–61 (1) the modern world 112 (2) WWII 210 (1), 211 (4)
Faesulae mod. Fiesole Italy early states 178 (1)
Failaka Southwest Asia (Iraq) first civilizations 24 (2), 25 (3)
Fairbanks North America (USA) US superpower 138 (1)
Faisalabad South Asia (Pakistan) postwar economy 253 (5)
Faiyum Egypt ancient Egypt 159 (2), (4) early agriculture 158 (1)
Faizābād, Faizabad see Fyzabad
Falaise France medieval states 186 (2)
Falisci people Italy early states 178 (1), (2)
Falkland Islands var. Falklands, Islas Malvinas colonial possession/state/island group South America Antarctic Exploration 287 (3) empire and revolution 151 (3) environment 153 (4) exploration 142 (1), 143 (3) historical geography 140–141 (1) politics 152 (1) see also Malvinas, Islas
Falklands see Falkland Islands, Malvinas, Islas
Fallen Timbers battle North America (USA) the growth of the US 129 (2)
Famagusta Southwest Asia (Cyprus) crusades 64–65 (2), 65 (3) economy 190 (1)
Fang state East Asia first cities 259 (3)
Fante var. Fanti state West Africa trade 167 (1)
Fanti see Fante
Fao oil terminal/settlement Southwest Asia (Iraq) 20th-century politics 235 (5) economy 234 (1)
Farawiyyn state West Africa trade 163 (4)
Far Eastern Republic state Siberia Communism 271 (8)
Farewell, Cape headland New Zealand colonization 283 (4)
Faro Iberian Peninsula (Portugal) Islam 192 (3)
Farrukhabad South Asia (India) economy 249 (4)
Farrukhabad state South Asia empire and revolution 249 (3)
Farruknagar state South Asia empire and revolution 249 (3)
Fars region/state Southwest Asia ancient Persia 225 (6) early Islam 56–57 (1) medieval Persia 231 (4)
Fars, Khalīj-e see Persian Gulf
Fartak state Southwest Asia Islam 163 (1)
Fashoda East Africa (Sudan) colonization 167 (4)
Fatehgarh rebellion South Asia (India) empire and revolution 249 (3)
Fatehpur South Asia (India) colonialism 247 (3)
Fatimid Caliphate state Egypt crusades 64–65 (2), 65 (3) Seljuks 228 (1)
Fatimids dynasty Egypt/Southwest Asia early Islam 57 (2) Islam 227 (5) medieval states 185 (3)
Faventia see Faenza
Faxaflói fjords Iceland exploration 172 (2)
Fayetteville North America (USA) US Civil War 131 (7)
Fazzān see Fezzan
Færøerne see Faeroe Islands
Fehrbellin battle Central Europe (Germany) early modern states 197 (3)
Felicitas Julia see Lisbon, Olisipo
Fellin Est. Viljandi Eastern Europe (Estonia) early modern states 195 (3)
Fell's Cave archaeological site/settlement South America (Chile) early cultures 144 (1)
Felsina var. Bononia; mod. Bologna Italy early states 178 (2) see also Bononia, Bologna
Feltre Italy WWI 207 (5)
Feng East Asia (China) first cities 259 (4) Mongols 68–69 (1)
Fengtian region East Asia Chinese revolution 271 (5) imperialism 270 (2)
Fengtian Clique movement East Asia Chinese Civil War 271 (6)
Fengtien see Mukden, Shenyang
Fengyuan East Asia (China) medieval states 263 (6)
Fengzhou East Asia (China) medieval states 263 (5)
Feni Islands island group Pacific Ocean early cultures 280–281 (3) medieval voyages 60 (2)
Fenni see Fenny
Fenny var. Fenni South Asia (Bangladesh) postwar politics 252 (3)
Feodosiya see Kaffa, Theodosia
Fère France WWI 206 (2), (3)
Fergana see Ferghana
Fergana Valley physical region Central Asia biological diffusion 73 (1)
Ferghana region/state Central Asia/East Asia ancient trade 44–45 (1) colonialism 269 (3) early Islam 56–57 (1) first states 260 (1) medieval states 261 (6), 262–263 (1) world religions 49 (3)
Fernandia North America (USA) US Civil War 131 (6)
Fernando de Noronha island South America the modern world 110–111
Fernando Po var. Bioko; prev. Macías Nguema Biyogo; Sp. Fernando Póo; island West Africa exploration 156 (3) trade 164 (2)
Ferozepore rebellion South Asia (India) empire and revolution 249 (3)
Ferrara anc. Forum Alieni Italy early modern states 193 (4) economy 190 (1) medieval states 188 (1)
Fertile Crescent region Southwest Asia early agriculture 174 (1)
Fès see Fez
Fetegar state East Africa the world in 1200 62–63
Fetterman's Defeat battle North America (USA) the growth of the US 129 (2)
Feyzābād see Fyzabad
Fez var. Fès North Africa (Morocco) biological diffusion 72–73 (1) crusades 64–65 (2), 65 (1) early Islam 56–57 (1) exploration 156 (3) Islam 163 (1) medieval states 185 (3) Mongols 68 (2) Ottomans 231 (3)
Fezzan mod. Fazzān; anc. Phazania region/state North Africa Ottomans 232–233 (1)
Field of Blood battle Southwest Asia (Syria) crusades 65 (3)
Fiesole see Faesulae
Fifth Cataract Waterfall Egypt ancient Egypt 159 (5)
Fiji state/island group Pacific Ocean colonization 284–285 (1) decolonization 285 (3) early cultures 280–281 (3) environmentalism 285 (2) exploration 276–277 (1), 279 (3) global immigration 101 (3) medieval voyages 60 (2) the modern world 113 (3)
Filitosa fort France Bronze Age 175 (3)
Finanj Mainland Southeast ASia (Malaysia) trade 230 (2)
Finca Arizona Central America (Mexico) first civilizations 123 (2)
Fingira Southern Africa (Malawi) early agriculture 158 (1)
Finland colonialpossession/region/state Scandinavia early modern states 197 (3) economy 205 (4) empire and revolution 202 (1) interwar 209 (3) medieval states 189 (3) postwar economy 213 (5), 214 (1) postwar politics 212 (3) Soviet Union 208 (2), 213 (4) the modern world 112 (2), 113 (4) WWI 207 (4), 208 (1) WWII 104 (1), (2), 210 (1), 211 (2), (3), (4) Cold War 108 (3) early 20th century 206 (1)
Finland, Gulf of Est. Soome Laht, Fin. Suomenlahti, Ger. Finnischer Meerbusen, Rus. Finskiy Zaliv, Swe. Finska Viken gulf Scandinavia early modern states 197 (3) WWI 207 (4)
Finnic Peoples people Eastern Europe/Scandinavia the world in 750 CE 54–55 the world in 1000 58–59
Finnischer Meerbusen see Finland, Gulf of
Finno-Ugrians people Eastern Europe/Scandinavia the world in 750 BCE 30–31 passim.
Finns people Scandinavia crusades 186 (1) Mongols 68–69 (1)
Finska Viken, Finskiy Zaliv see Finland, Gulf of
Firat Nehri see Euphrates
Firenze see Florence, Florentia
Firmum var. Firmum Picenum Italy early states 178 (1)
Firmum Picenum see Firmum
First Cataract Waterfall Egypt ancient Egypt 159 (2), (3), (4), (5)
First Riel Rebellion battle North America (Canada) the growth of the US 129 (2)
Firuzukh South Asia (Afghanistan) early medieval states 244 (2)
Fisher North America (USA) cultural groups 122 (5)
Fishguard Wel. Abergwaun British Isles (United Kingdom) economy 204 (1)
Fitzroy river Australia colonization 282 (1) prehistoric culture 17 (5)
Fiume see Rijeka
Flagler Bay North America (Canada) cultural groups 123 (3)
Flaminia, Via road Italy ancient Rome 181 (2) early states 178 (1)
Flaminia, Via road Italy early states 178 (1)
Flanders province/region Low Countries crusades 64–65 (2) early modern states 197 (5) economy 190 (1) medieval states 192 (1) Reformation 195 (5)
Flathead people North America colonization 126 (1)
Flensborg Ger. Flensburg Central Europe (Germany) empire and revolution 199 (3)
Flensburg see Flensborg
Fleurus battle Low Countries (Belgium) empire and revolution 199 (4)
Flinders river Australia colonization 282 (1) exploration 279 (2) prehistoric culture 17 (5)
Flint Run North America (USA) the world in 5000 BCE 18–19
Flitsch mod. Bovec; It. Plezzo Central Europe (Slovenia) WWI 207 (5)
Florence North America (USA) cultural groups 122 (5) US Civil War 131 (7)
Florence anc. Florentia; It. Firenze Italy early modern states 193 (4) economy 190 (1) Franks 184 (2) medieval states 188 (1) Napoleon 200–201 (1), 201 (2), (3) Reformation 194 (2)
Florence state Italy Reformation 194 (2)
Florentia mod. Florence, Firenze Italy ancient Rome 180–181 (1) see also Florence
Flores island Maritime Southeast Asia colonialism 247 (4) decolonization 251 (4) early medieval states 245 (6) exploration 239 (1), (2) Islam 243 (6) postwar economy 253 (5) postwar politics 253 (4) world religions 243 (5) WWII 251 (3), 272 (1), 273 (2)
Flores Sea sea Maritime Southeast Asia colonialism 247 (4) early medieval states 245 (5), (6) European imperialism 97 (3) exploration 239 (1), (2) Islam 243 (6) world religions 243 (5)
Floreşti Southeast Europe (Moldova) early agriculture 174 (1)
Florianópolis see Desterro
Florida state North America the growth of the US 129 (1) US Civil War 130 (2), (3), (4), (5), 131 (6), (7) US economy 134 (2), 139 (3) US society 137 (6) US superpower 139 (5)
Florina battle Greece WWI 207 (6)
Florisbad archaeological site Southern Africa (South Africa) first humans 13 (2)
Flossenbürg concentration camp Central Europe WWII 211 (3)
Foča Southeast Europe (Bosnia and Herzegovina) postwar economy 215 (3)
Foix France crusades 186 (1)
Folkestone British Isles (United Kingdom) economy 204 (1)
Folsom North America (USA) the world in 5000 BCE 18–19
Fongafale Pacific Ocean (Tuvalu) decolonization 285 (3)
Fontbrégoua Italy early agriculture 174 (1)
Font-de-Gaume archaeological site France prehistoric culture 17 (3)
Foochow see Fuzhou
Forbes goldfield Australia colonization 282 (2)
Forbes Quarry archaeological site Iberian Peninsula (Spain) first humans 13 (2)
Forlì anc. Forum Livii Italy economy 190 (1)
Former Shu state East Asia medieval states 263 (3)
Formosa mod. Taiwan, Republic of China island/state East Asia biological diffusion 72–73 (1) colonialism 247 (4) the world in 1925 98–99 trade 267 (3) world religions 243 (5), 49 (3), (4) WWII 104 (1), (2), 272 (1), 273 (2) see also China, Republic of, Taiwan
Føroyar see Faeroe Islands
Fort Albany North America (Canada) colonization 126 (1)
Fortaleza prev. Ceará, Villa do Forte de Assuppeãs South America (Brazil) environment 153 (4) see also Ceará
Fort Ancient burial mound/settlement North America (USA) cultural groups 122 (5) first civilizations 121 (4)
Fort Augusta fort North America (USA) empire and revolution 127 (2)
Fort Beauséjour fort North America (USA) empire and revolution 127 (2)
Fort Chambly fort North America (USA) empire and revolution 127 (3)
Fort Churchill North America (Canada) colonization 126 (1)
Fort Dauphin see Fort Liberté
Fort Dearborn battle North America (USA) the growth of the US 129 (2)
Fort Detroit fort North America (USA) empire and revolution 127 (2), (3)
Fort Donelson fort North America (USA) US Civil War 131 (6)
Fort Duquesne fort North America (USA) empire and revolution 127 (2)
Fort Fisher fort North America US Civil War 131 (7)
Fort Frontenac fort North America (USA) empire and revolution 127 (2)
Fort Gaines battle North America (USA) US Civil War 131 (7)
Forth and Clyde canal British Isles economy 204 (1)
Fort Hatteras fort North America (USA) US Civil War 131 (6), (7)
Fort Henry battle North America (USA) empire and revolution 127 (3)
Fort Henry fort North America (USA) empire and revolution 127 (3) US Civil War 131 (6)
Fort Hill burial mound North America (USA) first civilizations 121 (4)
Fortín Balliván fort South America (Paraguay) politics 152 (2)
Fortín Boquerón fort South America (Paraguay) politics 152 (2)
Fortín Nanawa fort South America (Paraguay) politics 152 (2)
Fort Jackson fort North America (USA) US Civil War 131 (6)
Fort James see Accra
Fort James Island West Africa (Gambia) slave trade 165 (4)
Fort Kaministikwia North America (USA) colonization 126 (1)
Fort Kearney battle North America (USA) the growth of the US 129 (2)
Fort Kosmo North America (USA) imperial global economy 93 (3)
Fort Liberté var. Fort Dauphin West Indies (Haiti) empire and revolution 89 (3)
Fort Louis Central Europe (Germany) early modern states 197 (5)
Fort Macon fort North America (USA) US Civil War 131 (6), (7)
Fort Malden fort North America (USA) empire and revolution 127 (3)
Fort Maurits South America (Brazil) colonization 149 (3), (4)
Fort Mellon battle North America (USA) the growth of the US 129 (2)
Fort Mims battle North America (USA) the growth of the US 129 (2)
Fort Monroe fort North America (USA) US Civil War 131 (6), (7)
Fort Necessity fort North America (USA) empire and revolution 127 (2)
Fort Niagara fort North America (USA) empire and revolution 127 (2), (3)
Fort Ninety Six fort North America (USA) empire and revolution 127 (3)
Fort Orange North America (USA) colonization 126 (1)
Fort Oswego fort North America (USA) empire and revolution 127 (2), (3)
Fort Pickens fort North America (USA) US Civil War 131 (6), (7)
Fort Pitt var. Fort Pittsburgh North America (USA) empire and revolution 127 (3)
Fort Pittsburgh see Fort Pitt
Fort Pontchartrain see Detroit
Fort Pulaski fort North America (USA) US Civil War 131 (6), (7)
Fort-Repoux see Akjoujt
Fort St Andries see New Amsterdam
Fort St David South Asia (India) empire and revolution 88 (1)
Fort St John fort North America (USA) empire and revolution 127 (2)
Fort St John's fort North America (USA) empire and revolution 127 (3)
Fort St Phillip fort North America (USA) US Civil War 131 (6)
Fort Sedgewick battle North America (USA) the growth of the US 129 (2)
Fort Selkirk North America (Canada) imperial global economy 93 (3)
Fort Stanwix fort North America (USA) empire and revolution 127 (3)
Fort Sumter fort North America (USA) US Civil War 131 (6), (7)
Fort Ticonderoga battle North America (USA) empire and revolution 127 (3)
Fort Ticonderoga fort North America (USA) empire and revolution 127 (2), (3)
Fortunatae Insulae island group Atlantic Ocean ancient trade 44 (2)
Fort Walton North America (USA) cultural groups 122 (5)
Fort Willam Henry fort North America (USA) empire and revolution 127 (2)
Fort William North America (Canada) the growth of the US 129 (2)
Fort William H Seward North America (USA) imperial global economy 93 (3)
Fort Worth North America (USA) Cold War 108 (2) the growth of the US 132 (1)
Fort Wrangell mod. Wrangell North America (USA) imperial global economy 93 (3)
Fortymile North America (Canada) imperial global economy 93 (3)
Forum Alieni see Ferrara
Forum Julii var. Cividale Italy medieval states 183 (4) see also Cividale
Forum Julii mod. Fréjussee also Fréjus archaeological site France ancient Rome 180–181 (1)
Forum Livii see Forlì
Forum Romanum Italy ancient Rome 181 (2)
Fossa Claudia see Chioggia
Fossoli ghetto Italy WWII 211 (3)
Fountains major cistercian house British Isles (United Kingdom) medieval states 187 (3)
Fourth Cataract waterfall Egypt ancient Egypt 159 (4), (5)
Fou-shan see Fushun
Fouta-Djallon see Futa Jallon, Serram Geley
Fouta-Toro see Futa Toro
Foveaux Strait sea waterway New Zealand colonization 283 (5)
Fowltown battle North America (USA) the growth of the US 129 (2)
Fox people North America colonization 126 (1)
Foxe Basin sea North America exploration 287 (2) the growth of the US 129 (2)
France anc. Gaul; Lat. Gallia; Fr. Gaule state France biological diffusion 72–73 (1) 109 (1) crusades 186 (1), 64–65 (2) early modern states 193 (4), (5), 194 (1), 197 (5) economy 190 (1), 205 (4) empire and revolution 199 (3), (4), 202 (1), (1i), (2), (3), 88 (1), 88–89 (2) European expansion 80–81 (1) European imperialism 97 (4) Franks 184 (2) Islam 192 (3) medieval states 185 (3), 186 (2), 187 (3), (4), 188 (1), (2) medieval voyages 60–61 (1) Napoleon 200–201 (1) Ottomans 231 (3) postwar economy 213 (5), 214 (1), (2) postwar politics 212 (1), (3) Reformation 194 (2), 195 (5), 196 (1), (2) Soviet Union 213 (4) the modern world 112 (1), (2), 113 (3), (4) imperial global economy 92 (1) interwar 209 (3), (4), (5) US superpower 138 (1) WWI 206 (2), (3), 208 (1) WWII 104 (1), 211 (2), (3), (4) Cold War 108 (3) early 20th century 206 (1) see also Gallia, Gaul, French Empire
Franche-Comté state Central Europe/France early modern states 193 (4), 194 (1), 197 (5) Reformation 194 (2), 196 (1)
Franchthi Greece early agriculture 174 (1)
Francia see Frankish Kingdom
Franciscans religious group South America exploration 143 (2)
Franconia region Central Europe medieval states 185 (3), 188 (1)
Frankfort North America (USA) the growth of the US 129 (2) US Civil War 131 (6)
Frankfurt var. Frankfurt am Main Central Europe (Germany) early modern states 193 (4) economy 190 (1), 205 (4) Franks 184 (2) medieval states 189 (3) Napoleon 201 (2) postwar politics 212 (1) Reformation 196 (1) WWII 211 (4)
Frankfurt am Main see Frankfurt
Frankfurt an der Oder Central Europe (Germany) empire and revolution 199 (3)
Frankhthi Greece the world in 5000 BCE 18–19
Frankish Empire state France early Islam 56–57 (1), 57 (2)
Frankish Kingdom var. Francia, Carolingian Empire, Frankish Empire, Kingdom of the Franks state France great migrations 53 (2) Islam 184 (1) see also Frankish Empire, Franks, Kingdom of the
Franklin battle North America (USA) US Civil War 131 (7)
Franks people Central Europe ancient Rome 181 (4)
Franks, Kingdom of the state France ancient Rome 182 (1) Franks 183 (6) medieval states 182 (2), 183 (4)
Franz Josef Land island group Arctic Ocean exploration 257 (2)
Fraser Cave Australia exploration 280 (1)

H

M

INDEX-GAZETTEER: Manuae – Misisil

Manuae island Pacific Ocean exploration 278 (1)
Manus island Pacific Ocean WWII 251 (3)
Manyakheta South Asia (India) early medieval states 244 (2)
Manzhouli var. Man-chou-li East Asia (China) colonialism 269 (4)
Manzikert Southwest Asia (Turkey) crusades 65 (1) early Islam 57 (2) Seljuks 228 (1)
Mao Khe battle Mainland Southeast Asia (Vietnam) postwar politics 251 (5)
Maoris people New Zealand the world in 750 CE 54–55 the world in 1000 58–59 the world in 1200 62–63 the world in 1300 66–67 the world in 1400 70–71 the world in 1500 74–75 the world in 1600 78–79 the world in 1700 82–83 the world in 1800 86–87
Mao Shan mountain East Asia first religions 37 (4)
Ma-pa see Maba
Mapungubwe state Southern Africa the world in 1200 62–63
Maputo prev. Lourenço Marques Southern Africa (Mozambique) economy 168 (2) see also Lourenço Marques
Maracaibo South America (Venezuela) colonization 148 (2) empire and revolution 150 (1), (2), 151 (3) environment 153 (4) European expansion 85 (2) Incas 148 (1) politics 152 (1)
Maracaibo, Gulf of see Venezuela, Gulf of
Maracaibo, Lago de see Maracaibo, Lake
Maracaibo, Lake Sp. Maracaibo, Lago de inlet South America colonization 148 (2) early cultures 145 (2), 146 (1) Incas 148 (1)
Maracanda var. Samarkand, Samarqand Central Asia (Uzbekistan) Hellenistic world 40–41 (1) see also Samarkand
Maradi West Africa (Niger) Islam 167 (3)
Maradi state West Africa the world in 1850 90–91
Maragheh Southwest Asia (Iran) Mongols 68–69 (1)
Marajó region/people South America the world in 1 CE 42–43 the world in 250 CE 46–47 the world in 500 CE 50–51 the world in 750 CE 54–55 the world in 1000 58–59 the world in 1200 62–63
Marajó archaeological site South America early cultures 145 (2)
Marajoara region South America early cultures 145 (2)
Marakanda Central Asia (Uzbekistan) ancient trade 44–45 (1)
Maralinga nuclear test Australia environmentalism 285 (2)
Marama people South America early cultures 281 (4)
Maramba see Livingstone
Maranhão region South America colonization 149 (3)
Maranhão see São Luís, São Luiz do Maranhão
Marañón river South America colonization 148 (2) early cultures 144 (1), 145 (2), (3), (4), 146 (1) economy 153 (3) empire and revolution 150 (2) environment 153 (4) exploration 143 (2) Incas 147 (3), 148 (1) narcotics 153 (5) politics 152 (1)
Marash Southwest Asia (Turkey) Islam 227 (4)
Maratha Confederacy state South Asia the world in 1800 86–87
Marathas state South Asia colonialism 248 (1)
Marathon battle Greece ancient Persia 223 (4)
Maravi state Southern Africa Islam 163 (1)
Marburg see Maribor
Marcellus, Theater of building Italy ancient Rome 181 (2)
March see Morava
Marcia, Aqua aqueduct Italy ancient Rome 181 (2)
Marcianopolis Christian archbishopric Southeast Europe (Bulgaria) world religions 48 (1)
Marcomanni people Central Europe ancient Rome 180–181 (1), 181 (4)
Marcus Island var. Minami-tori-shima island Pacific Ocean US superpower 138 (1) WWII 272 (1)
Mar del Plata South America (Argentina) empire and revolution 151 (3)
Mardi var. Mardoi region Southwest Asia Hellenistic world 40–41 (1)
Mardoi see Mardi
Margarita Island island West Indies European expansion 85 (2)
Mari Southwest Asia (Iraq) first cities 220 (2), 28–29 (1) first civilizations 221 (4), 24 (2), 25 (3)
Maria Island penal center Australia colonization 282 (1) environmentalism 285 (2)
Mariana Islands var. Marianas island group Pacific Ocean colonization 284–285 (1) early cultures 280–281 (3) exploration 279 (3) imperialism 270 (2) medieval voyages 60 (2) US superpower 138 (1) WWII 104 (1), 105 (3), 272 (1), 273 (2)
Marianas see Mariana Islands
Maria-Theresiopel see Subotica
Ma'rib Southwest Asia (Yemen) early trade 225 (3)
Maribor Ger. Marburg Central Europe (Slovenia) postwar economy 215 (3)
Marica see Maritsa
Maricopa people North America colonization 125 (4)
Marie Galante var. Ceyre island West Indies the world in 1800 86–87
Mari El region Eastern Europe Soviet Union 214–215 (4)
Marienburg mod. Malbork Central Europe (Poland) early modern states 195 (3) medieval states 188 (1)
Marietta burial mound North America (USA) first civilizations 121 (4)
Marifa oil field Southwest Asia economy 234 (1)
Marignano mod. Melegnano battle Italy early modern states 194 (1)
Marinids dynasty North Africa economy 163 (2), 190 (1)
Marion North America (USA) US society 137 (6)
Mariqua battle Southern Africa (South Africa) colonization 166 (2)
Maritime Territory Rus. Primorskiy Kray region Siberia colonialism 269 (3)
Maritsa var. Marica; anc. Hebrus Gk. Évros, Turk. Meriç river Southeast Europe WWI 207 (6)
Maritsa see Chernomen
Maritzburg see Pietermaritzburg
Marj Dabik see Marj Dabiq
Marj Dabiq var. Marj Dabik Southwest Asia (Syria) Ottomans 231 (3)
Mark region Central Europe empire and revolution 199 (3)
Marka East Africa (Somalia) economy 163 (2)
Markland region North America medieval voyages 60–61 (1)
Marksville burial mound/region/settlement North America (USA) first civilizations 121 (4) first religions 36 (1)
Marksville Culture people North America the world in 1 CE 42–43 the world in 250 CE 46–47 the world in 500 CE 50–51
Marlborough region New Zealand colonization 283 (5)
Marlik Southwest Asia (Iran) first civilizations 24 (3)
Marmara Denizi see Marmara, Sea of
Marmara, Sea of var. Marmara Denizi sea Southwest Asia ancient Greece 177 (2), (3) first civilizations 175 (4), 177 (1) WWI 207 (6)
Marne battle France WWI 206 (3)
Marne river France WWI 206 (3)
Maroc see Morocco
Maronea state Greece ancient Greece 177 (2)
Maroni Southwest Asia (Cyprus) ancient Egypt 159 (5)
Marquesas Islands Fr. Îles Marquises island group Pacific Ocean colonization 284–285 (1) early cultures 280–281 (3) environmentalism 285 (2) exploration 278 (1), 279 (3) medieval voyages 60 (2)
Marquises, Îles see Marquesas Islands
Marrakech see Marrakesh
Marrakesh prev. Morocco; Fr. Marrakech North Africa (Morocco) biological diffusion 72–73 (1) economy 163 (2) exploration 156 (3), 157 (4) Islam 163 (1) Mongols 68 (2)
Marree Australia colonization 282 (1)
Marrucini people Italy early states 178 (1)
Marruecos see Morocco
Marsala see Lilybaeum
Marseille anc. Massalia, Massilia; Eng. Marseilles academic center/settlement France ancient Rome 182 (1) biological diffusion 72–73 (1) crusades 186 (1), 64–65 (2) early modern states 197 (5) economy 190 (1), 205 (4) empire and revolution 199 (4), 202 (1) European expansion 84–85 (1) Franks 183 (5), (6), 184 (2) global immigration 100 (1) medieval states 182 (2), 185 (3) Napoleon 200–201 (1), 201 (2), (3) prehistoric culture 17 (3), (4) WWII 210 (1), 211 (2), (4) see also Massalia, Massilia
Marseilles see Marseille, Massalia, Massilia
Marshall Islands island group/state Pacific Ocean colonization 284–285 (1) decolonization 285 (3) early cultures 280–281 (3) environmentalism 285 (2) exploration 278 (1), 279 (3) imperialism 270 (2) medieval voyages 60 (2) WWII 273 (2)
Marsi people Italy early states 178 (1)
Martaban var. Moktama Mainland Southeast Asia (Burma) colonialism 247 (4) trade 230 (2)
Martinique colonial possession/state/island West Indies Cold War 108 (2) colonization 126 (1) empire and revolution 150 (1) European expansion 84–85 (1) the growth of the US 129 (2) the modern world 112 (1)
Martinique island West Indies empire and revolution 88 (1) European expansion 84–85 (1)
Martin Point headland North America exploration 287 (2)
Marton New Zealand colonization 283 (5)
Maru-Desa region South Asia world religions 242 (2)
Marutea island Pacific Ocean exploration 278 (1)
Marwar region South Asia early medieval states 244–245 (3)
Mary see Alexandria Margiana, Merv
Maryborough Australia colonization 282 (1)
Mary Island see Canton Island
Maryland state North America empire and revolution 127 (2), (3) the growth of the US 129 (1) US Civil War 130 (2), (3), (4), (5), 131 (6), (7) US economy 134 (2)
Marzūq see Murzuk
Masada Southwest Asia (Israel) ancient Rome 225 (4)
Más Afuera island Pacific Ocean exploration 278 (1)
Masan see Happo
Masawa see Massawa
Mascat see Muscat
Mascouter people North America colonization 126 (1)
Masena West Africa (Chad) exploration 157 (4)
Masina region/state West Africa Islam 167 (3) trade 164 (2)
Masishaka state South Asia first empires 241 (5)
Masjed Southwest Asia (Iran) 20th-century politics 235 (5)
Masjed-e Soleymān see Masjed Soleymān
Masjed Soleyman Southwest Asia (Iran) 20th-century politics 235 (5)
Masjed Soleyman var. Masjed-e Soleyman, Masjid-i Sulaiman Southwest Asia (Iran) economy 234 (1)
Masjid-i Sulaiman see Masjed Soleymān
Maskat see Muscat
Masqat see Muscat
Massa and Carrara state Italy empire and revolution 202 (1)
Massachusetts colonial possession/state North America empire and revolution 127 (2), (3) the growth of the US 129 (1) US Civil War 130 (2), (3), (4), (5) US economy 134 (2)
Massacre Canyon battle North America (USA) the growth of the US 129 (2)
Massalia mod. Marseille, Marseilles; Lat. Massilia France first civilizations 177 (1) ancient Rome 179 (3) exploration 172 (1) see also Marseille, Massilia
Massangano Southern Africa (Angola) exploration 157 (4)
Massawa var. Masawa; Amh. Mits'iwa East Africa (Eritrea) colonization 167 (4) Ottomans 231 (3) trade 165 (3)
Massif Central plateau France early modern states 197 (5) prehistoric culture 17 (3)
Massilia var. Massalia; mod. Marseille, Marseilles France ancient Rome 179 (5), 180–181 (1), 181 (3) ancient trade 44 (2), 44–45 (1) early cultures 161 (2) great migrations 52–53 (1) world religions 48 (1) see also Marseille, Massalia
Massilia mod. Marseille state France ancient Rome 179 (5)
Masterton New Zealand colonization 283 (5)
Masulipatam South Asia (India) ancient trade 44–45 (1) colonialism 247 (3) early medieval states 245 (4) economy 249 (4) Mughal Empire 246 (1) trade 267 (3)
Masulipatam battle South Asia WWII 272 (1)
Masurian Lakes battle Central Europe (Poland) WWI 207 (4)
Matabele see Ndebele
Matacanela Central America (Mexico) first civilizations 122 (1)
Matacapan Piedra Central America (Mexico) first civilizations 122 (1)
Matamba state Southern Africa slave trade 165 (4) trade 164 (2)
Matamorros battle Central America (Mexico) the growth of the US 129 (2)
Matanzas West Indies (Cuba) European expansion 85 (2)
Matara South Asia (Sri Lanka) colonialism 247 (3)
Matara East Africa (Eritrea) early cultures 160 (1)
Mataram Maritime Southeast Asia (Indonesia) colonialism 247 (4)
Mataram region/state Maritime Southeast Asia colonialism 247 (4) early medieval states 245 (5)
Mata-Utu Pacific Ocean (Samoa) decolonization 285 (3)
Matenkupum New Guinea (New Ireland) early cultures 280 (2) exploration 280 (1)
Mathila South Asia (India) world religions 242 (2)
Mathura Buddhist center/settlement South Asia (India) ancient trade 44–45 (1) early medieval states 244 (1) exploration 256 (1) first empires 241 (5) first religions 36 (2) world religions 242 (2), (3), 243 (4), 49 (3)
Mathurai see Madura, Madurai
Mathuru see Mathura, Muttra
Matianus see Urmia, Lake
Matjiesrivier Southern Africa (South Africa) early agriculture 158 (1)
Matmar Egypt ancient Egypt 159 (2)
Mato Grosso region South America colonization 149 (3)
Mato Grosso see Vila Bela
Mato Grosso, Planalto de plateau South America colonization 149 (3) early cultures 144 (1), 145 (2) empire and revolution 151 (3) environment 153 (4) exploration 142 (1), 143 (2), (3)
Matola archaeological site Southern Africa (Mozambique) early cultures 160 (1)
Matsu island Japan Cold War 109 (1) postwar economy 275 (3)
Matsubara var. Matubara Japan medieval states 264 (2), 265 (3)
Matsumae Japan early modern states 267 (4)
Matsuyama Japan WWII 273 (3) economy 270 (1)
Matsya region/state South Asia ancient India 242 (1) first empires 241 (5) first religions 36 (2) world religions 242 (2)
Matubara see Matsubara
Matupi Cave settlement/archaeological site Central Africa (Congo (Zaire)) early agriculture 158 (1) first humans 13 (2) prehistoric culture 17 (2)
Matuyama see Matsuyama
Mau var. Maunāth Bhanjan South Asia (India) colonialism 247 (3)
Maubeuge France WWI 206 (2), (3)
Mauer archaeological site Central Europe (Germany) first humans 13 (2)
Maui island Pacific Ocean exploration 278 (1)
Maule river South America Incas 147 (3)
Maulmain see Moulmein
Maunāth Bhanjan see Mau
Mauretania province/region North Africa ancient Rome 179 (5), 181 (4), 225 (5) ancient trade 44 (2), 44–45 (1) early cultures 161 (2) the modern world 113 (3) world religions 48 (1)
Mauretania Caesariensis province North Africa ancient Rome 180–181 (1)
Mauretania Tingitana province North Africa ancient Rome 180–181 (1)
Maurice see Mauritius
Mauritania region/state West Africa decolonization 168 (1) economy 168 (2), (3) European imperialism 96 (1) Islam 235 (4) the modern world 112 (1), 113 (4)
Mauritius Fr. Maurice colonial possession/state/island Indian Ocean decolonization 168 (1) economy 168 (2) European expansion 84–85 (1) European imperialism 96 (1) global immigration 100 (1), 101 (3) the modern world 112 (1), 113 (3)
Mauritsstad see Pernambuco, Recife
Mauryan Empire state South Asia the world in 250 BCE 38–39
Mauthausen concentration camp Central Europe (Austria) WWII 211 (3)
Mawhai Point whaling station New Zealand colonization 283 (4)
Mawlamyine see Moulmein
Maw Shans region Mainland Southeast Asia early medieval states 245 (6)
Maxwell Bay North America (Canada) cultural groups 123 (3)
Maya South Asia (India) early religions 48 (2)
Maya people Central America colonization 125 (4), 126 (1) first religions 36 (1)
Maya City States state Central America the world in 500 CE 50–51 the world in 1000 58–59 the world in 1200 62–63 the world in 1300 66–67 the world in 1400 70–71 the world in 1500 74–75
Mayapán Central America (Mexico) Aztecs 124 (1) first civilizations 122 (1)
Maya-Toltec region Central America first civilizations 123 (2)
Mayebashi see Maebashi
Mayence see Mainz
Maykop Eastern Europe (Russian Federation) the world in 1250 BCE 26–27
Maynas region South America colonization 148 (2) exploration 143 (2)
Mayotte colonial possession Indian Ocean the world in 1975 106–107 the modern world 110–111
Mayyafariqin Southwest Asia (Iraq) crusades 228 (2)
Mayyali see Mahe
Mazaca see Caesarea, Cappadocia, Kayseri
Mazagan mod. El-Jadida North Africa (Morocco) the world in 1600 78–79
Mazantzintamalco Central America (Mexico) Aztecs 124 (3)
Mazapil mine Central America (Mexico) colonization 125 (4)
Mazar-i Sharif Central Asia (Afghanistan) world religions 243 (4)
Mazatec people Central America colonization 125 (4)
Mazatlán Central America (Mexico) Mexican Revolution 133 (3)
Mazouro Iberian Peninsula the world in 10,000 BCE 14–15
Mazumbo A Kalunga state Southern Africa the world in 1700 82–83
Mazun state Southwest Asia ancient Persia 225 (6)
Mbailundu state Southern Africa slave trade 165 (4) trade 167 (1)
Mbakannas state South Asia early medieval states 244 (2)
Mbamba state Central Africa economy 163 (2)
Mbata state Central Africa economy 163 (2)
Mbwila state Southern Africa trade 164 (2)
McHenry County region North America 121 (4)
McLennan Creek battle North America (USA) the growth of the US 129 (2)
Meadowcroft North America (USA) the world in 10,000 BCE 14–15
Meath region British Isles medieval states 186 (2)
Meaux France medieval states 192 (2) WWI 206 (2)
Mecca Ar. Makkah Southwest Asia (Saudi Arabia) biological diffusion 72–73 (1) crusades 65 (1) early cultures 161 (3), (4), (5) early Islam 56–57 (1), 57 (2) early trade 225 (3) European expansion 84–85 (1) exploration 156 (3), 218 (2), 219 (4) Islam 163 (1), 226 (2), (3), 227 (4), (5), 235 (4) medieval voyages 61 (3) Mongols 229 (3), 68 (2) Ottomans 231 (3) trade 230 (2), 267 (3) world religions 226 (1), 49 (4) 20th-century politics 233 (4)
Mecca, Sharifs of state Southwest Asia the world in 1400 70–71
Mecklenburg state Central Europe empire and revolution 202 (2)
Mecyberna state Greece ancient Greece 177 (2)
Medan Maritime Southeast Asia (Indonesia) postwar economy 253 (5) WWII 272 (1), 273 (2)
Medellín South America (Colombia) empire and revolution 150 (2), 151 (3) environment 153 (4) narcotics 153 (5) the modern world 113 (4)
Medeshamstede see Peterborough
Media region/state Southwest Asia ancient Persia 223 (4) ancient Rome 224 (2) ancient trade 44 (2) first civilizations 222 (2) Hellenistic world 224 (1)
Media Atropatene state Central Asia ancient Rome 224 (2) Hellenistic world 224 (1)
Medias Aguas archaeological site Central America (Mexico) first civilizations 121 (3)
Medina var. Yathrib, Ar. Al Madinah Southwest Asia (Saudi Arabia) crusades 228 (2), 65 (1) early cultures 161 (3), (4), (5) early Islam 56–57 (1), 57 (2) early trade 225 (3) exploration 219 (4) Islam 163 (1), 227 (4) medieval voyages 61 (3) Mongols 229 (3) Ottomans 231 (3) WWI 233 (2) 20th-century politics 233 (4) see also Yathrib
Medina del Campo Iberian Peninsula (Spain) economy 190 (1)
Medina, Sharifs of state Southwest Asia the world in 1400 70–71
Mediolanum mod. Milan, Mailand, Milano settlement Italy ancient Rome 180–181 (1), 181 (4) great migrations 52–53 (1) world religions 48 (1) see also Milan
Mediomatrica see Metz
Mediterranean Sea Fr. Mer Méditerranée; Lat. Mare Internum sea Europe/Asia/Africa ancient Greece 179 (4) ancient Persia 223 (4), 225 (6) ancient Rome 179 (3), (5), 180–181 (1), 181 (3), (4), 224 (2), 225 (4), (5) ancient trade 44–45 (1) biological diffusion 72–73 (1) Bronze Age 175 (3) Copper Age 174 (2) crusades 186 (1), 228 (2) early 20th century 206 (1) early agriculture 174 (1), 20–21 (2), 220 (1) early cultures 160 (1), 161 (2), (3), (4), (5) early Islam 56–57 (1), 57 (2) early systems 223 (3) early trade 225 (3) economy 163 (2), (3), 190 (1), 205 (4) empire and revolution 202 (1) European expansion 84–85 (1) exploration 156 (3), 157 (4), (5), 172 (1), (2), 219 (3) first cities 220 (2), 28–29 (1) first civilizations 175 (4), 177 (1), 221 (4), (5), 222 (2) first humans 13 (2) first religions 36 (1), 37 (3) great migrations 52–53 (1), 53 (2) Hellenistic world 40–41 (1), 41 (2) interwar 209 (3) Islam 184 (1), 226 (2), 227 (4) medieval states 182 (2), 183 (4), 185 (3), (5), 188 (1) medieval voyages 60–61 (1) Mongols 229 (3) Napoleon 200–201 (1), 201 (3) Ottomans 230 (1), 231 (3), 232–233 (1) postwar economy 213 (5) postwar politics 212 (3) Reformation 194 (2), 196 (1), 196 (2) Seljuks 228 (1) slave trade 165 (4) the modern world 113 (4) trade 167 (1) world religions 226 (1), 49 (4) WWI 208 (1), 233 (2) WWII 104 (1), 105 (3) 20th century 234 (2) 20th-century politics 233 (3)
Méditerranée, Mer see Mediterranean Sea
Medja state Egypt ancient Egypt 159 (4)
Medlock river British Isles economy 204 (2)
Meeker Agency battle North America (USA) the growth of the US 129 (2)
Meerut South Asia (India) economy 249 (4) empire and revolution 249 (3) postwar economy 253 (5) world religions 49 (3)
Mega Chad lake Central Africa historical geography 154–155 (1)
Megáli Préspa, Límni see Prespa
Megalo-Vlachia state Greece medieval states 189 (4)
Megara Greece first civilizations 177 (1)
Megara-Hyblaea Italy first civilizations 177 (1)
Meghalaya region South Asia postwar politics 252 (1), (3)
Meghna river South Asia postwar politics 252 (3)
Megiddo Southwest Asia (Israel) ancient Egypt 159 (4), (5) first cities 220 (2), 28–29 (1) first civilizations 221 (5), 222 (1) battle WWI 233 (2)
Mehadia Southeast Europe (Romania) WWI 207 (6)
Mehdia see Mahdia
Meherpur South Asia (Bangladesh) postwar politics 252 (3)
Mehran Southwest Asia (Iran) 20th-century politics 235 (5)
Mehrgarh archaeological site/settlement South Asia (Pakistan) first cities 240 (2)
Meir Egypt ancient Egypt 159 (4)
Meissen region Central Europe medieval states 188 (1)
Mekong Cam. Mékôngk, Chin. Lancang Jiang, Lan-ts'ang Chiang, Lao. Mènam Khong, Thai. Mae Nam Khong, Tib. Dza Chu, Vtn. Sông Tiên Giang river Mainland Southeast Asia ancient India 241 (6) ancient trade 44–45 (1) biological diffusion 72–73 (1), 73 (3) Bronze Age 240 (3) colonialism 247 (4), 248 (1), 269 (4) early agriculture 20–21 (2), 258 (1) early medieval states 245 (5), (6) early modern states 266 (1) first humans 13 (2) first religions 36 (1) first states 260 (1) global immigration 100 (1) medieval states 263 (6) Mongols 68–69 (1) postwar economy 253 (5), 275 (3) postwar politics 251 (5) prehistoric culture 16 (1) the modern world 110–111 trade 230 (2) world religions 243 (5), 49 (3), (4)
Mékôngk see Mekong
Melaka Mainland Southeast Asia (Malaysia) early medieval states 245 (6)
Melaka, Selat see Malacca, Strait of
Melanesia island group Pacific Ocean WWII 272 (1), 273 (2)
Melbourne penal colony/settlement Australia colonization 282 (1), (2), 284–285 (1) decolonization 285 (3) environmentalism 285 (2) exploration 279 (2), (3) global immigration 100 (1) imperial global economy 92 (1) prehistoric culture 17 (5)
Melegnano see Marignano
Melilla anc. Rusaddir, Russadir North Africa (Spain) biological diffusion 72–73 (1) see also Rusaddir
Melilla see Rusaddir
Melita island Mediterranean Sea ancient Rome 179 (3)
Melitene mod. Malatya Southwest Asia (Turkey) ancient Rome 180–181 (1) Hellenistic world 40–41 (1) world religions 48 (1) see also Malatya
Melk Central Europe (Austria) medieval states 188 (1)
Melka Kunture East Africa (Ethiopia) the world in 5000 BCE 18–19
Mellifont major cistercian house British Isles (United Kingdom) medieval states 187 (3)
Melos Greece first civilizations 177 (1)
Melos island Greece ancient Greece 177 (2) first civilizations 175 (4)
Melrose major cistercian house British Isles (United Kingdom) medieval states 183 (3)
Meltus see Miletus
Melun France medieval states 192 (2)
Melville Island island/penal center Australia colonization 282 (1) environmentalism 285 (2)
Melville Koppies archaeological site Southern Africa (South Africa) early cultures 160 (1)
Mema state West Africa trade 163 (6)
Memel Lith. Klaipėda Eastern Europe (Lithuania) early modern states 197 (3) empire and revolution 199 (3) interwar 209 (5) WWI 207 (4) see also Klaipėda
Memel see Neman
Memorana North America (Canada) cultural groups 123 (3)
Mempawah see Mampava
Memphis Egypt ancient Egypt 159 (3), (4), (5) ancient Persia 223 (4) ancient Rome 180–181 (1) early cultures 160 (1), 161 (2) early Islam 56–57 (1) early systems 32 (1), 33 (2), (3) first cities 220 (2), 28–29 (1) first civilizations 222 (2) first religions 37 (3) Hellenistic world 40–41 (1) imperial global economy 93 (5) the growth of the US 129 (2), 132 (1) US Civil War 131 (7) US economy 136 (2) US politics 135 (6) US society 137 (6) world religions 48 (1)
Menado mod. Manado Maritime Southeast Asia (Indonesia) colonialism 247 (4) European expansion 84–85 (1) US Civil War 131 (6)
Mènam Khong see Mekong
Menasha Mounds burial mound North America (USA) first civilizations 121 (4)
Mende settlement/state Greece ancient Greece 177 (2) first civilizations 177 (1)
Mendes Egypt ancient Egypt 159 (2), (3)
Mendota Mounds burial mound North America (USA) first civilizations 121 (4)
Mendoza South America (Argentina) colonization 148 (2) empire and revolution 150 (1), 151 (3) environment 153 (4)
Mendut Maritime Southeast Asia (Indonesia) world religions 243 (5)
Menelaion palace Greece first civilizations 175 (4)
Mengtsz see Mengzi
Mengzi var. Mengtsz East Asia (China) colonialism 269 (4)
Meniet North Africa (Algeria) early agriculture 158 (1)
Menindee Australia exploration 279 (2)
Menindee Lake Australia exploration 280 (1)
Menominee people North America colonization 126 (1)
Menongue prev. Vila Serpa Pinto, Serpa Pinto Southern Africa (Angola) Cold War 109 (5)
Menorca anc. Balearis Minor; Eng. Minorca island Mediterranean Sea interwar 209 (4) see also Minorca
Menzies Australia colonization 282 (1)
Meran It. Merano Italy WWI 207 (5)
Merano see Meran
Mercia state British Isles medieval states 183 (3)
Mergui Mainland Southeast Asia (Burma) colonialism 247 (4), 248 (1)
Meriç see Maritsa
Mérida South America (Venezuela) empire and revolution 150 (1)
Mérida anc. Emerita Augusta Iberian Peninsula (Spain) early Islam 56–57 (1) Franks 184 (2) interwar 209 (4) see also Emerita Augusta
Mérida Central America (Mexico) colonization 125 (4), 126 (1) exploration 118 (1) Mexican Revolution 133 (3)
Merimda Egypt ancient Egypt 159 (2) early agriculture 158 (1)
Merina see Merina Kingdom
Merina Kingdom var. Merina state Southern Africa the world in 1800 86–87 the world in 1850 90–91
Merkits people East Asia/Siberia Mongols 68–69 (1)
Meroe archaeological site/settlement East Africa (Sudan) early agriculture 158 (1) early cultures 160 (1), 161 (3), (4), (5) early trade 225 (3) the world in 250 CE 46–47
Mersa Gawasis var. Sawu Egypt ancient Egypt 159 (4)
Merseburg Central Europe (Germany) medieval states 188 (1), 189 (3)
Mersin Southwest Asia (Turkey) early agriculture 174 (1) first cities 220 (2) first civilizations 221 (4), (5)
Merthyr Tydfil British Isles (United Kingdom) economy 204 (1)
Merv mod. Mary; anc. Alexandria Margiana Southwest Asia (Turkmenistan) ancient Persia 223 (4), 225 (6) ancient Rome 224 (2) ancient trade 44–45 (1) biological diffusion 72–73 (1) Hellenistic world 224 (1) Islam 226 (2), 227 (4), (5) medieval Persia 231 (4) medieval states 261 (6) Seljuks 228 (1) world religions 226 (1) see also Alexandria Margiana
Mesa Grande archaeological site North America (USA) cultural groups 123 (4)
Mesa Verde North America (USA) the world in 1200 62–63
Mesa Verde National Park archaeological site North America (USA) cultural groups 123 (4)
Mescalero people North America colonization 126 (1)
Mescalero Apache people North America colonization 125 (4)
Mesembria Southeast Europe (Greece) first civilizations 177 (1)
Meshan state Southwest Asia ancient Persia 225 (6)
Meshed Southwest Asia (Iran) Hellenistic world 40–41 (1) medieval Persia 231 (4)
Meskhetians people Southwest Asia Soviet Union 213 (4)
Mesoamerica region Central America biological diffusion 73 (2) early agriculture 120 (1)
Mesopotamia region Southwest Asia 20th-century politics 233 (4) ancient Rome 180–181 (1), 224 (2), 225 (5) Bronze Age 175 (3) crusades 228 (2) early agriculture 220 (1) early Islam 56–57 (1), 57 (2), (3) early systems 223 (3), 32 (1), 33 (3) exploration 218 (1), (2), 219 (3) first cities 220 (2) first civilizations 221 (4), 222 (2) first religions 36 (1) Hellenistic world 40–41 (1) Islam 226 (2), 227 (5) medieval Persia 231 (4) medieval states 261 (6) Ottomans 231 (3) world religions 226 (1) WWI 233 (2)
Messana mod. Messina; prev. Zancle Italy ancient Rome 179 (3), 180–181 (1), 181 (3) see also Messina
Messapii people Italy early states 178 (2)
Messene Greece ancient Greece 179 (4)
Messene see Messina
Messenia state Greece ancient Greece 179 (4)
Messina Italy crusades 186 (1), 64–65 (2) economy 190 (1) Islam 227 (4) medieval states 188 (1), 189 (4) WWII 211 (4)
Messina, Strait of sea waterway Italy ancient Rome 179 (3)
Messines France WWI 206 (2), (3)
Meta region South America narcotics 153 (5)
Meta river South America early cultures 146 (1) exploration 143 (2) narcotics 153 (5)
Metapontum Italy early states 178 (1) first civilizations 177 (1)
Metaurus, River battle Italy ancient Rome 179 (3)
Methone Greece ancient Greece 177 (3)
Methymna state Greece ancient Greece 177 (2)
Metis see Metz
Metz massacre/settlement France crusades 186 (1) early modern states 193 (4), 197 (5) economy 190 (1) empire and revolution 199 (4) Franks 183 (5), (6), 184 (2) medieval states 188 (1)
Metztitlan state Central America Aztecs 124 (1)
Meung academic center/settlement France medieval states 187 (3), 192 (2)
Meuniers, Pont aux bridge France economy 191 (2)
Meuse river Low Countries Bronze Age 175 (3) empire and revolution 202 (1), (2) Franks 183 (5) great migrations 52–53 (1), 53 (2) WWI 206 (2), (3)
Mexicaltzinco Central America (Mexico) Aztecs 124 (2), (3)
Mexico state Central America empire and revolution 88–89 (2) global immigration 100 (1), 101 (2) imperial global economy 92 (1) Mexican Revolution 133 (3) the growth of the US 129 (2), 132 (1), 133 (4) the modern world 112 (1), 113 (4) US economy 136 (2) US politics 139 (4) US superpower 138 (1) WWII 104 (2) Cold War 108 (2), 109 (1)
México var. Mexico City; prev. Tenochtitlan; Sp. Ciudad de México Central America (Mexico) colonization 125 (4) see also Mexico City, Tenochtitlan
Mexico City var. México; prev. Tenochtitlan; Sp. Ciudad de México Central America (Mexico) colonization 126 (1) European expansion 81 (3), 84–85 (1), 85 (2) exploration 119 (3) global immigration 100 (1) imperial global economy 92 (1) Mexican Revolution 133 (3) the growth of the US 129 (2) the modern world 113 (4) US economy 136 (2) Cold War 108 (2) see also México, Tenochtitlan
Mexico, Gulf of gulf North America Aztecs 124 (1) colonization 125 (4), (5), 126 (1) cultural groups 122 (5) early agriculture 120 (1), 20–21 (2) empire and revolution 88–89 (2) European expansion 84–85 (1), 85 (2) exploration 118 (1), 119 (2), (3) first civilizations 121 (2), (3), (4), 122 (1) global knowledge 76–77 (1) Mexican Revolution 133 (3) the growth of the US 129 (2), 132 (1) US Civil War 131 (6), (7) US economy 136 (2) Cold War 108 (2)
Mexiquito Central America (Mexico) first civilizations 122 (1)
Mezcala Central America (Mexico) first civilizations 121 (2)
Mezcalapa river Central America first civilizations 122 (1)
Mezhirich Eastern Europe the world in 10,000 BCE 14–15
Mézières France WWI 206 (2), (3)
Mezőkeresztes battle Southeast Europe (Hungary) Ottomans 195 (4)
Mfengu people Southern Africa colonization 166 (2)
Mfolosi river Southern Africa colonization 166 (2)
Miam see Aniba
Miami North America (USA) the growth of the US 133 (4) the modern world 113 (4) US economy 134 (1), 136 (2) US society 137 (6) Cold War 108 (2)
Miami people North America colonization 126 (1)
Miamisburg burial mound North America (USA) first civilizations 121 (4)
Miao rebellion East Asia empire and revolution 268 (2)
Miaodigou archaeological site East Asia (China) early agriculture 258 (2)
Michigan state North America the growth of the US 129 (1) US Civil War 130 (2), (3), (4), (5) US economy 134 (2)
Michigan, Lake lake North America colonization 126 (1) cultural groups 122 (5) early agriculture 120 (1) empire and revolution 127 (3) exploration 118 (1), 119 (2), (3) first civilizations 121 (4) the growth of the US 129 (2), 132 (1) US Civil War 131 (6)
Michilmackinac North America (Canada) colonization 126 (1)
Michoacán var. Tavascan state Central America Aztecs 124 (1) Mexican Revolution 133 (3) the growth of the US 129 (2)
Micmac people North America colonization 126 (1)
Micronesia island group Pacific Ocean WWII 272 (1), 273 (2)
Micronesia, Federated States of state Pacific Ocean environmentalism 285 (2)
Middelburg Southern Africa (South Africa) European imperialism 96 (2)
Middelburg battle Low Countries (Netherlands) Reformation 195 (5)
Middle Angles people British Isles medieval states 183 (3)
Middle Congo see Congo
Middle East region Southwest Asia US economy 138 (2)
Middleport North America (USA) cultural groups 122 (5)
Middlesbrough British Isles (United Kingdom) economy 204 (1)
Midhe mod. Meath state British Isles medieval states 188 (2) see also Meath
Midway Islands battle/colonial possession/island group Pacific Ocean Cold War 109 (1) decolonization 285 (3) exploration 276–277 (1) the growth of the US 133 (4) US superpower 138 (1)
Mie prefecture Japan economy 270 (1)
Mien state Mainland Southeast Asia medieval states 263 (6)
Miguel de Aguayo jesuit mission Central America (Mexico) colonization 125 (4)
Mihambo East Africa (Tanzania) exploration 157 (4)
Mikindani East Africa (Tanzania) exploration 157 (4)
Miklagard see Byzantium, Constantinople, Istanbul
Milan anc. Mediolanum; Ger. Mailan, It. Milano Italy crusades 186 (1) early modern states 193 (4), 194 (1) economy 190 (1), 205 (4) empire and revolution 202 (1), (3) Franks 184 (2) medieval states 182 (2), 183 (4), 185 (3), (5), 188 (1) Napoleon 200–201 (1), 201 (2), (3) postwar politics 212 (3) Reformation 194 (2), 196 (1) WWII 210 (1), 211 (2), (3), (4) Cold War 108 (3) see also Mediolanum
Milan state Italy early modern states 194 (1) Reformation 194 (2), 196 (1), (2)
Milano see Mediolanum, Milan
Miletos see Miletus
Miletus settlement/state Southwest Asia (Turkey) ancient Greece 177 (2), (3) ancient Persia 223 (4) ancient Rome 180–181 (1) exploration 172 (1) first civilizations 175 (4), 177 (1), 221 (5), 222 (2) Hellenistic world 40–41 (1)
Miller burial mound North America (USA) first civilizations 121 (4)
Miller region North America first civilizations 121 (4)
Millstream Australia the world in 5000 BCE 18–19
Milne Bay battle New Guinea (Papua New Guinea) WWII 104 (2)
Milpitas North America (USA)
Milton New Zealand colonization 283 (5)
Milwaukee North America (USA) the growth of the US 132 (1) US economy 134 (1), (3)
Mimana state East Asia medieval states 264 (2)
Mimana see Kaya
Mimbreo Apache people North America colonization 125 (4)
Mimbres Valley archaeological site North America (USA) cultural groups 123 (4)
Min state East Asia medieval states 263 (3)
Mina archaeological site South America (Brazil) early cultures 144 (1), 145 (2)
Minab Southwest Asia (Iran) economy 234 (1)
Mīnā Baranīs see Berenice
Minami-tori-shima see Marcus Island
Minangkabau region Maritime Southeast Asia early medieval states 245 (6)
Minas Gerais region South America colonization 149 (3)
Minas Novas South America (Brazil) colonization 149 (3) empire and revolution 151 (3)
Minca South America (Colombia) early cultures 146 (1)
Mindanao island Philippines colonialism 247 (4) European imperialism 97 (3) exploration 239 (1) historical geography 236–237 (1) Islam 243 (6) postwar politics 253 (4) world religions 243 (5) WWII 272 (1), 273 (2)
Minden anc. Minthun Central Europe (Germany) medieval states 189 (3)
Minden region Central Europe empire and revolution 199 (3)
Mindoro island Philippines European imperialism 97 (3) WWII 273 (2)
Minfeng see Niya
Ming Empire state East Asia early modern states 266 (1), (2), 267 (4) European expansion 80–81 (1) trade 230 (2), 267 (3) see also China
Minisink North America (USA) cultural groups 122 (5)
Minneapolis North America (USA) the growth of the US 132 (1) US economy 134 (1), (3)
Minnesota state North America the growth of the US 129 (1) US Civil War 130 (5) US economy 134 (2)
Minnesota Territory region North America US Civil War 130 (2), (3), (4)
Minong, Lake lake North America the world in 10,000 BCE 14–15
Minorca var. Menorca; anc. Balearis Minor island Mediterranean Sea empire and revolution 88 (1) see also Menorca
Minshat Egypt ancient Egypt 159 (2)
Minsk ghetto/settlement Eastern Europe (Belorussia) empire and revolution 198 (2) postwar politics 212 (3) Soviet Union 208 (2), 214–215 (4) WWII 207 (4) WWII 211 (2), (3), (4)
Minthun see Minden
Minyue province/state East Asia first cities 259 (5) first states 260 (1)
Mirabib archaeological site Southern Africa (Namibia) early cultures 160 (1)
Miraflores South America (Colombia) narcotics 153 (5)
Miraflores South America (Chile) politics 151 (4)
Mirambo state East Africa colonization 167 (4)
Miran East Asia (China) world religions 49 (3)
Miriwun Australia exploration 280 (1)
Miru people South America early cultures 281 (4)
Mirzapur South Asia (India) economy 249 (4)
Misasa Japan early modern states 265 (5)
Misenum archaeological site Italy ancient Rome 180–181 (1)
Misisil Melanesia (New Britain) early cultures 280 (2) exploration 280 (1)

Mississippi *state* North America imperial global economy 93 (5) the growth of the US 129 (1) US Civil War 130 (2), (3), (4), (5), 131 (6), (7) US economy 134 (2), 139 (3) US society 137 (6) US superpower 139 (5)
Mississippi *river* North America colonization 125 (4), 126 (1) cultural groups 122 (5) early agriculture 120 (1), 20–21 (2) empire and revolution 127 (3), 88 (1) European expansion 84–85 (1) exploration 118 (1), 119 (2), (3) first civilizations 121 (4) first religions 36 (1) imperial global economy 92 (1) prehistoric culture 16 (1) the growth of the US 129 (2), 132 (1) US Civil War 130 (5), 131 (6), (7)
Mississippian Cultures *people* North America the world in 1200 62–63 the world in 1300 66–67 the world in 1400 70–71 the world in 1500 74–75
Missoula, Lake *lake* North America the world in 10,000 BCE 14–15
Missouri *state* North America the growth of the US 129 (1) US Civil War 130 (2), (3), (4), (5), 131 (6), (7) US economy 134 (2)
Missouri *people* North America colonization 126 (1)
Missouri *river* North America colonization 126 (1) cultural groups 122 (5) early agriculture 120 (1), 20–21 (2) exploration 118 (1), 119 (2), (3) first civilizations 121 (4) first religions 36 (1) the growth of the US 129 (2) US Civil War 130 (5)
Mistra Greece medieval states 187 (5), 189 (4)
Miswar Southwest Asia (Yemen) early trade 225 (3)
Mitanni, Kingdom of *state* Southwest Asia first civilizations 221 (5)
Mitau *Latv.* Jelgava; *Rus.* Mitava Eastern Europe (Latvia) early modern states 195 (3) *see also* Mitava
Mitava *Latv.* Jelgava; *Rus.* Mitau Eastern Europe (Latvia) WWI 207 (4) *see also* Mitau
Mithila South Asia (India) ancient India 242 (1) world religions 242 (3)
Mithraeum *building* Southwest Asia (Iraq) first cities 220 (3)
Mitla Central America (Mexico) first civilizations 122 (1)
Mitrovica *var.* Kosovska Mitrovica Southeast Europe (Yugoslavia) postwar economy 215 (3)
Mits'iwa *see* Massawa
Mitte Central Europe (Germany) postwar politics 212 (2)
Mitte *region* Eastern Europe WWII 211 (2)
Mitterberg *mine* Central Europe Bronze Age 175 (3)
Mittimatalik North America (Canada) cultural groups 123 (3)
Mitylene
Miwa *mountain* Japan medieval states 265 (3)
Mixcoac Central America (Mexico) Aztecs 124 (2), (3)
Mixco Viejo Central America (Guatemala) Aztecs 124 (1)
Mixincan Central America (Mexico) Aztecs 124 (3)
Mixquic Central America (Mexico) Aztecs 124 (2)
Mixtlan Central America (Mexico) Aztecs 124 (1)
Miyagi *prefecture* Japan economy 270 (1)
Miyanouchi Japan early modern states 265 (5)
Miyazaki *prefecture* Japan economy 270 (1)
Mizda North Africa (Libya) exploration 157 (4)
Mizoram *region* South Asia postwar politics 252 (1), (3), 253 (4)
Mizquic Central America (Mexico) colonization 125 (5)
Mizu-shima *battle* Japan early modern states 265 (5)
Mladec *archaeological site* Central Europe (Czech Republic) the world in 10,000 BCE 14–15
Mlozi *state* East Africa colonization 167 (4)
Mo *people* East Asia first cities 259 (4)
Moab *state* Southwest Asia first civilizations 222 (1)
Mobile North America (USA) Cold War 108 (2) European expansion 84–85 (1) the growth of the US 129 (2) US Civil War 131 (7) US society 137 (6)
Mobile *battle* North America (USA) US Civil War 131 (7)
Mobile *people* Central America colonization 125 (4)
Mobutu Sese Seko, Lac *see* Albert, Lake
Moçambique *see* Mozambique, Portuguese East Africa
Moçâmedes *see* Mossamedes, Namibe
Moccassin Bluff North America (USA) cultural groups 122 (5)
Moche South America (Peru) early cultures 145 (4)
Moche *region/state* South America early cultures 145 (4)
Moche *river* South America early cultures 145 (3), (4)
Moche/Chan Chan *state* South America the world in 1000 58–59
Moctezuma *river* Central America first civilizations 121 (2)
Modder River *Afr.* Modderrivier *battle* Southern Africa (South Africa) European imperialism 96 (2)
Modderrivier *see* Modder River
Modena *anc.* Mutina Italy economy 190 (1) Franks 184 (2) medieval states 188 (1) *see also* Mutina
Modena *state* Italy empire and revolution 202 (1), (3) Reformation 194 (2), 196 (1), (2)
Modon Greece economy 190 (1) medieval states 187 (5)
Moeraki *whaling station* New Zealand colonization 283 (4)
Moero, Lac *see* Mweru, Lake
Moers *see* Mörs
Moesia *province/region* Southeast Europe ancient Rome 180–181 (1), 181 (4) ancient trade 44 (2) world religions 48 (1)
Moesia Inferior *province* Southeast Europe ancient Rome 180–181 (1)
Moesia Superior *province* Southeast Europe ancient Rome 180–181 (1)
Mogadishu *early Chin.* Mo-ku-ta-shu, *Som.* Muqdisho East Africa (Somalia) biological diffusion 72–73 (1) colonization 167 (4) economy 163 (2) European expansion 80–81 (1) exploration 156 (3) global immigration 100 (1) Islam 163 (1) medieval voyages 61 (3) Mongols 68 (2) trade 165 (3), 230 (2), 267 (3)
Mogador *mod.* Essaouira North Africa (Morocco) early cultures 160 (1) exploration 157 (4)
Mogilev Eastern Europe (Belorussia) economy 190 (1) Soviet Union 208 (2) WWI 207 (4) WWII 210 (1), 211 (4)
Mogollon *archaeological site* North America (USA) cultural groups 123 (4)
Mogollon Culture *region/state* North America/Central America cultural groups 123 (4)
Mogontiacum *mod.* Mainz *settlement* Central Europe (Germany) ancient Rome 180–181 (1), 181 (4) great migrations 52–53 (1) *see also* Mainz
Mogul Empire *see* Mughal Empire
Mohács Central Europe (Hungary) Ottomans 231 (3)
Mohács *battle* Southeast Europe Ottomans 195 (4)
Mohammerah *see* Khorramshahr
Mohelnice Central Europe (Czech Republic) early agriculture 174 (1)
Mohenjo-Daro *archaeological site/settlement* South Asia (Pakistan) early systems 223 (3) first cities 240 (2) first civilizations 24 (2), 25 (3)
Mohican *see* Mahican
Mojave *people* North America colonization 125 (4), 126 (1)
Mojave Desert *desert* North America cultural groups 123 (4)
Moji Japan economy 270 (1)
Mojos *people* South America colonization 148 (2) exploration 143 (2)
Mokpo *Jap.* Moppo East Asia (South Korea) Cold War 109 (4) early modern states 267 (4) Russo-Japanese War 270 (4)
Moktama *see* Martaban
Mo-ku-ta-shu *see* Mogadishu
Moldavia *var.* Moldova *region/state* Southeast Europe early modern states 193 (4) empire and revolution 198 (2), 202 (1) medieval states 189 (3), (4) Napoleon 200–201 (1) Ottomans 195 (4), 231 (3) postwar economy 214 (1), (2) Reformation 194 (2) Soviet Union 213 (4) the modern world 112 (2) WWI 207 (4)
Moldova *see* Moldavia
Mollendo South America (Peru) empire and revolution 151 (3)
Mologa *river* Eastern Europe Mongols 68–69 (1)
Molokai *leper colony* Pacific Ocean environmentalism 285 (2)
Molopo *river* Southern Africa European imperialism 96 (2)
Molotov Eastern Europe (Russian Federation) Soviet Union 213 (4)
Moluccas *prev.* Spice Islands; *Dut.* Molukken, *Eng.* Moluccas *island group* Maritime Southeast Asia ancient trade 44–45 (1) biological diffusion 72–73 (1) Bronze Age 240 (3) European expansion 80–81 (1), 81 (3) exploration 239 (1), (2) Islam 243 (6) trade 230 (2), 267 (3)
Molucca Sea *Ind.* Laut Maluku *sea* Maritime Southeast Asia Bronze Age 240 (3) early medieval states 245 (6) Islam 243 (6)
Molukken *see* Moluccas
Mombasa East Africa (Kenya) colonization 167 (4) economy 163 (2) European expansion 81 (3), 84–85 (1) European imperialism 96 (1) exploration 156 (3), 157 (4), (5) global immigration 100 (1) Islam 163 (1) Mongols 68 (2) slave trade 165 (4) trade 164 (1), 230 (2), 267 (3)
Mon *state* Mainland Southeast Asia world religions 49 (4)
Monacan *people* North America colonization 125 (4), 126 (1)
Monaco *var.* Monaco-Ville; *anc.* Monoecus *state* France empire and revolution 202 (1), (3) the modern world 112 (2), 113 (4)
Monaco *see* Munich
Monaco-Ville *see* Monaco
Mon and Malay States *state* Mainland Southeast Asia the world in 250 CE 46–47 the world in 500 CE 50–51
Monastir *var.* Bitolj; *mod.* Bitola *fort/settlement* Southeast Europe (FYR Macedonia) early Islam 56–57 (1) WWI 207 (6) *see also* Bitola, Bitolj
Moncastro Eastern Europe (Ukraine) economy 190 (1) medieval states 189 (4)
Mondidier France WWI 206 (2), (3)
Mondovi *battle* Italy Napoleon 200–201 (1)
Monemvasia Greece medieval states 187 (5) Ottomans 230 (1), 231 (3)
Monfalcone Italy WWI 207 (5)
Monghyr *var.* Munger South Asia (India) economy 249 (4)
Mongol Empire *state* East Asia medieval states 263 (5)
Mongolia *prev.* Outer Mongolia; *Mong.* Mongol Uls *region/state* East Asia biological diffusion 72–73 (1) Chinese revolution 271 (5) colonialism 269 (4) early modern states 266 (2) economy 274 (1) exploration 257 (3) historical geography 275 (5) Islam 275 (4) medieval states 261 (6) postwar economy 275 (3) postwar politics 271 (7), 274 (2) Soviet Union 208 (2), 213 (4) the modern world 113 (3), (4) world religions 49 (4) WWII 104 (1), (2), 272 (1), 273 (2) Cold War 109 (1) Communism 271 (8) *see also* Oirats, Khanate of the, Outer Mongolia
Mongolia, Plateau of *plateau* East Asia Mongols 68–69 (1)
Mongols *people* East Asia/Siberia early modern states 266 (1) Mongols 68–69 (1) trade 267 (3)
Mongol Uls *see* Mongolia, Oirats, Khanate of the, Outer Mongolia
Monkchester *see* Newcastle-upon-Tyne
Mon-Khmer Peoples *people* Mainland Southeast Asia ancient trade 44–45 (1)
Monkwearmouth *religious building* British Isles (United Kingdom) medieval states 183 (3)
Monmouth North America (USA) empire and revolution 127 (3)
Monmouth Court House *battle* North America (USA) empire and revolution 127 (3)
Monoecus *see* Monaco
Monopoli Italy economy 190 (1)
Monrovia West Africa (Liberia) economy 168 (2) US superpower 138 (1)
Mons Low Countries (Belgium) WWI 206 (2), (3)
Montagnais *people* North America colonization 126 (1) cultural groups 123 (3)
Montana *state* North America the growth of the US 129 (1) US economy 134 (2)
Montauban France early modern states 197 (5) Reformation 194 (2)
Mont-Dauphin France early modern states 197 (5)
Monte Alban *region* Central America first civilizations 122 (1)
Monte Albán Central America (Mexico) Aztecs 124 (1) first civilizations 121 (2), 122 (1) first religions 36 (1)
Monte Alegre *archaeological site* South America (Brazil) early cultures 144 (1)
Monte Alto Central America (Mexico) first civilizations 123 (2)
Monte Bello Islands *nuclear test* Australia environmentalism 285 (2)
Monte Cassino Italy Franks 184 (2) medieval states 183 (4) WWII 211 (4)
Montecristi West Indies (Dominican Republic) European expansion 85 (2)
Monteleone di Calabria *see* Hipponium
Montenegro *SCr.* Crna Gora *state/vassal state* Southeast Europe early modern states 193 (4) economy 205 (4) Napoleon 200–201 (1), 201 (2) Ottomans 195 (4), 232–233 (1) Reformation 194 (2) WWI 207 (6) WWII 211 (2), (4) early 20th century 206 (1)
Montenegro-Serbia *region* Southeast Europe postwar economy 215 (3)
Montenotte *battle* Italy Napoleon 200–201 (1)
Montereau *battle* France Napoleon 200–201 (1)
Monterey North America (USA) the growth of the US 129 (2)
Monterey *see* Monterrey
Monterrey *var.* Monterey Central America (Mexico) exploration 119 (2), (3) Mexican Revolution 133 (3) the growth of the US 129 (2) US economy 136 (2) Cold War 108 (2)
Montespan *archaeological site* France prehistoric culture 17 (3)
Monte Verde *archaeological site/settlement* South America (Chile) early cultures 144 (1)
Montevideo South America (Uruguay) colonization 148 (2) empire and revolution 150 (1), 151 (3) environment 153 (4) exploration 143 (3) global immigration 100 (1) imperial global economy 92 (1) politics 152 (1)
Montezuma Castle *archaeological site* North America (USA) cultural groups 123 (4)
Montferrat *state* Italy Reformation 196 (1)
Montgaudier *archaeological site* France prehistoric culture 17 (3)
Montgomery British Isles (United Kingdom) medieval states 188 (2)
Montgomery North America (USA) the growth of the US 129 (2), 132 (1) US Civil War 131 (7) US society 137 (6)
Montmaurin *archaeological site* France first humans 13 (2)
Montmirail France WWI 206 (2), (3) *battle* 200–201 (1)
Montpelier North America (USA) the growth of the US 129 (2)
Montpellier *settlement/university* France early modern states 197 (5) economy 190 (1) empire and revolution 199 (4) medieval states 187 (3), 192 (1)
Montreal *var.* Hochelaga; *Fr.* Montréal North America (Canada) colonization 126 (1) empire and revolution 127 (2), (3), 88 (1) European expansion 84–85 (1) exploration 119 (2), (3) imperial global economy 92 (1) the growth of the US 129 (2), 132 (1) US economy 136 (2) *see also* Hochelaga
Montréal *fort* Southwest Asia (Jordan) crusades 65 (3)
Montreuil France WWI 206 (2)
Montserrat *var.* Emerald Isle *colonial possession* West Indies the world in 1975 106–107 the modern world 110–111
Monza Italy medieval states 183 (4)
Mook *battle* Low Countries (Netherlands) Reformation 195 (5)
Mooloya Estate *rebellion* South Asia (Sri Lanka) decolonization 250 (1)
Moose Factory North America (Canada) colonization 126 (1)
Mootwingee *archaeological site* Australia prehistoric culture 17 (5)
Moppo *see* Mokpo
Moquegua South America (Peru) politics 151 (4)
Moradabad South Asia (India) economy 249 (4)
Morat *Ger.* Murten *battle* Central Europe (Switzerland) early modern states 193 (5)
Morava *var.* Glavn'a Morava, March, Velika Morava; *Ger.* Grosse Moravavar *river* Central Europe WWI 207 (6) *see also* Velika Morava
Moravia *region/state* Central Europe early modern states 193 (4) empire and revolution 199 (3) medieval states 189 (4) Napoleon 200–201 (1) Ottomans 197 (4)
Moravians *people* Central Europe Franks 184 (2)
Mordovia *region* Eastern Europe Soviet Union 214–215 (4)
Morea *vassal state* Greece Ottomans 230 (1)
Morelos *state* Central America Mexican Revolution 133 (3)
Moreruela *major cistercian house* Iberian Peninsula medieval states 187 (3)
Moreton Bay *bay* Australia exploration 279 (2)
Moreton Bay *penal center* Australia colonization 282 (1) environmentalism 285 (2)
Morgan Hill North America (USA)
Morgarten *battle* Central Europe (Switzerland) early modern states 193 (5)
Mori *region* Japan early modern states 267 (4)
Morimond *major cistercian house* France medieval states 187 (3)
Morioka Japan economy 270 (1)
Mormon Trail *wagon train route* North America (USA) the growth of the US 129 (2)
Morocco *Ar.* Al Mamlakah, *Fr.* Maroc, *Sp.* Marruecos *region/state* North Africa colonization 167 (4) decolonization 168 (1)early Islam 57 (2) economy 168 (2), (3) European expansion 84–85 (1) European imperialism 96 (1), 97 (4) global immigration 101 (2) Islam 235 (4) Napoleon 200–201 (1) Ottomans 231 (3) slave trade 165 (4) the modern world 112 (1), 113 (3), (4) trade 164 (2), 167 (1) WWII 104 (1), 211 (4) early 20th century 206 (1) Cold War 109 (1)
Mörs *var.* Moers Central Europe (Germany) Reformation 195 (5)
Mörs *region* Central Europe empire and revolution 199 (3)
Moscow *Rus.* Moskva Eastern Europe (Russian Federation) biological diffusion 72–73 (1) colonialism 269 (3) economy 190 (1), 205 (4) empire and revolution 202 (1) exploration 257 (2), 286 (1) global immigration 100 (1), 101 (2) imperial global economy 92 (1) Mongols 68 (2), 68–69 (1) Napoleon 200–201 (1) postwar politics 212 (3) Reformation 196 (2) Soviet Union 208 (2), 213 (4) Timur 229 (4) WWII 104 (2), 210 (1), 211 (2), (3), (4) Cold War 108 (3)
Mosega *battle* Southern Africa (South Africa) colonization 166 (2)
Mosel *Fr.* Moselle *river* France Reformation 195 (5) *see also* Moselle
Moselle *Ger.* Mosel *river* France empire and revolution 199 (4), 202 (2) WWI 206 (2), (3) *see also* Mosel
Moskva *see* Moscow
Mosquito Coast *colonial possession/state* Central America colonization 126 (1) empire and revolution 88 (1)
Mosquito Protectorate *state* Central America the world in 1850 90–91
Mossamedes *var.* Namibe; *mod.* Moçâmedes Southern Africa (Angola) exploration 157 (4) *see also* Namibe
Mossel Bay *bay* Southern Africa exploration 156 (3)
Mossi *state* West Africa Islam 163 (1) trade 163 (4), (6), (7), 164 (2)
Mostagedda Egypt ancient Egypt 159 (2)
Mostar Southeast Europe (Bosnia and Herzegovina) Napoleon 200–201 (1) Ottomans 230 (1) postwar economy 215 (3)
Mosul *Ar.* Al Mawşil Southwest Asia (Iraq) 20th-century politics 233 (3), 235 (5) crusades 228 (2) early Islam 56–57 (1), 57 (2), (3) economy 234 (1) exploration 219 (3) Islam 227 (5) Mongols 229 (3) Seljuks 228 (1) Timur 229 (4) WWI 233 (2)
Mosyllon East Africa (Somalia) early trade 225 (3)
Motagua *river* Central America first civilizations 123 (2)
Motecuzoma Central America (Mexico) Aztecs 124 (3)
Motuhora *whaling station* New Zealand colonization 283 (4)
Motul *var.* Motul de Felipe Carrillo Puerto Central America (Mexico) first civilizations 122 (1)
Motul de Felipe Carrillo Puerto *see* Motul
Motu Marotiri *island* Pacific Ocean early cultures 281 (4)
Motu Nui *island* Pacific Ocean early cultures 281 (4)
Motupalli South Asia (India) colonialism 247 (3)
Motya Italy ancient Rome 179 (3) early states 178 (2) first civilizations 177 (1)
Mouhoun *see* Black Volta
Mouila *archaeological site* Central Africa (Gabon) early cultures 160 (1)
Moukden *see* Mukden, Shenyang
Moulins France early modern states 197 (5)
Moulmein *var.* Maulmain, Mawlamyine Mainland Southeast Asia (Burma) WWII 251 (3)
Mound Bottom North America (USA) cultural groups 122 (5)
Mound Building Villages *region* North America the world in 500 BCE 34–35
Mound City *burial mound* North America (USA) first civilizations 121 (4)
Mounds State Park *burial mound* North America (USA) first civilizations 121 (4)
Moundville North America (USA) cultural groups 122 (5)
Moun Hou *see* Black Volta
Mount Acay South America (Argentina) Incas 147 (3)
Mountain *people* North America cultural groups 123 (3)
Mountain View North America (USA)
Mount Burr Australia the world in 5000 BCE 18–19
Mount Cameron West *archaeological site* Australia prehistoric culture 17 (5)
Mount Isa Australia colonization 282 (1), 283 (3)
Mount Lyell *goldfield* Australia colonization 282 (2)
Mount Magnet Australia colonization 282 (1)
Mount Newham Australia exploration 280 (1)
Mount Olympus *religious site* Greece first religions 36 (1), 37 (3)
Mount Royal North America (USA) cultural groups 122 (5)
Mourzouk *see* Murzuk
Moxeke *early ceremonial center* South America (Peru) early cultures 144 (1), 145 (3)
Moyen-Congo *see* Congo
Mozambique *Port.* Moçambique Southern Africa (Mozambique) colonization 167 (4) European expansion 81 (3), 84–85 (1) exploration 156 (3) Islam 163 (1) slave trade 165 (4) trade 164 (1)
Mozambique *prev.* Portuguese East Africa, Moçambique *state* Southern Africa decolonization 168 (1) economy 168 (2), (3) European expansion 84–85 (1) European imperialism 96 (1), (2) the modern world 112 (1), 113 (3) trade 167 (1) Cold War 109 (1) *see also* Portuguese East Africa
Mozambique, Canal de *see* Mozambique Channel
Mozambique Channel *Fr.* Canal de Mozambique, *Mal.* Lakandranon' i Mozambika *sea waterway* Indian Ocean first humans 12 (1), 13 (2) slave trade 165 (4)
Mpangu *state* Central Africa economy 163 (2)
Mpondo *see* Pondo
Mrohaung *var.* Myohaung Mainland Southeast Asia (Burma) colonialism 248 (1) early medieval states 245 (6)
Msalala East Africa (Tanzania) exploration 157 (5)
Msiri *state* Central Africa colonization 167 (4)
Msiri *people* Central Africa trade 167 (1)
Msiris Southern Africa (Congo (Zaire)) exploration 157 (4)
Mtamvuna *var.* Orange River, Oranjerivier *river* Southern Africa colonization 166 (2) *see also* Orange River
Mtkvari *see* Kura
Mtskheta Southwest Asia (Georgia) world religions 48 (1)
Mubi West Africa (Nigeria) exploration 157 (4)
Muchiri South Asia (India) world religions 243 (4)
Mudgagiri South Asia (India) early medieval states 244 (2)
Muenchen *see* Munich
Muenster *see* Münster
Mughal Empire *var.* Mogul Empire *state* South Asia medieval Persia 231 (4)
Mughals *state* South Asia colonialism 248 (1)
Mugharet el-'Aliya *archaeological site* North Africa (Morocco) first humans 13 (2)
Mugi East Africa (Sundan) exploration 157 (5)
Muhammerah *see* Khorramshahr
Muhi *battle* Central Europe (Hungary) medieval states 189 (4)
Mühlberg Central Europe (Germany) Reformation 194 (2)
Mühlhausen *var.* Mühlhausen in Thüringen Central Europe (Germany) medieval states 189 (3)
Mühlhausen in Thüringen *see* Mühlhausen
Muju *region* East Asia medieval states 264 (2)
Mukalla *Ar.* Al Mukallā Southwest Asia (Yemen) 20th-century politics 233 (4)
Mukden *prev.* Fengtien; *Chin.* Shenyang, Shen-yang, *Eng.* Moukden East Asia (China) early modern states 266 (1) postwar politics 271 (7) Russo-Japanese War 270 (4) Sino-Japanese War 270 (3) Communism 271 (8) *see also* Shenyang
Mülhausen *see* Mulhouse
Mulhouse *Ger.* Mülhausen Central Europe (France) early modern states 193 (5)
Multan South Asia (Pakistan) biological diffusion 72–73 (1) colonialism 247 (3), 248 (1) decolonization 250 (1) early Islam 56–57 (1), 57 (2) early medieval states 244–245 (3) economy 249 (4) empire and revolution 249 (3) imperial global economy 93 (5) Mongols 68 (2), 68–69 (1) Mughal Empire 246 (1) world religions 243 (4), 49 (3)
Multan *region/state* South Asia early medieval states 244–245 (3)
Mumbai *see* Bombay
Mumhain *region* British Isles medieval states 188 (2)
München *see* Munich
Munda *region/state* South Asia first empires 241 (5) world religions 242 (2)
Mundigak *archaeological site/settlement* Central Asia (Afghanistan) first cities 240 (2) first civilizations 24 (2), 25 (3)
Mundus East Africa (Somalia) early cultures 161 (3), (5) early trade 225 (3)
Munger *see* Monghyr
Mu Nggava *see* Rennell
Munich *Ger.* München, Muenchen; *It.* Monaco Central Europe (Germany) early modern states 193 (4) economy 205 (4) empire and revolution 202 (1), (2) interwar 209 (5) Napoleon 200–201 (1), 201 (2) postwar politics 212 (1), (3) Reformation 196 (1) WWII 210 (1), 211 (2), (3), (4)
Munster *region* British Isles medieval states 186 (2)
Münster *var.* Muenster, Münster in Westfalen *rebellion/settlement* Central Europe (Germany) early modern states 193 (4) Franks 184 (2) medieval states 189 (3) Reformation 194 (2)
Münster in Westfalen *see* Münster
Muqdisho *see* Mogadishu
Murchison River *river* Australia colonization 282 (1) exploration 279 (2) prehistoric culture 17 (5)
Murcia Iberian Peninsula (Spain) economy 190 (1) Islam 192 (3)
Murderer's Bay *bay* Australia exploration 278 (1)
Muret *battle* France crusades 186 (1)
Mureybat Southwest Asia (Turkey) early agriculture 220 (1)
Murfreesboro North America (USA) US Civil War 131 (6)
Mürītāniyah *see* Mauritania
Murmansk Eastern Europe (Russian Federation) early modern states 197 (3) WWII 211 (4)
Muroran *bomb target* Japan WWII 273 (3)
Murray River *river* Australia colonization 282 (1), (2), 283 (3) exploration 279 (2) prehistoric culture 17 (5)
Murrumbidgee Australia exploration 279 (2)
Mursa Southeast Europe (Croatia) ancient Rome 180–181 (1)
Murshidabad South Asia (India) colonialism 248 (1) economy 249 (4) Mughal Empire 246 (1)
Murten *see* Morat
Murzuch *see* Murzuk
Murzuk *var.* Marzūq, Mourzouk; *Ar.* Murzuch North Africa (Libya) ancient trade 44–45 (1) colonization 167 (4) exploration 157 (4) Islam 163 (1)
Murzuq *see* Murzuk
Musang Cave Philippines the world in 5000 BCE 18–19
Musawwarat es Sufra East Africa (Sudan) early cultures 160 (1)
Musay'id *see* Umm Said
Muscat *var.* Maskat, Mascat; *Ar.* Masqaṭ Southwest Asia (Oman) biological diffusion 72–73 (1) early Islam 56–57 (1), 57 (2) economy 234 (1) European expansion 81 (3), 84–85 (1) exploration 219 (4) Islam 226 (2), 227 (4) medieval voyages 61 (3) Seljuks 228 (1) trade 230 (2) world religions 226 (1) 20th-century politics 233 (4)
Muscat and Oman *see* Oman
Muscoda Mounds *burial mound* North America (USA) first civilizations 121 (4)
Muscovy *region/state* Eastern Europe biological diffusion 72–73 (1)
Muskogean *see* Tallahassee
Mutapa *state* Southern Africa Islam 163 (1)
Mutina *mod.* Modena *mithraic site* Italy world religions 48 (1) *see also* Modena
Muttra *var.* Mathura, Mathuru South Asia (India) economy 249 (4) *see also* Mathura
Mu Us Shamo *see* Ordos Desert
Muza Southwest Asia (Yemen) ancient trade 44 (2) early cultures 161 (3), (4), (5) early trade 225 (3)
Muzaffarabad South Asia (Pakistan) postwar politics 252 (2)
Muziris South Asia (India) ancient trade 44–45 (1)
Muzumbo a Kalunga *state* Southern Africa trade 164 (2)
Mwanza East Africa (Tanzania) exploration 157 (5)
Myanmar *see* Burma
Mycale *battle* Southwest Asia (Turkey) ancient Persia 223 (4)
Mycenae Greece Bronze Age 175 (3) first cities 28–29 (1) first civilizations 175 (4)
Myitkyina Mainland Southeast Asia (Burma) WWII 272 (1), 273 (2)
Mylae Italy ancient Rome 179 (3)
Myohaung
Myongju *region* East Asia medieval states 264 (2)
Myos Hormus *var.* Myus Hormus Egypt ancient trade 44–45 (1) early cultures 161 (3), (5) early trade 225 (3)
Myra *Christian archbishopric/settlement* Southwest Asia (Turkey) ancient Rome 180–181 (1) world religions 48 (1)
Myrina Greece first civilizations 177 (1)
Mysia *region* Southwest Asia first religions 37 (3) Hellenistic world 40–41 (1)
Mysore South Asia (India) economy 249 (4) imperial global economy 93 (5)
Mysore *region/state* South Asia colonialism 248 (1), (2) postwar politics 253 (4)
Mytilene Greece ancient Greece 179 (4)
Mytilene *state* Greece ancient Greece 177 (2)
Myus Hormus *see* Myos Hormos
Mzimvubu *river* Southern Africa colonization 166 (2)

N

Nabataea *province/state* Southwest Asia early cultures 161 (3), (5)
Nabataeans *people* Southwest Asia ancient Rome 225 (4)
Nabesna *people* North America cultural groups 123 (3)
Nabta Egypt the world in 5000 BCE 18–19
Nabta Playa Egypt early agriculture 158 (1)
Nachi-san *mountain* Japan medieval states 265 (3)
Nadikagama South Asia (India) world religions 242 (3)
Nad-i-Ali Central Asia (Afghanistan) Hellenistic world 40–41 (1)
Nafplio *see* Nauplia
Naga ed-Der Egypt ancient Egypt 159 (2)
Naga Hills *mountain range* South Asia economy 249 (4)
Nagaland *region* South Asia postwar politics 252 (1), 253 (4)
Nagano *prefecture* Japan economy 270 (1)
Nagappattinam *var.* Negapatam *Buddhist center* South Asia (India) world religions 49 (3) *see also* Negapatam
Nagara Sridharmaraj *see* Nakhon Si Thammarat
Nagarjunakonda *settlement* South Asia (India) exploration 256 (1) world religions 49 (3)
Nagasaki Japan biological diffusion 72–73 (1) WWII 273 (3) early modern states 267 (4), (5) economy 270 (1) European expansion 80–81 (1) trade 267 (3) WWII 272 (1), 273 (2)
Nagasaki *prefecture* Japan economy 270 (1)
Nagata Japan medieval states 265 (4)
Nagelwanze South Asia (India) colonialism 247 (3)
Nagidus Southwest Asia (Turkey) first civilizations 177 (1) Hellenistic world 40–41 (1)
Nagorno-Karabakh *region* Eastern Europe Soviet Union 214–215 (4)
Nagoya Japan early modern states 267 (4) economy 270 (1) Islam 275 (4) medieval states 262–263 (1) WWII 273 (3)
Nagpur South Asia (India) colonialism 248 (1) decolonization 250 (1) economy 249 (4) Marathas 246 (2) postwar economy 253 (5)
Nagur South Asia (India) world religions 243 (4)
Nagysalló *battle* Central Europe (Hungary) empire and revolution 88–89 (2)
Nagyszeben *mod.* Sibiu Southeast Europe (Romania) early modern states 193 (4)
Nahr *see* Diyala
Naimans *people* East Asia/Siberia Mongols 68–69 (1)
Na'in *see* Nayin
Nairobi East Africa (Kenya) colonization 167 (4) economy 168 (2)
Naishadha *region* South Asia world religions 242 (2)
Naissus *see* Niš, Nish
Najd *see* Nejd
Najima *see* Fukuoka
Najran Southwest Asia (Saudi Arabia) early cultures 161 (3), (4), (5) early Islam 56–57 (1) early trade 225 (3) Islam 226 (2) world religions 226 (1)
Nakambé *see* White Volta
Nakhichevan Southwest Asia (Azerbaijan) medieval Persia 231 (4) Ottomans 231 (3)
Nakhon Pathom *settlement/temple* Mainland Southeast Asia (Thailand) early medieval states 245 (5) world religions 243 (5)
Nakhon Ratchasima *var.* Khorat, Korat Mainland Southeast Asia (Thailand) colonialism 247 (4), 248 (1)
Nakhon Si Thammarat *var.* Nagara Sridharmaraj, Nakhon Sithammaraj Mainland Southeast Asia (Thailand) colonialism 248 (2)
Nakhon Sithammaraj *see* Nakhon Si Thammarat
Naknek North America (USA) cultural groups 123 (3)
Nakum Central America (Mexico) first civilizations 123 (2)
Nal *archaeological site* South Asia (Pakistan) first cities 240 (2)
Nalanda South Asia (India) ancient trade 44–45 (1) first religions 36 (2) world religions 242 (3)
Nama *people* Southern Africa trade 164 (1)
Namen *see* Namur
Namibe *Port.* Moçâmedes, Mossamedes Southern Africa (Angola) Cold War 109 (5) *see also* Mossamedes
Namibia *prev.* German Southwest Africa, Southwest Africa *state* Southern Africa decolonization 168 (1) economy 168 (2), (3) the modern world 112 (1), 113 (4) *see also* German Southwest Africa, Southwest Africa
Namiquipa Central America (Mexico) Mexican Revolution 133 (3)
Namnetes *see* Nantes
Nam Tun East Asia (China) the world in 5000 BCE 18–19
Namu *island* Pacific Ocean exploration 278 (1)
Namur *Dut.* Namen Low Countries (Belgium) early modern states 197 (5) WWI 206 (2), (3)
Namur *province* Low Countries Reformation 195 (5)
Nan *province* East Asia first states 260 (1)
Nanagunas *river* South Asia ancient trade 44 (2)
Nana Mode *archaeological site* Central Africa (Central African Republic) early cultures 160 (1)
Nanchang *var.* Nan-ch'ang, Nanch'ang-hsien *rebellion/settlement* East Asia (China) biological diffusion 72–73 (1) early modern states 266 (1), (2), 268 (1) economy 274 (1) postwar politics 271 (7)
Nanch'ang-hsien *see* Nanchang
Nanchao *see* Nanzhao, Yunnan
Nan-chao *see* Nanzhao, Yunnan
Nan-ching *see* Jianye, Nanjing
Nancy France empire and revolution 199 (4) medieval states 192 (1), (2) WWI 206 (2), (3) *battle* early modern states 193 (4), 197 (5)
Nandivardhana South Asia (India) early medieval states 244 (1)
Nan Hai *see* South China Sea
Nanhai *var.* Canton, Guangzhou East Asia (China) ancient trade 44–45 (1) exploration 256 (1) first states 260 (1) medieval states 261 (6) *see also* Canton, Guangzhou
Nanhai *province* East Asia first states 260 (1)
Nan-han *state* East Asia medieval states 263 (3)
Nanjing *var.* Nan-ching, Nanking; *prev.* Chianning, Chian-ning, Kiang-ning East Asia (China) colonialism 269 (4) early modern states 266 (1) economy 274 (1) empire and revolution 268 (2) first religions 37 (4) Islam 275 (4) medieval states 263 (5) Mongols 68–69 (1) postwar politics 271 (7), 274 (2) trade 267 (3) WWII 272 (1), 273 (2) Chinese revolution 271 (5)
Nanjing *province* East Asia early modern states 266 (1), (2)
Nankaido *region* Japan medieval states 265 (3)
Nanking *see* Jianye, Nanjing
Nanning *var.* Nan-ning; *prev.* Yung-ning East Asia (China) biological diffusion 72–73 (1) colonialism 269 (4) WWII 272 (1), 273 (2)
Nansei-shotō *see* Ryukyu Islands
Nan Shan *mod.* Qilian Shan *mountain range* East Asia exploration 257 (3) *see also* Qilian Shan
Nansha Qundao *see* Spratly Islands
Nantes *anc.* Condivincum, Namnetes; *Bret.* Naoned France crusades 186 (1) early modern states 197 (5) economy 205 (4) empire and revolution 199 (4) Franks 184 (2) medieval states 185 (3), 187 (4), 192 (1), (2) medieval voyages 60–61 (1) Reformation 194 (2)
Nantong East Asia (China) postwar politics 274 (2)
Nanyang *Buddhist center* East Asia (China) world religions 49 (3)
Nanyue *state* East Asia first cities 259 (5)
Nanzhao *var.* Nan-chao; *mod.* Yunnan *region/state* East Asia early medieval states 245 (5) medieval states 262–263 (1) Mongols 68–69 (1) world religions 49 (3), (4) *see also* Yunnan
Nanzheng *var.* Hanzhong, Han-Chung East Asia (China) first cities 259 (5) *see also* Hanzhong
Naoned *see* Nantes
Napata *var.* Gebel Barkal East Africa (Sudan) ancient Egypt 159 (5) early cultures 160 (1) *see also* Gebel Barkal
Napier *settlement/whaling station* New Zealand colonization 283 (4), (5)
Naples *anc.* Neapolis; *It.* Napoli, *Ger.* Neapel *settlement/university* Italy biological diffusion 72–73 (1) crusades 186 (1) early modern states 194 (1) economy 190 (1), 205 (4) empire and revolution 202 (1), (3) Franks 184 (2) global immigration 100 (1) medieval states 182 (2), 183 (4), 187 (3), (5), 188 (1), 189 (4) Napoleon 200–201 (1), 201 (2), (3) Ottomans 230 (1) postwar politics 212 (3) Reformation 194 (2) the modern world 113 (4) *see also* Neapolis
Naples *colonial possession/state* Italy early modern states 193 (4), 194 (1) medieval states 185 (3), 189 (4) Napoleon 201 (2) Ottomans 195 (4), 230 (1), 231 (3) Reformation 194 (2), 196 (1), (2)
Napo *river* South America early cultures 144 (1), 145 (4), 146 (1) empire and revolution 150 (2) exploration 142 (1) Incas 147 (3) politics 152 (1)
Napochi *people* North America colonization 125 (4)
Napoli *see* Naples, Neapolis
Naqa East Africa (Sudan) the world in 500 BCE 34–35
Naqada Egypt ancient Egypt 159 (2), (3) first civilizations 24 (2)
Nara Japan early modern states 265 (5), 267 (4) medieval states 262–263 (1), 264 (2), 265 (4) world religions 49 (4)
Nara *prefecture* Japan economy 270 (1)
Naranjo Central America (Mexico) first civilizations 123 (2)
Narasapur *var.* Madapallam South Asia (India) colonialism 247 (3)
Naravaranagara *mod.* Angkor Borei Mainland Southeast Asia ancient India 241 (6)
Narbo *mod.* Narbonne *settlement* France ancient Rome 179 (3), 180–181 (1), 181 (3), (4) early cultures 161 (2) great migrations 52–53 (1) world religions 48 (1) *see also* Narbonne
Narbonensis *province* France ancient Rome 180–181 (1)
Narbonne *anc.* Narbo *settlement* France Franks 184 (2) Islam 184 (1) medieval states 182 (2), 187 (3), 192 (1) *see also* Narbo
Narbonne *battle* France early Islam 56–57 (1)
Narce Italy Bronze Age 175 (3)
Narev *Pol.* Narew *river* Central Europe WWI 207 (4)
Narew *see* Narev
Nargund *state* South Asia empire and revolution 249 (3)
Nariokotome *archaeological site* East Africa (Kenya) first humans 13 (2)
Narmada *archaeological site* South Asia (India) first humans 13 (2)
Narmada *river* South Asia colonialism 247 (3), 248 (1), (2) decolonization 250 (1) early medieval states 244 (1), (2), 244–245 (3), 245 (4) economy 249 (4) first cities 240 (2) first empires 241 (4), (5) first religions 36 (2) Marathas 246 (2) Mughal Empire 246 (1) postwar politics 252 (1) world religions 242 (2), 243 (4)
Narni *see* Narnia
Narnia *mod.* Narni Italy early states 178 (1)
Narosura *archaeological site/settlement* East Africa (Kenya) early agriculture 158 (1) early cultures 160 (1)
Narraganset *people* North America colonization 126 (1)
Narva Eastern Europe (Estonia) early modern states 195 (3)
Narvik Scandinavia (Norway) WWII 104 (2), 210 (1), 211 (4)
Narym Eastern Europe (Russian Federation) exploration 257 (2)
Nasarpur South Asia (Pakistan) colonialism 247 (3)
Nashikya South Asia (India) world religions 242 (2)
Nashville *battle/settlement* North America (USA) the growth of the US 129 (2), 132 (1) US Civil War 131 (6), (7) US society 137 (6)
Nasik South Asia (India) decolonization 250 (1) exploration 256 (1)
Naskapi *people* North America cultural groups 123 (3)
Nassau West Indies (Bahamas) Cold War 108 (2)

INDEX-GAZETTEER: Possession Island – Rio

Possession Island island Pacific Ocean exploration 278 (1)
Potano people North America colonization 126 (1)
Potchefstroom Southern Africa (South Africa) colonization 166 (2)
Potidaea var. Potidea settlement/state Greece ancient Greece 177 (2), (3) first civilizations 177 (1)
Potidea see Potidaea
Potomac river North America colonization 126 (1) empire and revolution 127 (3)
Potosí South America (Bolivia) colonization 148 (2) empire and revolution 150 (1), 151 (3) exploration 143 (2) politics 151 (4)
Potrero Nuevo archaeological site Central America (Mexico) first civilizations 121 (3)
Potsdam Central Europe (Germany) empire and revolution 199 (3)
Poverty Point Central America (Mexico) the world in 1250 BCE 26–27
Powder River battle North America (USA) the growth of the US 129 (2)
Powhatan people North America colonization 126 (1)
Powys region British Isles medieval states 183 (3)
Poyang Hu lake East Asia early modern states 266 (1)
Poygars see Polygar Kingdoms
Poznań Ger. Posen, Posnania Central Europe (Poland) early modern states 193 (4) medieval states 188 (1), 189 (3), (4) see also Posen
Pozo Almonte South America (Chile) politics 151 (4)
Pozsony mod. Bratislava; Ger. Pressburg Central Europe (Slovakia) early modern states 193 (4) medieval states 188 (1), 189 (4) see also Bratislava
Pozsony battle Southeast Europe medieval states 185 (3)
Prabang see Lan Chang
Prabhasa South Asia (India) world religions 242 (2)
Prachya region South Asia ancient India 242 (1) first empires 241 (4)
Pracya/Purva-Desa region South Asia early religions 48 (2)
Praeneste Italy early states 178 (1)
Praenestina, Via road Italy ancient Rome 181 (2)
Prag see Prague
Praga see Prague
Pragjyotisapura South Asia (India) early medieval states 244 (1) first empires 241 (4)
Pragjyotisha region South Asia world religions 242 (2)
Prague Cz. Praha, Ger. Prag, Pol. Praga Central Europe (Czech Republic) crusades 186 (1) early modern states 193 (4) economy 190 (1), 205 (4) empire and revolution 199 (3), 202 (1), (2) interwar 209 (5) medieval states 185 (3), 188 (1), 189 (3), (4) Napoleon 200–201 (1), 201 (2), (3) postwar politics 212 (3) Reformation 194 (2), 196 (1) WWII 105 (3), 210 (1), 211 (4) Cold War 109 (1)
Prague, Defenestration of riot Central Europe Reformation 196 (2)
Praha see Prague
Prambanan Maritime Southeast Asia (Indonesia) world religions 243 (5)
Prasodes Mare sea Indian Ocean ancient trade 44 (2)
Prasum Promontorium headland East Africa ancient trade 44 (2)
Prathet Thai see Siam, Thailand
Pratichya region South Asia ancient India 242 (1)
Pratisthana South Asia (India) early medieval states 244 (1) first empires 241 (4) world religions 242 (2)
Pravarapura South Asia (India) early medieval states 244 (1)
Prayaga South Asia (India) early medieval states 244 (1) early religions 48 (2) first empires 241 (4) first religions 36 (2) world religions 242 (2), (3), 243 (4)
Predmostí Central Europe (Slovakia) the world in 10,000 BCE 14–15
Prenzlauer Berg Central Europe (Germany) postwar politics 212 (2)
Preservation Bay sealing station New Zealand colonization 283 (4)
Presidente Stroessner see Ciudad del Este
Presidi, Stato Dei state Italy Reformation 194 (2)
Prespa battle Southeast Europe (Serbia) WWI 207 (6)
Prespa, Límni see Prespa
Prespës, Liqeni i see Prespa, Lake
Pressburg see Bratislava, Pozsony
Preston British Isles (United Kingdom) economy 204 (1) imperial global economy 93 (4)
Pretoria var. Epitoli, Tshwane Southern Africa (South Africa) colonization 166 (2) economy 168 (2) European imperialism 96 (2)
Preussen see Prussia
Preveza Greece Ottomans 231 (3)
Priene Southwest Asia (Turkey) first civilizations 177 (1) Hellenistic world 40–41 (1)
Primorskiy Kray see Maritime Territory
Prince-Edouard, Île-du see Prince Edward Island
Prince Edward Island Fr. Île-du Prince-Edouard; prev. Ile St Jean, Eng. Isle St John province North America the growth of the US 129 (2), 132 (1) US economy 136 (2)
Prince of Wales Island island North America imperial global economy 93 (3)
Prince's Island see Príncipe
Princeton battle North America (USA) empire and revolution 127 (3), 88–89 (2)
Príncipe var. Príncipe Island, Eng. Prince's Island island West Africa exploration 156 (3)
Príncipe Island see Príncipe
Pripet Bel. Prypyats', Ukr. Pryp"yat' river Eastern Europe WWI 207 (4)
Pripet Marshes wetland Eastern Europe early agriculture 174 (1) Napoleon 200–201 (1) WWI 207 (4)
Priština settlement/battle Southeast Europe (Yugoslavia) Ottomans 197 (4) postwar economy 215 (3) WWI 207 (6)
Prizren Alb. Prizreni Southeast Europe (Yugoslavia) postwar economy 215 (3) WWI 207 (6)
Prizreni see Prizren
Progreso Central America (Mexico) Mexican Revolution 133 (3)
Prome Mainland Southeast Asia (Burma) world religions 243 (5), 49 (4)
Prospect Farm archaeological site East Africa (Kenya) early cultures 160 (1)
Provence region France early modern states 193 (4) Franks 183 (6), 184 (2) medieval states 192 (2)
Providence North America (USA) empire and revolution 127 (3) the growth of the US 129 (2), 132 (1)
Providence, Cape headland New Zealand colonization 283 (4)
Provins France crusades 186 (1) economy 190 (1)
Prusa later Brusa, Brussa; mod. Bursa Southwest Asia (Turkey) ancient Rome 180–181 (1) see also Brusa, Bursa
Prussia state Central Europe/Eastern Europe early modern states 195 (3) empire and revolution 198 (2), 202 (1), (2) Napoleon 200–201 (1), 201 (2) Reformation 194 (2), 196 (1), (2)
Prussians people Central Europe crusades 186 (1), 64–65 (2) medieval states 185 (3)
Prut see Pruth
Pruth var. Prut river Eastern Europe WWI 207 (4)
Pryp"yat' see Pripet
Prypyats' see Pripet
Przemyśl Central Europe (Poland) postwar politics 212 (3) WWI 207 (4)
Przheval'sk see Karakol
Pskov Ger. Pleskau; Latv. Pleskava Eastern Europe (Russian Federation) early modern states 195 (3) economy 190 (1) medieval states 189 (3) postwar politics 212 (3) Soviet Union 208 (2) WWI 207 (4)
Pskov Ger. Pleskau; Latv. Pleskava state Eastern Europe medieval states 189 (3)
Ptolemaic Empire state Egypt/Southwest Asia ancient Rome 179 (5) Hellenistic world 224 (1)
Ptolemais Southwest Asia (Syria) ancient Rome 225 (4)
Ptolemais North Africa (Libya) ancient Rome 180–181 (1)
Ptolemaïs var. Acco, Acre Southwest Asia (Israel) world religions 48 (1)
Ptolemaïs see Acco, Acre
Ptuj see Poetovio
Pucará South America (Peru) early cultures 146 (1)
Pucará de Andalgalá South America (Argentina) Incas 147 (3)
Pu-chou see Puzhou
Puduchcheri see Pondicherry
Puebla var. Puebla de Zaragoza Central America (Mexico) colonization 125 (4) Mexican Revolution 133 (3)
Puebla state Central America Mexican Revolution 133 (3) the growth of the US 129 (2)
Puebla de Zaragoza see Puebla
Pueblo Grande archaeological site North America (USA) cultural groups 123 (4)
Pueblos region North America the world in 750 CE 54–55
Puelche people South America early cultures 147 (2)
Puerto Bello var. Porto Bello; mod. Portobelo Central America (Panama) empire and revolution 150 (2) see also Portobelo
Puerto Cabello South America (Venezuela) empire and revolution 150 (1), (2)
Puerto Casado fort South America (Paraguay) politics 152 (2)
Puerto Deseado see Port Desire
Puerto Hormiga archaeological site South America (Colombia) early cultures 144 (1)
Puerto Montt South America (Chile) empire and revolution 151 (3)
Puerto Plata West Indies (Dominican Republic) European expansion 85 (2)
Puerto Presidente Stroessner see Ciudad del Este
Puerto Príncipe mod. Camagüey West Indies (Cuba) European expansion 85 (2)
Puerto Rico colonial possession/island West Indies colonization 125 (4), 126 (1) empire and revolution 150 (1) European expansion 85 (2) global immigration 100 (1) historical geography 140–141 (1) the growth of the US 133 (4) the modern world 113 (4) US politics 139 (4) Cold War 108 (2), 109 (1)
Puerto San Julián var. San Julián South America (Argentina) European expansion 80–81 (1)
Pukapuka island Pacific Ocean exploration 278 (1)
Puket see Phuket
Pulicat var. Pālghāt, Geldria South Asia (India) colonialism 247 (3)
Pulinda region/state South Asia first empires 241 (5) world religions 242 (2)
Pumpo South America (Peru) Incas 147 (3)
Punakha South Asia (Bhutan) colonialism 248 (1)
Puna Pau archaeological site Pacific Ocean early cultures 281 (4)
Pundra South Asia (Bangladesh) first empires 241 (4)
Pundra region/state South Asia (Bangladesh) early religions 48 (2) first empires 241 (5) world religions 242 (2)
Pundravardhana South Asia (Bangladesh) early medieval states 244 (1) world religions 242 (2)
Pune prev. Poona South Asia (India) postwar economy 253 (5) see also Poona
Punjab region/state South Asia colonialism 247 (3), 248 (2) economy 249 (4) empire and revolution 249 (3) postwar politics 252 (2), 253 (4) world religions 243 (4)
Punjab, (East) region South Asia postwar politics 252 (1)
Punjab, (West) region South Asia postwar politics 252 (1)
Punjab States state South Asia colonialism 248 (2)
Punkuri archaeological site South America (Peru) early cultures 145 (3)
Punneikayal see Kayalapattinam
Puno South America (Peru) empire and revolution 150 (1) politics 151 (4)
Punta Arenas prev. Magallanes South America (Chile) empire and revolution 151 (3) environment 153 (4)
Punta de Angamos battle South America (Chile) politics 151 (4)
Puntutjarpa Australia exploration 280 (1)
Pura mod. Iranshahr Southwest Asia (Iran) Hellenistic world 40–41 (1)
Puranadhisthana var. Shrinagara South Asia (India) first empires 241 (4)
Puri South Asia (India) biological diffusion 72–73 (1)
Puritjarra Australia the world in 10,000 BCE 14–15
Purosottama-Puri South Asia (India) world religions 243 (4)
Purus Sp. Río Purús river South America colonization 149 (3) early cultures 144 (1), 145 (2), (4), 146 (1) environment 153 (4)
Purusapura mod. Peshwar South Asia (Pakistan) Hellenistic world 224 (1)
Purush Khaddum Southwest Asia (Turkey) first civilizations 221 (4)
Purús, Río see Purus
Pusan var. Busan; Jap. Fusan East Asia (South Korea) early modern states 267 (4) Islam 275 (4) Russo-Japanese War 270 (4) Sino-Japanese War 270 (3) trade 267 (3) Cold War 109 (4)
Pushkar see Puskara
Pushkari archaeological site Eastern Europe (Russian Federation) the world in 10,000 BCE 14–15
Pusilha Central America (Mexico) first civilizations 123 (2)
Puskalavati South Asia (Pakistan) world religions 242 (2)
Puskara mod. Pushkar South Asia (India) early medieval states 244 (1) world religions 243 (4)
Pusyabhutis state South Asia early medieval states 244 (2)
Putan Maya state Central America Aztecs 124 (1)
Puteoli Italy ancient Rome 180–181 (1), 181 (3)
Puttalam South Asia (Sri Lanka) colonialism 247 (3)
Putumayo region South America narcotics 153 (5)
Putumayo var. Rio Içá river South America colonization 148 (2) early cultures 145 (4), 146 (1) empire and revolution 150 (2), 151 (3) environment 153 (4) Incas 148 (1)
Puyang East Asia (China) first religions 37 (4)
Puye archaeological site North America (USA) cultural groups 123 (4)
Puyo East Asia (Korea) medieval states 264 (1), (2)
Puzhou var. Pu-chou East Asia (China) Mongols 68–69 (1)
Pydna battle Greece ancient Greece 179 (4)
Pygela state Greece ancient Greece 177 (2)
Pylos Greece ancient Greece 177 (3), 179 (4) Bronze Age 175 (3) early systems 223 (3) first cities 28–29 (1) first civilizations 175 (4)
Pyongyang prev. Luolang; var. P'yŏngyang-si, P'yŏngyang East Asia (North Korea) Cold War 109 (4) early modern states 267 (4) Islam 275 (4) Sino-Japanese War 270 (3) world religions 49 (3) see also Luolang
P'yŏngyang-si see Luolang, Pyongyang
Pyramid Lake battle North America (USA) the growth of the US 129 (2)
Pyrenaei Montes see Pyrenees
Pyrenees Fr. Pyrénées, Sp. Pirineos; anc. Pyrenaei Montes mountain range France/Iberian Peninsula ancient Rome 179 (3), 180–181 (1), 181 (3) Bronze Age 175 (3) crusades 186 (1), 64–65 (2) early agriculture 174 (1) early Islam 56–57 (1), 57 (2) early modern states 197 (5) economy 190 (1), 205 (4) exploration 172 (1) first religions 37 (3) Franks 183 (5), (6), 184 (2) great migrations 52–53 (1) historical geography 170–171 (1) Islam 192 (3) medieval states 185 (3), 192 (1), (2) Napoleon 200–201 (1) prehistoric culture 17 (3), (4) world religions 48 (1) WWII 210 (1), 211 (4)
Pyrrha state Greece ancient Greece 177 (2)
Pyu region/state Mainland Southeast Asia medieval states 262–263 (1) the world in 750 CE 54–55 world religions 49 (3), (4)

Q

Qābis see Gabès
Qadesh Southwest Asia (Lebanon) first cities 28–29 (1)
Qadisiya battle Southwest Asia (Iraq) early Islam 56–57 (1)
Qafzeh archaeological site Southwest Asia (Israel) first humans 13 (2)
Qaidam Pendi see Tsaidam Basin
Qalat mod. Kalat South Asia (Pakistan) Mughal Empire 246 (1) see also Kalat
Qalat state South Asia Mughal Empire 246 (1)
Qalhat see Kalhat
Qalqut var. Kalikod; mod. Calicut, Kozhikode South Asia (India) early medieval states 244–245 (3) see also Calicut, Kalikod
Qânâq see Thule
Qandahar mod. Kandahar South Asia (Pakistan) early medieval states 244–245 (3) Mughal Empire 246 (1) see also Kandahar
Qandahar state South Asia Mughal Empire 246 (1)
Qandahār see Kandahar, Qandahar
Qannauj South Asia (India) early medieval states 244–245 (3)
Qaqortoq see Julianehaab
Qarabagh mod. Karabakh region Southwest Asia medieval Persia 231 (4)
Qaraghandy see Karaganda
Qarakhanids var. Karakhanids state Central Asia early Islam 57 (2) see also Karakhanids
Qarmatians dynasty Southwest Asia early Islam 57 (2) Islam 227 (4), (5)
Qarmatis dynasty South Asia the world in 1000 58–59
Qars see Kars
Qatar colonial possession/state Southwest Asia economy 234 (1) Islam 235 (4) the modern world 113 (3) US economy 138 (2) 20th-century politics 233 (4), 235 (5) Cold War 109 (1)
Qatna Southwest Asia (Syria) ancient Egypt 159 (4), (5)
Qaw Egypt ancient Egypt 159 (2)
Qaw el-Kebir Egypt ancient Egypt 159 (4)
Qazaqstan see Kazakhstan
Qazris see Cáceres
Qazvin var. Kazvin Southwest Asia (Iran) early Islam 56–57 (1) Mongols 229 (3), 68–69 (1) 20th-century politics 235 (5) see also Kazvin
Qeshm Southwest Asia (Iran) economy 234 (1)
Qeshm var. Jazīreh-ye Qeshm, Qeshm Island island Southwest Asia economy 234 (1)
Qeshm Island see Qeshm
Qeshm, Jazīreh-ye see Qeshm
Qi var. Ch'i region/state East Asia first cities 259 (4), (5) first religions 37 (4)
Qian East Asia (China) medieval states 263 (6)
Qiang East Asia (China) first cities 259 (4)
Qiang state East Asia first cities 259 (3)
Qiang people East Asia first cities 259 (4) first states 260 (1), 261 (2) medieval states 261 (4), (6), 262–263 (1)
Qiantang East Asia (China) first states 260 (1)
Qiemo see Cherchen
Qi Empire var. Ch'i state East Asia the world in 500 CE 50–51 see also China
Qift Egypt ancient Egypt 159 (4)
Qilian Shan mountain range East Asia early agriculture 258 (1) early modern states 266 (1) first cities 259 (5) first religions 37 (4) first states 260 (1) trade 267 (3)
Qin state East Asia first cities 259 (4), (5) first religions 37 (4)
Qin Empire state East Asia the world in 250 BCE 38–39 see also China
Qing see Qinghai
Qingdao var. Ching-Tao, Ch'ing-tao, Tsingtao, Tsintao; Ger. Tsingtau East Asia (China) economy 274 (1) imperialism 270 (2) Islam 275 (4) postwar politics 274 (2) Russo-Japanese War 270 (4)
Qingdao var. Tsingtao colonial possession East Asia colonialism 269 (4)
Qing Empire mod. China state East Asia colonialism 248 (1), (2), 269 (3), (4) decolonization 250 (2) economy 249 (4) empire and revolution 249 (3), 88–89 (2) European imperialism 97 (3), (4) Russo-Japanese War 270 (4) Sino-Japanese War 270 (3) see also China
Qinghai var. Chinghai, Qing, Tsinghai province/state East Asia Chinese revolution 271 (5) early modern states 266 (1), (2), 268 (1) empire and revolution 268 (2) postwar economy 275 (3) postwar politics 271 (7), 274 (2)
Qinghai Hu var. Ch'ing Hai, Tsing Hai, Mong. Koko Nor lake East Asia early modern states 266 (1) first states 260 (1)
Qingjiang East Asia (China) medieval states 263 (6)
Qingliangang archaeological site East Asia (China) early agriculture 258 (2)
Qingtang Xiang state East Asia medieval states 263 (3)
Qingyang rebellion East Asia early modern states 266 (2)
Qingzhou prev. Yidu rebellion/settlement East Asia (China) early modern states 266 (2) medieval states 263 (4)
Qinhuangdao var. Chinwangtao East Asia (China) colonialism 269 (4) postwar politics 274 (2)
Qiong see Hainan
Qiongzhou var. Kiungchow East Asia (China) colonialism 269 (4)
Qita Ghazzah see Gaza Strip
Qizhou military base East Asia early modern states 266 (1)
Qom var. Kum, Qum Southwest Asia (Iran) economy 234 (1) see also Qum
Qomul see Hami
Quadi people Eastern Europe ancient Rome 180–181 (1), 181 (4)
Quang Tri battle Mainland Southeast Asia (Vietnam) postwar politics 251 (5)
Quanrong state East Asia first cities 259 (3)
Quanzhou East Asia (China) ancient trade 44–45 (1) medieval states 263 (5) Mongols 68 (2), 68–69 (1) trade 267 (3)
Quapaw people North America colonization 126 (1)
Quarai archaeological site North America (USA) cultural groups 123 (4)
Quban Egypt ancient Egypt 159 (4), (5)
Quebec var. Quebéc North America (Canada) colonization 126 (1) empire and revolution 127 (2), (3) empire and revolution 88 (1)European expansion 84–85 (1) exploration 118 (1), 119 (2), (3) global immigration 100 (1), 101 (3) the growth of the US 129 (2), 132 (1) the world in 1800 86–87 US economy 136 (2)
Quebec colonial possession/province North America empire and revolution 127 (3) the growth of the US 129 (2), 132 (1) US economy 136 (2)
Queen Elizabeth Islands see Parry Islands
Queensland region Australia colonization 282 (1), (2), 283 (3)
Queenstown New Zealand colonization 283 (5)
Quelimane var. Kilimane, Kilmain, Quilimane Southern Africa (Mozambique) exploration 157 (4) Islam 163 (1) trade 164 (1)
Quelpart Jap. Saishū; Kor. Cheju-do island East Asia Sino-Japanese War 270 (3) see also Cheju-do
Quemoy var. Chinmen Tao, Jinmen Dao island East Asia Cold War 109 (1) postwar economy 275 (3)
Quentovic France medieval states 185 (3)
Que Que see Kwekwe
Quera see Chur, Curia
Querero South America the world in 10,000 BCE 14–15
Queres people North America colonization 126 (1)
Querétaro state Central America Mexican Revolution 133 (3) the growth of the US 129 (2)
Quetta South Asia (Pakistan) Hellenistic world 40–41 (1) postwar politics 252 (1)
Quetzaltepec Central America (Mexico) Aztecs 124 (1)
Qufu East Asia (China) first cities 259 (5) first religions 37 (4)
Quiahuac Central America (Mexico) Aztecs 124 (3)
Quiahuitztlan Central America (Mexico) colonization 125 (5)
Quiauhteopan state Central America Aztecs 124 (1)
Quiberon Bay battle France empire and revolution 88 (1)
Quierzy France Franks 184 (2)
Quilimane see Quelimane
Quilon var. Kolam, Kollam South Asia (India) biological diffusion 72–73 (1) colonialism 247 (3)
Quimbaya state South America the world in 1200 62–63
Quimbaya Chiefdoms state South America early cultures 146 (1)
Quimper anc. Quimper Corentin France Franks 184 (2)
Quimper Corentin see Quimper
Qui Nhon battle Mainland Southeast Asia (Vietnam) postwar politics 251 (5)
Quintana Roo state Central America Mexican Revolution 133 (3)
Quirigua Central America (Guatemala) first civilizations 122 (1), 123 (2)
Quirinal Hill Lat. Collis Quirinalis hill Italy ancient Rome 181 (2)
Quirinalis Collis see Quirinal Hill
Quito South America (Ecuador) colonization 148 (2) empire and revolution 150 (1), (2), 151 (3) environment 153 (4) exploration 142 (1), 143 (2), (3) Incas 147 (3), 148 (1) politics 152 (1)
Quito, Presidencia of region South America colonization 148 (2)
Qujialing archaeological site East Asia (China) early agriculture 258 (2)
Qum mod. Qom Southwest Asia (Iran) medieval Persia 231 (4) Mongols 229 (3), 68–69 (1) see also Qom
Qumis Southwest Asia (Iran) early Islam 56–57 (1)
Quonset North America (USA) WWII 104 (2)
Qŭqon see Kokand
Qurein see Kuwait
Qus var. Assouan, Assuan, Aswân; anc. Syene Egypt crusades 228 (2) see also Aswân, Syene

R

Rabat var. al Dar al Baida North Africa (Morocco) early Islam 56–57 (1) economy 168 (2)
Rabaul military base/settlement New Guinea (Papua New Guinea) WWII 104 (2), 251 (3), 272 (1), 273 (2)
Rabbah Ammon see Amman
Rabbath Ammon see Amman
Rabeh people Central Africa trade 167 (1)
Racibórz see Ratibor
Radom Central Europe (Poland) empire and revolution 198 (2)
Rae Bareli region South Asia decolonization 250 (1)
Raeti people Italy early states 178 (2)
Raetia var. Rhaetia province Central Europe ancient Rome 180–181 (1) Franks 184 (2) see also Rhaetia
Rafa see Rafah
Rafah var. Rafa, Rafaḥ; Heb. Rafiaḥ, Raphiah Southwest Asia (Gaza Strip) 20th century 234 (2)
Rafiaḥ see Rafah
Ragusa mod. Dubrovnik Southeast Europe (Croatia) early modern states 193 (4) economy 190 (1) medieval states 188 (1), 189 (4) Ottomans 195 (4) Reformation 196 (2) see also Dubrovnik
Ragusa state Southeast Europe early modern states 193 (4), 194 (1) Ottomans 195 (4), 230 (1), 231 (3) Reformation 194 (2)
Rahanagar South Asia (Bangladesh) postwar politics 252 (3)
Rahovec see Orahovac
Rai see Rayy
Rajagriha South Asia (India) first empires 241 (4) first religions 36 (2) world religions 242 (3)
Rajamahendri South Asia (India) early medieval states 244–245 (3), 245 (4)
Rajarattha region South Asia first empires 241 (4)
Rajasthan region/state South Asia postwar politics 252 (1) world religions 243 (4)
Rajgir religious site South Asia (India) first religions 36 (2)
Rajputana region/state South Asia colonialism 247 (3), 248 (1), (2)
Rajputs people South Asia early medieval states 244–245 (3)
Rajput States state South Asia the world in 1500 74–75
Rakka see Raqqa
Rakvere see Wesenberg
Raleigh North America (USA) the growth of the US 129 (2), 132 (1) US Civil War 131 (7) US society 137 (6)
Ramagama South Asia (India) world religions 242 (3)
Ramazan state Southwest Asia the world in 1400 70–71 the world in 1500 74–75
Rameshwaram South Asia (India) world religions 243 (4)
Ramhormoz Southwest Asia (Iran) 20th-century politics 235 (5)
Rampur South Asia (India) colonialism 248 (1) economy 249 (4)
Rampur state South Asia colonialism 248 (2)
Ramsay's Mill North America (USA) empire and revolution 127 (3)
Ramsgate British Isles (United Kingdom) WWI 206 (2), (3)
Rana Ghundai archaeological site South Asia (India) first cities 240 (2)
Ranas Central America (Mexico) first civilizations 122 (1)
Ranchillos South America (Argentina) Incas 147 (3)
Rancho la Chua North America (USA) colonization 125 (4)
Rancho Peludo archaeological site South America (Venezuela) early cultures 144 (1), 145 (2)
Rangiroa island Pacific Ocean exploration 278 (1)
Rangoon var. Yangon; anc. Dagon Mainland Southeast Asia (Burma) colonialism 247 (4), 248 (1), 269 (4) economy 249 (4) European expansion 84–85 (1) European imperialism 97 (3) Islam 275 (4) postwar economy 253 (5) US superpower 138 (1) world religions 243 (5) WWII 251 (3), 272 (1), 273 (2)
Rangpur archaeological site/settlement South Asia (Bangladesh) colonialism 247 (3) first cities 240 (2) postwar politics 252 (3)
Rano Kao see Rano Kau
Rano Kau var. Rano Kao volcano Pacific Ocean early cultures 281 (4)
Rano Raraku archaeological site South America (Chile) early cultures 281 (4)
Rapa Nui var. Isla de Pascua, Easter Island island Pacific Ocean early cultures 280–281 (3), 281 (4) medieval voyages 60 (2) see also Easter Island
Raphiah see Rafah
Raqqa var. Rakka Southwest Asia (Syria) early Islam 56–57 (1)
Raroia island Pacific Ocean exploration 278 (1)
Ra's al Junayz Southwest Asia (Oman) first civilizations 25 (3)
Ras al Khaimah Ar. Ra's al Khaymah Southwest Asia (United Arab Emirates) economy 234 (1)
Ra's al Khaymah see Ras al Khaimah
Ras Dashen mountain East Africa (Ethiopia) exploration 157 (5)
Rashtrakutas dynasty South Asia early medieval states 244 (2) the world in 750 CE 54–55
Ra's Shamrah see Ugarit
Ras Tannura oil terminal Southwest Asia (Saudi Arabia) economy 234 (1)
Rasulids dynasty Southwest Asia economy 163 (2)
Ratiaria Christian archbishopric Southeast Europe (Bulgaria) world religions 48 (1)
Ratibor mod. Racibórz Central Europe (Poland) medieval states 189 (3)
Ratisbon anc. Castra Regina, Reginum; hist. Ratisbona; Fr. Ratisbonne, Ger. Regensburg massacre/settlement Central Europe (Germany) crusades 186 (1) early modern states 193 (4) Franks 184 (2) medieval states 188 (1), 189 (3), (4) Napoleon 200–201 (1) see also Castra Regina, Regensburg
Ratisbona see Castra Regina, Ratisbon, Regensburg
Ratisbonne see Castra Regina, Ratisbon, Regensburg
Ratnagiri South Asia (India) exploration 256 (1)
Ratomagus see Rotomagus
Raukawa see Cook Strait
Ravenna Italy ancient Rome 180–181 (1), 181 (4), 182 (1) economy 190 (1) Franks 184 (2) great migrations 52–53 (1) medieval states 182 (2), 183 (4) Ottomans 230 (1) world religions 48 (1) early modern states 194 (1)
Ravenna, Exarchate of state Italy medieval states 183 (4)
Ravensberg region Central Europe empire and revolution 199 (3)
Ravensbrück concentration camp Central Europe WWII 211 (3)
Ravi river South Asia colonialism 247 (3) early medieval states 244 (1), (2), 244–245 (3) economy 249 (4) Marathas 246 (2) Mughal Empire 246 (1)
Rawak Buddhist center East Asia (China) world religions 49 (3)
Rawalpindi South Asia (Pakistan) postwar economy 253 (5)
Rawson South America (Argentina) empire and revolution 151 (3)
Ray see Rayy
Rayigama South Asia (Sri Lanka) early medieval states 244–245 (3)
Raysut Southwest Asia (Oman) early Islam 56–57 (1) medieval voyages 61 (3)
Rayy var. Rai, Ray, Rey; anc. Rhagae Southwest Asia (Iran) biological diffusion 72–73 (1) Islam 227 (5) Mongols 229 (3), 68–69 (1)
Real Alto archaeological site/settlement South America (Ecuador) early cultures 144 (1)
Reao leper colony Pacific Ocean environmentalism 285 (2)
Reate Italy early states 178 (1)
Recife var. Pernambuco; Dut. Mauritsstad South America (Brazil) colonization 149 (3), (4) economy 153 (3) environment 153 (4) exploration 142 (1), 143 (2) politics 152 (1) see also Pernambuco
Recuay South America (Peru) early cultures 145 (4)
Recuay region South America early cultures 145 (4)
Reddis dynasty South Asia the world in 1400 70–71
Red River river North America colonization 125 (4) cultural groups 122 (5) early agriculture 120 (1) exploration 118 (1), 119 (2) first civilizations 121 (4) the growth of the US 129 (2) US Civil War 131 (6), (7)
Red River var. Yuan, Chin. Yuan Jiang, Vtn. Sông Hông Hà river East Asia ancient India 241 (6) Bronze Age 240 (3) colonialism 247 (4), 248 (1) early medieval states 245 (5), (6) postwar politics 251 (5) world religions 243 (5)
Redruth British Isles (United Kingdom) economy 204 (1)
Red Sea anc. Sinus Arabicus sea Africa/Asia ancient Egypt 159 (2), (3), (4), (5) ancient Persia 223 (4) ancient Rome 180–181 (1), 181 (4), 224 (2), 225 (5) ancient trade 44–45 (1) biological diffusion 72–73 (1) crusades 65 (3) early agriculture 158 (1) early cultures 160 (1), 161 (2), (3), (4), (5) early Islam 56–57 (1), 57 (2) early systems 223 (3) early trade 225 (3) economy 163 (2), (3) exploration 156 (3), 157 (5), 172 (1), (2), 219 (3), (4) first cities 220 (2), 28–29 (1) first civilizations 222 (2) first humans 12 (1), 13 (2) first religions 37 (3) Hellenistic world 224 (1), 41 (2) Islam 163 (1), 226 (2), (3), 227 (4) medieval states 261 (6) medieval voyages 61 (3) Mongols 229 (3) Ottomans 231 (3), 232–233 (1) Seljuks 228 (1) slave trade 165 (4) Timur 229 (4) trade 165 (3), 167 (1), 230 (2) world religions 226 (1), 49 (4) WWI 233 (2) 20th century 234 (2) 20th-century politics 233 (4)
Redstone Fort North America (USA) empire and revolution 127 (3)
Reefton see Reef Town
Reef Town mod. Reefton New Zealand colonization 283 (5)
Reged region British Isles medieval states 183 (3)
Regensburg anc. Castra Regina, Reginum; Eng. Ratisbon; hist. Ratisbona; Fr. Ratisbonne Central Europe (Germany) crusades 64–65 (2), 65 (1) economy 190 (1) see also Castra Regina, Ratisbon
Reggio var. Reggio di Calabria; anc Rhegium Italy economy 190 (1) medieval states 188 (1) Ottomans 231 (3) see also Rhegium
Regillus Lacus lake Italy early states 178 (1)
Regina North America (Canada) the growth of the US 129 (2)
Reginum see Castra Regina, Ratisbon, Regensburg
Reichenau Central Europe (Poland) Franks 184 (2)
Reichskommissariat-Ostland region Eastern Europe WWII 211 (2)
Reichskommissariat-Ukraine region Eastern Europe WWII 211 (2)
Reims see Durocortorum, Rheims
Reindeer Lake lake North America the growth of the US 129 (2)
Reine-Charlotte, Îles de la see Queen Charlotte Islands
Reine-Élisabeth, Îles de la see Queen Elizabeth Islands
Reinickendorf Central Europe (Germany) postwar politics 212 (2)
Reka see Rijeka
Reka Ili see Ili
Remedello archaeological site Italy Copper Age 174 (2)
Remedios military base West Indies (Cuba) Cold War 108 (2)
Remi see Rheims
Remojadas Central America (Mexico) first civilizations 121 (2), 122 (1)
Remojadas region Central America first civilizations 122 (1)
Ren state East Asia first cities 259 (3)
Rennell var. Mu Nggava island Pacific Ocean early cultures 280–281 (3) medieval voyages 60 (2)
Renner burial mound North America (USA) first civilizations 121 (4)
Rennes anc. Condate; Bret. Roazon France empire and revolution 199 (4) Franks 184 (2) medieval states 187 (4)
Resolute North America (Canada) cultural groups 123 (3)
Réunion prev. Bourbon colonial possession/island/state Indian Ocean European expansion 84–85 (1) European imperialism 96 (1) global immigration 101 (3) see also Bourbon
Reval var. Revel; mod. Tallinn; Rus. Tallin Eastern Europe (Estonia) crusades 186 (1) early modern states 195 (3) economy 190 (1) medieval states 189 (3) see also Revel, Tallin
Revel Eastern Europe (Estonia) early modern states 197 (3) Soviet Union 208 (2)
Revillagigedo Islands see Revillagigedo, Islas
Revillagigedo, Islas Eng. Revillagigedo Islands island group North America the modern world 110–111
Rewardashur Christian archbishopric Southwest Asia (Iran) world religions 48 (1)
Rey see Rayy
Reykjavik Europe (Iceland) exploration 287 (2) medieval voyages 60–61 (1) WWII 104 (2)
Reẕā'īyeh, Daryācheh-ye see Urmia, Lake
Rha river Eastern Europe ancient trade 44 (2)
Rhaetia var. Raetia province/region Central Europe Franks 183 (6) world religions 48 (1) see also Raetia
Rhagae Southwest Asia (Iran) Hellenistic world 40–41 (1)
Rhapta East Africa (Ethiopia) ancient trade 44 (2)
Rhegium var. Reggio; mod. Reggio di Calabria Italy ancient Rome 179 (3), 180–181 (1) early states 178 (1) first civilizations 177 (1) see also Reggio
Rheims academic center/settlement France ancient Rome 182 (1) economy 190 (1) Franks 183 (5), (6), 184 (2) medieval states 185 (3), 188 (1), (2) Napoleon 200–201 (1) WWI 206 (2), (3)
Rhein see Rhine
Rhenus see Rhine
Rhin see Rhine
Rhine Dut. Rijn, Fr. Rhin, Ger. Rhein; Lat. Rhenus river Central Europe, Low Countries ancient Rome 180–181 (1), 181 (3), (4) ancient trade 44–45 (1) biological diffusion 72–73 (1) Bronze Age 175 (3) Copper Age 174 (2) crusades 186 (1), 64–65 (2) early agriculture 174 (1), 20–21 (2) early Islam 56–57 (1) early modern states 193 (4), (5) economy 190 (1) empire and revolution 199 (3), (4), 202 (1), (1i), (2) exploration 172 (1) first humans 13 (2) Franks 183 (5), (6), 184 (2) great migrations 52–53 (1), 53 (2) medieval states 182 (2), 185 (3), 188 (1), (2) Napoleon 200–201 (1), 201 (2) prehistoric culture 16 (1) Reformation 195 (5), 196 (1) world religions 48 (1) WWI 206 (2), (3) WWII 210 (1), 211 (4)
Rhine, Confederation of the state Central Europe Napoleon 201 (2)
Rhodanus see Rhône
Rhode Iberian Peninsula (Spain) ancient Rome 179 (3)
Rhode Island colonial possession/state North America empire and revolution 127 (2), (3) the growth of the US 129 (1) US Civil War 130 (2), (5) US economy 134 (2)
Rhodes Greece (Rhodes) ancient Greece 177 (3), 179 (4) early Islam 56–57 (1) economy 190 (1) Hellenistic world 40–41 (1) medieval states 187 (5) Ottomans 231 (3) world religions 48 (1) Islam 226 (2)s
Rhodes var. Ródhos; Gr. Ródos; Lat. Rhodus, It. Rodi state/island Greece ancient Greece 177 (2), (3), 179 (4) ancient Persia 223 (4) ancient Rome 179 (5) crusades 64–65 (2) first civilizations 175 (4), 177 (1), 221 (5) Islam 226 (2) medieval states 187 (5) Ottomans 230 (1) postwar politics 212 (3)
Rhodesia mod. Zimbabwe; prev. Southern Rhodesia state Southern Africa the world in 1975 106–107 see also Southern Rhodesia, Zimbabwe
Rhodos see Rhodes
Rhodus Greece ancient Rome 180–181 (1)
Rhône Lat. Rhodanus river France ancient Rome 180–181 (1), 181 (3) ancient trade 44–45 (1) biological diffusion 72–73 (1) Bronze Age 175 (3) Copper Age 174 (2) crusades 186 (1), 64–65 (2) early agriculture 174 (1) early Islam 56–57 (1) early modern states 193 (4) economy 190 (1), 205 (4) first civilizations 177 (1) Franks 183 (5), (6), 184 (2) great migrations 52–53 (1), 53 (2) medieval states 185 (3), 187 (4), 188 (1) prehistoric culture 17 (3) world religions 48 (1)
Rialto Bridge bridge Italy economy 191 (3)
Ribe Scandinavia (Denmark) medieval voyages 60–61 (1)
Ribeira Grande var. Concelho de Ribeira Grande island Atlantic Ocean the world in 1500 74–75
Richmond North America (USA) colonization 126 (1) empire and revolution 127 (3) European expansion 84–85 (1) the growth of the US 129 (2), 132 (1) US Civil War 130 (5), 131 (6), (7) US society 137 (6)
Rievaulx major cistercian house British Isles (United Kingdom) medieval states 187 (3)
Rift Valley see Great Rift Valley
Riga Latv. Rīga settlement Eastern Europe (Latvia) biological diffusion 72–73 (1) crusades 186 (1) early modern states 193 (4), 195 (3) economy 190 (1) empire and revolution 198 (2), 202 (1) medieval states 189 (3) Napoleon 200–201 (1), 201 (2) postwar politics 212 (3) Reformation 194 (2) Soviet Union 214–215 (4) WWI 207 (4) WWII 211 (2), (3), (4) Cold War 108 (3)
Rigaer Bucht see Riga, Gulf of
Riga, Gulf of Est. Liivi Laht, Ger. Rigaer Bucht, Latv. Rīgas Jūras Līcis, Rus. Rizhskiy Zaliv; prev. Est. Riia Laht gulf Eastern Europe WWI 207 (4)
Rīgas Jūras Līcis see Riga, Gulf of
Riia Laht see Riga, Gulf of
Rijeka anc. Tarsatica; Ger. Sankt Veit am Flaum; It. Fiume; Slvn. Reka Southeast Europe (Croatia) postwar economy 215 (3)
Rijn see Rhine
Rijssel see Lille
Rim archaeological site/settlement West Africa (Burkina) early agriculture 158 (1) early cultures 160 (1)
Rimini anc. Ariminum Italy economy 190 (1) medieval states 183 (4), 188 (1) see also Ariminum
Rinaldone Italy the world in 2500 BCE 22–23
Rinan province Mainland Southeast Asia first states 260 (1)
Ringsted Scandinavia (Sweden) medieval voyages 60–61 (1)
Rio see Rio de Janeiro

INDEX-GAZETTEER: **Riobamba – Santo Domingo**

Riobamba South America (Equador) Incas 147 (3)
Rio Barbate *battle* Iberian Peninsula (Spain) early Islam 56–57 (1)
Rio Bec Central America (Mexico) first civilizations 123 (2)
Rio Branco South America (Brazil) politics 152 (1)
Rio de Janeiro *var.* Rio; *hist.* São Sebastião de Rio de Janeiro South America (Brazil) colonization 149 (3), (4) economy 153 (3) empire and revolution 151 (3) environment 153 (4) European expansion 84–85 (1) exploration 143 (2), (3) global immigration 100 (1) imperial global economy 92 (1) politics 152 (1)
Rio de Janeiro *region* South America colonization 149 (3)
Río de la Hacha South America (Columbia) European expansion 85 (2)
Rio de la Plata, Viceroyalty of *colonial possession* South America colonization 148 (2) empire and revolution 150 (1) European expansion 84–85 (1)
Rio de Oro *later* Spanish Sahara; *mod.* Western Sahara *state* North Africa the world in 1900 94–95 the world in 1925 98–99 *see also* Spanish Sahara, Western Sahara
Rio Grande *var.* Rio Grande do Sul; *hist.* São Pedro do Rio Grande do Sul South America (Brazil) colonization 149 (3) empire and revolution 151 (3) environment 153 (4)
Rio Grande do Sul *region* South America colonization 149 (3)
Riom France early modern states 197 (5)
Rio Muni *state* Central Africa European imperialism 96 (1)
Ripuarian Franks *people* Central Europe Franks 183 (5)
Riverton *settlement/whaling station* New Zealand colonization 283 (4), (5)
Rivière au Vase North America (USA) cultural groups 122 (5)
Rivoli *var.* Rivoli Veronese *battle* Italy Napoleon 200–201 (1)
Rivoli Veronese *see* Rivoli
Riyadh *Ar.* Ar Riyāḑ Southwest Asia (Saudi Arabia) economy 234 (1) exploration 219 (4) 20th-century politics 233 (4), 235 (5)
Rizhskiy Zaliv *see* Riga, Gulf of
Roanoke *river* North America empire and revolution 127 (3)
Roazon *see* Rennes
Roccastrada Italy economy 190 (1)
Roc de Sers *archaeological site* France prehistoric culture 17 (3)
Rochdale Canal *canal* British Isles economy 204 (2)
Rochefort France early modern states 197 (5)
Rock Eagle North America (USA) cultural groups 122 (5)
Rockhampton Australia colonization 282 (1), 283 (3)
Rocks Point *sealing station* New Zealand colonization 283 (4)
Rocky Mountains *mountain range* North America colonization 125 (4), 126 (1) early agriculture 120 (1), 20–21 (2) exploration 118 (1), 119 (2), (3), 286 (1), 287 (2) imperial global economy 92 (1) prehistoric culture 16 (1) the growth of the US 129 (2)
Ródhos *see* Rhodes
Rodi *see* Rhodes
Ródos *see* Rhodes
Rodrigues *var.* Rodriquez *island* Indian Ocean the modern world 110–111
Rodriquez *see* Rodrigues
Roebourne Australia exploration 279 (2)
Roebuck North America (USA) cultural groups 122 (5)
Rohilkhand *region/state* South Asia colonialism 247 (3), 248 (1) empire and revolution 249 (3)
Rojadi South Asia (India) first civilizations 24 (2)
Roma var. Rome. Italy ancient trade 44 (2)
Romagna *state* Italy empire and revolution 202 (3)
Romanelli Southern Europe (Italy)
Roman Empire *state* Europe/Africa ancient Persia 225 (6) ancient Rome 181 (4), 224 (2), 225 (5) ancient trade 44–45 (1) early cultures 161 (3), (4) early trade 225 (3) great migrations 53 (2) medieval states 261 (6) world religions 226 (1), 49 (4)
Romania *Bul.* Rumŭniya, *Ger.* Rumänien, *Hung.* Románia, *Rom.* România, *SCr.* Rumunjska, *Ukr.* Rumuniya; *prev.* Roumania, Rumania, Romînia *state/vassal state* Southeast Europe early 20th century 206 (1) economy 205 (4) interwar 209 (3), (5) medieval states 187 (5) Ottomans 202 (4), 232–233 (1) postwar economy 213 (5), 214 (1), (2), 215 (3) postwar politics 212 (3) Soviet Union 208 (2), 213 (4) the modern world 112 (2) WWI 207 (4), (6), 208 (1) WWII 104 (2), 210 (1), 211 (2), (3), (4) Cold War 108 (3), 109 (1)
Rome *var.* Roma. Italy ancient Rome 179 (3), (5), 180–181 (1), 181 (3), (4), 182 (1), 225 (5) ancient trade 44–45 (1) crusades 186 (1), 64–65 (2), 65 (1) early cultures 161 (2) early Islam 56–57 (1), 57 (2) early modern states 193 (4), 194 (1) early states 178 (1), (2) early systems 32 (1), 33 (2), (3) economy 190 (1), 205 (4) empire and revolution 202 (1), (3) European expansion 84–85 (1) exploration 172 (1) first religions 36 (1), 37 (3) Franks 184 (2) great migrations 52–53 (1) imperial global economy 92 (1) interwar 209 (5) Islam 184 (1), 227 (4) medieval states 182 (2), 183 (4), 185 (3), (5), 188 (1) medieval voyages 60–61 (1) Napoleon 200–201 (1), 201 (2), (3) Ottomans 195 (4) postwar politics 212 (3) Reformation 194 (2) world religions 48 (1), 49 (4) WWII 210 (1), 211 (2), (4) Cold War 108 (3) *see also* Roma
Rome *state* Italy the world in 250 BCE 38–39
Rome, Duchy of *state* Italy medieval states 183 (4)
Romînia *see* Romania
Roncesvalles *battle* Iberian Peninsula (Spain) Franks 184 (2)
Rong *state* East Asia first cities 259 (3), (5)
Rong *people* East Asia first cities 259 (4)
Ronne Ice Shelf *ice feature* Antarctica Antarctic Exploration 287 (3)
Roonka Australia exploration 280 (1)
Roque River *battle* North America (USA) the growth of the US 129 (2)
Rorke's Drift *battle* Southern Africa (South Africa) European imperialism 96 (2)
Rosario South America (Argentina) empire and revolution 151 (3) environment 153 (4)
Rosario *var.* Rosario de Tezopaco *mine/settlement* Central America (Mexico) colonization 125 (4) Mexican Revolution 133 (3)
Rosario de Tezopaco *see* Rosario
Rosenkrans *burial mound* North America (USA) first civilizations 121 (4)
Roskilde Scandinavia (Denmark) early modern states 197 (3) medieval states 185 (3)
Ross New Zealand colonization 283 (5)
Ross Ice Shelf *ice feature* Antarctica Antarctic Exploration 287 (3)
Rossiyskaya Federatsiya *see* Russia, Russian Empire, Russian Federation, Soviet Union, Union of Socialist Republics
Ross Sea *sea* Antarctica Antarctic Exploration 287 (3)
Rostock Central Europe (Germany) economy 190 (1), 205 (4) empire and revolution 202 (2) medieval states 189 (3)
Rostov *var.* Rostov-on-Don Eastern Europe (Russian Federation) biological diffusion 72–73 (1) medieval states 185 (3) Soviet Union 208 (2), 214–215 (4) WWI 207 (4) WWII 210 (1), 211 (4)
Rostov-on-Don *see* Rostov
Rotomagus *var.* Ratomagus; mod Rouen *Christian archbishopric/settlement* France ancient Rome 180–181 (1) world religions 48 (1) *see also* Rouen
Rotterdam *air raid* Low Countries WWII 210 (1)
Rottweil Central Europe (Germany) early modern states 193 (5)
Rouad *see* Aradus
Rouen *anc.* Ratomagus, Rotomagus France crusades 65 (1) early modern states 197 (5) economy 190 (1) empire and revolution 199 (4) Franks 184 (2) medieval states 185 (3), 186 (2), 187 (4), 192 (1), (2) medieval voyages 60–61 (1) Napoleon 200–201 (1), 201 (2) WWI 206 (2), (3) *see also* Rotomagus
Roumania *see* Romania
Roussillon *region/state* France/Iberian Peninsula early modern states 197 (5) medieval states 192 (2)
Rovereto *see* Rovreit
Rovine *battle* Southeast Europe (Romania) medieval states 189 (4)
Rovreit *It.* Rovereto Italy WWI 207 (5)
Rovuma *see* Ruvuma
Roxolani *people* Southeast Europe ancient Rome 180–181 (1)
Royal Military Canal *canal* British Isles economy 204 (1)
Royal Palace *building* France economy 191 (2)
Royal Prussia *region* Central Europe early modern states 193 (4), 195 (3)
Rozwi *state* Southern Africa slave trade 165 (4) trade 164 (1)
Ruanda *see* Rwanda
Ruanda-Urundi *mod.* Burundi, Rwanda *state* East Africa WWII 104 (1)
Ruanruan *var.* Avars *people* East Asia medieval states 261 (4), (6) *see also* Avars
Ruanruan, Empire of the *var.* Juan-juan *state* East Asia the world in 500 CE 50–51
Ruapuke Island *whaling station* New Zealand colonization 283 (4)
Rubuga East Africa (Tanzania) exploration 157 (4)
Rudolf, Lake *var.* Lake Turkana *lake* East Africa early agriculture 158 (1) economy 163 (2) exploration 157 (4), (5) first humans 12 (1) Islam 163 (1) slave trade 165 (4) trade 165 (3)
Rufiji *river* East Africa exploration 157 (5)
Ruhr *region* Central Europe economy 205 (4) WWI 208 (1)
Rum *state* Southwest Asia economy 190 (1)
Rumania *see* Romania
Rumänien *see* Romania
Rummelsburger See *lake* Central Europe postwar politics 212 (2)
Rum, Seljuks of *state* Southwest Asia crusades 228 (2) Mongols 229 (3) Timur 229 (4)
Rumŭniya *see* Romania
Rumunjska *see* Romania
Runan *province* East Asia first states 260 (1)
Runzhou *var.* Janchou East Asia (China) medieval states 262–263 (1)
Ruo *see* Yanying
Rupar *archaeological site* South Asia (India) first cities 240 (2)
Rupella *see* La Rochelle
Rupert House North America (Canada) colonization 126 (1)
Rupert's Land *var.* Hudson Bay Company *state* North America colonization 126 (1) *see also* Hudson Bay Company
Rusaddir North Africa (Spain) ancient Rome 179 (3), 180–181 (1) early cultures 161 (2)
Ruschuk *mod.* Ruse Southeast Europe (Romania) WWI 207 (6)
Ruse *see* Ruschuk
Rusellae Italy early states 178 (2)
Ruseştii-Noui *archaeological site* Southeast Europe (Romania) Copper Age 174 (2)
Rush Creek *battle* North America (USA) the growth of the US 129 (2)
Ruspina *see* Monastir
Russadir *see* Melilla, Rusaddir
Russell New Zealand colonization 283 (5)
Russell *see* Kororareka
Russia *region/state* Eastern Europe/Siberia Chinese revolution 271 (5) crusades 65 (1) early modern states 195 (3) empire and revolution 202 (2), 88 (1) exploration 257 (3), 286 (1), 287 (2) imperialism 270 (2) Ottomans 195 (4) Reformation 194 (2) Russo-Japanese War 270 (4) the growth of the US 129 (2), 132 (1), 133 (4) *see also* Russian Empire, Russian Federation, Russian Principalities
Russian America *see* Alaska
Russian Empire *state* Eastern Europe/Southwest Asia colonialism 269 (3), (4) early 20th century 206 (1) economy 205 (4) empire and revolution 198 (2), 202 (1), 88–89 (2) European expansion 84–85 (1) European imperialism 97 (4) global immigration 100 (1), 101 (2) imperial global economy 92 (1) Napoleon 200–201 (1), 201 (3) Ottomans 202 (4), 231 (3), 232–233 (1) WWI 207 (4), (6), 233 (2) *see also* Russia, Russian Federation, Russian Principalities
Russian Federation *var.* Russia; *prev.* Russian Empire, Soviet Union, Union of Soviet Republics; *Latv.* Krievija, *Rus.* Rossiyskaya Federatsiya *state* Eastern Europe/Southwest Asia economy 190 (1) historical geography 275 (5) Islam 235 (4) postwar economy 214 (1), (2), 275 (3) postwar politics 274 (2) Soviet Union 214–215 (4) the modern world 112 (2), 113 (4) *see also* Russia, Russian Empire, Soviet Union, Union of Soviet Republics
Russian Principalities *state* Eastern Europe crusades 186 (1), 64–65 (2) medieval states 187 (3) Mongols 68–69 (1) *see also* Russia, Russian Empire, Russian Federation
Russian steppes *region* Siberia first cities 28–29 (1)
Rustenburg Southern Africa (South Africa) colonization 166 (2)
Rutanzige, Lake *see* Edward *Lake*
Ruvuma *Port.* Rovuma *river* East Africa exploration 157 (4) trade 164 (1)
Rwanda *prev.* Ruanda *state* Central Africa colonization 167 (4) decolonization 168 (1) economy 168 (2), (3) the modern world 112 (1) trade 167 (1) Cold War 109 (1) *see also* Ruanda-Urundi
Ryazan' Eastern Europe (Russian Federation) Mongols 68–69 (1) Soviet Union 214–215 (4)
Ryazan' *state* Eastern Europe the world in 1400 70–71 the world in 1500 74–75
Ryojun *see* Port Arthur
Ryssel *see* Lille
Ryukyu Islands *prev.* Loochoo Islands; *Jap.* Nansei-shotō *island group* East Asia colonialism 269 (4) Communism 273 (3) early modern states 265 (5) imperialism 270 (2) trade 267 (3) WWII 272 (1), 273 (2)
Ryzan *state* Southwest Asia Islam 163 (1)

S

Saami Hunter-Gatherers *people* Eastern Europe the world in 2500 BCE 22–23
Saar *region* Central Europe postwar politics 212 (1) WWI 208 (1)
Saare *see* Ösel
Saaremaa *see* Ösel
Saarlouis Central Europe (Germany) early modern states 197 (5)
Saba East Africa (Eritrea) early cultures 161 (4)
Saba *var.* Sheba *state* East Africa/Southwest Asia the world in 500 BCE 34–35
Šabac Southeast Europe (Serbia) WWI 207 (6)
Sabah *prev.* British North Borneo, North Borneo *region* Maritime Southeast Asia postwar economy 275 (3) *see also* British North Borneo
Sabarmati *river* South Asia first cities 240 (2) Mughal Empire 246 (1)
Sabatinus, Lacus *lake* Italy early states 178 (1)
Sabe *state* West Africa trade 164 (2)
Sabine North America (USA) US Civil War 131 (6), (7)
Sabini *people* Italy early states 178 (1), (2)
Sabotiers *battle* France Reformation 196 (2)
Sabrata North Africa (Libya) ancient Rome 180–181 (1) first civilizations 177 (1)
Saccopastore *archaeological site* Italy first humans 13 (2)
Sachsen *see* Saxony
Sachsenhausen *concentration camp* Central Europe WWII 211 (3)
Sacramento North America (USA) the growth of the US 129 (2)
Sá da Bandeira *see* Lubango
Sado *var.* Sadoga-shima *island* Japan Communism 273 (3) early modern states 265 (5), 267 (4) economy 270 (1) medieval states 264 (1), (2), 265 (3), (4)
Sadoga-shima *see* Sado
Sadowa *battle* Central Europe (Czech Republic) empire and revolution 202 (2)
Sadras South Asia (India) colonialism 247 (3)
Saena Julia *see* Siena, Sena Iulia
Safad *see* Safed
Safavid Empire *state* Southwest Asia Islam 163 (1) medieval Persia 231 (4) Mughal Empire 246 (1) Ottomans 231 (3)
Safed *Ar.* Safad, *Heb.* Zefat Southwest Asia (Israel) crusades 65 (1)
Safety Harbor North America (USA) cultural groups 122 (5)
Saffarids *dynasty* Southwest Asia early Islam 57 (2) Islam 227 (4)
Safi North Africa (Morocco) exploration 157 (4)
Safinaya *oil field* Southwest Asia economy 234 (1)
Saga *prefecture* Japan economy 270 (1)
Sagartia *province* Southwest Asia ancient Persia 223 (4)
Sagrajas Iberian Peninsula (Portugal) Islam 192 (3)
Sagua la Grande *military base* West Indies (Cuba) Cold War 108 (2)
Sagunto *see* Saguntum
Saguntum *var.* Sagunto Iberian Peninsula (Spain) ancient Rome 179 (3), 180–181 (1)
Sahagún Iberian Peninsula (Spain) Napoleon 200–201 (1)
Sahajati South Asia (India) world religions 242 (3)
Sahara *desert* North Africa ancient Persia 223 (4) ancient trade 44–45 (1) biological diffusion 72–73 (1), 73 (3) Bronze Age 175 (3) early agriculture 158 (1), 20–21 (2) early cultures 160 (1), 161 (2), (3), (4), (5) early Islam 56–57 (1), 57 (2) economy 163 (2) European expansion 84–85 (1) European imperialism 96 (1) exploration 156 (1), (2), (3), 157 (4) first humans 12 (1), 13 (2) imperial global economy 92 (1) Islam 163 (1) prehistoric culture 16 (1) slave trade 165 (4) trade 164 (2)
Sahara el Gharbîya *see* Western Desert
Saharan Peoples *people* Central Africa/West Africa the world in 500 BCE 34–35 the world in 250 BCE 38–39 the world in 1 CE 42–43 the world in 250 CE 46–47 the world in 500 CE 50–51 the world in 750 CE 54–55 the world in 1000 58–59 the world in 1200 62–63
Sahel *physical region* West Africa ancient trade 44–45 (1) slave trade 165 (4) trade 164 (2)
Sahul *var.* Sahul Shelf *physical region* Australia exploration 276–277 (1) historical geography 254–255 (1)
Sahul Shelf *see* Sahul
Saidpur *var.* Syedpur South Asia (Bangladesh) postwar politics 252 (3)
Saigon *var.* Hô Chi Minh, Ho Chi Minh City, Mainland Southeast Asia (Vietnam) colonialism 247 (4), 248 (1), 269 (4) European imperialism 97 (3) exploration 239 (1) trade 230 (2) US superpower 138 (1) WWII 251 (3) postwar politics 251 (5) *see also* Ho Chi Minh City
Saigon-Cholon *military base* Mainland Southeast Asia (Vietnam) WWII 272 (1), 273 (2)
Sai Hun *see* Jaxartes, Syr Darya
Saikaido *region* Japan medieval states 265 (3)
St Agostin *see* St Augustine, San Agostin, San Austín
St Augustine *prev.* San Agostin, St Agostin, San Agustín North America (USA) colonization 126 (1) European expansion 85 (2) US Civil War 131 (6) *see also* San Agostín, San Agustín
Saint Augustine North America (USA) colonization 126 (1)
St Botolph's Town *see* Boston
St. Catherine, Cape *headland* Central Africa exploration 156 (3)
St. Césaire *archaeological site* France first humans 13 (2)
Saint Christopher-Nevis *see* St. Kitts and Nevis
St Clairís Defeat *battle* North America (USA) the growth of the US 129 (2)
St. Denis France economy 190 (1)
Saint Domingue *colonial possession* West Indies empire and revolution 89 (3) *state* West Indies colonization 126 (1)
St Francis North America (USA) empire and revolution 127 (2)
St Gall Central Europe (Switzerland) Franks 184 (2)
St. Gallen Central Europe (Switzerland) early modern states 193 (5)
St. Gilles France crusades 186 (1) economy 190 (1)
St Gotthard *battle* Southeast Europe (Austria) Ottomans 197 (4)
St. Gotthard Pass *pass* Central Europe economy 190 (1)
Saint Helena *colonial possession/island* Atlantic Ocean exploration 156 (3)
St. Helena Bay *bay* Southern Africa exploration 156 (3)
St Jago de Vega West Indies (Jamaica) colonization 125 (4)
St James River *burial mound* North America (USA) first civilizations 121 (4)
Saint-Jean-d'Acre *see* Acco, Acre
St Jean, Ile *see* Prince Edward Island
St John, Isle *see* Prince Edward Island
St John's North America (Canada) the growth of the US 132 (1)
St. Kitts and Nevis *var.* Saint Christopher-Nevis *state* North America the modern world 112 (1) US economy 136 (2) US politics 139 (4)
St. Lawrence *river* North America colonization 126 (1) early agriculture 20–21 (2) empire and revolution 127 (2), (3) European expansion 80–81 (1) exploration 118 (1), 119 (2) first religions 36 (1) medieval voyages 60–61 (1) the growth of the US 129 (2)
St. Lawrence, Gulf of *gulf* North America colonization 126 (1) empire and revolution 127 (2) the growth of the US 129 (2)
Saint Lawrence Island *island* North America exploration 287 (2)
Saint Lawrence Island Inuit *people* North America cultural groups 123 (3)
Saint-Louis *settlement/island* West Africa (Senegal) empire and revolution 88 (1) European expansion 84–85 (1) slave trade 165 (4)
St Louis North America (USA) empire and revolution 127 (3) exploration 119 (2), (3) the growth of the US 129 (2), 132 (1) US Civil War 130 (5), 131 (6), (7) US economy 134 (1), (3), 136 (2) US politics 135 (6) Cold War 108 (2)
St Lucia *island/state* West Indies empire and revolution 88 (1) European expansion 84–85 (1) US economy 136 (2) US politics 139 (4) WWII 104 (2) Cold War 108 (2)
St-Malo France early modern states 197 (5)
St. Marks *battle* North America (USA) the growth of the US 129 (2)
St Martin *Dut.* Sint Maarten *island* West Indies the world in 1700 82–83 the world in 1800 86–87 the world in 1850 90–91 the world in 1900 94–95 the world in 1925 98–99 the world in 1950 102–103
St. Mary, Cape *var.* Cape Lobo *headland* West Africa exploration 156 (3)
St Michael North America (USA) imperial global economy 93 (3)
St Mihiel France WWI 206 (2), (3)
St Nazaire France WWII 104 (2)
St. Omer France economy 190 (1)
St. Paul North America (USA) the growth of the US 129 (2)
St. Peter, Patrimony of *state* Italy Franks 184 (2)
St Petersburg *prev.* Leningrad, Petrograd; *Russ.* Sankt-Peterburg, *Fin.* Pietari; Eastern Europe (Russian Federation) colonialism 269 (3) colonization 126 (1) early modern states 197 (3) economy 205 (4) empire and revolution 202 (1) exploration 257 (2) global immigration 100 (1) Napoleon 200–201 (1) Soviet Union 214–215 (4) WWI 207 (4) *see also* Leningrad, Petrograd
Saint Petersburg *see* Leningrad, Petrograd, St Petersburg
St. Pierre and Miquelon *colonial possession/island group* North America empire and revolution 88 (1) the growth of the US 129 (2)
St-Pierre et Miquelon, Îles *see* St Pierre and Miquelon
St Pol France WWI 206 (2), (3)
St Quentin France WWI 206 (2), (3)
Saint Thomas *see* São Tomé
St. Thomé South Asia (India) colonialism 247 (3)
St. Valéry France medieval states 186 (2)
St Vincent *island* West Indies empire and revolution 88 (1) European expansion 84–85 (1)
Saint Vincent *see* São Vicente
St. Vincent and the Grenadines *state* North America US economy 136 (2) US politics 139 (4)
Saipan *island/military base* Pacific Ocean decolonization 285 (3) WWII 104 (2), 251 (3), 272 (1), 273 (2)
Sais Egypt first cities 28–29 (1)
Saishū *see* Cheju-do, Quelpart Island
Saitama *prefecture* Japan economy 270 (1)
Saitobaru *state* Japan medieval states 264 (1)
Sai Yok *archaeological site* Mainland Southeast Asia (Thailand) Bronze Age 240 (3)
Saka *state* Central Asia first empires 241 (5)
Sak'art'velo *see* Georgia
Sakata Japan economy 270 (1)
Sakchu *region* East Asia medieval states 264 (2)
Saketa South Asia (India) world religions 242 (3)
Sakhalin *island* East Asia colonialism 269 (3), (4) exploration 257 (2) first states 260 (1) imperialism 270 (2) medieval states 263 (6) WWII 272 (1), 273 (2)
Sakiz-Adasi *see* Chios
Salado *river* South America colonization 148 (2) early cultures 146 (1) Incas 147 (3) politics 152 (1)
Saladoid *people* South America early cultures 145 (2)
Salaga West Africa (Ghana) Islam 163 (1)
Salala Southwest Asia (Oman) 20th-century politics 233 (4) exploration 219 (4)
Salamanca Iberian Peninsula (Spain) interwar 209 (4) Islam 192 (3) medieval states 187 (3) Napoleon 200–201 (1)
Salamantica *mod.* Salamanca Iberian Peninsula (Spain) ancient Rome 180–181 (1) *see also* Salamanca
Salamaua *air raid* New Guinea (Papua New Guinea) WWII 272 (1)
Salamis Southwest Asia (Cyprus) ancient Rome 180–181 (1) first civilizations 177 (1) Hellenistic world 40–41 (1) world religions 48 (1)
Salamis *battle* Greece ancient Persia 223 (4)
Salang *see* Phuket
Salaria vetus, Via *road* Italy ancient Rome 181 (2) early states 178 (1), ancient Rome 181 (2),
Saldae *mod.* Bougie North Africa (Algeria) ancient Rome 179 (3) *see also* Bougie
Salduba *see* Saragossa, Zaragoza
Salekhard *see* Obdorsk
Salem South Asia (India) colonialism 247 (3)
Salem North America (USA) the growth of the US 129 (2)
Salerno *settlement/university* Italy Franks 184 (2) medieval states 183 (4), 187 (3)
Salerno, Principality of *state* Italy medieval states 185 (3)
Salford British Isles (United Kingdom) economy 204 (2)
Salghurids *dynasty* Southwest Asia Mongols 68–69 (1)
Salian Franks *people* France Franks 183 (5)
Salina Cruz Central America (Mexico) Mexican Revolution 133 (3)
Salinas la Blanca Central America (Mexico) first civilizations 123 (2)
Salisbury Southern Africa (Zimbabwe) colonization 167 (4)
Salisbury *var.* New Sarum British Isles (United Kingdom) economy 190 (1)
Sallentini *people* Italy early states 178 (1)
Salmon *archaeological site* North America (USA) cultural groups 123 (4)
Salona Southeast Europe (Croatia) world religions 48 (1)
Salonae *mod.* Solin *settlement* Southeast Europe (Croatia) ancient Rome 180–181 (1), 181 (3) early cultures 161 (2) world religions 48 (1)
Salonica *var.* Salonika; *mod.* Thessaloníki; *prev.* Thessalonica; *SCr.* Solun, *Turk.* Selânik Greece economy 198 (1) empire and revolution 202 (1) medieval states 187 (5), 189 (4) Napoleon 200–201 (1) Ottomans 195 (4), 230 (1) Reformation 194 (2) WWI 207 (6) *see also* Thessalonica
Salonica *state/region* Greece medieval states 187 (5) WWI 207 (6) WWII 211 (2)
Salonika *see* Salonica, Thessalonica
Salsette Island South Asia (India) colonialism 247 (3)
Salta South America (Argentina) empire and revolution 150 (1), 151 (3) politics 151 (4) empire and revolution 88–89 (2)
Salţanat 'Umān *see* Oman
Saltillo Central America (Mexico) Mexican Revolution 133 (3)
Salt Lake City North America (USA) the growth of the US 129 (2), 132 (1) US economy 136 (2)
Salt River *river* North America cultural groups 123 (4)
Saluum *state* West Africa the world in 1400 70–71 trade 163 (6)
Salva *state* South Asia first empires 241 (5)
Salvador *prev.* Bahia, São Salvador South America (Brazil) environment 153 (4) European expansion 84–85 (1) politics 152 (1) *see also* Bahia
Salvador *mod.* El Salvador Central America, *state* the world in 1900 94–95 WWII 104 (1) *see also* El Salvador
Salvador *see* Bahia
Salween *Bur.* Thanlwin, *Chin.* Nu Chiang, Nu Jiang *river* Mainland Southeast Asia ancient India 241 (6) Bronze Age 240 (3) colonialism 247 (4) early medieval states 245 (5), (6) first states 260 (1) Mongols 68–69 (1) world religions 243 (5)
Salzburg *anc.* Juvavum Central Europe (Austria) early modern states 193 (4) Franks 184 (2) medieval states 185 (3), 188 (1), 189 (4) postwar politics 212 (1) Reformation 196 (1)
Salzkammergut *mine* Central Europe Bronze Age 175 (3)
Sama *state* West Africa the world in 1200 62–63
Samana South Asia (India) colonialism 247 (3)
Samanids *dynasty* Central Asia/Southwest Asia early Islam 57 (2) Islam 227 (4), (5)
Samapa South Asia (India) first empires 241 (4)
Samar *island* Maritime Southeast Asia exploration 278 (1)
Samara *prev.* Kuybyshev Eastern Europe (Russian Federation) colonialism 269 (3) Soviet Union 208 (2), 214–215 (4)
Samara Egypt ancient Egypt 159 (2)
Samarang *see* Semarang
Samaria Southwest Asia (Israel) Hellenistic world 40–41 (1)
Samaria *province* Southwest Asia ancient Rome 225 (4)
Samarkand *anc.* Maracanda; *Uzb.* Samarqand Central Asia (Uzbekistan) biological diffusion 72–73 (1) colonialism 269 (3) crusades 65 (1) early Islam 56–57 (1), 57 (2) exploration 218 (2), 256 (1) Islam 226 (2), 227 (4), (5) medieval Persia 231 (4) medieval states 261 (6) Mongols 229 (3), 68–69 (1) Ottomans 232–233 (1) Soviet Union 214–215 (4) Timur 229 (4) trade 267 (3) world religions 49 (3), (4) *see also* Maracanda
Samarobriva *see* Amiens
Samarqand *see* Maracanda, Samarkand
Samarra Southwest Asia (Iraq) early Islam 56–57 (1), 57 (2), (3) Islam 227 (4) WWI 233 (2)
Sambas Maritime Southeast Asia (Indonesia) colonialism 247 (4)
Samhar Southwest Asia (Oman) early cultures 161 (3), (5) early trade 225 (3)
Samkashya South Asia (India) first religions 36 (2) world religions 242 (3)
Sam Neua *mod.* Xam Nua *region* Mainland Southeast Asia postwar politics 251 (5)
Samnites *people* Italy early states 178 (1), (2)
Samoa *state/island group* Pacific Ocean the modern world 110–111, early cultures 280–281 (3) exploration 278 (1) medieval voyages 60 (2)
Sāmoa-i-Sisifo *see* Western Samoa
Samori *state* West Africa colonization 167 (4)
Samos *prev.* Limín Vathéos Greece first civilizations 177 (1)
Samos *state* Greece ancient Greece 177 (2)
Samosata *mod.* Samsat *settlement* Southwest Asia (Turkey) ancient Rome 180–181 (1) first cities 220 (2)
Samothrace *island/state* Greece ancient Greece 177 (2), 179 (4)
Samoyeds *people* Eastern Europe/Siberia trade 267 (3)
Samsat *see* Samosata
Samsun *see* Amisus
Samun Dukiya *archaeological site* West Africa (Nigeria) early cultures 160 (1)
San *river* Eastern Europe WWI 207 (4)
Sana *var.* Şan'ā', San'a Southwest Asia (Yemen) ancient trade 44–45 (1) early Islam 56–57 (1) early trade 225 (3) exploration 156 (3) medieval voyages 61 (3) 20th-century politics 233 (4)
San Agostín *fort* North America (USA) colonization 125 (4)
San Agustín North America (USA) European expansion 85 (2) exploration 119 (2)
San Agustín *state* South America the world in 1 CE 42–43 the world in 250 CE 46–47
San Ambrosio *island* South America the world in 1950 102–103 the modern world 110–111
Sanandita *oil field* South America politics 152 (2)
San Antonio North America (USA) Cold War 108 (2) Mexican Revolution 133 (3) the growth of the US 129 (2)
San Antonio *fort* North America (USA) colonization 125 (4)
San Carlos de Ancud *mod.* Ancud South America (Chile) colonization 148 (2)
San Casciano Italy medieval states 188 (1)
Sanchi *Buddhist center/settlement* South Asia (India) early religions 48 (2) world religions 242 (3)
San Cristóbal South America (Venezuela) empire and revolution 150 (1), (2) politics 152 (1)
San Cristóbal *var.* San Cristóbal de la Barranca Central America (Mexico) Mexican Revolution 133 (3)
San Cristóbal *var.* Makira *island* Pacific Ocean exploration 278 (1)
San Cristóbal *military base* West Indies (Cuba) Cold War 108 (2)
San Cristóbal de Havana West Indies (Cuba) colonization 125 (4)
San Cristóbal de la Barranca *see* San Cristóbal
Sancti Spíritus West Indies (Cuba) European expansion 85 (2)
Sanctuary of Ammon *var.* Siwa Oasis Egypt Hellenistic world 40–41 (1)
Sand Creek *battle* North America (USA) the growth of the US 129 (2)
San Diego North America (USA) exploration 119 (2), (3) the growth of the US 129 (2) US economy 136 (2)
Sandomierz Russ. Sandomir Central Europe (Poland) medieval states 189 (3) Mongols 68–69 (1)
Sandomir *see* Sandomierz
Sandu'ao *var.* Santuao East Asia (China) colonialism 269 (4)
Sandwich Islands *see* Hawaii, Hawaiian Islands
Sandy Creek *archaeological site* Australia prehistoric culture 17 (2)
Sandy Hill *burial mound* North America (USA) first civilizations 121 (4)
San Felice Circco *see* Circei
San Felipe Central America (Mexico) first civilizations 123 (2)
San Félix, Isla *island* Pacific Ocean the modern world 110–111 the world in 1950 102–103
San Fernando *see* San Fernando de Apure
San Fernando de Apure *var.* San Fernando South America (Venezuela) empire and revolution 150 (1), (2)
San Francisco *prev.* San Francisco de Asís North America (USA) exploration 119 (2), (3) global immigration 100 (1), 101 (3) imperial global economy 92 (1) the growth of the US 129 (2), 132 (1) US economy 134 (1), (3), 136 (2)
San Francisco de Asís *see* San Francisco
San Francisco de Macorís West Indies (Dominican Republic) empire and revolution 89 (3)
San Francisco de Selva *see* Copiapó
Sanga *archaeological site* Central Africa (Congo (Zaire)) early cultures 160 (1)
Sangamas *dynasty* South Asia early medieval states 244–245 (3)
Sangela South Asia (India) Hellenistic world 40–41 (1)
Sangiran *archaeological site* Maritime Southeast Asia (Indonesia) first humans 13 (2)
Sangju *region* East Asia medieval states 264 (2)
San Ignacio de Ostimuri *mine* Central America (Mexico) colonization 125 (4)
Sanindo *region* Japan medieval states 265 (3)
San Isidoro *archaeological site* South America (Ecuador) the world in 5000 BCE 18–19
San Isidro Piedra Parada Central America (Guatemala) first civilizations 121 (2)
Sanjayani South Asia (India) world religions 243 (4)
San Jerónimo Central America (Mexico) first civilizations 121 (2)
San Jorge, Golfo de *var.* Gulf of San Jorge *gulf* South America colonization 148 (2)
San Jorge, Gulf of *see* San Jorge, Golfo de
San Jose North America (USA)
San José Central America (Mexico) first civilizations 123 (2)
San José Central America (Costa Rica) the growth of the US 129 (2)
San José de Cúcuta *see* Cúcuta
San José Mogote Central America (Mexico) first civilizations 121 (2)
San Juan West Indies (Puerto Rico) Cold War 108 (2) colonization 125 (4), 126 (1) US economy 136 (2) WWII 104 (2)
San Juan Central America (Mexico) exploration 118 (1)
San Juan Bautista *mod.* Villahermosa Central America (Mexico) colonization 125 (4)
San Juan Bautista Tuxtepec *see* Tuxtepec
San Juan del Rio Central America (Mexico) first civilizations 122 (1)
San Juan de Ulna Central America (Mexico) colonization 125 (5)
San Juan de Vera *see* Corrientes
San Julián *see* Puerto San Julián
Sankt-Peterburg *see* Leningrad, St Petersburg, Petrograd
Sankt Veit am Flaum *see* Rijeka
Sanliqiao *archaeological site* East Asia (China) early agriculture 258 (2)
Sanli Urfa *see* Edessa
San Lorenzo Central America (Mexico) first civilizations 121 (2), (3), 122 (1) first religions 36 (1)
San Luis South America (Argentina) empire and revolution 151 (3)
San Luis Potosí *mine/settlement* Central America (Mexico) colonization 125 (4) the growth of the US 129 (2)
San Luis Potosí *state* Central America Mexican Revolution 133 (3) the growth of the US 129 (2)
San Marco Italy economy 191 (3)
San Marco, Canale di *canal* Italy economy 191 (3)
San Marcos de Arica *see* Arica
San Marino *state* Italy empire and revolution 202 (3)
San Martín Pajapán *archaeological site* Central America (Mexico) first civilizations 121 (3)
San Miguel South America (Peru) Incas 148 (1)
San Miguel Central America (Mexico) first civilizations 123 (2)
San Miguel Allende Central America (Mexico) first civilizations 122 (1)
San Miguel de Culiacan Central America (Mexico) colonization 125 (4)
San Miguel de Tucumán *var.* Tucumán South America (Argentina) environment 153 (4) exploration 143 (2) *see also* Tucumán
Sannār *see* Sennar
San Pedro *jesuit mission* North America (USA) colonization 125 (4)
San Pedro de Lagunas *jesuit mission* Central America (Mexico) colonization 125 (4)
San Salvador Central America (San Salvador) the growth of the US 129 (2)
San Salvador De Jujuy *see* Jujuy
San Sebastián Iberian Peninsula (Spain) interwar 209 (4)
Sanshui East Asia (China) first states 260 (1)
Santa Ana de Coro *see* Coro
Santa Barbara North America (USA) exploration 119 (3)
Santa Catarina *region* South America colonization 149 (3)
Santa Clara North America (USA)
Santa Clara *jesuit mission* North America (USA) colonization 125 (4)
Santa Clara *military base* West Indies (Cuba) Cold War 108 (2)
Santa Croce Italy economy 191 (3)
Santa Cruz Central America (Mexico) first civilizations 121 (2)
Santa Cruz *mod.* Santa Cruz Cabrália South America (Brazil) colonization 149 (4) empire and revolution 151 (3)
Santa Cruz *var.* Santa Cruz de la Sierra South America (Bolivia) empire and revolution 151 (3) environment 153 (4) narcotics 153 (5) politics 152 (2)
Santa Cruz Cabrália, Santa Cruz de la Sierra *see* Santa Cruz
Santa Cruz Islands *island group* Pacific Ocean early cultures 280–281 (3) exploration 278 (1) medieval voyages 60 (2) the world in 1900 94–95 WWII 272 (1), 273 (2)
Santa Cruz Valley *region* North America
Santa Elena *fort* North America (USA) colonization 125 (4)
Santa Fe South America (Argentina) environment 153 (4) exploration 143 (2), (3)
Santa Fe North America (USA) colonization 125 (4), 126 (1) exploration 118 (1), 119 (2), (3) the growth of the US 129 (2)
Santa Fé, Audiencia of *region* South America colonization 148 (2)
Santa Fé de Bogotá *mod.* Bogotá South America (Colombia) colonization 148 (2) exploration 142 (1), 143 (2) Incas 148 (1) *see also* Bogotá
Santa Fe Trail *wagon train route* North America the growth of the US 129 (2)
Santa Lucia *fort* North America (USA) colonization 125 (4)
Santa Maria de Belém *see* Belém do Pará
Santa Maria del Buen Aire *see* Buenos Aires
Santa Marta South America (Colombia) colonization 148 (2) empire and revolution 150 (1), (2), 151 (3) exploration 142 (1) Incas 148 (1)
Santa Monica North America (USA)
Santana de Riacho *archaeological site* South America (Brazil) early cultures 145 (2)
Santander Iberian Peninsula (Spain) economy 205 (4) interwar 209 (4)
Santarém Iberian Peninsula (Portugal) Islam 192 (3)
Santarém South America (Brazil) economy 153 (3) empire and revolution 151 (3)
Santarém *state* South America the world in 1000 58–59 the world in 1200 62–63 the world in 1400 70–71
Santarém *see* Tapajoso
Santa Rita Central America (Mexico) first civilizations 122 (1), 123 (2)
Santa Rosa Central America (Mexico) first civilizations 123 (2)
Santee *people* North America colonization 126 (1)
Santiago West Indies (Dominican Republic) empire and revolution 89 (3)
Santiago Central America (Cuba) exploration 119 (2), (3)
Santiago *var.* Gran Santiago South America (Chile) colonization 148 (2) empire and revolution 150 (1), 151 (3) environment 153 (4) exploration 142 (1), 143 (2), (3) imperial global economy 92 (1) Incas 147 (3) politics 152 (1)
Santiago *see* Santiago de Compostela
Santiago de Compostela *var.* Santiago, *Eng.* Compostella; *anc.* Campus Stellae Iberian Peninsula (Spain) crusades 186 (1) interwar 209 (4) Islam 192 (3) medieval states 185 (3)
Santiago de Cuba *var.* Santiago West Indies (Cuba) colonization 125 (4) exploration 118 (1) US imperialism 133 (5) Cold War 108 (2) *see also* Santiago
Santiago de Guayaquil *see* Guayaquil
Santiago del Estero South America (Argentina) empire and revolution 151 (3)
Santiago de Saltillo Central America (Mexico) colonization 125 (4)
Santo *see* Espiritu Santo
Santo Domingo West Indies (Dominican Republic) colonization 125 (4), 126 (1)

Sunomata battle Japan early modern states 265 (5)
Süntel battle Central Europe (Germany) Franks 184 (2)
Suomenlahti see Finland, Gulf of
Suomen Tasavalta see Finland
Suomi see Finland
Suomussalmi Scandinavia (Finland) WWII 210 (1)
Supara South Asia (India) medieval voyages 61 (3)
Superior, Lake lake North America colonization 126 (1) cultural groups 123 (3) early agriculture 120 (1) exploration 118 (1), 119 (2), (3) first civilizations 121 (4) the growth of the US 129 (2), 132 (1) US Civil War 131 (6)
Suqutra see Socotra
Sūr see Syria
Surabaja see Surabaya
Surabaya prev. Soerabaja, Surabaja military base/settlement Maritime Southeast Asia (Indonesia) exploration 239 (2) Islam 275 (4) postwar economy 253 (5) trade 267 (3) WWII 272 (1)
Surasena region/state South Asia ancient India 242 (1) first empires 241 (5) first religions 36 (2) world religions 242 (3)
Surashtra region/state South Asia first empires 241 (4), (5) world religions 242 (2)
Surat South Asia (India) colonialism 247 (3) decolonization 250 (1) early medieval states 244–245 (3) economy 249 (4) empire and revolution 88 (1) trade 230 (2)
Surgut Eastern Europe (Russian Federation) colonialism 269 (3) exploration 257 (2)
Surinam var. Suriname; prev. Dutch Guiana, Netherlands Guiana state South America colonization 149 (4) economy 153 (3) empire and revolution 150 (1), 151 (3) environment 153 (4) global immigration 101 (3) politics 152 (1) the modern world 112 (1), 113 (3) see also Dutch Guiana
Suriname see Dutch Guiana, Surinam
Sūriya see Syria
Surkotada archaeological site South Asia (India) first cities 240 (2)
Surparaka South Asia (India) early religions 48 (2) first empires 241 (4)
Surt see Sirt
Susa mod. Shūsh; Bibl. Shushan Southwest Asia (Iran) ancient Persia 223 (4), 225 (6) ancient Rome 224 (2), 225 (5) early Islam 56–57 (1) early systems 223 (3) early trade 225 (3) exploration 218 (1) first cities 220 (2), 28–29 (1) first civilizations 221 (4), 24 (2), 25 (3) Hellenistic world 224 (1) Islam 227 (4), (5)
Susia Central Asia (Turkmenistan) Hellenistic world 40–41 (1)
Susiana province/region Southwest Asia ancient Persia 223 (4) Hellenistic world 40–41 (1)
Susquehanna var. Conestoga people North America colonization 126 (1)
Susquehanna river North America empire and revolution 127 (3)
Sussex state British Isles medieval states 183 (3)
Sutkagen Dor archaeological site South Asia (Pakistan) first cities 240 (2)
Sutlej river South Asia ancient India 242 (1) colonialism 247 (3), 248 (1), (2) decolonization 250 (1) early medieval states 244 (1), (2), 244–245 (3) economy 249 (4) Marathas 246 (2) Mughal Empire 246 (1) world religions 242 (2), 243 (4)
Sutrium Italy early states 178 (1)
Sutton Hoo British Isles (United Kingdom) medieval states 183 (3)
Suva (Fiji) decolonization 285 (3) WWII 104 (2)
Suvarnagiri South Asia (India) first empires 241 (4)
Suvla Bay battle Southwest Asia (Turkey) WWI 207 (6)
Suways, Khalīj as see Suez, Gulf of
Suways, Qanāt as see Suez Canal
Suzdal Eastern Europe (Russian Federation) Mongols 68–69 (1)
Suzhou var. Soochow, Su-chou, Suchow; prev. Wuhsien East Asia (China) colonialism 269 (4) early modern states 266 (1) imperialism 270 (2) medieval states 263 (6)
Svalbard var. Spitsbergen, Spitzbergen colonial possession/island group Arctic Ocean exploration 286 (1), 287 (2) see also Spitsbergen
Sverdlovsk Eastern Europe (Russian Federation) Soviet Union 213 (4)
Sverige see Sweden
Svizhden state Eastern Europe medieval states 189 (4)
Svizzera see Helvetia, Helvetian Republic, Swiss Confederation, Switzerland
Svobodnyy Eastern Europe (Russian Federation) Soviet Union 214–215 (4)
Swabia region Central Europe crusades 64–65 (2) medieval states 185 (3), 188 (1)
Swahili City-States region/state East Africa/Southern Africa economy 163 (2)
Swanscombe archaeological site British Isles (United Kingdom) first humans 13 (2)
Swansea Wel. Abertawe British Isles (United Kingdom) economy 204 (1)
Swartkrans archaeological site Southern Africa (South Africa) first humans 12 (1)
Swatow see Shantou
Swazi people Southern Africa the world in 1850 90–91
Swazi see Swaziland
Swaziland prev. Swazi state Southern Africa decolonization 168 (1) economy 168 (2), (3) European imperialism 96 (1) trade 167 (1)
Sweden Swe. Sverige state Scandinavia colonialism 269 (3) crusades 186 (1), 64–65 (2) early 20th century 206 (1) early modern states 193 (4), 195 (3) economy 190 (1), 205 (4) empire and revolution 198 (2), 199 (3), 202 (1), (2) imperial global economy 92 (1) interwar 209 (3), (5) medieval states 185 (3) medieval voyages 60–61 (1) Mongols 68–69 (1) Napoleon 200–201 (1), 201 (2) postwar economy 213 (5), 214 (1), (2) postwar politics 212 (3) Reformation 194 (2), 196 (1), (2) Soviet Union 208 (2), 213 (4) the modern world 112 (2) WWI 207 (4), 208 (1) WWII 104 (1), 211 (2), (4) Cold War 108 (3)
Swedes people Scandinavia medieval states 185 (3) the modern world 112 (2)
Swedish Pomerania colonial possession Central Europe empire and revolution 199 (3) Napoleon 200–201 (1)
Swiss Confederation var. Switzerland; Fr. La Suisse, Ger. Schweiz, It. Svizzera; prev. Helvetia, Helvetian Republic; anc. Helvetia state Central Europe early modern states 193 (4), 197 (5) empire and revolution 199 (3), (4) Napoleon 200–201 (1) Reformation 194 (2), 196 (1), (2) see also Helvetia, Helvetian Republic, Switzerland
Switzerland var. Swiss Confederation, Fr. La Suisse, Ger. Schweiz, It. Svizzera; prev. Helvetia, Helvetian Republic; state Central Europe early 20th century 206 (1) economy 205 (4) empire and revolution 202 (1), (2), (3) interwar 209 (3), (5) postwar economy 213 (5), 214 (1), (2) postwar politics 212 (1), (3) Soviet Union 213 (4) the modern world 112 (2), 113 (3), (4) WWI 206 (2), (3), 207 (5), 208 (1) WWII 104 (1), 211 (2), (3), (4) Cold War 108 (3) see also Helvetia, Helvetian Republic, Swiss Confederation
Sword Brothers crusade Eastern Europe crusades 186 (1)
Syagrius, Kingdom of state France Franks 183 (5)
Sybaris Italy first civilizations 177 (1)
Sycaminum see Haifa
Sydney settlement Australia colonization 282 (1), (2), 283 (3), 284–285 (1) decolonization 285 (3) environmentalism 285 (2) exploration 279 (2), (3) global immigration 100 (1) imperial global economy 92 (1) prehistoric culture 17 (5)
Syedpur see Saidpur
Syene var. Assouan, Assuan, Qus; Ar. Aswān Egypt Hellenistic world 40–41 (1) see also Aswān, Qus
Sylhet South Asia (Bangladesh) postwar politics 252 (3)
Synnada Southwest Asia (Turkey) world religions 48 (1)
Syracusa, Syracusae see Syracuse
Syracuse mod. Siracusa; Lat. Syracusae; It. Syracusa settlement Italy ancient Rome 179 (3), (5), 180–181 (1), 181 (3), (4), crusades 186 (1) early cultures 161 (2) early states 178 (2) economy 190 (1) first civilizations 177 (1) first religions 37 (3) Islam 184 (1), 227 (4) medieval states 183 (4)
Syr Darya region Central Asia colonialism 269 (3)
Syr Darya var. Sai Hun, Sir Darya, Syrdarya, Kaz. Syrdariya, Rus. Syrdar'ya, Uzb. Sirdaryo river Central Asia ancient trade 44–45 (1) biological diffusion 72–73 (1) colonialism 269 (3) early Islam 56–57 (1) exploration 257 (3) first humans 13 (2) Mongols 68–69 (1) the world in 1500 74–75 see also Jaxartes
Syrdar'ya see Jaxartes, Syr Darya
Syria var. Siria, Syrie, Sūriya region/state Southwest Asia ancient Persia 225 (6) ancient Rome 180–181 (1), 224 (2), 225 (4), (5) ancient trade 44–45 (1) crusades 65 (3), 228 (2) early cultures 161 (3), (5) early Islam 56–57 (1), 57 (2) early trade 225 (3) economy 234 (1) exploration 219 (4) first religions 37 (3) Hellenistic world 224 (1), 41 (2) Islam 226 (2), 227 (4), (5), 235 (4) medieval states 187 (5) Mongols 229 (3) Napoleon 200–201 (1) Ottomans 231 (3), 232–233 (1) Seljuks 228 (1) Soviet Union 208 (2), 214–215 (4) the modern world 113 (3) Timur 229 (4) US economy 138 (2) world religions 226 (1), 49 (4) WWI 233 (2) WWII 104 (1), (2), 210 (1), 211 (2), (4) 20th century 234 (2) 20th-century politics 233 (3), (4), 235 (5) Cold War 109 (1) see also Aram
Syrian Desert Ar. Al Hamad, Bādiyat ash Shām desert Southwest Asia ancient Persia 223 (4) ancient Rome 180–181 (1), 181 (4) early agriculture 220 (1) economy 234 (1) exploration 219 (4) first cities 220 (2), 28–29 (1) first civilizations 221 (4), 222 (1), (2), 25 (3) Hellenistic world 40–41 (1)
Syrie see Syria
Szabadka see Subotica
Száva see Sava
Szczecin see Stettin
Szechuan, Szechwan see Sichuan
Szeged Ger. Szegedin, Rom. Seghedin Central Europe (Hungary) early modern states 193 (4) medieval states 189 (4)
Szegedin see Szeged
Székesfehérvár anc. Alba Regia; Ger. Stuhlweissenberg Central Europe (Hungary) medieval states 188 (1)
Szemao see Simao
Szigetvár Central Europe (Hungary) Ottomans 231 (3)
Sziszek see Sisak
Szlovákia see Slovakia

T

Tabaristan state Central Asia early Islam 56–57 (1)
Tabariya, Bahr, Tabariya, Bahrat see Galilee, Sea of
Tabasco state Central America Mexican Revolution 133 (3) the growth of the US 129 (2)
Tabon Cave Philippines (Philippines) the world in 10,000 BCE 14–15
Tábor Central Europe (Czech Republic) early modern states 193 (4)
Tabora var. Unyanyembe, Kazeh East Africa (Tanzania) exploration 157 (4), (5)
Tabriz Southwest Asia (Iran) biological diffusion 72–73 (1) exploration 218 (2), 219 (3) Islam 226 (2), 227 (4), (5) medieval Persia 231 (4) Mongols 68 (2), 68–69 (1) Ottomans 231 (3) Seljuks 228 (1) Soviet Union 208 (2) Timur 229 (4) world religions 226 (1) WWI 233 (2) 20th-century politics 233 (3), 235 (5)
Tabuk Philippines (Philippines) early Islam 56–57 (1)
Tabun archaeological site Southwest Asia (Israel) first humans 13 (2)
Tacna South America (Peru) empire and revolution 150 (1), 151 (3) politics 151 (4)
Tacna region South America politics 151 (4)
Tacuba Central America (Mexico) Aztecs 124 (2) colonization 125 (5)
Tacubaya Central America (Mexico) Aztecs 124 (2)
Tadmor Southwest Asia (Syria) first civilizations 222 (1)
Tadmor, Tadmur see Palmyra
Tadzhikistan see Tajikistan
Taegu East Asia (South Korea) Cold War 109 (4)
Taehan-haehyŏp see Korea Strait
Taehan Min'guk see South Korea
Taejon Jap. Taiden East Asia (South Korea) Cold War 109 (4)
Taensa people Central America colonization 125 (4)
Tafahi island Pacific Ocean exploration 278 (1)
Taforalt archaeological site North Africa (Algeria) first humans 13 (2)
Taga Japan early modern states 265 (5) medieval states 264 (2), 265 (3), (4)
Taghaza West Africa (Mauritania) exploration 156 (3) Islam 163 (1)
Tagish people North America cultural groups 123 (3)
Tagliacozzo battle Italy medieval states 188 (1)
Tagliamento river Italy WWI 207 (5)
Tagus Port. Rio Tejo, Sp. Río Tajo river Iberian Peninsula ancient Rome 180–181 (1) Bronze Age 175 (3) Copper Age 174 (2) crusades 64–65 (2) early agriculture 174 (1) economy 190 (1), 205 (4) first civilizations 177 (1) Franks 184 (2) great migrations 52–53 (1), 53 (2) interwar 209 (4) Islam 192 (3) Napoleon 200–201 (1), 201 (2) prehistoric culture 17 (3)
Tahert North Africa (Algeria) early Islam 56–57 (1) Islam 163 (1)
Tahirids dynasty Central Asia Islam 227 (4)
Tahiti island Pacific Ocean colonization 284–285 (1) early cultures 280–281 (3) environmentalism 285 (2) exploration 278 (1), 279 (3) medieval voyages 60 (2)
Tahltan people North America cultural groups 123 (3)
Ta'if Ar. Al Ta'if Southwest Asia (Saudi Arabia) early Islam 56–57 (1) Islam 226 (3) world religions 226 (1) 20th-century politics 233 (4)
Tai Hu lake East Asia early modern states 266 (1) first states 260 (1)
Taiji var. Imperial Palace palace East Asia (China) medieval states 262 (2)
Taimataima archaeological site/settlement South America (Venezuela) early cultures 144 (1)
Taimyr Peninsula see Taymyr, Poluostrov
Taipei East Asia (Taiwan) Islam 275 (4)
Taiping military campaign East Asia empire and revolution 88–89 (2)
Taira Japan economy 270 (1)
Tairona state South America the world in 1200 62–63
Tairona Chiefdoms state South America early cultures 146 (1)
Tai Shan var. T'ai Shan mountain East Asia first religions 37 (4)
Taiwan prev. China, Republic of island/state East Asia ancient trade 44–45 (1) colonialism 269 (4) decolonization 251 (4), 285 (3) early agriculture 258 (1) early modern states 266 (2), 268 (1) economy 274 (1) empire and revolution 268 (2) European imperialism 97 (3) first cities 259 (4), (5) first religions 37 (4) first states 260 (1), 261 (2), (3) historical geography 236–237 (1) imperialism 270 (2) Islam 275 (4) medieval states 261 (4), (5), 262–263 (1), 263 (3), (4), (5), (6) Mongols 68–69 (1) postwar economy 253 (5), 275 (3) postwar politics 271 (7) the growth of the US 133 (4) the modern world 113 (4) WWII 251 (3) Chinese revolution 271 (5) Cold War 109 (1) see also China, Republic of
Taiwanese rebellion East Asia empire and revolution 268 (2)
Taixicun East Asia (China) first cities 259 (3)
Taiyuan prev. T'ai-yuan, T'ai-yüan, Yangku East Asia (China) biological diffusion 72–73 (1) early modern states 266 (1) economy 274 (1) Islam 275 (4) medieval states 262–263 (1), 263 (4), (5) postwar politics 271 (7), 274 (2)
Tajikistan Rus. Tadzhikistan, Taj. Tojikiston state Central Asia Islam 235 (4) postwar economy 275 (3) Soviet Union 214–215 (4) the modern world 113 (3)
Tajiks people Central Asia historical geography 275 (5)
Tajo, Río see Tagus
Takamatsu battle Japan early modern states 267 (4)
Takaoka Japan economy 270 (1)
Takapoto island Pacific Ocean exploration 278 (1)
Takaroa island Pacific Ocean exploration 278 (1)
Takeda region Japan early modern states 267 (4)
Takedda West Africa (Mali/Niger) exploration 156 (3)
Ta Kieu Mainland Southeast Asia (Vietnam) ancient India 241 (6)
Takkola Mainland Southeast Asia (Thailand) ancient India 241 (6)
Takla Makan Desert Chin. Taklimakan Shamo desert East Asia ancient trade 44–45 (1) biological diffusion 72–73 (1) colonialism 269 (4) early agriculture 258 (1) empire and revolution 268 (2) exploration 256 (1), 257 (3) first cities 259 (5) first states 260 (1) medieval states 261 (6), 262–263 (1), 263 (6) Mongols 68–69 (1) trade 267 (3) world religions 49 (3), (4)
Taklimakan Shamo see Takla Makan Desert
Takoradi West Africa (Ghana) colonization 167 (4)
Takrur var. Toucouleur state West Africa Islam 163 (1) trade 163 (4), (6), (7)
Taksashila var. Taxila South Asia (Pakistan) early medieval states 244 (1) first empires 241 (4) see also Taxila
Takume island Pacific Ocean exploration 278 (1)
Takushan see Dagushan
Talasea island Pacific Ocean early cultures 280–281 (3) medieval voyages 60 (2)
Talas River battle Central Asia (Kazakhstan) early Islam 56–57 (1) Islam 226 (2)
Talavera var. Talavera de la Reina Iberian Peninsula (Spain) Napoleon 200–201 (1)
Talavera de la Reina see Talavera
Talca South America (Chile) empire and revolution 150 (1), 151 (3) environment 153 (4) Incas 147 (3)
Talcahuano battle South America (Chile) empire and revolution 150 (1)
Talgai Australia exploration 280 (1)
Ta-lien see Dairen, Dalian
Tal-i Ghazir Southwest Asia (Iran) first cities 220 (2)
Tal-i Iblis Southwest Asia (Iran) first civilizations 24 (2)
Tal-i Malyan Southwest Asia (Iran) first cities 220 (2)
Tallahassee prev. Muskogean North America (USA) the growth of the US 129 (2) US Civil War 131 (6), (7) US society 137 (6)
Tallasahatchee battle North America (USA) the growth of the US 129 (2)
Tallin see Reval, Revel, Tallinn
Tallinn prev. Revel; Ger. Reval, Rus. Tallin Eastern Europe (Estonia) postwar politics 212 (3) Soviet Union 214–215 (4) see also Reval, Revel
Tall-i Qaleh Southwest Asia (Iran) first civilizations 25 (3)
Taltal South America (Chile) politics 151 (4)
Tamanrasset var. Tamenghest North Africa (Algeria) colonization 167 (4)
Tamar see Palmyra, Tadmor
Tamar Hat archaeological site North Africa (Algeria) prehistoric culture 17 (2)
Tamathli people North America colonization 125 (4)
Tamatsukuri Japan early modern states 265 (5)
Tamaulepec people Central America colonization 125 (4)
Tamaulipas state Central America Mexican Revolution 133 (3) the growth of the US 129 (2)
Tamazultec people Central America colonization 125 (4)
Tambo Colorado South America (Peru) Incas 147 (3)
Tambora island Maritime Southeast Asia European expansion 84–85 (1)
Tambov Eastern Europe (Russian Federation) Soviet Union 208 (2)
Tambo Viejo South America (Peru) early cultures 145 (4)
Tambralinga Mainland Southeast Asia (Thailand) ancient India 241 (6) early medieval states 245 (5)
Tambralinga region Mainland Southeast Asia early medieval states 245 (5)
Tame South America (Colombia) empire and revolution 150 (1)
Tamenghest see Tamanrasset
Tamil Nadu region/state South Asia postwar politics 252 (1) world religions 243 (4)
Tamils people South Asia the world in 250 CE 46–47
Ta-ming see Daming
Tamluk religious site/settlement South Asia (India) ancient trade 44–45 (1) first religions 36 (2)
Tammaulipeco people Central America colonization 126 (1)
Tampa North America (USA) Cold War 108 (2)
Tampico Central America (Mexico) colonization 125 (4), 126 (1) exploration 118 (1) Mexican Revolution 133 (3) the growth of the US 129 (2) Cold War 108 (2)
Tamralipti South Asia early medieval states 244 (1) early religions 48 (2) first empires 241 (4) world religions 242 (3)
Tamuin Central America (Mexico) first civilizations 122 (1)
Tamworth British Isles (United Kingdom) medieval states 183 (3)
Tana Eastern Europe (Russian Federation) economy 190 (1) Ottomans 195 (4)
T'ana Hāyk' see Tana, Lake
Tanais see Don
Tana, Lake var. T'ana Hāyk' lake East Africa early cultures 161 (3), (4), (5) early trade 225 (3) exploration 157 (5) first humans 12 (1), 13 (2) trade 165 (3)
Tanana people North America cultural groups 123 (3)
Tanana river North America imperial global economy 93 (3)
Tanasari Mainland Southeast Asia (Burma) trade 230 (2)
Tancah Central America (Mexico) first civilizations 123 (2)
Tanchon East Asia (North Korea) Cold War 109 (4)
Tanchou see Tanzhou
Tanegashima island Japan early modern states 265 (5) Communism 273 (3)
Tang vassal state East Asia first cities 259 (3)
Tangana state South Asia first empires 241 (5)
Tanganhuato Central America (Mexico) first civilizations 122 (1)
Tanganyika mod. Tanzania; prev. German East Africa colonial possession East Africa WWII 104 (1) Cold War 109 (1) see also German East Africa, Tanzania
Tanganyika, Lake lake East Africa early agriculture 158 (1) early cultures 160 (1) economy 163 (2) European imperialism 96 (1) exploration 156 (3), 157 (4), (5) first humans 12 (1), 13 (2) Islam 163 (1) slave trade 165 (4)
Tang Empire state East Asia medieval states 262–263 (1) world religions 49 (4)
Tanger, Tánger, Tangerk see Tangier, Tingis
Tanggula Shan see Tangha Range
Tangier var. Tangiers; anc. Tingis; Fr./Ger. Tangerk, Sp. Tánger North Africa (Morocco) early Islam 57 (2) economy 163 (2) European imperialism 96 (1) exploration 156 (3), 157 (4) interwar 209 (4) Islam 163 (1), 192 (3) Mongols 68 (2) Napoleon 200–201 (1), 201 (2) slave trade 165 (4) see also Tingis
Tangiers see Tangier, Tingis
Tangjin battle East Asia (South Korea) Sino-Japanese War 270 (3)
Tangla Range Chin. Tanggula Shan mountain range East Asia exploration 257 (3)
Tang Protectorate see Fergana
Tanguts people East Asia early modern states 266 (1) medieval states 263 (3) trade 267 (3)
Tangxiang state East Asia medieval states 263 (3)
Tanis var. Avaris Egypt ancient Egypt 159 (5) first civilizations 221 (5) see also Avaris
Tanjavur South Asia (India) early medieval states 244–245 (3)
Tanjore var. Thanjāvūr South Asia (India) colonialism 248 (1) economy 249 (4) Mughal Empire 246 (1)
Tanjore region/state South Asia colonialism 248 (1) Marathas 246 (2) Mughal Empire 246 (1)
Tanjungpura Maritime Southeast Asia (Indonesia) early medieval states 245 (6) exploration 239 (1) world religions 243 (5)
Tanna island Pacific Ocean exploration 278 (1)
Tannenberg var. Grunwald battle Central Europe (Poland) early modern states 193 (4) WWI 207 (4)
Tannu Tuva region/state Siberia colonialism 269 (3) Communism 271 (8) Soviet Union 208 (2), 213 (4) WWII 104 (1)
Tan-Tan state Maritime Southeast Asia ancient India 241 (6)
Tan-tung see Andong, Dandong
Tanzania prev. German East Africa, Tanganyika and Zanzibar, state East Africa decolonization 168 (1) economy 168 (2), (3) the modern world 112 (1), 113 (3), (4) see also German East Africa, Tanganyika, Zanzibar
Tanzhou var. Tanchou East Asia (China) medieval states 262–263 (1), 263 (4), (6)
Taodeni Fr. Taoudenni, Taoudenit West Africa (Mali) Islam 163 (1)
Taos North America (USA) colonization 126 (1) exploration 119 (3)
Taos people North America colonization 126 (1)
Taoudenit see Taodeni, Taoudenni
Taoudenni var. Taoudenit, Taodeni West Africa (Mali) colonization 167 (4) see also Taodeni
Taourirt North Africa (Morocco) Islam 163 (1)
Tapajó people South America early cultures 147 (2)
Tapajós state South America the world in 1500 74–75
Tapajós var. Tapajóz river South America colonization 149 (3) early cultures 144 (1), 145 (2) empire and revolution 151 (3) environment 153 (4) exploration 142 (1), 143 (2)
Tapajoso var. Santarém region South America early cultures 145 (2)
Tapajóz see Tapajós
Tapasha region South Asia world religions 242 (2)
Taprobane var. Sarandib, Saylan, Sri Lanka island South Asia ancient trade 44 (2) world religions 49 (3) see also Ceylon, Lambakannas, Lanka, Simhala, Sri Lanka
Taquira Tradition people South America the world in 1000 58–59
Tara Eastern Europe (Russian Federation) exploration 257 (2)
Tarābulus see Tripoli
Ţarābulus al Gharb see Oea, Tripoli
Ţarābulus ash Shām see Tripoli, Tripolis
Taradavadi South Asia (India) early medieval states 244 (2)
Tarahumara people Central America colonization 125 (4)
Tarakan military campaign Maritime Southeast Asia WWII 273 (2)
Taranaki region New Zealand colonization 283 (5)
Tarangambadi see Tranquebar
Taranto var. Tarantum, Tarentum Italy crusades 186 (1), 64–65 (2) economy 190 (1) medieval states 187 (5) see also Tarantum, Tarentum
Tarantum var. Tarentum; mod. Taranto Italy ancient Rome 180–181 (1), 181 (4) see also Taranto, Tarentum
Tarapacá region South America politics 151 (4)
Tarawa military campaign Gilbert Islands WWII 273 (2)
Tarazona Iberian Peninsula (Spain) medieval states 187 (3)
Tardanizats battle France Reformation 196 (2)
Tarentaise France Franks 184 (2)
Tarentum var. Tarantum; mod. Taranto Italy ancient Rome 179 (3), (5) early states 178 (1), (2) first civilizations 177 (1) see also Taranto, Tarantum
Târgovişte see Tûrgovişte
Târgu-Jiu battle Southeast Europe (Romania) WWI 207 (6)
Târguşor prev. Tîrguşor, Tërguşor Southeast Europe (Romania) world religions 48 (1) see also Tîrguşor
Tari East Asia (China) first cities 259 (5)
Tarifa Iberian Peninsula (Spain) Islam 192 (3)
Tarija South America (Bolivia) narcotics 153 (5)
Tarim river East Asia exploration 257 (3) first states 260 (1) medieval states 262–263 (1) Mongols 68–69 (1)
Tarka Southern Africa (South Africa) colonization 166 (2)
Tarkhan Egypt ancient Egypt 159 (2)
Tarma South America (Peru) Incas 147 (3)
Tarnow Central Europe (Poland) WWI 207 (4)
Taroudannt var. Taroudant North Africa (Morocco) Islam 163 (1)
Taroudant see Taroudannt
Tarquinia see Tarquinii
Tarquinii mod. Tarquinia; hist. Corneto Italy early states 178 (1), (2) first civilizations 177 (1)
Tarraco mod. Tarragona settlement Iberian Peninsula (Spain) ancient Rome 179 (3), 180–181 (1), 181 (3), (4), 225 (5) early cultures 161 (2) great migrations 52–53 (1) world religions 48 (1) see also Tarragona
Tarraconensis province Iberian peninsula ancient Rome 180–181 (1)
Tarragona Iberian Peninsula (Spain) ancient Rome 182 (1) interwar 209 (4) Islam 192 (3) medieval states 182 (2)
Tarsatica see Rijeka
Tarsus settlement Southwest Asia (Turkey) ancient Rome 180–181 (1) crusades 228 (2), 65 (3) early Islam 56–57 (1) first civilizations 221 (4), 24 (2) Hellenistic world 40–41 (1) Islam 226 (2), 227 (4) medieval states 185 (3) Mongols 229 (3) world religions 48 (1)
Tartars see Tatars
Tartu see Dorpat
Taruga archaeological site/settlement West Africa (Nigeria) ancient trade 44–45 (1) early agriculture 158 (1) early cultures 160 (1)
Taruma state Maritime Southeast Asia ancient India 241 (6)
Tarut Southwest Asia (Saudi Arabia) first civilizations 24 (3)
Tarvisium see Treviso
Tarxien (Malta) the world in 2500 BCE 22–23
Tases state Central America Aztecs 124 (1)
Tashauz see Dashkhovuz
Tashi Chho Dzong see Thimphu
Tashihkiao see Dashiqiao
Tashi Lhunpo East Asia (China) exploration 257 (3)
Tashkent Uzb. Toshkent Central Asia (Uzbekistan) biological diffusion 72–73 (1) colonialism 269 (3), (4) Communism 271 (8) exploration 256 (1), 257 (3) global immigration 100 (1) Hellenistic world 40–41 (1) medieval Persia 231 (4) medieval states 261 (6) Mongols 68–69 (1) Ottomans 232–233 (1) Soviet Union 208 (2), 214–215 (4) trade 267 (3)
Tasmania prev. Van Diemen's Land region/island Australia colonization 282 (1), (2), 283 (3) early cultures 280–281 (3) exploration 276–277 (1), 279 (2), (3) medieval voyages 60 (2)
Tasman Sea sea Pacific Ocean colonization 282 (1), 283 (4), (5) early cultures 280–281 (3) environmentalism 285 (2) exploration 279 (2) medieval voyages 60 (2) prehistoric culture 17 (5)
Tatars var. Tartars people East Asia/Siberia historical geography 275 (5) Mongols 68–69 (1)
Tatarstan state Eastern Europe Soviet Union 214–215 (4)
Tatta South Asia (Pakistan) colonialism 248 (1)
Tatta see Thatta
Ta-t'ung, Tatung see Datong
Tauchira North Africa (Libya) first civilizations 177 (1)
Taung archaeological site Southern Africa (South Africa) first humans 12 (1)
Taunton British Isles (United Kingdom) economy 204 (1)
Taunum Central Europe (Germany) world religions 48 (1)
Taupo, Lake lake New Zealand colonization 283 (5)
Tauranga New Zealand colonization 283 (5)
Tauroggen region Eastern Europe empire and revolution 199 (3)
Taurus Mountains var. Toros Dağları mountain range Southwest Asia ancient Persia 223 (4), 225 (6) crusades 64–65 (2) early agriculture 220 (1) exploration 218 (1), (2), 219 (3) first cities 220 (2), 28–29 (1) first civilizations 221 (4), (5), 222 (2) Hellenistic world 224 (1) Ottomans 231 (3), 232–233 (1) Seljuks 228 (1) WWI 233 (2)
Tau'u Island island Pacific Ocean exploration 278 (1)
Tavascan see Michoacan
Tawahi Mainland Southeast Asia (Burma) trade 230 (2)
Tawakoni people North America colonization 125 (4)
Taxila Buddhist center/religious site/settlement South Asia (India) ancient Persia 225 (6) ancient Rome 224 (2) ancient trade 44 (2), 44–45 (1) exploration 256 (1) first religions 36 (2) Hellenistic world 224 (1), 41 (2) medieval states 262–263 (1) world religions 49 (3), (4)
Taxla Central America (Mexico) first civilizations 121 (2)
Tayasal Central America (Guatemala) Aztecs 124 (1)
Taylor's Battle battle North America (USA) the growth of the US 129 (2)
Taymyr, Poluostrov Eng. Taimyr Peninsula headland Siberia exploration 257 (2)
Tayspun see Ctesiphon
Taz river Eastern Europe exploration 257 (2)
Tazoult see Lambaesis
Tazumal Central America (Mexico) first civilizations 123 (2)
T'bilisi Eng. Tiflis Southwest Asia (Georgia) Soviet Union 214–215 (4) see also Tiflis
Tchad see Chad
Tchefuncte Culture people North America the world in 250 BCE 38–39
Tchongking see Chongqing
Te Anau, Lake lake New Zealand colonization 283 (5)
Teano see Teanum
Teanum var. Teanum Sidicinum; mod. Teano Italy early states 178 (1)
Teanum Apulum Italy early states 178 (1)
Teanum Sidicinum see Teanum
Tebuk Southwest Asia (Saudi Arabia) 20th-century politics 233 (4)
Tecama Central America (Mexico) Aztecs 124 (2)
Tecklenburg region Central Europe empire and revolution 199 (3)
Tecoac Central America (Mexico) colonization 125 (5)
Tédèllis North Africa (Algeria) economy 190 (1)
Tegasta fort North America (USA) colonization 125 (4)
Tegel airport Central Europe (Germany) postwar politics 212 (2)
Tegeler See lake Central Europe postwar politics 212 (2)
Tegucigalpa Central America (Honduras) the growth of the US 129 (2)
Teheran see Tehran
Tehran var. Teheran; Pers. Tehrān Southwest Asia (Iran) colonialism 269 (3) economy 234 (1) Islam 235 (4) medieval Persia 231 (4) Ottomans 231 (3), 232–233 (1) 20th-century politics 235 (5) Communism 271 (8)
Tehri Garhwal state South Asia colonialism 248 (2)
Tehuacán Central America (Mexico) first civilizations 122 (1) Mexican Revolution 133 (3)
Tehuacan Valley valley Central America early agriculture 20 (1)
Tehuantepec var. Santo Domingo Tehuantepec Central America (Mexico) first civilizations 122 (1) Mexican Revolution 133 (3)
Tehuantepec, Golfo de see Tehuantepec, Gulf of
Tehuantepec, Gulf of var. Tehuantepec, Golfo de gulf Central America Aztecs 124 (1) Mexican Revolution 133 (3)
Tehuantepec, Isthmus of var. Istmo de Tehuantepec coastal feature Central America Aztecs 124 (1)
Tehuantepec, Istmo de see Tehuantepec, Isthmus of
Tehuelche people South America early cultures 147 (2)
Tejo, Rio see Tagus
Teke state Central Africa the world in 1700 82–83 the world in 1800 86–87 the world in 1850 90–91
Tekesta people North America colonization 125 (4), 126 (1)
Telanaipura see Jambi
Tel Aviv Southwest Asia (Israel) 20th-century politics 235 (5)
Tel Aviv-Yafo Southwest Asia (Israel) 20th century 234 (2)
Telingana region/state South Asia early medieval states 244–245 (3)
Tell Agrab var. Tell Ajrab settlement/temple Southwest Asia (Iraq) first cities 220 (2) first civilizations 24 (2), 25 (3)
Tell 'Asmar, Tell Asmar see Eshnunna
Tell Aswad Southwest Asia (Iraq) first cities 220 (2)
Tell Brak Southwest Asia (Syria) early systems 223 (3), 32 (1) first cities 28–29 (1) first civilizations 24 (2)
Tell el-Ajjul Southwest Asia (Israel) ancient Egypt 159 (4)
Tell el-Amarna see Akhetaten
Tell el 'Ubaid Southwest Asia (Iraq) early agriculture 220 (1) first cities 220 (2)
Teller North America (USA) exploration 287 (2)
Tell es Sawwan Southwest Asia (Iraq) early agriculture 220 (1)
Tell Halaf Southwest Asia (Syria) early agriculture 220 (1)
Tell Ibrahim Awad Egypt ancient Egypt 159 (2)
Tellicherry var. Thalassery South Asia (India) colonialism 247 (3)
Telloh Southwest Asia (Iraq) first cities 220 (2)
Tell Sleimeh Southwest Asia (Iran) first civilizations 24 (3)
Tell 'Uqair settlement/temple Southwest Asia (Iraq) first cities 220 (2) first civilizations 221 (4)
Teloapan Central America (Mexico) Aztecs 124 (1)
Teloloapan Central America (Mexico) first civilizations 122 (1)
Telo Martius see Toulon
Telugucodas state South Asia Mongols 68–69 (1)
Temazcalpan Central America (Mexico) Aztecs 124 (2)
Temesvár battle Southeast Europe (Romania) Ottomans 197 (4)
Tempelhof Central Europe (Germany) crusades 186 (1)
Tempelhof airport Central Europe (Germany) postwar politics 212 (2)
Tenango Central America (Mexico) first civilizations 122 (1)
Tenanitla Central America (Mexico) Aztecs 124 (3)
Tenasserim state/colonial possession Mainland Southeast Asia colonialism 269 (4) European imperialism 97 (3)
Tenayuca Central America (Mexico) Aztecs 124 (3)
Tenayucan Central America (Mexico) Aztecs 124 (2)
Tenerife battle South America (Colombia) empire and revolution 150 (1)
Ténès North Africa (Algeria) economy 190 (1)
Teng East Asia (China) first cities 259 (5)
Teng state East Asia first cities 259 (5)
Tenganapatam var. Ft. St. David South Asia (India) colonialism 247 (3)
Tengasseri South Asia (India) colonialism 247 (3)
Teng-chou see Dengzhou
Tengchung see Dengyue
Tennant Creek Australia colonization 282 (1), 283 (3) exploration 279 (2)
Tennessee state North America the growth of the US 129 (1) US Civil War 130 (2), (3), (4), (5), 131 (6), (7) US economy 134 (2), 139 (3) US society 137 (6) US superpower 139 (5)
Tennessee river North America cultural groups 122 (5) first civilizations 121 (4) the growth of the US 129 (2) US Civil War 131 (6)
Tenochtitlan mod. Ciudad de Mexico, México, Mexico City archaeological site/settlement Central America Aztecs 124 (1), (2), (3) colonization 125 (5) exploration 118 (1) first civilizations 121 (3) see also México, Mexico City
Tenos mod. Tinos island Greece Ottomans 230 (1)
Teodomiro state Iberian Peninsula the world in 750 CE 54–55
Teos settlement/state Greece ancient Greece 177 (2) first civilizations 177 (1)
Teotihuacan Central America (Mexico) Aztecs 124 (2) first civilizations 122 (1)
Teotihuacan region Central America first civilizations 122 (1)
Teotitlan Central America (Mexico) first civilizations 122 (1)
Teotitlan del Cassino state Central America Aztecs 124 (1)
Tepahue people Central America colonization 125 (4)
Tepeacac Central America (Mexico) first civilizations 122 (1)
Tepeacac state Central America Aztecs 124 (1)
Tepecano people Central America colonization 125 (4)
Tepecuacuilco state Central America Aztecs 124 (1)
Tepe Gawra settlement/temple Southwest Asia (Iraq) early agriculture 220 (1) first cities 220 (2)
Tepe Giyan Southwest Asia (Iran) early agriculture 220 (1) first civilizations 24 (2)
Tepe Guran Southwest Asia (Iran) early agriculture 220 (1)
Tepe Hissar Southwest Asia (Iran) first civilizations 24 (3)
Tepehuan people Central America colonization 125 (4), 126 (1)
Tepe Sabz Southwest Asia (Iraq) early agriculture 220 (1)
Tepetlacalco Central America (Mexico) Aztecs 124 (3)
Tepetlatzinco Central America (Mexico) Aztecs 124 (3)
Tepetzinco Central America (Mexico) Aztecs 124 (2)
Tepexic Central America (Mexico) first civilizations 122 (1)
Tepexpan Central America (Mexico) Aztecs 124 (2)
Tepeyacac Central America (Mexico) Aztecs 124 (2), (3) colonization 125 (5)
Tepe Yahya Southwest Asia (Iran) first civilizations 24 (3)
Tepic Central America (Mexico) Mexican Revolution 133 (3)
Tepoatlan Central America (Mexico) first civilizations 122 (1)
Tepotzotlan Central America (Mexico) Aztecs 124 (2)
Tequexquinahuac Central America (Mexico) Aztecs 124 (3)
Tequisistlan Central America (Mexico) Aztecs 124 (2)
Terevaka, Cerro mountain Pacific Ocean early cultures 281 (4)
Tërguşor see Târguşor, Tîrguşor
Ternate Maritime Southeast Asia (Indonesia) colonialism 247 (4) colonization 284–285 (1) trade 267 (3)
Ternate island Maritime Southeast Asia colonialism 247 (4) early medieval states 245 (6) exploration 239 (2) Islam 243 (6) world religions 243 (5)
Ternopol' Eastern Europe (Ukraine) WWII 211 (4)
Terranova di Sicilia see Gela
Terranova Pausania see Olbia
Terre-Neuve see Newfoundland
Terror, Mount mountain Antarctica Antarctic Exploration 287 (3)
Teruel anc. Turba Iberian Peninsula (Spain) interwar 209 (4) Islam 192 (3)
Tešetice-Kyjovice Central Europe (Czech Republic) early agriculture 174 (1)
Teshik Tash archaeological site Central Asia (Uzbekistan) first humans 13 (2)
Tete Southern Africa (Mozambique) colonization 167 (4) exploration 157 (4) Islam 163 (1) trade 164 (1)
Tetecpilco Central America (Mexico) Aztecs 124 (3)
Tetelco Central America (Mexico) Aztecs 124 (2)
Teton people North America colonization 126 (1)
Tetzcoco Central America (Mexico) colonization 125 (5)
Teul people Central America colonization 125 (4)

U

V

INDEX-GAZETTEER: **Vientiane – Xiuhtetelco**

Vientiane Mainland Southeast Asia (Laos) colonialism 247 (4), 248 (1) postwar economy 253 (5) postwar politics 251 (5) world religions 243 (5)
Vientiane state Mainland Southeast Asia the world in 1800 86–87
Vierzon France medieval states 192 (1)
Vietnam state Mainland Southeast Asia (Vietnam) Bronze Age 240 (3) colonialism 248 (1) decolonization 251 (4) economy 274 (1) Islam 275 (4) postwar economy 253 (5) postwar politics 251 (5), 253 (4), 274 (2) the modern world 113 (4) US superpower 138 (1) Cold War 109 (1)
Vigo Iberian Peninsula (Spain) Napoleon 200–201 (1)
Viipuri see Viborg, Vyborg
Vijaya mod. Binh Đinh Mainland Southeast Asia (Vietnam) ancient India 241 (6) early medieval states 245 (5), (6)
Vijayanagar state South Asia the world in 1400 70–71 the world in 1500 74–75
Vijayanagara region/settlement South Asia colonialism 247 (3) early medieval states 244–245 (3), 245 (4)
Vijayans dynasty South Asia the world in 1 CE 42–43
Vijayapura South Asia (India) early medieval states 244 (2)
Vijayapura state Maritime Southeast Asia ancient India 241 (6)
Vijayawada prev. Bezwada South Asia (India) postwar economy 253 (5)
Vijosa, Vijosë see Vjosë
Vikings people Scandinavia medieval states 185 (3)
Vila Artur de Paiva see Cubango
Vila Bela var. Mato Grosso South America (Brazil) colonization 149 (3)
Vila da Ponte see Cubango
Vila do Zumbo see Zumbo
Világos mod. Şiria battle Central Europe (Hungary) empire and revolution 88–89 (2)
Vila Henrique de Carvalho see Saurimo
Vila Marechal Carmona see Uige
Vila Serpa Pinto see Menongue
Vilcas South America (Peru) Incas 147 (3)
Vilcas Huamán South America (Peru) Incas 148 (1)
Viljandi see Fellin
Villa Alta var. S.I. Villa Alta Central America (Mexico) first civilizations 122 (1)
Villach Central Europe (Austria) WWI 207 (5)
Villa Concepción see Concepción
Villa da Barra see Manáos, Manaus
Villa de la Veracruz Central America (Mexico) colonization 125 (5)
Villa do Forte de Assumpeão see Ceará, Fortaleza
Villahermosa see San Juan Bautista
Villa Montes South America (Bolivia) politics 152 (2)
Villa San Luis Central America (Mexico) colonization 125 (4)
Villefranche-de-Conflent France early modern states 197 (5)
Vilna mod. Vilnius; Ger. Wilna, Pol. Wilno Eastern Europe (Lithuania) early modern states 193 (4), 195 (3) empire and revolution 198 (2) medieval states 189 (3), (4) Napoleon 200–201 (1) WWI 207 (4) see also Vilnius, Wilno
Vilnius prev. Vilna; Ger. Wilna, Pol. Wilno Eastern Europe (Lithuania) postwar politics 212 (3) Soviet Union 214–215 (4) see also Vilna, Wilno
Vilno see Vilna
Vimeiro Iberian Peninsula (Portugal) Napoleon 200–201 (1)
Viminacium legion headquarters Southeast Europe (Yugoslavia) ancient Rome 180–181 (1)
Viminal Hill Lat. Collis Viminalis hill Italy ancient Rome 181 (2)
Viminalis Collis see Viminal Hill
Viña del Mar South America (Chile) empire and revolution 151 (3)
Vińca Southeast Europe (Yugoslavia) early agriculture 174 (1)
Vincennes fort North America (USA) empire and revolution 127 (3)
Vindava Ger. Windau, Lat. Ventspils Eastern Europe (Latvia) WWI 207 (4) see also Windau
Vindhya Mountains see Vindhya Range
Vindhya-Prstha region South Asia early religions 48 (2)
Vindhya Range var. Vindhya Mountains mountain range South Asia colonialism 247 (3), 248 (1) early medieval states 244 (1), 244–245 (3) first empires 241 (4) Mughal Empire 246 (1) world religions 243 (4)
Vindobona mod. Wien; anc. Vindobona; Eng. Vienna, Hung. Bécs, Slvk. Vídeň, Slvn. Dunaj legion headquarters Central Europe (Austria) ancient Rome 180–181 (1) see also Vienna
Vine Mound burial mound North America (USA) first civilizations 121 (4)
Vinh Thai Lan see Siam, Gulf of; Thailand, Gulf of
Vinh Yen battle Mainland Southeast Asia (Vietnam) postwar politics 251 (5)
Vinjha region South Asia world religions 242 (3)
Vinland region North America medieval voyages 60–61 (1)
Vinot South Asia (Pakistan) world religions 243 (4)
Virginia colonial possession/state North America empire and revolution 127 (2), (3) the growth of the US 129 (1) US Civil War 130 (2), (3), (4), (5), 131 (6), (7) US economy 134 (2), 139 (3) US society 137 (6) US superpower 139 (5)
Virginia Capes battle North America (USA) empire and revolution 127 (3)
Virgin Islands state/island group West Indies Cold War 108 (2) empire and revolution 88 (1) the growth of the US 133 (4)
Virgin Islands of the United States see American Virgin Islands
Virgo, Aqua aqueduct Italy ancient Rome 181 (2)
Virú river South America early cultures 145 (3)
Virunum Central Europe (Austria) ancient Rome 180–181 (1)
Visakhapatnam South Asia (India) postwar economy 253 (5)
Visby Ger. Wisby Scandinavia (Sweden) economy 190 (1) see also Wisby
Višegrad Southeast Europe (Bosnia and Herzegovina) WWI 207 (6)
Visigoths people Southeast Europe/Southwest Asia ancient Rome 181 (4) great migrations 52–53 (1)
Visigoths, Kingdom of the state France/Iberian Peninsula ancient Rome 182 (1) early Islam 56–57 (1) Franks 183 (5), (6) great migrations 52–53 (1), 53 (2) medieval states 182 (2)
Vistula Pol. Wisła, Ger. Weichsel river Central Europe Bronze Age 175 (3) Copper Age 174 (2) crusades 64–65 (2) early agriculture 174 (1) early modern states 193 (4) economy 205 (4) empire and revolution 198 (2), 199 (3), 202 (2) exploration 172 (1) great migrations 52–53 (1) medieval states 189 (3), (4) Mongols 68–69 (1) Napoleon 200–201 (1), 201 (2), (3) prehistoric culture 17 (4) WWI 207 (4)
Vitcos South America (Peru) Incas 147 (3)
Vitebsk var. Vitsyebsk Eastern Europe (Belorussia) early modern states 195 (3) economy 190 (1) Soviet Union 208 (2)
Viterbo anc. Vicus Elbii Italy economy 190 (1) medieval states 188 (1)
Vitez Southeast Europe (Bosnia and Herzegovina) postwar economy 215 (3)
Viti Levu island Pacific Ocean early cultures 280–281 (3) environmentalism 285 (2) medieval voyages 60 (2) US superpower 138 (1)
Vitim river Eastern Europe early modern states 268 (1) first states 260 (1)
Vitoria Iberian Peninsula (Spain) Napoleon 200–201 (1)
Vitória prev. Victoria South America (Brazil) colonization 149 (3) see also Victoria
Vitsyebsk see Vitebsk
Vittorio Veneto Italy WWI 207 (5)
Viye state Southern Africa slave trade 165 (4) trade 167 (1)
Vizagapatam air raid/settlement South Asia (India) colonialism 247 (3) decolonization 250 (1) WWII 251 (3), 272 (1)
Vizcaíno, Desierto de desert Central America cultural groups 123 (4)
Vjosë var. Vijosa; Vijosë, Gk. Aóos river Southeast Europe WWI 207 (6)
Vladimir var. Volodymyr-Volyns'kyy; Pol. Włodzimierz Eastern Europe (Russian Federation) medieval states 189 (4) Mongols 68–69 (1) see also Włodzimierz
Vladimir state Eastern Europe medieval states 189 (4)
Vladimir-Galich see Galicia-Volhynia
Vladivostok Siberia (Russian Federation) colonialism 269 (3), (4) Communism 271 (8) exploration 257 (2) global immigration 100 (1) imperialism 270 (2) Islam 275 (4) Russo-Japanese War 270 (4) Soviet Union 208 (2), 214–215 (4) Cold War 109 (4)
Vlonë, Vlora, Vlorë see Valona
Vogelherd archaeological site Central Europe (Germany) prehistoric culture 17 (2)
Vojvodina Ger. Wojwodina province Southeast Europe postwar economy 215 (3)
Volaterrae Italy early states 178 (1), (2) first civilizations 177 (1)
Volcae people France ancient Rome 179 (5)
Volcano Islands Jap. Kazan-rettō island group Pacific Ocean US superpower 138 (1) WWII 273 (2)
Volci var. Vulci Italy first civilizations 177 (1) see also Vulci
Voldtofte Scandinavia (Denmark) Bronze Age 175 (3)
Volga river Eastern Europe ancient trade 44–45 (1) biological diffusion 72–73 (1) early agriculture 20–21 (2) early Islam 56–57 (1) early modern states 197 (3) economy 205 (4) empire and revolution 202 (1) exploration 172 (1), 218 (2), 219 (3) first humans 13 (2) global immigration 100 (1) great migrations 52–53 (1), 53 (2) Islam 163 (1) medieval states 185 (3), 261 (6) medieval voyages 60–61 (1) Mongols 68–69 (1) Ottomans 231 (3), 232–233 (1) prehistoric culture 16 (1), 17 (4) Soviet Union 208 (2) Timur 229 (4) WWII 210 (1), 211 (4)
Volga Bulgaria state Eastern Europe medieval states 185 (3)
Volga Bulgars var. Bulgars, White Bulgars people Eastern Europe Mongols 68–69 (1)
Volga Germans people Eastern Europe Soviet Union 213 (4)
Volgograd prev. Stalingrad, Tsaritsyn Eastern Europe (Russian Federation) Soviet Union 214–215 (4) see also Stalingrad, Tsaritsyn
Vol'mar see Wolmar
Volodymyr-Volyns'kyy see Vladimir, Włodzimierz
Vologda mod. Kirov Eastern Europe (Russian Federation) Soviet Union 208 (2)
Volsci people Italy early states 178 (2)
Volsiniensis, Lacus lake Italy early states 178 (1)
Volsinii Italy early states 178 (1), (2) first civilizations 177 (1)
Volta river West Africa Islam 163 (1)
Volta Blanche see White Volta
Volta, Cape da var. Dias Point headland West Africa exploration 156 (3)
Volta, Lake reservoir West Africa economy 168 (2), (3)
Volta Noire see Black Volta
Volterra see Volaterrae
Volturno see Volturnus
Volturnus mod. Volturno river Italy early states 178 (1)
Volubilis mithraic site North Africa (Morocco) world religions 48 (1)
Vorkuta Eastern Europe (Russian Federation) exploration 287 (2)
Voronezh Eastern Europe (Russian Federation) Soviet Union 208 (2), 214–215 (4)
Vorskla river Eastern Europe WWI 207 (4)
Vosges mountain range France early modern states 197 (5) WWI 206 (2), (3)
Vouillé battle France Franks 183 (5)
Vrijji see Vrjji
Vrjji var. Vrijji region South Asia first religions 36 (2)
Vrshni state South Asia first empires 241 (5)
Vryburg Southern Africa (South Africa) European imperialism 96 (2)
Vukovar Hung. Vukovár Southeast Europe (Croatia) postwar economy 215 (3)
Vulci Italy early states 178 (1), (2)
Vungu state Central Africa economy 163 (2)
Vyadhapura Mainland Southeast Asia (Cambodia) ancient India 241 (6) medieval states 261 (6)
Vyatka mod. Kirov Eastern Europe (Russian Federation) Soviet Union 208 (2)
Vyborg Eastern Europe (Russian Federation) early modern states 195 (3) WWI 207 (4) WWII 211 (4)

W

Waalo state West Africa trade 167 (1)
Wabash river North America US Civil War 131 (6), (7)
Waccamaw people North America colonization 125 (4)
Wadai var. Ouadaï, Ouaddaï state Central Africa colonization 167 (4) slave trade 165 (4) trade 167 (1)
Wad Al-Hajarah see Guadalajara
Wadan West Africa (Mauritania) biological diffusion 72–73 (1)
Wadi Halfa var. Wādī Ḥalfā' Egypt colonization 167 (4)
Wadi Maghara Southwest Asia (Saudi Arabia) ancient Egypt 159 (5)
Wagadugu state West Africa trade 167 (1)
Wagram Central Europe (Czech Republic) Napoleon 200–201 (1)
Wągrowiec major cistercian house Central Europe medieval states 187 (3)
Wahabites Rising rebellion Southwest Asia empire and revolution 88–89 (2)
Wahgi Valley New Guinea (Papua New Guinea) early cultures 280 (2)
Wahhabi Expansion historical period 20th-century politics 233 (4)
Wahhabi Territory region Southwest Asia 20th-century politics 233 (4)
Wahran see Oran
Waicuri people Central America colonization 125 (4)
Waikanae New Zealand colonization 283 (5)
Waikawa whaling station New Zealand colonization 283 (4)
Waikouaiti settlement/whaling station New Zealand colonization 283 (4), (5)
Waimate New Zealand colonization 283 (5)
Wairagarh South Asia (India) colonialism 247 (3)
Wakayama Japan economy 270 (1)
Wakayama off. Wakayama-ken prefecture Japan economy 270 (1)
Wake Island colonial possession/ island Pacific Ocean exploration 276–277 (1) imperialism 270 (2) the growth of the US 133 (4) US superpower 138 (1) WWII 272 (1) Cold War 109 (1)
Walachei, Walachia see Wallachia
Walata West Africa (Mauritania) exploration 156 (3)
Waldensians people Italy crusades 186 (1)
Wales Wel. Cymru state British Isles empire and revolution 202 (1) medieval states 188 (2) the modern world 112 (2)
Walhalla goldfield Australia colonization 282 (2)
Walkunder Arch Australia exploration 280 (1)
Wallachia var. Walachia; Ger. Walachei, Rom. Valachia, Turk. Eflâk region Southeast Europe early modern states 193 (4) empire and revolution 202 (1) medieval states 189 (4) Napoleon 200–201 (1), 201 (2) Ottomans 195 (4), 230 (1), 231 (3) Reformation 194 (2)
Walla Walla battle North America (USA) the growth of the US 129 (2)
Wallis and Futuna colonial possession/island group Pacific Ocean decolonization 285 (3) environmentalism 285 (2)
Wallis, Îles var. Wallis Islands island group Pacific Ocean colonization 284–285 (1) exploration 278 (1), 279 (3)
Walnut Canyon archaeological site North America (USA) cultural groups 123 (4)
Walo state West Africa slave trade 165 (4)
Walvisbaai see Walvis Bay
Walvis Bay Afr. Walvisbaai Southern Africa (Namibia) colonization 167 (4) economy 168 (2) European imperialism 96 (1), (2)
Walvis Bay Afr. Walvisbaai state Southern Africa the world in 1900 94–95 the world in 1925 98–99
Walvis Bay bay Southern Africa exploration 156 (3)
Wambu state Southern Africa slave trade 165 (4) trade 167 (1)
Wan var. Nanyang East Asia (China) first cities 259 (5) first states 260 (1) see also Nanyung
Wan see Anhui
Wandel Sea sea Arctic Ocean exploration 287 (2)
Wandiwash battle South Asia (India) empire and revolution 88 (1)
Wandu state Southern Africa slave trade 165 (4)
Wang vassal state East Asia first cities 259 (3)
Wanganui New Zealand colonization 283 (4), (5)
Wangchenggang archaeological site East Asia early agriculture 258 (1)
Wanhsien see Wanxian
Wankarani state South America the world in 500 BCE 34–35
Wanxian var. Wanhsien East Asia (China) colonialism 269 (4)
Warangal South Asia (India) colonialism 247 (3) early medieval states 244–245 (3), 245 (4)
Warash Southwest Asia (Turkey) early Islam 56–57 (1)
Warka Southwest Asia (Iraq) the world in 5000 BCE 18–19
Warmia Ger. Ermeland region Central Europe early modern states 195 (3)
Warrnambool Australia colonization 282 (1), 283 (3)
Warsaw Central Europe (Poland) economy 205 (4) empire and revolution 198 (2), 199 (3), 202 (1), (1i) global immigration 101 (2) medieval states 189 (3), (4) Napoleon 200–201 (1), 201 (2), (3) postwar politics 212 (3) prehistoric culture 17 (4) Reformation 194 (2) Soviet Union 208 (2) WWI 207 (4) WWII 210 (1), 211 (2), (3), (4) Cold War 108 (3)
Warsaw, Grand Duchy of state Central Europe Napoleon 201 (2)
Warschau, Warszawa see Warsaw
Warwick British Isles (United Kingdom) medieval states 187 (4)
Washington var. Washington Territory state/settlement/settlement/settlement/settlement/road/region North America empire and revolution 127 (3) the growth of the US 129 (1), (2), 132 (1) US Civil War 130 (4), (5), 131 (6), (7) US economy 134 (1), (2), (3), 135 (4), 136 (2) Cold War 108 (2)
Washington DC North America (USA) Cold War 108 (2) the growth of the US 132 (1) the modern world 113 (4) US economy 134 (1), (3), 136 (2)
Washita battle North America (USA) the growth of the US 129 (2)
Washshukanni Southwest Asia (Iraq) first civilizations 221 (5)
Wasserburg mod. Wasserburg am Inn Central Europe (Germany) Bronze Age 175 (3)
Wasserburg am Inn see Wasserburg
Wateree people North America colonization 125 (4)
Waterford Ir. Port Láirge British Isles (Ireland) medieval states 185 (3), 187 (4)
Waterloo battle France Napoleon 200–201 (1)
Watom island Pacific Ocean early cultures 280–281 (3) medieval voyages 60 (2)
Wattasids dynasty North Africa Islam 163 (1), 192 (3)
Wattignies battle France empire and revolution 199 (4)
Waverley major cistercian house British Isles (United Kingdom) medieval states 187 (3)
Wawat state Egypt ancient Egypt 159 (4)
Wearmouth see Sunderland
Weddell Sea sea Antactica Antarctic Exploration 287 (3)
Wedding Central Europe (Germany) postwar politics 212 (2)
Weeden Island settlement/state North America (USA) cultural groups 122 (5)
Weeden Island Culture state North America the world in 500 CE 50–51
Weenen Southern Africa (South Africa) colonization 166 (2)
Wei province/state East Asia first cities 259 (3), (4), (5) first states 261 (2), (3)
Weichou see Weizhou
Weichsel see Vistula
Weihaiwei East Asia (China) Russo-Japanese War 270 (4)
Weihaiwei battle East Asia (China) Sino-Japanese War 270 (3)
Weihaiwei colonial possession East Asia (China) colonialism 269 (4)
Wei, Long Wall of wall East Asia (China) first cities 259 (5)
Weissenburg see Apulum, Gyulafehérvár
Weissensee Central Europe (Germany) postwar politics 212 (2)
Weissenstein Est. Paide Scandinavia (Sweden) early modern states 195 (3)
Weizhou var. Weichou East Asia (China) medieval states 262–263 (1)
Wejh Ar. Al Wajh Southwest Asia (Saudi Arabia) 20th-century politics 233 (4)
Welle see Uele
Wellington New Zealand colonization 283 (4), (5), 284–285 (1) decolonization 285 (3) environmentalism 285 (2) exploration 279 (3)
Wellington region New Zealand colonization 283 (5)
Wellington penal colony Australia colonization 282 (1)
Welsh Principalities state British Isles crusades 64–65 (2) medieval states 183 (3), 186 (2)
Welsh States state British Isles medieval states 187 (4)
Wen-chou, Wenchow see Wenzhou
Wenden mod. Cēsis; Latv. Cesis Eastern Europe (Latvia) early modern states 195 (3) medieval states 189 (3)
Wends people Central Europe crusades 64–65 (2)
Wenzhou var. Wen-chou, Wenchow East Asia (China) colonialism 269 (4) medieval states 263 (5) postwar politics 274 (2)
Wesenberg Est. Rakvere Eastern Europe (Estonia) early modern states 195 (3)
Weser river Central Europe empire and revolution 199 (3) Franks 184 (2)
Wessex state British Isles medieval states 183 (3)
West Alaskan Inuit people North America cultural groups 123 (3)
West and Central Punjab region South Asia decolonization 250 (1)
West Antarctica see Lesser Antarctica
West Asia region Asia biological diffusion 73 (2)
West Atlantic Peoples people West Africa early cultures 160 (1)
West Bank region Southwest Asia 20th century 234 (2)
West Bengal region South Asia postwar politics 252 (1), (3), 253 (4)
West Berlin Central Europe (Germany) postwar politics 212 (2)
West Bihar region South Asia decolonization 250 (1)
West Coast physical region South America early cultures 144 (1)
West Coast see Westland
West Dawson North America (Canada) imperial global economy 93 (3)
Westeregeln Central Europe (Germany) early agriculture 174 (1)
Western Australia region Australia colonization 282 (1), (2)
Western Bug see Bug
Western Christendom region Western Europe global knowledge 77 (5)
Western Cree people North America cultural groups 123 (3)
Western Desert var. Aş Şaḩrā' al Gharbīyah, Sahara el Gharbîya desert North Africa ancient Egypt 159 (2), (3), (5)
Western Dvina Bel. Dzvina, Ger. Düna, Latv. Daugava, Rus. Zapadnaya Dvina river Eastern Europe economy 190 (1) medieval states 185 (3) Timur 229 (4)
Western Europe region Europe US economy 138 (2)
Western Ghats mountain range South Asia colonialism 247 (3), 248 (1) early medieval states 244 (1), 244–245 (3) economy 249 (4) first empires 241 (4) first religions 36 (2) Mughal Empire 246 (1)
Western Liang state East Asia first states 261 (3)
Western Pomerania region Central Europe empire and revolution 199 (3)
Western Port penal center Australia colonization 282 (1) environmentalism 285 (2)
Western Regions region Central Asia first states 260 (1)
Western Sahara region/state North Africa decolonization 168 (1) economy 168 (2), (3) Islam 235 (4) the modern world 113 (3)
Western Samoa var. Sāmoa-i-Sisifo; prev. German Samoa; mod. Samoa state Pacific Ocean decolonization 285 (3) environmentalism 285 (2) see also German Samoa, Samoa
Western Shoshoni people North America colonization 126 (1)
Western Sierra Madre see Madre Occidental, Sierra
Western Tarahumara people North America colonization 126 (1)
Western Turkestan region Central Asia medieval states 262–263 (1)
Western Turks people Central Asia medieval states 261 (4), (5), 262–263 (1)
Western Ukrainian Republic see West Ukraine
West Fjords fjords Iceland exploration 172 (2)
West Florida colonial possession North America empire and revolution 127 (3)
West Galicia region Central Europe empire and revolution 198 (2)
Westgate British Isles (United Kingdom) economy 204 (3)
West Germany state Central Europe Cold War 108 (3), 109 (1) postwar economy 213 (5), 214 (1) postwar politics 212 (3) Soviet Union 213 (4) US superpower 138 (1)
West Greenland Inuit people North America cultural groups 123 (3)
West India States state South Asia colonialism 248 (2)
West Indies island group North America colonization 126 (1) early agriculture 20–21 (2)
West Irian see Dutch New Guinea, Irian Jaya, Netherlands New Guinea
Westland mod. West Coast region New Zealand colonization 283 (5)
West Malaysia see Malaya
West New Guinea see Dutch New Guinea, Irian Jaya, Netherlands New Guinea
West Pakistan state South Asia decolonization 251 (4) postwar politics 252 (1)
Westphalia region Central Europe empire and revolution 202 (2)
West Point North America (USA) empire and revolution 127 (3)
West Pomerania region Central Europe early modern states 197 (3)
Westport New Zealand colonization 283 (5)
West Prussia region Central Europe empire and revolution 198 (2), 199 (3), 202 (2) WWI 207 (4)
West River burial mound North America (USA) first civilizations 121 (4)
West River see Xi Jiang
West Roman Empire state Europe/Africa great migrations 52–53 (1)
West Siberian Plain plain Siberia exploration 257 (2)
West Turkana archaeological site East Africa (Kenya) first humans 12 (1)
West Ukraine var. Western Ukrainian Republic region Eastern Europe empire and revolution 198 (2)
West Virginia state North America the growth of the US 129 (1) US Civil War 130 (5), 131 (6), (7) US economy 134 (2), 139 (3) US superpower 139 (5)
West Wales var. Wessex state British Isles medieval states 183 (3) see also Wessex
Wexford Ir. Loch Garman British Isles (Ireland) medieval states 185 (3), 187 (4)
Wey and Arun canal British Isles economy 204 (1)
Whakatane New Zealand colonization 283 (4)
Whales, Bay of bay Antarctica Antarctic Exploration 287 (3)
Whangarei New Zealand colonization 283 (4), (5)
Whitby religious building British Isles (United Kingdom) medieval states 183 (3)
Whitebird Creek battle North America (USA) the growth of the US 129 (2)
White Bulgars see Volga Bulgars
Whitehorse North America (Canada) the growth of the US 129 (2) US superpower 138 (1)
White Huns see Ephthalites; Hephthalites, Empire of the
White Lotus rebellion East Asia empire and revolution 268 (2)
White Mountain battle Central Europe (Czech Republic) Reformation 196 (1)
White Nile Ar. Al Baḩr al Abyaḑ, An Nīl al Abyaḑ, Bahr el Jebel river East Africa early agriculture 158 (1) economy 163 (2) exploration 157 (5) Islam 163 (1) slave trade 165 (4) trade 165 (3)
White Plains battle North America (USA) empire and revolution 127 (3)
White Russia state Eastern Europe Soviet Union 208 (2)
White Sea Rus. Beloye More sea Arctic Ocean exploration 257 (2) historical geography 170–171 (1)
Whitestone Hill battle North America (USA) the growth of the US 129 (2)
White Temple temple Southwest Asia (Iraq) first cities 220 (3)
White Volta var. Nakambé, Fr. Volta Blanche river West Africa Islam 163 (1) trade 163 (4), (5), (6), (7), 164 (2)
Whittier North America (USA)
Whydah mod. Ouidah; Eng. Wida West Africa empire and revolution 88 (1) slave trade 165 (4) see also Ouidah
Wichita people North America colonization 125 (4), 126 (1)
Wichita Village battle North America (USA) the growth of the US 129 (2)
Wida see Ouidah, Whydah
Wien see Vienna, Vindobona
Wigan British Isles (United Kingdom) economy 204 (1)
Wight, Isle of island British Isles medieval states 186 (2)
Wigorna Ceaster see Worcester
Wila state Southern Africa trade 164 (2)
Wilkes-Barre North America (USA) empire and revolution 127 (3)
Wilkes Land physical region Antarctica Antarctic Exploration 287 (3)
Willandra Lakes Australia exploration 280 (1)
Will County region North America
Willendorf archaeological site Central Europe (Switzerland) prehistoric culture 17 (4)
Williamsburg North America (USA) empire and revolution 127 (2), (3)
Willkawain South America (Peru) early cultures 146 (1)
Wilmersdorf Central Europe (Germany) postwar politics 212 (2)
Wilmington North America (USA) empire and revolution 127 (2), (3) US Civil War 131 (6), (7)
Wilna see Vilna, Vilnius, Wilno
Wilno Eastern Europe (Lithuania) WWII 210 (1), 211 (4)
Wilson Butte Cave North America (USA) the world in 10,000 BCE 14–15
Wilson's Creek battle North America (USA) US Civil War 131 (6)
Wilson's Promontory Australia the world in 5000 BCE 18–19
Wilton archaeological site/settlement Southern Africa (South Africa) early agriculture 158 (1) early cultures 160 (1)
Wiluna Australia colonization 282 (1)
Wilzi people Central Europe Franks 184 (2)
Winburg Southern Africa (South Africa) colonization 166 (2)
Winburg-Potchefstroom, Republic of state Southern Africa the world in 1850 90–91
Winchester hist. Wintanceaster; Lat. Venta Belgarum British Isles (United Kingdom) economy 190 (1) medieval states 183 (3), 186 (2), 187 (4)
Windau var. Vindava, mod. Ventspils; Eastern Europe (Latvia) medieval states 189 (3) see also Vindava
Windhoek Ger. Windhuk Southern Africa (Namibia) colonization 167 (4) economy 168 (2) European imperialism 96 (2)
Windhuk see Windhoek
Windward Coast physical region West Africa slave trade 165 (4)
Windward Islands colonial possession/state West Indies the world in 1900 94–95 the world in 1925 98–99 the world in 1950 102–103
Winneba West Africa (Ghana) empire and revolution 88 (1)
Winnebago people North America colonization 126 (1)
Winnipeg North America (Canada) the growth of the US 129 (2), 132 (1) US economy 136 (2)
Winnipeg, Lake lake North America colonization 126 (1) cultural groups 123 (3) exploration 118 (1), 119 (2), (3) the growth of the US 129 (2)
Wintanceaster see Winchester
Winterville North America (USA) cultural groups 122 (5)
Winwaed battle British Isles (United Kingdom) medieval states 183 (3)
Wisby mod. Visby Scandinavia (Sweden) medieval states 189 (3) see also Visby
Wisconsin state North America the growth of the US 129 (1) US Civil War 130 (2), (3), (4), (5) US economy 134 (2)
Wisła see Vistula
Wismar Central Europe (Germany) economy 190 (1) medieval states 189 (3)
Wismar region Central Europe early modern states 197 (3)
Wittenberg Central Europe (Germany) Reformation 194 (2)
Wittstock battle Central Europe (Germany) Reformation 196 (1)
Włodzimierz var. Volodymyr-Volyns'kyy; Rus. Vladimir Eastern Europe (Russian Federation) medieval states 189 (3) see also Vladimir
Woccon people North America colonization 125 (4)
Woju people East Asia first states 260 (1)
Wojwodina see Vojvodina
Wollongong Australia colonization 283 (3)
Wolmar Latv. Valmiera; Rus. Vol'mar Eastern Europe (Latvia) early modern states 195 (3)
Wolof state West Africa Islam 163 (1) trade 163 (4), (6), (7)
Wolverhampton British Isles (United Kingdom) economy 204 (1)
Wonju Jap. Genshū East Asia (South Korea) Cold War 109 (4)
Wonsan East Asia (North Korea) early modern states 267 (4) Russo-Japanese War 270 (4) Sino-Japanese War 270 (3) Cold War 109 (4)
Wood Lake battle North America (USA) the growth of the US 129 (2)
Woodland Culture people North America/South America the world in 1000 58–59 the world in 1200 62–63 the world in 1300 66–67 the world in 1400 70–71 the world in 1500 74–75 the world in 1700 82–83
Worcester anc. Wigorna Ceaster British Isles (United Kingdom) medieval states 183 (3)
Workington British Isles (United Kingdom) economy 204 (1)
Wormatia see Worms
Worms anc. Augusta Vangionum, Borbetomagus, Wormatia settlement Central Europe (Germany) ancient Rome 182 (1) crusades 186 (1) economy 190 (1) Franks 184 (2) medieval states 182 (2), 187 (3) Reformation 194 (2) see also Borbetomagus
Wounded Knee battle North America (USA) the growth of the US 129 (2)
Wrangel Island island Arctic Ocean colonialism 269 (3) exploration 257 (2)
Wrangell see Fort Wrangell
Wrocław Ger. Breslau Central Europe (Poland) economy 190 (1) medieval states 188 (1) see also Breslau
Wu East Asia (China) first cities 259 (4), (5) first religions 37 (4)
Wu region/state East Asia first religions 37 (4) first states 261 (2) medieval states 263 (3)
Wubei East Asia (China) first states 260 (1)
Wuchang var. Wu-ch'ang settlement East Asia (China) biological diffusion 72–73 (1) early modern states 266 (1), (2) medieval states 263 (6) world religions 49 (3)
Wuchang see Hankou, Wuhan
Wucheng East Asia (China) first cities 259 (3)
Wu-chou, Wuchow see Wuzhou
Wuci East Asia (China) first states 260 (1)
Wudahai East Asia (China) Mongols 68–69 (1)
Wudang Shan var. Wu Tang Shan mountain East Asia first religions 37 (4)
Wudu province East Asia first states 260 (1)
Wuhan var. Hankou, Han-kou, Han-k'ou, Hanyang, Wuchang, Wu-han; prev. Hankow East Asia (China) Chinese revolution 271 (5) Communism 271 (8) economy 274 (1) Islam 275 (4) postwar economy 275 (3) postwar politics 271 (7), 274 (2) see also Hankou
Wuhsien see Suzhou
Wu-hsing see Wuxing
Wuhu var. Wu-na-mu East Asia (China) colonialism 269 (4)
Wuhuan people East Asia first states 260 (1), 261 (2)
Wuling province East Asia first states 260 (1)
Wulu East Asia (China) first states 260 (1)
Wu-lu-k'o-mu-shi, Wu-lu-mu-ch'i see Urumchi, Ürümqi
Wu-na-mu see Wuhu
Wupatki archaeological site North America (USA) cultural groups 123 (4)
Wuqie Mainland Southeast Asia (Vietnam) first states 260 (1)
Württemberg state Central Europe early modern states 193 (5) empire and revolution 202 (1), (2)
Wusuli Jiang, Wusuri see Ussuri
Wu Tang Shan see Wudang Shan
Wuwei Buddhist center/settlement East Asia (China) ancient trade 44–45 (1) first states 260 (1), 261 (3) world religions 49 (3)
Wuwei province East Asia first states 260 (1)
Wuxing var. Wu-hsing Buddhist center East Asia (China) world religions 49 (3)
Wuyi Buddhist center East Asia (China) world religions 49 (3)
Wuyi Shan mountain range East Asia historical geography 254–255 (1)
Wuyne state East Asia medieval states 263 (3)
Wuyuan East Asia (China) first states 260 (1)
Wüzburg Central Europe (Germany) medieval states 189 (3)
Wuzhong people East Asia first cities 259 (4)
Wuzhou var. Wu-chou, Wuchow East Asia (China) colonialism 269 (4) medieval states 262–263 (1)
Wye Wel. Gwy river British Isles economy 204 (1)
Wyndham Australia colonization 282 (1), 283 (3)
Wyoming state North America the growth of the US 129 (1) US economy 134 (2)
Wyoming battle North America (USA) empire and revolution 127 (3)

X

Xacalta Central America (Mexico) first civilizations 122 (1)
Xalpan Central America (Mexico) Aztecs 124 (3)
Xaltenco Central America (Mexico) Aztecs 124 (3)
Xaltocan Central America (Mexico) Aztecs 124 (2) colonization 125 (5)
Xaltocan, Lake lake Central America Aztecs 124 (2) colonization 125 (5)
Xam Nua see Sam Neua
Xanthus Southwest Asia (Turkey) first civilizations 177 (1) Hellenistic world 40–41 (1)
Xäzär Dänizi see Caspian Sea
Xeloc Central America (Mexico) Aztecs 124 (2)
Xhosa people Southern Africa the world in 1800 86–87
Xia state East Asia first states 261 (3)
Xiaguan see Dali
Xiamen var. Hsia-men; prev. Amoy East Asia (China) colonialism 269 (4) economy 274 (1) empire and revolution 88–89 (2) imperialism 270 (2) postwar politics 274 (2) trade 267 (3) WWII 251 (3)
Xi'an var. Changan, Ch'ang-an, Hsi-an, Sian, Signan, Siking, Singan, Xian East Asia biological diffusion 72–73 (1) early agriculture 258 (2) early modern states 266 (1), (2), 268 (1) economy 274 (1) Islam 275 (4) Mongols 68–69 (1) postwar economy 275 (3) postwar politics 271 (7), 274 (2) trade 267 (3) see also Chang'an
Xianbei people East Asia first states 260 (1), 261 (2) medieval states 261 (6)
Xianbi var. Hsien-pi, Sienpi, Tungus people East Asia the world in 250 CE 46–47
Xiang vassal state East Asia first cities 259 (3)
Xianggang see Hong Kong
Xiangping East Asia (China) first cities 259 (5)
Xiangyang var. Hsiang-yang settlement East Asia (China) early modern states 266 (2) medieval states 263 (4), (5) Mongols 68–69 (1) world religions 49 (3)
Xiangzhou var. Hsiangchou East Asia (China) medieval states 262–263 (1)
Xianrendong archaeological site East Asia early agriculture 258 (1)
Xianyang East Asia (China) first cities 259 (5)
Xianyun people East Asia first cities 259 (4)
Xiapi East Asia (China) first states 260 (1)
Xico Central America (Mexico) Aztecs 124 (2) first civilizations 122 (1)
Xicochimalco Central America (Mexico) colonization 125 (5)
Xie East Asia (China) first cities 259 (5) first religions 37 (4)
Xie state East Asia first cities 259 (5)
Xigazê see Shigatse
Xiiqtepec state Central America Aztecs 124 (1)
Xi Jiang var. Hsi Chiang, Eng. West River river East Asia early modern states 266 (1), (2) first cities 28–29 (1) first religions 37 (4) first states 260 (1) medieval states 261 (6), 262–263 (1), 263 (4), (6) Mongols 68–69 (1) postwar politics 274 (2)
Xi Jiang Delta region East Asia first cities 28–29 (1)
Xin see Sin Kiang, Turkestan, Xinjiang
Xing vassal state East Asia first cities 259 (3)
Xingan East Asia (China) first states 260 (1)
Xingging Palace palace East Asia (China) medieval states 262 (2)
Xingkai Hu see Khanka, Lake
Xingqingfu East Asia (China) medieval states 263 (4), (5)
Xingtai East Asia (China) first cities 259 (3)
Xingu river South America colonization 149 (3) early cultures 144 (1), 145 (2) economy 153 (3) empire and revolution 151 (3) environment 153 (4) exploration 142 (1), 143 (2)
Xingyuan East Asia (China) medieval states 263 (4)
Xingzhong East Asia (China) medieval states 263 (5)
Xining East Asia (China) economy 274 (1)
Xinje state Southern Africa trade 164 (2)
Xinjiang var. Sinkiang, Sinkiang Uighur Autonomous Region, Xin, Turkestan province/state East Asia ancient trade 44–45 (1) colonialism 269 (3), (4) Communism 271 (8) early modern states 268 (1) empire and revolution 268 (2) exploration 257 (3) medieval states 261 (6) postwar economy 275 (3) postwar politics 252 (2)
Xinjiang see Sinkiang, Turkestan
Xinye var. Hsin-yeh Buddhist center East Asia (China) world religions 49 (3)
Xinzheng East Asia (China) first cities 259 (4), (5) first religions 37 (4)
Xiong'er Jiang river East Asia first cities 29 (4)
Xiongnu var. Hsiung-nu, Huns people East Asia ancient trade 44–45 (1) first cities 259 (5) first states 260 (1), 261 (2) medieval states 261 (6)
Xiongnu, Empire of the var. Hsiung-nu, Hun tribal confederacy state East Asia the world in 250 BCE 38–39
Xi Shan mountain East Asia first religions 37 (4)
Xiuhquilpan Central America (Mexico) first civilizations 122 (1)
Xiuhtetelco Central America (Mexico) first civilizations 122 (1)

BIBLIOGRAPHY

World history

Atlases:

Atlante Storico De Agostini Novara, 1995
Atlante Storico del Cristianesimo Andrea Duè, Juan Maria Laboa, Milan, 1997
Atlas Historico Universal y de Espagna Santillana Madrid, 1995
Atlas of Ancient Archaeology Jacquetta Hawkes (ed.), London, 1974
Atlas of Atlases: The Map Makers Vision of the World Phillip Allen, New York, 1992
Atlas of Disease Distributions: Analytical Approaches to Epidemiological Data Andrew D. Cliff and Peter Haggett, Oxford, 1988
Atlas of Food Crops J. Bertin (et al.), Paris, 1971
Atlas of Islamic History H.W. Hazard, Princeton, 1952
Atlas of Jewish History Dan Cohen-Sherbok, London and New York, 1996
Atlas of Modern Jewish History (revised from the Hebrew edn.) Evyatar Friesel, Oxford, New York,1990
Atlas of the Christian Church Henry Chadwick and G.R. Evans (eds.), Oxford, 1987
Atlas of the Jewish World Nicholas de Lange, Oxford, 1995
Atlas zur Geschichte V.E.B. Hermann Haack, GDR, 1988
Atlas zur Kirchengeschichte H. Jedin, K.S. Latourette, J. Martin, Freiburg, 1970
Cambridge Illustrated Atlas: Warfare, Renaissance to Revolution 1492–1792 Jeremy Black,Cambridge, 1996
Cambridge Illustrated Atlas: Warfare, The Middle Ages 768–1487 Nicholas Hooper and Matthew Bennett, Cambridge, 1996
Cassell Atlas of World History John Haywood, Brian Catchpole, Simon Hall, Edward Barratt, Oxford, 1997
Chambers Atlas of World History, Edinburgh, 1975
Collins Atlas of Twentieth Century World History Michael Dockrill, 1991
Grand Atlas Historique Georges Duby, Paris,1996
Grosser Atlas zur Weltgeschichte, Braunschweig, 1997
Grosser Historischer Weltatlas (3 vols.) Bayerischer Schulbuch-Verlag, Munich, 1981
Hammond Atlas of World History, Maplewood, New Jersey, 1997
Historical Atlas of Islam William C. Brice (ed.), Leiden, 1981
Historical Atlas of the Muslim Peoples R. Roolvink, London, 1957
Historical Atlas of World Mythology Vol. I: The Way of the Animal Powers J. Campbell, New York, 1984
Historical Atlas of World Mythology Vol. II: The Way of the Seeded Earth, Part I: The Sacrifice Joseph Campbell, New York, 1988
Historical Atlas of the World's Religions, Isma'il Ragi al Faruqi, New York, 1974
New Cambridge Modern History Atlas, H.C. Darby, Harold Fullard (eds.), 1970
Past Worlds: The Times Atlas of Archaeology C. Scarre (ed.) London, 1988
Philip's Atlas of Exploration, London, 1996
Putzger Historische Weltatlas, Berlin, 1997
Rand McNally Atlas of World History 1993 (published in England as **Philip's Atlas of World History**, London, 1992)
Review and Atlas of Palaeovegetation: Preliminary Land Ecosystem Maps of the World Since the last Glacial Maximum J.M. Adams and H. Faure (eds.), Quaternary Environments Network, www.soton.ac.uk/~tjms/adams4.html
Soguatlas, Stockholm, 1992
Társadalom – És Művelődéstörténeti Atlasz Budapest, 1991
The World...its History in Maps W.H. McNeill, M.R. Buske, A.W. Roehm, Chicago, 1969
Times Atlas of Exploration Felipe Fernandez-Armesto (ed.), London, 1991
Times Atlas of the 20th Century Richard Overy (ed.), London, 1996
Times Atlas of the Second World War J. Keegan (ed.), London, 1989
Times Atlas of World History Geoffrey Barraclough (ed.), London, 1993
Times Concise Atlas of World History Geoffrey Barraclough (ed.), London, 1994
Tortenelmi Vilagatlasz, Budapest, 1991
WDTV Atlas zur Weltgeschichte (2 vols.) H. Kinder & W. Hilgemann, Stuttgart, 1964 (Published in English as **The Penguin Atlas of World History** London, 1974 and 1978)
WWF Atlas of the Environment Geoffrey Lean and Don Hinrischsen, Oxford, 1992
West Point Atlas of American Wars: Volume II, 1900-1953 Vincent J. Esposito (chief ed.), New York, 1959
West Point Military History Series: Atlas for the Arab-Israeli War and the Korean War Thomas E. Greiss (series ed.), Wayne, New Jersey,1986
West Point Military History Series: Atlas for the Great War Thomas E. Greiss (series ed.), Wayne New Jersey, 1986
West Point Military History Series: Atlas for the Second World War (vols. I–III) Thomas E. Greiss (series ed.), Wayne, New Jersey,1985

Other works:

A History of Discovery and Exploration: The Search Begins London,1973
A History of Islamic Societies I.M. Lapidus, Cambridge, 1988
A History of World Societies John P. McKay, Bennett D. Hill, John Buckler, Boston, 1997
A Study of History Arnold Toynbee, Oxford, 1972
Asia Before Europe: Economy and Civilization of the Indian Ocean from the Rise of Islam to 1750 K.N. Chauduri, Cambridge, 1991
Before European Hegemony: The World System AD 1250-1350 J.L. Abu-Lughod, Oxford, 1991
Claudius Ptolemy: The Geography Translated and edited by Edward Luther Stevenson, London, 1991
Columbia Lippincott Gazetteer of the World Saul B. Cohen (ed.), New York, 1999
Cross-cultural Trade in World History P.D. Curtin, Cambridge, 1984
Encyclopedia of World History, revised edn. W.L. Langer (ed.), London, 1987
Heck's Pictorial Archive of Military Science, Geography and History J.G. Heck, New York, 1994
Into the Unknown National Geographic Society: Washington, 1987
Maps and History J. Black, New Haven, 1997
Maps and Politics J. Black, London,1997
Maps from the Age of Discovery, Columbus to Mercator Kenneth Nebenzahl, London, 1990
Navies and Nations: Warships, Navies and State Building in Europe and America 1500-1860 J. Glete, Stockholm, 1993
Peoples and Places of the Past National Geographic Society: Washington, 1983
Plagues and Peoples W.H. McNeill, New York, 1992
Portugaliae Monumenta Cartographica Lisbon, 1960
The Atlantic Slave Trade P.D. Curtin, Madison, 1972
The Atlantic Slave Trade: Effects on Economy, Society and Population in Africa, America and Europe J.E. Inikori, S.L. Engerman, Durham, NC 1992
The Discoverers: An Encyclopedia of Explorers and Exploration Helen Delpar (ed.), New York, 1980
The Distribution of Wild Wheats and Barleys J.R. Harlan, D. Zohary, Science, 1966
The Earth and its Peoples: a Global History Richard W. Bulliet, Pamela Kyle, Crossley, Daniel R. Headrick, Steven W. Hirsch, Lyman L. Johnson, David Northrup, Boston, New York, 1997
The Evolution of International Business G. Jones, London, 1996
The First Imperial Age: European Overseas Expansion c. 1400–1715 G.V. Scammel London, 1992
The Geography behind History W.G. East, London, 1965
The History of Cartography (various vols.) J.B. Harley, D. Woodward, Chicago, 1987–
The Hutchinson History of the World, revised edn. J.M. Roberts, London, 1987
The Mapmaker's Art: A History of Cartography John Goss, London, 1993
The Osprey Companion to Military History Robert Cowley and Geoffrey Parker, London, 1996
The Oxford History of the British Empire II, the Eighteenth Century P.J. Marshall (ed.), Oxford, 1998
The Oxford History of the British Empire: The Origins of Empire Nicholas Canny (ed.), Oxford, 1998
The Oxford Illustrated History of Modern War C. Townshend (ed.), Oxford, 1999
The Plants and Animals that Nourish Man J.R. Harlan, Scientific American, 1976
The Revolutionary Age 1760–1791 H. Quebec Neaty, London, 1966
The Rise of Christianity: A Sociologist Reconsiders History R. Stark, Princeton, 1996
The Rise of the West: A History of the Human Community W.H, McNeill, Chicago, 1991
The Rise of Western Christendom: Triumph and Diversity 200–1000 P. Brown, Oxford, 1996
The Story of Archaeology Paul G. Bahn (ed.), London, 1996
The Wealth and Property of Nations D. Landes, London, 1998
The World since 1500: A Global History, 6th edn L.S. Stavrianos, Englewood Cliffs NJ, 1991
The World to 1500: A Global History, 5th edn L.S. Stavrianos, Englewood Cliffs NJ, 1991
The World: an Illustrated History Geoffrey Parker (ed.), London, 1986
The World's Religions Ninian Smart, Cambridge, 1992
War and the World: Military Power and the Fate of Continents 1450–2000 J Black, New York, 1998
War in the Early Modern World 1450–1815 J. Black (ed.), London, 1999
Why Wars Happen J. Black, London, 1998

North America

Atlases:

Atlas of American Indian Affairs Francis Paul Prucha, Lincoln, Nebraska, 1990
Atlas of Ancient America Michael Coe, Dean Snow, Elizabeth Benson, Oxford and New York, 1993
Atlas of Early American History L. Cappon (et al), Chicago, 1976
Atlas of Great Lakes Indian History Helen Tanner, Norman, Oklahoma, 1987
Atlas of North American Exploration: from Norse Voyages to the Race to the Pole William H. Goetzmann, Glyndwr Williams, New York, 1992
Atlas of the Civil War James M. McPherson, New York, 1994
Atlas of the North American Indian C. Waldman, M. Braun, New York, 1995
Atlas of Westward Expansion Alan Wexler, Molly Braun, New York, 1995
Civil War Newspaper Maps, a Historical Atlas David Bosse, Baltimore and London, 1993
Historical Atlas of Canada Donald Kerr and Deryck W. Holdsworth (eds.), Toronto, 1990
Historical Atlas of the American West Warren A. Beck and Ynez D. Haase, Norman, Oklahoma, 1989
Historical Atlas of New York E. Homberger, A. Hudson, New York, 1994
Historical Atlas of the United States: Centennial Edition National Geographic Society: Washington, 1988
Mapping America's Past: a Historical Atlas M.C. Carnes, P. Williams, J. A. Garraty, New York, 1997
Our United States...its History in Maps E.B. Wesley, Chicago, 1977
Penguin Historical Atlas of North America Eric Homberger, London,1995
The Settling of North America: the Atlas of the Great Migrations into North America from the Ice Age to the Present Helen Hornbeck Tanner (ed.), New York, 1995)

Other works:

A Guide to the Historical Geography of New Spain Peter Gerhard, Norman, Oklahoma, 1993
America in 1492: the World of the Indian Peoples before the Arrival of Columbus Alvin M. Josephy, New York, 1992
An Introduction to American Archaeology (vols. 1 & 2) Englewood Cliffs, NJ, 1970
Battle Cry of Freedom: the Civil War Era James McPherson, Oxford, 1988
Documents of American History Henry Steele Commager, 1973
European and Native American Warfare 1675–1815 A. Starkey, London, 1998
Encyclopedia of North America Indians Frederick E. Hoxie, Boston, 1996
Handbook of Middle American Indians Austin, Texas, 1964-76
Handbook of North American Indians Smithsonian Institution, Washington, D.C., 1978- (20 volumes projected)
Hispaniola; Caribbean Chiefdoms in the Age of Columbus S. M.Wilson, Tuscaloosa,1990
Native American Time: a Historical Time Line of Native America Lee Francis, New York, 1996
Oxford History of the American West Clyde A. Milner et al., Oxford and New York, 1994
Prehistory of North America, 3rd edn. J.D. Jennings, Mountain View, Calif., 1989
The American Century: the Rise and Decline of the United States as a World Power Donald W. White, New Haven, 1996
The Americans: Their Archaeology and Prehistory D. Snow London, 1976
The Fur Trader and the Indian L.O. Saum London, 1965
The Limits of Liberty Maldwyn A. Jones, Oxford/New York, 1983
The Market Revolution America: Social, Political and Religious Expressions, 1800–1880 M. Stokes, S. Conway, Charlottesville, 1996
The Northern Frontier of New Spain Peter Gerhard, Norman, Oklahoma, 1993
The Slave Trade Hugh Thomas, London/New York, 1997
The Southeast Frontier of New Spain Peter Gerhard, Norman, Oklahoma, 1993
The Spanish Frontier in North America D.J. Weber, New Haven, 1992
The Maya Michael D. Coe, London, 1993

South America

Atlases:

Atlas of Ancient America Michael Coe, Dean Snow, Elizabeth Benson, Oxford and New York, 1993
Latin American History: a Teaching Atlas Cathryn L. Lombardi, John V. Lombardi, Kym L. Stoner, Madison, Wisconsin, 1983

Other works:

A History of Latin America: Empires and Sequels, 1450–1930 Peter John Bakewell, Gainesville, 1998
Anthropological Perspectives A. C. Roosevelt (ed.), Tucson and London, 1994
Ancient Mexico in the British Museum Colin McEwan, London, 1995
Ancient South America K. Bruhns, Cambridge 1994
Archaeology in the Lowland American Tropics P. W. Stahl (ed.), Cambridge, 1994
Cambridge History of Latin America Leslie Bethel (ed.), Cambridge, 1985
Chavín and the Origins of Andean Civilization R. L. Burger, London, 1992
Chiefdoms and Chieftaincy in the Americas E. M. Redmond (ed.), Malden Mass, 1997
Chieftains, Power and Trade: Regional Interaction in the Intermediate Area of the Americas C. H. Langebaek & F. C-Arroyo (eds.), Departamento de Antropologia, Universidad de los Andes: Bogota, Colombia, 1996
Moundbuilders of the Amazon. Geophysical Archaeology on Marajo Island, Brazil A. C. Roosevelt, New York, 1991
Parmana: Prehistoric Maize and Manioc Subsistence along the Amazon and Orinoco A. C. Roosevelt, New York, 1980
Prehistory of the Americas S. J. Fiedel, Cambridge, 1987
The Conquest of the Incas John Hemming, London, 1970
The Discoverie of the Large, Rich and Bewtiful Empire of Guiana by Sir Walter Ralegh N. L. Whitehead (ed.), Exploring Travel Series Vol. 1, Manchester University Press: Manchester, American Exploration and Travel Series Vol. 71, Oklahoma University Press: Norman, 1998
The Incas and Their Ancestors: The Archaeology of Peru M. E. Moseley, New York, 1992
The Meeting of Two Worlds: Europe and the Americas, 1492–1650 W. Bray (ed.), Proceedings of the British Academy 81, Oxford, 1993
The Penguin History of Latin America Edwin Williamson, London, 1992

Africa

Atlases:

An Atlas of African History J.D. Fage London, 1958
Atlas of African Affairs Ieuan LL. Griffiths, London and New York, 1994
Atlas of Ancient Egypt John Baines and Jaromir Malek, Oxford, 1996
Cultural Atlas of Africa Jocelyn Murray (ed.), Oxford, 1993
New Atlas of African History G.S.P. Freeman-Grenville, London, 1991
Penguin Historical Atlas of Ancient Egypt Bill Manley, London, 1996

Other works:

A History of West Africa (2 vols.) 3rd edn. J.F.A. Ajaya, M. Crowder, 1985
A Survey of West African History B.A. Ogot (ed.), London, 1974–1976
Africa and Africans in the Formation of the Atlantic World 1400–1680 John Thornton, Cambridge and New York, 1992
Africa and Asia: Mapping Two Continents Natalie Ettinger, Elspeth Huxley, Paul Hamilton, London, 1973
Africa in the Iron Age c.500 BC–AD 1400 R. Oliver, B. Fagan, Cambridge, 1975
Africa since 1800, 3rd edn. R. Oliver, A. Atmore, Cambridge, 1981
African Archaeology, 2nd edn. David W. Phillipson, Cambridge, 1993
An Economic History of Africa From Earliest Times to Partition P.L. Wickins, New York, 1981
Arab Seafaring in the Indian Ocean in Ancient and Medieval Times G.F. Hourani and J.Carswell, Princeton, 1995
Cambridge History of Africa J.D. Fage, R. Oliver (eds.), Cambridge, 1975–
Early Egypt: The Rise of Civilisation in the Nile Valley A.J. Spencer, London, 1993
Economic History of West Africa A.G. Hopkins, London, 1973
General History of Africa II: Ancient Civilizations of Africa G. Mokhtar (ed.), Paris and London, 1981
General History of Africa III: Africa from the Seventh to the Eleventh Century M. Elfasi (ed.), I. Hrbek (asst. ed.), Paris and London, 1981
General History of Africa VII: Africa under Colonial Domination 1880–1935 A.A. Boahen (ed.), Paris and London, 1981
Oxford History of South Africa (vols. 1 & 2) Oxford, 1969, 1971
The African Inheritance Ieuan L.L. Griffiths, London and New York, 1995
The Art and Architecture of Ancient Egypt, revised edn. W.S. Smith, London, 1981
The Changing Geography of Africa and the Middle East Graham P. Chapman and Kathleen M. Baker, London and New York, 1992
Wars and Imperial Conquest in Africa 1830–1914 B. Vandervort, London, 1998
West Africa under Colonial Rule M. Crowder, London, 1968

Europe

Atlases:

Atlas of Medieval Europe Angus Mackay, David Ditchburn (eds.), London, 1997
Atlas of the Classical World A.M. Van der Heydon, H.H. Scullard, London, 1959
Atlas of the Crusades Jonathon Riley-Smith, New York and Oxford, 1991
Atlas of the Greek World Peter Levi, Oxford, 1997
Atlas of the Roman World Tim Cornell, John Matthews, New York, 1982
Atlas Historyczny Polski Warsaw, 1967
Cultural Atlas of France John Ardagh and Colin Jones, Oxford, 1991
Cultural Atlas of Spain and Portugal Mary Vincent and R.A. Stradling, Oxford, 1994
Cultural Atlas of the Viking World J.Graham-Campbell (ed.), Oxford, 1994
Historical Atlas of East Central Europe: Volume I Paul Robert Magosci, Seattle and London, 1993
Penguin Historical Atlas of Ancient Greece Robert Morkot, London, 1996
Penguin Historical Atlas of Ancient Rome Chris Scarre, London, 1995
Penguin Historical Atlas of Russia John Channon with Robert Hudson, London, 1995
Penguin Historical Atlas of the Third Reich Richard Overy, London, 1996
Penguin Historical Atlas of the Vikings John Haywood, London, 1995
Russian History Atlas M. Gilbert, London, 1972
Times Atlas of European History London, 1994

Other works:

A History of Ancient Greece N. Demand, New York, 1996
A History of Business in Medieval Europe 1200–1550 E.H. Hunt and J. Murray, Cambridge, 1999
A Russian Economic History A. Kahan, Chicago, 1991
An Historical Geography of Western Europe before 1800, revised edn. C.T. Smith, London and New York

As the Romans Did: a Sourcebook in Roman Social History, 2nd ed. Jo-Ann Shelton, Oxford, 1997
Britain and Industrial Europe 1750–1870 W.O. Henderson, Liverpool, 1965
Britain as a Military Power 1688–1815 J. Black, London, 1999
Cambridge Economic History of Europe II: Trade and Industry in the Middle Ages, 2nd edn. A. Miller (ed.), Cambridge, 1987
Capetian France 987–1328 E. Hallam, London, 1980
Eighteenth Century Europe 2nd edn. J. Black, London, 1999
Eighteenth Century Europe: Tradition and Progress I. Woloch, London and New York, 1982
Enlightened Absolutism H.M. Scott (ed.), London, 1990
Europe in the Eighteenth Century, 2nd edn J. Black, London, 1999
Europe in the Fourteenth and Fifteenth Centuries D.Hay, London, 1966
Europe under Napoleon, 1799–1815 M.G. Broers, London, 1997
European Warfare 1453–1815 J. Black (ed.), London, 1999
Frederick II. A Medieval Emperor D.Abulafia, London, 1988
From Louis XIV to Napoleon: The Fate of a Great Power J. Black, London, 1999
From Tsar to Soviets C. Read, 1996
Gainful Pursuits: The Making of Industrial Europe 1600–1914 J. Goodman, K. Honeyman, London, 1988
Geography of the Soviet Union J.P. Cole, London, 1984
Germany and the Germans, after Unification John Ardagh, London, 1991
Germany in the Middle Ages 800–1056 T. Reuter, London, 1991
History of the Byzantine State G. Ostrogorsky, Oxford, 1969
History of the National Economy of Russia to the 1917 Revolution P.I. Lyaschenko, New York, 1949
Information USSR Oxford and New York, 1962
Ireland 1912–85 J.J. Lee, 1989
Louis XIV and the French Monarchy A. Lossky, London, 1995
Medieval England: Towns, Commerce and Crafts 1086–1348 E. Miller, J. Hatcher London, 1995
Medieval Trade in the Mediterranean World: Illustrative Documents R.S. Lopez and I.W. Raymond, reprinted New York, 1990
Money and its Use in Medieval Europe P. Spufford, Cambridge, 1988
Moorish Spain R. Fletcher, Phoenix, 1994
Napoleon and the Legacy of the French Revolution M. Lyons, London, 1994
Napoleon's Integration of Europe S.J. Woolf, London, 1991
National States and National Minorities C.A. Macartney, 1968
New Cambridge Medieval History, vol. V, c.1198–c.1300 David Abulafia (ed.), Cambridge, 1999
New Cambridge Medieval History, vol. VI, c.1300–c.1415 Michael Jones (ed.), Cambridge, 1999
New Cambridge Medieval History, vol. VII, c.1415–c.1500 Christopher Allmand Jones (ed.), Cambridge, 1998
Northern Europe in the Early Modern Period: the Baltic World 1492–1772 D. Kirby, London, 1990
Oxford Classical Dictionary, 3rd ed. Simon Hornblower and Antony Spawforth (eds.), Oxford, 1996
Oxford History of the Classical World J. Boardman (ed.), Oxford, 1989
Oxford Illustrated History of the Crusades J. Riley-Smith (ed.), Oxford, 1997
Oxford Illustrated History of the Vikings P. Sawyer (ed.) Oxford, 1997
Oxford Illustrated Prehistory of Europe B. Cunliffe, Oxford, 1994
Poverty and Capitalism in Pre-Industrial Europe C. Lis and H. Soly, Brighton, 1982
Roman Civilization (2 vols) 3rd ed. Naphtali Lewis and Meyer Reinhold (eds.), New York, 1990
Seventeenth-century Europe 1598–1700 T. Munck, London, 1990
Seventeenth–century Europe, 2nd ed. D.H. Pennington, London, 1989
Spain in the Middle Ages: from Frontier to Empire Angus Mackay, London, 1977
Textiles, Towns and Trade J.H. Munro, Aldershot, 1994
The British Revolution: British Politics 1880–1939 Robert Rhodes, London, 1978
The Cambridge Ancient History J.B. Bury, S.A. Cook, F.E. Adcock (eds.), Cambridge, 1923–; 2nd edn 1982–
The Civilization of Europe in the Renaissance J.R.Hale, London, 1993
The Creation of the Roman Frontier S.L. Dyson, Princeton, 1985
The Crusades: a Short History J.Riley -Smith, 1990
The Emergence of the Rus J. Shepherd, S. Franklin, 1996
The European Dynastic States 1494–1660 R. Bonney, Oxford, 1991
The German Hansa P.J. Dollinger, trans. D.S. Ault, S.H. Steinberg, London, 1970
The Habsburg Monarchy, 1618–1815 C. Ingrao, Cambridge, 1994
The Hundred Years War. England and France at War c.1300–c.1450 C.T. Allmand, Cambridge, 1988
The Huns E.A. Thompson, 1996
The Industrialization of Soviet Russia (3 vols.) R.W. Davis, Cambridge, 1989
The Italian City Republics, 3rd edn. D.Waley, London and New York, 1988
The Later Crusades 1274–1580: from Lyons to Alcazar N.Housley, Oxford, 1992
The Legacy of Rome: A New Appraisal Richard Jenkins (ed.) Oxford, 1992
The Making of Europe. Conquest, Colonization and Cultural Change 950–1350 R.Bartlett, London, 1993
The Making of Roman Italy Edward Togo Salmon, Ithaca, NY, 1982
The Mediterranean World in Late Antiquity AD 395–600 A.M. Cameron, London, 1993
The Merovingian Kingdoms 450–758 I.N. Wood, London, 1994
The Old European Order 1660–1800, 2nd ed. W. Doyle, Oxford, 1992
The Origins of the Second World War in Europe P.M.H. Bell, 1986
The Roman Empire, 27 BC–AD 476: A Study in Survival Chester G. Starr, New York, 1982
The State in Early Modern France J.B. Collins, Cambridge, 1995
The Struggle for Mastery in Germany, 1779–1850 B. Simms, London, 1998
The Thirty Years War Geoffrey Parker, London, 1984
The Transformation of the Roman World 400–900 L. Webster, M. Brown, London, 1997
The Two Cities. Medieval Europe 1050–1320 M.Barber, London and New York, 1992
The Wars of Napoleon C.J. Esdaile, London, 1995
The World in Depression 1929–1939 C. Kindleberger, 1973
Venice: A Maritime Republic F.C. Lane, Baltimore, 1973
War and Imperialism in Republican Rome 327–70 BC William V. Harris, Oxford, 1979
War in the Middle Ages P. Contamine, Oxford, 1984

West Asia:

Atlases:

Atlas of the Jewish World Nicholas de Lange, Oxford, 1984
Cultural Atlas of Mesopotamia and the Ancient Near East Michael Roaf, New York and Oxford, 1996
Historical Atlas of Islam William C. Brice (ed.), Leiden, 1981
Historical Atlas of the Middle East G.S.P. Freeman-Grenville, New York, 1993
Times Concise Atlas of the Bible James B. Pritchard (ed.), London, 1991

Other works:

A History of the Arab People A. Hourani, Harvard, 1991
A History of the Ottoman Empire to 1730 M.A. Cook (ed.), Cambridge, 1976
A Popular Dictionary of Islam Ian Richard Netton, Richmond, 1997
An Introduction to Islam David Waites, Cambridge, 1996
Arabia Without Sultans Fred Halliday, London, 1979
Cambridge Encyclopedia of The Middle East and North Africa Cambridge, 1988
Encyclopaedia of Islam (10 vols.) new edn. H.A.R. Gibb et al. (eds.), Leiden, 1960
Histoire de l'Empire Ottoman R. Mantran, Paris, 1989
History of the First World War B.H. Liddell Hart, London, 1979
Lords of Horizons: A History of the Ottoman Empire Jason Goodwin, Henry Hoh and Company, 1999
Middle East Sources: A MELCOM Guide to Middle Eastern and Islamic Books and Materials in the United Kingdom and Irish Libraries Ian Richard Netton, Richmond, 1998
Muhammed, Prophet and Statesman W. Montgomery Watt, London, 1961, 1967
Ottoman Warfare 1500–1600 R Murphy, London, 1999
Palestine and the Arab Israeli conflict C.D. Smith, 1994
The Age of the Crusades. The Near East from the Eleventh Century to 1517 P. M. Holt, London and New York
The Ancient Near East c. 3000–300 BC A.T.L. Kuhrt, London, 1995
The Arabs Peter Mansfield, London , 1997
The Birth of the Palestinian Refugee Problem 1947–1949 Benny Morris, Cambridge, 1988
The Cambridge History of Iran (vol. 3) E Yarshater (ed.) Cambridge, 1983
The Fifty Years War: Israel and the Arabs Ahron Bregman and Jihan el-Jahri, Penguin, London, 1996
The Lessons of Modern War: The Iran-Iraq War Anthony H. Cordesman and Abraham R. Wagner, Boulder and San Francisco, 1990
The Neolithic of the Near East J. Mellaart, London, 1975
The Ottoman Empire: The Classical Age 1300–1600 Halil Inalcik, London, 1973
The Ottoman Turks: an Introductory History to 1923 J. McCarthy, London, 1994
The Prophet and the Age of Caliphates: The Islamic Near East from the Sixth to the Eleventh Century Hugh Kennedy, London and New York, 1986
The Travels of Ibn Battuta AD 1325–1354 (4 vols.) Ibn Battuta trans. by H.A.R. Gibb and C.F. Beckingham, Cambridge, 1958–1984
The Venture of Islam (3 vols.) Marshall G.S. Hodgson, Chicago, 1974
The World of Islam Ernst J. Grube, London, 1966
The World of Islam Bernard Lewis, London, 1976

South and Southeast Asia

Atlases:

Historical Atlas of South Asia, 2nd edn. Joseph E. Schwartzberg, Oxford and New York, 1992
Historical Atlas of South-East Asia Jan M. Pluvier, Leiden, 1995
Historical Atlas of the Indian Peninsula C.C. Davies, London, 1959
Historical Atlas of the Vietnam War Harry G. Summers Jr., Boston and New York, 1995
Macmillan's Atlas of South-East Asia London, 1988

Other works:

A History of India M.A. Edwardes, London, 1961
A History of India Burton Stein, Oxford, 1998
A History of India Romila Thapar, London, 1967
A History of Malaya 1400–1959 J. Kennedy, London, 1967
A History of South-East Asia, 4th edn. D.G.E. Hall London, 1981
A History of Vedic India Z.A. Ragozin, Delhi, 1980
A New History of India S. Wolpert, Oxford, 1993
Cambridge Economic History of India, Vol. 1, c.1200–c.1750 Tapan Raycgaudhuri and Irfan Habib (eds.), Cambridge, 1981
Cambridge Economic History of India, Vol. 2, c.1757–c.1970 Dharma Kumar and Meghnad Desai (eds.), Cambridge, 1983
Early India and Pakistan to Ashoka M. Wheeler, London, 1968
In Search of Southeast Asia, revised edn. David Joel Steinberg, Honolulu, 1987
In Search of the Indo-Europeans: Language, Archaeology and Myth J.P. Mallory, London, 1994
India: A Modern History, new edn. Percival Spear, Ann Arbor, Michigan, 1972
New Cambridge History of India G. Johnson (ed.), Cambridge, 1989
Prehistoric India to 1000 BC S. Piggott, London, 1992
Prehistoric Thailand from Early Settlement to Sukhothai C.F.W. Higham, R. Thosarat, Bangkok, 1999
Prehistory of the Indo-Malay Archipelago P. Bellwood, Ryde, NSW, 1985
South-East Asia C.A. Fisher, London, 1964
Southeast Asia: An Introductory History, 2nd edn. M.E. Osborne
Southeast Asia: History, Culture, People, 5th revised edn. E. Graff, H.E. Hammond, Cambridge, 1980
Thailand: A Short History David Wyatt, New Haven, 1984
The Archaeology of Mainland Southeast Asia Charles Higham, Cambridge, 1989
The Archaeology of Mainland Southeast Asia from 1000 BC to the Fall of Angkor C.F.W. Higham, Cambridge, 1989
The Birth of Indian Civilisation B. and R. Allchin, London, 1968
The History of Post-War Southeast Asia: Independence Problems John F. Cady, Athens, Ohio, 1972
The Indianized states of Southeast Asia Georges Coedes, Honolulu, 1968
The Making of South-East Asia D.J.M. Tate, Kuala Lumpur, 1971
The Stone Age of Indonesia, revised edn. H.R. Van Heekeren, The Hague, 1972
The Traditional Trade of Asia C.F. Simkin, Oxford, 1968
The Vedic Age R.C. Majumdar, Bombay, 1951
The Wonder That Was India (2 vols.) 3rd revised edn. A.L. Basham, London, 1987
Trade and Civilization in the Indian Ocean: An Economic History of the rise of Islam to 1750 K.N. Chauduri, Cambridge, 1985
Vietnam S.C Tucker, London, 1999
War, Culture and Economy in Java 1677–1721 M.C. Ricklefs, The Hague, 1990

North and East Asia

Atlases:

Ajiarekishi chizu Matsui and Mori, Tokyo, 1965
Atlas of China Chiao-min Hsieh, USA, 1973
Cultural Atlas of China, C. Blunden and M. Elvin, Oxford, 1991
Historical and Commercial Atlas of China A. Herrmann, Harvard, 1935
Historical Atlas of China A. Herrmann, Edinburgh, 1966
Cultural Atlas of Japan, M. Collcutt, M. Jansen, Isao Kumakura Oxford, 1991
Nihon rekishi jiten Atlas Tokyo, 1959
Times Atlas of China P.J.M. Geelan D.C. Twitchett (eds.), London, 1974
Tubinger Atlas der Orients (various vols.) Wiesbaden, 1972-

Other works:

A Historical Geography of Russia H.Parker (ed.), London, 1968
A History of the Peoples of Siberia J. Forsyth, Cambridge, 1992
Cambridge Illustrated History of China P. B. Ebrey, Cambridge, 1996
Cambridge History of China D. Twitchett, M. Loewe (eds.), Cambridge, 1979–
China, Korea and Japan: The Rise of Civilization in East Asia, Gina L. Barnes London, 1993
The Early Civilization of China Yong Yap and A. Cotterel, London, 1975
Histoire du Parti Communiste Chinois J. Guillermaz, Paris, 1968, English translation 1972
Inner Asian Frontiers of China O. Lattimore, New York, 1951
An Introduction to Chinese History, B. Wiethoff London, 1975
Le Monde Chinois J. Gernet, Paris, 1969; English translation 1982
The Archaeology of Ancient China, 4th edn. K.C. Chang, New Haven, 1986
The Empire of the Steppes: A History of Central Asia R. Grousset, New Brunswick, NJ, 1970
World Prehistory, G. Clarke, Cambridge, 1977

Australasia and Oceania

Atlases:

Aboriginal Languages and Clans: An Historical Atlas of Western and Central Victoria J.D. Clark, Clayton, South Australia, 1988
Cultural Atlas of Australia New Zealand and the South Pacific Richard Nile and Christian Clerk, Oxford, 1996

Other works:

A Prehistory of Australia, New Guinea, and Sahul J.P. White and J.F. O'Connell, Sydney, 1982
Aboriginal Australians: Black Responses to White Dominance Richard Broome, Sydney, 1982
Australia Unveiled Günter Schilder, Amsterdam, 1976
Australian Civilisation Richard Nile (ed.), Melbourne, 1994
Blood on the Banner: Nationalist Struggles in the South Pacific D.Robie, London, 1989
Convict Workers: Reinterpreting Australian History Stephen Nicholas, Cambridge (UK), 1988
Culture and Democracy in the South Pacific Ron Crocombe et al. (eds.), Suva, Fiji, 1992
Dispossession: Black Australians and White Invaders Henry Reynolds (ed.), Sydney, 1989
Easter Island Studies Steven Roger Fischer (ed.), Oxford, 1993
Ethnicity, Class and Gender in Australia Gill Bottomley and Marie de Lepervanche (eds.), Sydney, 1991
European Vision and the South Pacific Bernard Smith, New Haven, Conn., 1992
Fatal Necessity: British Intervention in New Zealand Peter Adams, Auckland, 1977
Frontier: Aborigines, Settlers and the Land Henry Reynolds, Sydney, 1987
Historical Charts and Maps of New Zealand Peter B. Maling, Auckland, 1996
History of Australia John Malony, Ringwood, Victoria (Australia), 1987
History of New Zealand Keith A. Sinclair, Auckland, 1988
History of the Pacific Islands I.C.Campbell, Berkeley, 1989
Man's Conquest of the Pacific Peter Bellwood, Auckland, 1978
Native Lands: Prehistory and Environmental Usage in Australia and the South-West Pacific J. Dodson (ed.), Melbourne, 1992
New History of Australia Frank Crowley, Melbourne, 1974
New Zealand Politics in Perspective H. Gold, Auckland, 1985
Oxford History of Australia Geoffrey Bolton (ed.), Melbourne, 1994
Oxford History of New Zealand W.H. Oliver and B.R. Williams, Wellington, 1981
Oxford Illustrated History of New Zealand Keith Sinclair (ed.), Auckland, 1990
Pacific Navigation and Voyaging Ben F. Finney (ed.), Wellington, 1976
Social Change in the Pacific Islands A.D. Robillard (ed.), London, 1992
Sunda and Sahul: Prehistoric Studies in Southeast Asia, Melanesia and Australia J. Allen, J. Golson and R. Jones (eds.), London, 1977
The Australian Colonists K.S. Inglis, Melbourne, 1974
The Discovery of the Pacific Islands Andrew Sharp, Oxford, 1960
The Evolution of Highland Papua New Guinea Societies D.K. Feil, Cambridge, 1987
The Exploration of the Pacific J.C. Beaglehole, Stanford, 1966
The Journals of Captain James Cook on his Voyages of Discovery (4 vols.) Beaglehole, J.C. (ed.), Cambridge, 1955–1974
The Maori Population of New Zealand 1769–1971 Ian Pool, Auckland, 1977
The Pacific Islands: Politics, Economics and International Relations Te'o I.J. Fairburn et al., Honolulu, 1991
The Pacific Since Magellan O.H.K. Spate, Canberra, 1988
The People's History of Australia since 1788 Verity Burgman and Jenney Lee (eds.), Melbourne, 1988
The Polynesians Peter Bellwood, London, 1987
The Prehistoric Exploration and Colonisation of the Pacific Geoffrey Irwin, Cambridge, 1992
The Prehistory of Australia D.J. Mulvaney, Ringwood, Victoria (Australia), 1975
The Prehistory of Polynesia Jesse D. Jennings (ed.), Cambridge (USA), 1979
The Quiet Revolution: Turbulence and Transition in Contemporary New Zealand Colin James, Wellington, 1986
The South Pacific: An Introduction Ron Crocombe, Suva, Fiji, 1989 (revised edition)
The World of the First Australians: Aboriginal Traditional Life – Past and Present R.M. and C.H Berndt, Canberra, 1988
We, the Navigators: The Ancient Art of Land-finding in the Pacific David Lewis, Canberra, 1972

Chronologies

Chronology of the Ancient World E.J. Bickermann, London, 1968
Chronology of the Expanding World N. Williams, London, 1969
Chronology of the Modern World N. Williams, London, 1961
Encyclopedia of Dates and Events L.C. Pascoe (ed.), London, 1991

ACKNOWLEDGMENTS

The publisher would like to thank the following for their kind permission to reproduce the photographs.

A = Above, b = below, B = Bottom, C = Center, L = Left, R = Right, T = Top.

1 **© 1996 Visual Language**.

2/3 **© 1996 Visual Language**.

5 **E.T. Archive**: British Library, London TC

10/11 **© Michael Holford**: British Museum, London.

12 **The Natural History Museum, London**: TRb, CA, BRA, CR, CB; **Science Photo Library**: John Reader TL.

13 **The Natural History Museum, London**: TCL, TR; **Science Photo Library**: John Reader TCR.

14 **DK Picture Library**: CL, BCL; **Professor Joseph E. Schwartzberg**: TRb; **Dr David Price Williams**: BRA.

15 **DK Picture Library**: CRA; Ashmolean Museum, Oxford TR; British Museum, London TL; **Eye Ubiquitous**: John Miles CRb.

16 **CM Dixon**: CR; **DK Picture Library**: CLL, BL, BCR; University Museum of Archaeology and Anthropology, Cambridge TL; **Dr David Price Williams**: CL.

17 **Ancient Art & Architecture Collection**: Ronald Sheridan TCR; **Coo-ee Historical Picture Library**: Ron Ryan BR; **DK Picture Library**: University Museum of Archaeology and Anthropology, Cambridge CL, CR; **© Michael Holford**: TCL.

18 **Ancient Art & Architecture Collection**: Ronald Sheridan TRb; **James Mellaant**: BR; **Scala, Florence**: Archaeological Museum, Belgrade CL; **The Utah Museum of Natural History, University of Utah**: BL.

19 **British Museum, London**: TCRb; **Robert Harding Picture Library**: Bildagentur Schuster / Schenk BR; **© Michael Holford**: Ankara Museum TCL; **Catherine Jarrige**: Centre de Recherches Archéologiques Indus-Baluchistan, Musée Guimet, Paris CRb.

20 **DK Picture Library**: CL(round-based shape); British Museum, London TL, CL(flat-based beaker); Museum of London CLA.

21 **Bridgeman Art Library, London / New York**: Photograph: Mrs Sally Greene TL; **DK Picture Library**: TR, BCL; British Museum, London BC.

22 **DK Picture Library**: TR; **Robert Harding Picture Library**: John G Ross BRA; Karachi Museum, Pakistan / Photograph: R Harding CL; **Smithsonian Institute**: Presented by Mrs Alice K Bache, Purchased from James Judge and Eugenia Rodriquez / Photograph: David Heald BL.

23 **James Davis Travel Photography**: TC; **Robert Harding Picture Library**: TRb, CR; **© Michael Holford**: British Museum, London CRb.

24 **British Museum, London**: CLb; **DK Picture Library**: British Museum, London BL; **Werner Forman Archive**: Ashmolean Museum, Oxford TL; **Hirmer Verlag München**: Iraq Museum, Baghdad CbL.

25 **Bridgeman Art Library, London / New York**: Ashmolean Museum, Oxford BRA; British Museum, London TRb; **DK Picture Library**: British Museum, London C, CR, BR; University Museum of Archaeology and Anthropology, Cambridge BCRA.

26 **AKG London / Erich Lessing**: BL; **Bridgeman Art Library, London / New York**: National Archaeological Museum, Athens BL(insert); **E.T. Archive**: National Museum, Copenhagen TRb; **National Museum of the American Indian**: Smithsonian Institute / Collected by MR Harrington / Photograph: David Heald CL.

27 **AKG London**: Archaeological Museum, Heraklion TL; **AKG London/ Erich Lessing**: BCL; **© Michael Holford**: Musée Cernuschi CRA; **DK Picture Library**: British Museum, London TR; **The University of Auckland**: Department of Anthropology / Excavated by Prof. R.C. Green CRb.

28 **Bridgeman Art Library, London / New York**: Musée du Louvre, Paris TL; **DK Picture Library**: British Museum, London CAL; **Friedrich-Schiller-Universität Jena / Hilprecht Collection of Near Eastern Antiquities**: Prof. Dr. Manfred Krebernik CbL; **Turkish Information Office, London**: BLA.

29 **© Michael Holford**: BRA; Ashmolean Museum, Oxford BR; **The Institute of Archaeology, Beijing**: Professor Zheng Zhen Xiang CRA.

30 **Werner Forman Archive**: Anthropology Museum, Veragruz University, Jalapa TR; **Robert Harding Picture Library**: BCL; **South American Pictures**: Kathy Jarvis CL.

31 **Bridgeman Art Library, London / New York**: Royal Albert Memorial Museum, Exeter BCL; **DK Picture Library**: British Museum, London TCL; **E.T. Archive**: British Museum, London CRA; Historical Museum of Armenia, Erevn TCRb; **Robert Harding Picture Library**: CRb.

32 **Bridgeman Art Library, London / New York**: Musée du Louvre, Paris / Photograph: Peter Willi CLL; **DK Picture Library**: British Library, London C; British Museum, London TL, TCR, BL, BCL; **© Michael Holford:** British Museum, London CL; Musée du Louvre, Paris CR.

33 **Bridgeman Art Library, London / New York**: Ashmolean Museum, Oxford CR(Athenian coin); British Museum, London TL, TCR; **DK Picture Library**: Ashmolean Museum, Oxford CRb; British Museum, London CL, C, CR(counting stick); **Robert Harding Picture Library**: Adam Woolfitt CbR; **© Michael Holford**: British Museum, London CR(Heracles); **Ch. Thioc, Musée de la Civilisation Gallo-Romaine, Lyon**: CLb.

34 **British Museum, London**: CL; **E.T. Archive**: TCR; **N.J. Saunders**: CLb.

35 **DK Picture Library**: Ashmolean Museum, Oxford CRb; British Museum, London TLb, CRA; **© Michael Holford:** British Museum, London TCLb; **Robert Harding Picture Library**: BCL; ACI TR.

36 **AKG London / Erich Lessing**: Iraq Museum, Baghdad TL; **Ancient Art & Architecture Collection**: Brian Wilson TCR; **Werner Forman Archive**: BL.

37 **AKG London**: BR; The Israel Museum, Jerusalem CRA; **AKG London / Erich Lessing**: National Museum of Archaeology, Naples CLA; **DK Picture Library**: British Museum, London CbR; **E.T. Archive**: Olympia Museum, Greece TC; **Werner Forman Archive**: Musées Royaux du Cinquantenaire, Brussels CbL.

38 **E.T. Archive**: British Museum, London CL; **Werner Forman Archive**: David Bernstein Collection, New York BL; **© Michael Holford:** British Museum, London BCR; **Tony Stone Images**: Robert Everts TCR.

39 **E.T. Archive**: TL; The Hermitage, Leningrad CRA; National Archaeological Museum, Naples TR; **Hutchison Library**: Jenny Pate CRb.

40 **E.T. Archive**: National Archaeological Museum, Naples CL; **Robert Harding Picture Library**: Archaeological Museum, Istanbul / Photograph: Christina Gascoigne TL; R Ashworth TCR; **Scala, Florence**: Museo Capitolini, Rome BL.

41 **British Museum, London**: CRb; **Robert Harding Picture Library**: CRA; **Réunion des Musées Nationaux Agence Photographique**: Musée des Arts Asiatique-Guimet, Paris C; **Scala, Florence**: Museo di Villa Giulia, Rome TCR; Museo Gregoriano Egizio, Vatican TCb.

42 **Axiom**: Guy Marks TC; **Bridgeman Art Library, London / New York**: British Museum, London BRA; **E.T. Archive**: Archaeological Museum, Lima CL; **Scala, Florence**: Museo della Civilta' Romana, Rome BCL.

43 **Axiom**: James Morris CR; **Robert Harding Picture Library**: TCRb; Richard Ashworth CRb; **Novosti (London)**: TCL.

44 **Bridgeman Art Library, London / New York**: British Museum, London TR; **CM Dixon**: CLb; **E.T. Archive**: Archaeological Museum of Merida CL; **Robert Harding Picture Library**: TL, CA.

45 **Ancient Art & Architecture Collection**: B Crip TR; J Powell: CRA; **Chris Scarre**: BC.

46 **Ancient Art & Architecture Collection**: Ronald Sheridan BL; **Bridgeman Art Library, London / New York**: British Museum, London CL; Fitzwilliam Museum, University of Cambridge TC.

47 **Bruce Coleman Ltd**: Fred Bruemmer TL; **Robert Harding Picture Library**: TC; **© Michael Holford:** British Museum, London BCL; Museo Prenestino CR; **Réunion des Musées Nationaux Agence Photographique**: Musée des Arts Asiatiques-Guimet, Paris / Photograph: Richard Lambert BR.

48 **Bridgeman Art Library, London / New York**: British Museum, London TCb; Galleria e Museo Estense, Modena CRb; National Museum of India, New Delhi BCA; **British Museum, London**: TL.

49 **CM Dixon**: Victoria & Albert Museum, London BR; **Werner Forman Archive**: TCR.

50 **AKG London / Erich Lessing**: Musée Lapidaire, Arles TC; **Werner Forman Archive**: Private Collection, New York CLb; **© Michael Holford:** British Museum, London CRb.

51 **DK Picture Library**: British Museum, London TR; **Werner Forman Archive**: CRb; **Sonia Halliday Photographs:** CR; **Robert Harding Picture Library**: CbL; Chinese Exhibition TCL.

52 **Ancient Art & Architecture Collection**: Ronald Sheridan TL; **Bridgeman Art Library, London / New York**: Private Collection TC; **© Michael Holford:** British Museum, London BR.

53 **AKG London / Erich Lessing**: National Museum, Budapest CRb; **Ancient Art & Architecture Collection**: Ronald Sheridan TC; **E.T. Archive**: Archaeological Museum, Madrid BL.

54 **Bridgeman Art Library, London / New York**: San Vitale, Ravenna TC; **Werner Forman Archive**: National Museum of Anthropology, Mexico BR; **© Michael Holford:** Museum of Mankind, London CbL.

55 **Werner Forman Archive**: Idemitsu Museum of Arts, Tokyo CRA; **Robert Harding Picture Library**: Bildagentur Schuster / Krauskopf TL; **© Michael Holford:** British Museum, London BR; **Leiden University Library, The Netherlands**: (Or. 3101) TCR.

56 **Ancient Art & Architecture Collection**: Ronald Sheridan TL; **Bridgeman Art Library, London / New York**: British Library, London (Or.6810 f.27v) CL; **Werner Forman Archive**: TC.

57 **AKG London**: Bibliothèque Nationale de France, Paris (Arabe 5847, fol.84) TL; **Robert Harding Picture Library**: BC; D Kraus TCL.

58 **DK Picture Library**: British Museum, London CRb; **Robert Harding Picture Library**: Gavin Hellier TC; **Tony Stone Images**: Robert Frerck CLb.

59 **Bodleian Library**: (Ms. Marsh 144 P.167) CR; **Bridgeman Art Library, London / New York**: British Library, London TL; **British Library, London**: TC; **DK Picture Library**: British Museum, London CLb; **E.T. Archive**: British Museum, London CRb.

60 **Bridgeman Art Library, London / New York**: Science Museum, London C; **Coo-ee Historical Picture Library**: BL; **Werner Forman Archive**: State Historiska Museum, Stockholm TL; **© Trustees of the National Museums of Scotland**: TCR.

61 **AKG London**: Bibliothèque Nationale, Paris (Arabe 5847, fol.119) BL.

62 **Axiom**: Chris Bradley CRb; **Bodleian Library**: Pococke (Ms. fol. 3v-4r) CL; **Werner Forman Archive**: Maxwell Museum of Anthropology, Albuquerque, New Mexico BL; **Robert Harding Picture Library**: TC.

63 **Bridgeman Art Library, London / New York**: Bibliothèque Nationale de France, Paris (Fr 2630 f.111v) TC; **E.T. Archive**: National Palace Museum, Taiwan CR; **Robert Harding Picture Library**: CRb; **Hulton Getty:** (Ms. Bodleian 264) TL.

64 **Bridgeman Art Library, London / New York**: Château Roux, France TR; British Library, London (Roy 2A XX11 f.220) TL, (Add 42130 f.82) BC.

65 **E.T. Archive**: Bibliothèque Nationale de France, Paris TLb; **Robert Harding Picture Library**: C.

66 **DK Picture Library**: British Library, London BL; Museum of Mankind, London CL; **Robert Harding Picture Library**: Bodleian Library, Oxford TCR.

67 **Bridgeman Art Library, London / New York**: Bibliothèque Nationale de France, Paris CR; **DK Picture Library**: National Maritime Museum, London TR; **Robert Harding Picture Library**: BR; I Van Der Harst BCL; **© Michael Holford:** British Museum, London TL.

68 **Bridgeman Art Library, London / New York**: National Palace Museum, Taipei TL; Private Collection TR; **DK Picture Library**: British Library, London CL.

69 **Bridgeman Art Library, London / New York**: British Museum, London CR; Victoria & Albert Museum, London BR; **Werner Forman Archive**: Formerly Gulistan Imperial Library, Teheran CLA.

70 **Bridgeman Art Library, London / New York**: British Museum, London BL; **Werner Forman Archive**: University Library, Prague TC.

71 **Bridgeman Art Library, London / New York**: British Museum, London BL; **British Library, London**: (Harl.4379, fol.83v) TL; **Robert Harding Picture Library**: TR; MPH CR; Adam Woolfitt BR.

72 **Bridgeman Art Library, London / New York**: British Library, London (Harl 4380, f.22) BC; **Jean-Loup Charmet**: Musée d'Histoire de la Médecine, Lyon CLA; **DK Picture Library**: National Maritime Museum, London TL; **Scala, Florence**: State Archive, Lucca BL; **Science Photo Library**: John Burbridge BL(insert).

73 **Collections**: Liz Stares CA; **Katz Pictures**: The Mansell Collection / Time Inc. BLA; **Scala, Florence**: Galleria Sabauda, Torino TR.

74 **AKG London**: BC; **E.T. Archive**: TR; **Tony Stone Images**: Jerry Alexander CLb.

75 **AKG London**: TC; Pinacoteca Vaticana, Rome TL; **Ancient Art & Architecture Collection**: Ronald Sheridan BLA; **E.T. Archive**: CRb; **Sonia Halliday Photographs**: CAR.

76 **E.T. Archive**: Bibliothèque Nationale de France, Paris TL

77 **Bridgeman Art Library, London / New York**: Bibliothèque Nationale d France, Paris (Fr 2810 f.188) BCL; **E.T. Archive**: University Library, Istanbul BL; **Library of Congress, Washington, D.C.**: (GA 1124 1555 F.8 G&M RR Plate 43) BCR.

78 **Bridgeman Art Library, London / New York**: Kunsthistorisches Museum, Vienna TCR; **DK Picture Library**: BCL; **© Michael Holford**: British Museum, London BCR; **Peter Newark's Pictures**: CL.

79 **Bridgeman Art Library, London / New York**: Bibliothèque Nationale de France, Paris (Fr 2810, f.84) CRb; **DK Picture Library**: British Library, London TRb; **Sonia Halliday Photographs**: Topkapi Palace Museum, Istanbul TL.

80 **AKG London**: BL; **Bridgeman Art Library, London / New York**: British Library, London (Sloane 197 f.18) TL; **Werner Forman Archive**: Art Institute, Chicago BR.

81 **Bridgeman Art Library, London / New York**: Prado, Madrid / Index BC; **British Library, London**: C; Institut Amatller D'Art Hispànic, Barcelona: CR.

82 **Bridgeman Art Library, London / New York**: Château de Versailles, France / Giraudon TC; **Peter Newark's Pictures**: CLb.

83 **E.T. Archive**: Musée Guimet Paris TC; **Robert Harding Picture Library**: BCL; M Robertson CRb; **© Michael Holford:** Science Museum, London TCLb; **Royal Geographical Society Picture Library**: CR.

84 **Bridgeman Art Library, London / New York**: British Library, London BC; **DK Picture Library**: TL; **E.T. Archive**: National Maritime Museum, London CAR.

85 **AKG London**: CR; **DK Picture Library**: BL; **E.T. Archive**: Bibliothèque Nationale de France, Paris TCR; **Mary Evans Picture Library:** Cb; **Peter Newark's Pictures:** TL.

86 **DK Picture Library:** National Maritime Museum, London BCL; **Peter Newark's Pictures:** TC, CL.

87 **Bridgeman Art Library, London / New York**: Victoria & Albert Museum, London CRb; **British Library, London:** TC; **Werner Forman Archive:** British Museum, London BC; **National Maritime Museum, London:** TL.

88 **Bridgeman Art Library, London / New York**: Private Collection CA; **Hulton Getty**: TL; **Peter Newark's Pictures:** CR.

89 **The Granger Collection, New York**: TCR; **Hulton Getty:** BR; **Peter Newark's Pictures:** BL.

90 **Bridgeman Art Library, London / New York**: Private Collection CLb; **Image Select:** Ann Ronan TC; **Public Record Office Picture Library:** BCL; **Peter Newark's Pictures:** CL.

91 **Bridgeman Art Library, London / New York**: National Maritime Museum, London TL; Alexander Turnbull Library, National Library of New Zealand, Te Puna Mātauranga o Aotearoa CR; The Stapleton Collection BC; **DK Picture Library:** TCR.

92 **Mary Evans Picture Library:** TCR, CL; **Hulton Getty:** TL; **Library of Congress, Washington, D.C.:** C.

93 **Corbis:** Bettmann CA, CRA; **Mary Evans Picture Library:** CLb.

94 **Bridgeman Art Library, London / New York:** Historisches Museum der Stadt, Vienna TC; **Public Record Office Picture Library:** BC; **William L. Clements Library, University of Michigan** CL.

95 **AKG London:** BC; **British Library, London:** (Shelfmark No. 2443) TC; **Werner Forman Archive:** CD Wertheim Collection TL; **Peter Newark's Pictures:** CR.

96 **Jean-Loup Charmet:** CLb; **Mary Evans Picture Library:** TL, TCR, TR; **Hulton Getty:** BRA.

97 **Corbis:** BL; **Mary Evans Picture Library:** TCRb, TRb.

98 **Advertising Archives:** CL; **E.T. Archive:** BC; **Frank Spooner Pictures:** Roger Viollet TCR.

99 **AKG London:** TC; **Jean-Loup Charmet:** BC; **Corbis:** Bettmann / Underwood TL; **National Motor Museum, Beaulieu:** CR.

100 **Corbis:** Bettmann BCL; **DK Picture Library:** National Maritime Museum, London TL; **Mary Evans Picture Library:** CLA, BL.

101 **Corbis:** Bettmann CAL; **Peter Newark's Pictures:** CRb.

102 **Corbis:** Burs Can TCR; Hulton-Deutsch Collection BR; **Hulton Getty:** Keystone / Oscar Kersenbaum BC; **London Transport Museum:** CL.

103 **Hulton Getty:** TL, TR, BC.

104 **Rex Features:** TL.

105 - **Corbis:** UPI / Bettmann BL; **Topham Picturepoint:** C; Associated Press TLb.

106 **Robert Harding Picture Library:** David Lomax BC; **Hulton Getty:** TCR; **Tony Stone Images:** Earth Imaging CL.

107 **DK Picture Library:** TC, CR; **Hulton Getty:** TL; **Frank Spooner Pictures:** Cilo BC.

108 **Corbis:** Bettmann / UPI TL; **Hulton Getty:** BL; **Topham Picturepoint:** CA.

109 **Rex Features:** TC; Sipa-Press BL; **Topham Picturepoint:** A Young-Joon C.

110 **Robert Harding Picture Library:** R. Hanbury-Tenison BC; **Rex Features:** Sipa-Press TR; **Science Photo Library:** CNES, 1986 Distribution Spot Image CLA.

111 **Corbis:** Philippe Wojazer / Reuter BC; **Rex Features:** Setboun / Sipa-Press TL; **Frank Spooner Pictures:** Xinhua-Chine TCb; **Tony Stone Images:** Robert Mort CR.

112 **PowerStock Photolibrary / Zefa:** N Solitrenick CLA; **Rex Features:** TL; Alexandra Boulat BR; **Frank Spooner Pictures:** Gamma / Tom Kidd CLb.

113 **Hutchison Library:** Carlos Freire TC; **Panos Pictures:** Chris Stowers CbR.

114/115 **© 1996 Visual Language**.

117 **Robert Harding Picture Library:** Robert Frerck / Odyssey / Chicago BC; **Tony Stone Images:** Tom Bean Cb; Jake Rajas CRb.

118 **Bibliothèque Nationale de France, Paris:** BC; **Bridgeman Art Library, London / New York:** British Library, London BR; **Robert Harding Picture Library:** New York Historical Society TL; **Musée de L'Homme, Paris:** D Ponsard TCR.

119 **DK Picture Library:** C, BL, CRb; **Robert Harding Picture Library:** TCb; **Peter Newark's Pictures:** TLb.

120 **DK Picture Library:** CL; **E.T. Archive:** BL; **Werner Forman Archive:** Field Museum of Natural History, Chicago TL; **Robert Harding Picture Library:** Robert Frerck / Odyssey / Chicago TCR.

121 **Werner Forman Archive:** British Museum, London TC; Ohio State Museum BR.

122 **Bridgeman Art Library, London / New York:** British Museum, London TL; **James Davis Travel Photography:** Cb; **E.T. Archive:** CLb; **Robert Harding Picture Library:** Robert Frerck / Odyssey / Chicago BR; **© Michael Holford:** CAR; **Hutchison Library:** Edward Parker TCR.

123 **DK Picture Library:** Museum of Mankind, London TL; **Werner Forman Archive:** Arizona State Museum C; Museum of the American Indian, Heye Foundation, New York CR.

124 **Ancient Art & Architecture Collection:** Ronald Sheridan TR; **E.T. Archive:** Antochiw Collection Cb; National Library, Mexico TL; **Werner Forman Archive:** British Museum, London CA.

125 **Ancient Art & Architecture Collection:** G Tortoli TL; **Robert Harding Picture Library:** Mexican Museum of Natural History BR; **Peter Newark's Pictures:** CRA.

126 **E.T. Archive:** TC; **Peter Newark's Pictures:** TL, CR.

127 **Bridgeman Art Library, London / New York:** Trinity College, Cambridge BR; **Peter Newark's Pictures:** CLA, BC.

128 **Bridgeman Art Library, London / New York:** City of Bristol Museum and Art Gallery TL; **Corbis:** Bettmann TCR; **Peter Newark's Pictures:** BCL.

129 **Bridgeman Art Library, London / New York:** Photograph: D.F. Barry, Dakota TRb; **Mary Evans Picture Library:** BR; **Robert Harding Picture Library:** National Gallery of Art, Washington CR.

130 **Corbis:** Bettmann TR, C; **Mary Evans Picture Library:** TL.

131 **Corbis:** Bettmann BL; **Peter Newark's Pictures:** CRb; Alexander Gardener TC.

132 **Bridgeman Art Library, London / New York:** Liberty Island, New York TL; **Corbis:** Bettmann / UPI TCR; **Peter Newark's Pictures:** TRb, BR.

133 **AKG London:** Photograph: Agustin Victor Casasola, (1874-1938) TLb; **Peter Newark's Pictures:** CL.

134 **Corbis:** CAL, Cb, BL; Bettmann TL; **Hulton Getty:** TCR.

135 **Corbis:** TR; **Mary Evans Picture Library:** CRb; **Ronald Grant Archive:** CA, © Disney CRA; **Peter Newark's Pictures:** CbL.

136 **Corbis:** Grant Smith TCR; **Robert Harding Picture Library:** D Lomax BR; **Peter Newark's Pictures:** CRb; **Frank Spooner Pictures:** Hulton Getty Liaison TL.

137 **Corbis:** CLA; UPI TC, BL; **Redferns:** Elliot Landy CRb.

138 **Corbis:** Bettmann / UPI CL, C; **Rex Features:** JFK Library TL.

139 **Corbis:** Bettmann / UPI TCR, CR; **Rex Features:** Sipa-Press C.

140 **Robert Harding Picture Library:** Christopher Rennie CLb; **N.H.P.A.:** M Wendler Cb; **South American Pictures:** Tony Morrison BC.

142 **E.T. Archive:** Biblioteca Estense, Modena CL; **Mary Evans Picture Library:** TL; **Robert Harding Picture Library:** Cartes et Plans, Bibliothèque Nationale de France, Paris TC.

143 **Bridgeman Art Library, London / New York:** Royal Geographical Society, London BCR; **DK Picture Library:** BR; **Robert Harding Picture Library:** National Gallery, East Berlin CbR; **Royal Geographical Society Picture Library:** TLb.

144 **Bridgeman Art Library, London / New York:** British Museum, London BR; **E.T. Archive:** University Museum, Cuzco BL; **Robert Harding Picture Library:** Robert Frerck / Odyssey / Chicago TRb; **South American Pictures:** Tony Morrison TL.

145 **Ancient Art & Architecture Collection:** Mike Andrews BR; **Bridgeman Art Library, London / New York:** British Museum, London BC; **Werner Forman Archive:** David Bernstein Fine Art, New York CL.

146 **Bridgeman Art Library, London / New York:** British Museum, London BR; **Dumbarton Oaks Research Library and Collections, Washington, D.C.:** BC; **© Michael Holford:** Collection of Señor Mujica Gallo, Lima TL, BL; **South American Pictures:** Kimball Morrison CbL.

147 **Ancient Art & Architecture Collection:** Museo Oro del Peru, Lima / Photograph: R Sheridan CbR; **E.T. Archive:** Museo del Oro, Bogota CL; **Werner Forman Archive:** Museum fur Volkerkunde, Berlin BCA; **Robert Harding Picture Library:** BLA; **South American Pictures:** Tony Morrison TC.

148 **Jean-Loup Charmet:** TR; **E.T. Archive:** Archbishop Palace Museum Cuzco TL; **Mary Evans Picture Library:** BL; **Robert Harding Picture Library:** British Museum, London Cb; **South American Pictures:** CL.

149 **Bridgeman Art Library, London / New York:** Harold Samuel Collection, Corporation of London BC; **Jean-Loup Charmet:** Bibliothèque des Arts Decoratifs CL; **E.T. Archive:** BL; **Royal Geographical Society Picture Library:** CLA.

150 **AKG London:** TL, CL; **DK Picture Library:** TCR.

151 **Bridgeman Art Library, London / New York:** British Library, London CL; **DK Picture Library:** BRA; **Mary Evans Picture Library:** CR.

152 **Rex Features:** Sipa-Press / Arias TL; **Sygma:** A Balaguer TC; **Topham Picturepoint:** CR.

153 **Panos Pictures:** Michael Harvey Cb; **Rex Features:** Sipa-Press CRb; Sipa-Press / Poveda TR.

154 **Bruce Coleman Ltd:** Christer Fredriksson CLb; **Tony Stone Images:** Hugh Sitton CRb; **World Pictures:** BC.

156 **DK Picture Library:** TL; **E.T. Archive:** British Library, London BR; **Katz Pictures:** The Mansell Collection / Time Inc. CL.

157 **AKG London:** TR; **Bridgeman Art Library, London / New York:** Royal Geographical Society, London CbL; **Royal Geographical Society Picture Library:** TC, BL; **Topham Picturepoint:** BR.

158 **AKG London / Erich Lessing:** Egyptian Museum, Berlin, SMPK TL; **Robert Estall Photo Library:** David Coulson CRA; **Dr David Price Williams:** TCR.

159 **Axiom:** James Morris CR; **Robert Harding Picture Library:** Gavin Hellier CLb.

160 **Werner Forman Archive:** Courtesy Entwistle Gallery, London TL; **Sonia Halliday Photographs:** James Wellard CAR; **Dr David Price Williams:** CAL.

161 **AKG London / Jean-Louis Nou:** TR; **Ancient Art & Architecture Collection:** Ronald Sheridan TC; **Werner Forman Archive:** Cb.

162 **Ashmolean Museum, Oxford:** Hebreden Coin Room TL; **Werner Forman Archive:** TC; Tanzania National Museum, Dar Es Salaam TCb; **© Michael Holford:** British Museum, London TRB.

163 **Musée de L'Homme, Paris:** BCL.

164 **Bridgeman Art Library, London / New York:** British Library, London (Sloane 197 f.225v-6) TCb; **British Library, London:** TL, BC; **DK Picture Library:** CL.

165 **Axiom:** Chris Bradley TR; **Jean-Loup Charmet:** Bibliothèque de L'Arsenal, Paris BLA.

166 **Mary Evans Picture Library:** TL, CL, CRb; **Sonia Halliday Photographs:** Africana Library, Durban / Photograph: Jane Taylor BC.

167 **Chester Beatty Library, Dublin:** (Ms 1599 fols 1v-2r) TCb; **Corbis:** Bettmann BR.

168 **Corbis:** Bettmann CAL; UPI Photo TL.

169 **PA News Photo Library:** EPA Photo / Lusa / Joao Relvas CL; **Panos Pictures:** Betty Press BR.

171 **The J. Allan Cash Photolibrary:** BCR; **Bruce Coleman Ltd:** Dr Eckart Pott Cb; **World Pictures:** CRb.

172 **AKG London:** Postmuseum, Berlin BR; **DK Picture Library:** Danish National Museum CLb(Insert); Statens Historika Museum, Stockholm CLb; **© Michael Holford:** Science Museum, London TL.

173 **Bridgeman Art Library, London / New York:** British Library, London C; Hereford Cathedral TC; **British Library, London:** BL, BC; **DK Picture Library:** National Maritime Museum, London TR; **E.T. Archive:** Musée Carnavalet CR; **Ordnance Survey © Crown Copyright:** BR; **Royal Geographical Society Picture Library:** CLb.

174 **DK Picture Library:** CL; British Museum, London TC, CRb; **© Michael Holford:** British Museum, London TL; **Images Colour Library:** The Charles Walker Collection BR.

175 **Bridgeman Art Library, London / New York:** Archaeological Museum, Iraklion / Lauros-Giraudon BCL; **DK Picture Library:** Museum of London CR; **E.T. Archive:** Historical Museum, Sofia TC.

176 **Ancient Art & Architecture Collection:** Mike Andrews CLb; Dr S Coyne BC; **Bridgeman Art Library, London / New York:** British Museum, London TCR; **© Michael Holford:** British Museum, London TL.

177 **Ancient Art & Architecture Collection:** Ronald Sheridan BL; **DK Picture Library:** British Museum, London C; **Scala, Florence:** National Archaeological Museum, Madrid TL.

178 **Robert Harding Picture Library:** Robert Frerck / Odyssey / Chicago BC; **© Michael Holford:** British Museum, London TL; **Scala, Florence:** Musei Capitolini, Roma TC; Museo di Villa Giulia, Roma Cb.

179 **E.T. Archive:** CLA(Insert); **Robert Harding Picture Library:** Gascoigne BL; **© Michael Holford:** CbR; British Museum CLA.

180 **Werner Forman Archive:** TL; **Sonia Halliday Photographs:** BL; **© Michael Holford:** TCRb.

181 **Ancient Art & Architecture Collection:** Ronald Sheridan BR; **DK Picture Library:** TL; **Sonia Halliday Photographs:** The Hatay Museum, Antioch, Turkey BL; **© Michael Holford:** TC, CRb.

182 **Ancient Art & Architecture Collection:** Ronald Sheridan CbR; **DK Picture Library:** British Museum, London TL; **E.T. Archive:** San Apollinare Nuovo, Ravenna CLA; **Sonia Halliday Photographs:** TR.

183 **Bibliothèque Nationale de France, Paris:** BC; **E.T. Archive:** Medieval Museum, Rome TC; **© Michael Holford:** British Museum, London TLb.

184 **AKG London / Erich Lessing:** Musée du Louvre, Paris TL; **Bridgeman Art Library, London / New York:** Musée Goya, Castres (PF 2826, f.106r) / Photograph: Giraudon C; **E.T. Archive:** Palatine Chapel, Aachen CL.

185 **Ancient Art & Architecture Collection:** Ronald Sheridan BL; **Bridgeman Art Library, London / New York:** Musée Condé, Chantilly (PE 7887, Ms. 14) TLb; **© Michael Holford:** Statens Historiska Museum, Stockholm TC.

186 **AKG London:** Biblioteca Apostolica Vaticana, Rome TL; **E.T. Archive:** Templar Chapel, Cressac CL; **© Michael Holford:** Musée de Bayeaux C.

187 **Bridgeman Art Library, London / New York:** Private Collection BLA; **E.T. Archive:** Bibliothèque de L'Arsenal, Paris CbR; **Robert Harding Picture Library:** TRb.

188 **AKG London:** San Benedetto Monastery, Subiaco (Sacro Speco) TCRb; **Ancient Art & Architecture Collection:** Ronald Sheridan TL; **Bridgeman Art Library, London / New York:** British Library, London CL.

189 **AKG London:** CRb; **Robert Harding Picture Library:** K Gillham TC.

190 **Archiv der Hansestadt Lübeck:** TL; **Bridgeman Art Library, London / New York:** Bibliothèque Nationale de France, Paris (Fr 12420 f.71) BL.

191 **AKG London / Cameraphoto:** CRb; **E.T. Archive:** Bibliothèque Nationale de France, Paris TCRb; **Scala, Florence:** Museo Correr, Venezia TCLb; Santa Francesco, Prato TC.

192 **Bridgeman Art Library, London / New York:** Archives Nationales, Paris / Giraudon TL; Bibliothèque Nationale de France, Paris (Fr 2643 f.165v) TCb; **Robert Harding Picture Library:** Simon Harris BR.

193 **AKG London:** Burgerbibliothek, Bern (Mss hist.helv I, 1, fol.70) BL; **DK Picture Library:** Wallace Collection, London CL; **E.T. Archive:** TLb; National Gallery of Art, Budapest BR.

194 **AKG London:** National Museum, Stockholm TL; **Bridgeman Art Library, London / New York:** Musée de Sibiu, Rumania / Giraudon CLb; **E.T. Archive:** Capodimonte, Naples C.

195 **Bridgeman Art Library, London / New York:** British Library, London (Add 33733 f.9) C; Nationalmuseet, Copenhagen TL; **Mary Evans Picture Library:** CR.

196 **AKG London:** CL; Musée du Louvre, Paris TL; **Bridgeman Art Library, London / New York:** Private Collection BCR; **DK Picture Library**: BRA.

197 **AKG London:** Historische Museum der Stadt Wien, Vienna TR; Musée des Beaux-Arts, Arras BL; **Mary Evans Picture Library:** BCL; **Scala, Florence:** Museo Statale Russo, Leningrad C.

198 **Bridgeman Art Library, London / New York:** Private Collection / Giraudon BRA; The Stapleton Collection BR; Tretyakov Gallery, Moscow TL; By kind permission of the **Earl of Leicester and the Trustees of the Holkham Estate:** CLA.

199 **Bildarchiv Preußischer Kulturbesitz:** Kunstbibliothek Preußischer Kulturbesitz, Berlin CR; **Bridgeman Art Library, London / New York:** Musée Carnavalet, Paris BL.

200 **Bridgeman Art Library, London / New York:** Bibliothèque Nationale de France, Paris / Lauros-Giraudon TL; Musée du Louvre, Paris / Giraudon CLA; **Mary Evans Picture Library:** CLb.

201 **Bridgeman Art Library, London / New York:** Musée du Louvre, Paris / Giraudon TCR; **E.T. Archive:** Musée de Versailles CRb; **Mary Evans Picture Library:** BL.

202 **AKG London:** TR; Slg. E. Werner, Berlin TL.

203 **AKG London:** TCLb; **E.T. Archive:** Palazzo Pubblico, Siena BL; **Mary Evans Picture Library:** TLb, C.

204 **AKG London:** TCR; **Corbis:** Bettmann CLA; **DK Picture Library:** TL; **E.T. Archive:** BR.

205 **AKG London:** BL, BR; **DK Picture Library:** The Science Museum, London TR.

206 By kind permission of **The Trustees of The Imperial War Museum, London:** CLA, CR, CRb; **Topham Picturepoint:** TL.

207 **Corbis:** Bettmann TCb; **Hulton Getty:** CL; **Topham Picturepoint:** BR.

208 **Corbis:** Bettmann BR; **Hulton Getty:** CL; **Rex Features:** Sipa-Press TL.

209 **Hulton Getty:** CRA; **Topham Picturepoint:** CLb, BC.

210 **Bridgeman Art Library, London / New York:** The Stapleton Collection TL; **Corbis:** CLA; **Robert Hunt Library:** BC.

211 **Corbis:** UPI / Bettmann CLb; **Rex Features:** BL.

212 **AKG London:** TL; **Corbis:** Jerry Cooke CLb; **Hulton Getty:** Keystone Munich CLA.

213 **Corbis:** Bettmann BLA; **David King Collection:** TRb; **Topham Picturepoint:** CR.

214 **Panos Pictures:** Jeremy Hartley Cb; **Rex Features:** TL; Darryn Lyons BL; Pensjo CA.

215 **Rex Features:** Sipa-Press / Alexandra Boulat CLA.

216 **James Davis Travel Photography:** CLb; **Robert Harding Picture Library:** CRb, BC.

218 **Bibliothèque Nationale de France, Paris:** (Ms Arabe 5847.f.19) BL; **Bridgeman Art Library, London / New York:** Bibliothèque Nationale de Cartes et Plans, Paris TL; **British Library, London:** (Maps 856.(6.)) BR.

219 **Bridgeman Art Library, London / New York:** Bibliothèque Nationale de France, Paris TR; **E.T. Archive:** Naval Museum, Genoa TCb; Richmond Borough Council BC; **Koninklijke Bibliotheek, The Hague:** (76 F 5: fol. 1r) CR; **Royal Geographical Society Picture Library:** CRb, BL.

220 **Bridgeman Art Library, London / New York:** Ashmolean Museum, Oxford TCRb; British Museum, London C; Reconstruction by **Mrs James Mellaant:** CL; **Scala, Florence:** The Iraq Museum, Baghdad TL.

221 **Caroline Chapman:** TRb; **Robert Harding Picture Library:** CRb; **© Michael Holford:** British Museum, London CLb.

222 **AKG London / Erich Lessing:** British Museum, London BR; Musée du Louvre, Paris TCR; **Caroline Chapman:** CL; **Topham Picturepoint:** TL.

223 **British Museum, London:** TCb; **Robert Harding Picture Library:** CL, CR; **© Michael Holford:** British Museum, London TRb.

224 **Bridgeman Art Library, London / New York:** British Museum, London TCR; Private Collection / Ancient Art and Architecture Collection Ltd BL; **© Michael Holford:** British Museum, London TL.

225 **Ancient Art & Architecture Collection:** Ronald Sheridan CR; **Bibliothèque Nationale de France, Paris:** BR; **DK Picture Library:** British Museum, London CLb; **Werner Forman Archive:** Coptic Museum, Cairo TCb.

226 **Ancient Art & Architecture Collection:** Ronald Sheridan TC; **Bridgeman Art Library, London / New York:** Institute of Oriental Studies, St Petersburg (Ms.E-4/322a) / Giraudon CL; **British Library, London:** (Add 27261 f.363) CbL; **DK Picture Library:** British Museum, London TL.

227 **Bildarchiv Preußischer Kulturbesitz:** C; **Werner Forman Archive:** BR; **Robert Harding Picture Library:** Ellen Rooney BL.

228 **E.T. Archive:** Forrester / Wilkinson TL; Victoria & Albert Museum, London BC; **Robert Harding Picture Library:** TCR; **Peter Newark's Pictures:** BL.

229 **AKG London:** Bibliothèque Nationale de France, Paris (Add. 18866, fol.140) CLA; **Bildarchiv Preußischer Kulturbesitz:** Staatsbibliothek zu Berlin Preußischer Kulturbesitz Orientabteilung (Ms. Diez A.Fol.70) C; **Robert Harding Picture Library:** CLb.

230 **Bridgeman Art Library, London / New York:** Victoria & Albert Museum, London BR; **Sonia Halliday Photographs:** Topkapi Palace Museum, Istanbul (Ms. 3109) TL, (Ms. H1523 p.165A) CL.

231 **Werner Forman Archive:** CLb; **Sonia Halliday Photographs:** TL; Topkapi Palace Museum, Istanbul (Ms. H.1523 p.19A) C.

232 **AKG London:** TL; **Bridgeman Art Library, London / New York:** Château de Compiegne, Oise / Lauros-Giraudon BC; **Jean-Loup Charmet:** TCR; By kind permission of **The Trustees of The Imperial War Museum, London:** BR.

233 **Corbis:** Bettmann / UPI TR; **Hulton Getty:** BLA, BCL; **Royal Geographical Society Picture Library:** Capt. W.I. Shakespear CR.

234 **Hulton Getty:** BC; **Rex Features:** Sipa-Press TL; **Frank Spooner Pictures:** Halstead / Liaison C.

235 **Rex Features:** Sipa-Press C, CRb; **Frank Spooner Pictures:** Eslami Rad TRb; Van der Stockt BR.

236 **Eye Ubiquitous:** David Cumming BC; **Robert Harding Picture Library:** Thomas Laird Cb; **Tony Stone Images:** Hugh Sitton CLb.

238 **British Library, London:** CRA, BR; (Egerton 1018 fol.335) BL; **E.T. Archive:** British Library, London TCR; **Robert Harding Picture Library:** C; © Free Gallery of Art Washington BC; **The History of Cartography, University of Wisconsin:** Bharat Kala Bhavan, Varanasi TL; **Professor Joseph E. Schwartzberg:** CLb.

239 **British Library, London:** TRb; (Sloane 197, fol.395v-396) CA; **DK Picture Library:** CR, BRA; **Robert Harding Picture Library:** Jim Thompson Collection CRA; **Royal Geographical Society Picture Library:** CbL, BL, BC.

240 **British Museum, London:** BR; **Robert Harding Picture Library:** CLb; HRH Princess Chumbhot Collection BRA; Karachi Museum, Pakistan TL, TC; **Scala, Florence:** New Delhi Museum, India Cb.

241 **Bridgeman Art Library, London / New York:** Oriental Museum, Durham University CL; **Robert Harding Picture Library:** BR; Adam Woolfitt TCR.

242 **DK Picture Library:** Ashmolean Museum, Oxford BL; **Robert Harding Picture Library:** TL; Adam Woolfitt CbR; **© Michael Holford:** Musée Guimet, Paris CAL.

243 **British Library, London:** CbL; **Werner Forman Archive:** Private Collection TRb; **Robert Harding Picture Library:** BR; Gavin Hellier CR.

244 **Robert Harding Picture Library:** TL; Nigel Cameron CL; A Kennet TC, C; Adam Woolfitt BC; **Hutchison Library:** Christine Pemberton BCR.

245 **Robert Harding Picture Library:** TR, CA; Bangkok National Museum, Thailand BCL; Rolf Richardson BC.

246 **Ancient Art & Architecture Collection:** Chebel Sotun Palace, Isfahan / Photograph: Ronald Sheridan BCL; **Bridgeman Art Library, London / New York:** Metropolitan Museum of Art, New York TL; Private Collection / The Stapleton Collection CLb; **Robert Harding Picture Library:** TCR; Gavin Hellier CLA.

247 **Bridgeman Art Library, London / New York:** Private Collection / The Stapleton Collection CR, CLb; **British Library, London:** TR, BR.

248 **Bridgeman Art Library, London / New York:** Victoria & Albert Museum, London BC; **DK Picture Library:** British Library, London TCRb; **E.T. Archive:** India Office Library BR; Zoological Society of London TL.

249 **Bridgeman Art Library, London / New York:** British Library, London TLb, (As10 Vol.52 ff.3 4896.cat.201 i-iv) CR; **Mary Evans Picture Library:** BR.

250 **Corbis:** UPI BC; **Robert Harding Picture Library:** Alain Evrard TL; **Hulton Getty:** CLA.

251 **Hulton Getty:** CL; **Rex Features:** Tim Page TCR; **Topham Picturepoint:** CRA.

252 **Hulton Getty:** BC; Bert Hardy TL; **Frank Spooner Pictures:** Gamma CL.

253 **Robert Harding Picture Library:** J Bright BL; **Pictor International:** BCL; **Frank Spooner Pictures:** Olivier Duffau / Gamma TR; Gamma CRA; Xinhua-Chine / Gamma TC.

254 **Robert Harding Picture Library:** Cb, BC; Nigel Blythe CLb.

256 **British Library, London:** TL, CR, BR; **Werner Forman Archive:** Archaeological Museum, Teheran CRb; **Ninnaji Temple, Kyoto:** TRb.

257 **Fotomas Index:** CR; **Réunion des Musées Nationaux Agence Photographique:** Musée des Arts Asiatiques-Guimet, Paris / Photograph: Arnaudet CLb; **Royal Geographical Society Picture Library:** Compiled by T.G. Montgomerie from the work of Nain Singh BL.

258 **Bridgeman Art Library, London / New York:** British Museum, London TL; **Werner Forman Archive:** Art and History Museum, Shanghai BL; **Robert Harding Picture Library:** Gavin Hellier TCR.

259 **Bridgeman Art Library, London / New York:** Tomb of Qin Shi Huang Di, Xianyang, China BL; **DK Picture Library:** British Museum, London C; **E.T. Archive:** British Museum, London TR.

260 **Bridgeman Art Library, London / New York:** Private Collection BR; **DK Picture Library:** British Museum, London TL; **E.T. Archive:** British Museum, London TC.

261 **Bridgeman Art Library, London / New York:** Bonhams, London CR; **Werner Forman Archive:** TCR; **Peter Newark's Pictures:** Landesmuseum, Halle, Germany C.

262 **Ancient Art & Architecture Collection:** Ronald Sheridan TL; **Werner Forman Archive:** Christian Deydier, London BCL; **Collection of the National Palace Museum, Taiwan, Republic of China:** BL.

263 **Ancient Art & Architecture Collection:** Kadokawa TLb; Ronald Sheridan CAR, BCR; **Fotomas Index:** BRA.

264 **DK Picture Library:** National Museum of Scotland, Edinburgh TL; **E.T. Archive:** National Museum of Tokyo CL; **Robert Harding Picture Library:** Nigel Blythe BR.

265 **AKG London:** National Museum of Tokyo BL; **Ancient Art & Architecture Collection:** Ronald Sheridan TR; **E.T. Archive:** Forrester / Wilkinson CRb.

266 **Robert Harding Picture Library:** Michael J Howell TC; **Collection of the National Palace Museum, Taiwan, Republic of China:** TL; **Philadelphia Museum of Art, Pennsylvania:** Given by John T. Dorrance CR.

267 **Bridgeman Art Library, London / New York:** National Museum of India, New Delhi CLA; Private Collection CRb; **DK Picture Library:** National Maritime Museum, London CA; **Robert Harding Picture Library:** Gavin Hellier BL.

268 **Christie's Images:** TL; **E.T. Archive:** School of Oriental and African Studies, London Cb; **Peter Newark's Pictures:** TC.

269 **Bridgeman Art Library, London / New York:** Taylor Gallery, London BR; **Topham Picturepoint:** CLA.

270 **AKG London:** TL; **Bridgeman Art Library, London / New York:** British Museum, London CL; **E.T. Archive:** Postal Museum, Frankfurt Cb; **© Michael Holford:** Print by Kokyo BC.

271 **David King Collection:** CLb; **Smithsonian Institute:** Freer Gallery of Art / Arthur M Sackler Gallery Archive / Photograph: Hsun-Ling TC.

272 **Robert Hunt Library:** TL; **Rex Features:** Sipa-Press CL; **Topham Picturepoint:** Associated Press Photos TCR.

273 **Robert Hunt Library:** BR; **Topham Picturepoint:** TR.

274 **Corbis:** Bettmann / UPI BR; **E.T. Archive:** TC; **David King Collection:** CL; **Tony Stone Images:** TL.

275 **Rex Features:** Sipa-Press / Photograph: East News BL; Sipa-Press / Photograph: Ben Simmons CbR; **Frank Spooner Pictures:** Gamma / Photograph: Xinhua TR.

276 **Bruce Coleman Ltd:** Nicholas de Vore BC; **Robert Harding Picture Library:** Nick Servian CLb; **Planet Earth Pictures:** Frank Krahmer Cb.

278 **Bridgeman Art Library, London / New York:** Mitchell Library, State Library of New South Wales BR; **DK Picture Library:** Museum of Mankind, London TR; **E.T. Archive:** National Library, Canberra, Australia TL; **Maritiem Museum 'Prins Hendrik', Rotterdam, The Netherlands:** BCR.

279 **British Library, London:** CRA; **Coo-ee Historical Picture Library:** CLb, BL; **Mary Evans Picture Library:** TL.

280 **Bridgeman Art Library, London / New York:** British Museum, London TL; **Robert Harding Picture Library:** Richard Ashworth C; Robert Francis TR; David Holdsworth BL.

281 **Bridgeman Art Library, London / New York:** British Museum, London TC; Royal Geographical Society, London CR; **Peter Crawford:** TRb; **Robert Harding Picture Library:** Geoff Renner BRA.

282 **Coo-ee Historical Picture Library:** TL; **Corbis:** Gleason's Pictorial Drawing-Room Companion BC; **State Library of New South Wales:** TRb.

283 **Panos Pictures:** Penny Tweedie TL; **Tony Stone Images:** Paul Chesley CRb; **Topham Picturepoint:** CL.

284 **Bridgeman Art Library, London / New York:** National Library of Australia, Canberra BL; **Hulton Getty:** TCRb; **Tony Stone Images:** Warren Bolster TL.

285 **Hutchison Library:** CR; **Science Photo Library:** US Department of Energy TRb.

286 **Corbis:** Bettmann TL; **E.T. Archive:** BR; British Museum, London CbR.

287 **Corbis:** Underwood & Underwood CR; **Mary Evans Picture Library:** TR, BL; **Hulton Getty:** TCR;

Jacket:

Front **Bridgeman Art Library, London / New York:** British Library, London (Add 33733 f.9) CL; British Museum, London CLb; Hereford Cathedral, Hertfordshire Globe L; **DK Picture Library:** Globe R; British Museum, London CRb, BLA; **Werner Forman Archive:** Anthropology Museum, Veracruz University, Jalapa BRA; **Robert Harding Picture Library:** Simon Harris BL; **National Maritime Museum, London:** Globe C; Popperfoto BR; Rex Features: CR.

Back **Bridgeman Art Library, London / New York:** Tomb of Qin Shi Huang Di, Xianyang, China TR; **DK Picture Library:** British Museum, London CR; Museum of Mankind, London CL; **Rex Features:** Tim Rooke TL.

Front Flap **Bridgeman Art Library, London / New York:** Royal Geographical Society, London T; **Werner Forman Archive:** Idemitsu Museum of Arts, Tokyo B.

Endpapers **© 1996 Visual Language**.

Dorling Kindersley Photography:

David Ashby, Geoff Brighting, Tina Chambers, Andy Crawford, Geoff Dann, Mike Dunning, Lynton Gardiner, Steve Gorton, Peter Hayman, Chas Howson, Ivor Kerslake, Andrew McRobb, Gillie Newman, Nick Nicholls, Laurence Pordes, James Stevenson, Linda Whitman, Peter Wilson, John Woodcock.

Dorling Kindersley would like to thank:

Alice Whitehead at Bridgeman Art Library, Ute Krebs at AKG London, Caroline Haywood and all staff at E.T. Archive, Themis Halvantzi at Werner Forman Archive, Michael Holford, all at Robert Harding Picture Library and Mark Vivian at Mary Evans Picture Library for all their assistance with picture research.

Venti Variabiles

I. de Dina et
Marseven

I de Tristan
de Cunha

Caput Terræ
Australis

Terra
Vitæ

MARE AUSTRALE

RUM qui et o HORIZON RATIONALIS P

q

parantur unius Circuli majoris itaque in superficie telluris, cujus
deprehenditur. Veterum itaque Orbis terrestris descriptiones ad su
diligentissima delineationes propius scilicet accedentes
Sole Terra minor est Tychora. 140 Ricciolo 38600. imo su